International Politics

International Politics

THE WESTERN STATE SYSTEM IN TRANSITION

by

FREDERICK L. SCHUMAN

*Woodrow Wilson Professor of Government, Williams College;
Sometime Lecturer in International Relations, the
University of Chicago, Harvard University,
the University of California*

THIRD EDITION
SIXTH IMPRESSION

McGRAW-HILL BOOK COMPANY, Inc.

NEW YORK AND LONDON

1941

INTERNATIONAL POLITICS

THE MAPLE PRESS COMPANY, YORK, PA.

TO

KARL AUGUST

PREFACE TO THE THIRD EDITION

ON THE thirteenth day of March, 1941, the General Assembly of North Carolina passed a resolution prepared by Mr. Robert Lee Humber of Greenville and endorsed by Governor J. M. Broughton. By its terms the legislators registered their "profound belief and irrevocable conviction: That governments are essential to the existence of communities and that the absence of government is anarchy. That there exists an international community, encompassing the entire world, which has no government and which is destined, as a consequence of the present war, either to be ruthlessly dominated and exploited by totalitarianism or to be federated by democracy upon the principle of freedom for all nations and individuals. That all human beings are citizens of this world community, which requires laws and not treaties for its government. That the present conflict is one whose issue involves the survival of free institutions throughout the world, and that it is morally incumbent upon all free peoples, before the war proceeds further, to write the definitive Treaty of Peace in terms of the Constitution of the Federation of the World, in order that those who are called to give their lives and fortunes for the triumph of democracy may have positive knowledge of the incorruptible utility of their sacrifice. . . . Communities without governments perish. Either this community must succumb to anarchy or submit to the restraints of law and order."

These propositions, thus stoutly championed by the lawmakers of the State which was the first to declare its independence from the British Crown in 1775, were not new. In their essentials they have been advocated through the centuries by all thoughtful observers, from Dante and Kant to Wilson and Streit, who have reflected upon the problem of peace on earth, good will among men. The tragedy of our time is that the freemen of the North Atlantic communities less than a generation ago won for themselves at infinite cost an opportunity to undertake the governance of mankind—and then threw that opportunity away in the belief that safety was to be had by avoiding risks and that peace was attainable through evading responsibilities. "Isolation," "neutrality," "nonintervention," "national sovereignty," "national defense," and all the slogans of the tribal gods became the catchwords of self-defeated peoples who have all but lost their heritage. Yet today's world will in the end be politically united, in whole or in part, since its inhabitants can no longer survive disunity and anarchy. If democrats shrink from the challenge and shirk the task, the conquering disciples of despotism, already brought to formidable power by democracy's default, will do what must be done.

This starkly simple issue is the central issue of the Second World War. Of necessity it is the *leitmotif* of the following pages, as it was of the two preceding editions of this work. This revision has been prepared in the conviction that teachers and students of international relations throughout the English-speaking world are now more than ever under an imperative obligation to understand the dynamics of *Realpolitik*. They owe it to themselves and to posterity to seek out the causes of the catastrophes which have overtaken them. They are summoned by disaster to redefine the faith they live by. They are called upon to dedicate themselves with high resolve and adequate knowledge of people and events to the task of building a new world order which will convert the nightmare of the present into the dawn of a more hopeful future.

If these chapters contribute in any way toward this goal, they will have served their purpose. Whether, in comparison with earlier editions and the several other praiseworthy texts published in recent years, these rewritten pages represent progress or retrogression in the assembling of data and in the functional analysis of world politics is for others to say. They at least constitute a revaluation of the subject matter in the light of the international developments anticipated in the previous versions of this work. They are enriched with many new maps. They include enlarged and modernized bibliographies and sundry other aids to study. The diplomacy of aggression, appeasement, and war is dealt with in considerable detail. Further documentary evidence behind such judgments as may seem controversial will be found in my other books of recent vintage.

To what degree the experiences and experiments of the wasted years between 1919 and 1939 are still worthy of close attention is a matter on which opinions will differ. While giving major emphasis to the Second World War, I have chosen to retain much of the earlier material. If the fortunes of battle give ultimate victory to the hosts of the democracies and thereby make possible the rebuilding of a democratic world polity, the successes and failures of the men and women of yesterday who struggled valiantly but vainly toward this objective will demand the most searching reexamination. If, conversely, the armed terrorists of the totalitarian Triplice are able to impose their "New Order" on the world by violence, then the whole study of the community of nations as it has hitherto been envisaged in institutions of higher learning will be at an end, in America as elsewhere.

The savage combat between freemen and tyrants for mastery of the future was *in medias res* as these pages went to press. The analysis here attempted is not "objective" in the sense of expressing no preferences. Those without preferences are doomed to be the unwitting agents of their own destroyers. I cherish the hope that this work may help in a modest way to influence the outcome of the struggle by aiding those who read it to clarify their purposes and understand their tasks. But it is no part of its function to predict that outcome. Victory will go to those with most courage, endurance, and imagination. Liberals learned little and forgot much during the lost decades of uneasy "peace." They have since learned much in the brutal school of blood, tears, toil, and sweat. Whether they had learned enough and in time was unclear in the spring of 1941. Their fitness to survive was still to be fully tested in the crucible of war.

In the epoch of the *Blitzkrieg* all chroniclers are at once engulfed in the thundering torrent of tomorrow's headlines. Suffice it to say that the narrative portions of this volume have a purely arbitrary terminal point: the opening of the spring campaign of 1941. At 6:30 A.M. of April 6, Joachim von Ribbentrop, in accordance with well-established Nazi custom, summoned foreign correspondents to Wilhelmstrasse to inform them that "England is about to commit another crime against Europe. . . . Germany has watched this intrigue and tried to bring Greece and Jugoslavia to see reason and accept Germany's friendship. But all German attempts to establish friendship were without avail. Our Führer, Adolf Hitler, has now given his answer. The Germany Army is marching." He enumerated the "crimes" of "the clique of brigands" in Belgrade who "continuously threatened" Germany and Italy with war. Hitler's order of the day declared: "Since early this morning the German people are at war with the Belgrade government of intrigue. We shall only lay down arms when this band of ruffians has been definitely and most emphatically eliminated. . . . The criminal usurpers of the new Belgrade government took the power of the State unto themselves, which is a result of being in the pay of Churchill and Britain. . . . We shall fight shoulder to shoulder with our allies until the last Briton has found his Dunkirk in Greece." Again in accordance with custom, Nazi envoys in Athens and Belgrade presented demands at dawn—after Nazi bombers had begun to drop their deadly cargoes and Nazi *Panzer* divisions had plunged across the frontiers.

The "crime" of Greece was to resist when attacked, that of Jugoslavia was to decline cooperation in the German invasion of Greece. Prince Paul, Premier Cvetkovitch, and Foreign Minister Cincar-Markovitch, paralyzed by fear and bewitched by the proffered bribe of Salonika, had signed the Triplice pact in Vienna on March 25. They had been ousted from power two days later by patriotic Serbian officers led by General Dushan Simovitch, who received the belated support of Vladimir Matchek, the Croat leader. The new Cabinet asked only "peace" and "neutrality." For such defiance of Caesar's desires, Jugoslavia was condemned to conquest. Its fall was less dishonorable than that of Hungary, Rumania, and Bulgaria, where deluded leaders voluntarily delivered their countrymen into the hands of the Reichswehr and the Gestapo. In Budapest Premier Paul Teleki, "the tight-rope walker," put a bullet through his head on April 3 rather than make Hungary an open accomplice in the murder of her neighbor. His successor, Laszlo Bardossy, and his Regent, Admiral Nicholas Horthy, had no such scruples. Hungarian forces began occupying Jugoslav border areas while *Stukas* reduced Belgrade to wreckage and Nazi divisions slashed into Skoplje and Salonika. Again in accordance with a familiar pattern, Berlin announced the formation of an "independent" Croat "government" at Zagreb, headed by Sladko Kvaternik and Anton Pavelitch, the Axis-protected terrorists who had plotted the murder of Alexander and Barthou at Marseilles in 1934.

In the larger arena of combat, Britain confronted the foe's new blows with a doubtful mixture of military assets and liabilities. Mussolini's East African Empire was all but conquered with the fall of Addis Ababa on April 6 and of Massawa on the eighth. The victors were freed to move northward to defend Suez. But to the West Nazi armored divisions, ferried to Libya under the protection of the *Luftwaffe* and with the probable connivance of Vichy, retook Bengazi on the third, Derne on the eighth, and Bardia on the thirteenth, wiping out in a few days all the gains of the British winter campaign and driving furiously into Egypt. And to the East in Bagdad an Axis-inspired *Putsch* deposed Regent Emir Abdul Illah and Premier Taha Al-Hashimi and installed Regent Sherif Sharaf and Premier Rashid Ali Beg Gailani as rulers of Iraq. Turkey clung to a suicidal "neutrality." Despite British aid, Jugoslavia and Greece were apparently doomed to swift subjugation. The whole Near Eastern nexus of British imperial communications was thus in dire peril. Should the Nazi offensive come within striking distance of the Red Sea and the Persian Gulf, the Tokio warlords would be strongly tempted to attack Singapore and the East Indies. In the "Battle of the Atlantic," moreover, 5,000,000 tons of British and Allied shipping has already been sunk, with the rate of new losses exceeding 500,000 tons per month.

Under these circumstances it seemed possible that Britain might be defeated without an invasion of the "Sceptred Isle" save perhaps as a *coup de grace*—unless the United States and/or the U.S.S.R. acted to forestall such a result. America's spokesmen, still inhibited from forthright action by popular mythology, proposed to defend Greenland (April 10); opened the Red Sea to American shipping through a Presidential proclamation (April 11), declaring it no longer a "combat zone"; conferred on the joint defense of Singapore and the Indies; and cast about for ways and means of relieving Britain's shipping shortage without risking Axis attack. With the American defense industries going into high gear and steel production approaching an annual output of 90,000,000 tons, the United States could still assure its own security by averting British defeat—if Britain survived the attacks of her enemies during 1941. But many Americans still shrank from war and hoped wishfully for Soviet intervention against the Axis.

As for Moscow, the Soviet leaders made gestures of empty protest to Sofia and Budapest and pledged "neutrality" to a Jugoslavia already lost and a Turkey which might soon be completely at the mercy of Berlin. The survival of Britain required full support from either the United States or the U.S.S.R. The victory of Britain over the Reich might well require full support from both. The fall of Britain would foredoom both to impotent isolation in a world whose masters would show no mercy either to Russians or to Americans. On April 13, 1941, Molotov, Ambassador Tatekawa, and Foreign Minister Matsuoka, fresh from Rome and Berlin, signed a five-year Soviet-Japanese nonaggression pact in Moscow. Each Power pledged itself to peace and friendship and to respect for "the territorial integrity and inviolability" of the other. Should either "become the object of hostilities on the part of one or several third Powers, the other will observe neutrality throughout the duration of the conflict." By an appended declaration Tokio agreed to respect the integrity and inviolability of Outer Mongolia, and Moscow assumed a similar obligation toward Manchukuo. The Kremlin thus registered its confidence in Britain's capacity for survival and gave *carte blanche* to Japan's southward drive, apparently on the assumption that this would hasten American involvement in war against the Triplice. Russians preferred, not unnaturally, that Japan and the Reich should be checkmated and beaten by Americans rather than by Russians. It remained to be seen whether this type of "appeasement," which out-Chamberlained Chamberlain with a vengeance, would serve Soviet interests better or worse than its earlier counterpart had served Anglo-French interests.

Would the United States or the Soviet Union or both act in time to save themselves from a Triplice victory in 1941? Russians and Americans were alike fearful, hopeful, and mutually suspicious. They had given no final answer by mid-April. They would be forced to answer by autumn. Upon their answers would hang the verdict of arms in the contest between Germany and Britain, and upon that verdict would hang all the future of all the world for all the days and years ahead. As these words were written the judgment of Mars was mercifully obscured in the fog of doubts still unresolved and the smoke of battles still unfought.

The following pages will serve in some sense as a guide to the future only if the legions of Fascist totalitarianism are vanquished. Whether or not this comes to pass, these chapters will at least, I trust, illuminate the recent past of world order and international anarchy. For all errors of fact and of judgment I am alone responsible. For new maps and for revisions of old maps my heartfelt thanks are due to Mr. George Brodsky of Chicago. For indispensable aid in typing and indexing I am deeply grateful to Sally Carlton Foote of Williamstown. For the constant stimulation of friendly comment and criticism I am more indebted than words can tell to my own best teachers: my students. May they learn, along with all the youth of the lands still free, how to face bravely their broken world and how to refashion it boldly into a dwelling place worthy of their hopes.

FREDERICK L. SCHUMAN.

WILLIAMSTOWN, MASS.
April 15, 1941.

PREFACE TO THE SECOND EDITION

IN AN epoch of insecurity and conflict, general treatises on politics, unless confined to abstractions, are soon overtaken by the stream of events. The present work, when first published four years ago, purported to describe, analyze, and evaluate the game of power politics as played by the members of the Western State System. The author therein attempted a somewhat fresh approach to the field, based on historical backgrounds and prospects and on the principles of *Realpolitik*, as well as on familiar legal and institutional orientations. It was his hope that such an approach might lead to conclusions and viewpoints of enduring validity. In the judgment of reviewers, teachers, students, and other readers, these aspirations were apparently realized in part. The result was well received—if not with cheers, then at least without jeers or indifference. This verdict, coupled with the diplomatic realignments which have taken place in the interim, has encouraged me to venture a new version of the book, retaining the original structure and conceptual framework but including many rewritten chapters and much new material on the recent and contemporary international scene.

Many friends, critics and collaborators, old and new, have contributed to whatever measure of merit this new edition may possess. Scholars and teachers too numerous to mention have generously submitted corrections and suggestions for improvement, to which I have endeavored, wherever possible, to give full consideration. My own students at the University of Chicago and, more recently, at Williams College have added much in the way of helpful comment. I am indebted for fruitful exchanges of views to my new colleagues at Williams; to many other observers in academic life, in public service, and in journalism; and, above all, to my colleagues at Chicago—more particularly to Professors Charles E. Merriam, Quincy Wright, Harold D. Lasswell, Harold F. Gosnell, Harry D. Gideonse, and Melchior Palyi, to mention but a few. To Mr. George Brodsky I am grateful for preparing new maps and revising old ones. Mr. Emil Lang, despite other arduous research and writing activities, assisted in gathering and compiling some of the new data. To him, and to Mr. Leonard W. Stearns, I owe no small degree of stimulation and many useful suggestions as to general organization and treatment. I am especially grateful to Miss Sally Carlton of Williamstown for clerical and stenographic aid. Last, but far from least, my thanks are due to my wife for her patience, encouragement, and invaluable assistance with the index.

The general conception of international politics set forth in the earlier edition has been confirmed, rather than invalidated, by the developments of recent years. It has, I venture to think, gained wider acceptance than it then enjoyed. The interpretation of the current and persisting world crisis has required modification only in details. It is assumed in the following pages that the preservation of a reasonable degree of material well-being and of tolerable conditions of living for most of the peoples of the western world is definitely jeopardized by the political fragmentation of western civilization into rival national States competing with another, by diplomacy and by arms, for power, prestige, and profits. It is assumed, further, that the necessary integration and unification of the world society into a stable community, offering to its members the benefits of orderly cooperation and justice under law, is rendered impossible for the present by the stubbornly irreducible division of the world into jealous tribes, devoted exclusively to the worship of local gods, and by the continued clash between the disciples of hostile and mutually intolerant ideologies. It is assumed, finally, that the decisive international issues of the immediate future will revolve about the diplomatic and military offensive of the Fascist Powers and the indisposition of the democratic States to offer effective opposition to this drive toward hegemony.

In terms of *Realpolitik*, the consequence of the irresponsible diplomacy of the 1930's has been a constant enhancement of the fighting capacity of the "dynamic," "unsatiated" States and a corresponding diminution of the relative power of France, Great Britain, the U.S.S.R., and the United States. The "diplomatic revolution" of 1934–1936 has made the Soviet Union an ally of France and Czechoslovakia, driven Germany and Japan into one another's arms and aligned Italy with Berlin and Tokio. But the new balance of power between the Fascist Triplice and the French bloc remains highly unstable, since one side has thus far yielded to the other in every clash of wills. Passive acceptance in Geneva, Paris, London, and Washington of the Japanese conquest of Manchuria has been followed by acquiescence in the rearmament of the Reich, the Italian conquest of Ethiopia, the remilitarization of the Rhineland, the formation of a Fascist coalition, and, more recently, in Fascist attempts to destroy democracy in Spain and to use a Fascist Spain as a pawn against the western democratic Powers.

The sequel illustrates admirably Machiavelli's dictum that "the prince who contributes toward the advancement of another power, ruins his own." The French bloc has partially disintegrated, with Czechoslovakia now defenseless and Belgium, Poland, Rumania, and Jugoslavia "allies" of dubious loyalty and uncertain value. Frenzied preparations for war have taken the place of astute and far-sighted diplomacy. The Fascist Powers are driven to aggression by their cults of glory and their internal dilemmas. At some point their prospective enemies must offer armed resistance or lose their independence. No amount of evasion, irresponsibility, "neutrality," or desperate hopefulness in London, Washington, or Geneva will alter this result. It follows that war between Great Powers will almost certainly break out before the time arrives for a third edition of this work. This melancholy conclusion is not the product of congenital pessimism on the part of the author, but of the inescapable consequences of the forces at work today in the Western State System. The first edition of this volume appeared at the end of the post-war epoch. The second appears in the midst of a pre-war epoch. While there is nothing "inevitable" in this dialectical process, there is no present evidence to suggest that the States capable of averting war will be able or willing to do what is requisite to keep the peace. The power game has therefore reverted to its pre-Sarajevo pattern, characterized by unprecedented competition in armaments, by periodical diplomatic crises, and by complex manoeuvering for favorable strategic positions for attack or defense. The diplomacy of 1933–1936, like the diplomacy of 1909–1914, is intelligible only in terms of preparations in all countries for "M-day." . . .

Ultimately—if western culture does not descend into the shades—reconstruction will be undertaken and the efforts of the peace-seekers to build an ordered world will be resumed. These pages will serve their purpose ill if they merely constitute an "objective" analysis of political behavior patterns and a series of academic analyses of international law and organization, of nationalism, imperialism, and foreign policies, and of the causes of war. They will also, I trust, contribute to an understanding of the problems of peace, of economic recovery, of political appeasement, and of the social and psychological prerequisites of human fraternity. In this faith, at any rate, they have been written. And in this faith I trust they may be read by a generation which is not yet lost, however dark appears its destiny.

FREDERICK L. SCHUMAN.

WILLIAMSTOWN, MASS.
April, 1937.

PREFACE TO THE FIRST EDITION

. . . The study of international relations has traditionally been monopolized by historians and by international lawyers. The historians have dealt with the phenomena in question in terms of time sequences and the simple cause-and-effect relations of diplomatic chronology. The lawyers and jurists have dealt with international relations in terms of the principles of public international law. In recent years the historians of diplomacy have been primarily concerned with the question of "war guilt"—and such general treatments of international politics as they have presented have for the most part been characterized by the usual word jugglery and the intellectual acrobatics habitually indulged in by those who conceive of social science as a vehicle for dispensing moral judgments. This procedure has been fruitful in so far as it has promoted scholarly investigation into the facts of diplomatic history. It has not, however, resulted in any significant formulation of concepts which can be utilized for the description and analysis of the great dynamic forces moving States to action in the international arena. The lawyers and jurists, on the other hand, have been primarily interested, in the post-war period, in formal and legalistic dissections of the contemporary fabric of international organization—or "international government," as some prefer to call it. This procedure has likewise been fruitful in that it has clarified the legal nature of the structural forms of international cooperation. But legal concepts and principles also offer no clue to the inner nature and significance of the established patterns of behavior in the relations between States.

In the present study an effort has been made to escape from the limitations of the traditional approaches and to deal with the subject from the point of view of the new Political Science. The adjective is used advisedly, since the old Political Science—still all-too-prevalent in the centers of higher learning—has been circumscribed by barren legal and historical concepts. The approach adopted here assumes that Political Science, as one of the social sciences, is concerned with the description and analysis of relations of power in society—i.e., with those patterns of social contacts which are suggested by such words as rulers and ruled, command and obedience, domination and subordination, authority and allegiance. An adequate treatment of these patterns would require the invention of new concepts and the devising of a new vocabulary, for the

[xvii]

old Political Science has little to offer which is helpful. The political scientists of the old school who have dealt broadly with international relations have either wandered up the blind alley of legalism or have contented themselves with elaborate fact gathering on a variety of scattered topics which they are unable to put together into any unified scheme of interpretation. The present work does not pretend to offer the new concepts and the new vocabulary which are necessary to escape entirely from these frustrations. This is a task for the future—and one not to be undertaken in a work intended for fairly wide consumption. The vocabulary employed in the following pages will not sound strange, even to the uninitiated. But a certain degree of originality may, in all modesty, be claimed for the general orientation of the study.

This orientation assumes that the phenomena of international politics can be dealt with most fruitfully if they are envisaged as aspects of the whole pattern of political behavior and power relations which has developed in western civilization. This pattern may be designated as the "Western State System"—i.e., the total complex of attitudes, values, habits, and behavior patterns which have a bearing on the contacts between the States of the western world. This State System has had its antecedents in earlier cultures, and it will doubtless have its successors in future civilizations as yet unborn. The particular and specific problems of contemporary international politics can be dealt with meaningfully only if they are considered in the light of the whole State System of modern world society.

The function of the present work is to describe the Western State System realistically and objectively in terms of its cultural origin, its institutionalized forms, its dynamic forces, and its apparent prospects. The four major divisions of the volume are devoted to these several tasks. This conception furnishes a framework for the analysis and interpretation of all the major events of international relations. The framework is broader than the traditional orientation of the diplomatic historian and international lawyer, for it enables the student and the observer to view diplomatic history and international law in their proper perspectives, as parts of a vast design. The nature and meaning of the design itself become clear only when it is looked upon as an indivisible whole, the various parts of the whole are significant only as aspects of the total cultural context. It is the author's conviction that all of the existing general works on international relations fall short of their objective, because they are fragmented, particularistic, and limited by the partial views inherent in narrow traditional concepts and approaches. It is the author's hope that this work will be judged, by reviewers and readers alike, by the extent to which it accomplishes its purpose of synthesizing and interpreting the raw data, of presenting a whole picture of the field, and of stimulating thought regarding the implications of particular institutions, forces, and problems in terms of the whole pattern of the Western State System. . . .

No preface is complete without the usual acknowledgments and confessions of guilt for sins of omission and commission. The author can make only general acknowledgments for stimulating and fruitful exchanges of views with that fraternity of scholars which constitutes the University of Chicago. More specific expressions of appreciation are due to a small and alert group of youthful collaborators, all at Chicago: to Miss Dorothy Blumenstock—for spending endless hours in close cooperation with the writer in gathering factual material, in preparing tables and charts, in criticizing content and style, in reading proof, and in concocting the index; to Miss Brita Berglund—for invaluable and invariably efficient stenographic and clerical assistance; to Mr. Gabriel Almond—for incidental assistance with the appendices; to a host of students, graduate and undergraduate, in the author's classes, from whose "term papers" he has cheerfully filched many useful data and a few suggestive thoughts; and, more particularly again, to Mr. David Blumenstock for assisting with the index and drawing outline maps, and to Mr. George Brodsky for the lettering and shading of the maps under the author's direction. To Mr. Brodsky is largely due whatever merit the maps may possess.

It goes without saying (but by the traditions of the profession, it must always be said nevertheless) that the author is solely accountable for all mistakes of fact or of interpretation. In a work of such wide scope and large size the possibilities of error are multitudinous, despite the most painstaking care in checking facts and weighing conclusions. The author would, in any case, not wish to deprive reviewers of the pleasure of pointing out that a word here is misspelled, that a date there is in error, and that a figure elsewhere is of dubious validity. These opportunities, it is hoped, will not be numerous. But the author accepts full responsibility for all lacunae, all misstatements, and all misjudgments. For the rest, the readers to whom this preface is addressed must arrive at their own verdict.

FREDERICK L. SCHUMAN.

THE UNIVERSITY OF CHICAGO,
  April, 1933.

[xix]

CONTENTS

CONTENTS

BOOK THREE—WORLD ANARCHY

CHAPTER VII

CHAPTER VIII

CHAPTER IX

CHAPTER X

CONTENTS

MAPS, CHARTS, AND TABLES

BOOK ONE
THE RISE OF THE WORLD SOCIETY

Chapter I

STATE SYSTEMS OF YESTERDAY

1. THE DESTINY OF MAN

Life is a plaything and a wandering in the wilderness and a passing show. . . . This is the work of Fate and Chance, who ever so softly escort us human beings in order to make the lives of some of us happy and the lives of others unhappy without rhyme or reason. So life travels its wandering and brutal course. . . . For Fate has enacted, to operate in the lives of each of us, an unalterable series of irrevocably accomplished facts. . . . As the actors on the stage change their makeup to fit the words of the book and play with a professional propriety, sometimes kings, sometimes brigands, and sometimes yokels or cockneys or gods, in the same way we too ought to play the parts with which we are invested by Fate, and to conform to them without capitulating morally to the chances and changes of Life. If any man rebels, he will have disgraced himself without having modified his destiny by one jot.—VETTIUS VALENS.

THOSE who live through great disasters commonly regard themselves as the unluckiest of mortals and look upon the dangers they face as the worst in the annals of man. Each generation, in good times or bad, is tempted to regard itself as the culmination of the history of the race. Its achievements are greatest. Its hopes are fairest. And if its dreams and its self-esteem are shattered, it cannot but believe that its failures are more heart-rending and its despair blacker than any experienced in past time.

In the fifth decade of the twentieth century after the birth of Christ, men and women everywhere over the planet are victims of bitter disenchantment. They seek peace and find war. They strive for abundance and suffer want. They attempt to recapture vanished landmarks and the half-forgotten hopes of lost faiths. Since these efforts are vain more often than not, they readily lose all sense of values and all awareness of meaning in their lives—unless they forget themselves in a blind and brutish struggle for mere survival or, like the holy men of old, renounce the world and retire from its disappointments to commune with God. Those who are still of the world and yet above the battle are tempted to mutter with Hamlet: "The time is out of joint;—O cursed spite, That ever I was born to set it right!"

Braver spirits are moved by adversity to reexamine the fundamentals of their beliefs and their way of living in order to win fortitude for the future. They are driven to scan more searchingly the world whose misfortunes they share and to look more deeply into the past as a means of discovering what is possible and what is necessary in their own time. The search is seldom fruitless. For the student and scholar, the consolations of philosophy are no less heartening than they were to Boetius amid the tumult of the fifth century. The consolations of history, reflectively considered, offer light even when the day's cause is lost—and perhaps that light is brightest when vanquished hope weeps for what seems forever gone. Formulas and panaceas for salvation are empty in periods like our own. But new wisdom and new promise always flow from perspective on the human adventure and understanding of what has been, what is, what will be, and what can never be.

If the belief of our fathers in the inevitable and endless "progress" of man from primeval slime and the brutishness of *Pithecanthropus erectus* to the glories of "modern civilization" is no longer tenable, new knowledge of the life of the race at least offers hope of a different order. Man lives and has ever lived not by bread alone but by his hopes, his beliefs, his faith in himself and his fellows, and by the arts and skills of his own devising whereby he has sought to translate his purposes into tangible form. In his striving, he has fashioned diverse and successive Cultures each of which, plantlike, has pushed itself upward from the dark earth to blossom and bear fruit and finally to wither and return to the soil. Never yet has collective man in his attempt to be master of his fate and captain of his soul outwitted or transcended this life cycle of his own social artifacts, any more than any individual has ever escaped, save by sudden death, his predetermined march from infancy and childhood through puberty, adolescence, and maturity toward old age. What is true of human individuals would appear to be true of human societies and of whole Cultures. To acknowledge this truth is not to become a fatalist, but only to recognize that the problems and opportunities of each generation are shaped by its place in the march of mankind through the phases of each great civilization. Here, as always, freedom lies in the recognition of necessity. If twentieth-century man has lost, or seems to be losing, his freedom to build the future to his heart's desire, his loss is largely a consequence of his inability or refusal to face the necessities of the age in which he finds himself.

That age is the age of the Great Society, spreading proudly and richly over the planet. Mankind is one as never before, thanks to man's skill as explorer, pioneer, inventor, engineer, producer and distributor of goods and services on a world scale for a world market. Such a society can flourish and escape demoralizing poverty and devastating conflict only if it is governed as a unit. In such a society, statesmanship must direct finance, industry, commerce, agriculture. In such a society, world organization must supersede local jealousies and feuds. The art of effective politics under these conditions is the art of planning and utilizing productive resources on a world scale, since planning on any lesser scale will fail or spell chaos, and of organizing and enforcing order and law on a world scale, since any lesser law and order is too little or too late for the needs of a world civilization. These statements of preference, long scoffed at as the dreams of utopian "socialists" or of visionary "internationalists," have never been faced by men in the mass as the inescapable prerequisites of their own survival. In such an age as our own, however, they are not preferences but necessities. Events bear tragic witness. Men have preferred to seek plenty through untrammeled profit making, free of "government interference," or they have sought prosperity through State action within national frontiers. The result is poverty. They have preferred to seek peace through pacifism or irresponsibility or tribal armaments wherewith other tribes were to be frightened into good behavior. The result is war. And many who weep and wail at these results are unable or unwilling to face the fact that no other results are possible until the unity of the world is recognized by all and made the basis for a reordering of man's economic and political life on a world scale.

Modern mankind must unite or die. The disciples of "democracy" and "capitalism" refused to face the issue or to redefine their beliefs and habits in the light of it. But men cling to life and usually do, in one fashion if not in another, what must be done in order to live. The task of unifying the world has perforce been assumed by the sworn enemies of capitalism and democracy. What the Pen and the Word failed to do, the Sword is in process of doing. What men of good will and men of tolerance and reason would not do, men of barbaric vigor and ruthlessness are accomplishing. The new Caesars, like those of ancient days, may conquer the earth and bring peace to humanity. They may plunge the planet into a dark and unending night of blood and chaos. They may reawaken the surviving capitalist democracies into resuming the role they have abdicated. Which of these possibilities is most likely to be realized cannot yet be said. Yet in any event, in the very midst of ruin and death, the necessities of the twentieth century are somehow being met.

The manner of meeting them is unpleasant. Men learn slowly and with difficulty. Where persuasion fails, the bludgeoning of outrageous fortune is often necessary. Business is enslaved by politics because business developed no statesmanship. Democracy is destroyed by tyranny because democrats were blind and tyrants had vision. Nations are broken by conquest because nations would not unite. But the end at least is union— on a continental, if not yet on a world scale. The end is government that governs, industry that produces, statesmanship that sees the world as one, even when its eyes are the eyes of greed and hatred rather than those of human sympathy.

Out of the wreckage of illusion, out of the welter of violence, the Great Society may well be born anew in a world united by force as was the world of ancient Rome. To anticipate a new Augustan age as the sequel to today's misery may appear as fantastic as the earlier Augustan age would have appeared to the Romans and Carthaginians who fell at Cannae or Zama or to the embattled partisans of rival tyrants struggling for power after the murder of the first Caesar. Yet the sequence is equally probable —indeed more so, since Western mankind has far greater need of world unity than did Classical mankind if it is to fulfill its destiny. To know what is necessary is to know how to keep on the road to the goal. Those who decline to learn in the school of reason will learn in the school of adversity or perish. In strange and ugly ways the process of learning goes on. Western humanity has failed several courses, received its last warning, and suffered a broken heart. But it has not yet "flunked out" of the university of history. The very barbarians who storm the gates and provoke turmoil within may yet be the instruments to teach the new wisdom and courage needed for the work of better days.

2. FROM CITY-STATE TO EMPIRE

The State, completely in its genesis, essentially and almost completely during the first stages of its existence, is a social institution forced by a victorious group of men on a defeated group, with the sole purpose of regulating the dominion of the victorious group, and securing itself against revolt from within and attacks from abroad. Teleologically, this dominion had no other purpose than the economic exploitation of the vanquished by the victors. . . . From war to peace, from the hostile splitting up of the hordes to the peaceful unity of mankind, from brutality to humanity, from the exploiting state of robbery to the Freeman's citizenship—this has been the path of suffering and of salvation of humanity, its Golgotha and its resurrection into an eternal kingdom.—FRANZ OPPENHEIMER, *The State*.

Every "social institution" in every Culture, whatever its trappings of mystery and ritual, is no more (and no less) than a widely accepted and persistent habit of dealing with human relations. Three "institutions" have endured through many Cultures from the dawn of recorded time: the Family, the Church, the State. Through them in their various forms, man has "solved" his problems of love and child rearing, of worship and communion with his fellows and with God, of the ends and means of command and obedience in society. Every "State" is a mosaic of habits whereby the few issue orders to, and secure obedience from, the many. In the words of Rousseau, "It would be contrary to nature for the many to command the few." This is so whether the purposes of command be exploitation or service; whether the few be tyrants, oligarchs, or elected officials; whether the many be slaves or serfs or free citizens. The State is the set of devices whereby power is wielded by rulers over the ruled. Politics is rivalry for control of the instruments of power. The typical weapons of politics are might, myths, and money—*i.e.*, physical coercion to induce fear, the manipulation of symbols to induce loyalty, the granting or withholding of benefits to induce self-interested deference to governors from the governed.

The prevalence of violence in political relations, within States and between States, is not unrelated to the circumstance that in all likelihood the State itself was originally a product of violence. Most certainly it was not created by a voluntary agreement as the "social contract" theorists once imagined. Most certainly it was not invented by sages and conferred as a blessing upon mankind as the philosophers of ancient China believed. Its origins are shrouded in mists of magic and religion. Yet there is much reason to believe that the historic State originated out of the conquest of primitive farmers by primitive hunters and herdsmen. Prior to this event, each group undoubtedly had simple forms of authority among its members, as do the surviving preliterate and prepolitical tribes of today in the far corners of the earth. But the historic State (envisaged as an institutionalization of power relationships involving a definite territory, a claim by rulers to universal obedience, and a successful assertion by power holders of a monopoly of legality and of force within the community) undoubtedly had its genesis in the relations between victors and vanquished in "old, unhappy, far-off things and battles long ago."

Once upon a time nomadic herdsmen learned that wealth was to be had by war as well as by work. They descended from the hills to rob the tillers of the soil in the valleys and plains. So long as the robbers slew the robbed, no political relationship between them was established. When the robbers became clever as well as ruthless and carried off the robbed as captives, the rudiments of class distinctions and of "government" began to emerge. Later the conquering robbers settled down upon the land, reduced the conquered to slavery or serfdom, and built strongholds from which they could rule and exploit the vanquished, while they defended their spoils from new raiders and organized the conquest of adjacent territories for their further enrichment. At this point the historic State was born.[1]

Most early States are city-states, with the city—*polis* or *civitas*—usually growing up about a military stronghold built for defense against the outer barbarians. Every early State has sharp class distinctions, with subjugated slaves or serfs tilling the soil for the benefit of nobles and priests who afford protection and spiritual solace, and demand obedience

---

[1] See Franz Oppenheimer, *The State*, 1912; Robert H. Lowie, *The Origin of the State*, 1927; W. C. MacLeod, *The Origin and History of Politics*, 1931; and R. M. MacIver, *The Modern State*, 1926.

and piety in return. Magician-kings or god-kings become leaders and symbols of the land-holding élite descended from the original conquering nomads. Laws are made and administrative procedures are invented by kings and prophets to regulate and perpetuate the social hierarchy. The maintenance of internal peace and order and the organization of defense against external aggression were the first functions of government. As cultural assimilation progressed, the community became solidified. The relationship between killers and killed, conquerors and conquered, masters and slaves, lords and serfs was transformed into a relationship between rulers and ruled reciprocally advantageous to both.[1]

Whether this process took place first in a single place, such as pre-historic Egypt, and spread elsewhere by cultural diffusion, whether class cleavages and urbanism grew everywhere out of conquest situations or sometimes out of the internal economic development of an already established community, whether some early States came into being by a totally different process are questions which remain unanswered. But primitive States for the most part bear upon their face the imprint of their origins in conquest. And the early and persistent type of social organization known as *feudalism*, wherein land is held in return for labor or military service and a propertied aristocracy of fighters lives by the toil of an unfree peasantry, likewise tends to confirm the war-and-conquest theory of the origin of the State.

States, once established, had commercial relations with other States and often waged war upon their neighbors. War, by accentuating in-group *versus* out-group animosities and by making solidarity the price of survival, normally promoted cohesion among all the inhabitants of the community. War led to the subjection of enemies by powerful States and thus enlarged the areas within which order, peace, and justice could be established by the ruling class of the victors. As great territorial States developed and fought with one another for dominance, a State System evolved. All early State Systems ultimately gave way to great empires in which peace and order were made to prevail over vast regions, first by the sword and later by the extension of legal and administrative institutions over the subdued populations. The "World State" became the end point of political evolution, and with its establishment international relations and war came to an end.

The State System of Western Culture has obviously not progressed to this end point which all earlier State Systems attained. It remains an aggregation of independent sovereignties, competing with one another for power by diplomacy and by violence. In the absence of central institutions

[1] "The State owes its origin to war. . . . Agriculture, slavery, and territoriality are the primary factors underlying State formation, but the force which actually welded them together to produce the State was war." M. R. Davie, *The Evolution of War*, 1929, pp. 174–175.

through which a world-ruling class wields world-wide authority, the units of the system repeatedly clash with one another in combat. International politics in any such State System is a contest for power in which the players are not subordinate to any superior authority. The law of the jungle still prevails among them. That a "world government" or a new "world empire" will ultimately emerge out of the conflicts of the nation-states is more than likely, since every earlier State System has come to an end in this fashion. But for the present the community of nations remains an imperfect society in which international government is an aspiration rather than a reality.

In the present configuration of the System, force is utilized as a weapon of authority not by a central power against lesser powers, but by States against States. Fraud, *i.e.*, propaganda, mysticism, duplicity, is an instrument of ruling élites within States and a tool of States in their struggle with other States for larger shares in the distribution of available satisfactions. Favors and material benefits are not apportioned among the members of the System by a central agency or distributed among each by the common deliberation of all, but are haggled over and fought for by competing independent sovereignties, each pursuing its own ends. The modern community of nations thus remains one in which political relations are still in large degree those of coercion and exploitation, not those of orderly cooperation in a régime of law. The State System stands precariously poised between the anarchic brutality from which it emerged (and to which it may return) and a vision of an ordered world which perhaps will remain forever a mirage enchanting and tantalizing the victims of violence.

A brief treatment of early State Systems and of the genesis of the world society of today will serve to place the contemporary scene in its historical setting. The earliest States known to modern scholars were the small city-states which appear at the dawn of written history in the fertile river valleys of the Nile, the Tigris-Euphrates, the Indus, and the Yangtze-Kiang. The oldest remains of these communities suggest that their inhabitants had already advanced far along the road from the primitive tribal group to the civilized territorial State generations before their development became a matter of written record. Somewhere between the Stone Age and the period of the use of metals, groups of farmers, dominated by the heirs of conquering nomads, had gathered together in towns and had become members of already complex societies, with kings, warriors, jurists, and administrators, nobles, priests, commoners, and slaves. These early city-states of Egypt and Mesopotamia were almost invariably despotic in government, with supreme power vested in a sacred kingship, supported by a landed aristocracy and an established church.

The attitudes and policies which such communities adopted toward one another seem to have been much the same in all early State Systems. The normal relations between the city-states were those of war. The first States, and most of the later and larger kingdoms of the ancient world, were little centers of culture, surrounded by a wilderness peopled by barbarian nomads only too eager to descend from their hills or deserts to sack the cities of the fruitful valleys. "Stranger" meant "enemy." Between the city-states, as between the forces of civilization and savagery, conflict was incessant. Each local ruler, with his landed warriors, sought additional wealth and power by subjugating his neighbors and plundering and enslaving near-by peoples unable to defend themselves. War was customary and peace exceptional.

International politics among these early city-states, however, was not entirely a struggle for power between them through war. Peace prevailed from time to time when neighboring cities found it expedient to establish alliances or pacific relations between themselves by treaty. And it may be assumed that at such times commerce flourished and political contacts were maintained through the exchange of diplomatic emissaries. Little is known, however, of the peacetime practices of these States, since their annals are filled with tales of war and conquest. But it is clear that treaty agreements were frequently concluded and furnished the basis for peaceful relations. The earliest treaty of which any written record remains is one concluded about 3000 B.C. between the kings of Umma and Lagash who were involved in a boundary dispute. The controversy was submitted to the arbitration of Mesilim, King of Kish, who, with the aid of the appropriate deities, was successful in adjusting the difference between his neighbors. The stone-carved text of a somewhat later treaty between the same States is preserved upon the "stele of the vultures" in the Louvre.[1] Knowledge of these early treaty negotiations is confused and fragmentary, but enough is known to justify the conclusion that treaties were regularly entered into between the city-states and that arbitration for the pacific settlement of disputes was not an unfamiliar procedure.

Following the political unification of the city-states of the great river valleys and of the plateaus of the Near East, there developed a larger State System and a new balance of power between the early Oriental monarchies—Egypt, Assyria, the smaller States of the eastern Mediterranean littoral such as Mitanni, Syria, and Phoenicia, and the Hittite State in Asia Minor whose armies overwhelmed Babylon about 1750 B.C. For several centuries these States engaged in chronic conflicts with one another, each seeking its place in the sun through the conquest of its neighbors. The weaker States preserved their independence by playing off the more powerful against one another. Coalitions and alliances formed

[1] See L. W. King and H. R. Hall, *Egypt and Western Asia*, 1910, pp. 170–173.

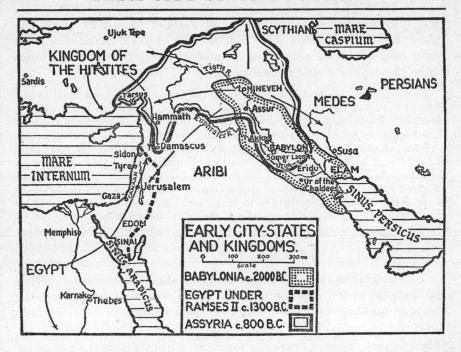

and dissolved in anarchical confusion within the area between the Sahara and the Caucasus, the Black Sea and Arabia. The borderlands and buffer States between the major contestants were frequently the scenes of bloody combats between rival hosts. The Egyptians and the Hittites were the most formidable of the empire builders, and war between them for control of the eastern Mediterranean seacoast was ever recurrent, with neither side enjoying a decisive advantage. After many changes of fortune, Hattushilish III, King of the Hittites, negotiated a treaty with Rameses II, in order that he might be at peace with his southern enemies in the face of attacks upon his dominions by the Assyrians from the east.

This Hittite-Egyptian treaty, which was apparently concluded about 1280 B.C., is of unusual interest, less so because of its political significance at the time than because of the fact that it is one of the few early treaties of which the text has been preserved. Two incomplete copies of the Egyptian version and a fragment of the Hittite version are extant, both taken from the original in Babylonian, which was seemingly the diplomatic language of the day. It was a treaty of peace and alliance, "witnessed by the thousand gods, by the male gods and the female gods." Like most early treaties, including those of the early modern period of the Western State System, it provided for perpetual peace between the parties. The obvious impermanence of such a pledge led to the general abandonment of this formula in the nineteenth century, though it was revived in modified form in the Pact of Paris of August 27, 1928. The treaty between Rameses and Hattushilish reveals these monarchs renouncing war as an instrument of national policy thirty-two centuries before the days of Kellogg and Briand.

There shall be no hostilities between them forever. The great chief of the Hittites shall not pass over into the land of Egypt, forever, to take anything therefrom; Rameses, the great chief of Egypt, shall not pass over into the land of the Hittites to take anything therefrom, forever. . . . If another people (or state) shall come, as an enemy, against the lands of Rameses, the great chief of Egypt, and he shall send to the great chief of the Hittites, saying "Come with me with your army against him," the great chief of the Hittites shall come, and the great King of the Hittites shall slay his enemy. But if it shall not be the desire of the Great Chief of the Hittites to come, he shall send his infantry and his chariotry, and shall slay his enemy. Or, if Rameses, the great chief of Egypt, be provoked against delinquent subjects, when they have committed some other fault against him, and he shall come to slay them, then the great chief of the Hittites shall act with the lord of Egypt.

This obligation, constituting a treaty of alliance for mutual defense and the suppression of revolution, was made reciprocal, as was also the provision for the extradition of fugitives from justice.

If any of the great men of the land of Egypt shall flee and shall come to the great chief of the Hittites, from either town, or . . . of the lands of Rameses, the great chief of Egypt, and they shall come to the great chief of the Hittites, then the great chief of the Hittites shall not receive them, but the great chief of the Hittites shall cause them to be brought to Rameses, the great chief of Egypt, their lord.

This arrangement evidently contemplated the extradition of political offenders, who were regarded then as more dangerous than common criminals, though they are now usually exempted from the operation of extradition conventions.[1] Some years after the conclusion of this agreement, Hattushilish paid a state visit to the land of the pyramids and his daughter was married to the Egyptian monarch. International peace was thus reinforced by matrimonial bliss—an arrangement which has commended itself to many reigning houses in other periods and civilizations.

In all probability the treaty of 1280 B.C. was in no way unique but was typical of similar agreements between these and other States, the records of which have been lost. Here, as always, contacts between independent political communities led to the evolution of a more or less elaborate system of treaty relationships and a high development of the art of diplomacy, as well as of the science of war. The passing generations brought great changes in the equilibrium of power between the units of this State System, with old States giving way to new and the uncontrolled

---

[1] See on the text of this treaty the article by Langdon and Gardiner in the *Journal of Egyptian Archaeology*, VI, 1920, pp. 179ff.

ebb and flow of international politics creating new situations with the
unrolling years. The Hittite Empire in Asia Minor collapsed at the end
of the thirteenth century B.C. under the assaults of migrating hordes from
the west. Egypt itself narrowly escaped conquest by invaders from the
Libyan desert. It declined in power until it became a mere appanage of
the new Asiatic empires of a later period. Freed from the pressure of
stronger rivals, the Aramaeans, the Philistines, and the Hebrews established States in Syria and Palestine which warred upon one another in
traditional fashion. The long reign of Solomon (c.975–935 B.C.) found the
Israelites masters of this region under the rule of a monarch who achieved
as much by diplomacy as by war. He brought brief glory to his State by
exploiting the subject peoples of his realm, promoting trade, and forming
astute political engagements with his neighbors. His kingdom disintegrated after his death, however, and the rising star of Assyria began to
cast its light over·the entire international arena. The ambitious kings of
these eastern peoples conducted a long series of successful military campaigns, extending over several centuries, and ultimately reduced to
vassalage most of the surrounding States, which failed to combine effectively against the newcomer. In this fashion the whole State System of the
Near East came temporarily to an end and gave way to the first of the
"world empires"—an imposing military and administrative structure
which, in its palmiest days, extended from the Persian Gulf to southern
Asia Minor and from the mountains south of the Caspian Sea to the first
cataract of the Nile.

The Assyrian Empire, to be sure, disintegrated under the combined
attacks of new enemies, among whom the Medes who came out of the east
were the most formidable. The capture and destruction of its capital,
Nineveh, in 606 B.C., completed the process of dissolution. Assyria proper
was annexed to the Median Empire. Egypt and Babylon resumed their
independence and fought for the control of Syria which the Babylonians
finally conquered. In 586 B.C. Jerusalem was stormed, sacked, and razed
by the great Babylonian monarch Nebuchadnezzar, and from that day to
this Palestine has remained under foreign rule. Many decades of confused
conflict followed between States, principalities, and nomad hordes, until
the military might of the Persians, under Cyrus, Cambyses, and Darius,
enabled them to build a new "world empire," even larger than that of
Assyria and covering all the civilized world from the Indus to the Aegean.

The end point in the evolution of the early State Systems of the Near
East was thus the military conquest and the destruction as independent
political entities of all the weaker States by the most powerful. World-
wide imperialism became in fact the prevalent form of political organization as an alternative to a system of competing independent States
struggling with one another for territory and power.

3. FROM DEMOCRACY TO CAESARISM

Our responsibility is to see that in this new world the dignity and worth of the individual shall be respected, the equality of men and races shall be recognized, the freedom of all shall be safeguarded; in short, that it shall be a world in which democracy will grow and peace will be assured. Such a world cannot come in any easy way, not by soft living nor by minding our business; it will come only through a hard struggle, through many sacrifices, and through unflinching courage and devotion. Only thus can the great heritage of western civilization that springs from Athens and Jerusalem be preserved and transmitted to future generations, enriched and purified by the thought and toil, by the suffering and striving, of our generation.—HANS KOHN, June, 1940.

During the centuries of war and empire building in western Asia there had developed in the eastern Mediterranean another great culture—the fairest and brightest of all in the ancient world in the memory of later ages. Sir Henry Maine doubtless exaggerated when he said that everything that lives and moves in the modern world, excepting only the blind forces of nature, is Greek in its origin. Nevertheless, the debt of Western civilization to the culture of ancient Greece is enormous. As later artists, poets, and philosophers all found inspiration in the aesthetic and intellectual legacy of the Greeks, so statesmen, diplomats, and political theorists have similarly found much that is worthy of their close attention in the political life and international relations of these remarkable people of the Aegean.

Existing evidence indicates that the Greek city-states emerged as definite political entities through war and that the exigencies of war largely dictated their social and political organization. The original tribal organization of the Greek peoples disappeared as they settled down to agricultural life and the primitive monarchy gave way to an aristocracy of landowners. Before their coming a great pre-Hellenic civilization had arisen in the eastern Mediterranean, with its center on the island of Crete, and had flourished for a thousand years (c.2400–1400 B.C.). In the days of its decline, successive waves of seminomadic peoples entered the region from the north, came into contact with the more highly developed Minoan culture, and created in course of time the civilization of the Homeric period, so called from the great epic poems of the *Iliad* and the *Odyssey* in which are described, presumably by Homer, the heroic episodes of the war with Troy and its aftermath. It was this civilization, imposed upon Minoan-Mycenean society, which prevailed in the peninsula when the earliest city-states became known to written history. The early Spartans, in the building of their communistic military State, became the ruling class in the commonwealth which they had created by conquering their neighbors and reducing them to the rank of *helots*, or peasant serfs, and of

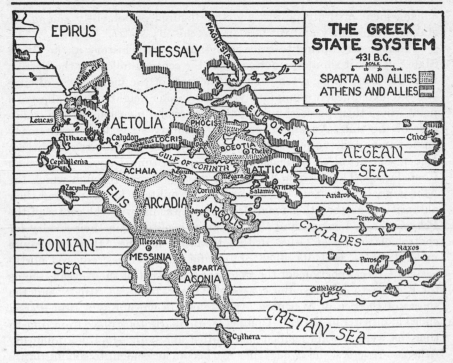

THE GREEK
STATE SYSTEM
431 B.C.
SCALE
SPARTA AND ALLIES
ATHENS AND ALLIES

perioikoi, or merchants. These subject classes had no political rights in a State ruled by the citizen-warriors who owned the land. By war and diplomacy Sparta eventually created a confederacy of city-states within the region over which Spartan power could be effectively exercised. Athens similarly seems to have emerged out of the fusion of petty communities and the extension by military means of the power of the dominant group over all of Attica.

The relationship of the classes within these early States, in terms of the distribution of wealth and political power, reflects the military origins of the States themselves. Politics within the State revolved about the forms of institutionalized authority through which the wealthy aristocracy of the nobles, descendants of the original conquerors, administered public affairs. The subject classes and the poor wrested privileges from their rulers from time to time; but, even in the brightest days of Athenian "democracy," Greek society was a hierarchy of classes resting at bottom upon slavery. Politics between the city-states, here as in every State System composed of independent political entities, was a struggle for power in which the larger units strove to conquer the smaller and the weak combined against the strong for mutual protection. Commercial advantages throughout the eastern Mediterranean and overseas colonies, scattered as far as Sicily and the coasts of Italy and Spain, were means to the enhancement of State power; and they figured prominently among the stakes of diplomacy and warfare among the city-states.

Without attempting to trace in detail the later history of the Greek State System, it should be noticed that the century following the Persian wars was marked by a tendency on the part of the more powerful city-states to extend their dominion over their weaker neighbors and allies to a point where their possessions assumed imperial dimensions by the standards of the time. An almost incessant military struggle for supremacy ensued among the various leagues and "empires" which were established. Under Themistocles, Athens built up a maritime league—the Delian Confederacy. This ultimately became an instrument through which the Athenians, by adroit use of diplomacy and military force, imposed their authority upon the other members. Sparta was likewise the center of the Peloponnesian League; and the two great coalitions, in their rivalry for control of the lesser cities, drifted toward war. The Athenian Empire under Pericles, with its allied States and dependencies, covered northeastern Greece, portions of the Peloponnesus, most of the Aegean islands for Euboea to Rhodes, the coasts of Thrace and Asia Minor, and the shores of the Sea of Marmora. An attempt to wrest Egypt from Persia ended in disaster in 454 B.C. Conflicts with Sparta took place from time to time, as well as wars against disgruntled allies. In 445 B.C., following Athenian reverses, the two leagues reached an agreement to submit future disputes to arbitration. The attempt of Pericles to establish a powerful land empire ended in failure, but the Athenian empire of the sea was increased by new conquests and colonies.

In 431 B.C. the truce was broken and the great Peloponnesian War began, with the Athenians striving to establish their hegemony and the Spartans professing to fight to free the Greeks from enslavement by Athens. Some States joined Athens, others Sparta; a few remained neutral. After many vicissitudes of battles, sieges, blockades, and diplomatic moves and countermoves, the Athenian cause was weakened by the disastrous expedition against Syracuse, the Sicilian colony of Corinth. Finally the Peloponnesian land and sea forces, under Lysander of Sparta, overcame the Athenians and obliged them to surrender in 404 B.C. Spartan hegemony was transitory, however, for the discontent of her allies, coupled with new wars with the Persians, led to a coalition against Sparta and her confederates on the part of Athens, Corinth, Argos, and Thebes. The last-named State achieved a position of equally temporary supremacy, followed by further chaos throughout Hellas which opened the way to foreign conquest by the Macedonians to the north. After preliminary conquests and diplomatic maneuvers, Philip of Macedon crushed the Greek forces at Chaeronea in 338 B.C. and established his power throughout the peninsula. With this event the Greek cities lost their independence for all time and the Greek State System came to an end.

Although the most obvious characteristic of this State System was the incessant struggle for power among its members and the constant resort to military coercion and diplomatic trickery to attain the ends of State, it developed certain international practices and institutions for pacific collaboration which were far in advance of their counterparts in earlier State Systems. The Greeks all acknowledged primary allegiance to their local State and were jealous of its sovereignty and power, but they were also aware of themselves as members of one race, with the same gods and a common culture, quite distinct from that of the outer "barbarians." This circumstance promoted intimate relations between them even when they were not threatened by a common enemy. The network of treaties which the States concluded with one another brought them at times very close to the conception of peace as a normal relationship between them. Treaties were always, in form at least, between equal and independent sovereignties and were sanctioned by Zeus, the guardian of oaths. They established the conditions of peace between the parties, sometimes in perpetuity, sometimes for a term of years. Commercial treaties were common, and a great variety of other subjects was dealt with in the numerous agreements which the city-states entered into. As early as the remote period of the Homeric epics, ceremonials had developed about the making of treaties which are described in the *Iliad* in the account of the compact between the Trojans and the Achaeans setting forth the conditions of the combat between Menelaus and Alexander for the love of Helen.[1] The divine sanction of treaties was always recognized by solemn oaths and imprecations. Heralds, ambassadors, secretaries, and a technical terminology became a regular part of the proceedings. Negotiations were usually public, though private conferences and even secret treaties were not unknown. Each party retained a copy in its own dialect, duly signed by the negotiators and stamped with the public seal of the signatory States. Treaty texts were often engraved on marble or bronze and kept in the temples. Hostages were frequently exchanged, especially in treaties of alliance, to ensure the execution of the compact. Treaties might legitimately be broken by one of the parties only if an inconsistency existed between two engagements, if enforcement would lead to hostilities with a friendly third State, or if a complete change of circumstances had taken place.

[1] The ceremonial embodied (1) a preliminary announcement by the heralds, (2) an invocation to the gods to bear witness to the transaction, (3) a declaration of oath, (4) a recital of the conditions of the engagement, (5) the offering of a sacrifice, (6) a libation of wine, (7) joining of hands, (8) the utterance of the imprecation: "Zeus, most glorious, most mighty, and ye other immortal gods! Whosoever shall first commit wrong contrary to their

The principles and procedures governing the exchange of diplomatic representatives also reached a high degree of development in the Greek State System. Though permanent embassies were not exchanged, a hierarchy of diplomatic agents developed in terms of rank and prestige. Only fully independent States had the right to send and receive ambassadors. Refusal to receive an envoy was analogous, in modern terms, to non-recognition of the sending State or to a rupture of diplomatic relations foreshadowing war. Envoys were received and dispatched by the popular assemblies, which likewise drew up their instructions. Only persons of distinction, wisdom, and ripe years were chosen. From an early period, all diplomatic representatives and their attachés enjoyed inviolability and exemption from local authority and were recognized to have the right to come and go as they pleased in the execution of their duties. A rudimentary consular service was likewise developed in the form of the institution of the *proxenoi*, who were permanent officials appointed to furnish commercial information to their home State and to give advice and assistance to its citizens abroad.

Though Greek scholars, jurists, and writers, including the prolific and versatile Aristotle, never treated in systematic form any body of law and custom comparable with modern international law, the actual practices of the city-states, as has already been suggested, were based upon general recognition of a body of rules and principles binding up the members of the State System. There was assumed to exist a universal "law of nature" or of reason to which all men were bound. Although there was, in regard to many matters, one law for the Greeks and another for the barbarians, the relations among the Greek States themselves were regulated by principles which closely approximate modern international law. The details of this somewhat inchoate system of jurisprudence cannot be dealt with here, but it covered such subjects as personal and property rights as affected by conflicting laws of various States ("private international law" in modern terminology), naturalization, status of aliens, right of asylum, extradition, alliances, treaties, diplomatic privileges and immunities, and the like. The international law of war was no less developed than that of peace.

Another feature of the Greek State System deserving of special mention was the extensive development of arbitration and of permanent institutions and agencies of international cooperation, foreshadowing what has come to be described as "international organization" in the Western State System of the contemporary period. The pacific settlement of disputes by submission to an impartial third party was a procedure

---

pledges, may their brains and their children's be dispersed on the ground, like this wine, and may their wives prove faithless." See Coleman Phillipson, *The International Law and Custom of Ancient Greece and Rome*, I, pp. 386–387.

familiar to the Greeks from the earliest times. It came to be resorted to so frequently and was developed to a point so far in advance of previous practice that it may well be regarded as one of the most significant contributions of the Greek State System to its successors. Disputes were often submitted to the arbitration of the Delphic oracle, the Amphictyonic Council, a third State, or a tribunal of individuals picked by the litigants. Treaties of alliance frequently contained "compromise clauses" providing for the submission to arbitration of such disputes as might arise between the parties. From an alliance to a confederation was but a step, and the Greek confederations and leagues often served as agencies for the peaceable adjustment of controversies among their members and for the promotion of cooperation in dealing with matters of common interest. The earliest confederations, or amphictyonies, were religious in character and were devoted to worship in common temples and the communal celebration of religious festivals. The antiquity of the Delphian Amphictyony, later called the Amphictyonic League, is attested by the fact that it was an association not of cities but of the twelve kindred tribes of the Greek peoples, each with two votes in the semiannual councils at Delphi and Thermopylae. This organization has sometimes been described, not without reason, as the Greek prototype of the League of Nations. In the course of its long history, it promoted religious unity among the Greeks, diminished the barbarities of war, arbitrated disputes, and subsequently became an instrument of Macedonian, and later of Roman, hegemony over the peninsula. The other Greek leagues and confederacies were true organizations of city-states, though in some cases they were approximations to modern federal governments and in others they were the means through which a powerful State dominated its weaker allies.[1] Such were the first and second Athenian leagues, the Peloponnesian League, and the Achaean League.

That the Greek State System never attained stability, unity, and peace and finally collapsed before foreign foes was due to the fact that its members, despite their common cultural heritage, were never capable over any long period of time of subordinating the special and particular interests of the local *polis* to the general interests of the Greek peoples as a whole. Under these circumstances the collectivity of States was incapable of harmonizing rival claims to power on the basis of the general interest. Although the clash of arms and the exaltation of city-state patriotism which accompanied it undoubtedly contributed to the rich profusion and fertility of Greek civilization, they rendered impossible the development of a type of inter-state political organization which could assure perma-

[1] In 1863 the English historian, E. A. Freeman, published his *History of Federal Government from the Establishment of the Achaean League to the Dissolution of the United States of America.*

nence to the System. In their days of decadence and exhaustion, when the bright radiance of the great creative period had burned itself out, the city-states fell easy victims to the power of Philip and Alexander of Macedon, rulers of a younger and more vigorous people to the north. Amid all the political changes of the ensuing centuries in the eastern Mediterranean, they never fully recovered their independence; and the peace between them was kept by the foreign conqueror.

This transition followed a design, unplanned but inexorable, which has reproduced itself in other Cultures, most notably in the modern West of our own age. On the surface the design was a product of the incapacity of the Greek commonwealths to combine effectively against external aggression. Below the surface, it was a manifestation of a slow process of change whereby the once vigorous and equalitarian mercantile democracy of the city-states was corroded by the complacency of the wealthy and by the unrest and indifference of the poor. This cleavage created a market for demagogues and despots. By destroying internal unity, it rendered the Greek States ripe for conquest. If Macedonia succeeded in doing what Persia had failed to do, the cause lay less in superiority of fighting power than in the inner enfeeblement of Greek democracy itself.

The confident faith of the Athenians in their own ideals, before the obvious advent of decline, was nowhere better expressed than in the oration of Pericles over the graves of those who first fell in the war with Sparta in 431 B.C.

Our military system is different from that of other peoples. Our city is open to the world; we have no laws excluding aliens; they can come here and learn and see what they like. It is true that an enemy may occasionally profit by this liberality, but we rely, when it comes to war, upon our own spirit rather than the devices of material armament. It is the same principle in our education. The Spartans from their childhood are laboriously drilled to become brave; we are free to live as we please, but are no less ready to face the same dangers. We combine love of beauty with simplicity and pursue things of the intellect without becoming unmanly. We set no store on wealth except as a means to an end. We consider it essential that public men should be ordinary citizens and that every ordinary citizen should play a part in the life of the community; for we differ from other people by regarding those who take no part in public life not as "quiet" but useless. Our method of government is government by discussion, for we believe that failure in action is not caused by discussion but by precipitate action not based on the knowledge which only discussion can give. The strongest-hearted are those who with the clearest vision of both the pleasant and unpleasant things in a situation do not shrink from facing it. Finally we have a standard of generosity peculiar to ourselves; we do good to our neighbors, not from calculations of self-interest, but from a fearless trust in freedom.

The Athenians of the age of Pericles responded quickly to such appeals and stood ready to defend themselves and the principles in which they believed. Thermopylae and Salamis were still living memories. The Greek way of life still seemed good to those who lived it. They deemed it worth living for and therefore worth dying for. Yet Athens was defeated by Sparta; and less than a century later the descendants of heroes, Athenians and Spartans alike, listened apathetically to Demosthenes (384–322 B.C.) when he warned them of the dangers of compromising and temporizing with Philip of Macedon. His words are still fresh.

Men of Athens, you must fix this firmly in your minds, that Philip is at war with us and has broken the peace. Let there be no more wrangling over that question. He is ill-disposed and hostile to the whole city and to the very soil on which the city stands and, I will add, to every man in the city, even to those who imagine that they stand highest in his good graces. If they doubt it, let them look at Euthycrates and Lasthenes, the Olynthians, who thought they were such bosom friends of his and then, when they had betrayed their city, met the most ignominious fate of all. The chief object, however, of his arms and his diplomacy is our free constitution: on nothing in the world is he more bent than on its destruction. And it is in a way natural that he should act thus. For he knows for certain that even if he masters all else, his power will be precarious as long as you remain a democracy; but if ever he meets with one of the many mischances to which mankind is liable, all the forces that are now under restraint will be attracted to your side. For nature has not equipped you to seek aggrandizement and secure empire, but you are clever at thwarting another's designs and wresting from him his gains, and quick to confound the plots of the ambitious and to vindicate the freedom of all mankind. Therefore he does not want to have the Athenian tradition of liberty watching to seize every chance against himself. Far from it! Nor is his reasoning here either faulty or idle.

This then is the first thing needful, to recognize in Philip the inveterate enemy of constitutional government and democracy, for unless you are heartily persuaded of this, you will not consent to take your politics seriously. Your second need is to convince yourselves that all his activity and all his organization is preparing the way for an attack on our city, and that where any resistance is offered to him that resistance is our gain. . . . But alas, ours is the one city in the world where immunity is granted to plead on behalf of our enemies, and where a man who has been bribed can safely address you in person, even when you have been robbed of your own. . . . You have passed from honor to dishonor, from affluence to destitution. For a city's wealth I hold to be allies, credit, good will, and of all of these you are destitute. Because you are indifferent to these advantages and allow them to be taken from you, Philip is prosperous and powerful and formidable while you are deserted and humiliated, famous for your well-stocked markets, but in provision for your proper needs, contemptible. . . .

At present our system is a mockery, and by heaven I do not believe that even Philip himself would pray that Athens might act otherwise than she is acting. You are behind your time and waste your money; you look round for someone to manage the business and then quarrel with him; you throw the blame on one another. . . . Never yet, Athenians, have you instituted or organized a single plan of action properly at the start, but you always follow in the track of each event, and then, when you find yourselves too late, you give up the pursuit; when the next event occurs, you are again in a bustle of preparation. But that is not the way. . . . You ask yourselves, "What is Philip going to do next?" The time has come when Philip should be asking himself, "What are the Athenians going to do next?" . . .

When men overthrow free constitutions and change them to oligarchies, I urge you to regard them as the common enemies of all who love freedom. Then again, Athenians, it is right that you, living under a democracy, should show the same sympathy for democracies in distress as you would expect others to show for you, if ever—which God forbid!—you were in the same plight. . . . Alliance and respect are willingly offered by all men to those whom they see ready and prompt to take action. And you too, men of Athens, if you are willing to adopt this principle, now if never before, if each citizen is ready to throw off his diffidence and serve the State as he ought and as he best may, the rich man paying, the strong man fighting, if, briefly and plainly, you will consent to become your own masters, and if each man will cease to expect that while he does nothing himself his neighbor will do everything for him, then, God willing, you will recover your own, you will restore what has been frittered away, and you will turn the tables upon Philip. . . . This Philip has not grown great through his own unaided strength so much as through our carelessness. . . .

I contend that we must send supplies to the forces in the Chersonese and satisfy all their demands, and while we make preparations ourselves, we must summon, collect, instruct, and exhort the rest of the Greeks. That is the duty of a city with the reputation such as yours enjoys. But if you imagine that Greece will be saved by Chalcidians or Megarians, while you run away from the task, you are wrong. For they may think themselves lucky if they can save themselves separately. But this is a task for you; it was for you that your ancestors won this proud privilege and bequeathed it to you at great and manifold risks. But if every man sits idle, consulting his own pleasure and careful to avoid his own duty, not only will he find no one to do it for him, but I fear that those duties that we wish to shirk may all be forced upon us at once.

These are my views and these are my proposals, and if they are carried out, I believe that even now we may retrieve our fortunes. If anyone has anything better to propose, let him speak and advise. But whatever you decide, I pray heaven it may be to your advantage.[1]

These appeals, like those of the opponents of appeasement in the Western democracies in the 1930's, fell on deaf ears. The Athens of the age of Philip, like France, Britain, and America in the age of Hitler, would do nothing in self-defense save what was too little and too late. The result was defeat and enslavement at the hands of Philip, Alexander, and later Caesars. Demosthenes took his own life when his countrymen were overwhelmed by the fate against which he had vainly sought to warn them.[2]

The two centuries which elapsed between the death of Philip of Macedon in 336 B.C. and the establishment of the supremacy of Rome saw the emergence of a new State System in the Near East out of the fragments of the great empire created by Philip's son, Alexander the

---

[1] These excerpts are taken from the Philippics and from other orations, all reproduced in Greek and in English in the Loeb Classical Library, *Demosthenes*, translated by J. H. Vince, New York, G. P. Putnam's Sons, 1930, *passim*.

[2] See "Isolationism: A Case-History" by Frederick H. Cramer, *Journal of the History of Ideas*, October, 1940.

Great. This extraordinary young man was perhaps the most spectacular military and administrative genius of all time. In his hands the art of war became for the first time an applied science. His Macedonian phalanxes overthrew and destroyed the might of Persia, and made him master of Greece, Asia Minor, Syria, Mesopotamia, Egypt, Babylonia, and a vastly greater territory to the east extending through what is now Persia, Turkestan, and Afghanistan to the borders of India. As ruler of the greatest empire thus far brought under the control of a single State, he sanctioned the deification of the royal office and became as a god. The interpenetration of cultures which followed his conquests led to the Hellenization of the western Orient and the partial orientalization of Greece. But death claimed this youth in 323 B.C., and the vast imperial structure which he had reared went with him to the tomb. Out of its ruins arose the Kingdom of the Ptolemies in Egypt, the realm of the Seleucids north of Arabia, the Kingdoms of the Arsacids and the Bactrians farther east, and a number of smaller States in Asia Minor. Macedonia remained the Great Power of the west, still dominating the Greek city-states. which were now divided into two rival federations, the Aetolian League and the Achaean League. Out of the struggles between the Succession States of the Alexandrine Empire a new balance of power emerged. The turbulent and colorful international politics of the Hellenistic Age led to a further development of the procedures and practices which earlier States had evolved in their relations with one another. An effete cosmopolitanism accompanied the intermingling of the decadent cultures, and the passing generations saw the twilight of a long decline slowly settling down over the peoples of the eastern Mediterranean basin.

Meanwhile, far to the west, a new sun was rising which was eventually destined to shine over the whole of the western civilized world. The remoter origins of the Roman State are obscure. It would appear that between the eighth and the fifth centuries B.C., when central Italy was dominated by the Etruscans, an alien community established itself on the banks of the Tiber. Myth and tradition later attributed its creation to the fabled Romulus and Remus or to wandering Trojans, survivors of the war with the Greeks, whose probably imaginary exploits were so beautifully described, many centuries later, in the great epic of Rome's greatest poet, the *Aeneid* of Virgil. The villages and towns of the Tiber achieved political unity under a monarchy whose later kings were conquering Etruscan despots.

Although the internal history of Rome during the ensuing period was a story of the foundation of Roman law and the gradual increase in political power of the plebeians at the expense of the ruling patrician class, its external history revolves about the great contest with Carthage and the subsequent extension of Roman power over the Mediterranean.

The Roman conquest of Italy disrupted the balance of power among the other States of the Mediterranean area. Carthage, empire of merchants and sailors, dominated the north African coast from Gibraltar to Egypt and exercised power over southern Spain, Malta, Sicily, and part of Sardinia. Roman intervention in the affairs of Syracuse led to the first clash of arms in 264 B.C. After prolonged hostilities, during which Hannibal, the great Carthaginian commander in the second Punic War (218–201 B.C.), invaded Italy and almost destroyed the Roman State, the legions at length triumphed. Spain was wrested from the enemy by Scipio, who carried the war into Africa and compelled the Carthaginians to sue for peace in 202 B.C. Carthage was compelled to pay a huge indemnity, to be spread over fifty years, was deprived of Numidia and all her non-African possessions, and was forbidden to wage any future wars without Rome's permission. Rome was now master of the middle sea and had achieved the position of the greatest military power of the ancient world.

Had the remaining independent States of the Mediterranean basin appreciated the ultimate menace to themselves which the Roman victory over Carthage represented, had they combined their forces against the strongest unit of the State System as balance-of-power considerations dictated, the legions of Rome might not have been able to achieve triumph after triumph along the road of empire and deprive them, one by one, of their independence. But this union of the weak against the strong was never consummated. Macedonia and Syria conspired to deprive Egypt of her possessions, and in the resulting complications Rome found her opportunity to interfere in the East. In 200 B.C. war was declared on Macedonia, with Rhodes, Pergamum, and the Greek leagues on the Roman side. In 197 B.C. the phalanx was conquered by the legion at Cynoscephalae and Macedonia was compelled to accept a Roman peace. When the Aetolian League invited Antiochus, King of Syria, to assist it in checking the power of Rome, war followed once more, with Rhodes and Pergamum again Roman allies (191). Antiochus was defeated and deprived of Asia Minor. In 146, following further conflicts, Macedonia was destroyed as an independent State and became a Roman province, and Rhodes and Pergamum were shortly afterward reduced to a similar status. The Greek leagues were dissolved; and though the fiction of the independence of certain of the city-states was retained for another century, Roman power was supreme in the Hellenic world. In 146 B.C. there also took place the last Punic War, culminating in the complete destruction of Carthage. The insistent injunction of Cato in the Senate— *Carthago delenda est!*—was thus at last fulfilled, and the territory of Rome's erstwhile enemy became the province of Africa.

Internal constitutional struggles among parties, factions, and classes within the metropolis hampered the further progress of imperial expansion, but only temporarily. In the Jugurthine War (112–106 B.C.), Numidia was almost lost and Italy itself was menaced by a new invasion of the Gauls from the northern forests. In both cases the day was saved by Marius, seven times consul of the Republic. The revolt of Mithridates VI, King of Pontus, led to a general rebellion of the Greeks against Roman rule; but under the leadership of Sulla the legions reestablished Rome's power in the Near East. Pompey completed the task which Sulla had begun and formed the First Triumvirate with Caesar and Crassus as its other members. Caesar, operating in Gaul (58–49 B.C.), carried Roman power to the Rhine and the Channel and even led his soldiers into Germany and Britain. Like his predecessors and rivals, Caesar used his military prestige to advance his political fortunes, overthrowing Pompey and making himself master of the Roman State. At the time of his murder in 44 B.C. Rome was already a world empire. At the close of the civil war which ensued, Octavius Augustus made himself *princeps*, or "First Citizen" (27 B.C.–A.D. 14). He extended Roman power over Egypt and the region south of the Danube and restored peace, order, and prosperity to the Roman world. The simplicity of the early Republic had already given way to the gaudy glory of military imperialism. "Princeps" became "Imperator." The name "Caesar" was taken as an imperial title, and the government of the Roman State became more and more absolutist. During the middle period of the third century, Franks, Goths, Moors, and other barbarians made damaging incursions into the Empire, but the great World State was reorganized, on the basis of the personal depotism of the emperor, by Diocletian (A.D. 284–305). Under Constantine (306–337) the capital was transferred to Byzantium (Constantinople), and in 392 Theodosius made Christianity the state religion. Three years later the Empire was completely divided into east and west, each with its own emperor, with one capital at Constantinople and the other at Milan or Ravenna.

As a universal State, Rome had no international relations. It had no contacts with the States of the Far East and few with those of India, and its relations with the quasi-states of the outer barbarians were never on a basis of equality. During its earlier history, however, before its legions had transformed the Mediterranean State System into a world empire, it had developed certain procedures and practices in its dealings with other States which are worthy of brief notice. Like most ancient peoples the Romans for a long period regarded themselves as being at war with all States with which no treaty of peace had been concluded. From the early days of Rome decisions of war and peace and the negotiation of treaties were entrusted to the College of Fetials (*collegium fetialium*). All wars were "just wars," declared and conducted in accordance with elaborate ceremonial rules and only after efforts at a pacific solution of the controversy had failed. If the *pater patratus* of the Fetials, acting as negotiator, failed to achieve a peaceful settlement, he so reported to the Senate. In the event of a decision for war, he hurled a bloody spear on the soil of the enemy to the accompaniment of appropriate oaths and invocations to Jupiter and other deities. As Rome expanded, the Fetials were represented by envoys and the ceremony of hurling the spear was performed, in purely symbolic fashion, on the Campus Martius or, later, before the temple of Bellona. The Fetials were also entrusted with the conclusion of treaties, but foreign envoys had audiences with the Senate during the month of February in the *Grecostiasis*, an open tribune near the Capitol. In the imperial period, the Emperor took over these functions. Almost all Roman treaties were unequal and in perpetuity in the sense that they imposed upon the other party a permanent status of dependence. The *ius gentium* of the Romans was not a body of true international law, but a set of legal principles adapted to the problems arising out of the relations of Roman citizens with citizens of other States which were friends or allies of Rome.

Despite the influence of Greek models upon them, the Romans never developed any conception of international law or relations based upon a system of independent States dealing with one another as equals. All was judged by Roman standards. The vision of world dominion was at all times, consciously or unconsciously, inherent in the attitudes and practices of the Roman State in its dealings with other peoples. The World Empire in its final form rested upon the extinction of the earlier States and State Systems by Roman military power. Though it was a huge international or cosmopolitan structure made up of very diverse elements, its whole organization and indeed its very existence precluded the possibility of those customs, procedures, and institutions of international intercourse which inevitably develop within a society of equal and independent political entities.

It was not without cause that the people of later ages came to view this great World State of the Caesars as the most magnificent political structure ever reared by the hand of man. At the time of its greatest territorial extent, under Trajan (A.D. 98–117), its forty-four provinces stretched from the borders of Scotland to the frontiers of India, from the Pillars of Hercules to the Black Sea and the Caucasus, from the Danube to the sands of the Sahara. It included within its confines all the Western civilized world and had a population, in the time of its greatest wealth and prosperity, of perhaps 100 million souls. Throughout all this vast area, threaded by well-built roads, ruled by the imperial bureaucracy, guarded by the power of the legions, the *Pax Romana* prevailed. The admin-

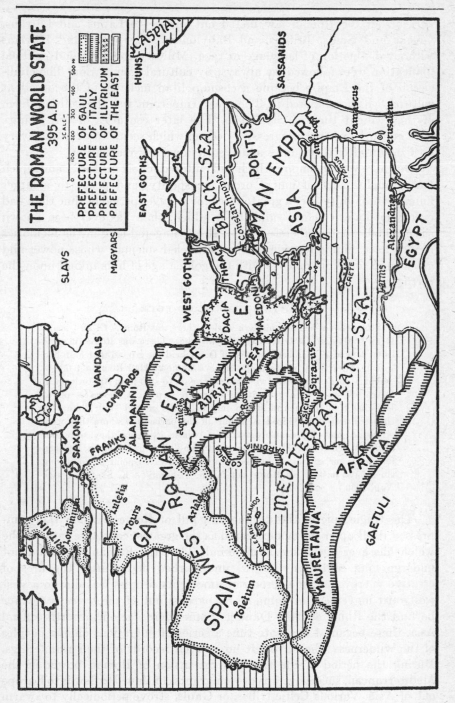

THE ROMAN WORLD STATE
395 A.D.

SCALE
0 100 200 300 400 500 M

PREFECTURE OF GAUL
PREFECTURE OF ITALY
PREFECTURE OF ILLYRICUM
PREFECTURE OF THE EAST

istrators of the Roman law meted out justice to Latins and Libyans, Greeks and Gauls, Britons and Babylonians, Egyptians and Illyrians without distinction of language or race. Military conquest and political unification were followed, as always, by cultural assimilation. The civilization of the Empire became a cosmopolitan mélange of the decadent cultures which composed it. The great Imperium was the political form of the twilight time of Classicism. The later centuries of the Empire were centuries of that progressive decline which seems to overtake every civilization after it has fully achieved its own self-realization.

But here was an empire which had endured for six centuries and which had brought more of unity, order, prosperity, and peace to a larger human community over a greater area for a longer period of time than had ever been known before—and, be it added, than has ever been known since. Small wonder, therefore, that Rome lingered long in the memories of men as a shining imperium of unparalleled splendor whose power and glory were contemporaneous with the golden age of humankind upon the earth.

4. THE SHADOW OF ROME

"Ours is not the first modern world—there was Rome." Of all I heard Dean Carlyle say at Oxford this I remember. There was Rome (it came to me long after) and had the men of Rome held the ground that Man had won then for Man, where might not we be now? Had Rome not fallen, would Man have needed two thousand years to step from Aristotle on to Descartes, and seven generations more to step from Descartes on to Darwin? Had the men of Rome only held this ground—but Rome fell, then fell not only civilized men, but all the barbarians whom they were civilizing, and American Redskins of whose existence they were not aware. When Rome fell, truly you and I and all of us fell down, for then fell down our species. It has not reached today the point it could long since have passed had Rome not fallen.—CLARENCE K. STREIT, *Union Now*, 1939.

The tragic epic of the decline and fall of Rome has inevitably impressed itself upon the modern mind as the greatest collective catastrophe which has ever overtaken humankind. That the Roman world did not undergo long centuries of slow, undisturbed decay after the fires of creative energy had smoldered out among its peoples was due to a vast westward movement of nomadic barbarians out of the *terrae incognitae* beyond the Rhine and the Danube. Somewhere, far off in north central Asia, there began at a remote time a series of migrations among peoples of the wilderness who have left no written records of their wanderings. During the period of the rise and expansion of Roman power in the Mediterranean, successive waves of migrants continued to flow into Europe out of Asia. Various Celtic tribes, or Gauls, strove periodically to swarm over the fertile countryside and into the gleaming cities of Greece and Italy, only to be beaten back by the superior military strength of the more civilized peoples of the south and to find their way finally into northwestern Europe. Behind the Gauls came the Germans—Teutons or Goths—behind the Germans the Slavs, and behind the Slavs the Finns, Huns, Avars, Magyars, Tartars, Mongols, and Turks.

The submergence of the Roman Empire by these wanderers from the east was a slow and gradual process, almost imperceptible in its early stages and finally completed in the fifth century only because the Empire itself had already become thoroughly permeated by barbarian peoples. From the time of Marcus Aurelius the Emperors had settled barbarian captives on the land as *coloni*, had taken them into the army when the Romans themselves had lost enthusiasm for military service, and had entered into alliances with the barbarians on the frontiers. When, in A.D. 376, the Emperor Valens admitted into the territory of the Empire a great horde of Visigoths who had been driven from their lands by the Huns, he was merely following the well-established policy of his predecessors. But the Visigoths rose in revolt, slew the Emperor and his legionaries, and ravaged Macedonia and Thrace to the gates of Constantinople. Theodosius made peace by settling them south of the Danube. Thirty year later, another Visigothic chieftain, Alaric, led his warriors across the Alps, devastated Italy, and sacked Rome (A.D. 410). The elevation of Alaric's successor, Atolf, to the command of the imperial armies by the Emperor Honorius is indicative of the impotence to which the Roman State had been reduced. Britain was evacuated by the legions, the distant frontiers crumbled before new foes, and barbarian hosts wandered almost unopposed through the provinces. Out of the east came the dreaded Huns under Attila, bent upon the complete destruction of the Empire and the creation of a great barbarian dominion. After Attila's hordes were beaten at Châlons-sur-Marne in 451, they invaded Italy, only to withdraw again into the eastern wilderness. The Vandals carried fire and sword through Gaul and Spain, occupied north Africa, crossed the sea, and sacked Rome once more in 455. In 476 the little six-year-old Emperor, Romulus Augustus, the last of the Emperors of the West, was deprived of his throne by Odoacer, chief of the mercenaries, and the imperial insignia were sent to Constantinople with the request that the Emperor Zeno permit Odoacer to administer Italy as a province of the Eastern Empire. This final "fall of Rome" was but an incident in a century of turmoil, but it marked the end of the Western Empire as a political entity.

But Rome dead was more powerful than Rome alive. The city itself remained the seat of the Papacy, which asserted and gradually established its spiritual supremacy over the Christianized barbarian kingdoms. The unity of western Christendom which had been disrupted by the collapse of the old Empire was revived by the growing power of the universal Church. The memory of the vanished universal State lingered on in the minds of the barbarians. The *Pax Romana* of the lost golden age became an ideal ever more desirable in the eyes of medieval mankind as it became ever more impossible of restoration. Catholic Christianity and this vision of order and peace under a universal State were the two great legacies which Classical civilization left to its heirs. The religious and political history of the long springtime of Western civilization—traditionally misnamed "the middle ages"—is largely the story of the Church and the "Empire"—the former a living reality of medieval life, the latter the unreal dream of a vanished past which could never be quite recovered. The new State System which rose on the ruins of Roman power was ever under the spell of the magic of the Popes and the legend of the world-wide Imperium of the Caesars.

At Byzantium the Eastern Empire was destined to endure for another thousand years until its mighty walls, often besieged and never breached, were pierced by the Osmanli Turks in 1453 and Constantinople (Istanbul) became the capital of the great Ottoman realm. At the beginning of the "Dark Ages" which followed the fall of the West the Eastern Empire was a beacon in the night. The Emperor Justinian (527–565) codified Roman law in its final form and sent his great general Belisarius to recover the Mediterranean world from the barbarians. Belisarius subdued the African kingdom of the Vandals (533–534), took Sicily and Rome (536), and reconquered Italy from the Gothic Kings. But the rescued provinces were soon inundated once more by hordes from the north, and the Byzantine Empire abandoned the West and looked to its own defenses against invaders from the Orient.

In time, however, as the barbarians settled on the land, absorbed the remnants of Roman culture, and embarked upon state building, new kingdoms and principalities emerged and conditions were ripe for the development of a new system of independent territorial States. But the vision of unity persisted and reached partial fulfillment three hundred years after the end of the Western Empire. The Kingdom of the Franks, established in what had been Roman Gaul, allied itself with the Papacy and gradually extended its power over its neighbors. The rise of the Frankish kingdom was contemporaneous with the appearance of a great new civilization in the Near East in the wake of the founding of Mohammedanism. When the armed apostles of Islam, having conquered Egypt, north Africa, and Spain with spectacular rapidity, pushed on to the north, it was the Franks who saved Christendom from Moslem conquest by defeating the Saracens at Tours in 732. At the end of the century the greatest of the Frankish kings, Charlemagne, had so widely extended his

control over the pagans that his realm reached from northern Spain
to the Baltic and from the Atlantic to the Oder. In 799 he restored Leo III
to the Holy See in Rome by frustrating the schemes of the Pope's rivals
and enemies. On Christmas day, A.D. 800, in the church of St. Peter at
Rome, the grateful Leo placed an imperial crown upon the head of
the Frankish monarch, while the populace shouted, "To Charles, the
Augustus, crowned by God, great and pacific emperor of the Romans, life
and victory!" Thus, with the sanction of the Papacy, the Empire was at
length restored by the power of Frankish arms and one emperor ruled
again over most of western Christendom.[1]

This restoration was ephemeral, however, and the medieval "empire"
was not finally established until another century and a half had elapsed.
The realm of Charles the Great fell to the weakest of his sons, Lewis the
Pious, in 814, and was promptly divided among the grandsons. Internecine
wars and further partitions followed, with the eastern, or German, portion
definitely separating itself from the western, or French, portion and with
both halves set upon during the ninth century by new invaders—Vikings
from the north, Magyars from the east, and Saracens from the south.
New rulers were crowned "Emperor" by the Popes, but their authority
was feeble. The imperial crown was finally transferred to a German king
in the person of Charles the Fat in 881. When Henry the Fowler, Duke of
the Saxons (the grave and stately monarch of Wagner's *Lohengrin*), was
elected king in 919 by the Saxon and Franconian nobles, he renounced
imperial ambitions and busied himself with beating back the Magyar
invaders and restoring some degree of order in his domains. His son Otto
continued the work with such success that he was able to extend his power
into Italy and in 962 was crowned Emperor by the Pope. The compact
between the Roman bishop and the German king laid the basis for what
later came to be called the "Holy Roman Empire of the German Nation"
(and still later the "First Reich")—a curious political structure with a
double sovereignty, resting upon the notion that the Empire and the

---

[1] David Jayne Hill aptly characterizes the significance of this ceremony as follows:
"The two figures before the high altar of St. Peter's on that Christmas day form a sym-
bolical picture of the whole course of history since the time of the Caesars. The Roman
and the German, the overshadowing past and the potential present, the universal and the
individual, the majesty of law and the vigor of liberty, the world of the spirit and the world
of actuality, imperial right and barbarian energy—all these are present, and all are henceforth to be combined as if swallowed up in one new creation. But it is the German who
kneels in pious devotion, the present which humbles itself before the past, the individual
who feels the power of the universal, the vigor of liberty which yields to the majesty of law,
the actual which seeks strength from the spiritual, and the barbarian who has been conquered by the Empire. It is the Roman who bestows the crown, the Roman who speaks in
the name of the divinity, the Roman whose transfigured republic is to profit by Rome's
latest conquest; for after centuries of suffering, toil, tragedy, it is the triumph of Rome's
work which is before us." *A History of Diplomacy in the International Development of Europe,*
I, pp. 95–96.

Papacy were respectively the temporal and spiritual agencies designated by the divine will for the governance of Christendom.

To trace through the subsequent history of this ramshackle creation of medieval statesmanship would be of little value here except to reveal the persistence with which the ideal of imperial unity was adhered to during many generations. The imperial crown passed to the House of Hohenstaufen and later to the House of Hapsburg, where it remained until the extinction of the Empire in 1806. The theory of the Empire as the successor of the Roman World State was not much modified either by the great conflicts between Popes and Emperors for supremacy or by the fact that the Empire had no effective authority outside of the German States and Italy. Even in these regions the imperial power was constantly flouted by the great dukes, the unruly principalities, and the turbulent free cities. Such powers as the Emperor wielded he derived less from his imperial office than from the lands and subjects which he controlled as a German king among many kings. It could almost be said of the Empire from the beginning what Voltaire said of it in the eighteenth century: that it was neither Holy nor Roman nor an Empire. It existed in the world of theological speculation and political metaphysics rather than in the world of fact. It was the most perfect expression of medieval mysticism and scholasticism applied to world politics. It was the ghost of ancient Rome which would not be laid but insisted upon stalking ceaselessly across the stage of the middle ages between classical and modern civilization. The firm hold which the theory of imperial unity secured on the hopes and imaginations of men is explicable in terms of a deep yearning for peace and order in a world of endless war and confusion. But the political and social structure of western society in medieval Europe doomed that yearning to perpetual frustration. The medieval political theorist and statesman became a new Tantalus, constantly groping for that which lay beyond his reach, constantly striving to realize an ideal which the conditions of the time put past all realization.

Nowhere in medieval political literature is this tragedy more poignantly expressed than in the *De monarchia* of Dante Alighieri, jurist, statesman, poet, and author of the immortal *Divine Comedy*. His great political essay has accurately been described by Lord Bryce as the "epitaph of the Holy Roman Empire." It is indeed a last cry of despair, a last plea for unity in a world of inescapable diversity. It represents both the culmination and the close of medieval political theorizing on international relations. A brief consideration of its message and of the circumstances which produced it will constitute an appropriate conclusion to this discussion of the medieval ideal of the world-wide Imperium.

The *De monarchia* was written about 1309, twelve years before Dante's death, at the period of the "Babylonian Captivity" of the

Papacy, when the Popes were residing at Avignon under the surveillance of the French monarchy, when no Emperor had visited Italy for over half a century, and when the Italian city-states were waging chronic war upon one another for power and territory. Great hopes were entertained that the newly elected Emperor, Henry VII, would come to Italy for his coronation and would restore peace to the land. Dante, as a practical student of law and government and as one who had served on several Florentine embassies and who was not, therefore, unfamiliar with diplomatic problems, shared this hope and wrote his famous essay as a defense of the Empire and as an appeal for general recognition of its supremacy. In allegorical and scholastic style, he presented the arguments in favor of his ideal.

Whole heaven is regulated by a single ruler—God. It follows that the human race is at its best state when it is ruled by a single prince and one law. So it is evidently necessary for the welfare of the world that there should be a single monarchy or princedom, which men call the Empire. Whenever disputes arise, there must be judgment. Between any two independent princes controversy may arise and then judgment is necessary. Now an equal cannot rule over his equal, so there must be a third prince of wider jurisdiction who is ruler over both, to decide the dispute. This third ruler must be the monarch or Emperor. And so monarchy is necessary for the world. . . . Moreover, the world is ordered best when justice is most powerful, and justice is most powerful under a monarchy or empire.

Dante cited the age of Augustus as the golden age of mankind and concluded with a dramatic exhortation, colored by pessimism and a half-confessed realization of the futility of the poet's aspirations.

But how the world has fared since that "seamless robe" (the Roman Empire) has suffered rending by the talons of ambition, we may read in books; would that we might not see it with our eyes. Oh, race of mankind! What storms must toss thee, what loss must thou endure, what shipwrecks must buffet thee, as long as thou, a beast of many heads, strivest after contrary things! Thou art sick in both thy faculties of understanding; thou art sick in thy affections. Unanswerable reasons fail to heal thy higher understanding; the very sight of experience convinces not thy lower understanding; not even the sweetness of divine persuasion charms thy affections, when it breathes unto thee through the music of the Holy Spirit: "Behold how good and how pleasant it is for brethren to dwell together in unity!"

But the hope was vain. Henry came to Italy and was crowned by agents of the Pope at Rome. He brought not peace, but a sword. Rome itself was torn by the struggles between Guelfs and Ghibellines. The Emperor and Pope, whom Dante had envisaged as two facets of a single perfect entity, quarrelled violently in words and in arms. Henry was placed under the ban of the Church by Clement V at Avignon, who was supported by the King of France in rendering aid to Robert of Naples and the cities of the north which resisted the imperial power. Henry laid unsuccessful siege to Florence and died in 1313, carrying with him to the grave all prospects of restoring the prestige of the Empire in Italy. The peninsula, like all Europe, was a welter of warring States, with the Empire but a specter of half-forgotten yesterdays.

5. THE DAWN OF THE WEST

> All nations of the west are of dynastic origin. In the Romanesque and even in Early Gothic architecture the soul of the Carolingian primitives still quivers through. There is no French or German Gothic, but Salian, Rhenish, and Suabian, as there is Visigothic (northern Spain, southern France) and Lombard and Saxon Romanesque. But over it all there spreads soon the minority, composed of men of race, that feels membership in a nation as a great historical vocation. From it proceed the Crusades, and in them there truly were French and German chivalries. It is the hallmark of Faustian peoples that they are conscious of the direction of their history.—OSWALD SPENGLER, *The Decline of the West*, II.

The plea of the great Italian poet for unity and peace through the reestablishment of the Empire was a typically medieval appeal in behalf of an ideal which had long since become something less than the shadow of a dream. Almost all the thinkers of the middle ages who indulged in speculation on international affairs looked backward in similar fashion to an age long dead and to a scheme of world organization which was never to be restored.

Here, as in so many phases of medieval thought, a wide chasm yawned between ideal and reality, theory and practice, literature and life, spirit and flesh. But the business of living went on, undisturbed by this dilemma, until finally the visionaries and scholastics returned to earth and awakened from their melancholy reminiscences to find themselves living on a new earth under a new heaven.

For a thousand years before this awakening, there had been developing a new State System and a new international life no less rich and colorful for having been largely ignored by the intelligentsia. As soon as the Western Empire dissolved into political fragments and the barbarian kingdoms were established in its stead, the stage was set for a drama not dissimilar to that which had been played by the independent States of the Mediterranean basin before Rome became supreme. Again there were contacts between States which were, for all practical purposes, independent, despite theories of imperial vassalage entertained by their rulers. Again geographically separated communities, uncontrolled by any single central authority, were free to bargain, trade, and fight with one another. Out of their relationships emerges the old design of the ancient State Systems, overlaid by the pattern of the dead Rome of the Caesars and the living Rome of the Popes.

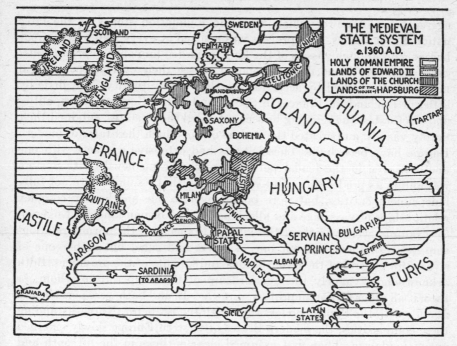

THE MEDIEVAL
STATE SYSTEM
c. 1360 A.D.
HOLY ROMAN EMPIRE
LANDS OF EDWARD III
LANDS OF THE CHURCH
LANDS OF THE HOUSE OF HAPSBURG

Following the rise of the institutions of feudalism throughout western Europe during the ninth and tenth centuries, the medieval State System became a congeries of feudal principalities whose contacts with one another were overlaid by complex feudal relationships. Feudalism was at once a form of land tenure, a scheme of government, and an economic and social system. With the disappearance of all central authority through internal conflicts and new barbarian invasions following the death of Charlemagne, political power in each locality passed to those who were mighty with sword and mace. The mass of the population sought safety from marauding bands by subordinating itself to those able to afford protection. The warrior class became the landowning class, and this new ruling caste transformed itself into a true feudal aristocracy. Barons, dukes, counts, and bishops administered their land like private estates. Royal authority almost vanished; and power rested with the local nobility, lay and ecclesiastical. Throughout Europe the fragmentation of economic and political power made war and diplomacy matters of concern to each noble and his neighbors rather than to well-defined political entities possessing the attributes of statehood. Each tiny unit was far smaller in size and power than the units of a city-state system, and the result was an incredibly complex and anarchical jungle of feudal confusion.

Despite these characteristics of the feudal age, the most powerful of the nobles became kings, established dynasties, and gradually built up aggregations of power which were the foundation stones of the later national monarchies. This process was resisted at every step by the great barons who, though vassals of the king, regarded him only as *primus inter pares* and were in no degree disposed to see their own power as local magnates diminished by accretions to the royal authority. Yet, little by little, in England, in France, in Spain, and in the German principalities and electorates, the reigning houses extended their estates, subdued their unruly vassals, and created the realms out of which the States of modern Europe have been built. These States had extensive contacts with one another, even in the feudal period, though the medieval State System was unlike its predecessors and successors in that its units were not fully independent entities, but were bound over to one another by complex relationships of vassalage and allegiance. The Norman kings of England, for example, were vassals of the king of France, but the normal relationship between them was not one of rulers and ruled but rather one of rivalry for control of the lesser barons and knights of the provinces. Both acknowledged vaguely the overlordship of the Emperor, to whom, in theory, all other Christian princes were vassals, and both were periodically at odds with the Papacy no less than with the Emperor. Notwithstanding these complexities, the modern States of western Europe slowly emerged out of feudalism. They first assumed clear outlines in the fifteenth and sixteenth centuries, when the kings, with the support of the burghers of the growing cities, demolished the power of the feudal baronage and made themselves absolute monarchs over unified nations. By this time the rudiments of international practice were well established, and the Western State System had been born.

The role of the Church in this process was of great significance. It long continued to symbolize the unity of the Christian world. The Pope was not merely the spiritual head of Christendom but exercised temporal powers as well, both as ruler of the Papal States in central Italy and as the Vicar of Christ upon earth with power over emperors, kings, and princes. As kings were crowned by the bishops of the Church, the Emperor was crowned by the Pope himself. He who gives is superior to him who receives. The Papacy not only asserted its authority over temporal rulers in all matters, both lay and ecclesiastical, concerning the administration of their realms, but offered its services as arbitrator to settle disputes between them. Such offers were often coupled with insistence upon acceptance, which gave to papal arbitrations the character of interventions. This arbitral procedure was widely utilized, particularly as between the princes of the Italian States. The national monarchies of the west likewise resorted to it. Among the more famous of the papal arbitrations were those between Philip le Bel and the English king (1298), between Philip le Long and the Flemings (1319), between the Emperor Maximilian and the Doge of Venice in the fifteenth century, and between Spain and Portugal regarding their claims in the New World in 1494. Nonecclesiastical arbitration was also developed as a means of settling disputes by the Swiss cantons, the cities of the Hanseatic League, the German States, and even by the English and French monarchies[1]; but the Papacy may properly be regarded as having made the greatest contributions to the institution of international arbitration during the period.

The Church likewise played an important part in the development of diplomatic practices and of the rudimentary international law which gradually came to be recognized by the various European States. From early times the Popes had dispatched envoys (*legati*) to attend Church councils and had regularly maintained ambassadors at the Byzantine court known as *apocrisiarii* until relations were severed between Constantinople and the Holy See in consequence of religious differences. Similar representatives were exchanged between the Vatican and the exarch at Ravenna. Later the Popes sent special envoys to the Emperor and to the courts of England, France, Naples, Hungary, Aragon, Castile, and other States. Ecclesiastical influence was also considerable in the development of Byzantine diplomacy which, in turn, greatly influenced the diplomatic practices of the Italian city-states in the fourteenth century. As regards international law, the Archbishop of Seville, St. Isadore, was writing as early as the seventh century, in his *Etymologies*, of the *ius gentium* of the Romans as a body of law having to do with "wars, captivities, enslavements, the recovery of rights of postliminy, treaties of peace and others, the scruple which protects ambassadors from violence, and prohibition of marriage between persons of different nationality." The efforts of the Church to restrict private warfare and protect noncombatants led to a marked development of what later came to be known as the international law of war and neutrality. In insisting upon the observance of the "Truce of God," the Church forbade fighting on Sunday. In the eleventh century efforts were made to extend the period of Sabbath peace from Wednesday evening to Monday morning and to apply it to religious holidays and to the whole period of Lent. In 1095 Pope Urban II decreed it for all Christendom in this form. The *pax ecclesiae* forbade fighting in the vicinity of church buildings or against clerics, pilgrims, merchants, women, or peasants, thus neutralizing certain areas and protecting certain categories of persons from the rigors of war.

If ecclesiastical anathemas and excommunications were not always effective in restraining the pugnacity of the embattled baronage, these efforts were nevertheless of great influence on later thought and practice and, coupled with certain other developments of the period, contributed

[1] See J. H. Ralston, *International Arbitration from Athens to Locarno*, 1929, pp. 176–178, for types of medieval arbitration treaties.

toward the weaving together of the warp and woof of customs, laws, practices, and institutions which are the fabric of modern diplomacy. As neighborhood warfare declined under the pressure of clerical persuasion and kingly power, towns grew and waxed prosperous through the wider commercial contacts which peace made possible. The Hanseatic trading cities of the north and the city-states of the Mediterranean maritime leagues built up a flourishing commerce which they fostered by exchanging commercial or consular representatives and by concluding numerous commercial treaties with one another. Political representatives followed on the heels of trading agents and therewith the modern diplomatic service was established. International maritime law also evolved out of these relationships and received its first clear statement in the *Consolato del Mare* of the fourteenth century, which the Italian mercantile States accepted as a guide in their trade relations. Another development contributing to the same result was the launching of the great Crusades to rescue the Holy Land from the infidels. These high adventures brought the rough warriors of western Europe into conflict with Saracen knights who fought like gentlemen. Chivalry was born and war became no longer a matter of cruel bludgeoning, rapine, and wanton destruction but a science and an art to be practiced in accordance with fixed rules. Travel increased with trading and crusading. Feudal provincialism declined and governments were brought into closer contact with one another. The dream of imperial unity gradually faded, and the new city-states and national monarchies dealt with one another as equal and independent political entities. Out of these new contacts between larger territorial units emerged a further development of the procedures and institutions of diplomacy, the usages and practices of international law, and the attitudes and values which underlie modern statecraft.

SUGGESTED READINGS

Bey, Essad: *Mohammed*, New York, Longmans, 1938.
Boas, Franz: *The Mind of Primitive Man*, New York, Macmillan, 1939.
Bryce, James: *The Holy Roman Empire*, New York, Macmillan, 1914.
Cambridge Medieval History, New York, Macmillan, 1913.
Davie, M. R.: *The Evolution of War*, New Haven, Yale University Press, 1929.
Graves, R.: *I, Claudius*, New York, Random, 1936.
———: *Claudius the God*, New York, Random, 1937.
———: *Count Belisarius*, New York, Random, 1938.
Hill, D. J.: *A History of Diplomacy in the International Development of Europe* (3 vols.), New York, Longmans, 1924.
Homo, L. P.: *Roman Political Institutions*, New York, Knopf, 1929.
Jouguet, P.: *Macedonian Imperialism*, New York, Knopf, 1928.
Lasswell, H. D.: *Politics—Who Gets What, When, How*, New York, McGraw-Hill, 1936.
Laski, H. J.: *The Foundations of Sovereignty*, New York, Harcourt, 1921.
Lowie, R. H.: *The Origins of the State*, New York, Harcourt, 1927.
MacLeod, W. C.: *The Origin and History of Politics*, New York, Wiley, 1931.
Merriam, C. E.: *Political Power—Its Composition and Incidence*, New York, McGraw-Hill, 1934.

Moret, A.: *From Tribe to Empire*, New York, Knopf, 1926.

Oman, C. W.: *A History of the Art of War in the Middle Ages* (2 vols.), London, Methuen, 1924.

Oppenheimer, F.: *The State*, Indianapolis, Bobbs-Merrill, 1912.

Phillipson, C.: *The International Law and Custom of Ancient Greece and Rome* (2 vols.), London, Macmillan, 1911.

Pirenne, H.: *Mohammed and Charlemagne*, trans. by Bernard Miall, New York, Norton, 1939.

Rostovtzeff, M.: *The Social and Economic History of the Hellenistic World*, 3 vols., New York, Oxford, 1941.

Sanford, E. M.: *The Mediterranean World in Ancient Times*, New York, Ronald Press, 1940.

Sellery, G. C., and A. C. Krey: *Medieval Foundations of Western Civilization*, New York, Harper, 1929.

Stevers, M.: *Mind through the Ages: A History of Human Intelligence*, New York, Doubleday Doran, 1941.

Thompson, J. W.: *Economic and Social History of the Middle Ages*, New York, Appleton-Century, 1928.

Tod, M. N.: *International Arbitration among the Greeks*, London, Clarendon Press, 1913.

Turner, R. E.: *The Great Cultural Traditions*, New York, McGraw-Hill, 1940.

Wilson, F. W.: *The Elements of Modern Politics*, New York, McGraw-Hill, 1936.

CHAPTER II

THE RISE OF THE WESTERN STATE SYSTEM

1. THE REBIRTH OF REALPOLITIK

We are much beholden to Machiavel and others, that write what men do, and not what they ought to do.—FRANCIS BACON, *Proficience and Advancement of Learning.*

MODERN diplomacy was born in northern Italy. Here there existed from the twelfth century onward a microcosmic State System that was in almost all respects a miniature of the larger State System of western Europe as a whole which made its appearance some two centuries later. The Italian city-states of the later middle ages and the Renaissance created the matrix in which modern statecraft was conceived.

After the thirteenth century the city-states of Italy were free alike from any effective threat of external control and from any possibility of unification by any one of their number. Under these circumstances they inevitably evolved a complex pattern of relationships with one another and developed the art of diplomacy to a higher level than had ever been known elsewhere in western Christendom. The Republic of Venice— "school and touchstone of ambassadors"—perhaps contributed most to this development because of its far-flung commercial interests and its contacts with the sophisticated, if decadent, Eastern Roman Empire. At a remote period the Venetian authorities began the practice of registering treaties, keeping diplomatic archives, and maintaining an elaborate system of commissions, written instructions, records, and dispatches in their contacts with diplomatic representatives abroad. By a law of 1268 a Venetian ambassador was forbidden to take his wife along on missions, lest she divulge his business, but required to take his cook along, lest he be poisoned. The *Consolato del Mare*, based upon the ancient "Tables of Amalfi," was solemnly approved by the Venetian representatives in Constantinople in 1255 as the basis of maritime international law and was later adopted by Pisa, Genoa, Naples, Aragon, and the States of northern and western Europe. The ceremonies which the Venetians developed for the reception and dispatch of diplomatic representatives influenced the practice of other States to a great degree. Envoys were carefully selected from the ranks of the nobility, until Venetian ambassadors became models of honesty, competence, and *savoir-faire*.

In other states as well the diplomatic profession attracted to it the service of distinguished and learned men. The diplomatic service of Florence during the thirteenth and fourteenth centuries included such illustrious names as Dante, Petrarch, Boccaccio, and Guicciardini. Diplomatic missions were at first limited to two or three months' duration and later extended to several years. Not until the middle of the fifteenth century did the practice become prevalent of maintaining permanent and regular diplomatic posts at the seats of foreign governments. The first clear instance of this kind was the establishment of a permanent embassy at Genoa by Milan in 1455. Various ranks of diplomatic agents were recognized, though there was much confusion on this point and no uniformity of practice.

This structure of diplomatic practices and usages was, of course, based upon the existence of a number of independent territorial States, free from external control and able to pursue their own interests by bargaining and fighting with one another. Here, as always in such a State System, each unit pursued such objectives as best served the interests of its ruling class; and these objectives involved in each case a maximum extension of the territory and power of the State at the expense of its rivals. International politics was a competitive struggle for power, a war of each against all, an uneasy equilibrium in which the weak combined against the strong in order to maintain a balance of power in which no one State could become so powerful as to threaten the independence of the others. Dante might deplore the resulting chaos and plead for unity. Other reflective souls might call, despairingly, for solidarity, as did an obscure priest of Milan: "And thou, Milan, thou seekest to supplant Cremona, to overthrow Pavia, to destroy Novara. Thy hands are raised against all, and the hands of all against thee. . . . Oh, when shall the day dawn in which the inhabitants of Pavia shall say to the Milanese: 'Thy people are my people,' and the citizen of Novara to the Cremonese: 'Thy city is my city'!"[1] All in vain. Each prince pursued his own interests. Each community was fired with local patriotism and looked upon its neighbor as a potential enemy or as a possible ally against an enemy still more dangerous. Republicanism gave way to princely absolutism as each city, in constant rivalry with its neighbors, perceived the advantages of concentrating diplomatic and military power in a single hand. Diplomacy and war were the means to power. War required money and the services of the *condottieri*. Diplomacy required secrecy, espionage, plot and counterplot, and a nice sense of the imponderable interrelationships and the fleeting opportunities for the enhancement of the power of the commonwealth. The prestige and power, the glory and aggrandizement of the local State became the supreme concern of government and all means thereto were justified.

[1] Quoted in D. J. Hill, *History of Diplomacy*, I, p. 359.

At last a great spokesman emerged who, first among political observers, comprehended the realities of the State System in which he lived. His name has become a symbol and his work may well be regarded as marking the conscious beginning both of modern diplomacy and of political science. Niccolò Machiavelli was born in Florence, May 5, 1469, into an ancient and honorable family which had long and faithfully served the State under whose authority it resided. He reached manhood near the close of the reign of the magnificent Lorenzo de' Medici. He was a republican who gladly entered the service of the Florentine Republic after the French invaders under Charles VIII had brought about the overthrow of the Medici in 1494. While the Florentines rallied to the puritanical Savonarola, then turned against him and put him to death, and engaged in a fierce and fascinating game of political intrigue among rival factions, young Niccolò turned his talents to defending and promoting the power of the Republic through the arts of diplomacy. He went on missions to Caterina Sforza, to Cesare Borgia, to Louis XII, to Pope Julius II, to the Emperor Maximilian. Little escaped his shrewd eye in the course of his work and his travels. In 1512 the forces of the Papacy drove the French from Italy. Florence was allied with France. In defeat the Republic perished. The Medici were restored. Thus Machiavelli "found himself at the age of 43 a dejected liberal without a job in a world that had come tumbling down about his ears."[1]

Machiavelli was suspect. An abortive conspiracy of 1513 led to his arrest and torture, though he was innocent. Upon his release from prison, he retired to a small farm near Florence. Since his efforts to return to public life by seeking the favor of the Pope and the Medici were fruitless, he wrote stories, plays, poetry, and several books filled with the distilled political wisdom of his own experience: *The Prince, The Art of War, Discourses on Livy, The History of Florence*. In 1527 soldiers of Charles V defeated the papal armies and sacked Rome. In Florence the Medici were temporarily ousted by the democratic faction. Despite his serious illness, Machiavelli hastened to the city to regain his post. The council, however, voted against his reappointment. But death came to him before he learned of this last failure of his hopes. And in death he found a place among the immortals not by the public service which he loved but by the writing with which he had relieved the ennui of his idle and lonely years.

The Prince has earned for its author the opprobrium of all right-thinking moralists and has come to be viewed as the most eloquent exhortation to the vices of trickery, treachery, unscrupulousness, and dishonesty to which modern diplomacy has fallen heir. In fact, it was nothing more than a realistic account of the behavior of States toward one another, with a

---

[1] Max Lerner, Introduction, p. xxvii, to *The Prince* and *The Discourses* by Niccolò Machiavelli, The Modern Library, New York, Random House, 1940.

wealth of contemporary and historical illustrations, coupled with a set of maxims for the guidance of rulers seeking power in the type of State System with which Machiavelli was familiar. It contains, in small compass, as he declares in his dedication to Lorenzo, grandson of the Magnificent, "all the experience I have acquired during many years of continual meditation and suffering in the school of adversity." Far from being immoral, it is entirely unconcerned with ethics and regards the State as beyond good and evil—an end in itself for the service of which all means are legitimate. Political expediency is the criterion of State action.

Machiavelli opens his most famous work with a description of different types of States and of the problems involved in state building. A prince may establish firm control over newly conquered lands by colonizing his own people on them, by establishing garrisons, by playing off neighboring princes against one another, and the like. Those who are injured thereby should be disposed of with dispatch, lest they become dangerous enemies —for a man "may revenge a slight injury, but a great one deprives him of his power to avenge." Desire for aggrandizement is a natural characteristic of rulers. "Nothing is so natural or so common as the thirst for conquest, and when men can satisfy it, they deserve praise rather than censure. But when they are not equal to the enterprise, disgrace is the inevitable consequence." And the power for which princes strive is a relative quantity. "The prince who contributes toward the advancement of another power, ruins his own." Monarchies must be conquered by superior force and then can be easily held, since once the reigning dynasty is disposed of, none remains to oppose the conqueror. Aristocracies can be conquered by intrigue among the nobles, but once in power the conqueror will encounter "an infinity of difficulty, not only from the conquered, but from those who have assisted in the enterprise." Free States may be subdued only by ruining them, by colonizing them, or by permitting them to remain in the enjoyment of their own laws. The difficulties of rulership which princes encounter vary with the means by which they have acquired power. "The usurper of a State should commit all the cruelties which his safety renders necessary at once, that he may never have cause to repeat them . . . for when time is allowed for resentment, the wound is not so deep; but benefits should be frugally dispensed, and by little at a time, that they may be the better relished." A wise prince will not only make himself a master of warfare but win over his subjects to him by being liberal, without being prodigal, and merciful without being weak. "It is safer to be feared than be loved, for it may truly be affirmed of mankind in general, that they are ungrateful, fickle, timid, dissembling, and self-interested." But the prince must avoid earning the hatred of his subjects. This can be achieved by respecting his subjects' property and the honor of their wives, "for it is certain that men sooner forget the death of their relations than the loss of their patrimony."

Since force and trickery are twin tools for the acquisition and retention of power, the prince must make the lion and the fox his models. "A prudent prince cannot and ought not to keep his word, except when he can do it without injury to himself, or when the circumstances under which he contracted the engagement still exist." It is unnecessary that a prince should possess many good qualities but indispensable that he should appear to have them, "as men in general judge more from appearances than from reality. All men have eyes, but few have the gift of penetration. . . . The vulgar are ever caught by appearances, and judge only by the event. And as the world is chiefly composed of such as are called the vulgar, the voice of the few is seldom or never heard or regarded." A prince should choose his ministers with care and avoid flatterers. The volume closes with an exhortation to Lorenzo to free Italy of foreigners, meaning the French invaders. "Every war that is necessary is just; and it is humanity to take up arms for the defense of a people to whom no other recourse is left."

The long shadow which *The Prince* of Machiavelli has cast down the succeeding centuries is attributable less to the influence of the work on the thought of its day or to the pungency of the author's wisdom than to the fact that his maxims reflected the fundamental nature of the new Western State System which existed in miniature in the Italy of the Renaissance. That State System rested upon the unlimited and uncontrolled sovereignty of the territorial State and upon the principle of the balance of power through which each State checkmated its rivals. The ruler of each unit inevitably strove to protect and further his own interests by force, when force was expedient, by trickery, when force was unnecessary. "To reign is to dissimulate," declared Louis XI of France. "If they lie to you," he admonished his ambassadors, "lie still more to them." The power of the State justified all means necessary for its enhancement. The political relations between States had again become a competitive struggle for power, and the vision of imperial unity receded into the past.

The old pattern, characteristic of all State Systems made up of independent territorial units, had reemerged, first in Italy and later throughout western Europe. The new national monarchies dealt with one another precisely as did the Italian city-states—and neither Pope nor Emperor could say them nay. The Empire was by now a phantom. The Papacy was impotent—in part because the Renaissance Popes were themselves rulers and diplomats who used the same methods for increasing their power as did the lay princes, in part because the forces of revolt against papal Catholicism were already gathering about the person of a German monk, Martin Luther, in preparation for the last great schism of the Reformation which was to shatter for all time the ecclesiastical unity of the Christian world. The great States of the modern age were in process of being born—and the politics which they practiced toward one another were then, and have ever since been, "Machiavellian politics" in the broadest sense of a much-abused phrase. In this fashion *The Prince* symbolized a new dispensation, and the humble servant of the Florentine Republic became the prophet of a new epoch.

2. SOVEREIGNTY AND LAW

With regard to the relations of States among themselves, their sovereignty is the basic principle; they are in that respect in the state of nature in relation to one another, and their rights are not realized in a general rule which is so constituted as to have power over them, but their rights are realized only through their particular wills.—GEORGE HEGEL.

The concept of State sovereignty, the principles of international law, and the politics of the balance of power may be regarded as the three cornerstones upon which the Western State System has come to rest. The first has been elevated to the dignity of a political theory and later to that of a juristic idea underlying the whole structure of modern international jurisprudence. The second has evolved into a system of public law in the community of nations. The third has become an avowed principle of foreign policy, accepted and acted upon so consistently by all the great States that it may well be viewed as the central theme about which the web of diplomacy is woven.

It was not until powerful aggregations of centralized power had been built up by the western dynasts that a systematic presentation of the philosophical basis of political authority became possible. The turbulent feudal aristocracy was gradually subordinated to the authority of absolutist kings and princes who preserved the ruling class and protected its interests without permitting it to interfere with an effective central administration. As soon as the new monarchs sought ethical justification for their policies, they found jurists and scholars at hand to supply them with the ideational paraphernalia requisite to make the cause of absolutism intellectually respectable. Though Machiavelli postulated the absolute sovereignty of the territorial State in relation to its neighbors, he did not discuss the location of sovereign power within the State, nor was he interested in the problem from a legal and juristic point of view. It fell to the French scholar, Jean Bodin, to formulate the first systematic presentation of the concept of sovereignty in its modern form in his *De republica* of 1586—a title which must be literally translated as "Concerning Public Affairs," since its author, far from being a republican, was an apologist of the purest absolutism. Bodin, in fact, devised the political theory upon which the French monarchy was to rest its case for unlimited

[45]

and autocratic central power. Sovereignty he defined as *unlimited power over citizens and subjects, unrestrained by law*. This power, he insisted, is by its nature absolute, unqualified, perpetual, and indivisible and resides not in the whole State but in the body of the citizenry in a democracy, in the estate of the nobility in an aristocracy, and in the person of the king in a monarchy. Rulers rule by divine right but are subject to the laws of God, of nature, and of nations, and also to the "laws of the kingdom"—a vague adumbration of constitutionalism. These limitations upon supreme power, however, are ethical rather than legal or political. The ideal form of government is a kingship in which unlimited sovereign power is exercised personally by the monarch.

Though Bodin's view of the nature of sovereignty became prevalent everywhere in Europe among the apologists of absolutism, it was not unchallenged. In fact, two conflicting schools of thought battled for supremacy until their differences were in part reconciled in the formulation of the concept suggested by Grotius. The first great challenge to absolutism came from that school of political philosophers known as the Monarchomachs—spokesmen for the most part of the persecuted sects of the period of the wars of religion who were anxious to justify resistance to tyranny and oppression. This group insisted upon the original and inalienable sovereignty of the people and argued that government had come into existence as a result of a written or tacit contract between rulers and ruled for the mutual convenience of both as an escape from the anarchy of a precivil state of nature. In the event of a ruler violating the compact by indulging in outrageous and despotic misgovernment, his subjects are *ipso facto* released from the obligation of obedience and may engage in revolution, depose the monarch, or even assassinate him under extreme provocation.

Johannes Althusius, one of the leading Monarchomach theorists, defined sovereignty in his *Politics Systematically Considered* (1609) as "the highest and most general power of administering the affairs which generally concern the safety and welfare of the soul and body of the members of the State." This power, according to his view, could be neither absolute nor supreme, since it is limited by the laws of God, the laws of nature, and the terms of the contract with the people, who remain the ultimate, original, and permanent source of sovereignty. This conception was obviously sharply at variance with that of Bodin, though Thomas Hobbes in his *Leviathan* (1651) later used the contract theory of the origin of the State as the basis for the most imposing intellectual justification of monarchical absolutism which has ever been presented.

Grotius resolved the issue, so far as international law and relations are concerned, by defining sovereignty as "that power whose acts are not subject to the control of another, so that they may be made void by the act of any other human will." For the great Dutch jurist, sovereignty was not absolute, but limited by divine law, by the law of nature, and by the law of nations, and also by agreements between rulers and ruled. It is likewise capable of division and resides simultaneously in the government and in the State. Subjects, however, may alienate their portion of sovereignty entirely to their ruler. The important thing to Grotius is the fact that a State is sovereign in relation to other States when it is free from outside control and capable of exercising its will without outside interference. This idea has become the foundation of the whole structure of modern international law.

This conception obviously grew out of the political realities of international contacts in the formative period of modern diplomacy. If carried to its logical extreme, it would result in a situation which can only be described as international anarchy. With the breakdown of the authority of Pope and Emperor, the national monarchies of the west, no less than the city-states and principalities of Italy and Germany, went their sovereign way, each striving against the others for territory, power, and prestige, each employing force, trickery, and bargaining in its quest. The provincial chaos of feudalism was replaced by an international chaos of national States, struggling with one another as the embattled knights and barons had once struggled in an earlier age. In this anarchic jungle of sovereign political communities, each State pursued its own ends in disregard of the interests of others, redressing its wrongs by self-help, acting as prosecutor, judge, jury, and sheriff combined, and hotly resenting any suggestion of allegiance or responsibility to any superior power. Here, indeed, was a precivil state of nature as Hobbes had described it, in which life was "solitary, poor, nasty, brutish, and short"—in which might makes right—in which power is to the strongest, and the devil takes the hindmost.

With the general acceptance of the concept of sovereignty by the States of western Europe, the foundations of the Western State System in its modern form were established. There remains to be noted the emergence of international law out of a confused and unformulated body of customs and usages into a definite system of jurisprudence regulating the relations between States. This development likewise took place in the later sixteenth and early seventeenth centuries, though it was foreshadowed by many centuries of preparation during which international law existed and evolved as a practical basis for defining the legal rights and obligations of States long before it attracted the attention of scholars and jurists.

International law as a distinct branch of legal science received almost no recognition among lawyers and jurists before the fifteenth century, despite the practical development of international customs and usages in the medieval State System. Vittoria (1480–1546) and Ayala (1548–1584) made early efforts to integrate these usages into a consistent system of law; and the Spanish Jesuit, Suarez (1548–1617), endeavored to discover the basis for such a system in "natural law" or reason. Gentilis (1552–1608) likewise attempted on a more pretentious scale to set forth the principles governing the relations between States. In this period of groping toward a logical basis for an international jurisprudence, two schools of thought were distinguishable: one looked for guidance to international practice and sought to make international law the written customs of States; the other tried to formulate principles on the basis of ethics, theology, reason, and common sense. The former school relied much upon the *ius gentium* of Roman law, while the latter searched for light in the *ius naturale*, or law of nature, which was the current symbolization of what seemed rational and just. These two fountainheads of wisdom have ever since been supplementary sources of international law in its subsequent development.

The task of reconciling the two schools and of erecting an imposing edifice of legal principles worthy of being called a true "law of nations" was first performed by the same versatile and erratic Dutch genius, Huig de Groot or Hugo Grotius, who contributed to the development of the concept of sovereignty. So significant was his contribution and so profound has been his influence that later generations of jurists conferred upon him the title of "the father of international law." Born at Delft, April 10, 1583, son of the burgomaster of Leyden, he wrote Latin verses at the age of nine, entered the university at twelve, and was a learned editor at fifteen, when he accompanied a Dutch embassy to Paris. After winning his LL.D. at the University of Leyden, he devoted himself to writing Latin dramas and poems and practicing law. At twenty he was appointed official historiographer by the States General, in which capacity he began work on his *De jure praedae* (1604) which was the basis of his later treatise. As advocate of the Dutch East India Company, he defended the capture of a Portuguese galleon in the Straits of Malacca by the Dutch captain, Heemskerk, with the argument that the Portuguese claim that all eastern waters were under Portuguese jurisdiction was unsound and contrary to the accepted practice of nations. His part in this early controversy over freedom of the seas won him further fame, and he embarked upon a promising diplomatic career which was rudely cut off in 1619—fortunately, perhaps, for posterity, for had he continued to occupy himself with the practical work of diplomacy he might never have found leisure to compile his monumental work.

Grotius' great treatise, *De jure belli ac pacis* ("Concerning the Law of War and Peace") was in part written in the prison fortress of Louvestein, where the poet-jurist was incarcerated in 1619 on a life sentence because of his unpopular religious views. The bloody Thirty Years' War had just broken out in Bohemia. It was to mark the culmination of the religious conflicts of the century. Young Hugo was a theologian no less than a lawyer and, like Erasmus a hundred years before, he pleaded for toleration and sought to mediate between the warring sects of Remonstrants and anti-Remonstrants. He was jailed for his pains and had his property conficated, but prison life was not unbearable, for he was permitted to live with his gifted wife and to continue his studies with the aid of many large chests of books which were periodically brought to him by his guards. In 1621 his wife nailed him up in a book chest and in this appropriate disguise he escaped from his cell and fled to Antwerp and Paris, where Louis XIII granted him a small pension. In 1625 his treatise was completed and published. It brought him no profits but ensured him immortal fame, for it was the most adequate and comprehensive statement of the principles of international law which had yet appeared. He subsequently became Swedish Ambassador to France and died at Rostock in 1645.

The *De jure belli ac pacis* was largely inspired by the author's revulsion at the horrors and excesses of the wars of religion which were devastating the Europe of his day. In his Prolegomena he declared:

> The civil law, both that of Rome, and that of each nation in particular, has been treated of, with a view either to illustrate it or to present it in a compendious form, by many. But international law, that which regards the mutual relations of several peoples, or rulers of peoples, whether it proceed from nature, or be instituted by divine command, or introduced by custom and tacit compact, has been touched on by few, and has been by no one treated as a whole in an orderly manner. And yet that this be done, concerns the human race. . . .
>
> I, for the reasons which I have stated, holding it to be most certain that there is among nations a common law of rights which is of force with regard to war, and in war, saw many and grave causes why I should write a work on that subject. For I saw prevailing throughout the Christian world a license in making war of which even barbarous nations would have been ashamed; recourse being had to arms for slight reasons or no reason; and when arms were once taken up, all reverence for divine and human law was thrown away, just as if men were thenceforth authorized to commit all crimes without restraint.

He therefore attempted, with signal success, to compile the principles by which States are, or ought to be, governed, deriving them from the law of nature or dictates of right reason, as set forth by philosophers, historians, poets, and orators, and also from the law of nations which he sharply distinguished from the other as consisting of the practices of States and the resulting principles of law binding upon them by virtue of their having consented to them.

Grotius here laid the foundations upon which subsequent jurists were to build. He combined custom and reason as sources of international law, as did such notable successors as Bynkershoek, Wolff, Vattel, and Wheaton. The Naturalist school, represented by Puffendorf, Thomasius, and Rutherford, continued to give precedence to reason or natural law, while the Positivist school of Selden, Zouch, Bentham, Martens, and others emphasized the actual customs and practices of States as the best possible criteria of their legal rights and obligations. The Grotian view, which was a synthesis of the two, has now come to prevail and has in turn influenced the practice of States and led to the erection of the imposing structure of modern international jurisprudence, the basic principles of which will be reviewed in a later chapter.

Many observers, particularly in recent years, have been struck by the apparent anomaly presented by a State System in which a great body of legal concepts has developed to define the rights, obligations, and procedures of States in their mutual relations and in which, at the same time, these States continue to be engaged in a competitive struggle for the stakes of diplomacy, involving the maintenance of an unstable equilibrium of power and periodical resorts to armed violence. This anomaly disappears, however, in the light of a fuller appreciation of the peculiar nature of international law. Within national societies, law is a substitute for force in the settlement of disputes. Private law defines the rights and remedies of individuals and groups and provides means for the pacific settlement of differences through litigation and adjudication. Public law defines the structure of the State and the procedures of government and makes of politics no longer an armed struggle for power as it was in the feudal period, but a peaceable process of competition, discussion, and compromise between parties, factions, classes, and other associations organized for political action. Domestic peace within the State is normally maintained by the coercive power of government, resting upon the acquiescence of the great mass of the governed who are willing to subordinate special interests to general interests and to submit to the result of the process of politics. International law has no such coercive power upon which to rely and it does not rest, except to a very limited degree, upon any willingness on the part of sovereign States to subordinate their interests to the interests of the whole society of States. It is not, therefore, a substitute for force in the relations between States, however much enthusiastic jurists would like to give it this function. Neither does it ensure the pacific settlement of disputes, though it supplies a set of concepts for the legal definition of the subject matter of disputes and it specifies what procedures are permissible, both in pacific and in nonpacific settlement. It consists merely of a set of rules which States have found it useful and expedient to observe.

These rules relate quite as much to the conduct of warfare, *i.e.*, to the application of violence by State against State, as to nonviolent discussion and compromise. Being based upon the actual behavior of sovereign

States, they take cognizance of the realities of that behavior. They are not concerned with the purposes, goals, and objectives of State behavior, but only with its forms. International law, unlike municipal law, does not deprive those to whom it is addressed of the right to protect their interests by their own power, though in recent years unsuccessful efforts have been made to outlaw war and to require States to resort only to pacific means of settlement. International politics, unlike national politics, has not yet been transformed from a violent to a pacific process by virtue of the evolution of a system of jurisprudence governing the relations between the contestants. The international law of the Western State System simply lays down the rules which the contestants are expected to follow. Within the limits of these rules there goes on as before that perpetual struggle for prestige and influence which is the distinguishing pattern of an international politics resting upon State sovereignty and a balance of power.

3. THE BALANCING OF POWER, 1500–1815

> The balance is a word that has subdued the whole world, by the light in which it was considered of its securing a constant possession; and yet, in truth, this same balance is no more than a bare word, an empty sound; for Europe is a family in which there are too many bad brokers and quarrelsome relations.—FREDERICK THE GREAT, *Confessions*.

If sovereignty is the mast to which the sails of modern statecraft are attached, the principle of the balance of power is the wind which drives the vessel over the stormy seas of international politics. The one has become the central concept of national political organization and of international law. The other has become the most important single pattern of political action in the international arena. Both existed in latent form in early State Systems. Both received their first clear formulation in the sixteenth century—tentatively at the hands of Machiavelli and more definitely from his successors.

The principle of the balance of power as an unformulated guide to State action is of great antiquity, as has been suggested in the preceding chapter. It has emerged more or less clearly in every system of States in which the units have engaged with one another in a competitive struggle for power. Apparently all States known to history have at one time or another striven to extend their power over the lands and peoples in their vicinity, for these are sources of additional wealth and power to the ruling class of the State. As such they furnish the basis for a further enhancement of State power which makes possible still greater conquests. It has been said truly that a large empire is the best possible reason for a larger empire. State power tends to spread outward from the central nucleus and to increase as it spreads. But power is local. Its efficacy within a given area varies inversely with the distance from the State which is wielding it. A single State, encountering no other obstacles, would normally extend its power over as wide an area as it could conquer and control effectively. But in practice obstacles are invariably encountered in the form of other States, similarly striving to expand their power. A struggle for power consequently arises, in which each State endeavors to overcome its competitors. The power of a State—*i.e.*, its ability to conquer other States or to bend them to its will—is necessarily relative to the power of its rivals. Since State power is a relative quantity, any enhancement in the power of one State automatically produces a diminution in the power of its neighbors.

It is because of this fact that the pattern of balance-of-power relationships emerges in every State System. Whenever three States are in contact with one another, the prerequisite conditions for its appearance are present. If one postulates a State System composed of the three units *A*, *B*, and *C*, it is obvious that an increase in the power of any one of them involves a decrease in the power of the other two. Should State *A* conquer State *B* or deprive it of a portion of its territory, State *C* would immediately be adversely affected, for *A* has now enhanced its power at the expense of *B* and is in a better position than before to impose its will upon *C*. If the authorities of State *C* are wise, therefore, they will attempt to forestall this result by coming to *B*'s assistance against *A*, not because of any sympathy or solicitude for the fate of *B*, but because considerations of self-interest make any enhancement of the power of *A* dangerous to *C* itself. In such a situation, *B* and *C* have a community of interests in opposing *A*, for each realizes that any increase in *A*'s power creates a potential threat to its own independence or existence. By the same token, any attempt by *B* to increase its power at the expense of *C* must be resisted by *A* and any enhancement of *C*'s power at the expense of either *A* or *B* must be resisted by the other. Consequently, each unit in this hypothetical State System will inevitably tend to throw its weight into the balance behind either of the other two States menaced by the third. If the principle is consistently applied by all three, no one State will be able to overcome another and all will preserve their independence. In its elementary form, therefore, the balance-of-power principle is designed not to preserve peace or to contribute toward international understanding, as later rationalizations would have it, but simply to maintain the independence of each unit of a State System by preventing any one unit from so increasing its power as to threaten the rest.

The wars of the middle ages, such as the Hundred Years' War between England and "France," waged while the latter was still an inchoate congeries of principalities, did not exhibit the characteristics of a true State System, since the contestants were not well-defined territorial units, but feudal structures, linked to one another in complex relationships of vassalage and fealty. But as soon as definite territorial States came into being and competed with one another for power, the balance-of-power pattern reemerged. This took place first, as has been noted, in Italy where the Kingdom of the Two Sicilies, the Papal States, Milan, Venice, Florence, Genoa, and lesser Powers struggled with one another and against outside invaders, German, French, or Spanish, who were attracted to the peninsula by the wealth of its cities. Each pursued its own interests, for, as Machiavelli observed, "the prince who contributes toward the advancement of another power, ruins his own." Invariably the weak combined against the strong, and no one power, whether local State or foreign invader, was able to bring the whole peninsula into subjection. The national monarchies of the west—England, France, and Spain—and the smaller States and principalities of central Europe were similarly engaged in a competitive struggle for power in which the same principle inevitably operated. When the House of Hapsburg under Charles V attained such vast domains that its power seemed a menace to other States, they combined to check its ascendancy. When Spain under Philip II aspired to hegemony, it was checked in turn by hostile coalitions. Later France became the most powerful State of Europe—a position which it held for over 200 years. International politics accordingly assumed the form of coalition after coalition against *la Grande Nation*, from the time of the league formed by William of Orange to frustrate the ambitions of Louis XIV, to the quadruple alliance which humbled Napoleon at Leipzig and Waterloo. Another balance of power, involving Sweden, Russia, Poland, Prussia, and Austria, developed in eastern Europe and became an integral part of the whole European State System in the latter half of the eighteenth century.

During the fifteenth and sixteenth centuries the States of western Europe pursued balance-of-power policies toward one another, without the principle itself receiving any clear and conscious formulation. In the early 1500's Francis I and Cardinal Wolsey, the great adviser of Henry VIII, both hinted at the principle in their declarations. But not until the time of Louis XIV does the concept emerge in definite form in the statements of diplomats and the literature of international relations. Lord Bolingbroke, who was responsible for English foreign policy during the last years of the War of the Spanish Succession (1701–1713), was one of the first English ministers to attempt to build his program with the deliberate purpose of preserving the continental equilibrium. In the negotiations which preceded the signature of the Treaty of Utrecht he was instrumental in arranging the solemn and public declarations of Philip V and the Dukes of Orleans and Berry by which, in the interest of maintaining a balance between the Powers of Europe, they renounced all ambitions of attempting to unite France and Spain under a single crown. In the words of one of Bolingbroke's friends, these renunciations "lay down the balance of power in Europe as their foundation, expressing that Spain ought not to be united either to France or to the House of Austria." Some years later the French philosopher and political writer, Fénelon, discussed the balance as essential to maintain the liberty, tranquillity, and public safety of Europe. At the opening of the War of the Austrian Succession (1741), Sir Robert Walpole stated the principle with even greater clarity.

The use of alliances . . . has in the last age been too much experienced to be contested; it is by leagues well concerted and strictly observed that the weak are defended against the strong, that bounds are set to the turbulence of ambition, that the torrent of power is restrained, and empires preserved from those inundations of war that, in former times, laid the world in ruins. By alliances . . . the equipoise of power is maintained, and those alarms and apprehensions avoided, which must arise from vicissitudes of empire and the fluctuations of perpetual contest. . . .

The firmest bond of alliances is mutual interest. Men easily unite against him whom they have all reason to fear and to hate, by whom they have been greatly injured, and by whom they suspect that no opportunity will be lost of renewing his encroachments. Such is the state of this nation (England) and of the Austrians. We are equally endangered by the French greatness, and equally animated against it by hereditary animosities, and contests continued from one age to another; we are convinced that, however either may be flattered or caressed, while the other is invaded, every blow is aimed at both and that we are divided only that we may be more easily destroyed (*Parliamentary History*, XII, pp. 168–169).

Frederick the Great likewise paid lip service to the principle, though his expansionist policies upset the balance and led to new wars to check Prussian power. The English philosopher, David Hume, in his *Political Discourses* (1751), dwells upon the efficacy of Britain's balance-of-power policy in checkmating French efforts to establish hegemony on the Continent. The Swiss jurist, Emeric de Vattel, who based his *Droit de gens* (1758) on the work of Wolff, was one of the first text writers to consider the principle as a problem of international law.

Europe forms a political system in which the nations inhabiting this part of the world are bound together by their relations and various interests into a single body. It is no longer, as in former times, a confused heap of detached parts, each of which had but little concern for the lot of the other, and rarely troubled itself over what did not immediately affect it. The constant attention of sovereigns to all that goes on, the custom of resident ministers, the continual negotiations that take place, make of modern Europe a sort of republic, whose members, each independent, but all bound together by a common interest, unite for the maintenance of order and the preservation of liberty. This is what has given rise to the well-known principle of the balance of power, by which is meant an arrangement of affairs so that no State shall be in a position to have absolute mastery and dominate over the others. (E. de Vattel, *The Law of Nations*, translation of edition of 1758, Washington, 1916, pp. 248f.)

Vattel argued that the balance of power could best be preserved through alliances and confederations to check the ascendancy of any one Power which seemed likely to upset the equilibrium. He denied that balance-of-power considerations give a State any absolute right of armed action against another, but he conceded that "one is justified in forestalling a danger in direct ratio to the degree of probability attending it and to the seriousness of the evil which is threatened."

If an unknown man takes aim at me in the middle of a forest, I am not yet certain that he wishes to kill me; must I allow him time to fire in order to be sure of his intent? Is there any reasonable casuist who would deny me the right to forestall the act? But presumption becomes almost equal to certitude if the prince who is about to acquire enormous power has already given evidence of an unbridled pride and ambition. In the imaginary case mentioned above, who would have dared counsel the European States to allow Louis XIV to make such a formidable addition to his power? (*Ibid.*)

Vattel also sought to present the balance of power as a guarantee of the liberty and independence of States. His wide influence led to general acceptance of this view. It is a substantially accurate characterization of the pattern, though it is obvious that the balance may sometimes be preserved by the partition of a weak State among its stronger neighbors, as happened in the extinction of the independence of Poland at the end of the eighteenth century by Russia, Austria, and Prussia. In any case, the balance-of-power principle has been recognized as an integral feature of the Western State System by Rousseau, Kant, and a host of later writers, as well as by the great majority of diplomats and statesmen.

* * * * *

International politics in Europe at the beginning of the sixteenth century and throughout the whole Baroque period of western European history was primarily a struggle for power, prestige, and territory between the rival dynasties which forged the States of modern Europe. Within each State the reigning house relied for support upon the new burgher class and upon that portion of the landed nobility which was willing to occupy the position of a titled ruling caste within the limits imposed by monarchical absolutism. Each dynasty strove to enforce its authority upon the still unruly remnants of the feudal aristocracy. Each king and prince endeavored to consolidate the power of his house over the realm by imposing unity upon the medieval, feudalized diversity of his heritage— ecclesiastical and religious unity, linguistic unity, judicial unity, fiscal unity, administrative unity, military unity. And between the rival dynasties of nation builders there was constant struggle, with each pursuing its own interests and seeking to expand its lands and its influence through marriage, war, and diplomacy.

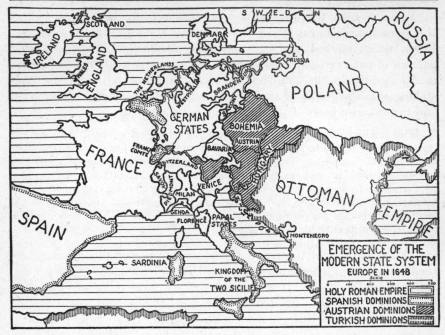

EMERGENCE OF THE
MODERN STATE SYSTEM
EUROPE IN 1648

HOLY ROMAN EMPIRE
SPANISH DOMINIONS
AUSTRIAN DOMINIONS
TURKISH DOMINIONS

By the second decade of the seventeenth century a definite pattern had emerged in the closely woven fabric of dynastic rivalry, religious conflict, and clashing national ambitions. Europe was in process of transition from an aggregation of separate States which had isolated and incidental contacts with one another to a State System in which each member is directly concerned with the relations between all the rest. This interdependence of political relations between the Powers was vaguely appreciated in the days of Elizabeth, Henry II, and Philip II. By 1648 it was a fixed feature of European international politics. The first general European war had intervened as a dramatic and bloody climax to the religious struggles of the preceding century. In its flames medieval Europe was consumed. The modern State System, fully matured, emerged from the ashes.

The causes and events of the Thirty Years' War are too involved to be dealt with here. Suffice it to say that it was at once a contest for supremacy between the Bourbon and Hapsburg dynasties, a death grapple between Protestantism and Catholicism, and a conflict (between the Emperor and the princes) over control of the German States. The Peace of Westphalia of 1648 was the first of the grand territorial and political settlements which have incorporated the verdict of arms into the public law of Europe after every general war among the Powers. At the close of the prolonged and tedious peace conference which opened in 1642, three treaties were concluded: one signed at Münster, January 30, 1648, between Spain and the Dutch; another signed at Münster, October 24,

1648, between the Empire, France, and the German princes; and a third of the same date, signed at Osnabrück, between the Empire and Sweden. Mutual toleration between Catholics and Protestants was provided for, and the wars of religion were at long last brought to a close. The independence of Switzerland and the Netherlands was acknowledged, and the boundary was drawn between the Dutch provinces and the Spanish Netherlands (Belgium). Sweden annexed territory in Pomerania; Brandenburg began that process of expansion which was to lead to the creation of the Kingdom of Prussia; France annexed Alsace, with the exception of the city of Strasbourg, and continued the war against Spain until the Treaty of the Pyrenees (1659) gave to her Artois to the north, Roussillon to the south, and a protectorate over Lorraine on the east. In this fashion, two new States were added to the System, the Empire was reduced to a shadow of its former self, the House of Hapsburg was humbled by the House of Bourbon, and an enlarged France stepped forward into the international arena as arbiter of the destinies of Europe.

Following the death in 1661 of Cardinal Mazarin, successor of the great Richelieu, the young French King, Louis XIV (1643–1715)—*le Grand Monarque*—assumed personal direction of policy and became the symbol of an epoch. Monarchical absolutism was now the prevalent form of State organization throughout Europe, though in England the Great Rebellion and the civil war of Cavaliers and Roundheads imposed limits upon the royal prerogative, despite the Stuart restoration of 1660. In France the old unruly aristocracy had become an ornamental and submissive ruling caste of titled and privileged nobles, who now perceived that their class interests were intimately bound up with the kingship. The bourgeoisie constituted willing servants and patient subjects of the great king who declared himself the State. The masses of peasants and artisans were inarticulate and politically of no consequence. The theory of divine-right monarchy was perfected and accepted by all men of substance save a few critics and cranks. The period was the great age of French letters. Artists, scientists, poets, and dramatists helped to make the Court at Versailles the envy and the model of the Western world. The able ministers and generals whom Louis XIV gathered about him—Colbert, Louvois, Vauban, Turenne, and Condé—led the French monarchy forward along the paths of power and glory in diplomacy and arms. France was the first State of Europe in peace and in war. The international politics of the age of Louis XIV therefore revolved about the attempts of France to impose its will upon the Continent and the counterefforts of numerous coalitions of weaker States to thwart this ambition and preserve the established equilibrium.

The development of the Western State System since the seventeenth century, however, is no longer the story of the States of an isolated

Europe. It is constantly complicated by the rivalries of the Powers for control of growing overseas possessions. Between northwestern Europe on the one side and Africa and Asia on the other lay the great Ottoman Empire, whose warriors had crossed the Dardanelles to seize Constantinople in 1453 and had subsequently extended their conquests over all of southeastern Europe, northern Africa, and the eastern Mediterranean. This circumstance played its part, though not such an important one as was once supposed, in causing the enterprising merchants of Italy and the Atlantic seaboard States of Europe to seek other routes to the distant Indies with which a profitable trade had already developed. The competition for the Eastern trade between the Italian, Spanish, and Portuguese merchants was also a factor encouraging the search for new sea routes to the Orient. Daring Atlantic captains sailed southward around the huge hulk of the Dark Continent and westward toward the setting sun. These first slender filaments were to link Europe to a vast new world. The Vikings, to be sure, had reached America in the middle ages; but the memory of their wanderings had been lost. Not until Columbus, under Spanish auspices, reached the Antilles in 1492 was there begun a systematic exploration of the great unknown across the Atlantic. The rounding of Africa by Vasco da Gama in 1497 and the first circumnavigation of the globe by Magellan shortly afterwards opened new seaways to southern Asia. Here an ancient and highly developed native civilization made easy conquest and settlement by Europeans impossible. But the Amerindian aborigines who lived in the wilds of the Western continents could offer no effective resistance to European explorers, conquerors, and colonizers, even where they had evolved great civilizations of their own as in Mexico and Peru. As tools for the exercise of political power the bow and arrow, the lance, and the canoe were no match for the blunderbuss, the horse, and the sailing vessel. The superior technology of European civilization enabled the Powers to conquer or disperse the native peoples of the new world and to carve out vast empires from the wilderness. Explorers, colonizers, treasure seekers, and empire builders jostled one another in quest of adventure, gold, and power; and their respective States were not slow to support claims to territory and to quarrel with one another for new dominions.

This clash of imperial aspirations played a major role in the long duel between the English and French which was about to open in Europe. In the middle period of the seventeenth century, when France was crushing the Hapsburgs and extending her frontiers to the Pyrenees, the Alps, the Rhine, and the Meuse, England was torn by the internal disturbances of the Great Rebellion, the civil war, the Commonwealth, and the Restoration. But when Louis XIV sought to acquire still more territory and to establish French hegemony over the Continent, England actively joined his enemies both to preserve the balance of power in Europe and to challenge French pretensions in Asia and America. In a series of far-flung combats, culminating in the War of the Spanish Succession (1701–1713), various coalitions thwarted the efforts of the French monarchy to establish its dominion over all of western Europe.

The peace conference at Utrecht (1712–1713) drew up another great international settlement, comparable with that of Westphalia in 1648, and destined to endure in its main features for more than a century. Philip of Bourbon, Louis' grandson, was recognized as Spanish king, but it was stipulated that France and Spain were never to unite, since "the most destructive flame of war which is to be extinguished by this peace arose chiefly from hence, that the security and liberties of Europe could by no means bear the union of the Kingdoms of France and Spain under one and the same King" (Article 6 of the Anglo-French treaty of April 11, 1713). The Spanish Netherlands were transferred to Austria, to which Louis was obliged to give up Ypres and Tournai. Austria also acquired Naples, Milan, and Sardinia, and England secured Gibraltar and Minorca from Spain. The Duchy of Savoy (Piedmont) was recognized as a kingdom and permitted to annex Sicily, which it later exchanged for Sardinia. The Elector of Brandenburg was similarly recognized as King of Prussia. As for America, England acquired Acadia (Nova Scotia), Hudson Bay, and Newfoundland, and trade concessions from Spain. With France checked and Spain stripped of portions of her territory, the other Powers were content to permit Bourbon kings to reign both at Paris and Madrid. The European equilibrium was preserved, though the contest between England and France for mastery of India and the New World was still undecided. It should be noted that the contemporaneous eastern wars between Charles XII of Sweden, and Russia, Denmark, and Poland were fought and terminated almost without reference to the relations between the western European States. After Utrecht, however, the European State System became an indissoluble unity and all States, east and west, were involved in every contest between any of its members.

The settlement of Utrecht was followed by an interlude, marked by new wars in the east (Austria against Turkey, 1715–1718, and Sweden against Russia, 1715–1721) which were not ignored by the Western Powers but in which they did not actively intervene. In 1719–1720 England and France joined forces to prevent Philip V from upsetting the terms agreed upon at Utrecht. The next general war arose out of international controversy over the election of a king of Poland. In the War of the Polish Succession (1733–1738), Austria and Russia, supporting the candidacy of the Elector of Saxony, defeated France which supported Stanislaus Leszczinski, father-in-law of Louis XV. England remained neutral and Spain seized the opportunity to wrest the Kingdom of the

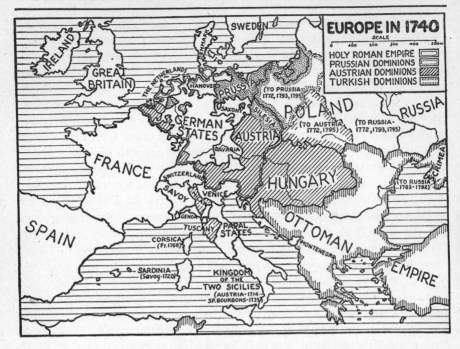

Two Sicilies from Austria and to place a Bourbon upon the throne of her recovered dependency. These conflicts, however, produced no fundamental changes in power relationships among the States of the European System. The next serious disturbance was a result, on the one hand, of rivalry between England, France, and Spain for colonial dominions and, on the other, of the rise of a new Power to ascendancy in north Germany— the Kingdom of Prussia under the Hohenzollern dynasty.

Great Britain fought a brief, indecisive, and localized war with Spain in the Caribbean in 1727. In 1739 the struggle was resumed in the "War of Jenkins's Ear" which opened in American waters and led to hostilities on the frontier between the British colony of Georgia and the Spanish colony of Florida. Walpole knew that the conflict could scarcely be localized because of the Bourbon "Family Compact" of 1733 which constituted an alliance between France and Spain. Difficulties were in the offing, moreover, regarding the throne of Austria; for there was little assurance that Great Britain, France, Spain, and Prussia would abide by the arrangement which they had made to guarantee the succession to Maria Theresa, daughter of Charles IV. In December of 1740, following the death of Charles, Frederick II of Prussia, surnamed "the Great," sent his armies into Austrian Silesia to expand Prussian power at Maria Theresa's expense. France, Bavaria, Saxony, and Spain joined Prussia in a league of plunder to despoil the young Queen of her possessions. England, supported by the Netherlands, joined Austria in the combat to preserve the Continental equilibrium and to continue the struggle against France and Spain in the new world. The War of the Austrian Succession (1740–1748), known to the transatlantic colonists as King George's War, was fought in America and in India as well as in central Europe. In all the arenas of conflict, it was indecisive. In the Peace of Aix-la-Chapelle of 1748, Great Britain and France restored the *status quo ante bellum* in India and America. Frederick managed to retain Silesia, and Austria also lost certain Italian dependencies, but Maria Theresa averted the partition of her realm. With Austria determined to check the Prussian menace in Germany and with Great Britain no less bent upon a final reckoning with France, the peace was but a truce. The great Prussian King perceived that Russia might be drawn into the coalition which Maria Theresa was striving to form against him. He therefore devoted himself to preparing for the inevitable, for, to him,

Politics is the science of acting always by convenient means conformably to one's own interests. To act conformably to one's interests, it is necessary to know what they are; and to arrive at this knowledge requires study, research, and application. The politics of sovereigns have two parts: one, which is concerned with internal government, comprises the interests of the State and the maintenance of its system of government; the other, which embraces all the System of Europe, labors to consolidate the safety of the State and to extend as much as is possible by customary and permitted means the number of its possessions, the power and consideration of the prince. (*Die politischen Testamente der Hohenzollern*, II, p. 33.)

Frederick likewise perceived that Anglo-French relations dominated the whole European scene.

Christian Europe is like a republic of sovereigns which is divided into two great parties. England and France have for a century given the impulse to all movements. When a warlike prince wishes to undertake anything, if both Powers are in agreement to keep the peace, they will offer their mediation to him and compel him to accept it. Once it is established, the political System prevents all great robberies and makes war unfruitful unless it be urged with greater resources and extraordinary luck. (*Ibid.*, p. 54.)

Under these circumstances the stage was prepared for the next general war, which was to decide whether Austria must permit Prussia to dominate north Germany and whether Britain or France should rule North America and India. In 1754 Anglo-French hostilities broke out in the Ohio valley in the so-called French and Indian War. In the "diplomatic revolution" of 1756, England became the ally of her erstwhile enemy, Prussia, which was now set upon from all points of the compass by Austria, France, Russia, and Sweden. The military genius of Frederick enabled him to defeat the French and Austrians at Rossbach and Leuthen (1757), but the Russians invaded East Prussia and occupied Berlin in 1759. After initial successes the French cause fared badly outside of Europe. Wolfe wrested Quebec from Montcalm in 1759. In India the British forces under Robert Clive outwitted Dupleix and seized most of the French strongholds. These failures, coupled with reverses in Brunswick, caused Louis XV to call to his aid the other Bourbon States, Spain and the Two Sicilies (1762). The Spanish intervention was overbalanced, however, by the accession to the Russian throne of the mad Tsar, Peter III, who deserted Austria, joined Prussia, and restored to Frederick the conquests of his predecessors. He was at once superseded by his wife, Catherine II, who refused to give active assistance to either side. Austria now despaired of recovering Silesia and ruining Prussia.

The Treaty of Hubertsburg (1763) put an end to the Seven Years' War in Europe, with Austrian acknowledgment of Prussian title to Silesia. European frontiers remained unchanged, but the House of Hohenzollern had successfully despoiled and defied the House of Hapsburg. With magnificent irony, Frederick placed upon the pinnacle of the New Palace at Potsdam three female figures supporting the Prussian Crown—Madame de Pompadour of France, Maria Theresa of Austria, and Catherine of Russia. The combined efforts of these ladies to consummate his destruction had left his State and his dynasty more powerful than ever. The Treaty of Paris, also of 1763, established peace between Britain and France. The English were masters of Canada and of the east coast of India. Louis XV was compelled to yield up to the victor almost the whole of New France in America east of the Mississippi, retaining only a few islands in the West Indies and off Newfoundland and French Guiana in South America. Spain was obliged to cede Florida to Britain and received as compensation from her ally all that remained of the French claims on the North American mainland, *i.e.*, the wilderness of Louisiana west of the Mississippi. French power in India was similarly broken by the peace terms. By the provisions of these settlements, Prussia attained the position of a new Great Power in the European galaxy, and England definitely triumphed over France in the long contest for commercial, colonial, and naval supremacy in America and the Orient.

Between the Seven Years' War and the great revolutionary upheaval of 1789–1815, which was temporarily to subvert the European State System, two developments took place which produced significant changes in the relationships between the Powers. One was to lead to the creation of a new State in the System on the other side of the Atlantic. The other was to lead to the extinction of an old State in eastern Europe. Such were the results of the American Revolution and the partition of Poland. In the former case the outbreak of rebellion against British rule in 1775 and the declaration of America's independence in the following year offered an opportunity to Britain's continental enemies to recover some of their lost prestige and to contribute toward the weakening of British power. France concluded a military alliance with the American rebels in 1778 and was soon joined in the war against England by Spain and the Netherlands. The British Government was at length obliged to sue for peace; and by the treaties of 1783-1784 the United States of America became an independent member of the family of nations, Spain recovered Florida, France reacquired minor possessions in the West Indies and Africa, and Holland lost to Britain a portion of her Asiatic empire. The British overseas dominions were thus reduced, but they still constituted an imposing imperial edifice. The United States, despite its vast territory and resources, was still too young and feeble to play a decisive role in the relations among the European Powers.

Meanwhile, Frederick of Prussia connived with the Tsarina Catherine in 1772 to relieve the weak and disorderly Kingdom of Poland of part of its territory. In order to counterbalance this enhancement of Prussian and Russian power, Austria intervened and annexed Polish Galicia. This bargain at Poland's expense was the means of preventing a general war threatened by Austrian resistance to Russian aggrandizement against the Turks in the Balkans. When Austria later made additional claims to Polish territory, Frederick objected. The balance of power was peaceably preserved by the extinction of the Polish State, Prussia and Russia taking fresh slices in 1792 and all three of the Powers dividing up the remainder in 1795.

By the last quarter of the eighteenth century, then, the Western State System comprised five major Powers on the European Continent, a large number of minor Powers, and a new State across the Atlantic, born of European colonialism. Of the States which might have been described as Great Powers in 1648, England, France, and Austria retained their former position. Spain had declined in wealth and in diplomatic and military prestige and had fallen to the rank of a second-rate Power, in spite of the vast colonies which she still held in the Americas and the East Indies. Holland and Portugal likewise retained extensive overseas possessions, but they had long since passed the halcyon days when they would cope with other Powers as equals. Following the failure of France to establish her supremacy over the Continent, the new State of Prussia, founded on the Mark of Brandenburg, had emerged in central Europe as the dynastic creation of a line of able kings. It had successfully withstood an assault by the other Powers upon the newcomer and had asserted its right to be regarded as their equal. In the more remote east, the Tsardom of Muscovy had extended its dominions eastward, southward, and westward. Under Peter the Great (1682-1725), Russia became partially "westernized" and made itself a member of the European System. Under Catherine the

Great (1762–1796), it became a Great Power. Its expansion pushed the Swedes from the eastern shores of the Baltic and the Turks from the northern shores of the Black Sea. Sweden fell to the rank of a third-rate Power; and the Ottoman Empire, never really a part of the European System, was already in decay. The end of Poland brought the enlarged States of Russia, Prussia, and Austria into closer relations with one another. The petty States of Italy and Germany remained pawns among their greater neighbors. The first great struggle for overseas empire was ended, and the Powers had achieved an equilibrium of power which seemed reasonably permanent and stable.

Beneath the surface of European society, however, there had long been germinating new forces and pressures now ready to burst forth in a political and social revolution which was not only to overturn the whole social and political structure of the Continent but also to demolish temporarily the whole European State System and replace it once more by universal empire. The slow expansion of industry and trade, the growth of cities, and the extension of commercial contacts among the States of Europe and between Europe and the world had all led to a great increase in numbers and wealth of those who were neither peasant serfs nor landowning nobles but who constituted the great urban middle class of the bourgeoisie. As this class in the European social order acquired economic power and became aware of its peculiar interests, it endeavored to secure political influence and to supersede the nobility and the clergy as a ruling caste. The political and social order of the *ancien régime*, resting upon monarchical absolutism and the privileges of the titled aristocracy, was rudely challenged by the will-to-power of the new class, whose intellectual weapons of assault were furnished by the philosophers of the eighteenth-century "enlightenment" and whose aspiration toward political power had already been reflected in the Great Rebellion in England and in the American Revolution. These upheavals preceded corresponding developments on the Continent. The first blow fell in 1789 where the old order was weakest and where the new forces were most powerful: the France of Louis XVI. Within three years the bourgeois revolutionaries had abolished the privileges of the nobles, confiscated the feudal estates, overturned the monarchy, executed the king, and involved themselves in war with all of Europe. The Republic was fighting not only Austria and Prussia, but Britain, Holland, Spain, and Sardinia, which constituted the "first coalition." The new energies which revolutionary enthusiasm gave to its people made France more than a match for her enemies. In 1795, after the French armies had conquered the Austrian Netherlands, reached the Rhine, and transformed Holland into the Batavian Republic, Spain sued for peace and Prussia withdrew from the conflict to complete the carving of Poland. War continued with Britain,

Austria, and Sardinia while the Reign of Terror waxed and waned in France and the National Convention gave way to the Directory.

In 1796–1797 a young commander of the revolutionary armies, Napoleon Bonaparte, swept the Austrians from north Italy, compelled Sardinia to cede Nice and Savoy to France, marched on Vienna, and imposed the Treaty of Campo Formio on the Hapsburg monarchy. France annexed the Austrian Netherlands; and Austria, in compensation, received Venice, whose ancient independence was thus extinguished. With England the only remaining enemy of the Republic, Bonaparte invaded Egypt in 1798 in a wild scheme to sever communications between the British Isles and India. When he returned, he found the Directory bankrupt and its armies hard-pressed by the forces of the Second Coalition of Great Britain, Austria, and Russia. Hailed as the savior of the Republic, he overthrew the Directory in 1799 and made himself First Consul. The French bourgeoisie, with the approval of the masses, sacrificed democracy and parliamentarianism upon the altar of militant national patriotism. Napoleon became the symbol of *la patrie* and high priest of the new cult of the nation in arms. Under his banner the people's armies of France set forth upon the paths of glory which were to lead to the conquest of Europe.

In the light of the historical evolution of the Western State System, the era of Napoleon is significant chiefly because it represents the most nearly successful effort at the restoration of universal empire which had ever been made by a single State. The power of earlier aspirants toward ascendancy over Europe—Charles V, Philip II, Louis XIV—was feeble and ineffective compared with the military might and diplomatic prestige of France under the first Bonaparte. Napoleon had at his back the richest and most populous nation of the Continent, welded into a solid phalanx by the new fire of patriotic fervor. His battalions were no longer the small, professional forces of the eighteenth century but were made up of conscript armies drawn from the man power of the whole population. His revolutionary predecessors had already invented military conscription as a means of defending France against Europe. His enemies were likewise obliged to resort to universal conscription, which has ever since been the basis of Continental military organization. But the mailed fists of his soldiery were so effectively supplemented by his own military genius and diplomatic astuteness that no State or combination of States could stand against him. The old balance of power was completely disrupted. In 1804 he made himself Emperor—and his Empire seemed likely to include all of western Europe within its limits. For a decade it appeared possible that the Western State System, like all its predecessors, had reached its end and was about to be superseded by a world-wide dominion of its most powerful member.

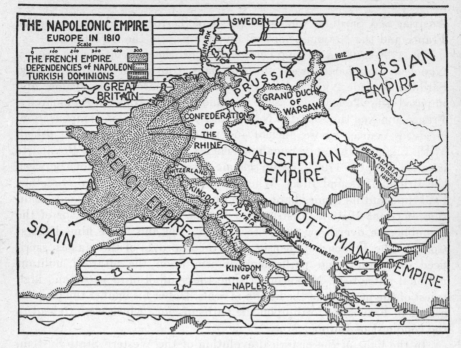

THE NAPOLEONIC EMPIRE
EUROPE IN 1810
Scale
THE FRENCH EMPIRE
DEPENDENCIES of NAPOLEON
TURKISH DOMINIONS

The temporary triumph and final failure of this imperial adventure throw a flood of light upon the fundamental nature of the State System which ultimately proved to be more powerful than its conqueror. From 1800 to 1812 French power rose dizzily in an almost uninterrupted ascent. The diplomacy of flattery induced Tsar Paul to withdraw Russia from the Second Coalition. Austria was crushed in Germany and Italy and obliged to come to terms. At Amiens (1802), England also made peace. But fourteen months later the British Government, with the support of the merchant classes, resumed the war in the conviction that British maritime, commercial, and colonial supremacy were dangerously menaced by French ambitions. Napoleon accepted the challenge in the equally firm conviction that the power of England must be broken before France could feel secure on the Continent. With England crushed, he could take up the task of rebuilding the French overseas empire and of winning for the French bourgeoisie a position of mercantile hegemony throughout the world. Pitt countered Napoleon's preparations for the conquest of England by strengthening British sea power and building up another continental coalition. The allied French and Spanish fleet was destroyed at Trafalgar (1805). Henceforth British naval predominance was assured, and Napoleon had no means at his disposal for the invasion of England. But the Third Coalition was smashed by the French armies. In December, 1805, the Austrian and Russian forces of the Emperor

Francis II and Tsar Alexander I were crushed at Austerlitz. By the Treaty of Pressburg, Austria was required to cede Venetia to the newly created French satellite kingdom of Italy and to surrender much of her territory in Germany to Bavaria and Württemberg, which were also Napoleonic puppet States. Prussia entered the lists, only to be defeated at Jena (1806).

Napoleon, who now entered Berlin, had already abolished the Holy Roman Empire and organized the west German States into the Confederation of the Rhine as a French protectorate. The Russians were in turn beaten at Friedland in 1807. At Tilsit, Napoleon met Alexander and the two Emperors almost literally divided Europe between them. The Third Coalition was destroyed. Austria was reduced to a second-rate Power, and Prussia was humbled to the dust. A truncated Poland was revived in the form of the Grand Duchy of Warsaw as a French dependency. Russia seized Finland from Sweden, and the latter State also became a French appanage. By 1808 Napoleon was Emperor of a France that extended from the Pyrenees and the Alps to the North Sea and the Rhine. He was also King of Italy; and his relatives, friends, or admirers held the thrones of Naples, Spain, Holland, Denmark, Sweden, and lesser States. Even England seemed likely to be brought to terms by the Continental System which was to close the European market to British goods and compel the "nation of shopkeepers" to sue for peace.

That Napoleon failed in this purpose and lived to see the destruction of the whole fabric into which he had woven so much blood and treasure was due primarily to the continued ascendancy of British sea power and to the intense national consciousness which foreign conquest evoked among the subject peoples of France. In 1808 Napoleon deposed the Spanish Bourbons and made his brother Joseph King of Spain. But a popular insurrection broke out almost at once against the usurper, which led Great Britain to occupy Portugal and send Wellington to assist the Spanish rebels in harassing the French in the Peninsular War (1808–1813). A national uprising took place in Austria in 1809 which Napoleon suppressed with difficulty. The Prussian Government introduced various internal reforms, civil and military, and bided its time. Napoleon was still master of Europe, nevertheless, and might have remained so had he not quarreled with Tsar Alexander and taken up arms against him in an effort to compel him to enforce the Continental System against Great Britain. By 1812 the French Emperor had gathered together an international army of 600,000 troops for the subjugation of Russia. The Russian forces withdrew before him, and he entered Moscow in September. But the capital was burned under his eyes. As the Russian-winter descended, the enemy soldiers and peasant irregulars assailed the French communications in the rear. The city was abandoned. The retreat from Moscow became a catastrophe. Only a ragged remnant of the Grand Army recrossed the Niemen in December.

Early in 1813 Alexander, now in alliance with Prussia, England, and Sweden, launched a counterattack which precipitated the German War of Liberation. Napoleon won further indecisive victories, but his rejection of mediation proposals from Vienna added Austria to the new coalition. At the great Battle of the Nations, fought near Leipzig in October, 1813, the Swedish, Russian, Prussian, and Austrian forces closed in on the French, defeated them, and compelled Napoleon to withdraw to the Rhine. His power in central Europe collapsed. France was invaded from the east by the allies and from the south by Wellington who had occupied all of Spain. Despite furious and brilliant resistance, Paris was surrounded in March, 1814. Napoleon was compelled to abdicate and was exiled to Elba. In the spring of 1815 he escaped and returned to power in France to play out the tragic farce of the "Hundred Days" to its dismal end at Waterloo.

The *ancien régime* had triumphed over the Revolution. The European State System had proved itself to be more powerful than its most powerful member. The forces of monarchical absolutism and feudal aristocracy, as represented by the Powers of the Coalition, had overcome those of bourgeois democracy and equality as represented by revolutionary and Napoleonic France. In France itself the old order was reestablished and the Bourbons were restored to the throne in the person of Louis XVIII. At the great international Congress of Vienna (September, 1814–July, 1815) emperors, kings, princes, and diplomats met in brilliant assemblage to restore dynasties in the name of legitimacy, to rebuild the Europe of 1789, and to consider "the disposal of the territories given up by his Most Christian Majesty (Louis XVIII) . . . and the relations from whence a real and permanent balance of power is to be derived" (Article I of the Separate and Secret Articles of the First Treaty of Paris, May 30, 1814).

Under the inspiration of the Austrian statesman, Metternich, the delegates set to work, only to discover that the old Europe had been smashed beyond all hope of complete restoration and that Humpty Dumpty could not, after all, be replaced in his old position on the wall. Bargains and compromises were necessary to adjust conflicting interests and ambitions. France was obliged to renounce her rights of sovereignty and protection over some 32 million people who had been brought under Napoleon's power; but she recovered the boundaries of 1792, with some slight additions. By the second Treaty of Paris, November 20, 1815, France was obliged to cede a number of strategic posts to the allies, to pay an indemnity of 700 million francs, and to submit to the occupation of eighteen fortresses for three to five years. Most of the Grand Duchy of

Warsaw was given to Russia, which also retained Finland and Bessarabia, conquered, respectively, from the Swedes and the Turks. Prussia received Swedish Pomerania, two-fifths of Saxony, and extensive territories on both banks of the Rhine. In the rest of Germany, it was scarcely feasible to restore either the defunct Holy Roman Empire or the hundreds of petty principalities which Napoleon had abolished. A German Confederation of thirty-eight States was therefore established, with Austria securing the presidency of its Diet. Austria gave up the Austrian Netherlands (Belgium), which were annexed by the Dutch, and also gave up a large part of her territories in Germany proper. In return, she was awarded north Italy (Lombardy-Venetia), Illyria, the Tyrol, and Salzburg. The Papal States and the Kingdom of Naples were restored and Italy remained a "geographical expression." In the north, Norway was taken from Denmark and joined to Sweden, under whose control it remained until it secured independence in 1905. Great Britain secured Heligoland in the North Sea, Malta and the Ionian Islands in the Mediterranean, and other fruits of victory overseas from the remnants of the French and Dutch colonial empires: Cape Colony in South Africa, Ceylon, St. Lucia, Tobago, Trinidad, etc.

A final word regarding events in the Western Hemisphere during the Napoleonic epoch: The new Republic of the United States embarked upon its spectacular career of territorial expansion by purchasing Louisiana from France in 1803—a region which the First Consul had reacquired from Spain in 1800 but which he was happy to sell when developments in Europe and the West Indies made a restoration of the French colonial empire impossible. American expansionists next turned their attention to Florida and Canada, but the issue was obscured by long and bitter controversies over blockades, impressments, contraband, and neutral trading rights between the United States on the one hand and Great Britain and France on the other. In 1812 the United States declared war on England in the name of "freedom of the seas" and moved at once to occupy Canada and Florida. In spite of Continental preoccupations, England was easily able to defend Canada from American attacks. The United States was invaded, its capital burned, and its commerce swept from the seas. The Treaty of Ghent (1814) restored the *status quo*. At no time since has the United States resorted to force in its controversies with Great Britain. Spain, however, was a weaker rival, and a skillful policy of browbeating and bargaining induced Madrid to sell the Floridas to the United States in 1819. Meanwhile the Latin American colonies of Spain had secured their independence, and a whole series of new nations was thus added to the Western State System. The United States, no less than Great Britain, was opposed to any restoration of these States to European control. Canning "called in the New World to redress the balance of the Old," as he put it; and the result was the Monroe Doctrine of 1823 by which the United States, with British approval, expressed its intention to resist any further colonization, interposition, or extension of control by European Powers over the American continents. At the very outset of Latin American independence, therefore, the United States asserted its claim to hegemony over the Western Hemisphere.

4. THE WORLD UNITED

> In the social production of the means of life, human beings enter into definite and necessary relations which are independent of their will—production relations which correspond to a definite stage of the development of their productive forces. The totality of these production relations constitutes the economic structure of society, the real basis upon which a legal and political superstructure arises and to which definite forms of social consciousness correspond. . . . With the change in the economic foundation, the whole gigantic superstructure is more or less rapidly transformed.—KARL MARX.

The century between Waterloo and Sarajevo will probably always remain, in a peculiar sense, a unique era. The population of the world doubled and that of Europe quadrupled during the 100 years between 1815 and 1914. The system of technology which had prevailed with few changes for many millennia was completely revolutionized. The old economic order was replaced by a new, the like of which had never before been known. The bourgeoisie, masters and beneficiaries of the new technology and the new economy, became the ruling class in almost all the States of the Western world. A new social group—the industrial proletariat, child of machine industry and the factory system—prepared to contest the dominance of its masters. Commerce and industry expanded with astounding rapidity in what appeared to be the triumphant and uninterrupted march of "progress." European civilization was carried throughout the five continents and the seven seas through a thousand new channels of travel and trade. New nations were born in the Near East, in Asia, in Africa, and in the Americas. In Europe two new Great Powers appeared on the international stage: Italy and Germany. Across the Atlantic the United States grew from a feeble infant to a young giant, with vast resources and an enormous population at its disposal. In eastern Asia another Great Power emerged: Japan. The European State System became a World State System. The entire globe was divided, partitioned, and subjected to the control of the Powers, whose citizens were fired with a new patriotism and whose governments struggled with one another for territory, for markets, and for a "place in the sun" until their rivalries culminated in the greatest and most destructive of all wars. All these developments were without parallel or precedent in the past. Out of them has evolved the world society of the twentieth century.

Fraternité, no less than *Liberté* and *Égalité*, was the battle cry of the bourgeois revolution. And as nationalism is always bred of war, the impact of people upon people in the great Napoleonic conflicts intensified national consciousness at the very time when the bourgeoisie was rising to grasp power from kings and aristocrats. The revolutions of the mid-century were led and supported by middle-class patriots for whom the achievements of national unity and of democratic constitutionalism were but two facets of the same liberal program. The tide of nationalism in almost every State rose in proportion to the economic and political ascendancy of the bourgeoisie. Nationalism and democracy were everywhere corollaries; for true national unity is impossible without that common participation in public life which political democracy implies, and democracy is unworkable on a national scale in a population whose members are not imbued with a sense of national consciousness and solidarity. In the era of the triumphant bourgeoisie, nationalism became a creed and a way of life, shaping the attitudes and actions of millions of people and scores of governments throughout the Western world.

The progressive dissolution of the Ottoman Empire presented an opportunity to the Slavic Christians of southeastern Europe to achieve liberation and statehood. The Serbs gained autonomy in 1815. The revolt of the Greeks began in 1821 and culminated a decade later in the attainment of Greek independence through the intervention of Great Britain, France, and Russia against the Turks. Belgium rose up against Dutch control in 1830, and nine years later her independence as a perpetually neutral and inviolate State was recognized by the mother country and by the Powers. In the 1830's Russia sought to establish a protectorate over Turkey but was frustrated by British and French opposition. The apprehension of the Western States over the extension of Russian power at the expense of "the sick man of Europe," as Turkey came to be called, led to the Crimean War (1854–1856) in which Great Britain and France, with the aid of little Sardinia, fought Russia to a draw in the Black Sea. Russian domination of Constantinople and the Straits was prevented by admitting the Sublime Porte to "the advantages of the public law and system of Europe" (Treaty of Paris, March 30, 1856) and by guaranteeing the independence and integrity of Turkey. In 1877 Russia waged war on Turkey again, now using the Slavic nationalities still under Turkish rule as pawns in her game of imperial expansion. The Powers again intervened, and Russia yielded once more, this time without a trial of armed strength. The Treaty of Berlin of 1878 created Bulgaria as an autonomous principality, and Serbia, Montenegro, and Rumania were all recognized as independent and granted additional territory at Turkey's expense. In 1912 the Balkan States waged war upon Turkey and further extended their frontiers, only to fall out among themselves to the detriment of Bulgaria which was set upon by Serbia, Montenegro, Greece, and Rumania in the Second Balkan War (1913) and deprived of many of her conquests. Balkan nationalism thus created six new States (Albania was established by the Powers in 1913) and made the Balkans an arena of the conflicting ambitions of the Great Powers. The interaction between Balkan nationalism and Great Power politics in this region furnished the immediate occasion of the Great War of 1914.

Nationalism effected even more significant changes in the political organization of central Europe after 1815. The people of Italy were divided into seven States and those of Germany into thirty-nine States. In both spheres Austrian power was predominant. In both, the impact of the Napoleonic wars had given rise to a rich growth of national sentiment under the influence of which middle-class patriots strove to attain political unity and nationhood. Since Austria refused to yield pacifically to such a disadvantageous modification of the *status quo*, war seemed the only road to unification, particularly after 1848, when the German liberals failed miserably in their efforts to create a German nation by peaceful means and when diplomatic efforts to achieve Italian unity proved of no avail. In both regions the new nation was forged in the heat of battle, with the Kingdom of Sardinia (Piedmont) under Cavour playing the same role in Italy as the Kingdom of Prussia under Bismarck was to play in

Germany. In 1858 the new Bonaparte Emperor at Paris, Napoleon III, formed an alliance with Sardinia against Austria on condition of the return to France of Nice and Savoy, conquered by the first Napoleon but lost in 1815. War followed in 1859, and Sardinia was able to annex Lombardy. Nationalist revolutions in central Italy increased the territory of the new State, and Garibaldi's filibusters added Naples and Sicily in the south. In 1861 King Victor Emmanuel of Sardinia took the title of King of Italy.

Three years later Prussia under the "Iron Chancellor" joined Austria in war against Denmark and promptly proceeded to quarrel with her ally over the spoils—Schleswig-Holstein. In the Seven Weeks' War of 1866 Prussia defeated Austria and assumed the presidency of the new North German Confederation, while Italy took her chance to wrest Venetia from the control of Vienna. This enhancement of Prussian power was veiwed with alarm by Napoleon III who played into Bismarck's hands by precipitating the Franco-Prussian war of 1870. With the withdrawal of French troops from the Papal States, Italy occupied Rome and the new Italian nation was complete, save for *Italia Irredenta* ("Italy Unredeemed"), *i.e.*, the provinces of the Tyrol and the Trentino, still under Austrian rule. The French armies were meanwhile crushed by the Prussian military machine. Napoleon III lost his throne, and the Third French Republic was compelled to return Alsace-Lorraine to German control. Since the South German States had joined Prussia in the war, the German Empire was proclaimed at Versailles during the siege of Paris, January 18, 1871. Two new Great Powers were thus created at the cost of the defeat and humiliation of France and the exclusion of Austria from German and Italian affairs. Austria and Hungary had already joined themselves together in the Dual Monarchy in 1867; but this political edifice, composed as it was of an incongruous congeries of German, Magyar, Latin, and Slavic peoples, was not a national State, but a composite structure which the rising tides of nationalism threatened to engulf.

The mid-century decades of national emancipation and unification, which completely upset the arrangements established by the Congress of Vienna, were followed by a new era of colonial expansion in which almost all of the non-European world was seized upon and partitioned by the Great Powers during a short span of thirty years. The great States of the West, old and new alike, took to the path of empire once more and gained larger territories and more imposing dominions in a single generation than their ancestors had won during the three centuries following the circumnavigation of Africa and the discovery of America. The impact of European culture upon the older civilizations of the East and upon the primitive peoples of the tropics resulted in almost every instance in the loss of political independence and in social and economic disorganization among the societies which were the victims of imperialism. One outstanding exception stood out in brilliant contrast. The medieval island empire of Japan was opened to Western influences by an American naval expedition under Admiral Perry in 1854—but, instead of falling prey to the Western Powers as did the other States of Asia, Japan adopted Western technology, Western economics, and Western nationalism and emerged forty years later as a great nation-state in her own right, the latest addition to the Western State System and the only one of the Great Powers whose population is not of European origin.

The course of empire building between 1881 and 1914 was marked by numerous minor wars between the European States and native African and Asiatic communities and by one open conflict between Great Powers: the Russo-Japanese War of 1904–1905, in which Japan ousted Russia from South Manchuria and the Liaotung peninsula. The minor wars are almost too numerous to list, but mention may be made of the French war against China of 1884–1885 which was inconclusive, of the Sino-Japanese War of 1894 in which Japan made her first successful bid for empire, the Italian war against Abyssinia of 1896 which was unsuccessful, the Boer War of 1898–1900 in which Great Britain finally conquered the stubborn Dutch settlers of South Africa in the face of heroic resistance, and the Italian war against Turkey of 1911 which resulted in the Italian annexation of Tripoli. These and innumerable other conflicts were waged by Great Powers against the feeble States of Africa and the Orient. The rival claims of the Powers themselves were usually adjusted by diplomacy and conference.

That the Americas did not also become an arena of imperialistic aggrandizement on the part of the European States was due primarily to the preponderant power of the United States in the Western Hemisphere. After the promulgation of the Monroe Doctrine in 1823, no European State made any permanent addition to its American possessions. The United States, on the other hand, annexed Texas in 1845, waged war upon Mexico, took from her almost half her territory in 1846, and purchased Alaska from Russia in 1867. Napoleon III had taken advantage of the American Civil War of 1861–1865 to attempt to carve out a French Empire in Mexico, but the venture failed dismally. In 1898 the United States resumed its expansion by annexing the Hawaiian Islands and by relieving Spain of Porto Rico, Cuba, and the Philippines after the Spanish-American War. It subsequently converted Cuba, Panama, Haiti, Santo Domingo, and Nicaragua into protectorates and made the Caribbean an American lake, much to the alarm of the Latin American Republics which bitterly resented the hegemony of the "Colossus of the North." The United States, no less than Great Britain, France, Germany, Italy, and Japan, thus carved out an overseas empire at the expense of weaker nations. By 1914 the political map of the world had largely become the map of the colonial possessions, protectorates, and spheres of economic influence of the great States which dominated the international scene.

These remarkable transformations of the Western State System, which was now literally a World System, greatly enhanced the power of its members, enormously extended their territories and resources, and knit them together into compact national units. But they did not modify the fundamental nature of the System or change the character of the competitive struggle for power among its members. They rather extended the struggle over the globe and intensified it to a great degree because the stakes of diplomacy were larger than ever before. The balance of power now depended less upon power relationships in Europe than upon developments all over the earth. The "Concert of Europe" operated fitfully to keep the peace in the race for empire, but rapid shifts in power relationships as a result of national unification and colonial expansion were constantly threatening to upset the equilibrium.

Bismarck's system of alliances to preserve the *status quo* of 1871 was superseded by new arrangements. Italy joined Germany and Austria-Hungary in the Triple Alliance of 1882 out of pique over the French seizure of Tunis; but her ambitions in the Near East and her hope of recovering Italia Irredenta made her an unreliable member of the combination. France, bent upon recovering the territory and the prestige lost in the war with Prussia, won Russia to her side in the Dual Alliance of 1894. After serious friction over the partition of Africa and Asia, France entered into the Entente Cordiale with England in 1904, which the Anglo-Russian agreements of 1907 converted into the Triple Entente. Through these arrangements and the alliance with Japan of 1902, Great Britain sought security from the menace of the growing commercial and naval power of Germany. France sought the *revanche*, and Russia strove to extend her influence in the Near East and the Balkans in competition with Germany and Austria-Hungary. The Central Powers in turn similarly hoped to achieve security, expansion, and a place in the sun by close cooperation with one another. The two great military coalitions, cemented by common interests and secret treaties, faced one another across the armed frontiers and competed with one another in a race of armaments and a struggle for colonial possessions. Each diplomatic conflict—the Franco-German controversies over Morocco of 1904–1905, 1908, and 1911, the Austro-Russian disputes in the Balkans of 1908, 1912, and 1913 and many lesser frictions—thus became crises between the alliances. An unstable equilibrium between these immense aggregations of power was maintained for some years, only to break down in a gigantic combat of nation-states in 1914, which marked the beginning of the end of an epoch.

5. THE WORLD AT WAR

The curse of political anarchy which comes from the distribution of sovereignty among a plurality of local States has afflicted other societies before ours; but, in all those other cases in which the same situation has arisen, it has always been transitory. For anarchy by its very nature cures itself sooner or later, by one means or another. The cure may come through a voluntary, pacific, rational constructive effort—such as we are making in our day—an effort to deprive the local States of their sovereignty for the benefit of society as a whole without at the same time depriving them of their existence. Alternately, the cure may come through the blind, violent, irrational, and destructive clash of material forces.—ARNOLD TOYNBEE.

The Great War marked the culmination of the struggle for power in which the coalitions had engaged for the preceding twenty years. From the ambitions of conflicting nationalisms, the strivings of competing imperialisms, the rivalries and tensions between hostile and acquisitive economies, the universal quest of the nation-states for power, profits, and prestige came the bloodiest and most catastrophic combat of recorded history, sweeping country after country into its vortex and shattering utterly, perhaps beyond all hope of repair, the great world society which Western civilization had created. The roots of war were deep and ineradicable in the very nature of the Western State System itself. The genesis of the conflict of 1914 lay in the irreconcilable aspirations of Teutons and Slavs, Frenchmen and Prussians, Britishers and Germans, struggling for empire, competing for armaments, searching for markets, dreaming of power, security, self-determination, and a brighter place in the sun. The spark was almost accidental: the murder of an archduke and his wife by an obscure patriotic terrorist in a remote Balkan town. Questions of moral responsibility are almost pointless after decades of frenzied debate, for none of the actors willed the war. Each national group of diplomats, imperialists, and militarists simply strove for certain ends which were valued above peace. The ends were those of good patriots everywhere. The striving was not villainy but an act of devotion—blind, stubborn, often muddled and stupid but seldom iniquitous or dishonorable. If the means to the ends spelled ruin and death, the guilt of arson and murder fell alike upon all or upon none.

The "Second Reich" of the Hohenzollerns was ruled by two élites: industrialists who feared British competition and dreamed of profits in overseas colonies; and noble Junkers who feared "encirclement" and saw visions of Pan-Europe under the Prussian sword. So long as Bismarck held the helm (1871–1890), German policy sought successfully to keep *revanchard* France in isolation and to avoid any challenge to Britain or Russia. The "Iron Chancellor" formed alliances with an Austria-

Hungary (1879) anxious over Russian ambitions in the Balkans and with an Italy (1882) resentful at French seizure of Tunisia the year before. He wooed St. Petersburg and concluded a "reinsurance" treaty with the Tsar in 1887. But the young Kaiser, William II, dismissed Bismarck in March, 1890. He alienated Russia and alarmed Britain by encouraging colonial and naval ambitions. The result was the conclusion of the Dual Alliance between France and Russia (1891–1894). Theophile Delcassé, French Foreign Minister from 1898 to 1905, has aptly been called the "Nemesis of Bismarck." He strengthened French ties with the Tsardom. He won Italy away from the Triple Alliance by securing secret pledges of neutrality in 1902 in return for benevolent acquiescence in Italian designs upon Tripoli. After the crisis at Fashoda in the Sudan in 1898, he compromised with Britain and fashioned the Anglo-French Entente Cordiale in 1904. The defeat of Russia by Japan and the intervention of Germany in Morocco compelled his retirement in the following year. But this German diplomatic victory only strengthened the Triple Entente. Britain and Russia composed their differences in 1907. London, Paris, and St. Petersburg made plans for common defense if the Berlin-Vienna axis should challenge them to war.

Each clash of Powers henceforth became a crisis between the coalitions. The first Moroccan crisis was resolved at Algeciras in 1906 where German interests in northwestern Africa were reluctantly recognized by France and Britain. A second and inconclusive crisis two years later was followed by a third in 1911 when Berlin granted Paris a free hand in Morocco in return for 100,000 square miles of French equatorial Africa, with a valueless strip of the German Cameroons going to France as sham "compensation." President Raymond Poincaré, "the Lorrainer," visited Russia in 1912 and again in 1914. He was resolved to resist further German demands. British Foreign Minister Sir Edward Grey was loyal to the Entente but suspected Russian purposes and hoped for compromise. Russian Minister Sazonov and his Ambassador in Paris, Izvolsky, had their eyes upon the Straits and hoped to realize pan-Slav ambitions in the Balkans through Entente solidarity against the Reich. The Dual Alliance had in fact been "Balkanized." Premier Viviani agreed with Poincaré that French interests demanded firm support of St. Petersburg and a solid front against Berlin.

Meanwhile Germany gave support to Austria-Hungary against Russia in the Balkans—"like a knight in shining armor," said the Kaiser. Austrian annexation of Bosnia-Herzegovina during the "young Turk" revolution of 1908 infuriated the Serbian irredentists who looked to Russia for support. Three years later Germany's "ally," Italy, despoiled Germany's "friend," Turkey, of Tripoli, with Anglo-French approval. Austro-Italian and Austro-Russian rivalry for hegemony in the Balkans

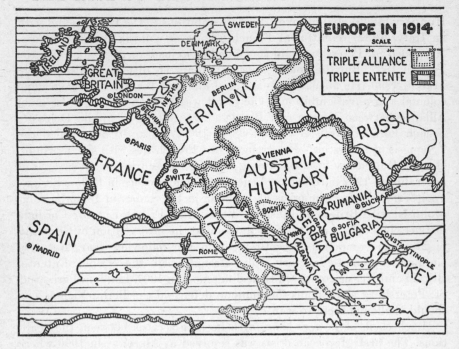

grew more acute during the Balkan wars of 1912–1913. The resultant compromises were no more than a truce between two groups of statesmen. Those in St. Petersburg championed Serbia against the Hapsburgs and hoped to acquire Constantinople. Those in Paris hoped to recover Alsace-Lorraine and felt obliged to support Tsar against Kaiser. Those in London feared German naval and colonial ambitions and supported Paris and St. Petersburg. Conversely, those in Vienna feared that Russian support of Serbia menaced the integrity of the Hapsburg Dual Monarchy, and those in Berlin felt that they must support Vienna, lest Germany's only reliable ally be weakened to the advantage of the Triple Entente.

Pan-Serbian terrorists, with the connivance of Serbian officials, assassinated the Archduke Francis Ferdinand, heir to the Hapsburg throne, at Sarajevo, capital of Bosnia, on June 28, 1914. The very existence of Austria-Hungary seemed to be at stake, for irredentist and autonomist agitation, encouraged by Serbia, threatened dissolution to an empire composed of diverse national elements. Following an unsatisfactory reply to the ultimatum of July 23, Austria-Hungary declared war upon Serbia on July 28. Two days later the Russian Government mobilized its armies against Austria-Hungary and her ally, Germany. To yield now to Russian pressure would destroy Austrian prestige in the Balkans and pave the way for the disintegration of the Dual Monarchy. If Germany refused to support Austria-Hungary, the Triple Alliance

[78]

would be weakened and Berlin would remain isolated within a circle of enemies. By the secret terms of the Franco-Russian alliance, mobilization was the signal for war. On July 31 the German Government dispatched a twelve-hour ultimatum to St. Petersburg, demanding the suspension of all Russian war measures. No reply was received. On August 1, 1914, Germany declared war on Russia. The French Government had failed to restrain the Russian mobilization, which transformed the Austro-Serbian war into a general war. France, as a loyal ally, stood as staunchly behind Russia as Germany stood behind Austria-Hungary. War was declared on France on August 3. The German invasion of Belgium as a means of attacking France resolved British hesitancy and led to a declaration of war on Germany on August 4. Italy remained neutral. All German patriots rallied to the sacred cause of the Fatherland, certain that Germany had been attacked by scheming enemies and that their only course was to hack their way to victory through encircling foes.

In the colossal combat which ensued, Germany revealed herself to be the most formidable of all the Powers in military might and more than a match for any three of her major enemies. The defection of Italy left Germany with Austria-Hungary as her only ally. Turkey joined the fray on the German side on November 5, 1914; and Bulgaria followed suit on October 14, 1915. But in this coalition of the four Central Powers, Germany was not only the keystone of the arch but the supporting pillars and the foundation stones as well. German industry and finance, German science and technology, German efficiency and morale proved equal to what seemed at the outset the impossible task of facing overwhelming odds. But here, as always in the Western State System, the coalition which proved itself the weaker was joined by one neutral State after another, alarmed at the prospect of the conquest of Europe by the most powerful State on the Continent. The blunders of German diplomacy contributed to this fatal result. The prodigious feats of German arms were in the end unable to rectify diplomatic mistakes and to turn the tide of battle against an anti-German coalition which included all of the other Great Powers of the world and half of the Minor Powers as well. Imperial Germany conquered vaster territories and won a position of military preponderance greater than that enjoyed by the first Napoleon, but in the end this military empire crumbled to pieces even more rapidly and completely than that of Bonaparte.[1]

The major phases of the struggle need only be sketched here. The "Schlieffen plan" of campaign contemplated a swift and decisive blow at France, which would release the German armies to face the Russian invasion from the east. French resistance was to be broken by a gigantic flank attack through Belgium to the north of the great border fortresses.

[1] The States at war with Germany and the dates of commencement of war were as

With crushing efficiency, fifty-three of the seventy-two divisions in the German Army poured into Belgium, pulverized the Belgian fortifications with heavy artillery, swept aside the Belgian army, defeated the French and English, and descended from the northeast upon Paris. At the Marne, however, the German onrush was stopped early in September, 1914, and the spearpoint of the invasion was deflected. In the race for the Channel ports the Allied armies retained possession of the French coast. The German lines were stabilized along the Aisne, and the conflict on the western front became a long-drawn-out war of attrition characterized by the costly and bloody futility of trench fighting. The decisive blow had failed, but the German armies held Belgium and the coal districts of northern France and could rest on the defensive, pending developments elsewhere.

Meanwhile the Russian invasion of East Prussia was crushed at Tannenberg on August 29, 1914,[1] and the war in the east carried into Russian Poland. On May 24, 1915, Italy joined the Entente against her erstwhile allies, but without any marked effect upon the combat. An Allied attack upon the Dardanelles ended in disaster, and the entrance of Bulgaria into the war enabled Germany and Austria-Hungary to conquer Serbia and establish communication with Turkey. While the German command remained on the defensive in the west, the Russian invaders of Austrian Galicia were driven out, Poland was conquered, and Russia itself was deeply invaded. In the spring of 1916 the German armies resumed the offensive on the western front, with a gigantic but unsuccessful assault upon Verdun, key to the southern half of the Allied lines. In the summer a great Allied offensive on the Somme similarly broke down.

follows:

1. Russia, August 1, 1914*
2. France, August 3, 1914
3. Belgium, August 4, 1914
4. Great Britain, August 4, 1914
5. Serbia, August 6, 1914
6. Montenegro, August 9, 1914
7. Japan, August 23, 1914
8. Italy, August 28, 1916†
9. San Marino, May 24, 1915‡
10. Portugal, March 9, 1916
11. Rumania, August 27, 1916§
12. Greece, November 28, 1916
13. United States, April 6, 1917
14. Panama, April 7, 1917
15. Cuba, April 7, 1917
16. Nicaragua, May 7, 1917
17. Siam, July 22, 1917
18. Liberia, Aug. 4, 1917
19. Brazil, Oct. 26, 1917
20. Guatemala, April 21, 1918
21. Costa Rica, May 24, 1918
22. Haiti, July 12, 1918
23. Honduras, July 19, 1918

* Separate peace, March 4, 1918.
† Declared war against Austria-Hungary, May 24, 1915.
‡ Against Austria-Hungary.
§ Separate peace, May 6, 1918.

[1] Ludendorff, Hoffmann, and François were the strategic geniuses of this remarkable victory, but Hindenburg received popular credit. This "myth" made Hindenburg an almost legendary figure and gained him election to the Presidency of the Republic in 1925 and reelection in 1932.

The war in the west remained a stalemate. In the east, Rumania joined the Allies by declaring war on Austria, August 27, 1916, but was promptly conquered by the forces of the Central Powers. The German lines were pushed deeper into Russia, and the defeated and discredited Tsarist régime collapsed in revolution in March of 1917. The war in the east went on, but with diminished intensity, for Russian powers of resistance were approaching the vanishing point.

The military ascendancy enjoyed by the Central Powers as a result of greater fighting efficiency, a unified command, and interior lines of communication was nullified by the diplomatic consequences of the war on the sea. Only one great naval battle between the British and German grand fleets was fought—off the coast of Jutland, on May 31, 1916. The German navy inflicted heavier losses on the enemy than it suffered, but the result was indecisive and the German fleet remained in port for the balance of the war. Allied naval superiority held the Central Powers in the grip of an unbreakable blockade, to which they responded by submarine blockades of Great Britain and France. The resulting controversies with neutral governments furnished the ground upon which the United States and other countries entered the war on the Allied side in the spring of 1917. Despite this enormous accession to the power of the Allies, German victory still seemed possible. The German armies remained on the defensive in France throughout 1917; but a disastrous defeat was inflicted on Italy at Caporetto in October, and a second revolution in Russia brought peace in the east. The Treaty of Brest-Litovsk of March 4, 1918, was a conqueror's peace, imposed by Berlin and Vienna on a prostrate foe.

If German military might could be concentrated for a decisive assault in the west before American fighting strength could turn the tide, there was still a possibility of success. In March of 1918 a terrific offensive was launched against the British lines in Picardy, which carried the German armies forward fifty miles toward Amiens and the Channel. In April another German attack in Flanders pushed the British back on Ypres. In May a third onslaught against the French resulted in a thirty-mile gain and carried the German forces to the Marne once more. Other attacks followed with less spectacular gains, and by July the struggle had again reached a deadlock. A final German effort to envelop Rheims in mid-July was checked at Château-Thierry. The German effort to break through the western front had failed. An allied counteroffensive was launched in July, and the German divisions were gradually forced back toward Belgium. Bulgaria, defeated by the Allied armies north of Salonika, sued for peace at the end of September. With Mesopotamia, Syria, and Palestine already lost, Turkey likewise surrendered. Austria-Hungary collapsed into chaos. On November 11, 1918, following a revolu-

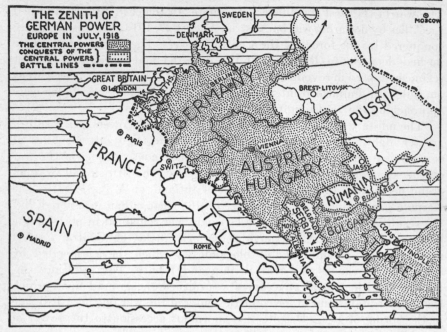

THE ZENITH OF
GERMAN POWER
EUROPE IN JULY, 1918
THE CENTRAL POWERS
CONQUESTS OF THE
CENTRAL POWERS
BATTLE LINES

tion and the overthrow of the Hohenzollern dynasty, the new German
Government acknowledged defeat and signed an armistice with Marshal
Foch and his young aide, Maxime Weygand. The ceremony took place in
Compiègne forest, near Rethondes.

On neither side had the military leaders been able to restore the
superiority of the offensive over the defense after the initial "war of
movement" degenerated into trench warfare. Casualties were therefore
colossal. The Napoleonic wars had taken the lives of 2,100,000 combatants, the American Civil War 700,000, and the Balkan wars 462,000.
The Great War, later renamed the First World War, took more lives
than all other wars of the nineteenth and early twentieth centuries
combined. The Allies mobilized in all 42,000,000 troops, of whom 5,157,-
000 were slain, 12,831,000 wounded, and 4,120,000 prisoners or missing.
Russia with 1,700,000 killed and France with 1,360,000 suffered most
heavily. The Central Powers mobilized 22,850,000 men, of whom 3,386,-
000 died, 8,380,000 were wounded, and 3,600,000 were prisoners or
missing. Germany lost 1,770,000 killed and Austria-Hungary 1,200,000.
Perhaps another 10,000,000 civilians lost their lives through battle,
famine, and pestilence. These appalling losses, followed by post-war
economic and financial chaos, hit the western Allies more heavily than
the Reich, whose territory was free from invasion even at the time of the
Armistice. They made for a vindictive peace, for the spread of pacifism
in the democracies, and for later cries in Germany for armed revenge.

The Treaty of Versailles of June 28, 1919, humbled Germany to the dust and imposed upon her terms so severe as to render her impotent in European international politics for many years. The Reich lost all its overseas colonies, Alsace-Lorraine, the Saar valley, Eupen and Malmédy, the Polish corridor, part of Upper Silesia, and a portion of Schleswig. German investments and property abroad were seized. Germany's coal production was reduced by one-third and her iron supplies by three-fourths. The German merchant marine was confiscated by the Allies. The German battle fleet was surrendered. The German army was limited to 100,000 men and was forbidden to possess tanks, heavy artillery, or airplanes. The new German navy was restricted to six battleships of not more than 10,000 tons, six light cruisers, twelve destroyers, and no submarines. The left bank of the Rhine and a fifty-kilometer zone on the right bank were demilitarized. The left bank and the bridgeheads were subjected to military occupation for fifteen years. A Reparation Commission was appointed to fix Germany's financial obligations to idemnify the victors for civilian damages, pensions, and the Belgian war debt, on the theory that the war was a result of "the aggression of Germany and her allies." The Kaiser was arraigned "for a supreme offense against international morality and the sanctity of treaties," and provision was made for bringing him to trial, along with other German "war criminals." Thanks to the collapse of Russia and the attitude of President Wilson, the terms of the secret inter-Allied treaties of 1915–1917 for the division of the spoils were not literally executed. But Germany was nevertheless crushed to earth and not permitted to join the League of Nations, which Wilson insisted on including in the peace settlement.

The Treaties of St. Germain with Austria, Trianon with Hungary, and Neuilly with Bulgaria furnished the basis for the relations between the victors and Germany's allies.[1] Among the defeated States was Russia which fell under the control of the Communists as a result of military disaster and social upheaval. The Allied Powers made an unsuccessful effort to destroy the revolutionary Soviet régime by armed intervention in the Russian civil war of 1918–1921. Despite the final triumph of the Red Army over the White Armies and the Allied forces, the Russian State lost sovereignty over Finland, the Baltic States, and Poland and also over Bessarabia which was annexed by Rumania with Allied approval. The Dual Monarchy of Austria-Hungary was completely destroyed as a political entity; and the House of Hapsburg, like the Hohenzollern and Romanov dynasties, passed into the shades. Republican

[1] The Treaty of Sèvres with Turkey was repudiated by the Turkish Nationalists who succeeded in driving the Greeks out of Asia Minor and in playing off the imperial ambitions of Great Britain and France against one another. The final Treaty of Lausanne of 1923 was consequently much more favorable to the new Turkish State than would otherwise have been the case.

Austria survived as the severed head of a truncated imperial body and was forbidden to join Germany. Hungary was reduced to the position of a small landlocked State, having lost most of its territory to its neighbors, Jugoslavia (Serbia), Rumania, and Czechoslovakia. Bulgaria was cut off from the Aegean Sea by the expansion of Greece; and Turkey was deprived of control over Arabia, Palestine, Syria, and Iraq (Mesopotamia).

A tremendous explosion of nationalism in 1918 and 1919 led to the political fragmentation of central Europe in the name of self-determination. As a means of further reducing the power of the defeated States, the Allies approved the resurrection of an enlarged Poland which was granted Austrian Galicia, part of German Upper Silesia, and the corridor to the sea between East Prussia and the rest of Germany. In 1920, Poland extended her frontiers eastward by waging war upon Russia and by annexing Vilna, the ancient capital of Lithuania. The Allies likewise sanctioned the restoration of the independence of Bohemia in the new State of Czechoslovakia. They acquiesced in the creation of a Greater Serbia, into which Montenegro was incorporated; and they approved the enlargement of Rumania at the expense of Hungary and Russia. To the north of the Succession States of Austria-Hungary appeared the new Russian border States, Lithuania, Latvia, Esthonia, and Finland, each with a total population smaller than that of the capital cities of the great States of the west, but each intensely jealous of its new sovereignty and independence.

In terms of power relationships, the chief effect of the war and the peace was to upset completely the old equilibrium between the pre-war coalitions and to replace it by the imposition upon the Continent of the military and diplomatic hegemony of France and her new allies in the east. The post-war alliances among the beneficiaries of the new distribution of power—France, Belgium, Poland and the Little Entente States of Czechoslovakia, Jugoslavia, and Rumania—created a new coalition for the preservation of the *status quo*. Germany, disarmed and diminished in size and population, was reduced to diplomatic impotence. Hungary and Austria were made powerless. Italy became master of the Adriatic by the annexation of territory at the expense of Austria and Jugoslavia and by the imposition of an Italian protectorate on Albania. She became a potential enemy of France and the Little Entente because of still unsatisfied territorial, colonial, and naval aspirations which could be fulfilled only by an alteration of the *status quo* disadvantageous to her neighbors. But she was incapable of realizing these ambitions unaided. Friction developed between Great Britain and France over colonies, debts, reparations, and armaments. A naval race started between France and Italy. Russia (the Union of Soviet Socialist Republics) held aloof from the international politics of the bourgeois States. These circumstances all made it impossible

for Great Britain and Italy either to support the dominant Continental bloc or to create effective counterweights against it.

But the hegemony of the French bloc was destined to pass away in the aftermath of world-wide economic and financial collapse—made almost inevitable by the progressive disruption of the world market and the world society after 1914. The universal insecurities and tensions engendered by the Great Depression destroyed whatever possibility may have existed during the relatively prosperous post-war years of establishing peace and plenty on firm foundations. The victors of 1919 would yield up few of their gains voluntarily. As years passed and difficulties accumulated, they became less and less disposed to resort to force to preserve the *status quo*. The vanquished (and the hungry States not among the vanquished) moved shrewdly, by devious diplomacy, by force, and by threats of force, to redress the balance. Japan seized Manchuria in 1931 in defiance of Washington, Geneva, Nanking, and Moscow. Germany succumbed to Fascism two years later. Under Hitler the Reich threw off the shackles of Versailles and prepared to make a new bid for mastery of the Continent. Fascist Italy conquered an empire in Africa in 1935–1936 and defied Great Britain and the League to keep the peace, enforce the law, or say her nay. In fear of Fascist aggression, the Soviet Union joined France and Czechoslovakia in a defensive coalition, but this enhancement of French power did not halt the disintegration of the system of alliances devised by the Quai d'Orsay. A hostile coalition began to take shape. The new balance of power was unstable. It promised wars and rumors of war in ever greater abundance. Less than two decades after Versailles, the work of the Paris Peace Conference was in large part undone. The State System moved fatalistically toward new conflicts and disasters. The cry for peace remained as empty as Dante's despairing pleas for unity six centuries earlier.

The genesis and course of the Second World War of the twentieth Century will be dealt with in detail in later pages. Here it is enough to note that the new Armageddon was rendered "inevitable" by the restoration of a balance of power between the victors and the vanquished of 1919 and that this result was due to miscalculations and delusions on the part of the Western democratic Powers which had no parallel in the earlier history of diplomacy. The United States failed to become a member of the League and sought peace through disarmament and paper pacts involving no entanglements, no responsibilities, and therefore, in theory, no risks. The unfortunate "National Government" of Britain (1931–1940) connived in the rearmament and in the aggressions of the Fascist Powers in the hope that peace could be had through "appeasement" and through the prospect of a Fascist attack on the U.S.S.R. Successive French cabinets betrayed the League and wrecked France's eastern alliances in the hope of pleasing Britain, appeasing Italy, placating Hitler, and turning the Third Reich toward the east.

The processes of Fascist aggrandizement and democratic defeatism marched in geometric progression from the plains of Manchuria to the Führerhaus in Munich. The refusal of Britain and the United States to take any effective measures to protect China from Japanese aggression in 1931 led to correct conclusions in Rome and Berlin. Nazi Germany left the League and the Disarmament Conference in October, 1933, and openly repudiated the military clauses of Versailles in March, 1935. In violation of the treaty, Britain concluded a naval accord with the Reich in June, 1935, whereby Germany was granted a new navy 35 per cent as large as the British fleet with 100 per cent parity in submarines. Mussolini, with a secret pledge of French acquiescence from Laval, attacked Ethiopia in October, 1935, and made good his conquest in the face of the hypocritical farce of League sanctions. Before his troops entered Addis Ababa,

Hitler sent the Reichswehr into the Rhineland (March, 1936) in violation of Versailles and Locarno. London and Paris contented themselves with paper protests. When Rome and Berlin openly supported Franco's Fascist rebellion in Spain in July, 1936, London and Paris organized an international "Nonintervention" Committee to deprive the Spanish Republic of arms for its defense. Washington adopted a similar policy. When Japan resumed aggression against China in July, 1937, the Western Powers wrote diplomatic notes and continued to permit their citizens to sell munitions and war supplies to the Japanese military machine. Warnings and appeals for action in resistance to the conquerors fell on ears as deaf as those to which Demosthenes had addressed like appeals twenty-two centuries earlier.

The cooperation of aggressors and appeasers reached its apogee in 1938. Hitler's seizure of Austria in March was viewed with secret approval by Downing Street and the Quai d'Orsay as foreshadowing the Nazi *Drang nach Osten*. His designs on Czechoslovakia were looked upon in a similar light. In the name of "self-determination" and "peace for our time," Chamberlain and Daladier rejected Soviet offers of military aid to Prague and compelled the Czech Republic to surrender the Sudeten areas, containing all the Czech border defenses, to the Reich. The "Peace" of Munich of September 29, 1938, was followed by Polish and Hungarian seizure of other bits of Czech territory and by Anglo-German (September 30) and French-German (December 6) "peace" declarations which were designed to leave the west secure while the Fascist Powers satisfied their appetites at the expense of small countries and the U.S.S.R.

This tragic miscalculation proved fatal. The willingness and ability of the U.S.S.R. to crush ruthlessly all internal traitors and agents of Berlin and Tokio, to resist Japanese attack on the borders of Manchuria and Mongolia, and to come to the armed aid of Czechoslovakia and the Western Powers (had they been willing to accept Soviet aid) convinced the Fascist Caesars that their path of least resistance lay elsewhere. The entire façade of the "Anti-Comintern" alliance was shrewdly and successfully designed to confuse the Western democracies. Cooperation among its members was directed toward purposes which could be realized only at the expense of France, Britain, and the United States. The original German-Japanese Anti-Comintern Pact of November 25, 1936, was signed by Italy on November 6, 1937. Manchukuo, Hungary, and Fascist Spain, each a satellite of one of the original signatories, signed later. On September 27, 1940, Berlin, Rome, and Tokio signed a ten-year alliance which threatened joint war against the United States if it attempted to save Britain or China from conquest.

Meanwhile the bitter fruits of appeasement had ripened. In mid-March, 1939, Hitler liquidated the remnant of Czecho-Slovakia, annexing

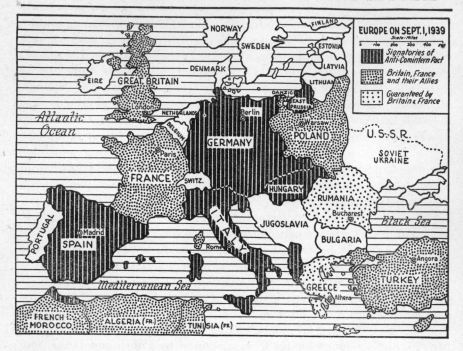

Bohemia and Moravia, converting Slovakia into a German protectorate, and tossing Carpatho-Ukraine to Hungary. This action belatedly convinced Chamberlain and Daladier that the Western Powers, rather than the Soviet Union, were in mortal danger of Fascist attack. Hitler seized Memel from Lithuania and threatened Poland. Mussolini annexed Albania and threatened Greece. London and Paris, having already thrown away the French alliance system and the French-Soviet mutual assistance pact of 1935, now sought to build a "peace front." During the spring and summer of 1939 the Western Powers guaranteed the "independence" of Poland, Rumania, Greece, and Turkey and ultimately secured reciprocal pledges of common defense from Poland and Turkey. These pledges, however, were strategically unworkable without Soviet cooperation. Chamberlain declined to pay Stalin's price for an alliance against the Reich—*i.e.*, Soviet military control of the Baltic States and military access to Poland. Moscow accordingly abandoned the Western Powers and concluded a nonaggression pact with Berlin on August 23, 1939.

With the Allies thus isolated, the Third Reich was free to strike. Poland was invaded on September 1, conquered in two weeks, and partitioned between Germany and the U.S.S.R. by the Moscow agreement of September 28, 1939. Britain and France declared war on Germany on September 3. The long winter stalemate, carefully designed by the Nazi leaders to demoralize the Western democracies, was marked by the imposition of Soviet protectorates on Estonia, Latvia, and Lithuania (all annexed to the U.S.S.R. in August, 1940) and by a Soviet attack upon Finland which finally compelled Helsinki to accept peace terms in March, 1940, involving territorial cessions to the Soviet Union. With incredible speed, made possible by a new technique of warfare, German divisions conquered Denmark and Norway on April 9, 1940, invaded and overran Luxemburg, Belgium, and the Netherlands on May 10, pierced the French defenses at Sedan on May 14, reached the Channel on May 21, drove the British Expeditionary Force from Dunkirk on June 3, crushed the French army south of the Somme on June 5–10, took Paris on June 14, and compelled the French Government to sign an armistice on June 23. The ceremony took place in the same dining car in the forest of Compiègne where the Second Reich had acknowledged defeat twenty-two years previously. Italy meanwhile declared war on France and Britain on June 10 and fifteen days later signed an armistice with a France already defeated by the Nazi hosts.

The fall of France caused the U.S.S.R. to seek safety by seizing Bessarabia and northern Bukovina from Rumania and incorporating Lithuania, Latvia, and Estonia into the Union. The United States was moved by the débâcle to give armed aid to Britain "short of war." to appropriate 13 billion dollars for armaments within the next four months, and to introduce military conscription during "peace" for the first time in the history of the Republic. Nazi plans to invade and subjugate Britain during the summer were frustrated. The Axis nevertheless dominated the Continent. Italian forces occupied Somaliland and invaded Egypt but were driven back into Libya, most of which was lost to the British by February, 1941. They met with equally humiliating defeat when they invaded Greece. Japan occupied French Indo-China and threatened Britain and America in the Far East. While London and other British cities suffered the agonies inflicted earlier on Shanghai, Addis Ababa, Madrid, Warsaw, and Rotterdam, a possibility developed that the conquest of the world by the Fascist Triplice might yet be averted by Soviet and American intervention. In the absence of such intervention, it appeared likely by the spring of 1941 that the world would be redivided by Berlin, Rome, and Tokio with the U.S.S.R. and the United States left in dangerous isolation promising neither security nor peace save on such terms as the Triplice might dictate.

This soul-shattering revolution in *Weltpolitik* constituted a transformation of the entire Western State System from a globe-girdling community of some threescore "sovereign" States into a structure of great Continental imperiums competing with one another for mastery of the earth. The restoration of the State System to its pre-war pattern, on the model of 1815 and 1919, appeared improbable whatever the verdict

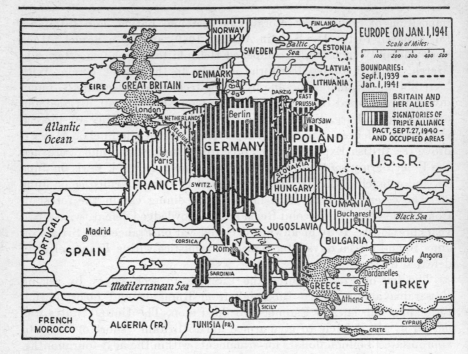

of arms might be. The unification of the world, or at least of the Continental land masses, promised to be permanent. This result might be the work of the conquering sword of the new Caesars. Or it might be the work of an anti-Fascist coalition tardily dedicated to world federation and perhaps capable at appalling cost of overthrowing the conquerors who had been brought to hegemony by the Western Munichmen. In either event the age of national sovereignty, of democratic capitalism, and of rivalries and conflicts among small nation-states was at an end, with no one certain whether the sacrifices of the morrow would bring a new Dark Ages or a final consummation of the political unity of Western mankind.

SUGGESTED READINGS

A. General Texts

Brown, F. J., Charles Hodges, and J. S. Roucek: *Contemporary World Politics*, New York, Wiley, 1939.

Buell, R. L.: *International Relations*, New York, Holt, 1929.

Hodges, Charles: *The Background of International Relations*, New York, Wiley, 1931.

Maxwell, B. W.: *International Relations*, New York, Crowell, 1939.

Middlebush, F. A., and N. L. Hill: *Elements of International Relations*, New York, McGraw-Hill, 1940.

Sharp, W. R. and G. L. Kirk: *Contemporary International Politics*, New York, Farrar, 1940.

Simonds, F. H. and Brooks Emeny: *The Great Powers in World Politics*, New York, American Book, 1939.

Steiner, H. A.: *Principles and Problems of International Relations*, New York, Harper, 1939.

B. General History

Banres, H. E.: *An Intellectual and Cultural History of the Western World*, New York, Random House, 1937.

Benns, F. L.: *European History since 1870*, New York, Crofts, 1938.

Burckhardt, C. J.: *Richelieu*, New York, Oxford, 1940.

Eyre, Edward (ed.): *European Civilization: Its Origin and Development* (4 vols.), New York, Oxford, 1936.

Gilbert, A. H.: *Machiavelli's Prince and Its Forerunners*, Durham, Duke University Press, 1939.

Gottschalk, L. R.: *The Era of the French Revolution (1715–1815)*, Boston, Houghton, 1940.

Hayes, C. J. H.: *A Political and Cultural History of Modern Europe* (2 vols.), New York, Macmillan, 1932.

Hick, A. C.: *Modern World History—1776–1926*, New York, Knopf, 1928.

King-Hall, Stephen: *Our Own Times, 1913–1934* (2 vols.), London, Nicholson, 1935.

Kohn, H.: *Revolutions and Dictatorships*, Cambridge, Harvard University Press, 1939.

Langer, W. H.: *Encyclopedia of World History*, Boston, Houghton, 1940.

Machiavelli, Nicollò: *The Prince and the Discourses* (intro. by Max Lerner), New York, Modern Library, Random House, 1940.

Laski, H. J.: *The Rise of Liberalism: the Philosophy of a Business Civilization*, New York, Harper, 1936.

Merriam, C. E.: *History of the Theory of Sovereignty*, New York, Columbia University Press, 1900.

Neurath, Otto: *Modern Man in the Making*, New York, Knopf, 1939.

Russell, F. M.: *Theories of International Relations*, New York, Appleton-Century, 1936.

Spengler, Oswald: *The Decline of the West* (2 vols.), New York, Knopf, 1928.

Swain, J. E.: *A History of World Civilization*, New York, McGraw-Hill, 1939.

Toynbee, A. J.: *A Study of History* (6 vols.), New York, Oxford, 1940.

White, W. W.: *The Process of Change in the Ottoman Empire*, Chicago, University of Chicago Press, 1937.

C. The Diplomatic Background of 1914

Bogart, E. L.: *Direct and Indirect Costs of the Great World War*, New York, Oxford, 1919.

Buchan, John: *A History of the Great War*, Boston, Houghton, 1940.

Fay, S. B.: *The Origins of the [First] World War* (2 vols.), New York, Macmillan, 1929.

Grey, Edward: *Twenty-five Years*, New York, Stokes, 1925.

Hart, Liddell: *The War in Outline, 1914–1918*, New York, Random House, 1936.

Langer, W. L.: *The Diplomacy of Imperialism, 1890–1902* (2 vols.), New York, Knopf, 1935.

Lloyd George, David: *War Memoirs of David Lloyd George, 1914–1915* (6 vols.), Boston, Little, Brown, 1933–36.

Nicolson, Harold: *Peacemaking, 1919*, London, Constable, 1933.

Schmitt, B. E.: *The Coming of the War—1914* (2 vols.), New York, Scribner, 1930.

Wolff, Theodor: *The Eve of 1914*, New York, Knopf, 1936.

D. Diplomacy, 1919–1939

Abend, Hallett: *Chaos in Asia*, New York, Washburn, 1939.

Almond, Nina and R. H. Lutz: *The Treaty of St. Germain*, Stanford University, Calif., Stanford University Press, 1934.

Angell, Norman: *Peace with the Dictators?*, London, Hamilton, 1938.

Armstrong, H. F.: *When There is no Peace*, New York, Macmillan, 1939.

Background of War, by the Editors of *Fortune*, New York, Knopf, 1937.

Benson, Oliver: *Through the Diplomatic Looking-glass*, Norman, University of Oklahoma Press, 1939.

Bethlen, Count Stephen: *The Treaty of Trianon and European Peace*, New York, Longmans, 1934.

Birdsall, P.: *Versailles Twenty Years After*, New York, Reynal and Hitchcock, 1941.

Birchall, F. T.: *The Storm Breaks*, New York, Viking, 1940.

Boothe, Clare: *Europe in the Spring*, New York, Knopf, 1940.

Carr, E. H.: *The Twenty Years' Crisis*, 1919–1939, New York, Macmillan, 1940.

Churchill, Winston L.: *The Aftermath 1918–1928*, New York, Scribner, 1929.

Dean, V. M.: *Europe in Retreat*, New York, Knopf, 1939.

Duff-Cooper, Alfred: *The Second World War: First Phase*, New York, Scribner, 1939.

Dutt, R. P.: *World Politics 1918–1936*, New York, Random House, 1936.

Grattan, C. H.: *Preface to Chaos: War in the Making*, New York, Dodge, 1936.

Hutton, Graham: *Survey after Munich*, Boston, Little, Brown, 1939.

Kain, R. S.: *Europe: Versailles to Warsaw*, New York, H. W. Wilson, 1939.

Keynes, J. M.: *The Economic Consequences of the Peace*, London, Macmillan, 1920.

Macartney, C. A.: *Hungary and Her Successors: The Treaty of Trianon and Its Consequences*, 1919–1937, New York, Oxford, 1937.

McInnes, Edgar: *The War: First Year*, New York, Oxford, 1940.

Millis, Walter: *Why Europe Fights*, New York, Morrow, 1940.

Morse, H. B., and H. F. MacNair: *Far Eastern International Relations*, Boston, Houghton, 1931.

Schuman, F. L.: *Europe on the Eve*, New York, Knopf, 1939.

————: *Night Over Europe*, New York, Knopf, 1941.

Seton-Watson, R. W.: *From Munich to Danzig*, London, Methuen, 1939.

Stephens, W. E.: *Revisions of the Treaty of Versailles*, New York, Columbia University Press, 1939.

Swing, R. G.: *How War Came*, New York, Norton, 1939.

Wiskemann, Elizabeth: *Prologue to War*, New York, Oxford, 1940.

Wolff, Theodor: *Through Two Decades*, London, Heinemann, 1936.

E. Current Guides

Events: the Monthly Review of World Affairs.

Foreign Affairs (quarterly).

Foreign Policy Association: *Bulletins* (weekly) and *Reports* (bimonthly).

Gunther, John: *Inside Asia*, New York, Harper, 1940.

————: *Inside Europe*, New York, Harper, 1939.

Horrabin, J. F.: *An Atlas of Current Affairs*, New York, Knopf, 1935.

International Conciliation Pamphlets, Carnegie Endowment for International Peace (monthly).

Mallory, W. H. (ed.): *Political Handbook of the World 1940*, New York, Council on Foreign Relations, 1940.

The Statesman's Year Book (annual).

Toynbee, A. J. and J. W. Wheeler-Bennett: *Survey of International Affairs* (annual), New York, Oxford.

Utley, Clifton (ed.): *Foreign Notes*, Chicago, Council on Foreign Relations (biweekly).

SOVEREIGN STATES OF THE WORLD
Jan. 1, 1941

NOTE.—Order of States within each group is by population. Dates indicate time of *de facto* annexation, conquest, "protection," or occupation of territories recently seized by the totalitarian Powers. Areas and populations of such territories are approximations where new frontiers do not coincide with old census districts.

State	Capital	Area, square miles	Population
A. Great Powers			
Union of Socialist Soviet Republics.........	Moscow	8,095,728	171,800,000
Eastern Poland, Sept. 28, 1939...........	....	80,000	13,000,000
Finnish territories, Mar. 12, 1940........	....	12,250	100,000
Bessarabia, June 28, 1940..............	....	17,146	3,110,000
Northern Bukovina, June 28, 1940.......	....	1,500	250,000
Estonia, Aug. 25, 1940.................	Tallinn	18,356	1,135,000
Lithuania, Aug. 25, 1940...............	Kovno	22,959	2,880,000
Latvia, Aug. 25, 1940..................	Riga	25,402	2,000,000
Grand total....................	....	8,273,341	194,275,000
Greater Germany.......................	Berlin	181,699	69,000,000
Austria, Mar. 12, 1938.................	Vienna	32,369	7,000,000
Sudetenland, Oct. 1, 1938.............	....	11,236	3,653,000
Bohemia, Mar. 15, 1939...............	Prague	12,525	5,000,000
Moravia, Mar. 15, 1939...............	....	6,533	2,500,000
Slovakia, Mar. 23, 1939...............	Bratislava	14,848	2,600,000
Memel, Mar. 22, 1939..................	....	200	150,000
Danzig, Sept. 1, 1939..................	....	754	415,000
Western Poland, Sept. 28, 1939..........	Warsaw	70,000	22,000,000
Denmark, Apr. 9. 1940.................	Copenhagen	16,576	3,813,000
Norway, Apr. 9, 1940..................	Oslo	124,556	2,910,000
Luxemburg, May 10, 1940..............	Luxemburg	999	300,000
Netherlands, May 15, 1940.............	The Hague	12,704	8,850,000
Belgium, May 28, 1940...............	Brussels	11,775	8,400,000
Occupied France, June 25, 1940..........	Paris	130,000	27,438,000
Rumania, Oct. 8, 1940.................	Bucharest	73,238	13,910,000
Grand total......................	....	700,012	178,939,000
United States of America................	Washington, D. C.	2,973,776	131,800,000
Japan.................................	Tokio	148,000	72,750,000
Great Britain..........................	London	89,041	47,500,000
Italy.................................	Rome	119,750	45,000,000
Albania, Apr. 9, 1939.................	Tirana	10,629	1,100,000
Total............................	....	130,379	46,100,000

SOVEREIGN STATES OF THE WORLD.—(*Continued*)

State	Capital	Area, square miles	Population
B. Secondary Powers			
China..................................	Chungking	4,000,000*	428,000,000*
Brazil.................................	Rio de Janeiro	3,275,000	46,500,000
Manchukuo............................	Hsinking	503,013	39,000,000
Spain..................................	Madrid	196,607	25,500,000
Mexico................................	Mexico City	763,944	20,000,000
Turkey................................	Ankara	294,416	17,840,000
Hatay, June 23, 1939..................	Alexandretta	200	273,000
Total.............................	....	295,616	18,113,000
Egypt.................................	Cairo	383,000	16,000,000
Jugoslavia............................	Belgrade	95,558	15,800,000
Thailand (Siam).......................	Bangkok	200,148	15,000,000
Iran (Persia)..........................	Teheran	628,000	15,000,000
Unoccupied France.....................	Vichy	82,659	14,500,000
Hungary...............................	Budapest	35,875	9,150,000
Southern Slovakia, Nov. 2, 1938........	....	4,605	1,045,000
Carpatho-Ukraine, Mar. 16, 1939.......	Chust	4,690	672,000
Northeast Transylvania, Aug. 30, 1940...	....	17,000	2,370,000
Total.............................	....	62,170	13,237,000
Argentina.............................	Buenos Aires	1,079,965	12,800,000
C. Minor Powers			
Colombia..............................	Bogota	448,794	8,800,000
Afghanistan...........................	Kabul	270,000	8,000,000
Portugal..............................	Lisbon	35,490	7,300,000
Greece................................	Athens	50,250	7,250,000
Peru..................................	Lima	482,133	6,600,000
Sweden................................	Stockholm	173,347	6,300,000
Bulgaria..............................	Sofia	39,825	6,200,000
Southern Dobrudja, Sept. 7, 1940.......	....	5,000	360,000
Total.............................	....	44,825	6,560,000
Nepal.................................	Kathmandu	54,000	5,600,000
Chile.................................	Santiago	285,133	4,650,000
Cuba..................................	Havana	41,164	4,235,000
Switzerland...........................	Bern	15,944	4,220,000
Saudi Arabia..........................	Mecca	320,000	4,000,000
Finland...............................	Helsinki	135,561	3,700,000
Iraq..................................	Bagdad	116,600	3,700,000

*Excluding Manchukuo, but including Mongolia, Tibet, Sinkiang, and coastal areas under Japanese occupation, with a population of perhaps 200,000,000.

SOVEREIGN STATES OF THE WORLD.—(*Continued*)

State	Capital	Area, square miles	Population
Yemen	Sanaa	75,000	3,500,000
Venezuela	Caracas	352,051	3,460,000
Bolivia	La Paz	537,500	3,450,000
Guatemala	Guatemala	45,452	3,100,000
Haiti	Port-au-Prince	10,204	3,000,000
Ecuador	Quito	275,936	2,800,000
Uruguay	Montevideo	72,153	2,100,000
Salvador	San Salvador	13,173	1,750,000
Dominican Republic	Ciudad Trujillo	19,332	1,550,000
Liberia	Monrovia	45,000	1,500,000
Honduras	Tegucigalpa	44,275	1,000,000
Nicaragua	Managua	60,000	1,150,000
Paraguay	Asuncion	321,000	1,000,000
Costa Rica	San José	23,000	625,000
Oman	Muscat	82,000	500,000
Panama	Panama	33,667	470,000
Iceland	Reykjavik	39,709	120,000
D. British Dominions			
India	Delhi	1,808,679	370,000,000
Canada	Ottawa	3,694,863	11,300,000
Union of South Africa	Pretoria	472,550	10,000,000
Australia	Canberra	2,974,581	7,000,000
Eire	Dublin	26,601	3,100,000
New Zealand	Wellington	103,934	1,700,000
Newfoundland	St. Johns	42,734	300,000
Labrador	St. Johns	110,000	4,800
E. Small States			
Monaco	Monaco	8	25,000
San Marino	San Marino	38	15,000
Liechtenstein	Vaduz	65	12,000
Andorra	Andorra	191	6,000
Vatican City	Vatican City	0.1	1,000

Note: Hungary became the highway for German troops moving into Rumania in the autumn of 1940. On March 1, 1941, Bulgaria signed the Triple Alliance pact and was occupied by the Reichswehr. If the areas and populations of these states are added to "Greater Germany," the Third Reich in the spring of 1941 had under its direct control some 807,000 square miles inhabited by 198,736,000 people.

BOOK TWO
WORLD ORDER

INTRODUCTION TO BOOK TWO

The present study is based upon the assumption that it is useful to view international politics in its cultural context, *i.e.*, the States of Western civilization and the totality of attitudes, habits, institutions, and procedures which they have evolved in their dealings with one another. This complex has here been designated as the Western State System. International politics revolves about the competitive struggle for power and prestige among the units of the System. It is therefore comprehensible only in terms of the general nature of the system and the specific patterns of action which have evolved out of the interrelationships between its units.

These habits and practices have been dealt with historically in the first section of the volume. They will henceforth be dealt with descriptively and analytically. For this purpose, they may be classified into two general types: those which make for "Order" in the community of nations and those which make for "Anarchy."

Between these extremes, all political societies oscillate, since the essence of every polity is a workable compromise between liberty and authority. Undiluted liberty spells license and chaos. Arbitrary authority spells tyranny. The modern community of nations is an imperfect polity. Its members are "sovereign" and "independent." Each is therefore a law unto itself, acknowledging no obedience to any higher power. Any community in which the members successfully assert such prerogatives is a community in a condition of anarchy, actual or potential. But the sovereign nation-states of the Western States System have developed rules of law, practices of diplomacy, procedures of orderly compromise, sundry institutions of collaboration which, however imperfect they may appear by comparison with their counterparts within any well-ordered State, are nevertheless important limitations upon anarchy. These rudimentary forms of world order will be discussed in the present book, with the forces making for anarchy reserved for later treatment.

CHAPTER III

THE LAW OF NATIONS

1. SOURCES AND SANCTIONS

It follows that we make enquiry into that most general and universal rule of human action, to which every man is obliged to conform, as he is a reasonable creature. To this rule custom hath given the name of natural law, and we may call it likewise the law universal or perpetual, the former in regard that it binds the whole body of the human race, the latter because it is not subject to change, which is the disadvantage of positive laws.— SAMUEL PUFFENDORF, *De jure naturae et gentium.*

Another species of law is positive (instituted or voluntary) law, which derives its origin from will and is either human or divine. Human positive law includes civil law, which proceeds from the power of the State, the law of nations, which receives its binding force from the will of all nations or of many, and law which does not emanate from the power of the State though subject to it, such as the commands of a father or a master.—HUGO GROTIUS, *De jure belli ac pacis.*

LAWLESSNESS is the son of anarchy and the brother of violence. These unpleasant companions flourish in all human communities where common purposes, implemented by an effective central power, are insufficient to enforce peace. In this generation the modern community of nations has entered upon a "time of troubles" in which the restraints of law upon brute force appear to be conspicuous by their absence. In an epoch of contending States, with the great contenders for mastery seeking to crush their rivals, a consideration of "international law" will appear to some to be wholly academic or to have only historical interest. This view, however, is shortsighted. Even in the midst of wars of annihilation, the older rules of the law of nations are still widely observed. Here (as elsewhere) respect for law attracts no attention, whereas violations "make the headlines." The painful processes of inter-state unification, moreover, whether achieved by the sword of tyranny or by the voluntary federation of those who survive the holocaust, will inevitably continue through the building of the world order of the future on foundations derived from the world public law of the present and the past. That law, therefore, cannot be dismissed as obsolete. So long as men and nations find it useful to act in accordance with established rules, international law will remain a living and growing body of legal principles, honored more in the observance than in the breach.

[99]

For the past three centuries the States of the Western State System have played the game of international politics in accordance with certain generally recognized rules which have usually been regarded as binding upon all the members of international society. These rules were first systematically formulated and set down as principles of the "Law of Nations" by Hugo Grotius at the beginning of the seventeenth century. Like many rules of law, however, they had been developing for many centuries before they were reduced to written form. Once put into writing and made the object of scientific study, they developed at a much more rapid rate than before. They became a well-defined and logically integrated set of principles indicating the rights and obligations of States in almost every conceivable international situation. The mere recital of these principles in any complete fashion would fill many hundreds of pages. Since the days of Grotius, innumerable scholars and jurists in all lands have written elaborate textbooks and treatises for the purpose of describing these rules and relating them to one another. Hundreds of judicial tribunals, both national and international, in countless thousands of cases, have developed international law by an endless process of adapting established rules to new situations. Thousands of treaties and conventions between States have made more specific the conceptions of rights and obligations which have grown out of custom and usage. This constant adaptation, reinterpretation, and elaboration of principles have created a vast body of international jurisprudence which could not be described adequately in many volumes, much less in one chapter of a single volume. This circumstance, coupled with the fact that the great textbooks are available in almost every part of the world, makes it unnecessary for the purposes of the present study to undertake more than a brief and simple sketch of the basic concepts underlying the whole structure.

Since the present study is concerned with the relations of States to one another, rather than with the legal rights and obligations of individuals, attention will be devoted only to that portion of international law which applies to States, *i.e.*, "public" international law, as distinct from "private" international law. The former has to do with States as legal and political entites. It consists of the rules and principles which the whole society of States habitually expects its members to observe in their relations with one another. It seeks to deduce from these rules and principles the legal rights and obligations of States in each particular situation. Private international law, on the other hand, is concerned primarily with individuals rather than with States. It has to do with the rights and obligations of individuals as they are affected by differences in the legislation of States. The name "conflict of laws" is often applied to this body of legal principles, for it deals with situations in which the legal status of persons or property is in doubt because of overlapping jurisdictions and divergencies of national legislation.

Inasmuch as public international law differs in many respects from other types of law, as has been suggested above, it will be useful to consider at the outset the problem of its sources and sanctions. Every statesman, diplomat, and jurist who is confronted with a legal problem concerning the relations among States must know where to look for the principles, precedents, and established rules and procedures which will indicate the rights and obligations of the parties in the particular situation. In dealing with problems of national, or "municipal," law, as it is sometimes called, this problem is comparatively simple; for lawyers and jurists can readily "find the law" in written constitutions, in statutes passed by national or local legislatures, or (in Anglo-Saxon countries) in past judicial decisions which furnish precedents for future cases. Once the law has been determined upon and a decision has been reached, the judgment will be carried out by the court, the sheriff, or, if need be, by the whole force of the State. In criminal cases, the convicted offender is fined, sentenced to jail, or sometimes executed for his crime. In civil cases, the injured party is awarded damages at the expense of him who has committed the injury. In international law, however, the situation is quite different. The law is not usually reduced to statutory form, and there is no judge, jury, sheriff, or police force to ensure its execution. In both its sources and its sanctions, *i.e.*, the means available to ensure its enforcement, it differs markedly from other types of law.

The sources of international law may be divided into four categories in order of their importance: (1) agreement, (2) custom, (3) reason, and (4) authority. In every international law case, the best and most conclusive sources of information regarding the rights of the parties are the written agreements, treaties, conventions, protocols, and the like, which the States involved have concluded with one another. Such written agreements, if properly signed and ratified, are unqualifiedly binding upon the parties. All modern States have hundreds of treaties with other States, dealing with an enormous variety of matters. The texts of these treaties are usually published by the signatory parties in a national treaty series.[1] There is also available a large number of privately published compilations of treaty agreements, though the best single source of recent treaties is the League of Nations Treaty Series. States are always free to make international law between themselves by treaty, provided that they do not violate the rights of third States. In this way, they agree upon the

[1] Treaties of the United States are issued in pamphlet form in the State Department Treaty Series. *Cf.* also Malloy (ed.), *Treaties, Conventions, Protocols, etc., of the United States* (2 vols.), 1909, and a third volume issued in 1923.

rules and principles which they propose henceforth to follow in dealing with one another. If such agreements cover the case in hand, it is unnecessary to look further for sources of law, for specific agreements supersede all other possible sources.

But if existing agreements do not cover adequately the situation under consideration, it is necessary to look further for enlightenment as to the rights and duties of the parties. The established customs, practices, and usages of States in dealing with analogous problems in the past furnish the next best guide. Differences of opinion are obviously more likely to arise regarding rights based exclusively upon customary international law than is the case where rights are specifically defined in written agreements. But the great bulk of modern international law is based upon custom and practice. When it can be clearly shown that a particular principle or practice has been generally observed by the majority of States over a long period of time, no question will ordinarily be raised regarding its legal validity. When, for example, the United States Supreme Court was obliged to pass upon the legality of the capture of a Spanish fishing smack by American gunboats during the Spanish-American War, it held the capture unlawful on the ground that "at the present day, by the general consent of the civilized nations of the world, and independently of any express treaty or other public act, it is an established rule of international law, founded on considerations of humanity to a poor and industrious order of men, and of the mutual convenience of belligerent States, that coast fishing vessels, with their implements and supplies, cargoes and crews, unarmed, and honestly pursuing their peaceful calling of catching and bringing in fresh fish, are exempt from capture as prize of war" (*The Paquete Habaña*, 175 U.S. 677). The court further held that a practice which had originally been a matter of custom or comity could readily become an established rule of law through securing the general assent of States. This view has been followed by practically all courts, arbitral tribunals, jurists, and text writers.

When appeals to agreements and to customs both fail to indicate the rights and obligations of States, recourse is had to reason and to authority, *i.e.*, to logical deductions from established general principles, and to arbitral awards, the decision of courts, and the opinions of text writers and jurists. Novel situations are constantly arising in contemporary international relations with regard to which no agreements have been concluded and no customs have developed. These are ordinarily dealt with by seeking to apply to the new facts a line of reasoning resting upon established general rules accepted as *a priori* premises. If, by this procedure, a definition of rights and obligations can be arrived at which appears to be in harmony with the whole body of international jurisprudence, it is more than likely to be accepted by the parties as a source of law in the novel situation. Similarly, the judgments of judicial tribunals, national or international, and the views of widely recognized authorities are constantly relied upon as guides to the law, chiefly to support the conclusions to which a consideration of agreements, customs, and reason has already led. Judicial decisions and arbitral awards are binding only upon the parties to the disputes of which they are settlements, but taken as a whole they indicate to all States the prevalent conception of rights and duties accepted in international society. Agreement and authority are written sources of international law. Custom and reason are unwritten only in the sense that they are not incorporated in treaties or decisions. The precedents, practices, and usages out of which they emerge, however, are to be found in the diplomatic correspondence and State papers maintained in governmental archives.

The sanctions of international law may be classified, in order of their importance, as (1) habit, (2) expediency, (3) good faith, and (4) organized force. Those rules and principles which have been habitually observed for the longest period of time are obviously most likely to be observed in the future, since the whole force of inertia lies behind them, and States, no less than individuals, are prone to do things in ways which are easy because traditional. The principle of the immunity and inviolability of diplomatic representatives, for example, has been generally observed by States for more than 2,500 years and is almost never willfully violated at the present time. Considerations of self-interest and political expediency are also influential in securing the observance of established principles, particularly as regards the international law of war. At the outbreak of the American Civil War there was some disposition in Union circles to treat captured members of the Confederate armies not as prisoners, in accordance with the laws of war, but as rebels who might be punished for treason, arson, murder, and other individual acts. Once it was realized, however, that the Confederacy would promptly retaliate on Federal prisoners and that the Union cause would be injured rather than aided by the contemplated departure from established rules, the intention was abandoned and the usual principles governing the conduct of hostilities were observed on both sides during the conflict. A more farsighted view of military and political expediency on the part of the German High Command would similarly have dictated observance of agreements forbidding the use of poison gas in the Great War. After the first use of gas by the Germans in 1915, events revealed that the Allied armies were not merely prepared to retaliate but possessed more adequate facilities for gas manufacture and enjoyed the advantage of the prevailing westerly winds on the Western Front.

Good faith as a sanction is doubtless of decreasing importance in the era of totalitarian aggression and lawlessness. More and more States adhere to the Machiavellian view that agreements and established customs should be observed only so long as it is expedient to do so. As for organized force, there has not as yet been developed in the Western State System any effective machinery for applying international coercion to lawbreaking States, in spite of the hypothetical scheme embodied in the Covenant of the League of Nations. Thus far, when force has been utilized to ensure observance of international law, it has always been the force of State against State, with the enforcer often pursuing ulterior political objectives disguised by a façade of morality and sanctimonious solicitude for the observance of international obligations. Organized force thus remains the least effective of the four types of sanctions mentioned.

2. STATE AND GOVERNMENT

> There is annexed to the sovereignty the right of making war and peace with other nations and commonwealths; that is to say, of judging when it is for the public good, and how great forces are to be assembled, armed, and paid for that end; and to levy money upon the subjects to defray the expenses thereof.—THOMAS HOBBES, *Leviathan.*

Since States are the persons of public international law, it follows that international law is concerned primarily with such sovereign political entities as are generally recognized as "States" within international society. With certain exceptions which will be noted below, no individual or corporation, no community or territorial group can claim rights under international law unless it is regarded by the members of the State System as a State, independent and coequal with other States. It is generally agreed that a State, in order to be worthy of the name, must possess citizens or subjects and a well-defined territory. Since land was the most important form of wealth and power, and sovereignty was associated with territorial property at the time when the foundations of international law were being laid, a territorial basis has always been regarded as a prerequisite to statehood. But the question of whether a particular political entity does or does not constitute a State in fact (*de facto*) is not, in itself, a problem of international law at all. A "State" may exist for a long period of time as a sovereign political entity, but it does not become a State in the legal sense until it has been received into the family of nations as a recognized member. Switzerland and the Netherlands before 1648, the United States between 1776 and 1778, Japan prior to 1854, and Turkey prior to 1856 all constituted *de facto* States without being persons of international law, *i.e.*, without being formally admitted as full-fledged members into the Western State System. States are initiated into the society of States only by the process of diplomatic recognition extended to them by other States.

When and under what circumstances established States shall recognize new States is entirely a matter of policy. That is to say, the granting of recognition of new States is entirely discretionary, and not mandatory, on the part of other States already established and recognized. It may be granted at once, it may be delayed, or it may be withheld indefinitely for legal reasons, for political reasons, for good, bad, or indifferent reasons. A new State seeking recognition has no means of compelling other States to grant it. Considerations of convenience and the obvious utility of maintaining diplomatic contacts with a *de facto* State, however, will usually dictate its recognition by other States as soon as its existence and independence are firmly established. New States may be recognized individually or collectively by other States. Greece was recognized collectively by the Powers at the London Conference of 1830. Belgium was likewise recognized collectively in 1831, Montenegro, Serbia, and Rumania in 1878, and Czechoslovakia and Poland in 1918. The Allied Powers jointly recognized the independence of the Baltic States of Estonia, Lithuania, and Latvia in 1919; but the United States, for reasons connected with its policy toward Russia, withheld recognition until 1922.

Recognition may be granted in a variety of ways, but once granted is irrevocable. When granted, it dates back, so far as legal rights and obligations are concerned, to the date of the establishment of the new State. Normally, one State recognizes another by a formal declaration to this effect, followed by an official exchange of diplomatic representatives. Either the dispatch or the reception of a diplomatic agent constitutes recognition. The reception of the consular agents of a new State through the granting to them of exequaturs authorizing them to assume their functions is also equivalent to recognition, though the sending of a consular agent to receive an exequatur from the authorities of a new State does not necessarily imply recognition on the part of the sending State.[1] The signature of an international agreement, a salute to the flag, or any other similar act authorized by the responsible authorities of the State whose officials take such action likewise constitutes recognition. In the United States, as in all other countries, the power to recognize new States and governments is vested in the executive, *i.e.*, the President and the Secretary of State. Congress has no power to grant, or to compel the granting of, recognition; and the courts never question executive discretion in such matters.[2] The United States has usually recognized new States by official proclamation of the President or Secretary of State.

If an outside State recognizes the independence of a new State during a period of conflict in which the new State's claim to independence is still

---

[1] See pp. 155–156 below.
[2] See *Williams v. Suffolk Insurance Co.*, 13 Pet. 415; *Jones v. U. S.*, 137 U.S. 202; *Foster v. Neilson*, 2 Pet. 253.

being contested by the State formerly having jurisdiction over its territory, the act of recognition takes on the appearance of intervention or unlawful interference in the domestic affairs of another State. The injured party may legitimately regard such premature recognition as a hostile act. France recognized the independence of the United States by signing treaties of alliance and commerce with American representatives at Paris on February 6, 1778, when Great Britain was still making active efforts to subdue her rebellious colonies. Great Britain consequently declared war against France. Had the European Powers recognized the independence of the Confederacy during the American Civil War, this action similarly would have been regarded as a *casus belli* on the part of the Union. The recognition of Mexico and the other Latin American republics by the United States in 1822 and 1823 was granted at a time when Spain still asserted claims to her lost empire but when all prospects of her recovering it had vanished. Japan's recognition of the Manchurian puppet State of Henry Pu-Yi on September 15, 1932, was a violation of the territorial integrity of China and might have been treated as an act of war by China had the latter been in a position to offer resistance. In every such case, the State whose rights are violated by premature recognition has a valid complaint against the recognizing State which has thus sanctioned the partition of its territory before the alleged new State has in fact established its independence.

Almost all the foregoing observations are also applicable to the recognition of new governments within States already recognized. A revolution within a State normally terminates its diplomatic relations with other States. The State continues to be a person of international law, but in the absence of the recognition of its new government by other governments it has no means of communicating with outside States. Recognition of revolutionary governments, no less than recognition of new States, is a question of policy on the part of other governments. During the period from 1793 down to the first Wilson administration, the United States usually adhered to the so-called *de facto* theory of recognition, which holds that new governments should be recognized as soon as they are in fact in control of the State, in contrast to the *de jure* theory, which denies the right of revolution and holds that only legitimate, constitutional governments are entitled to recognition. When Washington's Cabinet in 1793 granted an official reception to the new French Minister, Citizen Genêt, *i.e.*, extended diplomatic recognition to the revolutionary régime in France, it did so on the basis of Secretary of State Jefferson's view that the only relevant question was whether the new régime was in effective control of France and therefore in a position to represent the French State and discharge its international obligations. The *de facto* theory was followed by the United States quite consistently with respect to the various revolutions in Europe and Latin America throughout the nineteenth century.

These two divergent "theories" of recognition should not be confused with the two kinds or stages of recognition, *de facto* and *de jure*. The former phrase is applied to diplomatic recognition of a new State or government not followed at once by an exchange of diplomatic representatives. Great Britain, for example, extended *de facto* recognition to the Soviets by the trade agreement of March, 1921. *De jure* recognition was not granted until February, 1924, when diplomatic agents were exchanged between London and Moscow. The United States did not extend recognition of either kind to the U.S.S.R. until November 16, 1933, despite the fact that the Communists had been in control of the Russian State since November 7, 1917. This departure from the *de facto* theory of recognition was defended on the ground that the Soviet régime was unwilling to discharge the international obligations of the State, as shown by its repudiation of debts, its confiscation of property, and its revolutionary propaganda abroad.[1] The recognition granted in 1933 was *de jure*. All governments are free to grant or withhold recognition of revolutionary régimes at their option, though any general use of the power of recognition as a tool of diplomacy results in an unfortunate interruption of relations between States.[2] Premature recognition granted to a pretended revolutionary government when the lawful authorities are still fighting to suppress the uprising is, of course, a violation of the rights of the legitimate government. Thus the simultaneous German and Italian recognition of the Spanish Fascist rebels on November 18, 1936, was an act of intervention against the legal government of Spain, as was the earlier recognition extended by Guatemala on November 11, and the later recognition extended by France and Britain on February 27, 1939.

If the premature recognition of a revolutionary government or of a seceding State is a violation of the rights of those still asserting jurisdiction, the refusal of outside States to recognize *de facto* control of territory by those who have successfully asserted jurisdiction may also be deemed an injury. Where such a policy is utilized as a sanction to deter or punish

---

[1] See F. L. Schuman, *American Policy toward Russia since* 1917, 1928.

[2] In 1907, and again in 1923, the United States persuaded the Central American Republics to sign treaties in which they pledged themselves not to recognize governments set up in their territories by revolutionary means. The signatories thus bound themselves to accept the *de jure* theory of recognition. When a revolution broke out in Salvador in December, 1931, the other States withheld recognition from the new government. In December, 1932, Costa Rica and Salvador denounced the 1923 treaty, but it is still theoretically binding until three States denounce it. In January, 1934, all the Republics, as well as the United States, recognized the new government of Salvador. In dealing with the Latin American Republics the United States has often recognized governments of which it approves and denied recognition to governments of which it disapproved. Thus Wilson refused to recognize Huerta in Mexico in 1913–1915, and Roosevelt refused to recognize the "radical" régime of Grau San Martin in Cuba in 1933.

violation of earlier rights, however, it may be regarded as legally justified, whatever judgment may be passed upon its political expediency. Under the "Stimson Doctrine" of 1932 the United States and many members of the League refused to recognize territorial changes brought about by force in violation of the Nine Power Pact of 1922 and the Pact of Paris of 1928. Washington thus refused to recognize Manchukuo or the Wang Ching-wei puppet régime installed at Nanking in March, 1940, and recognized by Japan as the "government" of China on November 30. The United States recognized the German annexation of Austria. It granted recognition to the Franco régime in Spain on April 1, 1939. But it declined to recognize the conquests of Czechoslovakia, Albania, Poland, Denmark, Norway, Luxemburg, Belgium, and the Netherlands, preferring to maintain relations with the exiled governments of some of these States. Britain and France (before the collapse) followed a similar course. Roosevelt's reply of June 15, 1940, to Reynaud's last despairing appeal declared that the United States would "not consider valid any attempts to infringe by force the independence and the territorial integrity of France." When the French Republic fell, Washington evaded the issue of recognition of the new government by dealing with the Vichy régime as legally identical with its predecessor.

The granting or withholding of diplomatic recognition is by itself of no particular efficacy in promoting or discouraging revolution and aggression. In an organized community of nations, recognition would of course not be granted to "rights" acquired in violation of the law. But, in such a community, collective measures of prevention and punishment would be applied to prevent continued enjoyment of such alleged rights. In the absence of such measures, the wisdom of ignoring political or military facts and adhering to legal fictions is at best doubtful. In a world of hard and inescapable realities, which the champions of legal rectitude have neither the desire nor the power to change, Jefferson's *de facto* theory of recognition has much to commend it.[1]

---

[1] A *reductio ad absurdum* of the nonrecognition doctrine was achieved in Soviet-American relations. From 1917 to 1933 the United States denied recognition to the Soviet Government. From 1917 to 1922 the United States, in the name of preserving the "territorial integrity" of Russia, refused to recognize the independence of the Baltic States which had been promptly recognized by the unrecognized Soviet Government. In the Anglo-Soviet negotiations of 1939, London refused to meet Moscow's terms for an alliance at the expense of the "independence" of the Baltic States. By virtue of this refusal, Moscow came to terms with Berlin and forthwith extinguished the independence of Estonia, Latvia, and Lithuania. On July 23 Sumner Welles, apparently forgetting that the Baltic States had been early targets of the American nonrecognition policy, issued a statement declaring "From the day when the peoples of these republics first gained their independent and democratic form of government the people of the United States have watched their admirable progress in self-government with deep and sympathetic interest. The policy of this Government is universally known. The people of the United States are opposed to predatory activities no matter whether they are carried on by the use of force or by the

In summary, the rights and obligations of international law are in general applicable only to States recognized by the members of the family of nations, and States can deal officially with other States only through recognized governments. In both cases, recognition is a discretionary political act of the executive authorities of other States. There are, nevertheless, certain "persons" of international law which are not true States but which enjoy a certain qualified legal status. Members of confederations and other unions, though not sovereign States, may have their own diplomatic representation abroad and may be granted certain customary rights under international law by outside States. Such is the peculiar position of some of the self-governing Dominions of the British Commonwealth of Nations. Neutralized States, protectorates, and suzerainties are sovereign only in part, but they may be recognized as States by third parties. Insurgents and belligerents, *i.e.*, groups of armed individuals conducting hostilities for public purposes, are also entitled to the usual rights of the international law of war, provided that they observe the reciprocal obligations. When outside States recognize a condition of "insurgency" in a particular State, they take cognizance of hostilities in which they are bound to refrain from interference. The local State remains answerable for the acts of the insurgents. When a state of "belligerency" is recognized, on the other hand, either by the State confronted with civil war or by outside States, the international law of war applies in full to both combatants and the local State is released from responsibility. In these instances a qualified status under international law is granted to entities which are not genuine States.[1] With the exception of these special cases, however, international law is concerned only with recognized States and governments.[2]

threat of force. They are likewise opposed to any form of intervention on the part of one State, however powerful, in the domestic concerns of any other sovereign State, however weak." (U.S. Department of State *Bulletin*, July 27, 1940, p. 48.) Britain also declined to recognize Soviet annexation of the Baltic States. An empty legal formula thus became an obstacle to Anglo-American-Soviet collaboration, despite the desperate need of such collaboration to safeguard each of the three Powers from the Nazi threat.

[1] It is sometimes said that individuals have rights but no remedies in international law, in the sense that individual rights may be affected by State action but that the individuals so affected have no means of compelling observance of their rights unless they are protected by a State which takes diplomatic action in their behalf. In the Central American Court of Justice (1907–1917) the citizens of the five Central American Republics were granted the right of bringing suit in the court against the States themselves, but this arrangement is anomalous and exceptional.

[2] The severance of diplomatic relations, like the granting of recognition, is also an act of policy, usually resorted to as a protest or as a prelude to war. War automatically severs diplomatic relations between belligerents. Under the law of peace, a rupture of relations may lead to political retaliation but usually does not create a legal grievance. It has been contended that members of the League were legally bound to maintain diplomatic relations with one another. In becoming a member of the League a State did not by that fact recognize other States and governments which were signatories of the Covenant, but it may be argued

3. RIGHTS AND DUTIES

Nations being free, independent, and equal and having a right to judge according to the dictates of conscience, of what is to be done in order to fulfill its duties; the effect of all this is, the producing, at least externally, and among men, a perfect equality of rights between nations, in the administration of their affairs, and the pursuit of their pretensions, without regard to the intrinsic justice of their conduct, of which others have no right to form a definitive judgment; so that what is permitted in one, is also permitted in the other, and they ought to be considered in human society as having an equal right.—EMERIC DE VATTEL, *Droit des gens.*

In so far as the whole structure of public international law can be deduced from elementary principles, it may be said to rest upon certain broad concepts inherent in the idea of the sovereignty of the State which lies at the basis of the whole Western State System. A State which is sovereign is not subject to the will of any other State. It exists as an independent entity, coequal with other sovereignties and with exclusive jurisdiction over its territory. From this elemental fact, it follows that every State possesses certain fundamental rights and obligations with respect to other States. It possesses, for example, a right of existence or self-preservation and an obligation to recognize that other States enjoy the same right. It possesses a right of independence and an obligation to respect the same right in other States. It possesses a right of legal equality with other States and a right of exercising its power and enforcing its legislation within its frontiers, *i.e.*, a right of jurisdiction. It is sometimes said that States also possess fundamental rights of property and of intercourse. In view of the logical relationship between these fundamental rights and the whole superstructure of rules and principles, it will be legitimate for the purposes of the present survey to suggest the superstructure by an examination of the meaning of the fundamental rights.

The right of existence or self-preservation is obviously the most important and elementary of these fundamental rights. That every sovereign State is free to take any action which may be necessary to preserve its existence as a political entity, even to the extent of infringing upon the rights of other States, has long been recognized as an axiomatic principle. This right must be strictly construed, however, for no State can lawfully violate the rights of others on the basis of vague and general allegations that its existence is menaced by acts taking place outside its own frontiers. An attack upon an innocent third party, for example, can never be justified on the plea of self-preservation. The German invasion of Belgium in 1914, in violation of the neutralization treaty of 1839, was defended on the ground that it was the only procedure available to Germany for at-

that under Article 12 members were bound not to sever relations with governments which they had already recognized unless such governments refused to submit grievances likely to lead to a rupture to the established League procedures for settlement.

tacking France effectively and thus meeting the threat to Germany represented by the Franco-Russian alliance. But since the existence of Germany was by no conceivable stretching of the imagination jeopardized by any act of Belgium, the invasion was unlawful. The German Chancellor, Bethmann-Hollweg, recognized this in his address to the Reichstag of August 4, 1914, in which he declared, "We are in a state of necessity and necessity knows no law." Ribbentrop sought to justify German destruction of the independence of Czechoslovakia, Poland, Denmark, Norway, Luxemburg, Belgium, and the Netherlands in 1939–1940 by alleging that German minorities were persecuted or that the victim of aggression had forfeited his rights by conniving with France and Britain to attack Germany. These formulations, though ideologically interesting, are without juridical significance since none of the States mentioned had in fact, apart from alleged intent, violated German rights. Bethmann-Hollweg's attitude was more honest. A State can allege self-preservation as a justification for an infringement of the rights of other States only when it is directly and immediately menaced by some action in the other State which can be thwarted in no other way.

This principle was laid down in its classic form by Secretary of State Daniel Webster. During the Canadian rebellion of 1838 a body of insurgents gathered on the American side of the Niagara River, seized guns from American arsenals, occupied an island in midstream from which they fired shots into Canadian territory, and prepared to recross in the American ship *Caroline* to continue hostilities against the Canadian forces. In this emergency, British troops crossed into New York State, broke up the expedition, sent the *Caroline* over Niagara Falls, and returned to Canada. This violation of the territory of the United States evoked a strong protest from Webster in which he demanded an apology and reparation unless the British Government could "show a necessity for self-defense, instant, overwhelming, leaving no choice of means, and no moment for deliberation. It will be for it to show also that the local authorities of Canada, even supposing the necessity of the moment authorized them to enter the territories of the United States at all, did nothing unreasonable or excessive, since the necessity of self-defense must be limited by that necessity and kept clearly within it."[1] In this instance the British Government had no difficulty in justifying its action, since an instant and overwhelming necessity menacing the existence of the established government in Canada did undeniably exist and the action taken was limited to meeting this threat. Under such circumstances the right of self-preservation renders legitimate any reasonable action to safeguard the existence of the State or of its government.[2]

[1] See W. E. Hall, *International Law*, 1924, pp. 323–324.
[2] See also the case of the *Virginius*, *Foreign Relations of the United States*, 1894, pp. 922–1117, and Moore's *Digest*, II, pp. 895 f.

The right of independence entitles a State to formulate its own foreign policy within the limits of the rights of other States and to conduct its domestic affairs as it sees fit, provided that it does not ignore the obligations which international law imposes upon it. "Independence" as to domestic affairs is subject to the qualification that a State is responsible for injury to aliens within its territory, is required to maintain some degree of law and order, and is bound to maintain some authority answerable to foreign governments. A State must exercise due diligence in the protection of aliens, who are entitled to at least the same degree of protection as it affords to its own citizens. It is responsible for any obvious miscarriages of justice in its courts. An interesting case involving these questions arose between the United States and Italy in 1891. On March 14, 1891, eleven persons of Italian origin were taken from jail, where they were confined on charges of complicity in the murder of the chief of police, and were lynched by a mob in New Orleans. The local authorities made no effort to afford them protection. The Italian Foreign Minister at once instructed the Italian Minister in Washington "to denounce immediately to the United States Government the atrocious deed of New Orleans, requesting immediate and energetic steps . . . to protect the Italian colony endangered, and to punish severely the guilty." Secretary of State Blaine reminded the Governor of Louisiana that the treaty of 1871 guaranteed reciprocal protection of persons and property, but no action was taken to punish the lynchers and no indemnity was paid to the relatives of the victims. In protest, the Italian Minister was recalled from Washington, and Blaine intimated that the federal government of the United States had no constitutional authority to compel action by the State officials of Louisiana. The Italian Government denied the relevancy of this allegation; and, on April 12, 1892, Blaine offered an indemnity of 125,000 francs, the acceptance of which was followed by a full resumption of diplomatic relations.[1] Every State must maintain central authorities responsible for the fulfillment of its international obligations. Though the right of independence carries with it the reciprocal obligation of respecting the independence of other States, the Great Powers have frequently violated the independence of small and weak States when conditions of domestic disorder have led to damage to foreign lives and property. The extent to which States are justified in taking such action is much disputed, but the general principles indicated are universally accepted. The totalitarian Powers, however, have repeatedly extinguished the independence of small neighbors in the name of "self-determination," *Lebensraum*, protection against "Bolshevism," defense against "encirclement," etc.

---

[1] *Foreign Relations of the United States*, 1891, pp. 658–723.

The right of equality has reference only to legal rights and obligations and not, of course, to territory, population, power, or political influence. The sovereign States of the world differ enormously among themselves in these characteristics, with the Great Powers having power vastly disproportionate to that of the lesser countries. But, before the law, all sovereign States are equal. Nicaragua enjoys the same rights and is bound by the same obligations as those of the United States. The miniscule Vatican City occupies the same international legal status as the gigantic Soviet Union. All States have equal opportunities to assert their rights and to demand that other States observe their obligations. All have an equal right to make treaties, wage war, maintain or sever diplomatic relations with other States, and the like. From the principle of State equality is deduced the rule of unanimity in international conferences, according to which each State has one vote and no State can be bound without its consent. In practice, however, it has long been conceded that theoretical legal equality is inconsistent with actual political disparity. When controversies over conflicting claims lead to a resort to coercive measures, small, weak States are obviously less capable of protecting their rights than large powerful States. So long as self-help and coercion are the ultimate means of protecting State rights, equality under international law, in a system of unequal States, will remain almost as tenuous as individual equality in domestic law in societies in which economic power is unequally distributed among the citizenry. Anatole France once marveled at that majestic equality of the law whereby the rich and poor alike were forbidden to steal bread or to sleep under the bridges at night. This principle is paralleled by the comparable principle of equality among States in international law in a State System in which there appears at times to be one law for the Great Powers and another for the lesser nations. The principle of State equality is, nevertheless, a logical corollary of the concepts of sovereignty and independence, and States always resent hotly any suggestion that they are not the equals of their neighbors.

Any act by one State which infringes upon the sovereignty, the existence, the independence, or the equality of another State is an act of intervention and is *ipso facto* unlawful. Intervention is usually defined as any act of dictatorial interference by a State in the internal or foreign affairs of another State or any effort to coerce another State in its State action. "With the right of independence goes the correlative *obligation* of *nonintervention, i.e.,* of refraining from all acts that would forcibly limit the freedom of another State."[1] By its very nature, intervention is a violation of international law, unless it has been authorized by specific treaty agreements, as has sometimes been the case in the relations between the United States on the one hand and certain Caribbean States on the other—

[1] G. G. Wilson, *International Law*, 8th ed., 1922, p. 87.

notably Cuba, Haiti, the Dominican Republic, and Panama. In all other cases, intervention is necessarily unlawful, though under peculiar circumstances it may be justified if it is essential to protect the fundamental rights of the intervening State. It is generally agreed that a State may infringe upon the rights of another without incurring liability for paying damages to the victim if its existence or independence is menaced and it is acting, in Webster's words in the *Caroline* case, under an instant and overwhelming necessity of self-defense, leaving no choice of means and no moment for deliberation. If an act of intervention in such a situation is limited to meeting the immediate danger, it may be permissible, though the burden of proof is always on the side of the intervening State.

In spite of the indisputable logic of this principle, interventions have frequently been resorted to on a variety of other grounds. The colonial empires of the Great Powers were largely created by intervening in, and extinguishing the independence of, small or weak States incapable of resisting imperialistic aggression. The United States, before the advent of the "good neighbor" policy, intervened repeatedly in the affairs of the States of the Caribbean. Interventions, individual and collective, have been embarked upon by States in the name of upholding international law, enforcing treaty rights, preserving the balance of power, maintaining humanitarian principles, ensuring the payment of debts, affording protection to the lives and property of citizens abroad, etc. Since international law rests no less upon custom than upon reason, it might be contended that a general right of intervention had been established by these practices. This is scarcely a tenable position, however, since every act of intervention unauthorized by treaty terms is clearly a violation of the rights of the victim and no amount of practice can establish it as a principle of law that States have a right to violate the rights of other States. The doctrine laid down by Webster would appear to indicate the only legitimate grounds upon which intervention is justifiable. If this principle is not always adhered to, it is because States, in the pursuit of the objectives of high politics, do not always limit themselves to actions permitted by the accepted principles of law and because the existing machinery of international government is not yet adequate to ensure protection to the rights of States incapable of defending themselves by self-help.

A powerful State can usually thwart intervention and compel respect for its rights. Small States, like the Latin American Republics, or weak States, like China, are unable to protect themselves from intervention or to enforce payment of damages for violations of their rights. The rights are the same in both cases, and the interventions in question may be equally unlawful; but since international law is still enforced primarily by State action, the remedy which a State has available in such circumstances is likely to depend on its size and power. Other States may lend it moral support or may refuse to recognize the results of the intervention, as did the United States and the members of the League of Nations on behalf of China in the Sino-Japanese conflict of 1931–1932; but the time is not yet when a State can rely exclusively for the protection of its rights upon the organized force of international society.[1]

4. JURISDICTION

A thing may become our property by acquisition, original or derivative. Original acquisition formerly, when the human race could meet together and agree, might be made by division; at present it is only made by occupation.—Hugo Grotius, *De jure belli ac pacis.*

Jurisdiction—literally, authority to "say the law"—is the right to exercise State authority. It is a corollary of the rights already discussed. States have the right to exercise their jurisdiction, *i.e.*, to legislate and to impose their power, over the territories in which they are recognized as sovereign and over the persons who are their nationals. Conflicting claims put forward in the name of territorial jurisdiction and in the name of personal jurisdiction have been a fruitful source of international controversy in the past; for if States, as was once the case, insist both upon exclusive jurisdiction over their own territory, including all persons within it, and also over all their citizens or subjects, wherever they may be abroad, it is clear that difficulties will result. In the twentieth century the principle of the territorial basis of jurisdiction has in almost all countries been granted precedence over the idea of personal jurisdiction. A State, therefore, has jurisdiction over all persons within its territory, whether they be nationals or aliens, and possesses no general right to claim jurisdiction over its nationals who happen to be in the territory of other States. The two forms of jurisdiction, nevertheless, persist. It will be convenient to consider the various problems of jurisdiction in terms of (1) territorial jurisdiction, (2) personal jurisdiction, and (3) exemptions from jurisdiction.

A State may acquire territorial jurisdiction by discovery and occupation, by prescription, by accretion, by cession or leasehold, or by conquest.

[1] Under the good-neighbor policy proclaimed by President Franklin D. Roosevelt the United States renounced its former interventionist policy in Latin America. Article 8 of the Convention on Rights and Duties of States, signed at the Seventh International Conference of American States at Montevideo, December 3–26, 1933, declared, "No State has a right to intervene in the internal or external affairs of another." This principle was reaffirmed at the Inter-American Conference for Maintenance of Peace, held in Buenos Aires in December, 1936. At the Eighth Conference a "Declaration of Lima" (December 24, 1938) asserted that the signatories were resolved to "maintain and defend against all foreign intervention or activity" the principles of continental solidarity, absolute sovereignty, territorial integrity, peace, security, and the "juridical equality" of sovereign States. The "Declaration of American Principles" signed at the same time asserted, "1. The intervention of any State in the internal or external affairs of another is inadmissible. . . . 4. Relations between States should be governed by the precepts of international law."

Discovery of hitherto unknown and unclaimed land is no longer regarded as conveying valid title to the State of the discoverer unless it is followed by effective occupation. In the sixteenth century the maritime States of Europe laid claim to vast regions of the new world on the basis of discovery alone. England granted "sea-to-sea" charters to the Atlantic seaboard colonists who occupied only the coastal strip and had no notion whatever as to the location of the other sea or the extent of intervening land. As late as the nineteenth century, Germany sought, unsuccessfully, to lay down the "hinterland doctrine" with respect to Africa, according to which a State occupying a seacoast could claim all the unexplored interior region drained by its rivers. It is now conceded, however, that only effective and continued occupation conveys title to newly discovered lands. This basis of title differs little from prescription, which refers to a situation in which a State secures title to territory by virtue of long-continued occupation acquiesced in by other States. Similarly, if the natural processes of accretion build up deposits on a seacoast or create new land by other means in the immediate vicinity of an adjacent State, the latter has title to the new territory. The normal method of acquiring territorial jurisdiction during the past century, following the exploration and partition of the entire inhabitable globe by the colonial Powers, has been by treaties of cession. Such cessions may take the form of sales or exchanges of territory, with pecuniary or territorial considerations attached; or they may be the result of war and conquest, with the victors relieving the vanquished of their possessions.

Conquest, in the form of military occupation so prolonged as to be permanent, may confer title even when not followed by a treaty of cession, though the League of Nations Covenant, in protecting the territorial integrity of all members (Article 10), and the Kellogg-Briand Pact of August 27, 1928, in prohibiting recourse to nonpacific means in the settlement of disputes (Article 2), both sought to outlaw military conquest as a means of acquiring territory. In accordance with the new dispensation, the United States, on January 7, 1932, declared to the Chinese and Japanese Governments that "it cannot admit the legality of any situation *de facto* . . . and it does not intend to recognize any situation, treaty, or agreement which may be brought about by means contrary to the covenants and obligations of the Pact of Paris." On August 6, 1932, nineteen American Republics, including the United States, informed Bolivia and Paraguay that they would "not recognize any territorial arrangement of this controversy (over the Chaco) which has not been obtained by peaceful means nor the validity of territorial acquisitions which may be obtained through occupation or conquest by force of arms." The Argentine Anti-war Pact of October 10, 1933, pledged its signatories to similar obligations of nonrecognition of titles secured by conquest, as did the

Convention on Rights and Duties of States (Article 11) signed at Montevideo on December 26, 1933. Such efforts to deny recognition to titles secured by force have not thus far been effective in preventing resort to conquest by hungry States. Finally mention may be made of leaseholds as a means of acquiring territory. The status of the Panama Canal Zone, of certain ports and "concession" areas in China and of the Baltic naval base of Hanko (granted to the U.S.S.R. by Finland under the peace treaty of March 12, 1940) is based upon agreements by which the territories in question were leased to an outside State by the State originally having jurisdiction.

Almost all these methods of acquiring territory have been employed by the United States in the course of its expansion. The original boundaries of the new State were fixed by the treaty of 1783 with Great Britain, which recognized the independence of the United States and bounded it roughly by the Atlantic coast, the St. Croix-St. Lawrence-Great Lakes line, the Mississippi River, and the line of 31° on the south. The vaguely defined territory of Louisiana was secured by a treaty of purchase concluded with France in 1803, under the terms of which the United States paid $15,000,000 to the Government of the First Consul. East and West Florida, which were periodically subjected to American military occupation between 1806 and 1819, were acquired by treaty with Spain in 1819, on terms requiring the United States to meet claims of $5,000,000 on the part of American citizens against Spain. This treaty likewise defined the western boundary of Louisiana from the Sabine River northwestward to 42° of latitude and thence to the Pacific. This line was confirmed by the treaty of 1828 with Mexico. Texas, having declared independence of Mexico in 1836, was annexed by joint resolution of the American Congress in 1845, followed by similar action on the part of the Texan Congress. At the close of the Mexican War, during which the southwest was conquered and subjected to military occupation, the Treaty of Guadalope Hidalgo was signed, February 3, 1848. By its provisions, Mexico was obliged to cede a vast area of its northern provinces to the United States for $15,000,000, plus the assumption by the United States of claims of its citizens against Mexico to the amount of $3,250,000. This acquisition was rounded out in 1853 by the Gadsden purchase, for which the United States paid $10,000,000. Meanwhile the northeastern and northwestern boundary disputes with Great Britain were settled, respectively, by the Webster-Ashburton Treaty of 1842 and the Oregon Treaty of 1846. The first annexation of noncontiguous territory by the United States was provided for by the treaty of 1867 with Russia, by which the United States secured Alaska for $7,200,000. The Hawaiian Islands were acquired by joint Congressional resolution of July 7, 1898, acquiesced in by the independent local government, following the failure of earlier treaty negotiations. At the close of the Spanish-American War, Spain was obliged by the Treaty of Paris of December 10, 1898, to cede to the United States the Philippine Islands, Guam, and Porto Rico for $20,000,000. Tutuila, in the Samoan Islands, was acquired by a treaty of partition with Great Britain and Germany, signed December 4, 1899. The Panama Canal Zone was secured by the Hay-Bunau Varilla Treaty of December 7, 1903. By its terms the United States established a protectorate over the Republic of Panama, to which $10,000,000, plus $250,000 annually, were paid for sovereign rights in the Canal Zone. The Virgin Islands in the Caribbean were purchased from Denmark in 1917 for $25,000,000. A string of naval bases from the north Atlantic to the Caribbean were acquired by lease from Britain on September 2, 1940, in return for the transfer of 50 destroyers to the British navy. The American empire was thus created by a mixed process of occupation, conquest, purchase, and cession.

The next problem deserving of consideration is that of the extent of territorial jurisdiction, particularly with reference to air and water boundaries. The question of aerial jurisdiction has assumed great importance in the period of extensive international air communication, and many treaties have been signed regarding it.[1] All these are now based upon the universally accepted principle that a State has absolute jurisdiction over the air above its territory and its territorial waters, extending out into the farthest reaches of space. It is generally recognized, however, that as a matter of comity a State should grant a right of innocent passage through its air to foreign aircraft, subject to such reasonable regulations as are necessary to ensure observance of local laws relating to customs duties, immigration, public safety, national defense, and the like. Jurisdiction over the waters adjacent to a State, on the contrary, does not extend out indefinitely but is limited to a zone within three miles from the coast line. The three-mile limit of territorial waters or maritime jurisdiction, established at a time when three miles represented the effective range of coast artillery, is now recognized by almost all States. The waters beyond the three-mile limit are the "high seas" and are not subject to the jurisdiction of any State, except for purposes of punishing pirates, who may be proceeded against by all States. In accordance with the so-called *doctrine of hot pursuit*, however, coast-guard vessels may pursue foreign ships suspected of violating local laws out into the high seas, provided that the pursuit is begun within territorial waters and is continuous. Within territorial waters, privately owned foreign vessels are subject to local laws, though they are ordinarily granted a right of innocent passage and are exempt from interference by the local authorities except where a violation of local

[1] See Kenneth G. Colgrove, *International Control of Aviation*, 1930.

law occurs of such a nature as to disturb the peace of the port. Foreign public vessels, *i.e.*, war vessels and other ships owned by foreign governments and engaged in public business, are exempt from local jurisdiction and may not be boarded for any purposes by local authorities, since the foreign sovereign is directly responsible for their conduct which may, if objectionable, be made a matter of diplomatic representations.

Other water boundaries, like land frontiers, are usually defined by treaty. In the absence of treaty arrangements to the contrary, certain general rules are applied. River boundaries between two States follow the *thalweg*, or deepest navigation channel of the stream. If a boundary river shifts its bed gradually by accretion, the boundary shifts likewise; but where a sudden change by avulsion takes place, the boundary remains in its old position. Rights of navigation and of water diversion for irrigation or power purposes are always dealt with by treaty provisions. Rivers, lakes, and canals which are entirely surrounded by the territory of one State are completely within its jurisdiction in the absence of treaty arrangements to the contrary. The Boundary Waters Convention of 1909 between the United States and Great Britain opens navigation on Lake Michigan to British vessels. Straits less than six miles in width are within the jurisdiction of the shore State or States, though the vessels of other States have a right of navigation, subject to reasonable local regulations and duties for safety, the upkeep of lighthouses, and the like. The right of Denmark to levy tolls upon vessels passing through the Danish Sound connecting the North and Baltic Seas was successfully resisted by the United States and other Powers and abandoned in 1857, though it had been exercised since 1368. The Bosphorus and the Dardanelles, surrounded by Turkish territory, were opened to Russian merchant vessels by the treaty of 1774 and to foreign war vessels by the Treaty of Paris of 1856. The Treaty of Lausanne of 1923 made elaborate provision for the neutralization of these waterways and for freedom of navigation through them, but the right of Turkey to fortify the Straits once more and to close them, in certain contingencies, to foreign war vessels was acknowledged by the Powers in the Montreux Convention of July 20, 1936. The Suez Canal was partly demilitarized and opened freely to all vessels, public and private, both in war and in peace, by the convention of 1888. The Panama Canal is similarly open on a basis of equality to vessels of all States by the Hay-Pauncefote Treaty of 1901, though it is controlled and fortified by the United States. Gulfs, bays, and estuaries opening out onto the high seas are within the jurisdiction of the State enclosing them, with the line of maritime jurisdiction parallel to a line drawn from headland to headland, if the mouth is not more than six miles wide. Other arrangements have often been made by treaty, however, and more recently a 10-mile limit for width of mouth of territorial bays has been recognized.[1]

Jurisdiction over persons, as distinct from jurisdiction over land, sea, and air, has been claimed by States under two different theories which are still only partly reconciled. Under the rule of *ius soli* (right of the soil), States have claimed as nationals all persons born within their territorial limits. Amendment 14 to the American Federal Constitution declares, "All persons born or naturalized in the United States, and subject to the jurisdiction thereof, are citizens of the United States and the State wherein they reside." Under the rule of *ius sanguinis* (right of the blood), States have claimed that all children of their nationals, wherever born, are their nationals by virtue of parentage. The legislation of States regarding the bases of nationality varies considerably, and no general international agreement has yet been reached regarding these questions. Most States, however, now adhere to the rule of *ius soli*, with certain qualifications. American legislation, for example, bestows American citizenship on children born abroad of American parents provided that the parents have resided at some time in the United States. Almost all States now permit their citizens to expatriate themselves, *i.e.*, to become nationals of other States, and also provide for the "naturalization" of foreigners who desire to become citizens of the local State. Many States provide that women acquire the nationality of their husbands at marriage, though the American law of 1922 permits an American woman marrying a foreigner to retain her citizenship and does not automatically confer American citizenship on alien women marrying Americans. Foreigners who have resided in the United States for five years may become American citizens by taking out citizenship papers. Collective naturalization is often provided for in annexation treaties. Aliens, in general, are entirely subject to the jurisdiction of the State where they reside. Aliens who are fugitives from justice may be delivered up to the authorities of the State from which they have fled by the process of extradition. This procedure is almost invariably provided for by treaties which specify the crimes for which extradition shall be granted and the categories of persons subject to extradition. Political crimes, short of attempts at assassination, are normally exempted by specific provisions of such treaties.

Because of differences in the nationality laws of various States, it is possible for an individual to be a national of two States simultaneously, or to lose his nationality entirely by taking some action which forfeits his citizenship in one State without entitling him to citizenship in another. Such unfortunate individuals (*heimatlosen*, in the German phrase) have no

[1] See the award of the arbitral tribunal in the North Atlantic Fisheries dispute between the United States and Great Britain, 1910, in G. G. Wilson, *Hague Arbitration Cases*, pp. 180 *f.*

State to afford them diplomatic protection abroad. Such problems of personal jurisdiction make it desirable that the nationality laws of the various States be made more nearly uniform. Such uniformity can be achieved in this field, as in others, only through the process usually referred to as the "codification of international law," *i.e.*, the conclusion of general international conventions in which States agree upon the principles involved and pledge themselves to put their own national legislation in harmony with the agreement. The legal experts of the League of Nations prepared a draft nationality convention which was considered by the First Conference on the Progressive Codification of International Law which met at The Hague in March and April of 1930. The conference on April 12, 1930, adopted four instruments: (1) a convention on certain questions relating to the conflict of nationality laws; (2) a protocol relating to military obligations in certain cases of double nationality; (3) a protocol relating to a certain case of statelessness; and (4) a special protocol concerning statelessness. The first of these engagements has been signed by some forty States, but none of them has as yet received general ratification.

Certain common exemptions from local jurisdiction are universally recognized. Sovereigns traveling abroad in their official capacity are entirely exempt from the jurisdiction of the States through which they pass and may not be arrested, proceeded against, or interfered with on any ground, either as to their own persons, their families, their retinue, or their effects. Diplomatic representatives are similarly exempt from the jurisdiction of the State in which they reside. The buildings and grounds of embassies and legations are regarded as "extraterritorial," *i.e.*, as part of the territory of the foreign State maintaining them rather than of the local State. They may not be taxed or entered by the local police without permission, and local laws may not be enforced within their precincts. Diplomatic agents, along with their families, staffs, and servants, are immune from local laws and enjoy complete exemption from local civil and criminal jurisdiction, local police and administrative regulations, taxes and duties, jury and witness duty, and the like. They may not be arrested, subpoenaed, or otherwise interfered with in the exercise of their functions. Consuls ordinarily enjoy certain limited exemptions from local jurisdiction in order to enable them to carry on their work effectively. Foreign armies granted a right of passage through a State and foreign public vessels within its territorial waters are likewise exempt from local jurisdiction. In certain Oriental States, notably China, special treaty arrangements have been imposed by the Western Powers, whereby Western nationals, when defendants in cases brought by natives, are exempt from local jurisdiction and are usually tried in consular courts maintained by their own governments. The recent efforts of China to terminate extraterritoriality of this type have not yet met with success, except as regards the Soviet Union, which voluntarily relinquished this right for its nationals, and Germany, which was compelled to renounce the right by the terms of the Treaty of Versailles.

5. TREATIES

In contracts, nature requires equality, and in such a way that, from inequality, he who has the worse share acquires a right. This equality consists partly in the act, partly in the matter concerning which the act is, and in the acts both precedent and principal.—HUGO GROTIUS, *De jure belli ac pacis.*

The making of treaties between States regarding matters of mutual interest is a practice of great antiquity. It has been resorted to in all State Systems of which any record remains. The practice developed very early in the evolution of the Western State System and has been followed with increasing frequency by all its members during the past few centuries. The States of the world are now bound to one another by thousands of international agreements covering almost every conceivable subject of international interest and assuming a wide variety of forms. Early treaties were almost always bilateral, *i.e.*, between two States. More recently many treaties are multilateral, *i.e.*, among three or more States. The growing frequency with which States enter into treaty engagements is revealed by the treaty history of the United States. Since July 4, 1776—or, more accurately, since February 6, 1778, when the first treaties between the United States and a foreign State were signed—the United States has entered into no less than 1,000 formally ratified international engagements, exclusive of executive agreements.[1] Of these, only 59 were concluded prior to 1838, 110 during the next thirty years, 134 in the following three decades, and the remainder during the period since 1898. The record of most other States would show a comparable growth of treaty engagements during the past half century.

Since treaties and similar instruments constitute legally binding obligations between the signatory States, a large body of legal principles has developed with regard to their negotiation, conclusion, ratification, interpretation, and termination. The somewhat confusing problem of terminology may be considered first. The word "treaty" is sometimes loosely applied to all types of international engagement, other than executive agreements. The latter are not legally binding compacts between States, but merely arrangements entered into by executive authorities. An executive agreement binds only the administration which had concluded it, though it may be continued in force at the option of the succeeding

[1] See U. S. Department of State. *Treaty Series.*

administrations. The "Gentlemen's Agreement" of 1908 between the United States and Japan remained in force until 1924 when it was abrogated by the immigration act passed in that year by Congress. In the United States, executive agreements are easily distinguishable from treaties by the fact that they are concluded by the President or his agents and are not submitted to the Senate or formally ratified. They thus assume the character of personal promises, rather than of solemn contracts or "treaties" binding upon the State. In a narrower sense, "treaties" are State agreements relating to important political questions. "Conventions" are usually agreements relating to more specific and technical matters, though there is no uniformity of practice in this regard. A particular agreement may be designated as a treaty or a convention at the discretion of the negotiators. The term *protocol* is applied sometimes to any type of agreement less formal than a treaty or a convention, some times to preliminary drafts of agreements signed in anticipation of the preparation of more formal documents, and sometimes to the signed official minutes, or *procès-verbal*, of the sessions of an international conference. *Declarations* are multilateral engagements, setting forth a common conception of certain principles of international law, such as the Declaration of Paris of 1856, though the word is likewise applied to formal statements of policy on the part of particular governments. A declaration of the latter type, such as the Monroe Doctrine, is, of course, not an international agreement at all. *Sponsions* are agreements, subject to subsequent approval, signed by representatives who have not been properly commissioned or who have exceeded their authority. *Cartels* are agreements entered into between belligerents for such purposes as the exchange of prisoners of war. An *armistice* is an agreement between belligerents for the suspension of hostilities. A *compromis* is an instrument by which two States submit a dispute to arbitration. Letters, memoranda, and exchanges of notes may also under certain circumstances be given the effect of true international obligations.

The making of treaties and other inter-state instruments has been elaborately formalized and involves adherence, with minor variations, to a well-established sequence of procedures which must be followed if the resulting agreement is to be valid. The first step is (1) the meeting of the negotiators and the "exchange of full powers" between the plenipotentiaries. Upon meeting, the agents of each State submit documentary credentials to the agents of the other, showing that they have been regularly authorized (given full powers) to negotiate the contemplated agreement. Next follows (2) the actual negotiation and signing of the agreement. Prior to the nineteenth century, treaty texts usually began with an invocation of the Deity. A preamble ordinarily sets forth the general purposes of the agreement and gives the names of the heads of the signatory States and of the negotiators whom they have appointed to sign. There follow the numbered articles of the compact, the conditions of ratification, the place and date of signature, and the signatures and seals of the agents. Signatures are usually attached in accordance with the principle of the alternat, whereby each State receives a copy of the treaty signed first by its own delegates. Multilateral treaties are often signed by the delegates in alphabetical order of the names of the States, in French. Many treaties are drawn up in French, still the traditional language of diplomacy, as well as in the languages of the signatory States, either in separate versions or in parallel columns. The next step is (3) ratification of the signed agreement by the constitutionally designated authorities in the signatory States. Under the American Constitution, all treaties are ratified by the President, acting "by and with the advice and consent of the Senate . . . provided two-thirds of the Senators present concur" (Article II, Section 2, §2). Ratification may be withheld or amendments and reservations may be attached, if irregularities have taken place in the negotiations or if the agreement is regarded as unsatisfactory. In the latter case, however, friction and misunderstanding are likely to result, since States normally assume that a treaty which has been negotiated and signed by accredited representatives, in accordance with their instructions, ought to be ratified as a matter of course.[1] Amendments and reservations attached by one party are not binding unless accepted by the other. (4) The exchange of ratifications is a formal ceremony whereby the parties indicate to one another that ratification has taken place and solemnly guarantee to one another the execution of the terms of the contract. This ceremony consists in the exchange of the executive acts of ratification and the preparation of a *procès-verbal* registering this fact. Treaties subsequently ratified are normally binding from the date of signature, unless some other agreement is specified. (5) The execution of the agreement is the final step whereby the terms agreed upon are carried out by the parties. In the United States, execution is preceded by a formal proclamation of the treaty in the name of the President.

In order that an international agreement may be legally binding upon the signatory States, certain conditions are essential. The parties must first of all be legally competent to contract the engagement; *i.e.*, they must be free under the terms of their constitutions and of earlier treaties to enter into the agreement which has been made. The treaty, moreover, must in form and substance be a proper State agreement on the part of all

[1] On December 17, 1938, Count Ciano told French Ambassador André François-Poncet that the Laval-Mussolini accords of January 7, 1935 (under which the Duce had accepted minor territorial concessions and French acquiescence in the projected conquest of Ethiopia as a "final settlement" of Italian claims under the Treaty of London of 1915), were invalid because no exchange of ratifications had ever taken place. Rome hoped in this manner to wrest new concessions from Paris.

of the signatories. The plenipotentiaries must have been fully accredited and must have acted within the scope of their authority. There must be freedom of consent on the part of the negotiators, with no hint of fraud. bribery, or coercion. Coercion invalidates a treaty if it is applied against the persons of the negotiators, but not if it is applied against a State. Treaties of peace imposed by victors upon vanquished, like those of 1919, are usually accepted under duress; but so long as the coercion is of the State and not of its representatives, the agreement is binding. Finally, international agreements must be in conformity with international law and must not involve any infringement of the rights of third States. If, in any particular case, it can be shown that at any step in the proceedings these essential conditions have not been complied with, the agreement in question can be regarded as void by either party.

Here, as in other fields of law, the totalitarian States have deviated widely from accepted principles and practices. In the absence of any effective legislative assemblies in such States, the making of treaties is exclusively an executive act. Treaties among such States have often been declared binding upon signature with no formalities of ratification or exchange of ratifications. The "voluntary" character of treaties imposed by such States on their neighbors has often been doubtful, even as to the treatment of the delegates. Thus, Hitler compelled Chancellor Kurt Schuschnigg to admit Nazi agents into the Austrian Cabinet by browbeating him at Berchtesgaden on February 12, 1938, and threatening immediate invasion. President Emil Hacha of Czechoslovakia was summoned to Berlin on March 14, 1939, and there compelled to sign away the independence of his country by a process of threats and psychological torture of such a nature that he had to be revived by injections before he was able "voluntarily" to attach his signature to the "agreement." The question of whether such agreements are juridically valid, however, is entirely theoretical in the absence of any tribunal before which their validity can be questioned or of any capacity on the part of the victims and their allies, if any, to offer resistance to coercion.

States which are not parties to an international agreement are, of course, not bound in any way by its terms, since treaties are contracts which specify rights and obligations only for the signatory States. Outside States may protest against a treaty only if it violates their own treaty rights or is contrary to accepted principles of customary international law. States not parties to a treaty may express their *approbation* of the agreement, by which they indicate approval of its terms without in any way becoming a party to them; or they may announce their *adhesion* to it, by which they agree to abide by its principles, also without becoming a party; or, finally, they may announce their *accession* to the engagement, in which case they formally become parties to the engagement.

In the interpretation of treaties the real intention of the parties is usually accepted as a basis for definition of terms, rather than grammatical deductions from the language employed. The intention of the parties may be ascertained through *procès-verbaux*, notes, memoranda, and other exchanges of communications at the time of the negotiations. If such documents are exchanged and accepted by both sides prior to the exchange of ratifications, they bind the parties to the interpretation of the treaty terms which they set forth. In the controversy over the meaning of the Clayton-Bulwer Treaty of April 19, 1850, between the United States and Great Britain, relating to the rights of the parties in Central America with respect to a proposed interoceanic canal, it appeared that Bulwer on June 29 (five days before the exchange of ratifications) had written Clayton to the effect that the provisions of the agreement for reciprocal renunciation of territorial claims had no application to British Honduras "and its dependencies." The United States was obliged to accept this interpretation, in spite of its reluctance to do so. The language of treaties is construed in the ordinary sense of the words employed, unless evidence of a contrary intention is adduced. In conflicts between clauses of a single treaty, special clauses prevail over general clauses and prohibitory clauses prevail over permissive clauses. Cessions of sovereignty are always strictly construed. As between two conflicting treaties between the same States, the later one prevails. In general, treaties are so construed as to be self-consistent and as not to violate international law and the rights of third States.

Treaties may come to an end by the expiration of a specified time limit, by the complete fulfillment of their terms, by an express agreement of the parties, or by renunciation of the rights granted. A new treaty, expressly superseding an earlier one, is the most common and satisfactory form of termination. Treaties are likewise terminated by the disappearance of one of the parties. When the independence of a State is extinguished, all its treaties with other States are terminated unless provision to the contrary is made by the new State acquiring its territory. A declaration of war terminates political treaties between the belligerents, suspends all agreements of a permanent nature such as commercial and extradition treaties until the close of hostilities, and brings into operation such agreements as may relate to the conduct of war. Nonfulfillment of the terms of a treaty by one party, if persisted in despite diplomatic representations, makes it voidable by the other party. In all other cases, treaties cannot ordinarily be denounced by one party without the consent of the other, unless their terms make provision for such a procedure. Under the American Constitution the President or Congress or both may denounce a treaty without the consent of the other party. The French treaties of alliance and commerce of 1778 and the commercial convention with France of 1788 were abrogated by act of Congress of July 7, 1798. The Chinese exclusion acts of 1888 and 1892 were in violation of earlier American treaties with China relating to immigration. In 1911, in the face of congressional demands, President Taft abrogated the commercial treaty of 1832 with Russia. Under international law, however, it is doubtful whether one party to a treaty ever has a legal right to terminate it without the consent of the other unless the treaty itself provides for this. Under the principle of *rebus sic stantibus* (conditions remaining the same), it has been contended that fundamental changes of conditions authorize one party to a treaty to terminate it by unilateral action. Japan, for example, sought to deny the validity of the Nine Power Pact and other obligations to respect the "Open Door" in China on the ground that conditions had been altered fundamentally since ratification. The alteration referred to had been brought about by Japanese aggression in violation of the obligations which were alleged to have been invalidated by the change of conditions. Even when this is not the case the other party almost invariably protests against such a contention, and it cannot be said that this principle is part of accepted international law.

6. BELLIGERENCY AND NEUTRALITY

> "You will observe the rules of battle, of course?" the White Knight remarked, putting on his helmet too. "I always do," said the Red Knight, and they began banging away at each other with such fury that Alice got behind a tree to be out of the way of the blows.—LEWIS CARROLL, *Through the Looking Glass.*

From the point of view of international law, war may be defined either as a properly conducted contest of armed public forces, or as a condition or period of time during which inter-state relations are regulated by the law of war instead of by the law of peace. International law does not justify or sanction war but recognizes it as a fact of international politics and seeks to restrict and mitigate its cruel and destructive features. Any literal "outlawry of war" would be a step backward rather than forward, if, contrary to the hopes of the proponents of such schemes, armed conflicts between States continued under conditions permitting them to act as if the international law of war had become nonexistent. Such a development is quite unlikely, however. In many recent conflicts in which both sides refused to admit the existence of a legal state of war, the usual principles of international law governing the conduct of hostilities have been reasonably well observed, despite appearances to the contrary. Here, as in the Great War and in most other international conflicts, public attention tends to be centered on the occasional violations of international law which occur, creating the false impression that all customary restraints have been thrown to the winds and that the international law of war has been scrapped by the belligerents in their desperate efforts to overcome one another. In fact, the great body of rules and principles which have been developed to regulate the conduct of warfare are almost always fully observed because of considerations of expediency and fear of retaliation.

A state of war involves both an intention on one or both sides to wage war and overt acts of hostility. Hostile acts, unaccompanied by an intention to wage war, create a state of war in the legal sense only if they are regarded as inaugurating war by the victim or by third States. A legal state of war may exist without hostilities if the parties have expressed an intention to deal with one another as belligerents. But hostilities, unaccompanied by the intention and not treated as war either by the contestants or by outside parties, do not in themselves create a state of war. They constitute reprisals, retaliation, or intervention; but the rights and obligations of the parties continue to be determined by the law of peace.

In recent wars, it has been customary for States to issue formal declarations of war, making clear their intentions and specifying the time at which a legal state of war shall be regarded as having commenced. .The Hague Convention of 1907 with regard to the opening of hostilities[1] forbade the signatory States to commence hostilities without warning, through either a declaration or an ultimatum. At the opening of the Great War the belligerents in every case specified in a formal declaration the exact hour and minute of the commencement of war, a formality particularly useful to prize courts in determining the legality of captures. Germany invaded Poland on September 1, 1939, without a declaration of war and subsequently invaded Denmark, Norway, Luxemburg, Belgium, the Netherlands, and Rumania in the same fashion. Britain and France initiated hostilities against the aggressor by formal declarations following preliminary ultimata—the British declaration specifying 11 A.M., September 3, and the French 5 P.M. September 3, as the time of the commencement of belligerency. Italy entered the war by a formal declaration against France and Britain, effective at 12.01 A.M., June 11, 1940. Declarations of war usually require legislative action under democratic constitutions. In the United States, they require the approval of a majority of both houses of Congress; but such approval has never been withheld when the President has recommended war, nor has Congress ever declared war in opposition to the wishes of the executive.[2]

[1] Article 1. The contracting Powers recognize that hostilities between them must not commence without a previous and explicit warning, in the form of either a declaration of war, giving reasons, or an ultimatum with a conditional declaration of war.

Article 2. The existence of a state of war must be notified to the neutral Powers without delay, and shall not be held to affect them until after the receipt of a notification, which may, however, be given by telegraph. Nevertheless, neutral Powers may not rely on the absence of notification if it be established beyond doubt that they were in fact aware of the existence of a state of war.

[2] On the effects of the Pact of Paris of 1928 on the legal status of war, see p. 469 below.

As for the general principles underlying the law of war, it may be said that war suspends all nonhostile intercourse between the belligerent States and their citizens. Diplomatic and consular relations are severed, along with contacts of trade and travel. Political treaties between the belligerents are terminated, other treaties are suspended for the duration of the conflict, and agreements relating to the conduct of hostilities are put into operation. Relations between the belligerents are henceforth subject to the international law of war, and their relations with outside States not participating in the struggle are governed by the international law of neutrality. From the legal point of view, the purpose of war is to bring about the complete military subjection of the enemy in the shortest possible time with the least possible loss of life and property. This conception of the objective of hostilities is shared by the jurist and the strategist, but under modern conditions differences of opinion necessarily arise as to the implications of such a statement. It is agreed that mere wanton destruction and slaughter, having no reasonable relation to the military subjection of the enemy, is unlawful. The older view of the Continental States of Europe was that war should, as far as possible, be limited in its effects to armed public forces. Great Britain, and more recently the United States, have regarded it as permissible to attack the commercial resources and the food supplies of the whole enemy population through naval blockades, a view which has now received general acceptance. During the Great War, Germany developed the theory of *Schrecklichkeit*, or frightfulness, according to which, in its extreme form, it is legitimate to attack the entire civilian population of the enemy State by all possible means in order to break its will to resist. In spite of the general condemnation of this view at the time, it is the logical corollary of universal military conscription, of the mobilization of industrial resources, and of the decisive importance of civilian morale in a long-drawn-out war of attrition. It therefore continues to be applied.

This development is tending to break down the well-established legal distinction between soldiers and civilians. Nevertheless, it is still correct to say that for the purpose of ascertaining the legal rights and obligations of individuals in wartime they are divided into the two general categories of combatants and noncombatants. Combatants may be fired upon at sight and if taken alive are entitled to be treated as prisoners of war. In this category are members of the regularly authorized military, naval, and air forces of the State, officers and crews of merchant vessels resisting capture, and members of levies en masse and of popular civilian uprisings against invaders, provided that they carry arms openly, obey the laws of war, wear emblems or uniforms, and are under a definite command.[1] Noncombatants are all persons not participating in hostilities, not members of

---

[1] *Cf.* Hague Convention of 1907 on Laws and Customs of War on Land, Article 1.

fighting forces, and not belonging to any of the special classes mentioned below. Civilian enemy aliens found within a State at the outbreak of war may be expelled, interned, permitted to depart, or permitted to remain unmolested. Since 1914, belligerent States have commonly interned enemy aliens within their jurisdiction, sometimes for their own protection against mob violence. Noncombatants in occupied territory or in the zone of military operations are free from violence, constraint, or injury except what is dictated by military necessity or what may befall them through actual hostilities. Finally, notice should be taken of certain exceptional classes of persons who are neither combatants nor noncombatants, but are subjected to special treatment. Officers and crews of merchant vessels taking offensive action against other merchant vessels may be punished by death for piracy since the abolition of privateering by the Declaration of Paris in 1856. Guerrillas, *i.e.*, individuals not in the armed forces of the State who engage in military operations without State authorization, may likewise be punished for their individual acts. They are not entitled to be treated as prisoners of war but may be tried and sentenced for murder, arson, and other crimes which are not individually punishable when committed by soldiers, sailors, or aviators acting under orders. Similar treatment is accorded to spies, *i.e.*, individuals in disguise who act under false pretenses behind the lines or in occupied territory to secure information for the enemy. They are entitled to a trial and if found guilty are usually executed.

As regards the treatment accorded to property in wartime, the general rules applied are relatively simple, though their specific application in complex situations often involves tangled legal problems. Public real property in an enemy State or in occupied territory, *i.e.*, property owned by a belligerent government within the jurisdiction of an enemy belligerent or in a region under hostile military occupation, may be taken over and administered during the war for the benefit of the State in control but may not be confiscated. Public movable property, with the exception of works of art, science, or education, is subject to confiscation; but enlightened opinion has been increasingly averse to the exercise of this right, except in occupied territory. During the Great War, however, the American Government seized the German patents in the United States under conditions which amounted to confiscation. Private property of enemy nationals was formerly considered to be subject to confiscation wherever found. This harsh rule has now been modified in a variety of ways. Private property of enemy aliens found within a State at the outbreak of war is now usually unmolested or held under bond by the local government for the duration of the war to prevent its being used to the advantage of the enemy State. Private enemy property in occupied territory may no longer be taken by the occupying forces without compensation, though if military necessity requires its destruction no compensation need be paid. The Treaty of Versailles, however, required Germany to pay compensation to the victors for all civilian damages, on the theory that the Great War was a result of German aggression.[1] Forces of military occupation may levy taxes on the local population for local purposes and may assess fines and penalties on communities where it is clear that the municipal authorities have been negligent in fulfilling their obligations to maintain order and to prevent civilian participation in hostilities. In all other cases, as in the levying of money contributions upon the local citizenry, the requisition of food and other materials needed by the occupying forces, or the sequestration of vessels, vehicles, and the like, a receipt must be given to the owner as a promise of eventual compensation.

Property at sea is dealt with in accordance with principles differing somewhat from those applicable to property on land. Enemy property at sea is, in general, subject to capture and condemnation. Save for ships engaged in humanitarian, educational, or scientific enterprises, there are no exceptions to this rule for public enemy property, *i.e.*, battleships and other vessels and goods owned by the enemy State. With regard to enemy property owned by private individuals, however, various qualifications to the general right of capture have received general acceptance. Enemy merchant vessels in port at the outbreak of hostilities were formerly accorded a specified number of days of grace within which they might escape to sea. Religious, scientific, and philanthropic vessels are exempt from capture, as are hospital ships, fishing vessels, and small coastwise vessels of all types. Under the Declaration of Paris of 1856,[2] it is no longer

[1] Article 231: The Allied and Associated Governments affirm and Germany accepts the responsibility of Germany and her allies for causing all the loss and damage to which the Allied and Associated Governments and their nationals have been subjected as a consequence of the war imposed upon them by the aggression of Germany and her allies.

Article 232: The Allied and Associated Governments recognize that the resources of Germany are not adequate, after taking into account permanent diminutions of such resources which will result from other provisions of the present treaty, to make complete reparation for all such loss and damage. The Allied and Associated Governments, however, require, and Germany undertakes, that she will make compensation for all damage done to the civilian population of the Allied and Associated Powers and to their property during the period of the belligerency of each as an Allied or Associated Power against Germany by such aggression by land, by sea, and from the air, and in general all damage as defined in Annex I hereto.

Under these provisions Germany was required to pay compensation for all civilian injuries and deaths and for all Allied military pensions. She was likewise obliged to assume the entire war debt of Belgium. Chancellor Hitler repudiated the "war guilt" clause of the Treaty in his address of January 30, 1937.

[2] The plenipotentiaries who signed the Treaty of Paris of the thirteenth of March, one thousand eight hundred and fifty-six, assembled in conference . . . have adopted the following declaration: (1) privateering is and remains abolished; (2) the neutral flag covers enemy's goods, with the exception of contraband of war; (3) neutral goods, with the exception of contraband of war, are not liable to capture under enemy's flag; (4) blockades, in order to be binding, must be effective—that is to say, maintained by a force sufficient really to prevent access to the coast of the enemy. . . . April 16, 1856.

lawful for belligerents to issue letters of marque and reprisal to private vessels (privateers) authorizing them to capture enemy merchant ships. The Declaration likewise specifies that goods of neutral ownership found on enemy ships shall be exempt from capture and that goods of enemy ownership found on neutral ships shall also be exempt, contraband of war being excepted in both cases. The signatory Powers further declared that a proclamation of a blockade cannot give an indiscriminate right of capture of neutral vessels unless it is, in fact, effectively enforced. Enemy vessels are subject to capture wherever found, even in the absence of a blockade. In the exercise of the right of capture, all vessels are regarded as enemy vessels which fly an enemy flag, which have been transferred to a neutral flag to escape capture, which are under convoy of belligerent war vessels, or which resist search. Captured enemy vessels may be destroyed if there is no means of taking them into port for condemnation, but provision must be made for the safety of passengers and crew. The inability of submarines to make such provision led to widespread criticism (from enemy and neutral governments) of their use by Germany. In the great commercial wars of modern times, the naval Powers have usually attempted, in accordance with the general right of capture, to sweep enemy commerce from the seas. The pursuit of this objective has usually led to attacks upon neutral commerce as well.

A large number of well-defined principles have grown up regarding the actual conduct of hostilities. The more important of these were codified in the Hague Conference Conventions in 1899 and 1907 relating to the laws and customs of war on land. They are for the most part designed to mitigate the horrors and cruelties of war as much as possible. They are usually well observed, since considerations of expediency dictate their observance on both sides of the battle line. Wanton and unnecessary destruction of life and property is forbidden, as is the use of poison, dumdum bullets, the refusal of quarter, resort to assassination, deliberate perfidy and treachery, and attacks upon undefended towns. Sick and wounded are to be cared for, and prisoners of war must be humanely treated. Civilian populations are, so far as possible, to be spared from the incidents of war. Hospitals, churches, schools, museums, public buildings, and the like, are to be spared, unless used for military purposes. Naval and aerial bombardment of undefended cities is usually viewed with disapproval. During the Great War the established principles dealing with the relations between the armed forces were reasonably well observed, in spite of the introduction of poison gas, liquid fire, and other novel weapons. The rules designed to protect civilians, however, were in many instances ignored, particularly by the Central Powers which were strategically in a position to strike at enemy centers of population through air raids and long-range artillery for the purpose of disorganizing manufacturing and transport and breaking down morale through terrorism. These departures from established rules designed to protect civilians are logically dictated by military necessity under the contemporary economic, social, and psychological conditions attending large-scale combats between national States. In the Second World War there were intensive and persistent attacks upon civilians by weapons of unprecedented destructiveness. If such catastrophes are to be averted, it will be through the abolition of war itself, rather than through further efforts at limiting weapons or setting up new legal safeguards which are certain to be brushed aside in modern "wars of annihilation."

In most of the wars between members of earlier State Systems and in the early wars in the Western State System as well, the notion that an outside State might refrain from participation in a conflict between its neighbors was an unfamiliar one. What is now known as the international law of neutrality developed very slowly and did not reach its modern form prior to the nineteenth century. As recently as the War of the American Revolution, it was regarded as legitimate for a "neutral" State to rent out its troops to belligerents without violating its obligations. The Hessian mercenaries of Great Britain were secured in this fashion. In the early period, text writers, from Grotius onward, emphasized the rights of neutral States to be free from interference by belligerents, since such rights were frequently ignored. Later, after neutral rights had been more clearly defined, emphasis was shifted to the obligations of neutral States to refrain from participation in hostilities. In the most recent period the great controversies over neutrality have again centered in neutral rights as related to trading privileges. The United States neutrality code of 1794 was one of the first clear formulations of the modern conception of neutral obligations. As the first member of the Western State System outside of the European continent, the United States could more easily hold itself aloof from European wars than could the States of Europe. It has accordingly played a large role in the subsequent development of the principles of neutrality.

Neutral obligations may be summarized in terms of abstention, impartiality, and prevention. It is now customary for States to declare their neutrality upon the outbreak of war by a formal proclamation issued by the head of the government.[1] A State which has declared itself neutral has a right to have its neutrality respected by the belligerents. It is correspondingly obliged to enforce its neutrality by conducting itself impartially toward the belligerents, by abstaining from any participation in the

[1] On September 5, 1939, President Roosevelt issued a conventional neutrality proclamation under international law and a second proclamation under the Neutrality Act of 1937 imposing an embargo on the exports of arms, ammunition, and implements of war to Germany, Poland, France, Britain, India, Australia, New Zealand, South Africa (September 5), and Canada (September 10).

conflict, and by preventing its citizens from engaging in certain acts regarded as breaches of neutral obligations. A neutral State may not permit its territory to be used as a base of hostile operations by either belligerent against the other. It may not permit its armed forces to be employed to the advantage of either belligerent, nor may it officially loan money or sell war supplies to warring governments. It is not obliged, however, to prevent its nationals from lending money or selling war supplies, provided that they are legally free to sell to both sides on equal terms. Between 1914 and 1917, the period of American neutrality in the Great War, hundreds of millions of dollars worth of Allied war bonds were sold in the United States, and billions of dollars worth of munitions were sold to the Allied Governments by American manufacturers and exporters. The German Government complained that in fact this trade was entirely one-sided, since the Allied blockade prevented American munitions from reaching the Central Powers. In law, however, there was no breach of neutral obligations on the part of the United States, since the American Government was not responsible for the Allied blockade and Americans were free to sell to both sides on equal terms at their own risk.

A neutral State must prevent the enlistment of troops for war purposes on its territory, and it must intern belligerent troops and aircraft forced into its jurisdiction. It may grant a right of innocent passage through its territorial waters, however, to belligerent warships. Neutral governments are likewise obliged to prevent their nationals from making their territory a base of hostile operations. Neutral nationals may be permitted to sell war supplies to warring States, but they must be prevented from fitting out, in neutral ports, vessels designed to take part in the war. The failure of Great Britain to fulfill this obligation during the American Civil War caused the Geneva Arbitration Tribunal, created by the Treaty of Washington of 1871, to award $15,500,000 to the United States for damages committed by the *Alabama*, the *Florida*, and other Confederate cruisers constructed in British ports. A neutral State may not, in the course of a war, modify its neutrality regulations to the advantage of one belligerent. It must use due diligence to insure observance of its obligations; and it cannot extend its protection to its citizens who engage in "unneutral service," *i.e.*, who commit hostile acts against belligerents and thereby render themselves liable to treatment as enemy nationals.

During the past century the most acute controversies over neutral rights have arisen as a result of the efforts of belligerent States to cut off commercial contacts between the enemy State and neutral States. A belligerent State is recognized to have a right to intercept such commerce on two grounds. It may proclaim a blockade of enemy ports; and if such a blockade is effectively enforced, *i.e.*, if it is not merely a "paper blockade," it entitles war vessels of the blockading State to capture neutral vessels seeking to enter or leave the blockaded ports. At the same time, in the absence of any blockade, belligerent war vessels may capture neutral goods and ships falling in the category of contraband of war, *i.e.*, goods of neutral ownership, found on the high seas, of use in war, and destined for the enemy. Neutral vessels may be condemned if more than half the cargo consists of contraband, as measured by volume or by value. All other neutral commerce with States at war is theoretically legitimate and not to be interfered with. Neutral commercial States have always insisted vehemently upon "freedom of the seas" and neutral trading rights. Belligerent States, on the other hand, have always been disposed to interpret their rights to intercept neutral commerce as broadly as possible, through the extension of the contraband list and the "doctrine of continuous voyage."

The doctrine of continuous voyage, or "ultimate destination," was developed by Great Britain at the end of the eighteenth century, utilized by the Union in the American Civil War, and employed by both the British and American Governments in the Great War. It holds that neutral vessels going from one neutral port to another may be captured if there is presumption of eventual enemy destination of the cargo.[1] In the Great War and again in 1939 the British Admiralty applied this doctrine both to contraband and to blockade. It went so far as to allot quotas of foodstuffs and other supplies to the Scandinavian neutrals and to confiscate all neutral cargoes bound for Scandinavian ports in excess of the quotas, on the ground that there was reasonable presumption that the cargoes were destined for transshipment to Germany, either as contraband goods or in violation of the blockade. The retaliatory measures of the German Government took the form of a submarine blockade of the Allied States. By their very nature, the U-boats were obliged to strike and flee, without regard to the safety of life and property aboard torpedoed vessels. The ensuing controversies with neutrals over the legitimacy of this method of enforcing a blockade furnished the occasion for the entrance of the United States into the war in 1917. In addition to devising novel methods of enforcing blockades and applying the doctrine of continuous voyage, belligerent States in recent wars have extended the list of contraband goods to a point where almost all neutral commerce with the enemy is swept from the seas. Originally, only war supplies were regarded as contraband; but the British contraband lists of 1914 and 1915 included practically every conceivable commodity. This procedure was defended on the ground that all the industrial and commercial resources of Germany had been mobilized for war purposes. The Allied navies cut off the Central Powers from almost all commercial contacts

[1] *Cf. The Maria*, 5 C. Rob. 365, 368; *The Kim*, L. R. 215 (1915); *The Hart*, 3 Wall. 559–560.

with the outside world. Neutral ships and cargoes of every nature, destined either for German ports or for other neutral ports near Germany, were captured and condemned in wholesale fashion. The United States and other neutrals protested against these practices but resorted to them with even greater enthusiasm after becoming belligerents.

The major controversies between belligerents and neutrals in 1939–1940 revolved around similar issues. On September 3, 1939, the British liner *Athenia* was sunk without warning with heavy loss of life, including twenty-five Americans. Germany disclaimed responsibility, however; and in the absence of proof the United States refrained from protest. On October 9, 1939, before American vessels were forbidden to go to belligerent ports, the British-bound American freighter *City of Flint* was captured by the *Deutschland*. The prize crew took the vessel to Norway, then to Murmansk, U.S.S.R., and then back to a Norwegian port. On the principle that a neutral may not permit a belligerent to bring enemy prizes into its ports except temporarily for fuel, provisions, or repairs,[1] the United States demanded the release of the vessel. Norway complied. Germany protested. Oslo rejected the protest on November 5. In the same month, German naval forces began sowing magnetic mines in British waters, in violation of the Hague Convention of 1907, allegedly in retaliation for Allied blockade practices and contraband lists which Berlin held were unlawful. Early in December the Allies, in counter-retaliation, ordered the seizure of enemy exports in neutral vessels, contrary to the Declaration of Paris. The United States protested to London at this order and also protested against Allied interference with American mails and undue delay in contraband inspection and control at Gibraltar. The argument, as usual in such cases, was inconclusive.

The Allies subsequently contended that Norway was permitting the abuse of its territorial waters by the Reich. On February 16, 1940, the British destroyer *Cossack* violated Norwegian waters by entering Joesing Fjord, boarding the German naval supply ship *Altmark*, and releasing 300 British seamen who had been captured by the *Graf Spee*. Oslo protested to London. Berlin protested to Oslo. On April 5, London threatened action to close Norwegian waters to German shipping on the ground that Norway was permitting abuse of the right of innocent passage. Three days later, British vessels sowed mines along the Norwegian coast to intercept Swedish ore shipments to Germany via Narvik. The Nazi invasion of Norway, launched April 9, had been prepared long in advance but was "justified" by Berlin on the pretext that Norway was not safeguarding its neutrality and was about to be invaded by the Allies and used as a base of operations against the Reich.

[1] *Cf.* the case of the *Appam, Berg v. British and African Steam Navigation Company*, 243 U.S. 12 (1917) and Articles 21–23 of the Hague Convention (XIII) concerning the Rights and Duties of Neutral Powers in Naval Warfare (1907).

These developments raise serious and still unsettled questions regarding the status of neutral commerce in modern wars. The use of submarines and airplanes to enforce blockades, the enormous expansion of the contraband list, and the application of the doctrine of continuous voyage to both contraband and blockade are all devices whereby desperate belligerents seek to establish legal justification for a policy of severing all trading relations between the enemy and neutral States. They may be resisted by neutrals; but the law is still much confused and such protests are usually of little avail except to embroil the neutrals in controversies and sometimes in war with the belligerents. Until recently the traditional American championship of "freedom of the seas" and neutral trading rights had raised doubts as to whether members of the League of Nations could even apply economic sanctions to a Covenant-breaking State without involving themselves in a serious risk of diplomatic difficulties with the United States. The League of Nations Covenant and the Kellogg-Briand Pact, if taken literally, went far in the direction of abolishing neutrality completely as a feasible policy and a defensible legal status. Neutrality implies a large degree of isolation and aloofness from the issues of a war on the part of a neutral State. In a world of interdependent States, in which no State can view with indifference a war between any other two States, such isolation and aloofness are no longer possible. Here, again, international law as a means of protecting the rights of States appears to have reached the limits of its development, pending the effective outlawry of war itself.

In recent years, neutral governments have tended to restrict their rights and to enlarge their obligations beyond what is required by customary international law. After 1935 the United States warned its nationals that they would travel on belligerent vessels at their own risk and forbade them to sell arms or lend money to belligerents. Such embargoes limit somewhat the economic entanglement of neutrals in war but usually operate to the disadvantage of victims of aggression.[1] In the Spanish civil war, the Powers, though legally free to sell arms to the established government and bound to prevent any aid to the rebels, voluntarily agreed in August, at the suggestion of Britain and France, to forbid all arms shipments to either side. The United States did not join this pact but informally declared its neutrality on August 15, 1936, and refused to license arms shipments.[2] The "nonintervention" agreement was, by

---

[1] See p. 644 below.

[2] In December, 1936, Mr. Robert Cuse demanded, and received, a license to export 3 million dollars worth of aircraft to the Spanish Loyalists. In order to forbid such exports, Congress extended the neutrality legislation to the Spanish civil strife in an amendment signed by the President on January 8, 1937. Thus a lawfully constituted government, having correct and even friendly diplomatic relations with the United States, was, in the name of "neutrality," denied the right of buying arms from private American sources for the suppression of a rebellion. This provision was abandoned in the Act of 1939.

implication, a recognition of the belligerency of the rebels, though this was later denied by the British Government. Here, paradoxically, neutrality was unneutral in its practical effects and nonintervention was an act of intervention, both in law and in fact, since the signatories denied to Madrid its customary right to purchase arms to suppress rebellion and thus aided the insurgents. Germany, Italy, and Portugal, though parties to the agreement, surreptitiously sent war materials to the rebels. The London Nonintervention Committee, headed by Lord Plymouth, ignored Soviet charges of violations and whitewashed the culprits, thus conniving at outside support of the rebellion while continuing to insist that all aid be withheld from the legal government of Spain.[1] A neutral arms embargo, whether in international or civil war, inevitably strengthens the best-armed belligerent. The "new" neutrality, which is inconsistent both with earlier conceptions of nonintervention and impartiality and with the notion of outlawing war by penalizing aggressors, thus tends to encourage revolution wherever rebels have army support and to promote aggression by strong States against weak ones.

In 1939–1940 there occurred an almost complete breakdown of traditional conceptions of neutrality. The aggressor States encouraged bilateral nonaggression pacts with their weak neighbors and strict observance of neutrality by other States in order to thwart any common action against aggression and to facilitate the conquest of their neighbors one by one. The smaller neutrals and even the United States fell in with this design under the delusion that they could have peace by adhering to traditional neutrality. In this manner the Baltic States, Denmark, Norway, the Netherlands, Belgium, and Luxemburg ensured their own destruction.[2] The greatest of the neutrals, the United States, vacillated among formulae to "keep out of other peoples' wars" by enlarging neutral obligations, attempts at enlarging neutral rights for a similar purpose, and, ultimately, efforts to aid the Allies by abandoning "neutrality" in favor of "nonbelligerency" on the model of Fascist Italy (September 3, 1939–June 10, 1940) and of Fascist Spain after the fall of France.

At the outbreak of the war in 1939 the United States applied the Neutrality Act of 1937 forbidding Americans to send ships or sell arms to belligerents—a course which Assistant Secretary of War Louis Johnson

---

[1] See pp. 542–546 below.

[2] Thus Lithuania on March 22, 1939, Denmark on May 31, and Estonia and Latvia on June 7 signed bilateral treaties with Germany pledging the signatories "under no circumstances to go to war or employ force of any kind against one another. Should action of the kind specified be taken by a third Power against one of the contracting parties, the other contracting party will in no way support such action." All the Oslo States (Luxemburg, Belgium, the Netherlands, Denmark, Norway, Sweden, and Finland, united in an "economic entente" by the Oslo conventions of December 22, 1930) adhered to a similar conception with consequences that were almost uniformly disastrous.

said was equivalent to presenting Germany with an Atlantic fleet. President Roosevelt, whose earlier efforts to secure amendment of the Act had been thwarted by an isolationist Congress, declared, "I regret that Congress passed that Act. I equally regret that I signed that Act." At his suggestion, Congress enacted a Joint Resolution, signed by the President on November 4, 1939, "to Preserve the Neutrality and Peace of the United States and to Secure the Safety of its Citizens and their Interests." The new statute reasserted American neutral rights under international law and then proceeded forthwith to abandon them by continuing the embargo on private loans to belligerents, forbidding American ships and citizens to go to belligerent ports or combat zones, and requiring that all exports to States at war, including arms (sale of which was now permitted), must be paid for in advance and carried in foreign vessels. In the name of "cash and carry" the Great Power which had taken up arms in 1798, 1805, 1812, and 1917 to defend "freedom of the seas" and the right of its citizens to trade with belligerents thus gave up its rights in 1939 in the interests of keeping out of war.

This conception was supplemented by a strange corollary limited to the Western Hemisphere. By the Declaration of Panama of October 3, 1939, the twenty-one American Republics asserted "as of inherent right" and "as a measure of continental self-protection" that they were entitled to keep "free from the commission of any hostile acts by any non-American belligerent nations" a vast area of open sea, covering 5 million square miles and including the waters around the American continents extending from 300 to 1,000 miles from the shore. This denial of "freedom of the seas" and assertion of *mare clausum* was not accepted by the belligerents, none of which respected the "neutrality zone." The German pocket battleship *Admiral Graf Spee* raided enemy shipping in the south Atlantic. While pursuing the French merchantman *Formose* off the coast of Brazil well within the zone, it was overtaken on December 13, 1939, by the British cruisers *Ajax*, *Achilles*, and *Exeter* which drove it into the harbor of Montevideo and caused its captain to scuttle his ship and take his life when the seventy-two hours' grace granted by Uruguay had expired. This and other belligerent operations within the zone caused the twenty-one American Republics on December 21 to protest, through the President of Panama, to Britain, France, and Germany. London, Paris, and Berlin all denied the right of the American Republics to close the high seas to their vessels by unilateral action. The Allies offered to respect the zone if the American Republics would lay up all German vessels within it for the duration of the war and guarantee that no other German vessels would enter it. Germany offered to respect it if given a guarantee that British and French possessions within the zone, including Canada, would not be used as war bases. Neither the United States nor its neighbors could fulfill these conditions. They were unwilling to use force against belligerent vessels operating within the zone. The entire scheme, therefore, remained an empty gesture without legal validity and is significant only as a revelation of the length to which isolationist neutrals were prepared to go in departing from established law for the sake of "keeping out" of war abroad and "keeping war away" from their own shores.

When the disastrous results of such a policy became apparent amid the terrifying events of the spring of 1940, the United States departed once more from traditional conceptions of neutrality—this time in the interest of aiding Britain by measures "short of war." In his Charlottesville speech of June 10, denouncing Mussolini's "stab in the back," and in his reply to Reynaud's last plea, Roosevelt pledged all possible aid to the Allies. So long as such aid took the form of "private" sales of weapons and war supplies, it was consistent with conventional "neutrality." But governmental sales, gifts, or transfers of arms from a neutral to a belligerent had long been forbidden by established law. On August 18, 1940, however, the American President and Canadian Prime Minister Mackenzie King announced an agreement to establish a "permanent joint board of defense" to plan common action in defense of both countries. And on September 3, 1940, Roosevelt informed Congress that Secretary Hull and British Ambassador Lothian had exchanged letters on the preceding day whereby the United States acquired the right to lease for ninety-nine years naval and air bases in Newfoundland and in Bermuda "as gifts, generously given and gladly received," and to lease other bases for a similar term in the Bahamas, Jamaica, St. Lucia, Trinidad, Antigua, and British Guiana "in exchange for 50 of our over age destroyers. . . . This is not inconsistent in any sense with our status of peace. . . . Preparation for defense is an inalienable prerogative of a sovereign State."

This executive agreement made hash of old-fashioned "neutrality." Attorney General Robert Jackson's learned opinion argued that it was consistent with the obligations of neutrality. But the argument rested on the simple device of ignoring the basic distinction between "private" and "governmental" sales and twisting into meaninglessness the well-worn rule that neutrals must not permit their nationals to fit out and sell to belligerents any vessels designed to take part in hostilities. The nation applauded. When the "enemy" replied with the Rome-Berlin-Tokio alliance of September 27, 1940, threatening war against America, the President at Dayton on October 12 asserted that "no combination of dictator countries of Europe and Asia will stop the help we are giving to almost the last free people fighting to hold them at bay. . . . Our decision is made. We will continue . . . to help those who resist aggression and who now hold the aggressors far from our shores."

Few tears were shed over this scrapping of traditional neutral obligations save in the camps of isolationism and in the totalitarian capitals, whose rulers had already reduced neutrality to a farce. The exigencies of *Realpolitik*, here as in other fields, superseded the requirements of a jurisprudence which had its origin in an epoch when wars were designed to achieve limited objectives rather than to annihilate rivals and conquer the earth. The strategy of terror employed by the new Caesars had demolished the distinction between "peace" and "war" and between "neutrality" and "belligerency." For neutrals to adhere in law to concepts already meaningless in fact was simply to connive at their own defeat and destruction. Here, as always, self-preservation takes precedence over rules of law which have reality only when questions of survival are not raised.

To conclude, however, that such developments as these foreshadow "the end of international law" would be premature. They merely indicate the impossibility of maintaining the breath of life in concepts of juridical rights and obligations among equals in a community in which many members recognize no right save might and fulfill no obligations save those of aggrandizement. The community of nations in this generation, if it survives at all, will be unified—politically, administratively, and juridically—either by the sword of the aggressors or by the sword of those resisting aggression. In either case the victors will adapt international law to the needs of the world order that will emerge with victory. The new international law will be brought into harmony with the demands of world unity and will again rest, as the old law once rested, on common purposes and practices. It will therefore differ sharply from the old. Yet it will be an outgrowth of the old, even though the central concept of the "sovereign State" vanishes in the process. Indeed, it is more than probable that there will be no law among nations in the days to come unless "sovereignty" itself is relegated to the limbo of forgotten myths.

SUGGESTED READINGS

Borchard, E. M.: *The Diplomatic Protection of Citizens Abroad,* New York, Banks Law Publishing Company, 1915.

Briggs, H. W.: *The Law of Nations,* New York, Croft, 1938.

Deak, F., and P. C. Jessup (ed.); *Collection of Neutrality Laws, Regulations and Treaties of Various Countries,* New York, Columbia University Press, International Documents Service, 1940.

Dickinson, E. D.: *The Law of Nations,* New York, McGraw-Hill, 1929.

Fenwick, C. G.: *International Law,* New York, Appleton-Century, 1924.

Freeman, A. V.: *The International Responsibility of States for Denial of Justice,* New York, Longmans, 1939.

Hall, W. E.: *A Treatise on International Law,* New York, Oxford, 1924.

Hershey, A. S.: *Essentials of International Public Law and Organization,* New York, Macmillan, 1927.

Hudson, M. O.: *International Legislation* (6 vols.), Washington, Carnegie Endowment 1937.

Hyde, C. C.: *International Law, Chiefly as Interpreted and Applied by the United States* (2 vols.), Boston, Little, Brown, 1922.

Jessup, P. C. (ed.): *Neutrality: Its History, Economics and Law* (4 vols.), N. Y., Columbia University Press, 1936.

Keeton, G. W., and Georg Schwarzenberger: *Making International Law Work*, London, Peace Book Company, 1939.

Lauterpacht, H.: *The Function of Law in the International Community*, New York, Oxford, 1933.

Lawrence, T. J.: *The Principles of International Law*, Boston, Heath, 1923.

Malloy, W. E. (ed.): *Treaties, Conventions, International Acts, Protocols and Agreements between the United States and Other Powers*, Washington, Government Printing Office, vol. I, and II, 1909, vol. III, 1923.

Miller, Hunter (ed.): *Treaties and Other International Acts of the United States* (4 vols. to 1846), Washington, Government Printing Office, 1935.

Moore, J. B.: *A Digest of International Law* (8 vols.), Washington, Government Printing Office, 1906.

Oppenheim, L.: *International Law* (2 vols.), New York, Longmans, 1928.

—— (ed. by H. Lauterpacht): *International Law*, vol. I, Peace, New York, Longmans, 1937.

Padelford, N. J., *International Law and Diplomacy in the Spanish Civil Strife*, New York, Macmillan, 1939.

Rafuse, R. W.: *The Extradition of Nationals*, Urbana, University of Illinois Press, 1939.

Robson, W. A.: *Civilization and the Growth of Law*, New York, Macmillan, 1935.

Vali, F. A.: *Servitudes in International Law*, London, King, 1934.

Westlake, John: *International Law*, London, Cambridge University Press, vol. I, 1910, vol. II, 1913.

Wild, P. S., Jr.: *Sanctions and Treaty Enforcement*, Cambridge, Harvard University Press, 1934.

Wilson, G. G.: *International Law*, New York, Silver, Burdett, 1922.

Chapter IV

THE PRACTICE OF DIPLOMACY

1. THE PROFESSION OF NEGOTIATOR

The late Duke of Tuscany, who was a remarkably wise and enlightened prince, once complained to the Venetian Ambassador, who stayed over night with him on his journey to Rome, that the Republic of Venice had sent as resident at his court a person of no value, possessing neither judgment nor knowledge, nor even any attractive personal quality. "I am not surprised," said the Ambassador in reply; "we have many fools in Venice." Whereupon the Grand Duke retorted: "We also have fools in Florence, but we take care not to export them."—M. DE CALLIÈRES, *On the Manner of Negotiating with Princes*, 1716.

EARLY in the seventeenth century Sir Henry Wotton inscribed in Christopher Flecamore's album a definition of an ambassador which has since become famous. "An ambassador," he wrote, "is an honest man sent to lie abroad for the good of his country." This conception of the function of diplomacy is reminiscent of Machiavelli and Louis XI. Though it is now frowned upon by those who urge openness and honesty in international relations, it nevertheless suggests the fundamental nature of the State System in which modern diplomacy has arisen. In a System of independent sovereign units, engaged in a perpetual struggle with one another for territory, power, and prestige in an ofttimes violent if not entirely lawless fashion, diplomacy and war are inevitably regarded as means to the greater glory of the State. A State may enhance its power at the expense of its rivals through violent coercion or through discussion, compromise, and bargaining which may well involve unscrupulous trickery, deception, and misrepresentation. The end is the same. Which means it is most expedient to use in a given situation depends upon circumstances. But in any case modern diplomacy, like military might, is a weapon for the enhancement of State power quite as much as a means for the orderly discussion of international problems.

In the present chapter, however, attention will be directed to the mechanisms of diplomacy rather than to its purposes. The mechanisms have been created to achieve the purposes, for in the process of political and administrative invention, no less than in technology and organic evolution, structure reflects function. But the purposes of diplomacy are no longer limited to the enhancement of the power of the State at the expense of its neighbors. The functions of diplomats have become varied and multitudinous to the same degree to which the contacts among States in the machine age have become enriched and bewilderingly complicated. Sir Ernest Satow, in his great work, *A Guide to Diplomatic Practice*, defined diplomacy as "the application of intelligence and tact to the conduct of official relations between the governments of independent States" (2d ed., 1922, I, p. 1). In the contemporary period the number of problems which fall within the purview of the official relations among governments is enormously greater than it has ever been before. A correspondingly complex set of diplomatic procedures and institutions has been developed to meet the needs of the international world society of the modern age of Western civilization.

Modern diplomacy, invented in Renaissance Italy and embellished and enriched by the practice of the national monarchies of western Europe in the epoch of the great discoveries and of the Reformation, was first subjected to a crucial test of its efficacy as an instrument of international collaboration at the Peace Congress of Westphalia which concluded the Thirty Years' War. The circumstances attending this first great gathering of European diplomats revealed clearly the necessity of establishing fixed rules of diplomatic etiquette and ceremonial. The long delay of six years in the conclusion of the peace was due in large part to the absence of such fixed rules in the international practice of the period. A Venetian offer of mediation was ignored because the Republic had addressed Queen Christina of Sweden as "Sérénissime" and had failed to add "Très-Puissante" to her title. The Venetian Ambassador at Paris apologized for this omission to Grotius, then Swedish Ambassador to France, but the war went on. Not until the close of the year 1641 were arrangements made between the belligerents for the summoning of a peace conference. Innumerable procedural difficulties arose at once. The Swedes refused to send delegates to Cologne as the Pope had suggested or to any other place where Sweden's ally, France, might be regarded as having precedence. The mountain refused to go to Mohammed, and Mohammed refused to go to the mountain. After much wrangling, it was decided that the Swedes would negotiate with the enemy at Osnabrück and the French at Münster, both cities in Westphalia about thirty miles apart and roughly halfway between Paris and Stockholm. While the war continued, the two towns, as well as the route between them, were neutralized by international action to afford security to the delegates. New controversies arose over the forms of the documentary credentials of the plenipotentiaries. The Count d'Avaux, representing France, refused to accord the title of Emperor to Ferdinand III; and Salvius, the Swedish delegate, would not have the King of France named before his Queen. Finally, each delegate in his credentials gave first place to his own rulers. Next the Emperor refused to ratify the preliminary treaty which was concluded. It recognized the rulers of France and Sweden as his equals, he complained; his own name did not appear first in the document; the neutralization of Westphalia was derogatory to his dignity.

Not until July of 1642 were arrangements for the Congress finally completed, and another thirteen months elapsed before any of the delegates arrived on the scene. Since the full powers of some of them were questioned, no business was done till June of 1645. "If," wrote Ogier, friend of the French delegate, Abel Servien, "they create in the substance of the business delays proportioned to those hitherto, I do not know that the unborn child Madame Servien is expecting can hope to see the end of a treaty to which our adversaries create such extraordinary obstacles."[1] Long wrangles ensued over titles, places of honor in processions, and seating arrangements at the conference. Most of the States of Europe were represented, except England, Russia, and Turkey. So numerous were the delegates that one observer declared that "one could not look out the door without seeing ten ambassadors." Each delegate stood upon his dignity at all costs. All wanted to be at the head of the conference table. When a round table was at length agreed upon, more quarrels arose over the honor of occupying the place nearest the door. So tedious and complicated were all the details of the negotiations that the records fill many volumes. Eight years elapsed before the terms of peace were finally settled and embodied in the treaties of 1648.

Each succeeding international conference of European States has accomplished its work in a progressively shorter period of time. The congress at Utrecht (1713–1714) required only two years to complete its task. The Congress of Vienna of 1814–1815 lasted only fourteen months. The Paris Peace Conference of 1919 required less than six months to draw up the treaties of peace which closed the Great War, despite the fact that the problems under consideration were of world-wide significance and the issues were enormously more complex than in earlier negotiations. The expediting of the business of international conferences was made possible by the gradual development of established rules of precedence, etiquette, and ceremonial which may appear needlessly elaborate and even silly to the layman, but which are essential to ensure the conduct of diplomatic business with dispatch.

Among the most important of these rules are those relating to the ranks and titles of diplomatic representatives. During the fifteenth century, States began the practice of exchanging permanent diplomatic agents with one another. With the appearance of diplomats of lesser rank than ambassadors, such as envoys, ministers resident, and the like, confusion and controversy arose over questions of dignity and precedence, until general agreements could be reached regarding the principles to be

[1] D. J. Hill, *History of European Diplomacy*, II, p. 594.

applied to such problems. At the Congresses of Vienna and Aix-la-Chapelle of 1815 and 1818, respectively, rules were formulated regarding the relative rank of State agents which have since been accepted by all States. Four classes of diplomatic agents are now recognized in order of rank:

1. Ambassadors extraordinary and plenipotentiary and papal legates or nuncios, accredited to Sovereigns or heads of States.

2. Envoys extraordinary and ministers plenipotentiary, also accredited to Sovereigns or heads of States.

3. Ministers resident, likewise accredited to Sovereigns.

4. *Chargés d'affaires, ad hoc* when the agent so named is the permanent head of a diplomatic mission, *ad interim* when he is an official left temporarily in charge of an embassy or legation; accredited to the Minister of Foreign Affairs.

These ranks are significant chiefly for ceremonial purposes and serve to prevent most of the difficulties and embarrassments which hampered the work of the Congress of Westphalia. The third rank has now become of minor importance, since most States now confer the title of envoy extraordinary and minister plenipotentiary upon their ministers abroad, whether they are sent on special missions or reside permanently at their posts. In general, only sovereign States may send diplomatic agents. When States not fully sovereign are accorded this privilege, it is usually on the basis of the treaty arrangements which limit their sovereignty. Since the Great War, certain British Dominions have exchanged diplomatic agents of their own with a considerable number of foreign States. The Papacy from time immemorial has likewise enjoyed the right to send diplomatic agents (nuncios and legates) who have usually been accorded the position of "doyen," or "dean" of the diplomatic corps in States receiving papal representatives. The doyen is otherwise the senior diplomat of highest rank. Although the Papacy was not a sovereign State between 1870 and 1928, it again has jurisdiction over territory and subjects (the Vatican City) under the Lateran Treaty with the Italian Government concluded in 1929. President Roosevelt pleased Roman Catholics and displeased many Protestants by appointing Myron C. Taylor on December 23, 1939, as his "personal representative" to the Vatican with the rank of "Ambassador without Portfolio"—a category of diplomatic agent hitherto unknown.

Before diplomatic agents are appointed, it is customary to ascertain whether the person about to be chosen is personally acceptable to the Sovereign and Foreign Minister to whom he is sent. A diplomatic agent who, for any reason, is displeasing to those with whom he is expected to maintain friendly relations can obviously be of no great utility. All States are free to refuse diplomatic agents of other States on the ground of their being *persona non grata*. No reasons need be given for such refusal; and if trivial or irrelevant reasons are offered, irritation is likely to result. The rule of reciprocity is followed by States in the rank of diplomatic representatives exchanged. Ambassadors are exchanged between the Great Powers and between some of the Secondary Powers. Since they were once regarded as representatives of royalty, the republican government of the United States sent only representatives of lesser rank, *i.e.*, ministers and chargés d'affaires, for over a century after its establishment. In view of the fact that such representatives were literally obliged "to take a back seat" at foreign courts in deference to agents of the first rank, Congress authorized the President to exchange ambassadors with foreign States in 1893. Every diplomatic representative is entitled to bring with him to the capital to which he is sent a suite, the members of which share his privileges and immunities. The official suite of an ambassador or minister usually comprises a counselor, various secretaries, military, naval, and commercial attachés, interpreters and dragomans, clerks and accountants, a chaplain, a physician, etc. The unofficial suite includes the family, servants, private secretaries, etc., of the head of the mission. The totalitarian States in recent years have often sent large diplomatic suites to countries destined for destruction, consisting of spies, propagandists, saboteurs, professional conspirators, and the like, all of whom have been enabled to accomplish their tasks by virtue of the immunity accorded to them.

Every diplomatic agent receives a letter of credence, a special passport, and a set of instructions before starting on his mission. The letter of credence is issued by the head of the State to ambassadors and ministers and by the Minister of Foreign Affairs (Secretary of State in the United States) to chargés d'affaires. It authorizes the agent to undertake his duties. A diplomatic mission is commenced with the formal ceremony of the presentation and acceptance of the letter of credence. The agent is received for this purpose by the head of the local State, if he is an ambassador or minister, and by the Minister of Foreign Affairs if he is a chargé d'affaires. Diplomats of the first and second rank are usually received in a solemn public audience. They present their letters and make a short address, to which a formal reply is given. Deviations from established ceremonial are frowned upon. When Ribbentrop, then German Ambassador to Britain, was first received by King George VI in 1936, he failed to bow, as prescribed, and gave the Fascist salute, at the same time bellowing, "Heil Hitler!" When the King failed to reciprocate, he twice repeated his gesture and then shook the Sovereign's hand. The British press declared "Nazi insults King" and henceforth referred to him as "Brickendrop." By the time of his appointment as German Foreign Minister in February, 1938, he was a fanatic Anglophobe.

A diplomatic mission may be terminated in various ways, as by the expiration of the period for which the letter of credence or full power is granted, the change of grade of the representative, or the fulfillment of the purposes of a special mission. In all of these conjunctures, as well as in the case of the death of a diplomat, his resignation, or his recall or dismissal for personal reasons, a new letter of credence is required by his successor. Diplomatic missions are also terminated by a declaration of war or by recall or dismissal for political reasons in a situation of strained relations leading to a rupture. Such a severance of diplomatic contacts is not always followed by war, but war is invariably preceded or accompanied by a diplomatic rupture. On August 3, 1914, Ambassador von Schoen, German representative in Paris, appeared at the Quai d'Orsay for the last time to inform Foreign Minister Viviani of the declaration of war against France by Germany and to ask for his passports. On February 3, 1917, Count von Bernstorff, the German Ambassador in Washington, was handed his passports by President Wilson as a protest against the resumption of unrestricted submarine warfare on the part of Germany four days previously. At the same time, James W. Gerard, American Ambassador in Berlin, was recalled to Washington. On April 6, 1917, the American Congress declared war on Germany in accordance with the President's recommendations. At 1 P.M., September 1, 1939, the Polish Ambassador in Berlin, Josef Lipski, sent Chargé Prince Lubomirski to Wilhelmstrasse to ask for his passport. At 9 A.M., Sunday, September 3, Sir Nevile Henderson, British Ambassador to the Reich, delivered a two-hour ultimatum to the German Foreign Office. No reply was received by 11; but at 11.30 Ribbentrop delivered to Henderson a long memorandum rejecting the ultimatum. At 12.30 Robert Coulondre, the French Ambassador, saw Ribbentrop, who told him of the rejection of the British note. The British and French declarations of war took effect, respectively, at 11 A.M. and 5 P.M. On Monday the two Allied Ambassadors asked for their passports and took their leave.

The outbreak of a successful revolution, either in the home State of a diplomat or in the State where he is serving, also terminates his mission under ordinary circumstances and raises the question of the diplomatic recognition of the new government as a prerequisite to the resumption of relations between the States. Sometimes, however, this principle is not observed. On March 17, 1917, David R. Francis, American Ambassador to Russia, reported to the State Department the overthrow of the Imperial Government and the abdication of the Tsar. His request that he be authorized to recognize the new Provisional Government was granted by Secretary of State Lansing two days later. On March 22, Francis called on Miliukov and the new Council of Ministers and presented his new credentials. Shortly afterward, George Bakhmetiev, Tsarist Ambassador in Washington, resigned his post and was replaced by Boris Bakhmetiev (no relation to his predecessor) whose credentials were received by Lansing on June 19. On November 7, 1917, however, the Provisional Government was overturned by the Bolshevist coup d'état which set up the present Soviet régime in Russia. In this instance, recognition of the new government was withheld. Francis received no new credentials to the Soviet authorities, and his mission was presumably terminated, though he remained in Russia and continued to enjoy diplomatic privileges and immunities until his departure on July 25, 1918, from Vologda to Archangel, already held by forces hostile to the Soviet Government. The new revolution would normally have been regarded as terminating the diplomatic missions of the agents of the defunct Provisional Government abroad, but the State Department in Washington continued until 1922 to deal with Boris Bakhmetiev as the accredited and official representative of the State of Russia, though he represented no authority in Russia save, for a time, that of the counterrevolutionary White Guard leader, Admiral Kolchak, who was executed after the destruction of his régime in Siberia by the Red Army. Bakhmetiev's financial attaché, Serge Ughet, appeared on the rolls of the State Department as Russian diplomatic representative until 1933. This situation is anomalous and contrary to general practice. When, in 1919, Mr. Martens, the newly appointed Soviet Ambassador to the United States, sought to present his credentials to the State Department, they were refused and he was arrested and deported.

A diplomatic representative who is officially received is entitled to the benefit of the usual privileges and immunities during his entire mission. As a matter of general practice and comity, he is usually accorded the same privileges during the interval between his departure from his own State and his arrival in the foreign capital and likewise, in the event of his return, dismissal, or recall to his own State, during the interval between his departure from his post and his safe arrival home. Diplomatic ceremonial at the present time has been somewhat simplified as compared with the current practice in the eighteenth century. No diplomat can claim honors above other diplomats of the same rank. As among diplomats of the same rank, the one who has served longest at his post receives precedence. At diplomatic dinners, the host sits at the head of the table. The first place on his right is the place of honor accorded to the ambassador who has served longest; the next ambassador in order of service occupies the first place on the left, the third the second place on the right, and so on. When all the ambassadors are thus placed, the ministers plenipotentiary are seated in the same order, followed by the ministers resident and the chargés d'affaires. In processions the place of honor is sometimes the first place and sometimes the last. Diplomats of the first rank are entitled to be addressed as "Your Excellency," to remain covered in the presence of the Sovereign or head of the State, to use a coat of arms over the door of the embassy, to receive military and naval honors, to be invited to all court functions, and the like. Ambassadors traditionally receive salutes of 19 guns, ministers plenipotentiary of 15, ministers resident 13, and chargés d'affaires 11.

The legal privileges of diplomatic agents comprise inviolability of person, family, suite, and residence, extraterritoriality and exemption from local civil and criminal jurisdiction, freedom from personal and general property taxes, and liberty of worship. Diplomatic premises are seldom invaded by local authorities, even when political refugees seek safety in them. This "right of asylum," comparable to that accorded to the Church in the middle ages, is widely recognized and has been insisted upon emphatically by Latin American States. In the spring of 1939 Chile refused to authorize the surrender of a group of Loyalist refugees who had been harbored in the Chilean Embassy in Madrid. The Franco régime retaliated by severing diplomatic relations on the ground that Chile was protecting criminals and "Reds." On October 11, 1940, relations were resumed without a final settlement of the point at issue.

The rules relating to the conduct of international conferences are relatively flexible. The conference method of dealing with international problems was largely limited in the formative period of the Western State System to issues of war and peace. It has now become a normal and institutionalized procedure for dealing with questions of all kinds. In peacetime the United States participates commonly in 40 to 60 conferences each year. The number of States represented at such conferences depends upon circumstances. The first Hague Conference of 1899 consisted of representatives of 28 States, and the second Conference of 1907 was participated in by 44 States. The London Naval Conference of 1908–1909 was restricted to 10 States. At the Paris Peace Conference of 1919, 27 States were represented, in addition to the British Dominions and India. The 4 defeated States were not permitted to participate in the negotiations but sent agents to accept the terms of peace dictated to them by the victors. The Washington Arms Conference of 1921–1922 was participated in by the 8 States accepting the invitation of the American Government. The annual Assemblies of the League of Nations were participated in by the representatives of 50 or more States, and the General Disarmament Conference of 1932 had practically all the sovereign States of the world represented at its sessions.

The State or States issuing invitations to an international conference must assume responsibility for the membership and for the proposing of a list of topics to be dealt with. On the basis of such proposals every international conference draws up an "agenda," representing the consensus of opinion among the delegates present as to what subjects should be discussed. Every conference similarly determines its own organization and rules of procedure. Usually the organization of an international conference resembles that of a national legislative body, with presiding officers, secretaries, committees, plenary sessions, and committee meetings. The principle of State equality, however, requires that each State have one vote and that all action be by unanimity, since no sovereign State can be bound to an agreement without its consent. In most cases, the agreements reached are subject to ratification on the part of the participating States.

2. THE WORK OF DIPLOMATS AND CONSULS

A correct man punctually executes the orders he has received; but to this quality must be joined ability. Now, in order to execute a political commission well, it is necessary to know the character of the prince and those who sway his counsel; to attach himself to those who can procure him ready access to the prince, for there is nothing difficult to an ambassador who has the prince's ear; but it is above all things necessary to make himself esteemed, which he will do if he so regulates his actions and conversation that he shall be thought a man of honor, liberal and sincere.— NICCOLÒ MACHIAVELLI TO RAPHAEL GIROLAMI, Ambassador to the Emperor.

Modern States maintain official contacts with one another through far-flung networks of agents scattered over the globe. Each of the sovereign entities of the Western State System sends permanent diplomatic and consular officers to foreign capitals and cities and receives similar officers into its own territory from other States. The number of such officers has greatly increased during the last century with the growth of contacts among States and the transformation of the Western State System into a world system. Into the foreign office of every State come reports, queries, and official dispatches from agents scattered over the six continents and the seven seas. Out of each foreign office go elaborate instructions to the widely dispersed field agents in scores of foreign States. To use a familiar analogy, the foreign offices constitute the brains and higher nerve centers of the States in their dealings with one another. The field agents are the nerve endings and sense organs, through which impressions of the outside world are received and impulses are transmitted and translated into action in the game of world politics. According to the Department of State of the United States an efficient foreign service officer

Creates good will and common understanding, and, with restrained and critical leadership born of mature experience and profound knowledge of men and affairs, uses these as instruments for enhancing international confidence and cooperation among governments and people.

Promotes and protects the interests of the United States and of its citizens.

Negotiates, with tact, sound judgment, and intimate knowledge of conditions at home and abroad, protocols, conventions, and treaties, especially regarding international intercourse, tariffs, shipping, commerce, preservation of peace, etc., in strict conformity to Government instructions.

Establishes and effectively utilizes personal contacts in farsighted ways for the benefit of his Government and of American citizens.

Analyzes and reports on political and economic conditions and trends of significance to the United States.

Exercises skill in following prescribed form and routine procedure when possible; and displays discriminating judgment, as may be necessary in more complicated situations requiring investigations, careful accumulation of information, or professional understanding of laws, customs, conditions, etc.

Administers an office in a business-like and efficient manner.[1]

To revert to the well-established distinction between diplomatic and consular agents, the former may be described broadly as political representatives and the latter as commercial representatives, although there are certain functions performed by both. Diplomatic agents maintain contacts between governments, i.e., between the foreign offices; consular agents are entrusted with duties relating to trade relations, the protection of citizens abroad, the enforcement of customs and immigration laws, and the like. At the present time a diplomatic representative is entrusted in general with the business of directing the internal business of the embassy or legation of which he is in charge, of conducting negotiations with the proper authorities of the State to which he is accredited, of making reports to his home government, and of rendering various services to the nationals of his own State. These duties are likely to prove extremely arduous and expensive at an important foreign post, as Walter Hines Page, Ambassador to Great Britain a generation ago, discovered shortly after assuming the functions of his office. In a much-quoted letter of December 22, 1913, he described his impressions as follows:

If you think it's all play, you fool yourself; I mean this job. There's no end of the work. It consists of these parts: Receiving people for two hours every day, some on some sort of business, some merely to "pay respects"; attending to a large (and exceedingly miscellaneous) mail; going to the Foreign Office on all sorts of errands; looking up the oddest sort of information that you ever heard of; making reports to Washington on all sorts of things; then the so-called social duties—giving dinners, receptions, etc., and attending them. I hear the most important news I get at so-called social functions. Then the court functions; and the meetings and speeches! The American Ambassador must go all over England and explain every American thing. You'd never recover from the shock if you could hear me speaking about education, agriculture, the observance of Christmas, the navy, the Anglo-Saxon, Mexico, the Monroe Doctrine, co-education, woman suffrage, medicine, law, radio-activity, flying, the Supreme Court, the President as a man of letters, the hookworm, the Negro—just get down the encyclopaedia and continue the list! I've done this every week-night for a month, hand running, with a few afternoon performances thrown in. I have missed only

[1] *The American Foreign Service*, State Department Publication 235, 1931, pp. 4–6.

one engagement in these seven months; and that was merely a private luncheon. I have been late only once. I have the best chauffeur in the world—he deserves credit for much of that. Of course, I don't get time to read a book. In fact, I can't get time to keep up with what goes on at home. To read a newspaper eight or ten days old, when they come in bundles of three or four—is impossible. What isn't telegraphed here, I miss! and that means I miss most things.[1]

This firsthand account of the functions of a diplomat would undoubtedly receive the hearty endorsement of foreign representatives of the first rank in all the great capitals of the world. Social functions, speeches, routine duties, and favors done to fellow countrymen consume the major portion of a diplomat's time, despite the popular notion that he is primarily concerned with high affairs of State. Though negotiations among States are now almost incessant and cover a bewildering variety of topics, the diplomat as negotiator is much less important than he was a century ago. He is no longer isolated at his post and obliged to make important decisions at his own discretion as he was in the days of the sailing vessel and the stagecoach, when instructions from his government came slowly, infrequently, and sometimes not at all. The diplomat is now in daily—sometimes in hourly—communication by cable and telephone with those from whom he receives his orders. In Mr. Dooley's phrase, he has become "merely a highly paid messenger boy, and not always a very efficient one at that!" Very seldom is he placed in a situation where he must make an important decision without being able to consult the foreign office in his own capital. His importance is further diminished by the current practice of having treaties negotiated by special representatives chosen for the purpose, rather than by the regularly accredited diplomatic representatives. Foreign ministers and heads of States, moreover, are now in much more frequent and direct communication with one another than was ever possible before the Industrial Revolution. Under such circumstances the professional diplomat ceases to be the formulator of policy and the master of the destinies of nations that he was some generations ago. Nevertheless, he still serves as a permanent official who transmits communications between governments, who discusses current problems and differences of interests and policies with responsible authorities, and who still plays a not insignificant role in negotiations.

The less spectacular functions of the diplomatic agent, on the other hand, have expanded steadily during the same period. The duties connected with supervising the administration of embassies and legations have grown with the increase in the staffs of diplomatic missions. An ambassador or minister at an important foreign capital will frequently have a score or more of subordinates working under his direction, comprising a counselor, various grades of secretaries, military, naval, financial,

[1] See *The Life and Letters of Walter Hines Page* for other interesting comments on the diplomatic function.

and commercial attachés, interpreters, translators, clerks, stenographers, doormen, janitors, flunkies, and lesser fry. He is responsible for organizing and coordinating their activities in order that the work of the mission may be performed with neatness, dispatch, and economy. He has minor disciplinary authority over his subordinates; and he is answerable for the custody of the archives, the handling of diplomatic correspondence, and the keeping of records of the work of the mission. He is likewise responsible for reporting regularly to his home government the policies of the State to which he is accredited and the current political and economic developments affecting the relations between the States. His relations with his fellow nationals consume most of his time and that of his subordinates. He is constantly being called upon to do them all sorts of favors, from getting them out of jail to giving them letters of introduction to local officials, entrées to libraries and museums, and admission cards to the sessions of the national parliament of the State where he resides. He visas passports of aliens contemplating journeys to his own State; and he may issue passports, certifications of nationality, and travel certificates to his own fellow citizens under certain circumstances. He transmits, from his own government to the government to which he is accredited, requisitions for the extradition of fugitives from justice who have fled into the State where he resides. In cases of extraditions from his own State of nationals of the State to which he is accredited, he transmits the certification that the papers submitted as evidence are properly and legally authenticated. He may likewise be authorized to perform certain notarial acts; and he must, in general, strive to be of service in every possible way to his fellow citizens traveling or residing in the State where he is performing his duties.

The functions of consular representatives are, if possible, even more varied. From the point of view of the historical development of the foreign service, the States of the Western State System exchanged consular representatives before they exchanged diplomatic agents, for merchants had contacts with one another across political boundaries before governments entered into negotiations with one another regarding high affairs of State. Here, as in so many other respects, politics was the handmaiden of economics. The first consuls of the medieval period were apparently chosen by communities of merchants residing abroad to exercise extraterritorial jurisdiction over them and to represent their interests in dealing with the State where they resided. The office of consul was fully established by A.D. 1200. The Hanseatic city-states and the Mediterranean trading States exchanged consuls at an early period, with the national monarchies of western Europe presently following their example. The political functions of consuls were gradually diminished, however, with the development of a diplomatic service; and they have lost their extraterritorial jurisdiction except in a few Oriental countries. On the other hand, the constant growth of commercial contacts among States has increased the duties of consular officers and led to a great multiplication of their numbers.

The duties of consuls are determined by custom, treaty stipulations, and the provisions of exequaturs, or consular credentials. A consular officer, unlike a diplomatic agent, does not act as the spokesman of his government to a foreign government, though he may sometimes exercise quasi-diplomatic functions. He labors primarily to serve the business interests of his own State abroad and to perform incidental services for his fellow citizens. His concern is with markets, sales opportunities, and profits for traders and investors. In the epoch of economic nationalism and keen competition among rival merchant groups, each enlisting governmental support in its quest for the elusive dollar, pound, franc, or mark, even diplomatic agents must keep a sharp eye open for bargains. But this has been consuls' work for centuries. A consul makes detailed reports to his home government on economic opportunities, tendencies of trade, transportation, navigation, price trends, conditions of competition, etc. These reports are published for the information and guidance of exporters and investors who may be interested in foreign markets. The consul is expected to exert himself to insure the observance of commercial treaties and to make certain that invoices of shipments going to his own State are properly submitted and that shipments are made in accordance with the laws and regulations of his own State. He has also such supervision over merchant vessels of his own State in the port where he is serving as custom and the laws of his State grant to him. The papers of such ships are deposited in his office while the ship remains in port. He usually has authority to supervise the transportation, wages, relief, and discharge of seamen, the recovery of deserting seamen, the care of the effects of deceased seamen, and sometimes the adjustment of disputes among masters, officers, and crews. The function of protecting citizens abroad is shared by consular and diplomatic agents, though in situations not involving political questions the problems which arise are handled by consular representatives. Consuls arbitrate private disputes voluntarily submitted to them, intercede with local authorities on behalf of citizens, administer property of deceased citizens of their own nationality, assist in the enforcement of the immigration laws of their own States, and perform sundry minor services for such of their fellow citizens as solicit them. In certain Oriental States, consuls also have extensive civil and criminal jurisdiction in cases involving fellow citizens under the provisions of extraterritoriality treaties.

Consular agents enter upon their duties when they have been granted an exequatur by the authorities of the State to which they are sent. These documents correspond to the credentials of diplomatic representatives, except that they are issued by the State receiving the consul instead of by the sending State. When a consul is appointed, his commission or patent is transmitted to the diplomatic representative of the appointing State who applies to the foreign office for an exequatur for the consul. The issue of an exequatur may be refused for cause. It may subsequently be revoked, though it is more usual to request the recall of the consul who gives offense. Exequaturs are usually issued in the name of the head of the State.

The granting of a consular exequatur usually signifies diplomatic recognition of the State or government of the recipient by the granting State, but the reception of a consular exequatur does not have this effect. Should American consuls in Manchukuo, for example, receive exequaturs from the Manchukuo foreign office, this action would not constitute diplomatic recognition of Manchukuo by the United States. If, however, the President of the United States should issue exequaturs to Manchukuo consuls in the United States, this would constitute diplomatic recognition of Manchukuo by the United States. In fact, there are at present no consular agents of either State in the other. A severance of diplomatic relations between States, either through a rupture or through revolution followed by nonrecognition of the new régime, usually terminates consular as well as diplomatic missions. Both are normally terminated by war. Consular missions may likewise be terminated by the recall of the agent by the sending State or by the revocation of the exequatur by the receiving State.

Consular privileges and immunities are less extensive than those of diplomatic agents, particularly when, as is still sometimes the case, the consular officer is a citizen of the State where he exercises his functions. Certain immunities, however, are well defined by custom and are frequently extended by treaty. These include the inviolability of the archives and other official property, exemption from arrest save on criminal charges, exemption from witness duty, taxation, military charges and service, etc. In general, consuls are entitled to those privileges and immunities which will enable them to perform their duties without personal inconvenience. In Oriental States where extraterritoriality prevails, consuls usually enjoy the same privileges and exemptions from local jurisdiction as diplomatic representatives.

To describe the organization of diplomatic and consular services in an epoch of world-wide war and revolution is an impossible task, since States here today are gone tomorrow and all foreign services are in constant flux. An outline of the foreign service of the United States, however, will prove useful by way of suggesting how a Great Power organizes the work of its agents abroad. At the close of the year 1940 the United States maintained

53 active diplomatic posts abroad. Of these 33 were headed by ministers and 20 by ambassadors.[1] The United States exchanges ambassadors with all the Great Powers: Britain, France, Germany, Italy, the U.S.S.R., and Japan. It likewise exchanges ambassadors with Argentina, Brazil, Chile, Peru, Colombia, Venezuela, Panama, Cuba, and Mexico and with China, Turkey, Spain, Poland, and Belgium. The total number of diplomatic and consular officers sent from Washington to foreign posts is well over 1,300. In small States, only a few officials are required—e.g., 12 in Bolivia and 8 in Afghanistan. In Great Britain and its possessions, more than 150 American foreign service officers are normally stationed, as compared with 87 in Canada, 72 in Mexico, 89 in China, 45 in Japan, 24 in Argentina, 17 in the U.S.S.R., etc.[2] Foreign governments maintain some 670 diplomatic agents in Washington, exclusive of consuls scattered over the country.[3] Each embassy staff in a great capital ordinarily comprises, in addition to the ambassador, a counselor; sundry secretaries; military, naval, air, commercial, agricultural, and financial attachés and their assistants; and a score or more of clerks, stenographers, messengers and other employees.

The administration of the small army of civil servants in the United States Foreign Service involves difficult problems of recruitment, salary classification, promotion, retirement, and efficiency ratings. All foreign service officials are formally appointed by the President and confirmed by the Senate, though in practice the President no longer names appointees to any except the highest diplomatic posts. During the nineteenth century, foreign posts were frequently filled by incompetent local politicians who received such appointments as their share of the loaves and fishes distributed by the party in power in accordance with the "spoils system." Early in the present century the necessity of professionalizing the service in the interests of efficiency was appreciated, and steps in this direction were taken through executive orders issued by the President. In 1906 the consular service was placed under civil service rules, and in 1909 the lower positions in the diplomatic service were similarly classified. The most important measure for the professionaliza-

[1] On January 11, 1941 the Department of State announced the elevation of the United States Legation in Montevideo, Uruguay, to an Embassy, thus bringing the number of ambassadorial posts to 21. At the same time Britain and the United States resorted to the somewhat unusual practice of elevating to the rank of minister the highest permanent official, next to the ambassador, in their respective embassies.

[2] Cf. Foreign Service List, July 1, 1940, issued quarterly by the U. S. Department of State. Hugh Wilson, Ambassador to Berlin, was recalled to "report" in November, 1938, as a gesture of protest over the Nazi pogrom of that month. He had not returned to his post at the time of writing. William C. Bullitt (Paris), Anthony Biddle (Warsaw), Mrs. Harriman (Oslo), and various other heads of missions returned to the United States in 1939–1940 when the countries to which they were accredited were conquered and became German-occupied territory.

[3] The Diplomatic List, published monthly by the U. S. Department of State.

tion of the foreign service was taken by Congress when it passed the Rogers Act of May 24, 1924. This statute was designed to replace the spoils system by the merit system and to lay down principles of personnel administration which would enable the American Government to have at its disposal diplomats and consuls who might compare favorably in competence, experience, and professional *savoir-faire* with those of other Great Powers. Perhaps the most significant contribution of the act was the amalgamation of the diplomatic and consular services into a single "Foreign Service of the United States," within which capable individuals may achieve a life career and may transfer from consular to diplomatic posts, and *vice versa*, as their own inclinations and the needs of the service dictate.

Under the terms of the Rogers Act and of supplementary executive orders, all "classified" foreign service officers (*i.e.*, all officers below the heads of embassies and legations, who are still political appointees, and above the grade of vice consuls, who are unclassified) are selected on the basis of competitive civil service examinations. Since ambassadors and ministers are expected to represent the views of the administration in power, there is much to be said for having them appointed on a political basis. But the lesser officials perform administrative duties of a routine nature and have no policy-determining functions. It is more important, therefore, that they be professionally competent than that they be sympathetic with the political party in office at Washington. Considerations of professional efficiency have led to an increasing tendency to fill even the higher posts by promotion from the lower ranks. The lower posts are filled, in order of merit, by those who pass competitive examinations designed to test the applicants' knowledge of international, maritime, and commercial law, arithmetic, modern languages, history, economics, and economic geography. Above 70 per cent of the present foreign service officers of the United States are college graduates. Less than 7 per cent have had no college training. The examinations are given periodically (usually once a year) in the principal cities of the United States and are open to all persons between the ages of twenty-one and thirty-five who have been American citizens for at least fifteen years.[1] As for salaries, ambassadors receive $17,500 annually and ministers $10,000, though the heads of missions at important foreign capitals are likely to spend a good deal more than they receive and must usually be persons of independent means. The foreign service officers proper are divided into nine classes, with salaries ranging from $2,500 to $10,000. The senior clerks are divided into five classes, with salaries from $3,000 to $4,000, and the junior clerks into three classes,

---

[1] The rules and regulations governing admission to the foreign service, as well as copies of sample examination questions, are contained in the pamphlet, *The American Foreign Service*, which is mailed out to applicants by the U. S. State Department upon request.

with salaries from less than $2,500 to $2,750. Compensation is increased with years of service, and allowances are granted for travel and living quarters. Retirement is obligatory at sixty-five, with a variable pension paid out of a retirement fund. Promotions from one class to another are based upon efficiency ratings. Appointments are made not to particular posts or positions but to one or another of the designated classes, the members of which are assigned their posts at the discretion of the President and the Department of State.

The tasks of recruitment and personnel administration in the American foreign service are entrusted at present to four agencies which are part of the State Department. The board of examiners, under Executive Order 5642 of June 8, 1931, consists of three assistant secretaries of state, the chief of the division of foreign service personnel, and the chief examiner of the Civil Service Commission. It prepares the written and oral examinations which candidates for admission to the service are required to take. The board of foreign service personnel prepares and submits to the Secretary of State lists of foreign service officers, graded as to their efficiency and value to the service, recommends promotions and transfers, considers controversies and delinquencies and recommends disciplinary action, and passes upon recommendations for dismissal from the service made by the division of foreign service personnel. The latter agency interviews applicants for admission to the service, collects data relating to personnel, recommends appointments to subordinate positions, keeps efficiency records, and, in general, acts in a supervisory capacity for the development and improvement of the service. The foreign service officers' training school is maintained for the instruction of new appointees and is open only to those who have successfully passed the entrance examinations. The other agencies of the Department of State concerned with administrative problems are the office of the chief clerk and administrative assistants, the division of foreign service administration, the foreign service buildings office, the office of coordination and review, the division of accounts, the board of appeals and review, and the office of fiscal and budget affairs.

This general scheme of organization is paralleled in other foreign services, although those of the European Powers have long been professionalized, whereas sound principles of personnel administration have been introduced into the American service only comparatively recently. In the United States, Great Britain, and France the diplomatic and consular services, as well as the foreign office staff, have been amalgamated into a single, unified foreign service for purposes of recruitment, promotion, and personnel administration. This arrangement likewise prevails in the foreign services of most other States. Though the distinction in functions between diplomatic and consular agents is still maintained, the fusion of the services for personnel purposes has the advantage of enabling experienced officials to transfer their activities from one field to the other as the requirements of the service may dictate. An efficient foreign service must be so organized as to afford opportunities for a life career in which capable officials may work their way to the highest positions. These opportunities are now provided in the professionalized foreign services of almost all States.

The number of officials employed in the consular services is in every case much larger than the number in the diplomatic services. This is due to the fact that consular agents, as indicated in the preceding section, are commercial representatives sent by each government to all the principal ports and cities of the world, whereas diplomatic agents need be maintained only in foreign capitals. The United States has some 350 consular posts scattered over the globe. These posts consist of one or two individuals in a few remote places to full staffs of appreciable size in ports and cities of major commercial importance. All the Great Powers maintain a similar network of consular representatives at the principal cities and ports of all other States, and the lesser Powers send abroad as many consuls as their commercial interests appear to warrant.

Since there is no general international agreement in regard to consuls corresponding to that of 1815–1818 in regard to diplomatic agents, each State is free to determine for itself the ranks of its consular representatives and the organization of the service. The United States divides its consular representatives into five categories: (1) consuls general at large, who are traveling inspectors of consular posts; (2) consuls general, most of whom reside at the 36 supervisory consular offices to oversee the work of the consular service in their respective areas; (3) consuls; (4) consular agents, exercising consular functions at posts other than those at which full officers are located; and (5) vice consuls, acting as subordinate officers, assistants, and substitutes at the principal consulates. Most officers in the first two categories fall into Classes I to IV of the foreign service and receive $6,000 to $10,000 a year. Most of the consuls are placed in Classes IV to VIII and receive $3,500 to $6,000. Consular agents were abolished by the Rogers Act, but a few still survive and are for the most part paid out of fees. The vice consuls are unclassified and receive $2,500 to $3,000 a year. In the British consular service the ranks are: inspectors-general or consulates, consuls general, consuls, vice consuls, consular agents, and proconsuls. The last are individuals appointed to administer oaths, take affidavits or affirmations, and perform notarial functions. Most of the British proconsuls, consular agents, and vice consuls and some of the consuls are unsalaried. The French consular service consisted of consuls general, consuls of three classes, and deputy consuls. These variations in the organization and rank of consular representatives seldom give rise to difficulties, since consuls are ordinarily nonpolitical agents who are not hedged about with the pomp and ceremony attaching to diplomats.

3. FOREIGN OFFICES

> No diplomatist can succeed in his foreign task unless he is well supported by his own government and given every opportunity to understand its policy. . . . Without such knowledge he will certainly go astray, and without a constant contact with his home government the conduct of diplomacy cannot possibly prosper in his hands.—M. DE CALLIÈRES, *On the Manner of Negotiating with Princes.*

Consuls and diplomats of all States perform their work under the direction of the department of their own government charged with the administration of foreign affairs. They may be assisted and supplemented by agents maintained abroad by other departments of the national administration. Military attachés are sent out by ministries or departments of war, naval attachés by navy departments, financial attachés by treasury departments, and commercial attachés by departments of commerce. Departments or ministries of commerce frequently maintain extensive foreign services of their own with far-flung commercial agents scattered over the globe to assist businessmen and perform sundry functions not very different from those of consuls. These recent developments represent a devolution of authority over the foreign representatives of States away from the departments expressly charged with foreign affairs to other branches of the national administration. But it still remains true that each State maintains a single department or ministry which is primarily answerable for the conduct of the State's relations with other sovereignties. This department or ministry is under the control of the head of the State—President, Premier, King, or Emperor—and is directed by a minister or secretary who always occupies first place in the Cabinet in terms of honor and prestige. Into the foreign offices, state departments, or ministries of foreign affairs, as they are variously designated, go all the diplomatic and consular reports from abroad; out of them go the instructions to the hundreds of field agents in scores of foreign cities. Within the foreign offices are formulated the foreign policies of the States of the world. Between them the great game of international politics is played. Here again, for illustrative purposes, it will be sufficient to deal with the American Department of State as an example, for the functions performed and even the administrative pattern of divisions, boards, and bureaus is much the same in all States.

The Department of State of the United States is headed by the Secretary of State, who is appointed by the President, with the confirmation of the Senate. He is first in rank among the members of the Cabinet, and he succeeds to the presidency in the event of the death of the President and Vice President. He has at his disposal a personal assistant, two special assistants, a private secretary, a stenographer, a chauffeur, and a small staff of aides. Next in authority under him is the under-secretary of state who acts for the Secretary in matters not requiring his personal attention and who is acting secretary in the absence of his superior. The under-secretary and the counselor aid in the formulation and execution of policies and direct the work of the department and of the foreign service, in cooperation with the legal adviser and the advisers on political relations and economic affairs. The first assistant secretary of state is charged with the general administration of the department and the foreign service, and with supervision of matters relating to personnel and management. He is also the fiscal officer of the department who prepares estimates of necessary appropriations, submits them to Congress, and makes allotments of appropriations which have been approved. He likewise has supervision over consular affairs, passports, visas, foreign service buildings, and international conferences. He is chairman of the foreign service personnel board, the board of examiners for the foreign service, and the board of the foreign service school. The other assistant secretaries of state are charged with such duties as are assigned to them by the Secretary.

The subordinate agencies of the Department, which employs almost a thousand persons in Washington, are indicated, as of 1941, on the accompanying chart, with their duties in most cases suggested adequately by their names. The four geographical divisions receive, compile, digest, and interpret the daily flood of information coming in from diplomatic and consular posts abroad in their respective areas. Their chiefs advise the Secretary and his staff regarding current problems and policies throughout the world.[1]

This general pattern of organization is found, with minor variations, in other foreign offices. The British Foreign Office is headed by the Secretary of State for Foreign Affairs, who is assisted by a permanent under-secretary of state, two parliamentary under-secretaries of state (both members of the House of Commons), a deputy under-secretary of state, two assistant under-secretaries of state, three legal advisers, a finance officer, a press officer, twelve counselors, and sundry other high assistants and secretaries. The French Ministry of Foreign Affairs, located on the Quai d'Orsay, Paris, was similarly headed by the Minister of Foreign Affairs, who brought into office with him a secretarial staff or "Cabinet," charged with the direction of the cabinet service, the information and

[1] The U.S. Department of State was extensively reorganized by gradual stages between 1937 and 1939. For a good account of these changes and of the work of, and interrelations between, the present divisions and bureaus, cf. August C. Miller, Jr., "The New State Department," American Journal of International Law, July, 1939. With the death of R. Walton Moore in February, 1941, the post of counselor was left vacant and seemed likely to be abolished.

FOREIGN OFFICES

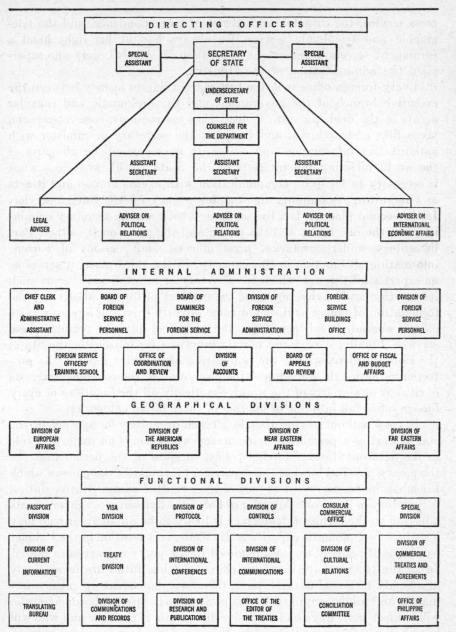

DIRECTING OFFICERS

SPECIAL ASSISTANT — SECRETARY OF STATE — SPECIAL ASSISTANT

UNDERSECRETARY OF STATE

COUNSELOR FOR THE DEPARTMENT

ASSISTANT SECRETARY — ASSISTANT SECRETARY — ASSISTANT SECRETARY

LEGAL ADVISER — ADVISER ON POLITICAL RELATIONS — ADVISER ON POLITICAL RELATIONS — ADVISER ON POLITICAL RELATIONS — ADVISER ON INTERNATIONAL ECONOMIC AFFAIRS

INTERNAL ADMINISTRATION

CHIEF CLERK AND ADMINISTRATIVE ASSISTANT — BOARD OF FOREIGN SERVICE PERSONNEL — BOARD OF EXAMINERS FOR THE FOREIGN SERVICE — DIVISION OF FOREIGN SERVICE ADMINISTRATION — FOREIGN SERVICE BUILDINGS OFFICE — DIVISION OF FOREIGN SERVICE PERSONNEL

FOREIGN SERVICE OFFICERS' TRAINING SCHOOL — OFFICE OF COORDINATION AND REVIEW — DIVISION OF ACCOUNTS — BOARD OF APPEALS AND REVIEW — OFFICE OF FISCAL AND BUDGET AFFAIRS

GEOGRAPHICAL DIVISIONS

DIVISION OF EUROPEAN AFFAIRS — DIVISION OF THE AMERICAN REPUBLICS — DIVISION OF NEAR EASTERN AFFAIRS — DIVISION OF FAR EASTERN AFFAIRS

FUNCTIONAL DIVISIONS

PASSPORT DIVISION — VISA DIVISION — DIVISION OF PROTOCOL — DIVISION OF CONTROLS — CONSULAR COMMERCIAL OFFICE — SPECIAL DIVISION

DIVISION OF CURRENT INFORMATION — TREATY DIVISION — DIVISION OF INTERNATIONAL CONFERENCES — DIVISION OF INTERNATIONAL COMMUNICATIONS — DIVISION OF CULTURAL RELATIONS — DIVISION OF COMMERCIAL TREATIES AND AGREEMENTS

TRANSLATING BUREAU — DIVISION OF COMMUNICATIONS AND RECORDS — DIVISION OF RESEARCH AND PUBLICATIONS — OFFICE OF THE EDITOR OF THE TREATIES — CONCILIATION COMMITTEE — OFFICE OF PHILIPPINE AFFAIRS

Organization of the Department of State of the United States.

[163]

press service, the dispatch and receipt of correspondence, and the telegraphic and telephonic service. He always had at his right hand a permanent secretary-general (in 1939–1940 M. Alexis Leger) who supervised the administration of the Ministry.

Every foreign office is in the first place a liaison agency between the executive branch of the government and the diplomatic and consular agents in the field. As such, it dispatches instructions, receives reports, keeps files and archives, and furnishes the secretary or minister with authoritative information and advice on developments in all parts of the world affecting the interests of the State. It likewise does what is necessary to facilitate communication with agents abroad and it acts as a recruiting, examining, and training agency for the foreign service. In the second place, it is a liaison agency between the secretary or minister, on the one hand, and the public and the press on the other. Parliamentary under-secretaries, press officers, and sections of current information all function in this capacity. In the third place, it serves as an expert staff through which the secretary or minister may secure such information and advice regarding the conduct of foreign affairs and the formulation of policy as does not come directly from the foreign service officers abroad. Legal, economic, and historical advisers perform these services. Finally, it performs certain functions for citizens of the State: the issuance of passports, the publication of consular reports, the protection of nationals abroad, and the promotion of the economic interests of citizens in all parts of the world. Practically all the functions of every foreign office fall into one or another of these broad categories.

It goes without saying that in all well-organized foreign offices the staff is part of a permanent bureaucracy which plays an important role in the determination of foreign policy, in spite of the fiction that the temporary political head of the department formulates the policies which his subordinates carry out as part of their routine administrative duties. A Secretary of State or a Minister of Foreign Affairs in most governments adhering to the forms of democracy is likely to be an amateur who may have had no diplomatic experience. He secures his position in the Cabinet by virtue of political services rendered to the party or parties in power. In all the technical duties of his office (and his duties are increasingly of a highly technical nature), he is, therefore, dependent upon the information and advice supplied by his professional expert subordinates who will in most cases have had extensive diplomatic experience and who will have become the custodians of tradition and the keepers of precedents. Since in most governments (though less so in the United States than elsewhere) there is an interchangeability of personnel between the foreign office and the foreign service, and since both are increasingly professionalized, the officials in the capital and the officials in the field are likely to see eye to eye on most important questions. The secretary or minister is usually constrained to accept the advice offered to him or to run the risk of making blunders or of creating friction between himself and his subordinates. The heads of important divisions often change with changes of administration, just as do ambassadors and ministers abroad; but the constant and insidious pressure of the permanent bureaucracy upon the formulation of policy can scarcely be overestimated. This is no less true at Washington than at Downing Street, Wilhelmstrasse, or the Quai d'Orsay. Those who are nominally charged with the formulation of foreign policy are thus hedged about on all sides by those who are in theory simple administrators. It is not astonishing then that the secretaries or ministers frequently become rubber stamps and that the permanent bureaucrats, acting behind the scenes, really determine policies. Here is one among many sources of power and pressure lying beneath the surface of foreign affairs which must be borne in mind constantly by all who would understand the dynamics of international politics.

Quite apart from the influences brought to bear upon a foreign minister from within the ranks of his own subordinates and agents, there are pressures playing upon him constantly from without. These pressures operate through his colleagues in the Cabinet, the President, the Prime Minister, or head of the State, the national legislature, the courts, the press, private lobbying agencies of all kinds, and "public opinion." The nature of the process by which foreign policy is formulated through the interaction of these pressures will be examined later in connection with the forces which drive States to action. Here, however, notice may be taken of the constitutional and legal forms which have developed within States for the conduct of foreign affairs. These forms determine the relationship between the foreign office and the other branches of the national government, and they set up certain fixed patterns of procedure which must be complied with in the day-to-day handling of international business.

As has already been suggested, the foreign office in every State is always one of a dozen or more executive departments or ministries of the national administration. The head of it is always appointed by and is removable by the head of the national administration—by the President in the American governmental scheme, by the Prime Minister in the name of the king or president in parliamentary governments, by him who, in one capacity or another, wields the executive power in dictatorships. In parliamentary governments the Prime Minister may assume the post of Foreign Minister himself if he so desires. In any case, the Foreign Minister is the first official in the cabinet even when he is not the head of it. In parliamentary governments, he will usually be a prominent leader of the party in power, or of one of the parties in a coalition, and he will have a seat in the national legislature. In so-called "presidential" governments, like that of the United States and most of the Latin American Republics, he will not be a member of the legislature, but he will be a prominent party leader close to the President. In either instance, he must perform the duties of his office in accordance with the provisions of the constitution and statutes dealing with the conduct of foreign affairs.

In almost all democratic States, the national legislature is given a considerable measure of control over foreign relations. In the period of monarchial absolutism, the handling of foreign affairs was normally an exclusive prerogative of the executive, i.e., of the king and his ministers. In the period of bourgeois democracy, the executive has been made responsible either to the legislature or to the voters and has been obliged to share this, as well as other functions, with representative, popularly elected assemblies. The American Constitution of 1787 was one of the first of modern constitutional documents to give large powers over foreign relations to the national legislature. Under its provisions, Congress has power over diplomatic appointments, treaties, and declarations of war. The President "shall nominate, and, by and with the advice and consent of the Senate, shall appoint ambassadors, other public ministers, and consuls" (Article II, Section 2, §2). Diplomatic and consular appointments are thus subject to the confirmation of a majority of the upper chamber of Congress, except where Congress, by statute, has vested this power in the President alone or in the Secretary of State, as has been done with regard to all the subordinate positions in the foreign service. The President has power "by and with the advice and consent of the Senate, to make treaties, provided two-thirds of the Senators present concur" (Article II, Section 2, §2). In practice the President and his agents in the Department of State and the foreign service negotiate treaties without legislative participation in the process, but he may not constitutionally ratify treaties without the approval of two-thirds of the Senators. The President is commander-in-chief of the army, the navy, and the militia; but Congress has power to raise and support armies, to provide and maintain a navy, and to declare war by a majority vote of both houses (Article I, Sections 8, 11, 12, 13). In all these respects, Congress is given express power over foreign affairs by the Constitution. Its general powers of legislation and appropriation have also been used to influence foreign relations. General congressional resolutions on foreign policy may be ignored by the President; but Congress may grant or withhold money for diplomatic missions and for the enforcement of treaties, and it may, by legislation, carry out treaties, refuse to carry them out, or abrogate them.

It is now well established as a matter of general constitutional practice that all powers over foreign affairs not expressly granted to the legislature by the Constitution are exercised by the executive.[1] The diplomatic recognition of new States or governments and the issuance of neutrality proclamations, for example, are both functions performed by the President and Secretary of State without congressional participation. Even with regard to those powers which the President must share with Congress, the course of developments has tended to place more and more power in the President's hands. President Washington, taking the Constitution very literally, endeavored to collaborate with the Senate in the negotiation of treaties as well as in their ratification. But when, in 1796, the Senators manifested a desire to have him withdraw his imposing presence from the chamber in order that they might consider by themselves the negotiation of an Indian treaty, he walked out and said he'd be damned if he ever came before them again on such business. None of his successors has ever consulted the Senate as a body during the course of treaty negotiations. Prior to 1815 the President submitted to the Senate for confirmation the names of special diplomatic representatives named to negotiate important treaties. But ever since the Senators embarrassed President Madison by refusing to confirm the appointment of Secretary of the Treasury Gallatin as one of the negotiators of the Treaty of Ghent, the President has ordinarily made such appointments without consulting the Senate. Treaties are now submitted to the Senate only after they have been signed. As Secretary of State Hay once observed, they are like bulls going into the arena, with no assurance that they will emerge alive. Friction between the President and the Senate over treaties has been chronic in the conduct of American foreign affairs, for two-thirds of the Senators are never of the President's party. But if an international engagement does not require legislation or appropriations, the President can escape the constitutional requirement of senatorial ratification by concluding an "executive agreement" which may achieve the same purpose. Similarly, the power of Congress over declarations of war means less in practice than in theory; for the President, as spokesman of the nation and as commander of the armed forces, can easily create diplomatic or military situations which leave Congress no genuine freedom of choice. In scores of instances,

[1] The Supreme Court has held that the Government of the United States is not a government of "limited powers" in the field of foreign affairs and that Congress may confer a large degree of discretion on the Executive in this field without unconstitutionally delegating its legislative authority to the President. Thus the familiar "separation of powers" principle and the rule that grants of power to federal authorities are restricted to specific constitutional authorizations do not apply to foreign affairs in the same sense in which they apply to domestic affairs. "Not only . . . is the federal power over external affairs in origin and essential character different from that over internal affairs, but participation in the exercise of the power is significantly limited. In this vast external realm, with its important, complicated, delicate and manifold problems, the President alone has the power to speak or listen as the representative of the nation." *The United States* v. *Curtiss-Wright Export Corporation*, 299 U.S. 304 (1936).

American forces have engaged in hostilities abroad without congressional authorization of any kind. All the formally declared wars in which the United States has engaged, with the possible exception of the Spanish-American War, were embarked upon at the initiative of the executive branch of the government.[1] In practice, therefore, the conduct of American foreign affairs is in the hands of the President, subject to constitutional checks which often lead to friction between the executive and legislature but which give Congress no real authority to initiate and direct diplomatic action.

Much the same situation prevails in parliamentary governments, though the responsibility of the executive to the legislature leaves less room for friction that is possible under the American check-and-balance system and the legislature is nowhere given such extensive control as in the United States. In Great Britain, the Cabinet has full authority over foreign affairs, though the House of Commons may, of course, vote it out of office if it is dissatisfied with its foreign policies. This is true of all parliamentary governments, but this power of the legislature is obviously not a very effective or subtle weapon for controlling foreign relations. Diplomatic appointments in Great Britain are not confirmed by the legislature. Treaties are made and ratified by the Cabinet in the name of the King, but important political treaties are sometimes submitted to Parliament for discussion and approval before the act of ratification takes place. Parliamentary objections to the Anglo-Soviet agreement of 1924 led to the fall of the first Labor Cabinet in the autumn of that year. Decisions of war and peace are also made by the Cabinet. As a matter of well-established convention, Parliament is always consulted before a formal declaration of war is issued, though hostilities are frequently embarked upon in the absence of a formal declaration without parliamentary authorization. The French Constitution of 1875 gave the President of the Republic, *i.e.*, the Cabinet, acting in the President's name, the power to negotiate and ratify treaties, to appoint diplomatic representatives, and to dispose of the armed forces of the State (Law of July 16, 1875, Article 8; Law of February 25, 1875, Article 3). Certain treaties were valid only when approved by a majority of the Senators and the Deputies: those

---

[1] With regard to the "Aid-to-Britain" bill before Congress in January and February, 1941, a perusal of constitutional precedents and Supreme Court decisions suggests that the powers asked for by the President were already available to him in his capacities as commander-in-chief of the armed forces and as spokesman of the nation in foreign affairs. The purpose of the bill was not to increase the President's powers but to make clear to the nation and the world that Congress and public opinion supported the exercise of these powers to keep aggression away from the Western Hemisphere. The bill was nevertheless debated in Congress and the press largely on the assumption that its purpose was to make the Chief Executive a "dictator" and to deprive Congress of authority. Cf. "Presidential Power and Congressional Control" by Walter Lippmann, *The New York Herald Tribune*, February 8, 1941.

relating to territory, peace, commerce, finances, and personal and property rights of Frenchmen abroad. It is significant that important political engagements, like treaties of alliance, did not require legislative approval and might even be kept secret for long periods of time. In France as elsewhere initiative and control in foreign affairs rested with the Executive, with legislative checks being of less practical importance than the Constitution might seem to indicate.

A word or two may be added regarding the position of the courts in foreign relations. The American Constitution (Article VI, Section 2) declares that all treaties made under the authority of the United States shall be regarded, along with the Constitution itself and laws of the United States which shall be made in pursuance thereof, as "the supreme law of the land; and the judges in every state shall be bound thereby, anything in the constitutions or laws of any state to the contrary notwithstanding." This means that all American courts, both state and federal, enforce treaties as law in cases which come before them requiring their application. State statutes contrary to treaties are held unconstitutional by the federal courts. As between a conflicting federal statute and a treaty, the courts enforce the most recent in point of time, since the Constitution places treaties and federal laws in the same category and Congress clearly has the right, under American constitutional law, to abrogate treaties by legislative act. In accordance with the "doctrine of political questions," however, the federal courts accept the interpretation placed upon treaties by the political branch, *i.e.*, the executive branch, of the government. The same applies to the enforcement of customary international law in American courts. In most other States, treaties and international law are likewise enforced in the courts, though sometimes only when they have been enacted into statutory form. In the absence of the judicial review of legislation in most other governments, the Executive and the legislature are fully responsible for the observance of the international obligations of the State.

In summary, the constitutional arrangements of most democratic States require some form of legislative participation in diplomacy, but initiative and control still remain for the most part in the hands of the Executive. Whatever degree of "democratization" of foreign policy has been attained has been achieved by imposing legislative checks upon the freedom of action of the Executive and by making the Executive responsible to the legislature, as in European parliamentary régimes, or to the electorate, as in the United States. Direct popular control over foreign affairs is by its nature unworkable. In Switzerland, to be sure, certain treaties must be ratified by popular referendum; and the utopian French Constitution of June 24, 1793, (which was never put into operation in this respect) required a vote of popular assemblies in the communes for all declarations of war. Popular referenda on questions of foreign policy are, by common consent, impracticable. Such responsibility to the electorate as exists is enforced through legislative action and through the popular election of policy-determining officials. In both cases, such responsibility is vague and intangible, and control continues to reside in the executive officials and in the diplomatic bureaucracy of the foreign offices and the field services.

SUGGESTED READINGS

Arnold, R.: *Treaty-making Procedure*, London, Oxford, 1933.

Cooper, R. M.: *American Consultation in World Affairs*, New York, Macmillan, 1934.

Corwin, E. S.: *The President's Control of Foreign Relations*, Princeton, Princeton University Press, 1917.

Dangerfield, R. J.: *In Defense of the Senate*, Norman, University of Oklahoma Press, 1933.

Dawes, C. G.: *Journal as Ambassador to Great Britain*, New York, Macmillan, 1939.

Dodd, W. E.: *Ambassador Dodd's Diary*, New York, Harcourt, 1941.

Dunn, F. S.: *The Practice and Procedure of International Conferences*, Baltimore, Johns Hopkins, 1929.

Flournoy, F. R.: *Parliament and War*, London, King, 1927.

Friedrich, C. J.: *Foreign Policy in the Making*, New York, Norton, 1938.

Hale, O. J.: *Publicity and Diplomacy*, 1890–1914, New York, Appleton-Century, 1940.

Hill, N.: *The Public International Conference*, Stanford University, Calif., Stanford University Press, 1929.

Hulen, B. D.: *Inside the Department of State*, New York, McGraw-Hill, 1939.

Lay, T. H.: *The Foreign Service of the United States*, New York, Prentice-Hall, 1932.

Mathews, J. M.: *American Foreign Relations: Conduct and Policies*, New York, Appleton-Century, 1938.

Nicolson, H.: *Diplomacy*, New York, Harcourt, 1939.

Poole, D. C.: *Conduct of Foreign Relations under Modern Democratic Conditions*, New Haven, Yale University Press, 1924.

Satow, E.: *A Guide to Diplomatic Practice*, New York, Longmans, 1922.

Schuman, F. L.: *War and Diplomacy in the French Republic*, New York, Whittlesey House, 1931.

Stuart, G. H.: *American Diplomatic and Consular Practice*, New York, Appleton-Century, 1936.

Takeuchi, T.: *War and Diplomacy in the Japanese Empire*, New York, Doubleday, 1935.

Tilley, Sir J. and Gaselee, S.: *The Foreign Office*, London, Putnam & Co., Ltd., 1933.

U.S. Department of State: *Bulletins* (weekly): *Register* (annual); *Foreign Relations* (annual).

Wright, Quincy: *The Control of American Foreign Relations*, New York, Macmillan, 1922.

CHAPTER V

THE SETTLEMENT OF DISPUTES

1. SELF-HELP

*Fury said to a mouse that he met in the house, "Let us both go to law:
I will prosecute you.—Come, I'll take no denial: we must have a trial;
for really this morning I've nothing to do." Said the mouse to the cur,
"Such a trial, dear sir, with no jury or judge, would be wasting our breath."
"I'll be judge, I'll be jury," said cunning old Fury; "I'll try the whole
cause and condemn you to death."—LEWIS CARROLL, Alice in Wonderland.*

RIGHTS and obligations of States received reasonably clear definition long before there existed any procedures for their enforcement. It is sometimes held to be a principle of private law that
there is no right without a remedy. If this notion were applied to international law, it would mean that States had no rights throughout the
whole formative period of modern international jurisprudence. It would
be more accurate to say, however, that the observance of the rights of
States depended upon their power to compel respect on the part of other
States. In the development of private law, remedies were established
simultaneously with rights and even in some cases antedated clear
definitions of rights. In international law, on the other hand, because
of the peculiar nature of the relations between independent sovereignties,
legal rights were recognized long before adequate remedies for their
protection came into being. In the absence of a superstate or a supreme
international authority to enforce international law, in the absence even
of settled procedures for the enforcement of rights between particular
States, all States were obliged to rely upon their ability to resist and
coerce their neighbors as means of protecting themselves. The prompt-
ings of ambition, the will-to-power, the lust for conquest, the pursuit of
national interests all dictated coercion as a method of dealing with other
States quite as much as did considerations of legal rights. States sought
(and still seek) security and the realization of their aspirations by efforts
to impose their will upon one another by force. Each State resorts to
self-help, *i.e.*, to its own power and resources, in its attempts to protect
its rights and interests.

War is obviously the ultimate means of coercion in inter-state relations. In war the belligerents each act as policeman, judge, jury, sheriff,
and executioner all in one. Questions of legal rights and obligations may

be raised on both sides at the beginning of war as excuses, rationalizations, pretexts, or plausible formulations of interests in the pursuit of which war seems preferable to surrender or compromise. War is a means of settling disputes only in the sense that, after an appropriate interval of bloodshed and destruction, the weaker party will be disposed to yield to the stronger or both will fall exhausted and agree to a compromise settlement which seemed unacceptable so long as each felt optimistic about imposing its will on the other. The terms of peace will set up new legal relationships between the disputants, reflecting the verdict of arms and destined to be more or less durable, depending upon the wisdom of the victors, the weakness of the vanquished, and subsequent shifts of power relationships. If neither side has succeeded in imposing its will on the other, the terms of the peace may make no reference to the original dispute at all. Such was the case with the Treaty of Ghent in 1814, which terminated the Anglo-American War of 1812. Under such circumstances, the dispute is "settled" by common agreement to say no more about it. That war is the most completely unsatisfactory method of settling disputes scarcely calls for demonstration in the fifth decade of the twentieth century. If war were to be judged on such grounds, it would have been banished long ago. But States generally resort to war not in the conviction that it represents the best mode of adjusting a controversy, but because armed coercion is an instrument of State power and a means of protecting and promoting the political interests of the State, quite apart from questions of legal rights.

There are various methods of hostile redress short of war which also involve an element of coercion. These may be broadly classified as threats of force, acts of retorsion, and acts of reprisal. Threats of force may take the form of military, naval, or aerial maneuvers, mobilization, the dispatch of an ultimatum, the severance of diplomatic relations, and the like. None of these is either injurious in fact to the other party or a violation of his legal rights but is a more or less violent gesture designed to frighten the other party into a more tractable frame of mind. Needless to say, most wars break out after one or both parties to a controversy have made threats of force which fail to produce the desired result. Acts of retorsion are definitely injurious to the other party, though not in violation of his legal rights. Such measures are always within the bounds of customary international law and are performed entirely within the jurisdiction of the State taking such action. Discriminatory tariff duties or penalties, the suspension of commercial intercourse, and the use of an economic boycott are common examples. In 1808–1809 the Jefferson Administration enforced an embargo on American trade with Great Britain and France as a means of bringing their governments to terms in the controversies over neutral rights. In this case the measure of retorsion was unsuccessful, and the United States suffered more than its victims. China's anti-Japanese boycott of 1931–1932 was an act of retorsion in retaliation for the Japanese military occupation of Manchuria. Such acts are not, in and of themselves, violations of the customary legal rights of the victim State, though they sometimes involve breaches of treaty obligations and often lead to violent incidents. When the victim retaliates in kind, grave consequences may easily ensue.

Acts of reprisal, as distinct from retorsion and threats of force, are in patent violation of the legal rights of the other party. Prior to the abolition of privateering by the Declaration of Paris of 1856,[1] it was usual for States to authorize private reprisals by issuing "letters of marque and reprisal" to their nationals with unsatisfied financial claims against a foreign State. Such individuals were then free to plunder the commerce of the other State up to the amount of their claims. In 1832 President Jackson urged Congress to authorize the seizure of goods from French vessels on the high seas as a means of compelling France to meet her financial obligations to the United States. Reprisals of this type are, happily, no longer permissible. Public reprisals, however, are still recognized as a legitimate method of redress. They may take the form of hostile embargoes, pacific blockades, acts of intervention, and acts of overt hostility indistinguishable from war in everything but name. An embargo is hostile, i.e., a violation of the rights of its victim and therefore an act of reprisal rather than of retorsion, when it takes the form of the seizure of the ships or goods of nationals of the other State. This practice is now looked upon with disfavor, and even on the outbreak of war enemy merchant vessels in port are usually allowed "days of grace" within which they may depart unmolested. A blockade consists of action by naval forces to intercept commerce. A war blockade may be applied to vessels of all States entering or leaving the blockaded ports. A "pacific" blockade, however, must be limited in its enforcement to the vessels of the parties to the controversy and cannot lawfully be extended to vessels of third States. The first modern instance of this practice was the pacific blockade of Greece by the Powers in 1827. This led to the great naval battle of Navarino, in which the Turkish-Egyptian fleet was destroyed, but war was not declared and the blockade was applied only to Greek and Turkish vessels and to those of the flag of the blockading States. New Granada was subjected to a pacific blockade by Great Britain in 1836, Mexico by France in 1838, Greece by Great Britain in 1850, China by France in 1884, Greece by Great Britain, Germany, Austria, Italy, and Russia in 1886, Zanzibar by Portugal in 1888, Crete by the Powers in 1897, Venezuela by Great Britain, Germany, and Italy in 1902, Soviet Russia by the other Powers

[1] See above, p. 131.

in 1918–1921, etc. Most pacific blockades are directed by Great Powers against small ones too weak to resort to war or to retaliate effectively. Those directed against strong States usually lead to war.

All acts of intervention are acts of reprisal when they are resorted to as a means of bringing diplomatic pressure to bear upon their victim and when they are unaccompanied by any intention of creating a legal state of war. In 1914 the United States bombarded and occupied Vera Cruz, and two years later it sent a military expedition into northern Mexico, in both instances disclaiming any intention of making war. The American interventions in the Caribbean States have been similar in character. The attack of the Powers upon the Shimonoseki forts (Japan) in 1863, the allied expedition against Pekin in 1901, and the Italian bombardment of Corfu in 1923 are other examples. The military occupation of the Ruhr valley in 1923 was likewise an act of reprisal for German nonpayment of reparations, though the French and Belgian Governments insisted that they were authorized to take such action by the Treaty of Versailles. In January and February of 1932 Japanese military and naval forces, in retaliation against the Chinese boycott, bombarded and occupied Shanghai, after several weeks of severe fighting. In every such case, the victim whose rights are violated may regard the act as a *casus belli* and resort to war. The act itself does not automatically create a state of war, regardless of how much fighting takes place, unless one party or the other expresses an intention to make war. These various forms of pressure may thus be indistinguishable in fact from actual war, but they are "pacific" in the sense that a legal state of war is not inaugurated by them.[1]

2. NEGOTIATION

> Every Christian prince must take as his chief maxim not to employ arms to support or vindicate his rights until he has employed and exhausted the way of reason and of persuasion. It is to his interest also to add to reason and persuasion the influence of benefits conferred, which indeed is one of the surest ways to make his power secure, and to increase it.—M. DE CALLIÈRES, *On the Manner of Negotiating with Princes.*

> If you wish to gain your ends by force, you must be strong; if you wish to gain them by negotiation, you must be twice as strong.—ADOLF HITLER.

If the parties to a dispute are disposed to discuss their differences rather than to threaten one another or to fight about them, they will resort to negotiation as a means of settlement. Negotiations may be conducted through diplomacy, through conference, or through the services of third States offering good offices or mediation. In the first instance the regular diplomatic channels may be utilized for an exchange

[1] On the present legal status of war see p. 469 below.

of views in an effort to reach an adjustment. The foreign minister of either State may call in the ambassador or minister of the other for consultation. Or the two foreign ministers may confer with one another directly. Or they may appoint special agents, publicly or secretly, to carry on discussions. If an agreement is reached it may be incorporated into an exchange of notes or some more formal international engagement. If negotiations are unsuccessful, other methods of settlement may be resorted to. The conduct of negotiations is essentially a bargaining process, for there can be no successful settlement by this method without give-and-take on both sides. Legal rights will be argued; but considerations of State power, equity, and political expediency will also be thrown into the scales. Each side will necessarily strive to attain maximum advantages with minimum concessions to the other. The respective foreign offices formulate their own claims and, by a more or less prolonged exchange of diplomatic correspondence, fence and parry with one another until some consensus of views is reached or until the negotiations break down in failure. In all negotiations the contending States remain judges of their own cases. The time consumed, however, allows an interval for popular passions to cool and facilitates compromise. When negotiations are conducted openly and irreconcilable claims are made public, it frequently becomes impossible for foreign ministers or diplomats to recede from the position which they have taken, particularly when patriotic zeal has been aroused over the controversy. Secret diplomacy obviates this difficulty, though it may lead to others even more undesirable. The great majority of international disputes are settled by diplomacy, and it may be viewed as the normal method of dealing with international differences.

In the settlement of disputes by conference, as distinct from diplomacy, recourse is had to special representatives, specifically chosen to deal with the particular controversy, rather than to the regular diplomatic service. It is also customary in international conferences to draw up an agenda or list of subjects to which the discussion is to be limited, whereas in diplomatic correspondence each side may draw into the case the whole range of national interests, including many matters subsidiary to, or even irrelevant to, the main question at issue. States participating in international conferences frequently insist upon the exclusion from the agenda of certain problems upon which they are especially sensitive. The United States, for example, has frequently refused to discuss the Monroe Doctrine or the international law of intervention at the Pan-American Conferences. In the Washington Conference of 1921–1922 Japan insisted upon excluding the status of Shantung and the famous twenty-one demands of 1915 from the discussion. This limitation of the agenda often serves to expedite a settlement, though it is not always easy to exclude extraneous questions from the proceedings and when they are so excluded irritation and resentment may be engendered rather than reduced. Settlement by conference has become increasingly common.

When two States are unable to reach any agreement with regard to a pending controversy and relations between them become "strained," it is permissible for outside States to offer their services in an effort to facilitate a settlement. If such interposition is dictatorial in character, it constitutes intervention. But if it is purely advisory, it cannot be regarded as an unfriendly act. Neither can the third State take offense if its offer is declined. A "tender of good offices" is usually nothing more than a mere polite inquiry as to whether the third State can be of service in preserving or restoring peace. It is often extended at the request of one of the parties to the controversy and is frequently made after a rupture of diplomatic relations or in the course of a war, as a means of restoring communication between the parties. If a tender of good offices is accepted on both sides, the third State may transmit suggestions for a settlement between the parties or may make such suggestions itself. In the latter case, true mediation occurs. Good offices consist of an invitation to resume discussions. Mediation, which normally follows an acceptance of good offices, consists of the actual transmission of suggestions. The mediating State does not seek to impose a settlement on the parties, but attempts rather to create the atmosphere and the means necessary for a settlement. In 1813 the Russian Government offered its mediation to Great Britain and the United States in an effort to terminate the war which had broken out in the preceding year. The United States at once accepted the offer and sent commissioners to St. Petersburg to negotiate, but the British Government declined to reciprocate. Peace negotiations were finally opened by direct conversations between the parties. In 1905 President Roosevelt made a tender of good offices to Russia and Japan, then at war. The offer was accepted on both sides. The United States then acted as mediator and arranged a peace conference at Portsmouth, New Hampshire. Its suggestions were instrumental in enabling the belligerents to come to an agreement and frame a peace treaty.

The first Convention of the first Hague Peace Conference of 1899 contained a number of provisions regarding good offices and mediation, in addition to providing for the creation of the Hague Permanent Court of Arbitration. In its revised form, as amended by the second Conference of 1907, it provided that the contracting Powers "agree to have recourse, as far as circumstances allow, to the good offices or mediation of one or more friendly Powers" in cases of serious disagreements or disputes between them. All Powers were recognized to have the right to offer good offices and mediation to disputants. "The exercise of this right shall never be regarded by one or the other of the parties in conflict as an unfriendly act." The function of a mediator was declared to be that of "reconciling the opposing claims and appeasing the feelings of resentment which may have arisen between the States at variance." It was made clear that mediation is purely advisory and that the function of the would-be mediator is at an end as soon as his suggestions are declined by either party. The convention likewise made provision for a plan of mediation (never subsequently utilized) whereby disputing States were to refer the controversy to two designated mediating Powers which would have exclusive control over efforts to achieve a settlement for a period of thirty days.

The term *conciliation* is frequently used to refer to the sequel of successful mediation, *i.e.*, to the process whereby an outside party promotes an agreement between contending States. This procedure was institutionalized in the League of Nations Covenant, which made the Council an agency of conciliation. The members of the League agreed by Article 15 to submit to the Council "any dispute likely to lead to a rupture which is not submitted to arbitration or judicial settlement." The Council was authorized to endeavor to settle the dispute. If its report was unanimously agreed to by its members, other than the representatives of the disputing States, the members of the League agreed that they would not go to war with any party to the dispute which complied with the recommendations of the report.

None of these permanent procedures was resorted to in the efforts made in 1939 to avert the outbreak of war. Only in the case of the hostilities between the U.S.S.R. and Finland did the victim of aggression appeal to the League of Nations. In the war crisis of August 4–September 3, 1939, The Hague and Geneva procedures were ignored, but various governments tendered their good offices to the disputants. On August 22, Chamberlain addressed a personal letter to Hitler urging direct German-Polish negotiations, with the aid of a neutral intermediary if desired by both sides. Hitler's reply of August 23 was inconclusive. While London and Paris pressed Warsaw to negotiate, King Leopold of Belgium, in the name of the Oslo States, broadcast a plea for peace on August 23. Pope Pius XII did likewise on the following day. At the same time, President Roosevelt appealed to King Victor Emmanuel of Italy to "formulate proposals for a pacific settlement of the present crisis." He also urged Chancellor Hitler and President Moscicki of Poland to refrain from all hostile acts "for a reasonable and stipulated period" and to seek a solution by way of negotiation or arbitration or conciliation through a moderator from one of the American Republics or one of the traditionally neutral European States. Warsaw agreed, but a second message from Washington to Berlin produced no reply until September 1 when Hitler merely said that Poland's attitude had nullified all his efforts to keep the peace. An appeal by the Prime Minister of Canada on August 26 and a tender of good offices by King Leopold and Queen Wilhelmina on August 29 were also without effect.

Hitler meanwhile offered an alliance to Britain on August 25 on condition of a German-Polish settlement satisfactory to the Reich. The British Ambassador, Sir Nevile Henderson, flew to London with this proposal and returned on August 28 with suggestions for a settlement and assurances that Poland was "prepared to enter into discussions." The Nazi leaders later declared that this was a lie and that London had sought to trick Berlin by pretending that Warsaw was ready to negotiate when in fact Warsaw had no such intention. The fact was that Warsaw was quite willing to "negotiate" on a basis of equality and compromise and had extended such assurances to Washington and London, but Berlin's conception of "negotiations" was one according to which Poland must send a special emissary to Berlin with full powers to accept German proposals at once. On August 29, Hitler and Ribbentrop told Henderson that they agreed to "accept the proposed intermediation of the British Government to send a Polish representative invested with plenipotentiary powers. They expect his arrival on Wednesday, August 30." The Ambassador said this "sounded like an ultimatum." This the Nazi leaders denied. Halifax promised "careful consideration" of the German reply but said " . . . it is, of course, unreasonable to expect that we can produce a Polish representative in Berlin today." Polish Foreign Minister Beck refused to go to Berlin, lest he be treated as Schuschnigg and Hacha had been treated. Warsaw ordered mobilization on August 30.

At midnight, August 30–31 (Wednesday–Thursday), Henderson saw Ribbentrop who said that German proposals for a settlement had been drawn up but that, since no Polish plenipotentiary had arrived by midnight, it was too late. He then read or, as the Ambassador put it, "gabbled through to me as fast as he could in a tone of the utmost scorn and annoyance," a plan of sixteen points whereby Germany was to annex Danzig and the status of the Corridor would be determined by a plebiscite. The proposals were not unreasonable, but the difference of views between Berlin on the one hand and London and Warsaw on the other as to the meaning of "negotiations" was never bridged. The sixteen points were not transmitted either to Poland or to Britain but were broadcast by Wilhelmstrasse during the evening of August 31. The Polish Ambassador, Josef Lipski, had seen Ribbentrop at 6.30 P.M. to tell him that his Government was "weighing favorably" the British suggestions and would give its formal reply within two hours. He did not have "full power" to accept the sixteen points. He did not ask for them. Ribbentrop did not offer them. An hour later the German Government severed all communications with Poland, so that no further discussions were possible. A last appeal by the Pope was without result. German armies invaded Poland at dawn on Friday, September 1, 1939.

Mussolini offered his mediation on August 31 in the hope of preventing war between the Allies and his own ally, Hitler. Even after the German invasion of Poland was launched, French Foreign Minister Georges Bonnet accepted the Italian proposal for a conference. His willingness to compromise was the cause of the delay in Anglo-French action. The British and French notes to Berlin of September 1 were not ultimata but warnings and appeals. Beck was horrified. "We are in the thick of war, as the result of unprovoked aggression. The question before us is not one of a conference, but of the common action to be taken by the Allies to resist." Italian mediation efforts continued on Saturday. But Halifax would not consent to a conference unless Germany agreed to withdraw her troops from Poland and refrain from further attack. This condition Hitler was unwilling to accept. Bonnet was overruled in his efforts to arrange another Munich. He was obliged to phone Ciano Saturday evening that the French Cabinet, also, could not consent to a conference unless German forces would evacuate Polish territory. Rome thereupon informed Berlin that it could do nothing more. Allied ultimata to the Reich were delivered on Sunday. The Anglo-French declarations of war followed. When one Power is bent upon the destruction of another or upon the unilateral imposition of its terms under threat of force, there is obviously no possibility of settlement by "negotiation."

To return to the condition (once regarded as "normal") in which compromise is possible: With respect to certain types of international controversies, States are willing to resort to methods of settlement which are in advance of negotiation in the sense that recourse is had to more or less impartial tribunals of adjustment but which fall short of arbitration or adjudication in that the disputants are unwilling to bind themselves in advance to accept such recommendations as may be made. These procedures can conveniently be described as methods approaching arbitration. In every instance the parties remain free to accept or reject the solution proposed by the agencies which they have created. These procedures fall into the categories of mixed commissions, commissions of inquiry, and commissions of conciliation.

A mixed commission is a body of representatives chosen by two disputing governments to make recommendations for its settlement. It consists of an even number of delegates, half chosen by each side—an arrangement which compels the members either to agree to disagree or to come to a definitive settlement. The members of mixed commissions are usually technical experts, qualified to ascertain the facts of the controversy. A commission of inquiry differs from a mixed commission in that it usually consists of an odd number of members and limits itself to fact finding. Its findings are again purely recommendations. This method of settlement was first provided for by general international agreement in the Convention for the Pacific Settlement of International Disputes drawn up at the first Hague Conference. The convention declared in part,

In differences of an international nature involving neither honor nor vital interests, and arising from a difference of opinion on points of fact, the signatory powers recommend that the parties who have not been able to come to an agreement by means of diplomacy should, as far as circumstances allow, institute an international commission of inquiry, to facilitate a solution of these differences by elucidating the facts by means of an impartial and conscientious investigation. (Article 9.)

The scheme of settlement here proposed was based upon a procedure whereby the parties to a dispute would, by special agreement, set up a commission of inquiry, designate the questions to be put to it, and indicate the rules to be followed. The commission would make an investigation, hear both sides, call witnesses and experts, and prepare a report limited to a statement of facts, leaving the parties "entire freedom as to the effect to be given to the statement." This procedure was first applied in the Dogger Bank affair of 1904. A Russian squadron, proceeding through the North Sea on its way to the Far East in the course of the Russo-Japanese War, fired upon a number of British trawlers under the impression that they were Japanese torpedo boats. In Great Britain, ally of Japan since 1902, a popular clamor for war commenced at once, and the Government demanded immediate explanations and reparations from Russia. The two States agreed to submit the questions of fact connected with the incident to a commission of inquiry of five members, consisting of British, Russian, American, and French naval officers with a fifth member (an officer in the Austro-Hungarian navy) chosen by the other four. The commission met at Paris and published its report on February 25, 1905. It found the Russian squadron at fault, and the Russian Government paid an indemnity of £65,000. The same procedure was resorted to by Germany and the Netherlands with regard to responsibility for the sinking of a Dutch steamer in 1916. The commission here found that the vessel was sunk by a torpedo fired by a German submarine, and an indemnity was likewise paid. Resort to the procedure outlined in the Hague Convention was not in any sense obligatory, and the commissions were not permanent agencies but merely *ad hoc* bodies set up for each particular controversy.

In an effort to institutionalize this procedure the United States, through Secretary of State Bryan, proposed to other States in 1913 the negotiation of a series of bilateral treaties which should set up permanent boards or commissions of conciliation to which all disputes, without exception, should be submitted. These commissions were to consist of five members: two nationals of the parties, two chosen by the parties from among foreign nationals, and the fifth selected by agreement. The commissions were to be given a year's time to report, during which period the parties agreed not to resort to hostilities. Thirty of the so-called Bryan "cooling-off" treaties were negotiated and twenty-one came into force—nine with European States, eleven with Latin American States, and one with China. Only ten commissions were set up. None of them was ever utilized for the settlement of any dispute and the entire scheme has been allowed to lapse. This effort to create permanent commissions of conciliation thus bore no immediate fruits, although the principle in question reappears in a number of post-1919 treaties. For example, the Saavedra Lamas Antiwar Treaty of Nonaggression and Conciliation, signed at Rio de Janeiro, October 10, 1933, provided for Conciliation Commissions of 5 members, 3 of whom should be non-nationals of the disputing States. The signatories undertook to submit disputes to such commissions, but their reports "shall in no case have the character of a final decision or arbitral award."

3. ARBITRATION

It is impossible to attack as a transgressor him who offers to lay his grievance before a tribunal of arbitration.—ARCHIDAMUS, King of Sparta.

If a difficulty should arise between the aforesaid cities, which cannot easily be settled by themselves, it shall be decided by the arbitration of the Sovereign Pontiff; and if one of the parties violates the treaty, we agree that His Holiness shall excommunicate the offending city.—Treaty between Venice and Genoa, 1235.

In all of the procedures sketched above, the disputing States remain free to accept or reject the recommendations made. It is of the essence of true arbitration that the parties bind themselves in advance to submit their differences to an impartial arbitrator or to an arbitral tribunal and to accept the award as binding. Article 37 of the Hague Convention for the Pacific Settlement of International Disputes defined arbitration as follows:

International arbitration has for its object the settlement of disputes between States by judges of their own choice, and on the basis of respect for law. Recourse to arbitration implies an engagement to submit in good faith to the award. (Article 37 of the first convention of 1907.)

This definition involves four elements which are the distinguishing features of genuine international arbitration: (1) settlement of disputes between States through their own voluntary action, (2) by judges of their own choice, (3) on the basis of respect for law, and (4) with an obligation to accept the award as binding. The last-named element distinguishes arbitration sharply from the methods dealt with above, in which recommendations are purely advisory. The phrase "respect for law" implies that arbitrators are free to consider extralegal aspects of a controversy, if this will contribute toward a settlement, and are not bound to apply the strict letter of international law to the case before them. C. C. Hyde defines international arbitration as "an impartial adjudication according to law, and that before a tribunal of which at least a single member, who is commonly a national of a state neutral to the contest, acts as umpire."[1] This suggests that the process of arbitration is identical with that of adjudication except as to the method of choosing judges. In practice, arbitral tribunals have usually acted as judicial bodies and have applied the principles of international law to the controversies submitted to them. It remains true, nevertheless, that arbitrators have more discretion than judges of a court and may apply principles of equity and justice, as well as political considerations, in making their award—a procedure inadmissable in a genuine judicial body.

Arbitration as a method of settling international disputes is of great antiquity. The earliest treaty of which any record remains was an arbitration treaty. The practice of arbitration was extensively resorted to in the State Systems preceding the present one, particularly among the Greeks. During the medieval period there were numerous papal arbitrations and an appreciable number of secular arbitrations between temporal rulers. Between 1500 and 1800, however, arbitration went out of fashion as a mode of adjusting differences, except for a few seventeenth century English arbitration treaties negotiated by Cromwell. The practice was revived in the Jay Treaty of 1794 between Great Britain and the United States. By this instrument, four commissions were set up: to locate the source of the Mississippi, to settle the St. Croix River boundary, to pass upon the claims of British subjects for prerevolutionary mercantile debts confiscated by the United States, and to judge of reciprocal claims arising out of the seizure of American vessels by British cruisers and the capture of British merchantmen by French privateers fitted out in American ports. These commissions were really arbitral tribunals, with the exception of the first, which might be better described as a commission of inquiry. The first failed in its object. The second located the St. Croix River to the satisfaction of both parties, subject to certain later readjustments of the boundary. The third failed to agree upon an award, but by the convention of 1802 the British Government agreed to accept $2,664,000 in settlement of the claims in question. The fourth awarded $11,650,000 to the American claimants and $143,428 to the British claimants. Between 1794 and 1900 it has been estimated that there were no less than 400 international arbitrations, of which the most spectacular was doubt-

[1] *International Law Chiefly as Interpreted and Applied by the United States*, II, pp. 111–112.

less the arbitration at Geneva, under the terms of the Treaty of Washington of 1871, of the claims of the United States against Great Britain for violations of neutral obligations during the American Civil War.[1] Since 1900 recourse to arbitration has become even more frequent, until it is now one of the best established procedures for the settlement of international controversies.

In its simplest form arbitration involves the negotiation by the parties to the dispute of a bilateral treaty, known as a *compromis*, in which they state clearly the question to be arbitrated, name the arbitrators or specify the method of their selection, and set forth the rules of procedure and the principles of law or equity to be applied. This arrangement is still used in many instances, particularly for the settlement of financial claims. General rules of arbitral procedure have gradually been developed, however, which now render it unnecessary to specify in detail how a particular tribunal shall act. In 1875 the Institute of International Law drew up a code of arbitral procedure and in 1889 the first Pan-American Conference prepared a complete scheme of arbitration, which was not adopted, however, at that time. When a dispute is not submitted to the judgment of a single arbitrator, such as the sovereign of a third State, a tribunal is set up consisting usually of one or two nationals of each of the disputing States, plus one or more nationals of outside States. These may be named in the *compromis* or chosen by the other members of the tribunal. One of the outsiders usually acts as umpire. The tribunal—almost invariably consisting of an odd number of members—meets at some designated place, organizes itself, and proceeds to hear both sides of the controversy. Each party argues its case through attorneys, who present briefs in the form of cases and counter-cases. The exchange of written arguments may be followed by oral pleading and the summoning of witnesses, though there is no use of a jury. The tribunal then reaches its decision by a majority vote and submits a written statement of the award, with the reasons therefor, to the respective disputants. Minority opinions may be rendered by the members of the tribunal who differ with the majority, but they are without legal effect.

An arbitral award is binding upon the parties and constitutes a final settlement of the controversy. States sometimes expressly reserve in the *compromis* the right to demand a reconsideration on the basis of the discovery of some new fact of vital importance, unknown to the tribunal or to the party making the demand at the time of the award. Arbitral awards may also be rejected on certain other grounds. If the arbitrators exceed their authority under the *compromis*, the award is not binding. In 1827 the United States and Great Britain submitted to the arbitration of the King of the Netherlands the question of the location of the "highlands"

[1] See p. 134 above.

mentioned in the treaty of 1783 as marking the American-Canadian boundary between Maine and Quebec. The arbitrator drew a compromise line through a valley located between two sets of highlands and both parties rejected the award on the ground that "highlands" could not be situated in a valley and that the arbitrator had exceeded his instructions. The subsequent discovery of fraud, bribery, or coercion in the course of an arbitration also invalidates the award, but such cases are rare. In general, arbitral awards are almost always accepted in good faith and loyally carried out, for States refrain from submitting questions to arbitration unless they are prepared to accept whatever settlement the tribunal may reach.

In the development of arbitral procedure, the next step beyond *ad hoc* agreements providing for the submission of a particular dispute to a particular tribunal was the inclusion in other treaties of provisions for the submission to arbitration of disputes arising thereunder. In addition to this arrangement, States also began to negotiate general arbitration treaties, specifying that all future controversies of a designated character between the signatories would be submitted to arbitration. During the nineteenth century the number of general arbitration treaties and of arbitral clauses in other treaties steadily increased. Prior to 1855 only 6 such treaties were in operation. Thirty were negotiated between 1865 and 1894, 50 in the ensuing decade, and 123 between 1905 and 1914. Such treaties provide for what is known as "compulsory" or "obligatory" arbitration. These adjectives are somewhat misleading, since the treaties referred to merely constitute a voluntary pledge that the parties will in future submit to arbitration certain specified types of disputes. They frequently contain such broad qualifications and exceptions as to leave the parties almost complete liberty of action with regard to any particular controversy. Many pre-1914 general arbitration treaties, modeled after the Anglo-French treaty of October 14, 1903, specified that all cases should be excluded from their operation which involved "national honor, independence, vital interests, or the interests of third parties." "These phrases are vague and indefinite and lend themselves to the purposes of any statesman who may desire to proceed to extremities. An interest becomes vital when a government chooses to consider it as such, and there is no fixed criterion of national honor."[1] Prior to 1917 thirty-six bilateral treaties had been signed providing for the submission to arbitration of any dispute whatever between the parties, without qualification. The first of these was the treaty of May 28, 1902, between Argentina and Chile. Nineteen other treaties provided for the arbitration of any dispute not involving constitutional questions. But no general treaty of this kind had been entered into between any two of the Great Powers.

[1] T. J. Lawrence, *The Principles of International Law*, 7th ed., 1923, p. 579.

Projects of general compulsory arbitration treaties were defeated at both the first and second Hague Conferences of 1899 and 1907. The Hague Convention for the Pacific Settlement of International Disputes bound the parties to resort to arbitration only "in so far as circumstances permit" (Article 38, convention of October 18, 1907).

Despite American championship of arbitration, the actual practice of the United States has been measurably behind that of other Powers. This has been due in part to the divergent attitudes of successive administrations and in part to the opposition of the Senate. The American Government has arbitrated numerous controversies, particularly with Great Britain, through *ad hoc compromis* agreements. It has likewise included arbitration clauses in numerous other treaties but has not always availed itself of the opportunities provided in this fashion. Article 21 of the Treaty of Guadalupe Hidalgo with Mexico of February 2, 1848, for example, specified that the parties would "consider" the arbitration of all future difficulties not settled by diplomacy; but when Mexico in 1916 proposed the arbitration of current controversies between the two governments, the United States declined the suggestion and instead resorted to reprisals by capturing and occupying Vera Cruz. Again, in 1927, when the dispute over the alleged confiscatory effects of Mexico's land and oil laws became acute, a widespread popular demand for arbitration appeared in the United States and even won the support of the Senate, but the administration declined to resort to this mode of settlement. The United States proposed arbitration of the controversies of 1938 arising out of Mexican expropriation of American oil properties, but Mexico declined. Arbitrators usually apply existing laws. When one of the parties to a dispute challenges the justice of established law, arbitration offers little promise of a settlement.

As for general treaties providing for "compulsory" arbitration, so many obstacles have been encountered that the United States has long been in the rear of the procession of States entering into arrangements of this kind. In 1896, following the successful arbitration of the boundary dispute between Great Britain and Venezuela, the British Government proposed to the United States a general treaty providing for obligatory arbitration. Secretary of State Olney, who insisted that arbitration should be made "automatic," was even more enthusiastic than Lord Salisbury; and on January 11, 1897, a treaty was signed which went far in the direction of such an arrangement. The Senate, however, rejected the treaty, and nothing came of the proposal at the moment. The American delegates to the first Hague Conference of 1899 were instructed to champion arbitration and to work for the establishment of an international court of justice; but anything in the nature of compulsory arbitration was ruled out by the Conference. Following the Russo-Japanese War of 1904–

1905 and the Anglo-French arbitration treaty of 1903, the United States signed a number of general treaties for the obligatory arbitration of questions of a legal nature, which, with the exception of controversies involving national honor, independence, vital interests, or the interests of third States, were to be submitted to the Hague Permanent "Court" of Arbitration. Here, as in all such treaties, it was of course contemplated that each *compromis* for the submission of a particular dispute to arbitration would be not a formal treaty requiring ratification, but merely an administrative agreement under the terms of the general treaty. But the Senate insisted that each *compromis* must be expressly approved by it as a "treaty" before the arbitration could proceed. President Roosevelt declared that this was "mere nonsense" which made the general treaties "shams." The administration therefore withdrew the treaties from Senate consideration and abandoned the whole enterprise. In Europe the formulation of a *compromis* under general arbitration treaties has always been regarded as a merely procedural matter, for unless it is so regarded there is no value in the general treaties.

In 1908 Secretary of State Root revived the negotiations and concluded some twenty-five treaties containing the provisions demanded by the Senate. In fact, as John Bassett Moore pointed out, the treaties represented a step backward in one sense, since prior to 1908 pecuniary claims had often been arbitrated without concluding a formal treaty with the foreign government, whereas under the new arrangement a treaty had to be concluded for each arbitration.[1] This feature, added to the exceptions of independence, national honor, and vital interests, made the treaties little more than meaningless gestures. In 1911–1912, another group of general arbitration treaties was negotiated by President Taft and Secretary of State Knox. They abandoned the exceptions of vital interests and national honor and pledged the parties to arbitrate all differences "which are justiciable in their nature by reason of being susceptible of decision by the application of the principles of law and equity." These treaties provided for a joint high commission of inquiry to determine whether a particular controversy was "justiciable." The Senate objected to this arrangement, struck it out, and inserted numerous reservations prohibiting the arbitration of a whole series of cases—with the result that President Taft declared of the treaties, after the Senate had finished with them, that "their own father would not recognize them." In disgust, he dropped the whole project. Except for the Bryan conciliation treaties, nothing more was done by the United States, prior to the outbreak of the Great War, in the direction of perfecting international machinery for the pacific settlement of disputes.

[1] See his *Principles of American Diplomacy*, p. 331, and *International Law and Some Current Illusions*, p. 86.

The post-Versailles arbitration treaties of the United States are for the most part based upon the treaty with France of 1928. They omit the exceptions of national honor and vital interests but contain exceptions of cases within the domestic jurisdiction of the parties, involving the interests of third parties, depending upon or involving "the maintenance of the traditional attitude of the United States concerning domestic questions, commonly known as the Monroe Doctrine," or involving the observance of obligations under the Covenant of the League of Nations. Each *compromis*, moreover, must take the form of a separate treaty which must be submitted to the Senate. The exceptions are almost as flexible as those in the pre-war treaties. In other words, the United States in its general arbitration treaties has said no more than that it will enter into special treaties for the arbitration of particular disputes if it regards them as suitable for arbitration, *i.e.*, not falling within the exceptions, and if the Senate, in its wisdom, sees fit to approve ratification of such special treaties. The American Government is obviously not prepared to commit itself to arbitrate particular controversies automatically, unless the language employed is so vague and flexible that loopholes can readily be discovered through which disputes can be excluded from the operation of the general treaties if considerations of political expediency dictate such action. Though many other States have entered into general arbitration treaties which really pledge them to arbitrate certain types of disputes, the United States has reserved its liberty of action to such a degree that its general arbitration treaties are little more than empty words.

The most important step thus far taken toward the institutionalization of arbitration was the creation of the Permanent Court of Arbitration by the first Hague Conference of 1899. This agency is neither "permanent" nor a "court," for its members are not required to reside and work at The Hague, nor do they collectively constitute a judicial body. Its name is due to the confusion between arbitration and adjudication which prevailed at the time of its establishment. It came into being through the signature and ratification by a large number of States of the Convention for the Pacific Settlement of International Disputes. This multilateral engagement required each of the signatory Powers to designate for a term of six years "four persons of known competency in questions of international law, of the highest moral reputation, and disposed to accept the duties of arbitrators." The list of arbitrators so compiled is kept at the international bureau of the "court" at The Hague as a panel from which States may pick an arbitral tribunal for the settlement of particular controversies. A new tribunal is picked for each dispute by means of a *compromis* between the parties. Only the panel is permanent. Resort to this procedure is entirely optional and voluntary. At the second Hague Conference of 1907, it was provided that of the two arbitrators appointed by each party, "only one can be its national, or chosen from among the persons selected by it as members of the Permanent Court." This ensures a majority of neutral members on each tribunal.

This institution is nothing more than a list of arbitrators and a secretariat. It has doubtless received more attention than its practical importance warrants. It did, nevertheless, stimulate general interest in arbitration; and it has performed a useful, if limited, function in disposing satisfactorily of a number of disputes submitted to it. Between 1903, when the United States and Mexico established the first tribunal to deal with the "Pious Funds" case, and 1914, fifteen cases had been arbitrated in accordance with the procedure outlined in the convention. These included international claims against Venezuela, the right of the dhows of Muscat to fly the French flag in the face of British objections, the Norway-Sweden maritime boundary dispute, the Anglo-American North Atlantic Fisheries controversy, a Dutch-Portuguese boundary dispute on the island of Timor, the Franco-German dispute over the Casablanca deserters, two Franco-Italian disputes, a Russo-Turkish dispute, and other cases of lesser importance. Most of these disputes were of little political significance, though arbitration achieved a settlement where diplomacy had failed. Since 1922, most of the cases which would have been arbitrated in this fashion have been adjudicated by the World Court. From the record of the years, as well as from the logic of arbitral procedure itself, it is clear that arbitration, taken by itself, is no substitute for war, but merely a convenient device for settling certain types of controversies with regard to which the parties are willing to accept the decision of an impartial third party. The international controversies which lead to war are precisely those involving questions which States are unwilling to submit to arbitration or to adjudication or, for that matter, to any form of pacific settlement which obliges the contestants in advance to subordinate their special and exclusive interests to the will of impartial international agencies.

Recent "arbitrations" imposed by totalitarian Powers on weak neighbors scarcely deserve to be regarded as falling within the usual meaning of the term. Thus Germany and Italy "arbitrated" the boundary dispute between Hungary and truncated Czechoslovakia and handed down an "award" from Vienna on November 2, 1938, by which Budapest was given a generous slice of Slovakia and the lowlands of Ruthenia. In similar fashion, Ribbentrop and Ciano "mediated" in the dispute between Hungary and Rumania over Transylvania and on August 30, 1940, "pronounced an arbitral sentence" whereby Hungary was given the northeastern half of Transylvania and the Axis "guaranteed" the remnant of Rumania. In the first case, Germany occupied what was left of Czechoslovakia within five months. In the second case, Germany occupied what was left of Rumania within five weeks. In both cases the alleged "arbitration" was not voluntary nor by judges chosen by the disputants nor on the basis of respect for law. Such "arbitrations," however, promise to become more and more frequent in an epoch of undiluted power politics.

4. ADJUDICATION

> In concerning the office of an arbiter, we must consider whether he be elected into the place of a judge, or with some laxer power, which Seneca speaks of as the proper power of an arbiter: "The judge is limited by rules of law: the umpire is left quite free, and can soften law and justice by kindness and mercy." So Aristotle says, "that a fair man will rather go to an arbiter than to a judge, because the arbiter looks to equity, the judge to law."—HUGO GROTIUS, *De jure belli ac pacis*.

If it be true, as seems likely, that arbitration in the future will not progress much beyond its present status, the cause is to be found both in the unwillingness of States to submit politically important disputes to arbitral tribunals and in the fact that disputes which are regarded as suitable for such treatment will be increasingly settled by adjudication rather than by arbitration. The two procedures have in the past been much confused. But it is now permissible, and indeed essential for clarity of thought, to distinguish sharply between them. Arbitration and adjudication are both modes of settlement whereby disputing States voluntarily submit their differences to an impartial outside agency. In both cases the parties agree in advance to abide by the award or decision. But in arbitration, even under The Hague procedure, the agency of settlement is an *ad hoc* tribunal specifically chosen by the parties for the purpose of dealing with a single controversy. The tribunal gathers evidence, hears arguments, and makes an award on the basis of respect for international law, taking into account such extralegal and political considerations as the arbitrators may think useful to achieve a settlement. In true adjudication, on the other hand, the agency of settlement is a permanent and continuous judicial body, not chosen by the parties but existing independently of them, and not weighing considerations of equity or politics but applying quite literally to the cases before it the established principles of international law. A true court proceeds from case to case, builds up precedents, and gradually creates a consistent body of case law. Arbitral tribunals, lacking continuity and corporate existence, are unable to act in this fashion.

The adjudication of international disputes is obviously impossible without the prior creation of a permanent international court to which they may be submitted. Numerous unofficial proposals were put forward in various States during the nineteenth century for the creation of an international judicial tribunal. But apparently insuperable obstacles stood in the way of the fulfillment of the vision. The principle of State equality seemed to require that all States be represented on any world court—an arrangement which would require a court of impossible size. Regional courts would have only regional utility. There were disputes, moreover, arising from differing national interpretations of certain moot points of international law. What legal principles should such a court apply? How were cases to be brought before it if it were created? What authority, if any, would such a body have to enforce its decisions?

These problems were discussed at the first Hague Conference, but without result. The Permanent Court of Arbitration there established was a court in nothing but name. They were again discussed, more fruitfully but again unsuccessfully in the final event, at the second Hague Conference of 1907. Elihu Root, Secretary of State of the United States, instructed the American delegates to work for the "development of the Hague tribunal into a permanent tribunal composed of judges who are judicial officers and nothing else, who are paid adequate salaries, who have no other occupation, and who will devote their entire time to the trial and decision of international causes by judicial methods and under a sense of judicial responsibility." This proposal met with the support of the British and Russian delegates, who likewise presented projects for a world court. A plan was drawn up for the creation of a Permanent Court of Arbitral Justice which should be a true judicial agency sitting permanently at The Hague. Unfortunately, however, no agreement could be reached regarding the number of the judges and the method of their selection. For all of the forty-four participating States to be "represented" on the court was out of the question and the minor Powers were unwilling to establish a court which might be dominated by the Great Powers. The whole scheme therefore failed, with the Conference recommending the adoption of the plan when an acceptable method of selecting the judges could be devised. A similar fate overtook the project of an international prize court which was also discussed at the second Hague Conference. An agreement was reached to set up a court to pass upon the legality of captures in naval war. The tribunal was to consist of fifteen judges, with the eight Great Powers having permanent appointees on the bench and the lesser Powers sharing the remaining seats by a process of rotation. The court was to hear appeals from national prize courts, with both States and individuals having a right of recourse to it. Thirty-three States signed the convention for its creation, but difficulties developed over the fact that much of the international law of prize is unsettled. The British Government rejected the plan for this reason, and the lesser naval Powers and the land Powers accordingly suspended further action. The London Naval Conference of 1908–1909 sought to codify the law of prize and drew up the Declaration of London. But this in turn was rejected by the House of Lords and failed of ratification. Both of these efforts to establish an international court thus failed, in one instance because of disagreement as to the method of choosing judges, in the other because of disagreement over the international law to be applied.

The first genuine international court to be fully established on a working basis was the creation of the United States and five Republics of Central America. Under the inspiration of the American State Department, the Central American Peace Conference of 1907 set up the Central American Court of Justice, consisting of five judges, one each for Costa Rica, Nicaragua, Salvador, Honduras, and Guatemala. The signatory States agreed to submit all questions to it for decision, without qualifications or reservations, unless they could be settled by negotiations. Its jurisdiction was thus "compulsory." This remarkable international agency had an even wider jurisdiction than the Supreme Court of the United States in that private citizens might bring suits against States before it. It was established for a ten-year period and went out of existence in 1917, after a decade of useful service, under somewhat peculiar circumstances. Costa Rica and Salvador had brought suit against Nicaragua, whose puppet government, supported by American marines, had negotiated the Bryan-Chamorro Treaty of 1916 with the United States. By this agreement the "Colossus of the North" was given canal rights along the San Juan River, which divides Nicaragua from Costa Rica, and also the right of fortifying Fonseca Bay, which commands the Pacific coast not only of Nicaragua, but also of Salvador and Honduras. The other States alleged that Nicaragua was legally incompetent to conclude such a treaty without their consent, since it affected their rights adversely and Nicaragua could not lawfully cede away what she did not possess. The court accepted this view and decided the suit against Nicaragua. The latter, however, with the tacit approval of the State Department at Washington, refused to abide by the decision. The other States then took the entirely reasonable view that there was nothing to be gained by maintaining a court if its members were free to ignore its judgments. They accordingly declined to renew the arrangement. What Washington had created it likewise destroyed, and this fruitful experiment thus suffered an untimely demise. The Conference on Central American Affairs at Washington in 1923 put into effect a new scheme; but this is modeled after the Hague Permanent Court of Arbitration and is not a true court in any sense.

Not until the Paris Peace Conference at the close of the Great War was it possible to create a permanent international judicial agency of wide jurisdiction. President Wilson regarded the creation of a world court as a necessary feature of the peace settlement. Article 14 of the Covenant of the League of Nations entrusted to the Council of the League the task of formulating and submitting to its members plans for the establishment of a "Permanent Court of International Justice." The court was to be competent to hear and determine any dispute submitted to it by the parties and to give advisory opinions upon any question referred to it by the Council or Assembly of the League. In accordance with this provision, the Council in 1920 appointed a commission of jurists, upon which Elihu Root served for the United States. The commission prepared a "Statute" or constitution of the proposed court, which was submitted first to the Council and then by the Council to the Assembly and the members of the League. The Statute became effective not through any action of the Council or Assembly, but through its ratification on the part of the member States. The first panel of judges was elected in September of 1921. On February 15, 1922, the judges convened at The Hague, and the ceremonies of its official establishment were performed in the Great Hall of Justice of the Peace Palace which had been erected by Andrew Carnegie for the Hague tribunal of arbitration created twenty-three years before. The same strange irony which made President Wilson a prophet without honor in his own land has made the United States, long an ardent proponent of international adjudication, one of the few States not members of the Court.[1]

The thorny problem of the selection of judges was ingeniously solved in the Statute. Eleven judges and four deputy judges were originally provided for; but the amendments of 1930 increased the number of judges to fifteen, and in February, 1936, the deputy judgeships were abolished. All had nine-year terms. Candidates for these positions were nominated by the national groups of the Hague Permanent Court of Arbitration, each group having the right to name four candidates, only two of whom might be of its own nationality. The Secretary-General of the League prepared an alphabetical list of the persons so nominated and transmitted it to the Council and Assembly of the League. These bodies, each voting independently, elected the judges by majority vote. In the event of disagreement, recourse was had to a conference of six members, three from the Council and three from the Assembly, for the purpose of submitting to their respective bodies one name for each vacant seat. If it was still impossible to reach an agreement, the judges already chosen filled vacancies from the candidates who had been voted for in the Assembly or in the Council. Large and small States alike thus had an equal voice in the selection of judges, and the dilemma of 1907 was resolved without creating a court of unwieldy size. At the first election of September, 1921, eighty-nine candidates were nominated and all places were filled by majority vote of the Council and Assembly after three days of balloting. At the second election (1930), sixty candidates were nominated.

[1] See p. 630 below.

Eleven ballots were cast by the Council and Assembly for judges and six ballots for deputy judges before an agreement was reached.[1]

The equally difficult question of the jurisdiction of the Court was solved with equal ingenuity. The commission of jurists which drafted the Statute recommended compulsory or obligatory jurisdiction with respect to the disputes mentioned in Article 13 of the League Covenant and Article 36 of the Statute, *i.e.*, disputes as to (1) the interpretation of a treaty; (2) any question of international law; (3) the existence of any fact, which if established, would constitute a breach of an international obligation; or (4) the nature or extent of the reparation to be made for the breach of an international obligation. This arrangement was rejected by the Council and the Assembly on the ground that Article 14 of the Covenant contemplated a court with voluntary jurisdiction. In general, the Court had jurisdiction only over such disputes as member States were willing to submit to it. Article 36 of the Statute, however, was transformed into an "optional clause" which member States might accept or reject as they wished. Those accepting it recognized the jurisdiction of the Court to be compulsory, without special agreement, for the four categories of disputes mentioned, provided that both parties to the dispute had adhered to the "optional clause." In other words, they agreed in advance to submit all disputes in these categories to the Court for settlement. States not accepting the clause remained free to submit, or refuse to submit, such disputes to the Court as they chose. Almost fifty States adhered to Article 36 of the Statute for varying terms of years.

The Permanent Court of International Justice represented the most important and successful effort thus far made to establish an international judicial tribunal for the adjudication of controversies between States. Its record during the seventeen years of its existence revealed it to be a body of very great value, both as a tribunal to render judgments between litigating States and as an agency to advise the Council of the League on the legal aspects of international problems. All its judgments and advisory opinions were accepted in good faith; and only rarely, as in the Austro-German customs union opinion of September 5, 1931, were its members criticized for placing their national prejudices above the impartial logic of the law. It built up a body of legal precedents of great utility for the solution of future international cases of a justiciable character. If it was not a panacea for war or a means of settling all international disputes—and assuredly it was neither—the cause lay in the fact that States do not regard all disputes as justiciable and that the

[1] Article 9 of the Statute provided, "At every election, the electors shall bear in mind that not only should all the persons appointed as members of the court possess the qualifications required, but the whole body also should represent the main forms of civilization and the principal legal systems of the world." Professor Manley O. Hudson (United States) was a judge of the Court at the time of the outbreak of the Second World War.

realm of international law is not coterminous with the realm of international politics.

* * * * *

The years between 1919 and 1939 were marked by the conclusion of more international agreements for the pacific settlement of international disputes than were negotiated during many decades prior to the Great War. Between November 11, 1918, and November 11, 1928, no less than 130 treaties of investigation, conciliation, arbitration, or adjudication were signed, exclusive of those between the U.S.S.R. and its neighbors. The great majority of these engagements were signed after 1924 and were eloquent testimony to the worldwide yearning for peace and security. The texts of these agreements fill almost 1,000 pages of a good-sized book.[1]

Regional arrangements in the Western Hemisphere paralleled these more general engagements. At the Fifth Pan-American Conference, held in 1923 at Santiago, Chile, the Gondra "Treaty to Avoid or Prevent Conflicts between American States" was signed. It authorized submission of all controversies to *ad hoc* Commissions of Inquiry and set up two permanent diplomatic committees to initiate pacific settlement. On January 5, 1929, at the Pan-American Conference on Conciliation and Arbitration in Washington, a General Convention on Inter-American Conciliation was signed, authorizing the committees to exercise conciliatory functions and permitting the Commissions to attempt conciliation as well as investigation. A supplementary General Treaty of Inter-American Arbitration (1929) outlined arbitral procedure whereby the signatories would submit "juridical" questions to arbitration by special treaty, subject to reservations of questions affecting domestic jurisdiction and third States. A Protocol of Progressive Arbitration sought to encourage the signatories to withdraw numerous other exceptions and reservations. The Argentine Antiwar Pact of October 10, 1933 (the Saavedra Lamas Treaty) condemned wars of aggression, pledged nonrecognition of territorial arrangements effected by nonpacific means, and contemplated inter-American cooperation to preserve neutrality. This complex system of conciliation and *ad hoc* arbitration, buttressed by numerous bilateral agreements, left much to be desired.

The lacunae were in part remedied at the Inter-American Conference for the Maintenance of Peace, originally proposed and opened in person by President Roosevelt at Buenos Aires on December 1, 1936. Secretary Hull attended throughout the sessions which were presided over by Señor Saavedra Lamas. The "good-neighbor" policy of the United States made possible a greater degree of good will and mutual understanding than had

---

[1] See Max Habicht's excellent compilation and analysis of *Post-war Treaties for the Pacific Settlement of International Disputes*, 1931, 1,103 pages.

hitherto been achieved in Pan-American gatherings. Prior to adjournment on December 23, delegates from all the American Republics signed no less than 69 conventions, resolutions, and recommendations providing for more intimate economic and cultural relations. A "collective security" convention pledged consultation in the event of any war or threat of war, in the Americas or elsewhere, with the object of achieving a common policy for the preservation of peace. A "declaration of solidarity" condemned territorial conquest, intervention, and forcible efforts to collect pecuniary claims and provided for consultation in the event of "any act of an unfriendly nature" toward any of the American Republics—thus, in principle, making the Monroe Doctrine a multilateral rather than a unilateral statement of policy. A separate protocol condemned all acts of intervention and provided for consultation in the event of such acts. A neutrality convention pledged discussion in the event of any conflict between the signatories in order to promote "a common and solidary attitude" among them as neutrals.

These instruments furthered friendship but did not create any new peace machinery or pledge the parties to anything beyond consultation and abstract condemnation of war, conquest, and intervention. The neutrality convention was limited to American wars. The arms and loans embargoes against belligerents which the signatories agreed to "consider" were to be subject to domestic legislation and the League Covenant. Argentina made a further reservation exempting foodstuffs and civilian raw materials from embargo and reserving freedom of action even with regard to arms exports in wars of aggression. With the exception of Brazil, all the larger Latin American States were members of the League and were unprepared to follow the United States in embargoing impartially all belligerents in future wars with no distinction between aggressors and victims of aggression. Proposals for an "American League of Nations" were without immediate result. Yet the way was paved at Buenos Aires for a large measure of inter-American collaboration which could reasonably be expected to promote the pacific settlement of controversies in the Western Hemisphere.

The verdict of time on this amazing proliferation of procedures for pacific settlement was unkind. Many peace seekers supposed that peace could be had cheaply, with no assumption of risks or responsibilities for the organization and enforcement of peace, simply by multiplying agreements and agencies for the settlement of disputes. The diplomats of appeasement in the Western democracies supposed that peace could be had by using these procedures to grant the demands of the new Caesars. Both suppositions were tragically mistaken. By 1937 the League of Nations had been reduced to a hypocritical farce and the World Court to a panel of almost idle jurists, thanks to the policies of democratic governments which professed their championship of order and law in international relations. By 1939 all the procedures of pacific settlement among the Great Powers had become empty forms. By 1941 they had become a memory. That they would ever be revived in their old guise was contrary to all reasonable probability.

Here, as elsewhere, men have ever been deceived by words without content and by forms without substance. War is seldom the result of the lack of procedures to settle differences pacifically. Its roots lie far below this thin veneer of conciliation, arbitration, and adjudication which has been spread over the Western State System in its later days. The clashes of wills which lead to war revolve about goals and purposes and great dynamic forces driving States to action which are not to be constrained within the confines of forms, written documents, and ingenious artifices. These goals, purposes, and forces (and the interests and values which lie behind them) are scarcely touched as yet by the new dispensation. The struggle for power proceeds along its accustomed channels, bending the new barriers to its ways or brushing them aside in the excitement and passion of great international crises. Until the fundamentals are altered, the new rules and principles of pacific settlement tend to resemble certain branches of classical economics in that they are addressed to hypothetical situations which never come to pass in the world of reality. The network of peace pledges prevented only such wars as would never have occurred and had no value in the great conflicts of interests and policies which were not "disputes" at all, justiciable or otherwise, but life-and-death combats for power and profits between the nation-states. Nevertheless, the threads of the net were spun. In the fabric lay the hope of an ordered and peaceful world. But the cloth was not cut to fit the wearer. The wearer refused to don the garment permanently for his own protection, preferring to relapse into the traditional bloody rags and tatters of self-help, coercion, and war.

SUGGESTED READINGS

Borchard, E. M.: *Distinction between Legal and Political Questions*, Washington, Government Printing Office, 1924.

Cory, H. M.: *Compulsory Arbitration of International Disputes*, New York, Columbia University Press, 1932.

Dunn, F. S.: *Peaceful Change*, New York, Council on Foreign Relations, 1937.

Habicht, M.: *Post-war Treaties for the Pacific Settlement of International Disputes*, Cambridge, Mass., Harvard University Press, 1931.

The Hague: *The Permanent Court of International Justice; Ten Years of International Jurisdiction*, Leyden, A. W. Sijthoff, 1932.

Hudson, M. O.: *The Permanent Court of International Justice*, New York, Macmillan, 1934.

Hull, W. I.: *The Two Hague Conferences*, Boston, Ginn, 1908.

Manning, W. R.: *Arbitration Treaties among American Nations to the Close of the Year 1910*, New York, Carnegie Endowment, 1924.

———: *Arbitration Treaties among the American Nations*, New York, Oxford, 1924.

ADJUDICATION

The Mexican Claims Commissions, 1923–1934, A. H. Feller (ed.), New York, Macmillan, 1936.

Moore, J. B.: *International Arbitrations* (5 vols.), Washington, Government Printing Office, 1898.

Morris, R. C.: *International Arbitration and Procedure*, New Haven, Yale University Press, 1911.

Ralston, J. H.: *The Law and Procedure of International Tribunals*, Stanford University, Calif., Stanford University Press, 1926.

——: *International Arbitration from Athens to Locarno*, Stanford University, Calif., Stanford University Press, 1928.

Scott, J. B. (ed.): *The Hague Court Reports* (second series, 1915–1930), N.Y., Oxford, 1931.

Wilson, G. G. (ed.): *The Hague Arbitration Cases* (to 1915), Boston, Ginn, 1915.

CHAPTER VI

THE DREAM OF WORLD UNITY

1. THE PARLIAMENT OF MAN: UTOPIA AND REALITY

These things are certain: (1) whatever may have been the case in the past, the modern world of economic and social interdependence, which represents in some respects the flowering of centuries of development, cannot forever endure the impact of frequent, large scale destruction; (2) a condition of human liberty protected by the rule of law, which is rightly regarded as a prime requisite of civilized life, cannot long prevail against either the demands of modern totalitarian warfare or the profound distress resulting from economic disorganization and human incompetence; (3) unless therefore the wisdom and wills of men can be mobilized to the exercise of control over international violence and economic depression, the twilight of this age is at hand, and the shadows ahead offer no prospect of a better one.—WILLIAM P. MADDOX, March, 1940.

THE development of international law, the evolution of diplomatic practice, and the elaboration of procedures for the settlement of disputes have all been stimulated by the quest for a warless world. Of equal significance in the building of these forms of international intercourse have been the practical exigencies of cooperation among States in dealing with common problems not always directly related to questions of war and peace. On the one hand, pacifists and idealists have theorized about the law of nations, the functions of diplomats, and the utility of arbitration and adjudication as a means of promoting peace. On the other hand, the growth of commerce, travel, and communication among States has obliged practical statesmen to face new problems of common interest to all States and to devise agencies for their solution. The forms which the members of the Western State System have created to facilitate their dealings with one another all reflect these two sources of inspiration: theory and practice, spirit and substance, ideal and reality. In international affairs, no less than in other human relations, the patterns of social action which men devise to achieve their purposes embody both Utopian aspirations and the concrete experience of the past.

Certain of the State Systems of the past developed the rudiments of international organization. The Amphictyonic Council and the various confederations of the Greek city-states were noteworthy prototypes of their modern counterparts. The State Systems of ancient China and India also had approximations to Leagues of Nations and other forms of institutionalized international cooperation. The world State of Rome and the medieval ideal of imperial unity both precluded the possibility of genuine international organization. Dante's speculations on world organization were overshadowed by the imperial ideal. His contemporary, Pierre Dubois, to be sure, was more realistic. His *De recuperatione sanctae terrae*, published in 1305, was the first clear formulation of a plan for permanent inter-state cooperation. He proposed a temporal union of the princes of Europe with a council and a court and cooperative action to rescue the Holy Land from the infidel. But it was not possible to envisage the creation of common agencies of cooperation among States until sovereign territorial units had emerged out of feudal confusion and built up through their contacts with one another a new system of independent political entities. Even after this development had taken place, the States of the Western State System were for centuries so exclusively occupied in struggling with one another for power and prestige that they had no common interests requiring institutionalized cooperation. The periodical wars to which this struggle gave rise, however, caused scholars and thinkers in many States to reflect upon the possibility of establishing international institutions to keep the peace. The result was the fabrication of a long series of theoretical and Utopian schemes to link together the States of the world into some kind of conference or league.

Two of these schemes appeared about the time that Hugo Grotius published his great treatise on international law. An obscure monk, Emeric Crucé, issued *Le nouveau Cynée* in 1623 as the first significant proposal for international organization since Dubois. Crucé's scheme contemplated the formation of a world union of States, including China, Persia, and the Indies, which should strive to promote freedom of trade among its members, foster the construction of interoceanic canals, and keep the peace through an elaborate structure of negotiation and arbitration, embodying a world assembly and a world court. The other scheme—the "Grand Design" of Henry IV—is described by the Duc de Sully in his memoirs and is attributed by him to the great French King who assumed the throne in 1593 and died by the dagger of Ravaillac in 1610. It was based upon the assumption that no State of Europe could permanently establish its ascendancy over the others and that all should therefore cooperate to keep the peace. This was to be achieved by dividing Europe into fifteen Powers which would have nothing for which to envy one another. These States would form a general council modeled after the Amphictyonic Council of the Greeks. The council would consist of four commissioners for each of the Great Powers and three for each of the lesser ones, all to be chosen for a three-year term. This body of commissioners would discuss all problems and pacify all quarrels among the nations and would be supplemented by six regional councils, from whose decision appeal could be taken to the general council. The latter would have at its disposal an international army and navy to enforce its decisions and keep the peace. Premiers Tardieu and Herriot of France made this same proposal for the League of Nations at the General Disarmament Conference of 1932. The scheme of King Henry was aimed primarily at reducing the power of the House of Hapsburg. The Tardieu proposal was aimed at preventing any forcible revision of the 1919 peace settlement by Germany, Austria, or Hungary. Both projects failed of adoption.

Toward the end of the seventeenth century the Quaker missionary, theologian, and colonizer, William Penn, propounded an even more ingenious, if less practicable, plan of international organization in his *Essay toward the Present and Future Peace of Europe* (1693). He proposed a general diet, estates, or parliament of all European princes to meet periodically for the purpose of establishing rules of international law and settling international disputes. "If any of the sovereignties that constitute the imperial States shall refuse to submit their claim or pretensions to them, or to abide and perform the judgment thereof, and seek their remedy by arms, or delay their compliance beyond the time prefixed in their resolutions, all the other sovereignties, united as one strength, shall compel the submission and performance of the sentence, with damages to the suffering party, and charges to the sovereignties that obliged their submission." Since all war, argued Penn, is waged to keep, to recover, or to conquer territory, the imperial diet can keep the peace by adjusting territorial controversies. He suggested that representation and voting strength in the international parliament be based upon national wealth: twelve units for the Holy Roman Empire, ten each for France and Spain, eight for Italy, six for England, three for Portugal, ten each for Turkey and Muscovy, etc. This scheme would have numerous advantages. Peace would be preserved, friendship among princes would be promoted, they would be enabled to marry for love instead of for reasons of State, and, not least important, "the reputation of Christianity will in some degree be recovered in the sight of infidels." This scheme, too, needless to say, failed to receive serious consideration from any of the governments of the day.

At the time of the Conference of Utrecht the learned Abbé Saint-Pierre published his *Project of Perpetual Peace* which he communicated to the French minister, Fleury. The statesman commented drily: "You have forgotten an essential article, that of dispatching missionaries to touch the hearts of princes and to persuade them to enter into your views." The good Abbé proposed an alliance of all States which should guarantee the territory of all its members, suppress revolutions, and maintain monarchs on their thrones. The alliance would oppose by force of arms any Power which should refuse to give effect to its judgments or make treaties contrary to them. Utrecht was to be designated as the City of Peace. Each State would maintain agents there who would constitute an assembly, authorized to keep the peace and to enact, by majority vote, all laws necessary and proper to give effect to its decisions and to achieve the objects of the alliance.

Jean Jacques Rousseau, vagabond philosopher of Geneva, used the Abbé's essay as the basis for his own interesting contribution to the literature of international organization. In his *Extrait du projet de paix perpetuelle de M. l' Abbé de Saint-Pierre* (1761), he came closer to an accurate analysis of the fundamental problems involved in organizing the world for peace than any of his predecessors. The imperfections of governments, he declared, are due less to their constitutions than to their foreign relations. The care which ought to be devoted to internal administration and security is withheld owing to the need of external security. Men have prevented little wars only to kindle greater ones, and the only solution is a federation of nations by which States, no less than individuals, are made subject to laws. The balance of power is at best an uneasy and unstable equilibrium. Without a community of interests among States, asserted Rousseau, there can be no stability or lasting peace. All the Powers of Europe must therefore be brought together in a solid confederation, with a common tribunal to pass laws and regulations binding upon its members. The confederation must have coercive power to enforce its decisions, and it must be able to prevent members from seceding as soon as they imagine their particular interests to be contrary to the general interest. Rousseau accordingly proposed an international agreement of five articles for the purpose of achieving "A Lasting Peace through the Federation of Europe." The first article would establish a perpetual and irrevocable alliance, working through a permanent diet or congress where all disputes would be settled by arbitration or judicial pronouncement. The second would deal with membership, finances, and officers. Each State would have one vote in the diet, the presidency of which would be rotated, and each would contribute its share to the expenses. By the third article, the federation would guarantee to all its members their territorial integrity and present form of government. Article 4 specified that any State breaking the treaty would be placed under the ban of Europe, proscribed as a public enemy, and proceeded against in arms by all the other members. By Article 5, the plenipotentiaries in the congress would have power, by a three-quarters majority, to frame common rules for the guidance of all.

In his *Principles of International Law* (1786–1789) Jeremy Bentham, who was apparently the first to use the word "international" in 1780, followed Rousseau's footsteps. He argued that war, which he defined as "mischief on the greatest scale," can be prevented by defensive alliances, general guarantees, disarmament, and the abandonment of colonial imperialism. By agreement the forces of the several nations comprising the European System are to be reduced and fixed and the distant dependencies of each State are to be emancipated. Secret diplomacy and the deeper causes of war must be eliminated, and conditions must be created appropriate to the establishment of a tribunal of peace with power to enforce its decisions on refractory States. Tariff barriers, bounties, and colonies must alike be abolished. "Mark well the contrast," declared Bentham. "All trade is in its essence advantageous—even to that party to whom it is least so. All war is in its essence ruinous; and yet the great employments of government are to treasure up occasions for war, and to put fetters on trade." Unless governments can be induced to desist from these activities, there can be no hope of peace.

Not least in the list of contributors to the Utopias of international organization was the celibate philosopher of Königsberg, Immanuel Kant. In 1795 he published his essay *Zum ewigen Frieden* ("Toward Eternal Peace") which begins, in good Kantian fashion, with the postulate that the highest of all practical problems for the human race is the establishment of a civil society administering right according to law, *i.e.*, the reconciliation of power and liberty. The external relations of States must be regulated through an international federation. "Every State, even the smallest, may thus rely for its safety and its rights, not on its own power, nor on its own judgment of right, but only on this *foedus amphictionum*— on the combined power of this league of states, and on the decision of the common will according to laws." Man is civilized but not yet moralized. No true or lasting league of nations is possible without a long process of internal improvement within States to create the proper moral atmosphere. On the basis of these observations, Kant drew up articles of perpetual peace among States. His scheme rested upon the maintenance of the independence of all States, the acceptance of the principle of nonintervention, and the gradual abolition of standing armies. His articles provided for republican constitutions for all States, world citizenship, and a federation of free States for the protection of international rights. At the close of his *Rechtslehre*, Kant likewise dwelt on the necessity of a universal union of States, voluntary in character, through which the idea of public rights among nations might become real and differences might be settled by civil process instead of by war.

Since the beginning of the nineteenth century the number of theoretical plans of international organization has multiplied manyfold. If the recent thinkers who have formulated such programs have been less distinguished than their more famous predecessors, they have been no less earnest and ingenious in the presentation of their proposals. Every general war has given rise to a rich crop of plans for perpetual peace. Those referred to above were inspired, successively, by the wars of religion, the conflicts between Louis XIV and his neighbors, the Seven Years' War, and the American and French Revolutionary Wars. The Napoleonic Wars and the Great War led to such a profuse output of schemes to keep the peace that the mere enumeration of them would require many pages. It is significant that all these schemes were directed toward the prevention of war. All of them embodied some form of international league, confederation, or alliance, operating through a representative body of delegates for the discussion of international problems and the settlement of international disputes. Almost all of them envisaged the application of international coercion against peacebreaking States. And it is equally significant that "practical" statesmen and governments, traditionally engaged in the pursuit of exclusively national objects, were uniformly uninterested in such schemes except in situations where tangible political interests could be served by organizing international support behind them.

Prior to 1815 international organization was a vision of dreamers rather than a concern of statesmen. Only when the existing European System had been all but demolished by the impact of revolutionary and Napoleonic France did States perceive the necessity of permanent institutions of cooperation to avert a recurrence of catastrophe. The victors of Leipzig and Waterloo represented triumphant reaction. They were bent upon restoring what had been destroyed and determined to preserve what had been restored. To achieve these objects they banded themselves together into a rudimentary type of organization to maintain the *status quo*, keep the peace, and suppress revolution wherever it might raise its head. Under the provisions of the final act of the Congress of Vienna, June 9, 1815, and of the second Treaty of Paris, November 20, 1815, Great Britain, Prussia, Austria, and Russia established the Quadruple Alliance which became the Quintuple Alliance in 1818 through the admission of a chastened and reactionary France. For the first time, all the Great Powers of Europe had joined forces to serve their common interests. The organization which they created functioned through periodical congresses called to deal with emergencies as they arose. At the insistence of Tsar Alexander I the structure was crowned by the Holy Alliance agreement of September 26, 1815, among Alexander, Francis of Austria, and Frederick William of Prussia. In this romantic and religious document the three Sovereigns, "in the name of the Most Holy and Indivisible Trinity," pledged themselves "to take for their sole guide the precepts of that holy religion, namely, the precepts of justice, Christian charity, and peace," to "remain united by the bonds of a true and indissoluble fraternity," to consider themselves all as "members of one and the same Christian nation," and to receive "with equal ardor and affection into this holy alliance" all other Powers subscribing to its sacred principles.

Behind this façade of mysticism there existed here the first genuine approximation to international organization in the history of the Western

State System. The organization was partial, incomplete, fragmentary, and lacking in permanent agencies—legislative, executive, or judicial. Its purposes were reactionary and ran counter to the great dynamic forces of bourgeois nationalism and constitutionalism which were destined to undo its work and bring it to ruin. Nevertheless, it was a true international organization, existing in fact and not merely in the minds of Utopian theorists, and it did function successfully for a time under the leadership of Metternich, its guiding genius. Congresses were summoned at intervals to devise means of keeping the peace and suppressing revolution. At Vienna and Aix-la-Chapelle, European political problems were discussed and rules of diplomatic precedence and procedure were drawn up. At Troppau, in 1820, Metternich proposed international intervention to put down the revolts which had broken out in Naples and Spain. At Laibach, in 1821, Austria was granted a mandate by the Powers to intervene in Italy. With its action thus sanctioned by international authority the Austrian Government sent troops to restore monarchical absolutism in Naples and Piedmont. At Verona, in 1823, France was similarly given a mandate to suppress the constitutional movement in Spain. Great Britain withdrew from the organization, however, and joined the United States in opposing any extension of its activities to the Western Hemisphere. The organization failed to act in the Greek insurrection of 1821 and had become moribund by the time of the French and Belgian revolutions of 1830. The revolutions of 1848 led to its final collapse and disappearance.

If any "lesson" is to be drawn from this unsuccessful experiment, it is that the success of such an organization is determined by the extent to which its members feel themselves bound together by common purposes which can best be served by cooperative action. In the absence of common purposes and a disposition to cooperate, the organization can achieve nothing. Its efficacy, within these limits, depends upon the degree to which cooperative action is definitely institutionalized through permanent central agencies and upon the provisions made for the peaceful and orderly modification of the *status quo*. These are the criteria which must be applied to the evaluation of all international organization. The "Holy Alliance," when tested by these criteria, was found wanting and came to a timely end.

The disappearance of the Holy Alliance was followed by the development of a habit of consultation among the Powers which came to be referred to as the "Concert of Europe." Here was no international organization, but merely a disposition on the part of States to confer with one another in international conferences at such times as their interests dictated. The Concert of Europe emerged out of the efforts of the Powers to deal with the "Eastern Question," and it functioned fairly successfully in supervising the gradual dissolution of the Ottoman Empire. The independence of Greece was recognized by the Powers, acting jointly, in 1829. The Concert was disrupted by the Crimean War but was reconstituted at Paris in 1856 and at the Congress of Berlin in 1878. The Powers likewise acted in concert in the recognition and neutralization of Belgium and in the partition of Africa and Asia among the great imperial States. But the conflicting interests and policies led to discord. In crises, when its services were most needed, it was nonexistent; for it had no permanent organs or procedures, and each State determined for itself, in each situation, whether it would cooperate or not. In 1870, when Count Beust of Austria failed in his efforts to arrange a conference to prevent the Franco-Prussian War he exclaimed, "I cannot find Europe!" Whenever the exclusively national interests of the States of Europe reasserted themselves in the face of the general interests of all States, the Concert ceased to function. And yet it represented the only approximation to institutionalized cooperation among the Powers in dealing with questions of high politics during the whole period between the dissolution of the Holy Alliance and the outbreak of the Great War in 1914.

If the members of the Western State System were not sufficiently bound together by their political interests to make possible the building of an enduring structure of international organization to serve these interests, they were nevertheless constrained by the economic and social developments of the nineteenth century to cooperate closely with one another for the protection and promotion of interests of lesser importance. This cooperation developed rapidly after the middle of the century and assumed the form of the establishment of permanent international agencies of an administrative character, usually called *public international unions*. Problems of international communication were among the first to command the attention of governments. With the growth of trade and travel, the international regulation of waterways, railroads, telegraphy, and postal service became imperative. In 1856 a number of States established the bases of the European Commission of the Danube, composed of representatives of the members, for the purpose of facilitating and regulating traffic on the great waterway of southeastern Europe. The Commission was established by international agreement as a permanent administrative agency with authority to maintain and improve the navigability of the lower Danube, to fix, collect, and apportion tolls, to enforce navigation rules, and to license tugs, lighters, and pilots. On fundamental matters of principle, the Commission acts only by the unanimous consent of its members, but on administrative questions it acts by simple majority decisions. The organization has been modified by many subsequent agreements. The supplementary International Commission for the Danube, set up by the Treaty of Versailles, cooperated with the European Commission to improve transportation facilities. Many other commissions to deal in similar fashion with other waterways have been established from time to time. The Rhine River Commission, the Congo River Commission, the Straits Commission, the Elbe River Commission, and various Chinese river commissions have functioned successfully in the same way.[1] The International Commission for Air Navigation, set up in 1922, under the Air Convention of 1919, similarly functions as an international agency for the regulation of aerial navigation.

Telegraphic communication across national frontiers likewise involves numerous problems which can be dealt with effectively only by international action. These problems were first handled through bilateral treaties between neighboring States. Austria and Prussia concluded the first of such treaties in 1850. France, Belgium, and Prussia followed suit. In 1852 most of the Continental States signed a multilateral convention to regulate telegraphic communication. In 1856, at an international conference at Paris at which twenty States were represented, the International Telegraphic Union was established as a permanent regulatory agency. A multilateral convention set forth the general principles of the new structure, and a *règlement* specified in some detail the administrative rules to be followed by the signatories and applied by the organization. A conference of diplomatic representatives was provided for to discuss common problems and amend the *règlement* by unanimous vote as necessity might require. A permanent administrative bureau was established at Berne, Switzerland, to gather and distribute information regarding telegraphic communication and to carry out the provisions of the agreement. Most of the member States maintain government monopolies of telegraphic communication. Such States as the United States, in which telegraphy is in private hands, frequently send representatives to the conferences but are not members and have no vote. In 1906 twenty-nine States sent delegates to Berlin, where another convention and *règlement* were signed establishing the International Radiotelegraphic Union, consisting of a conference of plenipotentiaries to revise the convention, an administrative conference to deal with modifications of the *règlement*, and a bureau which is identical with that of the Telegraphic Union. The second conference of this organization was held in London in 1912 and, in view of the greatest of all sea disasters in peacetime—the sinking of the liner *Titanic* in April, 1912, as a result of its collision with an iceberg in the north Atlantic—devoted much attention to wireless communication on ships. The third International Radiotelegraphic Congress was held in

---

[1] On November 14, 1936, the German Government unilaterally denounced Part XII of the Treaty of Versailles and repudiated the authority of the Rhine, Elbe, Oder, and Danube River Commissions on the ground that they were incompatible with German sovereignty. On October 27, 1940, Berlin announced the establishment of a new "United Danube Commission" to replace the former bodies and to include Germany, Italy, the U.S.S.R., Rumania, Hungary, Bulgaria, Slovakia, and Jugoslavia. France and Britain were excluded.

Washington in 1927. It was attended by representatives of seventy-nine contracting administrations who drew up a new convention and two appended sets of regulations, allocating radio wave lengths to various services by international agreement and dealing in detail with various problems of broadcasting and transmission. The fourth Congress met at Madrid in 1932.

The problems of international postal communication led to the creation in 1874 of the best-known of the public international unions—the Universal Postal Union. In 1817, France and the Netherlands signed the first bilateral postal convention. Other treaties followed, but each State sought to place the burden of postal charges on the other. Rates were high and uncertain; and there was no uniformity of national regulations regarding charges, routes, weights, registry, etc. On August 4, 1862, Montgomery Blair, Postmaster-General of the United States, invited other postal administrations to take remedial action. "Many embarrassments to foreign correspondence," he wrote, "exist in this, and probably in other postal departments, which can be remedied only by international concert of action. . . . Without entering into details, it is evident that the international adjustment of a common basis for direct correspondence, and for intermediate land and ocean transit, and for an international registry system, and for the exchange of printed matter, is clearly of the first importance to the commercial and social intercourse between this and other nations." A meeting was held in Paris in May, 1863. No definite action was taken, but thirty-one regulatory articles were agreed upon and submitted to the governments represented. Many difficulties remained, however. The Austro-German Postal Union of 1850 was a model of successful cooperation; and in 1868 Herr Stephan, Director-general of Posts of the North German Confederation, proposed the organization of a universal postal union, embracing all civilized States. The Franco-Prussian War interrupted the negotiations, but a few years later the government of Switzerland, at the suggestion of the German, Belgian, and Dutch Governments, invited the Powers to send delegates to a conference at Berne. In September, 1874, representatives of twenty-two States assembled and began discussion of various projects and suggestions. Within a few weeks a convention and a *règlement* were drawn up and the General Postal Union (later renamed the Universal Postal Union) was created.

This remarkably successful organization is based upon the principle that all the member States form a single postal territory for the reciprocal exchange of mail. Uniform rates for foreign correspondence are fixed and charges are normally borne by the State of origin. Transit charges on mail matter passing through a State are based on total net weight and mileage. Detailed regulations deal with registered articles, return receipts, prepayment, reply coupons, exemptions from postage, prohibitions on sending certain articles through the mails, etc. Under the original arrangements a congress of plenipotentiaries, to meet every five years, was given authority to amend the convention or the *règlement*, and questions of technical detail were to be dealt with by a periodical conference of administrators. An international bureau was set up at Berne to collect, publish, and distribute information on postal questions, to issue a journal, and to act as an international clearinghouse for the settlement of accounts. The bureau also circulates proposals for changes in the convention or the *règlement*, which may be made by any administration during the intervals between the congresses and conferences, provided that two other administrations concur. Votes on such proposals are taken by the bureau. Sixteen of the thirty-nine articles of the convention can be amended only by unanimity and the rest by majority vote. Every State, colony, and territory in the world, with the exception of Northern Rhodesia, Nigeria, Afghanistan, and a few small islands, now belong to the union, though many of these are grouped together for purposes of voting in the congresses. The principle of State equality is departed from by giving additional votes to colonial postal administrations. Great Britain thus has seven votes, France four, Japan, the United States, Portugal, and the Netherlands three each, and Italy two. The expenses of maintaining the bureau are apportioned among the member States on the basis of area, railway mileage, and volume of postal traffic. States in Class I pay 25 units, those in Class II, 20 units, those in Class III, 15, and so on down to Class VII, the members of which pay only 1 unit.

In practice the conference has ceased to exist, and all the work of the organization is done by the congress and the bureau. At the periodical congresses, decisions are really arrived at by majority vote. Members may refuse to sign or ratify proposed amendments; but since the practical disadvantages of withdrawal are so great that small comfort can be derived from abstract rights of independence and sovereignty, this is a theoretical rather than an actual danger. The cooperating postal administrations frequently put proposed changes into operation without waiting for formal ratification on the part of the political authorities entrusted with treaty making. The congresses, of which the ninth was held in London in 1929, have always functioned through discussion and compromise and have shown a willingness to make exceptions to general rules in special cases. In 1906 Persia, for example, requested the right to levy charges on incoming mail as well as outgoing mail, contrary to the general principles of the union. The Persian postal authorities, it appeared, derived very little revenue from outgoing mail but were put to great expense to distribute by camel caravan the large quantities of Bibles sent into the country by Christian missionary societies. Persia was consequently granted the right to tax all incoming printed matter. The Universal Postal Union has kept postal rates throughout the world at a minimum level and has made possible what could never have been achieved by national action: cheap and rapid postal communication between all parts of the globe under the supervision of a permanent international agency capable of securing uniform regulations and of dealing effectively with all new problems as they arise.

Problems of health, sanitation, commerce, finance, and humanitarian reform have led to the creation of public international unions no less significant in their respective fields than those dealing with international communication. These organizations are far too numerous to be described here individually. Reinsch, in his book of 1911 entitled *Public International Unions*, listed forty-five such organizations, of which over half had permanent administrative bureaus or commissions. The term should not be applied, however, to international arrangements for cooperation which do not set up permanent central organs, for these differ in no particular from ordinary multilateral conventions. The *Handbook of International Organizations* published by the League of Nations listed some two dozen associations of States, outside of the League itself and its subsidiary agencies, which were true international organizations. All of these were established since 1850, nine of them since 1914. They covered a wide range of interests. Brief mention may be made of a few of the more important.

The International Bureau of Weights and Measures (the Metric Union) was established in 1875 for the purpose of maintaining at the common expense of the parties an international body of scientific experts at Paris, working under the direction of an international commission and a general conference, who should prepare and maintain standard prototypes of the meter, the centimeter, the millimeter, the kilometer, the gram, the milligram, the kilogram, and all units of the metric system. These are decimal multiples or fractions of the meter, originally considered one ten-millionth part of the earth's meridian quadrant through Paris. The international prototypes, prepared with the utmost care and kept under constant conditions of temperature and humidity, are constantly being compared with national standards, which are thus verified and made as accurate and uniform as possible. The Bureau of Trade Marks, Copyrights, and Patents makes possible the international registration at Berne of these industrial and literary property rights—a procedure which entitles them to legal protection in all the contracting States. The International Union for the Publication of Customs Tariffs publishes at the common expense "the customs tariffs of the various States of the globe and the modifications that may, in future, be made in these tariffs" (Article II of the convention of July 5, 1890). The International Institute of Agriculture, established in Rome in 1904, collects, publishes, and distributes information relating to the production and movements of crops and livestock, studies agricultural cooperation, credit, and insurance, and recommends measures for the protection of the economic interests of farmers. The Geneva conventions of 1864 and 1868 established the International Red Cross for the amelioration of the condition of the wounded in wartime. The Union for the Suppression of the African Slave Trade (1890), the Union for the Regulation of the African Liquor Traffic (1890), and the International Opium Commission (1909) were likewise created to deal with social and humanitarian problems.

The broader significance of the public international unions has given rise to considerable difference of opinion among students of these organizations. They are sometimes described as the forerunners of a new era in international relations in which all international problems will be considered by experts through permanent international institutions. By others, they are dismissed as convenient administrative devices to deal with technical problems which have little or no bearing upon the forces and frictions of world politics. Since the ultimate place of international organizations in the Western State System is not yet fixed, differing evaluations of what has already been achieved are inevitable. It may be suggested, however, that the international unions exhibit interesting departures from traditional attitudes and behavior patterns in a number of respects. In almost every instance the member States, by agreement, have in effect surrendered a portion of their sovereignty and independence and have transferred power to an international body over what was once a "domestic question." In the practical operation of the unions, moreover, the obstructive principles of State equality and action by unanimity have been largely abandoned and decisions are reached by majority vote of the member States. These concessions are prerequisites to successful international collaboration. The structure of the unions is such that broad questions of principle are dealt with by diplomatic representatives meeting in periodical congresses, and problems of administrative detail are dealt with by the actual administrators meeting in conferences or working through the permanent bureaus. The national administrations are geared together into an effective international administration. Problems which were formerly discussed and quarreled about by diplomats in terms of national honor, prestige, and sovereignty are removed from the sphere of *politics* and made problems of *administration*, to be considered by administrative experts in terms of efficiency, economy, and the progressive adaptation of means to ends. Organized social intelligence is applied to the fulfillment of human needs. An anarchic and individualistic system of relationships in which each State pursues its own interests, with resulting inconvenience and loss to all, is replaced by organization and planning through which all cooperate to serve the common interests.

It is clear, however, that this form of collaboration is not adaptable to all problems of international concern. The great sources of tension and conflict among States, the great problems of power, prestige, territory, armaments, and markets cannot readily be transferred from the political sphere to the administrative sphere so long as national attitudes toward these things remain what they have been in the past. The public international unions have functioned successfully in dealing with matters of no particular interest to patriots or politicians. States are quite prepared to regard questions of postal service, weights and measures, sanitation, and telegraphy as matters of international concern which they can safely and advantageously submit to international regulation. But they are not yet prepared to deal in the same fashion with questions of armaments, colonies, or economic opportunities in "backward" areas; and they are not at all prepared to submit to international control their decisions regarding tariffs, immigration, security, or territorial claims. The problems involving "national honor" and "vital interests" are those which States are unwilling to submit to arbitration or adjudication. They are the same problems which States are reluctant to submit to agencies of international organization and administration.

2. THE BIRTH OF THE LEAGUE OF NATIONS

. . . It would be a master stroke if those Great Powers honestly bent on peace would form a league of peace, not only to keep the peace among themselves, but to prevent, by force, if necessary, its being broken by others. The supreme difficulty in connection with developing the peace work of The Hague arises from the lack of any executive power, of any police to enforce the decrees of the courts. In any community of any size the authority of the courts rests upon actual or potential force; on the existence of a police, or on the knowledge that the able-bodied men of the country are both ready and willing to see that the decrees of judicial and legislative bodies are put into effect. In new and wild communities where there is violence, an honest man must protect himself; and until other means of securing his safety are devised, it is both foolish and wicked to persuade him to surrender his arms while the men who are dangerous to the community retain theirs. He should not renounce the right to protect himself by his own efforts until the community is so organized that it can effectively relieve the individual of the duty of putting down violence. So it is with nations. Each nation must keep well prepared to defend itself until the establishment of some form of international police power, competent and willing to prevent violence as between nations. As things are now, such power to command peace throughout the world could best be assured by some combination between those great nations which sincerely desire peace and have no thought themselves of committing aggressions. The combination might at first be only to secure peace within certain definite limits and certain definite conditions; but the ruler or statesman who should bring about such a combination would have earned his place in history for all time and his title to the gratitude of all mankind.—THEODORE ROOSEVELT, *International Peace*, an address before the Nobel Prize Committee, delivered at Oslo, Norway, May 5, 1910.

The establishment of the League of Nations at the Paris Peace Conference of 1919 represented the most ambitious effort ever made to extend the method of international organization into the sphere of political relations among States. Between the collapse of the Holy Alliance and the outbreak of the Great War, enormous numbers of people throughout the Western world organized themselves in their private capacities to promote cooperation across national frontiers in the pursuit of a great variety of economic, scientific, religious, and aesthetic interests. At the same time, States organized public institutions and agencies of cooperation among governments to deal with problems of transportation, communication, commerce, finance, health, sanitation, social questions, and the like. But during this period no effort was made to set up an international organization of States to deal with broader political questions. The Concert of Europe functioned fitfully, and the Hague Conferences of 1899 and 1907 offered vain promise of peace on earth, good will to men. No permanent procedures of political collaboration were set up, however, until the world-shattering cataclysm of 1914–1918 brought disaster to all nations alike and led to a world-wide demand for a league of States to keep the peace. This demand, personified in Woodrow Wilson and buttressed by the desire of the victors to create an international federation to maintain the new *status quo*, led to the framing of the Covenant of the League of Nations.

The League of Nations was founded by America's war President. If it was not his invention (and the process of political invention is at best ill understood), it was at any rate the project upon which he, more than any of the contemporary statesmen, had set his heart. He played a large part in writing into the Covenant the ideas of others and the experience of the past. He insisted emphatically, moreover, upon the creation of the League at the Peace Conference and upon the incorporation of the Covenant into the peace treaties. Had it not been for his active leadership, it is quite possible that the League would not have been established. In a broader sense, however, the League was the work of the long line of Utopian theorists whose work has been reviewed above. It was a synthesis of the ideas of many people in many lands, and it embodied in a single structure all the past experience of the States of the world in establishing and maintaining international organizations. That experience was supplemented by the efforts of the Allied Governments during the war to work out methods of joint action for the purpose of coordinating their activities in the fields of shipping, food supplies, munitions, and military affairs.[1] The League was not, then, the creation of a single man or of a

[1] Not until the spring of 1918, when the great German offensives threatened to break through the western front, did the Allied Governments finally agree to appoint a single commander-in-chief of their armies in the person of Marshal Foch. It was only in the face of this supreme emergency that the Allied Maritime Transport Council, the Munitions Council, the Food Council, and the other coordinating agencies began to function effectively. Here, as in the public international unions, success was attained when the problems

single generation of men, but the culmination of a long process of practical and theoretical preparation for the building of an enduring structure of cooperation among States.

Popular interest in the possibilities of a League began to manifest itself in the United States shortly after the outbreak of the great conflict and grew rapidly during the period of American neutrality. A "League to Enforce Peace" was established by a group of prominent public leaders, including many outstanding figures in the Republican party, headed by former President William Howard Taft. The organization held a conference in Independence Hall, Philadelphia, in June of 1915, and adopted a four-point program which received wide publicity. The program called for the submission of all justiciable international disputes to arbitration, the submission of all other disputes to a council of conciliation, the application of economic and military force by all States against any State resorting to war without submitting its disputes to pacific settlement, and the convocation of periodical congresses to codify international law. This program was a synthesis of the Hague arbitration system and the Bryan "cooling-off" treaties, with a new element of sanctions added to them. At the end of May, 1916, the organization held another conference in Washington "to devise and determine upon measures for giving effect" to these proposals. This meeting was widely attended by leaders in all walks of life. Mr. Taft, as president of the League, presided. Alton B. Parker, Democratic candidate for the presidency of the United States in 1908, was vice president of the organization, with Edward Filene, Hamilton Holt, and Theodore Marburg serving as vice chairmen. The speakers included the presidents of the United States Chamber of Commerce, of the American Federation of Labor, and of Harvard University, as well as Senator Henry Cabot Lodge, Secretary of War Baker, and President Wilson himself. The speeches, in retrospect, were not without a certain ironic significance, for Senator Lodge exhibited much more enthusiasm for a league of nations than did President Wilson. The Senator declared that "the limits of voluntary arbitration have been reached" and that international force must be placed behind peace.

I know the difficulties which arise when we speak of anything which seems to involve an alliance. But I do not believe that when Washington warned us against entangling alliances he meant for one moment that we should not join with the other civilized nations of the world if a method could be found to diminish war and encourage peace.[1]

President Wilson, though more restrained, definitely committed himself to the major purposes of the organization.

---

at stake were dealt with directly by administrators as administrative problems, instead of by diplomats as political problems. See Arthur Salter, *Allied Shipping Control*, 1921, *passim*.

[1] Full text in "League to Enforce Peace," *Enforced Peace*, 1916, *passim*.

"We are participants, whether we would or not, in the life of the world," asserted the American President. The peace of the world "must henceforth depend upon a new and more wholesome diplomacy. Only when the great nations of the world have reached some sort of agreement as to what they hold to be fundamental to their common interest, and as to some feasible method of acting in concert when any nation or group of nations seeks to disturb those fundamental things, can we feel that civilization is at last in a way of justifying its existence and claiming to be finally established." Right must prevail over selfish aggression. Co-operation and understanding must be achieved on the basis of certain fundamental principles. We believe, first, that "every people has a right to choose the sovereignty under which they shall live"; second, "that the small States of the world have a right to enjoy the same respect for their sovereignty and for their territorial integrity that the great and powerful nations expect and insist upon"; third, "that the world has a right to be free from every disturbance of its peace that has its origin in aggression and disregard of the rights of peoples and nations. . . . So sincerely do we believe in these things that I am sure that I speak the mind and wish of the people of America when I say that the United States is willing to become a partner in any feasible association of nations formed in order to realize these objects and make them secure against violation."[1]

The activities of the League to Enforce Peace were supplemented by those of a number of other organizations, both in the United States and abroad. The "League of Free Nations Association" was formed in New York as an organization of more liberal-minded people than those in the League to Enforce Peace. Both organizations cooperated, however, and finally endorsed the League of Nations Covenant as achieving their purposes. After the war the League of Free Nations Association transformed itself into the New York Foreign Policy Association. In England, the Fabian Society and the League of Nations Society both played active roles in organizing peace sentiment behind the project of a league, with George Bernard Shaw and James Bryce taking the initiative in the respective groups. In France a League of Nations Society was likewise formed under the leadership of Léon Bourgeois. The French group emphasized the necessity of military sanctions and defense against outside attack. A corresponding German group was led by Erzberger, and similar organizations appeared in the neutral countries.

On January 22, 1917, President Wilson addressed the American Senate on a "World League for Peace."[2]

---

[1] *Ibid.*

[2] See Congressional Record, Senate, January 22, 1917; International Conciliation, Official Documents Looking toward Peace, Series II, 111, February, 1917.

In every discussion of the peace that must end this war it is taken for granted that that peace must be followed by some definite concert of power, which will make it virtually impossible that any such catastrophe should ever overwhelm us again. Every lover of mankind, every sane and thoughtful man, must take that for granted. . . . It is inconceivable that the people of the United States should play no part in that great enterprise. To take part in such a service will be the opportunity for which they have sought to prepare themselves by the very principles and purposes of their polity and the approved practices of their Government, ever since the days when they set up as a new nation in the high and honorable hope that it might in all that it was and did show mankind the way of liberty. They cannot, in honor, withhold the service to which they are now about to be challenged. They do not wish to withhold it. But they owe it to themselves and to the other nations of the world to state the conditions under which they will feel free to render it. That service is nothing less than this—to add their authority and their power to the authority and force of other nations to guarantee peace and justice throughout the world.

In resounding Wilsonian rhetoric, the American Chief Executive proposed that the United States take the initiative in organizing the world for peace. A durable peace, he argued, must be a "peace without victory."

Victory would mean peace forced upon the loser, a victor's terms imposed upon the vanquished. It would be accepted in humiliation, under duress, at an intolerable sacrifice, and would leave a sting, a resentment, a bitter memory, upon which terms of peace would rest, not permanently, but only as upon quicksand. Only a peace between equals can last; only a peace the very principle of which is equality and a common participation in a common benefit. The right state of mind, the right feeling between nations, is as necessary for a lasting peace as is the just settlement of vexed questions of territory or of racial and national allegiance. . . . I am proposing, as it were, that the nations should with one accord adopt the doctrine of President Monroe as the doctrine of the world: That no nation should seek to extend its policy over any other nation or people, but that every people should be left free to determine its own policy, its own way of development, unhindered, unthreatened, unafraid, the little along with the great and powerful.

I am proposing that all nations henceforth avoid entangling alliances which would draw them into competition of power, catch them in a net of intrigue and selfish rivalry, and disturb their own affairs with influences intruded from without. There is no entangling alliance in a concert of power. When all unite to act in the same sense and with the same purpose, all act in the common interest and are free to live their own lives under a common protection.

I am proposing government by the consent of the governed; that freedom of the seas which in international conference after conference representatives of the United States have urged with the eloquence of those who are the convinced disciples of liberty; and that moderation of armaments which makes of armies and navies a power for order merely, not an instrument of aggression and selfish violence.

These are American principles, American policies. We can stand for no others. And they are also the principles and policies of forward-looking men and women everywhere, of every modern nation, of every enlightened community. They are the principles of mankind and must prevail.

Less than a week after these brave words were uttered, the German Government announced the resumption of unrestricted submarine warfare and President Wilson responded by severing diplomatic relations between Washington and Berlin. On April 6, 1917, the American Congress, on the President's recommendation, declared war against Germany. In his war message, President Wilson again insisted that peace in the future could never be maintained except by a world-wide partnership of democratic nations. "It must be a league of honor, a partnership of opinion." Wilson's facility at phrase making made him an invaluable asset to the Allied cause and the chief interpreter of Allied war aims to a weary and blood-sickened world. Throughout the summer and fall of 1917 he clarified his views regarding the purposes of the "war to end war" and the struggle to "make the world safe for democracy" in a series of public addresses. Early in January, 1918, he received two pleas for a concise restatement of war aims which would have popular propagandist value. One was from Lord Balfour, British Foreign Secretary, who was worried over the restlessness of the British trade unions. The other was from Edgar Sisson, representative in Russia of the United States Committee on Public Information, who was trying to feed peace propaganda into Germany and to inspire the exhausted peasants and workers of Russia to continue the hopeless battle against the Central Powers. In response to these appeals, President Wilson, on January 8, 1918, issued his famous program of fourteen points, the last of which declared, "A general association of nations must be formed under specific covenants for the purpose of affording mutual guarantees of political independence and territorial integrity to great and small States alike." In the following September, Wilson asserted "the constitution of that league of nations and the clear definition of its objects must be a part, in a sense the most essential part, of the peace settlement itself." On November 11, 1918, came the armistice and peace, not without victory, but with an overwhelming Allied triumph; and in January of 1919 the great Peace Conference opened in Paris.

By this time numerous plans for a league, both official and unofficial, had been put forward. In March, 1918, a committee of the British Foreign Office, with Lord Phillimore as its chairman, had prepared a draft convention for the creation of a league. Three months later, Colonel House, President Wilson's confidential adviser, prepared another draft on the basis of Wilson's own ideas. In July of 1918 Wilson typed out his own first draft. In December General Smuts of South Africa proposed a plan containing the germs of the Council and the Mandate System. At the same time Lord Robert Cecil prepared a new draft on the basis of the Phillimore report. Wilson prepared his second draft on January 10, 1919, and his third draft ten days later to submit to the Peace Conference. Meanwhile the British delegation to the conference had combined the Cecil and

Smuts drafts into an official British draft of January 20, 1919. Since the third Wilson draft and the British draft diverged at a number of points, they were submitted to Cecil Hurst, legal adviser of the British delegation, and to David Hunter Miller of the American delegation, for revision. The result was the composite Hurst-Miller draft of February 3, 1919, which was used as a basis for discussion by the League of Nations Commission of the Peace Conference.

Wilson insisted, in the face of the indifference or opposition of Clemenceau and Lloyd George, that the conference should give its attention to the League project before taking up territorial and political settlements. Following the adoption of the British resolutions of January 25, appointing a commission to work out the details of the constitutions and functions of the proposed organization, Wilson declared that the League is "the central object of our meeting. Settlements may be temporary, but the actions of the nations in the interests of peace and justice must be permanent. We can set up permanent processes. We may not be able to set up permanent decisions." A commission of nineteen was chosen, with the small Powers in a minority of one. Wilson assumed the chairmanship of the commission, and the work was rapidly pushed forward by the combined efforts of the British and American representatives. On February 14 the tentative draft of the Covenant was presented to the conference as a whole for its consideration. "A living thing is born," asserted the American President. "While it is elastic, while it is general in its terms, it is definite in the one thing we are called upon to make definite. It is a guarantee of peace. It is a definite guarantee by word against aggression. Armed force is in the background in this program, but it *is* in the background, and if the moral force of the world will not suffice, the physical force of the world shall. But that is the last resort, because this is intended as a constitution of peace, not as a league of war. . . . (But) it is not in contemplation that this should be merely a league to secure the peace of the world. It is a league that can be used for cooperation in any international matter."

A few subsequent changes were made in the Covenant; and on April 28, 1919, the revised document was accepted unanimously at a plenary session of the conference. The other terms of the victors' peace were gradually hammered out, and on June 28 the German delegates were called into the Hall of Mirrors in the great Château of Louis XIV and compelled to attach their signatures to the Treaty of Versailles. The first twenty-six articles of the Treaty contained the Covenant of the League of Nations. The Covenant was likewise incorporated into the Treaty of St. Germain with Austria of September 10, 1919; the Treaty of Neuilly with Bulgaria, November 27, 1919; the Treaty of Trianon with Hungary, June 4, 1920; and the Treaty of Sèvres with Turkey, August 10, 1920. The last-named agreement was repudiated by the Turkish Nationalists. The four other treaties were ratified. On January 10, 1920, the League of Nations came officially into existence with the deposit at the Quai d'Orsay of eighteen ratifications of the Treaty of Versailles. The preamble to the Covenant read as follows:

> The HIGH CONTRACTING PARTIES,
> In order to promote international cooperation, and to achieve international peace and security
>   by the acceptance of obligations not to resort to war,
>   by the prescription of open, just, and honorable relations between nations,
>   by the firm establishment of the understandings of international law as the actual rule of conduct among Governments,
>   and by the maintenance of justice and a scrupulous respect for all treaty obligations in the dealings of organized peoples with one another,
> Agree to this Covenant of the League of Nations.

The first four words of this statement of purposes and of means thereto made it clear that the League was a creation and agency of the States ratifying the Covenant. Emphasis was placed upon *international* cooperation and *international* peace and security. All domestic questions were thus excluded from the scope of action of the League, but in the sphere of international relations the language employed was broad enough to cover the whole field of contacts among States. The "obligations not to resort to war" have been suggested in the preceding chapter. The phrase "open, just, and honorable relations between nations" was reminiscent of the first of the fourteen points: "open covenants, openly arrived at." Article 18 of the Covenant provided for the registration and publication of all treaties concluded by member States. The proceedings of the League itself were public and are published in its *Official Journal*. The "understandings of international law" suggested the origins of international jurisprudence in custom and contract. "Respect for all treaty obligations" implied the perpetuation of the peace settlements of 1919, though Article 19 of the Covenant made provision for the reconsideration of treaties which had become inapplicable. As for the articles of the Covenant itself, the first seven dealt with membership and structure, 8 to 21 with the League as an agency to keep the peace, and 22 to 25 with the League as an agency of international cooperation.

If the League be defined functionally, it was in the first place an agency for the enforcement of certain provisions contained in the peace treaties and in other supplementary agreements following the Great War. In this capacity the League was intended to preserve and maintain the *status quo* established by the Peace Conference. It was entrusted with certain administrative and supervisory functions usually exercised by the victors themselves at the close of a war but here conferred upon an international agency. Among these were the protection of national minorities, the supervision of the Free City of Danzig, the administration of the Saar valley, and the operation of the Mandate System. In the second place, the League was a means of promoting international cooperation in dealing with problems of health, social questions, finances, transportation, communication, and the like. In this capacity it served to integrate and coordinate the activities of the existing public international unions. In the third place, the League was an agency for the prevention of war and the pacific settlement of disputes. All threats to peace were within its competence; and all controversies among its members were, in theory at least, submitted to the procedures of arbitration, adjudication, or conciliation provided for in the Covenant.

Article 1 of the Covenant provided for membership and withdrawal. The Covenant, as incorporated in the Treaty of Versailles, was signed by 31 of the 32 States named in the annex. The thirty-second, China, became an original member by signing the Treaty of St. Germain. Of these 32 signatories, 3 failed to ratify the treaties: Ecuador, the Hejaz, and the United States. By January 10, 1920, 19 ratifications had been deposited at the Quai d'Orsay; and by April of 1920 a total of 42 States had become original members of the League, comprising the 29 Allied and Associated Powers which ratified the peace treaties (including Canada, Australia, South Africa, New Zealand, and India along with the 24 fully sovereign Allied belligerents) and the 13 neutrals invited in the annex to accede to the Covenant. Mexico, Costa Rica, and the Dominican Republic were not mentioned in the list of neutrals, because their governments were not at the time recognized by all the Allied and Associated Powers. India and the self-governing Dominions of the British Empire were given full status as members, though by a curious error of phraseology in the annex Great Britain itself was referred to as the "British Empire," with the Dominions and India listed separately below. Twenty-one other States were subsequently admitted to membership.[1] Only six States of the world never applied for membership: Saudi Arabia, Yemen, Oman, Nepal, Manchukuo, and the United States of America.

The structure of the League can be described in terms of its major organs: the Assembly, the Council, and the Secretariat. The Assembly was the representative and deliberative organ of the League, consisting of all its members, with each entitled to one vote in accordance with the ancient principle of State equality. The Assembly met annually every September in Geneva and held several special sessions. Each member

[1] In 1920 Albania, Finland, Bulgaria, Austria, Costa Rica, and Luxemburg were elected as members; in 1922 Estonia, Latvia, and Lithuania were admitted; in 1923 Hungary, Ethiopia, and the Irish Free State; in 1924 the Dominican Republic; in 1926 Germany; in 1931 Mexico; in 1932 Turkey and Iraq; in 1934 Afghanistan, Ecuador, and the U.S.S.R.; and in 1937 Egypt.

State was entitled to have not more than three delegates and several alternates at the Assembly meetings. The delegates from each State collectively cast the vote to which the State was entitled, in accordance with their instructions. Delegates were ordinarily chosen, like other diplomatic representatives, by the executive authorities of the State, though in many Assemblies prime ministers and foreign ministers themselves acted as delegates. A number of States maintained permanent delegations at Geneva. The Assembly elected its own presiding officers and made its own rules in harmony with the provisions of the Covenant. Its agenda was prepared in advance by the Secretary-General and was subject to modification by the Assembly itself. Its organization resembled that of a legislative body in that it followed the usual principles of parliamentary procedure and operated through committees. It maintained six regular standing committees—on constitutional and legal questions, on technical organizations, on reduction of armaments, on budgetary matters, on social and humanitarian questions, and on political questions—and was free to appoint special committees for particular purposes.

The functions of the Assembly were very broad, even if somewhat vague. Article 3 of the Covenant declared that it "may deal at its meetings with any matter within the sphere of action of the League or affecting the peace of the world." In practice, it exercised three general types of powers: electoral, constituent, and deliberative. In the exercise of its electoral functions, it elected new members to the League by a two-thirds vote, as occasion arose; it elected annually three of the nine nonpermanent members of the Council by a majority vote; and, in conjunction with the Council, it elected every nine years by majority vote the fifteen judges of the Permanent Court of International Justice. It also approved by majority vote the Council's nominations for the post of Secretary-General. As a constituent body, it amended the Covenant in accordance with the provisions of Article 26. In this capacity, it acted by majority vote, but amendments had to be approved unanimously by the Council and were subject to the ratifications of the member States. As a deliberative body, the Assembly considered general political, economic, and technical questions of international interest, advised the reconsideration of inapplicable treaties under Article 19 (it never exercised this power), supervised the work of the Council and of the technical organizations, and prepared the annual budget of the League. The budget usually totaled about $6,000,000, which, it was pointed out by pacifists, was about one-fifth the cost of a single modern battleship. The budget was prepared by the Secretariat, subject to revision by the Assembly, and was divided into three major parts, one for the Secretariat and special organizations, one for the International Labor Office, and one for the Permanent Court of International Justice. The 1935 budget totaled $6,128,000 (gold) and the

1936 budget about $5,655,000[1]. The Assembly provided for the apportionment of these expenses among the members in accordance with a scale (1937–1939) totaling 923 units, on which Great Britain paid 108 units, France 80, the Soviet Union 94, Italy 60, India 49, China 42, Spain 40, and so on, down to one unit each for such small States as Albania, Haiti, Liberia, Luxemburg, etc. These important functions made the Assembly the dominant organ of the League, though because of its nature and size it could not act so swiftly and expeditiously as the Council.

The Council of the League was designed to be a small body on which the Great Powers should have permanent seats, with the other seats rotated among the lesser Powers. It was originally contemplated that it would consist of five permanent seats to be occupied by the United States, Great Britain, France, Italy, and Japan and four nonpermanent seats, assigned temporarily in 1920 to Belgium, Brazil, Spain, and Greece, with their successors to be chosen periodically by the Assembly. The refusal of the United States to join the League reduced the ratio of Great Powers to small Powers to 4:4. In 1922, two additional nonpermanent seats were added, making a Council of ten members. The admission of Germany to the League created a "Council crisis" which necessitated further reorganization. The German Government agreed to enter the League only on condition of being received on a basis of complete equality and of receiving a permanent seat on the Council. Brazil, Spain, and Poland presented demands for permanent seats at the same time, which were resisted by Germany and other States. Though Germany could be admitted to the League by a two-thirds vote of the Assembly, it could secure a permanent seat on the Council only by unanimous vote of that body. An impasse was created which the special session of the Assembly in March, 1926, was unable to resolve. On March 18 the Council set up a special committee to study the problem. In accordance with its recommendations, subsequently approved by the Council and the Assembly, the Council was enlarged by establishing nine nonpermanent seats, three to be filled annually for three-year terms by the Assembly. By a two-thirds vote the Assembly may declare nonpermanent members reeligible, may fix rules for the election of nonpermanent members, and may, if it chooses, elect *in toto* an entirely new group of nonpermanent members. Under the terms of this compromise, Germany was admitted to a perma-

[1] 28,279,901 Swiss francs, apportioned as follows: Secretariat and special organizations, 14,591,635; International Labor Office, 6,699,450; Permanent Court, 2,321,000: Nansen international office for refugees, 270,000; buildings at Geneva, 2,334,000; pensions, 1,544,-153; Permanent Central Opium Board, 119,463; and Assyrians of Iraq, 400,000. The 1937 budget (expenditures) totaled 29,184,128 Swiss francs. Owing to the devaluation of Swiss currency, income was set at 21,284,822 *gold* francs, net, representing a sum equal to expenditures, reduced by 20 per cent and by the distribution of a 1935 surplus. Expenditures for 1938 were 31,268,810 Swiss francs, and, for 1939, 32,234,012 Swiss francs. The last League budget (for 1940) was fixed at 21,615,484 Swiss francs.

nent seat on the Council. Poland was satisfied to be declared reeligible to a nonpermanent seat for another three-year term. Brazil and Spain, however, gave notice of their intention to withdraw from the League. Spain later reconsidered her intention, but Brazil ceased to be a member in 1928. In 1933 a tenth nonpermanent seat was provisionally created for three years and was assigned to Portugal (1933–1936). In 1936, two nonpermanent seats were created for the ensuing three years and assigned to Latvia and China (1936–1939). By 1939 the Council consisted of three permanent members, Britain, France and the U.S.S.R., and eleven nonpermanent members.[1]

The functions of the Council were as broad as those of the Assembly. It met four times a year, or oftener as occasion required. Like the larger body, it could deal "with any matter within the sphere of action of the League or affecting the peace of the world" (Article 4). Its powers could be expanded by treaty agreements among States. The minorities treaties conferred special powers on the Council in regard to the supervision of the enforcement of their obligations. The Treaty of Lausanne of 1923, between the Allied Powers and Turkey, similarly gave the Council jurisdiction over the Mosul dispute. The Council was free to refuse to assume such special duties but it never did so. In practice, the most important function of the Council was the settlement of international disputes. It shared this function with the Assembly, but the latter seldom intervened. The Council also had executive, administrative, and supervisory functions in connection with Danzig, the Saar valley, the Mandate System, etc. Under Articles 10 to 16 of the Covenant, it had authority to mobilize the sanctions of the League against a Covenant-breaking State. The Council likewise carried out recommendations of the Assembly, prepared plans for disarmament, nominated the Secretary-General, and approved his appointments to subordinate positions in the Secretariat. All other League functions were shared concurrently by the Council and the Assembly.

It should be noted that, although the Council and the Assembly were both, in theory, expected to reach decisions only by unanimity, many

[1] In 1926 Poland, Chile, and Rumania were elected for three years; Colombia, the Netherlands, and China for two years; and Belgium, Salvador, and Czechoslovakia for one year. In each subsequent year the three retiring members were replaced by three new members for three-year terms, as follows: 1927—Canada, Cuba, Finland; 1928—Spain, Persia, Venezuela; 1929—Poland, Jugoslavia, Peru; 1930—Irish Free State, Norway, Guatemala; 1931—Spain, China, Panama; 1932—Poland, Czechoslovakia, Mexico; 1933—Denmark, Argentina, Australia, with Portugal as an additional member for three years; 1934—Spain, Chile, Turkey; 1935—Poland, Rumania, Ecuador; 1936—Bolivia, New Zealand, Sweden, with Latvia and China as additional members for three years; 1937—Iran, Peru, Belgium; 1938—Jugoslavia, Greece, and the Dominican Republic; 1939—South Africa, Bolivia, Finland, with Egypt and China as additional members for three years. In 1940 the League ceased to function.

practical departures from this rule took place. Article 5 declared that on matters of procedure, as distinct from "decisions," action could be taken by majority vote. In practice, the moral pressure brought to bear on small minorities was frequently sufficient to compel acquiescence in action which technically was by unanimity, but in fact was by majority vote. In the Assembly, moreover, a clear distinction was made between recommendations and decisions. In the former case, action was by a simple majority. Most of the acts of the Assembly took the form of recommendations or *voeux* (wishes). There is likewise the well-established rule of law that no one shall be judge in his own case, which meant that in the consideration of international disputes the litigating parties were not permitted to vote. The Covenant itself made additional qualifications to the unanimity principle. Nonmembers were admitted to the League by a two-thirds vote of the Assembly. Amendments to the Covenant were passed by a majority vote of the States in the Assembly. Judges of the Permanent Court were elected by a majority vote. It could be argued that all League actions were in any case only recommendations, since the League could not bind any State without its consent and all League acts were legally subject to ratification by the members before they became binding obligations. In view of these developments, the rule of unanimity, which in the past constituted a serious obstacle to effective international cooperation, became of theoretical rather than of practical importance.

The Secretariat was the permanent administrative organ of the League and consisted of an international civil service of almost 600 expert officials and subordinates residing at Geneva. It bore the same relation to the League as a whole as do the bureaus of the public international unions to their respective organizations. The Secretariat was headed by a Secretary-General, appointed by the Council with the approval of the Assembly. Sir Eric Drummond of Great Britain held this office from 1920 to 1933 and was largely responsible for the establishment and organization of the Secretariat. He was succeeded by M. Joseph Avenol of France. The Secretary-General appointed his subordinates with the approval of the Council. His immediate subordinates were two Deputy Secretaries-General and two under-secretaries. One of each of these higher posts was held by a national of each of the Great Powers in the League. The body of the Secretariat was divided into sections, headed by directors. The officials of the Secretariat were not recruited by civil service examinations but were chosen by the Secretary-General on the basis of professional competence, with a proper regard for the distribution of posts among the various States. The officials were in no sense governmental representatives, however, but were responsible only to the Secretariat itself to which they made a declaration of loyalty. They were charged with the compilation and publication of information on all the complex problems which came before the League for consideration and with the secretarial work of the Council and Assembly, which included the preparation of agendas, the translation of speeches into French and English (the two official languages of the League), and the preparation and publication of the Assembly and Council minutes in the *Official Journal*.

There were organized around the League a number of technical agencies, commissions, and advisory committees. Two of these—the Permanent Advisory Commission on Armaments and the Mandates Commission—were provided for in the Covenant (Articles 9 and 22). The others were established by the Council as bodies of technical experts to supply information and give advice on the various complex problems falling within the sphere of the League's competence. These organizations worked in close cooperation with the corresponding sections of the Secretariat.

Four great technical organizations were set up in this fashion. The Economic and Financial Organization was composed of an economic committee and a finance committee, each consisting of twelve to fifteen experts, to which were added a fiscal committee and a committee of statistical experts. Under the general direction of the Council, the Economic and Financial Organization prepared reports on subjects submitted to it for examination. If it decided that there was a prospect of effective international cooperation with respect to a particular subject, it prepared a program and recommended that the Council call an international conference to draft a convention dealing with the problem. Such conventions as emerged from this procedure were, of course, subject to ratification by the participating governments before they went into effect.

The Organization for Communications and Transit consisted of a periodical general conference of technical representatives chosen by the members of the League and an advisory and technical committee on communications and transit, made up of experts chosen by the general conference and entrusted with the duties of carrying out conference decisions and preparing for future conferences. Three general conferences were held—at Barcelona in 1921 and at Geneva in 1923 and 1927. Six conventions were drawn up by the conferences, dealing with freedom of transit, navigable waterways, railways, ports, hydraulic power, and the international transmission of electric power, in addition to a number of conventions drawn up at special conferences on particular problems.

The Health organization consisted of the health committee of twenty members and the advisory council, which was identical with the permanent committee of the International Office of Public Health at Paris. The health committee drew up resolutions on international health problems on the basis of the data prepared by the health section and transmitted them to the advisory committee for consideration. The latter made recommendations to the Council. The organization was supplemented by numerous committees, joint commissions, subcommittees, subcommissions, and the like, dealing with health insurance, maternity, smallpox, tuberculosis, sleeping sickness, malaria, preventive medicine, etc. The public-health activities of the member States were thus coordinated and a basis laid for the conclusion of international conventions dealing with health problems. The Health Organization maintained an Eastern Bureau at Singapore and an International Leprosy Center at Rio de Janeiro. Its work as a whole was financed by the Rockefeller Foundation.

In 1922 the Council set up the International Committee on Intellectual Cooperation to coordinate the work of such bodies as the International Research Council, the International Academic Union, the Institute of International Law, etc. In 1924 the Council accepted an offer of the French Government to establish in Paris an International Institute of Intellectual Cooperation to act as the secretariat of the committee. The Institute, the Committee, various special committees, and forty-two national committees, coupled with the International Educational Cinematographic Institute, were later linked together into an Intellectual Cooperation Organization, comparable with the three mentioned above. Each of these organizations was served by the appropriate section of the Secretariat of the League.

In addition to the technical organizations, numerous permanent or temporary committees were set up from time to time by the Council, often on the basis of Assembly resolutions, to deal with special problems. The Committee of Experts for the Progressive Codification of International Law and the Preparatory Committee for the Disarmament Conference are good examples. The social and humanitarian work of the League also required the creation of the necessary organizations of experts. The first Assembly established the Advisory Commission on the Traffic in Opium and Other Dangerous Drugs, which was instrumental in securing more effective enforcement of the Hague Opium Convention of 1912 and organized international conferences in 1924 and 1925 at which a new opium convention (1925) was drawn up, to regulate the production and distribution of opium on a world-wide scale. In 1921 a conference on the so-called "white slave traffic" drew up a final act, later embodied in the International Convention for the Suppression of the Traffic in Women and Children. The Council created an Advisory Committee on the Traffic in Women and Children, reorganized in 1925 as the Advisory Commission for the Protection and Welfare of Children and Young People. Various other organizations were established to deal with the traffic in obscene publications, slavery and the slave trade, and the repatriation of war prisoners and refugees.

The judicial agency of the League—the Permanent Court of International Justice—has been referred to in the preceding chapter.[1] This tribunal rendered decisions and "orders" in such cases as were submitted to it by member States in accordance with the provisions of the Statute, and it also gave advisory opinions to the Council on the legal aspects of such questions as the Council wished to submit to it. The Assembly might also request advisory opinions but never in fact did so. The Court met annually at The Hague and consisted of fifteen judges elected by majority vote of the Council and Assembly. Nine judges constituted a quorum. All the judges were strictly international officials and in no sense representative of their State, though this principle was departed from in the provision that in every case the parties were entitled to have a judge of their own nationality on the bench. When no judge or deputy judge of the required nationality was a member of the Court, a "national" judge could be added to the body for the purpose of the case. The judges held office for nine years, and vacancies were filled by election for the unexpired term. The justices were expected to devote their entire time to the work of the Court and were forbidden to hold any political or administrative position, to engage in any other profession, or to act as agent or counsel in any case. The judges received 45,000 Dutch florins ($30,000) annually, plus traveling expenses and liberal allowances. The Court chose its own president for a three-year term and drew up its own rules of procedure. Each party in cases before it was represented by an agent; and the proceedings were both oral and written, with witnesses summoned, but no use of a jury. Decisions and opinions were reached by majority vote and were always publicly printed with a statement of the reasoning upon which the judgment was based. Judges who differed with the majority were free to publish dissenting opinions. Special chambers heard cases relating to communications and transit and to the International Labor Organization under Parts XII and XIII of the Treaty of Versailles. There was little difference in procedure as between decisions and advisory opinions. The latter were not legally binding but were usually accepted as a basis of settlement by the Council.

The International Labor Organization had its headquarters at Geneva and, though distinct from the League proper, was an integral part of the whole League system. Its creation was due to an effort on the part of the Paris Peace Conference to satisfy the demands of organized labor and to provide a mechanism for dealing internationally with labor problems which would present the appearance of fulfilling the pledges made to labor by the various belligerent governments during the war period. Article 23 of the Covenant of the League defined the general purposes of

[1] On the jurisdiction and method of election of the judges, see pp. 192-193 above.

the organization. Its constitution was embodied in Part XIII of the Treaty of Versailles. It could be amended by a two-thirds vote of the Conference, subject to ratification by all States on the League Council and three-fourths of the members of the League. The organization consisted of three parts. The General Conference consisted of four delegates from each State (two representing the participating governments, one chosen by the governments to speak for the most representative employers' organization in their respective countries, and one chosen to speak for the most representative workers' organization). The General Conference assembled annually at Geneva. The delegates voted individually and deliberated upon the items of the agenda prepared by the Governing Body. They drew up, by a two-thirds majority, recommendations or draft conventions on labor legislation which were supposed to be submitted within a year to the national legislatures for ratification. The Governing Body, which met every three months, consisted of 32 members chosen for a three-year term. Sixteen were appointed by the member governments, 8 of these representing the States of chief industrial importance (Great Britain, France, Germany, Italy, Japan, India, the Soviet Union, and the United States) and the remaining 8 being picked by the other government delegates at the Conference. The other 16 members of the Governing Body were chosen half by the employers' delegates at the Conference and half by the workers' delegates. The Governing Body prepared the agendas of the conferences, appointed the director of the International Labor Office, and supervised its work. The International Labor Office consisted of some 350 experts appointed by the director and was the secretariat of the organization. It gathered and published information on labor legislation and assisted the Governing Body in preparing for the Conferences. M. Albert Thomas was its director from its establishment until his death in April, 1932. Harold Butler was named his successor, and was succeeded in turn by John G. Winant. The expenses of the International Labor Organization were met out of the League Budget.

The primary purpose of the I.L.O. was to promote uniformity of labor legislation throughout the world. National governments are frequently reluctant to enact adequate protective legislation for wage earners because the States granting such protection are alleged to be placed at a competitive disadvantage in world markets in comparison with States where employers are free to exploit labor without legislative hindrances. The problem involved can be dealt with adequately only by international action. It cannot be said, however, that the International Labor Organization achieved very much in this direction. Draft conventions and recommendations were binding only when ratified by the member States. More than fifty such proposals were made; but many did not receive general ratification and some were not even submitted to the national legislatures.[1] The methods provided for ensuring the execution of such conventions as were ratified did not prevent violations. The Governing Body could give publicity to violations and it might ask the Secretary-General of the League to appoint commissions of inquiry to investigate alleged violations. If one of the parties was dissatisfied with the report of such a commission, appeal could be taken to the Permanent Court which had authority to render a final decision. Economic sanctions against a violating State could be authorized by the commissions or by the Court, but they were never applied. The organization provided an international forum for the discussion of labor legislation; it prepared the way for the formulation of international standards of labor legislation and constituted a useful agency for the collection and publication of labor statistics; it promoted the crystallization of attitudes and policies on the part of governments, employers' associations, and labor unions in the member States. But its actions were purely advisory and its achievements were scarcely proportionate to the time and energy devoted to its work.

Finally, mention may be made of the Bank for International Settlements. This was not a League organization, but its creation marked the beginning of an international coordination of the activities of central banks in various States. The Bank was created in 1930 as part of the Young Plan for the "final" settlement of Germany's reparations obligations under the Treaty of Versailles. Its primary function was that of acting as a trustee and agent for the creditor governments in the collection and allocation of indemnity payments. The Bank was located at Basle, Switzerland, and had a stock of 100 million dollars, underwritten by the central banks of Great Britain, France, Italy, Germany, and Belgium, a consortium of Japanese banks, and a syndicate of private banks in the United States. The American Government refused to permit the Federal Reserve Banks to participate, and the United States remained outside of the institution, as it was outside of the League of Nations and the Permanent Court. The Bank was controlled by a board of sixteen directors, made up of the govenors of the central banks and persons appointed by them. The suspension of all payments of reparations and interallied debts in June of 1931, under the Hoover moratorium, and the subsequent cancellation of the reparations obligations diminished the importance of the organization. On the other hand, it had already demonstrated its utility as an agency for international cooperation among central banks, and it continued to function in this capacity until 1939.

---

[1] By January 1, 1936, 49 conventions had been adopted by the Conference, of which only 1 (on equality of treatment for national and foreign workers in accident compensation, 1925) had secured as many as 34 ratifications. None of the conventions adopted during the preceding three years had secured more than 2 ratifications.

There thus came into existence after the Great War an elaborately integrated structure of international organization far in advance of anything which existed prior to 1914. This structure reflected an enormous multiplication of the common interests and purposes of States. It was without precedent or parallel in earlier State Systems. It represented a culmination of the forms which have been evolved in the Western State System for the regulation of the relations among States and the promotion of international cooperation. It provided an opportunity for the international control of a large number of technical, economic, and social problems through international conventions based upon the advice of professional specialists and through permanent institutionalized cooperation among the administrative officials of the nation-states. It likewise provided an opportunity for the constant discussion of international political problems and the pacific settlement of disputes among governments. It constituted an embryonic international government which might have developed into a true world federation if the members of the Western State System had been capable of integrating their particular national interests into world-wide international interests.

3. THE DEATH OF THE LEAGUE

The world is a stupendous machine, composed of innumerable parts, each of which being a free agent, has a volition and action of its own; and on this ground arises the difficulty of assuring success in any enterprise depending on the volition of numerous agents. We may set the machine in motion, and dispose every wheel to one certain end; but when it depends on the volition of any one wheel, and the correspondent action of every wheel, the result is uncertain.—NICCOLÒ MACHIAVELLI, *On Fortune, Chance*, etc.

Either the peace-makers of 1919, who seemed almost all powerful at the time, were aiming at goals that were inherently inaccessible, or they were mistaken in their choice of roads, or they were betrayed by their successors. Which was it? . . . The present plight of Europe is due less to the excessive ambitions of the men of 1919 than to the excessive debility of their successors. It would be fair to lay the blame on the former only if they could be made responsible for not foreseeing the feebleness of the latter.—WILLIAM E. RAPPARD, *The Quest for Peace*, 1940.

The States that have undertaken to preserve order in the world have demonstrated that they are completely incapable of doing so. They have no power and if they had it they would probably be too cowardly to use it. They have declared that they will not tolerate the use of force. When force was used in Ethiopia they followed along with muffled drums. The Ethiopian conflict was decided not by the League of Nations but by bombing squadrons.—PAUL JOSEPH GÖBBELS, July 5, 1936.

The task of safeguarding the interests of each by protecting the security of all was beyond the capacity, or at least beyond the will, of the statesmen who were responsible for the crucial decisions and indecisions in foreign policy during the years of the League's decay. The League and its associated agencies never became symbols of human brotherhood eliciting love and loyalty from large numbers of people in all lands and thereby developing the prestige and authority required by an incipient world government. The League remained a method of cooperation among sovereign governments. The subjects and citizens of governments remained patriots devoted only to national interests. In some States, they were bewitched by visions of tribal conquest; in others, frightened into passivity; in still others, befuddled and betrayed. Nowhere were they united in the effective service of common purposes. The governments of the democratic Great Powers, moreover, upon which the future of the League depended, fell into the hands of those who were utterly lacking in the loyalty, wisdom, and courage through which alone the League could survive by fulfilling the dreams of its founders. The League's white palace in Ariana Park, by the shores of Geneva's Lac Leman, therefore became a sepulcher of what later (and sadder and wiser) generations may well regard as the last best hope of Western mankind.

The outward symptoms of the League's demise are easily described. The rate of withdrawal of States from membership reflected the progress of a fatal disease. The first State to give the required two-year notice of resignation was Costa Rica, January 1, 1925. The reasons were financial. The result was unimportant. But Brazil gave notice on June 12, 1926, for reasons of "prestige." Japan followed (March 27, 1933) and then Germany (October 14, 1933) for reasons of *Realpolitik*. Paraguay did likewise (February 23, 1935) and then, after the destruction of one League member by another, Guatemala (May 15, 1936), Honduras (June 20, 1936), Nicaragua (June 26, 1936), Salvador (August 10, 1937), Italy (December 11, 1937), Chile (May 13, 1938), Venezuela (July 12, 1938), Peru (April 8, 1939), Albania (April 13, 1939), Spain (May 8, 1939), and Rumania (July 10, 1940).

By the close of 1938, the 62 States that had at one time or another been League members were reduced to 49. Two members, Ethiopia and Austria, had been destroyed and another, Czechoslovakia, half destroyed. In 1939–1940, more League members were extinguished by the aggressors: Czechoslovakia, Albania, Poland, Denmark, Norway, the Netherlands, Belgium, Luxemburg, France, Estonia, Latvia, Lithuania, Rumania, etc. The Soviet Union was "expelled." At the end, only 1 Great Power was left in the League, Great Britain, and only 31 scattered and insecure smaller States. On May 16, 1940, M. Avenol dismissed most of the employees of the Secretariat, and on June 25 he discharged the remainder. He himself resigned. A few "nonpolitical" officials found refuge in Princeton University over which Woodrow Wilson had once presided. A remnant of the I.L.O. fled to Toronto. The judges of the World Court were scattered to the winds. By summer's end of 1940 the whole League system had become a memory. Even the memory seemed all but lost in a panic flight before the horsemen of the Apocalypse.

This decease was obviously part of the death of the world. The larger tragedy will be dealt with elsewhere in these pages. Yet that tragedy was in many of its acts and scenes played at Geneva. Its *leitmotiv* was the refusal of the Anglo-French appeasers to use the League to enforce peace by protecting the weak against the strong and by preventing and punishing international lawbreaking. The League, being but a method of concerted action, could not act against aggressions when its leading actors were determined first to evade their own obligations and second to use the League as a vehicle for appeasing the aggressors. The League did not perish because of any defects within its organization or any shortcomings in its administration of economic and social problems. Its structure was well suited to its original purpose. Its humanitarian and technical work was admirably administered. It did not perish because of failure to perform duties connected with the execution of the peace treaties. The settlement of 1919 broke down, and carried the League to ruin with it, because the United States assumed no responsibility and Britain and France evaded their responsibilities. The League perished because its members failed to use it to compel the orderly settlement of disputes and to prevent lawless aggression. This bitter tale is too long to be retold here in its entirety. Yet a few episodes must be recounted to suggest the Nemesis which condemned the League, and much else, to death.

Early League efforts to cope with aggressors were not reassuring. When Italy bombarded and occupied the Greek island of Corfu in 1923 and Greece appealed to the League, the Italian delegate, Salandra, declared that Article 16 of the Covenant[1] could not be applied, since Italy

---

[1] 16. 1. Should any Member of the League resort to war in disregard of its covenants under Articles 12, 13 or 15, it shall *ipso facto* be deemed to have committed an act of war against all other Members of the League, which hereby undertake immediately to subject it to the severance of all trade or financial relations, the prohibition of all intercourse between their nationals and the nationals of the covenant-breaking State, and the prevention of all financial, commercial or personal intercourse between the nationals of the covenant-breaking State and the nationals of any other State, whether a Member of the League or not.

2. It shall be the duty of the Council in such case to recommend to the several Governments concerned what effective military, naval or air force the Members of the League shall severally contribute to the armed forces to be used to protect the covenants of the League.

3. The Members of the League agree, further, that they will mutually support one another in the financial and economic measures which are taken under this Article, in order to minimise the loss and inconvenience resulting from the above measures, and that they will mutually support one another in resisting any special measures aimed at one of their number by the covenant-breaking State, and that they will take the necessary steps to afford passage through their territory to the forces of any of the Members of the League

did not intend to commit an act of war. The League Council permitted the Conference of Ambassadors to settle the dispute on terms entirely favorable to Italy. In dealing with small States the League Powers were more resolute and more successful. A dispute between Sweden and Finland in 1920 over the Aaland Islands was resolved without violence, as was the dispute between Poland and Germany in 1921 over Upper Silesia. The Greek-Bulgar border clash of 1925 was effectively dealt with by a Council "stop-fight" resolution and a local enquiry, followed by a settlement whereby Athens paid Sofia an indemnity of $210,000 for having violated Bulgarian territory. When Peruvian troops in September, 1932, occupied the Colombian port of Leticia on the Amazon, the Council was able with the diplomatic support of the United States to induce the parties to refrain from hostilities and to bring about the eventual evacuation of the seized area. League efforts to deal with the Gran Chaco war (1928–1935) between Bolivia and Paraguay had no result save Paraguay's withdrawal from the League, thanks largely to inept meddling by the United States and complete lack of coordination between Pan-American peace machinery and that of the League. No sanctions were imposed in this instance, but the League members imposed an arms embargo against the belligerents. On January 16, 1935, following Paraguay's rejection of League peace proposals, the Assembly recommended that the embargo against Bolivia be lifted. This action had no visible effect in preventing Paraguay from winning the war or in influencing the terms of peace.

In their first great test in dealing with aggression by a Great Power, the League members failed to restrain the lawbreaker and protect his victim. Following Japanese occupation of central Manchuria on September 18, 1931, China invoked the Covenant, calling attention by stages to Articles 10, 11, 15, and 16.[1] Sir John Simon, then British Foreign Minis-

---

which are co-operating to protect the covenants of the League.

4. Any Member of the League which has violated any covenant of the League may be declared to be no longer a Member of the League by a vote of the Council concurred in by the Representatives of all the other Members of the League represented thereon.

[1] 10. The Members of the League undertake to respect and preserve as against external aggression the territorial integrity and existing political independence of all Members of the League. In case of any such aggression or in case of any threat or danger of such aggression the Council shall advise upon the means by which this obligation shall be fulfilled.

11. 1. Any war or threat of war, whether immediately affecting any of the Members of the League or not, is hereby declared a matter of concern to the whole League, and the League shall take any action that may be deemed wise and effectual to safeguard the peace of nations. In case any such emergency should arise the Secretary-General shall on the request of any Member of the League forthwith summon a meeting of the Council.

2. It is also declared to be the friendly right of each Member of the League to bring to the attention of the Assembly or of the Council any circumstance whatever affecting international relations which threatens to disturb international peace or the good understanding between nations upon which peace depends.

12. 1. The Members of the League agree that if there should arise between them any dispute likely to lead to a rupture they will submit the matter either to arbitration *or judi-*

ter, was determined to thwart any effective action by the League or by the United States against Japan. In this he was completely successful. A Council resolution of September 21, 1931, calling upon the disputants to withdraw their troops was ignored by Tokio. As the fighting spread, the United States, for the first time and the last, authorized a representative (Prentiss B. Gilbert) to sit with the Council in invoking the Pact of

cial settlement or to enquiry by the Council and they agree in no case to resort to war until three months after the award by the arbitrators *or the judicial decision*[1] or the report by the Council.

2. In any case under this Article, the award of the arbitrators *or the judicial decision* shall be made within a reasonable time, and the report of the Council shall be made within six months after the submission of the dispute.

13. 1. The Members of the League agree that whenever any dispute shall arise between them which they recognise to be suitable for submission to arbitration *or judicial settlement*, and which cannot be satisfactorily settled by diplomacy, they will submit the whole subject-matter to arbitration *or judicial settlement*.

2. Disputes as to the interpretation of a treaty, as to any question of international law, as to the existence of any fact which, if established, would constitute a breach of any international obligation, or as to the extent and nature of the reparation to be made for any such breach, are declared to be among those which are generally suitable for submission to arbitration *or judicial settlement*.

3. *For the consideration of any such dispute, the court to which the case is referred shall be the Permanent Court of International Justice, established in accordance with Article 14, or any tribunal agreed on by the parties to the dispute or stipulated in any convention existing between them.*

4. The Members of the League agree that they will carry out in full good faith any award *or decision* that may be rendered, and that they will not resort to war against a Member of the League which complies therewith. In the event of any failure to carry out such an award *or decision*, the Council shall propose what steps should be taken to give effect thereto.

14. The Council shall formulate and submit to the Members of the League for adoption plans for the establishment of a Permanent Court of International Justice. The Court shall be competent to hear and determine any dispute of an international character which the parties thereto submit to it. The Court may also give an advisory opinion upon any dispute or question referred to it by the Council or by the Assembly.

15. 1. If there should arise between Members of the League any dispute likely to lead to a rupture, which is not submitted to arbitration *or judicial settlement* in accordance with Article 13, the Members of the League agree that they will submit the matter to the Council. Any party to the dispute may effect such submission by giving notice of the existence of the dispute to the Secretary-General, who will make all necessary arrangements for a full investigation and consideration thereof.

2. For this purpose the parties to the dispute will communicate to the Secretary-General, as promptly as possible, statements of their case with all the relevant facts and papers, and the Council may forthwith direct the publication thereof.

3. The Council shall endeavour to effect a settlement of the dispute and, if such efforts are successful, a statement shall be made public giving such facts and explanations regarding the dispute and the terms of settlement thereof as the Council may deem appropriate.

4. If the dispute is not thus settled, the Council either unanimously or by a majority vote shall make and publish a report containing a statement of the facts of the dispute and the recommendations which are deemed just and proper in regard thereto.

5. Any Member of the League represented on the Council may make public a state-

[1] The amendments printed in italics relating to these articles came into force on September 26, 1924, in accordance with Article 26 of the Covenant.

Paris. On October 24 the Council called on Japan to withdraw its troops by November 16. By this date Japanese forces were fighting their way into northern Manchuria. On December 10 the Council appointed a commission of five members, headed by Lord Lytton, to study the situation. When Japan attacked Shanghai, China appealed to the Assembly, which adopted a resolution (March 4, 1932) calling for Japanese evacuation of Shanghai and another (March 11) reiterating the Stimson Doctrine. Tokio did indeed quit Shanghai under the armistice of May 5 but continued to hold Manchuria—now transmuted into "Manchukuo" under puppet-regent Henry Pu-Yi, whom Japan formally recognized by the signature of a

---

ment of the facts of the dispute and of its conclusions regarding the same.

6. If a report by the Council is unanimously agreed to by the Members thereof other than the Representatives of one or more of the parties to the dispute, the Members of the League agree that they will not go to war with any party to the dispute which complies with the recommendations of the report.

7. If the Council fails to reach a report which is unanimously agreed to by the members thereof, other than the Representatives of one or more of the parties to the dispute, the Members of the League reserve to themselves the right to take such action as they shall consider necessary for the maintenance of right and justice.

8. If the dispute between the parties is claimed by one of them, and is found by the Council, to arise out of a matter which by international law is solely within the domestic jurisdiction of that party, the Council shall so report, and shall make no recommendation as to its settlement.

9. The Council may in any case under this Article refer the dispute to the Assembly. The dispute shall be so referred at the request of either party to the dispute provided that such request be made within fourteen days after the submission of the dispute to the Council.

10. In any case referred to the Assembly, all the provisions of this Article and of Article 12 relating to the action and powers of the Council shall apply to the action and powers of the Assembly, provided that a report made by the Assembly, if concurred in by the Representatives of those Members of the League represented on the Council and of a majority of the other Members of the League, exclusive in each case of the Representatives of the parties to the dispute, shall have the same force as a report by the Council concurred in by all the members thereof other than the Representatives of one or more of the parties to the dispute.

17. 1. In the event of a dispute between a Member of the League and a State which is not a Member of the League, or between States not Members of the League, the State or States not Members of the League shall be invited to accept the obligations of membership in the League for the purposes of such dispute, upon such conditions as the Council may deem just. If such invitation is accepted, the provisions of Articles 12 to 16 inclusive shall be applied with such modifications as may be deemed necessary by the Council.

2. Upon such invitation being given the Council shall immediately institute an enquiry into the circumstances of the dispute and recommend such action as may seem best and most effectual in the circumstances.

3. If a State so invited shall refuse to accept the obligations of membership in the League for the purposes of such dispute, and shall resort to war against a Member of the League, the provisions of Article 16 shall be applicable as against the State taking such action.

4. If both parties to the dispute when so invited refuse to accept the obligations of membership in the League for the purposes of such dispute, the Council may take such measures and make such recommendations as will prevent hostilities and will result in the settlement of the dispute.

treaty of protectorate on September 15, 1932. After a leisurely visit to the Far East the Lytton Commission issued a report of 100,000 words on October 3, 1932, recommending—much too late—a reasonable compromise. On February 24, 1933, the Assembly adopted a resolution condemning Japan and accepting these recommendations. Tokio rejected them and left Geneva. The other League Powers did nothing apart from refusing to recognize Manchukuo.

Italians and Germans dreaming of empire were not slow to grasp the lesson of these events. In Europe the paralysis of the Western Powers (and therefore of the League) first manifested itself in the aftermath of the breakdown of the League of Nations Disarmament Conference. When the German Government repudiated the military clauses of Versailles and introduced conscription on March 16, 1935, London and Paris were content to take refuge in a long but wholly innocuous resolution of the League Council (April 17, 1935) condemning Germany, threatening in the event of further treaty breaking to "call into play all appropriate measures on the part of the members of the League," and appointing a committee to define "the economic and financial measures which might be applied, should, in the future, a State, whether a member of the League of Nations or not, endanger peace by unilateral repudiation of its international obligations." When Germany on March 7, 1936, repudiated Locarno and began remilitarizing the Rhineland, the Western Powers avoided any counteraction save another resolution (March 19, 1936) of the League Council, meeting in London, whereby it was discovered that Germany had "committed a breach of Article 43 of the Treaty of Versailles" and the Secretary-General was instructed so to inform the signatories of the Locarno Treaty—who were already well aware of the fact. Subsequent German moves of rearmament and aggression produced no echo at Geneva, since London and Paris preferred to act (or not to act) outside of the League.

Fascist designs upon Ethiopia put the League Powers to their crucial test. Here as before they were found wanting, despite the imposition for the first time, and the last, of feeble sanctions against the aggressor. This gesture was hypocrisy, for the responsible leaders of France and Britain had agreed not to offer effective opposition to the Duce's ambitions. They assumed that Italy could be won as an ally against the Reich by tacit support of Mussolini's African dream. They discovered too late that such tactics made Italy an ally of the Reich against the Western Powers— for the modern Caesars, like those of old, respect strength and despise weakness. The almost unanimous demand of the British electorate for a firm policy of support of the League and resistance to aggression was demonstrated in the "National Peace Ballot" conducted by the League of Nations Union in 1934–1935. This sentiment caused Stanley Baldwin and his fellow Tories, who stood for election on the slogan "Our Word Is Our Bond!" to go through the motions of sanctions. This maneuver was successful. In the polling of November 14, 1935, the Government won 431 out of 615 seats in the Commons. It then proceded to break its word in an ultimately successful effort to betray Ethiopia and the Covenant.

The role of the lesser members of the League in this sordid sequence of events was that of a flock of sheep deceived by jackals in sheeps' clothing. French Foreign Minister Pierre Laval was bent upon buying Italian "friendship" at any cost. He therefore opposed every effort at Geneva to act upon Ethiopia's original appeal of December 13, 1934. Eight days previously Ethiopian and Italian forces had clashed at Ual Ual in the Ogaden desert, well within the Ethiopian frontier. In fear of invasion, Haile Selassie, Emperor of Ethiopia, Negus Negusti (King of Kings), Chosen of God and Conquering Lion of the Tribe of Judah, instructed the ministers of his dusky medieval realm to invoke Article 11 of the Covenant on January 3, 1935. But Laval met Mussolini in Rome. On January 7 they signed a series of complex agreements. The Duce agreed to "consult" on the defense of Austria and to "concert" in the event of German repudiation of disarmament obligations. In "final" settlement of Italian claims on France, he accepted 2,500 shares in the Jibuti-Addis Ababa railway, 309 square miles of desert in French Somaliland, and 44,000 square miles of desert south of Libya. Laval, despite his subsequent denials, secretly agreed to look the other way when Mussolini should attempt the conquest of Ethiopia. Rome informed London of the bargain early in January. Downing Street appointed a Foreign Office Commission headed by Sir John Maffey to make recommendations. On June 18, 1935, it recommended that Britain should not oppose Italian designs on Ethiopia but should on the contrary "seize the occasion to obtain, if possible, rectifications of the frontiers of British Somaliland, Kenya, and the Sudan."

Under these circumstances (unknown at the time to all save the "insiders"), any effort to organize collective security against the aggressor was foredoomed. Through the spring and summer of 1935, while Italian troops, planes, tanks, and poison gas poured through the Suez Canal in preparation for the blow to come, Pierre Laval and Sir Samuel Hoare obstructed all Ethiopian efforts at Geneva to initiate League action. A Council resolution of May 25 dealt only with the arbitration of the Ual Ual incident. When the arbitral commission, appointed under the Italian-Ethiopian treaty of 1928 and consisting of Count Luigi Aldrovandi-Marescotti, Signor Raffaele Montagna, Professor Albert de La Pradelle, and Professor Pitman B. Potter, was deadlocked because of Italian objections to any examination of the question of title to Ual Ual, the Council (August 3) instructed it not to discuss frontier questions. The Commission finally selected Nicolas Politis as a fifth member and handed down an "award" on September 3 holding that neither Ethiopia nor Italy was responsible for the original clash at Ual Ual. Mussolini thus gave away his pretext. But he was resolved to invade Ethiopia without any pretext. The responsible leaders of Britain and France were resolved to connive in his plans.

The most they were disposed to do was to threaten feeble penalties for the benefit of the British electorate and neutral opinion in the event that Mussolini should resort to war. Meanwhile, they sought to deter him from doing so by offering him control of Ethiopia without war. The Western Powers, which were bulwarks of the League and had solemnly pledged themselves to protect the weak against the lawless, offered Ethiopia not protection but a choice between assassination and suicide. Anthony Eden went to Rome on June 24 to offer an "exchange" of territories whereby Ethiopia would cede land to Italy and Britain would make small cessions to Ethiopia. Mussolini rejected it. While the invaders gathered in Eritrea and Italian Somaliland, France, Britain, and other States forbade exports of arms to Ethiopia. The United States offered Haile Selassie "moral support" and promptly passed the "Neutrality" Act of August 31, 1935, barring arms to Ethiopia (and to Italy which had no need of them) if Caesar should strike. On August 15, at a three-Power conference in London, Laval and Eden offered Baron Aloisi a plan for "territorial adjustments" and "collective assistance" to Ethiopia, "particular account being taken of the special interests of Italy." Mussolini rejected it. On September 18 a League Commission of Five proposed "international assistance to Ethiopia"—*i.e.*, Italian domination. Mussolini was uninterested. "If you offered me all of Ethiopia on a silver platter," he is reported to have said to the French Ambassador, "I would refuse it, for I have resolved to take it by force."

Laval and Hoare reluctantly concluded that Mussolini would attack and that they must go through the motions at Geneva of imposing sanctions. Otherwise the voters of Britain and France, unfamiliar with the subtleties of *Realpolitik* as practiced by the appeasers and convinced that their own safety lay in support of the League and enforcement of the Covenant, might turn them out of office and elect honest men in their places. On September 10, 1935, Hoare and Laval secretly agreed at Geneva to rule out "military sanctions," "naval blockade," "closure of the Suez Canal—in a word everything that might lead to war." On the next day, Hoare declared publicly at Geneva that his Government stood "for the collective maintenance of the Covenant in its entirety, and particularly for steady and collective resistance [meaning "assistance"?]

to all acts of unprovoked aggression." Laval asserted, "France is faithful to the Covenant." Both men privately assured Mussolini that he had nothing to fear.

The Duce therefore safely threatened war against all who might oppose his designs. In the sacred name of "peace," the Anglo-French leaders told parliaments and publics that sanctions must be kept innocuous lest all Europe be plunged into bloodshed. Laval consented to feeble sanctions to aid the British Tories to win their election. But Hoare hedged and quibbled when his French friends solicited a pledge of sanctions against Germany in the event of further treaty breaking. "Article 16 is not made applicable as regards a negative act of failing to fulfill terms of a treaty. . . . There may be degrees of aggression. . . . Elasticity is part of security." London and Paris assured Rome that sanctions would be purely "economic" and would not impede the Italian conquest. Rome assured Laval and Hoare that Italy would not retaliate with force and would remain "on the defensive." Hoare assured Hitler that Britain would not join France in any future sanctions against the Reich. Hitler assured Hoare that Germany would not join Italy or move against France during the crisis.

On October 1, 1935, Mussolini ordered the invasion of Ethiopia. Rome informed the Council that Ethiopian mobilization was a threat and provocation, aggravated by the withdrawal of Ethiopian troops from the frontier, and that "the warlike and aggressive spirit of Ethiopia has succeeded in imposing war against Italy." On October 5 the Council reassembled to consider the report of the Committee of Thirteen which refuted the Italian charges and noted that Italy was solemnly bound to refrain from resorting to force by a variety of engagements. Aloisi contended that Italy was a victim of aggression and was acting within the Covenant. M. Tecla Hawariati for Ethiopia asked for action under Article 16. The Council appointed a Committee of Six which reported that "the Council has come to the conclusion that the Italian Government has resorted to war in disregard of its covenants under Article 12 of the Covenant of the League of Nations."

On October 7, 1935, with Italy in the negative, the Council unanimously adopted a report of the Committee of Thirteen. On a roll call, all the members expressed their agreement with the report of the Committee of Six. At the Assembly meeting of October 9, all the members save Italy, Albania, Austria, and Hungary accepted the Council's conclusions and subsequently voted to apply sanctions. Aloisi declaimed, "Caught as she is in the tide of her full spiritual and material development but confined within territorial limits that are stifling her, Italy must make her voice heard in this Assembly as the voice of the proletariat calling for justice." On October 11 the Assembly adjourned and its "Committee for Coordination of Measures under Article 16" appointed a smaller Committee of Eighteen to propose sanctions.

The sanctions themselves were ineffective and indeed aided Mussolini to make an unpopular war popular by pretending that he was successfully defying the British Empire and the world. On October 8, 1935, George Lansbury, "Christian pacifist" and Parliamentary leader of the British Labor Party, resigned his post in protest against sanctions to which his party as well as the British Cabinet were committed. On October 10, fifty-one governments in the League Assembly confirmed the Council's verdict that Italy had resorted to war in disregard of its covenants under Article 12 and established a "committee of fifty for coordination of measures under Article 16." Only Italy and her satellites, Austria and Hungary, voted in the negative, and only four other States—Switzerland, Chile, Uruguay, and Venezuela—attached reservations to their acceptance of sanctions. On October 11 the Coordination Committee established a smaller Committee of Eighteen which drafted five sanctions proposals. The first contemplated lifting the arms embargo against Ethiopia and its continued application against Italy. On October 14 the Committee voted a second proposal to ban all loans and bank credits to Italy. On October 19 the three remaining proposals were adopted, forbidding all imports from Italy, banning the export to Italy of certain raw materials, and providing for mutual assistance among League members to minimize losses entailed by sanctions. The appeal for sanctions met with a surprisingly unanimous response from the League members, many of whom put the arms and loan embargo into effect at once.

On November 18, 1935, the "economic siege" of Italy got fully under way with the adoption of the third and fourth proposals by practically all the League members. Shocked by Italian lawlessness and imbued with a common fear of attack from various quarters, they were willing to accept trade sacrifices in the interest of restraining the aggressor. The Baldwin Cabinet was victorious in the general election of November 14 in large measure because of its championship of sanctions. France followed Britain reluctantly. But it was clear that the sanctions already imposed would not suffice to halt the war in the near future. Hostilities could have been stopped easily by closing the Suez Canal, by imposing a naval blockade against Italy, or by barring oil exports to Italy, since the Italian tanks, trucks, and planes in Ethiopia were dependent upon foreign oil. The League Powers were not prepared to apply military sanctions against the aggressor. Were they prepared to tighten economic sanctions up to the point at which they might become effective and therefore dangerous?

This crucial question was soon answered in the negative. On November 24 London and Paris agreed to postpone a consideration of oil sanctions at Geneva. The Committee of Eighteen was called for December 12 to discuss this measure. Hoare's successor, Captain Anthony Eden, staunch advocate of collective security, moved in a direction which seemed to promise effective pressure on Italy. On December 4 and 5 the British Government had asked the Foreign Ministers of Turkey, Greece, Jugoslavia, Rumania, and Czechoslovakia how far they were prepared to go in assisting any sanctionist State attacked by Italy. These Governments agreed to grant full support to Britain against any Italian assault in the event of an application of oil sanctions. France angled for a pledge of British assistance against future German aggression in return for a French pledge of support against Italy. None was forthcoming. Downing Street intimated early in January that the American decision not to stop oil shipments to Italy would make oil sanctions useless. More delay ensued while Italy laid in huge oil supplies.

On January 22, 1936, Eden announced that Britain had received promises of armed support from France, Jugoslavia, Greece, and Turkey. Simultaneously the Committee of Eighteen decided to study the feasibility of oil sanctions. But it presently appeared that the British move, like the dispatch of the fleet to the Mediterranean in the preceding spring, was a bluff designed to frighten the Duce into a more tractable frame of mind. The bluff failed. Britain was in fact unwilling to jeopardize the Facist régime and therefore unwilling to press for an oil embargo. No other Power would run risks if Britain would not. Since Mussolini could be stopped only by superior force and since the League States were unwilling to use force, the effort to restrain aggression by halfhearted economic measures was doomed to failure.

On February 12 the experts' committee reported that oil sanctions might prove effective in three months, provided that they were universal and that the United States limited its oil shipments to Italy to normal levels. On March 3 the Committee of Thirteen, which the Council had appointed in September to prepare a report under Article 15, appealed to Italy to open peace negotiations "within the framework of the League and the spirit of the Covenant." A reply within one week was requested. The Committee agreed to meet again on March 10, presumably to consider an oil embargo if Mussolini persisted in the war. The Committee of Eighteen went so far as to set up a subcommittee to plan the embargo. But this "ultimatum" was wholly without result. On March 7 Hitler took advantage of the prevalent confusion to repudiate Locarno and occupy the Rhineland. This thunderbolt shattered all plans for further pressure on Italy. Geneva marked time while Italian armies penetrated ever deeper into Ethiopia. Britain's refusal to support France against the Reich made Paris more reluctant than ever to support further moves against Italy. On April 13 the British Cabinet announced that it had abandoned all thought of military or naval action to halt the aggressor.

On April 17 the Committee of Thirteen decided to report to the Council that it had failed in its peace efforts. Britain and France again agreed to defer oil sanctions. Meanwhile the Western statesmen, again in the name of "peace," had done all in their power to give Ethiopia to the aggressor.

No sooner were economic sanctions applied than the betrayal of Ethiopia by Britain and France began to assume organized form. On December 8 it became known that Hoare and Laval had agreed to a "peace plan" whereby the aggressor was to be rewarded with control of two-thirds of Ethiopia. The British and French Foreign Ministers did not see fit to communicate their plan to the Council until December 13, exactly a year after Ethiopia had first appealed for protection. Laval requested the Council to express no views until Rome and Addis Ababa had been heard from. The plan failed because of Italian indifference. A storm of British indignation unseated Hoare, but the Council on December 19 thanked the British and French Governments for their suggestions and requested its Committee of Thirteen to examine the situation as a whole.

During January the Council evaded Ethiopian proposals that it undertake an impartial inquiry into Italian bombardments of Red Cross units and that it extend financial aid to Ethiopia. On January 23 the Committee of Thirteen adopted a unanimous report, accepted by the Council, rejecting all inquiry or assistance. The Committee of Thirteen met in London and requested Chairman Madariaga to take steps to restore peace and to bring to Italy's attention Ethiopian allegations of Italian use of poison gas contrary to the Protocol of June 17, 1925. Italy invited Madariaga to Rome and accused Ethiopia of atrocities. During April the Committee considered, discussed, postponed, delayed, and equivocated in a mood of "watchful waiting." On April 20 the Council met. After debate, it expressed regret that conciliation had failed, recalled that both belligerents were bound by the gas convention, and at length, in desperation, addressed to Italy "a supreme appeal that . . . she should bring to the settlement of her dispute with Ethiopia that spirit which the League of Nations is entitled to expect from one of its original members."

Words and feeble gestures availed nothing against bombing planes spraying poison from the clouds. Addis Ababa fell to the new barbarians come to save it from barbarism. Haile Selassie fled. From Jerusalem he wired the Secretary-General on May 10, 1936, that he had left his capital to "avoid the extermination of the Ethiopian people" and to devote himself to "the preservation of the age-old independence of Ethiopia and the principles of collective security and the sanctity of international obligations, all of which were threatened by Italy." He asked the League not to recognize the conquest and to pursue its efforts to secure respect for the Covenant. The Council met on May 11. Aloisi withdrew in protest over the presence of an Ethiopian delegation. Ethiopia asked a full application of Article 16. Argentina condemned postponement. Ecuador, which had already abandoned all measures against Italy, asked that sanctions be lifted since the war was over. Chile agreed. The Council delayed a decision until June 16, however, and resolved to keep sanctions in force meanwhile. Argentina now called for an Assembly meeting which was convoked for June 30. The Council met four days beforehand, while Italy announced that she could take no part in its meeting or in Locarno negotiations so long as sanctions remained in force. Eden, now acting as President, prevailed upon the Council to throw all responsibility upon the Assembly. Beck announced that Poland had ended sanctions.

Among Haile Selassie's last words from Ethiopian territory before his flight was a prophetic utterance.

> Do the peoples of the world not yet realize that by fighting on until the bitter end I am not only performing my sacred duty to my people but standing guard in the last citadel of collective security? Are they too blind to see that I have my responsibilities to the whole of humanity to face? I must still hold on until my tardy allies appear. If they never come, then I say prophetically and without bitterness, "The West will perish."

Britain now assumed leadership in destroying the League. On June 5, as Eden welcomed Haile Selassie to his lonely exile in England, Sir Samuel Hoare reentered the British Cabinet as First Lord of the Admiralty. On June 10 Neville Chamberlain told the Nineteen Hundred Club, "There is no use for us to shut our eyes to realities. . . . If we have retained any vestige of common sense, surely we must admit that we have tried to impose on the League a task which it was beyond its powers to fulfill. . . . Is it not apparent that the policy of sanctions involves a risk of war?" Italy had lost half of its gold reserves. Italian imports had been reduced from $14,650,000 in February, 1935, to $8,239,000 in February, 1936, and exports from $10,775,000 to $5,666,000. A continuation of sanctions might well have undermined the Facist régime despite its Ethiopian victory. But precisely this was what the Anglo-French appeasers feared most. Sanctions failed to halt aggression because the leaders of the democracies were more desirous of placating the aggressor than of impeding the march of Fascism. They now scrambled with indecent haste to betray the victim of banditry and to embrace the bandit.

The Assembly of June 30–July 4, 1936, abandoned Ethiopia to her fate. President Van Zeeland, Premier of Belgium, read a note from Rome: "The Ethiopian populations . . . welcome the Italian troops as champions of freedom, justice, civilization, and order. . . . Italy views the work she has undertaken as a sacred mission of civilization and proposes to carry it out according to the principles of the Covenant of the League and of other international agreements which set forth the duties of civilizing Powers. . . . The Italian Government declares itself ready to give once more its willing and practical cooperation to the League. . . . It is in this spirit that Italy acceded to the Treaty of Rio de Janeiro [the Argentine antiwar pact] of October 10, 1933."

These words were not intended as satire, but as a plea for the lifting of sanctions. Eden had already announced British abandonment of sanctions to the House of Commons on June 18. He had declared, "No Ethiopian Government survives in any part of the Emperor's territory." An Ethiopian Government did survive at Gore, as Eden undoubtedly knew; but its cables to London were sent by the British transmitters not via Khartoum but via Asmara in Italian Eritrea where they were, of course, suppressed. British and French efforts to dissuade Haile Selassie from speaking in Geneva failed. They were not yet prepared, in view of the attitude of the small Powers, to appease Italy by moving the expulsion of Ethiopia from the League or the exclusion of her delegation from the Assembly. The Negus came. As he mounted the rostrum, Italian journalists in the press gallery shrieked curses and execrations until they were expelled by the police. Haile Selassie spoke to an Assembly shamed into silence.

I am here today to claim that justice that is due to my people, and the assistance promised to it eight months ago by fifty-two nations who asserted that an act of aggression had been committed in violation of international treaties. [He reviewed the agonies inflicted upon his subjects by Italian poison gas and the betrayal of his country by Powers pledged to defend its independence and integrity.] I decided to come myself to testify against the crime perpetrated against my people and to give Europe warning of the doom that awaits it if it bows before the *fait accompli*. . . . If a strong government finds that it can with impunity destroy a weak people, then the hour has struck for that weak people to appeal to the League of Nations to give its judgment in all freedom. God and history will remember your decision. . . . What answer am I to take back to my people?

The answer was desertion. Blum spoke of the beauties of peace, disarmament, and collective security. Eden spoke of the failure of sanctions and declared that the Covenant must be amended. Litvinov asserted that sanctions would have stopped aggression had they been vigorously enforced. The League must be strengthened and not be made safe for aggressors. M. Ter Waters of South Africa declared that the impending decision would "shatter for generations all international confidence and all hope of realizing world peace. . . . Order is losing to chaos: the spectacle of power has hypnotized the world." The prevailing despair was symbolized on July 3 by the suicide on the floor of the Assembly of Stefan Lux, a Czech journalist who shot himself with the cry "C'est le dernier coup!" to draw attention to the plight of the Jews in Germany. Ethiopia asked the Assembly to declare that it would recognize no annexation obtained by force and to recommend a loan of 10 million pounds to Ethiopia under conditions to be fixed by the Council. The latter proposal was rejected, 23 to 1 with 25 abstentions. As for the former, the Assembly virtually ignored it and closed its session of July 4 with the adoption of an ignominious resolution expressing "firm attachment to the principles of the Covenant," soliciting proposals for the 'reform of the League, and recommending "that its coordination committee shall make all necessary proposals to the governments in order to bring to an end the measures taken by them in execution of Article 16." Sanctions were abandoned. Ethiopia was abandoned. Collective security was abandoned.

Early in September Secretary-General Avenol went to Rome, like the Emperor Henry IV to Canossa, to beg Fascist forgiveness of the League and to arrange Italy's return to Geneva in exchange for the exclusion of Ethiopia. Mussolini agreed on condition that the Assembly which was about to meet should refuse to seat the Ethiopian delegation. The French "People's Front" Cabinet, created to save liberty and peace from Fascism, obligingly brought pressure on Professor Jéze to prevent him from acting as Ethiopian delegate. His law classes at the Sorbonne had already been broken up by riotous pro-Fascist students. His own government now forbade him to serve. Downing Street and the Quai d'Orsay made plans to have the Assembly's Credentials Committee invalidate Haile Selassie's entire delegation. When the seventeenth Assembly convened on September 21, 1936, the Anglo-French plan failed because of the opposition of the smaller Powers, supported by the U.S.S.R. which felt that an Anglo-Franco-Italian *rapprochement* with Germany in a new Locarno would be but a prelude to a Nazi attack upon the Soviet Union. Haile Selassie hurriedly summoned his former American advisor, Everett A. Colson, to replace Jéze. For the first time an American citizen sat as a delegate on the floor of the League Assembly. Haile Selassie flew from London to Geneva. Eden and Delbos in the Credentials Committee found a majority in favor of seating the Ethiopian delegation. Eden thereupon declared, with more shrewdness than honesty, that his government had no objection to seating the delegation. British diplomatic prestige, already irreparably shattered, fell to a new low. By a vote of 39 to 4 the delegation was seated. Italy withheld "cooperation."

The last curtain fell in the spring of 1938. London proposed that the League Council, holding its one hundred and first meeting in Geneva, scrap the Stimson Doctrine, and approve formal diplomatic recognition of Italian title to Ethiopia on the part of the League members as promised in the Ciano-Perth Accord of April 16, 1938—another tragic milestone along the appeasers' road toward disaster. Washington was silent. Haile Selassie sought to block this final betrayal by making a "token payment" of 10,000 Swiss francs on Ethiopia's defaulted dues. On May 12, 1938, Halifax declared,

We must not be afraid to face the facts squarely. . . . When, as here, two ideals are in conflict—on the one hand the ideal of devotion, unflinching but unpractical, to some high purpose; on the other hand the ideal of a practical victory for peace—I cannot doubt that the stronger claim is that of peace. . . . Nothing is gained and much may be lost by refusal to face facts. Great as is the League of Nations, the ends it exists to serve are greater than itself and the greatest of those ends is peace. . . .

Haile Selassie, small and dark, a ruler of barbarians but every inch a king, replied in words which pronounced the doom of the League and of the Western Powers.

The Ethiopian people, to whom all assistance was refused, are climbing alone their path to Calvary. No humiliation has been spared the victim of aggression. All resources and procedures have been tried with a view to excluding Ethiopia from the League as the aggressor demands. . . . Will law win as against force? Or force as against law? . . . Many Powers threatened with aggression and feeling their weakness have abandoned Ethiopia. They have uttered the cry of panic and rout: "Everyone for himself." . . . It is a certainty that they would be abandoned as Ethiopia has been, and between the two evils they have chosen one which the fear of aggression led them to consider the lesser. May God forgive them. . . . There are different ways to maintain peace. There is the maintenance of peace through right and there is peace at any price. . . . The League would be committing suicide if after having been created to maintain peace through right it were to abandon that principle and adopt instead the principle of peace at any price, even the price of immolation of a member state at the feet of its aggressor.

The Council chose suicide. Council President Wilhelm Munters of Latvia declared that each member should decide for itself whether to recognize Italian title to Ethiopia. Only four delegations objected: New Zealand, Bolivia, China, and the U.S.S.R. Britain and France recognized Italian title to Ethiopia in November. Seventeen months later, Mussolini reciprocated with a declaration of war.

The League never recovered from this perfidious act of stupidity on the part of its leading members. Five States, including Italy, gave notice of withdrawal. Chile did likewise when its proposal that all coercive provisions be deleted from the Covenant was ignored. Venezuela followed suit. On September 13, 1937, the Eighteenth Assembly had celebrated the opening of the magnificent new Assembly Hall. The League Palace cost 15 million dollars. The new Council Chamber was decorated with murals by Sert, donated by the Spanish Republic, depicting the liberation of mankind from tyranny, intolerance, and injustice. Aga Khan supplied 2,500 bottles of champagne. But the celebration was a wake. Spain, torn by war and Fascist invasion which the League Powers condoned, failed of reelection to the Council. China, torn by new Japanese invasion which the League Powers condoned, invoked the Covenant. A parley of signatories of the Nine Power Pact met in Brussels on November 3 and adjourned on November 24, 1937, without taking action. In Litvinov's words the conferees said to Japan, "Take your plunder and peace be with you," and to China, "Love your aggressor, resist not evil."

On May 14, 1938, Alvarez del Vayo pleaded with the Council to urge the end of the policy of "nonintervention," as the Assembly had threatened to do in its resolution of October 4, 1937, if foreign troops were not withdrawn from Spain. Halifax and Bonnet voted against his plea. Only Litvinov voted for it. Spain was abandoned. China was abandoned. Austria was already abandoned. On September 16, 1938, Earl De La Warr, Lord Privy Seal, came to the funereal Nineteenth Assembly to urge that the sanctions article be diluted. He hurried away without waiting to hear Wellington Koo's plea for the application of Articles 16 and 17 against Japan. The Chinese delegate asked whether the League was "to be no more than an Egyptian mummy dressed up with all the luxuries and splendors of the living but devoid of life." On September 28 the Council held that sanctions were inapplicable to Japan. On September 29, as the Western Powers abandoned Czechoslovakia at Munich, the Assembly passed a resolution expressing hope for European peace. On September 30, it voted to sever the Covenant from the tattered Treaty of Versailles while the Council resolved that sanctions against Japan were discretionary.

The ultimate immolation of the League by its makers was without dignity. Geneva's halls were silent during the crisis which led to war in the summer of 1939. For all their illusions, the last leaders of Poland had themselves done too much to destroy the League to suppose that any purpose would be served by appealing to Geneva for aid. Britain and France made no appeal. They were now at war with the Caesarism to which they had sacrificed the small and the weak on the League's altar. But on December 3, 1939, Joseph Avenol received a note from Finland to the members of the Council invoking Articles 11 and 15 against the Soviet Union whose armies had attacked the Finns four days before. Argentina at once demanded the expulsion of the U.S.S.R. from the League. The most flagrant aggressions of Japan, Italy, and the Reich had produced no such proposal in Geneva's heyday. But most of the members regarded Communist aggression as far more monstrous than Fascist aggression, despite the fact (or perhaps because of the fact) that up to 1939 the U.S.S.R. was the only Great Power which had observed its obligations under the Covenant and had striven to make the League an effective instrument of collective security.

Moscow contemptuously declined to discuss the issue. On December 14 the Assembly unanimously voted to approve the Argentine proposal. The Council concurred and found "in virtue of Article 16, paragraph 4 of the Covenant that by its act the U.S.S.R. has placed itself outside of the

League of Nations. It follows that the U.S.S.R. is no longer a member of the League." Wellington Koo whistled and exclaimed, "China got nothing like that." Nor had any of the earlier victims of aggression. But what Finland got was a hollow gesture. No other sanctions were proposed. Unlike Ethiopia, Finland was granted tangible aid by some of the League members. The aid, however, as Lloyd George put it, was "too little and too late." Helsinki accepted defeat and made peace on March 12, 1940. The Assembly and the Council never met again. Their futile words against Moscow were a swan song.

4. A WORLD DIVIDED

> The British electorate of this generation were the children of an age in which a ci-devant Christian Society had come to believe that its talent for clockwork (institutional as well as metallic) could dispense it from the need of holding convictions and of summoning up the courage to act upon them when the consequences of such action were likely to be unpleasant. . . . These children of the Enlightenment fell under the yoke of the Goddess Tyche or Fortune, who, under many different names, had repeatedly established her paralyzing dominion over the souls of men and women who had been called upon to live in periods of social decadence. . . . They made their momentous choice neither on the absolute criterion of morality nor on the relative criterion of expediency, but on that trivial distinction between this moment and the next which keeps the sluggard cowering between the blankets when the house is burning over his head.—Arnold J. Toynbee.

The wrecking of the League of Nations was the external sign of the inner incapacity of Western mankind to translate the Wilsonian dream of a united world into terms of viable reality. In the community of nations, as in other communities, the alternative to order is anarchy. The price of order is easily stated: common loyalties to common purposes; willingness to assume responsibilities and run risks to restrain lawbreakers and promote security; ability to set up workable judicial procedures for the settlement of legal disputes through the application of established law, to establish competent legislative processes to settle political disputes by changing established law, and to devise effective executive agencies to administer and enforce the will of the community. Western humanity in the twentieth century has not been lacking in skill in the invention of agencies and procedures. It has been lacking in common will and common purposes and courage to act upon its feeble decisions—thanks to the folly and blindness of isolationists, pacifists, appeasers, traitors, dunces, and dupes. None of these groups consciously preferred anarchy to order in inter-state relations. But all of them abandoned or betrayed the cause of order in the name of "peace," "justice," and other abstractions which are susceptible of implementation only when order is organized and enforced.

All of them have therefore fallen into the morass of anarchy and the slough of despond, with few lamps of hope lighting the dark horizon.

This most dismal failure of the most important enterprise of a whole generation has not, however, altered the fundamental nature of the Great Society of modern civilization. That society is technologically and economically one on a world scale. Its members are completely interdependent in a thousand ways they scarcely dream of. Travel time over the planet continues to contract. British ambassadors in Rome in the 1830's required as long to get to London (13 days) as the couriers of Julius Caesar. In the single century succeeding, distance has been all but annihilated. In 1812 the traveler from Berlin who used the fastest available means of transit needed 5 days to reach Vienna, 10 for northern Italy, 15 for Spain, 20 for North Africa, and a full month to reach the Caspian. In 1790 the traveler from Boston needed 1 day to reach Worcester, Providence, or Portsmouth, 2 for Portland or Hartford, 4 for New York, 5 for Philadelphia, 7 for Baltimore, 9 for Richmond, 18 for Savannah, and 20 (if he were lucky) for Knoxville. In 1938 any European could span all the Continent by air in little more than a single day. The hurrying Bostonian with one day to travel could reach Bermuda, Vancouver, or Mexico City. In 2 days Panama or Honolulu were attainable; in 5, London, Paris, Rio, or Guam; in 7, Hongkong, Moscow, or Istanbul; in 11, Mandalay, Irkutsk, Zanzibar, or Singapore; and in 15, Melbourne or Wellington, New Zealand. Orville Wright's plane at Kitty Hawk in 1903 flew about 30 miles an hour. The fastest planes of 1913 reached 126 miles; those of 1919, 162; those of 1922, 222; those of 1938, 440 miles per hour. The inauguration of regular trans-Atlantic air service in the summer of 1939 shortened the time between Europe and North America from 5 days to less than 2. Australia and New Zealand can now be reached from the United States in 4 days instead of the 15 needed at the time of the peace of Munich. In travel time, the entire planet is now only half the size of western Europe or the thirteen American States a century and a half ago.[1]

Ease and speed of travel are obviously but one of the indices of the unity of the world. Communication of messages, pictures, and voices has become almost instantaneous from each of the great centers of the globe to all the others. Modern man is not content to learn from the printed page at breakfast what happened in the Antipodes the preceding evening. He expects to be able to listen later in the day to the kings and captains of other continents speaking in his living room. He also takes it for granted that he can talk by telephone to almost anyone almost anywhere on the planet. As he talks, he may (or may not) reflect that the small device he speaks into and listens to contains chromium from Rhodesia, the U.S.S.R.,

[1] These figures are taken from Part I, "This Shrinking World," of Eugene Staley's admirable volume, *World Economy in Transition*, 1939.

or Turkey; cobalt from the Belgian Congo; nickel from Canada; antimony from China, Belgium, or Mexico; tin from the East Indies or Bolivia; rubber from Malaya; silk from Japan; gum enamel from New Zealand; hemp from the Philippines; wax from Brazil; shellac from Siam and India; asphalt from Trinidad; and sundry other ingredients from all over the globe.[1] If he lives in any of the great cities of the twentieth century, he spends every hour of his day in contact with objects of use or beauty which are his only because he is a member of a Great Society and a world economy wherein people, things, and ideas, in peacetime at least, can be moved quickly and cheaply from any point to any other of his now very small world.

These things have been judged good by most of modern mankind. These have been made possible only because inventors, explorers, entrepreneurs, scientists, financiers, and other purveyors of services and commodities have been able to live and work, not in cloistered seclusion in narrow market towns or in walled-in provinces or countries, but in all the outdoors of the great world. This opportunity in turn came into being because jurists, diplomats, and statesmen patiently and often enough unknowingly built up the principles of law, the practices of political relations, the institutions and agencies of inter-state collaboration through which ideas, things, and people were enabled to move more and more freely over the fences of a patchwork State System of national sovereignties.

These hard-won comforts and these indispensable services, without which the civilization of the machine age cannot endure, are now threatened because men and women everywhere, even while they are the beneficiaries of a world economy and a world community, have failed to become world citizens. In their hearts and minds, they have remained national patriots. They have therefore given support and approval to programs of national prosperity, national security, national aggrandizement on the erroneous supposition that they and their fellow patriots could enjoy larger material benefits, as well as heightened emotional satisfactions, through the promotion of anarchy and conflict rather than order and collaboration in the relations among the nations of men. It is not for the social scientist to quarrel with this choice. But it is for him to point out its costs and consequences.

There is no good reason for assuming that continued anarchy in inter-state relations is compatible with the continued existence of the Great Society. One or the other is likely to disappear before this generation passes from the scene. And when people are called upon to choose between the increasing perils of anarchy and the obvious benefits of organized

[1] *Cf.* "From the Far Corners of the Earth," published by the Western Electric Company, cited by Eugene Staley, *ibid.*, pp. 24*f*.

order in the community of nations, it is probable that they will choose order. What reason and persuasion fail to accomplish, the harsh school-teachers of adversity and the bludgeonings of outrageous fortune often achieve. Man's folly, to be sure, may be such that in his blind quest for security within the limits of his local tribes he may reduce the world once more to a chaos of feudal principalities in which the survivors of disaster live as best they can among the ruins on a primitive and brutish level of existence. At present it seems more likely, however, that the world econ-omy and the world community not only will survive but will be rebuilt and enriched through the effective political unification of the planet.

The issue of the 1940's is less an issue of whether the unity of the world will be attained than the issue of who will attain it. Two major contenders for the honor are struggling for ascendancy. On one side stand the youth-ful *élites* of the totalitarian States, bent upon world conquest and world empire, possessed of faith and courage and a consciousness of a mission, and content to risk all to reach goals which are defined clearly and pur-sued relentlessly. On the other side stand (or stood until yesterday) the old *élites* of the capitalist democracies—timid, confused, self-betrayed, uncertain and only half-supported by a youth whose purposes are blurred, whose devices are timorous, and whose convictions are more often than not all sicklied o'er with the pale cast of thought. The first group of power seekers is bent upon unifying the world by the sword of the conqueror, supplemented by the pen of the propagandist and the whip of the terror-ist. The second group had an opportunity presented to it by the victory of 1918 to unify the world by the pen of the educator and advocate, sup-plemented by the voice of the administrator and the firm hand of those who might have dedicated themselves to enforcing justice among all peoples everywhere. The opportunity was thrown away. Those to whom it was given were perhaps unfit for the privilege. They had lost so much and suffered such crushing disasters under the fixed delusion that they were not their brother's keeper and that the misfortunes of others were no business of theirs that it was doubtful by 1941 whether they still had the physical means of recapturing and reordering the world after their heart's desire. Whether they had the spiritual means of creating and utilizing the physical tools needed for the task was perhaps even more doubtful. No adequate vision of a new world order had won mass support among the democrats who still survived when these pages went to press.

But it may be taken almost for granted that one or the other of the contestants for hegemony will unify the world before it has grown much older. Thinkers and publicists in both camps have long since been engaged in propounding schemes of world unity fashioned after their respective needs, preferences, and prejudices. These schemes are too many to re-view. In the democratic camp during the years of disaster, they ranged from the plans of appeasers for emasculating the Covenant to Clarence Streit's *Union Now*. In the totalitarian States, they ranged from continued Communist dreams of world-wide proletarian revolution to the vague terminology of the new "Triple Alliance" of September 27, 1940.

Any revival of the League of Nations in its old form, even in the event of the ultimate victory of the democracies, appears unlikely, for nothing is more difficult than to breathe new life into old institutions that have been betrayed and discredited. On May 27, 1939, the League Council authorized a committee headed by S. M. Bruce, High Commissioner of Australia in London, to study a possible division of the League into a political organization and an economic organization, on the assumption that universality of membership and acceptable formulations of common purposes might prove possible in the latter sphere if not in the former. The Bruce Report was issued on August 22 and adopted by the Assembly in a resolution of December 14, 1939. It proposed the creation of a "Central Committee for Economic and Social Questions" to supervise and direct the work of the established League Committee dealing with such problems. This body was to be composed of representatives of twenty-four States chosen by the Assembly. Nonmember States would be invited to join.[1] This plan, which came to nothing because of the collapse of the League, was administratively interesting but highly unrealistic as to its broader purposes and presuppositions. There can be no effective economic and social cooperation among nations in the Great Society of the twentieth century without effective "political" government based upon common public purposes and having adequate coercive authority at its disposal for the enforcement of order.

More realistic was the statement issued in November, 1939, by the Swiss Committee of the International Peace Campaign proposing the transformation of the League into a genuine federation. "In the federation to come the so-called *sovereignty of States*, a fiction of absolute independence long since disproved by fact, will have to go. . . ." The British League of Nations Union Declaration also emphasized the need of abolishing "sovereignty" and subordinating State action to an effective central power. French suggestions of 1932 for an international police force likewise exhibited a grasp of the nature of the problem of world order, but these proposals evoked no echo among other States and were soon forgotten in France itself. The New Commonwealth Society, founded in Britain with branches later established elsewhere, insisted upon the necessity of an international police force and an international equity tribunal.[2]

[1] *Cf.* League of Nations, A23, 1939, *The Development of International Cooperation in Economic and Social Affairs: Report of the Special Committee*, Geneva, August, 1939.

[2] For an excellent summary of these and other schemes, see William P. Maddox, "European Plans for World Order," James-Patten-Rowe Pamphlet Series 8, American Academy of Political and Social Science, Philadelphia, 1940.

In 1922 Count Richard N. Coudenhove-Kalergi, who later became a Fascist, founded at Vienna the "Pan-European Union" to work for a federation of all European States to keep the peace and provide for common defense against "a Bolshevik invasion." The Hungarian publicist contemplated the division of the world into five great units: the British Empire, the Soviet Union, Eastern Asia, Pan-America, and Pan-Europe. Pan-Europeanism has been sponsored by industrialists, economists, and statesmen, as well as by propagandists and idealists. Messrs. Loucheur, Caillaux, and Herriot were no less interested in the project than was Briand. As subject matter for practical (or impractical) politics, the scheme was sponsored most warmly by the French Government. Briand advocated European union before the Tenth Assembly of the League in 1925.[1] In the same year the "Minister of Peace" told the French deputies, "It is my greatest wish to see the realization of the United States of Europe. And if I have devoted my energies . . . to the League of Nations, I have done so because in that great institution I have seen a rough draft of the United States of Europe."

The Pan-Europa idea, like the idea of the League itself, anticipated the integration of national interests into international interests and the setting up of a new political framework for the protection and promotion of such interests. But the idea cut across the lines of language, of economic interests, and of power politics. The common interests, values, attitudes, and ideologies which are the prerequisites of successful union were nonexistent—or were existent in insufficient degree to move men to effective action. Frameworks, commissions, mechanisms remained fruitless under these circumstances. There was no adequate social and psychological basis for successful organization. The verdict of history on these efforts at unity was "Too late!"

The most dramatic and challenging plan for reordering the world on democratic foundations was that eloquently propounded by Clarence Streit in *Union Now*, published in the United States in March, 1939, translated into many languages, and followed by the establishment of

---

[1] On September 9, 1929, Briand discussed the project at Geneva with representatives of other European governments; and on May 17, 1930, the Quai d'Orsay dispatched to the twenty-six European members of the League a "Memorandum on the Organization of a System of European Federal Union." It proposed a "regional entente within the terms of Article 21 of the Covenant and its self-functioning within the League." A European conference was suggested, and measures of economic collaboration were proposed. The replies were not unfavorable, though Great Britain and other States made reservations. The revisionist bloc insisted upon equality of rights and looked askance at the whole scheme as a new device to perpetuate French hegemony. In September, 1930, the League Assembly passed a resolution providing for a Commission of Inquiry of European Union, which convened in January, 1931. It decided to limit the project to economic cooperation and to invite Iceland, Turkey, and the U.S.S.R. to join in the enterprise. Various subcommissions were appointed, and the commission continued to meet periodically; but it accomplished nothing of political significance.

the Inter-Democracy Federal Unionists, with branches in most of the democratic States. Mr. Streit's point of departure was the American Constitution of 1787. He proposed that the fifteen founder democracies (United States, Great Britain, the British Dominions, France, Switzerland, the Low Countries, and the Scandinavian States) establish an international federal union in place of the League pattern of confederation. Within the union, there would be common citizenship, common money, a common defense force, a common postal and communications system, and free trade. Delegated powers over federal questions, including the maintenance of order and the enforcement of law, would be entrusted to a democratic Union Congress of two houses and exercised by a federal executive. The clear logic and the crying need of such a plan won thousands of followers. After Scandinavia and the Low Countries were subjugated by Hitler, Winston Churchill on June 16, 1940, offered "Union Now" to defeated France as a basis for continuing the war, but Reynaud was forced out of office the same evening by the Munichmen who preferred to surrender to the Axis. The plan was not again referred to in official statements of British war aims during the remainder of the year.

In the totalitarian camp the oldest scheme for unifying the world was that sponsored by Karl Marx and his disciples. Marxism proposed to abolish international conflict and economic maladjustment by proletarian social revolution on a world scale, aiming at the abolition of private property and profit, the organization of all enterprise by the great public monopolies of the Workers' State, and the brotherhood of mankind in a fraternity of toilers. The Communist Manifesto of 1847, issued by Karl Marx and Friedrich Engels, concluded its appeal with the memorable battle cry, "Workers of the world, unite; you have nothing to lose but your chains!" Those who respond to this appeal have ever contended that the common class interests of the proletariat transcend national frontiers. The proletarian revolutionary movement, inspired and led by Marx and his disciples, has from the beginning been world-wide and international in scope and emphasis.

Prior to 1914 this movement had attained a semblance of world-wide unity through the international trade unions of Europe and through the so-called "Second International"—the federation of Socialist parties, which maintained its headquarters at Brussels and endeavored, through periodical congresses, to promote the common purposes of Marxists in all countries. In the aftermath of Sarajevo, however, the allegiance of the workers of the world to the myths and symbols of bourgeois nationalism proved more powerful than their allegiance to proletarian internationalism. They quickly forgot the international solidarity which was to keep the peace, and the general strike which was to paralyze the efforts of the warmakers. They willingly fell to slaughtering one another in the name of defending their respective fatherlands from the foreign foe. The Second International was disrupted. With few exceptions, the Socialists in each country supported the war as loyal patriots, and sang hymns of hate as lustily as the most nationalistic of the bourgeoisie.

The exceptional Socialists, however, were by no means insignificant, and they denounced their colleagues as cowards, scoundrels, "social patriots," and traitors to the toiling masses and to the cause of world revolution. In the wake of war came economic collapse and social disintegration. Throughout central and eastern Europe the moderate or revisionist Socialist parties found an opportunity to seize power. But they were divided, impotent, enfeebled by decades of pacific parliamentarianism. In Russia they supported the war and strove to establish a bourgeois democracy upon the ruins of the Tsardom, until they were swept into oblivion by the Bolshevik uprising. In Germany, Austria, and Hungary they had power thrust upon them. They used that power to bolster up the tottering structure of capitalism and to enable the bourgeoisie to wreak bloody vengeance upon their more revolutionary comrades. In Italy they debated until they were suppressed by the Fascists. The golden moment came and passed. Outside of Russia the proletarian revolution was nowhere achieved.

These events led to an open split between the moderate and revolutionary Marxists. This cleavage had appeared long before the war in the congresses of the Second International, but it did not become an irreparable breach until the close of the great conflct. In all the national parties the bases of cleavage were much the same. The moderate revisionist Marxists were content with electoral and parliamentary tactics and contemplated "peaceful revolution" through the attainment of legislative majorities. The orthodox revolutionary Marxists insisted upon the inevitability of forcible bourgeois resistance to expropriation and upon the resulting necessity of revolutionary violence. In the Russian party the moderate minority (Menshevik) faction was at war with the revolutionary majority (Bolshevik) faction. In Germany the radical Independent Socialists separated themselves from the Social Democrats and gave birth in turn in 1918 to the ultrarevolutionary Spartacists, forerunners of the German Communist party. Similar splits took place elsewhere. Meanwhile the Russian Bolsheviks, under Lenin's leadership, seized power, expropriated the nobility and the bourgeoisie, and established a proletarian dictatorship. Soviet governments were likewise set up in Hungary and Bavaria in the spring of 1919, but they were quickly suppressed by military force and reactionary terrorism. In Russia the Bolsheviks—or "Communists," as they dubbed themselves in 1918—succeeded in destroying the enemy classes and parties and in beating off a world attack upon their régime. In March of 1919 they called their sympathizers in other countries into conference and established the Communist or Third International, with its headquarters at Moscow. This was an international federation of the Communist parties of the world, dedicated to the repudiation of bourgeois democracy and to the violent seizure of power by the world proletariat. The Second or Brussels International was reconstituted by the German Social Democrats, the British Laborites, the French Unified Socialists, and other revisionist groups elsewhere. Between the two Internationals a bitter and implacable feud raged for over a decade, with each seeking to win the workers over to its banner, and with the Communists making slow but steady inroads upon the Socialists in most of the Continental countries.

Communism's millenial vision of salvation through suffering, of peace through war and revolt, began to fade rapidly after 1929 along with Liberalism's earlier and less bloody dream of unity which Socialists of the Amsterdam persuasion had generally shared. During the preceding decade, the long shadows of Wilson and Lenin pointed rightward and leftward toward alternative conceptions of the brotherhood of man. Geneva and Moscow were the shrines of rival faiths, each professing to desire a world-wide reign of peace and justice. In the one it was hoped that the Liberal virtues of tolerance and reason, coupled with orderly collaboration among the nation-states, would lead to the new day. In the other it was hoped that the workers' revolution, violent and liberating, would spread from country to country and bind all toilers in a single cause. Both hopes were deferred in the 1920's—the one because unregenerate nationalisms, monopolistic capitalisms, power-hungry imperialisms were obstacles too great to be at once overcome, the other because the proletarian revolution failed to materialize in other lands or was miserably crushed wherever it raised its head. Hope deferred, however, was not hope abandoned. Only with the beginning of the lean years which followed the years of plenty, only with the final unfolding of the world crisis which had been postponed, did the Liberal and Communist hopes become empty and impossible of fulfillment. The international consequences of poverty and war have now blocked both the right and left exits from chaos.

Fascism is by profession anti-internationalist and dedicated to national and racial megalomania. Its road of conquest, however, points also toward the unification of the world by the sword. Mussolini's dream of a new "Roman Empire," Tokio's vision of a "New Order in Eastern Asia," Hitler's quest for *Lebensraum* were all reflections of a realization that the world is one and must be united. The inability or unwillingness of the democracies to accept and implement liberal programs of world unity offered opportunity for the constant enhancement of the power of the

[255]

Fascist States and for efforts to translate Fascist programs of a world Imperium into reality. These programs by the close of 1940 were by no means clearly defined or consistent with one another. Hitler's plans for the new Europe were sometimes couched in terms of a revived Holy Roman Empire, sometimes of *Grossraumwirtschaft* in a continental free trade area, sometimes of alliances and federations surrounded by small vassal States á la Bonaparte. Continued totalitarian victories threatened to lead to potential conflict among the would-be world conquerors dreaming and scheming in Berlin, Rome, Tokio, and Moscow. The tripartite pact of September 27, 1940, was forged in the heat of war and might cease to operate as a basis of collaboration in the event of ultimate military victory. Fascist dynamism, moreover, promised to drive its disciples into ever-new adventures in conquest, with the final result highly uncertain. All that was clear was that democratic weakness and defeatism had given to the Fascist Powers an opportunity to impose their hegemony upon Europe and the world and to essay the political unification of the Great Society according to their own plans.

Here as elsewhere the fittest survive. If the surviving democracies continue to prove unfit for the mission of unifying the world, it will be undertaken by their enemies, with results as yet unpredictable. Meanwhile the central question of *Weltpolitik* is the question of who will defeat whom and therewith undertake the role of world unifier. Either Germany, Italy, Japan, and their allies and satellites will destroy the power of Britain, the U.S.S.R., America, and China, or they will be destroyed by them. The victors will remake the world. The war which will lead to the building of a new world order is clearly a product of the breakdown of an old world order and of the persistence of a still older world anarchy. That anarchy may well continue for years or even decades before a decision is reached. The victors may fail in their mission or may be betrayed by their successors, as the leaders of the 1920's were betrayed by those of the 1930's. In this event, anarchy among nations will continue until the Third World War of the century reopens the issue once more. It is therefore fitting that the next book of this study should be devoted not to visions of unity and order but to the realities of anarchy and conflict.

SUGGESTED READINGS

Armstrong, Hamilton Fish: *We or They; Two Worlds in Conflict*, New York, Macmillan, 1936.
Bingham, A. M.: *The United States of Europe*, New York, Duell, 1940.
Coudenhove-Kalergi, R. N.: *Pan-Europe*, New York, Knopf, 1926.
Cresson, W. P.: *The Holy Alliance*, New York, Oxford, 1922.
Curtis, Lionel: *World Order (Civitas Dei)*, New York, Oxford, 1939.
Dawson. C. H.: *The Making of Europe*, New York, Macmillan, 1932.
Dulles, E. L.: *The Bank for International Settlements at Work*, New York, Macmillan, 1933.
Eagleton, C.: *International Government*, New York, Ronald, 1932.

Einzig, P.: *The Bank for International Settlements*, New York, Macmillan, 1930.

Eliot, T. S.: *The Idea of A Christian Society*, New York, Harcourt, 1939.

Graham, M. W.: *The League of Nations and the Recognition of States*, Los Angeles, University of California, 1933.

Highley, A. E.: *The First Sanctions Experiment*, Geneva, Geneva Research Center, 1938.

Hill, N. L.: *International Administration*, New York, McGraw-Hill, 1931.

Howard-Ellis, C.: *The Origin, Structure and Working of the League of Nations*, Boston, Houghton, 1928.

Hughan, J. W.: *A Study of International Government*, New York, Crowell, 1923.

International Labor Office, Geneva: *The International Labor Organization; the First Decade*, London, Allen & Unwin, 1931.

Jennings, W. I.: *A Federation for Western Europe*, New York, Macmillan, 1940.

Keeton, G. W.: *National Sovereignty and International Order*, London, Peace Book Company, 1939.

Ladd, William: *An Essay on a Congress of Nations*, New York, Oxford, 1916.

Lansing, Robert: *The Peace Negotiations*, Boston, Houghton, 1921.

League of Nations Information Section: *Essential Facts about the League of Nations*, Geneva, 1936.

League of Nations *Monthly Summary*.

League of Nations *Official Journal*.

League of Nations: *Ten Years of World Cooperation*, Geneva, 1930.

League of Nations *Treaty Series*.

McClure, Wallace: *World Prosperity as Sought through the Economic Work of the League of Nations*, New York, Macmillan, 1933.

Marburg, Theodore: *Development of The League of Nations Idea* (2 vols.), New York, Macmillan, 1932.

Marriott, Sir J. A. R.: *Commonwealth or Anarchy*, New York, Columbia University Press, 1939.

Miller, D. H.: *The Drafting of the Covenant*, New York, Putnam, 1928.

Mitrany, D.: *The Progress of International Government*, London, Allen & Unwin, 1933.

Morley, Felix: *The Society of Nations*, Washington, Brookings, 1932.

Morrison, H. S., and others: *The League and the Future of the Collective System*, New York, Oxford, 1937.

Mowrer, E. C.: *International Government*, Boston, Heath, 1931.

Niebuhr, Reinhold: *Christianity and Power Politics*, New York, Scribner, 1940.

Newfang, Oscar: *World Federation*, New York, Barnes & Noble, Inc., 1939.

Perigord, P.: *The International Labor Organization*, New York, Appleton-Century, 1926.

Phelan, E. J.: *The International Labor Organization*, Geneva, 1925.

Potter, P. B.: *An Introduction to the Study of International Organization*, New York, Appleton-Century, 1934.

———: *The Wal Wal Arbitration*, Washington, Carnegie Endowment, 1938.

Rappard, W. E.: *The Quest for Peace*, Cambridge, Harvard University Press, 1940.

Reinsch, P.: *Public International Unions*, Boston, Ginn, 1911.

Ridgeway, G. L.: *Merchants of Peace*, New York, Columbia University Press, 1938.

Russell, B.: *Freedom and Organization, 1814–1914*, London, Allen & Unwin, 1934.

Salter, Sir Arthur: *Security; Can We Retrieve It?*, New York, Reynal, 1939.

Salter, J. A.: *Allied Shipping Control*, New York, Oxford, 1921.

Sayre, F. B.: *Experiments in International Administration*, New York, Harper, 1920.

Scott, J. B.: *The United States of America*, New York, Oxford, 1920.

Shotwell, J. T.: *On the Rim of the Abyss*, New York, Macmillan, 1936.

Streit, C. K.: *Union Now*, New York, Harper, 1939.

Temperley, H. W.: *History of the Peace Conference* (6 vols.), London, Hodder, 1920–1924.

Thomas, A.: *The International Labour Organization*, London, Allen & Unwin, 1931.

Willoughby, W. W.: *The Sino-Japanese Controversy and the League of Nations*, Baltimore, Johns Hopkins, 1935.

Wilson, F. G.: *Labor and the League System*, Stanford University Press, 1934.

Woolf, L.: *International Government*, New York, Brentano's, 1916.

World Peace Foundation: *Statistical Year-book of the League of Nations*, 1933–1934, Boston, World Peace Foundation.

Wright, Quincy (ed.): *Neutrality and Collective Security*, 1936, Norman Wait Harris Memorial Foundation.

York, E.: *Leagues of Nations, Ancient, Medieval, and Modern*, London, Swarthmore Press, 1928.

Zimmern, A.: *The League of Nations and the Rule of Law*, 1918–1935, London, Macmillan, 1936.

BOOK THREE
WORLD ANARCHY

INTRODUCTION TO BOOK THREE

Anarchy is the absence of order. "Order" is the result of government. "Government" is the set of habits and practices by which the few who make the most important social decisions command obedience from the many, either for their own good or for the good of the governed. In either case, government maintains order and enforces law. It is improbable that any government anywhere ever commanded complete obedience from all its subjects, for there are always twisted souls given to crime or rebellious souls given to insubordination. It is equally improbable that any people anywhere have ever lived in complete anarchy. In a state of anarchy, said Thomas Hobbes, human life is "poor, solitary, nasty, brutish, and short." All peoples are agreed that they are happier when they live in some kind of order, however imperfect, and under some kind of law, however rough-and-ready, than when they live wholly without these devices for regulating their collective affairs.

In the society of nation-states, law and order (of a kind) have existed for a long period. The elements of that law and the institutions of that order have been discussed in the preceding pages. Ten years ago and more, hopeful students of the community of nations believed that these adumbrations of organized justice among States were sufficiently promising to warrant the writing of textbooks entitled *International Organization* or even *International Government*. These hopes have long since waned. The Western State System is obviously not a community enjoying "government," but a community suffering from "anarchy." Yet anarchy sooner or later cures itself, for its consequences in the long run are usually judged intolerable by the majority of men and women. Sometime, somewhere, however far off the divine event may be, anarchy among nations will doubtless give way to law, order, and government.

Meanwhile, anarchy remains the reality of international relations, and government remains an unrealized aspiration. The anatomy and physiology of international anarchy will be the subject matter of the following chapters.

CHAPTER VII

THE POLITICS OF POWER

1. THE WILL-TO-POWER

When Pyrrhus had retired into Epirus and left Macedonia, he had a fair occasion given him by fortune to enjoy himself in quiet and to govern his kingdom in peace. But he was persuaded that neither to annoy others nor to be annoyed by them was a life insufferably tedious and languishing. His anxiety for fresh employment was relieved by his preparations for war against Rome. A certain Thessalonian named Cineas, one of his trusted advisers and a man of sound sense, perceiving what was afoot, drew Pyrrhus into a conversation. "If it please heaven that we conquer the Romans," he inquired, "what use, Sir, shall we make of our victory?" Pyrrhus explained that the conquest of Rome would open the way to subduing all Italy. Cineas suggested that surely the triumphs were not to stop there. Pyrrhus then allowed his visions of conquest to extend to Sicily, to Carthage, to Libya, to all the other insolent enemies of his kingdom. "But," asked Cineas, "when we have conquered all, what are we to do then?" "Why, then, my friend," said Pyrrhus laughing, "we will take our ease, and drink and be merry." Cineas, having brought him thus far, replied: "And what hinders us from drinking and taking our ease now, when we have already those things in our hands at which we propose to arrive through seas of blood, through infinite toils and dangers, through innumerable calamities which we must both cause and suffer?" This discourse of Cineas gave Pyrrhus pain, but produced no change in his plans.—PLUTARCH, *Life of Pyrrhus.*

ALL politics is a struggle for power. People with power usually relish the joy of commanding others to do their will. They usually enjoy as well the tangible benefits which come from ability to make great decisions and to affect thereby the ever-changing answer to the question of who gets what among the sons and daughters of men. From time immemorial those who have sought power, those who have competed with other power seekers, and those who have resisted or challenged power holders have employed force or fraud or favors or some combination of these devices to thwart rivals, win friends, and influence people. Obedience is had by filling the governed with fear, with love, or with hope of gain. To do these things successfully is to be an effective politician.

Those who are successful in the quest for power frequently discover that their appetites grow with what they feed upon. Under the lash of

[261]

ambition and the expectations of followers, those who are powerful usually aspire to become more powerful—either by bringing those who already obey them into more complete subjection to their desires or by imposing their will on others who, if left alone, would obey other leaders and follow other gods.

Western mankind, so long as it despised conquering tyrants and thirsted after freedom, sought to impose limits on ambition (and therefore upon oppression) by restricting the power of public office holders and compelling them to obey fixed rules to the end that society might enjoy "a government of laws and not of men." This purpose was of the essence of democratic constitutionalism within States and of all strivings toward international law and order among States. The reconciliation of liberty and authority has ever been the most difficult of community problems, no less so in the community of nations than in the communities which are nations. Having achieved a large measure of freedom within national frontiers and attained a semblance of order in the relations among States, modern man in our time has once more lost his liberties over large areas of the earth and has lost peace as well over all the earth. Contemporary politics presents a picture, perhaps temporary but possibly permanent, of arbitrary despotisms within States and anarchic violence among States. Had political Liberalism realized its early dream, its disciples would have outlawed tyranny and made its restoration forever impossible. They would likewise have subjected the capricious and destructive "independence" of sovereign States to a régime of ordered justice and enforced peace in the Great Society. If Liberals ever recapture their dream and fulfill their mission, they will do these things. Meanwhile the dream lies in ashes. The State once more is force. International relations are again a war of each against all with the devil taking the hindmost.

Even in the heyday of democracy, however, diplomacy was a game in which power was sought ambitiously by the rulers of all States in competition with all others. No effective central power ever emerged to impose law and enforce peace upon the nations. In every community where an effective central power is lacking, politics tends to become a violent competition for power *per se* with force as the final arbiter. This characteristic of international politics has been always present, albeit hidden frequently behind a facade of forms and rituals. It is now glaringly obvious. It must be the point of departure for any realistic analysis of how States actually deal with one another in the topsy-turvy world of the mid-twentieth century.

Whereas power is sought in domestic politics as a means toward other ends, power is sought as an end in itself in international politics. "Power" means ability to impose one's will on others, capacity to dictate to those who are without power or who possess less power, opportunity to achieve the gains which power makes possible of attainment. In the political process within each of the nation-states a constant struggle for ascendancy goes on among political leaders, parties, factions, sections, classes, and other groups. Power means admission to public office, control of the machinery of lawmaking and administration, influence over the determination of public policy. Here, too, it sometimes seems to be sought for its own sake, *i.e.*, for the emotional satisfactions which accompany its exercise. But usually it is sought for the attainment of the ulterior purposes which can be served by its use. The politician desires patronage, profits, graft, honest or dishonest. The party desires to build up a machine which will afford jobs and profits to its members. The lobbyist desires to secure legislative and administrative favors and the profits which go therewith. In international politics it is likewise true that power, diplomatic preponderance, political hegemony, military or naval supremacy serve ulterior purposes. But foreign offices and patriots often pursue these goals as things good in themselves. The great clashes of power interests among States frequently center in values which have no immediate relationship to tangible objectives. "National honor" is impugned when a State's power is challenged. A State's "prestige" must be respected by its rivals; for prestige is reputation for power, and in power relationships reputations and appearances are as important as realities. "Vital interests" are as much related to power considerations as to material goals. These are the things for which men fight in the Western State System. These are the symbols and verbalizations of the universal quest for power in which the nation-states are engaged.

If power is sought as an end in itself, it is nevertheless true that the power interests of each State are expressed in terms of specific purposes which reflect the interests and attitudes of the politically dominant groups within the State. These purposes are formulated through the interaction of internal political forces. Once formulated, they are imposed upon the nation as a whole and become identified with the "national interests." The stakes of diplomacy arise from the interests of the ruling class in the State—or if there be no clearly defined ruling class, from the equilibrium of forces through which public policy is determined. These classes and forces grow out of social structures in which those with economic power are ultimately the rulers. An agrarian autocracy with a landed nobility as its ruling class, *e.g.*, pre-war Russia, will express its power interests in terms of land hunger and territorial aggrandizement. An agrarian democracy, *e.g.*, pre-Civil War United States, will similarly manifest a desire for territorial expansion in its foreign policy. A commercial State, *e.g.*, seventeenth century Holland or eighteenth century England, will be interested in commodity markets and sea power. An industrialized capitalistic State, *e.g.*, contemporary Great Britain, Germany, the United States, or

Japan, will seek investment markets, concessions, opportunities for profit through trade and finance. An industrialized Communistic State, *e.g.*, the U.S.S.R., will be interested in proletarian revolution, colonial emancipation, the creation of other Communistic States with which it may make common cause against capitalism. In every case, the economic and social structure of the State will determine the nature of the stakes of diplomacy which it pursues.

This is but another way of saying that the economically dominant classes within each State, which are likely to be politically preponderant because of their economic power, tend to dictate the specific purposes in terms of which the national interests of the State are expressed. In the contemporary period, the bourgeoisie is the economically dominant group in most Western societies. It determines public policies, domestic and foreign, subject to pressures from landed nobles, farmers, and urban workers. National patriotism in itself is bourgeois in origin and is distinctly of the period of the political ascendency of the bourgeoisie. The quest for power of the bourgeois States is couched in terms of bourgeois interests and objectives. Economic nationalism, imperialism, militarism, navalism, dollar diplomacy, and the like, are unintelligible save in terms of the interests of the ruling bourgeois group. States in which agrarian groups predominate or in which a dictatorship of the proletariat prevails pursue correspondingly different objectives in their quest for power. In every instance, in all times and places, the power interests of politically competing States are comprehensible only in terms of the interests, values, and ideologies of the ruling group within each unit of the State System.

In our own time the phenomenon of "totalitarianism" has brought to the seats of power in many States groups of political adventurers who have made a cult of the quest for power. Although for the most part of bourgeois origin and usually indebted for their victory to businessmen and aristocrats who fancied that their own interests were being served thereby, the new Caesars and their disciples have spurned all "bourgeois" values. They have therefore repudiated freedom, constitutionalism, and representative government. They have repudiated international law, international organization, and visions of peaceful collaboration. They have established streamlined despotisms, dedicated to war for the greater power and glory of conquering tyrants. Before their assaults the democratic nations have crumbled and the League of Nations has died. World politics has thus become a fierce combat between would-be conquerors and their intended victims, and between rival conquerors—each determined to take all. The ancient principles of the game of power have come once more into their own. Those who follow them win. Those who forget them perish.

2. THE DYNAMICS OF FOREIGN POLICY

> It very rarely happens, or perhaps never occurs, that a person exalts
> himself from a humble station to great dignity without employing either
> force or fraud, unless indeed he attains it by gift or hereditary succession.
> I do not even conceive that force alone ever sufficed; but we shall find that
> cunning alone has sometimes succeeded.—NICCOLÒ MACHIAVELLI, *Dis-*
> *courses on Livy.*

Foreign policy is an expression of a State's will-to-power. States consist of sundry millions of patriots who obey the leaders who decide how
and when and where power is to be pursued and against whom and with
whom. Leaders in democracies are elected representatives answerable
to their followers and periodically subject to reelection or retirement.
They therefore find it difficult to practice *Realpolitik*, for they are impeded not only by the stubborn facts of the international environment
to which they must adapt their ends and means, but also by the desires
and hopes and illusions of masses of voters who know little of the subtleties of diplomacy. Leaders in autocracies are more free because their
followers are less free. They may often say, with Louis XIV, "L'Etat,
c'est moi!" ("The State? That's me!") They may play the game of
power abroad with no checks at home so long as they win successes or at
least avoid disasters.

But in every State, whatever the inner form of its policy, diplomacy
is the work of particular persons among the high and mighty who have
become specialists in Machiavelli's art. Foreign policies present the appearance of being formulated, at each given moment of time, by particular
individuals occupying high executive posts in governments. The American
Secretary of State, the British Secretary of State for Foreign Affairs,
the French, German, Italian, and Japanese Ministers of Foreign Affairs,
the Peoples' Commissar for Foreign Affairs in the U.S.S.R.—these and
their counterparts in the sundry sovereignties of the world are charged
with the conduct of the foreign relations of their respective States. These
foreign ministers occupy, in every case, a position of preeminence in their
cabinets. In presidential governments, such as those prevailing in the
United States and the Latin American republics, the secretary of state is
appointed by a popularly elected president, by whom he may be removed.
In parliamentary governments the foreign minister is a popularly elected
member of the legislature who is a leader of his party and who is picked
by the prime minister in the name of the king or president. Sometimes
the prime minister will himself take the portfolio of foreign affairs. In
either case, the foreign minister is a leading member of a cabinet which
is answerable to parliament. In the despotisms the foreign minister is
likewise appointed by those with executive power, unless the tyrant him-

self assumes the post. In all forms of government the foreign minister works in close collaboration with the head of the cabinet and with the other ministers, particularly with the heads of the departments of war, navy, commerce, and colonies. To what degree he can impose his own views on his colleagues, and to what degree he is controlled by those with whom he works, depends largely on personal equations.

The relations, personal and political, between the foreign minister and the chief executive constitute only one factor influencing the determination of foreign policy. The minister is the head of the foreign office and of its field services. He is obliged to rely for information and advice upon the permanent civil servants under his direction. Theoretically, he gives orders to his subordinates. But the subordinates are experienced professional experts, while he is often a politician-amateur. In practice, therefore, the minister may easily become the slave of his servants, and the determination of policies may rest in the hands of professional bureaucrats who are answerable only to their consciences. For factual information about current political problems, the minister must rely upon diplomatic agents abroad and upon the geographical divisions of the foreign office. For knowledge of commercial and financial matters, he is dependent upon his economic adviser and upon consular agents abroad. Legal problems he must submit to the legal adviser of the foreign office. Problems of etiquette and ceremonial he refers to the division of protocol. Precedents, former policies, records of things past he derives from the historical adviser and the archives section. The experts in the foreign office are the custodians of the forms of international intercourse, and by these forms the foreign minister and his agents are rigidly bound. In these various ways the professional bureaucracy always exercises great influence over the nominal head of the ministry or department of foreign affairs. It is the custodian of tradition, the keeper of the seals, the preserver of the past. It resists innovation. It adheres to its habitual attitudes, purposes, and modes of behavior. It bends the foreign minister to its ancient ways more frequently than it is bent by him toward new departures. Here is an important cause of the stability and continuity of foreign policies in the face of changes in politicians and party alignments.

The foreign minister must likewise reckon with forces and influences outside of his own circle of superiors, colleagues, and subordinates, but still within the orbit of government machinery. In democracies the legislature must be considered, for in democratic States it will have certain constitutional powers over foreign affairs and will endeavor to exercise a certain supervision over foreign policy. Almost all national parliaments are entrusted with decisions of peace and war and with the ratification of treaties. In the United States, all treaties must be approved by two-thirds of the Senate. In some other governments, certain specified treaties must be approved by a majority of both branches of parliament. The legislature may also have a voice in diplomatic appointments, and it is always able to influence foreign affairs through its general powers of appropriating money and enacting laws. In parliamentary governments, where ministerial responsibility prevails, the legislature can turn out the cabinet on issues of foreign policy as readily as on questions of domestic import. In such governments the foreign minister will be a member of the legislature and will be always in intimate contact with it. But whether he is a member or not, he must at all times endeavor to secure legislative approval for such of his policies as cannot be executed without it. He must speak in explanation and defense before the chambers, or at least before their committees on foreign affairs. He must "wangle" the appropriations which his purposes require. He must treat legislative resolutions on foreign affairs with respect, even when he does not act upon them. He must secure support for such treaties as must receive parliamentary approval in order to be valid. The legislature is thus able to exercise an appreciable degree of influence upon foreign policy in most governments, despite the fact that initiative and control continue to rest with the executive.

The role of political parties is likewise not to be neglected—in all States where more than one is tolerated. In many States, foreign policy is supposed to be so stable, so continuous, so charged with the interests and welfare of the whole nation as to be above partisan politics. Even in this case, however, there may be a "right" foreign policy and a "left" foreign policy, with slight differences between them in methods and objectives. Foreign ministers are almost always party leaders. Issues of foreign policy are often grist for the mill of parliamentary debates and electoral contests. In most of the Great Powers, however, one is struck less by the differences in party programs on foreign affairs than by their similarity. Elections are seldom won or lost, candidates are seldom elected or defeated because of international questions. Although there has everywhere been more popular interest in foreign affairs since the Great War than before and although party politics in most States now has more significance for foreign policy than heretofore, it still remains true that these issues play a minor role in domestic political struggles and that changes in the partisan composition of government seldom lead to radical transformations of diplomatic purposes. This circumstance is due to many things: the continuity given to foreign policy by the permanent bureaucracy which administers it, the lack of popular interest in diplomatic problems as compared with domestic problems, the existence in each State of relatively fixed patterns of policy based upon the general power interests of the State in relation to other States, the propensity of patriots to view all criticism of foreign policy as "unpatriotic," etc. These considerations discourage innovation and keep foreign policy in its accustomed groove. Political expediency often dictates caution, circumspection, delay, and timidity. But it seldom dictates new departures.

If a foreign minister can, in many cases, hold himself aloof from party politics, he can never afford to ignore the daily press, either at home or abroad. In the twentieth century a "good press" is essential to diplomatic success in all ventures which cannot be conducted in secrecy. With the great metropolitan newspapers of the world's capitals influencing the thought and action of millions of readers, with "public opinion" and the moral imponderables spelling triumph or defeat for all far-reaching political schemes, it is of vital importance for foreign offices to gain the friendship of reporters, editors, and owners of the leading journals. Press conferences and press releases must be handled with extreme care. Foreign correspondents and foreign newspapers are particularly important, and various techniques of influencing them have been devised.

Most foreign offices are granted secret funds to be used in shaping opinion abroad. For many years prior to 1914 the great majority of the newspapers of Paris were in the pay of the Russian Government. In return for bribes, they influenced French opinion favorably toward Russian bonds, toward the Dual Alliance, toward the prospects and purposes of the Tsardom, toward the necessity of close Franco-Russian diplomatic and military collaboration. In the 1930's, many French papers were in the pay of Hitler and Mussolini. These are not isolated instances, for foreign offices everywhere resort to similar tactics for similar purposes. In a few cases, notably in France, it has even been alleged that such funds are utilized to bribe domestic newspapers. A free and independent press may often cause embarrassment to diplomats, either by jingoistic chauvinism or by attacks upon the power-and-profit motives of particular diplomatic enterprises. Foreign offices must therefore watch the world press constantly, and they must devise means of controlling those who have their price and of placating those whose influence is not for sale. It was no small advantage to the diplomats of the despotisms that they could influence the free press in democratic States (before open war began) in order to create the sympathies and antipathies they desired, whereas their home press, being owned, controlled, or rigidly censored by the group in power, was immune from foreign pressure and could be used to regiment opinion as the Caesars desired.

"Public opinion" is a vague, intangible force which must likewise be taken into account by foreign ministers and diplomatic representatives. Whether public opinion in the bourgeois democracies is reflected in the daily press or is manufactured by the daily press is an interesting subject of academic debate. For the foreign offices, it is enough to remember that newspapers print what editors and owners think people like to read and that people are likely to think in terms suggested to them by newspapers.

The daily press is doubtless the most significant mirror of opinion and the most important force shaping that opinion. A thousand other forces play their roles, and the skillful manipulator will finger them all like an organist at a huge keyboard. Every foreign office has need of such organists, for the state of the public mind may demand this diplomatic action and condemn that, it may overturn this government and support that, it may make success possible here and ensure failure there. This force operates through elections, through organized pressure groups and lobbies, and through the representative legislature. It is all-pervasive, insidious, fickle, changeable.

This "public," however, is no homogeneous mass of like-minded individuals. It is no mythical, manlike monster possessed of a single will and of power to enforce that will. The great body of voters (and of nonvoters) who constitute the public is divided into almost innumerable segments which join, separate, dissolve, coalesce, cooperate, and disintegrate in a dizzy waltz. Some lines of cleavage are relatively permanent, such as those arising out of economic class interests, religious affiliations, and sectional loyalties. Others are ephemeral and arise out of the whims and fancies and the particular problems of a given period of time. The public is a vast, complex aggregation of organized minorities of all kinds whose complex interactions account for the variability and the unpredictability of the final result. Here is a political chess game more intricate and fascinating than the game of Great Power politics itself.

In analyzing the public from the point of view of the forces determining governmental policies and the elements with which the formulators of policies must reckon, the cleavages rising out of economic class distinction would seem to be of fundamental importance. Vocational groupings in themselves are politically significant, for in every national society there are butchers, bakers, candlestick makers and a thousand other craftsmen, artisans, and professional people. But class groupings are broader than these. Rich men, poor men, beggarmen, and thieves all feel a certain camaraderie with their fellows and all have political axes to grind. The modern societies of the Western nation-states comprise four major economic groupings whose relations with one another vary greatly from country to country: a landed aristocracy surviving from the feudal nobility of the middle ages; an agrarian class of peasants or farmers descended from the medieval serfs; a bourgeois class of businessmen, shopkeepers, financiers, and industrialists, raised to immense power by the Industrial Revolution; and an urban wage-earning class slowly becoming aware of its interests and its potentialities. The nineteenth and twentieth centuries have been the epoch of private capitalism and the political ascendancy of the bourgeoisie. This class constitutes the ruling group in many lands. In Great Britain, in Germany, in pre-war Russia, in present-day Japan, it shares power with the older landed gentry. In France, only remnants of the old nobility have survived the revolution. In the United States, no true landed aristocracy has existed since the end of slavery in the South. In all these States and many others, peasants or farmers and industrial workers strive for political influence in competition with the predominant bourgeoisie, sometimes through political parties of their own, sometimes within the bourgeois parties. In Russia, where the old social order was demolished, bourgeoisie and nobility alike have been swept from power and destroyed. The process of politics in all nations is intelligible only in terms of the interests, attitudes, demands, and purposes of these socio-economic strata in the electorate. And governmental policies in foreign, no less than in domestic, affairs reflect at all times the prevailing political equilibrium between these forces.

An adequate understanding of the foreign policy of any State would require a detailed analysis of the forces within the nation which have been suggested. These forces can scarcely be reduced to measurable terms. They are so numerous, so complex in themselves and in their interrelationships, that all prediction regarding the future equilibrium between them is hazardous. But the determining factors in the total situation are fairly obvious. The dead hand of the past, moreover, always hangs heavy over the present and affords a stability and continuity which might otherwise be lacking. From the point of view of the formulation of foreign policy, these forces may be thought of as sources of pressures which beat in upon the foreign minister and drive him inevitably in a direction over which he has little personal control. Far from being a free agent, a foreign minister has most of his policies determined for him in advance by forces beyond his reach. Never can he escape from the principles of law, the institutional forms, the values, behavior, patterns, and standardized procedures which make up the art and science of diplomacy in the Western State System. Never can he successfully defy the patriotic sentiments and traditions of the great masses of his fellow countrymen. Never can he pursue goals radically different from those dictated by the existing political equilibrium of social classes within the nation. He is often bound hand and foot by party politics, by legislative interferences, by executive supervision, by the habits and opinions of the foreign office staff and the diplomatic bureaucracy. He is bound by the diplomatic patterns and traditions inherited from the Baroque period of the dynasts and the aristocracies. A weak leader will be controlled completely by these pressures. A strong leader will know how to play them off against one another, how to gauge their potency with intuitive perception, how to enlarge somewhat the extremely narrow range of questions with regard to which he may exercise his personal judgment. The art of politics is the art of what is possible. The limits of what is possible for a foreign minister are closely defined by the juxtaposition of forces operating behind and around and within and through his own personality.

Modern democratic theorists have generally assumed that in "popular" governments the mass of the citizenry, by a process of thorough study, orderly discussion, and reasonable compromise, arrive at a consensus of opinion regarding public policy and that this consensus, this "popular will," is carried out by representative lawmakers and administrators. It is contended that democracy in foreign affairs involves the rational formulation of a popular will as to how the nation's relations with other States should be conducted and the translation of this will into action by the elected servants of the people. These servants, it is argued, must act openly, honestly, frankly, in the full light of day, in order that the citizenry may at all times perceive whether its will is being carried out and may call to account those charged with this duty. Secret diplomacy and selfish intrigue are viewed as relics of the predemocratic age, to be discarded and rendered impossible of revival. This is to be achieved through the power of public opinion, as wielded by an enlightened electorate, and through popular and legislative control of foreign policy. Since the Great War, there has been universal agitation for democratic control of international politics, general condemnation of the "old" diplomacy, and championship of the "new"—all on the assumption that democratic foreign policies will necessarily be enlightened, pacific, and constructive.

But democracy in foreign policy can never mean control of decisions by the inarticulate, unorganized mass of voters, for this mass can exercise no control over anything. The exercise of political power requires concentration, organization, a clearly formulated purpose, and means to achieve that purpose. Special groups with specific interests to serve always tend to control the formulation of public policy.[1] Democratic control can mean only that all interested groups shall have an equal opportunity to organize, agitate, propagandize, lobby, and otherwise bring pressure to bear on behalf of their programs. These groups, whether they be based upon provincial loyalties, class allegiances, vocational interests, or other common bonds, are ceaselessly engaged, inside and outside of political party struggles, in a competitive contest for power, in rival efforts to impress their wills upon the key officials who formulate policy. In an autocracy or dictatorship, certain groups occupy a position of legal privilege and monopolistic power and are able to discriminate against, or even destroy, rival groups. In a democracy all groups have at least a theoretically equal right to strive for influence and power. But the groups which will actually wield power will consist of interested persons with purposes of their own to serve. These purposes may be selfish or "disinterested,"

[1] See Walter Lippmann, *Public Opinion*, 1922, and *The Phantom Public*, 1925.

but they must exist, they must be verbalized and appreciated by the members of the group before it can act to influence policy.

In the formulation of foreign policy the best organized groups are within the governmental machine: the foreign office staff and the diplomatic bureaucracy. These groups usually have their way, and since they naturally resent outside meddling they prefer to work in secrecy. Secrecy is desired not merely to prevent interference by other groups, public or private, within the State, but also to accomplish those results in the arena of international politics itself which are impossible of achievement if purposes and methods are made known to the world press, to the public, to legislatures, and to other governments. Negotiations must be conducted in obscurity if popular clamor is not to make advantageous compromises impossible. The results of negotiations, embodied in written agreements, are often kept secret for reasons of high policy. The exact terms and intentions of all the pre-1914 alliances and ententes were carefully guarded by the foreign offices, and no one can doubt that similar secret commitments exist in the post-1919 world. Diplomatic correspondence in archives is often kept secret until it is of only historical or archaeological significance. Since complete secrecy is impossible, partial publicity must be given to matters of general interest—coupled with misrepresentation, duplicity, and falsification when critical situations seem to demand such measures.[1] Those who control directly the machinery of diplomacy are necessarily in the strongest position to use that machinery as they think best.

The democratization of foreign policy involves "meddling" and interference with the professional diplomatic bureaucracy on the part of outsiders. The professional bureaucracy is never insulated from the pressures of politically influential groups interested in foreign policy. At times, it is the spokesman and servant of these groups. It uses for its own purposes, and is used by (for their purposes), journalists, merchants, investors, missionaries, industrialists, etc. People with axes to grind, people with special interests to serve, people who are high in the party in power and who occupy strategic economic positions in the ruling class will never be

---

[1] For example, the French Yellow Book of 1914 was deliberately falsified by the Quai d'Orsay to make it appear that Russian mobilization was ordered after, instead of before, general Austrian and German mobilization. The dispatch of Paléologue, French Ambassador in St. Petersburg, 10:45 A.M., July 31 (sent sixteen hours after the event) declared "the mobilzation of the Russian army has been ordered." The falsifiers in the French Foreign Office concocted the following statement in place of the dispatch. "As a result of the general mobilization of Austria and of the measures for mobilization taken secretly, but continuously, by Germany for the last six days, the order for the general mobilization of the Russian Army has been given, Russia not being able, without serious danger, to allow herself to be further outdistanced; really she is only taking military measures corresponding to those taken by Germany. For imperative reasons of strategy the Russian Government, knowing that Germany was arming, could no longer delay the conversion of her partial mobilization into a general mobilization." F.Y.B., 1914, No. 118.

ignored by those who formulate foreign policy. Another step removed from the centers of power are the unofficial lobbies of pacifists, militarists, peace pleaders, preparedness advocates, professional patriots, internationalists, women's organizations, reformist groups, and other organized minorities of all kinds. These groups can seldom achieve results by working directly upon the foreign offices. Sometimes they can bring effective pressure to bear by influencing the legislature and public opinion. The "public" itself is not fully in the picture, except in crises when particular demands become almost universal. The task of those who would democratize foreign policy is to educate and organize the public, to induce it to take an interest in foreign affairs, to enable it to become vocal and to express its will to those who wield power at the center.

It is of fundamental importance, however, to bear in mind that the chief common bond which creates this "public," which gives cohesion and unity to the manifold interest groupings composing the electorates of the modern nation-states, is national patriotism. Except in the Soviet Union, where revolutionary proletarian internationalism has replaced bourgeois nationalism as the basis of political and social cohesion, the populations of all States have only such general and collective interests in foreign policy as emerge from a sense of common nationality, of identification with the nation, of loyalty to the fatherland. Democratic government on a national scale became possible only when sectional, group, and class loyalties were merged in common allegiance to the nation. The operation of democratic government strengthens this allegiance constantly. Democracy and nationalism have until recently been inseparable components in the political structure of the bourgeois nation-states. This can only mean that a democratic or popularly controlled foreign policy is a patriotic foreign policy— a policy reflecting the values, ideologies, symbols, and purposes of national patriots. To the degree to which national patriotism postulates international conflict, to the degree to which patriots are irrational, emotional, unreflective in their reactions, to that degree will a democratic foreign policy be bellivolent and unenlightened. To suppose that democratic control of foreign offices ensures pacific inclinations and informed altruism is to mistake the implications of patriotism and to overlook the relationship, in the political process, between democracy and nationalism. It would in fact be no exaggeration to say that a foreign policy which directly reflected popular patriotic passions would probably be more bellicose, less reasonable, more uncompromising, more exclusively devoted to the pursuit of selfish national interests than a foreign policy controlled by mature and experienced professional diplomats far removed from the tumult and the shouting of the market place.

In the despotisms, the new Caesars and their skillful propagandists manufacture patriotic excitement to order. Power holders rule by inculcating hero worship and fanatical hatred against the enemy class, the enemy race, and all the enemies beyond the frontier. Each success in the quest for power is presented by the controlled press, radio, and cinema as a triumph over foreign devils menacing the very life of the fatherland. Each failure is depicted as a dangerous threat by foes bent upon the destruction of the homes and altars of the chosen people. In this fashion the arbitrary rule of the tyrant is rendered palatable to befuddled masses which are easily moved by deceptive appearances to hail their oppressors with delirious enthusiasm. Under these conditions the head of the State, while apparently free to do what he likes, tends to become the slave of his followers who must be placated and bewitched with ever more glorious victories.

3. COMPROMISE AND CONFLICT

For unto every one that hath shall be given, and he shall have abundance; but from him that hath not shall be taken away even that which he hath.—MATT. 25: 29.

Plenty begets Pride; Pride, Envy, Envy, Warre,
Warre, Poverty, Poverty humble Care;
Humility breeds Peace, and Peace breeds Plenty;
Thus around the World doth rowle alternately.
*—ROBERT HAYMAN, *The World's Whirlegigge*, 1631.

This universal quest for power goes on under the conditions imposed by the nature of the State System and by the technological differentials between its members. Each State left to itself tends to extend its power over as wide a sphere as possible. Its power flows outward from a central nucleus in all directions. It is directed toward control of territory and people. If the ruling class of the State is an agrarian aristocracy, as in most of the States of the ancient world, control over territory and people is sought in order that the agricultural resources of the territory may be utilized to the profit of the conquerors, and the labor power of the people may be exploited through slavery or serfdom. If the ruling class is a commercial bourgeoisie, as in Western Europe between the sixteenth and nineteenth centuries, conquests are sought in order that the import and export trade of the region conquered may be monopolized. If it is an industrial and financial bourgeoisie, as in the twentieth century Western world, commodity and investment markets are sought—and they may be obtained by methods of control more subtle and indirect than open conquest and annexation. If the revolutionary proletariat is in power, as in the Soviet Union, it may seek conquests in order to extend the scope of the revolution and weaken the power of its enemies. If the *élite*, as in the Fascist States, is a war-driven and power-hungry brotherhood, recruited from middle-class outcasts, the objective of action is glory and conquest

as e   all means thereto. These purposes are rationalized,
dis   and supplemented by others, in accordance with the
at   ents of the ruling group. But the enhancement of
S   the goal. The will-to-power necessarily expresses
i   ms, both because political control is often sought as
a me   c exploitation and because territories and populations
are useful i   urther enhancement of power only when their resources
and energies are harnessed to the victor's chariot.

In a State System in which the sovereign units are engaged in a constant competitive struggle, power is at all times a relative quantity. In a world of one State, power considerations would disappear unless that State were threatened by internal revolution or barbarian incursions. A State existing in complete isolation from all other States would have no "power interests," for such interests grow out of contact, competition, and conflict among States. The "power" of a State is a meaningless concept except in relation to the power of other States. The power of each State, moreover, is significant only in relation to the other Powers with which it is in geographical proximity. The power of Italy is important as compared with the power of Germany, Spain, or Great Britain, but not of much importance as compared with the power of Japan, Bolivia, or Afghanistan, for normally Italian power will not come into contact with Powers so far away. The power of the United States is important in relation to the power of Cuba, Nicaragua, Mexico, and Great Britain, but not important ordinarily in relation to the Soviet Union, Nepal, or Iraq, for it cannot be exercised effectively in such remote places. The power of lesser States has meaning only in relation to their immediate neighbors. Power has meaning only as against other Powers which can be reached by it.

In the extension of State power, natural barriers may constitute as important an obstacle as the power of neighboring rival States. The extent to which such barriers are obstacles to expansion depends largely on the technological devices available for overcoming them. Power is always local. Ability to exercise it at points remote from its center varies inversely with distance and directly with the level of technology. Waterways and sea channels which are insuperable obstacles to people with small sailing vessels become paths to empire for peoples with more effective modes of transportation. Deserts cease to be barriers and become sources of wealth for peoples acquainted with the science of irrigation. The tropical jungle which was an impassable wilderness in the sixteenth century is a rich source of rubber, woods, bananas, and other products in the twentieth, when railways, automobile roads, and steamships are available. Even Arctic wastes and high mountain walls yield to the airplane. Machine technology facilitates the surmounting of such barriers and makes possible an extension of State power over distances once regarded as fantastic. The world empires of today are existing realities made administratively possible by the new technology. The world government of the future is already technologically possible, whatever may be the psychological and cultural difficulties in the way of its creation.

More serious obstacles to the extension of State power are encountered in the form of other States. These obstacles may also be overcome with ease if the technological differential between these States is sufficiently great. The people of the bow and arrow, the spear, the canoe, the sailing vessel must yield to the people of the machine gun, the battleship, and the bombing plane. Most of the peoples of the world not equipped with Western technology have lost their independence to the Western Powers. But the Western Powers themselves, and the States of the non-European world which have adopted Western ways, are on a parity of power so far as technology is concerned. Power relations among them are determined by size, population, man power, natural resources, armaments, shipping, commercial and industrial development, economic efficiency, organizing capacity, etc. These things are political objectives and stakes of diplomacy, because they are the measures of power and the means of power. Geographical and technological considerations are no less important in overcoming other States than in overcoming natural barriers. Control of topographical vantage points may be of vital significance, for the strategy of diplomacy rests at bottom upon the tactics of war. From the days when a handful of Spartans blocked the Persian hordes at the mountain pass of Thermopylae to the days when the hosts of von Hindenburg crushed the Russian invaders in the Masurian Lakes region of East Prussia and the French at Verdun hurled back the assaults of the foe, control of strategic areas has been an element of decisive significance in power conflicts. Land power requires fortresses, mountain barriers, river boundaries, and forests as centers of defense and headquarters for attack. Sea power requires naval bases, fueling stations, domination of strategic waterways and of the great ocean channels. Many of the contests of Great Power politics are waged for control of points of strategic importance, though in prolonged combats between the Powers victory may depend less on tactics and strategy than on the economic organization and morale of whole populations.

The Western State System has developed in such fashion that no one of its members possesses at any time sufficient power to extend its control over all the others. In the interests of self-defense, the members tend to combine against any one which is a potential menace to all. Invariably the pretender to world power is repressed by a coalition of the prospective victims. Each Power thus retains its independence, and the State System is preserved. Under these circumstances, an equilibrium or balance of power results. Any enhancement of the power of one State is a disturbance of the equilibrium and a potential threat to the others. At times this equilibrium is intangible, imponderable, and in the background of diplomatic action. At other times, and more frequently, it is clearly and sharply defined in alliances and coalitions. Each member of an alliance has an interest in forestalling any enhancement of the power of some member of the opposing alliance. The two coalitions or groupings of Powers are thus held together by common power interests, and conflicts for power become issues between the alliances as a whole. This pattern of power relationships has characterized the Western State System from its earliest beginnings.

The role of small States in this system of relationships is a peculiar one. The very minute States of Europe are historical curiosities and play no part in Power relationships. But such States as Portugal, Belgium, the Netherlands, Denmark, Switzerland, Albania, and the like, are all adjacent to infinitely more powerful States which could easily impose their will upon them and extinguish their independence if granted a free hand. In some cases, this has happened: Ireland was conquered by England in the middle ages; Poland was partitioned among her great neighbors at the end of the eighteenth century; the Low Countries, Poland, and two of the Scandinavian Kingdoms are at the time of writing under the conqueror's heel. But usually this result is rendered impossible by the conflicting power interests of the great States themselves. The small States, being impotent, have no power interests of their own save the preservation of their independence; and this they are able to protect, not by their own power, but by fitting themselves into the power relations of their mighty neighbors. The small States are often "buffers." They stand at the focal points of tension between the Great Powers, with the result that each Power prefers the maintenance of the independence of the small State to the extinction of that independence at the hands of a rival Power. Portugal was long a buffer of this kind between Spain and England. The Low Countries lay between England, France, and Germany. Each of these States opposed control by either of the others of this strategically vital area containing the mouths of the Rhine and the Scheldt. During the past two centuries England has successively fought Spain, Austria, France, and Germany when these States threatened to dominate this region. Belgium and the Netherlands are (or were) thus relatively secure in their independence, because of the power relations between their larger neighbors. Denmark was similarly a buffer between Germany and Great Britain, for the sea-power interests of the latter moved the British Government to oppose control of Denmark by a powerful Continental State as vigilantly as it opposed such control of the Netherlands, Belgium, or Portugal. Switzerland is most secure of all, for it is completely surrounded by Great Powers: France, Germany, Italy, and formerly Austria-Hungary. In every case the buffer State is dependent for its security in peacetime upon the diplomatic rivalries of its neighbors. In a general war among the Powers, it may be able to remain neutral (*e.g.*, Switzerland, the Netherlands, and the Scandinavian States, 1914–1918), unless it becomes a theater of battle between the belligerents (*e.g.*, Belgium in 1914). In the latter case, it must align itself with that coalition which seems least likely to deprive it of independence in the event of victory, or else remain neutral and face ruin (*e.g.*, the Scandinavian States and the Low Countries, 1939–1940).

Considerations of a similar character serve to explain the continued independence of small or weak native States in the areas of imperialistic rivalries between the Powers. The native States which lay directly athwart the path of expansion of a Great Power, unopposed by other Powers, have all succumbed. Those which survive are located at the tension points between rival imperialisms. Neither of the rival Powers wishes the other to enlarge its territory by annexing the intervening buffer State. The latter is enabled by this circumstance to play off the imperialists against one another. Ethiopia was thus the vortex of converging drives of British, French, and Italian expansionists. These drives neutralized one another, and Ethiopia remained independent until 1936. Turkey has similarly profited by conflicts between Russia, Great Britain, France, Germany, and Austria-Hungary. Iran and Afghanistan have been buffer States between British and Russian imperialisms. China has retained nominal control of Tibet, because neither Russia nor Great Britain could afford to permit the other to acquire it. China itself has thus far escaped complete partition for similar reasons. Thailand lies at the focal point of rival imperialisms in southeastern Asia. The independence of the Latin American Republics was originally championed by the United States to forestall European conquest. By the same token, the remaining colonial possessions of the Minor Powers are relatively secure against appropriation by the Great Powers, because none of the latter can permit any of the others to acquire them. The Portuguese colonies in Africa were long buffers between Great Britain and Germany. For over half a century neither Great Britain nor France nor the United States nor Japan would permit either of the others to acquire the Dutch East Indies, for this would have upset completely the established equilibrium in the southwestern Pacific.

As regards the complex plays and counterplays of the Great Powers themselves in their constant efforts to maintain or upset the balance of power, it is useful to recall Bismarck's suggestive distinction between "satiated" and "unsatiated" States. At any given period of time, the existing equilibrium, the prevailing distribution of power, the established ratios of territories, populations, armies, navies, colonies, etc., will appear ideal to the States which are its beneficiaries and unendurable to the States which do not feel that they have received their just due. The satiated States, content with the *status quo*, will usually be those which have been victorious in the last armed conflict and have been able to create a *status quo* in accordance with their own interests. The unsatiated States, bent upon modifying the *status quo* to their own advantage, will normally be those defeated in the last war and deprived of power by the victors. Rival alliances and coalitions emerge out of these relationships, with the satiated States combining to protect what they have acquired and the unsatiated combining to acquire what they covet.

All States do not, of course, fall into these neat categories, for some have complex and contradictory interests which drive them in opposite directions. Great Britain and Italy are examples. But generally speaking, the broad currents of Great Power politics can be interpreted in these terms. Prior to 1870, France was a satiated State, determined to preserve the prevailing equilibrium. This equilibrium was upset by the unification of Italy and Germany. French efforts to thwart German unification ended in disaster; and after 1871 France became an unsatiated State, bent upon recovering what had been lost. Germany under Bismarck was content with the *status quo* and formed alliances with Italy and Austria-Hungary to preserve it. France sought allies as a counterweight. Insatiable Tsarist Russia, driving toward the Straits and the Balkans, was a logical partner in the anti-German coalition. Great Britain was won over when German colonial, commercial, and naval ambitions caused Downing Street to regard Germany as a menace to the established distribution of sea power, markets, and imperial possessions. Britain was more interested in preserving the *status quo* than in upsetting it. Italy desired upsets both at the expense of Vienna and Paris. These two Powers were, therefore, not "loyal" members of the coalitions which they had joined. Britain joined the weaker side in 1914 only after considerable hesitation. Italy deserted her allies and followed suit in 1915. After the Entente victory and the peace settlement of 1919, the new victors became *status quo* States and the vanquished became "revisionist," *i.e.*, *revanchard*, in their policies. By the same logic the Axis Powers, after their conquest of most of the Continent in 1939–1940, asked nothing more than "peace" on the basis of the "new order" which they were striving to establish, but Britain fought on to restore a balance, and the United States and the Soviet Union became potential challengers of the victors.

In this ceaseless and uneasy striving for power, States which benefit from the established *status quo* seek naturally to preserve that from which they benefit. States which feel humiliated, hampered, and oppressed by the *status quo* seek as naturally to modify it. Satiated States are therefore likely to appear to be "pacific." They are committed to peace. They demand "security," for they are content with the equilibrium which peace and security will perpetuate. Unsatiated States demand changes, rectifications of frontiers, a revision of treaties, a redistribution of territory and power. Insofar as the fulfillment of these demands is resisted by *status quo* States, insofar as this resistance makes possible their realization only through coercion and conflict, such States appear to be "aggressive" and lacking in enthusiasm for peace. If such States have been reduced to impotence, as was the case with France from 1871 to 1894 and with Germany after 1919, they must speak softly, conceal their aims, and refrain from challenges or provocations which would result only in further losses in the event of a test of force.

Diplomatic friction between States arises from the fact that the existing equilibrium, at any given moment, is unstable because it rests upon a series of shifting tensions between the satiated and the unsatiated. The balance is unstable because it is seldom based upon a distribution of territory and power satisfactory to all the members of the State System. At the close of each great contest the rapacity of the victors and the weakness of the vanquished invite punitive settlements which are resented by their victims to such a degree as to ensure new conflict. Each peace contains the seeds of the next war. Each war results in a new peace. Even when great moderation is shown and mutual adjustments and compromises are achieved, the resulting equilibrium is only temporary, for uncontrollable and unforeseen factors are constantly upsetting the delicately poised balance and creating new tensions. These tensions usually center in territorial questions; for control of territory means land, population, resources, wealth, in short, all the ingredients of power. In such situations, compromise is difficult, for power is relative and each State's gain is another State's loss. A constant struggle therefore goes on for control of the means of power: strategic centers, backward areas, markets, waterways, irredentas, and frontier provinces. In this unstable balancing of shifting forces there can be neither permanence nor peace.

In the struggle between "satiated" and "unsatiated," between "haves" and "have-nots," the States in the former category do not pursue "dynamic" or "aggressive" policies simply because of the relatively disadvantageous position they occupy in the total distribution of power. Such policies are a consequence of the hope of ultimately changing the distribution. Great Powers can entertain such hopes. Minor Powers usually cannot. Germany, Japan, and Italy pursued aggressive policies in the 1930's because such policies, though dangerous, offered hope of success. Bulgaria, Hungary, or Lithuania, if unaided by Great Powers, had no such hopes and were long obliged to acquiesce in the *status quo*. Aggressive policies are likewise a consequence of internal tensions, insecurities, and hatreds, driving rulers to adventures abroad as a means of mobilizing acquiescence at home. Unsatiated Powers are typically those in which collective deprivations, bred of diplomatic or military frustrations coupled with economic maladjustments and latent class conflict within the State, give rise to demands for *revanche* and to ruthless efforts to restore unity, self-respect, power, and prosperity by attacks upon other nations.

On the chessboard of power politics, each Power is typically the potential enemy of its neighbors and the potential ally of its neighbor's neighbors. States which are neighbors are "friends" only when they both fear a third neighbor (as Britain and France *vis-à-vis* Germany, 1904–1940) or when they have by mutual consent renounced the game of power (as the United States and Canada since 1815). Proximity otherwise breeds rivalry for control of border areas which, once controlled, will give the controller superiority of power over his neighbor. Since outflanking and encircling operations are of the essence of war and since diplomacy is potential war, it is advantageous for each Power to have allies on the flanks or in the rear of its foe. Thus France and Britain were aligned with Russia before 1914 and with Poland, Czechoslovakia, Jugoslavia, and Rumania after 1919. In the face of this bloc, Germany, Italy, Hungary, Bulgaria, and the Soviet Union had common interests which found expression in the "Axis" and in the partitions of Poland and Rumania in 1939–1940. In the larger arena of the world, Germany, Italy, and Japan are allies against the U.S.S.R. and the English-speaking Powers, while the United States, the Soviet Union, and Britain (as of 1941) are potential allies against the opposing coalition. Potential alignments become actual ones, however, only when those who shape the policies among prospective allies are willing and able to make common cause with the potential enemies of their enemies. When they are inhibited from so doing by pride or prejudice, or reluctance to pay the price of an alliance, or by fatuous hopes that their menacing neighbor will attack others and leave them in peace (*e.g.*, Chamberlain's Britain and Daladier's France *vis-à-vis* Germany and U.S.S.R. in 1938–1939), they are left in lonely isolation and often condemned to defeat.

In the balancing-of-power process, long-festering fears and hatreds lead to periodical explosions of violence because the process operates haltingly and ineffectively. Any increase in the power of unsatiated States, through heavier armaments or alliances, creates new insecurities among the satiated and causes them to seek to redress the balance by still heavier armaments or counteralliances. But the compensatory policies seldom restore the equilibrium to its old level. They create new insecurities among the "have-nots," driving them to further steps to enhance their ability to overthrow the *status quo* by force. The "haves," moreover, are committed to "peace" and are reluctant to risk conflict or meet a challenge by a war of prevention. They typically procrastinate, make excuses for inaction, and fall victims to depressing anxieties without taking decisive action until it is too late to restore the balance. Imperial Germany after 1871 thus permitted France to rearm and form a coalition against her, without counterattacking until the strategic moment had long since passed. The French bloc and Britain, after 1933, permitted Germany and Italy to increase their power to a point at which they could upset the *status quo* and render any effort to thwart their designs highly dangerous. Counteraction was postponed in proportion as it became more and more difficult. The instability of each equilibrium generates tensions that explode in cataclysmic readjustments through wholesale violence because the players of the game of power are unable or unwilling to achieve smooth and gradual readjustments by other means.

4. THE ASSUMPTION OF VIOLENCE

War is politics continued by other (*i.e.*, forcible) means.—CLAUSEWITZ, *On War.*

When I say that the principal cause of war is war itself, I mean that the aim for which war is judged worth while is most often something which itself affects military power. Just as in military operations each side aims at getting anything which will give it a military advantage, so in diplomacy each side aims at getting anything which will enhance its power. Diplomacy is potential war. It is permeated by the struggle for power and when potential breaks out into actual war, that is usually because irreconcilable claims have been made to some element of power, and neither side can claim such preponderance as to compel the other to give way by a mere threat.—R. G. HAWTREY, *Economic Aspects of Sovereignty.*

That the assumption of violence lies behind all diplomacy is a truism which would be too obvious to dwell upon, were it not so frequently forgotten, often with disastrous results, in piping times of peace. Diplomatic bargaining and armed coercion are complementary weapons in the struggle for power among the nation-states. In the Western State System, as in all the state systems which have preceded it, military force has ever been the decisive means by which State power has been created, increased, reduced, or destroyed. The competitive struggle for hegemony and survival in which States have always engaged has been carried on from time immemorial through the clash of fighting soldiery and ships of war. The "Gallery of Battles" in the great palace at Versailles, depicting the combats by which the French nation was created and its power enhanced, could be duplicated for every sovereign State of the world. The world historical drama of international politics is a pageant of strife. Assyrians descend like the wolf on the fold. Hittite and Egyptian war chariots clash on the Mediterranean shore. Greek triremes ram Persian fighting ships at

Salamis. Macedonian phalanxes conquer a world empire. The war elephants of Hannibal charge the legions of Rome. The hosts of the Caesars conquer a vast realm embracing all of Classical civilization. Barbarian hordes overwhelm the Roman world State. Feudal knights and barons fight one another and battle the infidels. Mercenary armies of ambitious monarchs carve out nations. Popular armies of the nation-states engage in intermittent conflicts for power. The mechanized war monsters of the machine age ride roughshod over Africa and Asia and cover with blood and destruction the fields of Flanders and Galicia, Picardy and Lombardy, Manchuria and Ethiopia.

This universality of violence in international politics has been explained by numberless commentators in terms of original sin, the punishments of Providence, the machinations of the devil, the "fighting instinct" of man, the cry for bread, the periodical reversion of *homo sapiens* to savagery, etc. Though certain of these explanations have suggestive value, it is perhaps more relevant to recall that international politics is essentially a competitive struggle for power among sovereign members of State Systems. War is an incident of this struggle. Military violence is the ultimate means resorted to by States in their pursuit of power. The present problem is not that of explaining why men fight in general, but why States habitually resort to force in their differences with one another. All politics is a struggle for power, but in the domestic or national arenas recourse is had to violence only rarely. In international politics, on the contrary, violence or threatened violence is customary. War is to international politics what revolution is to national politics: a resort to physical coercion to achieve political objectives, *i.e.*, to preserve the power of the user against attack, to enhance that power at the expense of a rival, to upset an established equilibrium of power, or to prevent it from being upset. To be sure, national law forbids the use of force as a political weapon, and international law does not. The League Covenant and the Kellogg-Briand Pact sought to make war in the legal sense unlawful, but they did not prevent recourse to force under other names. The question calling for answer is: Why is physical coercion more frequently resorted to by States in the struggle for power which constitutes international politics than by parties, factions, sections, and classes in the corresponding struggle within national frontiers which constitutes national politics?

The answer lies in the circumstance that States do not stand in the same relation to one another as do parties, factions, sections, and classes within States. These entities of national politics are normally bound together by a "constitutional consensus," by common interests, by a consciousness of being parts of a larger whole—the nation—to which all owe allegiance. This consciousness and these common interests furnish a frame of reference for the pacific settlement of particular differences. Special interests are subordinated to general interests and are couched in terms of general interests. Political leaders, trade-union officials, provincial spokesmen, and businessmen are not usually disposed to say, "My party right or wrong!", "My section right or wrong!", "My class right or wrong!" They are rather disposed to assert that the general interests will be served best by the promotion of their particular interests and by the acceptance of their particular demands. The assumption of violence is not ordinarily made. The assumption is rather that of discussion, compromise, acquiescence in the result of pacific processes of adjustment. Without this assumption, orderly government is impossible. When the assumption ceases to be accepted, when the constitutional consensus breaks down, when the parties in the struggle for power place particular interests above general interests, there is danger of a resort to violence, *i.e.*, of revolution, riots, coups d'état, and civil war. If the coercive power of the State, exercised in the name of the general interest, is insufficient to repress disorder, revolution breaks out. It is of the essence of revolution that particular interests are placed above general interests and that coercion is substituted for compromise. So long as the political process functions normally on the basis of the assumption suggested, violence is eschewed, a peaceable equilibrium of forces is maintained, and all acquiesce pacifically to the "general will."

Sovereign States do not deal with one another on the basis of these assumptions. They are not parts of a larger whole, except in a formal sense, for a State System is not comparable to a national society or a national government. It is an aggregation of separate entities, each of which pursues its own interests by self-help and keenly resents any suggestion that its interests are to be subordinated to the interests of other States or of the whole community of States. There is as yet no "international government" worthy of the name, despite the hopes of proponents of the League of Nations. There is no international "constitutional consensus." There is no international police force, no super-state monopolizing coercive authority, to be employed in the general interest. International law itself is only what States agree upon, and it is enforced by State action. Coercive power in international society resides not in central organs reflecting the general interests, but in particular States pursuing particular interests. "My country right or wrong!" is an accepted slogan of State behavior. Under these circumstances, it is difficult to bring about the peaceable adjustment of inter-state differences through procedures and principles laid down by an inchoate international community on the basis of general interests which are largely nonexistent. Each State must rely upon its own strength. The struggle for power tends to involve coercion or threats of coercion, for States take what they can and keep what they take. When coercion is threatened or openly resorted to, there is no effective international authority to repress the peacebreakers and preserve law and order. If anarchy involves the absence of government, the pursuit by each of his own ends, and the use of violence in the service of such ends, then the practice of international politics can indeed be described accurately as "international anarchy."

It is noteworthy that, by a singular paradox, the very faith which makes for peace and unity within modern States makes for friction and conflict between them. That faith is nationalism. A sense of common nationality, a consciousness of common national interests and of national solidarity, disposes all pretenders to political power within each nation-state to place the nation above party, section, or class and to adjust differences on the basis of a common patriotism. Prior to the emergence of nationalism, armed conflict between feudal barons, free cities, provinces, and religious sects was frequent. Only when these lesser allegiances were merged in a national allegiance did local and neighborhood warfare come to an end. But, as Jean Jacques Rousseau once observed, "Men have suppressed little wars only to kindle greater ones." The nationalism which unites nations disunites the community of States of which each nation is a part. The national patriot exalts his own State and holds others in contempt. He vigorously opposes any subordination of national interests to international interests. He gives his support to those policies of national self-seeking which breed war. The power interests of States are couched in the language of nationalism, and nationalism leads to conflicts more gigantic and disastrous than any which were possible before the nation-states became unified.

Since the assumption of violence prevails in international politics, since physical coercion of State by State is an ever-present possibility, all States must keep swords sharp and powder dry to meet all eventualities. Each State must strive to have ready for instant use weapons of sufficient caliber, in sufficient numbers, to protect itself from attack and to promote its own interests by armed action whenever that appears necessary. Armaments are the spear points of foreign policy and the prime measure of power. As power is relative, the efficacy of armaments is also relative to the enemy armaments against which they may be pitted. "Preparedness" is never preparedness to fight some hypothetical State X or to fight the entire world, but to fight some specific State or States with which conflict seems likely. Each State arms against its neighbors, by land, sea, and air. The increasing smallness of the world, resulting from modern techniques of transportation, communication, and warfare, greatly enlarges the number of a State's "neighbors" and requires ever heavier armaments to attain "security" and achieve national purposes. Not only must the number of soldiers, sailors, and aviators be increased, but their equipment must be as modern and effective as those of the prospective enemy. Man power is no longer decisive; for masses of men, however well trained and heroic, are mere cannon fodder and can readily be ground to bloody pulp by the machines of modern war. Soldiers must have rifles, machine guns, hand grenades, trench mortars, poison gas, gas masks, barbed wire, armored cars, tanks, and light and heavy artillery. Sailors must have dreadnaughts, cruisers, destroyers, submarines, and aircraft carriers. Aviators must have bombing planes, combat planes, pursuit planes, dirigibles, balloons, and all the accompanying paraphernalia of defense and destruction. Without these devices, armed forces are helpless against mechanized enemy forces, as is clearly revealed by the whole history of imperialism, by the defeat of Russia in the Great War, by the military impotence of contemporary China, by the fate of Poland and Finland in 1939, and of the northern "neutrals" and France in 1940.

Competition in armaments is the inevitable corollary of competition for power. Armaments are the means of power and the measure thereof. An increase in the arms of one State automatically diminishes the power of its neighbors, unless they make a like increase. No State can permit its neighbors to enlarge their armaments to a point where they could feel certain of victory in war and could impose their will by the pressure of military superiority. Preparedness does not ensure peace, but it may instill fear in other States and make them less likely to disturb the existing equilibrium and more disposed to yield to the demands of more heavily armed rivals. For precisely this reason, preparedness induces other States to strive for an equal or a superior measure of preparedness. Each State seeks preponderance over possible enemies. If it succeeds after a victorious war in disarming the enemy State, as the Allies disarmed Germany in 1919 and as Germany and Italy disarmed France in 1940, it will be so much closer to preponderance. But even this security is unstable and transient when the disarmed State still has available the economic means, if not the legal right, of rearming. No single State can attain permanent preponderance. When all States endeavor to attain it, the result is a competitive race in armaments which may end in war, in bankruptcy, or in international agreements to limit or reduce arms. Each State must watch closely the armaments of all others and must attempt as best it can to prevent itself from falling too far behind in the race, for if this happens it will be exposed to diplomatic dictation and military attack.

Armaments are instruments of national policy, in peace no less than in war, for they largely determine the success of efforts to attain objectives through diplomacy. A diplomacy which is unsupported by potential fighting power is usually impotent. This fighting power need not be put to the test of war for it to count in the scales of diplomatic balances. A test of force is unnecessary when one disputant possesses an obvious superiority in armaments. The weaker party will yield without risking further losses through inevitable defeat in an open contest of strength unless the stronger demands the extinction of the weaker as the price of peace. In such a case, *e.g.*, Italy and Ethiopia in 1935, Britain and the Boer Republics in 1898, the U.S.S.R. and Finland in 1939, Italy and Greece in 1940, a feeble contestant may fight desperately and hopelessly in preference to surrender before *force majeure*, for surrender means national annihilation and the accidents of war may, miraculously, afford salvation. But when the demands of strong Powers upon weak Powers are not pressed to this point, and still more when they do not include territorial cessions, weakness yields to strength without armed resistance, for resistance may lead to extinction whereas surrender, however humiliating, leaves the victim at least alive. By the same token a man set upon by thieves may give up his money to save his life; but one assaulted by known assassins may fight his foes furiously, even if only to sell his life dearly. A test of force through war is necessary between Great Powers only when an apparent parity of strength exists and each side can hope to impose its will on the other. When one side knows that it is hopelessly inferior, it yields to diplomatic pressure and renders actual physical coercion unnecessary. Diplomacy is war by another name. It differs from war, not in objectives, but only in methods.

Diplomacy and strategy must go hand in hand. Every Great Power must strive in peacetime to prepare for war. It must maintain its armaments at a level which will secure recognition for the demands of its diplomats. It must strive, by persuasion or by force, to safeguard its power interests in areas of vital importance to it. Its diplomacy must be directed toward the control of strategic points which will enable it to exercise its power effectively. Power begets more power, and more power begets the demand for still more to protect what is already acquired. Great Britain must secure the Suez Canal, because she must defend India. To defend the Suez Canal she must control Egypt. To defend Egypt, she must control the Sudan, Aden, Malta, Cyprus, and Gibraltar. To defend her vast empire she must maintain a navy second to none, control naval bases all over the world, and strive to dominate as many strategic waterways as possible. Japan must control Port Arthur and the Liaotung peninsula in order to protect Korea and dominate the Gulf of Pechili. To control Port Arthur, she must control the railways of the Manchurian hinterland. To control these she must control Manchuria. To defend Manchuria, she must dominate Mongolia. The United States must defend the Panama Canal. This requires American naval dominance in the Caribbean. This in turn demands the control of the passages of the Caribbean—Bahia Honda and Guantanamo in Cuba, Porto Rico, and the

Virgin Islands—and control of the island bases that control the passages: the West Indies, the Bahamas, Bermuda, Newfoundland. It likewise leads to the control of the Great Corn and Little Corn Islands off the east coast of Nicaragua and of Fonseca Bay on the west coast as strategic prerequisites to the defense of a possible Nicaraguan canal. The diplomacy of strategy and the strategy of diplomacy are inseparable.

In a crisis, when a test of force appears imminent, control of policy passes from diplomats to strategists. When war is being waged, diplomacy is conducted by armies, navies, and air fleets. In the summer of 1914, in all the belligerent States, a point in the crisis was sooner or later reached at which war became "inevitable." This was the point at which the general staffs and the army commanders insisted upon military measures which rendered further diplomatic conversations futile. These recommendations were at first refused by the diplomats, so long as a chance of peace remained, and then accepted after a decision for war had been reached. The pressure of the militarists in every instance influenced this decision. In Russia the Foreign Minister and the general staff agreed upon general mobilization on July 30. The Tsar hesitated but finally acquiesced in an action which made war unavoidable. In France, General Joffre asked the Cabinet on July 31 for permission to move troops to the frontier. The Cabinet granted the request, with reservations (the ten-kilometer "withdrawal") dictated by diplomatic considerations. On August 1, Joffre demanded the mobilization of the French army, and his demand was granted. Once the demands of the strategists were accepted, diplomatic maneuvers were replaced by military tactics. The same pattern was clearly revealed in Japanese policy toward China in 1931–1933 and in the European war crisis of 1939. As soon as physical coercion is openly resorted to, the formulation of policy passes into the hands of the masters of force. War is diplomacy by another name and with a different technique.

In summary, military violence is the ultimate weapon of State power. So long as this is true, State power is necessarily directed toward increasing its opportunities for the effective exercise of military violence. Power depends upon armaments. Armaments depend upon population, economic resources, and technology. In both diplomacy and war, attention is concentrated upon acquiring control of resources and strategic points which will enhance State power. The power interests of States are necessarily expressed in economic terms which reflect the interests of their ruling classes. These interests are defended and promoted by physical force, actual or potential. In diplomacy the apparent potentialities of the force of rival States determine the outcome of clashes of wills. In war the actual fighting power of the belligerents determines which will shall prevail. In both cases the assumption of violence lies beneath the surface of politics. In a system of sovereign nation-states, armed conflict between the units is an inevitable incident in the competitive struggle for power in which they are engaged, so long as each pursues its own interests by self-help.

This formulation of the cause of war, however, will not be complete unless cognizance is taken of the internal as well as the external sources of insecurity which predispose States to violence. In certain situations the generalizations here attempted seem not to hold and the players of the diplomatic game appear to act without reference to calculations of relative power. Normally, when power is sought as a means to ulterior ends or even as an end *per se*, war becomes a means toward power and a method, when all else has failed, of securing the realization of concrete aspirations or of resisting intolerable demands made by others. Occasionally, however, States seem to desire war (or peace) as an end in itself, almost regardless of objectives or consequences. War and peace here become not an instrument of diplomacy but a weapon of internal politics.

Dictatorial régimes usually arise under conditions of mass insecurity and deprivation. A dictatorship menaced with mass unrest can often mobilize general acquiescence by deflecting the aggressions of its domestic enemies and critics away from itself and onto foreign enemies. Obedience, self-sacrifice, and solidarity are manufactured by mobilizing the entire community against the external foe in the name of national defense or racial honor or salvation from real or imaginary perils beyond the frontier. This political technique is most successfully employed when the dictatorship is subjected to attack from without. If such a régime eventually reduces the sources of domestic dissatisfaction, it will have progressively less need for diversion abroad. But if unrest continues to accumulate and if no amount of propaganda or suppression suffices to ensure the stability of the dictatorship, the ruling group may find it expedient to direct popular resentments either against internal scapegoats, who are frequently denounced and persecuted in elaborate totalitarian cults of intolerance, or against enemies abroad, with a corresponding inculcation of international hatred and glorification of militarism, war, and heroic death.

War may thus be embarked upon not for tangible and rational objectives, but as a means of silencing domestic opposition, compelling patriotic support of the dictatorship, and affording a bloody catharsis for the festering resentments which might otherwise destroy those in power. Dictatorial or autocratic régimes require glory and victory for their survival. They languish when condemned to inactivity. They usually disintegrate when defeated in foreign war. The targets of aggression selected by desperate dictators ought preferably to be weak and defenseless rather than powerful and dangerous. Plausible pretexts and objectives must be invented. Cautious calculations must be made as to the probable military consequences of taking the sword. But the cult of military glory is here a protective device whereby insecure power holders seek to buttress their domestic position. War is here not a continuation of foreign policy by other means but a categorical imperative of internal political and economic exigencies.

Examples of this technique are numerous. In 1870 Napoleon III launched upon a suicidal conflict with Prussia as a means, so he hoped, of winning glory and restoring the crumbling foundations of his throne. In 1923 Mussolini, faced with widespread opposition to the Fascist régime, obtained cheap prestige and mass support by bombarding and occupying Corfu. In 1931, Japanese militarists attacked China, in part as a means of enhancing their influence at home and directing popular attention away from poverty toward grandiose dreams of empire. The Nazi despotism sought to protect itself from the consequences of impoverishment and unrest among the masses by persecuting Jews and by developing an extravagant crusading faith in heroism and combat in the name of recovering lost provinces, achieving a place in the sun, and saving civilization from Bolshevism. In 1935 Mussolini launched his attack on Ethiopia, preferring war to all compromise or concessions, not because of genuine grievances or tangible diplomatic objectives, but because the necessary imposition of greater sacrifices on the Italian proletariat and peasantry required glory and bloodletting and an exciting diversion from domestic misery. League sanctions served his purpose admirably by enabling him to pose as Italy's defender against a hostile world. For comparable reasons, Hitler was obliged to engage in dangerous adventures and to cast about for fresh fields of conquest. For every Fascist régime, war lost is ruin, war won is salvation, but tedious peace is slow decay and final collapse in the face of the bitterness of the hypnotized multitudes who must not be permitted to become disillusioned.

The desperation, fanaticism, and irresponsibility to which tyrants are driven by inner conflict and their own cults of glory tend to produce in decadent epochs a strange counterpart of their behavior, in reverse form, in democratic States. Here power holders are at the mercy of public opinion, and the multitudes become desperately fearful of war as the sword-rattling of prospective enemies become louder. Pacifist sentiment demands peace at almost any price. When diplomats and strategists find themselves obliged to yield to such demands, they are compelled to act as if the avoidance of conflict, rather than a protection and promotion of national interests, were the prime object of policy. If they are addicted to lethargy and passivity by virtue of divided loyalties, confused judgments, or inhibitions bred of timidity, they find it easy to excuse their own irresponsibility by contending that the masses demand "peace." After 1933, Downing Street and the Quai d'Orsay, in their dealings with Rome and Berlin, repeatedly yielded up invaluable components of power to dangerous potential enemies. Britain and France were not weak in a material sense. But domestic opinion demanded concessions (or was alleged by irresolute politicians to demand concessions) whenever Mussolini or Hitler seemed to threaten war. And the Anglo-French leaders permitted the Axis Caesars to persuade them that Bolshevism was the common enemy of all. Just as war, glory, and aggression are politically and psychologically indispensable to Fascist dictatorships faced with the unrest of anxious and insecure subjects, so peace, compromise, and surrender are indispensable to democratic governments faced with an anxious and insecure citizenry. Power begets prestige. Strength begets greater strength. Weakness begets humiliation. Feebleness leads to ultimate ruin. When these inexorable laws of *Realpolitik* are ignored by statesmen because of the exigencies of domestic politics, the consequences are likely to be disastrous.

5. THE MEASURE OF POWER

> Men, Yron, money, and breade be the strengthe of the warre, but of these fower, the first two be most necessarie; because men and yron find money and breade; but breade and money fynde not men and yron.—
> NICCOLÒ MACHIAVELLI, *The Art of War* (trans. of 1586).

Since the evolution of the Western State System has been shaped primarily by the relationships of power among its members and since there is no reason for assuming that its future will differ from its past in this respect, it should prove illuminating to conclude this survey of the politics of power with a brief consideration of the "power potential" of each of the great States at the present time. To the degree to which it is possible to guage accurately the power of these States, it is possible to estimate the probable outcome of present and future clashes among them and thus to prognosticate, in a general way, the probable course of Great Power politics in the decades which lie ahead. Accuracy is unattainable in such an effort, for the imponderables of international politics are often decisive. But a rough measure of State power can be attempted. In view of the fact that power depends ultimately upon fighting capacity and upon the ability of the State to apply physical coercion successfully against its enemies, the problem is one of estimating the "war potential" of the Great Powers.

The elements of national power, constituting the war potential of a State, are numerous, varied, and fluctuating. Armaments on land, sea, and air are the most obvious and direct measures of power. But the efficacy of a State's armaments depends upon its geographical location and upon the human and material resources which make armaments possible. The most important of these resources are population (or more specifically, military man power), merchant shipping, and iron and steel production. Without facilities for producing iron and steel in large quan-

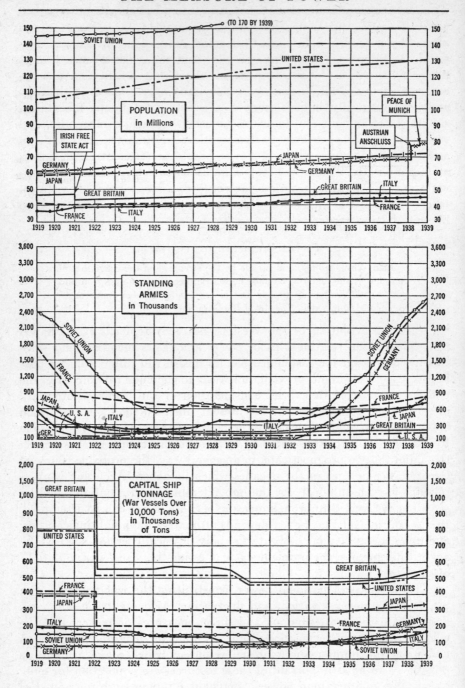

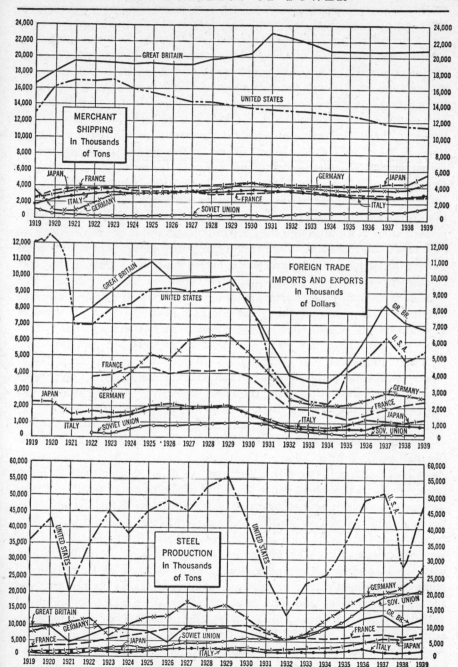

tities, no State can maintain modern armaments on an effective level, for iron and steel are the backbones of machine industry and of contemporary mechanized warfare. A State's foreign commerce is a measure of its economic productivity, though world trade may be a source of weakness rather than of strength for a State depending for its prosperity upon foreign markets which are vulnerable and exposed to attack by enemies. If communications with foreign markets can be maintained in wartime, however, these markets become a strategic asset of first importance. Other items could be utilized as criteria of power: foreign investments, gold reserves, national wealth and income, agrarian resources, total industrial production, productivity of chemical and other war industries, oil output, copper production, industrial and military efficiency, civilian morale, national unity or disunity, etc. These items will not be considered in the present survey, for although they are important and may even be decisive in a crisis, they are not susceptible of accurate measurement and comparison or, if measurable, are less constant and less revealing than the components of national power suggested above.

The accompanying charts are designed to indicate graphically the fluctuations in power of the great States during the twenty years between wars, as measured by population, standing armies, naval tonnage, merchant shipping, foreign trade, and production of iron and steel. By combining these and other figures into a single graph, an index of power could conceivably be worked out, but the results would be subject to so many qualifications that the effort is scarcely worth making. The charts themselves call for little comment. The preponderance of the United States and the constant rise in the power of the United States and Japan are noteworthy. The diminution and subsequent restoration of German power which followed the Great War are no less striking. The ascendancy of France over the European Continent prior to 1933 is not fully revealed, since there must be added to the power of France that of her eastern allies. The meteoric rise of revolutionary Russia is shown in the tables of population growth and iron and steel production. By the middle years of the third decade of the century, the population of the U.S.S.R. was still growing more rapidly than that of any other Power, with the United States second and with Japan outranking Germany and Italy outranking France. In the rush to increase armies, Germany and the U.S.S.R. took the lead. The great navies remained relatively stabilized until the expiration of the limitation treaties in 1936. The merchant shipping of all States, save the Soviet Union, tended to decline after 1930. All foreign trade diminished disastrously from 1929 until 1933 and then began to recover. The curves of steel production reveal the effects of the depression, the recovery after 1932, the steady crescendo of Soviet output, and the Nazi rearmament program.

[294]

On the Continent, the period after 1933 was characterized by a constant enhancement of the power of the unsatiated, or revisionist States and a corresponding diminution of the power of the French bloc. In 1932 France and her allies had some 1,573,000 troops under arms, 12,600,000 reserves, 28,860,000 potential soldiers (males between 15 and 49), and 5,250 military aircraft to cope with a possible enemy group of defeated Powers possessing only 175,000 troops and 21,480,000 potential soldiers, with no reserves, no heavy artillery, no tanks, and no military aircraft. France, moreover, ranked second to the United States in steel production and in addition could count on the output of Belgium, the Saar, and Czechoslovakia with a total production in 1930 (including France) of 16,882,000 tons. By the beginning of 1937 the French bloc had at its disposal some 1,657,000 troops, with 13,212,000 reserves, 30,265,000 potential soldiers, and 5,173 aircraft. Its new ally, the U.S.S.R., had an army of 1,300,000 with 15,000,000 reserves, 43,000,000 men of military age, and perhaps 7,000 military aircraft. On paper this combination seemed overwhelming.

There can be little doubt that this coalition, had it acted unitedly, could have prevented any restoration of German military power or have defeated the Reich in any open test of force. All these opportunities, however, were thrown away by the men of the Quai d'Orsay. Laval "appeased" Mussolini and thereby made him Hitler's ally, for those who aspire to be powerful despise the powerful who act like weaklings and admire the weak who know how to acquire power. Sarraut and Flandin yielded the Rhineland. Blum abandoned Spain to the Axis. Daladier and Bonnet acquiesced in the loss of Austria and actively joined Chamberlain in compelling Prague to surrender to Berlin. The Soviet alliance was thereby thrown away. Poland was rendered indefensible, Belgium was lost, Jugoslavia and Rumania were immobilized. The result was death. Many of the tanks that crushed the French army in 1940 were manufactured in the Czech Skoda works. This deliberate surrender of a position of overwhelming preponderance was without precedent in the annals of diplomacy. It was a product of blindness, treason, stupidity, pacifism, and empty hopes, assiduously cultivated by the Munichmen of Britain, that every enhancement of Axis power was to be welcomed as bringing closer the "inevitable" war between Germany and Russia.

Meanwhile the new Caesars made hay while the sun shone and made it so well that they continued to make it thereafter. Taking full advantage of democratic defeatism, they armed to the teeth and prepared their war against the West. Position and morale favored the Fascist coalition. With fortified frontiers and internal lines of communication, Germany was free to strike in any direction without fear of effective counterattack upon her defenses on other borders. Italy and Spain could blackmail

France from the south and, with sea and air forces based on the Balearic Islands, threaten French communications with North Africa, as well as menace British sea power in the Mediterranean. The Fascist masses were regimented, militarized, and imbued with a fervor for war quite unknown in the democratic countries. In a short conflict, every strategic advantage would lie with the "dynamic, unsatiated" Powers. French hegemony over the Continent came to its final end at Munich. British prestige and power were seriously damaged. The habit of compromise and surrender had become sufficiently well established in Paris, London, and Geneva to encourage the Fascist Powers to believe that they would deal separately with their foes without fear of common countermeasures. In the arms race, moreover, Britain and France were handicapped by huge public debts, whereas Germany, and to a somewhat lesser degree Italy and Japan, had reduced their internal obligations by inflation and drastic measures of currency control. Fascist imperialism perceived no serious obstacle in the way of its triumphant march toward power and glory save the armies and air squadrons of the Soviet Union. And with Moscow a "deal" was to be made.

The great riddle of military science, however, was precisely the question of whether war could be made short and decisive. In a swift war of movement, with machines which could deliver crushing blows within a few days or weeks, the Fascist Powers and their possible allies could count upon victory. But between mass armies in a long conflict of attrition, such as the Great War, they would almost inevitably be exhausted and defeated in the end. Autarchy and applied chemistry, coupled with organizational genius, unparalleled technological efficiency, and such resources as could be conquered during the first phase of hostilities might make the Reich relatively self-sufficient for war purposes for a period of months. But if fighting dragged on for years and degenerated into a test of mutual exhaustion, Germany would be vanquished, as in 1918, before the superior reserves of wealth and man power of her enemies. Italy similarly might hope to crush French and British sea power in the Mediterranean by a series of sudden blows but would face almost certain defeat in a prolonged conflict with antagonists far wealthier and more powerful than herself. Japan might conceivably seize Vladivostok, Chita, Hongkong, the Philippines, Guam, and even Singapore and the Dutch East Indies within a few months after the outbreak of war with either the United States, the U.S.S.R., or Great Britain, or even with some combination of foes. If the enemy failed to sue for peace because of his initial losses, however, the poverty of Japan would spell disaster.

Another consideration predisposed the Fascist Powers to seek a quick war of movement. Changes in military organization and technique affect internal social and political changes in ways which are of the utmost importance in the present balance of power. When highly specialized and expensive tools of war are decisive against foreign armies or domestic mobs, aristocracy and dictatorship are encouraged, for only privileged and propertied *élites* can afford to possess heavy armor, horses, chariots, and war elephants, or—in the twentieth century—tanks, aircraft, heavy artillery, and poison gas. When cheap and common weapons in the hands of multitudes decide the issue of battle, the masses have greater fighting power than the classes. The invention of gunpowder made useless the armor and horses of feudal knights and placed in the hands of burghers and peasants inexpensive weapons which contributed to the triumph of democracy. The inauguration of conscripted mass armies carried democracy to military victory in the era of the French Revolution and Napoleon. Monarchy and aristocracy in eastern and central Europe were destroyed in 1917–1918 by defeated and disintegrating mass armies. Small, highly skilled professional forces have ever been the bulwarks of oligarchy and absolutism. Tyrants imperil their power by arming *hoi polloi*—if the arms of the man in the streets are superior to those of the mercenaries and palace guards.[1]

The Nazi Führer solved his problems at home and abroad by forging a war machine and devising a strategy which enabled his mechanized troops to strike down Poland in two weeks and to turn all their might against the West, thanks to Berlin's pact with Moscow. After six months of *Sitzkrieg*, shrewdly designed to complete the demoralization of Britain and France which appeasement had begun, the *Blitzkrieg* struck north-

---

[1] It is usually true in class wars that the devotion of soldiers to the cause of the few against the many is in direct ratio to the degree of professional training they have acquired. Professional technicians, whether in war or business, identify themselves with their social superiors and hold the mob in contempt. In the Russian Revolution the Bolsheviks converted the infantry first, the cavalry later, and the artillerists, aviators, tank corps, etc., last—or not at all. In the Spanish civil war, part of the infantry remained loyal to the government while most of the artillery, aviation, and tank divisions joined the Fascist rebels. The entire Spanish army was small and professionalized and therefore sympathetic with the forces of social and political reaction. In the navy the commanders and technicians joined the rebels but were seized and shot by loyal proletarian seamen on most of the war vessels.

For a highly suggestive presentation of the general thesis indicated above, see Silas B. McKinley, *Democracy and Military Power* (Vanguard Press, 1934). The author concludes (p. 307), "It seems that infantry is no longer supreme nor are we positive that democracy is secure. The spear, the sword, the gun, each have been used by the infantryman in battle. In 1918 he was still relying upon the spear in its modern form, the bayonet, as he charged over No Man's Land, just as he did at Marathon and Bannockburn. He still rested his hope of victory upon the knife at the end of a stick, the weapon of the common man who must adopt some method of fighting that requires little training or equipment. But the new inventions may be destroying his effectiveness as the cavalry did in the past. Tanks can run him down, and airplanes bomb him from the air; gas can kill him at a distance. If these things can render him helpless either on the battlefield or as a revolutionary mob in the streets, then he will have only so much privilege and share in the affairs of his state as those who control the forces of destruction may be pleased to give him. And yet even today democracy and infantry have possibilities of renewing their ascendancy."

ward and westward. The ensuing victories overshadowed all achievements in the science of war since Napoleon. Denmark and Norway were conquered in a day, Luxemburg in another, the Netherlands in five, Belgium in eighteen, France in thirty-five. With Mussolini as belated ally and Franco as friend, the Third Reich controlled more of Europe by the close of 1940 than the first Bonaparte had ever conquered.

But Britain continued to defy the Caesars as it had defied the Little Corporal. And America came to the aid of Britain by all means "short of war." The Triple Alliance of September 27, 1940, enabled the Reich to use Japan to blackmail America and to threaten the U.S.S.R. But the Soviet Union gave only grudging "cooperation." The United States declined to be frightened. Britain's fleet retained control of the Mediterranean during the winter of 1940–1941 and (with American aid) of the north Atlantic seaways. The Axis could not conquer Europe and Africa, Japan could not conquer Asia, until Anglo-American sea power was broken or immobilized. By the spring of 1941 this was not in prospect. Unless the Triplice could speedily smash Britain, the vast industrial resources of America, slowly geared to the needs of war, would in the end be adequate to bring the conquerors to ruin.

The shape of the balance of power of the future obviously depends upon the outcome of the titanic struggle which was still unresolved as these words were written. A decisive military victory of the Triplice will mean the end of England, the partition of the British Empire, the carving of Africa, Asia, Oceania, and much of Latin America among the victors in a "new world order." Out of it may come a stable federation of tyrannies, in which there will be no struggle for power or balance of power in the old sense, or new and gigantic combats for mastery between Germany and Russia and between Japan and America. The defeat of the Triplice will give to the democracies their last opportunity to remake the world into an enduring federation of peoples in which a concert of power, skillfully contrived and used with daring to suppress violence and promote justice, will supersede the old order of *Realpolitik*. A stalemate will be but a truce, marked by new rivalries and conflicts between continental blocs —Fascist Europe, Anglo-America, the U.S.S.R., Greater Japan—until one of these destroys the other three, or two meet two in mortal conflict for mastery of the planet.

Which of these prospects becomes a reality will be decided by the god of battle. Since the war potentials of the contestants—*i.e.*, of the Triple Alliance and of Britain, America, and Russia—will be somewhat evenly matched in the event that each bloc acts together and is able to use its power to the full, it may well transpire that the decision will hinge upon the moral imponderables. The peoples who can take most punishment, who can face the worst with good cheer and the best with imagination, who can develop leaders rich in dynamic ideas and in soaring dreams of better days will win. The fearful, the discouraged, the thoughtless will perish.

SUGGESTED READINGS

Boggs, S. W.: *International Boundaries*, New York, Columbia University Press, 1940.

Colby, C. C. (ed.): *Geographic Aspects of International Relations*, Chicago, University of Chicago Press, 1940.

Engelbrecht, H. C.: *Merchants of Death*, New York, Dodd, Mead, 1934.

Fairgrieve, J.: *Geography and World Power*, New York, Dutton, 1915.

Foertsch, H.: *The Art of Modern Warfare*, New York, Viking, 1940.

Fullerton, W. M.: *Problems of Power*, New York, Scribner, 1918.

Hawtrey, R. G.: *Economic Aspects of Sovereignty*, New York, Longmans, 1930.

Knight, B. W.: *How to Run a War*, New York, Knopf, 1936.

Lasswell, H. D.: *Propaganda Technique in the World War*, New York, Knopf, 1927.

————: *World Politics and Personal Insecurity*, New York, McGraw-Hill, 1935.

League of Nations: *Statistical Year Book of the Trade in Arms and Ammunition*, Boston, World Peace Foundation, 1932.

League of Nations: *Armaments Yearbook* (annual), Geneva.

Lippmann, Walter: *The Stakes of Diplomacy*, New York, Holt, 1917.

Lowell, A. L.: *Public Opinion in Peace and War*, Cambridge, Mass., Harvard University Press, 1923.

Ludendorff, General Erich von: *The Nation at War*, London, Hutchinson, 1936.

Mahan, A. T.: *Retrospect and Prospect, Studies in International Relations, Naval and Political*, Boston, Little, Brown, 1902.

Marder, A. J.: *The Anatomy of British Sea Power* (1880–1905), New York, Knopf, 1940.

Merriam, C. E.: *Political Power—Its Composition and Incidence*, New York, Whittlesey House, 1934.

Noel-Baker, P.: *The Private Manufacture of Armaments* (2 vols.), London, Gollancz, 1936–1937.

Neumann, R.: *Zaharoff: The Armaments' King*, New York, Knopf, 1935.

Nickerson, H.: *The Armed Horde 1793–1939—A Study of the Rise, Survival and Decline of the Mass Army*, New York, Putnam, 1941.

Parmelee, M.: *Blockade and Sea Power*, New York, Crowell, 1924.

Pavlovitch, M.: *Foundations of Imperialist Policy*, London, Labour Publishing Company, 1922.

Pratt, F.: *Sea Power and Today's War*, New York, Harrison-Hilton, 1939.

Robbins, L.: *The Economic Causes of War*, London, Jonathan Cape, 1939.

Rosinski, H.: *The German Army*, New York, Harcourt, Brace, 1940.

Sprout, H. and M.: *The Rise of American Naval Power* 1776–1918, Princeton, N. J., Princeton University Press, 1939.

Stevens, W. O.: *A History of Sea Power*, New York, Doubleday, 1937.

Taylor, Griffith: *Environment and Nation*, Chicago, University of Chicago Press, 1936.

Vagts, A.: *A History of Militarism*, New York, Norton, 1937.

Van Valkenberg, S.: *Elements of Political Geography*, New York, Prentice-Hall, 1939.

Waller, W.: *War in the Twentieth Century*, New York, Dryden Press, 1940.

Whittlesey, D.: *The Earth and the State*, New York, Holt, 1939.

De Wilde, J. C., D. H. Popper, E. Clark: *Handbook of the War*, Boston, Houghton, 1939.

Chapter VIII

THE CULT OF THE TRIBAL GODS

1. PATRIOTISM AND PEOPLE

Our modern Western nationalism has an ecclesiastical tinge; for, while in one aspect it is a reversion to the idolatrous self-worship of the tribe which was the only religion known to Man before the first of the "higher religions" was discovered by an oppressed internal proletariat, this Western neo-tribalism is a tribalism with a difference. The primitive religion has been deformed into an enormity through being power-driven with a misapplied Christian driving-force. The Golden Calf—or Lion or Bear or Eagle, or whatever the tribal totem may happen to be—is being worshipped in our world today with an intensity of feeling and a singleness of mind which ought not to be directed by human souls towards any god but God Himself. And it is not surprising to find that we have been propitiating these blasphemously idolized tribal deities with the human sacrifices which they relish and exact.—Arnold J. Toynbee, *A Study of History.*

THE outstanding and distinctive characteristic of the peoples of the Western State System is their devotion and allegiance to the "nations" into which they have got themselves divided. The western world is a world of nations. The Western State System is a system of nation-states. The Western peoples and their Oriental and African imitators are keenly aware of themselves as "nationals" of particular nation-states, already in existence or striving to be born. Millions are influenced more in their emotions and behavior by a sense of national solidarity and fellow-feeling with their fellow-nationals than by their racial, religious, economic, aesthetic, or recreational interests. This becomes most apparent in wartime, when governments demand and usually receive unswerving and undivided allegiance to the nation. All other interests are in form, if not always in substance, subordinated to the supreme end of saving the fatherland, chastising the national foe, and enabling the nation to impose its will on the enemy nation. In 1914 and in 1939, throughout the European Continent, labor leaders forgot their slogans of class solidarity, pacifists forgot their crusade against war, churchmen forgot the Prince of Peace, socialists forgot the general strike of the workers of the world which would make war impossible. Merchants, munition makers, and militarists had less to forget. All rallied to the unfurled banners of the nations in arms. All hurled themselves into the fiery furnace, chanting hymns of hate against neighbor nations. But war merely brings to the surface and makes plain through pathological exaggeration what already exists in peace: an almost universal disposition to place the nation before all other human groupings, to give precedence to national interests above all other interests, to look upon national patriotism as the highest type of loyalty and allegiance.

THE MAKING OF PATRIOTS. The emotions and ideologies of patriotism are instilled into people in every nation by an elaborate process of inculcation. Nationalism is an inseparable component of the cultural heritage handed down from generation to generation in every modern society. Upon the eager minds of little children, as upon a blank slate, are written at an early age the large characters of "mother," "home," and "heaven," "flag," "fatherland," and "patriotism." The first impressions of the Great Society outside of the family, the neighborhood, and the kindergarten are associated with national emblems, heroes, myths, and traditions. Every child in the Western world, before he has learned how to read and write his national language, has learned how to respond to the gayly colored banner which is the flag of his fatherland, to the stirring rhythm of the song which is his national anthem, to the names and legends of the great nation builders who are revered as men like unto gods. Awe, respect, reverence, and enthusiasm toward the nation-state and its symbolic representations are inculcated from infancy in the home, in the school, and in the church.

Next comes the primer, with its quaint little tales of national glory and achievement, and after that the elements of national history and geography. In later childhood there is nationalistic history with a vengeance, patriotic exercises, flag-day celebrations, festivals and fun for independence day, or constitution day, or Bastille day, or Guy Fawkes' day. Puberty brings membership in the Boy Scouts or the Girl Scouts, outings and parties and training in citizenship. In adolescence the young citizen enters secondary school. He becomes acquainted with the alien tongues and customs of enemies and strangers. He studies the national literature, the national history, the national Kultur. He becomes politically conscious and emotionally inspired by a fuller appreciation of his identity with his fatherland. La patrie becomes father, mother, mistress, or lover in the heart of the youthful patriot; and he (or she) is taught to swear undying allegiance to that which is more sacred even than truth, honor, or life itself. And at length, in early adulthood, comes, in most lands, military service for the young man, romantic attachments to soldier lovers for the young woman, the right to vote and pay taxes, and a deep sense of loyalty and devotion to that half-real, half-mystical entity which is the nation-state. Thus, through the seven ages of the patriot, national sentiment is systematically inculcated into the citizens of every State—with the home, the church, the school, the army, the press, the political party, the business enterprise, and the State itself all contributing mightily to that process through which children and raw youths are transformed into ideally loyal and patriotic good citizens.

The mechanisms, procedures, and techniques of education and propaganda through which this result is attained have been analyzed in many States by a score of assiduous scholars.[1] The primitive initiation ceremonies of the tribe or clan through which the rising generation is made a participant in the social group are repeated with elaborate variation in the educational processes of every modern nation. Youth is conditioned to allegiance—no longer to the tribe, the clan, the class, the caste, the province, or the city, but to the nation which demands an allegiance above all other allegiances and a loyalty requiring, if need be, the supreme sacrifice on the altar of patriotism. What youth has been taught, age seldom forgets—and all modern States are nations of patriots whose rulers may ordinarily rely upon the unswerving devotion of the great masses of the citizens to the mighty traditions of the national past. Each State thus develops and enriches its own personality by perpetually recreating itself in its own image. Each State perpetually models its figures of earth and gets them more and more to its liking. Each State becomes symbolized as an anthropomorphic deity to which are attributed the national virtues and vices, the national achievements and frustrations. Each patriot, like a new Narcissus, is enthralled by the beauty of his own image, which he sees reflected in the national mirror; and he feels himself to be one with the nation. Here, beneath the world of forms and structures, beneath the external trappings of government and sovereignty, are the reality of the nation and the essence of nationhood instilled into the minds and hearts of the millions who make "France" because they feel themselves Frenchmen, the millions who make "Germany" because they feel themselves Germans, and the millions who make "America" because they feel themselves Americans.

THE GENESIS OF MODERN PATRIOTISM. An understanding of the process of manufacturing patriots, however, does not in itself serve to explain why national patriotism has come to occupy such an all-pervading place in the culture and ideology of Western civilization. This is perhaps one of the mysteries which Western man, in his ceaseless efforts to understand himself, can never quite comprehend.[2] Nation-

---

[1] See C. E. Merriam, *The Making of Citizens*, 1931, the concluding volume of the series which includes Elizabeth Weber, *The Duk-Duks;* C. J. H. Hayes, *France, a Nation of Patriots;* John Gaus, *Great Britain: a Study in Civic Loyalty;* S. N. Harper, *Civic Training in Soviet Russia;* Oscar Jaszi, *The Dissolution of the Hapsburg Monarchy;* and Paul Kosok, *Modern Germany: A Study of Conflicting Loyalties.*

[2] "What has given great vogue to nationalism in modern times? We really do not know. It is a pity that we do not know, for if we did, we could probably make some fairly accurate guess as to the future of nationalism. As it is, we have to content ourselves with hypotheses

alism may be regarded as an advanced form of ethnocentrism, in which the limits of social solidarity and cohesion are coterminous with the bounds of the language and culture of people in a large community inhabiting extensive territories. Ethnocentrism implies friendship with the members of the "in-group" and hostility toward members of all "out-groups." The in-group is the focus of all social life. Each new generation is initiated into the rituals and ceremonies which symbolize its solidarity. Law, language, art, religion, government, morality, family institutions, economic activities are all phases of the group culture, all strands in the ties which bind the individuals into a social whole. These fruits of social living are enjoyed only by the members of the group and are denied to outside groups, even though they may be extended to individual aliens in accordance with the ancient custom of hospitality. Through them the community is made aware of itself as a collective entity set apart from outside communities. "Stranger" is usually "enemy," and foreign cultures are strange and hostile.

A "nation" consists of a relatively large number of people spread over a relatively large area and bound together by common ties of language and culture. The communities which composed the civilizations of the Near East and the Mediterranean basin in ancient times were, for the most part, not nations in this sense. In their political organization they were city-states, military monarchies, or "world empires," consisting either of small communities of culturally homogeneous people or of large aggregations of culturally diverse peoples brought under unified control through war and political subjugation. The same was true of the peoples of the Western world in the early medieval period. Group solidarity, civic loyalty, and political organization rested, not upon national communities, but upon smaller or larger units. Nationalism appeared only as "nations" came into existence and attained awareness of their own identity.

It seems probable that conflicts among culturally divergent populations played a significant role in producing within each community that sense of its own identity, that feeling of solidarity and common interest, that conception of the personality or ego of the group which is of the essence of national patriotism. Contacts of war would seem to be more effective than any other kind in producing the type of group cohesion which lies behind nationalism. No emotion unifies a group so readily as hatred for a common enemy. Group hostility to the foreign foe arouses the most elemental types of defensive behavior which serve to give the

and suggestions. Of these the most plausible would appear to be the underlying tendency in modern times to regard the national state as the medium through which civilization is best assured and advanced." C. J. H. Hayes, *The Historical Evolution of Modern Nationalism,* 1931, p. 302.

primitive group a solidarity it could never attain otherwise. International relations in the formative period of nationalism were for the most part those of war. Anglo-Saxon England attained a degree of national unity for the first time when Alfred the Great rallied his subjects to resist the Danish invasion. Norman England was already an embryonic national State, with a national government of considerable power and authority and with a population increasingly impressed with its "English-ness" by virtue of chronic conflicts with the Scots, the Irish, and the French. In France, localism and provincialism gave way to a common consciousness of "Frenchness" in the course of the Hundred Years' War, when its inhabitants at last organized themselves for effective resistance against the English invaders and found a fitting symbol of the national cause in the person of the first great heroic figure of the French nation, Jeanne d'Arc. In Spain, constant warfare against the southern Saracens gave birth to Spanish nationalism and produced that blending of patriotic sentiment and crusading Catholicism which became its distinctive characteristic. In every case nationalism was born of war against alien groups.

All the later nationalisms between the fifteenth century and the twentieth were similarly born of conflict situations between societies already differing from one another in language, religion, and institutions and made more aware of these differences by increased contacts with aliens. Dutch nationalism attained full flower in the long struggle against Spanish rule of the Netherlands. Swiss nationalism emerged out of conflicts with Austria. Sweden became a nation through conflicts with Russians and Poles and Germans. American nationalism was generated by the War of the Revolution. In the nineteenth century, Italian nationalism attained political unity for Italy as a result of common resistance to foreign invasion and common conflicts against Austria. The German nation became a unified State through conflict with Danes, Austrians, and Frenchmen, after Napoleonic domination and the "war of liberation" earlier in the century converted Prussians and Bavarians and Suabians and Württembergers into "Germans." The peculiarly intense and fanatical nationalism of the Balkan peoples has been the product of armed revolt against the Turks and of the presence within the peninsula of a large number of divergent linguistic and religious groups, each of which became aware of itself through contact and conflict with its neighbors. Irish nationalism, Turkish nationalism, Japanese nationalism, Indian nationalism, and Chinese nationalism were likewise products of conflict against alien rulers, alien invaders, or alien foes across the frontier.

This suggests that the process whereby a community acquires a sense of its own identity and national personality bears a certain resemblance to the process whereby an individual growing up in society acquires a self or ego of his own. Social psychologists are generally agreed that an individual growing up to biological maturity in complete isolation from his fellows would not have a complete human "personality." The individual becomes humanized by social contacts and interactions with his fellows. His innate impulses are inhibited, directed, and conditioned through social pressure—until his personality becomes, in the language of the psychoanalyst, a fusion of instinctive biological drives (the "id"), the conscious thinking and acting self (the "ego"), and the unconscious controls and repressions of id and ego drives (the "super-ego").[1] The individual becomes aware of himself and develops distinctive personality traits by "taking the role of the other,"[2] by socialized experience with other persons.

Similarly, a nation acquires its ego by contacts with other nations; and it seemingly becomes acutely aware of its own identity to the degree to which such contacts are intimate, rich, and varied. Contacts of war would seem to promote national solidarity more effectively than contacts of peace, for war requires cooperation and cohesion in the interest of self-preservation. It emotionalizes and dramatizes the symbols, the flags, the songs, the slogans, the traditions, and the leaders which give unity to the group and distinguish it from other groups. National patriotism is the most complete expression of ethnocentrism. Its devotees are imbued with an intense consciousness of the collective personality of the national community, and this collective personality emerges out of social contacts and interactions between divergent groups not dissimilar to those contacts and interactions between single human beings which produce and enrich the individual personality. The history of this process remains to be written by social psychologists with historical training or by historians who are also social psychologists.

THE FAITH OF PATRIOTS. Nationalists everywhere exalt the nation-state as the highest form of political and social organization. The national community must achieve political independence. It must incorporate within its frontiers all peoples speaking the language and having the culture of the national society. It must compel conformity to the dominant language and culture on the part of alien groups within its frontier. It must attain unity, uniformity, solidarity. It must assert its rights vigorously and protect its interests energetically in contacts with other national groups. It is the all in all, the *ne plus ultra*, the final and perfect embodiment of social living for all loyal patriots. It is beyond good and evil, right or wrong; for its interests are supreme and paramount, and all means toward its greater glory and power are justified by the end. "A true nationalist places his country above everything; he therefore

---

[1] See Franz Alexander, *Psycho-analysis of the Total Personality*, 1930.
[2] This phrase was frequently used by the late professor George H. Mead in his lectures in social psychology at the University of Chicago.

conceives, treats, and resolves all pending questions in their relation to the national interest."[1] His object is "the exclusive pursuit of national policies, the absolute maintenance of national integrity, and a steady increase of national power—for a nation declines when it loses military might."[2] To the patriot the nation-state is a great goddess to be worshiped, to be loved, to be served—and all sacrifices in her service are noble and heroic. She calls out to her worshipers:

Citizens, it is I (the Great Mother, *la Patrie*) that undertakes to protect your personal safety, your peace, your property: What wilt thou give me in return for constant benefit? If it happens that I am in peril, if unnatural children torment my bosom . . . wouldst thou abandon me in these stormy moments for the price of my invariable protection? . . . No! . . . There are times when I would command the sacrifice . . . even of thy life which I have so steadily protected.[3]

The poetry of chauvinism transcends all the imperatives of morality and reason:

Our country! In her intercourse with foreign nations, may she always be in the right; but our country, right or wrong! (Stephen Decatur, April, 1816.)

The living expression of French nationalism is the result of the vigor of the good and pure blood which we have received from our fathers and mothers. . . . The cult of the sacred soil . . . has started; from year to year it will grow; it will be a factor in the renaissance of *la Patrie*. (Charles Maurras, *La Politique Religieuse*.)

Lord! Let the beautiful ships which are on their way to our Africa arrive safely at their port. Grant that our soldiers on the sunny roads on the other side of the sea have fortune as their guiding star and glory as their goal. Grant that they may crown with fresh laurels the old, glorious flags of Vittorio Veneto, which now wave under the tropic sky. Let the culture of the new Rome of Mussolini fuse with that of Caesar's Rome to a poem of greatness. Let the Italian Empire dreamed of by our great men and our martyrs become reality in the near future. Lord! Let our lives, if Mother Italy demand it, become a joyful sacrifice on the altar of Thy holy and just Will. (Prayer for the Ballila Boys, *L' Azione Coloniale*, Rome, 1935.)

It is not without significance that nationalism has flowered most luxuriantly in the period since the French Revolution, during which the bourgeoisie has risen to political power in most of the Western States. The nation-states of western Europe were originally dynastic creations of warrior-kings. Loyalty has been transferred from king to State, from monarch to fatherland only since the rise of modern mechanized economy.

[1] Charles Maurras, in *Action Française*, June 10, 1908, p. 969.

[2] Maurras, quoted in C. J. H. Hayes, *The Historical Evolution of Modern Nationalism*, p. 165.

[3] Barrère in *Procès-verbal de l'assemblée nationale*, No. 699, pp. 7–8, cited in Hayes, *op. cit.*, pp. 69–70. This and the preceding quotations all refer to French nationalism, but the values and ideology which they suggest are typical of all nationalisms.

Machine industry brought social integration and interdependence on a national scale. Bourgeois democracy and parliamentarism inspired the majority of the citizens of the nation-state with the attitudes, ideals, and values of popular patriotism. Of the three great passwords of the middle-class revolution—"liberty, equality, fraternity"—only fraternity, *i.e.*, national solidarity, was fully achieved, for liberty and equality in a social order of economic inequality and insecurity have remained dreams only partially fulfilled. Out of the gigantic efflorescence of mass patriotism in Napoleonic France, out of the military impact of Napoleonic France upon Europe, was born a nationalist awakening of the ascendant middle classes throughout the Continent. During all of the nineteenth century, liberalism and nationalism were the two faces of the bourgeois revolt against the *ancien régime* throughout the Western world. Only in the old Germany and the old Russia did the landowning aristocracy retain a large degree of political power—and even here the members of this class became more patriotic than the bourgeois patriots. The same observation might be made of contemporary Japan. Patriotism places allegiance to the whole national community and to its political symbol, the national State, above allegiance to caste or class or party. But it is nevertheless true that nationalism as a cult and a way of life became a mighty driving force in the hands of bourgeois patriot-liberals and that it has received general acceptance in the period during which merchants, bankers, and industrial entrepreneurs—the ruling classes in the epoch of capitalism—took political power unto themselves in the great nation-states. This historical coincidence need not be taken to mean that nationalism is of significance only as a manifestation of the attitudes and ideology of the bourgeoisie. But it is clear that this class has in most States played the largest role in the elaboration and inculcation of the attitudes and ideology of nationalism.

The more recent manifestations of this cult have been aptly characterized by Professor Hayes, astute student of patriotism in all its forms, as "integral nationalism." This doctrine differs not at all from earlier forms of nationalism in its fundamental postulates and values, but it requires its devotees to take their nationalism with deadly seriousness and to apply themselves in all earnestness to serving and glorifying the nation. Integral nationalism is best represented in the contemporary world scene by the *London Morning Post*, the *Action Française*, or French Royalists, the "National Socialism" of Germany, the Fascismo of Italy, and the military bureaucracy of Japan. American counterparts of these groups flourish in times of crisis. The various Fascist or semi-Fascist patriotic organizations in many lands are ordinarily made up of "integral" nationalists. The point of view of these organizations perhaps represents the logical development of nationalism to its ultimate end, and the latest and most extreme form of the nationalist philosophy. The germs of this final formulation of the gospel of the nation-state were latent in all the earlier manifestations. But the gospel has been purified of all irrelevancies, purged of all elements of thought or feeling running counter to the glorification of the nation, and applied as a categorical imperative to all phases of contemporary political and economic life.

Extreme nationalism of the Fascist variety has various faces in various countries, but it has everywhere certain common characteristics which deserve to be noted. Like nationalism in its earliest form, it is born of war and conflict among nations. It emerged out of the world-wide international bitterness and friction engendered by the Great War and it fed upon the intensified resentments among nations in the period preceding the war of 1939. It became most acute and widespread in "unsatiated" States like Italy, Germany, Hungary, and Japan, whose patriots were obsessed with a sense of national injustice or fascinated by ambitions of national expansion. It is everywhere directed against past, present, or future "enemy" nations. Perhaps its most striking characteristic is its divorce from nineteenth century bourgeois liberalism. It is still for the most part bourgeois in terms of the social and economic status of its devotees. But it is the bourgeois nationalism of an age in which the position of the bourgeoisie as a ruling class is everywhere challenged by enemies within and without. Since the challenge must be met and the enemies must be suppressed, emphasis is placed, not upon liberty, equality, and laissez-faire individualism, but upon law and order, discipline, national unity, and salvation through ultrapatriotic dictatorship.

Liberty is not an end but a means. As a means it must be controlled and dominated. This involves force . . . the assembling of the greatest force possible, the inexorable use of force whenever necessary—and by force is meant physical, armed force. . . . When a group or a party is in power it is under an obligation to fortify itself and defend itself against all comers. . . . Liberty is today no longer the chaste and austere virgin for whom the generations of the first half of the last century fought and died. For the gallant, restless, and bitter youth who face the dawn of a new history there are other words that exercise a far greater fascination, and these words are: order, hierarchy, discipline. . . . Fascism has already stepped over, and if it be necessary it will turn tranquilly and again step over, the more or less putrescent corpse of the Goddess of Liberty.[1]

In accordance with this philosophy, "strong" government is called for to suppress all "national enemies," in which category are usually placed all racial or linguistic minorities and all political groups aiming at changing the existing distribution of wealth and political power. The most common objects of attack are Socialists, Communists, labor leaders,

[1] Benito Mussolini in "Forza e Consenso," *Gerarchia*, March, 1923.

liberals, Jews, aliens of all kinds, and all who by virtue of race, language, religion, or political doctrines fail to conform to the highest standards of patriotic respectability. "Strong" government is likewise called for to discipline and organize the nation, to regulate and coordinate all economic activity, to regiment the entire population in order to give greater power to the State. Fascist Italy and Nazi Germany represent the most complete examples of the political and economic forms which extreme nationalism has devised to achieve its purposes.

No less marked is the close association between integral nationalism and military glory. Extreme nationalists are invariably advocates of military preparedness, of heavy armaments, of "strong" foreign policies, of the exclusive pursuit of national interests by military means. The army, the navy, and the air fleet are the visible symbols of the power of the nation and the instrumentalities through which it suppresses internal dissent and attains its goals in international politics. They are, therefore, the objects of particular solicitude on the part of ultrapatriots everywhere. On its negative side, extreme nationalism is antiforeign, ultrapatriotic, militaristic, and collectivistic to the degree required to preserve the established economic order and to enhance the power of the nation. Here, again, Fascism represents this doctrine in its purest contemporary form. Its greatest Italian spokesman, the Duce, contends that "with regard to the future development of humanity and aside from expediency and political considerations, Fascism does not believe either in the possibility or usefulness of perpetual peace and rejects pacifism as cowardice and renunciation of struggle. Only war carries human energy to the highest tension and prints the seal of nobility on the peoples which have the virtues to confront it. All other proofs of quality are substitutes which never make a man actually confront himself with the alternatives of life and death. Doctrine, therefore, which is prejudiced in favor of peace is foreign to Fascism."[1]

Comparable attitudes, in an exaggerated form, are to be found in the ideology of German Fascism. This *Weltanschauung*, born of lower middle-class insecurities, of national defeat and humiliation, of economic deprivations and anxieties afflicting businessmen, Junkers, and peasants, is anti-intellectual ("We think with our blood!"), anti-Marxist, antiliberal, antipacifist. But, in essence, it is a racial cult of collective paranoia and military megalomania. It attributes mystical virtues to "Blood and Soil." It translates anti-Semitism into a tribal faith of "Aryan" superiority and Pan-German imperialism. "National Socialism" interprets all history in terms of race: "Nordics" are the *élite* of the species, non-Nordics are inferior, Negroes are little removed from the ape, Slavs are "subhumans," and Jews are Oriental parasites, seeking to destroy the

[1] Benito Mussolini, in "Politics and Social Doctrine," *Popolo d'Italia*, August 4, 1932.

white race by intermarriage, capitalistic exploitation, parliamentarism, and internationalism. Liberalism begets Communism. The proletarian world revolution, contended Hitler and his high priests, is the end point of the "Jewish World Conspiracy." The Third Reich—a "racial" State cleansed of Marxists, liberals, and Jews; organized on the "Leadership" principle which gives all power to the Führer; and armed to the teeth—must save Aryan civilization from Bolshevism and extend its beneficence over all Mittel-Europa and the East.[1]

Hear Julius Streicher, Nazi potentate of Nürnberg, addressing the Hitler Youth on Hesenburg mountain, June 23, 1935:

Your proper gathering place is this mountain where, two thousand years ago, your forefathers gathered before the country had been infected by a race who at that time executed the greatest anti-Semite of all times, Jesus Christ, for high treason. Now this race is an enemy to all peoples and threatens the life of the German people. In front of this blazing fire dedicate yourselves to hatred. . . . Don't believe in priests as long as they defend people whom Christ called "sons of the Devil." Don't go to confessions. If you have any faults, cast them into the holy flame burning here on this holy mountain and I will absolve you. . . . The next war must be a crusade against the Jews.

Hear Baldur von Schirach, Nazi Youth Leader, addressing the *Hitler Jugend* in October, 1933, at the unveiling in Westphalia of a war memorial in the form of a monument to the Archangel Michael:

Here we will not speak the warm words of peace, the words "home" and "Fatherland." Our words are spoken in the face of the awful summons of war. Youths, your hands are now raised in an oath before this monument which is erected to the sublimity of bloodshed—and Michael is the Angel of Death—and you are swearing that your lives belong to the Reich, and your blood to Der Führer.

That nationalism and international conflict are concomitant and seemingly inseparable features of international politics in the Western State System is in no need of demonstration to those familiar with the past. States waged war on one another before nationalism in its modern form had come into being. The wars among the dynastic States of western Europe between the fourteenth and eighteenth centuries contributed powerfully to the development of nationalism among their subjects. In a State System of nation-states, wars are inevitably fought between nationalities made aware of their identity through conflict, imbued with national consciousness in the heat of battle, and fused into solidarity by bellicose symbols, gestures, and acts. Common opposition to an alien group, common resistance to an invader, common participation in an attack upon the enemy fuse national societies together much more

[1] See F. L. Schuman, *The Nazi Dictatorship*, 1936, pp. 95–130, for a more detailed account of the Nazi creed, with quotations from Nazi sources. *Cf.* Joseph Werlin, "The Pathology of Hyper-Nationalism," *Southwestern Social Science Quarterly*, December, 1939.

effectively than any amount of undramatic collaboration in the tasks of peace. National patriotism, by virtue of its origins, its faith, its deeds, and its symbols, is essentially bellicose and bellivolent. It puts the power interests of each State into terms of nationalistic aspirations. Peace-loving patriots are highly exceptional. A pacific nationalism is almost a contradiction in terms. If all patriots are not warlike, at least all wars are patriotic and serve to raise the enthusiasms of patriotism to fever heat. The cult of the nation-state is a cult of Mars, god of battles—and, even in a generation when all the world cries for peace, the various efforts to recondition patriots, to reeducate nationalists, to reform the whole nationalist ideology in the direction of international peace and coopera-tion have thus far given little promise of permanent success.

Whether a pacific patriotism is possible may well be doubted, in view of the long past of belligerent exaltation of the nation-state and in view of the current symbols, formulae, and attitudes which the cult of the nation-state has evolved. And it may likewise be doubted whether Western civilization, on its present level, can survive the continuation of inter-national strife which belligerent patriotism breeds. The reconditioning of patriots, the reeducation of intransigent nationalists, is perhaps the most critical problem of the twentieth century. Human nature is very flexible and adaptable, and it is quite conceivable that under appropriate condi-tions the attitudes and values of traditional patriotism may be modified in the direction of international and world interests, making for harmony among States. To substitute for nationalism a new set of emotional responses, associated with a new basis of social integration and affording equally adequate psychic satisfactions, is not, in the abstract, a task which is beyond all imagination and incapable of achievement. But little measurable progress toward its achievement has taken place thus far. On the contrary, the past two decades witnessed the intensification of belligerent patriotism through the Western world and its extension to the peoples of Africa and Asia. The rising tide of Fascist nationalism bodes no good for peace and international cooperation—for if patriots continue to sow the dragon's teeth, they will continue to reap the usual harvest of armaments, conflicts, and war.

RACE AND LANGUAGE. Everywhere, modern nationalism as a cult and a political dogma postulates the political independence of a national community as its original goal and its ultimate ideal. To all patriots throughout the world, no truth is more elementary than that the nation must be "free" to govern itself, to work out its own destiny, to formulate its own foreign policy. The nation must therefore attain state-hood, *i.e.*, become an independent and sovereign political entity. If existence and independence are the most fundamental rights of States under international law, they are likewise the most fundamental values of national patriotism. Nothing engenders patriotic fever among a people more effectively than foreign control or oppression. Nothing seems more supremely desirable to the patriot, or more in accordance with the most obvious principles of justice and common sense, than the political independence of the nation. The cry of national self-determination is accordingly the most poignant and insistent demand put forward by the nationalists of all countries. Each nationality demands political independence for itself, though it is seldom willing to grant the same right to the subject nationalities under its control. Each nation-state expresses its will to power in international politics no longer in terms of dynastic interests, but in terms of "national" interests. The nation must be served by enhancing its power and prestige in every way possible, and all its nationals rejoice in this adventure. The resulting tensions, the ensuing conflicts of interests and policies have been perhaps the most fruitful sources of international friction during the past century and the most important factors underlying the attitudes of governments and peoples toward one another.

This demand for self-determination, for the political independence of the national community, obviously raises questions, as soon as attempts are made to translate it into action, of what *is* the national community. Of whom does it consist? What persons are "nationals," to be included within the frontiers of the nation-state, and what persons are aliens? What territories shall the national community insist upon including within its political boundary? What is the criterion of nationality?

In the contemporary world, two criteria of nationality have received general acceptance: race and language.

The test of race is a wholly unworkable criterion of nationality; but it is frequently emphasized by patriots, largely as a result of their efforts to rationalize designs of aggrandizement or discrimination against disliked minorities. The veriest novice in biology knows that "racial purity" is entirely nonexistent among the nations of the earth and that mankind can be classified into races only in the crudest and most unscientific fashion. If "pure races" ever existed in the human family, they have long since disappeared as a result of migrations, wars, conquests, travel, intermarriage, and miscegenation on the grandest scale over thousands of years. And as for biologically pure national stocks, there are none. The population of every modern nation is made up of a large number of mingled strains, each of which was itself originally a mixture of earlier stocks.

Homo sapiens is hopelessly mongrel, and all attempts to dig up pure pedigrees for any of the sons of Adam are doomed to failure. Equally absurd are most popular notions of racial differences and race prejudice. People may easily be conditioned by their cultural environment to dislike members of an alien race, particularly where there is a clash of economic interests between the two groups. But that there is any inherent racial prejudice in the human animal is disproved by innumerable instances of perfect interracial harmony and cooperation. People of different races differ in their capacities and achievements, owing in large part to differences in economic opportunities, cultural background, climatic stimuli, and social environment. But individual differences are greater than racial differences, and glib generalizations of racial superiority or inferiority are little more than rationalizations of culturally inherited prejudices.

Yet men and women *are* white, black, red, yellow, or brown, with various shadings in between; and within each of these groups there are physical differences of stature, body build, hair, skin, and eye color, shape of skull, and the like. These differences are sufficiently marked to enable nationalist doctrinaires to spin finely woven theories of racial virtues and vices, of instinctive racial sympathies and antipathies, and of racial purity as the only proper criterion of nationality. The scientific unsoundness of these theories has not made them less effective in influencing attitudes and behavior. The cult of Aryanism was one of the earliest of the pseudo-scientific rationalizations to gain general acceptance. Professor Max Müller first developed the myth of the existence of an Aryan race on the basis of the resemblances among the various Aryan or Indo-European languages. Von Jhering, in his *Evolution of the Aryans*, carried this idea a step farther. Gobineau, in his *Essai sur l'inégalité des races humaines* (1884), developed the idea of Aryan superiority and of racial purity as a prerequisite of high civilization. Among the so-called Aryans, however, were obvious physical differences which led to the familiar division of the white race into categories of Nordic, Alpine, and Mediterranean. Houston Stewart Chamberlain, a Germanized Englishman, first presented persuasively the notion of "Teutonic" superiority. Teutonism, Gallicism, Anglo-Saxonism were all cut of the same cloth, as is the cult of "Nordic" supremacy which has flourished so amazingly in the backward areas of Anglo-Saxon North America. This most recent of the racial myths has also produced its pseudoscientific apologists[1] and has evoked in the hinterland the familiar patterns of anti-Semitic, antiforeign, anti-Negro, and anti-Catholic movements so well exemplified in the revival of the Ku Klux Klan during the 1920's. The Hitlerite movement in Germany, with its emphasis upon anti-Semitism, antiforeignism, and "Aryan" or "Teutonic" purity, is a similar phenomenon.

These efforts to link nationality with race, or to find in racial purity a new basis of social cohesion in contrast to nationality, have had consider-

[1] See Madison Grant, *The Passing of the Great Race*, 1918; Lothrop Stoddard, *The Rising Tide of Color*, 1920, *The Revolt against Civilization*, and *Racial Realities in Europe*, 1924; C. S. Burr, *America's Race Heritage;* etc.

able political significance. They have intensified racial and national prejudices. They have influenced the immigration legislation and population policies of national governments. They have lent popular support to imperialism and to the subjugation and exploitation of "backward" peoples by the "superior" races. But they have not resulted in any widespread cult of racialism comparable to nationalism. People in most parts of the world continue to identify themselves as Englishmen, Persians, Germans, Japanese, Italians, Bulgarians, etc., rather than as Nordics, Mediterraneans, Alpines, yellow men, black men, or brown men. Nationality or identification with the national group is an inherent feature of man's cultural heritage in many regions of the globe. It is the product of centuries of political contacts and cultural development, and it has become a part of the life and soul of people everywhere. Nations have been built by patriots and molded by constant efforts to remodel the nation to the patriot's liking. Efforts to lend reality to biological myths which have little relation to the content of national cultures are not likely to become a gospel and a way of life for any large number of men and women. People identify themselves much more readily with "nations," religious denominations, and economic classes than with largely imaginary racial groups.

If a race has not become the basis of nationality, the same can scarcely be said of language. Race and language obviously have no necessary connection with one another, since the one is a biological phenomenon and the other is part of the cultural legacy of the past. People are born with skin color, eye color, skull shapes, and the other physical marks of race. But the language they learn depends not on their heredity, but upon their cultural environment. Language, though no indication whatever of race, is everywhere the best index of an individual's cultural environment—of the linguistic and cultural group with which he identifies himself and of which he is a member. By the same token, one's mother tongue is everywhere taken as the best criterion of one's nationality. Most of the nations of the earth are nations, not so much because they are politically independent and socially unified, as because their peoples use a common speech which differs from that of other nations. Englishmen, Americans, and British colonials, it is true, all speak variants of a single language. Portuguese and Brazilians use a single language. So do Frenchmen and Haitians, and likewise Spaniards, Mexicans, Chileans, Argentinians, Peruvians, and the other Spanish-Americans. For these people, varying dialects, rather than language, may indicate nationality. On the other hand, Swiss nationals may speak French, German, or Italian and still be Swiss; and Belgians may speak French or Flemish without ceasing to be Belgians. For the most part, however, distinctions of nationality, in the social and cultural rather than in the legal sense, are coterminous with distinctions of language. With few exceptions, Germans are Germans because they *sprechen echt Deutsch*, Frenchmen are Frenchmen because they *parlent la belle langue française*, Englishmen are Englishmen because they speak the King's English. This association between language and national consciousness appear as natural and obvious as the association between race and nationality appears strange and false. The historical circumstances of the establishment of the older national groups have made the association inevitable. Language is almost universally regarded as the most important single criterion of national sentiment and allegiance. In the last analysis, however, nationality is a matter neither of race nor of language, but of social attitudes, sentiments, and ideologies.

THE DEMAND FOR "SELF-DETERMINATION." The fact that the national group is so generally regarded as coinciding with the language group has meant that the aspirations of nationalists are usually envisaged in terms of the common "national" interests of all who speak the same tongue. Common language has come to be the test of nationality—so much so that States like Switzerland or Belgium or the old Austria-Hungary, where more than one tongue prevails, are often spoken of as "nonnational" or "multinational" States. Whatever the location of political boundaries may be at any given time, "nations" in the nonpolitical sense are aggregations of people aware of themselves as units of virtue of linguistic and cultural ties. The national community whose independence is postulated by nationalism is a community whose members employ the same speech. If the language group does not possess independence, it must achieve it. If, having attained independence, it does not include within the nation-state all those who speak the mother tongue, efforts must be made toward their annexation, even at the cost of the dismemberment of neighboring States. If there are those within the State who do not speak the mother tongue, they must be taught, assimilated, and if necessary coerced into abandoning their own language and culture in the name of national unity and power. From these articles of faith of the national patriot flow many of the consequences of nationalism in the realm of international politics.

The most obvious consequence has been the fragmentation of the world into a large number of sovereign nation-states in the name of national self-determination and independence. Each linguistic group, as it has become infected with the nationalist germ (and the malady is extraordinarily contagious), has striven to attain its political independence, to achieve statehood, to set up national housekeeping for itself. The notion that a national language group can live contentedly under the political control of a government representing another and different group is anathema to the national patriot. Frenchmen have resisted English domination, Germans have resisted French domination, Poles have resisted

German domination, Lithuanians and Ruthenians have resisted Polish domination. Each national community has asserted its right to political independence as soon as national consciousness has taken root and flourished among its people. In the ancient world and in the middle ages, people differing in language and culture were content enough to live together under a common political control embodied in world empires or in complex feudal state forms. Not so in the modern era of Western civilization. Each distinct linguistic group must build its own State, win its own independence, have its own territory, flag, army, bureaucracy, and all the other trappings of sovereignty.

Demands for national self-determination and independence became peculiarly insistent during the Great War and were utilized by the Allied Governments as a means of encouraging the disruption of the enemy States and of convincing their own citizens that the Allied cause was the cause of justice and liberty. President Wilson, as the most eloquent phrasemaker among the statesmen who formulated "war aims" for popular consumption, constantly emphasized the "rights of small nations." Even before the United States entered the war, he laid it down as a principle "that no nation should seek to extend its polity over any other nation or people, but that every people should be left free to determine its own polity, its own way of development, unhindered, unthreatened, unafraid, the little along with the great and powerful."[1] The "fourteen points" address of January 8, 1918, demanded self-determination for the peoples of central and eastern Europe; and in February, 1918, the American President, in an address to Congress, said:

"Peoples and provinces are not to be bartered about from sovereignty to sovereignty as if they were mere chattels and pawns in the game. Peoples may now be dominated and governed only by their own consent. Self-determination is not a mere phrase. It is an imperative principle of action, which statesmen will henceforth ignore at their peril."

At the Paris Peace Conference of 1919 the newly emancipated nationalities of central Europe insisted that the slogan of self-determination be translated into political reality, and the Allied Governments gave effect to these demands wherever they found it politically advantageous to do so. It was clear, however, that in many cases political boundaries could not be made to coincide with language boundaries; for the intermingling of tongues in central Europe is so confused, as shown in the accompanying map, that this ideal is impossible of attainment. The independence of Poland, Czechoslovakia, Hungary, Austria, Jugoslavia, Albania, and Greater Rumania, and later of Finland, Estonia, Latvia, and Lithuania, was accepted as a matter of course. But the boundaries which the new States insisted upon and the boundary adjustments which the victors demanded for themselves were dictated quite as much by considerations of economics, strategy, and territorial aggrandizement as by the expressed desire to grant to the populations affected a right of self-determination. When "self-determination" threatened to thwart the territorial ambitions of the victors, it was denied to the

[1] Address to the Senate, January 22, 1917.

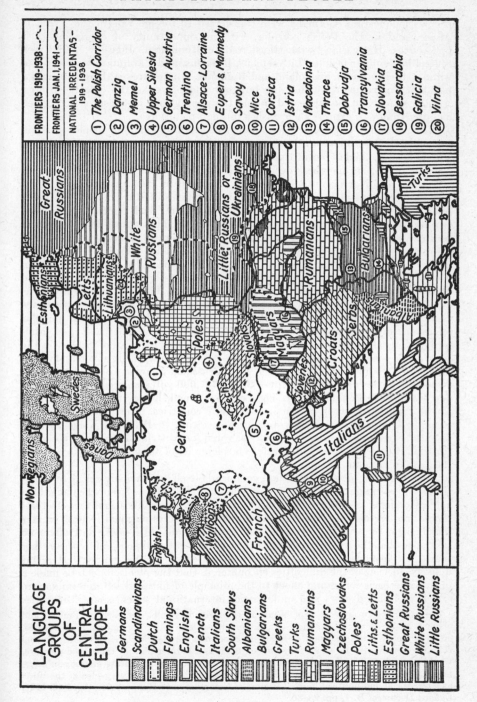

FRONTIERS 1919-1938 ~

FRONTIERS JAN.1,1941 ~

NATIONAL IRREDENTAS –
1919 - 1938

1. The Polish Corridor
2. Danzig
3. Memel
4. Upper Silesia
5. German Austria
6. Trentino
7. Alsace-Lorraine
8. Eupen & Malmedy
9. Savoy
10. Nice
11. Corsica
12. Istria
13. Macedonia
14. Thrace
15. Dobrudja
16. Transylvania
17. Slovakia
18. Bessarabia
19. Galicia
20. Vilna

LANGUAGE
GROUPS
OF
CENTRAL
EUROPE

Germans
Scandinavians
Dutch
Flemings
English
French
Italians
South Slavs
Albanians
Bulgarians
Greeks
Turks
Rumanians
Magyars
Czechoslovaks
Poles
Liths. & Letts
Esthonians
Great Russians
White Russians
Little Russians

peoples in question. Germans were transferred to foreign rule in the Tyrol, in Alsace, and in the Polish corridor, with no opportunity of expressing their preferences. Hungarians were transferred to Rumanian, Jugoslav, and Czech control in a similar fashion. Lithuanians, Russians, and Ukrainians were annexed without their consent by Poland and Rumania. But wherever there appeared a possibility of reducing further the territory and power of the defeated States, self-determination was appealed to and the populations in question were given an opportunity to express their wishes through plebiscites.

The plebiscite, or popular referendum, as a means of enabling peoples to attain national self-determination, has become an increasingly popular device. It has seldom been applied in recent times to an entire national community to determine whether or not its members desire political independence, though the division of Sweden and Norway into independent kingdoms in 1905 was sanctioned by a popular vote, and plebiscites were held in the States of Italy in 1860 and 1861 prior to their amalgamation into the present kingdom. Such referenda have been repeatedly held to ascertain the preferences of the inhabitants of a particular territory as between two outside States seeking control. Napoleon III held a plebiscite in Nice and Savoy prior to their annexation to France in 1859. The Treaty of Ancon in 1883 between Chile and Peru provided for a plebiscite in Tacna-Arica which was never held, in spite of efforts on the part of the United States to make arrangements for a vote in 1923–1925. The plebiscite principle, as a basis for allocating territory, received only partial recognition at the Paris Peace Conference, but the treaties of 1919 nevertheless provided for nine popular referenda: in Schleswig, Allenstein, Marienwerder, Upper Silesia, Eupen, Mal-médy, Klagenfurt, Burgenland, and the Saar valley. In most of Schleswig the population voted to remain under German, rather than Danish, sovereignty, and in Allenstein and Marienwerder the East Prussians likewise voted for German rather than Polish control. In Upper Silesia 707,000 votes were cast for Germany and 479,000 for Poland (1921). The League Council, however, divided the area to the great disgust of nationalists in both countries. Eupen and Malmédy, formerly German territories, voted for annexation to Belgium. Klagenfurt, in dispute between Austria and Jugoslavia, voted for Austria. Burgenland voted for Austrian rather than Hungarian rule. The plebiscite of January 13, 1935, restored the Saar to German sovereignty.

Although the plebiscite method commends itself to idealistic self-determinationists, it is fraught with numerous dangers and difficulties. Even when adequate neutral policing is provided and satisfactory suffrage qualifications and electoral procedures are devised, the referendum itself embitters national feeling, creates temptations to bribery, coercion, and terrorism on both sides, and offers no assurance that the voters will record their permanent national preferences rather than their fears, prejudices, and economic interests at the moment. It seems unlikely, in view of the difficulties encountered, that the plebiscite can be made a practicable basis for giving effect to the principle of national self-determination, except in isolated cases and under strict international supervision.[1] Territories

---

[1] In refusing to approve a plebiscite in the Aaland Islands, occupied by Finland and claimed by Sweden, the League Council committee declared, "To concede to minorities, either of language or of religion, or to any fractions of a population the right of withdrawing from the community to which they belong, because it is their wish or their good pleasure, would be to destroy order and stability within States and to inaugurate anarchy in international life; it would be to uphold a theory incompatible with the very idea of the State as a territorial and political unity." Report of Commission of Rapporteurs, April 16, 1921, *Council Document* B. 7, pp. 28–30.

and peoples continue to be transferred from State to State, and to be granted or denied national independence, in accordance with the dictates of political expediency and the verdict of force. Whenever the outcome fails to correspond to the demands of the peoples themselves, local dissatisfaction, international tension, and controversies between neighboring States invariably ensue.

NATIONAL IRREDENTISM. Another phenomenon of nationalism, which may conveniently be characterized as "irredentism," is closely related to the cry for self-determination and has been an equally fruitful source of conflict among the nation-states. The term is of Italian origin. In 1861 Italian nationalists at length achieved the goal which they had pursued for decades. A United Kingdom of Italy was created through the annexation to Piedmont of the lesser States of the south. Venetia was wrested from Austria in 1867 and Rome was added to the new nation in 1870. But a large Italian-speaking community in Trentino and the Tyrol remained under Austrian rule. No Italian patriot could regard the task of national unification as completed until these regions were likewise "liberated." They came to be known as *Italia Irredenta* ("Italy Unredeemed"). Toward them were turned the eyes of all patriots. Their annexation became one of the major objectives of Italian foreign policy. The French annexation of Tunis in 1881 threw Italy into the arms of Germany and Austria-Hungary, for Italian patriots had regarded the North African province as a future Italian colony. But in the Triple Alliance of 1882, Italy remained an ally of dubious loyalty, for the demands of nationalism were more appealing than the demands of imperialism. So long as Austria-Hungary retained control of Italia Irredenta, the Italian government could not rest content with the prevailing arrangements. In 1914 Italy remained neutral and sought to bargain with her neighbor and erstwhile ally for possession of the unredeemed provinces as the price of her entrance into the war on the side of the Central Powers. But the Allies were more generous in promises; and by the secret Treaty of London of May, 1915, they pledged Italy the realization of her irredentist ambitions at Austria's expense, on condition of her joining their cause. Italy accordingly declared war upon Austria-Hungary and in the peace settlement was awarded the coveted territories and considerably more besides. National irredentism was thus the guiding star of Italian foreign policy for over half a century.

Such aspirations are almost universal among patriots. Irredentist nationalists invariably strive to incorporate into the nation-state such territories as are inhabited by kinsmen of common speech and culture across the frontier. The claims of nationality and the cry of self-determination supersede the claims of legal right and are assumed to justify annexationist ambitions in such situations. Numerous "irredentas" of this character existed in pre-1914 Europe. Alsace-Lorraine under German rule was France irredenta; for every French patriot prayed and hoped for the *revanche* which would enable the Republic to take back to its bosom the "lost provinces," snatched away by Bismarck in 1871. Bosnia, Herzegovina, and the Dalmatian coast under Austrian rule were Serbia irredenta; and Serbian patriots were determined, by fair means or foul, to incorporate the South Slav inhabitants of these regions into a Greater Serbia. Transylvania, under Hungarian rule, and Bessarabia, under Russian rule, were Rumania irredenta, for they were in large part inhabited by Rumanian-speaking peoples whose control by an alien government was intolerable to the people themselves and to their fellow patriots within Rumania. Macedonia and Silistria, under Serbian and Rumanian rule, respectively, were Bulgaria irredenta for similar reasons. The post-1919 irredentas were even more numerous. Germany now had her own "lost provinces" and her own irredentas: Upper Silesia, Pomerelia and Netze (the Polish corridor), Danzig, Memel, German-speaking Austria, the German Tyrol, the German-speaking areas of Czechoslovakia, and even, in the eyes of the more extreme German nationalists, Alsace-Lorraine itself. No German patriot could regard as permanent the loss of these areas, nor could he rest content until they were recovered, at least in part. Hungarian nationalists were similarly embittered over the dismemberment of the ancient Magyar State and strove to incorporate into a resurrected Hungary the millions of Magyars annexed by Czechoslovakia, Jugoslavia, and Rumania. The Aaland Islands were an irredenta for Sweden, eastern Karelia for Finland, Vilna for Lithuania, the Dodecanese Islands for Greece. Bulgaria had her old grievances and a new irredenta as well in western Thrace, taken from her by Greece. If a nationalist government had existed in Russia, the eastern provinces of Poland and Rumanian Bessarabia, with their White Russian and Ukrainian populations, would have become a new Russia irredenta—as indeed they did in 1939–1940. Such attitudes tend to prevail wherever political frontiers fail to follow the boundaries of language, and they are obviously among the most productive causes of tension and conflict among the nations.

These attitudes and aspirations lie at the root of the various pan-nationalistic movements which have flourished so abundantly. "Pan-Germanism" in the pre-1914 period contemplated the annexation to a united Germany of all German-speaking peoples in adjacent foreign States. The Pan-German League, established in 1894, strove "to quicken the national sentiment of all Germans and in particular to awaken and foster the sense of racial and cultural kinship of all sections of the German people." Germany's defeat in the Great War led to additional losses of German territory, and the terms of the peace treaties forbidding any *Anschluss* or union of German-speaking Austria with Germany constituted a new obstacle to the realization of Pan-German ambition. Pre-1914 Pan-Slavism was a similar movement, sponsored by Russian patriots and by certain South Slav groups. It aimed at the "liberation" of the Slavic peoples living under German, Austrian or Turkish rule and the formation of a Slavic confederacy dominated by Russia. As early as the seventeenth century, the Croat, Krijanitcha, urged a political union of Slavic peoples. Pan-Slavic congresses were held in 1848, 1867, and 1908. These ambitions played a large role in the pre-1914 foreign policy of imperial Russia. Combined with annexationist designs on Constantinople and the Straits, they caused Russia to come to the defense of Serbia against Austria-Hungary and thus precipitated the Great War. The Russian Revolution and the political independence of Poland, Czechoslovakia, and Jugoslavia deprived Pan-Slavism of much of its significance. The "Norden Movement" in Sweden, Norway, and Denmark was a comparable Pan-Scandinavian movement. Pan-Anglianism has striven to encourage closer political relations between the English-speaking peoples. Joseph Chamberlain in 1898 advocated an Anglo-American alliance as part of this program. The English-speaking Union endeavored to promote closer cultural and economic contacts between the United States and the British Empire. Pan-Americanism is a movement of a somewhat different character, for any political union of the Latin peoples of South and Central America with the Anglo-Saxon peoples of the United States runs counter to the national aspirations of all Latin Americans. Pan-Latinism and Pan-Hispanism, however, are much more solidly grounded in national sentiment. They do not reflect irredentist ambitions so much as a feeling that linguistic and cultural ties should be made the basis for closer political and economic relations. Pan-African-ism, Pan-Islamism, Pan-Arabianism, Pan-Turanianism, Pan-Asianism, and other movements reflect similar sentiments and ambitions.[1]

The nationalistic aspirations of self-determination and irredentism breed inevitable discontent with all national boundaries which are at variance with the lines of language and culture. Very rarely can these lines by ascertained to the satisfaction of both parties. When they are ascertained, they are often unacceptable for economic or strategic reasons. Italy, for example, recovered Italia Irredenta in 1919 but insisted also on acquiring the Brenner Pass and the southern slope of the Tyrolean Alps for reasons of defense, with the result that 250,000 German-speaking peoples around Bozen (Bolzano) were placed under Italian rule. Boundaries drawn to conform to considerations of strategy and economics are criticized by patriots as violating the wishes of the population. Boundaries drawn to conform to the wishes of the population are criticized by other patriots (or even by the same ones) for other reasons. In such a situation, no rational basis exists for the demarcation of frontiers. Efforts to mini-mize tension are frustrated by annexationist ambitions. Each State exerts its power to gain all the territory possible as a means to greater power, wealth, and security. Power considerations are rationalized in terms of self-determination or irredentism or, when these are inapplicable, in terms of other catchwords and symbols. "Historic" frontiers are insisted upon. "Natural" boundaries are demanded. "Manifest destiny" is called upon to justify annexation. When the line of linguistic cleavage is gained, then the next river or mountain range becomes the goal; and when that is attained, some line beyond becomes the natural and neces-sary frontier. Boundaries are fixed by the clash, in peace or war, of the rival wills-to-power of the nation-states. Nationalism spurs the rivalry and furnishes formulae and slogans, in terms of which each national community can reassure itself of the justice and rectitude of its ambitions.

THE TREATMENT OF NATIONAL MINORITIES. Not only is each nation-state anxious, in its quest for territory and power, to extend its control over the peoples beyond its frontier who speak its language, but it is equally anxious to achieve linguistic and cultural

[1] See R. L. Buell, *International Relations*, 1929, pp. 76–95.

homogeneity among the peoples within its frontiers. "Self-determination" is a phrase used by nationalists only with reference to the oppressed subject peoples of other States. Their "liberation" will weaken the power of the State controlling them and thus enhance that of its neighbor. The neighbor is accordingly solicitous over their fate, particularly when they speak his own language and constitute an irredenta. Patriots are concerned in quite a different way, however, with the minority groups in the population of their own State. These groups must under no circumstances be liberated or granted a right of self-determination. They must be assimilated in the name of national unity and patriotic solidarity. They must be induced or compelled to abandon their own identity and their ties with other peoples beyond the frontier. They must learn the prevailing language, adopt the prevailing customs, and make themselves one with their fellow citizens.

The "problem of national minorities" arises from such nationalistic efforts at assimilation and from the counterefforts, supported by the national consciousness of the minorities, to resist assimilation at all costs. Except for the sentiments, attitudes, and ideologies of nationalism, there would be no problem. Peoples heterogeneous in language, race, and religion might dwell together peaceably under a single sovereignty, as in the Roman Empire, with no attempts made on the part of the government to impose uniformity of tongues and creeds on its subjects, and consequently no attempts at resistance to such efforts on the part of minorities. But in the age of nationalism, any such rational arrangements are regarded by all patriots as highly undesirable and even dangerous. Unassimilated minorities are viewed with alarm; for they are presumed to be of doubtful loyalty, to constitute an alien and possible hostile element in the population, and to be peculiarly susceptible to secret conspirings with neighboring enemy nations of their own blood and language. These suspicions may be at first unjustified, but they find justification as soon as efforts are made to extinguish the identity of the minority. People cling doggedly to their language and culture—never more so than in the era of nationalism, when these things are closely associated with the social cohesion and political self-respect of the community. Efforts at assimilation are vigorously resisted with an energy and determination equivalent to the pressure brought to bear by the assimilators. Resistance assumes the appearance of disloyalty; and this in turn justifies the national government, in the eyes of its patriots, in applying more coercion. The greater the coercion, the greater the resistance; and the greater resistance, the greater the coercion. The outcome of the cycle is persecution, revolt, international complications, and often war. In view of these consequences, the problem is not merely a domestic one but is of increasingly vital international concern.

In pre-1914 Europe, the prevalent policy pursued by governments toward minorities might be described as one of forcible assimilation. This policy was adopted, with minor variations, by the four governments of Europe which had the largest minority groups living under their control—those of Russia, Germany, Austria-Hungary, and Turkey. It was, almost without exception, unsuccessful in suppressing the identity of the minorities or in compelling them to adopt the language, culture, creeds, and institutions of the majority group. Indeed, it more frequently intensified to the point of desperation the solidarity of the oppressed groups and thus rendered impossible the achievement of its own purposes. The failure of this policy had already received a certain degree of recognition in various treaties which protected minority rights and made forcible assimilation difficult. Religious minorities were the first to receive international protection in this fashion, following the wars and persecutions of the Reformation period. The Peace of Augsburg (1555) and the Treaties of Westphalia both gave to minority religious groups a degree of protection from efforts at persecution on the part of the majority denomination. Here, as always, intolerance gave way to tolerance only when persecution had brought disaster and when the folly of achieving conversion by coercion was evident at all. The Powers exacted pledges regarding the protection of religious minorities in Holland and Greece in 1815 and 1830, respectively, on the occasions of the union of Belgium with Holland and of the recognition of Greek independence. Ethnic and linguistic minorities were in no need of such protection before nationalism became a new religion and led in turn to new efforts at conversion and persecution. By the late nineteenth century, however, the problem was a pressing one. The Treaty of Berlin of 1878 required Bulgaria, Montenegro, Serbia, Rumania, and Turkey to refrain from discriminating against religious minorities. As early as 1839, Turkey had been obliged to pledge equal treatment of its subjects regardless of religion, race, or language. The failure of the Turkish Government to observe this and subsequent pledges led to repeated diplomatic representations and interventions by the Powers. From time to time, international inspectors and supervisors were dispatched to Turkish territory to guarantee the protection of minorities in Armenia and Macedonia. These efforts at treaty protection and international guarantees were largely ineffective, however, and were utilized by interested Powers to further their own designs. They were not applied, moreover, to such powerful States as Russia, Austria-Hungary, and Germany, where the minorities were entirely at the mercy of the national patriots bent upon assimilating them.

The Great War and its aftermath created new minority problems and led to the development of alternatives to forcible assimilation. The breakup of Austria-Hungary and the partial dissolution of the Russian, Turkish, and German Empires, coupled with the redrawing of frontiers in the name of self-determination, reduced the minorities of Europe from 54 million to about 17 million. But the new frontiers were based upon economic and strategic considerations and did not in every case follow the lines of language. They were designed to cripple the defeated States as much as possible. Seven and a half million Germans, 3 million Magyars, and 1½ million Bulgarians were placed under alien rule in France, Poland, Czechoslovakia, Jugoslavia, Rumania, Italy, and Greece, along with ½ million Jugoslavs in Italy, 4½ million Ruthenians and Ukrainians in Poland, Czechoslovakia, and Rumania, and several million Russians along Poland's eastern frontier. One-fourth of Jugoslavia's population, one-third of Poland's population, two-fifths of Czechoslovakia's population (not counting the Slovaks as a minority), and over one-tenth of Italy's population consisted of linguistic minorities. To permit a reversion to policies of forcible assimilation on the part of the overenthusiastic patriots of the new States would create widespread domestic disorder and international tension throughout central Europe.

The most drastic solution of the problem was adopted in the case of certain minorities in the Balkans and the Near East. In 1914 Greece and Turkey entered into an agreement for the voluntary exchange of minorities across the new frontiers resulting from the Balkan wars, but the outbreak of the Great War prevented the execution of this plan. In 1919 Greece and Bulgaria signed a treaty for the exchange of minorities under the supervision of a mixed commission of one Greek, one Bulgar, and two members appointed by the League Council. In January, 1923, at the suggestion of Dr. Nansen, refugee commissioner of the League of Nations, a Turco-Greek convention was signed, providing for the compulsory exchange of their respective minorities, also under the supervision of a mixed commission of four Turks, four Greeks, and three neutral nationals chosen by the League Council. The individuals thus exchanged were to receive property in their new State equivalent to that left behind in the old. This arrangement rooted up hundreds of thousands of people from their ancestral homes. It led to the ruthless expulsion of Greeks from Turkey and of Turks from Greece. The Greek Government was obliged to care for almost a million refugees, and the entire proceeding was characterized by an enormous amount of hardship and disorder. The exchange of minorities is obviously a permanent solution of the problem only if the eternal permanence of existing frontiers is postulated—an assumption which is, to say the least, rash. The suffering and the social and economic disorganization to which it leads are out of all proportion to the benefit gained. The confused intermingling of linguistic groups in southeastern Europe, moreover, makes this method quite inapplicable as a general solution.

The Peace Conference, in considering the broader aspects of the problem, devised a new method of international regulation, involving the incorporation of protective guarantees in treaties between the new States and the Allied Powers, and the provision of international machinery through the League of Nations to insure the observance of these obligations. The first of the minorities treaties was imposed upon Poland and signed June 28, 1919. Other treaties followed, with Czechoslovakia (September 10, 1919), Jugoslavia (September 10, 1919), Rumania (December 9, 1919), Greece (August 10, 1920). The Treaty of St. Germain with Austria, of September 10, 1919 (Articles 62 to 69), of Trianon with Hungary, of June 4, 1920 (Articles 54 to 60), of Neuilly with Bulgaria, of November 27, 1919 (Articles 49 to 57), and of Lausanne with Turkey of July 24, 1923 (Articles 37 to 45), likewise contained clauses for the protection of minorities, largely modeled upon the Polish treaty. The Baltic States and Albania were subsequently induced to accept the same obligations.[1] Fifteen States of central and southeastern Europe, including Finland

[1] A resolution of the First Assembly, December 15, 1920, declared "in the event of Albania, the Baltic and Caucasian States being admitted into the League, the Assembly requests that they should take the necessary measures to enforce the principles of the minorities treaties and that they should arrange with the Council the details required to carry this object into effect" (League of Nations *Records of Assembly*, 1920, I, pp. 568–569).

Danzig, and Greece, were thus obliged to renounce their efforts at forcible assimilation and to protect the rights of minorities living within their frontiers.

In all these arrangements, six general principles were set forth. (1) The States in question must protect the life and liberty of all inhabitants "without distinction of birth, nationality, language, race, or religion" (Polish Treaty, Article 2). (2) "All inhabitants . . . shall be entitled to the free exercise, whether public or private, of any creed, religion, or belief whose practices are not inconsistent with public order or public morals" (Polish Treaty, Article 3). (3) All persons born within the territory of these States are entitled to rights of citizenship. "All persons born in Polish territory who are not born nationals of another state shall *ipso facto* become Polish nationals" (Polish Treaty, Article 6). (4) "All . . . nationals shall be equal before the law and enjoy the same civil and political rights without distinction as to race, language, or religion. Differences of religion, creed, or confession shall not prejudice any national in matters relating to the enjoyment of civil or political rights, as for instance admission to public employments or the exercise of professions and industries" (Polish Treaty, Articles 7 to 9). (5) "No restrictions shall be imposed on the free use by any . . . national of any language in private intercourse, in commerce, in religion, in the press or in publications of any kind or at public meetings. Notwithstanding any establishment of an official language, adequate facilities shall be given for the use of their [the minorities'] language either orally or in writing before the courts" (Polish Treaty, Articles 3 and 4). (6) The States involved must grant educational facilities for instruction in their own language to minorities in districts where a considerable proportion of the population is of minority speech (Polish Treaty, Article 9). Among these items (1), (2), (3), and (5) are essentially guarantees of individual rights, and (4) and (6) protect the minorities as groups by giving them schools and a share of public funds where they constitute a "considerable proportion" (in practice usually one-fifth) of the population. Lines of race, religion, and language do not of course always coincide; and the ultimate test of whether a group is a minority is historical, social, and psychological.

Two means were provided for ensuring the observance of these obligations: The guarantees were declared in the treaties to be part of the fundamental law of the States concerned. The minorities were placed under the protection of the League of Nations.[1] The Council of the League, in a series of resolutions, worked out a procedure for dealing with minority problems. Only States represented on

[1] The clauses of the treaties "so far as they affect persons belonging to racial, religious, or linguistic minorities constitute obligations of international concern and shall be placed under the guarantee of the League of Nations. They shall not be modified without the assent of the majority of the Council of the League of Nations. . . . Any member of the Council of the League of Nations shall have the right to bring to the attention of the Council of the League of Nations any infraction or danger of infraction, of any of these obligations. The Council may thereupon take such action and give such direction as it may deem proper and effective in the circumstances. . . . Any difference of opinions as to questions of law or fact arising out of these articles between the government concerned and any one of the principal Allied and Associated Powers or any other Power, a member of the Council of the League of Nations, shall be held to be a dispute of an international character under Article 14 of the Covenant of the League of Nations. . . . Any dispute shall, if the other party thereto demands, be referred to the Permanent Court of International Justice. The decision of the Permanent Court shall be final and shall have the same force and effect as an award under Article 13 of the Covenant." Polish Treaty, Article 12.

the Council could bring such problems officially before the body. But States not on the Council and organizations of the minorities themselves could call attention to infractions of the treaties by sending petitions to the Secretariat. The Secretary-General passed upon the receivability of petitions on the basis of five criteria: The petitions must have in view the protection of minorities in accordance with the treaties; they must not be submitted in the form of a request for the severance of political relations between a minority and the State of which it is a part; they must not emanate from an anonymous or unauthenticated source; they must abstain from violent language; and they must contain information not recently the subject of a petition.[1] When a petition was found receivable, it was sent to the interested governments for observations, which were transmitted along with the petition to the Council. Under a Council resolution of October 25, 1920, such petitions, if acted upon by the Council, were submitted to a minorities committee of three members, consisting of the president and two other members of the Council, none of whom is to be a representative of the States concerned or of neighboring States. The committee, in cooperation with the minorities section of the Secretariat, proceeded to investigate the complaint (resolution of June 10, 1925). Most petitions never got beyond the committee of three, for investigation, publicity, and suggestions usually sufficed to ameliorate the situation. When the case seemed to warrant further action, however, the committee referred the question to the Council with recommendations. On September 21, 1922, the Assembly passed four resolutions in which it urged: (1) friendly and informal communication as an alternative to direct recommendations by the Council; (2) resort to the Permanent Court for decisions on questions of law or fact; (3) the recognition by the minorities of their obligation to act as loyal citizens of their State;[2] and (4) adoption by States not bound by the minorities treaties of a standard of justice and toleration toward their minorities at least as high as that expected by the Council from the signatory States.

The minorities fared better than would have been the case in the absence of such international protection. On the other hand, it could not be said, nor could it be reasonably expected, that all discrimination and persecution were eliminated. States not bound by the minorities treaties were free to treat their minorities as badly as they like. A Lithuanian proposal of 1925 to make these obligations universal was rejected. Even in treaty States, minorities in which no government on the Council was particularly interested did not receive a full measure of protection. Such was the situation of the Jews in Rumania and Hungary, the Hungarians in Rumania, and the Ukrainians in Poland. Prior to 1926, the Council took official cognizance of only three petitions. It never asked a State to withdraw objectionable measures but merely expressed the hope that the State would observe its obligations. After the admission of Germany to the League, the Council acted on minority questions more frequently and

---

[1] *Official Journal of the League of Nations*, November, 1923, p. 1426.

[2] "While the Assembly recognizes the primary right of the minorities to be protected by the League from oppression, it also emphasizes the duty incumbent upon persons belonging to racial, religious, or linguistic minorities to cooperate as loyal fellow citizens with the nation to which they now belong." *Records of Assembly*, 1922, I, p. 186, Resolution II.

with greater energy. The largest number of petitions came from the German minority in Polish Upper Silesia, which was perhaps the best-organized and most articulate of the minority groups. The petitions, most of which were considered by the Council in 1929, related primarily to minority schools, language instruction, and property rights. Some of these grievances were remedied by Council action, but permanent harmony was not achieved. All such disputes, the Council insisted, were subjects of discussion between the Council and the State concerned, never between governments. But since the Council was a political body, it proceeded with great circumspection and was often tempted to side-step embarrassing issues or to make innocuous or ineffective recommendations.

In contrast to the relatively unsuccessful method of protecting minority rights by international guarantees, the United States exhibits on the largest scale the most successful application of still another method of dealing with minorities—one which may be termed *voluntary assimilation*. The original American Indian population of the United States has been largely confined to reservations where it is cared for (or neglected) by the federal government. The population groups in the United States whose members are of European ancestry have never been regarded as "minorities" in the European sense. The United States has proverbially been the melting pot of all nations, and millions of immigrants from overseas poured into its territories during the period of its greatest agricultural and industrial development. The peoples in question were not subjected to American governmental authority, American laws, American language and culture by virtue of transfers of territory and changes in boundaries which they have no hand in bringing about. They came voluntarily for their own economic advancement. Most of them did not contemplate returning to their home States, nor did they cherish hopes that the new lands which they occupied would eventually be annexed to their fatherlands. Neither did they cherish aspirations of national independence. No problem of irredentism or of self-determination arose under these circumstances. "Americanization" was rapid and amazingly successful because on the one hand it was not coercive in character and on the other it did not encounter the resistance of national sentiment among those being Americanized. This process is now, of course, of only historical interest. By 1940 almost 80 per cent of the population of the United States consisted of native-born whites, less than 10 per cent of foreign-born whites, 9 per cent of Negroes, 1 per cent of Mexicans, and less than half of 1 per cent of American Indians, Japanese, and Chinese combined.

The "quota law" of 1921 restricted the numbers of each foreign nationality which might enter the United States annually to 3 per cent of foreign-born persons of the same nationality residing in the United States in 1910. The 1924 act reduced the quotas to 2 per cent of those residing in the United States in 1890, in the interest of cutting down immigration still further and of admitting a larger proportion of northern and western Europeans and a smaller proportion of southern and eastern Europeans. The Rumanian and Italian Governments protested against this disguised discrimination, but without result. The "national origins" plan which went into effect in 1929 provides for the admission of some 150,000 aliens annually on this quota basis. The new immigrants entering the United States are far too few in number to constitute a problem. Since the onset of the economic depression and the prevalence of widespread unemployment in the United States, American immigration has been reduced almost to the vanishing point by administrative action. The aliens already here are in process of speedy assimilation.

If aliens of European extraction in the United States have not constituted a minority problem, the same cannot be said of the Asiatics and Africans. The 12 million Negroes in the United States are descendants of the slaves of pre-Civil War days who were brought to the New World against their will for purposes of economic exploitation. Their emancipation in 1863 and the granting to them of constitutional protection in the Thirteenth, Fourteenth, and Fifteenth Amendments of the federal Constitution have not been followed by their reception into American society on a basis of equality. In most of the Southern States, they are denied the right to vote; and, throughout the nation, they are subjected to so many forms of discrimination and oppression, social and economic if not political and legal, that they continue to constitute a degraded and outcast pariah community. Here again there is no problem of irredentism or self-determination, and the serious problem of racial adjustment is in no sense an international one, for the Negro States of the world—Haiti, Liberia, and formerly Abyssinia—are such feeble midgets compared with the United States that they are in no position to act in a protective capacity, even were they inclined to do so. The only treaties which the United States has ever entered into regarding Negro rights relate to the African slave trade. The colored population of the nation continues to be "kept in its place" by the white "Nordic" masters; and the poverty, indignity, and occasional violence and persecution to which it is subjected is a domestic question with which no outside State and no international organization concerns itself.

The situation with regard to Asiatics in the United States is somewhat different. Considerable numbers of Chinese were welcomed into the country in the mid-nineteenth century, when labor was scarce in the west. Many of the western railroads were built with the aid of Chinese coolie labor. Later Japanese came to the Pacific Coast as workers and farmers, along with a smaller number of Hindus. Race prejudice and friction developed as soon as changed economic conditions created competition for land and jobs between white and Asiatic workers. The latter were regarded as "unassimilable" because of their physical characteristics. They were prevented from becoming American citizens by the provisions of American naturalization laws, which open citizenship rights to white persons, Amerindians, and persons of African descent, but bar them to all the yellow and brown peoples of Asia. Following outbreaks of mob violence against Chinese in a number of western towns, Congress barred all Chinese immigration to the United States in a series of acts passed in 1882, 1888, and 1892. This legislation was in violation of American treaties with China of 1868 and 1880, but Chinese diplomatic protests were of no avail. Slightly over 70,000 Chinese now reside in the United States.

Diplomatic controversies between the United States and Japan later developed over California legislation barring Japanese children from public schools in San Francisco and forbidding Japanese to own land. In 1907, by the Gentlemen's Agreement concluded between President Roosevelt and the Japanese Government, the latter voluntarily agreed not to issue passports to laborers desiring to go to the United States. This arrangement achieved its purpose without offending Japan. The Japanese population of the United States (111,000 in 1920) continued to increase through natural multiplication, but the increase by immigration was only about 500 a year. In 1924, however, Congress placed in the immigration act a provision declaring that "no alien ineligible to citizenship shall be admitted to the United States" (Act of May 26, 1924, §13, Part C). This was an obvious discrimination against Asiatics. It was a violation of the Gentlemen's Agreement, was opposed by the Administration and the State Department, and was needlessly offensive to Japanese sensibilities. Had Japan been treated equally with other foreign States and placed on a quota basis, fewer than 200 Japanese could have entered the United States annually. But patriotic fervor and white supremacy dictated discriminatory exclusion despite its evil effects on Japanese-American relations.[1] American treatment of Asiatic minorities has thus created diplomatic friction, though here again there is no problem of self-determination, irredentism, or international protection.

Finally, brief notice may be taken of the solution of the Russian "nationalities problem" arrived at by the Communist Government of the Soviet Union. This solution was that of complete cultural autonomy within the political and economic framework of the proletarian State. All efforts at "Russification" were abandoned, at least in theory, and each of the many nationalities of the U.S.S.R. was not only permitted, but encouraged, to use its own language, develop its own culture, and pursue its own way of life. So long as the content of the national cultures and the political and economic institutions of the nationalities were "proletarian"

---

[1] On May 31, 1924, Ambassador Hanihara presented to Secretary of State Hughes an official protest from the Japanese Government against this provision. This protest concluded, "Unfortunately . . . the sweeping provisions of the new act, clearly indicative of discrimination against Japanese, have made it impossible for Japan to continue the undertakings assumed under the Gentlemen's Agreement. An understanding of friendly cooperation reached after long and comprehensive discussions between the Japanese and American Governments has thus been abruptly overthrown by legislative action on the part of the United States. The patient, loyal, and scrupulous observance by Japan for more than sixteen years of these self-denying regulations, in the interest of good relations between the two countries, now seems to have been wasted.

"It is not denied that, fundamentally speaking, it lies within the inherent sovereign power of each State to limit and control immigration to its own domains, but when, in the exercise of such right, an evident injustice is done to a foreign nation in disregard of its proper self-respect, of international understandings, or of ordinary rules of comity, the question necessarily assumes an aspect which justifies diplomatic discussion and adjustment.

"Accordingly, the Japanese Government consider it their duty to maintain and to place on record their solemn protest against the discriminatory clause in §13 (C) of the Immigration Act of 1924 and to request the American Government to take all possible and suitable measures for the removal of such discrimination."

in spirit and substance, the forms could be "national." The 1923 federal constitution of the Soviet Union incorporated this solution into the political structure of the State, consisting of eleven federated Soviet Republics, each of which was politically independent and had a theoretical right of secession from the Union. The Central Executive Committee ("Supreme Soviet" since 1936) consists of the Council of the Union and the Council of Nationalities. In the latter chamber each constituent republic has five members and each autonomous district, one member. Political unity and social cohesion are given to Soviet society by the All-Union Communist Party which, like the Soviet Government itself, rests upon complete equality for all nationalities and races. These arrangements put an end to the minorities problem in Russia. In the absence of efforts at assimilation by the majority groups, there is no basis for irredentist or secessionist aspirations among the minorities. In the absence of political, economic, or social discrimination based on lines of race and language, there is no problem of interracial relations.[1]

THE TRIUMPH OF INTOLERANCE. The whole post-Versailles system of protecting minorities broke down in the face of a resurgence of racial and national intolerance long before 1939. The Polish Government proposed in 1934 that all the members of the League accept identical obligations to protect minorities. On September 13, 1934, M. Beck told the Fifteenth Assembly that Poland would refuse all further cooperation in protecting minorities until a general and unifom system had been accepted.[2] On September 14 the delegates of Great Britain, France, and Italy (cosignatories of the Polish minorities treaty) declared that no State could release itself from such obligations by unilateral action. In the Sixth Committee, it became clear that certain governments were not willing to accept universal obligations. The Polish proposal was therefore dropped. The rising tide of anti-Semitism in Poland indicated that minority rights were no longer being protected with even a semblance of adequacy. Other States followed the Polish example in ignoring their obligations and refusing to cooperate with the League.

[1] In the U.S.S.R. the Russians number barely 50 per cent of the population, the Ukrainians about 20 per cent, the White Russians 3 per cent, the Jews 1.7 per cent, the Georgians 1.2 per cent, the Turks, Armenians, and Mordvins 1 per cent each, and the Germans, Ostiaks, Turcomans, Tadzhiks, Kirghisians, Bashkirs, Kalmuks, Ossetins, etc., less than 1 per cent each.

[2] "Pending the introduction of a general and uniform system for the protection of minorities, my Government is compelled to refuse, as from to-day, all cooperation with the international organisations in the matter of the supervision of the application by Poland of the system of minority protection. I need hardly say that the decision of the Polish Government is in no sense directed against the interests of the minorities. Those interests are and will remain protected by the fundamental laws of Poland, which secure to minorities of language, race and religion free development and equality of treatment." In his visit to London, April 3 to 6, 1939, M. Beck attempted without visible success to use the Nazi technique of blackmail to compel the Western Powers to aid Poland to expel Jews.

Germany was not bound by treaty to refrain from persecuting the Jews of the Reich. No effective action was taken through the League either to halt Nazi anti-Semitism or to provide a refuge for its victims. Here an old problem was posed in a new setting. Since the *Diaspora*, or dispersion of the Jews over the ancient world, the Jews have ceased to be a "nation" and their descendants have nowhere constituted a "national minority" in the usual sense of the term. Until the French Revolution they were almost everywhere in the Western world discrminated against as a religious minority and confined in ghettos. Religious anti-Semitism was a characteristic feature of both Catholic and Protestant Christianity until the nineteenth century. As it waned under the impact of Liberalism, many Jews lost the age-old religious and cultural heritage which they had so persistently cherished in the face of persecution. Many became fully assimilated with the people among whom they lived. Where discrimination ceased, the Jews ceased to be a political or social minority in any sense. Nationalism made most Jews loyal and patriotic citizens with no irredentist or self-determinationist aspirations. But no sooner had medieval religious anti-Semitism disappeared than modern racial anti-Semitism was born. Jews began to be persecuted once more not because they were non-Christians but because they were falsely alleged to constitute a "race" bent upon exploiting the populations among whom they lived.

Racial anti-Semitism is a product of the insecurities of decaying social systems. Its sources are not to be found in the attitudes or behavior of Jews, but in the fears of powerholders anxious to deflect mass resentments at injustices away from themselves and onto a scapegoat minority. Thus, in Tsarist Russia, the imperial bureaucracy incited mobs to pogroms in order that impoverished peasants might discharge their aggressions against the Jews rather than the landlords, and exploited workers might relieve their wrath at the expense of Israelites instead of employers and officials. In the last decades of the nineteenth century, the socially insecure *Kleinbürgertum*, or lower middle class, in central Europe began to show symptoms of increasing anti-Semitism. This class suffered from a sense of oppression induced by its weak economic position between big business and finance on the one hand and organized labor on the other. In Jew baiting and racial mysticism, it found a release for its tensions. That the Jews are not a race, that Aryanism is a fiction, that the "Jewish world conspiracy" is a myth were without significance, for these things have no relevance to the social and psychological roots of modern anti-Semitism. Belief in the preposterous is ever the true test of faith.

This resumption of persecution produced its inevitable reaction the rise of a Jewish counternationalism. In 1896, Theodore Herzl published *Der Judenstaat*. "The Jews have but one way of saving themselves—a return to their own people and an emigration to their own land." Herzl's followers held the first Zionist Congress in Basle in 1897. Herzl died in 1904; but political Zionism, aiming at the creation of a Jewish State in Palestine, continued to spread among those who saw no refuge elsewhere. In the Balfour Declaration of November 2, 1917, the British Government yielded to the plea of the Zionist leader, Dr. Chaim Weizmann, and pledged itself to the establishment of a Jewish National Home in Palestine. The Mandate indeed became a thriving community and a useful center of Jewish culture. But it was scarcely a substitute for tolerance. Neither did the other Jewish "home" in remote Siberia, Biro-Bidjan, created by the U.S.S.R., offer any hope of ultimate salvation to the 16½ million Jews of the world. Nationalistic Semitism breeds more anti-Semitism.

In the Third Reich of Adolf Hitler, anti-Semitism has received its most complete contemporary expression. The Jews of Germany had not constituted a minority. They were more indifferent to Zionism and more completely assimilated than most Jews in other countries. They had become good Germans.[1] But anti-Semitism became the basis of the Nazi *Weltanschauung*, the source of the Nazi racial philosophy, the inspiration of the swastika flag, and the alpha and omega of Nazi racial legislation. In the National Socialist dictatorship, *Junkers* and industrialists were protected from the bitterness of peasants, workers, and petty burghers by Jew baiting. The politicians in power deflected the aggressions of the masses onto Jewish scapegoats. On April 1, 1933, a one-day boycott of all Jewish businesses and professions initiated the "cold pogrom." There followed a series of laws barring Jews from the civil service, the army, and a constantly enlarged number of private vocations. As economic and social insecurity in the Nazi State gave rise to increasing popular unrest, the attack upon the Jews was intensified. The "Nürnberg Laws" of September, 1935, deprived the Jews of citizenship, forbade intermarriage between Jews and "Aryans," and barred Jewish children from the public schools. The Jews, having already been driven from the professions in large numbers, were driven from business likewise and became a pariah caste. The nationwide pogrom of November, 1938, shocked all the democratic world.

[1] In 1925 there were 564,379 professing Israelites in Germany, or 0.9 per cent of the population. Extensive intermarriage had created perhaps 2 million more Germans who were partly Jewish by ancestry. During the Great War, 12,000 German Jews gave their lives for the fatherland and three Jewish geniuses helped make possible Germany's long resistance to a world in arms: Fritz Haber, the chemist, who invented the processes of fixing nitrogen from the air in 1915 and thus made Germany independant of foreign nitrates; Erich von Richthofen, greatest of war aces; and Walter Rathenau, organizer of the German war industries, Richthofen was killed in battle and was thus spared the sight of his subordinate, Hermann Goering, becoming a leader of an anti-Semitic movement and Minister of Air in the Nazi Cabinet. Rathenau was assassinated by anti-Semitic nationalists in 1922. Haber, a broken man, died in exile in Switzerland, January 29, 1934.

With their livelihood destroyed and all living made intolerable, thousands of Jews fled Germany. Other governments could do little to avert the tragedy. Since no minority treaty protected the Jews, their fate was a German "domestic" matter. But the international problem created by Nazi persecution could not be escaped. On October 26, 1933, the League Council appointed James G. McDonald as High Commissioner for Refugees coming from Germany. McDonald sought to coordinate relief and resettlement activities, but neither he nor the League had any public funds for this purpose. Private contributions were totally inadequate. On December 27, 1935, the High Commissioner resigned. He condemned the Nazi régime for pauperizing hundreds of thousands of its subjects and made a plea for League pressure on Berlin "by all pacific means" to bring the persecutions to an end. "The League must ask for a modification of policies which constitute a source of unrest and perplexity in the world, a challenge to the conscience of mankind and a menace to the legitimate interests of these States affected by the immigration of German refugees." In the sequel the League neither assumed responsibility for caring for the fugitives nor took any steps to check Nazi anti-Semitism at its source. Thousands of German Jews with means went to Palestine, France, England, America, and other lands. Other thousands faced starvation in exile, and the majority, having no means to go abroad, remain in Germany to face a living death. Meanwhile, other Fascist groups in Poland, Rumania, Hungary, and other countries strove to follow the Nazi example by persecuting the Jews and attempting to drive them out into an inhospitable world.[1]

International efforts to cope with the problem outside of the League produced meager results. On the initiative of the United States, delegates of thirty-two countries met at Evian, France, July 6 to 15, 1938, to facilitate the emigration of political and racial refugees. Financing of the enterprise was to be in private hands, however, and no State was asked to liberalize its existing restrictions on immigration. At the opening of the conference, Myron C. Taylor, Chairman of the United States delegation, condemned "the forced and chaotic dumping of unfortunate peoples in large numbers" and urged the establishment of an organization to supplement the work of the League and to deal ultimately with all fugitives

[1] McDonald was succeeded by Sir Neill Malcolm, whose mandate was extended by the seventeenth Assembly to the close of 1938. He estimated that, of the 115,000 refugees from Germany since 1933, 100,000 were Jews. Meanwhile, the Nansen Office, under M. Michael Hansson (President of the Governing Body) sought to aid the 445,000 Russian refugees, the 234,000 Armenians, the 15,000 Syrians and Assyro-Chaldeans, the 4,000 Saarlanders, etc., who fled revolution or persecution. During 1936, 112,000 were given aid. In 1938 the Nansen Office and the Office of High Commissioner were combined under a single High Commissioner. On September 30, 1938, the Assembly appointed Sir Herbert Emerson to this post for a five-year term, beginning January 1, 1939. His activities virtually ceased with the outbreak of war and the collapse of the League.

from persecution. All agreed in principle. None (save the Dominican Republic) was willing in practice to admit any additional refugees. An Intergovernmental Committee was nevertheless established in London with Earl Winterton as Chairman and George Rublee as Director. It sought to secure the cooperation of the Nazi authorities in promoting the transfer of refugees with their property rather than without it. The Nazi régime was admittedly engaged in the robbery of its victims. It was therefore willing to "cooperate" only on condition that funds taken out by refugees be used exclusively to buy German exports. Since other States had no more desire for increased imports from Germany than for additional immigrants, this effort to cope with persecution by cooperating with the persecutors came to nothing.

Another heavy blow at Jewish hopes was the British White Paper of May 17, 1939, declaring that His Majesty's Government had no intention of making Palestine a Jewish State and would henceforth appease the Arabs by restricting land sales and limiting Jewish immigration to 10,000 per year for five years, with an additional 25,000 admissible at the discretion of the British High Commissioner. With the coming of war, the last doors were all but closed. Millions of people hitherto free, Jews and non-Jews alike, became victims of Nazi intolerance. With no place to flee, with no one to protect them, they were swallowed in black night with only the faintest echo of their futile lamentations reaching the outer world.

THE DUSK OF THE GODS. The great "breaking of nations" which marked the Second World War doubtless foreshadows the twilight of nationalism in its old guise. The war itself, like that of 1914, grew out of issues of irredentism and national minorities. The western Munichmen acquiesced in Austrian *Anschluss* and compelled Czechoslovakia to cede Sudetenland to Germany in the name of national "self-determination." Said the Führer, "We don't want any Czechs." When Berlin annexed Czechs and Slovaks in March, 1939, Chamberlain and Daladier complained that Hitler was now violating his promise. German efforts to recover Danzig and the Polish corridor (both of which, unlike Sudetenland, had been under German sovereignty for many generations) were resisted by Warsaw, Paris, and London not for "nationalistic" reasons but because it was feared that any such enhancement of German power would spell the doom of Germany's neighbors. The Nazi leaders manufactured the war crisis of 1939, like that of 1938, with loud outcries that German "racial comrades" were being "persecuted" by Slavic oppressors. The German minorities in Poland, France, Denmark, and elsewhere, like those in Czechoslovakia and Rumania, were firmly organized by Nazi party agents from Berlin and used as "Trojan Horses" to destroy the States in which they lived.

Once this object was accomplished, whether by internal intrigue or by *Blitzkrieg*, the leaders of the Reich developed a conception of the German role which far transcended Pan-Germanism and contemplated the permanent subjugation of the conquered peoples in a Holy Reich in which political independence should be reserved to the ruling race. Allied war aims in 1939–1940 were couched in terms of national self-determination once more, with promises to restore Austria, Czechoslovakia, Poland, Denmark, Norway, etc. Hopes of this kind were long entertained by all the "governments in exile." There seemed little reason for supposing, however, that Humpty Dumpty could ever be put back on the wall. Political nationalism, having "Balkanized" Central Europe after 1919, reached its logical *reductio ad absurdum* in 1933–1939 in the refusal of isolationist patriots in democracies to permit common action against a common threat to the independence of all nations, and in the deliberate use by the Axis Powers of minority claims to "self-determination" in order to befuddle democratic diplomats and encompass the political destruction of all their neighbors.

By the spring of 1941 all the smaller nation-states of Europe had lost their independence with the exception of Switzerland (which is not a nation-state) and with the doubtful exceptions of Finland, Sweden, Spain and Portugal. All others willy-nilly had surrendered or been conquered or were under such pressure from powerful neighbors, enemies, or allies that their "independence" had become a fiction. Germany, Italy, the Soviet Union, and Japan were great multilingual and transnational empires, bearing no resemblance in their structure or extent to the modern model of the national state. The victory of the Triplice promised to perpetuate the new dispensation indefinitely. Allied victory was all but unthinkable in terms of attempts to restore the world of 1939 or 1919. Only a program of European and world federation which would substitute international interdependence for national independence and thereby abolish "sovereignty," "self-determination," and political patriotism of the old variety offered any prospect of peace with victory for the democratic Powers. In either case the tribal totems of the nations, having exacted their last full measure of tears and blood, were passing into the twilight which finally engulfs all local deities. The flickering lights on the horizon of a new dawn were heralds of an age to come in which men and women would live not by allegiance to their national land patches but by loyalty to great continental empires or federations, giving political unity to many lands and many peoples.

2. PATRIOTISM AND PROFITS

I understand by economic nationalism the point of view that it ought to be the object of statesmanship in economic matters to increase the power rather than the economic well-being of a given society.—T. E. GREGORY.

"Butter makes us fat, but iron makes us strong!"—GENERAL HERMANN GOERING.

The economic consequences of national patriotism are no less significant for international politics than its "political" manifestations. The traditional division of human motives and activities into "economic" and "political" is at best somewhat artificial and misleading. The "political animal" of Aristotle is no less an imaginary creature than the "economic man" of the classical economists. Men and women in their private capacities have, from time immemorial, striven to gain for themselves the necessities of life, to create wealth, and to increase their material well-being. They have likewise striven to exercise power over one another and to set up common procedures and institutions for the exercise of power, through which their "public" affairs could be regulated and administered. But the line between "private" and "public" affairs is purely arbitrary and relative. The distinction between economics and politics, business and government, profit motives and power motives is useful only for purposes of academic division of labor and not for purposes of analyzing realistically the whole complex of human interrelationships and social behavior. In contemporary Western civilization there is no form of economic activity which is not affected by governmental action, and there is no type of political or governmental activity which is not intimately connected with the production and distribution of wealth. These relationships in our own age have been profoundly affected by the cult of the nation-state.

ECONOMIC NATIONALISM. The national patriot necessarily thinks of international economic relations, as he thinks of international political relations, in terms of "national interests." He regards the sovereign nation-state not merely as the normal basis of political organization, but likewise as the basis of economic activity. The fatherland to which he grants supreme loyalty is the land which produces his meat and drink, his corn and cabbage, his potatoes and peas. Its fields and farms and vineyards give employment to him or to many of his fellow citizens. Its factories, mills, and mines, its shops and stores and business offices, its ships and railways and air lines are the bases of national prosperity. The maintenance and promotion of this prosperity are the primary concern of government, for the nation which is prosperous presumably becomes wealthy and strong and politically influential in world affairs. The government is accordingly called upon to enact such legislation as will contribute to prosperity and economic power. It is expected to administer its relations with foreign governments in such fashion as will be most advantageous to the national economy. These assumptions and ideas, and the governmental policies which flow therefrom, can conveniently be described by the phrase "economic nationalism."

In a rational world, governmental regulation of economic activity would be directed toward welfare rather than power. In the world of the Western nation-states, the reverse is the case. If the power of the State and the economic welfare of its inhabitants do not coincide, the patriot must insist that the power and security of the State are paramount and that economic sacrifices are necessary on the altar of the fatherland. It must not run the risk of being cut off from essential sources of raw materials or manufactured goods in war time. It must not run the risk of defeat through lack of cannon fodder. It must not permit investments to be made where they will be jeopardized by war, with a resulting diminution of national power and prestige. In anticipation of war the State must maintain its own military industries and have its own sources of supply. It must strive to attain economic self-sufficiency, to make itself as far as possible a strong and self-contained economic system. This may involve a heavy cost, but the exigencies of war require that welfare be sacrificed to power.

The relative political influence of producers and consumers, moreover, leads to similar results. Generally speaking, all producers are also consumers, and *vice versa*, and in a sane world there would be no clash of interests between them. But in the salesman's and advertiser's world of capitalistic industry, production is organized and managed by a relatively small number of persons whose control over the productive process is out of all proportion to their consuming capacity. The great mass of consumers are employees who work for wages or salaries and who have no control over production. They have an interest in low prices, cheap goods, reduced living costs, and more abundant goods and services of all kinds from whatever source, domestic or foreign. But they are inarticulate, unorganized, unaware often of the effect upon them of governmental policies and economic measures. They have no political power or influence over domestic legislation proportionate to their numbers.[1] Those who con-

[1] "Power depends for its habits upon a consciousness of possession, a habit of organization, an ability to produce an immediate effect. In a democratic state, where there are great inequalities of economic power, the main characteristics of the poor are exactly the want of these. They do not know the power that they possess. They hardly realize what can be effected by organizing their interest. They lack direct access to those who govern them. Any action by the working classes, even in a democratic state, involves risk to their economic security out of all proportion to the certainty of gain. They have rarely in their hands the instruments necessary to secure their desires. They have seldom even learned how these may best be formulated and defended. They labor under the sense of inferiority

trol production, on the other hand, are the great entrepreneurs, the captains of industry, the business leaders, the owners of the means of production, the bankers, capitalists, and employers of labor. These persons organize production and produce goods and services for profit. Profits are dependent upon prices. Prices are dependent upon the well-known "law of supply and demand." If foreign goods can be shut out or heavily taxed, if domestic industries can be "protected" and subsidized, the domestic producers can monopolize the domestic market and raise prices to enhance profits. Protective tariffs, bounties, and indirect governmental assistance of various kinds are instrumental in bringing about this result. The producers are few, highly organized, well aware of their interests, and politically influential in proportion to their economic power. They can usually bring effective pressure to bear to secure governmental aid. In the name of patriotism, national self-sufficiency, and the "full dinner pail" for the workingman, they can determine public policies in their own interests and persuade the consumers to acquiesce or even to imagine themselves to be benefited by the process. The patriot and the profiteer work hand in hand. Nationalism, which is a creation of the ideology and the class interests of the bourgeoisie, *i.e.*, the owners and managers of production, continues to serve its creators.

In summary, economic nationalism has become the universal policy of the nation-states, because those who profit by it are politically influential and able to control governmental policy and because all good patriots place national power above economic welfare for reasons of high politics and war. This policy promotes national self-sufficiency, national political power, and producers' profits rather than economic specialization and consumers' welfare through a world-wide exchange of goods and services. It tends increasingly to divide up the world into small, self-contained economic units coinciding in area and population with the political frontiers of the nation-states. Each unit strives desperately to free itself from economic dependence upon the others, and each suffocates behind its tariff walls to the common economic detriment of all.

POPULATION POLICIES. Though population and man power have always been an extremely important element in the fighting strength and political influence of nations, they have usually not been susceptible of any very effective control through governmental action. The size of a

which comes from perpetual obedience to orders without any full experience of the confidence which comes from the habit of command. They tend to confound the institutions they have inherited with the inescapable foundations of society. There is, in fact, every reason to expect that a state built upon universal suffrage will be responsible for wider concessions to the multitude than will be granted under any alternative form; but there is no historic reason to suppose that such a state will be able of itself directly to alter at the root the social results of an economically unequal society." Harold J. Laski, *Politics,* 1931, pp. 26–27.

State's population is determined by birth rates, death rates, and immigration and emigration. These things in turn depend upon resources, economic opportunities, fecundity, and a variety of other uncontrollable factors. The composition of a State's population is similarly dependent upon relative birth and death rates among the various groups which compose it. These things are little affected by legislation and administration—so little, in fact, that it may be doubted whether there has ever been a single clear instance of a nation's population being radically changed, either as to size or composition, through deliberate governmental policies. Governments have nevertheless attempted from time to time to regulate population growth for economic and political reasons. They have sought to subject to organized social intelligence the ebb and flow of peoples, the size and movements of families, the number of births and deaths—not through the impossible method of intervening in the private affairs of each of the millions of homes comprising a nation's population, but through various legislative and administrative devices intended to influence the underlying causal factors determining population growth. These measures are part of the policies of economic nationalism, since they have to a large degree been motivated, not by any rationally devised program of social and economic amelioration, but by power considerations and by various prejudices, superstitions, inhibitions, and stupidities which have furthered the purpose of patriots.

Early in the nineteenth century the English economist Thomas Malthus promulgated the discouraging hypothesis (which helped to earn for economics the name of the "dismal science") that there is everywhere a constant pressure of population on resources which tends to keep the living standards of the masses down to a bare subsistence level. According to Malthus, population increases in geometric ratio (1, 2, 4, 8, 16, 32, etc.), whereas the means of subsistence increase in arithmetic ratio (1, 2, 3, 4, etc.). He could perceive, therefore, nothing but prospects of increasing misery in the rapid growth of population which he saw taking place around him. The Malthusian formulation was in error in that it assumed a constant rate of reproduction and overlooked the effects of technological improvements and industrialization in providing better means of subsistence for vastly greater populations than any ever seen before the age of the machine. It is quite true that the reproductive capacity of the human species is enormously greater than its capacity to provide the means of livelihood for its swarming broods. Given favorable economic conditions, any human population group can double its numbers every twenty-five years. It has been calculated that if a single pair of human beings, at the time of Christ, began reproducing at this rate and if all their descendants had reproduced at the same rate, the entire land surface of the globe would furnish standing room only for one-eleventh of the living progeny. If the population of the earth had doubled only every fifty years for the past twenty centuries, the descendants would now number one thousand times the world's present population.[1] But the ultimate possibilities of human fecundity are never attained. Positive checks on population growth always operate through famine, disease, and war. Preventive checks likewise operate through birth control and perhaps through a decline in fecundity with higher standards of living and urban life. The population which a given area can sustain does not depend so much on the resources of the area as on the technological devices employed for utilizing those resources. Population growth is thus determined, not by any simple relationship between reproduction and resources, but by (1) the birth rate, which is affected by the number and fecundity of childbearing mothers, by birth control, and by social habits and customs; (2) the death rate, which is affected by longevity, war, and the control of disease; (3) the natural resources at the command of a given population, which influence both the birth rate and the death rate; and (4) the level of technology, which has a bearing upon all of the three other factors.

Such phrases as "overpopulation," "underpopulation," or "surplus population," glibly bandied about by nationalists and imperialists, have no meaning except as they are related to these factors. Overpopulation in a given area has nothing to do with the size, density, or resources of the population but can only refer to a situation in which there is sufficient pressure of population on resources to cause a reduction of living standards or to retard their improvement. Underpopulation can only mean a situation in which the number of people available to exploit natural resources is too few for the most profitable exploitation possible. Overpopulation—or underconsumption, or underdeveloped technology (these are all the same thing)—has long existed in large parts of Asia, where the level of technology has been constant for centuries, where contraception has never been generally practiced, and where living standards have been kept down to a bare subsistence level. Famines, pestilences, unemployment, and extensive emigration are typical symptoms of overpopulation of this kind. But an improvement in technology may make it possible for a given area to sustain an enormously greater population on a higher standard of living than was possible on a lower technological level. The present territory of the United States sustained only 1 million or so Indians in pre-Columbian days, because hunting and fishing and very primitive agriculture were the only means of livelihood. It now sustains 132 million people through intensive agriculture, industry, and commerce. Germany, with 30 million in the mid-nineteenth century, was overpopulated, as shown by low living standards and wholesale emigration. Germany, with 60 million people in the early twentieth century,

[1] See E. B. Reuter, *Population Problems*, 1923.

was no longer overpopulated, for the industrialization of the country had intervened. It has long been alleged that Japan and Italy are over-populated, but no deterioration of living standards had taken place in either country prior to the Great Depression. Density of population per square mile is also no index to overpopulation. The Netherlands has 669 people to the square mile, Belgium 755, Great Britain 500, Germany 371, Italy 350, and Japan 476. On the other hand, the United States has 34 people to the square mile, the Soviet Union 21, Argentina 7, Brazil 9, Canada 2, and Australia less than 2. These figures by themselves do not in the least prove that the first group of States is overpopulated or that the second group is underpopulated, if one measures these conditions by living standards. One can properly speak of overpopulation only in relation to numbers, resources, technology, and standards of living. This phrase is more frequently a rationalization of expansionist ambitions than a statement of economic and social facts.

A rational and scientific population policy, it may be agreed, would be one aimed at securing an economic optimum population, *i.e.*, a population of such size in relation to resources and technology that all of its members could enjoy the highest possible standard of living. Such a policy might call for a larger population in such States as Russia, Australia, and Argentina, in order that existing resources might be more adequately utilized. It might call for a smaller population in highly developed industrial States. Though expert opinion is not unanimous on this point, it is probable that, if economic well-being were the sole test of wisdom in such matters, it would follow that a substantial reduction of population in most of the great States of the world would be advantageous to succeeding generations. Such a reduction is, in fact, impending in northwestern Europe and in North America, but it is viewed with alarm by governments and has taken place in spite of governmental efforts to check it. It is apparently due to a decline of birth rates more rapid than the decline in death rates. The higher the standard of living of a population, the more nearly stationary it becomes. This circumstance, which is sometimes mysteriously attributed to a decline in fecundity, is more probably due, in the Western world at least, to the increasingly prevalent practice of contraception on the part of parents for the purpose of limiting voluntarily the size of families.

It is scarcely necessary to point out that the population policies of national governments are not based on welfare considerations. Military and political power, rather than social and economic well-being, is the immediate objective of the economic nationalists who so largely dictate governmental policies. The patriot tends to regard the size of his country's population as the measure of its power and prestige. He favors all governmental measures that seem likely to increase the rate of population growth. He condemns all that threaten to limit the unchecked growth of population. He is joined in condemnation by many churchmen, who are opposed to birth control for theological reasons. He is also joined by moralists and reformers, to whom liberty means license and to whom compulsions, inhibitions, and prohibitions are preferable to organized intelligence and freedom of choice as roads to the good life. He is joined by many others: the employer of labor who wants labor to be cheap and who knows that it can be cheap only when it is abundant; the military expert who feels that men rather than machines win wars; the physician who would keep the laity in ignorance and profit from the esoteric mysteries of his trade; the timeserving politician who shouts with the crowd and who would sell his soul to the devil before he would offend the religious and moral sensibilities of his constituents; and by a few sincere sociologists and economists, who view an impending decline of population with apprehension for reasons not directly connected with the economic welfare of the next generation. This combination is overwhelming and decisive, and the voices of the more farsighted physicians, politicians, economists, sociologists, social workers, and labor leaders are lost in the storm.

In consequence of these combined pressures, the population policies of almost all the nation-states are directed toward discouraging or suppressing the practice of birth control and toward promoting the largest possible growth of population. Great Britain is one of the few States where contraceptive information may be freely distributed and contraceptive devices freely sold. In practically all the Continental countries and in Latin America, these things are forbidden by legislation. The prohibitive laws of the United States, both federal and state, are among the most severe in the world, imposing heavy fines and jail sentences for their violation, but like other American laws are observed more in the breach than in the enforcement. In the Orient, where birth control is desperately needed, it is just beginning to make headway in the face of governmental opposition. Even in the U.S.S.R., where parenthood was at first made genuinely optional by the maintenance of governmental birth-control clinics and by the legalization of abortion, prizes began to be offered in 1936 for large families, and legalized abortion was abolished.

On the positive side, national governments have striven with indifferent success to promote large families. President Theodore Roosevelt's vigorous denunciation of "race suicide" finds responsive echoes elsewhere. French political and military leaders bemoaned France's stationary population for half a century and from time to time offered tax exemptions and bounties to fathers of numerous children. German patriots are similarly concerned over every indication of a decline in the German birth rate. In Fascist Italy, with its combination of extreme nationalism and Roman Catholicism, the government has made the most determined effort to raise the birth rate. The birth-control movement is rigidly suppressed. Bachelors are penalized by heavy taxes. Heads of large families are rewarded for their labor. Reduced rates on railroads are granted to honeymooners, to encourage matrimony. Early in January, 1935, when 4,000-lire prizes were distributed by Mussolini to champion mothers, it appeared that the leading *madre prolifica* of the province of Rome was the wife of an unemployed laborer whose twelve children lived in one room on three pounds of beans and spaghetti per day. "My children are my greatest and almost my only joy," she declared. "Only with no work it is so difficult to feed them." The Fascist reasoning is perhaps the most complete *reductio ad absurdum* of economic nationalism as applied to population problems. It holds, in effect, that Italy is over-populated, that it must have more land and colonies for its surplus population, that these can be gained only by war, that success in war requires a large army, and that a large army requires a still larger population! This logic is not different in kind from that of economic nationalists elsewhere.

That these legislative and administrative devices have had any appreciable influence in promoting population expansion may be doubted.[1] The factors entering into population growth are too complex and too ill understood to be much affected by such measures. But it is possible that legal restrictions on birth control have had some influence on the rate of reproduction of different classes of the population in certain countries and have contributed to what is sometimes described as a progressive deterioration of population. When the acquisition of birth-control information is made difficult and when the sale of contraceptive devices is made unlawful, those who are ignorant and poverty-stricken are deprived of the means of limiting their families, whereas those who are wealthy or clever can easily evade the law. In Italy, which has a birth rate of over 20 per 1,000, the greatest increase of population takes place in the most backward, impoverished, and illiterate areas such as Calabria, Basilicata, and Apulia, whereas progressive and industrialized Piedmont has a birth rate of only 16 per 1,000. In most countries, those sections of the population which from a eugenic point of view ought to contribute the largest contingent to each new generation contribute the smallest, whereas a less desirable stock breeds without restraint. General dissemination of birth-control information would do much to change this situation. But States and churches alike remain obdurate and continue to cooperate, the one in the name of national power, the other in the name of conventional morality, to make population restrictions as difficult as possible even in a period of world-wide poverty and unemployment.

A final word may be to the point by way of showing the failure of such policies in the Western nations and of suggesting future trends of population growth. The present total population of the world is usually estimated at about 2,000,000,000, of which, in round numbers, perhaps 900,000,000 are white, 600,000,000 yellow, 400,000,000 brown or red, and 100,000,000 black. The white race has in the past century multiplied more rapidly than any of the others and is apparently still in the lead. Authorities are agreed, however, that the unprecedented population growth of the nineteenth and early twentieth centuries will not continue in the

[1] In 1922 the Italian birth rate was 30.2 per 1,000. By 1930 it had fallen to 26.7 and by 1934 to 23.2. On the other hand, Nazi efforts to stimulate population growth in Germany have greatly increased the marriage rate with a corresponding rise of the birth rate from 14.7 in 1933 to 18.9 in 1934. More recently a new decline has set in. By contrast, the U.S.S.R. had a birth rate of 43.8 in 1928 and an annual increase of population of 24.9 per 1,000, compared with 10.1 for Italy, 3.5 for Germany, 13.8 for Japan, 5.9 for the United States, 2.1 for Great Britain, and 0.5 for France (1933). The Soviet birth rate has since fallen, but the death rate (highest among the Great Powers) has fallen more rapidly, with the result that the population of the U.S.S.R. is growing with phenomenal rapidity.

future, though the world's population is still increasing at the rate of five-eighths of 1 per cent annually, which means an annual excess of births over deaths of about 11,500,000. Future increments of population depend not upon a simple calculation of the present ratio between deaths and births, but upon the age composition of society and specifically upon the reproduction rate of childbearing mothers. In northwestern Europe, on the basis of a 1926 calculation, every 100 mothers gave birth to only 93 future mothers.[1] Although this population continues to grow slowly because of its age composition, it is already failing to reproduce itself and soon will become stationary or will decline. The same situation exists in North America and in Australia. The populations of Italy and Japan, however, show few signs of a diminished rate of growth, and the Slavic peoples of eastern Europe continue their rapid expansion. The next half century, therefore, will lead to a stationary or declining population in the Western countries and to a growing preponderance of the Slavic stocks over the Teutonic and Romance stocks of the white race.

RAW MATERIALS. If population is the most elementary foundation of national power, the great primary commodities which are indispensable to the operation of modern industry are of almost equal importance in the calculation of statesmen, businessmen, and economic nationalists. Prior to the Industrial Revolution, the economic foundations of State power were to be found in local agriculture, forestry, shipbuilding, and such simple industries as could be supplied with needed raw materials from the national economy. Economic activity was simple and diversified. People traded with one another across political frontiers; but each State was largely sufficient unto itself, for the raw materials of its industries could be found within its boundaries. But the introduction of machinery and steam power created an economic order demanding coal and iron in large quantities. The States possessing abundant amounts of these mineral resources—Great Britain, Germany, and the United States— passed more rapidly and completely through the transition from agricultural to industrial society. This transition involved the progressive utilization, for a bewildering variety of productive purposes, of an ever greater number of raw materials—cotton, rubber, sugar, oil, nitrates, copper, etc. That industrialized States can with great speed bring enormously greater power to bear in a distant area than is possible for agricultural States is a natural result of the new technology. The fact itself has been amply demonstrated in every great contest of power among States during the past century. Agrarian States have therefore striven to industrialize themselves, quite as much for political and military reasons as for reasons related to wealth production and living standards. The

[1] See Robert R. Kuczynski, *The Balance of Births and Deaths in Western and Northern Europe,* 1929.

struggle for power and for diplomatic and strategic advantages has played a role in promoting economic competition among national societies quite as important as that played by "economic" motivations in a narrower sense. Competition has been especially keen with regard to basic raw materials, and governmental policies have been particularly directed toward deriving maximum political and economic advantages from the control of such materials. The resulting relationships constitute one of the most interesting phases of economic nationalism in the world economy of the twentieth century.

The problem which arises here can be put in quite simple terms. It is due to the uneven distribution of basic raw materials over the globe, to the determination of competing private producers to derive maximum profit from such materials, and to the determination of national governments to regulate production and trade in such materials in the interests of national power and profits. The basic materials are available only in certain areas and in restricted amounts. The great mineral resources—coal, iron, petroleum, and a variety of metals—are found only in certain regions of the earth and are obviously present in definitely limited quantities. The great vegetable resources—rubber, cotton, sugar, wheat, etc.—can be produced continuously, but only in the regions which are suitable to their cultivation by virtue of soil and climate.[1]

No international struggle would take place if producers and consumers throughout the world were left free to buy and sell in accordance with their needs and inclinations, for such goods would then flow as easily across national frontiers as they now do across provincial or district frontiers within the nation. But large producers, in their quest for profit, and large consumers, in their quest for cheap sources of supply, call for governmental intervention or assistance. And patriotic governments are the more willing to render such assistance out of a desire, inspired by considerations of national power, to utilize such material as they control for purposes of diplomatic bargaining. They seek to acquire, if possible, independent sources of supply in order to be secure in wartime and in order to prevent other governments and national producing groups from charging monopolistic prices. The result is a welter of monopolistic combinations, price-fixing arrangements, export and import duties, quotas, prohibitions, and valorization schemes.

To review all these measures for all the basic commodities would take more pages than are included in this volume. The fundamental patterns

---

[1] The United States, which is most nearly self-sufficient in basic raw materials, is obliged to import all its rubber, chromite, antimony, and tin and almost all its manganese, nickel, tungsten, mica, and mercury. On the other hand, it has export surpluses of coal, oil, copper, sulphur, zinc, and phosphates. The U.S.S.R. is in the next most advantageous position, with Germany, Italy, and Japan most dependent on foreign sources of supply. See Brooks Emeny, *The Strategy of Raw Materials*, 1936.

of policy, with the purposes lying behind them and the results ensuing from them, are more important than the details of special cases.

In general, governmental regulation of raw materials takes the form either of control of exports and imports or of restrictions on production and marketing. Customs duties or import taxes on goods entering a country are frequently levied for the purpose of barring out foreign raw materials and of raising prices in the domestic market to the advantage of the "protected" domestic producers. Export duties are constitutionally impossible in the United States and are seldom imposed by industrialized countries, but they are much in vogue in colonial regions and in States which are sources of important raw materials for the outside world. Such duties are usually intended to raise revenue or to conserve resources; but they may also be used, by States enjoying a monopolistic position, to raise world prices. India, for example, enjoys a monopoly in the production of jute, used in the manufacture of burlap bagging, and its government imposes an export duty on this commodity, both to raise revenue and to keep up the price. Chile has long raised a large proportion of her public revenues from export taxes on mineral nitrates, the production of which is monopolized by the Cosach combine (*Compania Saliterera de Chile*), formed in 1931 under the leadership of the Anglo-Chilean Consolidated Nitrate Corporation, controlled by the Guggenheim interests. The British East Indies produced a large proportion of the world's rubber supply, most of which was purchased by the American tire industry. The decline of rubber prices led to the adoption of the Stevenson plan of 1922, which provided for a sliding scale of export duties for the purpose of limiting production and raising the price. American rubber importers secured the support of the United States Government in protesting against this arrangement and attempted to find independent sources of supply in the Philippine Islands and in Liberia. In part as a result of American defensive measures, the Stevenson plan failed and was abandoned in 1928. British interests, in cooperation with the Bolivian multimillionaire, Simon Patiño, likewise controlled the world supply of tin, most of which is produced in the Federated Malay States, Australia, Bolivia, and British Africa. The Malay export duties were preferential as regards tin shipped to Singapore, Great Britain, and Australia. These duties also aroused opposition in the United States, the world's largest consumer of tin. Complete prohibitions or embargoes on the import or export of certain products are sometimes resorted to. After the Great War, Great Britain forbade the importation of coal-tar dyes to cripple the German industry and foster domestic production. Various Canadian provinces have forbidden the export of pulpwood.

In recent years taxes and embargoes, as means of governmental control of raw materials, have been supplemented by various devices to regulate production and marketing. In many instances, these schemes are designed to prevent overproduction and to keep up prices. In some cases, governments have themselves gone into business and established State monopolies for purposes of raising revenue and serving "national interests." The Japanese Government maintains a practical monopoly of the output of camphor, the bulk of which is produced in Taiwan (Formosa). It restricts production, licenses producers, fixes prices, and makes allotments of exports to other countries. The Spanish Government has at times produced and marketed mercury. More frequently, production of basic raw materials has remained in private hands in States in which private capitalism is the prevailing form of economy, with the government assisting or regulating the activities of the producers, both to increase the power of the State and to enhance producers' profits at the expense of consumers, either within the State or in the world market. In 1902 the government of São Paulo, largest coffee-producing State of Brazil, passed a law limiting coffee planting as a means of reducing exports and keeping up the world price. Subsequently, taxes were levied on exports, and government loans were provided for the purchase and storage of coffee in times of surplus supply. In 1921 the Brazilian federal government took over these functions and established an Institute for Permanent Coffee Protection, which purchases and stores coffee in order to control prices, makes loans to producers, and advertises coffee abroad to promote greater consumption. Since 1931 it has likewise resorted to burning coffee or dumping it into the sea. This "valorization" scheme has at times had an appreciable effect in raising coffee prices. Ecuador has evolved a similar scheme for pegging cocoa prices, Greece for currant prices, the Mexican State of Yucatan for sisal prices, Spain and Portugal for pyrite, Italy for sulphur and citric acid, Chile for nitrates, etc. Efforts by national governments to fix world prices can obviously be effective only when a State enjoys a monopoly or a quasi monopoly of the goods in question. As regards goods produced in many countries, the world price of which is determined by a variety of uncontrollable factors, purely national efforts to fix prices are likely to be unsuccessful.

Governmental policies dictated by economic nationalism have been directed toward the acquisition of independent sources of basic raw materials as well as toward price fixing and the exploitation of monopolistic advantages. The currency of such phrases as "oil diplomacy," "oil imperialism," "rubber imperialism," and the like, is indicative of general recognition of the fact that the territorial and political ambitions of States are greatly influenced by such considerations. The fascinating and intricate story of the international struggle for petroleum resources is too long to be recounted here, but a few of its salient features may be suggested. The rapid adoption of petroleum for power, light, and lubrication and the amazingly large number of products resulting from its distillation have led to its rapid and wasteful exploitation in all parts of the world where it is found. The United States normally produces 70 per cent of the total world production, with Russia, Venezuela, Mexico, Persia, Rumania, the Dutch East Indies, Colombia, and Peru following next in order. The United States and the Soviet Union are the only Great Powers which have sources of supply within their own territory adequate to meet their own needs. The oil business was long conducted on a world-wide scale by a small number of huge industrial combinations, including the Standard Oil (American), the Royal Dutch Shell (Anglo-Dutch), the Anglo-Persian Oil Company (British), etc. The British Government owned the controlling stock in the Anglo-Persian Oil Company and frequently gave diplomatic support to the Royal Dutch Shell, as did the American Government to the Standard Oil and other American oil interests. The United States protested against the British policy of excluding aliens from the control of petroleum supplies within the Empire. The Dutch Government pursued a similar policy in the East Indies. French legislation virtually excluded from the French sources of supply all companies not under French control. Powerful governments are able to enforce such policies in the face of foreign protest. Weaker governments, like that of Mexico, are often compelled to abandon such monopolistic efforts under pressure of the Great Powers. The United States has not pursued a discriminatory exclusion policy, except in retaliation against particular States, and has demanded an Open Door policy throughout the world as a means of enabling Americans to enter foreign fields.

The Near East has been a theater of acute international friction for the control of oil resources. The unsuccessful British intervention against the Soviet Government in the Russian civil war was in part inspired by a desire to secure possession of the rich Caucasian oil fields. Prior to 1914 Anglo-German rivalry in the Near East centered about the oil fields of Mesopotamia. On April 14, 1920, at San Remo, the British and French Governments, acting in the interests of military security and on behalf of the prospective profits of their oil corporations, reached an agreement for the division between them of rights to exploit oil resources in Rumania, Russia, Mesopotamia, and elsewhere. The United States protested against this horse trading in oil-bearing areas, on the ground that it contemplated exclusion of Americans and other foreign nationals from the opportunities for profit in these regions. At the Lausanne Conference of 1923, the local hotels housed more representatives of oil companies than of governments, and the resulting treaties were oleaginous in the extreme. Great Britain insisted successfully upon the abandonment of Turkish claims to the Mosul district, reputed to be rich in oil reserves, in favor of Iraq, under British mandate. The British and French Governments were unable to validate all their contested claims, but the great game of oil imperialism still goes on, with private producers posing as patriots in order to enlist governmental support for their profit-making schemes and with governments granting such support for reasons of strategy and Great Power politics. The story of oil diplomacy in Mexico, Colombia, and other regions reveals the same basic motives at work, creating the same types of governmental policies. The story of the international struggle for other basic resources differs only in degree and not in kind from that already suggested.

NEO-MERCANTILISM. The policies of economic nationalism, directed toward exclusive national control and monopolistic exploitation of the world's raw materials, are but a phase of the competitive struggle for markets carried on by the nation-states. Trade carried on by producers and merchants would be of little direct significance for international politics if it went on without governmental interference or regulation. But international trade, even more than domestic trade, has almost always been subjected to various forms of State control. Competition in international trade is not competition among the governments of the nation-states, for governments seldom engage in commerce. It is competition among private merchants who receive governmental support in their search for profit. Such support is extended because the profit seekers possess sufficient political influence to control governmental action and because government seeks to enhance national power through striving after markets abroad and economic self-sufficiency at home. In the twentieth century, ambassadors, consuls, and commercial agents have often acted as advertisers and promoters of private business.

During the seventeenth and eighteenth centuries, the prevailing school of economic thought in western Europe was that of the mercantilists, who held that government should regulate trade for the purpose of enhancing national wealth and prosperity. This early philosophy of economic nationalism was based upon a number of serious misconceptions. Trade was regarded less as a mutually advantageous exchange of commodities than as a process in which one party lost what the other gained. Gold was regarded less as a convenient symbol of value and a useful medium of exchange than as an embodiment of riches. A nation's wealth was assumed to be equivalent to its stock of gold. All that would increase the gold stock was therefore good; all that diminished it was bad. It was observed that when a nation's exporters sold more goods abroad than its importers purchased the surplus of exports over imports was paid for in gold instead of goods. Since this situation produced a flow of gold into the country, it was looked upon as "favorable"—and, ever since, an excess of national exports over imports has been called a "favorable balance of trade." On the other hand, it was observed that when importers purchased more goods abroad than exporters sold, gold flowed out of the country. An excess of imports over exports was consequently described as an "unfavorable balance of trade." Inasmuch as gold was assumed to be wealth, governmental policies were directed toward encouraging exports by bounties and subsidies of various kinds and discouraging imports by tariffs, embargoes, and prohibitions. At the same time, colonial trade was monopolized by the nationals of the mother country in order that it too might contribute as much as possible to the national wealth. Domestic trade was likewise subjected to numerous restrictions and regulations.

The decline of mercantilistic policies at the end of the eighteenth century was due less to the demonstrated fallacies of mercantilist logic than to the political ascendancy of the new bourgeoisie born of the Industrial Revolution. The new manufacturers and merchants found the old restrictions a burdensome interference with free profit seeking. The publication of Adam Smith's *Wealth of Nations* in 1776 and the work of the Continental economists known as the *Physiocrats* revealed clearly the *lacunae* in mercantilist reasoning and furnished intellectual respectability to the demand for an end of governmental interference with trade. Gold, it was pointed out, is not wealth, but simply a medium of exchange in terms of which commodities are priced. An inflow of gold into a nation tends to raise the price level, for the purchasing power of gold varies inversely with its quantity. An outflow of gold lowers prices for the same reason. If an excess of exports over imports leads to an inflow of gold, prices rise, domestic costs of production increase, and the nation's exporters are less and less able to compete effectively in foreign markets with producers in other nations where prices are lower. At the same time, foreign exporters, attracted by the higher prices, send in goods in increasing volume. The export surplus consequently tends to vanish and to be replaced by an import surplus, as a result of the effect upon trade of changing national price levels due to gold movements. Conversely, an excess of imports over exports causes gold to flow out, lowers prices, and places exporters at a competitive advantage and importers at a competitive disadvantage, with the result that the movement is in course of time reversed. In short, gold movements and price levels tend to keep foreign trade at an equilibrium. It is impossible for a nation, in the long run, to export more than it imports. In the long run a nation's imports and exports, including in these terms not merely commodities, but all the items in the international balance such as shipping charges, insurance premiums, investments, and immigrant remittances, must attain parity. Governmental efforts to prevent this are ineffective and mischievous.

Out of this reasoning developed the "free-trade" doctrine of the classical laissez-faire economists, which the new bourgeois governments adopted quite generally. In 1846 the Corn Laws (import duties on grain) were abandoned in Great Britain, which then became a free-trade country. The United States adopted lower tariffs between 1830 and 1860. The Anglo-French Cobden Treaty of 1860 provided for French tariff reduction. German tariff duties were almost completely abandoned in the mid-century. The period of untrammeled individualism, with governmental regulation of economic activity reduced to a minimum, was marked by the general abandonment of mercantilist restrictions on foreign trade and the progressive adoption of free-trade policies by many governments. In the absence of governmental interference with foreign trade, producers, importers, and exporters will buy and sell freely across national frontiers in accordance with the dictates of price and the opportunities for profit. Each nation will specialize in the production of those commodities which, by virtue of climate, resources, and technical skill, it can produce most cheaply. It will sell these goods abroad and receive in exchange goods which can be produced more cheaply abroad than at home. World-wide geographical specialization develops, and each nation gains economically by free exchange with all others. The resulting trade is advantageous to all concerned, even to those to whom it is least so.

In spite of the fact that the logic of free trade has never been successfully refuted, the governments of the nation-states have progressively abandoned it since 1870 and have once more erected higher and higher tariff walls in a new quest for prosperity and economic self-sufficiency. As soon as production began to outrun the market, as soon as competition in all markets became increasingly keen, entrepreneurs began to perceive possibilities of profit through governmental action. They abandoned their former laissez-faire attitude and looked to government to bar out competitors from the domestic market and to assist them in conquering foreign markets. In the United States the tariff "for revenue only" was replaced during the Civil War by a tariff designed to protect national producers from foreign competition and to encourage home industry. The McKinley Tariff of 1890 was enacted to prevent the importation of various foreign goods or to make their prices so high in the American market that they could not compete successfully with similar American goods. The Dingley Tariff of 1897 and the Payne-Aldrich Tariff of 1909 raised duties to still higher levels. The (Democratic) Underwood Tariff of 1913 lowered import duties, but only temporarily. The Fordney-McCumber Tariff Act of 1922 carried American tariff duties to unprecedentedly high levels, and the Smoot-Hawley Tariff (1930) of the Hoover administration carried protectionism to a point which threatened the complete strangulation of American import trade. In Germany, Bismarck's protective tariff of 1879 inaugurated a permanent policy of high duties on both agricultural and industrial imports. The Third French Republic adopted moderate protectionism in 1881 and subsequently imposed higher and higher duties on imports. These three States set the pace, and others followed step by step, until almost all nations in retaliation and self-defense had become protectionist by the turn of the century. The general economic disorganization following the Great War and the determination of the new States of Europe to become economically self-contained led to the erection of higher tariff barriers everywhere, until finally even Great Britain, the last citadel of free trade, abandoned its ancient faith and embraced protectionism in 1931. A large section of the British Liberal party, along with Ramsay MacDonald and the renegade members of the Labor party, followed the example of the American Democratic party in abandoning traditional convictions and championing neo-mercantilism.

Broadly speaking, protectionist and prohibitive customs duties on imports are in most cases economically indefensible, for they diminish national wealth and prosperity rather than increase them. But such duties may be politically justified if it is assumed that the legitimate objective of governmental regulation of foreign commerce is the enhancement of State power, regardless of the economic cost. It is arguable that the promotion of uneconomical home industries and the attainment of national economic self-sufficiency are politically advantageous to a State, since they diminish its dependence upon foreign sources of supply, lessen the dangers of loss from an economic blockade in wartime, and perhaps increase its fighting power by making it self-contained. These political gains are always paid for in economic losses, but the economic nationalists may contend that power and security are worth whatever they cost in welfare.

But this is only a partial explanation of the paradox of neo-mercantilism. Tariff protectionists invariably insist that restrictions on imports are *economically* advantageous as well as politically desirable, and they have succeeded in convincing a politically effective majority in most modern States that this is really the case. Tariff-making politicians (and this includes most politicians) are perpetually at odds with free-trade economists (and this includes most economists). When a thousand American economists petitioned President Hoover not to sign the Tariff Act of 1930, on the ground that it would bring ruin to American foreign trade, the Chief Executive showed himself to be a politician rather than an economist by ignoring the plea and signing the act. The explanation of such situations is to be found in the domestic economic effects of tariffs and in the nature of the domestic political process as it affects tariff making.

Almost every tariff is a device whereby privileged and protected domestic producers are enabled to exploit the domestic market more effectively by charging their customers monopoly or quasi-monopoly prices. It likewise enables inefficient and uneconomical domestic producers to continue production by antiquated methods, since they are protected from more efficient foreign competitors who produce better goods at lower cost. Now it so happens, as has already been suggested, that in bourgeois democracies or despotisms organized producers are politically influential. They are few in number. They know exactly how they may profit from protective duties. They possess wealth and prestige. They contribute to campaign funds, maintain powerful lobbies, and control the acts of legislators and administrators. The ultimate consumers, who pay the bill, are inarticulate, unorganized, multitudinous, without political power, often unaware of where the burden falls, and easily persuaded that their interests as consumers are identical with those of profit-seeking producers attempting to enlist governmental support in exploiting them. Governmental policies are dictated by the few privileged producers who are enabled to profit at the expense of the many. This fact, coupled with considerations of patriotic duty and national self-sufficiency, serves to explain why all important governments are now protectionist. What is an economic loss to the country as a whole is not merely a political gain for the power of the State, but an economic gain also (at the expense of consumers) for the influential producers who rule the State and shape its policies.

Under these circumstances, tariff making becomes a process in which ever larger numbers of interested producers call loudly for protection, *i.e.*, for higher prices in the domestic market, and pose as patriots promoting national prosperity. Once a tariff wall is set up, vested interests arise behind it and assume that they possess an inalienable right to the profits of patriotic protectionism. They demand more and more protection as a means to greater and greater profits, and other producers' groups soon demand the same privilege. These demands cannot be ignored by politicians, for these groups control political parties. Legislators and executives cannot ignore their master's voice and continue to enjoy the profits and perquisites of holding public office. To raise tariff duties is always politically easy, for those who profit thereby pay generously for such services and those who lose are dumb and voiceless. To lower tariff duties is almost always politically impossible, for the vested interests which profit from them are too powerful to be defied. The resulting process of log rolling, horse trading, and patriotic profiteering is most beautifully illustrated in the tariff history of the United States. When the Fordney-McCumber Act of 1922 required three additional votes in the

Senate for its passing, they were gained by adding duties on sugar, fruits, nuts, and other products of California and Louisiana. Senator Hiram Johnson and the Democratic senators from Louisiana then voted for the bill. The Smoot-Hawley Act of 1930 was passed by a combination of Republican and Democratic senators and representatives, each interested in securing protection for the industries of his own state.

At the same time that the protectionist governments of the world have endeavored to exclude imports, they have attempted to promote exports by a variety of devices. The mercantilist doctrine, which regarded an outflow of goods as "favorable" and an inflow of goods as "unfavorable," has received new recognition at the hands of entrepreneurs anxious to enhance profits, both by monopolizing the domestic market and by selling their surpluses in foreign markets. Government aid has been solicited by profit seekers to achieve both of these purposes. It has been freely granted by patriotic legislators who find economic nationalism politically expedient. Government bounties have frequently been paid to exporters. Austria-Hungary began paying bounties on exported beet sugar in 1888, Germany in 1891, and France in 1897. In this instance the importing countries levied retaliatory duties on sugar imports to nullify the effects of the bounties. A general agreement was finally reached in the International Sugar Convention of 1902 to make bounties unprofitable by the systematic imposition by each State of countervailing duties on sugar imports coming from States which paid bounties on exports. Government bounties on exports are often nullified by such retaliatory action. The payment of "drawbacks" is a device with a similar purpose. Manufacturers who import raw materials to be used in the fabrication of goods for export are refunded the tariff duties paid on such materials. More recently, as in the American tariff acts of 1922 and 1930, such manufacturers are often permitted to import goods for eventual export without paying any duty in the first place.

Bounties and drawbacks are only two of the innumerable methods employed by governments to subsidize and encourage export trade. Railway freight rates on exported goods are often reduced. Financial aid from governments to shipping lines is now customary in most commercial States, as a means both of promoting exports and of making available a large tonnage of merchant shipping for use in war. This aid may take the form of direct bounties, of large payments for mail services, or of various disguised subsidies. During the Great War, the American Government operated merchant shipping lines directly, through the United States Shipping Board. Since the passage of the White-Jones Act of 1927, it has subsidized shipping indirectly, following the rejection by Congress of the Ship Subsidy Bill of 1922. Governments have likewise loaned money to other governments or have encouraged private capitalists to lend money to private enterprises abroad, on condition that the proceeds be used for purchasing goods in the lending country. "Concessions" obtained in "backward" countries for railroad construction or other industrial purposes often specify that the goods in question are to be purchased in the country of the concessionaire. Favorable credit facilities and legal privileges of one kind or another are frequently made available to exporters. The United States, France, Spain, Sweden, and other States refuse foreign vessels permission to engage in their coastwise trade. The American Webb-Pomerene Act of 1918 exempts export-trade associations from the operation of the antitrust laws. These and other devices frequently make profitable the practice of "dumping," *i.e.*, of selling goods in foreign markets at a price lower than that charged in the domestic market, for the purpose of disposing of surpluses, conquering new markets by swamping competition, or limiting domestic supplies to raise prices in the home market.

The logical end of these policies is reached when the government of each State makes it impossible for its nationals to purchase anything from foreigners and does all in its power to enable them to sell goods to foreigners. Each national unit seeks to sell without buying. International trade is progressively impeded, and each nation-state finds its efforts to promote exports thwarted by the determination of all other States to bar out imports. Out of this situation have emerged commercial treaties, international tariff bargaining, import and export quotas, and the acute strangulation of world commerce which developed after 1930. The nature of this economic dilemma will be examined below, along with national and international efforts to solve the problem. Here it is enough to have noticed how national economic policies in the era of neo-mercantilism have produced a crisis as a result of the collaboration of patriots and profiteers.

INVESTMENT POLICIES. In the epoch of world economy, of large-scale production and immense accumulations of wealth in the hands of those who look further and further afield for profitable investment opportunities, it is natural that governments should concern themselves with movements of capital across frontiers, no less than with movements of goods. Capitalists and investors, as well as manufacturers and merchants, early perceived the possibility of increasing their profits through enlisting governmental support in their behalf. And politicians and statesmen similarly perceived the possibility of increasing national prestige and achieving diplomatic objectives through an adroit use of investments and loans as weapons of power politics. Governmental regulation of capital movements has accordingly become the order of the day, and the diplomacy of high finance has, like Jehovah, moved in mysterious ways its wonders to perform.

This outward movement of capital began first, naturally enough, in Great Britain, the cradle of modern industrial capitalism. By 1914, private British capital to the value of about $19,500,000,000 had been invested abroad, with British investments increasing at the rate of $1,000,000,000 a year. In the case of Germany, about $6,700,000,000 had been invested abroad, with an annual increase of perhaps $250,000,000. France was less industrialized and therefore less wealthy in liquid capital than her neighbors; but the stockings of the peasant, the artisan, and the *petit bourgeois* were long and deep. About $8,600,000,000 of French private capital had found its way abroad by 1914, with an increase of perhaps $500,000,000 a year. Belgian, Dutch, Swiss, Italian, and other investors likewise found it possible to get more for their money by sending it abroad to remote and exotic places than by investing it in domestic industry. From northwestern Europe there flowed outward a golden stream of capital, running like the blood of life through the veins of industry and commerce all over the world. And from the backward and capital-hungry regions there flowed back a steady stream of dividends, premiums, interest payments, and commissions to enrich the lenders from the profits of the borrowers. In the United States, until recently a new, undeveloped country, more foreign capital was absorbed that was exported. Some $4,000,-000,000 of European capital were invested in the United States by 1914, though it should be noted that over $2,500,000,000 of American capital had already gone into the Caribbean area, Canada, and Europe.

The Great War and its aftermath produced a complete reversal in the international position of the United States from the point of view of movements of private capital. The American colossus was transformed from the greatest debtor to the second greatest creditor country in the world. One of the first effects of the war was to cause European investors in the United States to sell their stocks and bonds in American industries to Americans, who became increasingly eager to purchase them with the onset of the feverish flush of war prosperity. Some $2,500,000,000 worth of American securities held abroad were repurchased in this fashion. Private investors in the United States, moreover, reaped a rich harvest by lending money to enterprises of all kinds abroad and to the Allied Governments through the purchase of their war bonds. Under the influence of an unprecedented European demand for goods and services at almost any price, American industry, commerce, and finance entered upon a "boom" period which lasted, with minor interruptions, until the great crash of 1929. Twenty-one thousand new American millionaires emerged from the most profitable of all American wars. The newly accumulated hoards of capital in the United States fed the automobile industry, the motion-picture industry, the radio industry, and the stock market—and then looked abroad for still greater profits. After 1924, American loans flowed to Europe, particularly to Germany, in a great flood, and it became possible in the United States to sell at lucrative prices almost any foreign security, public or private, printed on good paper with the requisite gilt edge. American loans and investments in Europe increased from about a third of a billion dollars to over $5,500,-000,000, in Canada from $750,000,000 to almost $4,500,000,000, in South America from $100,000,000 to $3,000,000,000, in the Caribbean area from $1,250,000,000 to almost $3,000,000,000. So large was this flow of capital that American investors, by 1931, had exported about $18,000,000,000 abroad, exclusive of intergovernmental debts. After 1931, in the face of world-wide defaults and bankruptcies, the outward movement of American capital practically ceased, and many of the loans of the boom epoch became worthless.

In a report submitted to President Roosevelt on May 5, 1935, George N. Peek estimated that new foreign securities issued in the United States, between July 1, 1914, and December 31, 1933, totaled $18,864,000,000 and that this amount had been reduced through retirement, repurchase, or refunding to $5,270,000,000 by December 31, 1934, of which total $1,940,000,000 was in default in whole or in part. The Foreign Bond-holders' Protective Council, Inc., estimated on May 18, 1936, that of the $5,345,000,000 of foreign dollar bonds outstanding at the end of 1935, $1,825,403,000, or 34 per cent, were in default as to interest or principal or both. Meanwhile short- and long-term foreign investments in the United States had increased to $6,235,000,000 by the close of 1935.[1]

European capital-exporting countries also suffered a reduction of their investments abroad. British foreign investments fell from $19,500,-000,000 in 1914 to $18,200,000,000 in 1929; French from $8,600,000,000 to $3,500,000,000; and German from $6,700,000,000 to $1,100,000,000. At the beginning of the Great Depression the Netherlands had $2,300,-000,000 invested abroad, Switzerland $2,000,000,000, Belgium $1,500,-000,000, Japan, $1,000,000,000, Sweden $500,000,000, and other States smaller sums, making an estimated world total of foreign investments of $47,500,000,000 before the crash. These figures were substantially reduced after 1929, though subsequent estimates are difficult because of the fluctuating value of securities and currencies.

Quite apart from governmental efforts to control these great capital movements, they produce in themselves economic and social effects with political ramifications. Some of these effects will be considered below in connection with imperialism, Great Power politics, and the contemporary crisis of capitalism. From the point of view of economic nationalism, the most significant aspect of capital exports and imports is that they have frequently been regulated by governments for the purpose of promoting national power and prestige and attaining diplomatic objectives having no direct relation to the immediate interests of borrowers or lenders. If "free trade" prevailed in the world's investment markets, i.e., if governments permitted investors and borrowers to do as they pleased and if investors and borrowers made no appeals for governmental assistance or support, loans would be made and investments would be placed in accordance with pure profit considerations. Mistakes of judgment would cer-

[1] Estimate of Amos E. Taylor of the U. S. Department of Commerce, New York *Times*, June 5, 1936. For a critical discussion of various estimates of foreign investments, see Eugene Staley, *War and the Private Investor*, 1935, pp. 523–539. The figures in the text are in part taken from Professor Staley's estimates and are in gold dollars. In July 1940, the U. S. Department of Commerce estimated that United States private investments abroad totaled $11,759,000,000 at the close of 1939, a decline of 3.3 per cent from 1938. Of this total, direct investments were estimated at $6,985,000,000 and portfolio investments at $3,785,000,000. United States investments in Canada totaled $3,781,000,000, in Latin America $4,134,000,000, and in Europe $2,278,000,000.

tainly occur, and frauds and swindles might be even more frequent, for brokers and investment bankers are not distinguished from ordinary mortals by excessive wisdom or honesty. But governments would not be at once involved in the results, and capital movements would scarcely deserve consideration in a treatise on international politics. In fact, however, this situation seldom prevails, for the governments of capital-exporting States are disposed to point with pride to a swelling volume of foreign investments and to use the money power of their financiers for political purposes, whereas the governments of capital-importing States often view with alarm the invasion of the domestic market by foreign capitalists and seek to check their influence in various ways.

The methods employed to control capital exports vary considerably from State to State. The devices used are both positive and preventive. They aim to encourage private investments in certain States and to discourage them in others. In almost every case some form of official approval is required before foreign stocks and bonds may be listed and sold in the local market. In France all foreign flotations on the Paris Bourse had to be approved by the Minister of Finance and the Minister of Foreign Affairs. In Italy, Belgium, Germany, and certain other Continental States, similar regulations were enforced. In Great Britain, informal contacts are regularly maintained between investment houses and the Foreign Office, and loans disapproved by Downing Street are seldom made. In March of 1922 the American State Department announced "the desire of the Government to be duly and adequately informed regarding (loan) transactions before their confirmation, so that it might express itself regarding them if that should be requested or seem desirable. . . . Subsequently, the President was informed by the bankers that they and their associates were in harmony with the Government's wishes and would act accordingly." This American loan-supervision policy is not based upon legislative enactment, nor does the State Department have any authority to compel bankers to heed its advice. But it would be a rash banker indeed who would float a foreign loan not approved by his government. The implication of governmental supervision is that the government will grant diplomatic support to approved lenders if their interests are jeopardized, whereas it may withhold such support from loans which have not met with official approval. This fact alone is usually sufficient, in most capital-exporting States, to ensure a large degree of governmental control over foreign loans and investments, regardless of the particular devices utilized.

The purposes for which such control is exercised are various and sundry. Considerations of economic welfare would dictate governmental supervision to prevent fraud, dishonesty, and undue risks and to safeguard borrowers and lenders alike. But considerations of patriotism, power, and profits lead to quite different motives and purposes. At least four specific political objectives have been sought by governments in their regulating objectives.

1. Loans are often encouraged to strengthen an ally.

The French government pursued this objective on the grandest scale. Almost one-quarter of the French foreign investments in 1914 were placed in Russia, either in government bonds or in private Russian enterprises. This was due less to considerations of profit and security than to the deliberate policy of the Quai d'Orsay in bolstering up the Tsardom in order that Russia might push forward her industrialization and her military preparations and thus become a more trustworthy ally. All these investments were lost in the revolutionary holocaust of 1917. After the Great War the Quai d'Orsay similarly encouraged French bankers to loan money to governments or private enterprises in France's new eastern allies. During 1931 French capital to the amount of $21,560,000 was invested in Poland, $22,540,000 in Rumania, $23,520,000 in Czechoslovakia, and $38,220,000 in Jugoslavia.

2. Loans are frequently discouraged to weaken a past or prospective enemy State.

Prior to 1914, the Quai d'Orsay vetoed participation by French banks in the proposed Bagdad railway consortium because of German interests in the project. After 1918 the French Government discouraged investment in the defeated States—Germany, Austria, Hungary, and Bulgaria. Such capital boycotts are frequently ineffective, since funds can ordinarily be secured elsewhere, but they have at times been successfully used as a tool of high politics.

3. Loans are often encouraged or forbidden as a means of obtaining political, economic, or financial concessions from the government of another State.

The post-Versailles financial diplomacy of France, in its dealings both with ally and enemy States, repeatedly sought to achieve its purposes by offering or withholding loans from French banks. In the spring of 1931, for example, the Quai d'Orsay made it clear that French participation in a loan to the Austrian Government was contingent upon the abandonment of all efforts at treaty revision or *Anschluss* with Germany.[1] In the summer of 1932, Austria was obliged to renounce for twenty years the project of a customs union with Germany as a condition of receiving a new League of Nations loan of $43,000,000. Germany was refused French loans for similar reasons, whereas French loans to Poland and Czechoslovakia cemented the alliances with these States and brought their policies into harmony with those of France.

In 1921 the American State Department brought pressure on European governments to refund their war debts to the United States by requesting American bankers to withhold loans. As funding agreements were signed with the debtor governments, the embargo on private capital exports was lifted. By 1928 it remained in force only against the U.S.S.R. With the subsequent default of the debts, it was revived. By the Johnson Act of April, 1934, Congress made it a criminal offense to sell in the United States any securities of defaulting governments or of the subdivisions thereof. Loans to private indi-

---

[1] In accepting the international League of Nations loan of 1922, the Austrian Government was obliged to pledge itself "not to alienate its independence; it will abstain from any negotiations or from any economic or financial engagement calculated directly or indirectly to compromise this independence." Austria also agreed that in customs matters "she shall not violate her economic independence by granting to any State a special régime or exclusive advantages calculated to threaten this independence" (Protocol I, *League of Nations Official Journal*, November, 1922, p. 1471). It was on the basis of this protocol that the Permanent Court of International Justice, on September 5, 1931, denied Austria the right to form a customs union with Germany.

viduals and corporations were not included in these embargoes. The Neutrality Acts of 1936–1939 made it unlawful to purchase or sell within the United States any securities of a belligerent government or its subdivisions, although the President was authorized to make exceptions for ordinary commercial credits and short-term obligations. This embargo was inspired by the belief that the loans extended by American bankers to the Allies, after Secretary Bryan's objections had been swept aside by Wilson and Lansing in 1915, had played a major role in involving the United States in the Great War. In 1925 Herbert Hoover, then Secretary of Commerce and an ardent foe of raw-material monopolies, induced the State Department to disapprove the flotation of a Brazilian loan for coffee valorization and a German loan of the monopolistic Potash Syndicate. Under the legislation of 1934, information designed to assist purchasers of domestic and foreign securities must be filed with the Securities Exchange Commission before such obligations can be sold. The United States has thus regulated capital exports as a means of protecting investors, discouraging monopolies, preserving American neutrality in future wars, and inducing payment of past war debts to the American Government.

4. Loans have frequently been encouraged by governments as a means of securing economic and political control of "backward" areas.

Governments have protected investors in such regions, and investors have served the purposes of government. Bankers in capital-exporting States have loaned money to impecunious governments or have invested in private enterprises in backward regions, often on usurious terms calculated to exploit the borrower to the limit of endurance. When the repayment of such obligations has been endangered through bankruptcy or local revolution, the lenders have appealed for diplomatic or military support to their own governments, which in many instances have encouraged the original loan in order to create such opportunities. Diplomatic support is extended, and the result in many cases is the landing of marines, the collection of customs duties by agents of the bankers' government, and the imposition of a financial and political protectorate upon the defaulting State.[1] This pattern of "dollar diplomacy" is a familiar one in the imperialistic expansion of all the Great Powers.

Having learned from painful experience that imports of foreign capital often lead to diplomatic pressure from the lenders' governments, and sometimes to loss of political independence, the governments of capital-importing States frequently seek to impose restrictions upon the rights of foreign investors and property owners with resulting diplomatic complications of various kinds.

Such efforts naturally arouse resentment among the investors who feel that their acquired rights—whether honestly obtained or not—are deserving of protection. Their resentment usually manifests itself in agitation in the public press of the local State and of the investors' State against the régime which proposes to interfere with property rights. Revolutions are sometimes organized

[1] President Taft declared in 1912, "The diplomacy of the present administration has sought to respond to modern ideas of commercial intercourse. This policy has been characterized as substituting dollars for bullets. It is one that appeals alike to idealistic humanitarian sentiments, to the dictates of sound policy and strategy, and to legitimate commercial aims. It is an effort frankly directed to the increase of American trade upon the axiomatic principle that the Government of the United States shall extend all proper support to every legitimate and beneficial American enterprise abroad." Annual Message to Congress, December 3, 1912.

against it, and appeals are made to the investors' home government for protection. Such appeals are usually heeded, both because bankers and investors are politically influential and because the resulting diplomatic controversies offer opportunities for imperialistic expansion. The governments of capital-exporting States may bring varying degrees of pressure upon the governments of backward States in the interests of investors and concessionaires. They may, in the first place, refuse to extend diplomatic recognition to governments which confiscate property, repudiate debts, or otherwise reduce the profit of foreign nationals. American recognition policy in the Caribbean has been largely motivated by such considerations. The United States withheld diplomatic recognition from the Obregon Government in Mexico until 1923, when it agreed not to apply retroactively Article 27 of the constitution providing for the nationalization of mineral resources. The United States has acted in the same fashion toward Nicaragua, Costa Rica, Honduras, Colombia, Peru, and other Latin American States. The governments of such States are chronically in a condition of financial embarrassment and are usually unable to secure foreign loans without diplomatic recognition. The withholding of such recognition is therefore an effective weapon in the hands of the American State Department. The Huerta régime in Mexico was compelled to abdicate in 1915 for this reason. The United States withheld diplomatic recognition from the Soviet Union on similar grounds, but without effecting a change of régime or a modification of policy at Moscow.

Governments of capital-exporting States may go a step further in the protection of the interests of their investors by engaging in intervention against the State complained of.

Armed intervention and military or naval demonstrations for the collection of debts have been the usual weapon of the Great Powers in their dealings with backward States. Between 1800 and 1927 the United States engaged in no less than seventy interventions in Latin America, many of them for the purpose of protecting investments and collecting debts. Interventions by other Powers in Asia and Africa have been even more numerous. Such interventions are often accompanied by efforts to overthrow the local government and replace it by one more acceptable to foreign interests. Where the victim is weak, the intervening Powers usually achieve their purposes. Where the victim is strong or is supported by another Power, success is less likely. The French intervention in Mexico, culminating in the setting up of the Archduke Maximilian on the throne of a new French-Mexican empire in 1863, was frustrated by internal insurrection, the exigencies of European politics, and the hostile attitude of the United States. The Allied and American intervention in the Russian civil war (1918–1921) was designed to overturn the Soviet régime and replace it by a government disposed to pay its debts, recognize foreign property rights, and make Russia safe for capitalism. It was beaten back by the Red Army and failed to achieve its purposes. Seldom can a Great Power, or even a combination of powers, intervene successfully in the affairs of another Great Power. But in dealing with small and weak States such interventions have been frequent and effective. The Latin American Governments have endeavored, with little success, to secure general recognition of the principle that all armed interventions for the protection of nationals abroad are illegal (the "Calvo doctrine") or, failing this, that there should be no resort to intervention for the collection of debts (the "Drago doctrine"). At the Hague Conference of 1907 a convention was drawn up in which the signatories bound themselves "not to have recourse to armed force for the recovery of contract debts claimed from the government of one country by the government of another country as being due its nationals," unless arbitration of the dispute was refused. This agreement has had no visible effect in reducing the frequency of such action.

The most extreme measure of protection which a State may take on behalf of the property rights or financial claims of its nationals is to impose its control upon the weak State whose conduct is an object of complaint.

Intervention has often led to this result. The degree of control established varies with circumstances. In its mildest form it may involve only the appointment of customs collectors or financial advisers by the intervening Power, coupled with whatever action is necessary—usually the landing of marines— to compel the local government to accept their services. In its ultimate form it involves the extinction of the sovereignty and independence of the victim State and its annexation by the intervening Power. All possible variations between these extremes are observable in the history of financial imperialism. The Caribbean policy of the United States has led to the exercise of financial control over backward countries on the largest scale. The finances of Cuba have from time to time been supervised by an American representative in Havana. The treaty of 1915 between the United States and Haiti authorized the United States to "nominate" a general receiver of customs and a financial adviser who collects revenues to pay the salaries of American officials, to meet the interest and principal on the public debt, to maintain the American controlled constabulary, and finally, if any revenue remains, to meet the expenses of the Haitian Government. By the treaty of 1907, the United States likewise appointed a general receiver of customs for the Dominican Republic. In 1916 the Republic, along with Haiti, was occupied by American marines. Between 1905 and 1922 the American receiver collected $67,000,000 in customs duties, of which $33,000,000 went to foreign bankers. Under the Bryan-Chamorro Treaty of August 5, 1914, Nicaragua also became a financial protectorate of the United States, which was given authority to supervise the expenditure of the $3,000,000 paid annually by the United States to Nicaragua for canal rights and for the lease of islands as naval bases. In 1922 Bolivia borrowed $33,000,000 from New York bankers at 8 per cent and was obliged to pledge certain revenues for repayment under the supervision of a banker's commission. Salvador is under similar control. Financial experts named by the American State Department have likewise been employed from time to time by Colombia, Guatemala, Honduras, Panama, Peru, and Persia. International financial control was imposed upon Egypt in 1876, upon Turkey in 1881, upon Greece in 1897, and upon China at various times for limited purposes. Through the League of Nations a degree of international financial control was established over Austria, Hungary, Bulgaria, Greece, Danzig, and Esthonia.

The implications of these phenomena in the development of modern imperialism will be discussed in the following chapter. Consideration will also be given elsewhere[1] to the problem of inter-Allied debts and reparations. These problems involve loans from government to government or financial claims advanced by governments against other govern-

[1] See pp. 452f. below.

ments. Intergovernmental loans constitute an unusual arrangement in international finance, resorted to ordinarily only in time of war. During peace, governments in need of money borrow it by selling bonds to private investors at home or abroad. All that has been said in the present discussion applies not to intergovernmental loans, but only to loans extended by private individuals or corporations to foreign individuals, corporations, or governments. Here it is sufficient to emphasize again that the power of private bankers and investors to lend or withhold money, to export or to refuse to export capital has been regularly employed by the governments of the Great Powers as an instrument of national policy to achieve diplomatic purposes. These purposes have sometimes reflected directly the pecuniary interests of the lenders and investors; they have almost always served these interests even when they have been inspired by patriots and politicians rather than by entrepreneurs and profiteers.

But more often than not the purposes have been those of *haute politique*, involving larger stakes of diplomacy than interest payments and premiums and reflecting the power, prestige, and profit goals of the patriotic bourgeoisie as a whole. The interests of particular entrepreneurs, concessionaires, and coupon clippers have been utilized by governments to serve these larger purposes quite as often as they have themselves been the objects of governmental solicitude. In the words of one commentator describing the political role of capital exports in pre-war Europe,

Capital was called upon to abstain from investment in the lands of potential enemies. It was urged or commanded into the service of allies. It was encouraged to develop the areas that were within the political system of the country where it accumulated. It was upheld in ventures which sustained a national political ambition or hope. In France and Germany, and within the alliances which they headed, it came to be commonly regarded as a servant of national purposes rather than as ordinary private possession to be disposed of in accordance with the private judgment and on the private risk of the owner.[1]

Though nationalistic bankers and investors have found it lucrative to wrap themselves in the national flag, to call upon governments to protect their interests abroad, and to drink deeply of the profits of patriotism, patriotic statesmen in the pursuit of diplomatic prestige, political influence, and imperial possessions have at the same time found bankers and investors willing tools of the politics of power. Here, again, a mutually advantageous combination of patriots and profit seekers shapes the policies of economic nationalism and impels the nation-states to action in the international arena.

POLITICS CONQUERS ECONOMICS. The rise and spread of "totalitarianism" and the advent of the Second World War of the present

[1] Herbert Feis, *Europe: The World's Banker* 1870–1914, 1930, pp. 465–466.

century have everywhere accelerated the trend toward economic nationalism and profoundly altered, beyond all hope of restoration, the relationships between private business and Great Power politics. Soviet totalitarianism abolished all private business in Russia in favor of State-controlled enterprise. A Socialist State has no problem of bribing or coercing private entrepreneurs to serve the higher purposes of *Realpolitik*. All goods are bought and sold abroad by State trusts. Money is loaned or borrowed by State banks. Tariffs, bounties, and other devices to regulate private business disappear. A central agency, possessed of effective control over investment, production, and distribution, directs the flow of goods, services, and money across frontiers as well as within them. Economic decisions are made by politicians. Their motivations, like those of all politicians, revolve around the protection and promotion of their own power and that of the Great Power which they rule, rather than around the economic welfare *per se* of their subjects.

The new Socialism has spread itself over the world and led everywhere to the imposition of political controls upon all economic activity, in sharp contrast to the hidden control of government by business which often prevailed in the heyday of competitive capitalism. "Communism," to be sure, is still restricted to Russia, and Fascism in theory and pretense is "anti-Communist" and solicitous of the interests of private property and profits. In fact, Italian Fascism, German National Socialism, and Japanese militarism have developed a degree of State control over business, and particularly over foreign trade, which differs little from that prevailing in the U.S.S.R. "Private" capitalists and industrialists are still tolerated, provided that they yield unquestioning obedience to the new political *élite*. If they do not (like Fritz Thyssen, the German steel magnate who originally subsidized the Nazi party and helped put Hitler in power), they are expropriated, imprisoned, or deported. Politicians fix prices and wages, establish quotas of production exports and imports, manage money and credit, suppress competition, promote monopoly, and administer the entire national economy as a unit.

The purpose of these operations—invariably in the case of the Fascist Powers, frequently in the case of the U.S.S.R.—is to enhance the power of the State and to use business and finance to serve diplomatic and military ends. Under these conditions the last vestiges of the free market disappear. Totalitarian States, by controlling and rationing foreign exchange and putting international trade on a barter basis, oblige their merchants to buy and sell not where goods and services can be bought most cheaply or sold most profitably, but where high policy dictates the conferring of benefits or the imposition of penalties. By such devices, Dr. Hjalmar Schacht and his successor as German Minister of Economics and Reichsbank president, Walter Funk, set Germany's Anglo-American creditors by the ears, invaded Latin American and Oriental markets, and brought all of southeastern Europe into economic subjection to the Reich long before any armies marched or any planes left their hangars with loads of bombs.

The enormous diplomatic and military advantages accruing to the totalitarian States from these methods (so long as they dealt with private businessmen in other lands) compelled democratic governments to resort to comparable practices in self-defense. Many steps in this direction had been taken after 1930 in attempts to cope with the Great Depression. More steps followed with the approach of war. The leaders of France, however, never learned how to meet the business strategy of the Reich. The slow-minded aristocrats and businessmen who governed England in the 1930's learned only slowly how to adapt their behavior to the dangers and opportunities of a changed world. In America, where "individualism" persisted longest and public regulation of business was most vigorously opposed, the transition came by stages after 1933—first in governmental control of money, credit, and the securities market, later in the promotion of exports through government loans to foreign purchasers, still later in the control of exports through embargoes and in the actual conduct of certain foreign trade operations, particularly in strategic raw materials, by public agencies. The Export-Import Bank, originally established as a subsidiary of the Reconstruction Finance Corporation to help develop Soviet trade (in which field it had done no business up to the time of writing), later became a vehicle for public loans to actual or prospective victims of aggression, particularly China.[1]

Under the impact of hostilities, Great Britain and the British Dominions developed measures of economic mobilization and economic warfare involving as complete control over business by government as anything to be found in Germany, Italy, or Japan. America moved more slowly in the same direction. Whether these steps would enable Britain and America to resist the Triplice successfully was not clear by the advent of 1941. But certain other things were quite clear. One was that no measures less than these, no reliance on "private initiative" or "business as usual," would suffice either to keep the economies of the democratic Powers functioning or to meet the threat of totalitarian war. Another was that there would be no post-war return to "normalcy" in any perceptible future, whatever the verdict of Mars might be. The new Socialism, whether democratic or despotic in its philosophy, had come to stay —at least in the sense that all business enterprise, and all activities of farmers and workers as well, would henceforth be publicly controlled for public purposes defined by political leaders.

[1] *Cf.* Benjamin H. Williams, *Foreign Loan Policy of the United States since* 1933, New York, Council on Foreign Relations, 1939.

By a singular paradox, however, these developments, which carried economic nationalism to its logical terminal point, coincided with the waning of the nation-state as a politico-economic unit and with the passing of both "nationalism" and "economics" as these things were understood before 1914. In the world society of the future the currency and trade areas within which the State will control international business and command it to serve the ends of politics will not be areas defined by national boundaries. They will be at least great continental blocs and at most a world federation. Within each area the purposes of such control may be, as in the recent past and present, the waging of economic and military wars of annihilation against other areas, with the vanquished enslaved by the victors. Or the purposes of control may be the maintenance of productivity and the promotion of a safer and richer life for all. The answer to this riddle is still hidden in the fog of dubious battle and in the doubtful wisdom of the leaders of men. In either case the power and glory of the nation-state will be forgotten goals, superseded by the broader purposes of more daring minds. And if the enrichment of nations is still possible in the world of tomorrow, it will be achieved not by each seeking its own good at the expense of its neighbors but by cooperating with its neighbors in a common program which will leave to the national states of today a role as small as that now enjoyed by the provinces, principalities, and city-states of yesterday.

SUGGESTED READINGS

Angell, N.: *Raw Materials, Population Pressure and War*, Boston, World Peace Foundation, 1936.

Barzun, J.: *Race: A Study in Modern Superstition*, New York, Harcourt, 1937.

Benedict, Ruth: *Race: Science and Politics*, New York, Modern Age, 1940.

Boaz, F.: *Race, Language and Culture*, New York, Macmillan, 1940.

Brown, F. J. and J. S. Roucek: *Our Racial and National Minorities*, New York, Prentice-Hall, 1937.

Burr, C. S.: *America's Race Heritage*, New York, National Historical Society, 1922.

Buthman, W. C.: *The Rise of Integral Nationalism in France*, New York, Columbia University Press, 1939.

Carr-Saunders, A. M.: *World Population: Past Growth and Present Trends*, New York, Oxford, 1936.

Condliffe, J. B.: *The Reconstruction of World Trade*, New York, Norton, 1940.

Coon, C. S.: *The Races of Europe*, New York, Macmillan, 1939.

Culbertson, W. S.: *Reciprocity: A National Policy for Foreign Trade*, New York, Whittlesey House, 1937.

Davenport, E. H., and S. R. Cooke: *The Oil Trusts and Anglo-American Relations*, New York, Macmillan, 1924.

Davie, M. R.: *World Immigration*, New York, Macmillan, 1936.

Dietrich, E. B.: *World Trade*, N. Y., Holt, 1939.

Drucker, P. F.: *The End of Economic Man: A Study of the New Totalitarianism*, New York, Day, 1939.

Einzig, P.: *Finance and Politics*, New York, Macmillan, 1932.

———: *World Finance, 1914–1935*, New York, Macmillan, 1935.

Elliott, W. Y., and others: *International Control in the Non-ferrous Metals*, New York, Macmillan, 1937.

Ellsworth, P. T.: *International Economics*, New York, Macmillan, 1939.

Fairchild, H. P.: *People: The Quantity and Quality of Population*, New York, Holt, 1939.

Feis, H.: *The Changing Pattern of International Economic Affairs*, New York, Harper, 1940.

———: *Europe—the World's Banker*, New Haven, Yale University Press, 1930.

Fraser, H. F.: *Foreign Trade and World Politics*, New York, Crofts, 1932.

Gaus, J. M.: *Great Britain: A Study in Civic Loyalty*, Chicago, University of Chicago Press, 1930.

Greaves, H. R. O.: *Raw Materials and International Control*, London, Methuen, 1936.

Gregory, T. E. G.: *Tariffs: A Study in Methods*, Philadelphia, Lippincott, 1921.

Hayes, C. J. H.: *Essays on Nationalism*, New York, Macmillan, 1926.

———: *The Historical Evolution of Modern Nationalism*, New York, Smith, 1931.

Heilperin, M. A.: *International Monetary Economics*, New York, Longmans, 1939.

Hodgson, J. G. (ed.): *Economic Nationalism*, New York, H. W. Wilson, 1934.

Jaszi, O.: *The Dissolution of the Hapsburg Monarchy*, Chicago, University of Chicago Press, 1929.

Killough, H. B.: *International Trade*, New York, McGraw-Hill, 1938.

Kohn, H.: *A History of Nationalism in the East*, New York, Harcourt, 1929.

Kuczynski, R. R.: *The Balance of Births and Deaths*, New York, Macmillan, 1928.

———: *Population Movements*, New York, Oxford, 1936.

Ladas, S. P.: *The Exchange of Minorities, Bulgaria, Greece and Turkey*, New York, Macmillan, 1932.

Leith, C. K.: *World Minerals and World Politics*, New York, McGraw-Hill, 1931.

Lippincott, L.: *The Development of Modern World Trade*, New York, Appleton-Century, 1936.

Lowenthal, M.: *The Jews of Germany*, New York, Longmans, 1936.

Merriam, C. E.: *The Making of Citizens*, Chicago, University of Chicago Press, 1931.

Norman Wait Harris Memorial Foundation, *Population*, Chicago, University of Chicago Press, 1930.

Playne, C. E.: *The Neuroses of the Nations*, New York, Boni, 1925.

Radin, P.: *The Racial Myth*, New York, McGraw-Hill, 1934.

Reuter, E. B.: *Population Problems*, Philadelphia, Lippincott, 1923.

Riegel, O. W.: *Mobilizing for Chaos*, New Haven, Yale University Press, 1934.

Ruppin, A.: *Jewish Faith and Future*, New York, Macmillan, 1940.

Sachar, A. L.: *Sufferance is the Badge*, New York, Knopf, 1940.

Samuels, M.: *The Great Hatred*, New York, Knopf, 1940.

Schattschneider, E. E.: *Politics, Pressures, and the Tariff*, Wesleyan University, Prentice-Hall, 1936.

Simpson, K.: *Introduction to World Economics*, New York, Harper, 1934.

Spengler, J. J.: *France Faces Depopulation*, Durham, N. C., Duke University Press, 1939.

Spurr, J. E.: *Political and Commercial Geology and the World's Mineral Resources*, New York, McGraw-Hill, 1920.

Staley, E.: *War and the Private Investor*, New York, Doubleday, 1935.

Stone, J.: *International Guarantees of Minority Rights*, New York, Oxford, 1932.

Taussig, F. W.: *Tariff History of the United States*, New York, Putnam, 1922.

———: *International Trade*, New York, Macmillan, 1927.

Tawney, R. H.: *Religion and the Rise of Capitalism*, New York, Harcourt, 1926.

Thompson, Dorothy: *Refugees: Anarchy or Organization?*, New York, Random House, 1938.

Thompson, E. T. (ed.): *Race Relations and the Race Problem*, Durham, N. C., Duke University Press, 1939.

Thompson, W. S.: *Population Problems*, New York, McGraw-Hill, 1930.

Trevor, J. B.: *Japanese Exclusion: A Study of the Policy and the Law*, Washington, Government Printing Office, 1925.

Viner, J.: *Dumping: A Problem of International Trade*, Chicago, University of Chicago Press, 1923.

———: *Studies in the Theory of International Trade*, New York, Harper, 1937.

Wambaugh, S.: *Plebiscites since the World War*, Washington, Carnegie Endowment, 1933.

Wright, F. C.: *Population and Peace*, New York, Columbia University Press, 1939.

CHAPTER IX

THE STRUGGLE FOR EMPIRE

1. COLONIALISM, OLD AND NEW

Take up the White Man's Burden—Send forth the best ye breed—Go bind your sons to exile To serve your captives' need; To wait in heavy harness, On fluttered fold and wild—Your new-caught, sullen peoples, Half-devil and half-child.—RUDYARD KIPLING, 1899.

The legions which [America] sends forth are armed not with the sword but with the Cross. The higher State to which she seeks the allegiance of all mankind is not of human but of divine origin. She cherishes no purpose save to merit the favors of Almighty God. . . . We extended our domain over distant islands in order to safeguard our own interests and accepted the consequent obligation to bestow opportunity and liberty upon less favored people.—Inaugural Address of CALVIN COOLIDGE, March 4, 1925.

A new spirit inspired by the policy of the good neighbor was born at Montevideo. It was the spirit of the Golden Rule. . . . We must sell abroad more of our surpluses.—CORDELL HULL, February 10, 1934.

THAT patriotism and economic nationalism have contributed to the pursuit of policies of territorial aggrandizement on the part of the nation-states has been suggested in the preceding chapter. These policies have, until recently, led to most spectacular results in the backward regions of the globe, where native governments have been unable to offer effective resistance to Great Powers. The latter have succeeded in partitioning most of the non-European world among themselves, sometimes by peaceful bargaining, sometimes by war. More than half of the world's land surface and almost half of its population are included in the colonies, protectorates, mandates, and spheres of influence of the imperial States. *Imperialism* is the collective and all-embracing term usually applied to these and related phenomena. This term, like most words ending in "ism," has a multitude of meanings, none of them clear and precise. Historians apply it generally to all situations in which States acquire colonies or build empires. They usually distinguish this process from that of simple conquest by limiting the application of the term to instances where the conquered are alien in language, culture, or race to the conquerors or where noncontiguous overseas territory is acquired. Patriots employ "imperialism" as an epithet of opprobrium to describe the territorial ambitions of enemy States. Communists apply it to the historical epoch which they regard as marking the last stage of capitalism.

From the point of view of the present study, imperialism is chiefly significant as a phase of the competitive struggle for power among the sovereign units of the Western State System. That struggle typically takes the form of efforts on the part of the nation-states to increase their power by extending their control over new land. In the modern period of Western civilization, it has been easier for the States of Europe—and for the non-European States which have adopted the technology of Europe— to acquire new land at the expense of the small weak States or of the politically unorganized natives of the non-European world than to wrest contiguous territory from powerful neighbors. Conquest has followed the paths of least resistance and has reflected the dictates of interest and opportunity. The political partition and the economic exploitation of America, Asia, Africa, and the islands of the seven seas at the hands of the great States constitute the most grandiose and characteristic expression of the will-to-power in modern times. It is this process, with all its political, economic, and cultural ramifications, to which the term *imperialism* will be applied in the following pages.

THE OLD COLONIALISM. In the second half of the fifteenth century the peoples of western Europe invented or adapted to their own uses a number of devices which enabled their governments to exercise military and political power overseas much more effectively than had been possible hitherto. The general employment of gunpowder in warfare was perhaps the most significant of these developments. The invention of printing, the construction of larger, sturdier, and more seaworthy sailing vessels, the progress made in the sciences of navigation, geography, and astronomy, the improvements in road building, carriage construction, and fortifications, and the elaboration of the institutions of banking and commerce also played their part in producing those economic and social changes usually associated with the transition from "medieval" to "modern" times. These devices greatly altered the technological differential between the European and non-European world to the advantage of the former. When competing Mediterranean merchants sought new routes to the Indies in order that they might import more cheaply and sell more profitably the spices, precious stones, drugs, dyes, perfumes, woods, and rare fabrics of the Orient, they found ships and navigators at their service capable of doing what had not been done before—sailing around Africa, crossing the Atlantic, exploring distant sea routes, and finally circumnavigating the globe.

The governments of the European States at once perceived the possibilities of increasing their power and wealth by assisting their merchants in the quest for profits, their missionaries in the quest for converts, their navigators and explorers in the quest for adventure, fame, and fortune. They accordingly organized commercial and colonizing companies, fitted out exploring expeditions, and developed their sea power as a means to the attainment of this purpose. And when Negroes, Hindus, Arabs, South Sea Islanders, or Amerindians offered resistance to conquest, the European States sent out military and naval expeditions to confer upon them by force the blessings of Christianity, to save them from temptation by relieving them of their riches, or in some cases to exterminate them in order that white men might take their lands. The establishment of political control over the newly conquered regions seemed a necessary step to foster commerce and promote economic exploitation. Each European State was determined to monopolize for itself and for its subjects as many of the new opportunities as possible. The tools of resistance available to the victims of these ambitions were no match for the tools of the conquerors. The bow and arrow, the spear, the lance, the canoe, and the small sailing craft could not cope with the blunderbuss, the cannon, the galleon, and the armed man-of-war. The non-European peoples were consequently vanquished, and great colonial empires were established by the Atlantic seaboard States which possessed navigators, ships, and sea power and had direct access to the great ocean highways.

If European technology in the sixteenth and seventeenth centuries was superior to that of the non-European peoples, it was still feeble and ineffective by the standards of the twentieth century. The path of empire was arduous and beset with difficulties, delays, and detours of all kinds. Empire building was accordingly a slow and painful process, requiring not years or decades, but generations and centuries. The old colonial empires were created very gradually. Portugal first rose to brief commercial ascendancy and conquered the Spice Islands in the East Indies, Angola on the West African coast, a strip of East Africa opposite Madagascar, Brazil in South America, and other scattered possessions. Portuguese sea power was unequal to the task of maintaining this empire, however, and it suffered partial dissolution at the end of the sixteenth century. Spain conquered most of the new world, as well as various Pacific islands, and waxed wealthy and powerful with the gold and silver of the Aztecs and the Incas. The old Spanish empire was the largest, richest, and most imposing of the colonial domains; but Spanish power rapidly declined in the sixteenth century, owing to policies of ruthless exploitation, mercantilistic monopoly, and religious intolerance. The destruction of the Armada by the English and the elements in 1588 foreshadowed the end of Spain's overseas domain.

In the first half of the seventeenth century, the Netherlands rose to a position of commercial and naval supremacy. The Dutch conquered most of the Portuguese possessions in the East Indies and established settlements on the Atlantic coast of North and South America. But Dutch sea power was worsted in contests with England, and the Netherlands soon fell to the rank of a second- and then of a third-rate power. France entered the lists later and established footholds in Canada, the Great Lakes region, the Mississippi valley, and India. This large empire was not settled by Frenchmen, but was feebly held by scattered military posts unsupported by adequate sea power. England, having vanquished Spain and the Netherlands, entered the arena last of all, in the early seventeenth century. But the English colonies of North America were settlement colonies with a large and growing white population, and the constant growth of English sea power ensured English colonial supremacy. In the long combat with France, England finally triumphed, both in India and in North America. The first great epoch of European imperialism thus came to an end with England holding North America east of the Mississippi and north of the Great Lakes, much of India, and various possessions in the East and West Indies, Africa, and the Pacific. Spain still held most of South America, all of Central America and Mexico, North America west of the Mississippi, the Philippine Islands in the East Indies, and smaller scattered islands. Portugal retained Brazil, the Azores, the Madeiras, the Cape Verde Islands, and portions of the African coast line; and the Dutch held the major portion of the East Indies and the Cape of Good Hope in South Africa. The French colonial empire had all but disappeared.

THE FIRST RETREAT. The period between 1763 and 1880 was a century of the decline of commercial and naval imperialism, the partial dissolution of the old empires, the agrarian expansion of Russia and the United States, and the full flowering of industrialism and nationalism in Europe. Great Britain lost her Atlantic seaboard colonies in the American Revolution. Spain and Portugal lost their Western empires in the Latin American Revolutions. Mercantilism and the doctrines of the old colonialism fell into disrepute. France, to be sure, conquered Algeria in the 1830's; and Great Britain took control of Australia, New Zealand, South Africa, and other overseas regions. But, in general, European governments lost interest in colonies and came to regard them as a wasteful and unprofitable extravagance. While the old empires decayed, two new empires—or, more accurately, two States of continental proportions—came into prominence in world politics. Tsarist Russia continued its land-hungry, military imperialism, pushing eastward and southward into central Asia and toward the Pacific. At the same time, the young giant of the new world, the United States, extended its power across the North American continent at the expense of France, Spain, and Mexico. Other Powers remained quiescent.

Viewed in retrospect, this century was but an interlude between the old and the new imperialism. It was a period during which the Western States were revolutionizing their technology and gathering their energies for another epoch of overseas expansion, destined to overshadow completely all earlier achievements. The new drives to imperialism came from the Industrial Revolution and the cult of the nation-state, from the new capitalism and the new nationalism, from entrepreneurs, exporters, and investors, and from patriots, thirsty for national power and glory. The advent of the machine industry produced a direct effect upon the technological differential between the Western States and the non-European world. In the realm of transportation, the wooden sailing vessel, the stagecoach, and the mud highway were in course of time replaced by the steel steamship, the steam railway, the concrete road, the bicycle, the motorcar, the electric line, and the airplane. In the realm of communication, the old modes of dispatching messages by horseback, stagecoach, or ship gave way to the telegraph, the telephone, the radio, and modern postal services. In the realm of warfare, the pistol, the blunderbuss, and the muzzle-loading cannon were replaced by revolvers, rifles, machine guns, heavy mobile artillery, armored cars, tanks, dreadnoughts, submarines, bombing planes, and other strange weapons. Formerly difficult or insuperable problems of distant military operation and remote colonial administration became child's play for those with the new technology at their disposal. The non-European peoples now found European technology to be not two or five or ten times more effective than their own, but one hundred or five hundred or even one thousand times more effective. A single modern cruiser could destroy with ease a vast squadron of sailing vessels. A single battery of modern artillery could demolish the strongest fortification of the premachine age. A single machine-gun company or a few airplanes could put to flight an enormous army equipped with more antiquated weapons. In short, the Industrial Revolution placed at the disposal of the Western States tools of colonial conquest and administration of a range and potency inconceivable in any earlier period.

The indirect economic effects of the new technology have been as significant for imperialism as its direct effects upon the political and military power of governments. The productivity of the new industry was many times greater than that of the old handicraft economy. An enormous flood of goods of all kinds poured out of the mills and factories, seeking purchasers wherever they might be found. Population in the industrial States doubled, trebled, and quadrupled. Standards of living ascended dizzily. Home markets soon became glutted, in spite of increasing populations and rising living standards. Farmers and manufacturers turned abroad for an outlet. The total foreign trade of the world, estimated at

$1,400,000,000 in 1800, grew to $4,000,000,000 by 1850, $10,000,000,000 by 1870, $20,100,000,000 by 1900, $40,400,000,000 by 1913, and $65,200,-000,000 by 1927. The great markets of the Orient and of Latin America became spheres of keen competition among rival national groups of entrepreneurs and exporters. The rich natural resources of Africa, Asia, and the Americas were demanded in ever greater quantity to feed the seemingly insatiable hunger of the god of the machine. As fortunes were accumulated by the profit makers, as great sums of liquid capital were piled up, the new captains of industry and finance turned abroad for investment markets as well as for commodity markets. The backward areas of the earth—rich in resources or in labor power or in consumptive capacity, but poor in capital and undeveloped industrially and commercially—became happy hunting grounds for the profit seekers of Western capitalism. From western Europe, from the United States, from westernized Japan, there poured forth a deluge of ships, goods, and money, inundating the rest of the world.

THE NEW IMPERIALISM. Within the brief period of three decades —roughly from 1880 to 1910—the imperial Powers partitioned the world among themselves. Within a single generation, larger colonial empires were established than had been created during the three centuries of the old imperialism. Great Britain conquered an imperial domain upon which the sun never sets. France created the second largest colonial empire of the world. Imperial Russia pushed onward into Asia. Two new Powers, Italy and Germany, entered the field belatedly and carved out empires of their own in regions not yet seized by their rivals. The United States reached out into the Pacific and the Caribbean for new territory, power, and profits. The new Japan created a colonial empire in eastern Asia and the western Pacific. Lesser States kept what they had (*e.g.*, Portugal and the Netherlands) or carved out new empires (*e.g.*, Belgium). Only Spain lost her remaining overseas possessions. By 1914 the process of peaceful partitioning was practically completed and the new epoch entered upon the phase of armed combat among the empires for world supremacy.

To retell the tale of the building of the new empires and to describe the way in which they are governed would require many more pages than can be devoted to the task in a work of this kind. But some general conception of the colonial possessions and the imperial interests of the Great Powers is indispensable to an understanding of the patterns of contemporary international politics. A brief survey of the empires will suffice for this purpose.

The British Empire, or, more accurately, the "British Commonwealth of Nations" as it has been officially designated since 1926, was by far the largest of the imperial domains. It was scattered over the six continents and the seven seas and included within its frontiers something like one-fifth of the land area of the globe and one-quarter of its population. It differed from the other empires in that its largest units were self-governing Dominions, largely inhabited by the descendants of those who emigrated overseas from the mother country. Viewed as a whole, however, it represented not an empire created by outward-moving settlers, colonizing empty land, but an empire built up by conquest and by the imposition of British rule upon alien peoples. Fewer than 80 million of its 500 million inhabitants were of the white race, and of these 47 millions lived in the mother country. Of the white British subjects, several millions were of non-English stock, such as the French in Canada, the Dutch in South Africa, and the Irish of the Irish Free State. If the Empire was not precisely built up inadvertently in periods of absence of mind, as some have alleged, it nevertheless represented the result of a long process of accretion, expansion, and internal evolution.

The richest and most populous unit of the Empire was India.

Early in the seventeenth century trading posts were established along the coasts by the British East India Company, an organization of private merchants who received a charter from the Crown, giving them a monopoly of British trade with India and authorizing them to rule over the natives within their sphere of commercial operation. Since the disintegration of the Empire of the Great Mogul, India had been divided into warring principalities in whose quarrels the Europeans found an excellent opportunity for intervention. The British East India Company and the French East India Company became rivals for commercial and political supremacy, with the former triumphing over the latter in the Seven Years' War (1756–1763) and undertaking all of the functions of government in the portions of the country under its control. Huge profits were made by the members of the company and by its agents, who were almost completely free from governmental supervision prior to 1784 and were then subjected to merely a loose control by parliamentary commissions. The area of British power was gradually extended by conquest. In 1818 the Mahratta Confederacy of Princes was overthrown and its land in central and western India annexed. In 1849 the Sikhs of the Punjab were similarly conquered and brought under British rule. A series of wars on the eastern frontier culminated in the annexation of Burma in 1886. Baluchistan became a province of British India in 1903.

Meanwhile, native resentment at alien control had flamed out in the great Sepoy Rebellion of 1857, which was crushed two years later after extensive fighting and the customary atrocities on both sides. An act of Parliament of 1858 abolished the East India Company and transferred its powers to the Crown. A large part of the country was left under the control of the native princes, with British advisers directing them. The administration of the remainder was placed in the hands of a viceroy, assisted by executive and legislative councils, both appointed by the British Government and acting under the supervision of the Secretary of State for India. Under the pressure of Indian nationalist agitation for autonomy, a limited degree of native participation in the government was subsequently permitted.

If any consciously formulated and consistently pursued purpose played a part in the creation of the empire, that purpose was to safeguard the channels of trade between India and Great Britain. Considerations of trade and strategy along the line from Manchester to Calcutta played a prominent part in the acquisition of coaling stations, naval bases, colonies, and protectorates along the two routes from England to India—one around Africa and the other through the Mediterranean, the Red Sea, and the Arabian Sea. Both routes, before they divide west of Gibraltar, lie along the coast of Portugal, and Portugal had been more or less under British influence since the early eighteenth century. The southern route circumscribed the African continent. Along its course, Great Britain controlled Sierra Leone, the Gold Coast, South Africa, Tanganyika territory, Kenya colony, and scattered islands in the south Atlantic and in the western Indian Ocean. The shorter Mediterranean-Red Sea route was of even greater strategic significance. British hegemony in the Mediterranean was assured by the possession of Gibraltar, Malta, and Cyprus, and in the Red Sea by possession of Aden, British Somaliland, and the Sudan, and by effective control of Egypt and the Suez Canal.[1] In the region between the Mediterranean and the Persian Gulf, British power was secured through control of Palestine and Iraq. The security of north-south communications between the two routes was attained by acquiring Rhodesia, Uganda, and other points in Africa between Cairo and the Cape. The vital line of imperial defense was extended eastward in two directions to include Malacca, Singapore, Sarawak, North Borneo, British New Guinea, Australia, and New Zealand, on a line from India to the southern Pacific; and Hongkong and Weihaiwei on a line curving northeastward around Asia from Singapore to the Yellow Sea. In the Western Hemisphere the Empire included Canada, Newfoundland, British Honduras, Jamaica, the Bermudas, the Bahamas, a string of Caribbean islands, British Guiana in South America, and sundry islands in the south Atlantic and the south Pacific.

These segments of the globe-girdling arcs of British imperial power were put together through a mixed process of settlement and conquest, involving the imposition of British rule upon native peoples, the granting of autonomy to British settlers, or the seizure of territories of other States. From a stategic point of view, Egypt and South Africa were the two most important links in the line of imperial defense, for they commanded the two routes to India. The Suez Canal, the construction of which was begun in 1859, lies entirely within Egyptian territory. The government of the country was heavily indebted to European bankers, who encouraged its extravagant borrowing. In 1876, the Khedive offered to sell a large number of shares of his Suez Canal stock as a means of extricating himself from his difficulties. The British Prime Minister, Disraeli, with an eye open for imperial bargains, purchased the shares for the British Government. In the following year, Great Britain and France took over the management of Egyptian finances. In 1882 the disgruntled natives, under the leadership of Arabi Pasha, rallied to the cry of "Egypt for the Egyptians!" and rose in revolt against the Khedive and the foreign bankers. France failed to act; and a British army marched in, quelled the uprising, took control of military as well as financial affairs, and seemingly prepared for an indefinite sojourn. Under Mohammed Ahmed—the "Mahdi"—the fanatical Moslems of the Sudan attacked the invaders in 1885, massacred Gordon and the British garrison at Khartoum, and defied British power for more than a decade, until the dervishes were crushed by Kitchener at Omdurman in 1898. The Sudan became an Anglo-Egyptian

[1] In a note of October 7, 1924, Prime Minister Ramsay MacDonald declared " . . . it is no less true today than in 1922 that the security of the communications of the British Empire in Egypt remains a vital British interest and that absolute certainty for the free passage of British ships is the foundation on which the entire defensive strategy of the British Empire rests." Parliamentary Command Papers 2269, 1924.

"condominium." France relinquished her claims in 1904; and Egypt, still nominally under the suzerainty of the Sultan, passed under British control. It was officially proclaimed a protectorate in 1914.

South Africa was settled by Dutch colonists in the seventeenth century and remained a Dutch colony until 1814, when it was awarded to Great Britain at the Congress of Vienna.

As a result of constant friction between the old Dutch and the new English settlers, the Dutch packed up bag and baggage in 1836 and migrated northward, where they established the two independent Boer Republics of Transvaal and the Orange Free State. In 1877, Great Britain announced the annexation of the South African Republic (Transvaal). The Dutch successfully resisted this attack, and Great Britain again recognized their independence in 1884. But the discovery of the Rand gold deposits led to a rush of Englishmen into the Transvaal and resulted in the Boers being outnumbered by the Uitlanders, or foreigners, who sought to control the government and transfer authority to Great Britain. Cecil Rhodes, millionaire gold and diamond prospector, conspired with Joseph Chamberlain, British Colonial Secretary, to bring on a war which would result in the annexation of Transvaal to the Empire. The spectacular "Jameson raid" of 1895 failed in its purpose but convinced the Boers that they must prepare to resist British aggression. When they refused a British demand that suffrage rights be granted to the Uitlanders, war broke out in 1899. Under the leadership of Paul Kruger, the tiny Boer Republics defeated the British and compelled the British Government to mobilize a large army and to send her ablest generals, Roberts and Kitchener, to South Africa. A British force of 250,000 troops was required to overcome the 40,000 Boer soldiers. The conflict, which Lloyd George called "a war for 45 per cent dividends," cost Great Britain 250 million pounds and 30,000 lives. Not until 1902 was Boer independence extinguished and the Transvaal and Orange Free State reduced to colonial status. In 1906–1907 the new Liberal Ministry granted responsible government to the Boers, and in 1909 the Union of South Africa was created as a federation of the four provinces of the Cape of Good Hope, Transvaal, Orange Free State, and Natal. This grant of dominion self-government to the Boers has ensured their loyalty to the Empire, though the future of the Union is clouded by growing unrest among the native Negro population, which greatly outnumbers the whites and is subjected to a status of political, economic, and social inferiority.

The other self-governing Dominions of the Empire, with the exception of Ireland, are "settlement" colonies rather than conquests.

Canada, to be sure, was conquered from the French in 1763, but the French Canadians remained loyal during the American Revolution and were subsequently outnumbered by English-speaking immigrants. Following the suppression of the rebellion of 1837, self-government was gradually introduced. On the basis of the report of Lord Durham (1839), the British North America Act of 1867 united all of the colonies except Newfoundland into the present federation of the Dominion of Canada, which consists of nine self-governing provinces and a central government independent in all important respects. Newfoundland is a self-governing Dominion in its own right. New Zealand and the arid island continent of Australia were claimed for the British Crown by Captain Cook at the end of the eighteenth century. Australia was first used as a penal colony and was gradually settled by immigrants from England. In 1900 the six Australian colonies of New South Wales, Queensland, Victoria, South Australia, West Australia, and Tasmania were united into a self-governing federal union. New Zealand was formally annexed to the Empire in 1839. In 1907, it was organized as a self-governing Dominion. Ireland received Dominion status in the Irish Free State Act of 1921. The six Dominions of the Empire were all theoretically subject to control by the Parliament at Westminister, in which they had no representation, and in form their constitutions were simply parliamentary statutes. In fact, however, the constitutions were quasi treaties which conferred upon the Dominions rights of complete local autonomy and self-government. The British Crown remained the symbol of imperial unity, but the royal governors-general in the dominions occupied the same position with respect to the Dominion parliaments and cabinets that the King occupied with respect to the Parliament and Cabinet of the United Kingdom, *i.e.*, that of a figurehead with power to recommend and to admonish, but with no power to control policy and administration. The Dominions all became independent members of the League of Nations and maintained their own diplomatic services, entered into treaties with foreign governments, and in general conducted themselves like sovereign States.

The Empire as a whole, including Great Britain, India, the Dominions, the Crown colonies, the protectorates, and the mandates, gradually evolved away from the form of political organization prevailing before the American Revolution, when Parliament claimed the right to tax and legislate for all the parts, and became a federation of self-governing units. The new colonial policy of the nineteenth century repudiated the monopolistic economic doctrine of mercantilism and sought to achieve imperial unity through compromise and cooperation rather than through dictation by the home government. That imperial loyalty was attained is shown by the fact that in the Boer War, in the Great War, and in the War of 1939 the Dominions fully supported Great Britain. At the end of the nineteenth century, Joseph Chamberlain pleaded eloquently for imperial federation. In 1887 the first Imperial Conference was held as a means of discussing common problems of trade and defense. Such conferences were held at fairly regular intervals thereafter. The 1926 Conference took cognizance of the new constitutional structure of the Empire and gave it its present official name of the British Commonwealth of Nations. This title suggests that the Empire, like the Trinity, was both singular and plural at the same time. At the 1930 Conference the Statute of Westminster recognized the equality of the Dominions with Great Britain in the Commonwealth. The Imperial Economic Conference at Ottawa in the summer of 1932 adopted measures designed to make the Empire more nearly self-sufficient commercially, but the divergent interests and the protectionist policies of its several units made "imperial preference" a slogan rather than a reality and precluded any complete customs union.

The colonial empire of France was the second largest in the world in area and population. Unlike the British Empire, it represented less a reconstruction and expansion of the old imperial dominions of the eighteenth century than a creation *de novo* of the nineteenth century. The old French colonial empire collapsed under the blows of Britain in the Seven Years' War. By 1815, French overseas possessions included only five Indian ports, French Guiana in South America, Guadaloupe and Martinique in the West Indies, and a few scattered islands. The building of the new empire began with the conquest of Algeria in North Africa in the 1830's. In the face of stout resistance and numerous revolts, French power was pushed into the interior. French settlements were established along the Ivory and Guinea coasts in the 1840's. Under the Second Empire (1852–1870), control of Algeria was consolidated, New Caledonia and adjacent islands in the Pacific were acquired (1853), expeditions were sent into Cochin-China and Annam (1858) to avenge the murder of missionaries, and a French protectorate was established over Cambodia (1863). The attempt to conquer Mexico (1863–1866) ended in disaster.

Upon the foundations laid by its predecessors, the Third French Republic built an imposing colonial edifice to compensate itself for its loss of power and prestige in Europe and to protect merchants, missionaries, investors, and concessionaires. The major fields of French imperial expansion were north and central Africa, the southwestern Indian Ocean, and southeastern Asia. In 1881, French troops descended upon Tunis in the name of protecting Algeria from raiding tribesmen. The interests of investors and of holders of Tunisian bonds were safeguarded by the conversion of the country into a French protectorate. From the foothold already established in Senegal, on the west African coast, expeditions were sent up the Senegal River toward Timbuktu and westward along the Niger valley. French Equatorial Africa north of the Congo was acquired in 1884. By 1899 Mauretania, Dahomey, and the central Sudan were secured, and a broad belt of French power stretched across the Sahara from the Guinea Coast on the south to Algeria and Tunis on the north. On the eastern coast of the Dark Continent, France held a small but strategically valuable strip of Somaliland at the head of the Gulf of Aden. The agents of French imperialism pushed westward from Somaliland across Abyssinia and eastward from the French Sudan to converge on the headwaters of the Nile. But this was already a British sphere of influence. Following the meeting at Fashoda between Marchand and Kitchener in 1898, French ambitions yielded before British power and the two segments of the French empire in north Africa remained separated by Ethiopia and the Anglo-Egyptian Sudan. If British resistance to French encroachments in the Sudan was effective, German resistance to French encroachments in Morocco was not; and, after several diplomatic crises, most of this remnant of the Moslem world became a French protectorate in 1912.

Meanwhile, ancient claims to Madagascar, the huge island lying off the southeast coast of Africa, were vigorously pressed at the instigation of French property owners, naval officers, and expansionist diplomats. In 1885 a treaty of protectorate was concluded which led to endless difficulties, culminating in annexation in 1896. The conquest of Madagascar was completed by the ruthless repression of the native Hovas' resistance to the invaders. In southeastern Asia the government of the Republic utilized its position in Cambodia and Cochin-China to establish a protectorate over Annam and Tonkin in 1884, a procedure which led to an indecisive war with China. The annexation of Laos in 1892 completed the creation of French Indo-China. Among France's other Oriental possessions were five ports in India, Kwangchow-wan in China, New Caledonia, Tahiti, and Syria, the last acquired as a mandate in 1922.

Italy's imperial career was begun belatedly and was hampered by Italy's relative weakness as compared with Great Britain and France.

Italian patriots and imperialists bitterly resented the French conquest of Tunis but were unable to prevent its successful completion. Italy established a foothold in Eritrea on the Red Sea coast, north of French Somaliland, and in 1889 acquired a larger colony in Italian Somaliland, on the easternmost tip of the African shore line. Italian designs against Ethiopia were frustrated by the crushing defeat of the invaders at the hands of the natives in the battle of Adowa (1896). A decade later, Italy, France, and Great Britain all agreed to respect the independence of the Ethiopian Kingdom. The French Government pledged itself not to oppose Italian ambitions in Tripoli, and in 1911 Italy waged a war upon Turkey which ended in the annexation of Tripoli and Cyrenaica. These provinces were united in the colony of Libya, which was held with considerable difficulty and at great expense in the face of Arab rebellions. After the Great War, its boundaries were extended westward with the consent of France and eastward with the consent of Great Britain. The successful invasion and conquest of Ethiopia in 1935–1936 increased the size of the Italian colonial empire by one-quarter, more than quadrupled its population, and created a broad belt of Italian power in East Africa from the Red Sea to the Indian Ocean.

The colonial empire of imperial Germany was likewise created belatedly and was lost in its entirety in the Great War. Between 1884 and 1890 Germany acquired Togoland on the Guinea Coast, Cameroon between Nigeria and French Equatorial Africa (extended to the Congo in the Franco-German settlement of 1911), German Southwest Africa between Portuguese Angola and British South Africa, and German East Africa between Lakes Victoria, Tanganyika, and Nyasa on the west and the Indian Ocean on the east. A general native rebellion in German East Africa in 1905 led to great loss of life before German authority was restored by the customary blood-and-iron methods of imperialists everywhere. In Asia and Oceania, Germany acquired Kiaochow in the Shantung peninsula as a leasehold from China (1899), the Bismarck Archipelago (1884), the Marshall Islands (1885), the Caroline Islands (1899), the Pelew Islands (1899), the Ladrone Islands (1899), and two of the Samoan group (1899). In 1884 Germany annexed the northeastern section of New Guinea (Kaiser Wilhelm's Land). These territories were all seized by the Allies in the Great War, and by the peace settlement they passed to the victors as mandates of the League of Nations. Togoland and Cameroon were divided between Great Britain and France. Southwest Africa became a mandate of the Union of South Africa. German East Africa became a British mandate (Tanganyika), with the small western section known as Ruanda-Urundi becoming a Belgian mandate. Kiaochow, seized by Japan in 1914, was restored to China in 1922. The German Pacific islands north of the Equator became Japanese mandates, and those to the south became mandates of Great Britain, New Zealand, and Australia. Kaiser Wilhelm's Land likewise became an Australian mandate. Post-Versailles Germany thus remained without overseas possessions of any kind.

The only other States of western Europe with colonial empires were Spain, Portugal, the Netherlands, Belgium, and Denmark. Spain, once mistress of the greatest of all colonial empires, lost the last of her possessions in America and the Far East in 1898–1899. As a somewhat pathetic and expensive compensation for her losses, she obtained three strips of African coast: Spanish Morocco, opposite Gibraltar, Rio de Oro, opposite the Canary Islands, and Rio Muni on the Guinea Coast. The enormous losses of men and money incurred in the effort to suppress the revolt of Abd-el Krim in Morocco (1920–1925) contributed to the overthrow of the Spanish monarchy in April of 1931. Portugal, whose navigators and explorers first opened Africa to Europe in the fifteenth century, retained only Portuguese East Africa (Mozambique and Zambesia), Portuguese West African (Angola), Portuguese Guinea, and St. Thomas, Prince's Island, the Cape Verde Islands, the Azores, and the Madeiras off the west coast. Portuguese efforts to unite the east and west African possessions were frustrated by Cecil Rhodes and the British Government in 1891. Portugal retained none of her American possessions and had in Asia only the ports of Goa in India and Macao in China. The Netherlands retained a larger proportion of their old colonial empire, including Dutch Guiana in South America and, in southeastern Asia, Java, Sumatra, most of Borneo, the Celebes, and Dutch New Guinea, with the adjacent islands. The African empire of Belgium was the creation of King Leopold II, who became interested in the explorations of Livingstone and Stanley in the Congo basin and who took the initiative in the formation of the "International Association for the Exploration and Civilization of Africa" in 1876. A Belgian commercial company, the International Association of the Congo, was formed two years later; and in 1885 the "Congo Free State" with Leopold as its personal sovereign was recognized by the Powers. Through the atrocious exploitation of native forced labor, Leopold and his fellow investors made millions from the trade in rubber, ivory, and palm oil. In 1908, after numerous scandals, "reforms" were introduced and the shrewd Leopold surrendered the Congo to the Belgian Government for a liberal compensation. The Belgian mandate of Ruanda-Urundi lay just west of the Belgian Congo. Denmark retained a somewhat controversial title to Greenland and was united with Iceland in a personal union under a common king.

Of the other empires of the Powers, the largest was that of Russia. The expansion of the Russian State differed from that of the States of western Europe in that it represented the spreading out over contiguous territory of a land-hungry agrarian population, rather than an imperialism of commerce, sea power, and investments over the ocean highways. The only noncontiguous possession ever acquired by Russia was Alaska, sold to the United States in 1867. This process of expansion brought under Russian power a large number of non-Russian peoples, some of them on a primitive cultural level. The power of the Tsardom was extended over a vast realm stretching from the Baltic and Black Seas to the Pacific, covering eastern Europe and northern Asia and comprising one-sixth of the land surface of the globe. The original Grand Duchy of Muscovy brought most of European Russia under its control by the end of the sixteenth century. The early Tsars of the Romanov dynasty (1613–1917) pushed Russian power eastward across Siberia and reached the Pacific before the end of the seventeenth century. Continued pressure westward and southward for outlets to the sea led to the founding of St. Petersburg in 1721, the annexation of Estonia and Latvia from Sweden in the same year, the expulsion of the Turks from the north coast of the Black sea, the partition of Poland at the end of the eighteenth century, the acquisition of Finland in 1809, and the occupation of Bessarabia in 1812. These conquests were followed in the nineteenth century by the penetration of Trans-Caucasia, central Asia, the Amur River region of the Pacific coast, and Manchuria. Further Russian expansion in eastern Asia was checked by Japan, in central Asia by Great Britain, and in the Balkans and the Near East by Great Britain, France, Turkey, and later by Austria-Hungary and Germany. The Russian Revolution led to the independence of Finland, Estonia, Latvia, Lithuania, and Poland and the loss of Bessarabia to Rumania. The new Soviet Union remained, however, the largest of the Great Powers next to the British Empire, both in territory and in population. In Asia, it extended its control beyond the old limits, for the new Soviet spheres of influence include Outer Mongolia and an undefined area of Chinese Turkestan north of Tibet. In Europe, it recovered the Baltic States, Eastern Poland, Bessarabia, and a slice of Finland in 1939–1940.

The expansion of the United States prior to the twentieth century resembled that of Russia in that it was the expansion of an agrarian population across a contiguous territory of continental dimensions. Alaska was the only noncontiguous possession of the United States prior to 1898. In the last two years of the nineteenth century the United States annexed the Hawaiian Islands and Samoa, and seized Puerto Rico, the Philippine Islands, and Guam as the fruits of victory of the Spanish American War. After 1900 the United States embarked upon an active career of commercial and financial imperialism in the Western Hemisphere. In 1903, Cuba became an American protectorate as a condition of its independence, and Panama accepted a similar status. The construction of the Panama Canal and the growth of American commerce and investments in the Caribbean led to the imposition of American protectorates upon the Dominican Republic (1905) and upon Haiti (1915), the purchase of the Virgin Islands from Denmark (1917), and chronic interventions in the Central American States for reasons of strategy, commerce, and "dollar diplomacy." The American islands in the Pacific and American trade in the Far East led to the projection of a policy of establishing American naval supremacy in the Pacific, but this policy was abandoned and replaced by one of cooperation and consultation with the other Pacific Powers in 1922.

The great rival of the United States for control of the Pacific is, of course, Japan, whose new empire in eastern Asia made her one of the great imperial Powers. Following the reopening of Japan to contacts with the West in the middle of the nineteenth century, her peoples imported, along with other elements of Western culture, industrial capitalism, militarism, and imperialism. In 1894, Japan waged war on China, defeated her, annexed Formosa and the Liukiu Islands, and detached Korea from Chinese control. She was compelled to give up Port Arthur and the Liaotung peninsula under Russian pressure, supported by Germany, France, and Great Britain. Russo-Japanese conflict for control of South Manchuria culminated in war in 1904–1905. A second Japanese victory enabled the empire to annex southern Sakhalin, acquire Port Arthur and the Liaotung peninsula by leasehold from China (on whose lands the war was fought), and free Korea and southern Manchuria from Russian influence. Korea was annexed in 1910. Japan, in alliance with Great Britain after 1902, declared war upon Germany in 1914 and seized Kiaochow, Shantung, and the German islands in the north Pacific. The islands she retained as mandates; but she was obliged, under Chinese, Russian, and American pressure, to give up Shantung, to relinquish her design to establish a protectorate over China, and to evacuate the Russian territory occupied by Japanese troops during the Allied intervention in the Russian civil war. In the fall of 1931 Japanese troops ousted the Chinese authorities from Manchuria and subsequently set up the independent State of Manchukuo as a Japanese protectorate. The most important issues of international politics in the Pacific and the Far East revolve around the future of Japanese imperialism in eastern Asia.

This brief survey of the empires[1] has dealt primarily with territories

---

[1] The outcome of the Second World War, still in progress as these words are written, will inevitably alter the colonial empires of 1939 beyond all recognition. The Fascist Powers, if victorious, may confidently be expected to partition the British, French, Dutch, Belgian, Portuguese, and American empires among themselves. The Western Powers, if victorious, will doubtless put an end to the Italian, Spanish, and Japanese colonial empires and reorganize their own colonial domains, probably under some form of international administration. Early in 1941 the French colonial empire was in chaos, the British colonies were threatened with invasion and were in turn threatening Italy's colonial

which have been openly annexed or brought under the direct control of the imperial Powers. Mention must also be made of the indirect forms of imperialism through which varying degrees of foreign control have been imposed upon States still nominally independent. The leasehold has been a device commonly resorted to for this purpose. The German "colony" of Kiaochow in China was acquired in 1898 through a ninety-nine-year lease from the Chinese Government. China was likewise compelled to lease Port Arthur and Dairen to Russia in 1898 for twenty-five years. In 1905 Russia was obliged to transfer these leases to Japan, which coerced China into extending them until 1997 in the twenty-one demands of 1915. Great Britain still holds the leases of Weiheiwei (acquired in 1898 for as long as Russia should hold Port Arthur) and of Kowloon (acquired in 1898 for ninety-nine years). France leased Kwangchow-wan in 1898 for the same period. The United States has also leased naval bases from Cuba, Nicaragua, and Panama. In 1903 the Republic of Panama, established by a revolution against Colombia, instigated in Washington and supported by American naval forces, leased to the United States in perpetuity the Canal Zone for a consideration of $10,000,000 and an annual payment of $250,000. The same agreement made Panama a protectorate of the United States, by giving the American Government the right to use its forces to protect the canal and maintain order. The treaty agreements between the United States and Cuba, Haiti, the Dominican Republic, and Nicaragua also made these States semiprotectorates.

The protectorate as a form of imperial control usually involves the retention of agencies of local self-government on the part of the "protected" State, with the "protecting" State assuming control of the foreign relations, the defense, and sometimes the financial affairs of the victim. "Spheres of influence" represent another device of imperial control. This phrase is usually applied to areas in which imperial Powers are granted economic privileges and the native States retain sovereignty and political authority. It is also loosely used to describe a situation in which an imperial Power exercises an appreciable degree of control over a region which it has not formally annexed or converted into a protectorate. By the agreements of 1896 and 1904, Great Britain and France divided Siam into spheres of influence. The Anglo-Russian agreement of 1907 divided Persia into British and Russian spheres, with an intermediate zone between them. Manchuria, Tibet, and the southern provinces of China were at various times spheres of influence, respectively, of Japan,

domain, and the other colonial empires were in flux. Under these circumstances, it would be futile to list colonial possessions with areas and populations or to include special maps of the colonial domains. For such lists and maps on the eve of the war, cf. the second edition of this work, pp. 310–11, 314, 316, 318, 320, 322f. Cf. also current issues of The Statesman's Yearbook and The World Almanac.

Great Britain, and France. The territories of Turkey have from time to time been divided into spheres of influence among Great Britain, France, Germany, and Italy. In Africa and Asia, annexations and the establishment of protectorates have usually been preceded by the creation of such spheres. In other instances, imperial control has been established over backward States through various devices of financial supervision, tariff regulation, extraterritoriality, military intervention, etc.

The most significant result of the new imperialism for international politics has been the partition of most of the non-European world among the colonial Powers of the Western State System. Only two non-European States possess colonial empires—the United States and Japan—and these are the only States of the world not located on the European continent which can be regarded as Great Powers. Of the colonial States of Europe, all save Belgium and Denmark are, or have once been, Great Powers. Between 1860 and 1914 the non-European peoples have been progressively deprived of their territory, their freedom of action, and often of their independence by the empire builders. On the African continent, only Liberia and Egypt remained even nominally independent by 1939. Egypt was for all practical purposes a British protectorate. Liberia remained independent only because of the interest of the United States in its fate. In Asia, only Japan, China, Thailand, Nepal, Afghanistan, Iran, Turkey, and the Arabian States remainded independent. Japan became an imperial Great Power. The other States remained nominally independent only because their size, resources, or strategic location made them objects of competition among several Powers, no one of which has been willing to permit another to absorb them. All suffered losses of territory and were subjected to greater or lesser degrees of foreign control. No independent States remain in the South Sea Islands. The States of Latin America remained free from efforts of the European Powers to control them primarily because of the British navy and the hegemony of the United States in the Western Hemisphere.

It is worthy of note that although this new conquest of the world involved innumerable wars against weak States and native peoples on the part of the imperialistic governments, it was for the most part achieved without war among the imperial Powers themselves. The Crimean War of 1854–1856 and the Russo-Japanese War of 1904–1905 were the only open clashes of arms between the Great Powers for control of backward areas prior to 1914. The Spanish-American War of 1898 was waged by a Great Power against a third-rate Power. All other conflicts and controversies among the empire builders were adjusted pacifically by diplomacy, conference, bargaining over pawns, and horse trading in territory and populations. War, rebellion, and repression there were in abundance, for the path of empire is red with the blood of its victims. Britishers fought and beat Hindus, Egyptians, Arabs, Turks, Afghans, Boers, Bantus, Bushmen, Chinese, and Polynesians. Frenchmen fought and beat Arabs, Syrians, Hovas, Chinese, Siamese, etc. Americans fought and beat Filipinos, Haitians, Mexicans, Nicaraguans, etc. But before 1914, with the exceptions noted, the Great Powers did not fight one another so long as native States remained to be conquered and new lands remained unclaimed. But when the world became filled with jostling imperialists, friction between the Powers increased to a dangerous degree. The Great War of 1914 initiated a life-and-death struggle among the great States themselves, interrupted in 1919 and resumed in 1939. It is not impossible that the twentieth century may witness a series of suicidal combats among the imperial nation-states for world mastery.

THE ART OF EMPIRE BUILDING. If the process of imperialism is to be understood in terms of its actual functioning rather than in terms of preconceived dogmas and theories of interpretation, it must be studied, not through a consideration of abstract generalizations, but through a careful examination of men, motives, facts, and events in particular situations. To examine in detail the process of empire building in all its manifestations would obviously be impossible even in a work of many volumes. It is quite out of the question in the present study. A reflective consideration of the way in which the Great Powers acquired their colonial domains, however, reveals notable uniformities of motives, techniques, and results which can justifiably be made the basis for certain observations more or less applicable to all the empire builders. With minor variations of time, place, circumstances, and personalities, the sequence of events is much the same whether one studies the United States in Nicaragua, Haiti, or the Philippines; Great Britain in Burma, Borneo, or Hong Kong; France in Siam, Syria, or Madagascar; Belgium in the Congo; the Netherlands in Java; Portugal in Angola; Spain in Morocco; or Japan in Manchuria. All show much the same pattern. Should some new Machiavelli, capable of looking objectively and realistically at this pattern, attempt to set forth the maxims which modern statesmen must follow if they would be successful in empire building, his precepts might read somewhat as follows:

Choose as your field of operation some area, preferably rich in resources, which is weakly held by a feeble State or has a weak independent government of its own. If your capitalists, traders, and investors already have interests in this area, make a great show of protecting these interests and complain bitterly over every infringement upon them, real or imaginary. If no interests exist, create some by inducing your profit seekers to enter the region. In either case, act in close cooperation with private business. Use the power of the State to serve business, and use business interests to further political designs. Look about you circumspectly to see what the interests and policies of other Powers are. If they conflict with yours, if they are certain to oppose you when you endeavor to acquire control of the territory, decide whether you can safely defy them or must come to terms. Defiance is dangerous unless you have a great preponderance of power and your rivals are weak or only moderately interested. Coming to terms is more advantageous if you can offer a *quid pro quo* for their acquiescence or support. Diplomacy and war— bargaining and force—are essential means of preparing the ground for action.

When all is in readiness, manufacture a pretext, an incident, a grievance which will make your aggression appear defensive and thus justify it in the eyes of your patriots and of certain opinion groups in other States. Deceive your parliament and press, if necessary, as to your intentions, and make much of national honor, vital interests, the sanctity of the flag, the necessity of protecting the rights of your citizens abroad, the blessings of Christianity, and the duties of humanitarianism. It is often possible, by intrigues among the native politicians conducted by your businessmen, diplomats, and naval officers, to achieve your purposes by cleverly contrived revolutions without an open resort to force. If this seems too difficult, strike swiftly, decisively, with overwhelming strength, in order that you may paralyze resistance, impose your will, and confront your own people and the world with a *fait accompli*. Speak softly to foreign governments which object, but never yield to their objections unless you feel unable to defeat them if they should resort to extreme measures. Secure recognition of your new position in treaties, and use the treaty rights as a means of further extending your power if you do not gain all you desire at a blow. Whether you create a colony, a protectorate, or a dominion or merely establish financial and military control over the region depends upon circumstances. In any case, once in power, make firm your control by assisting your bankers to loan money to the local government, by securing concessions for your businessmen and investors, and by acquiring trading privileges for your merchants and exporters. This economic exploitation of the area will enhance the profits of your businessmen and make them disposed to cooperate with you in future ventures. Unless carried out too wastefully, it will make the territory a more valuable asset to the State. Placate the local inhabitants wherever possible by granting them small favors and benefits, or even the appearance of self-rule, for long-nursed grievances breed resentment and future trouble. When they will not be placated and offer resistance, stop at nothing to crush their will, for in the eyes of your businessmen and patriots yours is a mission of enlightenment and civilization.

These maxims of imperialist behavior are not offered in any spirit of cynicism or jesting but are presented in all seriousness as precepts which imperialist statesmen have followed. They are offered not as praise or condemnation, nor indeed as judgment of any kind, but simply as necessary prescriptions which successful empire builders must adhere to. These were the methods employed by Great Britain and France in Africa and southeastern Asia. These were the methods utilized by imperial Germany in Africa, Asia, and the South Seas during the creation of the original German colonial empire. These have been the methods used by the United States in the Caribbean, by Japan in China, by Italy in Africa.

WHY HAVE COLONIES? As soon as questions are raised regarding the ends behind the means, the deeper motives beneath the technique, the underlying purposes which are served by the practice of the art of empire building, complex problems of interpretation and evaluation present themselves for solution. These problems are usually resolved by glib formulae which express half truths but fail to explain imperialism in its totality. "Over-population," "the need for markets," "the white man's burden," "capital investments," "trade follows the flag," "exploitation of subject peoples," and "the monopolistic stage of capitalism," are among the formulae which have gained wide acceptance. Each emphasizes one element in the process whereby the Western nation-states have divided the world among them. Each seeks to explain the entire process in terms of this single element, which is regarded at the same time as a clue to motives and purposes and an explanation of results. The validity of each hypothesis can be demonstrated to the satisfaction of its proponents by a careful selection of evidence to prove a case, and each can be as readily disproved by a compilation of negative evidence. Every interpretation and evaluation in the fifth decade of the twentieth century must necessarily be tentative, for the Western State System is still in the midst of the epoch of imperialism. Whither the road which has been taken will finally lead no one can now say. As one commentator aptly puts it,

> The question is too complex, despite its brevity, to be disposed of neatly in a final formula or a facile phrase. The answer can be obtained only by summing up the profit-and-loss account in each of half a dozen departments of activity, and combining the net results. An exhaustive study of each item would require more than one volume and more than a single lifetime. In the end, some of the benefits and evils of imperialism would still be imponderable, and the final judgment would be subjective rather than scientific, for no scientific balance can be devised to weigh ships against schools, raw materials against wars, profits against patriotism, civilization against cannibalism.[1]

The problem of analyzing the purposes and fruits of imperialism is made peculiarly difficult by the fact that prior intentions are usually hopelessly confused with subsequent results, both in official apologies and in public discussions. Results are cited in explanation of original motives

[1] P. T. Moon, *Imperialism and World Politics*, p. 526.

with which they have no connection at the time of action. If the American occupation of Haiti leads to the construction of roads, schools, and hospitals, the occupation is defended in terms which suggest that its original purpose was to construct roads, schools, and hospitals, despite the fact that those who engineered the occupation had no such purpose in mind. The American annexation of Alaska is justified by gold discoveries, though the very existence of gold in the territory was unknown at the time of the purchase. Prior intentions, moreover, are frequently disguised in such ambiguous verbiage that the outside observer may well wonder whether those who framed and executed policies had any clear conception in their own minds of why they were acting. The arts of dissimulation, misrepresentation, and rationalization are so highly developed that the practitioners are deceived by their own cleverness. After naval strategists had dictated the annexation of the Philippine Islands for reasons of high politics, President McKinley justified the acquisition by solicitude for the little brown brothers "for whom Christ also died." After sugar, investments, and naval policy dictated the conversion of Cuba into an American protectorate, its "emancipation" from Spain was defended in the name of humanity and self-determination. In democratic States, profit motives and power motives must be skillfully concealed in terms of humanitarianism, civilizing missions, religious conversion, and material benefits conferred upon the backward peoples; for, as a distinguished Florentine diplomat pointed out some centuries ago, "the vulgar are ever caught by appearances and judge solely by the event." The multitudes of patriots and taxpayers are moved to enthusiasm and self-glorification by the tactics of interested minorities, and the shouts of the multitude move statesmen to action as a means of retaining public favor. In this jumble of slogans, catchwords, and emotional appeals to irrationality, it is next to impossible to separate the honest and the dishonest, the sincere and the insincere, the realities and the illusions.

The alleged motives may be divided into those which postulate benefits to the home country and those which postulate benefits to the colony. As for the first of these, it is argued that colonies are necessary as outlets for surplus population, as markets for goods produced in the home country, as markets for surplus capital seeking investment, and as sources for the raw materials essential to make the nation self-sufficient and secure. These arguments are at best of the *post hoc ergo propter hoc* variety. At worst they are pure rationalizations of quite other purposes or figments of too vivid imaginations skilled in wish-fulfillment thinking.

The establishment of political control over some backward area works no magic whereby the wealth of the area is appropriated and distributed piecemeal among the citizens of the imperial State. The type of imperialism which involves the seizure of the goods and chattels of the conquered and the distribution of the inhabitants as slaves among the conquerors has long since disappeared. When a modern State asserts title to a backward region, the property of the inhabitants remains in the hands of its former owners precisely as before, or it is bought up and exploited by interested investors of the conquering State for their own private profit. In the first case, the total population of the State which has asserted title derives no economic benefit whatever from the new status; and, in the second, the general benefit, if any, is entirely incidental and completely negligible. The direction of trade and investment, it is true, may be altered by political means, but it cannot be demonstrated that the masses of voters and taxpayers in the mother country gain anything thereby except additional satisfaction for their patriotic impulses.

The value of colonies to the imperial nation-states as outlets for surplus population has thus far been completely negligible, despite the large role played by this alleged purpose in imperialistic propaganda in Germany, Italy, Japan, and other supposedly "overpopulated" States. Since most of the empires are located in tropical or subtropical areas unsuitable for residence by Europeans and since emigrants prefer to go to congenial lands of easy economic opportunity, there has been no appreciable outflow of population from the nation-states to their colonies. During the past half century, fewer than 500,000 of the 20,000,000 Europeans who took up permanent residence outside of Europe went to the colonial territories of European governments. After 30 years of colonialism, only 20,000 Germans lived in Germany's colonies in 1914, compared with over three times this number on Manhattan Island alone. In 1931 all the Italian colonies in Africa contained only 55,000 Europeans, many of whom were not Italians. Twice as many Italians lived in New York City. In 1930 there were only 238,000 Japanese in all Manchuria. By 1935 the number was still under 750,000, though Japan's population had increased almost 5,000,000 in the interval and Manchuria's Chinese population had increased by 4,500,000. In 1933 there were 543,000 Japanese in Korea and 257,000 in Formosa. The "surplus population" argument for imperialism has played its part in convincing patriots of the necessity of expansion, for reasons, facts, and logic are usually conspicuous by their absence in the mental processes of emotional nationalists. It has therefore been utilized effectively by imperialists as a means of securing popular support for their policies. But in view of the results, it can be regarded as an honestly and consciously formulated purpose behind the quest for empire only on the assumption that statesmen are imbeciles or madmen.

It is likewise not difficult to show, despite appearances to the contrary, that most colonies are not acquired by States as markets for goods or for investments, though such motives may influence particular groups of politically influential imperialists and may be regarded as plausible by the citizenry. "Trade follows the flag," cries the imperialist—and the crowd believes and approves. In fact, trade does *not* follow the flag in most cases; and where it does, the economic results, though profitable for the traders involved, are of little significance to the people of the home State. The total trade of the colonial empires is reasonably impressive in round numbers—or was before the onset of the Great Depression. During the post-Versailles years when "prosperity" still prevailed, the total foreign commerce of the colonies of the world reached an annual figure of about 15 billion dollars, something less than one-quarter of the world's international trade. The British Empire accounted for three-quarters of this colonial trade, with the United States enjoying 10 per cent of it and the other colonial Powers smaller proportions. Efforts on the part of the imperial States to monopolize such trade for their own nationals in many cases led to an increased percentage of the foreign trade of the colonies being carried on with the mother country. But only two imperial Powers enjoyed over half of the trade of their colonies: the United States and Japan. Even in these cases, colonial trade was a negligible fraction of the State's total foreign trade and an infinitesimal fraction of the total domestic and foreign commerce of the State. The larger part of this fraction would in most cases be enjoyed by the imperial State without political control of the territories with which the trade is carried on. To a few industries in the colonial States, *e.g.*, cotton textiles, iron and steel, etc., colonial markets are of considerable importance. In the national economy as a whole, these markets are of minor significance.

The same statement may be made regarding exports of capital. Investment interests have often played a leading role in the process of imperialism. "Dollar diplomacy" suggests empire building on a grand scale. But most of the foreign investments and loans of the imperial States are made, not in their colonies, but in foreign countries. Accurate investment figures are difficult to obtain, but there is no question regarding the validity of this generalization for all the capital-exporting States. Again professions and facts are widely at variance. Again the professions must be regarded as rationalizations, superstitions, and shibboleths, not as accurate verbalizations of the purposes of imperialism. Between 1931 and 1937, for example, Japan had "invested" $682,000,000 in Manchukuo, but $312,000,000 of this sum represented the cost (wholly unproductive) of maintaining armed forces and suppressing "banditry" and only $40,000,000 represented private investments. Each dollar invested by Japanese capitalists thus cost the Japanese taxpayers $17.00 —and the ungrateful capitalists found other markets for investment more attractive.

Finally, it may be pointed out that the contention that colonies are acquired as sources of raw materials is also without foundation, either in the political process of empire building or in the economic results of the process. On the one hand, efforts on the part of imperial States to fix world prices of raw materials exported from their colonies, and thus make profits for their own nationals at the expense of foreign purchasers, have been largely unsuccessful. On the other hand, none of the imperial Powers derived the major portion of its required raw materials from its colonies. Colonial raw materials are sold to purchasers willing to buy them, and such purchasers are quite as likely to be found in foreign States as in the mother country. Purchasers needing raw materials buy them where they are to be had most cheaply, and the sources of supply are quite as likely to be found in foreign States or colonies as in the territories of the State of the purchasers. Self-sufficiency in raw materials is impossible even for Great Britain, with her vast and variegated Empire, and is quite out of the question for other States. If the empires were acquired to make the imperial States self-sufficient in such goods, the experiment failed miserably. In point of fact, this, too, is not a "purpose" of imperialism, but a phrase employed by profitseekers and by power-and-prestige politicians to bewilder the uninitiated and win popular approval for policies motivated by considerations of a different character.

If space permitted, it could be demonstrated statistically that the taxpayers of every imperial Power have been obliged to pour out blood and treasure for the acquisition and administration of colonies out of all proportion to any economic gains secured by the mother country from colonial areas or to any alleged "benefits" conferred upon the subject peoples. The most that can be said in support of the contention that colonies are "profitable" to the nation holding them is that the progressive fragmentation of the world into politically defined economic units, cut off from free-trading opportunities with other units, coupled with the collapse of the international gold standard, makes it economically advantageous for certain States to have colonies for the disposal of surplus goods and capital and for the purchase of raw materials. In a world of neo-mercantilism and autarchy, the absence of tariff obstacles, import quotas, and exchange difficulties are welcome features of trade among colonies and the States controlling them.[1] But these "advantages" are themselves by-products of the enormous losses accruing to world economy as a whole from restrictions upon the free flow of goods and services across frontiers. Where all States are alike impoverished, each can relieve its poverty slightly by controlling colonies. Starving men may fight for dry crusts. But the nourishment thus obtained does not demonstrate that dry crusts constitute an adequate diet. In terms of economic welfare, imperialism is almost universally a costly and wasteful luxury.

[1] See Hjalmar Schacht, "Germany's Colonial Demands," *Foreign Affairs*, January, 1937.

Each particular purpose, however, plays its role in the total complexity of purposes. The entire process has been so confused, anarchic, and disorderly that no clear, single purpose is discernible. The preceding observations have served their end if they have suggested (1) that no "single-purpose" explanation of imperialism is tenable, whether it be couched in political, economic, religious, or humanitarian terms, and (2) that the course of empire building has been one in which no single directing intelligence has ever played a controlling role, save in a few exceptional instances. Generally speaking, scores of divergent interests in the imperial States, by a more or less blind and uncoordinated pushing and pulling, have contributed to a final result not clearly foreseen at the outset by anyone and certainly not representing any consciously formulated and willfully executed program on the part of any single individual or group. Contemporary colonialism is a phenomenon of Western civilization in the age of private capitalism, bourgeois individualism, planless economy, parliamentary democracy, and demagogic politics. These aspects of Western culture suggest one of its dominant characteristics: pluralism, competition among a bewildering multitude of interests and forces, uncontrolled and uncontrollable economic and political drifting under the impact of pressures released by the Industrial Revolution and not yet brought under the control of organized social intelligence. Out of the interaction of interests and forces, certain consequences flow which take on the appearance—which are indeed deliberately given the appearance—of purpose and planning on the part of the whole community of the nation-state. But this is appearance only, for the forces which have produced the consequences are part of a chaotic jumble of interests and groups within each nation. "Imperialism" is such a consequence. Its "purposes" are intelligible only in terms of the nature of the political process within and between the nation-states themselves.

If imperialism is viewed as a phase of the struggle for power between States, its results must be judged in terms of its role in power politics. The most obvious result of the competitive quest for empire is war—war, first between the imperial States and the backward peoples, and then war among the imperial States themselves. Whether investors use foreign offices to enhance profits or foreign offices use investors to extend State power, the diplomatic influence of the State is placed at the disposal of the empire builders; and if diplomacy fails to attain the goal, it is supported by coercion and military force. This force has been used on innumerable occasions against the native States which resist conquest. There is scarcely a single colony of any of the Great Powers which was not won through bloodshed. Such wars are often costly (*e.g.*, the Boer War and the Manchurian hostilities of 1931–1933); they are sometimes disastrous to conquerors and conquered alike (*e.g.*, Spain in Morocco, France in

Mexico); they almost always involve atrocities, abuses, fierce resentment, and savage repression (*e.g.*, the United States in the Philippines and Haiti, France in Madagascar and Syria, Germany in Southwest Africa, Great Britain in India, Egypt, the Sudan, China, and elsewhere). In general, however, colonial wars do not, in and of themselves, upset the balance of power or bring the conquerors to ruin. They tend rather to increase the power of the imperial States and to enhance the profits of their immediate beneficiaries. The situation is quite different when the imperial States engage in war with one another for mastery of tropical lands or Oriental markets. Prior to the nineteenth century, even such wars normally had little effect upon the nation-states themselves, apart from changing titles to territories and bringing about redistributions of power and prestige. In the machine age, however, such conflicts have become enormously costly and destructive of life and property whenever Great Powers have been belligerents on opposite sides. The fruits of empire building, garnered by the war god, are destruction, death, bankruptcy, and national ruin. Yet these fruits are seldom weighed in the balances of those who tabulate profits and losses.

THE REVOLT OF THE SUBJECT PEOPLES. The fruits of imperialism must also be judged in terms of the increasingly bitter resentment on the part of the subject populations. Limitations of space do not permit a review here of the long and tragic tale of the exploitation of the "backward" races, of their gradual conversion to Western conceptions of racial and national pride, of their vehement demands for justice and freedom, of savage repressions and reprisals, and of grudging concessions slowly wrested from the masters by the sweat and tears and blood of colonial slaves in revolt. Colonies held by force alone are precariously held. To win the loyalty of the conquered is difficult so long as national aspirations for self-determination are denied. To induce acquiescence by distributing material benefits is equally difficult, since benefits are costly and are often received with resentment rather than with gratitude. The amelioration of the economic lot of the subjugated is frequently quite incompatible with the whole ideology of imperialism and with the success of the quest for profits by privileged exploiters who use diplomats and strategists (or who are used *by* diplomats and strategists) to further imperialistic purposes. To grant genuine independence to the victims of the game tends to make the game itself quite pointless. Here brief cognizance may be taken of some of the more striking manifestations of colonial revolt.

Islam

In Africa, the black peoples have, for the most part, not yet attained to such a degree of racial or national solidarity as would enable them to offer effective resistance to their white masters. The Arab peoples of the north coast, however, are held in subjection with difficulty. In Morocco the warlike native tribes almost succeeded in ousting their conquerors during and after the Great War. In the Spanish zone the Riffian warriors of Abd-el Krim inflicted such crushing defeats on the Spanish troops that Spanish authority was limited to the coastal areas, Spanish parliamentary government was discredited and replaced by the dictatorship of Primo de Rivera in 1923, and the Spanish monarchy itself was overthrown in 1931 as an aftermath. In 1925, following French encroachments on the valleys south of the Riff, Abd-el Krim's veteran forces invaded French Morocco and scored a series of victories over the French troops. Lyautey resigned as Governor, and by the end of the year the Riff war had cost France the lives of 11,419 troops and an expenditure of several hundred million francs. France and Spain joined forces, and Marshal Pétain finally drove Krim into the mountains and compelled him to surrender in 1926.

This momentarily successful defiance of the armed might of the imperial States sent a thrill of joy throughout Islam. It was not entirely a coincidence that the Druze revolt in Syria broke out at the same time. It was drowned in blood after much loss of life and destruction of property. Successive rebellions of the Arabs of Palestine and Iraq likewise availed nothing against European arms, though Iraq attained an "independence" comparable to that of Egypt. In the Greco-Turk war of 1922–1923, the Turkish Nationalists of Mustapha Kemal defeated the Greeks and tore up the Treaty of Sèvres. Turkey reconquered the hinterland of Smyrna as well as Adalia, Cilicia, and part of Armenia, all earmarked for foreign seizure. Persia, Afghanistan, and the Hejaz-Nejd (renamed the Saudian Arabian Kingdom in October, 1932) preserved a precarious independence, but the Moslems of India, once masters of that rich land in the days of the Mogul emperors, fell under British rule. Of the 227 million Moslems in the world, almost half were under British control, 25 million were subjects of France, and 30 million lived in the Dutch East Indies in 1939. Great Britain, for obvious reasons, has always been the *bête noire* of Islamic anti-imperialists.

In 1903 the Pan-Islam Society was established in London to unify the Moslem world. The Mohammedans were divided, however, into the orthodox Sunnis and the Shi'ahs, who refused to recognize the Caliphate at Constantinople. The Caliphate was abolished in 1924, with the separation of church and State in Turkey; but the Moslem world remained divided, ecclesiastically as well as politically. The anti-Turkish Pan-Arab Movement was supported by the Allies in the Great War. By the treaty of October 24, 1915, Emir Hussein of the Hejaz received a British pledge of support in establishing a Pan-Arabian State in return for entering the war against the Central Powers. The pledge was never fulfilled; for Iraq, Syria, and Palestine were detached as mandates, and Arab revolts against the new order were put down. Schemes of Arab confederation failed to bear fruit; and Ibn-Saud, rival and successor of Hussein, remained ruler of a truncated Arabian kingdom after 1924. If Pan-Islamism and Pan-Arabism have not achieved their goal, they remain forces to be reckoned with in the Near East. The ancient maxim of "divide and rule" has thus far been successfully applied by the imperial Powers in the Moslem world. But it is not improbable that the sword of Islam will again some day be unsheathed in the name of emancipation from Christian imperialism. The Moors whom General Franco employed in his effort to save aristocracy and Catholicism in Spain from liberal and radical anticlericalism learned how to use machine guns and artillery to kill Christians in 1936–1939. Some day they may use their new skill to achieve their own independence.

India

The native revolt against Western imperialism in India constitutes one of the most fascinating chapters of contemporary history. Only its outlines can be sketched here. This ancient land supports 370 million people—approximately one-sixth of the population of the globe. This population has for many centuries been sharply divided into social castes and hostile religious, racial, and linguistic groups. The Hindus, numbering about 250 million, and the 80 million Moslems of eastern Bengal, Punjab, and other regions are the largest sects. Hindi is spoken by one-third of the population, Bengali by one-sixth, and dozens of other tongues by the remainder. In 1931 there were no less than 2,300 distinct castes, with the degraded "untouchables" comprising about one-third of the Hindu population. Racially the population is a complex blend of Aryans, Afghans, Arabs, Mongols, Persians, Dravidians, and lesser groups, some of them highly cultured and others on a primitive level. There remain, alongside of the British provinces proper, hundreds of native States comprising about one-third of the area and population of the country. Here native autocrats and their aristocracies are used as instruments of British domination. These internal cleavages facilitated the British conquest. They rendered easy the continuation of British control and constituted obstacles to effective and united Indian resistance against foreign rule.

On the other hand, it may be said that India has been united by common opposition to Great Britain—for here, as everywhere, nothing so readily unites a heterogeneous community as conflict with an alien group. The great Sepoy rebellion of 1857 was crushed by British military power. In the decades which followed, opposition to British rule increased with the growing national consciousness and political awareness of the upper classes. Demands for *swaraj* (self-government) were put forward with increasing frequency and energy. In 1885 the first Indian National Congress assembled as a gathering of upper-class Hindus to criticize British administration and to work for greater native participation in the government of the country. In 1912 the Moslem League was established with a similar purpose. In 1916 the two movements joined forces. Two years later they agreed upon a program of complete self-government, to be attained gradually during the next fifteen years. Aspirations for independence were nurtured by specific grievances, which became the symbols of the Nationalist movement. British rule was autocratic and arbitrary and was maintained, in the classic phrase, as a "system of outdoor relief" for British upper classes which sent their sons to lucrative posts in the Indian civil service. British rule, moreover, was originally established and consistently maintained as a tool of commercial imperialism until fiscal autonomy led to tariffs against British goods.

When unrest in Bengal assumed the form of bomb throwing and assassination of officials during the administration of the high-handed Viceroy, Lord Curzon, appointed in 1905, the British Government began to make concessions. The "Morley-Minto" constitution of 1909 made natives eligible to posts in the viceroy's executive council and in the councils of the provincial governors. It likewise enlarged the "legislative councils," but they remained undemocratic and purely advisory, with power to propose and criticize but no power to control the administration. The Montagu-Chelmsford report of 1918 declared that the 1909 arrangements had become obsolete and recommended changes, which were incorporated into the Government of India Act of 1919. This new charter established a central legislature, consisting of a council of state of 60 members and a legislative assembly of 144, with a majority of native representatives in both houses.

The 1919 constitution was regarded by the leaders of the independence movement as a miserable makeshift. Under the inspiration of Mohandas Gandhi, the demand for *swaraj* was intensified. In Gandhi's view, "the government established by law in British India is carried on for the exploitation of the masses. No sophistry, no jugglery in figures can explain away the evidence which the skeletons in many villages present to the naked eye. I have no doubt whatsoever that both England and the town-dwellers of India will have to answer, if there is a God above, for this crime against humanity which is perhaps unequaled in history."[1] The 1919 arrangements gave voting rights to less than 1 million people, out of the 247 million of the British provinces. Representation was on a class basis. Under the "diarchy" principle, certain "transferred subjects"—education, agriculture, public health, etc.—were placed under the control of officials responsible to the native councils, and certain "reserved subjects"—law, order, police, justice—were left in the hands of the appointed British governors, uncontrolled by the legislature. The Nationalists were not content to remain half slave and half free. Gandhi advocated nonviolent noncooperation, *i.e.*, passive resistance, civil disobedience, an economic boycott of British goods, and a political boycott of the elections. His asceticism and his Tolstoyan doctrines made him a Mahatma or holy man in the eyes of millions of Hindus. The prospect of tariff protectionism against British goods in an independent India caused Bombay manufacturers to give financial support to the movement. Though Gandhi preached against violence, the British officials whose authority was defied by his followers necessarily resorted to force.

When several thousand unarmed natives assembled to hold a mass meeting at Amritsar on April 13, 1920, General Dyer ordered them mowed down with machine guns. This savage slaughter spurred the Nationalist movement to new efforts. Noncooperation was intensified. British cloth was boycotted, and Gandhi urged a return to the spinning wheel, the hand loom, and cottage industry. The Moplah rebellion of the fanatical Moslems of Madras was crushed in 1921. Other disorders were followed by similar repressions. When the civil disobedience campaign was launched, Gandhi was arrested and sentenced to a six-year prison term in March, 1922. He was released two years later, with his influence temporarily diminished by factional differences between Hindus and Moslems, extremists and moderates, in the National Congress. In April, 1926, Lord Irwin (later Lord Halifax, Foreign Minister) succeeded Lord Reading as Viceroy. Great Britain slowly began to yield before Nationalist pressure. In 1928 the Simon commission arrived to investigate the desirability of extending the principle of responsible government. Its report (1930) was cautiously conservative but recommended greater independence for the local governments and the creation of a federal government for India as a whole. A "Council of Greater India" was contemplated, in which representatives of the native States would join with representatives of the British provinces in discussing matters of common concern.

In March, 1930, Gandhi commenced another civil disobedience campaign by marching with his followers from Ahmadabad to Dandi to make salt from sea water, thus defying the government monopoly and evading the salt tax. Riots and disturbances spread once more, as the British police clubbed the noncooperationists with their lathis, and British troops battled border tribesmen on the northwest frontier. Gandhi and the other leaders of the Congress executive com-

[1] M. Gandhi, *Speeches*, pp. 753–754, quoted in P. T. Moon, *Imperialism*, p. 290.

mittee were arrested once more. On November 12, 1930, the first Round Table Conference opened in London to prepare the new federal constitution, with some eighty Indians present, representing the more important races, religions, classes, and parties—save the Congress, which boycotted the proceedings. The Conference adjourned inconclusively on January 19, 1931, pending further discussions. On March 4, 1931, Lord Irwin and Gandhi (again released from prison) signed a truce providing for the discontinuance of civil disobedience and of the boycott in return for the withdrawal of repressive ordinances and the freeing of arrested Nationalists. Moslem-Hindu riots continued, however, and the British continued to use religious cleavages as an excuse for making haste slowly with constitutional reform. After much vacillation, Gandhi agreed to attend the second Round Table Conference which met in London September 14–December 1, 1931. There, amid imperial splendors, his gaunt figure, clad only in a loin cloth and a sheet, seemed to the West to be a grotesque symbol of futility and to the East to be an inspiration and an embodiment of the silent power of the Oriental masses. The conference agreed on a federal structure, but Moslem-Hindu differences made an accord impossible on the question of minority representation in the legislatures.

Gandhi described the Conference as a "complete failure." Terrorism and repression began once more in Bengal, and the holy man was again arrested. While more than 30,000 political prisoners languished in jail and while Hindu-Moslem riots continued sporadically, the British authorities went forward with their plans for a federal State and an enlarged electorate, despite the failure of Gandhi's followers to cooperate. In October, 1932, Gandhi secured more favorable treatment of the "untouchables" by a sensational hunger strike. The new Viceroy, Lord Willingdon, and his colleagues proceeded to make plans for a third Round Table Conference, despite continued Nationalist resistance. The third Round Table Conference opened in London on November 17, 1932. The Nationalists refused to cooperate in any way. On December 23 the Conference closed with a report which was to be made the basis of a new constitution.

On August 2, 1935, the Cabinet approved a new Government of India Act, passed by a large majority in Parliament over the opposition of Laborites who demanded greater concessions and die-hard Tories who demanded fewer. On August 6 the Marquess of Linlithgow was appointed Viceroy of India. He succeeded the Earl of Willingdon on April 18, 1936. The Act created a federation embracing British India and the Native States, with considerable autonomy for the eleven provinces established by the statute. The Viceroy had a Council of Ministers answerable to a national legislature; but he had a broad veto power and could administer independently the "reserved" departments, including foreign affairs, defense, finances, internal law and order, and all the decisive spheres of power. In short, the new India had neither Dominion self-government nor a parliamentary régime responsible to the electorate. The new legislature consisted of an upper house, or Council of State of 156 elected representatives of the provinces and 104 representatives of the Native States, and a lower chamber, or House of Assembly of 250 representatives of the provinces and 125 of the States elected indirectly on a basis of "communal voting" whereby minority groups receive separate representation with the effect of perpetuating religious and caste divisions. The franchise in the eleven provinces was increased from 7 million votes to 35 million, including 6 million women—or about 14 per cent of the population, selected on the basis of property and educational qualifications.

Far from satisfying Nationalist demands for self-rule, the new constitution was resented by many native patriots. The New President of the Indian National

Congress, Pandit Jawaharlal Nehru, elected in May, 1936, represented the more aggressive and extreme wing of the movement which tended to reject Gandhi's plea for nonviolence. "Our members must fight, not spin," declared Nehru. From his retirement, Gandhi asserted, "My life work is ruined. . . . Still, in two or three years' time, this excitable and enthusiastic young leader will return to me. . . . India loves me. India trusts me. India needs me. I feel, therefore, that my life mission is not yet ended. I still hope to see India free from the domination of the foreigner."

By the time Britain drew the sword in 1939 to battle for its life and that of its Empire against Hitler's Reich, the riddle of India had received no answer. Between 1936 and 1939 membership in the National Congress grew from 457,000 to 5,000,000. The Congress rejected the Constitution of 1935 and refused to cooperate in putting it into effect. In the provincial elections of 1937, its candidates won almost half the seats, gaining absolute majorities in Madras, Bombay, the United Provinces, Bihar, the Central Provinces, and Lerissa and emerging as the strongest single party in Bengal and Assam. The new constitution was formally inaugurated on April 1, 1937. In July, Congress Ministries were formed in seven of the eleven provinces of British India. During the ensuing two years, these Ministries, though possessed of no genuine autonomy, enacted a series of moderate reform measures and brought about a relaxation of British military and police control. The Congress continued to demand independence and rejected uncompromisingly the federal section of the constitution. Subhas Chandra Bose, Congress President in 1938, was reelected in 1939 with the support of Left Nationalists, Socialists, and Communists against a moderate candidate favored by Gandhi. The Mahatma reasserted his leadership, however; and in April, 1939, Bose resigned. He later violated Congress discipline and was disqualified from holding office.

This growing split between moderates and radicals within the independence movement strengthened the hopes of some Britishers that acquiescence in the new dispensation would be forthcoming. But it also foreshadowed the possibility of a grave crisis. When the Viceroy made India a belligerent by executive action and sanctioned the Defense of India Ordinance of September 3, 1939, authorizing the Central Government to rule by decree, the Congress boycotted the Legislative Assembly and demanded self-determination. Increasing friction led to the arrest of Nehru and other radical leaders in the autumn of 1940. Gandhi had no desire to play into the hands of the Fascist Triplice by crippling Britain's fight for survival, but he was equally insistent that self-government for India should be made a part of Britain's war aims. As in 1914–1918, the demand was evaded with phrases.

It is improbable that Britain's defeat at the hands of the Axis will lead to India's emancipation. Such an eventuality is more likely to spell chaos and to precipitate a struggle among Germany, the Soviet Union, and Japan for mastery of India's millions. British victory is unlikely to be followed by a resumption of the status of 1939, for such a victory presupposes a revolutionary transformation of Britain and the Empire in the direction of a revitalized democracy. In India the transformation will have reality and thus offer promise of stability and progress, only if genuine Dominion status is granted and if the British authorities identify their purposes with the social aspirations of the masses instead of with the interest of the princes, aristocrats, and large property owners.[1]

[1] For an excellent "Left Wing" account, see R. Palme Dutt, *India Today*, London, Victor Gollancz, Ltd., 1940.

China

The rising flood of Asiatic nationalism in China has beaten not against a single foreign conqueror, but against the whole array of imperial Powers which have detached from China its outlying possessions, imposed upon it a status of political and juristic inferiority and subjected it to successive indignities and humiliations, leaving little of its theoretical sovereignty intact. China, like India, is a vast land of many peoples, with an area of 4,277,000 square miles and a population in excess of 450,000,000. China, like India, has undergone such a prolonged process of cultural and political disintegration under the impact of Western civilization that it seems doubtful to many whether there is any alternative to complete foreign domination or anarchy. Unlike India, China has from time immemorial exhibited a large degree of cultural unity. Unlike India, China has never been subjected as a whole to any one of the Western Powers. For countless millennia China—the great human sea that salts all rivers flowing into it—has absorbed all her conquerors, for they were for the most part roving barbarian nomads swallowed up in a rich and ancient culture. The Mongol hordes of Genghis Khan overran the country in the thirteenth century, much as the Mongol Turkish conquerors later subdued India and created the Mogul Empire. In the seventeenth century the Manchus imposed their power upon China and established the Manchu dynasty (1644–1911). In both cases the victors were largely assimilated by the vanquished. Only with the coming of the Western white man and his machines did China become helpless.

Soon after the Celestial Empire was first compelled to open its doors to the West, antiforeignism emerged out of traditional isolationism and aloofness. The great Taiping rebellion of 1850–1864 was directed more against the Manchu dynasty than against the alien. It was suppressed with foreign assistance. The partial dismemberment of China followed. In the Boxer Rebellion of 1899–1900 the Government made common cause with the rebels in attempting to expel the Westerners. The more farsighted spokesmen of the new Chinese nationalism soon perceived that China could resist the West only with the weapons of the West, and they began to advocate the adoption of Western technology, Western economics, Western political ideas and institutions. Their pleas were entirely academic until economic and social changes increased the numbers of the Chinese business classes and urban working classes to a point where they furnished a fertile field for revolutionary agitation. Sun Yat Sen (1866–1924) became the spiritual father and the political organizer of the Chinese revolution. The Nationalist revolutionary movement was at first directed against the corrupt and decrepit Manchu dynasty. It later aspired to the political and social regeneration of China as a means of resisting imperialistic aggression.

In 1911 the Manchus were overthrown—but the presidency of the new republic passed, not to Sun Yat Sen, who retired to Canton, but to the opportunist adventurer, Yuan Shih Kai, who aspired to become emperor. Followers of Sun, organized into the Kuomintang, or National People's Party, were committed to a Western bourgeois program of parliamentary democracy, tinctured with Socialist elements. Yuan's subservience to foreign bankers, his surrender to Japan in 1915, and his assumption of royal honors in the following year led to a new revolution and to the commencement of an epoch of prolonged civil war. This state of affairs was due to the impotence of the Central Government, the uncontrolled greed of the semi-independent provincial tuchuns, or "war lords," the emergence of a mass of undisciplined mercenary soldiery, and the progressive disintegration of all the social and economic bases of political unity and cohesion.

Only the international aspects of these endless disorders can be outlined here. In June, 1916, Yuan Shih Kai died amid a ferment of revolutionary disturbances. There followed years of turmoil, marked by chronic struggles for the control of the central government among the war lords: Wu-Pei-fu of the Chihli clique, Chang Tso Lin of Manchuria, Feng Yu-hsiang, the "Christian general" of Shansi, and other lesser feudal chieftains. Chang's sphere of power was Manchuria and he was at all times dependent upon the whim of Japan for the continued rulership of his satrapy. Feng centered his power in Mongolia and looked toward Moscow. While the north was torn by these internecine conflicts, the Kuomintang followers of Sun Yat Sen remained in power at Canton and prepared themselves for the mission of unifying China on the basis of Sun's "three principles": people's nationalism, people's democracy, people's livelihood. In 1921 Sun was "elected" President of the Republic by a group of 1913 rump parliamentarians at Canton, but he encountered constant resistance from the militarists and led a most precarious existence. In his search for foreign aid, Sun received much sympathy from the anti-imperialist rulers of Communist Russia.

In September, 1923, Michael Borodin arrived from Moscow to act as the chief adviser of the Kuomintang. His leadership, strengthened by a naval demonstration on the part of the Western Powers against Sun's threat to seize the Canton customs receipts, initialed a four-year period of successful Soviet-Kuomintang cooperation. Russian military officers trained the new Nationalist army. The Kuomintang was reorganized on the model of the Russian Communist party as a rigidly disciplined brotherhood designed to assume dictatorial power and thus to achieve the purposes of the revolution. In 1924 the Chinese Communists, who were increasing in numbers, were admitted to the party. With this, there began the internal struggle between the bourgeois elements and the peasant-proletarian elements, which was later to lead to disaster. For the moment, however, the movement was greatly strengthened by this alliance with Soviet advisers and native Communists. It launched upon a career which offered a brief hope of uniting the entire country under its rule.

Despite Sun's death in April, 1924, Chiang Kai-shek, with the assistance of Borodin, assumed control in Canton after a period of disorder. He continued the Communist-Kuomintang alliance. A political and military campaign was now launched to convert and conquer the entire nation. This campaign was directed as much against Chinese and foreign bourgeois interests as against the northern war lords. By March, 1927, the Yangtse valley and the Shanghai area had fallen to the southerners. But success brought the inevitable break between Chiang and Borodin, each of whom had sought to use the other for his own ends. While Chiang now summoned anti-Communist, bourgeois, and militarist elements to his aid, the Communistic left wing of the Kuomintang occupied Nanking and began a general assault upon foreign interests which led to the bombardment of part of the city by American and British war vessels. Chiang now allied himself with the merchants and bankers of Shanghai. In April, 1927, he purged Shanghai and Canton of Russians and Communists by wholesale arrests and executions. Feng Yu-hsiang, also supported by Moscow, now intervened and joined the right-wing Nationalists.

In July Borodin retired to Russia, after thousands of labor leaders, peasants, students, and radicals had been put to death by the now thoroughly bourgeois Kuomintang under Chiang's military domination. Borodin's Chinese followers, including Mme Sun Yat Sen, now denounced Chiang as a renegade and a betrayer of the social and agrarian revolution. Chiang himself retired in August, 1927, in the face of new rivalries and disorders. The "retirement" of Chinese leaders from public life is never to be taken seriously, however. Chiang has "retired" repeatedly, but he remains master of the "purified" and reactionary Kuomintang. He returned to power in January, 1928, and set up a personal dictatorship at Nanking, while the closing of Soviet consulates and the slaughter of Communists continued in the principal cities of the south. The Nationalist armies now moved on Peking, controlled by Chang Tso-lin; but they were delayed by an armed clash with Japanese troops at Tsinan. In June the Manchurian war lord, under Kuomintang pressure and on the advice of the Japanese minister, left Peking for Mukden. He was killed by a bomb explosion during the journey and was succeeded by his son, Chang Hsueh-liang. At the same time Yen Hsi-shan's troops occupied Peking in the name of the Kuomintang, and all of China was seemingly united under the Nationalist government of Chiang Kai-shek at Nanking.

This unity, however, was entirely illusory and transitory. The party program of abrogating the unequal treaties, abolishing extraterritoriality, occupying the foreign concessions, and ousting foreign interests was soon paralyzed by new dissensions within the ranks and by the stubborn refusal of the innumerable war lords to be reformed. In October, 1928, an Organic Law of the National Government of the Republic of China was promulgated, providing for the indefinite perpetuation of the one-party dictatorship of the Kuomintang. But all efforts to demobilize the predatory armies of the tuchuns failed. In February, 1929, civil strife broke out in Shantung and Hunan. Chiang waged war on the Wuhan-Kwangsi faction and sent a punitive expedition against the now rebellious Feng, who "resigned" shortly afterward. In July, 1929, young Marshal Chang seized the Chinese Eastern Railway, with the result that Soviet forces under General Blucher, formerly Borodin's colleague and military adviser at Canton, entered Manchuria and compelled the war lord to observe established treaties. This incident led to the final rupture of diplomatic relations between Moscow and Nanking.

The unstable balance of power among independent war lords, self-seeking provincial governors, and rival Kuomintang factions could not long be maintained. Mutinies, riots, and coups d'état brought the Nanking Government to the verge of destruction by the end of 1929. Early in 1930 a large-scale civil war broke out between Chiang on the one side and Feng and Yen Hsi-shan on the other, allied in a new northern coalition. By October, Chiang was again victorious, after tens of thousands of lives had been lost, much property destroyed, and the country reduced to bankruptcy. Chang Hsueh-liang cooperated with Chiang in crushing Feng and Yen, but he was removed from the scene by the Japanese occupation of Manchuria in 1931 and the setting up of the new State of Manchukuo in 1932 in what had formerly been his domain. The Sino-Japanese hostilities which accompanied these events brought no unity to the country. Though Japanese trade was ruined by a nationwide boycott, the Chinese Government was helpless against Japanese military power and Chiang was more interested in keeping himself in power than in organizing the nation for resistance. Diplomatic relations with the Soviet Union were resumed, but the days of Soviet-Kuomintang collaboration had long since passed. By the end of 1932, half a dozen new civil wars had broken out, and the restoration of peace and order seemed as remote as ever. Chiang's passivity in the face of new Japanese aggression generated a widespread demand among patriots, students, and intellectuals for war against Tokio in the spring of 1936. This movement culminated in the rebellion of several southern war lords, dependent upon Canton; but the uprising soon collapsed in the face of the bribery of the leaders and the mobilization of overwhelming force against them.

Protests continued, however. Chiang's annual crusade against the Communists, whose local Soviets rules some 50 million people in scattered provinces, were costly and futile enterprises that precluded any possibility of national unity in the face of Japanese aggression. When he visited Sianfu in Shensi, Chiang Kai-shek found himself "kidnapped" (December 12 to 24, 1936) by followers of Chang Hsueh-liang who released him only on condition that he cease his wars against Red China, work for an anti-Japanese "united front," and cooperate with the Communists and the northern military leaders against Japan. When it appeared that genuine unity might develop on this basis, the Japanese army leaders launched a new and murderous assault upon China in July, 1937. The resulting conflict dragged on through dark and bloody years and finally became part of the Second World War. Subsequent developments will be reviewed below in connection with Japanese policy. The new aggression not only brought death to hundreds of thousands of Chinese and left millions homeless, but it resulted in a new Kuomintang-Communist coalition, in the emergence of a peoples' army, in the growth of cooperative industry and agriculture in the interior provinces, and in a genuine national regeneration of the Chinese masses. Despite the seizure of the coastal cities and the Yangtse valley, the invaders were balked by peasant partisans and by the ill-clad and ill-armed divisions which Chiang's government at Chungking was able to muster.

China's future, like that of India and indeed of all the subject peoples, depends at the time of writing on the decision of the sword. If Britain continues successful resistance, if American and Soviet aid flows to Chungking in sufficient amount, if Tokio is entangled in costly adventures elsewhere and ultimately defeated, a new and free Chinese nation will emerge from today's misery. If, conversely, Tokio establishes successfully its "New Order" in "Greater East Asia," if the Axis conquers Europe and Africa and brings Britain to ruin, China must either become a slave State or align itself completely with the U.S.S.R. in a possible war of liberation.

EFFORTS AT INTERNATIONAL CONTROL. The "white man's burden" in the twentieth century is promising to break the back of the bearer. The imperial nation-states have come into increasingly acute and disastrous conflict with one another over control of backward regions. The revolt of the colonial peoples has threatened the destruction of the empires. The efforts of the empire builders to meet this double danger have assumed a variety of forms, ranging from a deliberate repudiation of imperialism and the grant of complete or partial independence to subject populations, to belated (and ultimately futile) attempts on the part of rival imperial governments to compose their differences and evolve common programs of cooperative action.

Among the earlier efforts to diminish international frictions arising out of imperial rivalries were proposals to "internationalize" areas of tension, with economic opportunities open on equal terms to the nationals of all States or partitioned by agreement in some mutually satisfactory fashion. The port of Tangier, commanding the western entrance to the Mediterranean, was long a focal point of international rivalries. The "Convention Regarding the Organization of the Statute of the Tangier Zone," signed December 18, 1923, left "sovereignty" in the hands of the Sultan of Morocco (controlled by France), but placed the government of the city in the hands of a committee of control and an international legislative assembly. The seizure of the zone by Franco's Spain in June, 1940, terminated these arrangements, at least temporarily. In 1906 joint Anglo-French control was established over the New Hebrides, with a joint high commission, a joint court, and a joint naval commission. The Samoan Islands were under a joint Anglo-German-American condominium from 1889 to 1899, when they were partitioned. The Anglo-Egyptian Sudan was under the joint administration of Great Britain and Egypt. International control of this type is almost always unsatisfactory and is usually unsuccessful in the long run. Either one of the participating States secures a controlling voice in the administration, as at Tangier and in the mandates, or the checks and balances provided for lead to endless friction in which the interests of the natives are forgotten.

The Open Door represents an alternative solution which may be applied either to the possessions of colonial powers or to the regions of imperialist competition which are still independent. As an abstract principle, it means simply equality of economic opportunity in backward regions and equal treatment to nationals of all States without favors or discriminations. It is to trade and investment in colonial areas what most-favored-nation treatment is to the commerce among the Western States. As a concrete policy, the Open Door was championed most vigorously by States fearing the exclusion of their merchants and investors from some lucrative field of profit making. In principle, it was accepted by most States, since each State desires to prevent others from barring out its nationals from attractive preserves. In practice, it was ignored by most States in certain areas where the profits of special privilege and discimination were large. In theory, it tends to minimize political friction arising out of economic rivalries for markets by keeping such markets open on a basis of equality to all—"open" here meaning that customs tariffs, port duties, taxes, railway, steamship, and telegraph rates, judicial procedure, and law enforcement shall afford equal privileges for, and impose equal burdens upon, the nationals of all countries. Markets will then be conquered by price and quality, rather than by the sword or by political and economic favors and discriminations. But the policy was accepted less because of its theoretical advantages than because each State, in its quest for power and profits, had a tangible interest in keeping open trading opportunities in the colonies of other States and in preventing its rivals from converting independent areas into spheres of monopolistic exploitation.

Various efforts have been made to ensure by treaty the observance of the Open Door in colonies. The General Act of Berlin of 1885 provided for the maintenance of equality of economic opportunity in the Congo basin. Originally no tariff duties whatever were permitted in this area. In 1890 a 10 per cent ad valorem tariff was permitted by international agreement. In 1919 all limitations on the height of tariff walls were removed, subject to the condition that duties must be applied equally and in a nondiscriminatory fashion. At the same time an effort was made to apply the Open Door to other parts of Africa, but without success. In 1885 Germany and Great Britain agreed to observe the Open Door in their possessions on the Gulf of Guinea, and in 1898 Great Britain and France made a similar agreement for West Africa. The Anglo-German agreement of 1886 guaranteed the Open Door in the Pacific possessions of the two Powers. The Anglo-German-American agreement of 1899 contained a like provision for Samoa. But such arrangements are frequently violated, either openly or through various subtle favors and discriminations contrary to the spirit of the Open Door.

In the backward regions which are not colonies but are still held by native States, the scramble for markets and concessions led to the setting up of "spheres of influence" by the imperial Powers, in order that their nationals may enjoy exclusive opportunities for profit making in these areas. International agreements for the creation of such spheres usually contemplate the closing of the door to nationals of outside States. The Anglo-Russian compact of 1907 over Persia, the Franco-German agreement of 1914 relating to Turkey, the inter-Allied secret treaties of 1915–1917 dealing with the Near East, and sundry agreements concerning Africa and the Pacific were of this character. The pressure of outside States and the interests of the participating States have led, in some of these situations, to treaties for the preservation of the Open Door. The German-Russian agreement of 1910 pledged the parties to observe the Open Door in their respective spheres in Persia and Turkey. The Anglo-Franco-Italian agreement of 1906 over Ethiopia pledged equality of treatment in harbor and railway matters and cooperation in the acquisition of concessions. The Act of Algeciras of 1906 provided for "economic liberty without inequality" in Morocco. The United States was a party to this act. It has been the most consistent champion of the Open Door everywhere, save in the Caribbean and in its own possessions. The geographical position of the United States makes it difficult for the American Government to acquire exclusive spheres of interest for its nationals in Africa or Asia. In order to prevent their exclusion from the spheres of other Powers on these continents, it has striven to secure general recognition of the Open Door principle in treaties. These efforts, too, have been only moderately successful, since each Power is tempted to favor its own citizens in areas where it possesses influence and there is as yet no general agreement as to what does or does not constitute the Open Door in each concrete situation.

In recent decades the most acute diplomatic controversies over the Open Door have centered in China. In the nineteenth century the problem was primarily one of trading privileges. When such privileges were forcibly wrested from China by the European Powers in the first and second Opium Wars (1839–1842 and 1858–1860), the United States secured the same favors for its own citizens by the simple device of concluding most-favored-nation commercial treaties with the Chinese Government, obliging it to grant to the United States as favorable treatment as had been granted, or might in the future be granted, to other States. American commerce in China was protected in this fashion by the Cushing Treaty of 1844[1] and the Burlingame Treaty of 1868. Later the outlying dependencies of the empire—the Amur River provinces, the Liu-kiu Islands, Formosa, Hongkong, Korea, Annam, Tonkin, etc.— were detached and annexed by more powerful neighboring States. Following the Sino-Japanese War of 1894, there began that scramble for lease-holds and concessions which seemed to foreshadow the partitioning of the entire country into colonial possessions or spheres of foreign influence. Within each of these a particular Power would monopolize opportunities for trade, investment, and railway construction for its own mercantile and financial groups. Under these circumstances, the United States could hold itself aloof and thus lose its Chinese market, it could participate in the scramble—which would have been difficult in view of the inability of the United States to exercise its power effectively in the Far East—or it could seek to induce all the Powers to accept the Open Door principle.

[1] Caleb Cushing's instructions declared, "You will signify in decided terms and in a positive manner that the Government of the United States would find it impossible to remain on terms of friendship and regard with the Emperor if greater privileges or commercial facilities should be allowed to the subjects of any other government than should be granted to citizens of the United States." The Treaty of Wang-hsia of July 3, 1844 (Article 2), provided, "Citizens of the United States . . . shall in no case be subject to other or higher duties than are or shall be required of the people of any nation whatever. . . . And if conditional advantages or privileges, of whatever description, be conceded hereafter by China to any other nation, the United States and the citizens thereof shall be entitled thereupon to a complete, equal, and impartial participation in the same." Secretary of State Fish commented on the Burlingame Treaty of 1868, "The general principle which underlies the articles of July, 1868, is the recognition of the sovereign authority of the imperial Government at Peking over the people of the Chinese Empire and over their social, commercial, and political relations with the western Powers. . . . While it confirms the international jurisdiction conferred by former treaties upon European and American functionaries over the persons and properties of their countrymen, it recognizes at the same time the territorial integrity of China and prevents such a jurisdiction from being stretched beyond its original purpose."

It chose the latter course for obvious reasons. In spite of her Oriental possessions and spheres of influence, Great Britain had a similar interest in blocking French and Russian monopolistic designs on China. In 1898 the British Associated Chambers of Commerce dispatched a mission to China, headed by Lord Beresford, who subsequently championed the Open Door and the territorial integrity of China in his speeches in the United States. American commercial interests engaged in Chinese trade likewise brought pressure to bear upon the State Department.

On September 6, 1899, Secretary of State John Hay issued his famous circular letter, calling upon the Powers to subscribe to the principle that they would not interfere with Chinese tariff duties, harbor dues, or railway rates or with treaty ports or vested interests in their spheres of influence in China. Great Britain agreed at once, with France, Italy, Germany, Japan, and finally Russia following suit. On March 20, 1900, Hay announced that the American Government would regard the acceptance of the principle as "final and definitive." On July 3, 1900, following the outbreak of the Boxer Rebellion, Hay despatched a second circular note to the Powers in which he urged action to "bring about permanent safety and peace to China, preserve Chinese territorial and administrative entity, protect all rights guaranteed to friendly Powers by treaty and international law, and safeguard for the world the principle of equal and impartial trade with all parts of the Chinese Empire." In the Root-Takahira Agreement of November 30, 1908, Japan and the United States agreed to maintain the *status quo* and to "preserve the common interest of all Powers in China by supporting by all pacific means at their disposal the independence and integrity of China and the principle of equal opportunity for commerce and industry of all nations in that Empire." American friction with Japan over these issues became acute during the Great War. The Lansing-Ishii Agreement of November 3, 1917, reiterated the principles already agreed upon; but the United States recognized that "territorial propinquity creates special relations between countries" and that "Japan has special interests in China, particularly in the part to which her possessions are contiguous." This admission was withdrawn in 1923, following the Washington Conference. Here the United States was successful in securing for the first time the incorporation of the Open Door doctrine into a general treaty to which China itself was a party. The Nine Power Pact of February 6, 1922, entered into by the United States, Japan, Great Britain, France, Italy, China, Belgium, Portugal, and the Netherlands, declared (Article I),

The contracting Powers, other than China, agree: (1) to respect the sovereignty, the independence, and the territorial and administrative integrity of China; (2) to provide the fullest and most unembarrassed opportunity to China to develop and maintain for herself an effective and stable government; (3) to use their influence for the purpose of effectually establishing and maintaining the principle of equal opportunity for the commerce and industry of all nations throughout the territory of China; (4) to refrain from taking advantage of conditions in China in order to seek special rights or privileges which would abridge the rights of subjects or citizens of friendly States, and from countenancing action inimical to the security of such States.

The Powers also agreed (Article III) not to support their nationals in seeking monopolies or preferences prejudicial to nationals of other Powers or "any general superiority of rights with respect to commercial or economic development in any designated region of China" or (Article IV) "any agreements . . . designed to create spheres of influence or to provide for the enjoyment of mutually exclusive opportunities in designated parts of Chinese territory." The treaty of the same date relating to the Chinese customs tariff likewise provided for equality of treatment. The resolutions of the Conference set up a board of reference to which questions arising out of these obligations might be submitted (third resolution) and provided for publicity of all treaties, agreements, and private contracts for concessions, franchises, and other privileges in China (tenth resolution). These agreements did not invalidate existing concessions and spheres or pass judgment as to whether they were in conformity with the Open Door principle. The board of reference was to deal only with future concessions and contracts. The publicity provisions were ineffective, and general abstract principles were not translated into definite and specific engagements accompanied by adequate international machinery to ensure observance of the Open Door.

It soon became clear that the future of the Open Door in China was by no means safeguarded by these treaty arrangements and that the door was in process of being gradually pushed shut in the Japanese sphere and, to a lesser degree, in the British and French spheres. The Japanese seizure of Manchuria and the creation of the puppet State of Manchukuo were regarded at Washington and Geneva as a violation of the Nine Power Pact. The Stimson doctrine of nonrecognition of agreements, situations, or territorial gains achieved by force was motivated as much by a desire to protect the American conception of the Open Door in China as by regard for the Kellogg-Briand Pact. The doctrine has to date been without visible effect upon Japanese policy. The only ultimate safeguard of the Open Door is China's own power to protect herself from aggression and to keep her territories open on equal terms to nationals of all States. The victory of Japanese imperialism in East Asia will inevitably spell the end of the Open Door—and of an independent China as well.

THE MANDATE SYSTEM. The most significant international effort to deal effectively with the double problem of imperialism—that of protecting native interests and that of keeping the peace among the empire builders—is to be found in the Mandate System, devised at the Paris Peace Conference of 1919 and administered by the League of Nations.

Out of a complex background of "trusteeship," "self-determination," "rights of small nations," political expediency, and humanitarian sentiments, there emerged on the eve of the Peace Conference the ideas which were subsequently incorporated into Article 22 of the League Covenant and into the mandate agreements. On December 16, 1918, General Jan Smuts of South Africa published a scheme for the international control of certain regions formerly belonging to Austria-Hungary and Turkey. He had no expectation that his plan would be applied to the former German colonies in Africa, since it was contemplated that these would be annexed by the victors. President Wilson enlarged upon this plan in his second draft of the Covenant (January 10, 1919) and argued vigorously for its general application to the outlying possessions of the defeated Powers. In his Fourteen Points of January 8, 1918, Wilson had declared that "the interests of the populations concerned must have equal weight with the equitable claims of the government whose title is to be determined" (fifth point) and that "the nationalities which are now under Turkish rule should be assured an undoubted security of life and an absolutely unmolested opportunity of autonomous development" (twelfth point).

At the Conference, however, these proposals encountered the annexationist aspirations which had been incorporated into the secret treaties negotiated during the war. Under the Sykes-Picot Agreement of 1916 and other inter-Allied commitments of the same period, the former Turkish possessions in the Near East were to be partitioned between Great Britain and France. These Powers had likewise agreed to the division of the German African colonies which their military forces had occupied, and Japan had secret treaties of February-March, 1917, with Great Britain, France, Italy, and Russia, whereby she was promised the German Pacific islands north of the Equator. But outright annexation was precluded by the pledges made during the war to certain native chieftains, notably in Arabia, and by the idealistic verbiage in which Allied war aims had been clothed. Complete independence for these regions was never seriously contemplated, and their restoration to Germany and Turkey was of course inconceivable. The distribution of the territories was already provided for in the secret treaties, and these would be followed in any case. The only question was the form in which the victors should take control. France desired to recruit black troops in the new African territories allotted to her. The British Dominions sought to close their new territories to foreign trade and immigration. Wilson secured general acceptance of the mandate principle only by yielding to the British Dominions on the Open Door, to France on the recruitment of native soldiers, and to all of the Allies on the maintenance of the territorial allocation provided for in the secret treaties.

Article 22 of the League Covenant in its final form referred to the former enemy territories, "which are inhabited by peoples not yet able to

Mandates	Area, square miles	Population	Mandatory
Class A Mandates			
Iraq....................................	116,600	3,700,000	Great Britain
Syria and Lebanon.......................	77,220	3,650,000	France
Palestine and Trans-Jordan...............	26,230	1,700,000	Great Britain
Class B Mandates			
Tanganyika............................	360,000	5,200,000	Great Britain
Ruanda-Urundi..........................	20,500	3,450,000	Belgium
Togoland (British).......................	13,041	340,000	Great Britain
Togoland (French).......................	21,893	750,000	France
Cameroons (British)......................	34,136	840,000	Great Britain
Cameroons (French)......................	166,489	2,520,000	France
Class C Mandates			
Southwest Africa........................	318,099	300,000	South Africa
New Guinea............................	93,000	670,000	Australia
North Pacific Islands.....................	960	100,000	Japan
Western Samoa..........................	1,130	60,000	New Zealand
Nauru..................................	9	3,400	Great Britain

stand by themselves under the strenuous conditions of the modern world." To these territories was to be applied the principle "that the well-being and development of such peoples form a sacred trust of civilization and that securities for the performance of this trust should be embodied in this Covenant." The "tutelage" of such peoples was to be entrusted to the "advanced nations" best able to assume this responsibility and was to be "exercised by them as mandatories on behalf of the League."

By Article 119 of the Treaty of Versailles, Germany was compelled to renounce her colonies to the principal Allied and Associated Powers. During the Peace Conference, they were distributed with few departures from the terms of the secret treaties. On May 7, 1919, the Pacific Islands were divided among Great Britain, Australia, New Zealand, and Japan, subject to an informal reservation by President Wilson regarding the Island of Yap, which he thought ought to be an internationalized cable center. German Southwest Africa was assigned to the Union of South Africa, German East Africa to Great Britain, and Togoland and Cam-

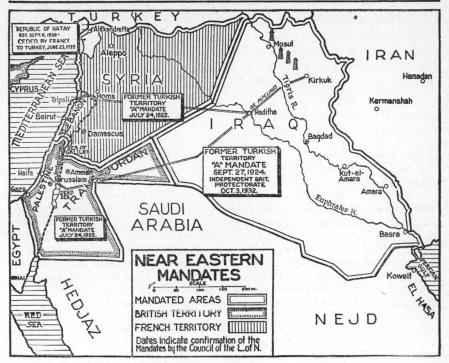

Near Eastern Mandates

eroons were partitioned between Great Britain and France. The French Government originally insisted upon full sovereignty but finally contented itself with annexing that portion of Cameroons ceded to Germany in 1911. France insisted, however, upon her right to recruit troops in her African mandates for general war purposes, in spite of Article 22 of the Covenant. Belgium objected to the transfer of all of East Africa to Great Britain and on May 30, 1919, was granted Ruanda-Urundi by the British Government. Portugal demanded a mandate but received merely recognition of her sovereignty over Kionga, a small territory adjacent to Mozambique which she had recognized as belonging to Germany in 1894. The Turkish territory was distributed at San Remo on April 25, 1920. The British and French Governments failed to cooperate with Wilson in his efforts to ascertain the wishes of the inhabitants. He had sent the King-Crane Commission to the Near East in June-July, 1919. Its report revealed that Arab sentiment favored an independent united Syria, including Palestine, and strongly opposed the Zionist project, sponsored by Great Britain, to convert Palestine into a new Jewish homeland. If independence could not be secured, the Arabs preferred the United States as mandatory, with Great Britain as second choice. This report was kept secret until 1922 and was ignored by the Allied Governments. France was assigned Syria and the Lebanon, and Great Britain received Palestine,

Trans-Jordan,* and Mesopotamia. The United States refused the proffer of a mandate over Armenia, which was subsequently divided between Turkey and the U.S.S.R. in defiance of the Allies. Under the abortive Treaty of Sèvres of 1920, Greece sought to annex the hinterland of Smyrna, and Italy and France had marked out Adalia and Cilicia, respectively, as annexations. But following the Turkish Nationalist victory over the Greeks these regions were restored to Turkey by the Treaty of Lausanne of 1923.

The actual "mandates" in the legal sense were the agreements concluded between the Allied and Associated Powers under the direction of the Supreme Council. It was here that the A, B, and C classification was made, in conformity with the three categories mentioned in Article 22 of the Covenant. Japan objected to the Closed Door in the British Pacific mandates. The United States objected that British oil interests had been granted exclusive privileges in Palestine and Mesopotamia. It expressed its regret over the San Remo oil agreement of December 23, 1920, whereby Great Britain granted France a 25 per cent share of the oil resources of Mesopotamia. The American Government reasserted the Open Door principle and declared that although it was not a member of the League it would not submit to the exclusion of its nationals from the benefits of equality of treatment. Lord Curzon agreed in principle to these contentions in February, 1921, but declared that American policy in the Philippines, Haiti, and Costa Rica was not consistent with the Open Door. In November, 1925, American oil interests (Rockefeller, Sinclair, and Doheny) were granted 25 per cent of the shares of the Turkish Petroleum Company, which secured from Iraq an exclusive concession for the exploitation of the oil resources of the Bagdad and Mosul areas. The United States likewise objected to the omission of the Yap reservation in the Japanese mandate. The United States subsequently concluded treaties with Japan, France, Great Britain, and Belgium, safeguarding the rights of American nationals to equal treatment. These negotiations delayed final action on the mandate agreements. All these instruments were subject to confirmation by the League Council. The C mandates were confirmed by the Council on December 17, 1920. The B mandates were similarly confirmed on July 20, 1922.

Additional delays occurred before the A mandates were finally approved. The Palestine mandate was objected to by the Papacy, the Moslems, the Jews, and the British House of Lords—all for different and mutually incompatible reasons. Italy objected to confirmation of both the Palestine and the Syrian mandates. These mandates were tentatively confirmed by the Council on July 22, 1922, and subsequently given full approval with the announcement of a Franco-Italian agreement on September 29, 1923. The Arabs of Mesopotamia revolted against the British mandate, with the result that Great Britain recognized the Kingdom of Iraq, with Feisal, son of King Hussein of the Hejaz, as its ruler. A British-Iraq treaty of October 10, 1922, to be in effect for four years, defined British power in the new State and raised doubts as to whether Iraq was still a mandate or not. On September 27, 1924, the Council approved a document which made Iraq a British mandate but accepted the new treaty provisions, along with supplementary British pledges defining the mandatory's obligations. The boundary dispute over the Mosul district between Iraq and Turkey was submitted to the League Council by the Treaty of Lausanne of July 24, 1923. The Council award granting the district to Iraq was contingent upon Great Britain's remaining

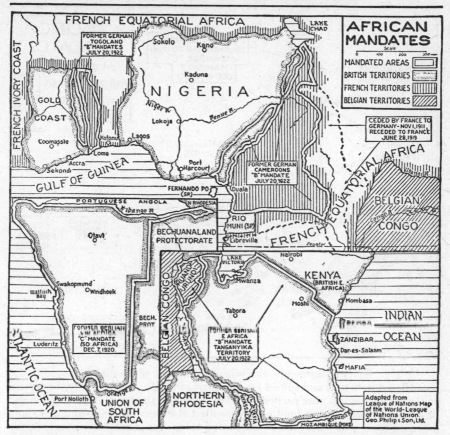

mandatory for twenty-five years, unless Iraq should be admitted earlier to the League. On March 11, 1926, the Council ratified the Mosul award, following a new British-Iraq treaty of January 13. On June 5, 1926, Turkey recognized the new boundary in return for the neutralization of the frontier and 10 per cent of the Iraq oil royalties. A third British-Iraq treaty of December 14, 1927, was not ratified; and on November 4, 1929, the British Government announced that it would recommend Iraq for admission to the League in 1932. On October 3, 1932, Iraq became the fifty-seventh member of the League of Nations by a vote of the Assembly and thus began its career as an independent State under British protection.[1]

[1] Nicholas Politis, President of the Assembly, characterized the admission as follows: "We see, with the consent and to the satisfaction of all, that a new State has come peacefully into existence, whereas in past centuries that State could probably only have come into existence by violent means. The League, therefore, once more has shown the error of those who think it merely exists to crystallize the present situation and prevent the normal development of the world. The admittance of Iraq shows that the League offers the possibility of carrying out peacefully what might otherwise have required revolution, and when, despite the difficulties and anxieties of the present time, we see a League of Nations doing its regular work so successfully, I think we realize that the crisis from which the League is supposed to be suffering is apparent rather than real" (Assembly meeting, October 3, 1932).

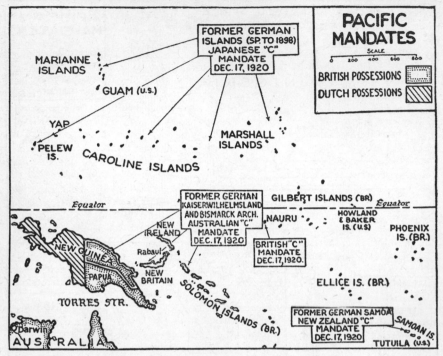

In these final arrangements, the original principle of the mandate system was "mutilated in details and sullied by the spirit of barter."[1] The essential purposes of the secret treaties were carried out. The wishes of the population were ignored in Palestine and Syria and not even consulted elsewhere. In Togoland and Cameroons, France was permitted to use native troops for general war purposes outside the territory. The Open Door, formerly maintained by Germany in the C mandates, was closed by the mandatories. It was protected in the A mandates neither by the Covenant nor by the mandate agreements, but only by subsequent treaties, negotiated largely at the insistence of the United States. Only in the B mandates was there a definite obligation laid upon the mandatories to maintain the Open Door. The Powers seemed to regard the mandates as annexations, as shown by the "compensations" granted to Italy in Jubaland (Kenya colony), in the Jarabud oasis, in Egypt, and in a strip of eastern Tunis. For all practical purposes, the C mandates were treated as annexations and the B mandate administration was scarcely distinguishable from that which would have been provided for outright conquest. The A mandates were also under the effective control of the mandatories.

In all these regions save Iraq, the aspirations of the inhabitants toward independence and self-determination were crushed with the same ruthlessness which has characterized imperialism everywhere. When, in 1922, the Bondelzwart tribe in Southwest Africa resisted governmental measures designed to further the economic interests of the white settlers at the expense of the natives, South Africa replied with machine guns and bombing planes, which slaughtered scores of men, women, and children in the native villages. In Palestine the chronic

[1] Quincy Wright, *Mandates under the League of Nations*, 1930, p. 63.

friction between Arabs and Jews, engendered by British and Zionist efforts to create a Jewish settlement in what is preponderantly a Moslem country, led to rioting and strife, with the British authorities (in the eyes of the Arab leaders) acting in accordance with the ancient principle of "divide and rule." The Syrians were subjected to French control against their wishes, and they indulged in insurrections almost annually until 1927. The Jebel Druze revolt of 1925 was repressed with the utmost severity by the French military forces, which attempted to terrorize the population into submission by destroying with artillery the whole central area of the ancient city of Damascus, with the loss of thousands of lives. Other disorders in Iraq, western Samoa, and elsewhere were likewise dealt with by punitive expeditions and violent reprisals, as seems inevitable where white imperialists rule natives, regardless of the form of administration. Africans and Polynesians were unable to distinguish the new modes of oppression and exploitation from the old. The Moslem leaders of the Near East waxed indignant over the new dispensation. Imperialist diplomats condemned the system as involving all the obligations of annexation, with few of the advantages. Germans, Americans, Turks, Russians, and Arabs jeered at the mandate principle as a hollow mockery. The mandatory governments usually refused to spend any more money on the mandates than they collected in local revenue, and they tended to treat the mandates as outright conquests. In the light of these circumstances, cynics and pessimists concluded that the system was a hypocritical sham, designed to disguise old imperialistic wolves in new sheep's clothing.[1]

Regardless of these shortcomings, the Mandate System represented a significant adventure in international supervision over backward areas.[2] The whole procedure of League supervision centered in the Permanent Mandates Commission (P.M.C.). In accordance with the provisions of Article 22 of the Covenant, this body was established by the Council to advise it on mandate questions. It was originally composed of nine members, with a majority of nationals of non-mandatory Powers. In 1924, M. Rappard, formerly head of the Mandates Section of the Secretariat, was made an "extraordinary member" and provision was also made for an advisory member from the International Labor Office (I.L.O.). In 1927 the number of regular members was increased to ten, in order to provide a place for a German national.

The observations of the P.M.C. were purely advisory, but in practice it became the agent of the Council, through which international supervision was exercised. The P.M.C. received its information from the annual reports of the mandatory powers, from questioning their representatives, and from petitions submitted by the inhabitants of the mandated regions. Such petitions, however, could be submitted only through the mandatory government, and the Commission refused to consider petitions opposing the mandate itself. In March, 1927, the Council decided that petitioners should not be granted oral hearing. The P.M.C. also received information from other League bodies, but it never visited the mandated areas nor dispatched investigators to them.

A survey of the Commission's proceedings leads to the conclusion that it was primarily dependent upon the mandatory Powers for information and that the

[1] See *ibid.*, pp. 64–98, "The Reception of the System," for a résumé of favorable and unfavorable evaluations.

[2] At the conclusion of an exhaustive discussion of the legal aspects of the Mandate System, Quincy Wright concludes that "sovereignty of the areas is vested in the League, acting through the Covenant-amending process, and is exercised by the mandatory with consent of the Council for eventful transfer to the mandated communities themselves." *Ibid.*, p. 530.

native populations, in whose interest the whole system was presumably established, had little opportunity for the independent presentation of grievances or for a full and impartial hearing. The Commission did serve to mobilize opinion and, by its suggestions, influenced the conduct of the mandatories to some degree and made a beginning of establishing international standards of colonial administration. But it cannot be said that the P.M.C. acted vigorously as a bold and independent agency determined to protect native interests, regardless of the prestige of the mandatories. Whether international friction in the backward regions was greater or less, whether the natives were better off or worse off than would have been the case under some alternative arrangement, no one can say with any degree of certainty. The collapse of the League and the war of 1939, which was, among other things, an "imperialist war," brought the system to an abrupt and ignoble end—possibly temporary, probably permanent.

In the last analysis, the essential nature of imperialism constitutes a stubborn and irreducible obstacle to the complete success of the efforts reviewed above. Imperialism is the imposition by force and violence of alien rule upon subject peoples, despite all moralizings and pretensions to the contrary. The empires of today are maintained by holding dissatisfied backward peoples in subjection. The empires of the future will be created by the same process. Force to the utmost has been and still is the final arbiter in disputes between subject peoples and imperial governments and among the imperial States themselves. Those who are ruled submit willingly to forcible control by rulers when they feel that the rulers represent themselves, or symbolize certain common interests of the whole community, or are acting disinterestedly on behalf of the welfare of their subjects. They resent coercion, and resist it when they have the means, in every situation in which the rulers are set apart from themselves by race, language, culture, or cleavages of economic interests. The first and most elementary defense reaction on the part of the imperial governments in the face of resistance from their subjects is to crush such resistance by force and to adopt policies designed to enfeeble their victims and to destroy their identity. Such States have frequently, though seldom successfully, adopted the nationalistic policy of cultural assimilation.

THE SECOND RETREAT. The almost uniform failure of this policy has led to the development of various forms of autonomy, protection, and native participation in local government. Native rulers and native institutions are retained as the basis of foreign control. Decentralization is substituted for bureaucratic authority at the center. Legislation for the colonies is enacted by local assemblies, subject to various limitations and controls. Executive power is entrusted to an appointed governor who is given considerable discretion. Local courts are maintained, and military and fiscal affairs are handled in such a fashion as to encourage local participation and local responsibility. This system was most extensively developed in the British Empire under the new colonial policy inaugurated after the American Revolution and the Canadian rebellion. In the native States of India and in Nigeria, Uganda, and Tanganyika, native princes or chieftains were used as agents of colonial government. In Morocco and Tunis, the French Government maintained in operation the native monarchies, whose rulers were aided by French "advisers." Where the impact of Western civilization has disintegrated native social and political institutions, this solution is of course unworkable. But in most of the colonial areas of Africa and Asia it is still quite feasible.

A more extreme policy is represented by the actual emancipation of colonial possessions or by the establishment of forms of control which are compatible with theoretical independence. The most significant instances of imperial States definitely relinquishing power over possessions without being compelled to do so by *force majeure* are to be found in the British Empire and the United States. The British Dominions became fully self-governing, with representative parliaments and responsible cabinets; and though still units of the British Commonwealth, acknowledging allegiance to the King and to the local governors-general of the crown, they became for all practical purposes independent. It is safe to say that they would all sooner or later have followed the example of the thirteen Atlantic seaboard colonies in 1776, had they not been granted self-government in this fashion. With the exception of South Africa, the Dominions were all inhabited by English immigrants, and in South Africa the native black majority was kept from political power by franchise restrictions giving the English and Dutch settlers effective control.

After the Spanish-American War, the United States "emancipated" Cuba as an independent State. The "Platt amendment" to the Army Appropriation Act of 1900, however, was incorporated into the Cuban Constitution of 1903 and the Cuban-American treaty of the same year. It forbade Cuba to alienate its independence, limited the public debt, and reserved to the United States the right to acquire coaling-stations and naval bases and to intervene to preserve order and protect Cuba's independence. The Hay-Bunau-Varilla Treaty of November 18, 1903, with Panama similarly made this State an American protectorate, without damaging its "sovereignty" save in the Canal Zone. American dollar diplomacy in the Caribbean has devised various schemes of financial advisers, customs collectors, and marine intervention which ensure effective American control without destroying the fiction of independence.

The Near East

In February, 1922, Egypt, formerly a British protectorate in form as well as in fact, was granted its "independence," *i.e.*, became a British protectorate only in fact but not in form. Great Britain reserved control over security of communication, defense, the protection of foreign interests and properties, and the

Anglo-Egyptian Sudan. The British Government declared, moreover, that it would "regard as an unfriendly act any interference in the affairs of Egypt by another Power, and it will consider any aggression against the territory of Egypt as an act to be repelled with all the means at their command." British troops continued to be stationed in the country, and the Egyptian army remained under the command of Sir Lee Stack, Governor-General of the Sudan, much to the disgust of the Egyptian Nationalists and of Zaghlul Pasha, the native Prime Minister. When Sir Lee was murdered on November 9, 1924, the British Government dispatched a stiff ultimatum to Cairo and compelled Egypt to accede to its demands (including a $2,500,000 indemnity) by occupying the customs house at Alexandria. When Egypt appealed to the League of Nations, the British Government successfully sustained its contention that this was a "domestic question" beyond the purview of Geneva. The Egyptian Constitution of April 19, 1924, did not expressly reserve British rights, but a British high commissioner and British civil and military advisers remained at the capital.

Following widespread unrest and disturbances during the Anglo-Italian crisis of 1935–1936, London felt obliged to make greater concessions to Egypt. By the terms of a new Anglo-Egyptian treaty of August 26, 1936, which was to run for twenty years, British military occupation was terminated, save for the temporary maintenance of small forces in the Canal area. Britain agreed to exchange ambassadors with Egypt, to support her application for membership in the League, and to cooperate in seeking abolition of the régime of capitulations. Egypt agreed to act as an ally of Britain, with each State coming to the aid of the other in war, subject to the obligations of the Covenant and the Pact of Paris. In 1940, Egypt severed diplomatic relations with Italy and welcomed British defense, but did not declare war—despite the presence of Italian invaders on her soil during the autumn, prior to their defeat and expulsion by General Wavell's "British and Imperial Army of the Nile."

This arrangement resembled the British alliance with Iraq, incorporated in treaties of 1922–1924 and 1930. It was a model for the French-Syrian treaty negotiated in September, 1936, which promised a comparable degree of qualified independence for Syria but was never ratified. Arab efforts to halt Jewish immigration to Palestine, culminating in bloodshed and a half-year "strike" in 1936, rendered any grant of independence to the Jewish homeland improbable. In any case, pipe lines from the Mosul oil fields of Iraq reach Mediterranean ports (Tripoli and Haifa) through Syria and Palestine. These regions, as well as Egypt, were the centers of British and French power in the Near East. With that power increasingly threatened by Italy, elementary considerations of strategy dictated concessions to the native population to quiet unrest and checkmate Italian intrigue. But they also forbade any grant of "independence" which might imperil military and naval control.

The Philippines

Perhaps the most striking instance of a voluntary abandonment of imperialistic policies on the part of any Great Power still committed to the promotion of private exports of goods and capital is furnished by the United States in the years of the Great Depression. Recent American policy toward the Philippines has been influenced less by those interested in maintaining American control—investors, exporters, diplomats, and strategists—than by economic-interest groups anxious to close the American domestic market to the islands by granting them independence. The American Federation of Labor has sought to bar Filipino workers from the United States. Beet sugar and cottonseed oil interests have striven to keep out Philippine cane sugar and coconut oil. These groups, buttressed by Democratic party leaders committed to anti-imperialism and to the pledge of independence contained in the Jones Act of 1916, succeeded in pushing through Congress over President Hoover's veto the Hawes-Cutting bill of January 7, 1933, which provided for independence in ten years. The Philippine legislature, however, demanded immediate independence and refused to accept the terms of the act. On President Roosevelt's recommendation, Congress passed the Tydings-McDuffie bill which became law on March 31, 1934. It likewise provided for independence after a ten-year period at the expiration of which the United States would abandon all military stations and negotiate as to the status of naval bases. During the transition period of the Philippine "Commonwealth," the number of Filipinos permitted to enter the United States annually was limited to fifty. The act further provided for annual duty-free quotas of 850,000 tons of sugar, 200,000 tons of coconut oil, and 3,000,000 pounds of cordage and fibers, with imports above these figures paying full American tariff duties. Between the sixth and tenth years, the Philippine Government is required to levy an export tax on products sent to the United States, beginning at 5 per cent of the American tariff and rising to 25 per cent. After 1946 the full American tariff will apply unless some alternative arrangement is made. Meanwhile, American goods shall be admitted to the islands free of duty. The Philippine Legislature accepted these terms on May 1, 1934. An additional Act of Congress imposed a processing tax of 3 cents per pound on coconut oil, thus striking another blow at Philippine imports into the United States.

The new Constitution of the Philippine Commonwealth, completed on February 8, 1935, was approved by President Roosevelt and ratified by the Filipino voters. It provided for a popularly elected president with a six-year term and an elected, one-chambered National Assembly. The new Supreme Court may declare laws unconstitutional only by a two-thirds vote. The United States retains financial powers, control of foreign affairs, a right of intervention, and authority to review legislation and judicial decisions. On November 15, 1935, Manuel Quezon was inaugurated as first President of the Commonwealth. Frank Murphy ceased to be "Governor-General" and became High Commissioner. On July 4, 1946, the completely independent Philippine Republic will presumably be launched. Meanwhile, measures are under way to train a Filipino army and to render the Commonwealth secure against possible attack—with Japan as an unnamed prospective aggressor. The Japanese threat may well lead to a modification of present arrangements before 1946.

The Caribbean

The retreat of the United States from its imperial position in the Caribbean has been scarcely less impressive. In March, 1930, the J. Reuben Clark Memorandum on the Monroe Doctrine, subsequently reiterated by Hoover and Stimson, Roosevelt and Hull, asserted that the Doctrine would not henceforth be used to justify intervention by the United States in Latin America. When the President-Dictator of Cuba, Gerardo Machado, was overthrown by revolution in August, 1933, the American Government refrained from landing marines, though it withheld recognition from the radical régime of Grau San Martin, established in September. When the more conservative Carlos Mendieta became President in a new overturn, the United States granted recognition on January 23, 1934. On May 29, 1934, a new treaty abrogated the "Platt Amendment" treaty of

May 22, 1903, and abolished all American rights of intervention or of military or fiscal control. The commercial reciprocity treaty of August 24, 1934, sought to restore the American market to Cuban exports. Dr. Miguel Gomez was elected to the Cuban Presidency on January 10, 1936, with Colonel Fulgencio Batista, the reactionary head of the army, remaining the real power behind the scenes. When Gomez refused to yield to Batista's demands for the militarization of Cuba's rural schools, Batista forced him out of office through impeachment proceedings and replaced him on December 24, 1936, with President Laredo Bru who was a pliant tool of the army. In 1940, Batista elevated himself to the Presidency. American "nonintervention" in Cuba thus had the somewhat paradoxical consequence of maintaining in power a semi-Fascist military dictatorship.

Haiti, to the east of Cuba, was under American military occupation since 1915. Following the rejection by the Haitian National Assembly of a Haitian-American treaty of September 3, 1932, by which the 1915 arrangements were terminated and the United States relinquished control of the Black Republic, the two Governments accomplished the same result by an executive agreement of August 7, 1933. The last of the marines withdrew on October 15, 1934, though American fiscal control was continued to ensure payment on the $14,150,000 worth of Haitian bonds, largely held by the National City Bank of New York. A Haitian-American trade agreement of March 28, 1935, promised to restore profitable commercial relations. American marines were similarly withdrawn in January, 1933, from Nicaragua where they had supervised the elections of 1928, 1930, and 1932, officered the Nicaraguan National Guard, and fought the rebel forces of General Augusto Sandino. With the American marines gone, Sandino laid down his arms, only to be murdered in February, 1934, with the connivance of Nicaraguan officials. The United States had never imposed on Nicaragua a formal treaty giving it a general right of intervention. But here as elsewhere in the Caribbean the policy of the "good neighbor" has meant an abandonment of intervention, a restoration of authority to the local government, and a return to a *de facto* policy of recognition.[1]

The new dispensation was motivated by a desire to regain Latin American good will and thereby to restore shrinking markets for American exports. Economic nationalism in the epoch of depression has dictated the emancipation of the Philippines as well as the surrender of control over Caribbean Republics. These gestures of withdrawal have not modified American political and strategic interests in the regions in question, nor do they necessarily imply any surrender of American economic and financial interests. Over half of the foreign trade of Central America is with the United States. American private capital investments remain impressive: in Cuba, $1,000,000,000; Mexico, $700,000,000; the Central American Republics, $234,500,000; Venezuela, $232,500,000; and Colombia, $124,000,000. This economic stake can be protected and increased without a resumption of the more obvious forms of imperial control only if internal stability and security prevail in the Caribbean States. This in turn is largely dependent upon that prosperity which can be provided only by a restoration of a profitable market in the United States for Caribbean products. Since no other Great Power threatens the position of the United States, Washington can afford to experiment

[1] "In the field of world policy I would dedicate this nation to the policy of the good neighbor—the neighbor who resolutely respects himself and, because he does so, respects the rights of others—the neighbor who respects his obligations and respects the sanctity of his agreements in and with a world of neighbors." Franklin D. Roosevelt, March 4, 1933.

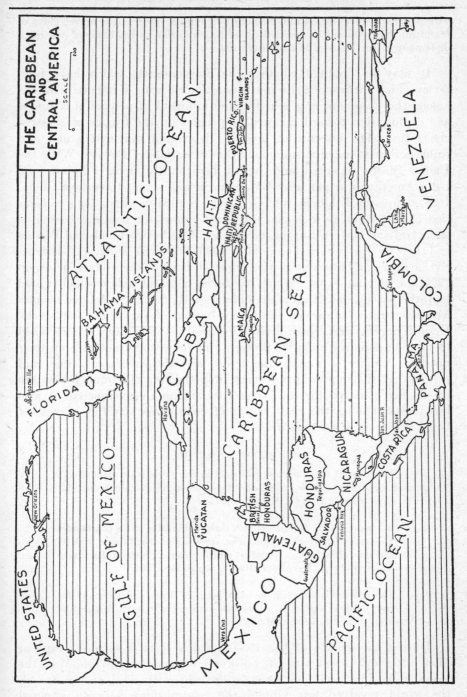

THE CARIBBEAN AND CENTRAL AMERICA

SCALE

with policies of moderation and cooperation. For the present the velvet glove of friendship has replaced the mailed fist of intervention on the hand of American diplomacy in the lands of the southern sea.

It may be doubted whether the developments which have been reviewed foreshadow any diminution on a world scale of imperial rivalries among the Powers or any general relinquishment of policies of conquest and exploitation toward the weaker peoples on the fringes of Western civilization. The insecurities bred by depression nurtured a new and ruthless Fascist imperialism among the "unsatiated" Powers. While the United States repented and smiled benignantly upon Filipinos and Latin Americans, Japan seized Manchuria and sought to enslave China, Italy conquered Ethiopia, and Germany coupled demands for a restoration of lost colonies with gigantic preparations for imperial conquests in central and eastern Europe. Savage conflicts between imperial Powers and their victims occurred anew after 1929. Far more savage and destructive armed combats among the imperial Powers themselves began in 1939 and put an end to efforts to devise a world policy which would keep the peace among the empire builders and protect the colored peoples who have thus far carried the heavy burden of the white man's rule. Despite hopeful gestures and pleas for sanity, the Western States failed to solve imperialism's double problem, for they would not give up their quest for empire or modify the credos and the social, economic, and political relationships which generate imperialism. The quest for empire breeds fierce hatred for the conquerors among the conquered. It also breeds war among the rival camps of conquerors. Its full harvest of blood and tears is yet to be reaped.

2. BLOOD AND SOIL

Never forget that the most holy right in this world is the right to soil, and that the most hallowed of sacrifices is the blood which one sheds for this soil.—ADOLF HITLER, *Mein Kampf.*

If I had the Ural Mountains with their incalculable stores of treasures in raw materials, Siberia with its vast forests, and the Ukraine with its tremendous wheat fields, Germany under National Socialist leadership would swim in plenty.—ADOLF HITLER, September, 1936.

The conflict is between the vital needs of Italy and Germany for territory and a régime of superfluous territory of Great Britain and France.—VIRGINIO GAYDA, May, 1939.

During the decade of the 1930's, which opened with the rape of Manchuria and closed with the outbreak of the Second World War, the issues of international politics most fraught with weal or woe for all the world revolved less around the relationships between imperial

Great Powers and colonial peoples than around those between the Powers with great colonial empires and the Powers which aspired to have great colonial empires. In Britain and France, debilitated and feckless leaders sought to meet the threat to their vast imperial domains by attempts to buy peace through concessions. This policy greatly strengthened the Fascist Powers and brought the Western States to war and disaster. The diplomacy of appeasement exhibited on the grandest scale the clash of rival imperial ambitions (if a contest in which one side always advances and the other always yields can be called a "clash") and the emergence of the new totalitarian imperialism which differed sharply from the old colonialism of dividends and markets in undeveloped areas.

The road to ruin for the Western Powers, down which the Fascist Caesars marched toward world hegemony, was lined with the great milestones of appeasement marking the times and places where France and Britain gave away other peoples' rights or territories, and occasionally their own, in an effort to bribe their enemies into good behavior. These agreements fell into two groups: those relating to totalitarian claims to new rights or territories in Europe (the Anglo-German naval accord of June 18, 1935; the Spanish "Nonintervention" agreements of August 1936; the Munich and post-Munich pacts of 1938), and those relating to totalitarian claims to overseas colonial territories (the Laval-Mussolini compact of January 7, 1935; the Ciano-Perth accord of April 16, 1938; the French-Turkish alliance of June 23, 1939; and the Anglo-Japanese agreement of July 24, 1939). The first group of agreements will be dealt with elsewhere in these pages. The second group deserves consideration here.

APPEASING JAPANESE IMPERIALISM. The paths of empire trod by the war lords of Nippon brought under Japanese control large numbers of Koreans, Manchurians, Mongolians, and Chinese. They also led to conflict, actual or potential, with the U.S.S.R., Britain, France, and the United States. Soviet policy after 1935 was one of resisting by force every Japanese effort to encroach upon the Maritime Provinces, the Amur River territories, or Outer Mongolia. This policy was sufficiently successful to prevent any extension of Japanese power at the expense of the Soviet Union or its protectorates. The Western democracies, on the other hand, coupled verbal protests with refusal to use force and with periodical concessions. They accordingly suffered "loss of face" and were obliged to yield position after position to Tokio.

This process was first displayed in the aftermath of the Japanese occupation of Manchuria in September, 1931. The efforts of Secretary of State Stimson to invoke the Nine Power Pact against Japanese aggression were repeatedly thwarted by Sir John Simon, British Foreign

Secretary. During February, 1932, Stimson telephoned Simon four times to plead for cooperation. Each time Simon refused. "I finally became convinced," wrote Stimson later, "that the British Government felt reluctant to join in such a démarche. . . . My plan was therefore blocked. . . . I seemed doomed to inaction, while a great tragedy was following its predestined course."[1]

The result of British policy was to enable Japan to retain Manchuria in defiance of the other signatories of the Covenant, of the Pact of Paris, and of the Nine Power Pact. Secretary Stimson felt that America could not act alone. He was forced to limit himself to a futile gesture in the form of the nonrecognition doctrine linked with his name. When Japanese aggression was renewed in 1933 and again on a larger scale in 1937, more verbal protests came from the Western Powers, but no action save futile resolutions at Geneva and at Brussels where a conference of signatories of the Nine Power Pact (other than Japan) assembled in futility and adjourned in despair in November, 1937. With no interference from their government, American citizens continued to supply the Japanese war machine with some 60 per cent of its imports of oil, scrap metal, planes, trucks, and other equipment. With no interference from their government, British subjects continued to supply another 20 per cent. Downing Street and Washington continued to protest to Tokio at violations of the Open Door. The Japanese military leaders continued to ride roughshod over British and American interests wherever

[1] *The Far Eastern Crisis*, New York, Harper & Brothers, 1936, pp. 164–165. The Tory press in Britain fully approved Simon's stand. Thus the *Morning Post*, November 16, 1931: "Nothing could be more foolish than any attempt on the part of the League Council to invoke against Japan the 'economic sanctions' stipulated in Article 16 of the Covenant. . . . A policy which risked embroiling the world for the sake of peace would be a mockery. What is at issue is something more important than the dignity of the League of Nations." And again, January 30, 1932: "For our part, although we do not believe in peace at any price, we value it enough to beware of entering into superfluous danger in a doubtful cause. Japan, broadly speaking, is the only element making for order and good government in the Far East." Also the *Daily Mail*, November 5, 1931: "Japan's presence in Manchuria has been a benefit to the world. . . . Not for a moment would the people of this country permit an attitude of hostility toward Japan." November 21, 1932: "The Japanese reply to the Lytton Report re Manchuria was issued last evening. It is an exceedingly able document which will convince all reasonable people that Japan has right on her side. . . . It would be an outrage on humanity to bring about such a solution [as the Lytton Report] in order to save the face of the League of Nations. But the misguided idealists who have so openly taken sides with the Chinese war lords and Communists mean to make strenuous efforts to force Great Britain into some wild scheme of economic and financial boycott of Japan which they hope would drive Japan from Manchuria." December 10, 1932: "Japan is rendering good service to civilization by restoring law and order in Manchuria. . . . Fortunately Sir John Simon's wise and moderate policy prevailed with the Assembly of the League of Nations." February 27, 1933: "Any embargo of arms to the combatants must be applied equitably to both sides. But any embargo would mean ominous interference with British industry." These and other excerpts are to be found in Norman Angell: *Peace with the Dictators?* (London: Hamish Hamilton; 1938), pp. 141–4.

their power reached and to harry China with fire and sword—with both swords and fire made in America or in Britain.

Fools and their empires are soon parted. Three weeks after Munich, Japanese troops occupied Canton, cut Hong Kong off from its hinterland, and closed the Yangtze to foreign shipping. On October 19, 1938, Poland followed the example of El Salvador, Italy, Germany, and Franco's Spain in recognizing Manchukuo. Japanese planes bombed British gunboats. Tokio threatened Paris with action against Indo-China unless arms shipments to China were halted. Chamberlain, however, told the Commons on November 2, 1938, that British capital would eventually be needed to reconstruct China and that no one need fear a Japanese monopoly of the China trade. The logical culmination of these developments was reached in 1939–1940. On June 14, 1939, Japanese forces instituted a "blockade" against the British concession in Tientsin to compel British "cooperation." Chamberlain denied that any change of British policy was contemplated. He declared that the beating of British gentlemen and the stripping of British ladies by Japanese soldiers made his "blood boil." He hinted darkly that "in certain circumstances" the fleet might be sent to the Far East. But on July 24, 1939, he told the Commons that the text of a "formula" had been agreed upon as a basis for continuing the discussions over Tientsin.

His Majesty's Government in the United Kingdom fully recognize the actual situation in China where hostilities on a large scale are in progress and note that as long as that state of affairs continues to exist the Japanese forces in China have special requirements for the purpose of safeguarding their own security and maintaining public order in the regions under their control and that they have to suppress or remove such causes or acts as will obstruct them or benefit their enemy. H. M. Government have no intention of countenancing any acts or measures prejudicial to the attainment of the above-mentioned objects by the Japanese forces and they will take this opportunity to confirm their policy in this respect by making it plain to British authorities and British nationals in China that they should refrain from such acts and measures.

But Tory hopes of securing American cooperation in arranging an Oriental Munich were disappointed. In belated recognition of the danger of continued connivance in Japanese aggression, the State Department on July 26, 1939, gave the required six-months' notice of termination of the Japanese-American commercial treaty of 1911. After January 26, 1940, the United States was legally free to impose embargoes on the export of war supplies to Japan. None was imposed, however, until July, and then only in a halfhearted and tentative fashion. Under further Japanese pressure, Prime Minister Churchill had meanwhile agreed in June to bar transit of war materials to China through Hong Kong and over the Burma Road for a period of three months. It is possible that, in the negotiation of the Anglo-American bargain of September over naval bases and destroyers, Washington invited London to reopen the Road, since America was now pledged to all aid "short of war" to Britain and China against the Axis and Japan. On October 17, 1940, the Burma Road was reopened.

Meanwhile, Tokio responded to British gestures of appeasement and to American lack of "understanding" by concluding the military alliance of September 27, 1940, with Germany and Italy. Japan had already capitalized upon French defeat and helped herself (with German approval) to the first installment of the spoils by compelling the authorities of French Indo-China to admit Japanese troops to the colony. Their function was to establish bases for further operations against China— and presumably against British, French, Dutch, and American territories in the East Indies. Further embargo moves at Washington, coupled with firm reiteration of the decision to aid China and Britain, produced hesitation in Tokio as to where and when the next blow should be struck at the Western Powers. When Tokio extended diplomatic recognition to Wang Ching-wei's puppet régime at Nanking on November 30, 1940, Washington retaliated at once by announcing a loan of 100 million dollars to China.[1] London followed suit with a loan of 10 million pounds announced on December 10.

That new blows would be struck at the first favorable opportunity admitted of no doubt. Japan had been the first ambitious Power to discover that the Western democracies possessed no will to fight for their

[1] Prior to the U. S. State Department order of October 8, 1940, calling United States citizens home from the Far East, Japanese spokesmen displayed no timidity in threatening the United States with war. Thus Prince Konoye declared on October 4,

"If the United States refuses to understand the real intention of Japan, Germany and Italy and persists in challenging those Powers, in the belief that the pact is a hostile action, there will be no other course open to it than to go to war." On the same day Mr. Suma, the Foreign Office spokesman, asserted that recent moves by the United States in the Far East "clearly indicate that it is taking step after step in a direction that may precipitate it into the vortex of armed conflict." Also on October 4, Foreign Minister Matsuoka, in a news interview, stated that Japan would declare war "if the United States entered the European struggle."

"I fling this challenge to America. If she in her contentment is going to stick blindly and stubbornly to the status quo in the Pacific, then we will fight America. For it would be better to perish than to maintain the status quo."

Hsin Min Pao, a Japanese-owned paper published in Peiping: "The American army is weak and the quality of her soldiers poor. They know more about comfort than about fighting and are, moreover, not brave enough to die. . . . As to the talk of America hampering Japan's policy in East Asia, that is a pure joke. . . . Should America, with her usual hypocrisy, attempt to interfere with the reconstruction of East Asia, we peoples of East Asia will fight her with all our resources and to the last man. It will be very unfortunate for her should she lightheartedly venture to embark on a trial of strength with us. After all, what have we to fear from her?"

AFTER: On October 9, Mr. Suma declared: "There is no reason to be so nervous. We wish Americans would understand that there is nothing to be alarmed about." Matsuoka, October 10: "The tripartite pact was not entered into with the intention of directing it 'against' the United States, but was directed, if at all, 'for' the United States."

interests unless they were directly attacked. Rome and Berlin had learned from Tokio's example. All three were now united to forge by the sword a "New Order" for the entire world. The foundations of this order were to be the seizure and partition of the colonial empires of France, the Netherlands, Belgium, Britain, and the United States. In the event of victory, Japan's share would be all of China, Indo-China, the Philippines, the East Indies, Australia, New Zealand, Thailand, and perhaps part of India. For such stakes as these the warriors of Nippon were prepared to risk much. Thanks to the policies of the Western Powers, they already had in their hands the means of victory—unless America or the Soviet Union or both should intervene in arms against them.

APPEASING ITALIAN IMPERIALISM. Simon and Chamberlain were the principal architects of the appeasement of Japan. The comparable process which enabled Mussolini's Italy to conquer a new empire and threaten the Western Powers was the contribution to the diplomacy of decadence made by Pierre Laval, Sir Samuel Hoare, and Lord Halifax. Following the failure of the initial Italian attempt (approved by Britain and opposed by France) to conquer Ethiopia in 1896, a stable balance of power had emerged in East Africa with each Power able and willing to protect its interests. By the accord of December 13, 1906, Britain, France, and Italy agreed to maintain the *status quo* and to make "every effort to preserve the integrity of Ethiopia." By the secret Treaty of London of April 26, 1915, Italy was promised "compensations" in the event of British and French acquisitions in Africa at the expense of Germany. The failure of the Allies at the Peace Conference to fulfill this pledge embittered all Italian imperialists. The small British cessions to Eritrea in 1924 and the larger Anglo-Egyptian cessions to Libya in 1934 were deemed wholly inadequate. Mussolini made it clear that more was expected and that no Italian cooperation with France and Britain against the Reich need be expected unless Paris and London paid in African real estate.

Pierre Laval, butcher's son from the Auvergne and Foreign Minister of France after the death of Barthou, fell into Caesar's trap. He admired Fascism. He hated Communism. He could see only one means to make France secure against Germany: an alliance with Italy. For such a bargain, no price seemed to him too high to pay. On January 5 to 7, 1935, he conferred with the Duce in Rome. The result was the signature of elaborate accords, pledging peace, friendship, and consultation and "settling" all issues.[1] Laval got no alliance but only a vague pledge to "consult" in case of any threat to Austrian independence or any danger of unilateral modification of disarmament obligations. Laval gave much

[1] Texts in *Europe on the Eve*, pp. 559–561.

more than he got, and more than the world then knew. The published accords called for collaboration in developing African colonies and Italian participation, to the extent of 7 per cent of the shares, in the French-owned railway from Jibuti (French Somaliland) to Addis Ababa, capital of Ethiopia; for a redefinition of the status of the Italian nationals in Tunisia; and for the cession by France to Italy of 44,000 square miles of desert in the Tibesti region south of Libya and of 309 miles of desert south of Eritrea. These concessions were accepted as a "definitive" settlement of Italian claims under the Treaty of London. The ceded deserts had no resources and almost no inhabitants. Those who were astonished at the modesty of Italian demands did not know that Laval had also agreed to acquiesce in Mussolini's projected conquest of Ethiopia. "Of course," said Laval privately to Jules Romains, "I gave him Ethiopia."[1] Despite his repeated public denials, Laval had given to the Duce precisely such a pledge—as became clear from the secret Maffey Commission Report of the British Foreign Office, dated June 18, 1935, and later stolen and published in Italy. Sir Samuel Hoare, British Foreign Secretary after June 7, 1935, secretly agreed with Laval that Caesar should be served at Ethiopia's expense, despite the desire of the British electorate to uphold collective security through the League.

The steps whereby Laval and Hoare sought to carry out their unholy bargain have already been reviewed. Ethiopia was the least of the victims. The League of Nations was the major victim—and ultimately France and Britain as well. Like all tyrants and would-be conquerors, Mussolini despised weakness and respected strength. Having induced Paris to grant him Ethiopia in exchange for an alliance with France against Hitler, he took Ethiopia and at once made an alliance with Hitler against France. The Duce added insult to injury by withholding ratification of the Laval-Mussolini accord, though the French Chambers, including even the Socialists, had promptly approved them. He hinted that French recognition of Italian title to Ethiopia was a prerequisite. The last leaders of the French Republic were like the Bourbons: they learned nothing and forgot nothing. Bonnet joined Halifax in betraying Ethiopia and the League anew at Geneva in May, 1938. After Munich, French Ambassador André François-Poncet was transferred from Berlin to Rome. He brought the gift of recognition of Italy's title to Haile Selassie's realm. The Italian deputies replied on November 30, 1938, with loud outcries of "Tunisia! Nice! Savoy! Corsica! Jibuti!"

The Ambassador was even more distressed when Ciano on December 17 handed him a note to the effect that the French attitude toward Italy had invalidated the accords which had "been rapidly outdated

[1] Jules Romains, *Seven Mysteries of Europe*, New York, Alfred A. Knopf, Inc., 1940, p. 229.

by the events that followed the application of sanctions. Further, creation of the Empire has established new rights and new interests of fundamental importance." Bonnet complained in his reply of December 26 that France had fulfilled all its pledges (to betray Ethiopia and the League) and that Mussolini's attitude savored of base ingratitude.[1] Even this blow produced no change of heart at the Quai d'Orsay. Bonnet sent Paul Baudouin as his confidential agent to Rome in February, 1939, to offer Caesar more concessions in spite of Daladier's loud defiance. Bonnet failed, but he persisted in his fatuous hopes even after the signature of the formal Axis alliance of May 22, 1939. Last-minute efforts to bribe Mussolini with further colonial promises also failed, since the Duce was now playing "winner take all."

British policy toward Italian imperial ambitions was, if possible, even more disastrous. Hoare was forced out of the Cabinet (for a brief six months) by the public and parliamentary storm which broke when the Hoare-Laval deal of December, 1935, became known. His successor, Anthony Eden, spoke eloquently about collective security and then cooperated with Paris in destroying Ethiopia, the League, and the Spanish Republic. Chamberlain's eagerness to appease both Germany and Italy, however, finally drove Eden to resign on February 20, 1938, along with his Parliamentary Under-secretary, Viscount Cranborne, rather than approve new negotiations with Rome. "Agreements that are worth while," he declared, "are never made on the basis of a threat. Of late the conviction has steadily grown upon me that there has been a too keen desire on our part to make terms with others rather than that others should make terms with us." Cranborne was succeeded by Richard A. Butler, Eden by Lord Halifax. After Munich, Eden observed, "We are constantly giving and they are constantly taking."

Britain's Ambassador in Rome was the Earl of Perth—formerly Sir Eric Drummond, First Secretary-General of the League of Nations. To this mild-mannered Roman Catholic Scotsman and bureaucrat was entrusted the task of giving to Caesar what Caesar said was his. After coming home for new instructions, he opened prolonged negotiations with Ciano, eventuating in the signature of eight agreements on April 16, 1938.[2] Britain agreed to acquiesce in Italian victory in the Spanish war and to take steps at Geneva to secure general recognition of Italian title to Ethiopia. Italy agreed to reduce troops in Libya to peace strength and to sign the naval treaty of 1936. Britain and Egypt signed a "good neighbor" agreement to prevent Ethiopians in the Sudan, Kenya, or British Somaliland from crossing the frontier to oppose Italian control of their native land. Rome and London pledged themselves to define

[1] Text in *Night over Europe*, pp. 84–87.
[2] Text in *Europe on the Eve*, pp. 565–573.

frontiers and exchange information on their military, naval, and air forces in the Near East. They agreed to respect the integrity and independence of Yemen and Saudi Arabia and to prevent any third Power from acquiring privileges within these States. The two Arab kingdoms, although not consenting to the bargain, thus became joint Anglo-Italian protectorates. Rome recognized London's protectorate over Hadramaut east of Aden and British water rights in Lake Tana. The Suez Convention of 1888 for unrestricted use of the Canal was reaffirmed.

The victims of this compact were Spain, Ethiopia, Yemen, Saudi Arabia, the League of Nations—and ultimately Great Britain. London at once pressed Paris and Prague to "cooperate." Czechoslovakia recognized Italian title to Ethiopia on April 20. War Minister Leslie Hore-Belisha visited Rome. Daladier and Bonnet went to London to be told what to do. At the one hundred first meeting of the League Council in May, Halifax urged "facing facts." On November 16, 1938, Britain recognized Italian title to Ethiopia. Chamberlain and Halifax visited Rome in January, 1939, but all their efforts to buy peace from Caesar at French expense were vain—not because Bonnet was unwilling, but because Caesar had been permitted to taste blood and would be sated with nothing less than everything.

If Anglo-French efforts to appease Italy at the expense of colonial subject peoples led only to catastrophe, the efforts made later to buy allies against the Axis had no happier results. Only one of these efforts directly involved a colonial people. The victims were the Syrians, suffering for twenty years from French misrule, thinly disguised as a "mandate." Anglo-French attempts to bring Turkey into the "peace front" of 1939 were complicated by Turkish desires to annex the Sanjak of Alexandretta which constituted the northwest corner of the Syrian mandate. On July 3, 1938, Paris and Ankara had concluded a pact under which Turkish troops were allowed to participate in the policing of the Sanjak during the election of a local constituent assembly. The League of Nations Commission which was to have supervised the election retired in haste. On September 6 the forty delegates chosen (22 Turks, 9 Alouites, and the balance Armenians, Greeks, and Arabs of other sects) voted a new constitution for the district, now rechristened the "Republic of Hatay"— a Turkish name indicating Hittite origin. The changed status of the Sanjak resembled a joint French-Turkish protectorate. Ankara had disclaimed all territorial designs and insisted that its only interest was self-determination for the Turkish inhabitants. In the negotiations of 1939, however, Turkey made clear its desire to annex Hatay as a condition of a new accord with France. The Quai d'Orsay was willing. Syrian protests were brushed aside. On June 23, 1939, two identical agreements were signed by Bonnet and Ambassador Suad Davaz and by Foreign

Minister Shukru Saracoglu and Ambassador René Massigli. One provided for the outright cession of Hatay to Turkey. The other was a mutual assistance pact of seven articles following the model of the Anglo-Turkish accord.

This purchase of Turkish aid savored of a new type of "appeasement," different from the old in that the party bribed was a friend turned ally rather than a rival turned enemy. The "bribe," however, was not the property of the briber. Bonnet's gift of Hatay to Turkey had as little ethical or legal justification as Laval's gift of Ethiopia to Italy. Hatay was part of Syria, to which France had promised independence by the unratified treaty of 1936. France as mandatory had no title to Hatay. Syrian nationalists fumed over the bargain. Members of the League Mandates Commission spoke of the French action as a flagrant violation of the mandate. The Axis press raged against French "perfidy" and "hypocrisy." But at least an ally had been bought. The means of the buying, like the *raison d'être* of British policy in Palestine, was dictated by Mussolini's self-appointed role as "Defender of Islam" and Hitler's pose as friend of the Arabs.

Even here, however, the final results of the bargain were unhappy. Turkey remained neutral throughout 1939 and 1940. Mussolini declared war on Britain and France on June 10, 1940. François-Ponçet complained bitterly, "It is the first case in history where a country offered a chance to receive all peacefully prefers to fight for it in a war dubious as to outcome." But rightly or wrongly the Duce had no doubts. France and Britain had demonstrated their incapacity to organize peace or defend their colonial interests. Caesar was certain that their leaders lacked all capacity to save their States from destruction. As to France, this view was correct. As to Britain, time would tell. To stab in the back those who have long faltered and now seem about to fall is good *Realpolitik* if one can pluck from their failing hands the rich booty of broken kingdoms and lost empires.

APPEASING GERMAN IMPERIALISM. The quotation from *Mein Kampf* at the head of this section appeared for several years on a large banner over the doors of the "German Colonial Exposition" on Potsdammerstrasse, Berlin. The Exposition was devoted to exhibits of the "stolen" German colonies of 1914 and urgent pleas for their restitution. An examination of *Mein Kampf*, however, reveals the significant fact that the quotation in question referred not at all to African or Asiatic colonies, but to new territories to be conquered by the Reich in eastern Europe.

Most of the Nazi leaders were from the beginning anticolonialists. *Mein Kampf* declares unequivocally that the major blunder of the Second Reich was to challenge Britain by seeking colonies and sea power. William II should have renounced overseas possessions and sought cooperation with London. An Anglo-German-Italian alliance would have sufficed to bring about the "annihilation" of France. Germany could then have achieved her destiny in the east at the expense of Russia.

Although this conception of the German future was never wholly abandoned, the course of events turned the Third Reich in a different direction. In any case, it was good propaganda, both at home and abroad, to make periodical demands for the return of the lost colonies. Such demands were presented with monotonous regularity after 1933 in speeches, books, and pamphlets and occasionally in diplomatic notes. None of the colonies had been returned by 1939; but the fruits of victory, if victory could be won, would surely include large slices of African and Asiatic territory as well as mastery of the European Continent.

The details of Anglo-German negotiations over colonial questions during the prologue to war are not yet public knowledge. On his mysterious visit to the Reich on November 16 to 17, 1937, undertaken over the objections of Foreign Minister Eden, Lord Halifax doubtless discussed colonies with Goering and Hitler. It seemed to be understood that, if Britain gave the Reich a free hand with Austria and Czechoslovakia, Berlin would not at once raise the colonial issue in acute form. On the day of Eden's resignation, however, Hitler declared that Germany's colonial demands would be "voiced from year to year with increasing vigor" and would not be silenced with promises or credits. On November 8, 1938, after Munich, he declared, "It only remains for us to agree over colonies which were taken away from us on pretexts which were contrary to justice. . . . We wish to negotiate, but if others decline to grant our rights, we shall secure them in a different way."

In the face of such threats, J. L. Garvin's *Observer* proposed that France cede Togoland and Cameroons to the Reich. Oswald Pirow, South Africa Defense Minister, made a Cook's tour of European capitals in October and November, negotiating "unofficially" over Germany's colonial "grievances." Rumors spoke of the possibility of satisfying Berlin with Portuguese Angola, the Belgian Congo, or possibly French Equatorial Africa. But Pirow was discouraged. Popular indignation at the November pogrom led Chamberlain to declare that no British mandates would be restored to the Reich. Despite Tory willingness to buy peace with colonial concessions, particularly if others could be induced to do the giving, no new bargain could be struck. In late July, 1939, it became known that Sir Horace Wilson and Robert S. Hudson had secretly discussed with Dr. Helmuth Wohlthat, Hitler's economic adviser, a British loan of a billion pounds to Berlin in return for acceptance of armament limitations. No British territory was to be given up; but the Reich, said Hudson, could join the Western Powers and the United States "in the economic development of China and of the vast regions of Africa." Chamberlain declared that this represented merely Hudson's "personal view."

On the eve of war, Hitler sought to buy British nonintervention by offering an alliance and a deal over colonies. On August 25, 1939, he told Sir Nevile Henderson that he was "a man of great decisions." He was therefore ready to "guarantee" the British Empire, once the Polish question was settled. His colonial demands must be met, but he was willing to concede "a most protracted time limit." Henderson flew to London with this offer on August 26 and returned on August 28 with a reply which expressed willingness to negotiate a "general settlement," but only if the Polish question were settled through an international guarantee without jeopardizing Polish independence. Hitler suggested immediate colonial concessions as an evidence of British good faith, but Henderson replied that "concessions were easier of realization in a good rather than a bad atmosphere." The issue was soon lost sight of amid the more immediate exigencies of the crisis. The war of 1939 was obviously not an "imperialist" war in the sense of being a conflict directly attributable to irreconcilable demands over colonial questions. But it was a war on the part of Britain to impose limits on the expanding power of the State which British policy had done so much to make formidable. And it was a war on the part of the Axis, plus Japan, to smash the British Empire and seize mastery of Europe, Asia, and Africa, colonies included.

THE FASCIST WILL-TO-EMPIRE. Here as elsewhere the appeasers of the Western Powers failed until too late to comprehend the motives and roles of the terrifying genii they had let loose upon the world. "The view of His Majesty's Government," said Sir Samuel Hoare before the League Assembly on September 11, 1935, "is that the problem is economic rather than political and territorial. It is the fear of monopoly— of the withholding of essential colonial raw materials—that is causing alarm. It is a desire for a guarantee that the distribution of raw materials will not be unfairly impeded that is stimulating the demand for further inquiry. So far as His Majesty's Government is concerned, I feel sure that we should be ready to take our share in an investigation of these matters." Eden and Halifax spoke later in similar vein. Sir Arthur Salter (*Peace and the Colonial Problem*) urged an international convention guaranteeing equality of access to colonial raw materials. All of these phrases, like the flowers that bloom in the spring, had nothing to do with the case.

The will-to-power of the totalitarian Caesars and of their counterparts in Japan had little in common with "capitalist imperialism" or, to use Lenin's phrase, with "imperialism as the last stage of capitalism." Fascist Italy, Nazi Germany, and militarist Japan were not States ruled by "capitalists," despite the initial delusions of the capitalists who brought political extremists to power to protect Property and Profits against "Communism." The imperialism of the late nineteenth century represented the competitive pushing and pulling in all the Western nation-states of diplomats, strategists, and chauvinists, concerned with national power and glory, and of bankers, exporters, and entrepreneurs, concerned with the profits of "backward" areas rich in resources or labor but poor in capital and military might. Colonial objectives were thus defined in limited fashion in terms of acquisitions which would improve the strategic position of the State *vis-à-vis* its rivals and contribute to the enrichment of favored merchants and investors. Totalitarian imperialism in the twentieth century is the imperialism of bellivolent political *élites*, drunk with grandiose dreams of world hegemony and with the heady wine of war. Profits are incidental or negligible. Power is the goal—at the expense, if need be, of profits and welfare. Limited and local enhancements of national power are but means to ends. The goal is not to improve one's position in relationship to rivals, but to destroy and enslave one's rivals and rule the world over the wreckage of their realms.

Under these circumstances, colonies in distant areas, access to raw materials, freedom of colonial trade, and the like, are also but means to ends. The great end is the creation of an invulnerable and invincible imperium, fashioned not after the model of Cecil Rhodes, Jules Ferry, Theodore Roosevelt, Crispi, or Bülow, but after the model of Napoleon, Charlemagne, Julius Caesar, or Alexander the Great. Selling shirts to Hottentots or clipping Congo coupons is irrelevant to such a goal. Smashing neighboring States and using them to smash rival Great Powers is the purpose all sublime of the new empire builders.

This purpose was acknowledged long before the outbreak of war. Nazi orators talked of "Living Space" (*Lebensraum*), Fascist orators of "Our Sea" (*Mare Nostrum*), and Japanese orators of the "New Order" in "Greater East Asia." So long as disguise was expedient, however, the purpose masqueraded in the garments of "Anti-Communism." For some of the Triplice leaders, this costume was not a disguise, for they dreamed in truth of carving out new empires on the Russian steppes. When they discovered that Moscow was willing and able to fight all invaders and even to fight in defense of Outer Mongolia, Czechoslovakia, and Spain, they decided rightly that the paths of least resistance led toward the Western Powers.

"Anti-Communism" then became more than ever a useful façade, for the Anglo-French Munichmen were at all times, until their last hour, ready and eager to believe that the U.S.S.R. would be the ultimate target of Fascist aggression. Hitler would take the Ukraine and the Caucasus. Japan would take eastern Siberia. Mussolini would be placated at the expense of Ethiopia, Spain, and perhaps France. Successive surrenders to the Triplice were good not because they meant "peace," but because they were believed to mean new steps toward the death grapple between Fascism and Communism which would leave the West in peace. In fact, they meant the death of the West. Those who contribute to the enhancement of another's power under the delusion that it will be turned against others thereby ensure their own destruction.

The imperialism of the Great Powers today and tomorrow is no longer a striving for distant colonies. It is a struggle of Briton's and Americans, at home and overseas, for political survival. It is a struggle of Germans, Italians, and Japanese for control of the continents and of the great seaways and therewith for mastery of the globe. The "backward" peoples of Asia and Africa, despite all their striving for independence, and the advanced peoples of Latin America (which is economically a "colonial" area) are more than ever pawns in a vast game of power, as are the less numerous national groups of Europe itself. The yellow, black, and brown peoples will inevitably be confronted in the future, not by the rival ambitions of half a dozen imperial Powers, all competing in exploiting and oppressing them, yet checkmating one another to the occasional advantage of the "lesser breeds without the law." They will be confronted with great continental empires, organized and coordinated for the single-minded pursuit of such ends as seem good to their rulers. If the rulers and rebuilders of the world are to be the disciples of the Fascist Caesars, the colonial subject peoples face a prospect of enslavement and degradation darker than any they have known in the darkest chapters of "plutodemocratic" imperialism. If world victory and world mastery is to go to an Anglo-American federation, joined by a liberated France and by other emancipated peoples of Europe, then Africans, Asiatics, and Latin Americans may conceivably look forward to a future of hope and progress in a world revolutionized and united by a revolutionary liberalism. In either case, imperialism's present halfway house will have been abandoned in favor of a new structure, containing many mansions and looking out upon new vistas in the relationships between those who use machines and those who are still learning to use machines.

SUGGESTED READINGS

Anderson, W. H.: *The Philippine Problem*, New York, Putnam, 1939.
Andrews, F. F.: *The Holy Land under Mandate*, Boston, Houghton, 1931.
Armstrong, H. C.: *Grey Wolf: Mustapha Kemal*, London, Barker, 1932.
Bau, M. J.: *The Open Door Doctrine in Relation to China*, New York, Macmillan, 1923.
Bentwich, N.: *England in Palestine*, London, Routledge, 1932.
———: *Palestine*, London, Benn, 1934.
Bonn, M. J.: *The Crumbling of Empire*, London, Allen & Unwin, 1938.
Brailsford, H. N.: *Rebel India*, New York, New Republic, 1931.

Buell, R. L.: *The Native Problem in Africa* (2 vols.), New York, Macmillan, 1928.

Carter, J. F.: *Conquest: America's Painless Imperialism*, New York, Harcourt, 1928.

Chiang, M. S., and Chiang Kai-shek: *Sian: A Coup d'Etat*, Shanghai, China Publishing Company, 1937.

Chiang Kai-shek, Mme: *China Shall Rise Again*, New York, Harpers, 1940.

Clark, G.: *The Great Wall Crumbles*, New York, Macmillan, 1935.

————: *The Balance Sheets of Imperialism*, New York, Columbia University Press, 1936.

————: *A Place in the Sun*, New York, Macmillan, 1936.

Clyde, P. H.: *Japan's Pacific Mandate*, New York, Macmillan, 1935.

Dawson, W. H.: *The Future of Empire*, London, Williams and Norgate, 1930.

Denny, H. N.: *Dollars for Bullets*, New York, Dial, 1929.

Dorn, W. L.: *Competition for Empire, 1740–1763*, New York, Harper, 1940.

Earle, E. M.: *Turkey, the Great Powers, and the Bagdad Railway*, New York, Macmillan, 1923.

Foster, H. A.: *The Making of Modern Iraq*, Norman, University of Oklahoma Press, 1935.

Gandhi, M.: *His Own Story*, London, Allen & Unwin, 1933.

Gerig, B.: *The Open Door and the Mandates System*, London, Allen & Unwin, 1930.

Giddings, F. H.: *Democracy and Empire*, New York, Macmillan, 1901.

Harris, J. H.: *Slavery or "Sacred Trust"?*, London, Williams and Norgate, 1926.

Hobson, J. A.: *Imperialism: A Study*, New York, Pott, 1905.

Hocking, W. E.: *The Spirit of World Politics*, New York, Macmillan, 1932.

Howard, H. N.: *The Partition of Turkey, 1913–1923*, Norman, University of Oklahoma Press, 1931.

Jenks, L. H.: *Our Cuban Colony: A Study in Sugar*, New York, Vanguard, 1928.

Johnston, Sir H. H.: *History of the Colonization of Africa by Alien Races*, London, Cambridge University Press, 1905.

Kirk, G. L.: *Philippine Independence*, New York, Farrar, 1936.

Lawrence, T. E.: *Seven Pillars of Wisdom*, New York, Doubleday, 1935.

Leeuw, H. de: *The Struggle for Colonies*, New York, Harrison-Hilton, 1939.

Lucas, Sir Charles P.: *Partition and Colonization in Africa*, New York, Oxford, 1922.

Macaulay, N.: *Mandates*, London, Methuen, 1937.

Main, E.: *Iraq: From Mandate to Independence*, London, Allen & Unwin, 1935.

Malcolm, G. A.: *The Commonwealth of the Philippines*, New York, Appleton-Century, 1936.

Margalith, A. M.: *The International Mandates*, Baltimore, Johns Hopkins, 1930.

Middleton, L.: *The Rape of Africa*, New York, Random House, 1936.

Mitchell, N. P.: *Land Problems and Policies in the African Mandates of the British Commonwealth*, Baton Rouge, Louisiana State University Press, 1931.

Moon, P. T.: *Imperialism and World Politics*, New York, Macmillan, 1926.

Morel, E. D.: *The Black Man's Burden*, New York, Viking, 1920.

Motherwell, H.: *The Imperial Dollar*, New York, Brentano's, 1929.

Nearing, Scott: *Dollar Diplomacy: A Study in American Imperialism*, New York, Viking, 1926.

Nehru, Jawaharlal: *Toward Freedom* (Autobiography), New York, Day, 1941.

Overlach, T. W.: *Foreign Financial Control in China*, New York, Macmillan, 1919.

Peffer, Nathaniel: *The White Man's Dilemma: Climax of the Age of Imperialism*, New York, Day, 1927.

Riesenberg, Felix: *The Pacific Ocean*, New York, Whittlesey, 1940.

Restarick, H. B.: *Sun Yat-Sen*, New Haven, Yale University Press, 1932.

Roberts, S. H.: *History of French Colonial Policy (1870–1925)* (2 vols.), London, King, 1929.

Salter, A., and N. Bentwich: *Peace and the Colonial Problem*, London, National Peace Council, 1936.

Schoonmaker, E. D.: *Democracy and World Dominion*, New York, R.R. Smith, 1939.

Schuster, M.: *The Strangling of Persia*, New York, Appleton-Century, 1912.

Stoddard, T. L.: *The Revolt against Civilization*, New York, Scribner, 1932.

Stoyanovsky, J.: *The Mandate for Palestine*, New York, Longmans, 1928.

Ware, E. E.: *Business and Politics in Far-East*, New Haven, Yale University Press, 1932.

Woolf, L. S.: *Empire and Commerce in Africa*, New York, Macmillan, 1920.

Wright, Quincy: *Mandates under the League of Nations*, Chicago, University of Chicago Press, 1930.

Chapter X

THE BREAKDOWN OF THE WORLD SOCIETY

1. POVERTY CONQUERS PLENTY

"Cheshire-Puss," Alice began . . . "would you tell me please which way I ought to go from here?" "That depends a good deal on where you want to go," said the Cat. "I don't much care where—" said Alice. "Then it doesn't matter much which way you go," said the Cat. "—so long as I get *somewhere*," Alice added as an explanation. "Oh, you're sure to do that," said the Cat, "if only you walk long enough. . . . In *that* direction lives a Hatter; and in *that* direction lives a March Hare. Visit either you like: they're both mad." "But I don't want to go among mad people," Alice remarked. "Oh, you can't help that," said the Cat, "we're all mad here. I'm mad, you're mad." "How do you know I am mad?" said Alice. "You must be," said the Cat, "or you wouldn't have come here."—LEWIS CARROLL, *Alice in Wonderland.*

FOR most of modern mankind the business of living in the early 1940's had become a panic flight before the Horsemen of the Apocalypse: Famine, Pestilence, War, and Death. This shocking and hideous state of affairs was entirely unanticipated by the optimists of the palmy days before 1914 when men could still believe in unending "progress" and feel confident that all was for the best in the best of all possible worlds. Man had conquered Nature. Man had in his hands the tools to bring peace and plenty to all the planet. Man had a future brighter than any preceding generation had ever dreamed of. To answer adequately the question of why these high hopes were so bitterly frustrated would be to retell the whole story of Western culture with a degree of insight and understanding not as yet vouchsafed to any participant observer. Yet an answer of a kind must be attempted, for without it the tragic drama of contemporary world politics becomes little more than "a tale Told by an idiot, full of sound and fury, Signifying nothing." And if it were no more than this, it would be unworthy of serious study.

Chaos and breakdown have their hidden "laws" and their secret "causes" no less than order and progress. The tragedy of modern man is the tragedy of Faust who sold his soul to Mephistopheles in order to recapture his youth—and then used the energies of youth to bring others to ruin and finally to encompass his own doom. In the language of sociologists, rather than poets, Western man has become a victim of "cultural lag." He perfected the skills and devised the gadgets required

[435]

to make the world an economic unity, a cultural unity, and, potentially at least, a political unity. But he had already learned how to live his life in a prescientific and premachine age in which the world was not a unity but rather a loose aggregation of national tribes in which each tribe was "independent" and more or less sufficient unto itself. Animals capable of learning often suffer from their inability or reluctance to forget or modify what they have learned. Solutions to old problems, once learned, are carried over into new situations and applied to new problems to which they are inapplicable. The result is frustration. If frustration provokes no effective adjustment to new needs in new ways, the result is madness and disaster.

CAPITALISM IN CRISIS. Poverty and war have become the external manifestations of the disorder of an ill-adjusted world. Their initial adumbrations in the twentieth century impinged first upon men's minds in the confusions of an economic order which once promised plenty for all and finally bred "crises," unemployment, bankruptcy, and impoverishment (or the fear of it) for all.

The contemporary tragedy of the new economy, insofar as it can be explained by a too-simple formula, arises out of the circumstance that competition tends to become self-destructive. When free competition wanes, the price mechanism no longer functions to preserve a balance. In its initial phase, capitalism operated in expanding markets in which competition was the life of trade and new enterprises were constantly being established to meet new demands. Subsequently markets expanded less rapidly and then began to contract in periodical deflations of increasing severity, caused in part by the fact that the unequal distribution of wealth and income left insufficient purchasing power in the hands of the masses of consumers to buy the output of the new industry and agriculture at prices profitable to the producers. In contracting markets, competition becomes destructive. To escape losses producers combine for protection, *i.e.*, for restricting output and for fixing prices at levels determined not by free competition but by agreement or decree. Entrepreneurs combine in corporations, cartels, and trusts and seek to establish monopolies. They demand from governments "protective" tariffs to bar out of the home market goods from abroad or to compel their sale at prices no lower than those profitable to domestic producers. Entrepreneurs further seek and secure aid from the State in the form of diplomatic protection and subsidies wherewith to win new foreign markets.

At a later stage comes governmental price fixing, production quotas, dumping or destruction of surpluses, and "planned economy." All these efforts to escape from the unhappy consequences of unlimited competition in shrinking markets tend to destroy competition, to make certain prices rigid and inflexible, and to disrupt the maintenance of economic equilibrium through price changes. Private monopoly in its various forms becomes the death of trade. Periods of prosperity become highly inflationary and speculative with all producers profiting from general and artificial price increases. Depressions become more acute and prolonged because the deflationary processes necessary to achieve a readjustment are interrupted by artificial price controls. In passing from its competitive phase to its monopolistic phase, capitalism passed into a vicious circle from which no escape has yet appeared.

The Great Depression exhibited in exaggerated form the general symptoms characteristic of all such depressions. Everywhere it grew out of the boom period of 1924–1928, marked by rising or stationary price levels, a great increase in almost all lines of production, high wages, huge profits, tremendous investments at home and abroad, credit expansion, and wild speculation in securities. Sales began declining in 1929 as markets became incapable of absorbing the flood of goods, even under the impetus of installment purchasing, long-term credits, and high-pressure advertising. Declining sales brought declining production and price cutting. The lofty structure of inflated credit and security values began to topple. The New York stock market panic of October–November, 1929, initiated a prolonged and progressive collapse of security prices which brought ruin to millions of speculating investors. Commodity prices and production began to decline rapidly. Factories closed, wages fell, unemployment increased, and purchasing power fell more swiftly than prices. In a desperate effort to save something of their vanishing markets, some producers and distributors cut prices still more severely, and others kept their prices artificially high and thus prevented deflation from restoring an equilibrium. All fixed obligations become increasingly difficult to meet. Banks closed, corporations became insolvent, tax revenues declined while millions of hungry unemployed clamored for relief. The collapse of the *Kredit-Anstalt* of Vienna in the spring of 1931 presaged new disasters in Europe. The great industrialized nations— Germany, Great Britain, and the United States—were gripped by economic paralysis.

The social and political consequences of economic maladjustment became so serious that governments were obliged to intervene. Their intervention was usually designed to halt the fall of values, to restrict output, to "stabilize" prices, and to put an artificial end to a process of deflation which had already become artificial and abnormal because of the disappearance of the automatic, competitive controls of an earlier epoch. The "cures" aggravated the disease by multiplying its causes. Governmental deficits became enormous. Emergency measures were of no avail, and even the abandonment of the gold standard and the inflation of the currency in many countries were within effect. By the summer of

1932, the fall of price levels had apparently stopped for certain commodities; but countless millions were without work and wages, and the subsequent recovery of production and trade was painful and slow.

To the workers struggling along on a dole or subject to the mercies of private and local charity, to the farmer whose mortgage is foreclosed because the prices of his crops net him no money with which to meet payments, to the businessman forced into bankruptcy, and to the banker whose folly or indiscretion has led to the disappearance of depositors' money in worthless investments, it may appear a far cry from the depression to international politics. But to the exporter, the importer, the foreign investor, the diplomat, and the reflective observer of world affairs the problems of the economic order and those of the political order, national and international, are inseparably linked. The economic crisis is deserving of the careful consideration of the student of international politics, not merely because the power of States rests upon economic resources and productivity, but because the crisis is both a cause and a result of the policies of governments in their dealings with one another. Economic nationalism in all its aspects played a large role in precipitating the crisis, and governments confronted with ruin reacted defensively by becoming more nationalistic and mercantilistic than ever. In this fashion, they aggravated the conditions they strove to ameliorate. The frenzied diplomacy of the depression period centered in problems created by the crisis: vanishing gold reserves, the postponement or repudiation of public and private debts, barriers to trade, disappearing markets, dumping, social unrest, and revolution. All national efforts to deal with the crisis not only failed to achieve the expected results but in many cases actually worsened the situation. There was general agreement that only international efforts could be effective. International efforts required cooperation among governments still primarily interested in national power and prestige and in the profits of their own nationals. Such cooperation was difficult to achieve and was often ineffective because of its halting and hesitant character.

THE MOST-FAVORED-NATION CLAUSE. The origins of neomercantilism and the increasing prevalence throughout the world of prohibitive tariff policies have been considered above. If protectionism is pushed to its logical limit, each State will exclude all imports from other States while it continues its efforts (obviously vain in such a situation) to market its own exports abroad. Under such circumstances, all international trade will be strangled and all the national economies will be left to suffocate within their closed compartments. In point of fact, this state of affairs has never quite been reached, though the Western States seemed to be approaching it at the close of 1932. Normally, each government has a sufficient interest in keeping foreign markets open for its own nationals to induce it to keep open its own markets for foreigners, provided that the requisite *quid pro quo* can be secured. Here is a basis for bargaining and a reciprocal exchange of favors. If in a particular case another State cannot be induced to grant tariff concessions, discriminatory or penalty duties may be resorted to. If the other State retaliates in kind, a "tariff war" results until one side or the other yields and strikes a bargain. As many such bargains and special arrangements can be entered into as there are States in the world and commodities entering into international trade.

Out of this situation there emerged at an early period the "most-favored-nation" clause of commercial treaties, as a partial solution of the problem. Commercial treaties, *i.e.*, agreements setting forth the conditions of trade between the two signatory States, are of great antiquity. In the ancient State Systems and in the medieval and early modern period of the Western State System, they usually consisted of special bargains between the parties. As trade expanded, the resulting confusion of bilateral favors and discriminations became increasingly burdensome. All States gradually recognized that this situation was advantageous to none and began incorporating into their commercial treaties reciprocal pledges whereby each signatory agreed to afford to the commerce of the other as favorable treatment as it granted to any "most-favored" third State. The purpose of the most-favored-nation clause was to minimize special bargains and favors and to eliminate discrimination. To the degree to which States were bound by such clauses, general equality of commercial treatment was assured. Each State was bound to accord equal treatment in tariff duties and commercial regulations to the trade of all other States with which it had concluded such treaties. Some commercial treaties have gone beyond this and provided for "national treatment," *i.e.*, treatment of aliens as favorable as that granted to citizens. But national treatment has been limited for the most part to taxation and navigation rules and has little direct bearing on import or export duties.

During the nineteenth and early twentieth centuries, the American Government always adhered to the so-called "conditional," or "American," form of the most-favored-nation clause, in contrast to the "unconditional," or "European," form. The first commercial treaty concluded by the United States—that with France of February 6, 1778—granted reciprocal most-favored-nation treatment, "in respect of commerce and navigation . . . freely, if the concession was freely made, or on allowing the same compensation if the concession was conditional." The American form of the most-favored-nation clause opened the door wide to extensive discriminations and to a large number of special bargains. The American State Department always reserved the right to decide for itself what compensation was identical or equivalent. This interpretation of the most-favored-nation clause led to endless wrangling over "equivalence of compensation." The tariff history of the United States and of other States adhering to the conditional interpretation is filled with special bargains, inequalities of treatment, diplomatic protests and recriminations, and an amount of friction and misunderstanding out of all proportion to the advantages derived from this evasion of the fundamental purpose of most-favored-nation treatment.

In 1923 the United States abandoned the conditional form of the most-favored-nation clause in its new commercial treaties with Brazil and Germany. The American Government has subsequently adhered to the European, or unconditional, form. Under this form, which is now almost universal, each party agrees to levy against the commerce of the other "no higher or other duties, conditions, or prohibitions" than are imposed on the same commodity imported from or exported to any other foreign country. Any favor granted to a third State "shall simultaneously and unconditionally, without request and without compensation, be extended" to the same commodity of the other signatory party. These provisions were incorporated in the usual language in Article 7 of the German-American treaty, signed December 8, 1923, and proclaimed on October 14, 1925.

> Each of the high contracting parties binds itself unconditionally to impose no higher or other duties or conditions and no prohibition on the importation of any article, the growth, produce, or manufacture, of the territories of the other than are or shall be imposed on the importation of any like article, the growth, produce, or manufacture of any other foreign country.
> Each of the high contracting parties also binds itself unconditionally to impose no higher or other charges or other restrictions or prohibitions on goods exported to the territories of the other high contracting parties than are imposed on goods exported to any other foreign country.
> Any advantage of whatsoever kind which either high contracting party may extend to any article, the growth, produce, or manufacture of any other foreign country shall simultaneously and unconditionally, without request and without compensation, be extended to the like article the growth, produce, or manufacture of the other high contracting party.[1]

It should be observed that the most-favored-nation clause is aimed at preventing discriminations and has no effect whatever upon the height of tariff walls. Under its provisions a State may levy as high duties on imports as it likes or prohibit them altogether, so long as the duties or prohibitions are applied equally to all States enjoying most-favored-nation treatment. The application of duties is dealt with in commercial treaties,

---

[1] This article makes the same arrangement for all advantages accorded by either party to the nationals, vessels, or goods of third States but excepts from these obligations purely border traffic within a ten-mile zone on either side of the customs frontiers and likewise excepts the commerce of the United States with Cuba, Panama, and other dependencies.

but the level of duties is ordinarily a "domestic question" beyond the control of other States. The most-favored-nation clause has been only partly effective in achieving even the limited objective of equality of treatment. Neighboring States still find it advantageous to make special bargains with one another involving discrimination against third States. Such discriminations can be effected either by exceptions incorporated in treaties or by sundry legislative and administrative expedients. Minute classifications of commodities in tariff acts are sometimes resorted to. Or a State may impose quotas on imports or limit foreign-exchange operations to attain the same objective. Universal equality of treatment has never been achieved. Meanwhile, tariff walls have risen steadily throughout the world.

The United States set the pace by enacting the Smoot-Hawley Tariff Act of 1930. This act was followed by foreign retaliation and by a catastrophic decline in international trade. During the first six months of 1929 the United States exported goods to the value of $2,623,200,000. During the same period of 1932 American exports amounted to only $841,800,000. American exports thus fell 67.8 per cent in this period, and imports fell 62.1 per cent. During 1931 as compared with 1930, American exports fell 36.9 per cent, British exports 31.8 per cent, French 29.0 per cent, German 20.2 per cent, and Japanese 22.9 per cent. Creditor countries generally experienced a larger loss of exports than imports, whereas debtor countries curtailed their imports by a larger percentage than their exports declined. In the American revenue act of 1932, additional import duties were imposed on lumber, copper, coal, and oil. Great Britain resorted to "temporary" protectionism in the autumn of 1931 and on March 1, 1932, imposed a general 10 per cent ad valorem duty on imports, with other increases to follow as a result of the agreements considered at the Imperial Economic Conference at Ottawa during the summer. The French Government not only increased its import duties but restricted imports by a system of quotas on a large variety of manufactured and semimanufactured articles. On September 6, 1932, Germany adopted a new scale of tariff duties, in many cases 100 per cent higher than those hitherto prevailing. Everywhere, among great and small Powers alike, similar prohibitions, quotas, licensing systems, foreign-exchange restrictions, and other insurmountable trade barriers were resorted to, all in the face of such a rapid rate of decline in international trade as to threaten its complete disappearance in the absence of a recovery of prices and markets.

This situation, which presents in exaggerated form the same tendencies operating in more normal times, led to a frenzied quest for salvation through the same remedies (again in exaggerated form) attempted earlier. These remedies may be classified into three categories: (1) purely national remedies, consisting for the most part of carrying economic nationalism to its logical conclusion; (2) international remedies through bargains of various kinds among particular States or groups of States; and (3) international remedies through efforts at world-wide agreements among all States to deal with world-wide problems.

The forms and purposes of purely national action have already been suggested. Each national government strives to safeguard the domestic market for its producers by restricting imports. It may likewise grant favors or subsidies to exporters in the hope of retaining its foreign markets. But exports will vanish in proportion as imports are made impossible, for it is an axiom of international trade that he who does not buy, neither shall he sell. Retaliatory tariffs and restrictive measures on the part of other States will tend to destroy export markets. Each State is thus compelled to see its foreign trade approach the vanishing point and to have national economic self-sufficiency thrust upon it whether it will or no. In the period of the Great Depression the term *autarchy* came into general use in Europe to describe such a self-contained national economy. It need scarcely be pointed out that this solution tends toward the abolition of international trade and is acceptable only to States which are prepared to forego the advantages of geographical specialization and to accept lower living standards for their populations. In the world economy of the twentieth century, no nation, however large and rich in resources, can sever its economic contacts with others without paying an enormous price. The United States is perhaps more nearly self-sufficient than any other country; but it is obliged to import tin, chromium, manganese, nickel, rubber, and dozens of other products not available in sufficient quantities in the United States to supply domestic needs. On the other hand, its economy is organized on the assumption that 20 per cent of its wheat crop, 40 per cent of its tobacco, 60 per cent of its cotton, and considerable proportions of other products will be sold in foreign markets. It has often been pointed out that less than 10 per cent of the total annual production of exportable commodities in the United States is sold abroad, but this margin is just sufficient to make the difference between prosperity and depression. The United States could not dispense with its foreign markets without disorganizing completely its whole economic structure and returning to a standard of life far below that now prevailing. Smaller and poorer States would obviously suffer even more severely from efforts at achieving autarchy. The uneven distribution of basic raw materials and the economic interdependence of nations render this solution impossible. Those who advocate it preach a counsel of despair.

CUSTOMS UNIONS. If national action is inadequate, international action must be resorted to. Tariff bargains between individual States have long been part of the established commercial policy of nations. In periods of crisis, such bargains become more advantageous than ever; for when all States are raising barriers to trade, special arrangements between neighbors may be the means of economic survival. The most extreme form of such action is the customs union in which two or more States abolish all tariffs between them and adopt a common tariff for outside States. Luxemburg maintained a customs union with Germany prior to the Great War and later formed a similar union with Belgium. Leichtenstein maintained a customs union with Austria-Hungary prior to 1914 and later joined Switzerland in such an arrangement. Such Unions have also existed between Italy and San Marino, and between France and Monaco. Other instances are to be found in the relations between Poland and Danzig, France and the Saar, the city of Geneva and the French districts of Gex and Savoy, Syria and Palestine, and certain States of the Baltic region and of Latin America.[1]

Projects for customs unions frequently fail because they seem to foreshadow political union between the parties, as did the German Zollverein of 1833 and the Austro-Hungarian union of 1851. On March 23, 1931, Austria and Germany announced a plan for a customs union in which each party would retain its political independence and other States would be invited to join. France, Italy, and the Little Entente opposed the project for political reasons and appealed to the League Council which requested the Permanent Court for an advisory opinion as to the legality of the plan. On September 5, 1931, the Court held by vote of 8 to 7 that the scheme was illegal under the financial protocol of 1922 and the Treaty of St. Germain. Under French pressure, Berlin and Vienna abandoned their design. Austria reluctantly accepted a new League loan of 43 million dollars and agreed to abandon all plans for union with Germany for twenty years. The decision of the Court was perhaps legally correct. But the opposition of the Governments was politically and economically shortsighted since it helped to perpetuate German and Austrian impoverishment, further discredited the German Republic, contributed to the rise of Hitler, and caused many Germans and Austrians to conclude that political union, achieved if need be in defiance of the Powers, was the only possible path to economic collaboration.

Many bilateral or multilateral reductions of trade barriers short of a complete customs union have been attempted. In June, 1932, Belgium, the Netherlands, and Luxemburg signed a five-year convention to reduce

[1] Representatives of the States of southern and central South America met in Montevideo in February, 1941, in a "Rio de la Plata Conference" to discuss measures of economic collaboration, but no agreement could be reached on the project of a customs union. Such an arrangement would have small value for these States, since they are economically dependent upon exports to Europe.

tariff duties among them by 10 per cent annually. On August 21, 1932, at the British Imperial Economic Conference at Ottawa, agreements were signed among the Dominions (long committed to protectionism) and the United Kingdom (newly converted to trade barriers) for a five-year period of intra-imperial quotas and preferences. On May 14, 1934, Italy, Austria, and Hungary signed eight agreements at Rome whereby Italy and Austria agreed to buy more Hungarian wheat, Hungary agreed to buy more industrial products from Italy and Austria, and all three States granted tariff preferences to one another. Such agreements may promote freer trade among the participants, but they tend to impose new barriers to trade between the signatories and outside States, since their advantages are necessarily restricted to the parties which expressly enter into them. The most-favored-nation clause is thus evaded and a régime of special bargains and discriminations restored.

RECIPROCAL TRADE AGREEMENTS. One of the most ingenious and notable efforts to meet these difficulties is found in the new commercial policy of the United States embodied in the Trade Agreements Act of June 12, 1934, which authorized the President for a period of three years to negotiate bilateral agreements for reciprocal reduction of tariffs, subject to termination or extension after three years' operation. In the agreements the President could increase or reduce established American tariff duties by not more than 50 per cent. The reductions would be extended to other States having most-favored-nation agreements with Washington but might be withheld from countries discriminating against American goods. The Executive was thus given power to bargain with other governments for lower duties without departing from the spirit of the most-favored-nation cause and without the necessity of securing congressional approval for each reduction or of submitting each agreement to the Senate before ratification.

The first agreement under the new act was signed with Cuba and became effective on September 3, 1934. The United States reduced its tariff on Cuban sugar from 2 to 0.9 cents a pound and granted reductions on tobacco, rum, pineapples, and other Cuban products in return for Cuban reductions on American manufactures and foodstuffs. Because of Cuba's special relations with the United States, these advantages were not extended to outside States. On February 2, 1935, an agreement was signed with Brazil by which the United States agreed to keep 90.8 per cent of its imports from Brazil on the free list and to reduce duties on Brazil nuts, castor beans, and manganese, while Brazil cut duties on American automobiles, machinery, fruits, and oatmeal. This and the subsequent agreements were extended by Washington to other States having most-favored-nation treaties. Agreements were signed with Belgium, February 27, 1935; Colombia, September 13, 1935; Canada,

November 15, 1935 (this agreement caused Mr. Peek to resign); Switzerland, January 9, 1936; Guatemala, April 24, 1936; France, May 6, 1936; Finland, May 18, 1936; Costa Rica, November 28, 1936; etc. By the beginning of the third Roosevelt Administration a score of such agreements had been signed. States which discriminated against American goods or subsidized exports—notably Germany, Japan, and Australia—were deprived of the advantages of the pacts or subjected to countervailing duties. The new policy stimulated trade and seemed to offer hope of reducing barriers by bilateral bargains within the framework of unconditional most-favored-nation treatment.[1]

INTERNATIONAL ECONOMIC COOPERATION. There remain to be considered the efforts made to deal with the problem on a worldwide scale, through established institutions and agencies of international cooperation. These efforts long centered at Geneva in the League of Nations. Since its establishment, the League strove to facilitate trade by removing barriers and discriminations. It championed economic interdependence, geographical specialization, capitalistic internationalism, and an unhindered flow of goods and services across national boundaries. It opposed nationalistic parochialism, national self-sufficiency, and prohibitive tariffs and embargoes. These statements may seem paradoxical, since the League was little more than the sum of its part and its parts were national States which usually championed what the League opposed and obstructed what it proposed. But the "League" may here be taken to mean not so much the sum of national governments as the international technical experts and economists, plus certain businessmen and diplomats who adopted a new orientation. The small degree of success which these efforts met with was in large part due to the reluctance of nationalistic governments and businessmen to sacrifice the immediate profits of economic nationalism for the less tangible benefits of international freedom of trade.

The early work of the League in this field was based upon what had already been done by the International Chamber of Commerce, organized in 1920. The first congress of this body was held in London in June, 1921. The League Council, acting under Article 23 of the Covenant, had already established the Financial and Economic Committee of the League in October, 1920. In April of 1921 an international conference on communications and transit was held at Barcelona. In October–November, 1923, a conference for simplification of customs formalities was held at Geneva, and in December of the same year a second conference on communications and transit took place. Six international conventions resulted from these early gatherings, but none of them touched the heart of the problem of

[1] In March, 1937, Congress by joint resolution extended the Trade Agreements Act to June 12, 1940. In April, 1940, it was extended to June 12, 1943.

tariff barriers. The first serious effort to grapple with the dilemma created by neo-mercantilism took the form of a World Economic Conference, held at Geneva May 4–27, 1927, under League auspices.

The Conference worked through three committees: on commerce, on agriculture, and on industry. M. Loucheur, whose views were shared by the Conference as a whole, pointed out that the delegates could do no more than recommend the facilitation of trade and the removal of prohibitions on imports and exports. "Neither this conference nor any other body can override State sovereignty. This conference can only provide the means of economic disarmament, it cannot achieve it." In the final report and resolutions of the Conference, the delegates declared unanimously that "each nation's commerce is today being hampered by barriers established by other nations, resulting in a situation, especially in Europe, that is highly detrimental to the general welfare." They further declared that "the time has come to put a stop to the growth of customs tariffs and to reverse the direction." These prescriptions were in every case merely recommendations, which were largely ignored by the governments of the participating States.

The subsequent history of League endeavors in this direction is a tale of almost unrelieved failure. During 1932, efforts were initiated, in the various European chancelleries, to summon a second World Economic Conference. It was clear from past experience, however, that nothing whatever could be achieved by the conference method if the conferees were unwilling to make concessions in the interests of an agreement on constructive measures. Since no general willingness to modify policies of economic nationalism was observable, the Conference was repeatedly postponed. In July the United States agreed to participate, only on condition that there be no discussion of tariff, debts, and reparations—a demand which would make the Conference resemble a wedding without the bride or, more appropriately, a funeral without the corpse. The Conference met in London in June, 1933, following the conclusion of a temporary world-wide tariff truce, but soon broke up in complete disagreement and futility because the United States, though originally conceding that monetary and tariff problems were inseparable, refused to limit the depreciation of its currency inaugurated in the preceding March. Without a currency agreement, other Powers refused to reduce tariffs. Efforts to reduce trade barriers by world-wide international agreement were now practically abandoned, pending a restoration of some stable international medium of exchange.

GOLD. The breakdown of the gold standard contributed to commercial chaos among the nations. Before 1914, almost all countries had currencies convertible into gold at fixed rates. They could be exchanged for one another at rates reflecting their gold value. When supply and demand in foreign-exchange marts fluctuated with variations of imports and exports, balances were met by gold movements. If State A exported to B more than it imported, B's debts would be met by sending gold to A. This access of gold, in theory and to some degree in practice, would tend to cause an expansion of currency and credit in A, and B's loss of gold would provide a corresponding contraction within its own economy. In the sequel, price levels in A would tend to rise and those in B to fall. This in turn would encourage buyers in A to purchase from B and would discourage sellers in A from selling to B; conversely, B's sellers could increase profits by greater sales to A because of rising prices, and B's buyers would normally buy less from A for the same reason. Thus an equilibrium in trade would be restored by the effects upon prices of the gold movements caused by the initial disequilibrium. The exchanges would return to par, and gold movements would cease. The international gold standard functioned effectively before 1914 without large gold movements so long as gold could be freely bought, sold, and transferred from country to country and so long as governments did not interfere extensively with foreign-exchange rates, gold movements, price levels, and imports and exports of goods.

The necessary conditions for the successful operation of the gold standard disappeared with the Great War. Belligerent governments forbade or controlled gold exports and ceased to exchange paper currency for gold. After the war the gold standard was restored at the pre-war level by Britain in 1925, at one-fifth of the old level by France in 1926, and at various other levels by other States. Here was the first element of maladjustment. Sterling was overvalued; *i.e.*, British costs and prices remained high in relationship to costs and prices elsewhere, with the result that British exports were discouraged, imports were encouraged, and Britain lost gold. Francs were undervalued; *i.e.*, French prices were low with the franc worth 5 cents in gold instead of 20 cents as in 1914, with the result that imports fell, exports increased, and France accumulated huge gold stocks which failed to raise internal prices proportionately or to lower prices in the countries whence the gold came. Governments and central banks, moreover, were anxious to promote domestic stability of price levels and were reluctant to permit gold movements to influence prices. Discount rates were changed to counteract the natural course of events. Britain failed to deflate her currency and price level to a point which would compensate for the pound's overvaluation. The United States with its enormous gold holdings failed to inflate currency and prices to a corresponding degree. Tariffs and other trade barriers made impossible a restoration of equilibrium through increased imports in the countries with high price levels and increased exports from countries with low prices. In addition, a large volume of short-term international obligations grew up because of uncertainty about long-term investments which were difficult to liquidate readily. The rapid movements of these obligations from country to country during each economic or political crisis contributed to instability of exchange rates.

The impact of the Great Depression on this already precarious structure was disastrous. In countries where prices fell first, compensatory exports could not be developed because of tariffs abroad. Short- and long-term investments were withdrawn in panic with resultant gold losses. To keep currencies convertible into gold and to permit continued gold exports meant the continued fall of prices in an endless spiral of deflation with consequent economic prostration and social and political unrest. Governments, by necessity or by choice, suspended gold payments and forbade gold exports, thus permitting their currencies to fall on the exchanges. Depreciation of currencies tended to raise domestic prices and thus halt deflation. But since domestic prices usually increased less rapidly than exchange rates fell, entrepreneurs in countries with depreciated currencies could undersell competitors in world markets with a resultant expansion of exports, a reduction of imports, a cessation of the outflow of gold, and a stimulus to an inflow of gold. Countries with currencies still on gold found their markets disappearing, their exports declining despite subsidies and other aid, their imports increasing despite new tariffs and quotas, their gold flowing out, and their national economies sinking ever deeper into a morass of seemingly endless deflation. The "automatic" balancing mechanisms no longer functioned because free competition, free trade, free gold movements were all at an end. In order to halt deflation at home by raising domestic price levels and to meet competition in foreign markets by lowering the prices of their goods in relationship to prices elsewhere, governments still on gold abandoned it and followed the procession in depreciating currencies. In the race to depreciate, trade advantages lay with the States whose currencies fell most rapidly.

This general formula applies with few qualifications to the actual course of events. In the summer of 1931 the political crisis, engendered by the Austro-German customs union project and the financial difficulties of the *Kredit-Anstalt* of Vienna, led to large-scale withdrawals of foreign capital from Central Europe, initiated by politically inspired French withdrawals designed to bring pressure to bear on the Austrian and German Governments. Since British banks held Central European obligations in large amounts, the rapid fall in the prices of these obligations menaced the solvency of London's financial institutions and precipitated a panic withdrawal of funds from London. Credits advanced by the Bank of France and the Federal Reserve system failed to stem the tide. Faced with huge gold losses and catastrophic deflation, the British Government suspended the gold standard on September 21, 1931. All the Dominions, except Canada and South Africa, followed suit, as did the Scandinavian countries and many Latin American States, constituting the "sterling bloc." The pound fell about 40 per cent in terms of gold currencies. British exports increased, and domestic inflation was halted. In December, 1931, Japan abandoned gold and allowed the yen to depreciate 66 per cent (June, 1935) with a resultant export boom and loud protests from foreign competitors. In the United States the banking crisis of March, 1933, was followed by the suspension of gold payments. The dollar fell, prices rose, deflation ceased, prosperity seemed at last to be just around the corner. President Roosevelt was therefore unwilling at the London Conference to stabilize currency. The Gold Reserve Act of January 30, 1934, authorized the President to devalue the dollar from 40 per cent to 50 per cent. On January 31 an Executive proclamation fixed the value of the dollar at 59.6 per cent of its former gold value. With this depreciation of 41 per cent, American exports could compete once more with British and Japanese goods in world markets.[1] On March 29, 1935, Belgium abandoned gold and depreciated her currency 25 per cent. Following steady losses of gold, France followed suit on September 26, 1936, and depreciated the franc 30 per cent from 6.63 to 4.66 cents. Switzerland and the Netherlands did likewise. Italy depreciated the lira 41 per cent. Germany, possessing almost no gold and imbued with a nationwide fear of renewed inflation, clung desperately to a gold standard which was wholly fictitious. By the close of 1936 the gold standard had ceased to exist as an international medium of exchange.

In October, 1936, the American Government expressed its willingness to buy gold in the world market at a fixed price of $35 per ounce as compared with $20 before depreciation. This policy, coupled with America's "favorable" balance of trade, produced a fantastic result. Since the world purchasing power of $35 was greater than that of an ounce of gold translated into any other currency, most of the world's gold gravitated

[1] Under the Silver Purchase Act of June 20, 1934, passed largely at the behest of domestic silver producers, the Treasury was authorized to buy silver in a world market to increase its price to $1.29 an ounce or to increase American silver stocks to one-quarter of the gold stocks. The Treasury purchased about 20 million ounces a week at approximately 65 cents an ounce without achieving either objective. In September, 1935, China, with her currency on a silver standard, protested that the drain of her silver and the rise of the world price of silver were lowering her price level and disorganizing her public finances and foreign commerce. By November $100 would buy 320 Chinese silver dollars as compared with 258 a month before. Having secured no redress, China experienced a banking crisis and abandoned silver payments on November 3, 1935, adopting thereafter a managed paper currency. Silver prices declined sharply in December. In May, 1936, the United States agreed to buy silver from China in exchange for gold. The American Government, however, had defeated its own purpose and had injured China in the imagined interests of American silver producers at the very time when the Department of State was interested in strengthening China against Japanese pressure.

to the United States. In the 1920's, Americans sold huge export surpluses abroad without buying any comparable quantities of imports through a heavy export (*i.e.*, "investment") of private capital to foreign markets. In the 1930's this outflow of capital came to an end. Export surpluses continued to grow, however, by virtue of imports of gold. Output of the world's gold mines was stimulated from $707,000,000 (paper) in 1934 to $1,000,000,000 (paper) in 1939. The French gold reserves declined from $5,445,000,000 in December, 1934, to $3,191,000,000 in November, 1939; the Italian from $518,000,000 to $193,000,000; the Japanese from $394,000,000 to $164,000,000; the German from $32,000,000 to $29,000,-000. By the end of 1940, American gold stocks had increased to $20,000,-000,000, representing about 80 per cent of the world's monetary gold. This growing hoard was for the most part buried in the hills of Kentucky and strongly guarded—in apparent imitation of the giant Fafnir who concealed the stolen Rheingold in a cave and transformed himself into a dragon to protect it. Whether America's gold hoard, like Fafnir's, would tempt some Siegfried to slay the guardian was uncertain. Its utility was not greater than that of the riches of Fafnir. It might indeed prove as much of a curse to its possessors as did the gold of the Ring of the Nibelungs —if, as was probable, all other lands ceased to use gold in any form for currency purposes.

Meanwhile, efforts to stabilize currencies by agreement (like the Anglo-French-American accord of September 26, 1936) offered no hope of a restoration of the international gold standard or even of fixed ratios of exchange. The outbreak of war in 1939 led to new Anglo-French currency arrangements but in the sequel demolished the remnants of what had once been a viable system of free international exchange. In no country was paper money any longer convertible into gold. All currencies were "managed"—*i.e.*, controlled—along with credit and foreign exchange, by political authorities, not by private banks or by the fluctuating needs of a competitive market. This at least promised to be a permanent innovation. What remained uncertain was whether in the years ahead each nation would retain a national currency not convertible into other currencies, with international trade therefore reduced to crude barter operations, or whether new "international" managed currencies would come to prevail in great continental regions and perhaps in the world as a whole. The political unification of the Continents and of the world implied common currencies in common market areas coextensive with the areas of imperial and world administration.

INTERGOVERNMENTAL DEBTS. Nothing revealed more clearly the breakdown of the old world economy than the fate of the huge intergovernmental debts left over from the Great War. These obligations fell into two categories: (1) loans among the Allied and Associated

Governments for the purpose of prosecuting the war and (2) indemnity payments or "reparations" imposed upon Germany by the victors. The total volume of these obligations was entirely unprecedented, and the economic and financial problems involved in their payment were of unparalleled magnitude and complexity. The story of fifteen years of negotiations and controversy over inter-Allied debts and reparations can be conveniently divided into five periods: (1) from the Peace Conference, 1919, to the Dawes Plan, 1924; (2) from the Dawes Plan to the Young Plan, 1929; (3) from the Young Plan to the Hoover moratorium, 1931; (4) from the Hoover moratorium to the Lausanne Conference, 1932; and (5) from the Lausanne Conference to the final collapse of the whole debt structure.

It is essential in the first instance to emphasize certain elementary economic facts regarding intergovernmental debt payments which were familiar enough to economists in 1919 but which were lost sight of by diplomats and politicians because of ignorance or the dictates of political expediency. If the government of State A is obliged to pay money to the government of State B, its first problem is that of raising the necessary funds within State A out of taxes or loans. State A's ability to accomplish this is obviously the primary measure of "capacity to pay." But the raising of the funds in State A does not of itself ensure payment. The funds will be in the currency of State A, but State B wishes payment in its own currency. If State B is willing to accept goods in payment, State A may place the funds at its disposal for the purchase of such goods within A's frontiers. They may then be transported to B, and the obligation will be discharged by this transaction. In all probability, however, state B will refuse goods in any large quantity, for an inflow of goods will lower prices and cause State B's producers to demand protection from such a catastrophe. State B's consumers will usually have nothing to say in reaching this decision. At the same time, State B's politicians and taxpayers will demand payment. State A must then pay in gold. But gold stocks are quite insufficient to meet payments of the magnitude of those in question. State A will, in fact, pay in bills of exchange, ultimately redeemable in gold, which are normally the only international medium and measure of value. With the funds it has raised in its own currency, the government of State A will purchase bills or drafts payable in B's currency, or in the currency of some third State, and ultimately redeemable in gold. Such bills will be available for purchase in State A in proportion as State A's exporters have sold abroad more than its importers have bought. Unless State A maintains a "favorable" balance of trade of sufficient magnitude to meet debt payments, its government cannot transfer funds to B by purchasing foreign exchange, without upsetting the exchange rates to its own disadvantage. If bills on B are not available in sufficient amount, the purchases by the government of A will increase their price, *i.e.*, will raise the value of B's currency as measured in A's currency on the international exchanges. A's currency will decline in international-exchange value; and A's whole monetary system will become demoralized, along with its commerce and industry. In the last analysis, payment can be made only in goods—if not in goods shipped to B, then in goods sold to outside States in excess of what is purchased. If international payments are not to prove disastrous to the payer, they must involve an export surplus. But an export surplus on the part of the payer is likely to be viewed with alarm by the payee, who erects tariff walls to keep out the payer's goods and resents any invasion of outside foreign markets by the payer in competition with his own exports. Here, in brief, is the riddle of international debts. By comparison, the old problem of eating one's cake and having it too is easy of solution.

The implications of this dilemma were scarcely appreciated at the Paris Peace Conference. Fantastic figures running into hundreds of billions of dollars were bandied about, but the absurdity of expecting Germany alone to pay for the colossal costs of the conflict was recognized, even by Clemenceau and Lloyd George. It was accordingly decided to leave the exact amount to be fixed by "experts" and to impose only a blanket obligation on Germany in the treaty

The indemnity was to be disguised as "reparations," on the popular assumption that Germany, as the aggressor, had inflicted the war upon her innocent victims. Reparation payments were to include all civilian losses, destruction of nonmilitary property, and military pensions. Germany was likewise required to make certain payments in kind and to pay 20 billion gold marks by May 1, 1921. The so-called "Dawes Plan," which was accepted on August 16, 1924, following the Ruhr adventure, was a stopgap arrangement, designed to give Germany a breathing spell without offending French sensibilities. It did not reduce the total of Germany's obligations or fix the number of annual payments. It did provide for the evacuation of the Ruhr, for foreign control over German finances, and for a reduced schedule of annual installments. This agreement temporarily removed the problem from the sphere of acute diplomatic controversy and paved the way for the Briand-Stresemann period of Franco-German *rapprochement*, marked by the Locarno treaties of 1925, the admission of Germany to the League in 1926, the formation of the Franco-German steel cartel, and the final evacuation of the Rhineland in June of 1930.

Meanwhile there had been much friction over the inter-Allied debts, followed by the conclusion of a series of debt-funding agreements. The United States was owed roughly 11½ billions and Great Britain about the same amount. The British debt to the United States reduced Britain's net credit to 3¾ billions. France owed 3½ billions net, Italy 4⅓ billions, and Russia 4½ billions. The Soviet Government repudiated the Russian war debts on the ground, among others, that Russia had not shared in the fruits of victory, and the other debtor governments manifested no enthusiasm for meeting their obligations. No interest or principal was paid to the American Government until 1923. The Allied Governments in general, and the French Government in particular, took the view that the debts should be canceled, since the United States had entered the war belatedly, grown wealthy therefrom, and suffered negligible losses. The Allied taxpayers were persuaded of the injustice of repayment and, in the event that payment was demanded, were disposed to support policies to wrest the necessary sums from Germany. In 1922 Lord Balfour, the British Foreign Secretary, offered to reduce Britain's claims on Germany, France, and Italy to the amount demanded from Great Britain by the United States. The implication of this proposal was that general cancellation might be made possible by American generosity.

These and similar suggestions fell upon deaf ears in America. Payment in full was demanded by the new Republican Administration. Secretary of State Hughes denied that any connection existed between the Allied debts to the United States and German reparation payments—a legal fiction, completely divorced from financial realities, to which the American Government has consistently attempted to adhere up to the present time. The Foreign Debt Funding Act, passed by Congress and approved February 9, 1922, created a debt commission of five members to refund or convert principal and interest into bonds "in such form . . . as shall be deemed for the best interest of the United States of America," provided that the maximum time of maturity should not exceed June 15, 1947, and the minimum rate of interest should be $4\frac{1}{2}$ per cent. These conditions proved unworkable; they were subsequently modified, with congressional approval. In 1921 pressure had been brought to bear upon the debtors by the State Department through a boycott on private loans to governments refusing to refund their obligations. Negotiations commenced first with Great Britain and were pursued with other debtors on the basis of "capacity to pay." The terms of the Liberty Loan Acts and of the Foreign Debt Funding Act were departed from. The principal sums were kept intact, but the reduction of interest rates and the spreading of the payments over a period of sixty-two years amounted to a cancellation of a substantial part of the original obligations. On a $4\frac{1}{2}$ per cent interest rate, the total indebtedness would have amounted to almost $33,000,000,-000. Nearly $11,000,000,000 of this total was canceled, since the debt-funding agreement provided for total principal and interest payments of $22,188,484,000.[1]

Country	Funded debt owed to U. S.	Principal plus interest
Austria............................	$ 24,614,885	$ 24,614,885
Belgium...........................	417,780,000	727,830,500
Czechoslovakia....................	115,000,000	312,811,433
Estonia...........................	13,830,000	33,331,140
Finland...........................	9,000,000	21,695,055
France............................	4,025,000,000	6,847,674,104
Great Britain.....................	4,600,000,000	11,105,965,000
Greece............................	18,125,000	20,330,000
Hungary...........................	1,939,000	4,693,240
Italy.............................	2,042,000,000	2,407,677,500
Latvia............................	5,775,000	13,958,635
Lithuania.........................	6,030,000	14,531,940
Poland............................	178,560,000	435,687,550
Rumania...........................	44,590,000	122,506,260
Jugoslavia........................	62,850,000	95,177,635
Total.............................	$11,565,093,885	$22,188,484,877

The various agreements were signed between 1923 and 1926, and during the same period the Allied Governments adjusted their debts to one another. The United States refused to deal with the debtors collectively and applied no consistent principles in negotiating the agreements, apart from the vague criterion of "capacity to pay." Great Britain, which was the first to offer to pay, was charged 3.3 per cent interest. France, which delayed longest, was charged 1.6 per cent interest. Italy, which likewise delayed negotiations, was charged only 0.4 per cent. Poland, Czechoslovakia, and Rumania paid 3.3 per cent, Belgium 1.7 per cent, and Jugoslavia 1 per cent.

No sooner were these agreements concluded than it became apparent that Germany could not meet the Dawes Plan annuities, even out of new American (private) loans. A new committee of experts, headed by Owen D. Young of the United States, was appointed; and, after months of arduous and acrimonious negotiations, its report—the Young Plan—was accepted by the Powers on June 9, 1929. The plan was designed to be "complete and final." Total German indebtedness was scaled down to $26,500,000,000, with payments to run until 1988. With interest figured at 5½ per cent, the principal of the German debt would be about

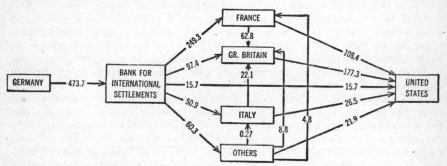

The stream of intergovernmental payments in millions of dollars of average annual payments under the Young Plan and the Interallied Debt Agreements. (*Adapted from Charles Merz, "The War Debts Puzzle," New York Times, Nov. 1, 1931.*)

$8,800,000,000 under this scheme. Germany was to pay variable annuities, ranging from 1,707,900,000 gold marks in 1930–1931 to 2,428,800,000 gold marks in 1965–1966. The payments were so adjusted that the sums owing to the United States by the Allies would equal 65 per cent of the annual German payment. The Reparation Commission was abolished and a Bank for International Settlements was created to handle reparation transactions. Germany recovered financial autonomy and was made responsible for transfers, with a right to postpone transfers or payments for a period not exceeding two years, subject to investigation by a special advisory committee. With slight modifications, the plan was approved at the conference at The Hague of August, 1929, and was incorporated into a final act, signed at The Hague on January 20, 1930. The annual schedule of intergovernmental payments, based on the Young Plan and the inter-Allied agreements, is indicated in the diagram, as shown on the following page, with figures in millions of dollars and fractions thereof, as of 1931, when the whole structure broke down.

These "final" settlements proved to be no more final than their predecessors. Whether the payments could have been made had "prosperity" continued to prevail is an academic question. Germany borrowed more in private loans from the United States between 1924 and 1930 than she paid in reparations, and the whole process at bottom was one whereby the American Government collected money paid to the Allies by Germany out of funds borrowed from American bankers and American purchasers of foreign securities. The enormous sums involved represented no transfers of tangible goods and services across frontiers, but only the scribbling of the mad bookkeepers of frenzied international finance. When this process of paying debts by incurring still greater debts came to its inevitable end in the crash of 1929–1931, the whole intergovernmental debt structure collapsed, along with private credit.

American private lending to Germany came to an end in 1930. Symptoms of the depression appeared in Germany as early as the summer of 1928. The stream of American capital was already drying up as the result of the diversion of funds for speculative purposes during the American stock-market boom. The Wall Street débâcle in the autumn of 1929 and the onset of the Great Depression were followed by widespread bankruptcy and unemployment. By the spring of 1931 it was clear that a gigantic financial panic was impending in Germany and that all debts, public and private, were jeopardized. Germany could borrow no more, and her foreign creditors were liquidating both short-term credits and long-term investments. Further reparation payments were out of the question. Allied debt payments to the United States likewise became impossible in the face of budgetary deficits and disturbed exchange rates. The German Government could apply for a moratorium under the Young Plan, but an open confession of default at Berlin might have precipitated a financial catastrophe. Early in June Chancellor Bruening and Foreign Minister Curtius conferred with Ramsay MacDonald at Chequers—from which Paris deduced that Berlin was seeking diplomatic aid from London against France, Germany's chief creditor. Andrew Mellon, American Secretary of the Treasury, was also in England at the time, French irritation was increased by the fact that the Bank of England extended a temporary loan to the Austrian Government after the Quai d'Orsay had refused to permit French banks to participate in this project unless Austria definitely renounced her customs-union proposal. For Germany to seek aid from Great Britain or the United States was like the lame seeking guidance from the blind, for British and American banks were heavily involved in the impending insolvency of Germany. Of the German long-term foreign debt of $2,272,000,000, 55.2 per cent was held in the United States, 11.5 per cent in Great Britain, and only 5 per cent in France. Of the German short-term indebtedness of $2,450,000,-000 (January 1, 1931), 37.1 per cent was held in the United States, 20.4 per cent in Great Britain, and only 6.5 per cent in France. The bankers and diplomats of London, New York, and Washington had a vital interest in maintaining German solvency. But the purse strings were now held by the Bank of France, which was relatively unscathed by the depression. The support of the French Government was essential to the success of any scheme of salvation.

In this critical situation, the Hoover moratorium proposal was announced, June 20, 1931. The panic among Germany's creditors had reached such proportions that it seemed clear that most of the German banks would be unable to open on Monday morning, June 22. American bankers brought pressure to bear on Washington. After receipt of an appeal from President von Hindenburg and hurried consultations with financiers, officials, and congressmen, President Hoover announced his plan, probably with considerable reluctance in view of congressional and popular opposition in the United States to any reduction or cancellation of war debts. In his announcement he proposed "the postponement during one year of all payments on intergovernmental debts, reparations, and relief debts, both principal and interest, of course not including obligations of governments held by private parties. Subject to confirmation by Congress, the American Government will postpone all payment upon the debts of foreign governments to the American Government payable during the fiscal year beginning July 1 next, conditional on a like postponement for one year of all payments on intergovernmental debts owing the important creditor Powers." The announcement listed the Senators and Representatives who had sanctioned the plan, mentioned Messrs. Dawes and Young as having approved, and sought to soothe provincial opposition by presenting the scheme as a step toward the restoration of prosperity. The old formulae were reiterated once more:

"The repayments of debts due to us from the Allies for the advances for war and reconstruction was settled upon a basis not contingent upon German reparations or related thereto. Therefore, reparations is necessarily wholly a European problem with which we have no relation. I do not approve in any remote sense of the cancellation of the debts to us."

Though the Hoover plan was hailed with enthusiasm in Germany, Austria, Great Britain, and Italy, it was resented by France and her allies. Next to the United States, France had most to lose by its acceptance and the French Government had not been consulted prior to its promulgation. The French reply of June 24 insisted that the Young Plan be kept intact and that Germany be required to pay into the Bank for International Settlements the nonpostponable part of her reparation debt, to be used for improving general credit conditions in all countries of Central Europe. There followed protracted and difficult Franco-American negotiations, ending in agreement on July 6. All intergovernmental payments were postponed from July 1, 1931, to June 30, 1932, and the German unconditional annuities were deposited in the Bank for investment in government-guaranteed German railway bonds, with the German railways passing the sums so received back to the German Government and thus relieving its budget. The shadow of the Young Plan was thus preserved, though its substance was already gone.

Not only was no progress made toward the abandonment of the unworkable policies of economic nationalism which made the debt problem insoluble, but rising tariff walls made the situation worse during the intervening months. The year of the Hoover moratorium witnessed an aggravation of the crisis and an intensification of the depression. As tariff walls rose higher throughout the world and commerce declined, the prospect for a resumption of payments on public and private debts became ever more dismal.

In December, 1931, the American Congress refused to act upon President Hoover's recommendation that the World War Debt Funding Commission be reestablished. It ratified the moratorium but declared that it did not approve, in any remote sense, of the cancellation or reduction of the debts and that its action was not to be construed as foreshadowing any future modification of this policy. The Allied Governments were persuaded to sign agreements for the repayment of the postponed installments in annual sums at 4 per cent interest, to be remitted over a ten-year period—presumably in addition to the regular installments falling due under the debt-funding agreement. When the moratorium year expired on June 30, 1932, no new arrangements had been concluded, despite the fact that the debtors were even less able to pay than they had been a year previously.

German reparations, however, were at long last wiped out, albeit conditionally, by the Lausanne Conference of June–July, 1932. The European Governments were given to understand by Washington that any readjustment of the inter-Allied debts must be preceded by a solution of the reparations question. Such a readjustment must be brought about by the European Powers, and the United States refused to take any part in their deliberations. The Lausanne accords made no mention of the inter-Allied debts, but a supplementary "gentlemen's agreement" of July 7 provided that ratification should be contingent upon a satisfactory settlement with the United States. This arrangement was apparently insisted upon by France. Herriot expressed his intention of not submitting the accords to Parliament for ratification until favorable trans-Atlantic developments should have occurred. "What must be clearly understood is that the link is now definitely established between the settlement of reparations and the solution of the debt problem with relation to the United States. Everything is now subordinated to an agreement with America."

The State Department expressed its pleasure at the Lausanne accords but declared that "on the question of war debts owing to the United States by the European Governments, there is no change in the attitude of the American Government" (press release of July 9, 1932). In a letter to Senator Borah, President Hoover declared on July 14, "While I do not assume it to be the purpose of any of these agreements to effect combined action of our debtors, if it shall be so interpreted, then I do not propose that the American people shall be pressed into any line of action or that our policies shall be in any way influenced by such a combination, either open or implied." Though many Senators and Representatives, with the support of a portion of the provincial press, professed to see a European "plot," Senator Borah declared himself in favor of a world conference to reduce or cancel all war obligations. Other public figures adopted a similar position, in some cases proposing that European disarmament be made the price of debt reduction.

But the Administration adhered to its established policy, apparently out of fear of arousing the resentment of isolationists and irreconcilables seeking to make political capital out of opposition to debt reduction. That policy consisted of doing nothing prior to the presidential election of November 8, 1932, unless the European governments should solicit a reconsideration of the funding agreement. Each appeal would then be dealt with individually on its merits, on the basis of a revised estimate of "capacity to pay." And since the European governments, out of fear of upsetting confidence by confessing their inability to pay, were reluctant to make such appeals, months of drifting ensued, with the Lausanne agreements unratified and with no government daring to raise embarrassing issues. The zenith of futilitarianism was reached when the United States insisted on excluding these problems from the agenda of the proposed World Economic Conference as the price of its participation. Out of deference to the American view, the official invitation extended to the United States declared that "the questions of reparations, of debts, and of specific tariff rates (as distinguished from tariff policy) will be excluded from the scope of the conference."

The end was now at hand. European requests for postponement of payments due on December 15, 1932, led to a futile conference between President Hoover and President-elect Roosevelt and to exchange of notes between Washington and foreign capitals. On December 15 Britain paid $95,550,000 in gold bars. Italy, Czechoslovakia, Lithuania, Latvia, and Finland also paid; but France, Belgium, Poland, Esthonia, and Hungary defaulted on payments totaling $24,996,511.85. Congressional and public insistence on payment in full tied the hands of the new President and made impossible any agreement for reduced payments, with the result that all payments were soon suspended. President

Roosevelt accepted small "token" payments from a number of debtors in June, 1933. Others defaulted. Only Finland paid in full. More tokens and defaults followed in December. Even token payments ceased after the passage by Congress in April, 1934, of Senator Hiram Johnson's bill to forbid private American loans to defaulting governments. The Attorney General ruled that States which had made no payments, including the U.S.S.R., were defaulters under the act but that Great Britain, Czechoslovakia, Italy, Latvia, Lithuania, and Finland were not defaulters and would not be so regarded if they paid in full the installments due on June 15. Following labored exchanges of notes, all the debtors defaulted in toto on the appointed day, save Finland which paid her installment of $166,538. This was all the Treasury received out of $174,647,439.19 due, with $303,196,-205.26 in accrued installments unpaid. On December 15, 1934, the United States received $228,538 from Finland and nothing from the other debtors. After that date only Finland stubbornly persisted in making payments until Congress in 1940 suspended Finland's obligations. German reparations were dead. Inter-Allied debts were dead. The American war debts were dead. The collapse of the intergovernmental debt structure of the 1920's was thus complete, thanks to the persistence of attitudes and policies making payments impossible.

This belated liquidation of intergovernmental obligations was not followed, however, by any sane reordering of international economic relations. On the contrary, it coincided with the growth of autarchy and with the swift descent of most of the capitalist economies toward complete breakdown. But a "cure" was at long last discovered, first by Adolf Hitler and Hjalmer Schacht. It enabled the German Government, and eventually others, to revive the capital goods industries, abolish unemployment, restore prosperity, and spend money in ever larger amounts. The cure consisted in colossal armament programs in preparation for Armageddon. Men who lacked wit and will to abolish poverty and achieve plenty through a reordering of resources and labor to serve human needs found it easy to attain both objectives by devoting resources and labor to preparations for war. International trade became more and more a weapon of *Realpolitik*.[1] National economies became more and more military economies, "socialist" rather than "capitalist" in their controls and their incentives to productivity.

The tribes of men, having reduced themselves to beggary by the efforts of each to enrich itself at the expense of others, refused to abandon old ways and meet new problems with imagination. As beggars, they once more made themselves rich—or fancied themselves rich—by beating idle plowshares into swords and idle pruning hooks into spears. At length they again devoted themselves wholeheartedly to mutual slaughter and destruction. Out of chaos a new world economy will emerge, along with a new world polity—or else another feudal age in which miserable bands of survivors will live from hand to mouth in their poor and broken

[1] *Cf.* Thomas Brockway, *Battles without Bullets: The Story of Economic Warfare*, Foreign Policy Association, 1939.

provinces and relieve the ennui of want by robbery, arson, and neighborhood warfare in a world without end, sans hope and sans meaning.

2. WAR CONQUERS PEACE

A condition of peace is the realization in international relations of a system of law intolerant of violence except as a legally controlled instrument of execution. While the use of force under authority of the society as a whole to prevent or remedy illegal acts by its members is consistent with a regime of law, the use of violence to change the law is not. Statesmen or jurists who tolerate war as a necessary instrument of legislation in the society of nations, are in part denying the existence of international law altogether.—QUINCY WRIGHT, *The Causes of War and the Conditions of Peace.*

In the downward course of a broken-down civilization's career there may be truth in the Ionian philosopher Heracleitus's saying that "War is the father of all things." The sinister concentration of the society's dwindling powers upon the absorbing business of fratricidal warfare may generate a military prowess that will place the neighbouring societies at the war-obsessed society's mercy, and may strike out a military technique that will serve as a key to the acquisition of a far-reaching technical mastery over the Material World. Since the vulgar estimates of human prosperity are reckoned in terms of power and wealth, it thus often happens that the opening chapters in the history of a society's tragic decline are popularly hailed as the culminating chapters of a magnificent growth; and this ironic misconception may even persist for centuries. Sooner or later, however, disillusionment is bound to follow; for a society that has become incurably divided against itself is almost certain to "put back into the business" of war the greater part of those additional resources, human and material, which the same business has incidentally brought into its hands. —ARNOLD J. TOYNBEE, *A Study of History.*

O Lord our God, help us to tear their soldiers to bloody shreds with our shells; help us to cover their smiling fields with the pale forms of their patriot dead; help us to drown the thunder of the guns with the cries of the wounded, writhing in pain; help us to lay waste their humble homes with a hurricane of fire; help us to wring the hearts of their unoffending widows with unavailing grief; help us to turn them out roofless with their little children to wander unbefriended through the wastes of their desolated land in rags and hunger and thirst, sport of the sun flames of summer and the icy winds of winter, broken in spirit, worn with travail, imploring Thee for the refuge of the grave and denied it—for our sakes, who adore Thee, Lord, blast their hopes, blight their lives, protract their bitter pilgrimage, make heavy their steps, water their way with their tears, stain the white snow with the blood of their wounded feet! We ask of One who is the spirit of love and who is the ever faithful refuge and friend of all that are sore beset, and seek His aid with humble and contrite Hearts. Grant our prayer, O Lord, and Thine shall be the praise and honor and glory, now and ever. Amen.—MARK TWAIN, *War Prayer.*

The men and women of the Great Society between 1919 and 1939 struggled more earnestly and desperately for "peace on earth, good will to men" than any generation before them. The fruit of their struggle was fraticidal bloodshed and devilish destruction of a scope and fury unknown since the Thirty Years' War and perhaps since the barbarian invasions. To retell in detail the story of this tragic failure is a heartbreaking task. Yet it is imperative, if anything is to be saved from the wreckage, to "reason why" rather than blindly "do or die." The reasons for the failure, however, are not complex or esoteric. They are, on the contrary, starkly simple.

Human beings, like other organisms, experience frustration and ultimately destroy themselves when they are incapable of adapting their habits to the new problems created by environmental change. The "problem" of war among nations has never been "solved" since the disintegration of the Roman Empire largely because there was no great incentive for solving it during the many centuries of local agrarian and mercantile economies throughout the Western world. War was the sport of kings, the adventure of restless youth, the business of professional soldiers. With rare exceptions, it brought little woe to the common run of men. Never before the advent of the machine did it threaten "civilization" with "destruction." Since the Industrial Revolution, however, war itself was revolutionized along with all the ways of peace in the Great Society of a changed world until a state of affairs was reached in which it could be truly said that civilization would abolish war or war would abolish civilization.

Those most concerned with avoiding the latter outcome and attaining the former strove mightily for peace. But the attitudes and habits which they brought to bear upon the central problem of the twentieth century were inherited from the smaller, safer, and simpler world of the eighteenth century. The nature of the problem was therefore not perceived. All problem solvers, whether they be rats, monkeys, or men, see in new problems only what they have learned to see from experience with old problems. Some organisms, when convinced by new experience that old solutions will not solve new problems, are intelligent enough to devise new solutions which are relevant and successful. Other organisms, usually destined for extinction, love their old and familiar ways so devotedly that they persist, contrary to all reason, in futile efforts to make them work until they are completely unstrung and undone. Western mankind in this century obviously belongs to the second group of animals rather than to the first.

The price of peace in any State System, or in any community of lesser size, is the clear definition and general acceptance of common purposes and the subordination of all to one for the service of those purposes, whether the one be a conquering Caesar or a democratic central power created by the common will and resting upon consent. The price of peace is *E Pluribus Unum*. The purpose of the payment is the replacement of anarchy by order. The price of order in the community of nations is the end of national patriotism, national sovereignty, national isolation, neutrality, and independence and the substitution of effective organized force in the hands of guardians of the peace who are able and willing to apply the law, to enforce justice, and to suppress peacebreakers at whatever cost or risk. On no other terms can peace be had. Modern man has striven for "peace" through clever solutions and formulae whereby he sought to retain what must be abolished and to avoid establishing what must be created if peace is to become a reality. He has therefore failed, as almost all of his great leaders and thinkers assured him he would fail. Good intentions and wishful thinking do not suffice. Who pays the piper may call the tune. Who does not pay the piper will have no music. Who seeks to cheat the piper will end up with a broken head or worse.

THE "OUTLAWRY OF WAR." All the panaceas for war propounded by the organized peace movement,[1] save only the Wilsonian League and Clarence Streit's *Union Now*, have come to nothing and will, if persisted in, continue to breed frustration and disaster. The reason is that the propounders refused to face the issue or to pay the price that must be paid if the purposes of peace seekers are ever to be attained. A brief sketch of the major panaceas which led to governmental action will suggest the physiognomy of failure.

The solution of the problem of peace through international agreements, wherein the signatories pledge themselves to refrain from war, is not distinctive of the post-Versailles period. Early treaties pledging eternal peace and friendship among the parties constituted, by implication, a renunciation of war, as do all treaties providing for the pacific settlement of disputes. The League Covenant was such a treaty, as were the Locarno agreements of 1925.

In the Treaty of Mutual Guarantee (the "Rhine Pact"), Germany and Belgium, and likewise Germany and France, agreed "in no case to attack or invade each other or to resort to war against each other" except (1) in self-defense, which includes resistance to a flagrant breach of the articles of the Treaty of Versailles demilitarizing the Rhineland, (2) in the course of action under Article 16 of the League Covenant, and (3) in action resulting from a decision of the Council or Assembly of the League of Nations. The four Treaties of Conciliation, Arbitration, and Compulsory Adjudication (Germany-Belgium, Germany-Czechoslovakia, Germany-France, and Germany-Poland) provided unqualifiedly that "all disputes of every kind between Germany and (the other signatories) with regard to which the parties are in conflict as to their respective rights, and which it may not be possible to settle amicably by the normal methods of diplomacy, shall be submitted for decision either to an arbitral tribunal or to the Permanent Court of International Justice as laid down hereafter. It is agreed that the disputes referred to above include in particular those mentioned in Article 13 of the Covenant of the League of Nations" (Article 1). A permanent conciliation com-

[1] *Cf.* pp. 562–587 of the second edition of the present book.

mission was established by each of the treaties. To this body all disputes not settled by adjudication or arbitration were to be submitted, with the right of appeal to the Council of the League. All the parties were thus bound to resort to pacific means of settlement. This *implied* a negative obligation not to resort to force but did not expressly say as much, save for the Treaty of Mutual Guarantee applying to Germany's western frontiers. The latter instrument was a definite renunciation of war, subject to the broad and somewhat ambiguous exceptions noted. The other treaties renounced the use of force only by implication. Germany was unwilling to accept her eastern frontiers as definitive, and Great Britain and Italy were unwilling to guarantee them. Germany agreed not to attack or invade France and Belgium, and they accepted the same obligation toward Germany. But with regard to Poland and Czechoslovakia, the German Government merely agreed to settle all disputes by pacific means.

The conclusion of the Locarno Pacts was followed by negotiations, initiated by the Soviet Union, for similar pacts in eastern Europe. On December 17, 1925, the first of these treaties was concluded at the Soviet embassy in Paris between the U.S.S.R. and Turkey. Article 1 provided for the neutrality of each party in the event of the other party being attacked by any third party or parties. In Article 2 each party undertook not to attack the other and not to participate in hostile acts or agreements with third parties directed against the other, including financial and economic boycotts. The appended protocols provided for pacific means of settlement. "The best proof of the peaceable intentions of the agreement," declared Litvinov, "is the fact that the Soviet Government is ready to conclude an analogous agreement with all countries with which it has normal relations." Similar nonaggression pacts were concluded between the U.S.S.R. and Germany (April 26, 1926), Lithuania (September 28, 1926), Afghanistan (August 31, 1926), Persia (October 1, 1927), Estonia (May 2, 1932), Latvia (February 5, 1932), Finland (January 21, 1932), Poland (July 25, 1932), France (November 29, 1932), and—ironically—with Germany once more (August 23, 1939).

The Soviet Union supplemented its nonaggression pacts by efforts to define aggression. At the London Economic Conference of 1933, Litvinov signed a multilateral convention defining aggression with Afghanistan, Estonia, Latvia, Persia, Poland, Rumania, and Turkey (July 3), another with Czechoslovakia, Rumania, Turkey and Jugoslavia (July 4), and a third with Lithuania (July 4). Finland adhered later. These agreements were based upon the Politis Report (May 24, 1933) of the Security Committee of the League of Nations Disarmament Conference, which in turn was based upon the proposals of the Soviet delegates at Geneva. They declared that the aggressor in an international conflict would be considered that State which first declares war, invades foreign territory, attacks the territory, naval vessels, or aircraft of another State, imposes a naval blockade, or aids armed bands to invade the territory of another State.

These agreements and various others to be noticed below were all regional in character and provided for the renunciation of war by bilateral or multilateral agreements. The Covenant of the League of Nations, on the contrary, was a general renunciation of war by world-wide agreement. Article 11 of the Covenant made any war or threat of war a matter of concern to all members of the League. Article 12 obliged all members to submit disputes to arbitration, adjudication, or inquiry by the Council. "They agree in no case to resort to war until three months after the award by the arbitrators, or the judicial decision, or the report by the Council." The members further agreed (Article 13) "that they will not resort to war against a member of the League which complies" with any award or decision or (Article 15) with the Council's recommendations. Under the Covenant, war was still possible three months after an award, decision, or Council report, in the event of the rejection of the settlement by one or both parties. It was likewise permissible if the Council failed to make a unanimous recommendation, if there was unreasonable delay in arriving at an award, decision, or recommendation, if a dispute was found to be "domestic," if the dispute was between nonmember States, and if sanctions were applied against a Covenant-breaking State. These obligations, therefore, constituted a renunciation of war which was partial and incomplete, with many loopholes remaining open.

Following the establishment of the League, a long series of efforts was embarked upon to plug up the loopholes in the Covenant and to render more specific and effective the obligations not to resort to war. The first of these was embodied in the Cecil-Requin Draft Treaty of Mutual Assistance of 1923, which declared (Article 1) that "aggressive war is an international crime and (the contracting parties) severally undertake that no one of them will be guilty of its commission." The knotty problem of defining aggression was to be left to the League Council, which would designate the State which was the victim of aggression in a particular conflict and therefore entitled to assistance from the other signatories. After the rejection of this arrangement, the Geneva Protocol of 1924 appeared. Its preamble asserted that "a war of aggression constitutes a violation of [the solidarity of the members of the international community] and an international crime." It contemplated the amendment of the Covenant and provided that the signatory States would agree "in no case to resort to war," except in resistance to aggression or with the consent of the Council or Assembly. The signatories also agreed to "abstain from any act which might constitute a threat of aggression against another State." An aggressor State was defined as one going to war after refusing to accept the procedures for pacific settlement provided for, or rejecting a decision. In doubtful cases the Council would designate the aggressor and apply sanctions. The British Government failed to ratify the Protocol, and it was abandoned. The Locarno pacts followed as a regional substitute for general agreement.

The negotiations preceding the Kellogg-Briand Pact (the General Treaty for the Renunciation of War) had been initiated in June, 1927, by a proposal from M. Briand to Secretary of State Kellogg for a bilateral Franco-American treaty solemnly renouncing war as an instrument of national policy. Mr. Kellogg, with the support of peace seekers everywhere, proposed making the treaty multilateral and general. Briand agreed, provided that it should be restricted to "wars of aggression." Kellogg dissented, and the French Government finally agreed to general renunciation. Great Britain agreed to become a party on condition of reserving its liberty of action in "certain [undefined] regions of the world, the welfare and integrity of which constitute a special and vital interest for our peace and safety." This British "Monroe Doctrine" was accepted, though the Canadian and Irish Governments and subsequently the Egyptian, Turkish, and Persian Governments declared themselves not bound by it. The Pact was signed at the Quai d'Orsay on August 27, 1928, by representatives of fifteen States. By the close of 1930 it had been adhered to by sixty-one States, Argentina and Brazil being the only important abstinents. After considerable wrangling over ratification and some subsequent interpretations and understandings, President Hoover proclaimed the Pact in force on July 24, 1929. Its text follows:

. . . Deeply sensible of their solemn duty to promote the welfare of mankind;
Persuaded that the time has come when a frank renunciation of war as an instrument of national policy should be made to the end that the peaceful and friendly relations now existing between their peoples may be perpetuated;
Convinced that all changes in their relations with one another should be sought only by pacific means and be the result of a peaceful and orderly process, and that any signatory Power which hereafter seeks to promote its national interests by resort to war should be denied the benefits furnished by this treaty;
Hopeful that, encouraged by their example, all the other nations of the world will join in this humane endeavor and by adhering to the present treaty as soon as it comes into force bring their peoples within the scope of its beneficent provisions, thus uniting the civilized nations of the world in a common renunciation of war as an instrument of their national policy; [the high contracting parties]
Have decided to conclude a treaty and for that purpose have appointed as their respective plenipotentiaries. . . .

Article 1

The high contracting parties solemnly declare in the names of their respective peoples that they condemn recourse to war for the solution of international controversies, and renounce it as an instrument of national policy in their relations with one another.

Article 2

The high contracting parties agree that the settlement or solution of all disputes or conflicts, of whatever nature or of whatever origin they may be, which may arise among them, shall never be sought except by pacific means.

Article 3

The present treaty shall be ratified by the high contracting parties named in the preamble in accordance with their respective constitutional requirements, and shall take effect as between them as soon as all their several instruments of ratification shall have been deposited at Washington.

This treaty shall, when it has come into effect as prescribed in the preceding paragraph, remain open as long as may be necessary for adherence by all the other Powers of the world. Every instrument evidencing the adherence of a Power shall be deposited at Washington and the treaty shall immediately upon such deposit become effective as between the Power thus adhering and the other Powers parties hereto.

It shall be the duty of the Government of the United States to furnish each Government named in the preamble and every Government subsequently adhering to this treaty with a certified copy of the treaty and of every instrument of ratification or adherence. It shall also be the duty of the Government of the United States telegraphically to notify such Governments immediately upon the deposit with it of each instrument of ratification or adherence. . . .

The Soviet Union was the first to ratify the Pact, despite the fact that it was denounced in Moscow for its indefiniteness and irrelevance. On December 29, 1928, the Soviet minister in Warsaw proposed that the two Powers, along with Lithuania, should sign a protocol (the "Litvinov Protocol") making the Pact effective between them at once without waiting for the general exchange of ratifications. The Soviet note deplored Poland's earlier refusal to sign a non-aggression and neutrality agreement. The Polish Government accepted in principle but made formal objections and counterproposals for the inclusion of Rumania and all the Baltic States. Litvinov accepted these suggestions at once. Lithuania had already accepted the Soviet proposal on January 3, 1929, and suggested to Latvia and Estonia that they should adhere to the protocol. On February 9, 1929, the protocol was signed at Moscow by representatives of the U.S.S.R., Poland, Latvia, Estonia, and Rumania. Lithuania and Turkey adhered on April 1, Danzig on April 30, and Persia on July 4. Simultaneous efforts to "close the gap in the Covenant" by incorporating the Kellogg Pact into amendments failed.

It was at once pointed out that the Pact was purely negative and contained no provisions for its enforcement. What were the "pacific means" of settlement which the signatories were to utilize? What in particular would the attitude of the United States be in the event of a violation of the Pact? Resolutions were introduced in the American Congress, suggesting that American aid be refused to aggressor States, but none of these was passed or acted upon. In the summer and autumn of 1929, in the course of Sino-Soviet hostilities in northern Manchuria, Secretary of State Stimson consulted with the other signatories as to what should be done. After much discussion, identic notes were despatched to Moscow and Nanking by the United States, Great Britain, France, and Italy in December, 1929. They arrived when the hostilities had ended and a new agreement had been signed. Litvinov failed to comprehend how the American Government, which then refused to recognize the U.S.S.R., could undertake to advise it on the conduct of its foreign affairs. The lack of established procedures of consultation which was partly responsible for this embarrassing situation led Mr. Stimson to suggest to M. Claudel, French Ambassador in Washington, that machinery be set up in the form of an impartial conciliation commission for consultation and for the mobilization of public opinion against an aggressor State. At the London Naval Conference of 1930 the question was again raised, since France refused to reduce her armaments without assurances of international support against an aggressor State. Mr. Stimson tentatively considered the conclusion of a "consultative pact," but a great hue and cry was at once raised in the American hinterland against this "foreign entanglement" and the proposal was dropped, like the proverbial hot potato. No agreement could be reached on guarantees of security, and France and Italy refused to become parties to the whole of the naval treaty. On November 11, 1930, President Hoover spoke of the desirability of "strengthening and buttressing" the Pact by agreements for negotiation, conciliation, and arbitration. Later in the month, however, the State Department, again bowing to American isolationist sentiment, denied that any negotiations to this effect had been opened.

The Sino-Japanese crisis of 1931–1932 produced a new emergency and led to a definite crystallization of opinion in the United States and at Geneva as to the means by which the Pact was to be enforced. On October 9, and again on October 12, 1931, Secretary Stimson urged the League of Nations to do all in its power to settle the dispute and ensure observance of obligations not to resort to war on the part of the contestants. The United States subsequently recalled the obligations of the Pact to both Japan and China. On October 16 Mr. Prentiss Gilbert, American Consul General at Geneva, took a seat at the Council table with instructions from Washington "to take part in the discussions when they relate to the possible application of the Kellogg-Briand Pact." A month later Ambassador Dawes was instructed to hover in the vicinity of the Council meeting in Paris for the same purpose, though he was ordered not to sit in on the sessions. This informal procedure of consultation did not produce any visible effect on the course of events in Manchuria. On January 7, 1932, in identic notes to Japan and China, the American Government formulated the "Stimson Doctrine" as a statement of the means to be employed in ensuring observance of the Kellogg Pact.

"In view of the present situation and of its own rights and obligations therein, the American Government deems it to be its duty to notify both the Government of the Chinese Republic and the imperial Japanese Government that it cannot admit the legality of any situation *de facto* nor does it intend to recognize any treaty or agreement entered into between these Governments, or agents thereof, which may impair the treaty rights of the United States or its citizens in China, including those which relate to the sovereignty, the independence, or the territorial and administrative integrity of the Republic of China, or to the international policy relative to China, commonly known as the Open Door policy; and that it does not intend to recognize any situation, treaty, or agreement which may be brought about by means contrary to the covenants and obligations of the Pact of Paris of August 27, 1928, to which treaty both China and Japan, as well as the United States, are parties."

In a letter to Senator Borah of February 24, 1932, Mr. Stimson expressed the hope (after the British Government had declined to invoke the Nine Power Pact or take other joint action with the United States) that a similar decision would be reached by the other governments of the world, in order that "a caveat will be placed upon such action which, we believe, will effectively bar the legality hereafter of any title or right sought to be obtained by pressure or treaty violation, and which, as has been shown by history in the past, will eventually lead to the restoration to China of rights and titles of which she may have been deprived." On March 11, 1932, the League Assembly accepted this means of enforcement in a resolution.

"The Assembly . . . declares that it is incumbent upon the members of the League of Nations not to recognize any situation, treaty, or agreement which may be brought about by means contrary to the Covenant of the League of Nations or to the Pact of Paris."

In the summer of 1932, Dr. Charles Saavedra Lamas, Argentinian Foreign Minister, proposed a draft Antiwar Treaty on Nonaggression and Conciliation. This agreement was signed by Argentine, Brazil, Chile, Mexico, Paraguay, and Uruguay on October 10, 1933, and was later adhered to by the other American Republics, including the United States, and also by Italy, Portugal, Bulgaria, Greece, Turkey, Czechoslovakia, Rumania, Jugoslavia, Spain, and Norway. The Pact once more condemned wars of aggression and provided procedures of conciliation. Its importance, if any, lies in the fact that it provides for nonrecognition of the spoils of conquest and thus buttresses the Stimson Doctrine. It further stipulates that in the event of its violation the contracting States will undertake to maintain peace "but will in no case resort to intervention, either diplomatic or armed." They will, however, "adopt in their character of neutrals a common and solidary attitude." The former provision penalizes aggressors by a moral and legal boycott and the latter presumably contemplated a neutral "united front" in future conflicts.

In summary, then, the States of the world renounced war and agreed to enforce this renunciation by refusing to recognize any advantage, territorial or otherwise, achieved by one State through warlike coercion of another. Why, then, was peace not assured? The explanation of this paradox is to be found in part in the meaning attached to the Pact in the interpretative notes and understandings which preceded its ratification. No technical "reservations" were made. At French insistence, however, the Pact was expressly understood not to apply to wars of self-defense or to obligations under existing military alliances. At British insistence the Pact was understood not to interfere with a State's liberty of action in areas vital to its interests—and these areas were purposely left undefined in the British "Monroe Doctrine." In the United States, it was understood (at least by the State Department) that the Pact in no way interfered with the right of the United States to enforce the American Monroe Doctrine—likewise undefined—in the name of self-defense. During the negotiation of the Pact, representatives of the United States at Havana strongly opposed the nonintervention resolution sponsored by the Latin Americans. It was agreed by all parties that the Pact forbade only "wars of aggression" and did not apply to defensive hostilities, to hostilities against a State violating its obligations under the agreement, or to hostilities required by the League Covenant, the Locarno treaties, or other engagements of alliance or neutrality.[1]

The Pact, moreover, lacked any effective means of enforcement. It was understood that if one signatory violated the Pact the others were released from it. The Pact was no stronger than its weakest link. But a State resorting to force to protect or promote its interests can always argue, with much show of reason, that the Pact does not apply, since it is acting in "self-defense." It can also argue, with equal reason, that all measures of "settlement" unaccompanied by a declaration of war are "pacific," as indeed they are in a technical, legal sense. Other States may dissent and "world opinion" (if one admits its possibility in a world of multitudinous diversity and discord) may condemn. But a State which is strong and determined will not be restrained by verbal censure. It will be restrained only by superior force.

The efficacy of the Stimson Doctrine as a restraining influence was negligible. The foreign office at Tokio, in its note to the United States of January 16, 1932, commented dryly,

The Government of Japan takes note of the statement by the Government of the United States that the latter cannot admit the legality of matters which might impair the treaty rights of the United States or its citizens or which might be brought about by means contrary to the treaty of August 27, 1928. It might be the subject of an academic doubt, whether in a given case the impropriety of means necessarily and always voids the ends secured, but as Japan has no intention of adopting improper means, that question does not practically arise.

In reality the Stimson Doctrine failed of its purpose. On February 24, 1933, the League Assembly adopted a report of the Committee of Nineteen which provided that the members of the League would "continue not to recognize this régime (Manchukuo) either *de jure* or *de facto*." An advisory committee, with which the United States cooperated, recommended the exclusion of Manchukuo from international conventions, the nonacceptance of Manchukuan passports, and a number of postal, currency, and consular restrictions on relations with the new State. But on March 3, 1934, Salvador granted formal recognition to Manchukuo; and on April 29, 1936, Germany concluded a commercial agreement constituting at least *de facto* recognition. The United States continued to provoke Japanese resentment by adhering to the Stimson Doctrine in the Far East, but neither the United States nor the League Powers formally applied the Doctrine to the Italian conquest of Ethiopia. Indeed the Italian decision to annex Ethiopia, rather than to set up a puppet State,

[1] Under the Pact and comparable instruments, an aggressor may be legally defined as a State which persists in resorting to force contrary to obligations it has assumed and in violation of procedures it has accepted for implementing such obligations. See Quincy Wright, "The Concept of Aggression in International Law," *AJIL*, July, 1935, pp. 373–395.

was perhaps influenced by the Stimson Doctrine. This decision left other States with no practical means of withholding recognition from the *fait accompli*. The United States and certain other governments, to be sure, continued for a time to maintain fictitious diplomatic posts at Addis Ababa, accredited to a nonexistent Ethiopian government, and pretended to receive Italian diplomats only as representatives of Victor Emanuel as "King of Italy" and not as "Emperor of Ethiopia." Germany, on the other hand, accepted the conquest by reducing her legation at Addis to a consulate general on July 25, 1936, and on October 25 expressly recognized Italian title. Austria, Hungary, and Japan followed suit. In May, 1938, the League Council renounced the Stimson Doctrine. General recognition of Italian title to Ethiopia followed. The device of the legal boycott did not outlaw war, restrain aggression, or prevent conquest. The underlying assumption of the Doctrine was as naïve and as far removed from the realities of international politics as was the whole theory of the outlawry of war itself.

The Kellogg Pact and other agreements for the renunciation of war, however, had one legal effect of considerable significance. They rendered it expedient for States to refrain from formal declarations of war or from the expression of any intention to inaugurate a state of war in the legal sense. Even this myth, however, soon became a thing of shreds and patches. After years of armed combat, Paraguay abandoned the pretense of "peace" and declared war on Bolivia on May 10, 1933. Neighboring States declared their neutrality. In 1935–1936 Italy, the only European Great Power which had signed the Argentine Antiwar Treaty of 1933, openly violated that compact, as well as the Kellogg Pact, the League Covenant, and other engagements by waging war upon and destroying the last independent kingdom of Africa. Although the Covenant was invoked against Italy, the other agreements were conveniently forgotten, as was the Stimson Doctrine. The United States, before the outbreak of hostilities, merely expressed the hope that Italy and Ethiopia would both observe their obligations. In October, however, the American Government recognized the existence of a state of war and proclaimed its neutrality. But it did not adopt any "common and solidary attitude" with other neutrals. Here the renunciation of war broke down completely, and the status of belligerents and neutrals in an anarchic State System resumed its ancient sway. The assumption of violence and the law of the jungle in international politics are not to be uprooted by pious hopes, however solemn are the pacts in which such hopes are incorporated.

THE FAILURE OF DISARMAMENT. Attention may now be given to efforts to achieve peace through disarmament. Such efforts must, by their nature, be "international," *i.e.*, based upon agreements among States, for no State can safely discard or reduce its armaments while its rivals and potential enemies remain armed. At the Paris Peace Conference of 1919, lip service was paid to disarmament as one of the major "war aims" of the Allies. The Allied statesmen incorporated into the treaty provisions for the disarmament of the defeated States. The forcible disarmament of vanquished by victors was not new (in 1808, Napoleon compelled Prussia to limit her armies to 42,000 men for ten years), but it was carried out more completely in the peace treaties concluding the Great War than ever before. The German general staff was abolished, military conscription in Germany was forbidden, and the German army was limited to 100,000 men. These soldiers had to be enlisted for 12 consecutive years, and not more than 5 per cent of the total effectives could be discharged in any one year—a device designed to prevent a repetition of the Prussian tactics of the Napoleonic period, whereby a large trained reserve was built up by successive installments. Tanks, poison gas, heavy artillery, and aircraft were forbidden to the German army. Munition plants were dismantled or converted to peace purposes, and Germany was subjected to the supervision of inter-Allied military, naval, and aeronautical commissions to ensure observance of these terms. The Rhineland was demilitarized and Germany was forbidden to maintain forts or garrisons within a 50-kilometer zone east of the Rhine. For 15 years the Rhineland and the Rhine bridgeheads were to be subjected to Allied military occupation, though the last of the occupying forces were in fact withdrawn in 1930. The imperial German navy was surrendered—and scuttled by its crews at Scapa Flow on June 27, 1919. For the future the German navy was limited to 6 battleships not to exceed 10,000 tons, 6 light cruisers, and 12 destroyers. Germany was denied the right to construct or use submarines or military and naval airplanes (Articles 173 to 210 of the Treaty of Versailles). The supervisory commissions were later dissolved, but, by Article 213 of the Treaty, "German undertakes to give every facility for any investigation which the Council of the League of Nations, acting if need be by majority vote, may consider necessary." Austria was limited to an army of 30,000, Hungary 35,000, and Bulgaria 33,000. Similar efforts to disarm Turkey were frustrated by the repudiation of the Treaty of Sèvres, but by the Straits Convention of 1923 the Turkish garrison at Constantinople was limited to 12,000 men, the Bosphorus and the Dardanelles were demilitarized, and the number and size of war vessels to be admitted to the Black Sea were limited.

Pending the realization of the general disarmament which was anticipated in the peace settlement, the naval Powers began considering the possibility of putting an end to the new armaments race which had already begun. President Harding invited the other naval Powers—Great Britain, Japan, France, and Italy—to attend a conference, which was broadened to include China, the Netherlands, Belgium, and Portugal, for the discussion of Pacific and Far Eastern problems. The measure of success achieved by the Washington Conference, which met on November 12, 1921, has never been equaled by any succeeding disarmament conference. Its success was due to the fact that none of the participants had any political purposes to serve by establishing its naval superiority over any of the others and that all of them had both a political and a financial interest in stabilizing armaments at the existing levels. If naval armaments were limited or reduced proportionately for all, the "security" and the fighting potential of each would be unaffected. In the opening address of the Conference, Charles Evans Hughes, the American Secretary of State, offered to abandon the American building program in return for concessions from Great Britain and Japan. He proposed limitation and reduction on the basis of the *status quo*, through the scrapping of certain ships and the abandonment of building plans.

This bold proposal was at length accepted; Great Britain, the United States, and Japan agreed on a 5:5:3 ratio in capital ships, *i.e.*, battleships and battle cruisers. France and Italy later accepted a ratio of 1.67 each. The Five Power Treaty Limiting Naval Armament, signed February 6, 1922, provided for the scrapping of 68 ships, built or planned. The United States was left with 18 capital ships of 525,850 tons, Great Britain with 20 ships (most of them smaller and older than the American) of 558,950 tons, Japan with 10 of 301,320 tons, France with 10 of 221,170 tons, and Italy with 10 of 182,800 tons. The treaty likewise limited aircraft carriers to a total of 135,000 tons each for Great Britain and the United States, 81,000 for Japan, and 60,000 each for France and Italy. No agreement could be reached on other types of vessels. Great Britain urged the abolition of submarines, but the other Powers refused to consider this. The French Government announced its intention of constructing 90,000 tons of submarines.[1] The British then refused to consider any limitation of destroyers, which in turn made cruiser limitation impossible. A draft treaty forbidding the employment of submarines as commerce destroyers was signed, but it failed of adoption because of French refusal to ratify it. No agreements were reached regarding aircraft and land forces.

The Washington Conference likewise formulated a number of agreements relating to the Far East and the Pacific. The prospective increase of American fortifications in Guam and the Philippine Islands had been viewed with the greatest apprehension by Japan, since these bases constituted a direct threat to Japanese naval ascendancy in the western Pacific. Persistence on the part of the United States in a policy of establishing its naval hegemony west of Hawaii would probably have led to war as certainly as would Japanese efforts to acquire and fortify bases in the eastern Pacific. The Japanese Government demanded the limitation of Pacific fortifications as the price of agreeing to the 5:5:3 ratio and of relinquishing the Anglo-Japanese alliance. Despite opposition from American

[1] The French Government likewise resented the implication of naval parity with Italy and declared in July, 1923, when it ratified the treaty, "The French Government considers, and always has considered, that the ratios of total tonnage in capital ships and aircraft carriers allowed to the several contracting Powers do not represent the respective importance of the maritime interests of those Powers and cannot be extended to the categories of vessels other than those for which they were expressly stipulated."

naval officers, Secretary of State Hughes accepted this bargain. Article 19 of the Naval Treaty provided that the United States, Great Britain, and Japan "agree that the *status quo* at the time of the signing of the present treaty, with regard to fortifications and naval bases, shall be maintained in their respective territories and possessions specified hereunder." The United States agreed to maintain the *status quo* in all its Pacific possessions save Hawaii and the islands adjacent to the coast of the United States, Alaska, and the Panama Canal zone; Great Britain accepted the same obligations for its possessions east of 110° longitude (just east of Singapore, the site of an important projected naval base) save for Australia, New Zealand, and the coasts of Canada; Japan agreed not to change the *status quo* of its fortifications in the Kurile Islands, the Bonin Islands, Amami-Oshima, the Liu-Kiu Islands, Formosa, and the Pescadores.

The Four Power Pact, concluded at the same time among the United States, Great Britain, France, and Japan, specified that "with a view to the preservation of the general peace and the maintenance of their rights in relation to their insular possessions and insular dominions in the region of the Pacific Ocean" the parties "agree as between themselves to respect their rights" in these possessions. It further stipulated that any future controversies among the signatories over these territories would be submitted to a conference and that in case of any outside threat the parties would communicate with each other "in order to arrive at an understanding as to the most efficient measures to be taken, jointly or separately, to meet the situation." The Nine Power Treaty of February 6, 1922, relating to principles and policies in matters concerning China, reiterated the principle of the Open Door and bound the signatories to respect the sovereignty, the independence, and the territorial and administrative integrity of China as well as to use their influence to maintain equality of economic opportunity. The other Conference agreements and resolutions also related to Chinese problems.

If the Washington Conference had reduced the number of capital ships and terminated competition in their construction, it left the Powers quite free to construct whatever other types of vessel they desired. On February 10, 1927, President Coolidge invited Great Britain, Japan, France, and Italy to participate in a conference with the United States to limit construction of the types of vessel not covered by the Washington agreement. Great Britain and Japan accepted, but France and Italy refused, the former on the ground that outside conferences would hinder the disarmament work of the League of Nations, the latter on the ground that Italy's geographical situation made further limitation unwise.

The Geneva, or Coolidge, Conference which met on June 20, 1927, was thus a three Power conference, with the participants represented by their delegations to the League of Nations Preparatory Commission for the Disarmament Conference. These gentlemen were largely admirals and naval experts with no great enthusiasm for abolishing their own jobs. The problems to be dealt with were highly complex. Great Britain objected to the American proposals for a global limitation on cruiser tonnage, contending that the proposed tonnage was too low for British needs and that 8-inch gun cruisers and 6-inch gun cruisers should be limited separately and not lumped together. The British Government desired a large number of small cruisers, for it had naval bases scattered over the world and was perhaps reluctant, in any case, to concede cruiser parity to the United States. The American Government, lacking such bases, championed large cruisers, insisted on parity, and viewed with skepticism the British notion of "absolute" naval needs unrelated to the naval strength of other Powers. On August 4 the Conference broke up in failure. On February 13, 1929, the American Congress authorized the President to construct fifteen 10,000-ton cruisers and one aircraft carrier at a cost of 274 million dollars.

On April 22, 1929, Mr. Hugh Gibson, at the Preparatory Commission for the Disarmament Conference, took the first step toward allaying the new friction by declaring that the United States was prepared to consider further limitation and reduction on the basis of the French thesis: global limitation by tonnage and division of total tonnage for each State into the four categories of capital ships, aircraft carriers, surface vessels below 10,000 tons, and submarines, with maximums fixed for each category. The way was gradually prepared for a new agreement. The British Government, in view of the Kellogg Pact, decided to reduce its cruiser demands from seventy to fifty units. On October 4 MacDonald arrived in New York on a good-will tour, and on October 8 invitations to a new naval conference were dispatched by the British Government to the United States, Japan, France, and Italy after the Prime Minister had spent a week end with Hoover at Rapidan.

The London Naval Conference opened on January 21, 1930. The British representatives expressed their desire to bring down to the lowest possible level the building programs of all the participants and to prevent future competition in the building of all types of vessel, as the Washington Treaty had done for capital ships. The United States concurred in this aspiration but insisted on parity with Great Britain. Japan demanded a 70 per cent ratio in large cruisers, as compared with Great Britain and the United States, and the retention of her existing strength in submarines. The French delegation dwelt on the absolute naval needs of France in defending her colonial empire and proposed global limitation once more as a solution which would permit each State to specialize in whatever types of vessel it required. The French delegation later accepted a compromise, involving limitation by six categories of ships, with the possibility of transferring tonnage from one category to another. The Italian Government repeated its willingness to reduce its naval armaments to any level, provided that it was granted parity with other Continental Powers, *i.e.*, France. The United States supported Great Britain in advocating the abolition of the submarine, but France and Japan refused to agree.

The London Naval Treaty of April 22, 1930, was divided into five parts, of which Part III—the essence of the agreement—was not signed by either France or Italy. According to Part I, all five signatories agreed not to exercise their rights under the Washington Treaty of 1922 to lay down the keels of capital ship replacement tonnage during 1931–1936. Great Britain agreed to scrap 5 capital ships, the United States 3, and Japan 1. Armaments on aircraft carriers were limited to 6.1-inch guns. Submarines in the future were to be limited to 2,000 tons, with 5.1-inch guns, though each signatory retained the right to not more than 3 submarines of 2,800 tons, with 6.1-inch guns. The limitation on cruisers and destroyers (binding only on Great Britain, the United States, and Japan) divided cruisers into two categories: those carrying guns above 6.1-inch caliber and those carrying guns of less than 6.1-inch caliber. As for the first category, the United States was allotted 18 totaling 180,000 tons, the British Empire 15 of 146,800 tons, and Japan 12 of 108,400 tons. As for the second category, the United States received 143,500 tons, the British Empire 192,200 tons, and Japan 100,450 tons. The United States and the British Empire were each granted 150,000 tons of destroyers, as compared with Japan's 105,000; and all three Powers were granted 52,700 tons of submarines each. Limited transfers of tonnage from one category to another were permitted. In view of French and Italian abstention and the resulting danger to Great Britain from growing Continental navies, a "safeguarding clause" was inserted whereby these limits might be exceeded if necessary. Part IV of the treaty required submarines operating against merchant ships to place passengers and crews in a place of safety before sinking the vessel. Part V specified that the treaty would endure until December 31, 1936, except for Part IV, which was given an indefinite duration. A new conference in 1935 was provided for. This modest achievement was scarcely a triumph for disarmament and was doomed to frustration within five years. The ultimate failure of the naval Powers to continue the task of limitation, begun in 1921, followed upon the even more complete failure of efforts to promote general disarmament through the League of Nations.

The painful story of League efforts toward disarmament begins with the appointment by the Council in 1920 of a body known subsequently as the Permanent Advisory Commission, composed of a naval, a military, and an air representative of each State on the Council. This group of technical experts was ill adapted to its purpose;[1] and in November, 1920, the Assembly decided to supplement it with a Temporary Mixed Commission, appointed by the Council and consisting of six civilians of recognized authority in political, social, and economic matters, as well as representatives of the Permanent Advisory Commission, the economic and financial committees, and the governing body of the I.L.O. In September, 1921, the Second Assembly requested the Temporary Mixed Commission to prepare a draft treaty for disarmament. Between February and September of 1922 the Temporary Mixed Commission considered a plan for general disarmament submitted by Lord Esher, based upon the limitation of peacetime

---

[1] "It was as foolish to expect a disarmament convention from such a commission as a declaration of atheism from a commission of clergymen. . . . The military profession cannot recognize any duty above that which constitutes its very essence: the insuring the safety of its country. A military delegation sent to discuss disarmament problems cannot and should not envisage them—as it is implicitly requested to do—in a somewhat general and abstract light." Salvador de Madariaga, *Disarmament*, 1929, p. 91.

standing armies by ratios in units of 30,000 men, excluding reserves and overseas colonial forces and likewise excluding all consideration of weapons. In September, 1922, the Commission reported that no agreement had been reached and that the problem of disarmament was not to be solved directly by international limitation, but only indirectly by providing that security without which States were unwilling to disarm.

The 1922 Assembly accepted this view in Resolution XIV, which asserted that "in the present state of the world, many governments would be unable to accept the responsibility for a serious reduction of armaments unless they received in exchange a satisfactory guarantee of the safety of their country." The subsequent League efforts to promote disarmament were all based upon this assumption. They were therefore directed toward providing security. When this endeavor failed, the General Disarmament Conference of 1932, representing the culmination of League efforts, returned to the method of direct limitation and failed once more to accomplish anything thereby.

The Temporary Mixed Commission sought to achieve security as a step toward disarmament by implementing Articles 10 and 16 of the Covenant. The first fruit of its labors was the adoption by the Fourth Assembly (1923) of a Draft Treaty of Mutual Assistance for international aid to victims of aggression. Following the failure of this instrument to win general favor, the element of arbitration was introduced as a substitute for war and a test of aggression. The formula had been "Disarmament → Security → Arbitration." The formula now became "Arbitration → Security → Disarmament." The Fifth Assembly (1924) unanimously adopted the Geneva Protocol for the Pacific Settlement of International Disputes and laid plans for a General Disarmament Conference to meet on June 15, 1925. But the Geneva Protocol failed of adoption, just as the Draft Treaty had failed, because certain States, notably Great Britain, were unwilling to accept general and indefinite obligations to come to the defense of other States in controversies in which they had no immediate interests. General solutions having failed, special ones were attempted, and the Locarno treaties of 1925 resulted. The Sixth Assembly (1925) resolved, "In conformity with Article 8 of the Covenant [the Assembly] requests the Council to make a preparatory study with a view to a Conference for the Reduction and Limitation of Armaments, in order that, as soon as satisfactory conditions have been assured from the point of view of Resolution XIV of the Third Assembly, the said conference may be convened and a general reduction and limitation of armaments may be realized." The Council accordingly abolished the Temporary Mixed Commission and replaced it by the "Preparatory Commission for the Disarmament Conference," composed of representatives of States on the Council, plus certain other League members, and the U.S.S.R., the United States, and Germany from among the non-League States. Argentina and Chile were invited to become members in 1926, Greece in 1927, and Turkey in 1928. Representatives from the Soviet Union did not attend the sessions until 1927, after the Swiss Government had made appropriate reparation and apologies for the assassination of Vorovsky, Soviet delegate to the Lausanne Conference of 1923. The other non-League Powers, including the United States, accepted membership at once.

The seven sessions of the Preparatory Commission for the Disarmament Conference revealed clearly the difficulties of its task and foreshadowed the obstacles encountered later by the Conference itself. The first session met on May 18, 1926, and considered an elaborate questionnaire, already prepared by the Council. The later sessions of the Preparatory Commission were devoted to the elaboration of a draft convention to serve as the framework upon which the General Disarmament Conference would hang its achievements. The preliminary draft convention, drawn up and approved on April 26, 1927, was little more than a record of disagreements.[1]

Meanwhile, the Soviet delegates had appeared and had thrown the Commission into consternation by suggesting that the way to disarm was to disarm. On November 30, 1927, Litvinov proposed the complete abolition of all land, sea, and air armaments within one year, the abolition of conscription, of general staffs, and of war ministries, and the suppression of all war appropriations. Consideration of this proposal was deferred; and at the fifth session, on March 15, 1928, Litvinov presented a draft convention of sixty-three articles, embodying the Soviet project for immediate and complete disarmament. For the first time, the other members of the Commission were almost unanimous. They rejected the Soviet proposal. Only the German and Turkish delegates supported it. Litvinov then produced a second draft convention for partial and gradual disarmament, based upon the disarmament of the defeated States in the peace treaties. This was likewise rejected. The President of the Commission, M. Loudin, called upon the Soviet delegates on March 24 "in all seriousness to attend our next and any ensuing meetings in a constructive spirit, and not with the idea of destroying the work we have already done." On April 19, 1929, the Commission finally decided (with Turkey abstaining, and China and the U.S.S.R. voting in the negative) that it could not accept the Soviet plan but that the Disarmament Conference itself might consider its principles.

The seventh and final session of the Preparatory Commission met on November 6, 1930. It closed its work on December 9, 1930. Germany made a formal reservation to Article 53 and failed in her efforts to persuade the commission to set a date for the General Disarmament Conference. In January the League Council fixed the opening date for February 2, 1932, despite German pleas for November, 1931. In May the Council appointed Arthur Henderson, then British Foreign Secretary, President of the Conference. The Draft Convention—incom-

---

[1] The Belgian delegate, M. de Brouckère, characterized this outcome as follows: "We began with that celebrated trilogy which has aroused such enthusiasm: Arbitration, Security, and Disarmament. We then said: 'We are not concerned with disarmament but with reduction.' Then in a subsequent stage of our work it was pointed out that it would perhaps be too ambitious to attempt reduction, and thus we should have to content ourselves with limitation. Well, we have now reached a point when we may even have to erase this last word."

plete, emasculated, and devoid of any assurance of armament reduction—was a document of sixty articles, accompanied by blank tables of ratios and quotas, to be filled in by the Conference. It provided for budgetary limitation, limitation of the period of military service, limitation of effectives of land, sea, and air forces, the London Treaty method of naval limitation, and the creation of a Permanent Disarmament Commission. The Convention contained no provision for limiting trained reserves, none for direct limitation of war materials of armies and navies, and none for the limitation of the cost of materials of air forces.

The General Disarmament Conference of the League of Nations—the culmination of a decade of international efforts to attain disarmament and ensure peace—met at Geneva on February 3, 1932, with Arthur Henderson presiding over 232 delegates, representing 57 States. By an ironic coincidence, open warfare was going on at Shanghai while the delegates deliberated at Geneva. Five main committees were created to deal with budgetary limitation, political problems, and land, air, and naval armaments. The delegates brought with them no less than 337 separate proposals. On February 5 André Tardieu, head of the French delegation and, perhaps not inappropriately, Minister of War, presented a sensational scheme for the creation of a "preventive and punitive international police force" through action by the various States to place at the disposal of the League of Nations civil aircraft over a specified tonnage, bombing planes, and all other "offensive" weapons such as capital ships, batteries of long-range artillery, submarines, etc. This scheme was to be accompanied by compulsory arbitration and a new definition of aggression. The proposal at once encountered strong American, British, and German opposition. This and other proposals got nowhere. The Conference was stillborn.

No useful purpose would here be served by reviewing the painful tale of the subsequent efforts to breathe life into the Conference and of its slow decline and miserable demise. Stresemann had died on October 3, 1929. Briand died on March 7, 1932. Failure greeted all efforts to prevent the Conference from following him to the grave. Neither President Hoover's dramatic proposals of June 22, 1932, nor Chancellor von Papen's obscure schemes of a Franco-German alliance, nor the "Benês Resolution" of July 23 recording "progress" achieved, nor Germany's threat to withdraw of September 14, nor the "equality formula" offered to Berlin on December 6 nor MacDonald's appeal of March 10, 1933, nor Roosevelt's plea of May 16, 1933, nor even Norman Davis's pledge of May 22, 1933, promising no American obstruction to collective sanctions against peacebreakers, was able to break the deadlock.

The Nazi revolution of 1933 delivered the *coup de grace*. The refusal of the French bloc to grant arms equality to Germany had contributed to the triumph of German Fascism. The destruction of the Republic by Hitler's belligerent followers convinced the French bloc of the wisdom of having refused arms equality to Germany. German Fascism would take by force what German democracy had been unable to obtain by bargaining. The France which had not hesitated to send troops against the disarmed Germany of 1923 would not dare to send troops against the rearmed "Third Reich." The new German rulers were not interested in equality of armaments rights save in so far as the slogan of *Frieden und Gleichberechtigung* could serve the purposes of propaganda at home and abroad. Their new objectives in foreign policy called for the militarization of the nation on such a scale as to dwarf Hohenzollern militarism into insignificance. They moved at once to create a colossal war machine. They were deterred from repudiating immediately the League, the Disarmament Conference, the Treaty of Versailles, the Locarno Engagements, and all other legalistic impedimenta in the way of Fascist imperialism only by considerations of diplomatic expediency. To proceed step by step, to becloud the issue on each occasion with reassuring promises and specious "peace" proposals, to play upon British and French fears, sympathies, and anxieties—these were the techniques which would involve few risks and open the road for the downfall of the French bloc, the conquest of Czechoslovakia, the Danube valley, and the Ukraine, and the establishment of German military hegemony over Europe.

All discussion of reducing armaments now became utterly futile. When the General Commission of the Conference reassembled on February 2, 1933, a French plan of the preceding November was reexamined. France and the Little Entente demanded security pacts as a prerequisite to disarmament. Germany and Italy demanded disarmament (of France and the Little Entente) as a prerequisite of security. Britain and America would assume no further commitments. Autumn brought no harvest, but only the cold approach of death. During the summer Arthur Henderson had journeyed wearily to London, Paris, Berlin, Rome, and Prague, hoping against hope for some basis of agreement. The breakdown of the London Economic Conference was an ill omen. The march of Nazi legions echoed menacingly along the borders of Austria. On the fatal morning of October 14, 1933, Sir John Simon presented to the bureau of the Conference a statement, approved by France and the United States, designed to meet German demands for arms equality and French demands for security. The essence of the compromise was a four-year transitional period during which Germany would be content with her inferior status and after which the heavily armed Powers would begin to reduce their armaments. The reply from Berlin came within three hours: without warning or discussion, Germany announced her withdrawal from the Disarmament Conference and from the League of Nations. Hitler's first venture in the rude diplomacy of the *fait accompli* was a success. The other Powers gasped and did nothing. The German electorate almost unanimously endorsed the policy of isolation and defiance in the referendum of November 12. The Conference at Geneva expired.

Corpses are not interred when no one will assume responsibility for burial. The dead body of the Disarmament Conference long remained exposed to view at Geneva with the assembled diplomats ever and anon addressing it as though it lived and shuddering slightly at their macabre humor. On January 31, 1934, London sought to induce Berlin to return to the Conference by proposing that the Reich be permitted to have military aircraft, heavier artillery, and more numerous battalions. Mussolini made a similar gesture. He also proposed the abolition of chemical warfare and prohibition of bombardment of civilian populations. (Two years later, his bombing planes were raining poison gas on defenseless Ethiopians!) France spurned such schemes, demanded security, and pointed in alarm to the Nazi Stormtroops.

In June, 1934, the Bureau of the Conference met once more. Mr. Henderson's resolution for adjournment, pending Germany's return, was withdrawn. A French resolution, providing for continuance while the governments should seek separately to induce Germany to return, was adopted. The General Commission appointed committees on June 11 and adjourned till October. In September Litvinov proposed that the Conference be brought to an end and replaced by a small permanent commission. The League Assembly tabled his plan. On November 20 the United States submitted the draft of a convention for the international control of the private manufacture and trade in armaments. With this as a last reed to lean upon, the Conference, reduced to a skeleton, stumbled toward its grave. It had postponed everything, including its own death. On March 16, 1935, Germany repudiated Part V of the Treaty of Versailles and reintroduced military conscription. Arthur Henderson died on October 20, 1935. On March 7, 1936, Germany repudiated Articles 42 and 43 of the Treaty of Versailles, denounced Locarno, and sent troops into the demilitarized Rhineland. After sixteen years, the circle of frustration was closed. Efforts at world disarmament through the League had begun with the unilateral disarmament of Germany. The efforts ceased with the unilateral rearmament of Germany. The collective intelligence of Europe, having failed to achieve security, turned toward preparations for suicide.

Simultaneously the great sea Powers reached a similar impasse. Naval disarmament had begun in 1921 with the termination of an Anglo-American-Japanese naval race. Naval disarmament ended in 1936 with the resumption of the race. This melancholy tale of failure—as menacing to peace in the Pacific as was the failure at Geneva to peace in Europe—revolved about American opposition to Japanese demands for naval parity. Preliminary conversations looking toward a new naval agreement to replace the Washington and London Treaties were initiated in the winter of 1933–1934. Washington proposed the continuation of established ratios. Tokio proposed the abolition of long-range battleships and cruisers and equality between reduced Japanese and American fleets. Neither government receded from this position in later discussion. In June, 1934, tripartite negotiations in London revealed that no basis existed for an agreement. Japan contended that the increased cruising radius of battleships, the increased range of guns, and the development of transoceanic aircraft threatened Japanese security under the 5:5:3 ratio. She proposed parity and a reduction of navies to purely defensive forces. The United States contended that parity of navies would not afford parity of security, since the United States, unlike Japan, had two continental coast lines to defend and had vulnerable positions in the far Pacific. The result was a deadlock.

An unsuccessful disarmament conference is always worse than none at all, for it increases suspicions and insecurity and promotes preparation for war. Wisdom would have dictated that no new naval conference be held when it became clear that the Washington and London Treaties were doomed and that the Japanese and American positions were irreconcilable. But Downing Street and the State Department were imbued with the Anglo-Saxon conviction that talk around a table is always desirable. They pressed for a conference, promised in the 1930 settlement. The preliminary negotiations ended in December, 1934, with Britain and the United States opposing the Japanese plea for parity and maneuvering to put the blame for a breakdown on Tokio. On December 29, 1934, Ambassador Hirosi Saito submitted a communication to Secretary of State Hull:

In accordance with Article 23 of the Treaty concerning the limitation of naval armament signed at Washington on the 6th February 1922, the Government of Japan hereby gives notice to the Government of the United States of America of their intention to terminate the said treaty, which will accordingly cease to be in force after the 31st December 1936.

The London Treaty of 1930 was scheduled to expire on the same date. Washington moved at once to build its fleet up to full treaty strength by 1942. President Roosevelt expressed his conviction that the United States must keep pace in building with other naval powers so as to maintain the 5:5:3 ratio. The British Government eyed the new German navy with some apprehension. On June 18, 1935, in the name of "realism," Sir Samuel Hoare announced a naval pact with Joachim von Ribbentrop whereby the Reich was granted a navy 35 per cent of the strength of the British navy in all categories of vessels save submarines, which Germany might build up to 45 per cent or even 100 per cent of the British strength. This agreement, so far as Britain was concerned, superseded the naval limitations imposed upon Germany at Versailles. It was negotiated by

Downing Street three months after London had protested against German violation of the armaments clauses of the Treaty of Versailles. It was negotiated, moreover, without consultation with France and the U.S.S.R., both of which felt that they had been betrayed by Britain and were directly menaced by German sea forces. Moscow and Paris moved to increase their fleets in the face of this threat, just as the United States increased its navy in the face of Japan's demand for parity.

Despite these inauspicious developments, delegations from the United States, Great Britain, Japan, France, and Italy met in London on December 9, 1935. Neither the American-Japanese nor the Franco-Italian deadlock over parity had been resolved. Each delegation reiterated the proposals already made by its government. Speeches, appeals, and counterproposals effected no compromise. An American plea for a 20 per cent reduction in navies with existing ratios continued met with no support. The Japanese plea for a "common upper limit" was rejected. On January 15, 1936, the Japanese delegation withdrew from the conference. Negotiations continued among the four remaining Powers. On March 25, 1936, a new naval treaty was signed by Great Britain, France, and the United States. Japan would have none of it. Italy refused to sign in the face of League sanctions and British naval threats in the Mediterranean.

The new treaty provided neither for reduction nor quantitative limitation of naval armaments. Its only contribution was an agreement on the tonnage and guns of war vessels. Capital ships were limited to 35,000 tons and to 14-inch guns—or to 16-inch guns in the event of Japanese nonadherence. No capital ship of less than 17,500 tons would be laid down prior to January 1, 1943. Aircraft carriers were limited to 23,000 tons and 6.1-inch guns, light surface vessels to 8,000 tons and submarines to 2,000 tons. The signatories agreed to exchange information on future building programs. Numerous "safeguarding" and "escape" clauses opened the way for departure from even these limited restrictions. The American and British Governments reiterated their adherence to the principle of parity between themselves. London and Tokio availed themselves of the escape clauses of earlier agreements to enlarge their fleets before the close of 1936.

By the beginning of 1937, all treaties imposing quantitative restrictions on the three great naval Powers were at an end. Britain, France, and the United States had agreed to (but had not yet ratified) certain qualitative restrictions, none of which was likely to be observed in the event of other naval powers ignoring them. Britain and Germany had agreed (June 18, 1935) that the German navy should be 35 per cent as large as the British. Anglo-Soviet negotiations for a naval pact came to nothing, in part because of German opposition to any increase of the Red navy in the

Baltic. The United States proceeded to strengthen the fortifications of its bases in the western Pacific and rejected British suggestions that Article 19 of the Washington Naval Treaty be kept in force as a means of maintaining the *status quo* of fortifications. By March, 1937, the British Government had announced plans for constructing 238,000 tons of new battleships, including three 35,000-ton dreadnoughts, and for expending over 100 million pounds in the ensuing year on naval armaments. The United States followed suit, and Japan struggled desperately to keep pace with her wealthier rivals in a naval race which was far costlier and more dangerous than that which preceded 1914. On April 28, 1939, Hitler denounced the Anglo-German Naval Pact of 1935 on the ground that Britain's alliance with Poland was hostile to the Reich and a violation of the purpose of the agreement.

Disarmament at sea had become a memory of the fading past and a feeble hope of the remote future. Disarmament on land and in the air had never amounted to more than the temporary reduction to helplessness of the vanquished of 1918. Even this was now gone with the victors helpless to prevent the vanquished from arming to the teeth for revenge. Japan and America drifted toward conflict. Germany armed for the day of glory, and her neighbors armed desperately in self-defense. Each Power sought safety in matching its potential enemies regiment for regiment, bombing plane for bombing plane, battleship for battleship. In this there could be no security but only the promise of disaster. On the walls at the feast of Belshazzar, the destruction of his kingdom was foretold by the cryptic words *mene, mene, tekel, upharsin*. The letters of FAILURE, written large over the portals of successive disarmament conferences during the two decades after Versailles, became letters of impending catastrophe for the Western world.

SECURITY AND SANCTIONS. International efforts to renounce war and to limit armaments obviously failed to assure peace. The roots of this failure lay deeply embedded in the very foundations of power politics in the Western State System. On the surface the failure was attributable to a lack of "security." Governments refused to give up armaments or to abstain from armed attacks on other States on the ground that their "security" required weapons and demanded the vigorous defense of jeopardized interests. In the abstract all States are equally concerned with security. In practice, however, security has been the peculiar concern of insecure States. In international politics, as in all politics, the insecure are not necessarily the weak and the poor, but rather those whose vested interests in the *status quo* are challenged. Weak States threatened with aggression by strong States clamor for security. Strong States whose strength rests on the spoliation of defeated rivals clamor for security when the rivals recover their power and menace the established distribution of satisfactions. Such States seek to organize the whole community of nations for their own protection. "Security" thus becomes a problem of international guarantees and sanctions on a world-wide scale to replace or supplement national armaments and military alliances.

The problem of sanctions lies near the heart of all international efforts to prevent war. The problem is not new, although it was never dealt with seriously by governments before 1919. It has already been pointed out that international law differs from national law in that there is no collectively organized, coercive authority in the existing structure of international government to restrain lawbreakers and preserve order. The "sanctions," i.e., methods of enforcement, of international law were described as habit, expediency, good faith, and organized force. The first three of these involve individual action by separate States—with each State protecting its rights by self-help, holding others responsible for violations of its rights, and observing the rights of others to the degree dictated by custom, honor, or fear of reprisals and retaliations. These national sanctions rely ultimately upon national power or upon force exercised by a State or a group of States with common power interests. The application of physical coercion becomes the ultimate means of enforcing law. But the result is not peace and justice, which the observance of law is designed to promote, but war, which is the negation of justice and the essence of lawlessness. Almost all observers, save the most ardent advocates of military preparedness, agreed in the post-Versailles period that purely *national* sanctions of a coercive character offered no hope of preventing war in the future. They differed fundamentally, however, regarding the deductions to be drawn from this conclusion.

Some peace seekers argued that no sound analogy could be drawn between police forces within States and the instruments of physical coercion in the relation among States; that peace could never be preserved by force; and that the whole effort to ensure peace through war or threats of war was doomed to failure. Those who accepted this view sought to provide noncoercive sanctions: "public opinion," a sense of duty, reciprocal respect for rights, moral obligations, etc. Others—including the Governments of the French bloc—contended that coercion is undesirable as a sanction only when it is applied nationally by single States or groups of States against other States. They argued that the sanction of general *international* organized force offered the only hope of preserving peace. In this way, war makers would be restrained through the application of coercion against them on the part of the whole community of States. All the States of the world must therefore be organized to preserve peace by force—and since no single State could defy the entire world, acts of aggression would become so inexpedient as to compel their abandonment.

This cleavage between the advocates and the opponents of collective international coercion frustrated all post-war efforts to achieve security. At the Paris Peace Conference the view prevailed that peace could be assured only by organized force on a world-wide scale. This notion had been developed by the American "League to Enforce Peace," the British League of Nations Society, and other groups of peace seekers interested in the problem of international political organization. It had been accepted by Wilson, Lloyd George, Clemenceau, and the Allied Governments generally. Pre-war experience was rich in instances of the successful application of international force by the Powers against small, weak States. As early as 1904 Theodore Roosevelt had spoken of the necessity of an international police force, and in 1910 he declared that the weakness of the Hague peace machinery "arises from the lack of any executive power, of any police power to enforce the decrees of the court."[1] An American congressional resolution of the same year (Resolution 43, June 25, 1910) proposed the combining of the navies of the world into "an international force for the preservation of universal peace." In 1916 Senator Henry Cabot Lodge had declared that force must be placed behind international peace.[2] In view of these developments, it was natural that the framers of the Covenant of the League of Nations should have incorporated into that document provisions for the application of international force against Covenant-breaking States.

Article[3] 16 obviously contemplated the application of international economic pressure and military force against peacebreakers, under the direction of the League Council. Nonmember States which resorted to war against League members could be proceeded against in the same fashion as members (Article 17, §3). These provisions were at once criticized by the advocates of international sanctions as being too weak and by its opponents as being too strong. At the Peace Conference the French Government made a much more far-reaching proposal for an international police force under an international general staff, with the Council empowered to entrust enforcement of League decisions to particular States. This plan, which amounted to a revival of the procedure of the Holy Alliance, was rejected by the other Allies. The sanctions article as written into the Covenant was further weakened by the interpretations attached to it. It was discussed in connection with Article 10, guaranteeing the League members against external aggression and authorizing the Council to "advise upon the means by which this obligation shall be fulfilled." At the Fourth Assembly (1923) an interpretative resolution was introduced, declaring that the Council, in recommending the application of military measures, "shall be bound to take account, more particularly, of the geographic situation and of the special conditions of each State. It is for the constitutional authorities of each member to decide, in reference to the obligations of preserving the independence and the integrity of the territory of members, in what degree the member is bound to assure the

---

[1] Nobel Prize speech of May 5, 1910.
[2] See pp. 213f. above.
[3] See pp. 231–232 above.

execution of this obligation by employment of its military forces." Each State would thus determine for itself whether it would cooperate in the application of sanctions. In the vote on the resolution, twenty-nine States approved, thirteen abstained, and one (Persia) disapproved.

The interpretation given to Article 16 itself led in the same direction. In 1921 the Second Assembly adopted a resolution making the application of an economic boycott against a Covenant-breaking State optional and discretionary, rather than obligatory and automatic, on the part of other members. "The unilateral act of the defaulting State cannot create a state of war; it merely entitles the other members of the League to resort to actual war or to declare themselves in a state of war with the Covenant-breaking State; but it is in accordance with the spirit of the Covenant that the League of Nations should attempt, at least at the outset, to avoid war, and restore peace by economic pressure." Moreover, "it is the duty of each member of the League to decide for itself whether a breach of the Covenant has been committed." The Council was further authorized to "postpone the coming into force of any of these measures for a specified period where it is satisfied that such postponement will facilitate the attainment of the object of the measures . . . or that it is necessary to minimize the loss and inconvenience which will be caused to such members." This resolution was unanimously adopted and incorporated into a proposed amendment to Article 16, which, however, was never approved. It was clear that in the view of the League members the Council could merely "advise" (Article 10) or "recommend" the application of sanctions, military or economic. It could not mobilize the sanctions and command States to apply them, since each State would decide its obligations for itself. The final betrayal of Article 16 has already been reviewed.[1]

When it was perceived that the Covenant was inadequate in this regard and that disarmament was impossible because of the insistence of the French bloc on security through some alternative arrangement, efforts were launched to supplement the Covenant with other instruments. The Draft Treaty of Mutual Assistance, considered by the Fourth Assembly in 1923, proposed to give the Council definite authority to designate the "aggressor" State in each conflict and to decide what military forces each State should be required to place at the disposal of the victim of aggression. This proposal proved quite unacceptable to the States outside the French bloc, as had its predecessors. The Geneva Protocol of 1924 laid greater emphasis upon compulsory arbitration, adjudication, or decision by the Council. States refusing to resort to this procedure, or violating such decisions as might be reached, would be presumed to be aggressors unless the Council unanimously held otherwise. The Protocol failed of adoption. Despite the fact that it conferred less authority upon the Council than the Draft Treaty, it was nevertheless regarded as limiting freedom of State action too rigidly and as involving States in conflicts in which they had no direct interest. This view was taken by the British Government, which urged special and regional agreements in place of such general arrangements.

[1] *Cf.* pp. 235–245 above.

The Locarno Treaty of Mutual Guarantee, initialed on October 16, 1925, represented the first significant effort to create a regional security pact which should cut across established lines of international rivalry and afford genuinely collective guarantees of protection to the signatories. Despite temporary apprehensions in Moscow, there was here formed not an alliance among Germany, France, Belgium, Great Britain, and Italy against an outside enemy but an arrangement for mutual aid among the signatories. They collectively and severally guaranteed the maintenance and inviolability of the Franco-German and Belgian-German frontiers and also the observance of the stipulations of Articles 42 and 43 of the Treaty of Versailles concerning the demilitarized zone of the Rhineland (Article 1).[1] Germany and France and Germany and Belgium agreed (Article 2 and 3) not to attack, invade, or resort to war against each other and to settle all questions of every kind by peaceful means: diplomacy, adjudication, conciliation, or appeal to the League Council. In the event of alleged violation or breach, appeal would be had to the Council. Should it find that a breach had been committed, it would notify the signatories "who severally agree that in such case they will each of them come immediately to the assistance of the Power against whom the act complained of is directed." In the event of a flagrant violation of the Treaty or of Articles 42 or 43 of the Treaty of Versailles, "each of the other contracting parties hereby undertakes immediately to come to the help of the party against whom such a violation has been directed as soon as the said Power has been able to satisfy itself that the violation constitutes an unprovoked act of aggression and that by reason either of the crossing of the frontier or the outbreak of hostilities or of the assembly of armed forces in the demilitarized zone immediate action is necessary" (Article 4).

The ultimate fate of this agreement indicated the difficulty of committing States to aid other States against aggression when the States thus committed are not moved to act by national self-interest. On March 7, 1936, the German Government repudiated the Locarno Treaty and Articles 42 and 43 of the Treaty of Versailles and sent the Reichswehr into the Rhineland, alleging that the Franco-Soviet Pact had violated Locarno and released Germany from her obligations. This was precisely one of the contingencies which the Locarno commitments were designed to cover. Britain and Italy were bound to come to the military assistance of France to prevent German remilitarization of the Rhine frontier. But the obligations in question were as much scraps of paper in London and Rome as in Berlin. France and Belgium took no military action against Germany because they feared to alienate Britain. Italy, occupied in Ethiopia and beleaguered by sanctions, would do nothing to aid Paris against Berlin.

[1] "Article 42: Germany is forbidden to maintain or construct any fortifications either on the left bank of the Rhine or on the right bank to the west of a line drawn fifty kilometers to the east of the Rhine. Article 43: In the area defined above the maintenance and the assembly of armed forces, either permanently or temporarily, and military manoeuvres of any kind, as well as the upkeep of all permanent works for mobilization, are in the same way forbidden. Article 44: In case Germany violates in any manner whatever the provisions of Article 42 and 43, she shall be regarded as committing a hostile act against the Powers signatory of the present Treaty and as calculated to disturb the peace of the world."

Downing Street spurned all French pleas for joint military measures and even for economic sanctions against Germany. Despite the plain language of the 1925 agreement the British Foreign Office denied that Germany had committed any "flagrant violation" or any "unprovoked act of aggression." Was not the Reichwehr, after all, merely occupying German territory? With this sophistry, Britain evaded her obligations. Locarno collapsed and none of its guarantors would act to save it.

Mussolini's Four Power Pact of July 15, 1933, was similarly doomed to futility. This was not a pact of mutual assistance and guarantee but was designed to promote security by pledging the four western European Powers to pacific collaboration and by promising treaty revision and arms equality to Germany. In deference to French desires the original project was modified to include a reference in a preamble to Locarno and to exclude any specific reference to treaty revision and arms equality. The Pact as signed declared that the High Contracting Parties would "consult together as regards all questions which appertain to them"; would "pursue, within the framework of the League of Nations, a policy of effective cooperation between all Powers with a view to the main-tainance of peace"; would "examine between themselves, and without prejudice to decisions which can only be taken by the regular organs of the League of Nations, all proposals relating to methods and procedure calculated to give new effect to" Articles 10, 16, and 19 of the Covenant; would strive to ensure the success of the Disarmament Conference and would reexamine collectively any questions it might leave in suspense; and would consult on economic questions. This consultative agreement committed no one to anything. Despite this fact, it was never ratified.

The ill-fated "Eastern Locarno" project, with its significant sequel, represented another unsuccessful effort to devise a regional mutual assistance arrangement contrary to the dictates of national self-interest. This project of Louis Barthou and Maxim Litvinov contemplated a pact of territorial guarantees and mutual assistance against aggression as a means of freezing the *status quo* in eastern Europe against Nazi attempts at revision or aggrandizement. France, Germany, and the Soviet Union would sign an agreement to aid any one of their number attacked by another. The U.S.S.R., Poland, Germany, the Baltic States, and Czechoslovakia would sign a similar pact with France as guarantor. It was hoped that Italy, Jugoslavia, Greece, and Turkey would conclude a Mediterranean Locarno and that a further agreement would link the three regional systems of collective security and place them under the aegis of the League of Nations, with Germany and the U.S.S.R. among its members. Such was the scheme which Barthou urged in London in July, 1934. Sir John Simon approved, since Britain was not called upon to accept any new obligations. On September 10, 1934, Berlin rejected the proposal on the ground that peace in eastern Europe could best be assured by bilateral treaties of nonaggression and that Germany could not pledge assistance to her neighbors. Poland refused to join if the Reich would not.

The project thus failed to materialize. The German counterproposal, if accepted, would forbid any of Germany's neighbors to come to the defense of any other in the event of a Nazi attack. On both sides security schemes were but means toward the attainment of ulterior objectives in the game of power. Paris and Moscow, however, were too concerned over Nazi designs to drop the plan completely. On September 12, 1934, Estonia, Latvia, and Lithuania, with Moscow's blessing, signed a ten-year pact of consultation and cooperation in foreign affairs. On September 15 the U.S.S.R. was admitted to the League. Barthou moved to negotiate mutual-assistance pacts against Germany if none could be had including Germany. On October 9, 1934, however, he and King Alexander of Jugoslavia were assassinated at Marseilles by a Croatian terrorist. His successor, Pierre Laval, was indifferent toward collaboration with the U.S.S.R. and preferred to bargain for Italian support against Germany. But Paris and Moscow were again brought together by Berlin's repudiation of the disarmament clauses of the Treaty on March 16, 1935, coupled with Anglo-Italian friction and Britain's disposition to acquiesce in Hitler's *fait accompli*. On May 2, 1935, Ambassador Vladimir Potemkin and Foreign Minister Laval signed a five-year pact of mutual assistance at the Quai d'Orsay. On May 16 Czechoslovakia signed a similar pact with Moscow, subject to the provision that mutual support would be rendered only if the victim of aggression received aid from France.

The Franco-Soviet Pact was belatedly ratified at Paris after Hitler's remilitarization of the Rhineland. It went into effect on March 27, 1936. In content and purpose, it was a defensive military alliance of the traditional type. In form it reflected the new conception of collective security. The signatories agreed, in the event of their being threatened with aggression by any European State, to consult regarding measures to enforce Article 10 of the Covenant. They further agreed to come immediately to each other's assistance in the event of actual unprovoked aggression and also to lend each other aid in application of Article 16 of the Covenant. A Protocol of Signature made it clear that the parties were bound to come to one another's assistance, even if the League Council failed to act, in the event of aggression against either of the contracting Powers' own territory. Other States were invited to join, specifically Germany, Poland, Czechoslovakia, and the Baltic States bordering on the U.S.S.R. Although the alliance was plainly aimed at Germany, it was strictly defensive in character, open to German adherence, and perfectly compatible with the League Covenant and the Locarno Treaties, despite Nazi allegations to the contrary.

The Quai d'Orsay and the Narkomindel had no serious expectation that Germany would join an arrangement so inimical to her diplomatic objectives. Despite references to the League Covenant, France and the U.S.S.R. had pledged themselves to join military action against Germany in the event of German aggression against either of them. The alliance was open to other States and placed within the framework of the League partly to placate Britain and partly by way of lip service to the principle of collective security. These Pacts among Paris, Prague, and Moscow, unlike the Locarno Treaty and the Four Power Pact, were based upon an actual community of national interests. Three States menaced by aggression agreed to act together against the aggressor. In the sequel, however, one of them (France) compelled another (Czechoslovakia) to surrender to the common enemy (Germany) in the hope that the third (the U.S.S.R.) would become the ultimate victim of enemy aggression. The Franco-Soviet Pact was never formally denounced. But Moscow had no further interest in it after Munich.

There can be no security, collective or otherwise, among States whose leaders refuse to accept commitments to act against aggressors or who betray the obligations they have assumed. Whatever may have been true in earlier epochs, there can be no security or peace for anyone in this epoch without security and peace for everyone. In the age of the Caesars, those who refuse to hang together are all hanged separately. But those who urged collective action earlier were denounced in every country by good patriots and imperialists as "visionaries," "meddlers," "warmongers," "bellicistes," "internationalists," and "traitors." In the end each national tribe sought safety in a panic flight back to sovereignty, neutrality and isolation—like frightened cattle running back into the burning barn. By such devotion to outmoded myths the members of the Great Society brought their community to disaster and their nations to destruction.

3. CAESARISM CONQUERS DEMOCRACY

They that can give up Liberty to obtain a little temporary Safety deserve neither Liberty nor Safety.—BENJAMIN FRANKLIN.

Those who have been present at any deliberative assemblies of men will have observed how erroneous their opinions often are; and in fact, unless they are directed by superior men, they are apt to be contrary to all reason. But as superior men in corrupt republics (especially in periods of peace and quiet) are generally hated, either from jealousy or the ambition of others, it follows that the preference is given to what common error approves, or to what is suggested by men who are more desirous of pleasing the masses than of promoting the general good. When, however, adversity comes, then the error is discovered, and then the people fly for safety to those whom in prosperity they had neglected, as we shall show at length in its proper place. Certain events also easily mislead men who have not a great deal of experience, for they have in them so much that resembles truth that men easily persuade themselves that they are correct in the judgment they have formed upon the subject.—NICCOLÒ MACHIAVELLI, *The Discourses.*

The disintegration of the Great Society has been a process far vaster and more complex than is suggested by observing only the spread of poverty and war over the world. These scourges are but the symptoms of an inner and deeper disorder in human relations. Men starve and cure starvation with guns, men quarrel and slay their neighbors in battle because old ways of earning a livelihood no longer work in a new world, because old ideals and old devices of peace no longer bring results in the face of new and stubborn facts, because men lack capacity to learn, willingness to forget, talent to imagine and implement a new way of living in which their ancient hopes might be recaptured and realized. This lack is the earmark of decadence—of individuals, of nations, and of entire civilizations. The terrifying consequences of the lack are impoverishment and violence. These afflictions breed in turn new insecurities, new fears, new desperate expedients to escape from the need of taking thought and acting relevantly in the face of challenge.

One of the most striking concomitants of this process has been the breakdown of democracy in many of the Great States and the advent of a "new" political order which is in reality very old and appears in every Culture when men grow weary of freedom and no longer understand the world. When the burdensome responsibilities of liberty grow too heavy because the world becomes complex, when anxious men and women lose hope and feel intolerable fatigue of body and soul in the face of the necessity of meeting their problems by thought and talk, then democracy dies. In such situations the apostles of the "new order" denounce democracy and freedom as ignoble, unworkable, despicable, obsolete. Such situations, however, are never instances of the unworthiness of the ideal of freedom, but rather of the unworthiness of peoples who no longer deserve freedom. Those who have become slaves to outworn superstitions, those who no longer know what to do with their liberty because they are unwilling to face facts which are unpleasant and difficult, are seldom willing to acknowledge their own shortcomings. Vanity impels them to denounce others and to blame not their own blindness and fecklessness but the alleged inadequacies of a way of life and a set of values to which they are no longer able to give meaning. Tired of thinking and talking and failing in all they undertake, they look for a "Savior" who will think and talk for them and somehow make them happy again (no matter how) without obliging them to do anything more burdensome than Believe, Obey, Fight. Those who ask no questions, doubt no answers, and challenge no orders become robots and "heroes" in a mass which cheers and marches because the Leader commands. They have, after a fashion, "solved" the problems presented to them by the miseries and maladjustments of a disintegrating world.

The "new" form of political power which emerges from this development has been widely misnamed "dictatorship." The name is wrong because in classical usage and even in early modern usage a "dictatorship" was a temporary resort by the citizens of a democracy to the rule of one group, one party, or one man as a means not of destroying democracy but of preserving it in a crisis against external or internal threats. The so-called dictators of the twentieth century are not dictators in this sense. They are arbitrary rulers of people who have forever surrendered their freedom and often all desire for freedom. They are, in the political vocabulary of Greece and Rome, "despots" or "tyrants" who come to power after democracy has destroyed itself and with no thought or possibility of restoring it. They are the power-hungry whose will-to-power is ruthless, limitless, insatiable. They find their chance in the breakdown of democracy in crisis. They seize control of the State with the aid of their partisans and co-conspirators. They come with promises of salvation from crises and safety from real or imagined dangers. Like dictators, they are crisis rulers. But since they need crises to consolidate and perpetuate their rule, they are driven to manufacture one emergency after another in order that they may continue to "save" their subjects.

"Caesarism" is a better name for the "new" state form. It was in this fashion that the Roman Republic was destroyed and that Julius Caesar became the first of a long line of arbitrary rulers over people who had lost all desire to rule themselves. The later Caesars donned the garments of majesty and divinity. The first Caesar in every such transition from democracy to despotism is a political or military adventurer whose purpose is power as an end in itself. So it was before Rome in the Greek democracies in the period of their decay. So it was long after Rome in the nation-states of the West. The first adumbration in Western culture of the purely personal power of a self-appointed ruler came with Napoleon Bonaparte. His career was a premature microcosm of the twentieth century. He failed in the end either to unify the world or to found a permanent dynasty of despots because the will-to-freedom had in his time not yet died. The modern Caesars have faced fewer obstacles. A widespread rebirth of faith in freedom may yet bring them to ruin, but only if free men are themselves willing to pay the price of unifying the world and establishing a viable social order relevant to the needs of today and tomorrow.

The internal, or "domestic," anatomy of Caesarism can scarcely be discussed here. Suffice it to say that the social revolution in Russia which destroyed the old *élites* of land, money, and piety brought to power a group of daring men who, in the name of the "dictatorship of the prole-tariat," established the first "totalitarian," "one-party" State of our time. The Soviet State under Lenin moved perceptibly toward a recapture and redefinition of the values of Western liberalism. But Western liberals proved themselves incapable of reordering the world or their own affairs in such wise as to save themselves and serve their faith. Under Stalin the Soviet State became more and more a Caesar-State ruled by the will of one. In Italy the old *élites* of land, money, and piety destroyed democracy (in the name of "saving" Property and Religion from the menace of "Bolshevism") by delivering their nation and themselves into the hands of the adventurous Fascisti who blindly followed their Duce. In Germany, this process was repeated, with *Junkers* and industrialists imagining that they were protecting their power and privileges by making the Führer of the Nazis the Führer of the Reich. In Austria, Spain, Portugal, Jugo-slavia, Greece, Poland, Japan, Brazil, and defeated France the same process led to comparable results. In all cases the rulers of the totalitarian States finally deprived aristocrats, businessmen, and priests of many of their privileges and all of their influence and established a "socialist" tyranny of one party and one man.

The stages of this transition were clearly stated twenty-two centuries ago by the first great political scientist, Plato:

Tyranny naturally arises out of democracy, and the most aggravated form of tyranny and slavery out of the most extreme form of liberty. . . . The lead-ers of the poor deprive the rich of their estates and distribute them among the people, at the same time taking care to reserve the larger part for themselves. And the persons whose property is taken from them are compelled to defend themselves before the people as best they can. And then, although they may have no desire of change, the others charge them with plotting against the people and being friends of oligarchy. And the end is that when they see the people, not of their own accord, but through ignorance, and because they are deceived by informers, seeking to do them wrong, then at last they are forced to become oligarchs in reality.

This, and no other, is the root from which a tyrant springs; when he first appears above ground he is a protector. How then does a protector begin to change into a tyrant? . . . Having a mob entirely at his disposal, he is not restrained from shedding the blood of kinsmen. . . . Some he kills and others he banishes, at the same time hinting at the abolition of debts and the partition of lands: and after this, what will be his destiny? Must he not either perish at the hands of his enemies, or from being a man become a wolf—that is, a tyrant? . . . Then comes the famous request for a bodyguard, which is a device of all those who have got thus far in their tyrannical career. . . . At first, in the early days of his power, he is full of smiles, and he salutes everyone whom he meets; he is to be called a tyrant, who is making promises in public and also in private! liberating debtors, and distributing land to the people and his followers, and wanting to be so kind and good to everyone!

But when he has disposed of foreign enemies by conquest or treaty, and there is nothing to fear from them, then he is always stirring up some war or other, in order that the people may require a leader. . . . And if any of them are suspected by him of having notions of freedom, and of resistance to his authority, he will have a good pretext for destroying them by placing them at the mercy of the enemy; and for all these reasons the tyrant must be always getting up a war. Now he begins to grow unpopular. Then some of those who joined in setting him up, and who are in power, speak their minds. . . . And the tyrant, if he means to rule, must get rid of them; he cannot stop while he has a friend or an enemy who is good for anything. And therefore he must look about him and see who is valiant, who is high-minded, who is wise, who is wealthy; happy man, he is the enemy of them all, and must seek occasion against them whether he will or no, until he has made a purge of the state. . . . And the more detestable his actions are to the citizens the more satellites and the greater devotion in them will he require. . . .

If there are sacred treasures in the city, he will confiscate and spend them. . . . Then he is a parricide, and a cruel guardian of an aged parent; and this is real tyranny, about which there can no longer be a mistake: as the saying is, the people who would escape the smoke which is the slavery of freemen, have fallen into the fire which is the tyranny of slaves. (Plato's *Republic*, translated by Benjamin Jowett, in *Complete Dialogues*, New York, Random House, 1937, I, pp. 822–888 *passim*.)

Twenty years ago this process was also forecast for our own age by the German genius, Oswald Spengler, who saw most deeply into the meaning of history:

The more radical the political elimination of the matured old order of Estates and callings, the more formless and feckless the electoral mass, the more completely is it delivered into the hands of the new powers, the party leaders, who dictate their will to the people through all the machinery of intellectual compulsion . . . and treat public opinion merely as the weapon to be forged and used for blows at each other. But this very process, viewed from another angle, is seen as an irresistible tendency driving every democracy further and further on the road to suicide. . . . In the Late Democracy, *race* bursts forth and either makes ideals its slaves or throws them scornfully into the pit. It was so, too, in Egyptian Thebes, in Rome, in China—but in no other Civilization has the will-to-power manifested itself in so inexorable a form as in this of ours. The thought, and consequently the action, of the mass are kept under iron pressure—for which reason, and for which reason only, men are permitted to be readers and voters—that is, in a dual slavery—while the parties become the obedient retinues of a few, and the shadow of coming Caesarism already touches them. . . .

Through money, democracy becomes its own destroyer, after money has destroyed intellect. . . . Men are tired to digust of money-economy. They hope for salvation from somewhere or other, for some real thing of honor and chivalry, of inward nobility, of unselfishness and duty. And now dawns the time when the form-filled powers of the blood, which the rationalism of the Megalopolis has suppressed, reawaken in the depths. Everything in the order of dynastic tradition and old nobility that has saved itself up for the future, everything that there is of high money-disdaining ethic, everything that is intrinsically sound enough to be, in Frederick the Great's words, the *servant*—the hard-working, self-sacrificing, caring *servant*—of the State, all that I have described elsewhere in one word as Socialism in contrast to Capitalism—all this becomes suddenly the focus of immense life-forces. Caesarism *grows* on the soil of Democracy, but its roots spread deeply into the underground of blood tradition. . . . There now sets in the final battle between Democracy and Caesarism, between the leading forces of dictatorial money-economics and the *purely political* will-to-order of the Caesars. . . . [This is the] *final battle between Economics and Politics*, in which the latter *reconquers* its realm. (Oswald Spengler, *The Decline of the West*, New York, Alfred A. Knopf, Inc., 1928, II, pp. 457, 463f.)

The consequences of Caesarism for inter-state politics have become too obvious to require elaborate restatement. The specific forms of these consequences during the present decade will constitute much of the subject matter of the remainder of this volume. If Caesarism is the possible herald of a new and happy age and of a new world order, the prospect is still a hope and a wish, not a probability. Caesarism in its current manifestations is bred of anarchy and breakdown and promotes further anarchy. The devices by which the Caesars have already conquered much of the globe and the corollary devices by which the democracies have brought themselves to ruin may be conveniently summarized (with apologies to Machiavelli) in the remainder of the present chapter.

4. HOW TO BREAK NATIONS

A revolutionist must be able to do everything—to unchain volcanic passions, to arouse outbreaks of fury, to set masses of men on the march, to organize hate and suspicion with ice-cold calculation, so to speak with legal methods.—PAUL JOSEF GÖBBELS.

Faith is more difficult to shake than knowledge, love undergoes fewer changes than respect. Hate is more permanent than antipathy, and the impetus to the most powerful revolutions in this world lies at all times less in scientific cognition dominating the masses than in the fanaticism inspiring them and sometimes in the hysteria driving them forward. Who wishes to win the broad mass must know the key which opens the door to its heart. It is not called "objectivity," *i.e.*, weakness, but Will and Strength.—ADOLF HITLER, *Mein Kampf*.

The wise victor will, if possible, always impose his claims on the defeated people stage by stage, dealing with the people that has grown defeatist, and this is every people which has voluntarily submitted to force. He may then rely on the fact that in not one of these further acts of oppression will it seem sufficient reason to take up arms again.—ADOLF HITLER, *Mein Kampf*.

To be a perfect model of a modern Genghis Khan, it is first of all necessary for the would-be world conqueror to make himself absolute master of a large and powerful State. This can be done most readily in the twentieth century by founding a political party to win a mass following and by organizing a conspiracy against the government in power. Neither the conspiracy nor the party, however, should follow old patterns. The conspirators will fail of their purpose unless influential personalities in industry, commerce, finance, agriculture, the church, the army, and the civil service are enlisted, openly or secretly, in the cause. The party will fail unless it becomes a large military brotherhood of fanatics.

These problems are not difficult of solution in a period of economic crisis and social insecurity, particularly if full advantage is taken of demoralization and desires for revenge resulting from defeat in war. To admit openly that one is aiming at social revolution is to drive all the members of the upper classes together in common opposition and to force many middle class people into support of those one intends to destroy. This was the strategy of Lenin who built his brotherhood of followers almost exclusively from the ranks of workers, soldiers, and peasants. He achieved his goal, but only at the cost of bloody civil and foreign war precipitated by the propertied classes. The war left his country so exhausted that it was unable to give any effective aid to the revolution elsewhere or to conquer new lands by the sword. Mussolini and Hitler, in contrast, acted with, rather than against, the plutocracy and the aristocracy and won their mass followings among the little men of the middle class.

The delicate balancing and juggling which must be done to make effective use of the moneyed co-conspirators on the one hand and the marching mobs of fanatics on the other are difficult, but not beyond the talents of a shrewd tactician. Capitalists and nobles can be converted by promising to save them from radicalism. They are typically timid souls in perpetual quest of "confidence." They are often ignorant, knowing only how to manage their enterprises and having little conception of politics except in terms of how to manipulate democratic vote getters and how to secure favors from them once they are elected. They are often greedy and vicious, particularly when they are worried and believe that their privileges are threatened. They can therefore be won over with assurances of protection. They can easily be befuddled with the delusion that they can control all politicians who work with them because they have in the past controlled some. If one promises to "put labor in its place," to outlaw strikes, to get rid of reformers and crackpots in public office, the men of money will contribute generously to the cause.

The little people must be converted by other devices. They lead cramped and insecure lives. They fear and hate labor unions. They also fear and hate capitalists and aristocrats, partly out of envy, partly out of a sense of injustice and exploitation. These worried masses can be won by preaching "socialism," but it must be a patriotic socialism, "national" and anti-Marxist. They are easily frightened by the bogey of "Bolshevism" and will go to great lengths to save themselves. They can be persuaded to believe in any program (like the original Nazi platform of 1920) for abolishing trusts, breaking the power of the bankers, nationalizing industry, and dividing up large landed estates. Many workers and peasants will also be taken in by such pledges. This procedure is quite safe so long as the monopolists, the bankers, the industrialists, and the aristocrats are secretly given to understand that such programs are designed only to win followers and influence voters. Above all, the middle and lower classes in most countries can readily be bamboozled with the "socialism of fools"—i.e., anti-Semitism, for they are prone to simple and dramatic explanations of their troubles, and will readily believe that "capitalists," "labor agitators," "Reds," and other groups named with labels of dislike consist mostly of Jews or are led or secretly controlled by Jews. Once this poison is put to work in their minds and hearts, the battle is more than half won. These simple souls, moreover, live in drabness and crave excitement. The Party therefore should be full of music, marching, drama, pageantry, suspense, and hero worship. Here great artistry is needed in devising banners, symbols, uniforms, shirts, slogans, ceremonies, and other paraphernalia of mass mysticism. These masses also dislike the need of taking thought and are bitterly hungry for something to believe in. They must therefore be given a new faith and a "philosophy" which flatters their vanity. And they must be constantly assured that "the Leader is always right."

In the struggle for power it is important to make full use of all the opportunities of propaganda and political action afforded by democratic guarantees of civil rights and to avoid any open challenge by violence to the constituted authorities until the authorities can be counted upon to cooperate in destroying democracy. Between 1919 and 1922, Mussolini's Black Shirts, claiming full rights under the democratic constitution of Italy, marched and rioted throughout the peninsula, beating up enemies, raiding trade union and cooperative headquarters, demolishing newspaper offices, breaking up strikes, terrorizing liberals and radicals, and delighting many politicians and plutocrats. The "March on Rome" (October 28, 1922), however, was undertaken only after the King, the army leaders, and certain members of the Government had agreed to a Fascist regime. In the "Beerhall Putsch" in Munich on November 8 to 9, 1923, Hitler made the mistake of believing promises of cooperation from the Bavarian political leaders without having the means of compelling fulfillment. When they changed their minds during the night and called out police and troops, the Nazis were crushed—for a few years. Thereafter Hitler carefully avoided any open challenge to the Republic until he was able to seize power "legally" through friends and dupes on the inside. Franco's conspiracy in Spain was a carefully planned military coup organized by the army leaders. It failed through a series of accidents and through the courage of unconverted workers, peasants, and middle class people whose resistance was crushed only after two and a half years of bloody fighting.

To take power by fraud is always easier than to take it by force. The Führer won the German Chancellorship January 30, 1933, as the result of a plot against Chancellor von Schleicher hatched between Hitler and ex-Chancellor Franz von Papen with the connivance of the banker, Baron Kurt von Schroeder; Fritz Thyssen, steel magnate and leader of the *Reichsverband der Industrie;* the East Prussian *Landbund;* the great press and motion-picture magnate, Alfred Hugenberg; and old President von Hindenburg. Once in the Cabinet, although in a minority, the Nazis ordered an election. During the campaign their Stormtroopers terrorized most of the other parties. A week before the voting, they burned the Reichstag, blamed the Communists, shrieked that Red revolution was imminent, and panicked millions of German voters into voting Nazi as their only salvation. Hitler still won only 44 per cent of the votes on March 5, 1933; but the exclusion and arrest of all the Communists deputies gave his followers a "legal" majority and enabled them "legally" to suppress the trade unions and dissolve all other political parties by midsummer, thus accomplishing in three months what it had taken the pioneering Duce in Italy three years to accomplish a decade earlier.

Once in power, it will be found that the extension of these same devices to international politics will accomplish comparable results on the larger stage. Anti-Communism will befuddle the diplomats and the ruling classes of States earmarked for conquest. Anti-Semitism, skillfully propagated through appropriate agents, will befuddle the masses abroad. To win wars, allies are needed. But the most useful allies are not other friendly nations, but the appeasers, pacifists, isolationists, and political reactionaries in prospective enemy States. Some of these can be bought for cash. Others (*e.g.*, Laval, Flandin, Bonnet, Daladier) can be won over by adroitly playing on their sympathies and antipathies. Still others (*e.g.*, Chamberlain, Halifax, Simon, Hoare) will have the mentality of businessmen and will be easily persuaded that they can make "deals" and "bargains" like peddlers, even though it turns out each time in retrospect that they have given away much and got nothing in return. Still others (*e.g.*, Baldwin, Eden, Blum) will be weaklings who will hesitate and vacillate, being unable to decide on anything until all decisions have already been taken out of their hands by others.

In dealing with democracies, the conqueror-to-be must never neglect "public opinion," for democratic politicians are always dependent upon it. The wise tyrant will keep his own press under rigid control as well as his radio, motion pictures, school systems, and all other vehicles for the transmission of information and the shaping of mass attitudes. Thus no foreign government will have the slightest opportunity to use the tyrant's weapons of propaganda against the tyrant. But in democracies, where all the agencies of news, entertainment, propaganda, and education are free, nothing is simpler for tyrants abroad than to secure effective control of important elements shaping public opinion and to use them to propagate friendship, pacifism, appeasement, anti-Semitism, anti-Communism, and other programs which will confuse opinion and paralyze any action in opposition to the tyrant's aggression. In some democracies (*e.g.*, the Third French Republic), part of the press will be frankly for sale to the highest bidder. Bribes to owners, editors, and reporters, secretly and judiciously distributed, pay rich dividends. In other democracies (*e.g.*, Great Britain and the United States), this crude technique is less possible. But cordial relations can be readily established with the great magnates of the "yellow press" (*e.g.*, Rothermere, Beaverbrook, Hearst) who will be men of great wealth, easily persuaded until they are overtaken by catastrophe that their own interests and those of their class can best be served by denouncing "radicalism" and preaching "friendship" with foreign Powers whose rulers are preparing aggression under the mask of "anti-radicalism."

Another measure which is indispensable to conquerors who aim at maximum results at minimum costs is that of organizing disciplined and faithful groups of traitors inside of States earmarked for conquest. Such groups are of three kinds: high civil and military officials who are bought or converted to secret sympathy with the cause of the alien conqueror; revolutionary political parties, bribed and directed by the conqueror but acting ostensibly as patriotic organizations aiming at national renovation through exposure of corruption and abuses; and organized linguistic minorities seeking "autonomy," "self-determination," or "return to the fatherland." Members of the first category are useful for organizing coups d'état in crisis situations, manufactured to order by the diplomacy of the conqueror, and for paralyzing resistance to invasion. Those in the second category are able to discredit the leaders of the enemy State, to spread doubt and confusion, and, if they win an obedient mass following, to furnish popular support for appeasement, defeatism, or the direct subversion of the State. Members of national minorities, when they can be brought under totalitarian control and manipulated from abroad, are highly effective in provoking "persecution," winning democratic sympathy, and lending plausibility to irredentist and annexationist ambitions. Which type of group or which combination of groups can be organized and used most efficiently to disrupt the doomed State obviously depends upon circumstances.

Feeble and amateurish efforts toward the development of this technique of "boring from within" were made by the Bolshevik rulers of the U.S.S.R. almost as soon as they seized power in Russia in 1917. On the model of the Second, or Amsterdam, International of Socialist Parties, they sought to organize Communist parties in every country, federated in the Third, or Communist, International and subservient to Moscow. This world revolutionary conspiracy, however, failed completely of its purpose, for such parties either remained insignificant minorities (as in Great Britain and the United States) or else (as in Italy, Germany, and France) frightened all decent citizens into support of "anti-Communist" activities. Their chief importance was that of acting as foils or scapegoats for the far more widespread and efficient revolutionary conspiracy organized by the Fascist Caesars. Here all devices were successfully employed, and support was obtained from members of all classes. The aggressions of Japan in eastern Asia, of Italy in the Mediterranean and Africa, and of Germany in central and western Europe were all made possible by the successful use of the various types of "Trojan Horse" and "Fifth Column" here suggested.[1]

---

[1] See the following chapter for specific instances of the application of these techniques. According to Homer's Iliad the Greeks finally conquered long-besieged Troy in the legendary Trojan war by pretending to abandon the siege and leaving behind them a huge

All these devices are designed to "soften" resistance in order to make possible bloodless victories through coups d'état or "protective occupation" or "pacific" invasions. Overt violence should never be used save as a last resort. If circumstances permit of the effective use of the preparatory measures already indicated, violence will be unnecessary, for no possibility of effective counterviolence will remain. Totalitarian diplomacy (*i.e.*, bargaining, threats, intrigue, espionage, conspiracy, and the organization of revolution) is totalitarian war carried on by "pacific" means. The goal of diplomacy, as of strategy, is to outflank, encircle, and paralyze the enemy forces so as to induce nonresistance and surrender. The achievement of the goal requires that the enemy be disintegrated and demoralized from within, so that all will to resist is dissipated, and isolated from without, so that no allies will be available if resistance is attempted. The latter purpose is best promoted by making "deals" and concluding bilateral nonaggression and neutrality pacts with as many neighbors and friends of the intended victim as possible. Each may thus be dealt with in turn and conquered separately with no danger of opposition by a united coalition.

When the stage is appropriately set, it becomes feasible to strike with minimum risks. If the victim has already been sufficiently "softened" and deserted in advance by his prospective allies (*e.g.*, Austria in March, 1938), a sudden blow will often turn the trick. Such blows are best struck during the night or just before dawn and preferably on Fridays and Saturdays, since the attention of the victims and their friends will usually be turned elsewhere at such times. Once the blow is struck, other governments will find it easier to acquiesce in the *fait accompli* than to take counter measures which are already too late. Leaders of democracies can commonly be counted upon to take the course which is easiest or most popular. If the victim is disposed to resist, a prolonged crisis may be necessary to wear down his endurance. The arts of precipitating crises, managing their development, making threats and promises, feigning moderation or lunacy, spreading panic, increasing demands, and "saving peace" at the very last moment by an illusion of concessions are arts which the efficient conqueror must learn to employ with skill and subtlety. Under favorable conditions, these arts, properly practiced, may produce almost miraculous results—as when Hitler in 1938 induced Chamberlain and Daladier to

wooden horse filled with warriors. When the Trojans drew the horse into the city as a trophy of victory, the warriors leaped out and so confused and decimated the defenders that the city fell. The original "Fifth Column" was a group of rebel sympathizers in Madrid whose activities were expected to paralyze Loyalist resistance, thereby enabling the four advancing columns of Mola and Franco to take the city in October, 1936. Loyalist vigilance and Soviet military aid spoiled the plan. Madrid's Fifth Column had no opportunity to do its work successfully until all Loyalist military resistance collapsed in February and March, 1939.

believe that his designs upon Czechoslovakia were but the prelude to an assault upon the U.S.S.R. and thereby induced them, in the name of "peace" and "self-determination," to deceive their own people, to abandon Prague, and to compel Beneš to surrender to Berlin.

The wise conqueror will recognize, however, that the devices already reviewed may prepare the way for a total war of annihilation against once powerful foes but will never by themselves lead to the destruction of such foes. In the end, force must be used. But force should never be used until one has overwhelming superiority and the enemy is so weakened that his powers of resistance are at a minimum. This state of affairs is not difficult to achieve if one knows how to capitalize upon every weakness of the foe, how to befuddle and confuse his leaders, how to distract his attention and divide his people against themselves with irrelevancies (*e.g.*, anti-Semitism and anti-Communism), how to penetrate his military secrets, how to build a military economy and a military society dedicated to the single aim of conquest, how to develop new weapons, new tactics, new strategy, new commanders, above all how to restore in war the superiority of the attack over the defense. To attack is to conquer. To remain on the defensive is to invite defeat.

To break the resistance of the enemy, it is needful to keep at least a generation ahead of him in military science and two generations ahead of him in political science. The largest and most formidable enemy forces can readily be crushed at small cost by a 3 to 1 superiority in tanks, dive bombers, parachute troops, and armored divisions. It is well, however, to leave as little as possible to chance and to supplement the crushing technique of the *Blitzkrieg* with the well-coordinated action of spies, saboteurs, traitors, pacifists, appeasers, Trojan Horses, and Fifth Columnists behind enemy lines. In this fashion, political leaders can be seduced or bewildered, military commanders can be misled into actions certain to ensure the destruction of their forces, ports and fortresses can be rendered defenseless, air fields can be destroyed or occupied by local agents of the invader, bridges and roadways can be seized and made secure, enemy troops can be led to believe that they are deserted or betrayed, while mysterious and paralyzing terror is unleashed against the civilian population. Here again careful planning will produce almost miraculous results. Enterprises in conquest which formerly took months or years to carry through now become a matter of weeks, days, or even hours.

Once a country is broken and occupied, it will usually be found convenient to turn its civil administration over to a puppet régime, recruited from the ranks of the natives who have long been in the pay of the conqueror. Puppet rulers should not be raised to positions of prominence, however, before military victory is won, nor should it be assumed that a puppet can ever, by himself, rally a following and win a campaign. This was Stalin's mistake in recognizing Otto Kuusinen as "Premier" of Finland at the outset of the Finnish war and Tokio's mistake in setting up Wang Ching-wei at Nanking in March, 1940, and granting him diplomatic recognition in November. Mussolini acted more wisely in establishing Shefket Verlaci as "ruler" of Albania in April, 1939, *after* the country had been effectively occupied by Italian troops and King Zog driven out. The Duce, however was deceived in his hopes of setting up a puppet régime in Athens a year and a half later and was therefore led into military disaster. Hitler deemed the outright annexation of Austria preferable to a puppet régime under Austrian Nazis. He likewise annexed Sudetenland in preference to administering it through a puppet régime under Konrad Henlein. Father Josef Tiso, however, became a useful puppet ruler of Slovakia after March, 1939. It similarly proved advisable to keep King Christian on the throne of conquered Denmark and to employ Vidkun Quisling as administrator of Norway after King Haakon had rejected all inducements and fled the country. Puppets, however, are peculiarly allergic to assassins, and this difficulty cannot always be guarded against.

After each conquest is completed, it is wise to offer "peace" to remaining enemies and to make propitiatory gestures toward outside Powers whose people may be alarmed by the march of aggression. Such offers should be designed to bring about a cessation of hostilities on apparently moderate terms, couched in the language of compromise, justice, humanity, a new world order, and the like. Such offers will raise the morale of one's own people and create doubts among enemy and neutral populations as to the desirability of further resistance. If they are accepted, the resulting negotiations can easily be exploited to complete the demoralization of the enemy and the disillusionment of the neutrals in order to render all alike helpless before a new onslaught some months or years hence. If they are not accepted, they have still served the purpose of putting upon the foe the onus of continuing hostilities. Inducements to come to terms should be judiciously interspersed with threats. Terrorization of civilians is often more effective (and always safer) than attacks upon the armed forces of the foe. Threats of terrorization are sometimes more effective than the actuality. It is likewise useful to make "alliances" with as many other Powers as possible, even if they be empty of content, since some enemies can always be discouraged by the appearance of an overwhelming coalition and some neutrals can always be intimidated by like devices. Here again, however, it is fatal to confuse appearances with reality. Every delay, every truce, every possibility of a "negotiated settlement" must be utilized to prepare the new arms wherewith unconquered enemies can later be subjugated and to spread anti-Semitism, anti-Communism, and other poisons of disintegration in all countries from which resistance may be anticipated.

How long and how far these arts of conquest can be successfully applied is a question which can be answered only by experimentation. Other things being equal, the domestic victories won through these skills can be duplicated by diplomatic victories, and these in turn by military victories—first in local areas, then on a continental scale, and finally on a world scale. But the wise conqueror will realize that other things seldom remain equal. His own caution, his acuteness of perception, his intuitive sense of strategy and timing become dulled with the passing years and with an unbroken succession of triumphs. His very victories open eyes abroad that were hitherto closed. They lead to alarm in unexpected places, to the repudiation of old leaders and the emergence of new ones, to a growing ability on the part of prospective victims to see through the ideological and military tricks of the conqueror, to learn in the hard school of tears and blood, to adapt for their own purposes the weapons and tactics of the aggressor. It is a dangerous thing to convince any great people by threats and blackmail that its choice lies between conquering or being conquered. It is perilous to reawaken in any nation a passionate devotion to freedom. These sentiments break through the entangling cobwebs of illusion and summon to dynamic action reserves of wisdom and courage hitherto unsuspected.

Thus the people of Spain, although utterly unprepared to meet the assault upon their liberties launched against them by the Axis, fought heroically and successfully in defense of their rights for over two years. Despite large-scale military intervention against them by Germany, Italy, and Portugal, they would have triumphed over the Fascist rebels had it not been for the determination of Baldwin, Eden, Chamberlain, Halifax, Blum, Delbos, Daladier, Bonnet, Hull, and Roosevelt to deprive them of arms and ensure their defeat. Thus the Finns inflicted grievous losses upon the Soviet invaders of 1939 before they were finally compelled to sue for peace. Thus the British experienced a national awakening in the summer of 1940 and the Greeks, vastly inferior in numbers and materials, hurled back the Italian invaders in the autumn as their distant ancestors had once beaten back the hordes of Persia.

Most world conquerors of the past (but by no means all) were sooner or later brought to ruin by the forces of resistance which their conquests unleashed against them. In epochs of cultural decadence, however, the conquest of all the known world is quite within the capacity of a nation or a group of nations consecrated to war and led by ruthless adventurers. In such periods the victims of aggression each seek safety in flight and avoid any common action until it is too late. The balance of power is therewith destroyed. The victims, moreover, cling to the end to their beloved illusions and suffer the inevitable fate of the witless and the sightless. There is abundant evidence in the record of the recent past that the twentieth century of the Western world is precisely such an era. If so, then the conquerors of today need impose no geographical limits to the scope of their ambitions, for they may be certain that their larger and more distant victims will so behave as to bring down upon themselves a fate comparable to that which overtakes the initial victims in the first stages of the unification of the world by the sword.

5. HOW TO AVOID SURVIVAL

"Now! Now!" cried the Queen. "Faster! Faster!" And they went so fast that at last they seemed to skim through the air, hardly touching the ground with their feet, till suddenly, just as Alice was getting quite exhausted, they stopped, and she found herself sitting on the ground breathless and giddy.

The Queen propped her up against a tree, and said kindly. "You may rest a little now."

Alice looked around her in great surprise. "Why, I do believe we've been under this tree the whole time! Everything's just as it was!"

"Of course it is," said the Queen: "what would you have it?"

"Well, in *our* country," said Alice, still panting a little, "you'd generally get to somewhere else—if you ran very fast for a long time, as we've been doing."

"A slow sort of country!" said the Queen. "Now, *here*, you see, it takes all the running you can do, to keep in the same place. If you want to get somewhere else, you must run at least twice as fast as that!"— LEWIS CARROLL, *Through the Looking-glass*.

The new Machiavelli who would prescribe to the rulers of the doomed how they must conduct themselves to ensure self-destruction is performing a thankless task. Politicians and peoples seldom strive willfully for their own undoing. It is characteristic of lost souls that they regard each step toward damnation as the only possible means of salvation. They have no patience with those who suggest that their ways are in error and will produce consequences very different from those desired. They are intolerant of those who would open their eyes, for they prefer the comforts of blindness to the discomforts of facing realities. Yet the reflective student of politics whose purpose is not to state preferences but to describe and analyze how men act cannot refrain from depicting the process whereby States are done to death, for this is the inseparable counterpart of the process whereby conquerors win their triumphs.

The first prerequisite of self-destruction is to be conservative—not with the wise conservatism of those who know that old values can be saved only by constant redefinition and by courageous adventures in new solutions to new problems, but with the stubborn slowness of those who resent and resist the tides of change in the affairs of men. To learn nothing and to forget nothing is a formula which foredooms all peoples and rulers who follow it. This indeed is the earmark of decadence and the proud badge of all who are lost. This is the bright device of those who unwittingly welcome extinction: *in hoc signo, morituri salutamus.* This is the way of all hollow men in all epochs of decay—particularly of commercial ruling classes confronted by proletarian unrest from within and by conquering barbarians or Caesars from without.[1]

In our own times the businessmen and aristocrats of the Western capitalist democracies were for a long period (perhaps forever) unable or unwilling to forget or to learn. They remained patriots in a world society in which national patriotism could only spell world anarchy and the destruction of all they cherished. They refused to make the emotional and material sacrifices required to build a new world order. They likewise refused to make the sacrifices called for by the paralysis of their economies and by cries for "social justice" from the lower classes. They frequently preferred to meet their problems by employing the gangsters of the colored shirts, bred of lower class desperation, to preach hysterical chauvinism. They preferred to delude themselves with gangsters' promises to smash radicalism and trade unionism. They preferred to deliver the apparatus of the State to their own worst enemies in the name of protecting Property, Profits, and Piety against Bolshevism, Labor, and Atheism. In this wise the aristocrats and industrialists of Italy put Mussolini's Black Shirts in power in the early 1920's. In this wise, their counterparts in Germany put Hitler's Brown Shirts in power in the early 1930's. That these gentlemen of wealth and influence had thereby jeopardized their wealth and destroyed their influence to the advantage of a new political *élite* of fanatics, whose Caesar in the end would not respect Piety, Profits, or Property, did not occur to them until too late.

By the same token the business leaders (and the political leaders who spoke for business) in the France, Britain, and America of the late 1930's were quite unable to comprehend the consequences of playing diplomatic giveaway while the Caesars played cleverly at "heads I win, tails you lose." They behaved like Cardinal Innitzer of Vienna who welcomed the Nazis in March, 1938, as the God-sent protectors of religion and saviors of civilization from Bolshevism, only to discover in October that the saviors were sacking his palace and seeking him out for lynching. The Western *élites* devised a program based upon the postulate that Fascism was a useful bulwark against social radicalism and a foreordained destroyer of Communism and the U.S.S.R. This program of appeasement required not only that they render unto Caesar whatever Caesar claimed (particularly if it belonged to third parties), but that they rescue Caesar over and again from his own folly and strengthen him for their own destruction. This program was followed

[1] See the comments of Demosthenes, pp. 21–22, above, and of Plato, pp. 492–493.

with undeviating consistency from September of 1931 until the Ides of March of 1939—and indeed thereafter, despite the growth of doubts.

Appeasement of aggressors requires popular support. This is to be had by playing upon the patriotic and pacifist sentiments of the democratic masses. It is easy to convince voters that resistance means war, that connivance in aggression spells "peace for our time," that safety can best be had by isolationist neutrality, nonintervention, avoidance of foreign entanglements, "minding your own business," and "keeping out of other peoples' wars." It is easy to denounce each new victim of the aggressor as "Red" (even if he be black, yellow, or white) and to condemn as "warmongers," "interventionists," and "foreign propagandists" all critics who question the policy and demand a different course. The paid agents of the Caesars, and the bought press which serves their purposes, will gladly cooperate in such condemnation. The Caesars themselves will cooperate with democratic statesmen, as Mussolini did with Hoare and Laval in 1935–1936 and as Hitler did with Chamberlain and Daladier in 1938, in manufacturing war panics and convincing democratic electorates that concessions spell peace, that retreats are advances, that disastrous surrenders are great triumphs for justice, that defeats snatched from the jaws of victory are to be regarded as great successes. With proper collaboration, the democratic architects of such a catastrophe as the "Peace of Munich" will even be hailed upon their return as heroes.

Defeatist diplomacy, if it is to achieve its goal, must follow a few simple rules: Don't make alliances. Sabotage collective security. Refuse to cooperate with any other Power in preventing or suppressing aggression. Reject all commitments and obligations; or, still better, sign bilateral nonaggression pacts. Offer aggressors all they ask in return for avoidance of force. If they resort to force regardless, offer them more. Trust tyrants as if they were businessmen or gentlemen. Assume that they are interested in profits for themselves and their class and in prosperity for their people. Pay no attention to what they write, say, or do to the contrary. Ignore the content and direction of their heroic philosophies. Keep out of war by imposing impartial embargoes on aggressors and their victims alike, for this will help to make the world safe for aggression. Cling to isolationist neutrality and undiluted national sovereignty. If you have allies, desert them. If necessary, compel them to surrender to the enemy. Refuse to fight for anything except your own territory. If other Powers offer you alliances against aggression, spurn their offers or refuse to pay their price. This will drive them into collaboration with your enemy and thereby strengthen him enormously at your expense.

Don't rearm until too late. Don't tell the truth to your people. Confuse them with lies and comfort them with illusions. Help your enemies to rearm. Permit them to buy all they need in your markets for the creation of their own war machine. When they attack other States, proclaim your own neutrality and deny arms to the victims. If they promote rebellion in other States in order to bring them under control, sign solemn agreements and sponsor international committees to deny arms to the friendly government which the Caesars seek to destroy. When they have conquered other peoples, recognize their title to what they have seized (this will encourage them to seize more) and, if necessary, lighten their task of ruling the vanquished by feeding the conquered for "humanitarian" reasons, for this will aid the conquerors to prepare new conquests.

If, contrary to all your hopes, you are finally compelled to fight, remain on the defensive. Trust to fixed fortifications or to sea power or to money power or to "Maginot Lines," "hemisphere defense," passive resistance, and the like. Never wage war until your own territory is invaded, your cities bombed, and your houses burned over your heads. When waging war, never attempt an offensive. Leave the military and diplomatic initiative to the enemy. Appease and bribe his allies, so that when they later enter the war against you they will be strong and formidable. During war, keep appeasers and traitors in high office, fight radicalism at home more vigorously than the enemy abroad, protect Property and Profits first and the fatherland only later, if at all. When the enemy breaks through, change your leaders; put into high posts those who want the enemy to win. When he wins, surrender at once and offer to collaborate with him against such unconquered friends as you may still have left.

In all of this, it is essential above all for those seeking extinction to lose all faith in democracy and to seek salvation in tyranny or despotism. Tyrants can be counted upon ultimately to destroy all who oppose them and all who support them. Therefore it is well to bargain with them and to buy peace through compromise. They can be counted upon usually to destroy themselves in the end and reduce all men and all things to a vast chaos. In the words of Rudyard Kipling, "Here is nought unproven —here is nought to learn. It is written what shall fall if the King return. . . . He shall take a tribute, toll of all our ware; he shall change our gold for arms—arms we may not bear. . . . Hate and all division; hosts of hurrying spies; money poured in secret; carrion breeding flies. . . . We shall take our station, dirt beneath his feet, while his hired captains jeer us in the street. Cruel in the shadow, crafty in the sun, far beyond his borders shall his teachings run. Sloven, sullen, savage, secret, uncontrolled—laying on a new land evil of the old; long forgotten bondage, dwarfing heart and brain—all our fathers died to lose he shall bind again."[1]

[1] "The Old Issue," October 9, 1899, copyrighted 1899 as "The King," pp. 107–112 of Rudyard Kipling's, *The Five Nations*, Doubleday, Doran & Company, Inc., for *Review of Reviews*, 1914.

The danger to those who wish to be slaves or corpses, however, is that it is possible, as Lincoln put it, to fool some of the people all of the time and all of the people some of the time, but not all of the people all of the time. Simple men and women often have correct insights and intuitions, even when they lack knowledge. They have in greater measure than effete aristocrats and plutocrats a will-to-survive, a determination to preserve their liberties, and a disposition, when their eyes are open, to cry out, however senselessly, "Give me liberty or give me death!" They are therefore addicted to sacrifice and heroism and prone to violent resentments against their betrayers. Once awakened on a mass scale, they have been known to upset the best-laid plans and to snatch victory from the jaws of defeat. If the defeatists and appeasers blunder, a revolt of the masses may raise its ugly head and precipitate political or social revolution inspired with a fierce will-to-deeds against the foreign invader and his dupes and stooges at home. Chamberlain, Simon, and Hoare never quite solved this problem in Britain. Laval, Weygand, and Pétain solved it only temporarily in conquered France. In America the isolationists, pacifists, appeasers, and defeatists were not quite able in 1940 to prevent the masses from seeing reality and demanding effective national action against the enemies of the Republic.

This final obstacle in the way of complete success has baffled even the most efficient defeatists and their Caesarian allies. It has in some cases wrecked their highest hopes and brought them to ruin. It may yet in our age save the surviving democratic States through a new and revolutionary dynamism directed toward the reordering of economic and social relations within States and of the political relations among States. It may yet smash the would-be conquerors and their Trojan Horses and Fifth Columns among their prospective victims. Whether this will be so or no cannot now be forseen. All that is clear is that if leaders and masses alike in democratic States follow to the end the rules of action and inaction suggested above they will escape old age and discover that the paths of compromise lead most surely to the grave.

SUGGESTED READINGS

Allen, D.: *The Fight for Peace*, New York, Macmillan, 1930.
Angell, N.: *The Great Illusion*, New York, Putnam, 1913.
———: *The Unseen Assassins*, New York, Harper, 1932.
Ashton, E. B.: *The Fascist: His State and His Mind*, New York, Morrow, 1937.
Beneš, E., R. Coulborn, and A. Fuller: *International Security*, Chicago, University of Chicago Press, 1939.
Berber, F. J. (ed.): *Locarno: A Collection of Documents*, London, Hodge, 1936.
Bogart, E. L.: *The Economic History of Europe, 1760–1939*, New York, Longmans, Green, 1941.
Borgese, G. A.: *Goliath: The March of Fascism*, New York, Viking, 1937.
Briffault, R.: *Breakdown: The Collapse of Traditional Civilization*, New York, Coward-McCann, 1935.

Buell, R. L.: *The Washington Conference*, New York, Appleton-Century, 1922.
Carr, A.: *Juggernaut, The Path of Dictatorship*, New York, Viking, 1939.
Cassel, G.: *The Downfall of the Gold Standard*, New York, Oxford, 1936.
Curti, M.: *Peace or War. The American Struggle*, 1636–1936, New York, Norton, 1936.
Dawes, C. G.: *A Journal of Reparations*, New York, Macmillan, 1939.
Dennis, L.: *Is Capitalism Doomed?*, New York, Harper, 1932.
Dollard, J.: *Frustration and Aggression*, New Haven, Yale University Press, 1939.
Durbin, E. F. M., and J. Bowlby: *Personal Aggressiveness and War*, New York, Columbia University Press, 1939.
Ford, G. S. (ed.): *Dictatorship in the Modern World*, Minneapolis, University of Minnesota Press, 1939.
Glover, E.: *War, Sadism and Pacifism*, London, Allen & Unwin, 1933.
Graham, F. D., and C. R. Whittlesey: *Golden Avalanche*, Princeton, N. J., Princeton University Press, 1939.
Hutchins, R M. (chairman): *International Economic Relations*, Minneapolis, University of Minnesota Press, 1936.
Jones, F. E.: *The Defense of Democracy*, New York, Dutton, 1938.
Kemmerer, E. W.: *Money*, New York, Macmillan, 1935.
Kohn, H.: *Revolutions and Dictatorships: Essays in Contemporary History*, Cambridge, Mass., Harvard University Press, 1939.
League of Nations: *Records of the Conference for the Reduction and Limitation of Armaments*, Geneva, 1932–1934.
Lewis, C.: *America's Stake in International Investments*, Washington, D. C., Brookings, 1938.
Listowel, Earl of (introduction): *The Brown Network*, New York, Knight Publishers, Inc., Dial Press (Lincoln MacVeagh), Inc., 1936.
Madden, J. T., M. Nadler, and H. C. Sauvain: *America's Experience as a Creditor Nation*, New York, Prentice-Hall, 1937.
McMahon, M. M.: *Conquest and Modern International Law*, Washington, Catholic University Press, 1940.
Merriam, C. E.: *The New Democracy and the New Despotism*, New York, McGraw-Hill, 1939.
Miller, D. H.: *The Geneva Protocol*, New York, Macmillan, 1925.
———: *The Peace Pact of Paris*, New York, Putnam, 1928.
Morrison, C. C.: *Outlawry of War*, Chicago, Clark, 1927.
Moulton, H. G., and L. Pasvolsky: *World War Debt Settlements*, New York, Macmillan, 1926.
Parmelee, M.: *Bolshevism, Fascism, and the Liberal-Democratic State*, New York, Wiley, 1934.
Patterson, E. M.: *The Economic Bases of Peace*, New York, McGraw-Hill, 1939.
Pearson, D., and C. Brown: *The American Diplomatic Game*, New York, Doubleday, 1935.
Rauschenbusch, S.: *The March of Fascism*, New Haven, Yale University Press, 1939.
Reimann, G.: *The Vampire Economy: Doing Business under Fascism*, New York, Vanguard, 1939.
Robbins, L.: *Economic Planning and International Order*, New York, Macmillan, 1937.
Salter, J. A.: *Recovery—The Second Effort*, New York, Appleton-Century, 1932.
Sayre, F. B.: *The Way Forward*, New York, Macmillan, 1939.
Shotwell, J. T.: *War as an Instrument of National Policy and Its Renunciation by the Pact of Paris*, New York, Harcourt, 1929.
Staley, E.: *World Economy in Transition*, New York, Council on Foreign Relations, 1939.
Steed, Wickham, *Vital Peace: A Study of Risks*, London, Constable, 1936.
Wheeler-Bennett, J. W.: *The Pipe Dream of Peace*, New York, Morrow, 1935.
Williams, B. H.: *Foreign Loan Policy of the United States since 1933*, New York, Council on Foreign Relations, 1939.
Wright, Quincy: *Causes of War and Conditions of Peace*, New York, Longmans, 1935.

Chapter XI

THE MARCH OF THE CONQUERORS

Right without might is weakness. Might without right is tyranny. We must therefore combine right and might, making what is right mighty and what is mighty right.—Pascal.

WAR is less the product of evil within the hearts of men than of anarchy in the relations among men. When people murder their neighbors, burn their homes, and ravage their fields, they do so partly because collective fears and worries drive them to madness and brutishness. The primal beast in every man is civilized with difficulty. It breaks forth anew when inner anxieties and outer opportunities lend glamour to the guilty joys of pillage and butchery and enable men to externalize their aggressions with impunity. But aggressions flow from the maladjustments and frustrations of communities which are badly governed or governed in separate local areas not coterminous with the interests and needs of their inhabitants. Opportunities for collective crime result from ineffective enforcement of law. Where no central power exists to defend peace by restraining the use of force on the part of some against others and by imposing justice upon all, the result is anarchy. The inevitable fruit of anarchy in all civilized societies is war.

Anarchy is the absence of government. Where there is no government, each man fears and hates his fellows and protects his interests as best he can by his own strength. When government in an ordered society breaks down, all rivalries for power and all strivings for larger shares of available satisfactions sooner or later assume the form of violent conflict among individuals, classes, sections, parties, and factions. When, as in the world community of nations, government has not yet been established in a far-flung society which can no longer have order or peace without it, the local societies whose members have established peace and order within their frontiers become rivals among themselves—first for a brighter place in the sun and then for control of the tools of power which, once possessed, will enable each to coerce its neighbors and impose its demands and dreams upon them. Since trial by battle is the ultimate method of adjusting conflicts of claims among the members of such a society, each member is driven to seek superiority of fighting ability over his competitors in order that he may escape destruction at their hands and, if possible, destroy them lest he himself be destroyed.

The foreign policy of each Great Power is a formula for survival in an anarchic community wherein politics is a competition among "sovereignties" and a struggle of each against all. It consists of the attitudes and practices (and of the words which evoke them) whereby each State seeks to protect and promote "national interests." Diplomacy is the pursuit of power by bargaining and threats. War is the pursuit of power by overt violence designed to coerce rivals into compliance. The Powers whose leaders understand the stakes and rules of the game and comprehend the ever-changing chessboard on which the game is played usually achieve success by virtue of playing well. Failure and ruin are often the lot of those whose leaders are halt or blind or are restrained from "playing power politics" by pressures at home they cannot control. To play well is to survive and to win. To resolve not to play is to court disaster; for as long as some States play, all States are forced to play or forfeit their fortunes. The game itself must go on until anarchy gives way to order—either through one Power subjugating all its rivals or through the establishment of an enduring union of Powers with the will and the means to act as one. In either case, if war is to be abolished, the "balance of power" must be ended and further struggles for power by violence must be rendered impossible by the presence of a superior Power able and willing to enforce peace.

Until this point is reached (and in all the State Systems preceding our own it has at last always been reached), the cardinal principle of foreign policy for each Power desirous of survival is to conduct itself in such a manner that none of its rivals may secure a dangerous superiority of power and to arrange matters, if possible, so that it will acquire for itself a preponderance of power dangerous to its competitors. Armaments and allies are the normal weapons for upholding the balance to one's own advantage or upsetting it to the disadvantage of one's antagonists. Those who were least successful in the last contest and who are therefore the "unsatiated," or "have-not," Powers invariably strive in their weakness and humiliation to restore a balance and then to upset the restored balance by acquiring preponderance for themselves in preparation for the next contest. Those who were most successful in the last contest strive to maintain their own hard-won superiority and to thwart all efforts by the vanquished to restore an equilibrium. But success breeds complacency whereas failure breeds desperation. Since inaction is easier for those victorious (and therefore contented) than for those defeated (and therefore disgruntled), the "have-nots" are usually able, after an interval of time, to rebuild the balance and prepare new blows against their foes. The "haves" on the contrary are typically unsuccessful in the end in preserving their prestige, their power, and the fruits of their late victory.

In the course of this jockeying for position, the diplomatic game becomes a military game when the shifting equilibrium has reached a point at which the new aspirants for hegemony feel confident of their ability to defeat their rivals in arms, and the champions of the *status quo* feel constrained to resist rather than yield lest by yielding once too often they invite destruction. In the march of the years between major wars, the mid-point of the changing balance is reached when the victors of the last conflict cease to gain power and begin to lose it and when, conversely, the vanquished cease to lose power and begin to regain it. If the direction of the new trend is not reversed, the former winners are soon terrified with the prospect of defeat and the former losers are driven to new adventures by the hope of triumph. The terminal point in the sequence is war once more.

In the world-wide balancing of power between 1919 and 1939 the mid-point was reached in 1931 with the resumption of Japan's drive toward mastery of eastern Asia and the beginning of the long retreat of the Western Powers before the revived imperial ambitions of Tokio, Rome, and Berlin. Nine years of success in the quest for hegemony on the part of the unsatiated States, nine years of compromise and surrender on the part of the victors of 1918 brought all the Powers to the journey's usual end. The new war differed sharply from the old in that the challengers of the *status quo* were bent upon social revolution and a total subversion of the Western State System. It resembled the old in that one side (the Allies in 1914–1918, the Triplice in 1939–1940) was committed to a "new world order" in the aftermath of anticipated victory and the other (the Central Powers in 1914–1918, the Allies in 1939–1940) fought blindly for survival with no effective vision of rebuilding the world society. The verdict of arms would determine who would have the opportunity to remake the world. The aftermath of victory would determine whether the opportunity would again be thrown away in favor of a resumption of the game of power or would be utilized by the victors to destroy the balance of power for all time and unify the world.

1. JAPAN: "NEW ORDER IN EASTERN ASIA"

"There's glory for you!" "I don't know what you mean by 'glory,' " Alice said. Humpty Dumpty smiled contemptuously. "Of course you don't—till I tell you. I meant, 'there's a nice knock-down argument for you!" "But 'glory' doesn't mean 'a nice knock-down argument,' " Alice objected. "When *I* use a word," Humpty Dumpty said in a rather scornful tone, "it means just what I choose it to mean—neither more nor less." "The question is," said Alice, "whether you *can* make words mean so many different things." "The question is," said Humpty Dumpty, "which is to be Master—that's all."—LEWIS CARROLL, *Through the Looking-glass.*

In order to conquer the world, we must first conquer China. In order to conquer China, we must first conquer Manchuria and Mongolia. . . . Sooner or later we shall have to fight against Soviet Russia. . . . One day we shall have to fight against America.—*The Tanaka Memorandum,* 1927.

The spirit of the Japanese nation is, by its nature, a thing that must be propagated over the seven seas and extended over the five continents. Anything that may hinder its progress must be abolished, even by force.— GENERAL SADAO ARAKI, Minister of War, in *Kaikosha,* July, 1932.

That the youngest of the "Great Powers" should have taken the initiative in bringing the oldest of the Great Powers to the brink of ruin was perhaps the penalty which age must ever pay to youth when age teaches youth not virtue but vice. That the only Great Power which is non European in race and culture should have humiliated all the European Powers in turn and then aligned itself with the least European to bring the most European to disaster was the Nemesis of Western imperialism in the Orient. Whatever judgment may be passed upon the event, the fact remains that the revolutionary transformation of the world balance of power which deprived the victors of 1918 of the fruits of victory and brought them ultimately to war and catastrophe began with the open resumption in 1931 of Tokio's campaign for hegemony over the Asiatic mainland.

Within the memory of people still alive, Japan emerged from the status of an ancient kingdom of feudal barons and cherry blossoms, shielded from the world by voluntary isolation, and became a great State of industrial magnates and battleships, holding the reins of power in the western Pacific. Prior to the middle of the nineteenth century, the realm of the Mikado was a mysterious and picturesque medieval empire, remote from the centers of Western power and determined to safeguard itself from Western contamination. But the dynamic impact of the industrialized West was not to be resisted. In 1853–1854, Commodore Perry, bearing gifts and letters, led an American squadron into Tokio bay and in accordance with his instructions from Washington induced the Japanese authorities, partly by persuasion, partly by threats, to conclude a treaty with the United States opening the empire to American commerce. Other Powers took advantage of the opportunity thus created to secure trading privileges for their own nationals. In 1867 the nobility, perceiving the wisdom of adopting Western ways if Japan was to escape the fate already overtaking China, overthrew the Shogun, or regent, restored full power to the young Emperor Mutsu Hito, and embarked upon a program of transforming the country into a State capable of coping with the Western nations. All of the technological paraphernalia of the West were introduced: railways, telegraph lines, steamships, factories, and a modernized army and navy. This swift adoption of Western technology made Japan a Great Power and enabled her to make a successful bid for hegemony in eastern Asia.

Once supplied with the technical prerequisites of power, Japan proceded to exert her new might to extend her influence over the mainland. In 1894 the Japanese Government sent troops into the "hermit kingdom" of Korea, a dependency of the Chinese Empire, earmarked for seizure by the forces of the Mikado. War with China followed, and in less than a year Japan had overrun Korea and South Manchuria and was threatening Peking. By the Peace of Shimonoseki, April 17, 1895, China was compelled to recognize the independence of Korea, pay an indemnity of 150 million dollars, and cede to Japan Formosa, the Pescadores Islands, and the Liaotung peninsula, key to Manchuria and gateway to the Gulf of Pechili and the Chinese capital. At this point, Russia, Germany, and France intervened and obliged Japan to give up the Liaotung peninsula in return for an increased indemnity. Japanese expansion was thus thwarted by rival Western imperialisms. If Japanese power was to be extended over the Asiatic mainland, Japan must be prepared, not merely to participate in the dismemberment of an impotent and disorganized China, but also to defy the Western Powers. Russia was the first obstacle to be overcome. In 1902, Japan strengthened her position by concluding an alliance with Great Britain, Russia's hereditary enemy in Asia. In 1904, after appropriate preparation, Japan challenged the Muscovite giant to combat. The soldiers of Nippon captured Port Arthur and routed the Russian armies at Mukden, while the new Japanese fleet destroyed the Russian squadrons sent against it. By the Treaty of Portsmouth, September 5, 1905, Japan acquired southern Sakhalin as well as Russia's leaseholds to Port Arthur and the Liaotung peninsula, and Russian railway and coal mining rights in South Manchuria.

The outcome of the Russo-Japanese War enabled Japan to achieve the status of a Great Power without qualification and to prepare the way for a further extension of her empire. The Anglo-Japanese alliance was renewed in 1905, and by agreements with France and Russia in 1907 Japan became practically a fourth member of the Triple Entente. Japan achieved a free hand in Korea and South Manchuria; and if an occasion presented itself in war between Germany and the Entente, she could displace Germany in Shantung as she had already displaced Russia further north. The United States had acquired the Philippine Islands in 1898, and America came across the Pacific out of the east as the champion of the Open Door and Chinese territorial integrity. Here was a possible new rival to Japan in the Orient. But in July, 1905, Theodore Roosevelt, in a secret memorandum, agreed not to oppose Japan in Korea and to cooperate with Japan to maintain peace in the Far East in return for a Japanese disclaimer of any designs on the Philippine Islands. In the Root-Takahira agreement of November, 1908, the two Powers agreed to respect one another's possessions, maintain the *status quo* in the Pacific, and preserve the Open Door and the independence and integrity of China. In 1910 Japan annexed Korea. In 1913 Russia and Great Britain took advantage of the Chinese revolution to detach Outer Mongolia and Tibet from Chinese control. Further disintegration of China appeared imminent. Japan was already well along on the road to empire when the Great War broke out and provided an opportunity for further enhancement of Japanese power.

On August 15, 1914, Japan advised Germany to withdraw all her warships from the Far East and to deliver the Kiaochow leased territory to Japan "with a view to the eventual restoration of the same to China." In the absence of a reply, Japan declared war on Germany on August 23 and seized the area in question. On January 18, 1915, the Japanese Minister presented to the President of China twenty-one demands embodying Chinese acceptance of any disposition Japan might make of Kiaochow and Shantung, the granting to Japan of a ninety-nine year lease on Port Arthur and Dalny, along with mining, railway, and financial concessions in South Manchuria and eastern, or Inner, Mongolia and participation in the Hanyehping Company, the great Chinese iron and steel concern on the Yangtze. China was also asked to agree "not to cede or lease to a third Power any harbor, bay, or island along the coast of China." Group V of the twenty-one demands provided for Japanese supervision of Chinese political, financial, and military affairs, a joint Sino-Japanese police force in important places in China, the purchase of at least half of China's munitions from Japan, and the granting to Japan of a sphere of influence in Fukien, opposite Formosa. Under threats of coercion, the Chinese Government yielded, and the first sixteen of the demands were incorporated in treaties and notes on May 25, 1915. The preoccupation of the other Powers in the gigantic conflict in Europe enabled Japan to have her way: The Allies secretly agreed to support the Japanese claims at the Peace Conference; and even the United States, in the Lansing-Ishii agreement of November 2, 1917, recognized that "territorial propinquity" gave Japan "special interests" in China. In 1918, new concessions were wrested from China by the Japanese Government, despite the fact that China had entered the war on the Allied side.

At the close of the Great War, Japanese power in Asia reached its zenith. Tokio had secured control of Shantung, Fukien, all of Manchuria, Inner Mongolia, and the German islands north of the Equator. Revolution and civil war in Russia enabled Japan to extend her conquests to the north. In cooperation with the Allies and the United States, Japan launched upon a program of military intervention in Russia in the summer of 1918. Although the other intervening governments were interested primarily in aiding the counter-revolutionary White Armies and consummating the overthrow of the Soviet régime, Japan appeared to be concerned more with territorial acquisitions. Northern Sakhalin was occupied. Seventy thousand Japanese troops were poured into eastern Siberia, where they entrenched themselves with the apparent object of retaining permanent control of the Maritime Provinces, and perhaps of the whole vast area east of Lake Baikal. Friction developed between the American and Japanese forces in Siberia and between Tokio and Washington, but Japanese power was predominant in eastern Asia and the diplomatic representations of other States were unavailing.

Japan, however, had overreached herself in various directions and was subsequently obliged to abandon much of the territory which her troops had occupied. At the Peace Conference in 1919, she was persuaded, under American pressure, to agree to retain only economic rights in Shantung, though the treaty transferred German rights in this province to Japan. The United States protested against the continued Japanese occupation of Siberia and denounced Japan's retention of Shantung. Anti-Japanese sentiment increased in the United States, in China, in Russia, and in Canada and Australia as well. The United States had embarked upon a naval program with which Japan could not hope to compete. The intervention in Russia had failed, and Soviet troops were again east of Lake Baikal. At the Washington Conference of 1921–1922 the United States and Great Britain cooperated to bring Japan to terms. The Anglo-Japanese alliance was terminated. The Japanese Government found it expedient to compromise. By the Four Power Pacific Pact the United States, Great Britain, Japan, and France agreed "to respect their rights in relation to their insular possessions and insular dominions in the region of the Pacific Ocean" and to communicate with one another in the event of any threat of aggression. In the naval treaty of February 6, 1922, Japan was granted 315,000 tons of capital ships as against 525,000 tons each for Great Britain and the United States. The Powers agreed to maintain the *status quo* as regards naval bases and fortifications in the western Pacific. At the London Naval Conference of 1930 Japan achieved the right to maintain a naval strength in cruisers and auxiliary vessels in the ratio of

7:10:10 as compared with Great Britain and the United States. Japan was thus recognized as the third greatest naval Power. The United States renounced all ambitions of establishing its naval supremacy in the western Pacific. Japanese predominance in this area was assured. Japan was obliged to agree to the restoration of Shantung to China, however, and to sign the Nine Power Pact of 1922 for the preservation of the Open Door and Chinese territorial integrity. She also gave informal assurances regarding Siberia, and in 1925 northern Sakhalin and the Maritime Provinces were restored to the Soviet Union. Although the Japanese Government had surrendered much, it had achieved as much as the existing state of power relationships in the Far East permitted.

These developments constituted a postponement, not a renunciation, of efforts to enhance Japanese power on the Asiatic mainland. Japan, like all the other Great Powers in the Western State System, sought to extend its domination over as wide an area as possible. Japan's theater of action in eastern Asia was remote from the centers of power of other great States. Japan—Westernized and militarized—found the huge disintegrating hulk of the Celestial Empire an easy prey. She was able to dominate the western Pacific with her naval power and to dominate the Asiatic mainland with her army. The specific objectives of her quest for power reflected the interests of her ruling classes: the new bourgeoisie, the old nobility, and the military, naval, and diplomatic bureaucracy. The goals were the usual goals of imperialism everywhere in the age of competitive capitalism: markets for goods and investments, leaseholds, concessions, and other profit-making opportunities. "Surplus population" was a plausible rationalization of expansionist ambitions, for Japan was densely populated and the United States and the British Dominions closed their doors to Japanese immigration. Though China could furnish no outlet for Japan's millions, Australia and New Zealand contain enormous expanses of empty land. But Japanese policy was long directed more toward profitable economic opportunities for entrepreneurs and investors than toward land for peasants and workers.

The Great Depression created economic and social insecurities in Japan comparable with those experienced by other States with small margins of wealth and resources. It led, as elsewhere, to political extremism, to desperate efforts to recapture shrinking markets, and to a resurgence of militant imperialism. Industrialists and financiers, dominating a capitalistic economy which from the beginning has been highly monopolistic rather than competitive,[1] tended to control the Minseito party; the feudal landed aristocracy, closely linked with the army leaders (as in

---

[1] It is estimated that eight families—Mitsui, Mitsubishi, Asano, Sumitoma, Shibusawa, Yasuda, Okura, and Suzuki—control over one-quarter of Japan's insurance reserves, almost half of the bank deposits, and three-quarters of all trust properties. They dominate effectively the industrial, commercial, and financial life of the empire.

Prussia), was better represented in the Seiyukai party. Neither group had been firmly attached to the ideals of Western liberalism. The new lower middle class was long inarticulate in politics. The impoverished peasantry, heavily indebted to the landlords, demanded relief but did not embrace radicalism or lose its traditional reverence for the Emperor and the established social order. The growing urban proletariat was influenced somewhat by Communist doctrine, but did not become a significant factor in Japanese social politics.

After 1929 army leaders, with some support from industrialists, aristocrats, and peasants, leaned toward Fascist ideals and methods and repeatedly challenged the civil authorities and the parliamentary system. Just as Japan's fighting power is greater than is warranted by her resources because of her geographical position and the large proportion of the national income devoted to armaments, so the domestic political influence of the militarists is greater than is warranted by their numbers or wealth because of their social position and the great respect in which they are held by all patriots. They assailed the Minseito Cabinet in 1930, demanding an end of the "corrupt" alliance between politicians and capitalists and insisting on political leadership by the army, a "strong" foreign policy, the crushing of all radical agitation, and a kind of national socialism to control industry and relieve agriculture. Liberal Baron Shidehara, Foreign Minister during the 1920's, was committed to compromise with the Western Powers and conciliation of China as the best means of enlarging markets and promoting prosperity. Japanese bankers and merchants supported him. But the militarists, following more heroic gods, were interested less in welfare than in power. They denounced Shidehara's "weakness" and determined to achieve their ends by fair means or foul. Premier Hamaguchi was shot on November 14, 1930. Following a Seiyukai victory in the election of February, 1932, and Premier Inukai's assassination by patriotic terrorists, Admiral Makato Saito formed a coalition cabinet in May, which was replaced by the Okada cabinet in July, 1934. Both adopted much of the militarist-Fascist program in domestic and foreign affairs.

The internal struggle for power between the army leaders and the more liberal politicians and industrialists continued, with military extremists attempting to intimidate civil authorities by propaganda and terrorism. During 1935 moderate elements seemed in the ascendancy in the army. In December the liberal Saito succeeded the equally liberal Makino as Keeper of the Privy Seal and adviser to Emperor Hirohito. In the election of February, 1936, the Minseito party and its allies, supporting the Okada Cabinet, were victorious, the Seiyukai and the Fascist groups were repudiated, and the proletarian Shakai Taishuto, though still small, doubled its popular vote. Incensed at this defeat, the army terrorists attempted an armed *coup* on February 26. The rebels were beaten, but they murdered Saito, Finance Minister Takahashi, and General Watanobe. Makino was attacked but was unhurt. Okada escaped death by a ruse but resigned the premiership to Koki Hirota who also became Foreign Minister in a coalition cabinet. The assassins were repudiated by the army command and executed, but the prestige of the militarists was not markedly reduced. Unless their demands were granted, they remained ready to oppose the cabinet, to plot rebellion, and to encourage the assassination of liberal leaders.

The prime weapon of the militarists, however, was war. To precipitate conflict abroad is always the best means of promoting temporary unity at home and increasing the influence of ultrapatriots and professional warriors. Japan's foreign wars since 1931 have been less instruments of national policy than weapons of domestic politics in the hands of the warlords. Any war with any foreign foe could be made to serve their purposes at home, provided only that it were not too dangerous. Army leaders, looking northward and westward, envisaged the U.S.S.R. as their logical enemy. Navy leaders, looking southward and eastward, considered the United States to be their divinely appointed target. In either case the strategic prerequisite of greater things to come, whether by land or by sea, was control of Manchuria and domination of China. To strike once more at China would stir the Japanese masses to mystic patriotism, exalt the militarists, discredit the moderate businessmen and bankers, and pave the way for a domestic war economy. The adventure would be safe; for China was weak, and the Western Powers would not act in unison. Some of their leaders could easily be persuaded that Tokio's ultimate victim was the Soviet Union and that action against China was designed only to "save Asia from Communism." They would therefore applaud the saviors and denounce those who might seek to restrain Japanese aggression.

It was in this context that a bomb exploded on the tracks of the South Manchurian railway near Mukden on the night of September 18, 1931. Local Japanese commanders utilized the "outrage" as a pretext for occupying the cities of Southern Manchuria. Three days later China appealed to the League of Nations. Geneva asked Washington to cooperate in an investigation. In view of the temper of American opinion and the isolationist propensities of President Hoover, Secretary of State Stimson was reluctant to agree to joint action with the League. He believed, moreover, that the "civil" authorities in Japan would restrain the militarists if provocation were avoided by the Western Powers. (This illusion was to be carefully cultivated by Japanese and other aggressors in the years to come; for it was always useful, along with loud outcries of "anti-Communism," for paralyzing the Western States.) Stimson declined the

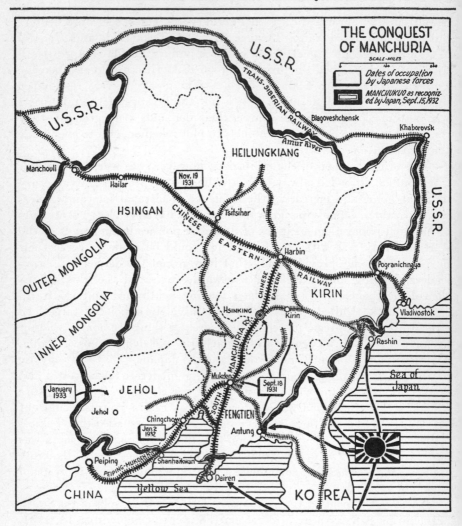

League invitation. When it appeared, however, that Tokio was ignoring all pleas from both Washington and Geneva, the United States joined the League Powers in invoking the Kellogg Pact, although declining all suggestions of cooperation in possible League sanctions against the aggressor. When this step likewise produced no results, Stimson formulated his "nonrecognition" doctrine and appealed to Sir John Simon to cooperate in a joint invocation of the Nine Power Pact. But Sir John was persuaded that Japan was merely fighting "Communism" and preparing to attack the U.S.S.R. He therefore refused to act.

Appeals from Geneva led to a truce at Shanghai, where thousands of civilians had already been slain by Japanese bombs and shells, and to

Japanese evacuation of the city in May, 1932. But neither Washington nor Geneva nor the leisurely Lytton Commission was able to bring about any withdrawal from Manchuria. Shidehara was gone. The Tokio militarists were climbing into the saddle. In March, 1932, they had set up as "Regent" (later "Emperor Kang Teh") of "Manchukuo" the forgotten Henry Pu-Yi, last of the Manchu rulers of China, who at the age of four had succeeded the Dowager Empress Tzu Hsi shortly before the revolution of 1911. By September Japan had recognized Manchukuo and made it a Japanese protectorate in defiance of the Western Powers.[1]

This resumption of Japanese aggression on the Asiatic mainland was engineered by army leaders in quest of land and glory. It was acquiesced in by business groups interested in markets and by patriots devoted to power and prestige. The seizure of Manchuria was followed by the penetration of China itself. During 1933, Jehol was annexed to Manchukuo. Japanese troops occupied Chahar to the west early in 1935. By summer, Chinese military forces were compelled to retire temporarily from the Peiping-Tientsin area. In November, 1935, the North China demilitarized zone was partly taken over by the independent "Autonomous Federation for Joint Defense against Communism" with its capital at Tungchow, twelve miles east of Peiping. Japanese pressure led to the establishment in December of an "autonomous" régime embracing Peiping, Tientsin, Chahar, along with Hopei and Shantung. During 1936, Manchurian forces with Japanese assistance invaded and occupied much of Suiyuan in Inner Mongolia, west of Chahar, and sought to establish here another "autonomous" régime, partly encircling Outer Mongolia. Japanese military and civil officials meanwhile ignored Chinese customs regulations and fostered the smuggling of Japanese goods into North China on a large scale, thus conquering new markets and further reducing the revenues of Nanking. During the course of protracted and inconclusive negotiations in the autumn of 1936, Japan endeavored to compel

[1] The protocol signed at Changchun September 15, 1932, by General Nobuyoshi Muto, representing the Emperor of Japan, and Cheng Hsiao-hsu, Premier of Manchukuo, was as follows: "Whereas Japan has recognized the fact that Manchukuo, in accordance with the free will of its inhabitants, has organized and established itself as an independent State, and Whereas Manchukuo has declared its intention of abiding by all international engagements entered into by China in so far as they are applicable to Manchukuo; Now the Governments of Japan and Manchukuo, each respecting the territorial rights of the other, and also in order to secure the peace of the Far East, agreed as follows: (1) Manchukuo shall confirm and respect, in so far as no agreement to the contrary shall be made between Manchukuo and Japan in the future, all the rights and interests possessed by Japan or her subjects within the territory of Manchukuo by virtue of Sino-Japanese treaties, agreements or other arrangements, or through Sino-Japanese contracts, private as well as public. (2) Japan and Manchukuo, recognizing that any threat to the territory or peace and order of either of the high contracting parties constitutes, at the same time, a threat to the safety and existence of the other, agree to cooperate in the maintenance of their national security, it being understood that such Japanese forces as may be necessary for this purpose shall be stationed in Manchukuo."

Chiang Kai-shek to "cooperate" through acceptance of Japanese advisers and Japanese army support in fighting the Chinese Soviets, the granting of economic privileges to Japanese concessionaires, and the suppression of all anti-Japanese agitation. The objectives of Tokio were clearly to detach from Chinese control as much of the northern portion of the country as possible and to subject the remainder to Japanese domination more complete than was contemplated in the Twenty-one Demands of 1915.

The aftermath of the Manchurian adventure had meanwhile turned out as the war lords of Nippon had hoped. Tokio rejected the report of the Lytton Commission in February, 1933. When the League Powers, with the independent concurrence of Washington, endorsed its recommendations, Tokio gave notice (March 27, 1933) of withdrawal from the League. Britain and France did nothing to impede the march of the Japanese soldiery south of the Great Wall. Secretary of State Hull sent mild notes of protest. In April, 1934, Tokio announced a "Japanese Monroe Doctrine" to the effect that henceforth Japan alone would be "guardian of the peace of the Pacific." The Japanese fire-eaters were encouraged by the Philippine Independence Act of March 24, 1934, and by the first of the new United States "neutrality" bills, enacted in August 1935. When Japanese demands for naval parity with Britain and America were refused, Tokio declined to renew the naval treaties of 1922 and 1930. As the new naval race got under way, Rome and Berlin borrowed a leaf from Tokio's book and initiated new adventures in conquest in Africa and Europe. Many leaders of the Western Powers continued to look favorably on Fascism as a bulwark against Communism. The conquerors were quite willing to encourage this hallucination. On November 25, 1936, Germany and Japan signed the "Anti-Comintern" Pact which Italy joined a year later, followed by Hungary, Manchukuo, and Franco's Spain.[1] The warriors of the Rising Sun thus further befuddled the Western Powers and won potential allies for despoiling them of their empires.

These developments, coupled with the effects of the Great Depression, admirably served the domestic purposes of the Japanese militarists. The problems of depression were in part met by a foreign-trade boom achieved by depreciating the yen. The Minseito Government's return to the gold

---

[1] On November 28, 1936, Japan and Italy agreed to reciprocal recognition of Manchukuo and the Italian conquest of Ethiopia. Three days previously, Berlin and Tokio announced an agreement to cooperate against the "Bolshevist menace." This was obviously a screen to mask a pretended alliance against the U.S.S.R. and perhaps also to conceal a German-Japanese agreement to divide the Dutch East Indies into spheres of influence, preparatory to future conquest and partition. The text of the published accord was as follows:

"The German Government and the Japanese Government, recognizing that the aim of the Communist International known as the Comintern is directed at disrupting and violating existing States with all means at its command and convinced that to tolerate the Communist International's interference with the internal affairs of nations not only en-standard early in 1930 resulted in severe deflation. Following British abandonment of gold in September, 1931, and the fall of the Minseito Cabinet, Japan followed the British example in December. By the summer of 1935 the yen had depreciated 66 per cent below gold parity—a greater decline than had been experienced by any other great commercial State. Japanese goods, already cheap because of low wages and the extensive rationalization and cartelization of industry, were thus further cheapened in world markets. Between 1931 and 1935, Japanese exports increased 71 per cent in volume and 118 per cent in yen value. Japanese textiles, toys, and other goods flowed into China, India, Africa, South America, and the United States. This expansion led to increased Japanese

dangers their internal peace and social well-being but threatens world peace at large, animated by a desire to work in common against Communist disruptive influences, have arrived at the following agreement:

I

"The high contracting parties agree to mutually inform each other concerning the activities of the Communist International, to consult with each other concerning measures to combat this activity, and to execute these measures in close cooperation with each other.

II

"The two high contracting States will jointly invite third parties whose domestic peace is endangered by the disruptive activities of the Communist International to embark upon measures for warding these off in accordance with the spirit of this agreement or to join in it.

III

"For this agreement, both the German and Japanese texts are regarded as original versions. It becomes effective the day of signing and is in force for a period of five years.

"The high contracting States will, at the proper time before expiration of this period, arrive at an understanding with each other concerning the form this cooperation is to take.

SUPPLEMENTARY PROTOCOL

"A. The competent authorities of both high contracting parties will cooperate most closely in connection with the exchange of information concerning the activities of the Communist International, as well as in connection with publicity and defense measures against the Communist International.

"B. The competent authorities of both high contracting parties will, within the framework of existing laws, take strict measures against those who, at home or abroad, directly or indirectly, are active in the service of the Communist International or lend a helping hand to its disruptive work.

"With a view to facilitating the cooperation of the competent authorities of both high contracting parties, specified in (A), a permanent commission will be created. In this commission the further defensive measures necessary for combatting the disruptive work of the Communist International will be considered and deliberated upon.

"Berlin, Nov. 25, 1936; that is, the Nov. 25 of the eleventh year of the Showa Period.

RIBBENTROP,
MUSHAKOJI."

It may be noted that Section B of the Protocol afforded a cloak for joint interventionist activities in the internal affairs of any state—China, Spain, Czechoslovakia, the Dutch East Indies, etc.—whenever Tokio and Berlin chose to allege that a "helping hand" was being given in such States to "agents" of the Comintern.

imports of raw materials from other countries; but this circumstance did not silence the outcries of American, British, Italian, and other producers whose markets were progressively invaded by Japanese competitors. The boom brought temporary gains to Japanese business, but did not relieve agriculture or bring satisfaction to the peasantry, the landlords, and the militarists.

Following sharp criticism of its policies in Parliament, the army, led by General Terauchi, overthrew the Hirota Cabinet on January 23, 1937, by refusing to supply a minister of war. The militarists demanded an end of rule by "politicians" and declined to approve a new cabinet headed by the moderate General Kazushigi Ugaki, named by the Emperor to replace Hirota. Ugaki gave up his efforts on January 29, asserting that "Japan is now standing at the crossroads of Fascism or parliamentary government." On February 2, 1937, General Senjuro Hayashi formed a compromise cabinet approved by the army. The political parties were powerless and militarist influence was in the ascendancy. The Cabinet dissolved the Diet on March 30. In the national election of April, 1937, all the major parties opposed Hayashi. The Minseito lost 26 seats but retained 179 and was still the largest party group. The Seiyukai, with a total of 175, gained 1 seat, the Independents increased their numbers from 25 to 34, and the anti-Fascist Shakai Taishuto, or "Social Mass," party increased its representation from 18 to 37. In the new House of Representatives, 421 of the 466 seats would be filled by anti-Hayashi candidates. The General-Premier nevertheless attempted to keep office with army support. On June 3, however, he gave way to Prince Fumimaro Konoye, who made Koki Hirota his Foreign Minister and announced cryptically that "our external policy will seek peace based upon justice, which is not the same thing as the mere maintenance of the *status quo*."

Under these circumstances the war lords had urgent need of a new diversion abroad to rally to their support an electorate which had repudiated their leadership. To attack the Western Powers would be unsafe until they should be effectively immobilized by Japan's allies in Europe. To attack the U.S.S.R. was a constant temptation, since the West would give its blessing and the propertied classes of both Japan and China would rally to the cause. On June 20, 1937, Japanese forces clashed with Soviet detachments along the Amur, seventy miles south of Blagovestchensk. A Japanese ultimatum to Moscow of June 29 demanded Soviet evacuation of several disputed islands. But in the end the Tokio militarists decided not to risk a large-scale test of force with the Red giant. In the years which followed they conducted successive military experiments along the Soviet frontiers. Like all wise conquerors, they were eager to expand in directions where resistance was likely to be least effective. All the experiments, however, had an identical outcome.

The Far Eastern Red Army defeated the Japanese on the Amur in June of 1937. On July 20–23, 1938, Japanese troops stormed the heights of Changkufeng (on the Manchurian border near Possiet Bay), claimed by Tokio but occupied by Red troops on July 11. On August 11, however, after Soviet forces had retaken most of the territory, fighting was terminated by an armistice which Litvinov and Ambassador Shigemitsu had signed in Moscow the day before. In early February, 1939, inconclusive hostilities broke out on the Argun River, northeast of Manchuli. In September, 1939, a fourth experiment was attempted. Japanese troops attacked Soviet detachments on the Manchu-Mongol frontier near the Khalka River. In the course of several weeks of heavy fighting the Japanese were once more defeated with numerous casualties. To fight those who are willing to fight and who fight too well to be beaten is always inexpedient if other and easier victims are at hand. The would-be conquerors in Tokio, like those in Berlin and Rome, decided to leave the U.S.S.R. in peace.

Meanwhile the Tokio war lords had temporarily solved their domestic problem by launching a new assault upon China. On July 7–8, 1937, a battalion of the Japanese North China garrison went out for "night maneuvers" southwest of Peiping, near Lukouchiao. At the Marco Polo Bridge over the Yungting River they clashed with part of the Chinese Twenty-ninth Army. Local truces, skirmishes, negotiations, and sieges followed in bewildering disorder. Japanese troops poured into North China from Manchukuo. Tokio refused to negotiate with the Chinese Government at Nanking and demanded that the authorities in North China withdraw all troops, suppress all anti-Japanese activity, and "cooperate against Communism." On July 27, Foreign Minister Hirota told the Diet that a new buffer State would be established south of the Great Wall. "The Japanese policy in east Asia is directed solely toward the realization of stability through conciliation and cooperation between Japan, Manchukuo, and China and by stopping the Communist invasion of the Orient." By the end of the month, general hostilities were in progress in the north. Japanese fliers slaughtered thousands of helpless noncombatants in Tientsin and harried the near-by provinces with fire and sword in a campaign of terrorization.

Chiang Kai-shek had no option but to resist. He declared on July 29, "It is obvious that the Peiping-Tientsin warfare marks the beginning of a war of invasion. . . . I am sure that our people, finding the fatherland at this crucial point, will fight to the finish like one man. I am confident that final victory will be ours." A month later, he announced a nonaggression pact with the U.S.S.R. In September the Chinese Communist party announced the dissolution of the "Soviet Republic of China," which had governed peasant soviets in scattered provinces, and the establishment of a united front with the Kuomintang in resistance to Japanese aggression.

In the appalling bloodshed which ensued, the invaders took city after city and province after province only to find that they had at last aroused the slumbering Chinese masses to fierce patriotism. Victories in the field over the ragged troops of Chiang Kai-shek and brutal massacres of Chinese civilians were alike futile in inducing surrender so long as a trickle of military supplies continued into central China from the Western world and the Soviet Union. Months and years of horror followed. A new Japanese attack on Shanghai was launched on August 13, 1937. While the Japanese fleet enforced a pacific blockade along the whole length of China's coast, Japanese warships, bombing planes, and land artillery turned much of the native city of Shanghai into a flaming charnel house. By mid-November Chinese troops were compelled to quit the vicinity of China's greatest port. The capital was moved from Nanking to Hankow and later to remote Chungking in Szechwan province. On December 10–15, 1937, Japanese troops, coming up the Yangtze, occupied Nanking. They pillaged and burned much of the city. They raped thousands of women. They slaughtered the aged, the infirm, the helpless, and even the children. They butchered thousands of disarmed soldiers and noncombatants with machine guns and artillery. In the gutted capital, they set up a provisional puppet régime, modeled after the one already established in Peiping.

When these evidences of loving-kindness produced no capitulation, Tokio sought through Nazi good offices to negotiate a peace with Chiang Kai-shek on the basis of Chinese repudiation of "Communism" and of the Soviet nonaggression pact, recognition of Manchukuo, payment of the costs of the war, and appointment of Japanese "advisers." When Chungking refused to yield, Konoye announced in January, 1938, that Tokio would have no further dealings with Chiang Kai-shek but would look forward to the establishment of a new Chinese régime.

The spring campaign of 1938 revolved about Japanese efforts to take Suchow in Kiangsu, junction of the Peiping-Nanking and Sian-Haichow railways. Chinese forces, aided by thousands of guerrillas operating all over North China, inflicted crushing defeats on the foe near Taierchwang in early April and again in May but were obliged to evacuate Suchow on May 20. Further south the invaders took Amoy (May 13) and slew thousands in air raids on Canton. But their efforts to take Chingchow, west of Suchow, and to cut the Peiping-Hankow railway were halted with heavy losses by the breaching of the dikes of the Yellow River. Foiled in the north, they resumed the invasion in the south, occupying Canton on October 21 and Hankow on October 25. On February 10, 1939, the island of Hainan was seized and on March 31 the Spratley Islands. These con-

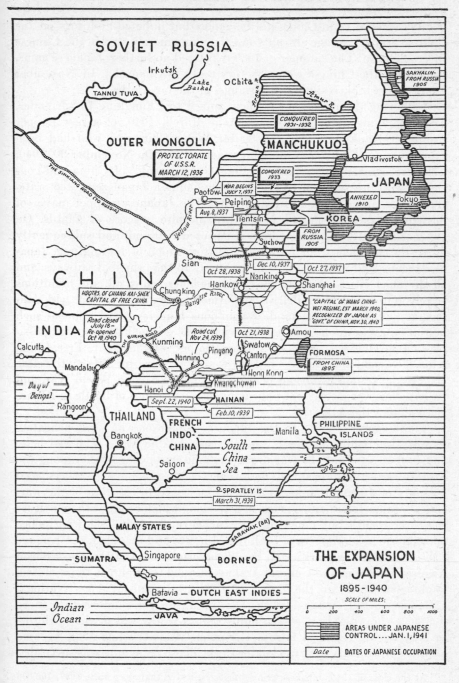

SOVIET RUSSIA

Irkutsk

Lake Baikal

O Chita

TANNU TUVA

Amur R.

Argun R.

SAKHALIN—
FROM RUSSIA
1905

OUTER MONGOLIA

*PROTECTORATE
OF U.S.S.R.
MARCH 12, 1936*

*CONQUERED
1931-1932*

MANCHUKUO

Vladivostok

JAPAN

*CONQUERED
1933*

*ANNEXED
1910*

Tokyo

THE SINKIANG ROAD (TO RUSSIA)

Paotow

*WAR BEGINS
JULY 7, 1937*

Peiping

Aug. 8, 1937

Tientsin

KOREA

*FROM
RUSSIA
1905*

Yellow River

C H I N A

Sian

Suchow

Dec. 10, 1937

Oct. 28, 1938

Nanking

Oct. 27, 1937

*HDQTRS. OF CHIANG KAI-SHEK
CAPITAL OF FREE CHINA*

Chungking

Hankow

Shanghai

Yangtze River

*"CAPITAL OF WANG CHING-
WEI REGIME, EST. MARCH 1940,
RECOGNIZED BY JAPAN AS
'GOVT.' OF CHINA, NOV. 30, 1940*

INDIA

*Road closed
July 18 –
Re-opened
Oct. 18, 1940*

*Road cut
Nov. 24, 1939*

Kunming

Oct. 21, 1938

Amoy

Calcutta

THE BURMA ROAD

Nanning

Pinyang

Swatow
Canton

FORMOSA

*FROM CHINA
1895*

Mandalay

Hong Kong

Bay of
Bengal

Hanoi

Kwangchowan

Rangoon

Sept. 22, 1940

HAINAN

Feb. 10, 1939

THAILAND

FRENCH
INDO-
CHINA

PHILIPPINE
ISLANDS

Bangkok

Manila

Saigon

*South
China
Sea*

SPRATLEY IS
March 31, 1939

MALAY STATES

SARAWAK (BR.)

SUMATRA

Singapore

BORNEO

Batavia — DUTCH EAST INDIES

*Indian
Ocean*

JAVA

THE EXPANSION
OF JAPAN
1895-1940

SCALE OF MILES

0   200   400   600   800   1000

AREAS UNDER JAPANESE
CONTROL...JAN. 1, 1941

Date   DATES OF JAPANESE OCCUPATION

quests menaced Indo-China and Singapore but inflicted no injury on the Chinese armies. Savage air raids on Chungking merely steeled the Chinese will to fight on. The summer of 1939 registered no further Japanese gains. In October the Chinese won a victory north of Changsha. In November the invaders took Nanning in Kwangsi in the far south.

Following the rejection of a new appeal to Chungking to surrender, Tokio announced the establishment in March, 1940, of a new puppet régime at Nanking under the traitor Wang Ching-wei who had been expelled from the Kuomintang in January, 1939. On November 30, 1940, Tokio recognized this régime as the "Government" of China and concluded with it a series of treaties making China a Japanese protectorate. But Wang Ching-wei had no authority. The Japanese puppet mayor of Shanghai was assassinated in his bed, despite a score of guards. On October 25, 1940, Chinese forces recaptured Nanning and subsequently drove the invaders from Kwangsi and from much of Kwangtung. Japanese troops held most of the Chinese coast, all the principal railways, and all the chief cities. With trucks, tanks, planes, guns, oil, and munitions largely purchased from British and American exporters, they had slain several million Chinese, made 50 millions homeless, and inflicted such bestial outrages upon their helpless victims as no one had supposed possible among civilized peoples.[1] But no victory was in sight. Free China refused to yield and looked to Moscow and the West for aid. By the close of 1940 the Chinese war had become part of the Second World War, and its outcome was clearly contingent upon the fortunes of battle in Africa, Europe, and the Atlantic.

The staggering costs to the Japanese people of what was delicately termed "the China incident" are too incalculable to be reviewed here. Suffice it to say that the war drove the militarists ever farther along the road toward totalitarianism and that the businessmen, workers, and peasants of Japan, thanks to their acquiescence in the rule of the warlords, became dehumanized cogs in a machine which brought them neither glory nor wealth but much misery. In February, 1938, following police raids on the headquarters of both the Minseito and Seiyukai, the Konoye Cabinet was bitterly criticized in a disorderly session of the Diet. Baron Kichiro Hiranuma and General Araki continued their efforts to promote a totalitarian state in the name of "Great Japanism." A "National Mobilization Bill," passed by the Diet in March, foreshadowed the more complete subordination of the industrialists to the will of the warlords. In May, Ugaki replaced Hirota as Foreign Minister while Araki became Minister of Education. A week later the bellicose Sugiyama was succeeded

---

[1] At the close of 1940, Japanese army sources estimated that since July, 1937, 100,000 Japanese had lost their lives in China, that 1,800,000 Chinese dead had been counted, and that 3,500,000 Chinese had been slain.

by the more bellicose Itagaki as Minister of War. But the "Quick Victory" Cabinet brought no victory. In the wake of acrimonious disputes over state control of corporation funds, Konoye resigned on January 4, 1939. Hiranuma assumed the Premiership with Arita as his Foreign Minister. A month later the "Social Mass" party merged with the ultra-imperialist Tohokai. Official consternation over the Nazi-Soviet pact led to the resignation of the new cabinet on August 28. General Abe became head of an interim cabinet which resigned in turn on January 14, 1940, with Admiral Mitsumasi Yonai succeeding as Premier and Arita displacing Admiral Kichisaburo Nomura at the Foreign Office.

On July 16, 1940, Prince Konoye returned to the Premiership in a purely militarist cabinet which included Yosuke Matsuoka as Foreign Minister. The new Premier now announced a program of undiluted totalitarianism. The Minseito was the first of the major parties to decree its own dissolution in the interest of a one-party system. In Japan, however, the monolithic party of twentieth-century despotism was slow in taking shape. No self-made Caesar emerged as the counterpart of the Führers, Duces, and Caudillos of other tyrannies. Yet it was clear that the last vestiges of democracy and parliamentary government in Japan were doomed, that the new business *élite* and the old aristocracy had been ousted from the seats of power by the warlords, and that Japan was irrevocably committed to a militant "national socialism" whose apostles would brook no compromise between world power and national ruin.

By 1941 the bellivolent adventurers who had drenched much of Asia in blood were well on their way toward hegemony over the Eastern Hemisphere. This result was due less to their own power than to the inane and insane policies, or lack of policies, of the Western Powers for the better part of a decade. The Japanese war machine regularly purchased 80 per cent of its imported supplies of fuel, oil, iron, arms, and other strategic materials from American and British sources, thanks to the isolationist delusion and the neutrality fixation of the United States, and thanks to Tory fantasies that Tokio's ultimate target was the U.S.S.R. and that a "deal" could be made with the warlords. At any time between 1931 and 1939 Great Britain and the United States could have crippled the Japanese Juggernaut by cutting off its supplies from abroad or by extending effective aid to China in cooperation with the Soviet Union. Despite repeated and extreme provocation, London and Washington preferred a course of suicide until long after the eleventh hour.

In the fighting at Shanghai in August, 1937, several Americans were killed, several American ships were damaged, and the British Ambassador, Sir Hughe Montgomery Knatchbull-Hughesson, was machine-gunned and gravely wounded by Japanese fliers. London and Washington sent notes of protest which evoked apologies but were otherwise without results. Despite Chinese complaints over such action, President Roosevelt on September 14, 1937, forbade vessels owned by the United States Government to ship arms or munitions to China or Japan and warned that privately owned vessels so engaged would be given no protection. Wordy protests at bombing outrages and eloquent pleas for "quarantining" aggressors (President Roosevelt, Chicago, October 5, 1937) were empty so long as Tokio knew that neither Britain nor America would run any risks to aid China or even to protect their own interests. Following a new epidemic of political paralysis at Geneva, London made the proposal on October 4 which Stimson had made (and London had rejected) six years previously: that the Nine Power Pact be invoked against Japan. Washington assented and followed the League in denouncing Japanese aggression. In November, 1937, the signatories of the Pact (sans Japan) met at Brussels in despair and adjourned in futility. No one would take action or assume responsibility. On December 13, 1937, Japanese aviators bombed and sank three American oil tankers on the Yangtze, along with the American gunboat U.S.S. *Panay*. Roosevelt protested to Emperor Hirohito and ultimately accepted an apology and indemnity. During 1938 Chamberlain furiously appeased Tokio as well as Rome and Berlin. Washington sent periodical notes of protest in the name of humanity, international law, and the Open Door. In June, 1939, Japanese forces blockaded the British concession in Tientsin, demanding the surrender of four Chinese, accused of murder, who had taken refuge therein. In August, London yielded. The outbreak of war in Europe enabled Tokio to threaten Britain, France, and the United States with greater impunity. The fall of France in 1940 enabled Tokio to impose an accord on French Indo-China (September 22) giving Japan military and air bases in the northern part of the colony.

Only at the twelfth hour, and quite possibly too late, did London and Washington move to thwart the march of Japanese conquest. On December 15, 1938, the Export-Import Bank authorized a credit of 25 million dollars to finance American exports to China. On July 26, 1939, Washington denounced its commercial treaty with Japan of 1911. On October 19, 1939, Ambassador Joseph Grew told the American-Japan Society in Tokio, "straight from the horse's mouth," that United States opinion "deeply resented" Japanese activities in China and was "profoundly shocked" by bombings of noncombatants. On September 25, 1940, another 25 million dollars' credit to China was announced in Washington. On October 17 the Burma Road, which had been closed to trade in arms with China by London's decision of June 17, was reopened. Partial embargoes on exports of oil and iron to Japan went into effect in the United States. By this time, Tokio was already installed in Indo-China, was cooperating with Thailand, and was openly menacing Singapore, the Philippines, and the Dutch East Indies.

The warriors of Nippon were not in doubt as to how to meet these belated counterthreats from the West. The obvious formula was to make an alliance with Italy and Germany and to menace Britain and America with war in two oceans. After much urging from Berlin, Tokio accepted the formula in the autumn of 1940. Earlier reluctance was due to hopes that Hitler might, after all, attack the U.S.S.R. and thereby create new opportunities for Japanese aggrandizement. Premier Hiranuma had said on January 13, 1939, "We will shake hands with those who agree to the establishment of a new order in East Asia by Japan, but we cannot shake hands with those who oppose such a policy." War Minister Itagaki, April 17, 1939: "I wish to express heartfelt homage to Germany and to Italy for their spirited endeavors in the cause of a projected new order in Europe." But on May 3, 1939, Hiranuma asserted, "There is a totalitarian bloc and there is a democratic bloc. Japan confronts neither." He expressed approval of the Axis alliance but declined to make Japan a signatory. The chagrin evoked by the Hitler-Stalin accord on the eve of Armageddon slowly waned with a realization of the opportunities which Nazi victory over the West would present to Tokio. Doubts faded with the fall of France, the warnings from Washington to respect the *status quo* in the East Indies, the Anglo-American destroyer deal of September 2, and the visit of Ribbentrop's special envoy Heinrich von Stahmer, bearing the gift of French Indo-China as advance payment. On September 27, 1940, Ribbentrop, Ciano, and Ambassador Saburo Kurusu attached their signature in Berlin to a new Triple Alliance:

The governments of Germany, Italy and Japan, considering it as a condition precedent of any lasting peace that all nations of the world be given each its own proper place, have decided to stand by and cooperate with one another in regard to their efforts in Greater East Asia and regions of Europe respectively wherein it is their prime purpose to establish and maintain a new order of things calculated to promote the mutual prosperity and welfare of the peoples concerned.

Furthermore, it is the desire of the three governments to extend cooperation to such nations in other spheres of the world as may be inclined to put forth endeavors along lines similar to their own, in order that their ultimate aspirations for world peace may thus be realized.

Accordingly, the governments of Germany, Italy and Japan have agreed as follows:

1. Japan recognizes and respects the leadership of Germany and Italy in the establishment of a new order in Europe.

2. Germany and Italy recognize and respect the leadership of Japan in the establishment of a new order in Greater East Asia.

3. Germany, Italy and Japan agree to cooperate in their efforts on aforesaid lines. They further undertake to assist one another with all political, economic and military means when one of the three contracting powers is attacked by a power at present not involved in the European war or in the Chinese-Japanese conflict.

4. With the view to implementing the present pact, joint technical commissions, members of which are to be appointed by the respective governments of Germany, Italy and Japan, will meet without delay.

5. Germany, Italy and Japan affirm that the aforesaid terms do not in any way affect the political status which exists at present as between each of the three contracting parties and Soviet Russia.

6. The present pact shall come into effect immediately upon signature and shall remain in force ten years from the date of its coming into force. At the proper time before expiration of said term the high contracting parties shall at the request of any of them enter into negotiations for its renewal.

In faith whereof, the undersigned, duly authorized by their respective governments, have signed this pact and have affixed hereto their signatures.

Done in triplicate at Berlin, the 27th day of September, 1940, in the eighteenth year of the Fascist era, corresponding to the 27th day of the ninth month of the fifteenth year of Showa [the reign of Emperor Hirohito].

Emperor Hirohito explained that Japan's mission was

. . . to enhance justice on earth and to make the world one household. . . . We fervently hope for a cessation of disturbances and hope a restoration of peace will be realized as swiftly as possible. Accordingly we commanded our Government to deliberate on the matter of mutual assistance and cooperation with the governments of Germany and Italy, which share the views and aspirations of our empire. We are deeply gratified that a pact has been concluded between these three Powers.

Kurusu opined,

The final aim of this pact is the establishment of general and lasting world peace based on right and justice. It is self-evident that we cannot deny our collaboration to those countries who share our views and endeavors, nor does this pact in any way affect the present political situation existing between Japan, Germany and Italy on the one hand and the Soviet Union on the other.

The chivalrous spirit of Japan was originally symbolized by the sword, but the essential principle of the proper handling of the sword does not consist in unthinkingly killing human beings but in protecting them with the sword.

I feel impelled to express the hope that this pact, in the hands of the champions of justice in Japan, Germany and Italy, may become a sword in the hand of the righteous warrior and will thus contribute to the reestablishment of universal peace.

The "peace" to come was obviously to be built upon the graves of China and the British Empire, with the United States and the Soviet Union immobilized and ultimately rendered ripe for defeat by threats of battle on two fronts. Moscow professed indifference and continued its aid to China. London retaliated by reopening the Burma Road. On October 8, Washington alarmed Tokio by calling home all Americans in the Far East. President Roosevelt at Dayton on October 12 declared, "No combination of dictator countries will stop the help we are giving. . . . Our decision is made." Tokio spoke more softly, blackmailed Indo-China and the East Indies, and recognized Wang Ching-wei on November

30. Washington at once took counteraction by extending a loan of 100 million dollars to China, moving warships and bombers west of Hawaii toward Manila, and secretly warning of worse to come if Japan did not desist.

In this game of thrust and parry the stakes were now quite simple. The crucial question for Tokio, and still more for London and Washington, was: To be or not to be. Several broad alternatives confronted the war makers who owed fealty to Hirohito, the "Son of Heaven" whose legendary ancestors had divinely ruled Japan for twenty-six centuries. China could not be crushed so long as any outside support was to be had by her defenders unless, as seemed possible early in 1941, a new civil conflict broke out between the Kuomintang and the Communists. China could be subjugated and all of "Greater East Asia," including Australia, New Zealand, and India, could be conquered if Britain were defeated by the Axis, and Washington and Moscow were immobilized by the triumphant hosts of the Caesars. Tokio could not run the risk of contributing directly to this outcome so long as the American navy and the Far Eastern Red Army were free to move against Japan, for both were superior to Japan's own forces.

Tokio, therefore, moved southward with caution. Japanese diplomats imposed a truce at the end of January, 1941, in the undeclared border war between Thailand and Indo-China. They pressed Vichy to yield Laos and Cambodia, east of the Mekong River, to Bangkok. They strove to bring Thailand under their domination. Japanese strategists occupied Cam-Ranh Bay and Saigon, concentrated war vessels in the Gulf of Siam, and threatened Anglo-Dutch-American outposts south of the China Sea. But this game of bluff and blackmail in cooperation with the Axis could not be pressed too far or too rapidly. Nomura, sent as new ambassador to Washington, was received coldly. Australian troops moved to Singapore and up the Malay peninsula to meet a possible attack by land through Thailand. Bombing planes moved from California and Hawaii toward the East Indies. The Powers, opined Matsuoka, should cede all of "Oceania" to Japan. Tokio waited upon events in Europe. If Britain fell in the sequel, then both the United States and the Soviet Union would be helpless to say Japan nay. But if the Axis should face defeat? In this dread event, Tokio could perhaps execute another major retreat on the model of 1919–1922. More probably, however, the warlords would stake their all on a desperate blow against Singapore, the Indies, the Philippines, and Australia.

If they should succeed, all the East would be theirs to enslave and exploit in preparation for the final defeat of America and Russia at the hands of the victorious Triplice. If they should fail, they and the dupes who obeyed their will would bring about the suicide of the Japanese

Empire. No viable middle road loomed between world conquest and hara-kiri. Which finale would conclude the play depended upon the ability or inability, the willingness or unwillingness, of the English-speaking Powers to do what Destiny demanded of them.

SUGGESTED READINGS

Bisson, T. A.: *Japan in China*, New York, Macmillan, 1939.

Chamberlin, W. H.: *Japan over Asia*, Boston, Little, Brown, 1940.

Falk, E. A.: *Togo and the Rise of Japanese Sea Power*, New York, Longmans, Green, 1936.

Hindmarsh, A. E.: *The Bases of Japanese Foreign Policy*, Cambridge, Harvard University Press, 1936.

Hishida, S.: *Japan among the Great Powers*, New York, Longmans Green, 1939.

Ishimaru, T.: *Japan Must Fight Britain*, New York, Telegraph Press, 1936.

Karig, W.: *Asia's Good Neighbor*, Indianapolis, Bobbs-Merrill, 1937.

Lattimore, O.: *Manchuria—Cradle of Conflict*, New York, Macmillan, 1935.

MacNair, H. F.: *The Real Conflict between China and Japan*, Chicago, University of Chicago Press, 1938.

Moulton, H. G.: *Japan—An Economic and Financial Appraisal*, Washington, Brookings Institution, 1931.

Quigley, H. S.: *Japanese Government and Politics*, New York, Appleton-Century, 1932.

Rea, G. B.: *The Case for Manchukuo*, New York, Appleton-Century, 1935.

Snow, Edgar: *Red Star over China*, New York, Random, 1938.

————: *The Battle for Asia*, New York, Random, 1941.

Steiger, G. N.: *History of the Far East*, New York, Ginn, 1936.

Stimson, H. L.: *The Far Eastern Crisis*, New York, Harpers, 1936.

Utley, Freda: *China at War*, New York, Day, 1939.

Vinacke, H. M.: *History of the Far East in Modern Times*, New York, Crofts, 1936.

Willoughby, W. W.: *Japan's Case Examined*, Baltimore, Johns Hopkins Press, 1940.

Yakhontoff, V. A.: *Eyes on Japan*, New York, Coward-McCann, 1936.

Young, A. M.: *Imperial Japan*, 1926–1938, New York, Morrow, 1938.

Young, C. W.: *The International Relations of Manchuria*, Chicago, University of Chicago Press, 1929.

2. ITALY: CAESAR AFRICANUS

Insatiable Italy, with furtive glances, roves restlessly hither and thither, instinctively drawn on by the odor of corruption and calamity—always ready to attack anybody from the rear and make off with a bit of plunder. It is outrageous that these Italians, still unsatisfied, should continue to make preparations and to conspire in every direction.—CHANCELLOR OTTO VON BISMARCK.

The Fascist State is a will to power and an empire. The Roman tradition is the idea of force. In the Fascist doctrine, the imperial idea is not only a territorial, military, and mercantile expression, but also one of spiritual and moral expansion. For Fascism, the tendency to the imperial idea means expansion of the nation and is a manifestation of vitality.—BENITO MUSSOLINI in *Popolo d'Italia*, August 4, 1932.

A Prince ought to take care never to make an alliance with one more powerful than himself for the purpose of attacking others . . . because if he conquers, you are at his discretion.—NICCOLÒ MACHIAVELLI.

When weighed in the scales of the arts and the skills of gracious living, Italy has long stood in the forefront of Western civilization. This was acknowledged by all during the glory of the Renaissance. This was also so, even if not so widely realized, during the *Risorgimento* and after the establishment of the House of Savoy in 1861 as the reigning family of a united nation. In the scales of power, however, the Kingdom of Italy was from the outset the weakest of the Great Powers. The ambitions of her patriotic and imperial politicians were often beyond attainment with the meager components of fighting capacity at the disposal of the new Rome. Italy's only military asset was a teeming population. Numbers count for little without coal, iron, capital, control of seaways, and possession of bases—and in these things Italy is poor. Italians, moreover, have always been (to their credit) the least bellicose of peoples. The peasantry of the south was long content with its colorful folk life and with the blessings of illiteracy and superstitious religiosity. The townspeople of the north have ever worshiped not at the bloody and barren altar of Mars but at the cheerful shrines of joy and beauty. Twenty years of imitation Prussianism, imposed upon them by a blind plutocracy and aristocracy and enforced by a boastful tyrant, did not change their character.

Under these conditions the inevitable quest of Italian diplomats and strategists for martial glory and the gaudy baubles of empire has ever had about it something incongruous and pathetic. From Bismarck's day to the present, Italy's role in *Realpolitik* has been that of jackal, attacking only the small and weak, mauling those already mortally wounded, or snatching bones from the feasts of the great carnivores. Italy was inferior to other Powers in the economic and strategic prerequisites of an effective role in power politics. She was consequently reduced to adroit maneuverings and complex bargainings to achieve her purposes—and she repeatedly met with failure and frustration.

The foreign policy of Italy after 1870 was pulled alternately in two directions by two sets of irreconcilable ambitions: the desire to secure Italia Irredenta, and the desire to create an African empire. The first could be achieved only at the expense of Austria, the second only at the expense of France. The French seizure of Tunis precipitated Italy into the waiting arms of Germany and Austria-Hungary in the Triple Alliance of 1882. But Italy remained an unreliable ally, for nationalistic aspirations in the north and in the Adriatic were more powerful driving forces behind foreign policy than hopes of imperialistic aggrandizement in Africa. France, for a price, was prepared to approve the fulfillment of at least a portion of these hopes. In 1896 Italy at last recognized the French protectorate in Tunis, in return for commercial concessions. In 1899 a commercial convention put an end to the long Franco-Italian tariff war. In 1900 France extended assurances that she harbored no designs on Tripoli, and Italy acquiesced in French designs on Morocco. By the agreement of 1902, Italy, acting contrary to the spirit if not the letter of her compacts with her allies, agreed to remain neutral in the event of an attack upon France, even if France should be obliged to take the initiative in a declaration of war. In 1909 Italy agreed to view with benevolence Russia's designs upon the Straits and Constantinople, in return for Russian approval of her project of seizing Tripoli (Libya) from Turkey, Russia's hereditary enemy and satellite of Italy's allies, Germany and Austria-Hungary. Libya was accordingly seized in the Italo-Turkish war of 1911. But in form Rome retained its commitments to Berlin and Vienna. Italy thus had a foot in both camps and was prepared to bargain for terms in the event of a crisis in which each of the great coalitions should seek her support.

When the Great War came, Italy remained neutral on the specious plea that the war was aggressive and not defensive on the part of her allies and thus did not involve the *casus foederis*. With her long, open coast line exposed to attack by the British and French fleets, Italy had more to lose than to gain by joining the Central Powers, even if eventual victory might enable her to seize a large portion of the French African colonies. During the winter of 1914–1915 the Italian Government, acting frankly on a policy of *sacro egoismo* (holy selfishness), bargained with both coalitions for promises of territorial compensation and agreed to enter the war on the side which promised most. Though Germany and Austria-Hungary were lavish with promises of French territory in Africa, they were unwilling to surrender Trieste, the Tyrol, and Trentino as the price of Italian aid. The Allies, on the other hand, promised Rome all these territories and part of the Dalmatian coast besides, plus compensations in the Near East and "rectifications" of the African frontiers. These terms were embodied in the secret Treaty of London of April 26, 1915. On May 24, Italy declared war on Austria-Hungary. Italy's military contribution to the Allied cause was not impressive; and when the Italian front collapsed in the disaster of Caporetto in the fall of 1917 and most of Venetia fell into the hands of the enemy, British and French divisions had to be sent to the Piave to stem the German invasion. In the summer of 1918, however, the Italian armies checked an Austrian offensive and counter-attacked with sufficiently telling effect (Vittorio Veneto) to claim a share in the glory of final victory.

At the Peace Conference, Italy found her claims thwarted by Wilsonian idealism, by Serbian aspirations in the Adriatic, and by French and British reluctance to permit Italy to dominate the Mediterranean. "Rectifications" of the Libyan frontiers were secured, but they were not of sufficient magnitude to satisfy Italian colonial hopes. In the north, Italia Irredenta was indeed acquired, plus the Austrian Tyrol south of Brenner Pass, which was demanded for strategic reasons. Fiume was likewise seized, as well as Zara and the island of Lagosta. But the Italian

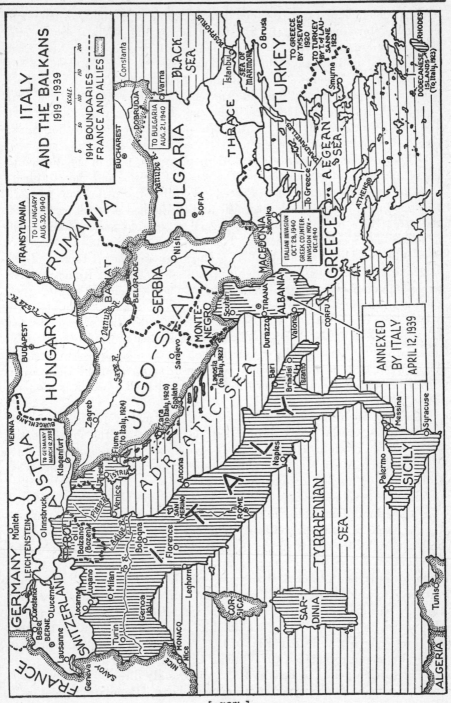

ITALY
AND THE BALKANS
1919 - 1939

SCALE.
50 100 150 200

1914 BOUNDARIES ------
FRANCE AND ALLIES

TO HUNGARY
AUG. 30, 1940

TRANSYLVANIA

TO BULGARIA
AUG. 21, 1940

TO GREECE
BY T.9 SEVRES
1920

TO TURKEY
BY T. of LAU-
SANNE
1923

DODECANESE
ISLANDS
(To Italy, 1923)

RHODES

TURKEY

BLACK
SEA

Constanta

BUCHAREST

Danube

DOBRUDJA

Varna

SOFIA

BULGARIA

THRACE

Istanbul

Sea of
Marmora

Brusa

Smyrna

BOSPHORUS

RUMANIA

BANAT

Danube R.

BELGRADE

SERBIA

Nish

MACEDONIA

Saloníka

Salonika

AEGEAN
SEA

Athens

GREECE

ITALIAN INVASION
OCT 28, 1940
GREEK COUNTER-
INVASION NOV-
DEC.1940

Budapest

HUNGARY

Save R.

JUGO-SLAVIA

Sarajevo

MONTE-
NEGRO

Scutari

TIRANA

ALBANIA

Durazzo

Valona

CORFU

To Greece

VIENNA

TO GERMANY
MARCH 18, 1938

BURGENLAND

AUSTRIA

Innsbruck

Klagenfurt

Zagreb

Fiume

Zara
(To Italy, 1924)

Lagosta
(To Italy, 1920)

Spalato

ANNEXED
BY ITALY
APRIL 12, 1939

GERMANY

Munich

LEICHTENSTEIN

SWITZERLAND

Lucerne

Constance

Basel

BERNE

Lausanne

Geneva

SAVOY

Lugano

Locarno

TIROL

Bolzano
(Bozen)

Brenner

Adige R.

Piave R.

Trieste

ISTRIA

Venice

Bari

Brindisi

Taranto

ADRIATIC SEA

Ancona

SAN
MARINO

Florence

ROME

Bologna

Po R.

Milan

Turin

MONACO

Nice

NICE

Genoa

Leghorn

I T A L Y

Naples

TYRRHENIAN

SEA

COR-
SICA

SAR-
DINIA

Palermo

Messina

SICILY

Syracuse

FRANCE

ALGERIA

Tunis

acquisitions included territory claimed by Serbia on grounds of language and self-determination. Italy was faced across the Adriatic by an embittered and resentful Jugoslavia in alliance with France. In the Near East Italy gained nothing save the Dodecanese and the confirmation of her occupation of Rhodes. While Kemal Pasha's Turkish Nationalists frustrated Italian aspirations in Anatolia, France retained Syria and Great Britain acquired Iraq and Palestine. All Italian patriots felt that Italy had won the war but had lost the peace. Italy, despite her gains, emerged from the Conference an unsatiated State.

This thwarting of patriotic ambitions played its part in the discrediting of parliamentary government, the rise of Fascism, and the establishment of a new despotism. The Fascist revolution was at bottom a resort to force on the part of the bourgeoisie and the landed proprietors to meet the threat of a peasant-proletarian social revolution under Communist and extreme Socialist leadership. The armed Black Shirts of Mussolini were subsidized by the industrialists of the north and the aristocrats of the south, and at first even supported by the weak Cabinet at Rome in their assaults upon Socialist and Communist party headquarters, their destruction of working-class papers, and their suppression of labor unions and cooperative organizations. In October of 1922, when the instrument for the suppression of the social revolution had become more powerful than its creators, the Fascist militia marched on Rome and Mussolini became Premier. In 1925 all the opposition parties were suppressed and the Italian Government became a tyrannical régime in which all power was monopolized by the Fascists.

The Fascist movement made its appeal not merely to the economic and social interests of the propertied classes, but to the nationalistic emotionalism of all ardent patriots. Its symbols were those of the Rome of the Caesars. Rome's ancient glories were to be restored. The Duce was to be the new imperator and conqueror. Italy was to be made strong, powerful, respected. A new empire was to be won. All other interests were to be subordinated to the supreme end of the power of the fatherland. In the name of national solidarity, the old trade unions were dissolved and the right to strike suppressed. Italian economic life was rigidly regimented, as a means of securing industrial peace and prosperity. In the name of unity and power, Italian youth was indoctrinated with a fervent antiforeign, militaristic patriotism. In the name of unity and power, the tyranny was defended, rationalized, and sanctified. In the name of unity and power, the Italian State concluded its long struggle with the Papacy and by the Treaty and Concordat of 1929 restored the temporal authority of the Pope and recognized the Vatican City as the new Papal State.

The foreign policy of Fascist Italy was frankly directed toward territorial expansion at the expense of her neighbors. "Population pressure" was advanced as the chief justification for territorial demands. During the four-year period before 1914, 3,500,000 Italians emigrated to foreign lands; and at present over 10,000,000 Italians live abroad. Italian immigration to the United States was later shut off by American legislation. Though Italians continued to go to France, South America, and elsewhere, emigration was no solution of the problem. In any case, the Duce desired to retain the sons of Italy, for Italy "must appear on the threshold of the second half of the century with a population of not less than 60,000,000 inhabitants. If we fall off . . . we cannot make an empire."[1] Empire building involves war. War requires man power. Man power requires not emigration or birth control, but a population which will grow to the bursting point. More colonies must be acquired at all costs. Italian power must be extended over the Mediterranean. Only in this way can Italy attain that "place in the sun" to which she has so long aspired.

Italy, however, could afford to use force only against small or weak States. When an Italian general was assassinated by Greek patriots near the Albanian frontier, Italy bombarded and seized the Greek island of Corfu on August 31, 1923, and defied the League of Nations to say her nay. An indemnity and an apology were exacted from Greece, but Corfu was evacuated under British pressure and Italy gained no conquests. By the Treaty of Tirana, November, 1926, Albania became definitely an Italian dependency, to the alarm of Jugoslavia and Greece. But against the prospective enemy in the Adriatic, Jugoslavia, Italy was obliged to proceed cautiously, for Jugoslavia was the ally of France and a member of the Little Entente. Fascist Italy was long obliged to modify Theodore Roosevelt's advice to "speak softly and carry a big stick," by speaking loudly and recognizing that the Italian big stick was ineffective against the bigger stick of French hegemony over the Continent.

Mussolini was nevertheless impelled by the gradual impoverishment of the Italian masses under Fascism to counteract popular unrest by fulfilling long-deferred promises of war and glory. The Nazi revolution in Germany indirectly furnished him with his opportunity, though its immediate effect was dangerous to Italian interests. He sponsored the futile Four Power Pact of July 15, 1933, whereby Italy, France, Britain, and Germany agreed to consult one another to promote peace and disarmament. He blocked Hitler's designs on Austria by subsidizing the Austrian Heimwehr and supporting the Dollfuss régime against Germany. He secured British and French diplomatic support against Berlin in championing Austrian "independence." In May, 1934, following the bloody suppression of the Austrian Social Democrats, he formed an "Italian bloc" by concluding a series of political and economic agreements with Hungary and Austria.

[1] Mussolini to Parliament, May 26, 1927.

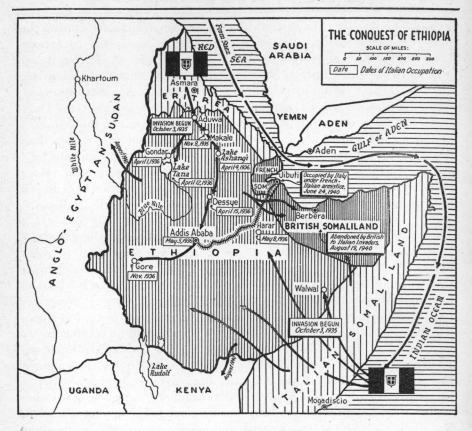

But glory had to be sought in other fields. Fascist Rome turned eyes toward Africa, calculating that Britain and France, out of fear of Germany, would consent to Italian expansion. An Anglo-Italian-Egyptian agreement of July 20, 1934, extended the frontiers of Libya at Egypt's expense. By the Laval-Mussolini accord of January 7, 1935, 44,500 square miles of the Tibesti Desert were ceded to Libya and a strip of French Somaliland was added to Eritrea, all in fulfillment of the Treaty of London of 1915. Laval and his successors blessed Italian designs against the ancient empire of Haile Selassie in the hope of securing continued Italian support against the Reich—at the cost of destroying the League of Nations as an agency of collective security. In October, 1935, the invasion of Ethiopia was launched. As it approached completion the following spring. Hitler's occupation of the Rhineland caused London and Paris to desert Ethiopia and the League completely in the hope of bringing Mussolini back into the "Stresa Front" of 1935. By July of 1936 Mussolini could celebrate the establishment of a new Italian empire and victory over Britain and the League as well as over Ethiopia.

This successful aggression placed Italy in a far stronger international position than she had hitherto enjoyed. Having effectively played off Berlin against Paris and London, Mussolini could retain a foot in both camps and bargain with each for concessions under threat of joining the other. The Austro-German accord of July 11, 1936, represented, at least on paper, an abandonment of Nazi designs against Vienna in return for Italian diplomatic support against France. The Italian-German accord of October 25, 1936, was appropriately negotiated by the husband of Edda, the Duce's daughter, Foreign Minister Galeazzo Ciano, who had won his laurels by bombing Ethiopians in the African war. It foreshadowed an alliance between the Fascist Powers. Austria became a bridge instead of a barrier between Rome and Berlin. Hungary's regent, Admiral Horthy, as well as Premier Julius Goemboes, was committed to a policy of cooperation with Italy, Germany, Austria, and Poland against the Little Entente. Goemboes's death on October 6, 1936, brought no change of Hungarian orientation. Foreign Minister Kanya continued to act in unison with the Fascist Powers in return for support of Hungarian irredentist ambitions. Italy alone could not dominate the Balkans through her ties with Austria and Hungary, but she might achieve much through the alliance with the Reich. Such a combination could split or defy the Little Entente and destroy French power in eastern Europe. Cooperation with a strong ally, however, often means subordination. To play Hitler's game was almost as dangerous for Italy as for Poland. But Fascism glorified danger. Mussolini was prepared to take the risk.

Italy's increased prestige in the Mediterranean offered opportunities in other directions. The British route to India through Suez and the Red Sea now seemed at the mercy of Italian bombers and cruisers. The Sudan and the headwaters of the Nile lay adjacent to Italian Ethiopia. French communications with North Africa could be severed by Italian air power, particularly in the event of cooperation with a Fascist Spain. Intrigues against Britain and France in Palestine, Syria, and Arabia offered hope of further weakening the influence of London and Paris in the Near East. Perhaps the Mediterranean could, after all, be made once more a Roman lake. Perhaps Libya and Italian East Africa could be united over the ruins of British imperial power. Perhaps in the coming European war German support of Italy would make possible the conquest of Corsica, Nice, and Savoy. Yemen, Turkey, and Greece were among the other prospective victims of Fascist imperialism.

Despite assertions that the conquest of Ethiopia had made Italy a satiated State, Mussolini was driven forward to new adventures by the economic dilemma of Fascism and by the psychological compulsion of a dictatorship obliged to give the masses circuses instead of bread. On August 30, 1936, the Duce declared, "We can mobilize 8,000,000 men.

. . . We reject the absurdity of eternal peace, which is foreign to our creed and to our temperament. We must be strong. We must be always stronger. We must be so strong that we can face any eventualities and look directly in the eye whatever may befall." And on November 1, at Milan: "Collective security never existed, does not exist and will never exist. . . . The League of Nations can perish. . . . Today we raise the banner of anti-Bolshevism. . . . For us Italians the Mediterranean is life."

Meanwhile, the next adventure in aggression had been launched. In Rome, as in Berlin, it was obvious to the tyrant in power that his ambitions could be furthered by converting Spain into a Fascist ally or vassal. To threaten Gibraltar from Algeciras and Ceuta, to menace French communications from the Balearic Islands, to control the coasts of Spain would enable the Axis to levy further blackmail against France and Britain and perhaps ultimately to destroy them. The means for the enterprise were at hand in the determination of the army officers, industrialists, feudal grandees, and priests of reactionary Spain to destroy the liberal Spain of the "People's Front" which won the election of February 16, 1936. Although there were neither Socialists nor Communists in the People's Front Cabinet, the Axis crusade could be readily disguised in terms of "saving Spain from Bolshevism." Mussolini and Hitler assumed correctly that most men of Property and Piety in France, Britain, and America would be deceived by this slogan and would therefore acquiesce or even cooperate in the destruction of the Spanish Republic.

As early as March, 1934, Spanish monarchist leaders were received by Mussolini and Balbo in Rome and encouraged to hope for Fascist support against the Republic. In the spring of 1936, Spanish generals and plutocrats made repeated visits to Rome and Berlin and laid their plans for a military uprising with Axis support. General Francisco Franco, dispatched to the Canaries because his loyalty to the Republic was suspect, conferred before his departure with Generals Mola and Varelo, millionaire Juan March, Colonel Yagüe, and José Primo de Rivera, son of the former Spanish dictator and leader of the Fascist *Falange Española*. On July 15, 1936, a private British plane arrived at Las Palmas in the Canaries. On the same day a squadron of bombers of the Royal Italian Air Force was ordered to be ready for duty in Spain. On July 17, Franco received a wire from Yagüe in Tetuán, Spanish Morocco. "The troops in Africa revolted on the 16th at 11 a.m." Franco boarded the plane, reached Tetuán on July 19, took command of the revolting Moors and Foreign Legion, and proclaimed that Spain was "saved." But this Nazi-Fascist *putsch* failed in its immediate purpose. General Sanjurjo, flying from Lisbon, was killed in an air crash. General Goded, flying from the Balearic Islands, was captured and shot. Mola was subsequently killed and Rivera executed. Army uprisings were successful in the south and in the north but were crushed in Madrid, Barcelona, and other centers by a hastily organized People's Militia which rallied to the defense of the Republic. What was to have been a military coup became a "civil war."

In reality this "civil war" at once assumed the form of an Axis invasion of Spain. Italian bombers were immediately placed at Franco's disposal. Nazi agents, technicians, and aviators poured into Rebel territory from German ships and from Portugal. Italian troops landed in Seville and at other points. The first joint diplomatic action of Rome and Berlin, following their secret agreement of October 25, was simultaneous recognition of Franco as ruler of Spain on November 18, 1936. The better to lend plausibility to the enterprise, Germany and Japan concluded the "Anti-Comintern" Pact of November 25. Italy adhered on November 6, 1937, and Franco's Spain on March 27, 1939. Britain and France in the name of "nonintervention," followed by the United States in the name of "neutrality," forbade their citizens to sell arms to Spain and thereby cooperated with the Axis Powers in the murder of Spanish democracy. An international "Nonintervention" Committee was set up in London with Lord Plymouth as chairman to supervise the enforcement of the obligations assumed. These obligations were well observed by France and Britain and systematically violated by Italy, Germany, and Portugal—and also, in retaliation for Fascist intervention, by the U.S.S.R. After the event, when all need for subterfuge was gone, Mussolini's *Popolo d'Italia* boasted, "We have intervened from the first moment to the last." In June, 1939, Italian and German troops returned to their homelands and enjoyed triumphal receptions in Rome and Berlin. Ciano and Göring revealed that Axis soldiers, sometimes disguised as "tourists," had gone to Spain at the outset of the rebellion and had been prepared for action long in advance.

The courageous struggle of the Spanish people to defend their liberties in the face of the united opposition of the Vatican, the Caesars of the Axis, and the appeasers and isolationists of Paris, London, and Washington was foredoomed to failure. No government, save only that of the U.S.S.R., would give or even sell them arms to resist their enemies. By mid-August, 1936, Franco's mercenaries had taken Badajoz, where they massacred several thousand helpless prisoners, and effected a junction with Mola's forces in the north. By the end of October they raised the Loyalist siege of the Alcázar in Toledo. In early November, four Rebel columns, supported by Italian and German planes, tanks, and artillery, advanced on Madrid, expecting a "Fifth Column" of sympathizers within the city to give them speedy mastery of the capital. But the Loyalist "International Brigade," assisted belatedly by Soviet arms, smashed the assault and compelled the invaders to lay siege to Madrid. On January 2, 1937, as

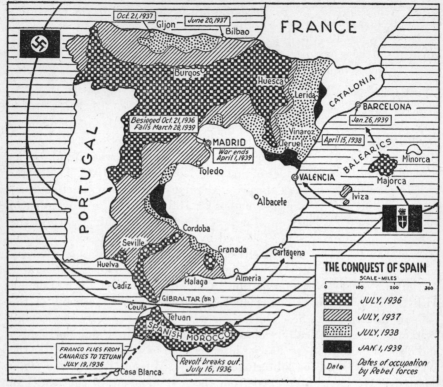

THE CONQUEST OF SPAIN
SCALE—MILES
0   100   200   300

JULY, 1936
JULY, 1937
JULY, 1938
JAN. 1, 1939
Date ● Dates of occupation by Rebel forces

German and Italian cruisers fired on Loyalist shipping, Ciano and Perth exchanged letters pledging respect for the *status quo* in the Mediterranean and the territorial integrity of Spain. Under the new "Nonintervention" plan of February 16, 1937, designed to "prohibit" volunteering and arms exports to both sides, Axis warships "patroled" the Loyalist coasts while British and French vessels did likewise off Rebel ports. The United States imposed its own unilateral arms embargo upon Spain on January 8, 1937. "President Roosevelt," declared Franco, "behaved in the manner of a true gentleman."

On March 13, 1937, an Italian armored column seeking to outflank Madrid from the north via Guadalajara was crushingly defeated by the defenders. Rome refused to withdraw its "volunteers." The London Committee and its local observers were at no time able to detect any violation of the "Nonintervention" agreements. In May, Loyalist planes bombed the Italian cruiser *Barletta* at Palma and the German pocket battleship *Deutschland* at Iviza. Hitler retaliated by ordering a naval bombardment of Almeria on May 31. Rome and Berlin announced their withdrawal from the sea "patrol." They resumed "cooperation" on June 16. Nazi dive bombers meanwhile destroyed Guernica, holy city of the Roman Catholic Basques, on April 26. Italian forces occupied Bilbao on June 19. On June 23, Mussolini and Hitler alleged further Loyalist outrages against their ships and withdrew permanently from the naval patrol, simultaneously demanding belligerent rights for Franco. The hypocritical tergiversations of the London Committee now became incredibly complex. Italian efforts to blockade Republican Spain by torpedoing merchant ships all over the Mediterranean were abruptly halted by a conference at Nyon in September, 1937, where it was agreed by nine Powers (not including Italy and Germany which refused to attend) that "unknown" submarines should be attacked and destroyed on sight as pirates.

Despite these setbacks, the Duce and Führer were enabled by Paris, London, and Washington to achieve their goal of victory for Caudillo ("Chief") Franco. Almost 100,000 Italian troops were operating in Spain. Rome acknowledged 40,000. A League Assembly resolution of October 2, 1937, declared "there are veritable foreign army corps on Spanish soil." It urged "immediate and complete withdrawal." Rome and Berlin refused to withdraw "volunteers" unless the Western Powers should grant Franco belligerent rights and thus enable the Axis navies to impose an effective blockade upon Loyalist ports. Downing Street and the Quai d'Orsay were willing to negotiate forever over this question while the Fascist conquest of Spain continued. Santander fell to the invaders on August 22 and Gijón in the Asturias on October 21, 1937. The summer offensive of the Loyalists in Aragon failed. The Republican capital was moved from Valencia to Barcelona on October 20. On St. Patrick's Day, 1938, Axis bombers raided Barcelona twelve times in twenty-four hours. The slain victims included 245 women and 118 children. In New York, Patrick Cardinal Hayes publicly prayed for a Franco victory. The Earl of Perth negotiated amiably with Ciano in Rome.

Franco's forces reached the Mediterranean at Vinaroz on April 15, 1938. On the following day Ciano and Perth signed the pacts whereby Britain agreed to recognize Italian title to Ethiopia and accepted an Italian pledge to withdraw volunteers from Spain only after the end of the "civil war." Chamberlain and Mussolini exchanged congratulatory telegrams. Roosevelt expressed "sympathetic interest." Daladier and Bonnet approved. Early in May Hitler visited Rome to return Mussolini's visit to Berlin of the preceding September. Austria was dead. Spain was dying. The Axis was "steel." In mid-May Alvarez del Vayo, Loyalist Foreign Minister, infuriated Halifax and Bonnet at Geneva by indelicately recalling the Assembly resolution on the withdrawal of volunteers. During June British ships and French towns were "accidentally" bombed by Franco's allies. Chamberlain went fishing. On July 5, 1938, the London Committee adopted an eighty-page "formula" for the withdrawal of volunteers. Franco rejected it. The Duce and Führer laughed. In the aftermath of Munich, Britain put into effect (November 16, 1938) the Ciano-Perth accord which had specified that "a settlement of the Spanish question" was "a prerequisite of entry into force" of the agreement.

The nature of this "settlement" was no longer in doubt. Chamberlain and Daladier were as eager for Fascist victory in Spain as were Hitler and Mussolini. The final Rebel offensive against Catalonia was launched two days before Christmas, 1938. Chamberlain and Halifax conferred with Mussolini, Ciano, and Pius XI in Rome, January 11 to 14, 1939. On January 18 Chamberlain and Daladier declared that "nonintervention" must continue to the end. On January 26, Barcelona fell to the Rebels. Mussolini shouted to cheering crowds outside the Palazzo Venezia, "Our enemies are biting the dust!" Early in March a group of defeatists and appeasers in Madrid, headed by General Sigismundo Casado, repudiated the authority of Loyalist Premier Juan Negrin, raised the banner of "anti-Communism," and asked Franco for peace terms. He demanded unconditional surrender. Casado fled. The Fifth Column in Madrid took over the ruined capital. Rebel forces entered on March 28, 1939. Bloody vengeance was visited on thousands of Loyalists. Half a million refugees were grudgingly admitted to France, there to be herded wretchedly into concentration camps and condemned to misery. Since Franco and his executioners, trained by the Gestapo and blessed by the bishops, would grant no amnesty, the fugitives could not be repatriated.

On February 27, 1939, Chamberlain and Daladier granted *de jure* recognition to the Franco régime. London sent as Ambassador to Burgos Sir Maurice Peterson, one of the authors of the Hoare-Laval plan to give Mussolini Ethiopia. Paris sent eighty-three-year old Marshal Henri Philippe Pétain, clerical reactionary and favorite hero of the French Fascist leagues. The United States recognized Franco on April 1 and lifted the arms embargo. The democratic Powers hoped to appease Franco with loans. The Caudillo's brother-in-law and Minister of the Interior, Ramón Serrano Suñer, leader of the Falange (who was to become Foreign Minister in October, 1940), hinted broadly that the new Spain would aid the Axis to destroy France and Britain and to combat the United States in Latin America. "Our enemies," declared the Duce, "are too stupid to be dangerous."

But victory in Spain was not an undiluted blessing for the Caesar of Rome. Italian losses had been heavier than in the Ethiopian campaign. No territories had been won. Fascist Spain was dominated more by Germany than by Italy. Franco was in no position to make an alliance for war in aid of the Axis. A million Spaniards had been slain. The vanquished were starving, sullen, bitter. The country was in ruins. Yet Mussolini had again demonstrated that the class prejudices of the Anglo-French ruling groups incapacited them for defending the interest of their States. He had likewise improved his opportunities for blackmailing the French Republic and further weakening British power.

When French Ambassador André François-Ponçet came to Rome in November, 1938, bearing the gift of French recognition of Italian title to Ethiopia, he was greeted in the Italian chamber with loud outcries for "Tunisia! Jibuti! Corsica! Nice! Savoy!" On December 17, Rome informed Paris that the Laval-Mussolini accord on 1935 was no longer regarded as binding. France must give more. Daladier breathed feeble defiance. Bonnet intrigued obscurely through his secret agents—Fernand de Brinon in Berlin, Paul Baudouin in Rome—to give away additional French territory, but he failed. The psychological and diplomatic aftermath of Hitler's seizure of Prague in mid-March rendered further appeasement inexpedient. The Duce's potent ally had won another major victory. The Roman Caesar was left empty-handed.

Mussolini sought solace by seizing Albania and concluding a formal military alliance with the Reich. On April 7 to 8, 1939, Italian troops drove King Zog and Queen Geraldine out of their backward Balkan kingdom. On April 15, King Victor Emmanuel assumed the Albanian crown. Although this action was a flagrant violation of the Ciano-Perth accord, France and Britain took no counteraction beyond extending guarantees to Greece and Rumania on April 13 and concluding an alliance with Turkey on May 12. On April 15, Roosevelt addressed an appeal to Hitler and Mussolini to refrain from attacking their neighbors. The Führer replied at length on April 28 with bitter and effective sarcasm. The Duce contemptuously refused to be moved by "Messiahlike messages." Ribbentrop conferred with Ciano at Milan on May 6. On May 22, 1939, the two Foreign Ministers affixed their signatures at Berlin to an apparently unlimited military alliance threatening the Western Powers with war should they continue to oppose Axis demands.[1]

But this "pact of steel" was in part compounded of *Ersatz*. Ciano admitted in December that Rome had told Berlin at the time of its conclusion that Italy would not be ready for war for three years. Hitler had

[1] The German Reich Chancellor and His Majesty the King of Italy and Albania, Emperor of Ethiopia, consider that the moment has come to bear testimony by a solemn act to the close relationship of friendship and community of interests existing between National Socialist Germany and Fascist Italy.

Now that a secure bridge toward mutual aid and support has been constructed by the common frontier, fixed for all time between Germany and Italy, both governments declare anew their faith in the policy, the foundations and aims of which have already at an earlier date been agreed upon and which has proven successful as well for the advancement of the interests of both countries and for rendering secure the peace of Europe.

Firmly bound to each other through the inner relationship of their philosophies of life and the comprehensive solidarity of their interests, the German and Italian peoples are

agreed not to raise issues likely to lead to armed conflict during this period. In the summer crisis of 1939, Rome sought to avert an open test of force. Mussolini was not favored with any advance information regarding the German-Soviet pact. When a general conflagration appeared imminent, Mussolini and Ciano cooperated with Bonnet in efforts to localize the German-Polish conflict and to arrange an armistice and a conference. Their plans foundered on German refusal to halt the *Blitzkrieg* and British refusal to negotiate unless it were halted. If Mussolini contemplated joining Germany in hostilities, he was dissuaded by his Chief of Staff, Marshal Pietro Badoglio, by the King, and perhaps even by Hitler, who realized full well that Italy as a belligerent would soon crack under the full brunt of Anglo-French attack. Much greater advantages were to be had by retaining the benefits of neutrality while cooperating secretly with the Reich. This policy presupposed that the Western

---

determined in the future also to stand side by side and with united strength to render secure their space for living (Lebensraum) and for the maintenance of peace.

Proceeding along this path pointed out to them by history, Germany and Italy desire in the midst of a world of unrest and disintegration to serve the task of rendering safe the foundations of European culture.

In order to formulate their principles in a treaty there have been designated as plenipotentiaries:

By the German Reich Chancellor, the Reich Minister for Foreign Affairs, Herr Joachim von Ribbentrop.

By His Majesty the King of Italy and Albania, Emperor of Ethiopia, the Minister for Foreign Affairs, Count Galeazzo Ciano di Cortellazzo, who, after an exchange of their credentials which were found to be in good and proper form, agreed upon the following provisions:

Article I

The contracting parties will remain in constant contact with each other in order to arrive at an understanding on all matters touching their common interests or the general European situation.

Article II

Should the common interests of the contracting parties be endangered by international events of any sort whatsoever they will immediately enter upon consultations concerning the measures to be taken for safeguarding these interests.

Should the security or other essential interests of one of the contracting parties be threatened from the outside the other contracting partner will give the threatened party his full political and diplomatic support in order to remove this threat.

Article III

If contrary to the wishes and hopes of the contracting parties it should happen that either of them should become involved in military entanglements with one other power or with other powers, the other contracting party will immediately rally to his side as ally and support him with all his military resources on land, at sea and in the air.

Article IV

In order in any given case to make sure that the duties of an ally undertaken in accordance with Article III shall be carried out speedily, the governments of the two contracting

Munichmen would be too timid and blind to force an immediate show-down with Rome. The assumption was correct.

On September 1, 1939, the Italian Government accordingly announced that it "would take no initiative whatever toward military operations." The Fascist formula was "nonbelligerency" which meant in practice all aid to Germany short of war and blackmail against the Allies. Early in March, 1940, Britain yielded on the issue of Italian imports of German coal. Ribbentrop conferred in Rome with Mussolini, Ciano, and Pius XII on March 10 and 11. Hitler and Ribbentrop conferred with Mussolini and Ciano at Brennero on March 17. Sumner Welles, departing from Rome on March 19 after a tour of the belligerent capitals, declared that he had neither received nor conveyed any peace plans and was not carrying any home to the President. The *Popolo d'Italia* asserted early in May, "Italy has been in the war from the beginning. When she changes her policy of waiting is a matter which concerns only him who has the responsibility of guiding and safeguarding the interests of the Italian people." The answer to the question of when depended upon calculations of safety. To attack while the Allies could still counterattack would be too soon. To attack after the Reich had won complete victory would be too late. To attack after the Allies had been decisively defeated but before they had capitulated would be to attack at the right moment.

As the moment seemed to be approaching in the wake of Allied disasters in the north and west, efforts were made from Paris, London, and

---

parties will further deepen their cooperation in the realm of the military and in the realm of war economy (Kriegswirtschaft).

In a similar manner the two governments will also constantly arrive at understandings concerning other measures necessary for the practical execution of the provisions of this act.

The two governments will form standing commissions for the purposes indicated above under Articles I and II. These commissions shall be under the jurisdiction of the two Foreign Ministers.

ARTICLE V

The contracting parties obligate themselves now, in the event of war conducted jointly, to conclude an armistice and peace only in full agreement with each other.

ARTICLE VI

The two contracting parties are conscious of the importance which attaches to their common relations to powers with whom they are on terms of friendship.

They are determined in the future too, to keep up these relationships and jointly to give them a form consonant with the mutual interests that bind these powers.

ARTICLE VII

This pact becomes effective immediately from the moment of signature.

The two contracting parties are in agreement to fix the first period of its effectiveness for ten years.

They will come to an understanding in sufficient time (rechtzeitig) before expiration of this period concerning the extension of the effectiveness of the pact.

Washington to bribe or cajole the Duce into continued neutrality. Reynaud made proposals. They were rejected. Laval went to Rome and returned empty-handed. On May 16, 1940, Churchill sent a secret message of good will, coupled with a plea and a warning. "Whatever may happen on the Continent, England will go on to the end, even quite alone as we have done before; and I believe, with some assurance, that we shall be aided in increasing measure by the United States and, indeed, by all the Americas. I beg you to believe that it is in no spirit of weakness or of fear that I make this solemn appeal, which will remain on the record. . . . Hearken to it, I beseech you in all honor and respect, before the dread signal is given. It will never be given by us." Mussolini replied weakly on May 18 with references to "grave reasons of a historical and contingent character which ranged our two countries in opposite camps [e.g., sanctions and Mediterranean "servitude"]. . . . The same sense of honor and of respect for engagements assumed in the Italian-German treaty guides Italian policy today and tomorrow in the face of any event whatsoever."[1] President Roosevelt through Ambassador William Phillips offered to Mussolini his good offices to adjust Anglo-Italian differences. "I proposed that if Italy would refrain from entering the war I would be willing to ask assurances from the other Powers concerned that they would faithfully execute any decision so reached and that Italy's voice in any future peace conference would have the same authority as if Italy had actually taken part in the war as a belligerent." Rome rejected all overtures.

By early June Mussolini and his advisers had decided that France was doomed and that Britain would be crushed by the end of the summer. On June 10, 1940, the Duce informed a cheering throng in the Piazza Venezia that Italy had declared war on France and Britain and that hostilities would begin at 12:01 A.M., June 11. "The hour destined by fate is sounding for us. The hour of irrevocable decision has come. . . . We want to break the territorial and military chains that confine us in our sea. . . . It is a conflict between two ages, two ideas. . . . Now the die is cast and our will has burned our ships behind us. I solemnly declare that Italy does not intend to drag other peoples bordering on her by sea or land into the conflict. Switzerland, Jugoslavia, Greece, Turkey, and Egypt take note of these words of mine. . . . We will conquer in order, finally, to give a new world of peace with justice to Italy, to Europe, and to the universe." On the same day, at the University of Virginia, Roosevelt asserted, "The hand that held the dagger has struck it into the back of its neighbor."

The calculation behind this decision was right as to France and wrong as to Britain. For his rightness, the Duce got small reward. For his wrongness, his subjects were to suffer grievously. On June 16, 1940, Pétain

---

[1] This exchange of communications was first revealed by Churchill in his broadcast of December 23, 1940.

telephoned Madrid to seek an armistice from Hitler. The Duce and the Führer met in Munich on June 18. On June 22 the French-German armistice was signed. A French-Italian armistice was made a condition of its execution. On June 23, Ciano, Badoglio, and Cavagnari met French emissaries near Rome. At 7:15 P.M., June 24, an agreement was signed. Hostilities in France ceased at 12:35 A.M., June 25, 1940. The twenty-six articles of the Italian armistice required French demilitarization of a fifty-kilometer zone on the European frontier and of comparable zones in Tunisia, Algeria, and French Somaliland, as well as disarmament of the French naval bases at Toulon, Bizerte, Ajaccio, and Oran. Italy secured control of Jibuti and the French railway to Addis Ababa. But Rome got nothing more. In the interest of "collaboration" with Vichy, Berlin denied to Mussolini the pleasure of immediate annexation of French territory. Despite Laval's intrigues, the French fleet did not pass to the Axis. The British navy remained master of "Mare Nostrum." Nazi assaults on England in the summer and autumn failed of their purpose.

Mussolini sought to solve his problem by joining Germany and Japan in the Triple Alliance of September 27, 1940, and by invading British Somaliland, Kenya, the Sudan, Egypt, and Greece. Only the first of these invasions attained its objective. With the evacuation of Berbera on August 19, British Somaliland passed into Italian hands. Attempts to invade Kenya and the Sudan from Ethiopia achieved only local successes. Marshal Rodolfo Graziani's Libyan army of 250,000 invaded "non-belligerent" Egypt in mid-September in a drive aimed at Alexandria and Suez. It quickly reached Sidi Barrani, some seventy-five miles from the border, only to be stalled on the narrow coastal plain pending the arrival of stores and equipment which never came in sufficient amounts because of control of the sea by Sir Andrew Cunningham's battle fleet. On October 28, Hitler and Mussolini conferred in Florence. On the same day the Italian army in Albania launched an invasion of Greece in an effort to strike toward Alexandria by way of the Aegean, Crete, and Rhodes. This adventure proved disastrous. The Duce had been deceived by the wily Greek dictator, John Metaxas, who had studied war and politics in Germany, into supposing that "Little John" and King George II would flee at the first blow and deliver Athens into the hands of a pro-Italian Fifth Column. Metaxas and his able Chief of Staff, General Alexander Papagos, had secretly made all preparations for a warm reception of the unwelcome guests.

The Italian ultimatum to Greece of October 28, 1940, asking "free passage" and "control of strategic points," was at once rejected. The invaders were thrown back. Albania was invaded in turn. British air and sea forces now had free access to Greek bases and used them to raid Naples, smash Italian battleships at Taranto (November 11), bomb

Valona and Durazzo, and harry communications across the Straits of Otranto. The Greeks took Koritza on November 22, Porto Edda on December 6, and Argyrokastron on December 8. On the next day, General Sir Archibald Wavell's "Army of the Nile" launched a motorized *Blitzkrieg* against Graziani's troops, retaking Sidi Barrani on December 11, invading Libya four days later, and taking Bardia, Tobruk, and Bengazi by February. Over 100,000 Italian troops surrendered to the victors. British forces invaded Eritrea and Ethiopia, occupied all of Italian Somaliland and retook Berbera on March 17, 1941.

These events brought Italy to the brink of disaster. Early in December, Marshal Badoglio, who had opposed the Greek adventure, resigned and was replaced by General Ugo Cavallero as Chief of Staff. Admiral Domenico Cavagnari, whose fleet had suffered successive defeats at British hands, was displaced by Admiral Arturo Riccardi. Other shifts of military and political personalities reflected confusion in Rome. On December 23, 1940, Churchill broadcast an appeal to the Italian people.

Our armies are tearing your African empire to shreds. . . . It is all because of one man—one man and one man alone has ranged the Italian people in deadly struggle against the British Empire. . . . After 18 years of unbridled power he has led your country to the horrid verge of ruin. . . . One man has arrayed the trustees and inheritors of ancient Rome upon the side of the ferocious pagan barbarians. There lies the tragedy of Italian history and there stands the criminal who has wrought the deed of folly and shame. . . . The people of Italy were never consulted. The army of Italy was never consulted. No one was consulted. . . . What hard choice is open now? It is to stand up to the battery of the whole British Empire on sea, in the air, and in Africa, and to the vigorous counterattack of the Greek nation. Or, on the other hand, to call in Attila over the Brenner Pass with his hordes of ravenous soldiery and his gangs of Gestapo policemen to occupy, to hold down and to protect the Italian people, for whom he and his Nazi followers cherish the most bitter and outspoken contempt that is on record between races.

President Roosevelt echoed Churchill on December 29. " . . . Even the people of Italy have been forced to become accomplices of the Nazis, but at this moment they do not know how soon they will be embraced to death by their allies. . . . I believe that the Axis Powers are not going to win this war."

Such hopes at the turn of the year 1940–1941 were possibly premature. But whatever the future might bring, one thing was certain: the role of Fascist Italy as a Great Power was ended. German defeat would leave Italy helpless before the victors and inevitably bring about the fall of the Fascist régime. German victory would leave Italy equally helpless as a Nazi vassal State, granted only such crumbs from the triumphal feast as Berlin might see fit to give. Meanwhile, unless the Reich could smash England in the spring of 1941, Italy might well lose her African empire and become the Achilles heel of the Axis. Since the Nazi warlords could not permit Italian capitulation, they would seek to save Italy by a Balkan campaign (involving grave risks of a clash with Moscow) or by pressure to put Vichy and Madrid into the war or, if worst came to worst, by occupying Italy and thereby discrediting Mussolini utterly and completing the demoralization of the Italian masses. For Italy, as for France, Britain, and America, the penalty of departing from policies designed to maintain the balance of power threatened to be catastrophic. And for Italian Fascism the paths of glory promised to lead only to the grave.

SUGGESTED READINGS

De Bono, E.: *Anno XIIII: Conquest of an Empire*, London, Cresset, 1937.
Boveri, M.: *Mediterranean Cross-currents*, New York, Oxford, 1938.
Farago, L.: *Abyssinia on the Eve*, New York, Putnam, 1935.
Finer, H.: *Mussolini's Italy*, New York, Holt, 1935.
Garratt, G. T.: *Mussolini's Roman Empire*, Indianapolis, Bobbs-Merrill, 1938.
Halperin, S. W.: *The Separation of Church and State in Italian Thought from Cavour to Mussolini*, Chicago, University of Chicago Press, 1939.
Macartney, M. H. H., and P. Cremona: *Italy's Foreign and Colonial Policy*, 1914–1937, New York, Oxford, 1938.
Megaro, G.: *Mussolini in the Making*, Boston, Houghton, 1938.
Monroe, E.: *The Mediterranean in Politics*, New York, Oxford, 1938.
Salvemini, G.: *Under the Axe of Fascism*, New York, Viking, 1936.
Schmidt, C.: *The Corporate State in Action*, 1939.
Schneider, H. W., and S. B. Clough: *Making Fascists*, Chicago, University of Chicago Press, 1931.
Seldes, G.: *The Vatican: Yesterday, Today, Tomorrow*, New York, Harper, 1934.

3. GERMANY: THE THIRD REICH

To harness slowly but to drive rapidly is in the nature of this people.—PRINCE OTTO VON BISMARCK.

One must be perfectly clear that the recovery of lost provinces is not achieved by solemn invocations of the Beloved Lord, nor through pious hopes in a League of Nations, but only through armed violence.—ADOLF HITLER, *Mein Kampf*.

God up to now has placed the stamp of approval on our battle. . . . It is the will of the democratic war-inciters and their Jewish-capitalistic wire-pullers that the war must be continued. . . . The year 1941 will bring completion of the greatest victory in our history.—ADOLF HITLER, December 31, 1940.

The inner life of nations is often revealed by their symbols of leadership. The history of Germany begins with a man symbol, continues with three successive dynasty symbols, and ends with a man symbol: Hermann, the Hohenstauffens, the Hapsburgs, the Hohenzollerns, Hitler. The first of these leaders, called by the Romans Arminius, was the chieftain of the Cherusci who led his pagan followers out of the long darkness of barbarism to butcher the legions of Varus in Teutoburger Wald (A.D. 9), thereby compelling Imperial Rome to abandon the dream of a frontier on the Elbe. The early dynasties typified the "First," or Holy Roman, Reich, established in its initial form eight centuries after Hermann by Karl der Grosse (Charlemagne) when the Germanic tribes had long since learned to revere and imitate the great world of ancient Rome which their ancestors had destroyed. Under Hohenstauffen and Hapsburg emperors, this curious realm endured as a living polity for eight centuries more, symbolizing the catholic universality of medieval Christendom and the common culture of Frenchmen, Germans, Czechs, Poles, Italians, and others—bound together by Church and Empire until the "seamless robe" of unity was torn beyond all mending by Protestantism and Nationalism. The life span of the Hohenzollern dynasty was the life span of the modern cult of the nation-state in Germany—from the Mark of Brandenburg through the Kingdom of Prussia to the German Empire (the "Second Reich") of 1871–1918. Hitler, the little man of Austria who became tyrant over Europe, symbolized the twilight time of Nationalism and Christianity when Germans returned to a debased cult of imperial power, reverted to barbarism and paganism, dreamed of a world State conquered by the sword of a "Third Reich," and surrendered themselves in their political and social relations to utter formlessness—violent, empty, and touched with the shadow of a long darkness to come.

The foreign policies of the Second and Third Reichs were similar in that a constant pattern of relationships with Russia to the east, Danubia, Balkania, and Italy to the south, and France and Britain to the west posed similar problems demanding similar solutions. The leaders of the Second Reich, however, pursued limited, national objectives and accepted European civilization and the Western State System as permanent concomitants of their thought and action. The leaders of the Third Reich, on the contrary, repudiated the basic values of European culture, aimed at the destruction of the State System, and worshiped gods who led them to limitless visions of imperial aggrandizement. In both cases the German State was the most powerful single member of the community of nations. European and world politics during the five decades preceding 1918 revolved around the Second Reich. In like manner, European and world politics during the decade following 1933 revolved around the Third Reich.

THE WEIMAR REPUBLIC. Between the fall of the Hohenzollern régime and the establishment of the Nazi despotism, fifteen years elapsed. These were the years when German Liberalism and Social Democracy belatedly came into their own. They were years of hope and of misery. The hope was always deferred and forever frustrated, since the democrats and socialists of the defeated Reich were never able to please patriots or convert to their cause the old ruling classes whose prerogatives they

GERMANY'S WESTERN FRONTIERS

SCALE

0   50   100   150   200 MI.

1919 FRONTIERS ———
1914 FRONTIERS ------
DEMILITARIZED ZONE
JUNE 28, 1919 – MARCH 7, 1936
① SAAR ② EUPEN ③ MALMEDY ④ RUHR

dared not disturb. They fought Communism on the Left (and defeated it in 1919–1920) but compromised endlessly with reaction on the Right. French insecurity, enhanced by British indifference and American isolationism, drove Paris to policies of oppression which the German Republic had no means of resisting. Its weakness promoted disloyalty; its hopelessness provoked desperation. For a few brief years (1924–1929), British and American loans brought to many Germans a feverish prosperity, but the Great Depression produced misery redoubled. By 1932, 6 million Germans were jobless and 60 million Germans were more or less convinced that nothing could restore national well-being and prestige save a return to "blood and iron."

Despite limited and belated diplomatic successes, the Weimar Republic never lived down its early associations with the military débâcle, the "Diktat" of Versailles, indemnities, disarmament, weakness, disgrace, inflation, disaster. In the struggle over reparations between victors and vanquished the Republic lost the first great battle in "the war after the war." On April 27, 1921, the Reparation Commission fixed the total bill at 132 billion marks, or about 31 billion dollars. Germany was compelled to accept this total, under threat of the occupation of the Ruhr. But the financial condition of the German Government led to huge budgetary deficits, which were met by inflation, with a resulting depreciation of the mark. A temporary moratorium had to be granted to Germany; but at the end of 1922 the determination of the Poincaré Government in France to use force and seize "productive guarantees" was reflected in the action of the Reparation Commission in declaring Germany in voluntary default on timber, coal, and cattle deliveries. In the face of British objections, the French and Belgian Governments ordered engineers and troops into the Ruhr in January, 1923. Germany countered by stopping all reparation payments and organizing passive resistance against the invaders. The forces of occupation resorted to reprisals, arrests, courts-martial, and other repressive measures; but coal could not be mined with bayonets, and the occupation was fruitless. The German Government, however, was reduced to bankruptcy, and in August of 1923 Chancellor Stresemann abandoned passive resistance and surrendered.

Germany's efforts to bring about the end of foreign military control and to secure equality in armaments were more successful. The Allied occupation of the Rhineland was terminated in June of 1930, five years before the expiration of the period specified in the treaty, and the Allied military and financial control commissions were withdrawn. This was a substantial gain and the fruit of the Briand-Stresemann era of *rapprochement*. By abandoning passive resistance and flirtations with the Soviet Union, by accepting as permanent the Reich's western frontier, guaranteed in the Locarno treaties of 1925, and finally by accepting the Young Plan, Stresemann gained membership in the League of Nations for Germany in 1926 and achieved the end of foreign supervision of German armaments. But this was a negative victory and only a small step toward that equality of military status which was the prerequisite of effective political equality with other Powers. Germany insisted upon the fulfillment of the pledge of the Treaty of Versailles that the unilateral disarmament of Germany would be followed by general disarmament. In the sessions of the Preparatory Commission for the Disarmament Conference between 1925 and 1929 and in the General Disarmament Conference of the League of Nations which met at Geneva in February, 1932, the German representatives pleaded eloquently for general disarmament to the German level or, as an alternative, the granting to Germany of the right to rearm to the level of her neighbors. France and her eastern allies, with qualified support from Great Britain, stood steadfast against both demands, for the acceptance of either would destroy the strategic bases of French hegemony and enable Germany to challenge the 1919 *status quo* in other respects.

In the matter of territorial readjustment, the German Republic achieved nothing. In the Locarno treaties, it accepted the loss of Alsace-Lorraine and of Eupen and Malmédy as permanent. But the loss of Danzig, the Polish corridor, and Upper Silesia remained a festering wound in the hearts of all patriots, and none could abandon hope of recovering

these territories in the future. Their recovery, however, demanded a new dismemberment of resurrected Poland—and behind Poland stood France and the Little Entente, firmly resolved to maintain frontiers as they were. Here was a stake of German diplomacy which could be attained only at the risk of war; and so long as Germany was impotent, war could not be risked under any circumstances. At Locarno, Germany refused to guarantee the eastern frontiers but agreed not to resort to forcible measures of revision. Stresemann and his successors were consequently obliged, like Gambetta, to cherish in silence the memory of the new "lost provinces" and to await a more favorable conjuncture of events before essaying their recovery. As for the lost colonies, the most that Germany was able to attain was a seat on the Permanent Mandates Commission of the League of Nations. German colonial aspirations remained unfulfilled. Efforts at *Anschluss* with Austria led to further humiliation, compelling Foreign Minister Curtius to resign under French pressure in 1931 and further weakening Chancellor Brüning, last hope of German democracy.

In summary, Republican Germany's foreign policy encountered a succession of defeats at the hands of France and attained none of its major objectives. This circumstance helped to discredit democracy. The psychic insecurities bred of national defeat and impotence were aggravated by social insecurities engendered by currency inflation and general impoverishment. Even in its early days, the Weimar Republic was bitterly assailed by monarchists, ultrapatriots, and adventurous leaders of disgruntled ex-soldiers. Liberals and Social Democrats, in the name of freedom, tolerated reactionary enemies of the Republic on the Right and Communist enemies of the Republic on the Left and were denounced by each for tolerating the other. *Junkers* and industrialists, unconverted to Liberalism and still in possession of much of their old power and prestige, dreamed of glory and profit and schemed with reactionary conspirators against the new régime. The dark years after Versailles created a following for anti-Republican plotters. The Kapp Putsch of March, 1920, was frustrated only by a general strike. In November, 1923, during the French occupation of the Ruhr, an obscure ex-corporal of Austrian birth, preaching anti-Semitism and the glory of the Treaty of Brest-Litovsk and leading a "National Socialist German Workers' Party," attempted a *Putsch* in Munich. It was suppressed. He was tried and lightly sentenced. He resumed political activity in 1925 but converted few to his cause so long as the new prosperity of the middle twenties caused the lower middle classes, the proletariat, and the peasantry to turn deaf ears to agitators and fanatics. His name was Adolf Hitler.

When the Great Depression descended upon the Reich, it created potentially revolutionary conditions once more. Jobless workers flocked to the Communist Party. The impoverished peasantry and *Kleinbürgertum*, terrified at the economic collapse and fearful of Communism, flocked to Hitler's Nazis who promised to save them from Bolshevism and the Jews. Industrialists and *Junkers* perceived an opportunity to use Hitler to destroy the trade unions and the liberal and radical parties. The forces of democracy were paralyzed. The Communists were incapable of undertaking proletarian revolution. The Nazi Messiah appealed to the masses by combining the vocabulary of socialism with the language of impassioned chauvinism and racial hatred. He and his aides cried from the housetops that the German armies were undefeated in 1918 but had been "stabbed in the back" by the Marxists and Jews; that democracy and Communism were destroying German *Kultur;* that the "Weimar Jew Republic" was shameful and corrupt; that the glories of the Hohenstauffen and Hohenzollern Empires must be recaptured in a glorious "Third Reich," strong, authoritarian, and ready to restore to Germany her rightful place in the sun.

THE NAZI REVOLUTION. With banners, drums, and trumpets the brown-shirted Nazi Stormtroopers, subsidized by businessmen and aristocrats, carried the *Hakenkreuz* flag of anti-Semitism throughout the land and shouted their battlecries: "Freedom and bread!" "Out with the Jews!" "Break the bonds of interest slavery!" and "Germany awake!" In the Reichstag election of September 14, 1930, they won 6,400,000 votes. In the presidential election of April 10, 1932, in which the "wooden

Titan," Hindenburg, was reelected by a slim margin, 13,400,000 votes were cast for Hitler. In the Reichstag election of July 31, 1932, 13,745,000 Nazi votes were cast—37 per cent of the total. Hitler seemed about to be swept into power by a great mass movement which would give him a majority of the electorate. But business conditions improved slightly in the autumn of 1932 and in the Reichstag balloting of November 6, 1932 (the last free election in Germany), the Nazis polled only 11,-737,000 votes—less than one-third of the total. By the end of the year their movement was bankrupt and disintegrating.

The Reich was delivered to Fascism not by an electoral victory but by a conspiracy, entered into against the last republican Chancellor, Kurt von Schleicher, whose old friend, Franz von Papen, resolved to use Hitler to put himself back in power. Papen, arch muddler of the German reaction, had been head of the "Baron's Cabinet" which Hindenburg had appointed after ousting Chancellor Heinrich Brüning in May, 1932. In January, 1933, Papen spun his plot. His tools, so he thought, were Hitler, the mob hypnotist; Hugenberg, the ultra-nationalist publisher; Fritz Thyssen, the steel magnate; the *Reichsverband der Industrie;* and the *Junker Landbund.* Hindenburg, who had been reelected to the Presidency nine months previously by the support of Brüning and of all the liberals and Socialists in order that he might save the Reich from Hitler, was persuaded to "save agriculture" (*i.e.*, the *Junkers*) from "agrarian Bolshevism" (*i.e.*, an exposure of the use to which they had put State subsidies) by dismissing Schleicher on January 30, 1933, and appointing Hitler Chancellor, Papen Vice Chancellor, Hugenberg Minister of Economics, and other reactionaries to the remaining posts. Hitler dissolved the Reichstag and ordered an election on March 5, 1933. Six days before the balloting the Reichstag building was burned. Hitler at once accused the Communists of arson and bloody revolution. He posed as the savior of the nation from the Red menace. He ordered the arrest of thousands of Communists and Social Democrats, suppressed the campaign activities of the anti-Nazi parties, induced Hindenburg to abolish civil liberties in the name of defense against the Communist peril, and threw the electorate into a panic. His followers polled 44 per cent of the vote. They promptly secured a majority in the new Reichstag by excluding and arresting all the Communist deputies. An "Enabling Act" transferred dictatorial powers to the Cabinet.

The story of how Hitler astutely tricked his non-Nazi colleagues, wiped out all other parties, suppressed the social radicals in his own ranks, and established the Nazi despotism cannot be reviewed here. Suffice it to note that the multitudes were exalted by the mass pageantry of great festivals, by the masterly propaganda of Göbbels and by the demagoguery of the Führer. They were prevailed upon to give the régime almost unanimous support in a series of referenda. Dissidence was suppressed by the ruthlessness of Göring and the espionage of Himmler. Heavy industry and the *Junkers* had paid the piper and were, to a considerable degree, able to call the tune. On "Bloody Saturday," June 30, 1934, critics within the ranks were silenced and old scores were settled. Among those shot for treason were Gregor Strasser, Ernst Röhm, Karl Ernst, and other Nazi radicals who resented Hitler's dependence on the propertied classes or who aspired to replace the *Junker*-controlled Reichswehr with the Stormtroopers as Germany's new army; the aides of the incautious Papen, who barely escaped death and was bundled off to Vienna as German Ambassador; Kurt von Schleicher and his wife; Erich Klausener, General von Bredow, and scores of others.

With Hindenburg's death on August 2, 1934, and Hitler's assumption of the powers of the Presidency, the Führer's control of the German State became absolute. Hjalmar Schacht remained his liaison with big business. Defense Minister Blomberg and the General Staff remained his liaison with the *Junkers*. With the trade unions abolished and strikes forbidden, with the press, radio, motion pictures, theater, and school system shackled and with all social organizations "coordinated" under Nazi control, the dictatorship was as unlimited as human ingenuity and lust for power could make it. Popular unrest was deflected into Jew baiting and into hatred of foreign enemies. Germany thus became a new citadel of Fascist totalitarianism, dedicated to militarism, revenge, and imperial expansion.

The Third Reich pursued the same general diplomatic objectives as the Weimar Republic but utilized in place of conciliation and compromise the methods of treaty breaking, threats, and defiance. But to these old objectives were added new ones far more alarming to Germany's neighbors. Mystical racial Pan-Germanism contemplated the ultimate "liberation" of all Germans abroad and the union with the Reich of Austria, German Switzerland, the Sudeten-Deutsch of Czechoslovakia, the Germans of Danzig, the Corridor, the Baltic States, and other irredentist areas. Beyond these lived other "Nordics" who ought also, willy-nilly, to join the Reich—the Flemings, the Dutch, the Scandinavians. The building of this greater Reich in the name of *Deutschtum* and *Grossraumwirtschaft* would require the partition or extinction of most of Germany's neighbors. In militant National Socialism, moreover, was a new *Drang nach Osten*—a dream of controlling the Danube valley and the Balkans. And here also, bred of middle-class hysteria and the fanatical thirst for revenge of Alfred Rosenberg and other Russian émigrés in the Nazi ranks, was a vision of a great crusade against Bolshevism, involving a restoration of the terms of Brest-Litovsk, with White Russia, the Baltic States, and the Ukraine in German hands. "To forge a mighty sword," Hitler had written in *Mein Kampf*, "is the task of the internal political leadership of a people; to protect the forging and to seek allies in arms is the task of foreign policy."

That these objectives meant war was fully realized by the Nazi leaders. But quite apart from specific diplomatic goals, German Fascism, like its Italian counterpart, set its face toward war for other reasons. Fascist ideology repudiates pacifism and internationalism and glorifies war as a thing good in itself. The ghosts of barbarian ancestors and the shades of Nietzsche, Treitschke, and Bernhardi here joined hands with the frenzied sadism and masochism of a people driven to desperation by real or imagined sufferings. War became a psychological necessity in the Nazi *Weltanschauung*. It also became a necessary political expedient to keep the tyranny in power. In order to impose further sacrifices on the population, to deflect mass resentments onto foreign foes, to conquer the markets and raw materials abroad without which the Fascist economic order cannot survive, the ultimate unsheathing of the sword becomes a categorical imperative.

REARMAMENT. War is seldom embarked upon, however, even by desperate autocrats, unless it offers at least a gambler's chance of victory. Hitler's problem was one of building up an overwhelming military force, dividing and weakening his prospective enemies, and finding allies. Rearmament was dangerous because it involved treaty violations and might precipitate a preventive war by the French bloc before the Reich was prepared to resist. Hitler moved cautiously and calculated correctly that French pacifism and British muddlement would prevent any concerted effort to coerce Germany. Amid loud protestations of peace and further pleas for "honor" and "equality," he announced Germany's withdrawal from the League and the Disarmament Conference on October 14, 1933. This gesture of protest against the refusal of other Powers to grant arms parity to the Reich won wide approval at home and provoked no retaliation from Paris or London. The second step was taken on March 16, 1935, with the announcement of the "Law for the Reconstruction of the National Defense Forces" which reintroduced military conscription and greatly enlarged the Reichswehr in open repudiation of Part V of the Treaty of Versailles. This led, after considerable fumbling and wrangling, to the Anglo-French-Italian "Stresa Front" of April and to Germany's condemnation by the League Council on April 17. There were warnings and threats but again no action, save the signature of the Franco-Soviet Pact on May 2 and of the Czech-Soviet Pact on May 16. The united front was soon shattered. On June 18, 1935, Downing Street connived in Hitler's treaty breaking by accepting his offer of a naval pact limiting the German fleet to 35 per cent of the British. Since Berlin was anxious to conciliate London, the agreement was most satisfactory. A German fleet one-third the size of the British could easily dominate the Baltic and thus aid in the projected crusade against Russia. Within three months, Britain and Italy were at swords' points in the Mediterranean and Hitler could proceed with his plans unhindered. The German General Staff was reestablished on October 15 with General Ludwig Beck as its Chief. Unemployment waned and munition profits mounted, as government loans financed an enormous production of guns, tanks, artillery, bombing planes, submarines, and battleships.

The third step toward military domination of the Continent was taken on March 7, 1936, while the Western Powers were hopelessly split over Italy's impending conquest of Ethiopia. Hitler announced the abrogation of the Locarno treaties of 1925 and the remilitarization of the Rhineland (in violation of Locarno and of Articles 42 and 43 of Versailles), alleging that the Franco-Soviet Pact violated the Locarno engagements. He proposed a twenty-five year nonaggression pact with France and Belgium, guaranteed by Italy and Britain; the reciprocal demilitarization of the frontier (involving the scrapping of the Maginot Line); bilateral non-aggression pacts with Germany's eastern neighbors (excluding the U.S.S.R.); and other ingenious devices designed to safeguard the western frontier and leave Germany free in the east. Had French armies moved into the Rhineland, the Reichwehr was prepared to withdraw, since it was not yet ready for war. But the French armies did not march. Again protests, warnings, and League condemnation were followed by inaction. Britain pledged France support against German invasion but pledged nothing as to eastern Europe where conflict would come first. The British memorandum of May 8, designed to discover Hitler's intentions in the east, was judged in Berlin unworthy of a reply. German troops remained in the Rhineland. Paris acquiesced.

Although German strategists perfected a new Schlieffen Plan to crush France through Holland and Belgium, Hitler's professed objective was to keep the peace in the west while he moved forward in the east. A Fascist or conservative France could be expected to abandon Moscow and strike a bargain with Berlin, however suicidal, at Russia's expense. A liberal or socialist France would be sufficiently pacifist to acquiesce in whatever Hitler might do, short of open war. In the event of French military aid to Czechoslovakia or the U.S.S.R., the Reichwehr would remain on the defensive in the west as a means of keeping Britain neutral. Such a defensive strategy, made possible by the refortification of the Rhineland, would render French aid to Prague or Moscow impossible. Britain would scarcely fight unless France or the Low Countries were invaded. With France checkmated and British neutrality assumed, the *Drang nach Osten* could be carried forward until the Western Powers should be outarmed, outmaneuvered, and made ripe for conquest.

On August 24, 1936, German military service was extended from one to two years. The Nürnberg Party Congress of September 1936 was devoted to denunciations of Bolshevism. The Führer declared wage increases impossible. He demanded new sacrifices and promised to make the Reich economically self-sufficient within four years. Rosenberg declared, "The Soviet Union's Government is controlled by Jewish interests and it is money stolen from the Russian people by the Jews which is being used in an attempt to awaken the underworld in all nations to march against European culture and against the holy traditions of all peoples." Said Göbbels, "Bolshevism must be annihilated. The idea of Bolshevism could have emanated only from the Jewish brain." Hitler, denouncing Russia and the "Bolshevist Jews" before massed thousands of marching troops, shouted, "We are ready any hour. . . . I cannot permit ruined States on my doorstep."

ANTI-COMINTERN AXIS. By such mouthings of anti-Bolshevism the leaders of the Western Powers were effectively anesthetized to their doom, precisely as the leaders of German liberalism had been a few years before. So long as the Anglo-French ruling classes could be induced to believe that the Third Reich was "saving civilization from the Reds" and arming only to attack the Soviet Union, so long could Hitler and Mussolini move from victory to victory. Their violations of treaties and their aggressions against the weak were not only tolerated by Downing Street and the Quai d'Orsay but were even encouraged. The Führer's threats against the U.S.S.R. were doubtless "sincere" up to the point at which his experimentation convinced him that the Soviet Union, far from being a weak State in process of reduction to helplessness by the "Jewish ferment of decomposition," was a strong State whose leaders and people were able and willing to fight not only in defense of their frontiers but in defense of their allies. The weak Powers were obviously France and Britain since their governments, despite the enormous resources at their disposal, had no will to fight and preferred to desert their allies so long as they believed that they could find safety by deflecting the Reich against Moscow. Hitler accordingly prepared for war against the West. For this a mighty sword was needed—and control of Austria, Czechoslovakia, and Poland to protect the German rear. For this allies were also needed. Hitler originally dreamed of a coalition with Britain and Italy to crush France before undertaking the conquest of Russia. Experience demonstrated that a formal alliance with Britain was not to be had. Berlin could merely rely on British opportunism to afford a strong likelihood of nonintervention in any war in eastern or central Europe. As for Italy, the fly in the ointment was Austria. Mussolini could not tolerate at the Brenner Pass a Germany of 75 million people pushing southward toward Bolzano and Trieste. Therefore he must oppose

German designs on Austria. Propaganda from Berlin and Munich converted perhaps 40 per cent of the Austrian electorate to the Nazi faith—and to union with the Reich—during 1933; but the conservative clerical Chancellor, Engelbert Dollfuss, established an Austrian Fascist State to block the Hitlerite menace. Spurning support against the Nazis from the Social Democrats who controlled the municipality of Vienna and another 40 per cent of the Austrian electorate, he placed himself in the hands of Mussolini and of the reactionary Heimwehr militia which was subsidized from Italy. At the behest of Rome and of the Heimwehr leaders, Emil Fey and Prince von Stahremberg, Dollfus crushed the Social Democrats in February, 1934, by accusing them of rebellion, bombarding the apartments of the Vienna workers, and executing or imprisoning their leaders. In May, he signed a series of political and economic protocols at Rome with Hungary and Italy.

Hitler journeyed to Italy to confer with Mussolini at Venice on June 15, 1934; but the two tyrants could come to no agreement. Seemingly in despair over the prospects of securing control of the Government by peaceful penetration, the Austrian Nazis resorted to force in the *Putsch* of July 25, 1934. Armed Nazis seized the Chancellory building, shot Dollfuss, and permitted him to bleed to death. But the uprising failed in the provinces. The Duce threatened to send troops over the border if Germany intervened or the Nazis seized Austria from within. Chancellor Kurt Schuschnigg succeeded Dollfuss and continued to enjoy Italian support.

At last, however, Hitler came to terms on July 11, 1936, and agreed to respect Austrian independence and to reopen German trade and travel with Vienna. In October, Schuschnigg dissolved the Heimwehr and subsequently dropped its representatives from the Cabinet. With the Nazi menace at least temporarily removed, he could afford to dispense with the support of Mussolini's mercenaries. The Duce acquiesced, for he had fallen into Hitler's arms. On October 25, Ciano struck a bargain with the Führer at Berlin and Berchtesgaden. Germany recognized the conquest of Ethiopia and was promised economic concessions. Italy agreed with the Reich that any new Locarno must be limited to western Europe, that Article 16 should be removed from the Covenant, and that the two Fascist Powers must cooperate against "Bolshevism." Both Powers expressed their approval of General Franco's cause in Spain. Both agreed to cooperate in the Danube valley within the framework of the Protocols of Rome and the Austro-German accord of July 11. This entente apparently signified Italian acquiescence in the German domination of an independent Austria and joint German-Italian support of Hungarian revisionism, tempered by continued efforts to isolate Czechoslovakia. After the discussions at Berchtesgaden in the Bavarian Alps,

Italy was, for all practical purposes, Germany's ally, even though Berlin would not forget that desertion of allies was an old Italian custom. An ally which might definitely place Britain in the enemy camp, moreover, was dangerous. But this could be risked in order to isolate France.

In other quarters, varying degrees of success were encountered in Nazi efforts to build a coalition. On January 26, 1934, a ten-year nonaggression pact with Poland was signed. Claims on the Corridor were deferred in return for Poland's detachment from the French bloc. But Nazi aggressiveness in Danzig, coupled with the alarming scale of German rearmament and the obvious fact that Germany could attack Russia effectively only through Poland, caused Warsaw to veer back toward Paris in the summer of 1936. Poland remained an incalculable factor. Hungary would be certain to cooperate in any attack on Czechoslovakia if protected against Rumania and Jugoslavia. The murder of Premier Duca of Rumania by pro-Nazi Iron Guardists in December, 1933, the toleration at Bucharest of anti-Semitic and pro-German conspirators, and the dismissal of Titelescu in August, 1936, all encouraged hopes at Berlin that Rumania might be won to the Fascist cause. Bulgaria's conservative régime, with irredentist ambitions scarcely less passionate than those of Hungary, was sympathetic. If Italy, Hungary, and Bulgaria became Germany's allies, Jugoslavia would be immobilized. The successful Fascist coup d'état of General John Metaxas in Greece on August 5, 1936, placed in power at Athens a régime sympathetic toward Germany. Nazi support of the Fascist Rebels in the Spanish civil war was based on the hope that a Fascist Spain could be used to complete the isolation and encirclement of France. In Asia, Turkey remained committed to a policy of friendship with Moscow; but Japan, with designs on Siberia, was prepared to enter into commercial, political, and military understandings with Germany and Italy promising an eventual assault upon the U.S.S.R. from the east and west simultaneously. The German-Japanese agreement of November 25, 1936, ostensibly against the Comintern but actually against the U.S.S.R., was a significant step in this direction, although Ribbentrop secretly envisaged it as so much dust thrown into the eyes of Britain and France to blind them to the blows being prepared against them.

VIENNA. The stage was thus set for territorial expansion. Prior to 1938, no "lost provinces" had been recovered save the Saar district which was restored to the Reich March 1, 1935, following an overwhelmingly pro-German plebiscite in January. Recovery of Danzig and the Corridor required that Poland be first rendered defenseless. This in turn required the liquidation of Czechoslovakia, since German armies in Bohemia and Slovakia could outflank Poland's Reich frontiers. The reduction of Czechoslovakia to helplessness (and its consequent destruction without war) required German control of Austria in order to outflank the Czech border fortifications. Italian acquiescence in the liquidation of Austria was already assured. Berlin felt confident of British acquiescence following the visit of Lord Halifax to the Reich in November, 1937. The war in Spain had demonstrated that the Western Powers were paralyzed and self-defeated. It had furnished a useful testing ground for the new Nazi arms. It had confirmed Axis hypotheses regarding the best slogans for befuddling London and Paris. Hitler thus began to outline the plot of the third and most terrifying volume of his *Kampf*, destined to be written in deeds rather than words.

In early February, 1938, Hitler made important changes in his entourage. Minister of Defense General Werner von Blomberg, then on his honeymoon with his secretary, was retired in disgrace. The Führer took his post and named General Wilhelm Keitel as his adjutant. General Werner von Fritsch, Commander-in-Chief of the Reichswehr (who was to die mysteriously in Poland twenty months later), was replaced by General Walter von Brauchitsch. Baron Constantine von Neurath, Foreign Minister since May 1932, was replaced by Joachim von Ribbentrop. Hjalmar Schacht was succeeded as Minister of Economics by Walter Funk. Henceforth the army command, the diplomatic bureaucracy, and the industrialists would be pliant tools in the hands of the Nazi radicals. On February 12 the last Chancellor of Austria, Kurt Schuschnigg, was invited to Berchtesgaden at Papen's suggestion. He was there browbeaten by Hitler's threats of invasion into granting amnesty and full freedom of action to the Austrian Nazis and admitting into his Cabinet several leaders of the Nazi Fifth Column in Vienna, including Edmund Glaise-Horstenau, Guido Schmidt, and Arthur Seyss-Inquart. On February 20 Hitler denounced Russia before the Reichstag, promised "protection" to all Germans outside the borders of the Reich, demanded a free hand in central Europe, and condemned British critics of National Socialism, in particular Foreign Minister Anthony Eden. The same night Eden resigned and was replaced by Lord Halifax. The Führer now felt that he could take Austria with few risks.

On March 9 Schuschnigg announced in desperation that a plebiscite would be held on March 13 on the question of Austrian independence. He was confident of overwhelming support from the older voters. On the same day the French Cabinet fell. Ribbentrop visited British leaders in London as he took his leave as Ambassador. On March 10 the German press and radio shrieked that a "Communist" uprising in Vienna was imminent and that Germany must act to protect its nationals. On March 11 Glaise-Horstenau returned from a visit to Berlin and delivered a Nazi ultimatum to Schuschnigg: Abandon the plebiscite, or face invasion. The same afternoon a second ultimatum arrived: Resign by 7:30, or face invasion. Nazi rowdies were already attacking Jews and rioting in the doomed capital. Schuschnigg was alone. He announced his resignation that evening. Seyss-Inquart assumed the Chancellorship and invited the Reichswehr to "protect" Austria. On March 12, 1938, after the German Minister in Prague assured himself and the Wilhelmstrasse that Czechoslovakia would not interfere, the German army poured into Austria, followed by Hitler who entered Vienna in triumph on March 14, named Seyss-Inquart *Statthalter* of the *Ostmark*, and ordered a "plebiscite" on *Anschluss* on April 10. In both Germany and Austria, 99 per cent of the electors voted "*Ja.*" Meanwhile, Schuschnigg was imprisoned and never heard from thereafter. Fey was found shot to death, along with his wife and dog. Stahremberg survived by virtue of being in Switzerland. The assassins of Dollfuss became heroes. Scores of liberals, Socialists, and Jews committed suicide. Thousands fled the country. More thousands stayed behind to face persecution, imprisonment, or death. Austria was conquered.

SUDETENLAND. The next victim was Czechoslovakia. Here the leader of the Nazi Fifth Column was Konrad Henlein, leader of the Nazified *Sudeten Deutsche Partei*, subsidized from Berlin and pretending to represent the $3\frac{1}{2}$ million German-speaking citizens of the Czech Republic. The Sudetens had lived within the Bohemian borderlands for centuries and had never been nationals of any North German State. They were perhaps better treated by Prague than any other national minority in central Europe. But Hitler found it useful to provoke disorders, to raise a great cry of "persecution," and ultimately to demand the "liberation" (and then the annexation) of Sudetenland in the name of a specious "self-determination." Chamberlain announced on March 24 that Britain would assume no commitments to defend Czechoslovakia. He intimated that Hitler could have his way if only he would refrain from force. In April Henlein (*i.e.*, Hitler) demanded "autonomy." In May Henlein visited London, and Hitler alarmed Britain and France and precipitated partial Czech mobilization by threatening force. On June 3, the London *Times* opined that "self-determination" for the Sudetens would afford "a welcome example of peaceful change. . . . It would be a drastic remedy for the present unrest, but something drastic may be needed."

The fantastic "war crisis" of the summer of 1938 and the even more fantastic "peace" which followed it scarcely admit of brief review.[1] The determining elements, however, were simple. Hitler was resolved to destroy Czechoslovakia. If Prague could be induced to yield Sudetenland, which included all the Czech border fortifications, the rest of the country would be indefensible. President Eduard Beneš, Premier Milan Hodza, Foreign Minister Kamil Krofta, and General Jan Syrovy were determined

---

[1] For a detailed and documented account of both, see the author's *Europe on the Eve*, 1939, New York, Alfred A. Knopf, Inc., pp. 358–489.

to fight rather than surrender. Czechoslovakia was guaranteed by France and the Soviet Union, allied with Rumania and Jugoslavia, and linked through France with Britain and Poland. Hitler was at no time prepared to risk war with any such combination. But he quickly perceived that no Power save the U.S.S.R. was prepared to come to Prague's defense. Daladier and Bonnet were groping for ways of evading French obligations. Chamberlain and Halifax were resolved to sacrifice Czechoslovakia on the altar of the Nazi *Drang nach Osten*. The Nazi bluff could be called and Czechoslovakia protected by accepting Soviet offers of joint defense. This, however, was the last thing desired by the Anglo-French appeasers. Their calculus was based on the assumption of an eventual Nazi-Soviet conflict, and for this Czechoslovakia must be sacrificed. To "sell" the sacrifice to the Western parliaments and publics, a war panic must be manufactured. Hitler was quite willing to cooperate. The result was the "Peace" of Munich.

Both Hitler and Chamberlain played their roles with consummate skill. On July 18, Hitler sent a confidential message to Halifax through Fritz Wiedemann, his aide-de-camp. It presumably suggested a non-violent "solution" of the Sudeten problem through a Four Power Pact. On July 25 it was announced that Chamberlain was sending Viscount Runciman to Prague as an "investigator" and "mediator" between Henlein and the Czech Cabinet. Runciman arrived on August 4, conferred with sundry persons, and pressed Beneš to yield. He departed on September 16. In a final letter dated September 21 he recommended the immediate cession of the Sudeten areas to the Reich without a plebiscite. He also urged that Prague forbid all anti-German agitation, terminate its alliances, accept a guarantee from the Powers against unprovoked aggression, and conclude a commercial treaty with the Reich on preferential terms. The war panic was meanwhile fully developed. On August 23 the Little Entente committed suicide by granting to Nazi-supported Hungary equality of rights in arms in return for projected nonaggression pacts which were to become effective only after Prague's "minority problem" was solved to Budapest's satisfaction. Each day the Nazi press and radio screamed more loudly about "Czech outrages," "barbarous persecutions," and the "Red menace." The Reichswehr gradually mobilized. Armored divisions and bombing squadrons gathered near the Czech borders. On September 6 the London *Times* unofficially urged the partition of Czechoslovakia. On September 12, last day of the Nürnberg *Parteitag*, Hitler shrieked terrifying threats and dedicated the Reich to the "liberation" of the Sudetens.

Immediately thereafter, Henlein's followers attempted a military *Putsch* in Sudetenland but were speedily dispersed. The leaders fled into Germany where they were received as "refugees" from the "Czech terror." On September 15 Chamberlain flew to Munich and conferred with Hitler in Berchtesgaden. There he made the "discovery" that Hitler was contemplating an immediate invasion of Czechoslovakia unless Chamberlain could promise "self-determination." The Prime Minister returned to London to confer with Simon, Hoare, and Halifax and then with the full Cabinet. On Sunday, September 18, Daladier and Bonnet flew to the British capital. The King, the Queen, and the Archbishop of Canterbury led England in prayers for peace. On September 19 an Anglo-French ultimatum was presented to Prague, demanding the surrender of Sudetenland and offering in return an international guarantee against unprovoked aggression to what would be left of the Czech Republic. A reply was asked "at the earliest possible moment." When Prague inquired of Paris whether France would honor its obligations in the event that a rejection of the ultimatum was followed by German aggression, Daladier and Bonnet made no answer. A new ultimatum demanding an immediate decision was presented to Beneš at 2:15 A.M., September 21, by the British and French Ministers, Basil Newton and M. De la Croix, warning that Britain and France would not only abandon Czechoslovakia in case of a German invasion but would even aid the Reich.

Despite all pretense to the contrary, then and later, Anglo-French policy was not dictated by military weakness. With the Soviet Union as ally, the Western Powers could crush the Reich, as Hitler well knew. Chamberlain and Daladier desired to save the Reich and turn its might against Moscow over the body of Czechoslovakia. The Soviet Union was not bound to defend Prague after the French desertion, but it nevertheless offered to do so and to compel Poland and Rumania to grant passage to the Red army. Beneš debated the offer with the party leaders. Rudolf Beran, leader of the reactionary Agrarians, threatened to call in the Nazis and precipitate civil war if Beneš relied on Communist support against Hitler. Brokenhearted, Beneš yielded and accepted the Anglo-French ultimatum. " . . . Nothing else remained, because we are alone." Said Minister Hugo Vavrecka, "It is a case without parallel. . . . We shall not blame those who left us in the lurch, but history will pronounce a judgment about these days."

MUNICH. The end was not yet, for more panic was needed to secure public acceptance in the West of so base a betrayal. Shame and indignation began to sweep British and French opinion. On September 22, Chamberlain flew to Godesberg on the Rhine where he conferred again with Hitler and Ribbentrop. He returned with dark hints that Hitler had enlarged his demands and was threatening immediate war unless they were met. The Czech army was mobilized. Daladier ordered partial mobilization in France. Gas masks were distributed in London. Air-raid shelters were hastily dug in public parks. Hitler's "Godesberg Memorandum" asked military occupation of certain Czech areas by October 1, with plebiscites to follow in others. Daladier, Bonnet, and Gamelin flew to London. Downing Street and the Quai d'Orsay belatedly pledged defense of Czechoslovakia if Germany attacked. Chamberlain pleaded with Hitler for a conference. The Führer breathed blood and fire. "If this problem is solved, there will be no further territorial problems in Europe for Germany. . . . We do not want any Czechs. . . . We are resolved! Let Herr Beneš choose!" Roosevelt pleaded for negotiations. Hitler intimated to Mussolini that he would invade Czechoslovakia on September 28. Chamberlain told the world on September 27 that it was "horrible, fantastic, incredible that we should be digging trenches and fitting gas masks because of a quarrel in a faraway country among people of whom we know nothing. . . . I was taken completely by surprise [by Hitler's demand for immediate military occupation]. I must say that I find that attitude unreasonable. . . . [But] if we have to fight it must be on larger issues than that. . . . But if I were convinced that any nation had made up its mind to dominate the world by fear of its force, I should feel that it must be resisted."

By September 28 all the democracies were in a frenzy of fear, precisely as Hitler (and Chamberlain) intended. The Commons met at 2:45. The Prime Minister spoke in funereal tones to a House fully expecting immediate war. He reviewed the negotiations lugubriously and revealed that he had appealed to Hitler and Mussolini for a conference to arrange the transfer of Czech territory. At 3:40 a messenger dashed madly to Lord Halifax in the balcony. The message was hurriedly relayed to Chamberlain. He paused, read it, and beamed: Hitler had invited him to Munich the next morning. The whole House burst forth in cheers. Chamberlain and Simon smiled and wept. Continental banking circles had known early the same day that a four Power conference would be held in Munich on the morrow. But Parliament, public, and all the Western world were led to believe that war had been averted at the very last moment.

During the afternoon and evening of September 29, 1938, Chamberlain, Hitler, Daladier, and Mussolini conferred in the Munich *Führerhaus*. Czech representatives were kept waiting in an anteroom. Shortly after midnight all four leaders attached their signatures to a document whereby German forces were to begin occupation of Czech territory on October 1 and continue their advance by stages until October 10. An "international commission" would fix the conditions governing the evacuation, prepare and supervise plebiscites in additional territories, and finally determine the frontiers. An annex declared that Britain and France "stand by the offer" of September 19 "relating to an international guarantee of the new boundaries of the Czechoslovak State against unprovoked aggression. When the question of the Polish and Hungarian minorities in Czecho-

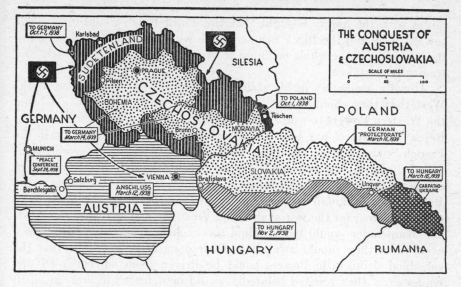

THE CONQUEST OF
AUSTRIA
& CZECHOSLOVAKIA

slovakia has been settled, Germany and Italy for their part will give a guarantee to Czechoslovakia." In bitterness and tears, Prague yielded to what Beneš knew was a death sentence. He resigned and was presently succeeded by weak and elderly Emil Hacha, with Beran as Premier. Chamberlain concluded his work by signing with Hitler a pledge "never to go to war again." He came home to announce that he had "saved" Czechoslovakia and brought "peace with honor. I believe it is peace for our time."

The Peace of Munich was the greatest triumph to date of Hitler's strategy of terror. It was the culmination of appeasement and the warrant of death for the Western Powers. The fate of the last surviving Continental democracy east of the Rhine was the smallest part of the price to be paid for the agreement signed in Hitler's house. Poland seized 400 square miles of Czech territory with a population of 240,000, including 160,000 non-Poles. Hungary seized 5,000 square miles with 1 million inhabitants, including a 250,000 non-Magyars. The "international guarantee" of the rump "Czecho-Slovakia" never materialized. The "international commission" became a farce. Ambassadors Henderson, François-Poncet, and Attolico yielded at once to Nazi demands (going far beyond even the "Godesberg Memorandum") as presented by Count Ernst von Weizsäcker, leaving Dr. Mastny, the Czech representative, helpless. Berlin groomed Carpatho-Ukraine as the nucleus of the Great Ukraine which was to be carved out of Poland and the U.S.S.R. Bonnet signed a nonaggression pact with Ribbentrop in Paris on December 6— interpreted in Berlin to mean that France had renounced all interest in eastern Europe. The Munichmen of Paris and London comforted them-

[571]

selves with the happy thought that the Third Reich would now strike toward Kiev and the Black Sea and clash with Moscow. In this assumption, which was the whole meaning of Munich, they were completely and tragically mistaken.

Hitler's genius lay in his ability to persuade the hollow men of the West that they should grant him the means wherewith he could bring the Western Powers to ruin. Munich left Poland more helpless before the Reich than *Anschluss* had left Czechoslovakia. Munich reduced the French-Soviet mutual assistance pact of 1935 to waste paper and compelled Stalin to seek new roads toward safety. Munich left Hitler free to complete the economic and military domination of the Danube and the Balkans, to blackmail Warsaw, and to make a bargain with Moscow to protect his rear for the war against the West. He assumed that the Western Munichmen would be too blind to conclude a new Russian alliance even when they should awaken to their danger. He assumed that the enfeebled democratic Powers could be driven from surrender to surrender or, if they resisted belatedly, could be defeated in arms at small cost. That most of these things were to come to pass was the measure of Hitler's astuteness and of the incredible folly of the Western appeasers.

PRAGUE. Whatever Ukrainian dreams were entertained by the Führer were abandoned or indefinitely postponed during the winter of 1938–1939. He likewise decided to liquidate the pitiable remnant of "Czecho-Slovakia." The technique was already perfected. Nazi agents fanned separatist sentiment in Slovakia and Carpatho-Ukraine. When Prague sought to hold the State together by curbing such agitation, the separatists appealed to Berlin against "Czech persecution." When Hacha on March 9 to 10 dismissed the Slovak Cabinet, ordered the Fascist "Hlinka Guards" disarmed, and discharged from his post Father Josef Tiso, pro-Nazi Premier at Bratislava, Tiso flew to Berlin to confer with Ribbentrop and Hitler. On March 14 he returned and proclaimed the "independence" of Slovakia. On the same day Hitler summoned President Hacha and Foreign Minister Frantisek Chvalkovsky to Berlin while German armored divisions gathered in Sudetenland. In the Chancellery building shortly after midnight, Hacha was given a document to sign placing Czecho-Slovakia under German "protection." When he refused Göring declared that Prague would be destroyed by Nazi bombers at 6 A.M. Hacha fainted and was revived by injections. The Nazi officials hounded him around the table with threats and imprecations. At 4:30 A.M. he signed.

German troops were already across the frontiers. They entered Prague at 9:15 A.M., March 15, followed by the Schutzstaffel (Black Guard) and the Gestapo. Hitler came in the afternoon and proclaimed from Hradčany Castle that Czecho-Slovakia was part of Germany's *Lebensraum.* Bohemia and Moravia were annexed, with Neurath as "Protector." Budapest was covetous of the Carpatho-Ukraine and a common frontier with Poland. Pro-Nazi and anti-Semitic Premier Bela Imredy had resigned in February on discovering that he had "Jewish blood." On March 16, with Berlin's consent, his pro-Nazi and anti-Semitic successor, Paul Teleki, announced the annexation of Carpatho-Ukraine to Hungary. "Independent" Slovakia was obliged to sign a treaty on March 23 making it a German protectorate. On the preceding day the Reich occupied Memel and signed a nonaggression pact with Lithuania.

TOWARD WAR. These events led to the belated abandonment of appeasement by London and Paris and to Anglo-French guarantees to Poland, Rumania, Greece, and Turkey. Hitler retaliated on April 28, 1939, by denouncing the Anglo-German Naval Accord of 1935 and the Polish nonaggression Pact of 1934. On May 22 he concluded his treaty of alliance with Italy. When the Western Powers in the course of prolonged negotiations with Moscow declined to pay Stalin's price for an alliance against Germany (*i.e.*, Soviet military control of the Baltic States and access to eastern Poland), Hitler secretly offered Stalin a nonaggression pact on the same terms. On August 23, 1939, the world was shocked by the signature in Moscow by Molotov and Ribbentrop of a ten-year pact of nonaggression and neutrality between the Third Reich and the U.S.S.R.[1] The self-appointed savior of European civilization from

[1] TREATY OF NONAGRESSION BETWEEN GERMANY AND THE UNION OF SOCIALIST SOVIET REPUBLICS, AUGUST 23, 1939

Guided by the desire to strengthen the cause of peace between Germany and the Union of Socialist Soviet Republics, and basing themselves on the fundamental stipulations of the Neutrality Agreement concluded between Germany and the Union of Socialist Soviet Republics in April, 1926, the German Government and the Government of the Union of Socialist Soviet Republics have come to the following agreement:

1. The two contracting parties undertake to refrain from any act of force, any aggressive act and any attacks against each other undertaken either singly or in conjunction with any other Powers.

2. If one of the contracting parties should become the object of warlike action on the part of a third Power, the other contracting party will in no way support the third Power.

3. The Governments of the two contracting parties will in future remain in consultation with one another in order to inform each other about questions which touch their common interests.

4. Neither of the two contracting parties will join any group of Powers which is directed, mediately or immediately, against the other party.

5. In case disputes or conflicts on questions of any kind should arise between the two contracting parties, the two partners will solve these disputes or conflicts exclusively by friendly exchange of views or if necessary by arbitration commissions.

6. The present agreement is concluded for the duration of ten years with the stipulation that unless one of the contracting partners denounces it one year before its expiration, it will automatically be prolonged by five years.

7. The present agreement shall be ratified in the shortest possible time. The instruments of ratification are to be exchanged in Berlin. The treaty comes into force immediately it has been signed.

Bolshevism proclaimed his friendship with Stalin. He thus rejected, at least for the immediate future, Alfred Rosenberg's wild visions of conquering Russia and returned to the Bismarck tradition of "reinsurance" in the East as a means of avoiding the danger of war on two fronts which had brought the Second Reich to disaster.

The fate of Poland was therewith sealed. Immediately after Munich, on October 24, 1938, Ribbentrop had asked Ambassador Josef Lipski to submit to Foreign Minister Josef Beck and Marshal Edward Smigly-Rydz a German proposal for the return of Danzig to the Reich and the creation of a German extraterritorial highway and railway across the Corridor. A reciprocal guarantee of the new frontiers was offered as a *quid pro quo*. The Polish leaders, who fancied that their State was a Great Power, refused. In January, 1939, Beck visited Berchtesgaden and Ribbentrop visited Warsaw without result. After the fall of Prague, Berlin became more insistent. Ribbentrop repeated the German proposals to Lipski on March 26. The first British guarantee to Poland of March 31 was inspired by fear of a swift Nazi blow at Danzig and the Corridor. Beck breathed defiance in his address to the Diet of May 5. Poland would not yield. Neither would Poland consider any defensive arrangement with the only Power which could possibly protect Poland: the U.S.S.R. The Polish Colonels and feudal gentry feared and hated Bolshevism no less ardently than Beran, Bonnet, Daladier, Halifax, and Chamberlain. Suicide was preferable to salvation at the hands of Moscow.

Hitler, no less than Stalin, drew the necessary conclusions. The Führer's well-known "patience" was now "exhausted." Beyond Danzig and the Corridor, he had again "no further territorial demands" to make. He discovered that the German minority in Poland was being outrageously persecuted. In Danzig the Nazi Senate President, Arthur Greiser, and the Nazi *Gauleiter*, Albert Forster, kept up a running fire of controversy with Warsaw while the Nazi press and radio fabricated a campaign of hatred and fear even more impressive than that unleashed against Prague a year before. Hitler doubtless assumed at the outset that a new Munich was possible. The Anglo-French Munichmen were already crying that "Danzig is not worth a war." Chamberlain and Daladier toyed with new appeasement schemes. Given half a chance to compel Poland to yield, they might have cooperated with Berlin once more. But in the end Hitler decided that the time had come to strike Poland down and to seek a reckoning by arms with the Western Powers. The Anglo-French leaders were neither able to defend Poland nor willing to make a bargain with Moscow whereby it might have been defended. Under these circumstances the Nazi war lords concluded that *Der Tag* had arrived.

The war crisis of August, 1939, began with a Danzig-Polish controversy over customs duties on herring and margarine and ended with an Anglo-German dispute over diplomatic etiquette and the meaning of "negotiations."[1] Amid the scurryings of the diplomats the central issue for Berlin was whether the Allies would compel Warsaw to yield to German demands. For London and Paris the issue was whether Berlin would abstain from force and refrain from jeopardizing Polish independence. Berlin half hoped that the announcement on August 21 of the impending Soviet pact would lead to capitulation, since Poland was now obviously beyond the power of the Allies to defend. Chamberlain addressed a letter to Hitler on August 22, however, declaring that "no greater mistake could be made" and that Britain would fight if Poland were attacked. But Britain was prepared to do all it could to promote a negotiated settlement. Hitler told Henderson that "he was 50 years old: he preferred war now to when he would be 55 or 60." He was really an artist, he said, and wanted to retire in peace to his studio. In his reply to Chamberlain, he insisted that Germany must have Danzig and the Corridor. He had always wanted Anglo-German friendship. If the Reich's just demands led to war with Britain, it would be Britain's fault. On August 25, he asked Henderson to fly to London with an offer of an alliance. On the same day the tentative Anglo-Polish Pact was converted into a binding commitment of mutual defense. On August 28, Henderson returned with a reply: The prerequisite condition of any Anglo-German understanding was a settlement of German-Polish differences which would not endanger Poland's independence. An effort should therefore be made for a negotiated solution to be guaranteed by the Powers. Warsaw was "prepared to enter into discussions on this basis." Hitler and Ribbentrop told Henderson on August 29 that they were quite ready for negotiations, provided that a Polish plenipotentiary should arrive on Wednesday, August 30. The Ambassador commented that this "sounded like an ultimatum." Hitler denied it. He stressed the urgency of the moment and accused Henderson of not caring "how many Germans were being slaughtered."

Halifax replied that it was "unreasonable" to expect Britain to produce a Polish plenipotentiary on Wednesday. Beck recalled the fate of Schuschnigg and Hacha and refused to go to Berlin. Warsaw ordered mobilization on August 30. London urged negotiations but did not envisage them in terms of acceptance of a Nazi ultimatum. At midnight of August 30, Henderson saw Ribbentrop again in a stormy interview. The Foreign Minister declared that everything was now too late, since the time limit had expired. But to show German good faith he hurriedly read a sixteen-point proposal which was amazingly moderate. Danzig should be forthwith returned to the Reich. The Corridor should be placed

---

[1] For a detailed and documented account, see *Night over Europe*, 1941, New York, Alfred A. Knopf, Inc., pp. 285–376.

under international supervision and a plebiscite held a year later. If the residents (as of 1918) voted to remain Polish, Germany should be granted an extraterritorial traffic zone to East Prussia. If Germany won, Poland should be granted a similar zone to Gdynia. All this was quite reasonable and implied neither a new Munich nor the destruction of the Polish State. But Ribbentrop declared contemptuously that the proposal was "outdated" since no Polish plenipotentiary had arrived by midnight. He refused to transmit a copy of it to either Henderson or Lipski. "I returned to the Embassy that night," wrote Henderson, "convinced that the last hope for peace had vanished."

The sixteen points were never officially delivered to Warsaw or to London. Lipski saw Ribbentrop at 6:30 P.M., August 31, not as a "plenipotentiary" but as Ambassador come to say, on Beck's instructions, that Warsaw was examining favorably British suggestions for direct German-Polish negotiations and would give its reply in a few hours. He did not ask for the sixteen points. Ribbentrop did not offer them. When Lipski tried to telephone Warsaw in the evening, he found the wires cut. At 9 P.M. the sixteen points were printed in the evening extras in Berlin and broadcast over the German radio as evidence of Nazi moderation. Weizsäcker told Henderson that the Führer had "now waited for two days in vain for the arrival of an authorized Polish delegate" and could not but regard his proposals "as having been once more virtually rejected." In the small hours of September 1, Halifax wired Warsaw to urge that the Polish Government receive German proposals, provided that they were not accompanied by any ultimatum. The British Ambassador replied later in the day that this would be useless since Poland had been invaded at dawn.

WARSAW. Hitler had in fact launched his *Blitzkrieg.* At 4 A.M. of Friday, September 1, 1939, Forster issued a decree proclaiming the incorporation of Danzig into the Reich. German troops had already entered the Free City. By 5 A.M. German cruiser *Schleswig-Holstein* was pouring shells into the near-by Polish fortifications on the Westerplatte. By 5:30, German bombs were falling on Polish air bases. Into the Corridor raced 29 German divisions, into southern Poland 40 divisions, all preceded by *Panzerdivisionen* of tanks and armored cars which tore through the Polish defenses and the half-mobilized Polish armies like deadly scythes. Göring's air force carried raids deep into Polish territory, destroying airdromes, railways, and mobilization centers and terrorizing noncombatants with fire, bullets, and bombs. There was no "front." The German High Command had devised the means of breaking the stalemate of 1914–1918. Mobile warfare was restored. The superiority of the attack over the defense was reestablished. Western strategists, hypnotized by the outdated doctrines of Liddell Hart and General Maginot, drew no con-

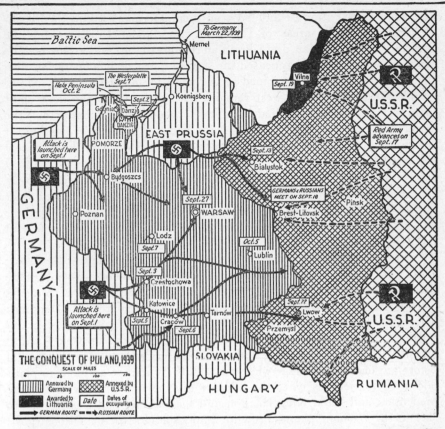

THE CONQUEST OF POLAND, 1939

SCALE OF MILES

Annexed by Germany
Annexed by U.S.S.R.
Awarded to Lithuania
Date — Dates of occupation
GERMAN ROUTE ＝＝＝RUSSIAN ROUTE

clusions from the Polish *Blitzkrieg* until their own vastly superior armies fell victims to identical tactics in the following spring.

Poland crumpled like a deflated balloon. Within two weeks, all the western provinces were lost, Warsaw was surrounded, and the Cabinet was fleeing toward Rumania. The Polish capital was besieged and all but demolished by artillery and dive bombers. Its defenders surrendered on September 27. How many scores of thousands of Poles perished in the holocaust may never be known. In a war of machines against men the casualties of the aggressor were negligible. A nation of 34,000,000 people with an army of 1,500,000 was completely conquered in three weeks at a cost of 10,572 German dead, 30,322 wounded, and 3,404 missing.

Britain and France had meanwhile declared war on the Reich on September 3. Moscow ordered the Red Army to enter eastern Poland on September 17—possibly by prearrangement with Berlin, probably because of alarm over the *Blitzkrieg* and a desire to prevent German occupation of all of the old Polish State. Ribbentrop again flew to Moscow on September 27. On September 28 the Reich and the U.S.S.R. reached an

[577]

agreement to partition Poland between them, Germany taking the Polish-speaking industrial areas of the west, the Soviet Union taking the agrarian, White Russian, and Ukrainian regions to the east. So perished the State whose leaders had appeased the Reich, spurned all cooperation with the U.S.S.R., and eagerly joined in the partitioning of Czechoslovakia.

That the war in the west remained stalemated for the next eight months was a result of Allied inability to penetrate or even attack the German West Wall. The Nazi war lords had means at their disposal for smashing the Maginot Line, as events were to show, but they wisely preferred to demoralize their victim with peace overtures and military inactivity which would cause Allied soldiers and civilians to wonder why they were fighting (or not fighting) and cause commanders to sink ever deeper into the fatal morass of a purely defensive strategy. The Führer and his fanatic followers had no doubts as to the outcome of the fearful miracles of war they were preparing.

OSLO. On April 9, 1940, Hitler struck his first great blow at the West. It was an operation of outflanking and diversion. Before dawn, strange events took place all along the far-flung coast of Scandinavia from the Arctic Circle to the Danish frontier. German troops poured into Denmark and at once occupied the whole kingdom without resistance. German bombers roared over Oslo. The *Blücher* brought troops up Oslo fjord to capture the Norwegian King and his Ministers and occupy the capital before anyone should know what was afoot. By a mere accident in plans laid with meticulous care, the *Blücher* and several other vessels were fired upon and sunk. King Haakon and his Cabinet had time to flee to the north. German planes brought 1,500 soldiers to the Oslo airport. Without opposition, they occupied the capital and installed a puppet régime under the Norwegian Nazi leader, Major Vidkun Quisling. At Kristiansand, Bergen, Stavanger, and Trondheim, German warships emerged out of the morning mists. German troops materialized as by magic from German "freighters" at the docks and from the ranks of German "tourists." Traitors and Fifth Columnists gave them aid. At Narvik a dozen German destroyers came out of a snowstorm, torpedoed two Norwegian gunboats, seized British vessels in the harbor, and landed 2,000 men. Ribbentrop explained that Norway had been "unneutral" and that Germany was acting in the nick of time to forestall a British invasion of Scandinavia. Between dawn and midday of April 9 the Reich conquered two kingdoms.

The Allied counterattack was brief and inglorious. The Swedish army could have ousted the invaders from their foothold. But Stockholm preferred neutrality. Small and ill-equipped British forces made landings along the Norwegian coast between April 15 and 19. A blow at Trondheim was planned and then abandoned. Nazi columns penetrated inland from

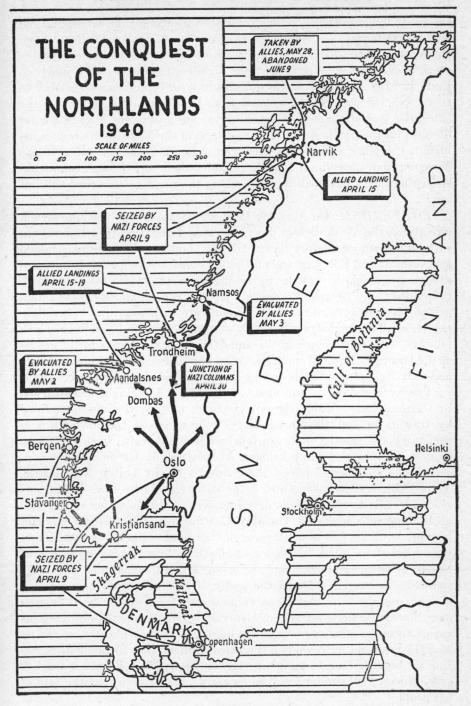

THE CONQUEST
OF THE
NORTHLANDS
1940

SCALE OF MILES

0   50   100   150   200   250   300

TAKEN BY
ALLIES, MAY 28,
ABANDONED
JUNE 9

Narvik

ALLIED LANDING
APRIL 15

SEIZED BY
NAZI FORCES
APRIL 9

ALLIED LANDINGS
APRIL 15-19

Namsos

EVACUATED
BY ALLIES
MAY 3

Trondheim

EVACUATED
BY ALLIES
MAY 2

Aandalsnes

Dombas

JUNCTION OF
NAZI COLUMNS
APRIL 30

Bergen

Oslo

Stavanger

Kristiansand

Stockholm

SEIZED BY
NAZI FORCES
APRIL 9

Skagerrak

Kattegat

DENMARK

Copenhagen

S W E D E N

F I N L A N D

Gulf of Bothnia

Helsinki

the coast to join other columns from Oslo ascending the Gudbrandsdal and the Osterdal. The feeble Norwegian army scattered before them. On April 25 the British rescuers were obliged to abandon everything south of Namsos. Five days later the invading forces effected a junction. Early in May the Allied forces quit Namsos and Aandalsnes. On May 28 to 29, Narvik was indeed wrested from the Nazis, but on June 9 the enterprise was abandoned. German naval units sank the aircraft carrier *Glorious* off the northern coast; the vestiges of the Norwegian army capitulated; the King and his Ministers fled to London; the last Allied troops departed from the ruins of Narvik, threaded their way through the wreckstrewn harbor, and sailed for home where their cause was already all but lost.

ROTTERDAM. On May 10, 1940, the German war machine struck directly at the West. Before dawn, German forces occupied Luxemburg without resistance. Before dawn, German bombers by hundreds raided the Netherlands, Belgium, and northern France, striking at airdromes and dropping parachute troops to cooperate with spies, traitors, Fifth Columnists, and German "tourists." Ribbentrop explained that Belgium and the Netherlands were about to cooperate with the Allies in invading the Ruhr. The fearful wonderwork of destruction and conquest which followed was truly unique in the annals of warfare, thanks to the genius of the German High Command and the prevalence of blindness, treason, and unmitigated ineptitude among those who led the Allied forces.

The Netherlands was subjugated in five days. The Hague was attacked by German agents inside the city. German motorized divisions, guided by traitors behind the Dutch lines, poured across the lowlands and decimated the small Dutch army before it could resist, open the dikes, or even destroy roads and bridges. At Rotterdam, German troops concealed in "freighters" joined the followers of the Dutch Nazi leader, Anton Mussert, in disorganizing the defenses of the city. When surrender was delayed, Göring's dive bombers went into action to terrorize all Holland into surrender. On May 14 a quarter of Rotterdam was laid in ruins within a few hours. Scores of thousands of helpless inhabitants were burned, crushed, or blown to death in the flaming wreckage of homes, apartments, offices, and factories. German cameramen filmed the spectacle, as they had filmed the agony of Poland, for the terrorization of other peoples who might contemplate resistance to the Nazi Juggernaut. Later the same afternoon, General Henrik Winkelman ordered his troops to cease fighting, save in Zeeland and at sea. The Hague fell on May 15. Zeeland surrendered. The Government fled to London. Seyss-Inquart became Nazi Commissar over the vanquished. From her English exile, Queen Wilhelmina resolved to carry on and lamented the fate of her people:

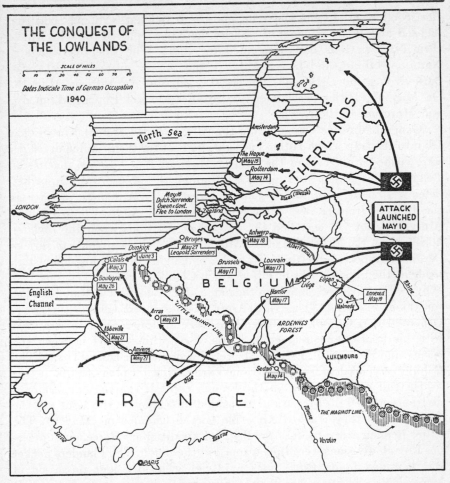

THE CONQUEST OF
THE LOWLANDS

SCALE OF MILES

Dates Indicate Time of German Occupation
1940

At this immensely grave moment in the history of mankind, black silent night has settled on yet another corner of this earth. Over free Holland the lights have gone out, the wheels of industry and the plows of the fields that worked only for the happiness of a peace-loving people have come to a dead stop. The voices of freedom, charity, tolerance and religion have been stilled. Where only two weeks ago there was a free nation there is now the desolation and stillness of death, broken only by the bitter weeping of those who have survived the extinction of their relatives and the brutal suppression of their rights and liberties.

Belgium suffered a like fate. Allied efforts to rescue the State whose King and Cabinet had insisted upon neutrality proved disastrous not only to Belgium but (as Brauchitsch intended) to the Allied cause in France as well. The invaders smashed through the Dutch province of Limburg to attack Maastricht and swarm across the heavily fortified Albert Canal, where bridges fell mysteriously into German hands. The

Rexist followers of Léon DeGrelle, apostle of Belgian National Socialism and self-appointed defender of "Christ the King," played the roles which their Nazi patrons had designated for them. The tide overwhelmed Namur, Malines, and Louvain, where the library burned in 1914 was burned once more. Brussels fell on May 17 and Antwerp on May 18. On May 19, Hitler proclaimed the reannexation of Eupen, Malmédy, and Moresnet to the Reich.

General Maurice Gamelin and the Allied High Command in France fell into the trap which Hitler's generals had set for them. Allied divisions were rushed from behind the "Little Maginot Line" to the defense of Belgium. The Sedan-Montmédy sector along the Meuse was stripped of defenders on the assumption that the forest of the Ardennes, just across the Belgian frontier, was impenetrable. General André Corap's Ninth Army had not yet occupied the evacuated positions when the invader appeared on the hither side of the Ardennes in the hideous guise of shrieking dive bombers, flame-throwing tanks, and eighty-ton armored monsters made at the Skoda works in Pilsen which Chamberlain and Daladier had delivered into Hitler's hands in the name of "peace for our time." Sedan was taken on May 14. The Ninth Army was destroyed. Corap's successor, General Henri Giraud, blundered into German forces and was captured with his staff. Panic reigned in Paris, for nothing stood between the enemy and the capital. Documents were burned at the Quai d'Orsay. The Cabinet prepared to flee. But the invader had other plans.

Instead of descending on the French capital, the German armored divisions crossed the Meuse and descended the valleys of the Aisne and the Somme until they reached Abbéville on the Channel on May 21. The entire Belgian army, most of the British Expeditionary Force, and numerous French divisions were thus trapped in the north. The Flanders pocket was hemmed in on three sides by Reichswehr divisions possessed of immense superiority of fire power, motorized units, heavy tanks, and air squadrons. King Leopold III, whose closest advisers were of ambiguous allegiance, ordered the surrender of the Belgian army on May 28, despite the opposition of his Cabinet which had taken refuge in London. The Belgian capitulation left the B.E.F. in a hopeless position. The armored divisions which had reached Abbéville tore up the Channel coast to cut off its only avenue of retirement. By a miracle of courage and organization, 335,000 British troops were safely evacuated from Dunkirk before its fall on June 3. All their arms and equipment were lost. Belgium was lost. Flanders was lost. France was also lost.

PARIS. Before dawn of June 5, 1940, the Reichswehr attacked the hastily improvised "Weygand Line" along a 100-mile front south of the Somme. The new French Generalissimo, Maxime Weygand, was bewildered by what he called "means of war of a hitherto unknown formula." Reynaud hoped for a "miracle." But the battle was lost before it was begun. The armored divisions with their escorts of dive bombers, acting as mobile artillery, cut the French armies to ribbons. By June 12, Weygand had given up hope. "All is lost." Vice Premier Pétain agreed. "There are no more military possibilities." The invaders took Paris on June 14. A week later, Adolf Hitler toured the lost capital and visited Napoleon's tomb. Italy entered the war in order to be in on the "kill." At Bordeaux a new French government sued for peace on June 16. The entire Western campaign had cost the Third Reich no more than 30,000 dead and 120,000 wounded. France was prostrate under the conqueror's heel.

In Compiégne forest near Rethonde, forty-five miles northeast of Paris, stands a monument bearing the inscription, "Here on November 11, 1918, perished the criminal arrogance of the Imperial German Reich, defeated by the free peoples whom it sought to enslave." Nearby was a railway coach in which Foch and Weygand had accepted the German capitulation. Here on June 21, 1940, Hitler, Keitel, Göring, Raeder, Hess, and Ribbentrop received the French armistice delegation. At 6:50 P.M., June 22, the document was signed. Hostilities ceased at 12:35 A.M., June 25, six hours after notification of the signing of an armistice with Italy. The terms defined the occupied territory and provided for French demobilization and disarmament. Vichy was required to pay the costs of the German forces of occupation and to surrender on demand all military and civil prisoners, as well as German anti-Nazi exiles still within its jurisdiction. Almost 2 million French prisoners remained in German camps. A definitive peace was to wait upon the expected defeat of Britain. Berlin decreed the reannexation of Lorraine in November.

NAZI "NEW ORDER." Hitler now proceeded to organize the conquered Continent for war against Britain, much as Napoleon had once sought to do. Hitler spoke confidently to his subjects on September 4:

Whatever may come, England will break down. I recognize no other termination than this one alone. The people of England are very curious and ask: "Why in the world don't you come?" We are coming. . . . All of England's allies will not help her—neither Haile Selassie, nor King Zog, nor King Haakon, nor even Queen Wilhelmina. . . . In the East we stand on the river Bug. In the North we stand at North Cape and Narvik, and in the South on the Spanish frontier. The fight is for existence or non-existence, to decide whether in the future a situation can be created in which it is possible for one nation to get a stranglehold on Europe. Both Germany and Italy will take care that this will never occur again.

Whatever the ultimate shape of the "new order" might be, its immediate purpose was to bring about British defeat. If this objective could not be achieved by frontal attack and invasion, it must be attempted by isolating and blockading Britain, by organizing as many Continental

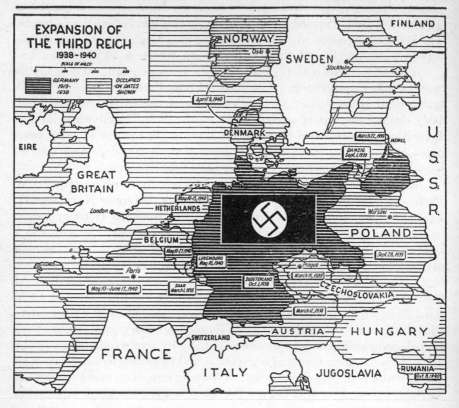

States as possible as the Reich's allies, by rescuing Italy from the full brunt of British attack in the Mediterranean, by attacking the life line of the Empire overland via France and Spain in the West and the Balkans and Turkey in the East, and by immobilizing the Soviet Union and the United States. These tasks were far more difficult of accomplishment than what had gone before, for they required sea power which was lacking and involved risks of a clash with Moscow or Washington, or both. The first step was German seizure of Rumania. In anticipation of such a move the U.S.S.R. occupied Bessarabia and northern Bukovina on June 28. On August 21, Bucharest agreed to restore southern Dobrudja to Bulgaria. The Axis "mediated" between Hungary and Rumania on August 30, granting northeastern Transylvania to Budapest and "guaranteeing" what was left of the Rumanian State. On September 6, Hohenzollern King Carol II abdicated and fled with his mistress Magda Lupescu. His son Michael took the tottering throne, and General Ion Antonescu, with the support of the Iron Guard, invited German "collaboration." On October 8 German troops began pouring into Rumania to "protect" the oil fields. As Iron Guardists indulged in an orgy of mass murder to avenge their murdered leader, Corneliu Zelea Codrianu, more and more Nazi divisions arrived through Hungary to menace Bulgaria, Jugoslavia, and Turkey and to warn the U.S.S.R. to acquiesce in Axis domination of the Balkans.

By the close of 1940, year of victory, this campaign in the southeast had not yet reached its goal. The Triple Alliance of September 27, 1940, designed to deter Moscow and intimidate the United States, led to increased American aid to Britain and increased Soviet opposition to the Axis. Berlin and Rome intimated that most of the Continental States would sign the new alliance. Hungary did so on November 20 and the remnant of Rumania on November 23. The enlistment of new signatories was temporarily halted, however, with the wholly unimpressive adherence of Slovakia on November 24. Bulgaria hesitated to join. Molotov's visit to Berlin, November 12 to 14, 1940, was followed by Soviet encouragement to Bulgaria and Turkey to resist Axis pressure and by heavy concentrations of Red troops along Rumania's shrunken frontier. Hitler's initial efforts in the West met with no better fortune. Franco did not dare take his sullen subjects into war and expose his famished land to the British blockade until he was convinced that British defeat was imminent. Laval's intrigues to take what was left of France into the war against Britain were impeded by his dismissal from office at the hands of Pétain on December 13. Weygand remained in North Africa with still formidable military forces at his disposal. Open German coercion of Vichy might set these forces in motion against Italian Libya, already invaded by the British from Egypt. The Führer hesitated in the face of his difficulties. But he promised new triumphs for 1941. As the new year opened, he poured still more troops into Rumania, induced Hungary to mobilize, and made plans for a frontal assault on the British Isles. Following the conclusion of an ambiguous Turkish-Bulgarian nonaggression pact in February, King Boris, Premier Bogdan Philov, and Foreign Minister Ivan Popov yielded to the Axis and made Bulgaria the seventh signatory of the Triple Alliance on March 1, 1941. German troops immediately swarmed over Bulgaria to rescue Italy by threatening Turkey and Greece and jeopardizing the British position in the Eastern Mediterranean. The result promised to be either the "peaceful" conquest of all the Balkans by the Reich or the conversion of all the Near East into a major theater of war.

A durable "new order" in Europe and the establishment of Triplice hegemony over the world required the conquest or capitulation of England. The "all-out" Nazi air assault of September and October, 1940, had not produced the desired result. If American aid to Britain continued on an ever-increasing scale, if Moscow continued to thwart the Axis in the Near East, victory over Britain would continue to be elusive. But if Britain could be successfully terrorized or invaded before American aid became effective and before the Kremlin precipitated a showdown in the

Balkans, all would yet be well with the Nazi dream. Even a prolonged stalemate during which Hitler remained master of the Continent might lead to eventual victory if Britishers grew weary and hopeless, if Americans and Russians shrank from the task of aiding in the reconquest of Europe, if London at last sued for a "negotiated" peace. Such a peace would merely postpone the final defeat of Britain unless followed by a binding Anglo-American-Soviet alliance and a new intercontinental balance of power. The fall of Britain, whether achieved by arms or by "negotiations," would pave the way to the conquest of Russia and the immobilization of America, since neither Washington nor Moscow would have effective means of opposing the Triplice if British sea power were broken and the British Commonwealth disintegrated.

As the war moved into its second spring, however, America prepared to use all its immense resources to defeat the Axis. Britain continued the demolition of Mussolini's African Empire. Hitler's drive through the Balkans led to the capitulation and occupation of Bulgaria on March 1. At Belgrade the Munichmen who made Jugoslavia a signatory of the Triplice were ousted on March 27 by the army which put 17-year old Peter II on the throne and defied the Axis to do its worst.[1] Nazi appeals for aid to Tokio brought Matsuoka to Berlin and Rome, but he was scarcely persuaded of the inevitability of Axis victory by the spectacle of Serbian peasants frustrating the plans of the Caesars.

The month of the war god, always lucky for Hitler, came to a close in 1941 with a series of reverses which deflated the Duce completely and confronted the Führer with two alternatives.[2] He could confess failure in the Balkans and attempt to invade Britain before American aid should render such an enterprise hopeless. Or he could open a new fighting front in southeastern Europe in an effort to save Italy and strike at Britain in the Near East at the risk of possible war with Turkey and the U.S.S.R. On April 6 he declared war on Jugoslavia and Greece. General Siegmund List's *Blitzkrieg* divisions in Bulgaria struck with invincible fury. Belgrade was laid in ruins. The invaders cut across southern Serbia. They swept down the Vardar valley and seized Salonika on the 9th. They effected a junction with the Italians in Albania and isolated the battered Jugoslav armies to the north. Nazi forces in Libya drove toward Egypt.

[1] See footnote on p. 684 below.

[2] Despite the death of Metaxas in January, the Duce's personally directed counter-offensive against the Greeks failed, March 20–25, 1941. Despite Nazi reinforcements and local gains, Graziani resigned his Libyan command on the 27th. British land forces invading Italian East Africa took Cheren and Harar on the 27th, cut the Jibuti railway at Diredawa on the 29th, and took Asmara, capital of Eritrea, on April 1. British sea forces in the Eastern Mediterranean sank 3 Italian cruisers and 2 destroyers on March 27. The United States, followed by the Latin American Republics, seized Axis shipping in American ports on March 30 in defiance of protests from Berlin and Rome.

Axis agents in Iraq organized an anti-British coup. The whole British position in the Near East was placed in grave jeopardy. The campaigns of 1941 would place the Reich within reach of world victory or ensure its ultimate doom.

SUGGESTED READINGS

Bayles, W. D.: *Caesars in Goosestep*, New York, Harper, 1940.

Baynes, N. (ed.): *Hitler's Speeches*, New York, Oxford, 1940.

Buell, R. L.: *Poland: Key to Europe*, New York, Knopf, 1939.

Deák, F. (ed.): *Papers and Documents Relating to the Foreign Relations of Hungary*, vol. I, 1919–1920, New York, Columbia University Press, 1940.

Documents on the Events Preceding the Outbreak of the War (1939), German White Book No. 2, New York, German Library of Information, 1940.

Dodd, M., and W. E. Jr. (eds.), *Ambassador Dodd's Diary*, New York, Harcourt Brace, 1941.

Ermarth, F.: *The New Germany: National Socialist Government in Theory and Practice*, Washington, American University Studies in International Law and Relations, No. 2, 1938.

Fodor, M. W.: *Plot and Counter-plot in Central Europe*, Boston, Houghton, 1937.

Gregory, J. D.: *Dollfuss and His Times*, London, Hutchinson, 1935.

Hambro, C. J.: *I Saw It Happen in Norway*, New York, Appleton-Century, 1940.

Hitler, Adolf: *Mein Kampf*, New York, Reynal, 1939.

Jones, F. E.: *Hitler's Drive to the East*, New York, Dutton, 1937.

Kolnai, A.: *The War against the West*, London, Gollancz, 1938.

Lennhoff, E.: *Last Five Hours of Austria*, New York, Stokes, 1938.

Loewenstein, K.: *Hitler's Germany*, New York, Macmillan, 1939.

Mowrer, E. A.: *Germany Puts the Clock Back*, New York, Morrow, 1939.

The Nazi Conspiracy in Spain, by the editor of "The Brown Book of the Hitler Terror," London, Gollancz, 1937.

Netherlands Documents: *The Netherlands Orange Book*, New York, Columbia University, Press, 1940.

Neumann, F. L.: *Behemoth: the Origins and Practice of National Socialism*, New York, Oxford, 1941.

Rauschning, H.: *The Revolution of Nihilism*, New York, Longmans, 1939.

———: *The Voice of Destruction*, New York, Putnam, 1940.

Schacher, G.: *Germany Pushes West*, London, Hurst, 1939.

Schuman, F. L.: *The Conduct of German Foreign Relations*, Annals of the American Academy, 1935.

———: *The Nazi Dictatorship*, New York, Knopf, 1936.

———: *Germany since 1918*, New York, Holt, 1937.

Schuschnigg, K.: *My Austria*, New York, Knopf, 1938.

Tolischus, O. D.: *They Wanted War*, New York, Reynal, 1940.

Van Kleefens, E. N.: *Juggernaut over Holland*, New York, Columbia, 1941.

Wheeler-Bennett, J. W.: *The Forgotten Peace: Brest-Litovsk*, New York, Morrow, 1939.

———: *Wooden Titan: Hindenburg in Twenty Years of German History*, 1914–1934, New York, Morrow, 1936.

Williams, F.: *War by Revolution*, New York, Viking, 1941.

Wiskemann, E.: *Czechs and Germans*, New York, Oxford, 1938.

Wolfe, H. C.: *The German Octopus*, New York, Doubleday, 1938.

Young, E. P.: *Czechoslovakia—Keystone of Peace and Democracy*, London, Gollancz, 1938.

CHAPTER XII

THE RETREAT OF THE VANQUISHED

1. THE FALL OF FRANCE

Sad tidings bring I to you out of France, of loss, of slaughter, and discomfiture; Guienne, Champagne, Rheims, Orleans, Paris, Guysors, Poictiers, are all quite lost. . . . . "How were they lost? What treachery was us'd?" No treachery but want of men and money. Amongst the soldiers this is muttered—that here you maintain several factions, and whilst a field should be dispatch'd and fought, you are disputing of your generals. One would have lingering wars with little cost; another would fly swift, but wanteth wings; a third thinks, without expense at all, by guileful fair words peace may be obtain'd. . . . Cropp'd are the flower-de-luces in your arms; of England's coat one half is cut away.—WILLIAM SHAKE-SPEARE, *King Henry* VI, Part I, Act I, Scene 1.

GREAT nations are seldom destroyed by foreign conquerors unless they are first self-defeated by disunity within. Napoleon's amazing victories were made possible not merely by a superior military technique but by the disruption of the other States of the Continent through class conflict between aristocrats and burghers. Hitler's career as "Aggrandizer of the Reich" was similarly made possible not only by superiority of arms and strategy but by inner conflict among his victims. During the years of democratic retreat preceding democratic defeat, influential elements among the propertied classes of all countries were favorably disposed toward Fascism as an imagined bulwark against proletarian radicalism. Conversely, many workers and some peasants and smaller business people suspected the political spokesmen of the wealthy and wellborn of being envious of the depotisms at Rome and Berlin and more than willing to sacrifice national safety upon the altar of class interest—narrowly defined and stupidly served. Such suspicions were in many cases justified. In capitalist democracies, most gentlemen and ladies of means were well-fed but worried lest they lose their privileges as the result of economic depression, war, and incipient social revolution. They therefore tended to be secretly sympathetic with the cause of the Caesars who had cured unemployment, outlawed trade unions and strikes, "put labor in its place," and loudly proclaimed their own devotion to Property and Profits and their determination to save "civilization" from "Bolshevism."

The result was democratic appeasement, pacifism, paralysis, and more often than not connivance in Fascist aggression up to the point at which catastrophe became inevitable. Decadent ruling classes frequently embrace their destroyers under the delusion that they are saviors. People of property in Italy, Germany, and Japan delivered themselves into the hands of a new military *élite* which they mistakenly believed they could control in their own interests. They thereby lost all political influence and ensured their own ultimate doom. Far from profiting from this spectacle, the people of property of France, Britain, and a dozen lesser States dealt with the Fascist Caesars in precisely the same fashion with similar results. Hitler and his agents assiduously spread the poisons of anti-Semitism and anti-Communism in every country earmarked for conquest. They profited richly from the bitter wrangling in the democracies between "isolationists" and "interventionists." They achieved their purposes through capitalizing on fear of labor, hatred of Russia, delusions of Fascist "protection" among men of property, piety, and privilege. The resulting disunity and confusion made the work of the Reichswehr easy.

The Third French Republic died in 1940, as the Second French Empire had died in 1870, because of incredible blindness on the part of its diplomats and strategists and because of appalling corruption and an incurable schism within French society. In the earlier instance the consequence was the débâcle of Sedan, followed by national defeat and the bloody class war of the Paris Commune of 1871. In the later instance, the consequence was a long period of inner strife between Munichmen and "*bellicistes*," reactionaries and liberals, rich and poor, pro-Fascists and anti-Fascists—followed by the second débâcle of Sedan, the capitulation at Bordeaux, and the establishment of the defeatist Vichy régime. France was betrayed from within, partly by isolationist stupidity, partly by malice prepense on the part of the well-to-do, long before France was crushed from without by the hereditary foe. The latter result was the product of the former cause. In this there is perhaps no "moral." In Hegel's phrase, the only lesson which history teaches is that history teaches no lesson. Degenerate *élites* (*e.g.*, the European aristocracies at the end of the eighteenth century, and the European plutocracies in the middle of the twentieth) typically learn nothing and forget nothing. The anatomy of disaster is nevertheless worthy of dissection.

The French nation-state is, with the possible exception of England, the oldest of the Great Powers in the Western State System. It was the first State of Continental Europe to attain political unity under its medieval kings. It was in France that royal absolutism and centralized power first triumphed over feudal anarchy and medieval particularism. It was in France, some three centuries later, that bourgeois democracy first triumphed over absolutism and the landed aristocracy. Corresponding changes had taken place earlier in England, but England was across the Channel and was no longer able to act effectively on the Continent after her knights and barons were driven out of Normandy, Aquitaine, and other "French" provinces in the Hundred Years' War (1337–1453). The same conflict which ousted England from the mainland launched France on her career as the largest, richest, and most populous State of Europe. For three centuries—roughly from 1500 to 1815—French kings, statesmen, and patriots took pride in the fact that *la belle France* was ranked first among the nations in military might, in diplomatic influence and prestige, and in the arts of civilization.

From the point of view of the traditional position of *la grande nation*, it was the tragedy of the nineteenth century that France ceased to be the most powerful State of western Europe. French policy under the Second Empire of Napoleon III (1852–1870) was directed toward imperial expansion and toward preventing the political unification of Germany. The effort to forestall this misfortune failed. The Franco-Prussian War of 1870–1871 spelled the end of French supremacy on the Continent. In the dust of Sedan and the agony of besieged and captured Paris, there perished the possibility of retaining in the hands of the Quai d'Orsay the reins of power which those hands were no longer strong enough to hold. The Rhine frontier was lost. Alsace-Lorraine was lost. Germany was a united nation. And Italy to the south was also a united nation. French foreign policy after 1871 sought to recover for France what had been lost and to reestablish traditional French hegemony over Europe. How this goal—seemingly impossible of realization—was attained and how French soldiers and diplomats finally achieved and for a time preserved a new position of uneasy preponderance over the Continent in the post-Versailles period need not here be told. It will suffice to suggest how and why that preponderance was thrown away and France was brought to ruin.

In 1918, after four years and three months of unprecedented bloodshed and destruction, France achieved the goal which her diplomats and soldiers had pursued since 1871. German military might had been as grossly underestimated as Russian fighting capacity had been exaggerated, and only a world in arms against the Central Powers enabled France to achieve victory. The Republic's Russian ally had been ground to pieces by the enemy and was in the throes of social revolution. Great Britain, Italy, the United States, and a host of lesser allies stood in the way of a purely French peace. They opposed French annexation of the Rhineland. They opposed outright annexation of the German colonies. They refused to conclude an alliance against Germany for the future. But much had been gained despite these obstacles. Austria-Hungary was destroyed. German military and naval strength was reduced to impotence by the Treaty of Versailles. The French army became the most powerful force on the Continent. French power and prestige were restored almost, if not quite, to their old status. French hegemony was successfully reasserted. A new distribution of territory and power, embodying the realities of this hegemony, was written into the public law of Europe. If Poincaré and other extreme nationalists were bitter over the "leniency" to the enemy of the most crushing peace settlement among Great Powers in modern times, at least the new Europe offered ample opportunities for the permanent humiliation of Germany and the perpetuation of French ascendancy.

Post-Versailles French foreign policy was directed almost exclusively toward the attainment of this end, although differences of opinion developed as to the best means thereto. "Security" became at once the guiding slogan of the Quai d'Orsay. "Security" meant assurance against invasion from the east. Assurance against invasion was not to be had, in the opinion of most patriotic Frenchmen, unless the prospective invader were kept in a position of political inferiority and military helplessness. No chances were to be taken with German good will, for France has been twice invaded in fifty years. Germany, moreover—defeated, truncated, disarmed—still possessed 63 million people to France's 40 million and a magnificent industrial establishment for the making of modern war. There could be no security unless the Republic possessed overwhelming power to paralyze at once any threatened resort to force on the part of the foe. Since the political, territorial, military, and reparations clauses of the Peace Treaty afforded a large measure of such security, it was natural that the French Government not only should insist upon their preservation intact but should interpret them as liberally as possible from the point of view of French interests.

The attainment of French security, *i.e.*, the maintenance of French hegemony over the Continent, required that Germany be kept weak and that France be kept strong. To achieve this goal, the dismemberment of the German federal State was at first contemplated. "Separatist" intrigues in the Rhineland were indulged in extensively between 1918 and 1925 and were then abandoned when it appeared that the Rhineland was not detachable. But the territorial clauses of the Treaty of Versailles were kept intact, and any union, political or economic, between the Reich and German Austria was prevented. Germany was kept disarmed, for a rearmed Germany, bent upon a counter-*revanche*, would be a formidable foe. Germany was kept diplomatically isolated, for if she gained allies she might conceivably at some future date undo the verdict of 1919, as France, with the aid of allies, was able earlier to undo the verdict of 1871. And Germany was kept economically and financially prostrate, for without capital and productive capacity no State can achieve military power or diplomatic influence. With this end in view, the French Government, between 1918 and 1924, insisted upon the full execution of the economic and financial clauses of the Treaty. A weak Germany could perhaps pay no reparations, but a strong Germany could threaten French security. Poincaré and his supporters preferred security to reparations. When payments were defaulted in 1923, French and Belgian troops occupied the Ruhr valley, the industrial heart of Germany, as a means of coercing the Reich.

If these and similar measures were adopted to keep Germany impotent, corresponding measures were devised to keep France powerful. New fortifications were erected along the eastern frontier, and the French army, though reduced in numbers, was maintained at what was believed to be the highest possible level of technical efficiency. The French Government steadfastly refused to reduce its armaments further, except in return for an international police force or some alternative arrangement which would afford an equal degree of security. New allies were sought to replace the old. Tsarist Russia was gone, and French efforts during the Russian civil war to bring about the overthrow of the Soviet régime were fruitless. But Belgium and Poland became allies of France, for both would be menaced even more directly by a German *revanche* than would France. In the southeast the Little Entente—Czechoslovakia, Jugoslavia, and Rumania—was no less resolved to maintain the *status quo*. All its members became allies of France, and under French guidance and with the aid of French loans they resolved to oppose all efforts to modify the existing distribution of territory and power, whether from Germany to the north, from Hungary or Austria within their midst, from Italy to the west, or from Russia to the east. These common interests stretched a broad cordon of French power around Germany's frontiers.

Not content to rely only upon this bulwark, the Quai d'Orsay sought overseas assistance from every possible source. In 1919 the French Cabinet reluctantly abandoned its plan for annexation of the Rhineland in return for a pledge of a Franco-Anglo-American security pact which never materialized. French interest in the League of Nations was largely motivated by the hope that it could be utilized to ensure enforcement of the peace treaties and place the power of all its members behind the victim of any aggression. The French Government attempted, without success, to secure a general British guarantee of European frontiers. Nothing would have been more welcome to it (or more improbable of attainment) than a pledge of diplomatic and military support from the United States, in the event of any forcible effort at treaty revision. Despite failures and disappointments, post-war France and her eastern allies established such a preponderance of power on the Continent that the old equilibrium between opposing coalitions disappeared and, for fifteen years, no aggregation of power emerged which could hope to challenge French ascendancy.

But this "security" was as uneasy as that of the proverbial head that wears a crown. Seventy million Germans remained in central Europe, and should they ever become politically united and armed, they could overwhelm Poland and Czechoslovakia. Should they ever secure Russian or Italian assistance, they could sweep through all barriers. It consequently seemed expedient to placate Germany to a certain degree. Following the failure of the Poincaré policy of coercion, the Herriot Cabinet of 1924 consented to the so-called Dawes Plan of reparation payments and to the evacuation of the Ruhr. Reparation obligations were further reduced in the Young Plan of 1930 and in the face of world-wide economic collapse were abandoned entirely in the Lausanne agreements of July 8, 1932. Under the leadership of Briand, a "new era" of Franco-German relations was inaugurated by the Locarno pacts of October, 1925, and by the admission of Germany into the League in 1926. The Rhineland was evacuated in 1930, five years before the required time. Extreme French nationalists condemned these concessions as an indication of weakness, a menace to security, and an invitation to Germany to make new demands for treaty revision. More moderate Frenchmen defended them as necessary steps toward security via conciliation and *rapprochement*. The "Locarno epoch" closed with the deaths of Briand and Stresemann, and new friction developed over *Anschluss*, armaments, and treaty revision in 1931–1932. In any case, French conciliatory gestures stopped at the point where equality in armaments and frontier revision began, for no French Government could permit any such enhancement of German power. Security demanded peace. Peace demanded the preservation of the *status quo* in its broad essentials. Preservation of the *status quo* demanded the maintenance of French hegemony and, paradoxically, France was prepared to fight to maintain peace, *i.e.*, French ascendancy, rather than yield the fruits of victory.

The year 1933 inaugurated a new and disastrous epoch in French diplomacy. Refusal to make larger concessions to the German Republic contributed to the collapse of Liberalism across the Rhine and to the rise to power of Hitler's Nazis, committed to a belligerent program of treaty revision and *revanche*. As German truculence increased and German military power grew, French willingness to resort to force to maintain the *status quo* diminished. French opinion was so firmly attached to peace that it would no longer approve recourse to preventive violence to meet the menace of the new militarism now dominant in the Reich. French refusal to act against the Third Reich drove Pilsudski into his non-aggression pact with Hitler in January, 1934.

An unstable balance between political extremes in parliament rendered difficult the development of any strong and consistent French policy. A desire to secure British and Italian support against Germany inhibited action likely to alienate London or Rome. The rise of Fascism in France, represented in the *Croix de Feu* of François de La Rocque, in the followers of the renegade Communist Jacques Doriot, and in a variety of other groups, was a further source of confusion and paralysis, as was the delayed but nevertheless damaging impact of the Great Depression on French economy. The great issue before the Republic was no longer that of keeping a weak Germany in subjection, but that of preserving the remnants of security and checkmating a strong, rearmed, and defiant Reich. Could liberal France prevent the establishment of Nazi hegemony over the Continent? Could liberal France protect itself from domestic Fascism? Upon answers to these questions depended the future of the French position in the game of power politics and the future of the Republic itself as a democratic state form.

La grande nation moved hesitantly and without clear guidance amid its new difficulties. Some positive steps were taken toward an affirmative answer to the questions posed. The "Maginot line"—a wall of steel and concrete, dotted with subterranean batteries and machine-gun nests—was rushed to completion along the German frontier. The Fascist riots in Paris of February 6, 1934, drew the powerful Socialist and Communist parties together into an anti-Fascist coalition, joined in January, 1936, by the large liberal party of the Radical Socialists. This "People's Front" frustrated the internal Fascist danger, at least temporarily. In the diplomatic field, Foreign Minister Louis Barthou had moved earlier to counterbalance the possible defection of Poland and the new might of Germany by a *rapprochement* with the U.S.S.R. In May, 1935, Franco-Soviet and Czech-Soviet Mutual Assistance Pacts were signed. In the elections of April and May, 1936, the People's Front parties won a sweeping victory and put in power a Left Cabinet headed by the Socialist leader, Léon Blum. French democracy was apparently saved. French security was apparently assured. In August, 1936, General Gamelin, Chief of the French General Staff, visited Warsaw. In September, General Edward Rydz-Smigly, who had succeeded Marshal Pilsudski (d. May 12, 1935) as dictator of Poland, visited Paris. The alliance was reaffirmed in the face of Polish fears of Nazi militarism and French promises of new loans. Perhaps Poland was to be saved for the French bloc. The U.S.S.R. was a new ally. Belgium and the Little Entente seemingly remained bulwarks of French power.

Counterbalancing these favorable developments was a series of diplomatic and strategic blunders which were ultimately to prove fatal. On October 9, 1934, Barthou and King Alexander of Jugoslavia were assassinated at Marseilles by a Croatian terrorist. This tragedy left France's ally on the Adriatic with a boy king, Peter II, and removed from the scene the only French foreign minister of great ability during the period of crisis. The retirement in 1933 and the death on November 22,

1934, of Philippe Berthelot, long Secretary-General of the Quai d'Orsay, removed another able diplomat from the helm. Barthou's successor, Pierre Laval, hesitated to ratify the Soviet Pact until Germany's *démarche* in March, 1936, compelled such action. Laval sought to conciliate Britain and Italy on the assumption that these Powers could be counted upon for support against Berlin. In order to placate Downing Street and "preserve peace," he acquiesced in German rearmament and supported Britain in imposing sanctions on Italy. In order to placate Rome and "preserve peace," he acquiesced in Italian designs on Ethiopia and undermined the League system of collective security. In the execution of this devious course, Paris fell between two stools. Rome and London were both alienated, Berlin was strengthened, and French power and prestige were diminished.

When on March 7, 1936, Hitler repudiated Locarno and remilitarized the Rhineland, the French General Staff perceived that effective military aid to Czechoslovakia or the U.S.S.R. in the event of Nazi aggression would be rendered impossible if Berlin were allowed to fortify the Rhine frontier. It urged French military occupation of the Rhineland, as was permitted by the Treaty of Versailles. But such a step would require expensive mobilization and would seem to threaten war. It would be highly unpopular in France and might lead to an open break with London. Gamelin did not insist. The Sarraut Cabinet consequently took no military action but limited itself to protests in accordance with the example set a year previously when the French Government acquiesced in Hitler's repudiation of the military clauses of the Treaty. The Blum Cabinet continued the same policy, hoping that French inaction in the Rhineland and French support of British initiative in deserting Ethiopia and abandoning sanctions against Italy would at least preserve an Anglo-French-Italian common front against Germany. Again the hope was vain. Britain refused to accept any commitments in central or eastern Europe. Mussolini at once reached an understanding with Hitler. The Quai d'Orsay was again betrayed by its own illusions.

The Little Entente was weakened by Czechoslovakia's relatively defenseless position and by growing German influence in the Balkans. On August 29, 1936, Nicholas Titulescu, for many years Rumanian Foreign Minister and a staunch advocate of solidarity with France, was forced out of office. The Jugoslav Government was also passing out of the French into the German orbit because Germany could supply a market for Jugoslav exports as France could not. Despite the efforts of President Eduard Beneš of Czechoslovakia,[1] the Little Entente continued to

[1] Beneš had been Foreign Minister since the establishment of Czechoslovakia. He was elected to the Presidency on December 18, 1935, following the retirement of the distinguished and venerated founder of the Republic, Professor Thomas Masaryk. Kamil Krofta succeeded as Foreign Minister.

.languish. Belgrade and Bucharest, united to Prague only by fear of Hungarian revisionism, began to spin a web of pro-German and anti-Soviet intrigue. French power on the Danube was rapidly becoming a memory. That it survived at all was due to Mussolini's championship of Magyar dreams of *revanche*. Meanwhile, Belgium was also lost. On October 14, 1936, King Leopold, in response to pressure from Flemish sources and from the Fascist followers of the "Rexist" leader, Léon Degrelle, announced the termination of Belgium's military alliances and her return to pre-war neutrality. A Belgium rendered defenseless by French acquiescence in Nazi remilitarization of the Rhineland could scarcely be expected to remain France's ally. The French bloc thus seemed on the point of collapse before the Fascist diplomatic offensive.

If Laval epitomized the blindness of the conservative French plutocracy in the face of mortal danger from the Caesars, Blum epitomized the paralysis of French liberals and radicals in the face of the same danger. The Right would do nothing to halt the aggressors because it feared the Left more than it did the aggressors. It hoped to make appeasement the means of protecting the class interests it represented. The Left would do nothing to halt the aggressors because its spokesmen were pacifists more interested in "social reforms" than in national security. Their enemies, moreover, were not above threatening civil war if the Left ventured either to attack the privileges of the wealthy "200 families" or to translate its anti-Fascist convictions into diplomatic and military action. On June 4, 1936, Léon Blum, leader of the French Socialist party, became Premier in a "People's Front" Cabinet of Radical Socialists and Socialists, supported in Parliament by these parties plus their Communist allies against Fascism. When the Spanish "Popular Front" was violently attacked by the generals and the propertied classes, aided by the Axis, the Socialist deputies in the French Chamber declared their solidarity with the Loyalists on July 24. On the next day, however, Blum and Foreign Minister Yvon Delbos persuaded the Cabinet in the name of "peace" and "nonintervention" to forbid all arms shipments to Spain. In deference to Tory Britain and the pro-Franco parties of the Right, Blum appealed to the Powers on August 1 to adopt "common rules of nonintervention." On August 15, Britain and France put a formal arms embargo into effect at once. Other States adhered with a variety of qualifications. The farcical London "Nonintervention" Committee was set up. The betrayal of the Spanish Republic was launched. Blum's own followers protested bitterly and demanded, "Planes for Spain!" But Blum was imperturbable. He told them on September 6,

There is not a single piece of circumstantial evidence to show that the [nonintervention] agreement has been violated. . . . Do you think my heart is not

torn when I think what is happening down there in Spain? . . . Undoubtedly
the legal government that has arisen from the expression of universal suffrage,
the government of the Spanish Republic, would assure us complete security on
our Pyrenees frontier, while it is impossible to foresee the ambitions of the Rebel
generals. On the one hand, safety; on the other, danger. . . . But should we
undertake a competition of armaments on Spanish soil? . . . If certain Powers
furnish arms and planes to the Rebels, should France furnish them to the Popular
Front? . . . No.

This decision was fatal not only to the Spanish Republic but to the
French Republic. France was to fall not because of the People's Front
"reforms," but because the diplomacy of the People's Front was identical
with that of the extreme Right. The ensuing collaboration with the Axis
in conquering Spain drove more nails into the coffin of France's eastern
alliances and left *la grande nation* discredited and weakened. It also
strengthened enormously the pro-Fascist element within France. In the
autumn of 1937 a series of outrages revealed the existence of a "Secret
Committee of Revolutionary Action," popularly known as the "*Cagou-
lards*," or Hooded Men, who were securing arms and money from Berlin
and Rome to set up a Fascist Directory—to be headed by Jacques Doriot,
Jean Chiappe, Pierre Laval, Maxime Weygand, and Henri Philippe
Pétain. Exposure of the plot was hastily hushed up. Too many "respectable" personages in the army and in high finance were implicated. Blum
had been succeeded in the Premiership in June, 1937, by anti-Socialist
Camille Chautemps of the Radical Socialists. To the Finance Ministry
went the sly and sinister figure of Georges Bonnet. The Chautemps
Cabinet fell on March 10, 1938. Blum tried in vain to form a new Ministry. On March 12 Hitler took Austria. Blum formed a cabinet on March
13—and did nothing. On April 8 he resigned once more. He was succeeded
by the weak and ignoble leader of the Radical Socialists, Edouard
Daladier, who, like so many French politicians, began his public life as
a radical (he was a baker's son) and finally acquired wealth and "wisdom"
and therewith became first a conservative and later a reactionary.
Daladier was to remain Premier of France until March, 1940. Although
brought to power by the People's Front, he kept power with the support
of the Right. His Foreign Minister (April 8, 1938–September 13, 1939)
was Georges Bonnet. The two men were destined to bring France and the
Republic to destruction.

Munich was the symbol of their folly. They made the Quai d'Orsay
completely subservient to Chamberlain's designs. They dreaded war or
threats of war to save Czechoslovakia because any such war would have
to be fought against Fascism in the name of democracy and the People's
Front and, *horribile dictu*, in alliance with Moscow. Bonnet publicly
pledged support of Prague and privately worked for an entente with
Hitler at Prague's expense. He denied (falsely) that France could rely

on British support. He exaggerated the weakness of the French army to London. He alleged (falsely) that Litvinov was abandoning Beneš. He cooperated with Pierre-Etienne Flandin (who sent Hitler a congratulatory telegram after the "peace") and with the defeatist press of the Right, much of it in the pay of the Axis. Bribed journalists denounced Prague and Moscow and shouted over and again to a befuddled public, "No war for Czechoslovakia." On his return from Munich, Daladier feared that the crowd at the airpoirt might denounce him for betraying France. But it had come to cheer the "savior of peace." He was joined by Bonnet and Gamelin. All were praised as heroes for having thrown away the victory of 1918 for which 1½ million Frenchmen had died. Gamelin was silent when a visitor remarked, "General, you have just lost 35 divisions!"—*i.e.*, the Czech army. "I accept my popularity," declared Daladier, "with the modesty that is only one of the forms my duty takes." Blum, in a mood he admitted was "cowardly relief," rejoiced that "peace was saved." Winston Churchill's judgment was more accurate: "France and Britain had to choose between war and dishonor. They chose dishonor. They will have war."

Bonnet and Daladier moved after Munich to surrender the Continent to Hitler's fancied *Drang nach Osten*, to wage war at home against "Communism," and to undermine the social reforms of the French "New Deal." Labor resisted and ordered a one-day general strike on November 30. It was broken. Daladier declared he had saved France from Bolshevism. On December 6, 1938, Bonnet signed with Ribbentrop a declaration of "pacific and good neighborly relations." "It is the struggle against Bolshevism," wrote Bonnet a week later, "which is essentially at the basis of the common German and Italian political conception and, without saying so formally, Ribbentrop perhaps wished to give us to understand that there is no other objective to be attributed to it. . . . In regard to Spain, it is again the struggle against Bolshevism which alone has inspired the German effort from the beginning." Ambassador Robert Coulondre in Berlin agreed: "To secure mastery over Central Europe by reducing Czecho-Slovakia and Hungary to a state of vassalage and then to create a Great Ukraine under German control—this is what essentially appears to be the leading idea now accepted by the Nazi leaders" (*French Yellow Book of* 1939, No. 33). Bonnet and Daladier were willing.

When Hitler yielded Carpatho-Ukraine to Hungary on March 16, 1939, immediately after the occupation of Prague, the last leaders of a doomed nation awakened belatedly to their error. "Will the Führer," asked Coulondre on March 19, "be tempted to return to the idea expressed by the author of *Mein Kampf* which, be it said, is identical with the classic doctrine held by the German General Staff, according to which Germany cannot accomplish her high destiny in the East until France has been crushed and, as a consequence, Britain reduced to impotence on the Continent? . . . The Reich will first turn against the Western Powers" (*ibid.*, No. 80). Paris joined London in belated effort to reconstruct the coalition which had been thrown away. The result was reaffirmation of the Polish alliance, support of Britain in guaranteeing Rumania and Greece, and the conclusion on June 23, 1939, of a French-Turkish alliance, paid for by the cession of Hatay to Ankara. But many of the Rightists were furious at such moves. "Danzig," wrote Flandin on May 7, "is merely an episode of the revision of the peace treaty. . . . If there were a new world war, in which Germany would doubtless be defeated, the German people would probably become Communist. . . . If the present crisis continues, revolution will come." The Quai d'Orsay, no less than Downing Street, was unwilling to pay Stalin's price for a new alliance against the Reich. The result was the collapse of the "peace front," the Nazi-Soviet Pact, the coming of war.

At the end, Bonnet made one last effort to arrange another Munich. On September 1 and 2, 1939, he accepted Italian proposals for "peace" through a conference, with German troops remaining where they were on Polish soil. He declined to join London in a common warning to Berlin and insisted upon separate action. Daladier vacillated but told Parliament on Saturday afternoon (September 2) that France must not abandon its ally. The Chambers voted a war budget and gave the Cabinet implied authority to declare war. Halifax insisted that there could be no conference without a cessation of the *Blitzkrieg* and German evacuation of Poland. The French Cabinet agreed. Bonnet reluctantly assented. Ciano replied that, since Hitler was unwilling to accept the condition, no further action could be taken. At 10:20 Sunday morning, Bonnet wired Coulondre of "the decision of the French Government" and instructed him to present an ultimatum at noon and to inform the Wilhelmstrasse in the event of a negative reply that Paris would be "compelled to fulfill as from today September 3 at 5 P.M. the engagements France entered into towards Poland." The British ultimatum was delivered at 9 and was followed by war at 11 A.M. At 11:20 Ribbentrop submitted a contemptuous note of rejection to Henderson. At 12:30 the Nazi Foreign Minister received Coulondre and told him that if France attacked the Reich "this would be on her part a war of aggression." At 5 P.M., September 3, 1939, war began between France and Germany. Bonnet had failed. He was obliged to yield the Quai d'Orsay to Daladier ten days later and content himself with the Ministry of Justice.

The Third French Republic entered upon its last war under leaders who were utterly inept. Its citizens were confused, baffled, and hopelessly divided against themselves. "Passive defense" was thought to be cheap in money and lives and was expected to save the State. No one was enthusiastic for war against the foe across the Rhine. Daladier, however, developed much enthusiasm for war against radicalism at home. On September 26, he decreed the dissolution of the Communist party and thereafter devoted much energy to combatting the "Reds." Bonnet schemed with Laval and Adrien Marquet to end the war and resume appeasement. After the outbreak of fighting in Finland, Daladier, Gamelin, and Weygand laid plans for war—not against Germany, but against the U.S.S.R. The débâcle of Allied policy in Finland, however, led to a parliamentary vote of nonconfidence on March 19, 1940. Daladier resigned but retained the Defense Ministry in the new cabinet of Paul Reynaud. Bonnet was out. Reynaud had long been an anti-Munichois and therefore anathema to the Right and to many of the Radical Socialists. "I have come too early," he remarked. He secured a majority of only one vote in his first test in the Chamber on March 21. He nevertheless decided to carry on.

In reality, Reynaud had come too late. Even he was self-defeated. He realized Gamelin's incompetence but was obliged by political considerations to keep Daladier in the Cabinet—and Daladier insisted on Gamelin's retention. His friend, the Countess Hélène de Portes, moreover, was a defeatist and a friend of Munichman Paul Baudouin. Reynaud and Daladier quarreled violently during the Nazi conquest of the Northlands and the Low Countries. Gamelin had no plan for meeting the *Blitzkrieg* save "Win or Die." All his calculations were based on the belief that the Maginot line was impregnable. Years before, Reynaud had urged in vain the thesis of Charles de Gaulle, an obscure officer who had been denied promotion by the conservative General Staff, that German tanks and planes could break through the line near Sedan and that France must have armored divisions and a powerful air force to meet the threat. They were not available. On May 18, Reynaud formed a new cabinet, putting Daladier at the Quai d'Orsay and appointing as Vice Premier the eighty-four-year-old Marshal Henri Philippe Pétain. He also took into the Cabinet the ultra-Rightists Louis Marin and Jean Ybarnégary, Vice President of the Fascist *Croix de Feu*. On May 19, he dismissed Gamelin and made seventy-three-year-old General Maxime Weygand Commander in Chief. These men were all clerical reactionaries, Anglophobes, anti-Bolsheviks, enemies of the Republic, and warm admirers of Franco and Mussolini if not of Hitler. If France was to be saved, it would not be by such artisans of disaster as these.

But France was now beyond saving. On June 5, as the full force of the invaders struck south from the Somme, Reynaud dropped Daladier and named Charles de Gaulle as Undersecretary at the War Ministry. Hélène persuaded him to name Baudouin as Under-secretary at the Quai

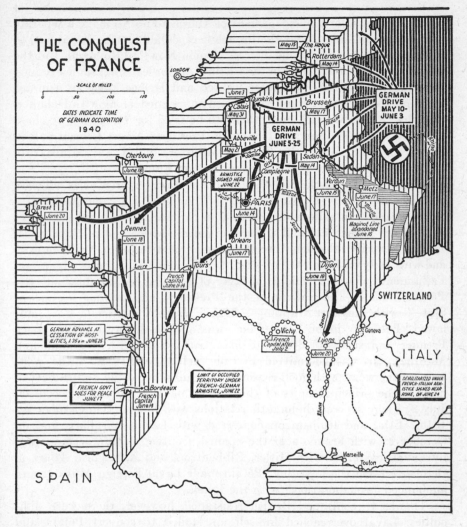

THE CONQUEST OF FRANCE

SCALE OF MILES

0   50   100   150

DATES INDICATE TIME
OF GERMAN OCCUPATION
1940

d'Orsay. Weygand was baffled. His armies were overwhelmed. "A modern retreat," he observed, "has no limits." The Cabinet fled to Tours (June 11 to 14) and then to Bordeaux. Weygand alleged (falsely) that Communists were "rioting" in abandoned Paris prior to the German occupation and that the Cabinet must surrender to "save France from Bolshevism." Pétain, Chautemps, Baudouin agreed, as did Bonnet, Laval, and Flandin. To move to London or to North Africa, to carry on the war with the fleet and the colonies and the unbroken might of the British Empire would have been quite feasible. But the Munichmen gave Britain up for lost and preferred surrender for reasons of class interest. Reynaud appealed in vain for immediate American aid and asked Churchill to release France from the engagement of March 28 not to make a separate peace. Churchill asked that the French fleet should first be dispatched to British ports. On June 16, he offered "Union Now" to Reynaud. But the capitulators won a majority in the Cabinet at Bordeaux the same evening. Reynaud resigned. He was later injured and Hélène killed in a motor accident. In August, he was arrested and imprisoned, along with Daladier, Gamelin, Blum, Mandel, and others, to be tried for "treason" by those who had betrayed France. Meanwhile, President Albert Lebrun named Pétain Premier, Baudouin Foreign Minister, and Laval Minister of Justice. They sued for peace at once through Franco.

In the aftermath the Republic died and France perished as a Power and as a free State. De Gaulle fled to London and became leader of a "Free France" in exile which carried on the war and secured control of part of the French colonial empire in central Africa and in the Pacific. Pétain authorized the signature of an armistice with Germany on June 22 and with Italy on June 24. At Vichy, to which the Cabinet moved, a rump Parliament committed suicide in favor of a projected "totalitarianism." Pétain assumed the powers of the President and became "Chief of State" with Royalist trappings. *Liberté, Egalité, Fraternité* were outlawed. The very name "Republic" was abolished. Laval became Vice Premier and successor-designate in a triumvirate with Weygand and Marquet. He was committed to full "collaboration" with the Axis. Fearing the worst with good reason, Churchill ordered the British fleet to destroy the principal units of the French navy at Oran, Morocco, on July 3. Vichy severed diplomatic relations with London. On October 22, 1940, Hitler and Ribbentrop conferred with Laval near Paris and on October 23 with Franco near the Spanish frontier. Pétain, accompanied by Laval, conferred with Hitler, Ribbentrop, and Keitel near Tours on October 25. On the next day, Pétain made Laval Foreign Minister and announced "collaboration" with the Reich.

Thanks to continued British resistance, however, there were difficulties. Laval overreached himself and failed to convert Pétain and Weygand (who went to North Africa) to his view that Vichy should join the Axis in war against Britain. On December 13, Pétain dismissed Laval from all his posts and named Flandin Foreign Minister. Otto Abetz, German Commissioner to France, went to Vichy to demand "explanations" but received little satisfaction despite threats of a Nazi military occupation of all of France. Berlin had ample means of carrying out such a threat but hesitated to do so lest the remnants of the French fleet and the French forces in Africa might openly join the British cause. By February, 1941, Pétain was yielding to German demands. Laval was not reinstated. Admiral Jean Darlan became Vice Premier and Foreign Minister. But the aged Marshal and the men around him had staked their fortunes on a Nazi victory over Britain and were prepared to do all they dared to do to ensure British defeat.

What future awaited the strange régime at the Hotel du Parc amid Vichy's bubbling waters? What future awaited France? "What we ask at this moment," said Churchill in a broadcast to the French people on October 21, 1940, "in our struggle to win the victory which we will share with you, is that if you cannot help us, at least you will not hinder us. . . . Remember, we shall never stop, never weary, and never give in, and that our whole people and Empire have bowed themselves to the task of cleansing Europe from the Nazi pestilence and saving the world from a new Dark Ages." In secrecy the men of Vichy pursued their devious course. But at least the aged Pétain and the scarcely less aged Weygand were beginning to learn that "peace with honor" was not to be bought by surrender or "collaboration"—and the people of property who had brought France to defeat were learning that Hitler was no respecter of property and no safeguard against radicalism. Vichy was but an interim régime. If the Axis should win its war, France would be partitioned, exploited, enslaved, and crushed to earth beyond all hope of resurrection. If the Axis should lose and the Third Reich should crumble, a new France would rise and share in the rebuilding of Europe and the world. It seemed probable, however, that no such destiny could be achieved unless France again became a united nation with a national will and a leadership worthy of its mighty past. Such a transformation, in turn, might well require civil war before the contest for mastery of the French soul should be resolved and a new opportunity created for the development of a healthy society and a viable and enduring State. Meanwhile, in the words of Baudelaire's *Flowers of Evil*, "wandering spirits whine mournfully without a Fatherland while vanquished Hope weeps vainly, and Anguish, atrocious and despotic, plants on bowed and weary heads its flag of night."

SUGGESTED READINGS

Armstrong, H. F.: *Chronology of a Failure*, New York, Macmillan, 1940.
Brogan, D. W.: *France Under the Republic*, New York, Harper, 1940.
Buckley, H.: *Life and Death of the Spanish Republic*, London, Hamish Hamilton, 1940.
Chambrun, René de: *I Saw France Fall*, New York, Morrow, 1940.
Daladier, Edouard: *In Defense of France*, New York, Doubleday, 1939.
Del Vayo, J. A.: *Freedom's Battle*, New York, Knopf, 1940.
The French Yellow Book: Diplomatic Documents (1938–1939), Published by authority of the French Government, New York, Reynal, 1940.
Gannes, H., and T. Repard: *Spain in Revolt*, New York, Knopf, 1936.
Haight, F. C.: *A History of French Commercial Policies*, New York, Macmillan, 1940.
Hayes, C. J. H.: *France—A Nation of Patriots*, New York, Columbia University Press, 1930.
Herriot, E.: *Eastward From Paris*, London, Gollancz, 1934.
Jellinck, F.: *The Civil War in Spain*, London, Gollancz, 1938.

Kerner, R. J., and H. N. Howard: *The Balkan Conferences and the Balkan Entente,* 1930–1935, Berkeley, University of California, 1936.

Machray, R.: *The Poland of Pilsudski,* New York, Dutton, 1937.

Manuel, F. E.: *The Politics of Modern Spain,* New York, McGraw-Hill, 1938.

Matthews, H. L.: *Two Wars and More to Come,* New York, Carrick and Evans, 1938.

Maurois, André: *Tragedy in France,* New York, Harper, 1940.

Paul, O.: *Farewell, France!* London, Gollancz, 1941.

Pol, H.: *Suicide of a Democracy,* New York, Reynal, 1940.

Pribichevich, S.: *World Without End: The Saga of Southeastern Europe,* New York, Reynal, 1939.

Romains, J.: *Seven Mysteries of Europe,* New York, Knopf, 1940.

Roucek, J. S.: *Politics of the Balkans,* New York, McGraw-Hill, 1939.

Schuman, F. L.: *War and Diplomacy in the French Republic,* New York, McGraw-Hill, 1931.

Selsam, J. P.: *The Attempts to Form an Anglo-French Alliance,* 1919–1924, Philadelphia, University of Pennsylvania Press, 1936.

Sforza, Count C.: *Fifty Years of War and Diplomacy in the Balkans,* New York, Columbia University Press, 1940.

Steer, G. L.: *The Tree of Gernika,* London, Hodder, 1938.

Stokes, R. L.: *Léon Blum: Poet to Premier,* New York, Coward-McCann, 1937.

Taylor, E.: *The Strategy of Terror,* Boston, Houghton, 1940.

Werth, A.: *The Destiny of France,* London, Hamilton, 1937.

———: *France and Munich,* New York, Harper, 1939.

2. THE DUSK OF BRITAIN

This royal throne of kings, this sceptred isle, this earth of majesty, this seat of Mars, this other Eden, demi-paradise; this fortress built by Nature for herself against infection and the hand of war; this happy breed of men, this little world, this precious stone set in the silver sea, which serves it in the office of a wall, or as a moat defensive to a house, against the envy of less happier lands; this blessed plot, this earth, this realm, this England, this nurse, this teeming womb of royal kings, fear'd by their breed, and famous by their birth, renowned for their deeds as far from home, for Christian service and true chivalry, as is the sepulchre in stubborn Jewry of the world's ransom, blessed Mary's Son: this land of such dear souls, this dear dear land, dear for her reputation through the world, is now leas'd out —I die pronouncing it—like to a tenement or pelting farm. England, bound in with the triumphant sea, whose rocky shore beats back the envious siege of watery Neptune, is now bound in with shame, with inky blots and rotten parchment bonds; that England, that was wont to conquer others, hath made a shameful conquest of itself. Ah, would the scandal vanish with my life, how happy then were my ensuing death!—WILLIAM SHAKESPEARE, *King Richard the Second,* Act II, Scene 1.

The agony of England, like the martyrdom of France, was in one sense self-inflicted. It flowed from a long series of tragic blunders and dishonesties on the part of an effete ruling class whose leaders were no longer able or willing to understand the world. They proved incapable either of comprehending their own interest or of serving the nation and the Empire they were sworn to defend. If Waterloo was "won on the playing fields of Eton," it was no less true a century and a quarter later that Madrid, Vienna, Prague, Warsaw, Oslo, Amiens, and Dunkirk were lost there. The myopia of the "upper classes" and of the sons of the wealthy who came from the "public schools" was far more responsible for what befell the realm than the ignorance or provincialism of the masses. In England there was not, as in France, any colorful Communist movement to frighten people of means. There was no important Socialist movement, for the Labor party remained politically impotent after its abandonment by Ramsay MacDonald. The forces of political Liberalism were feeble. During all of a dismal decade, Britain's destiny was entrusted by a confused electorate to the ultra-Tory wing of the Conservative party which dominated without challenge the catastrophic "National Government" of 1931. This régime of blind men made way for other leadership only on the brink of irreparable disaster in May, 1940. The disaster was the fruit of its toil.

The central error of Tory politics was to ignore a principle which all wise British statesmen had adhered to for many centuries: that of preserving a balance of power on the Continent by giving diplomatic and military support to the neighbors and possible victims of the most powerful Continental State. To permit any one Power to control the Continent had always been deemed highly dangerous to the British Isles and to its far-flung colonies and dominions. To prevent any such development, England had waged war upon, and raised successive coalitions against, the Spain of Philip II, the France of Louis XIV and Napoleon I, and the Germany of Wilhelm II. Only when a stable equipoise of rivals prevailed across the Channel could Britain safely follow a course of "splendid isolation." Such was the case between 1815 and 1904. When the growing power and ambition of the Second Reich threatened domination of the Continent, Britain joined forces with France and Russia to checkmate Berlin. This combination, even when joined by Japan and Italy, proved inadequate to defeat Imperial Germany. Only the addition of the United States made possible the victory of 1918. In the twenty years which followed, the leaders of Britain threw that victory away and finally permitted the Third Reich to enhance its power to a point at which it was able to conquer the Continent and menace Britain with destruction.

The question of why Britain's leaders so completely forgot the lessons of the past and brought upon their people so painful an aftermath of folly admits of various relevant answers, none of them having much relationship to the "explanations" offered by the chief actors during the years of retreat. In terms of *Realpolitik*, Britain after Versailles could have found security either by putting an end for all time to the Continental and world balance of power through giving full support to an effective League of Nations or by reverting to a policy of supporting the weaker Continental Powers against the stronger. The former policy would have required the assumption of far-reaching commitments of collective security and a firm resolve to honor all such obligations. The latter policy would have required enforcement of the military clauses of Versailles to prevent the rebuilding of a German war machine or, if this was not to be, then at least full British support of France, Poland, and the Little Entente and a *rapprochement* with the U.S.S.R. as a means of checkmating the Axis. Downing Street followed neither of these courses. It supported the League in a halfhearted manner and finally sacrificed it on the altar of appeasement. It supported Republican Germany in feeble fashion against the France of Poincaré and subsequently supported the Third Reich against the France of Barthou and Blum, meanwhile alienating the Soviet Union and firmly declining all obligations to defend Vienna, Prague, or Warsaw.

This policy, which was clearly suicidal in its consequences and apparently mad or muddled in its motivation, was not primarily a product of popular isolationism or pacifism, although these sentiments won public support for a program which otherwise might have been repudiated. The Tory line had a logic of its own in *Realpolitik*, albeit one seldom acknowledged. That logic presupposed that the great protagonists of the future would be Japan and the U.S.S.R. in Asia and the Reich and the U.S.S.R. in Europe. If these Powers were likely to checkmate one another and ultimately engage in a death grapple, Britain could well afford to stand aloof and to protect itself from involvement by pressing France to abandon the allies which stood in the way of the German drive to the east. If world revolutionary Communism, moreover, was the gravest of menaces to the British ruling classes and to the integrity of the Empire and if the Fascist Triplice promised to hold the menace in check, Britain could well afford to boycott the U.S.S.R. and lend comfort to Hitler, Hirohito, and Mussolini.[1] If the Triplice should attack and conquer the Soviet Union, it might, to be sure, become a danger to the Empire. But this danger was envisaged as negligible by comparison with the danger to the Empire of any extension of Communism beyond the Soviet frontiers or any major enhancement of the power of the Soviet State. Hence the wisdom of appeasement.[2]

[1] This view was put forward as early as 1921 by Viscount D'Abernon, post-Versailles British Ambassador in Berlin. *Cf. The Diary of an Ambassador: Versailles to Rapallo,* 1920–1922, pp. 21f. New York, Doubleday Doran & Company, Inc., 1929.

[2] The reasoning behind this view may be suggested by the following quotations. On September 22, 1933, Lloyd George declared:

If the Powers succeed in overthrowing Nazism in Germany, what would follow? Not a Conservative, Socialist or Liberal regime, but extreme Communism. Surely that could not be their objective. A Communist Germany would be infinitely more formidable than a Communist Russia. The Germans would know how to run their Communism effectively.

In Commons, November 28, 1934, Lloyd George asserted:

In a very short time, perhaps in a year or two, the Conservative elements in this country will be looking to Germany as the bulwark against Communism in Europe. She is planted right in the center of Europe, and if her defense breaks down against the Communists—only two or three years ago a very distinguished German statesman said to me: "I am not afraid of Nazism, but of Communism"—and if Germany is seized by the Communists, Europe will follow; because the Germans could make a better job of it than any

The only difficulty with this logic was that its premises were tragically false. If it be asked how so experienced and astute a group of men as ruled the world's greatest empire from Downing Street could have been so completely mistaken in their basic presuppositions about world politics, the only answer is that this group had come by the 1930's to reflect not the high political wisdom which had so often in the past enabled Britain to survive and prosper, but rather the narrow provincialism, class prejudices, and naïve ignorance of Tory squires, international financiers, and businessmen from the Midlands. David Low's immortal cartoon character, Colonel

---

other country. Do not let us be in a hurry to condemn Germany. We shall be welcoming Germany as our friend.

In 1934 Mr. L. Lawton wrote in the *Fortnightly Review*:

Whereas formerly German statesmen looked both to the East and to the West, Hitler at present looks to the East only. . . . No one who studies the map of Eastern Europe can doubt that there are immense possibilities of a German-Polish compromise at the expense of others. The idea of including Ukraine within the Western European system, and moving Russia on towards the East is certainly tempting. . . . With Ukraine as part of a democratic federated system there would, it is hoped, come into existence a grouping of States with which Great Britain could be on friendly terms. The moment is long overdue for the creation of some such grouping in Eastern Europe.

Mr. L. S. Amery, former Colonial Minister, wrote in *The Forward View* (1935):

The first condition of European peace today is the frank acknowledgment that Germany's armaments are now her own affair and nobody else's [p. 71]. . . . The time has come for such a revision of the Covenant as will get rid of all those clauses (more particularly 10 and 16) which give an encouragement to the super-State theory of the League [p. 272]. . . . The doctrine of the inevitable contagion of war is, of course, pure nonsense [p. 283]. . . . We do not regard ourselves as one of the nations of Europe [p. 285]. . . . It would be no concern of ours . . . to prevent Japanese expansion in Eastern Siberia [p. 288].

The Marquess of Londonderry, owner of many mines and large estates, differed from most of his collaborators in a somewhat naïve propensity to state his convictions in print, with the aid of Lady Desborough and Mr. G. Ward Price. Thus:

Our Foreign Office appears to condone the associations with Communism and Bolshevism through our affiliation with France, while paying but little regard to the robust attitude of Germany, Italy, and Japan which wholeheartedly condemn Communism and Bolshevism. Bolshevism is a world-wide doctrine which aims at the internal disruption of all modern systems of Government with the ultimate object of what is termed World Revolution. That Germany, Italy, and Japan condemn Bolshevism is an attitude of mind which is not properly appreciated in this country. . . . We fail to recognize that the present condition of Spain is mainly the result of Red machinations. We console ourselves with the reflection that, owing to the Conservatism of the French peasant, Bolshevism will not prevail to any serious extent among the urban industrial population of France, although the Communist representation in the Chamber has increased to the number which Herr Hitler personally prophesied to me over two years ago. Belgium is showing signs of Bolshevism. And Germany sees herself surrounded by Bolshevist countries and militarily and economically hemmed in with what may well be disastrous consequences. We watch this movement with strange equanimity. We throw in our weight under "non-intervention" on the side of the Reds in Spain. Belgium and France do the same. And we wonder why Germany and Italy appear more truculent and challenging as their strength and prestige increase [pp. 21–22].

I was at a loss to understand why we could not make common ground in some form or other with Germany in opposition to Communism. . . . The anti-Communist platform was (and still is) invaluable [p. 129].

Blimp, thought of *Weltpolitik* as a cricket game or a bargain counter. That it might be a fox hunt with himself as the fox never occurred to him. He was for "peace," against "foreign entanglements," apoplectic about Russia, half envious of Mussolini and Hitler, contemptuous of all "nonsense" about "collective security," and whole-heartedly devoted to "muddling through," Scotch and soda, and "business as usual." He loved pudgy Stanley Baldwin with his pipe and pigs. He respected lank and cadaverous Neville Chamberlain who left his father's screw business in Birmingham to bring balm to a troubled world. He stoutly and stubbornly denounced all those who argued that these attitudes would spell the ruin of his nation and his class in a world vastly changed and increasingly dominated by ruthless demagogue-despots whose fondest secret dream was the destruction of the British Empire.

Colonel Blimp found the atmosphere congenial in such places as Cliveden, country estate of Lord Astor who owned *The Observer* (edited by J. L. Garvin), whose brother Major John Jacob Astor owned the *Times*, and whose wife, Lady Nancy, sat in Commons and entertained other lords and ladies, along with "interesting" foreigners and intellectuals, at luncheon parties and pleasant week-end gatherings. Sir Montagu Norman, Governor of the Bank of England, was of like mind. So were many of the greater industrialists of the Midlands and the financiers of the City. So were the magnates of the yellow press, Lord Beaverbrook and Lord Rothermere. (The latter for a time openly championed Sir Oswald Mosley's British Black Shirts.) So were Dean Inge of St. Paul's, the Archbishop of Canterbury, many High Churchmen, many Catholics, and a host of others. "I often think," sighed Lord Halifax, "how much easier the world would have been to manage if Herr Hitler and Signor Mussolini had chanced to have been at Oxford." Multitudes of "Little Englanders" and isolationists cherished a picture of the world which led to similar conclusions. Such Laborite pacifists as George Lansbury and James Maxton helped to educate the masses to the necessity of seeking peace with tyrants through appeasement. Of such materials was Britain's bitterest tragedy fabricated.

The devious and dishonorable course of British diplomacy in the 1930's, from Sir John Simon's connivance in the rape of Manchuria to Chamberlain's betrayal of Ethiopia, Spain, Austria, and Czechoslovakia, was the product of the Tory mind at its worst. The second Labor Cabinet, constituted in 1929 with Ramsay MacDonald as Prime Minister, disintegrated in the financial crisis of August, 1931, and gave way to a coalition "National Government," predominantly Conservative but still headed by MacDonald and his "National Laborites." The latter had no following and were expelled from the Labor Party as traitors, with Labor and part of the Liberals going into opposition. The National Government won an overwhelming victory in the election of October, 1931, and carried on with the renegade MacDonald at its head. He resigned on June 7, 1935, and was replaced by the Conservative leader, Stanley Baldwin. The new Cabinet was a coalition in form, but for all practical purposes was a Conservative government. The death of George V and the succession of Edward VIII on January 30, 1936, was without consequence for foreign policy, as was the constitutional crisis of the autumn, precipitated by the Cabinet's refusal to approve the King's projected marriage to the twice-divorced American commoner, Mrs. Wallis Simpson. Edward abdicated on December 10, 1936, and was succeeded by his brother as George VI. Neville Chamberlain succeeded Baldwin as Prime Minister on May 28, 1937. Eden continued as Foreign Minister until his disgust at appeasement led him to resign on February 20, 1938. His place was taken by Edward Frederick Lindley Wood, third Viscount Halifax, who (as Baron Irwin) had been Viceroy of India, 1926–1931. Chamberlain's principal advisers, aside from Halifax and such confidantes as Sir Horace Wilson, were Hoare and Simon.

The *Leitmotifs* of appeasement have already been suggested. In the end the British public acquiesced in this policy in the mistaken conviction that it provided the only hope of escape from the war which the policy itself had made inevitable. But the electorate had not at the outset sponsored any such course and was in fact tricked into supporting those who did. In 1934–1935 the British League of Nations Union, under Lord Robert Cecil, conducted a "National Peace Ballot" in which no less than 11,500,000 votes were cast, giving an overwhelming majority for support of the League and disarmament and a heavy majority in favor of economic and military sanctions against aggressors. Accepting this result as an accurate index of what British voters wanted, Baldwin declared, "We value this support. . . . The League of Nations remains, as I said in a speech in Yorkshire, 'the sheet-anchor of British policy.' " The National Government's election manifesto of November, 1935, asserted, "The League of Nations will remain as before the keystone of British policy. . . . We shall continue to do all in our power to uphold the Covenant. . . . There will be no wavering." An election poster of the Conservative party showed Baldwin's fist squarely planted on the Covenant over the caption, "Our word is our bond." In the polling of November 15, 1935, the Government won 431 out of 615 seats in Commons. This was a popular endorsement not of appeasement but of collective security to which the Government had pledged itself. The voters did not know that Hoare and Laval had made a secret pact at Geneva in September to betray Ethiopia and the League and that an even more shameful bargain between them was to leak out three weeks after the election. It is fair to say that for the next four years a group of leaders, placed in power by a public convinced it was supporting the cause of world order and resistance to Fascist aggression, pursued a policy of connivance in aggression which was certain to produce world anarchy. These leaders progressively "sold" this policy to the public in the name of "peace."

The precedent established in dealing with Japan in China was faithfully followed in dealing with Italy in Ethiopia, Germany in the Rhineland, and the Axis in Spain. At each step, one eloquent voice was raised in protest and warning. Each time it was ignored by those who knew better. It was the voice of one of the rarest of animals, a Tory dissenter—Winston Churchill.[1] At each step the appeasers told Parliament and public that their decisions would insure peace. Once the new St. George had slain not the dragon but the Abyssinian maid and the League which might have protected her from the dragon, the Tory leaders explained that the League was "too weak" to be relied upon. Finally they argued that support of the League was not to be thought of since it might mean "war"—i.e., Mussolini might "attack" the British Empire, France, Jugoslavia, Greece, Turkey et al. "Is it not apparent," asked Chamberlain on June 10, 1936, "that the policy of sanctions involves a risk of war? . . . There is no use for us to shut our eyes to realities." Eden announced the abandonment of sanctions on June 18, 1936, one hundred and twentieth anniversary of Waterloo and first anniversary of the Simon-Hoare-Ribbentrop naval accord by which Britain had granted to the Reich 35 per cent parity in sea power and full parity in submarines. Simon asserted, "I do not think there is a single member of the League which is prepared to use force. . . . I am not prepared to see a single ship sunk even in a successful naval battle in the cause of Abyssinian independence." Government supporters shouted at the Labor opposition, "Do you want war?" Lord Cecil wrote in the *Times*, "We cannot escape war by running away from it. . . . There is no escape from blackmail by submission." But his voice was as lonely as Churchill's.

The formula thereafter was "no commitments" and "no entanglements." A clear indication was given to Berlin that Downing Street would not resist German expansion to the east by Anthony Eden's address to his constituents at Leamington on November 20, 1936.

---

[1] Thus Churchill, writing on December 30, 1938, wrote (*Step by Step*, G. P. Putnam's Sons, New York, 1939, p. 274), "The bulk of the Conservatives admire General Franco; all the forces of the Left are ardent for the Republic. The difference between the Duchess of Athol and the Scottish Tories in the Perth by-election began about Spain. The dominant element in those parts regarded her vehement sympathy for the Spanish Government as proof that she was almost ready to carry Bolshevism into Britain, to confiscate their property, pollute their churches and, if necessary, cut their throats. Nothing has strengthened the Prime Minister's hold upon well-to-do society more remarkably than the belief that he is friendly to General Franco and the Nationalist cause in Spain. But these sentiments on either side may be pushed beyond the bounds of British interest. It would seem that today the British Empire would run far less risk from the victory of the Spanish Government than from that of General Franco." *Cf.* also *Europe on the Eve*, pp. 332–46.

These [British] arms will never be used in a war of aggression. . . . They may, and if the occasion arose they would, be used in our own defense and in the defense of the territories of the British Commonwealth of Nations. They may, and if the occasion arose they would, be used in the defense of France and Belgium against unprovoked aggression in accordance with our existing treaty obligations. They may, and if a new Western European settlement can be reached, they would, be used in the defense of Germany were she the victim of unprovoked aggression by any of the other signatories of such a settlement. These, together with our Treaty of Alliance with Iraq and our projected treaty with Egypt, are our definite obligations. In addition our armaments may be used in bringing help to a victim of aggression in any case where, in our judgment, it would be proper under the provisions of the Covenant to do so. I use the word "may" deliberately, since in such an instance there is no automatic obligation to take military action. It is, moreover, right that this should be so, for nations cannot be expected to incur automatic military obligations save for areas where their vital interests are concerned.

On March 3, 1937, in Lords, Lord Halifax asserted that although the Government did not disinterest itself in these areas, "we are unable to define beforehand what might be our attitude to a hypothetical complication in Central or Eastern Europe."

Eden and Halifax were thus in agreement, at a time when Eden was Foreign Minister and posing as the champion of collective security, that Britain should assume no commitments to defend victims of aggression in eastern or central Europe. This was the only assurance which the leaders of the Third Reich required. It meant that, so far as London was concerned, they had a free hand in the east. Then and later, the only stipulation insisted upon by Downing Street was that Nazi imperialism must achieve its purposes without war, since war might involve Britain by involving France. The Tory *carte blanche* to Hitler with respect to the *Drang nach Osten* was thus given in the autumn of 1936—and by none other than Anthony Eden!

By 1938, more than passivity was required. After *Anschluss*, which had been passively sanctioned by persistent British refusal to come to Austria's defense, Halifax cried, "Horrible, horrible, I never thought they would do it!" But when Litvinov warned on March 17 that Czechoslovakia was in danger, London declined his proposal for a conference of League members and the United States to consider collective means of "checking the further development of aggression and eliminating an aggravated danger of a new world massacre." Chamberlain spoke to Commons on March 24, 1938:

I cannot imagine any events in Europe which would change the fundamental basis of British foreign policy, which is the maintenance and preservation of peace. However, that does not mean nothing would make us fight. . . . Our existing commitments which might lead to use of our arms for a purpose other than our own defense were, first of all, defense of France and Belgium against unprovoked aggression. Britain also has treaty obligations to Portugal, Iraq, and Egypt.

The question now arises whether we should go further. Should we forthwith give assurance to France that in the event of her being called upon by reason of German aggression on Czechoslovakia to implement her obligations under the Franco-Czech treaty we would immediately employ our full military force on her behalf? Or should we at once declare our readiness to take military action in resistance to any forcible interference with the independence of Czechoslovakia and invite any other nations which might desire to associate themselves with us in such a declaration?

From consideration of these two alternatives it clearly emerges that under either a decision as to whether or not this country should find itself involved in war would automatically be removed from the discretion of His Majesty's Government and the suggested guarantee would apply irrespective of the circumstances by which it would be brought into operation and over which His Majesty's Government might not have been able to exercise any control. This position is not one which His Majesty's Government could see their way to accept in relation to an area where their vital interests are not concerned in the same degree as they are in the case of France and Belgium. It certainly is not a position that results from the Covenant. For these reasons His Majesty's Government feel themselves unable to give the prior guarantee suggested.

But while plainly stating this decision I should add this: where peace or war is concerned legal obligations are not alone involved and if war broke out it likely would not be confined to those who have assumed such obligations. The [Soviet] proposal appeared to involve less consultation with a view to settlement than concerting of action against an eventuality that has not yet arisen. . . . [This] would aggravate a tendency toward establishment of exclusive groups of nations which must be inimical to the prospect of European peace. . . .

His Majesty's Government will at all times be ready to render any help in their power toward the solution of questions likely to cause difficulty between the German and Czechoslovak governments. In the meantime there is no need to assume the use of force or, indeed, to talk about it. Such talk is to be strongly deprecated. Not only can it do no good; it is bound to do harm.

There followed in logical order the Ciano-Perth accord of April 16 for appeasing Italy, Mr. Chamberlain's friendly gestures toward Japan, the Runciman mission to Prague, the ultimatum of September 19 to Beneš, and the "peace" at Munich. Chamberlain, like Daladier, was welcomed on his return from the *Führerhaus* as a conquering hero. Only one member of his Cabinet resigned in protest, Alfred Duff-Cooper, First Lord of the Admiralty, who said in Commons, "It was not for Serbia or Belgium we fought in 1914, though it suited some people to say so, but we were fighting then, as we should have been fighting last week, in order that one Great Power should not be allowed, in disregard of treaty obligations and the laws of nations and against all morality, to dominate by brutal force the continent of Europe. . . . I tried to swallow the Munich terms, but they stuck in my throat. I have perhaps ruined my political career . . . but I can still walk about the world with my head erect." Churchill also spoke: "We have sustained a total, unmitigated defeat. We are in the presence of a disaster of the first magnitude which has befallen Great Britain and France. Do not let us blind ourselves." No one cared. By a vote of 366 to 144, Commons upheld the Prime Minister who went to Scotland to fish. Mahatma Gandhi commented, "Europe has sold her soul for seven days of earthly existence."

The early events of 1939 did not change Chamberlain's view of the future. He observed with some anxiety the Japanese occupation of Hainan and the Spratley Islands. Earl Plymouth warned Tokio in December of the "incalculable consequences" of closing the Open Door and paved the way for the granting of credits to China in March. Downing Street welcomed the reciprocal trade agreement of November 17, 1938, with the United States and looked with approval on the death of the Spanish Republic. Mussolini's demands for French territory, which Chamberlain and Halifax failed to satisfy by their January journey to Paris and Rome, were disturbing. Also disturbing were German proposals to build submarine tonnage up to the British level. Yet this, obviously, was a means of meeting the "Soviet menace." The Wilhelmstrasse said so. The Nazi leaders, however, were slow in showing gratitude for appeasement. "I am still waiting for a sign," said Chamberlain in mid-December, "that they are prepared to make their contribution to peace." They were still slower in pushing toward the Ukraine. Montagu Norman visited Schacht early in January, but the safe and conservative President of the Reichsbank was unfortunately displaced a few weeks later by Walter Funk. Yet Chamberlain still had hopes.

His hopes were not at once shattered by Hitler's seizure of Prague in the Ides of March. This was doubtless the first step toward Kiev and the Caucasus. Halifax asked the press on March 13 not to "propagate rumors or spread distorted views." Bonnet and Sir Eric Phipps in Paris agreed that the Anglo-French "guarantee" to Czechoslovakia did not apply. "The proposed guarantee," explained Chamberlain, "was one against unprovoked aggression. No such aggression has yet taken place." When Ellen Wilkinson asked in Commons whether it was "unprovoked aggression for a country to provoke secession," the Speaker ruled her question out of order. On Wednesday, as Hitler entered the Hradčany in triumph, Chamberlain declared that this had not been contemplated by any of the signatories of the Munich agreement, but "I do not wish to associate myself today with any charges [of bad faith]. It is natural that I should bitterly regret what has occurred. But do not let us on that account be deflected from our course." Simon urged sympathy toward Czechoslovakia but said the guarantee did not apply. "It is really essential that we should not enter into any extensive, general and undefined commitment." The *Daily Mail* opined, "The final disintegration of Czechoslovakia was almost inevitable. . . . It was due to an internal split up, not external aggression."

On Thursday, March 16, Hitler gave Carpatho-Ukraine to Hungary. On Friday, at Birmingham, Chamberlain publicly denounced him for a breach of faith. Munich had been right but the Führer was now violating Munich and the principle of self-determination.

Is this the last attack upon a small State or is it to be followed by others? Is this, in fact, a step in the direction of an effort to dominate the world by force? . . . I am not going to answer [these questions] tonight but I am sure they will require grave and serious consideration. . . . While I am not prepared to engage this country by new and unspecified commitments operating under conditions which cannot now be foreseen, yet no greater mistake could be made than to suppose that because it believes war to be a senseless and a cruel thing, this nation has so lost its fibre that it will not take part to the utmost of its power in resisting such a challenge if it ever were made.

There followed belated and hesitant efforts to rebuild a coalition against the Reich upon the ruins of appeasement. On March 31, 1939, Chamberlain informed Commons that the British Government, pending the conclusion of the extensive negotiations under way, would give Poland all the support in its power "in the event of any action which clearly threatened Polish independence, and which the Polish Government accordingly considered it vital to resist with their national forces." At the conclusion of Beck's visit to London (April 3 to 6), it was announced that "the two countries were prepared to enter into an agreement of a permanent and reciprocal character to replace the present temporary and unilateral assurance." Meanwhile Poland would consider itself "under an obligation to render assistance to H.M. Government under the same conditions as those contained in the temporary assurance already given by H.M. Government to Poland." For the first time in twenty years, Downing Street had entered into a bilateral pledge of mutual defense with an eastern European State. On August 25, 1939, a formal five-year Anglo-Polish alliance was signed, pledging the parties to give one another all the support in their power in case of either "becoming engaged in hostilities with a European Power in consequence of aggression by the latter against that Contracting Party" or in consequence of a direct or indirect threat to the independence of either, requiring resistance. Provision was made for military consultation. In the event of hostilities, the signatories would conclude no armistice or peace save by mutual consent.

On April 13, 1939, following the Italian annexation of Albania, Chamberlain told Commons that he was "disappointed" but that "nothing that has happened has in any way altered my conviction that the policy of H.M. Government in signing the Anglo-Italian agreement a year ago was right." He announced, however, that the Government was prepared to lend Greece and Rumania all the support in its power "in the event of any action being taken which clearly threatened the independence of either, and which the Greek or Rumanian Governments respectively consider it vital to resist with their national forces."

On May 12, Chamberlain told Commons that, pending the conclusion of a definitive alliance with Turkey, "H.M. Government and the Turkish Government declared that in the event of aggression leading to war in the Mediterranean area they would be prepared to cooperate effectively and lend each other all aid and assistance in their power." On October 19, 1939, Turkey signed a fifteen-year treaty of mutual assistance with Britain and France who pledged aid to Ankara in case of attack by any European Power. All agreed to aid one another in case of aggression by a European Power leading to war in the Mediterranean. By Article 3,

So long as the guarantee given by France and the United Kingdom to Greece and Rumania by the respective declarations on April 13, 1939, remain in force, Turkey will cooperate effectively with France and the United Kingdom, and will lend them all aid and assistance in its power, in the event of France and the United Kingdom being engaged in·hostilities in virtue of either of the said guarantees.

This presumably meant that Turkey was pledged to keep open the Straits if France and Great Britain should be obliged to go to Rumania's aid. But a supplementary protocol asserted, "The obligations undertaken by Turkey in virtue of the above-mentioned treaty cannot require that country to take action having as its effect or involving as its consequence entry into armed conflict with the U.S.S.R." Moscow was thus left with a veto over Turkish policy if it chose to threaten war. Should Italy enter the war, Turkey would aid the allies, but only on condition that the guarantees to Greece and Rumania remained in force and that aid involved no conflict with Russia. This last success of Allied effort to complete the "peace front" was to prove as futile as earlier steps. The Italian declaration of war coincided with the collapse of France and the Rumanian repudiation of the British guarantee. Turkey, therefore, remained neutral.

On other fronts, this intended coalition failed completely of its purpose. It neither deterred the Axis from risking war nor did it afford to the Western Powers any allies sufficiently powerful to save them from defeat. Poland was to be crushed like an eggshell. Rumania and Greece had assumed no reciprocal obligations to come to the aid of France and Britain. The Allied guarantee to Bucharest proved wholly illusory. The kingdom was partitioned and its remnant occupied by the Reich without resistance in the autumn of 1940. When Italy invaded Greece, Britain was able, thanks to naval control of the Mediterranean, to come to the aid of Athens and strike heavy blows at the foe from Greek bases. Even the attack upon Greece did not move Turkey to enter the war. Whether a German assault through Rumania and Bulgaria would bring Turkey to Britain's side was uncertain during the early months of 1941.

The central difficulty in the projected coalition was that it bore no relationship to the obvious rules of arithmetic in the game of power politics. Poland, Rumania, and Turkey could be protected against the Reich only by the U.S.S.R. The considerations which prompted Chamberlain to guarantee Warsaw and Bucharest before opening negotiations with Moscow and to refuse Stalin's price for an alliance until it was too late were legacies of "appeasement" which proved fatal to the whole enterprise. As failure became apparent in the summer of 1939, the Tory leaders, far from adopting a more realistic program, sought to revert to appeasement. British spokesmen reiterated their willingness to settle all differences through "negotiation." In May, Chamberlain and Simon permitted the Reich, through the Bank of International Settlements, to secure control of some million pounds in Czech gold held in London. In July, Sir Horace Wilson and Robert S. Hudson entered into discussion with Hitler's economic adviser, Dr. Helmuth Wohlthat, for a British "disarmament loan" of a billion pounds sterling. Chamberlain declared the discussions wholly "unofficial." Nothing came of them, but they revealed a state of mind which brought no comfort to those who hoped for the establishment of a firm and powerful anti-Nazi coalition. Downing Street, moreover, would not even lend money to Poland unless Warsaw agreed to spend it in Britain. On July 24, Chamberlain recognized that "the Japanese forces in China have special requirements for the purpose of safeguarding their own security and maintaining public order in the regions under their control and that they have to suppress or remove such causes or acts as will obstruct them or benefit their enemies. . . . British authorities and British nationals in China should refrain from such acts and measures."

That the British negotiations with the only Power which could have served as an adequate counterweight to the Axis should have come to nothing was not unnatural, given such leadership as this. Lloyd George, Churchill, and other realists issued repeated warnings during the last spring of peace that all the Cabinet's efforts would be vain unless the Soviet Union were enlisted in the coalition. But Chamberlain and Halifax could never bring themselves to a realization of the urgency of securing Moscow's collaboration. They were therefore unable to overcome their chronic anti-Soviet prejudices and strike a viable bargain with the Kremlin. Litvinov's plea of March for a conference was rejected, as his similar plea after *Anschluss* had been. Not until mid-April were any negotiations undertaken. London desired no alliance and no offense to the anti-Comintern Powers. Litvinov's resignation on May 7 produced no awakening.

In the tedious discussions which dragged through five months,[1] Moscow demanded a binding alliance for mutual defense against any attack on the signatories or any attack or indirect aggression against the Baltic States. Moscow also demanded, as an elementary strategic necessity, military access to Polish territory if the U.S.S.R. was to assume obligations to defend Poland. Chamberlain and Halifax, however, having lightly sacrificed China, Ethiopia, Spain, Austria, Czechoslovakia, and Albania to the Fascist aggressors, now became inflexible champions of the "rights of small nations." Since the Baltic States wanted no guarantee, London would make no pact with Moscow granting them one. Since Poland's leaders would rather see their State perish at the hands of Hitler than accept military aid from the hands of Stalin, London could not or would not meet the terms of Molotov and Voroshilov. When the diplomatic discussions got nowhere, Chamberlain sent as special envoy to assist Ambassador Sir William Seeds one of his most devoted Munichmen, William Strang. When the *Strang nach Osten* also produced no results, an Anglo-French military mission (of wholly undistinguished personnel) was sent in August. In all cases, however, London and Paris would not meet Stalin's terms. But beggars cannot be choosers. Stalin, not being a beggar, had no need to conclude a pact with the Western Powers on conditions he regarded as strategically unworkable and highly dangerous to the U.S.S.R. Hitler was quite willing to grant him, in exchange for mere neutrality, what Chamberlain would not grant in exchange for an alliance. Despite their denials, Chamberlain and Daladier knew this early in May and throughout June. They still preferred to reject the Kremlin's terms. Stalin therefore made the obvious choice. His nonaggression pact with Berlin of August 23 left the Western Powers isolated in the face of a formidable foe.

Never did modern Britain embark upon a war under such perilous circumstances as prevailed in 1939. The cause had already been all but lost at Madrid and Munich and Moscow. To fight the Reich with no allies save a feeble Poland ruled by a Beck and a defeated France ruled by a Daladier and a Bonnet was to invite disaster. Yet not to fight was to invite destruction, for even a Chamberlain was now dimly aware of Hitler's objectives and methods. After two days of doubt, due primarily to Bonnet's intrigues to desert Warsaw, the Prime Minister did what had to be done. At 11:15 A.M. on September 3, Halifax delivered a note to German Chargé Kordt, informing him that, since no reply had been received to the British ultimatum, the two Powers were at war as of 11:00 A.M. Chamberlain told Commons,

> When I spoke last night to the House I could not but be aware that in some parts of the House there were doubts and some bewilderment as to whether there

[1] For detailed account, see this writer's *Night over Europe*, pp. 216–284.

had been any weakening, hesitation, or vacillation on the part of H.M. Government. In the circumstances, I make no reproach, for if I had been in the same position as hon. members not sitting on this Bench and not in possession of all the information which we have, I should very likely have felt the same. The statement which I have to make this morning will show that there were no grounds for doubt. . . . This is a sad day for all of us, and to none is it sadder than to me. Everything that I have worked for, everything that I have hoped for, everything that I have believed in during my public life, has crashed into ruins. There is only one thing left for me to do; that is, to devote what strength and powers I have to forwarding the victory of the cause for which we have to sacrifice so much. I cannot tell what part I may be allowed to play myself; I trust I may live to see the day when Hitlerism has been destroyed and a liberated Europe has been reestablished.

This was not to be. The man from Birmingham was not to survive the fearful misery he had brought upon his country. Whether his nation would survive was doubtful. Poland perished at once. For eight months thereafter the Tory Munichmen clung tenaciously to their posts and directed the war under the slogan of "business as usual." In the War Cabinet of September were included two major critics of their policies: Anthony Eden as Dominion Secretary, and Winston Churchill in his 1914 post of First Lord of the Admiralty. But no Liberals or Laborites would serve in any government headed by Chamberlain. Save for the displacement of Leslie Hore-Belisha by Oliver Stanley as War Secretary in January, 1940, no major changes took place in the Cabinet until the advent of catastrophe. The armaments with which Tory leadership had supplied Britain fell as far short of the requirements of waging effective war as Tory diplomacy had fallen short of the requirements of defending peace. Only the Navy remained in a high state of efficiency. The Royal Air Force, though qualitatively excellent and growing in size, was pitiably small. As for the Army, conscription had not been introduced until April, 1939. The B.E.F. in France was to find that it had no armored divisions capable of coping with the *Blitzkrieg* and no commanders who would have known how to use them had they existed. Yet Chamberlain expressed imperturbable confidence and held that Hitler had "missed the bus."

The débâcle of British arms in Norway foreshadowed what was to come. On May 7, 1940, the Prime Minister weakly defended his course in Commons. But it was clear that he was losing the war as he had lost the peace. Leopold S. Amery, rebel Conservative, drew cheers when he quoted Oliver Cromwell: "You have sat too long here for any good you have been doing. Depart, I say. Let us have done with you. In the name of God, go." But Chamberlain had no desire to go. His Tory majority, as always, voted "confidence." But the vote was 281 to 200. A majority of 81 was a defeat in a house normally conservative by a margin of 210. For two days Chamberlain sought in vain to persuade the Labor leaders to join the Cabinet. At dawn of May 10 the Nazi hosts struck at the Low Countries with irresistible force. Chamberlain resigned that night. He remained in the new Cabinet as Lord President of the Council but fell ill and resigned on October 3. On November 9, 1940, he died.

If England still lived, the credit for survival was due to Winston Churchill and to the millions of men and women whom he rallied to devotion and sacrifice in a cause they had all but forgotten under Churchill's puny predecessors. In the Ministry of May, Eden became War Secretary and Alfred Duff-Cooper Minister of Information. Liberal Sir Archibald Sinclair and Laborites Clement Attlee, Albert Alexander, Herbert Morrison, Ernest Bevin, and Arthur Greenwood all were included. Churchill told Commons on May 13, "I have nothing to offer but blood, tears, toil, and sweat. . . . Our policy? It is to wage war by land, sea, and air. War with all our might and with all the strength God has given us, and to wage war against a monstrous tyranny never surpassed in the dark and lamentable catalogue of human crime. . . . Our aim? It is victory. Victory at all costs—victory in spite of all terrors—victory, however long and hard the road may be, for without victory there is no survival."

On June 18, 1940, 125 years after Waterloo and immediately after the fearful débâcle on the Continent, Churchill warned his countrymen,

What General Weygand called the Battle of France is over. The Battle of Britain is about to begin. On this battle depends the survival of Christian civilization. Upon it depends our own British life and the long continuity of our institutions and our empire. The whole fury and might of the enemy must very soon be turned upon us. Hitler knows he will have to break us in this island or lose the war.

If we can stand up to him all Europe may be freed and the life of the world may move forward into broad sunlit uplands; but if we fail, the whole world, including the United States and all that we have known and cared for, will sink into the abyss of a new Dark Age made more sinister and perhaps more prolonged by the lights of a perverted science.

Let us therefore brace ourselves to our duty and so bear ourselves that if the British Commonwealth and Empire last for a thousand years, men will still say "This was their finest hour."

After a summer lull in which military operations paused and obscure peace overtures came to nothing, Goering's *Luftwaffe* opened an "all out" assault on London in the hope of "softening England for invasion." Endless relays of hundreds of bombers made day and night hideous, slaying thousands and tens of thousands of civilians, burning whole blocks of houses, smashing factories, schools, churches, palaces, tenements, and many of the architectural treasures of the centuries. The world's greatest city suffered a fate far worse than that of Barcelona. Coventry was blasted as completely as Guernica and probably by some of the same aviators. Manchester, Liverpool, Southampton, Birmingham, and a dozen lesser towns knew horrors hitherto known only to the people of Shanghai, Addis Ababa, Madrid, and Warsaw. British aircraft production and shipbuilding were retarded. But the people of Britain refused to be terrorized into submission. Their resistance hardened to steel, for they followed a great leader who promised them no comforts and told them no lies. "Death and sorrow will be our companions on the journey, hardship our garment, constancy and valor our only shield. We must be reunited, we must be undaunted, we must be inflexible. Our qualities and deeds must burn and glow through the gloom of Europe until they become the veritable beacons of its salvation."

To such summons the people of Britain and of all the Empire (save only neutral Eire) responded with a vigor and courage which caused Axis journalists to wonder anxiously whether their last unconquered foe consisted of "47 million Churchills." Faith begot works. Faithful work, inspired by new foresight and able leadership, begot local victories which might ultimately prove important. Greece was defended, Albania invaded, and the Italian fleet driven to cover. Graziani's Libyan army was ejected from western Egypt, whence it had hoped to push on toward Suez, by General Sir Archibald Wavell's mechanized "British and Imperial Army of the Nile," valorously aided by the R.A.F. and the mighty ships of war of the Mediterranean fleet. Sidi Barrani was retaken on December 11 and the important Libyan base of Bardia on January 5. Tobruk was next (January 22, 1941) and then Derne (January 30) and Bengazi (February 6). The next goal, Tripoli, was far off in the western desert. Haile Selassie returned to Africa to reconquer his kingdom with British aid. The liberation of all of Mussolini's African empire from Fascist rule seemed a possibility of the spring unless Hitler by some improbable miracle could save his ally. Beyond this prospect loomed the defeat of Italy, or its salvation through an unwelcome and dangerous German occupation. Evidences of a new democracy offered promise for the more distant future. The Munichmen slowly faded from the political scene—Hoare to Madrid, Simon to Lords, Halifax to the British Embassy in Washington in January, 1941, to replace the late Marquess of Lothian. Eden resumed his old post as Foreign Minister. There was little evidence during the second year of hostilities of any general awareness of the need of framing and defending a democratic "new world order" to meet the Triplice challenge, but this might come in the fullness of time.

All these hopes and every hope of victory, however, depended upon the possibility of thwarting the attempt at large-scale invasion which was all but certain to come from the Continent during 1941. This hope in turn depended upon American or Soviet aid. If such aid were too little or too late, all might be lost. If Britain stood fast, then the hope of final victory would depend even more on American or Soviet assistance, for it was improbable that the British Commonwealth alone could break the Nazi realm. This was a task for a united Anglo-Saxony or for a counter-Triplice of the United States, the British Empire, and the Soviet Union. Whether Britain would stand, and if so whether Americans and Russians would do what was requisite for their own safety and for the remaking of the world society, were the questions upon which the fate of Britain and of all of Western mankind depended at the fiery dawn of a new decade.

SUGGESTED READINGS

Adams, J. T.: *Empire on the Seven Seas*, New York, Scribner, 1940.
Angell, Norman: *For What Do We Fight?* New York, Harper, 1940.
Benham, F.: *Great Britain Under Protection*, New York, Macmillan, 1940.
Briffault, Robert: *The Decline and Fall of the British Empire*, New York, Simon & Schuster, 1938.
The British War Blue Book, 1939, New York, Farrar, 1939.
Catlin, G.: *Anglo-Saxony and Its Tradition*, New York, Macmillan 1939.
Chamberlain, Neville: *In Search of Peace*, New York, Putnam, 1939.
Churchill, Winston: *While England Slept*, New York, Putnam, 1938.
———: *Step by Step*, 1936–1939, New York, Putnam, 1939.
———: *Blood, Sweat and Tears*, New York, Putnam, 1941.
Dangerfield, G.: *The Strange Death of Liberal England*, New York, Random House, 1936.
Eden, Anthony: *Foreign Affairs*, New York, Harcourt, 1939.
Elliott, W. Y.: *The New British Empire*, New York, McGraw-Hill, 1932.
Garratt, G. T.: *Gibraltar and the Mediterranean*, New York, Coward-McCann, 1939.
Gedye, G. E. R.: *Betrayal in Central Europe*, New York, Harper, 1939.
Halifax, Lord: *Speeches on Foreign Policy, 1934–1939*, New York, Oxford, 1940.
Henderson, Nevile: *Failure of a Mission*, New York, Putnam, 1940.
Hindus, Maurice: *We Shall Live Again* (Czechoslovakia), New York, Doubleday, 1939.
Ingersoll, R.: *Report on England* (November, 1940), New York, Simon & Schuster, 1940.
Johnson, A. C.: *Anthony Eden*, New York, Washburn, 1939.
Kerner, R. J. (ed.): *Czechoslovakia: Twenty Years of Independence*, Berkeley, University of California, 1940.
Kraus, R.: *Winston Churchill*, Philadelphia, Lippincott, 1940.
Liddell-Hart, B. H.: *The Defense of Britain*, New York, Random House, 1939.
Lohrke, E. and A.: *Night over England: A Report*, New York, Harrison-Hilton, 1939.
Londonderry, the Marquess of: *Ourselves and Germany*, London, Robert Hale & Co., Ltd., 1938.
Maddox, W. P.: *Foreign Relations in British Labour Politics*, 1900–1924, Cambridge, Mass., Harvard University Press, 1933.
Marder, A. J.: *The Anatomy of British Sea Power*, 1880–1905, New York, Knopf, 1940.
Martin, K.: *The Magic of Monarchy*, New York, Knopf, 1937.
Petrie, Sir Charles: *The Chamberlain Tradition*, London, Dickson, 1938.
Temperley, H., and L. M. Penson: *Foundations of British Foreign Policy*, New York, Macmillan, 1939.
Viton, A.: *Great Britain: An Empire in Transition*, New York, Day, 1940.
Wolfers, A.: *Britain and France between Two Wars*, New York, Harcourt, 1940.

3. THE ISOLATION OF AMERICA

It is the duty of those who stand apart from a war to do nothing which may strengthen the side whose cause is unjust, or which may hinder the movements of him who is carrying on a just war; and in a doubtful case, to act alike to both sides.—HUGO GROTIUS, *De Jure Belli ac Pacis*, 1625.

It is very difficult to ascertain, at present, what degree of sagacity the American democracy will display in the conduct of the foreign policy of the country; and upon this point its adversaries, as well as its advocates, must suspend their judgment.—ALEXIS DE TOCQUEVILLE, *Democracy in America*, 1839.

A country is either well armed, as that of the Romans was, or as that of the Swiss is nowadays; or it is not well armed, as was the case with the Carthaginians, and is at present with France and Italy. In the latter case you must keep the enemy at a distance; for as your strength consists in your money, and not in soldiers, you are lost whenever you are prevented from availing of your financial resources, and nothing interferes so much with that as war within your own territory.—NICCOLÒ MACHIAVELLI, *The Discourses*.

The hidden civil war within the Western soul which paralyzed France and Britain during the Great Depression and rendered them ripe for conquest had its counterpart in the North American Republic. Fear of Communism on the part of people of property was no less acute than in the Western European democracies, despite the political insignificance of the noisy American section of the Communist International. Admiration for Fascism was less widespread, doubtless because of the absence of any aristocratic tradition in American society and the greater devotion of all classes to democratic ideals of tolerance. The cleavage between "isolationists" and "interventionists," however, was deeper than in Western Europe—with a significant reversal of roles. Anglo-French isolationists tended to be political conservatives or reactionaries, speaking for blue blood and large bank accounts, whereas proponents of collective security and world order were more frequently liberal or radical spokesmen for workers, peasants, and small businessmen. In America, on the other hand, "big business" was largely "internationalist" or "interventionist" whereas those who claimed to speak for urban workers, western farmers, and the lower middle class followed a tradition of Liberalism or "Progressivism" which was heavily charged with xenophobia, isolationism, and fear of foreign entanglements.

Thus, charges of "dragging the country into war" were hurled by Anglo-French aristocrats and industrialists against liberals and radicals, and by American liberals and radicals against arms manufacturers, Wall Street, and the "international bankers." Another difference was that in

France and Britain political power holders reflected the desires and prejudices of the monied *élite*, even during the interlude of the People's Front in France, whereas the American "New Deal" aroused bitter resentment among businessmen, large and small. The political scene in the United States was further confused by the circumstance that the isolationism of Harding, Coolidge, and Hoover was opposed by the business elements whose interests these administrations favored and was approved by the farmers and wage earners of the hinterland. The "internationalism" of Franklin D. Roosevelt, on the other hand, was approved by most of the businessmen who disliked him most cordially and was opposed by many of the provincial farmers and workers who elected him.

Such cleavages did not make for national unity until the eleventh hour. They served to obscure the central problem of American foreign policy in the 1930's and to prevent any relevant action until disaster was imminent. That problem was one of awakening Americans to the changed nature of the world and of their place in it. It was one of educating them out of the dangerous superstitions and delusions inherited from a past which few of them understood. It was one of moving them to support diplomatic and military policies which offered some hope of safeguarding the Republic from the designs of the world-conquering Caesars who had grown great through the indolence and paralysis of all the democratic States. Until the Year of Terror, 1940, most Americans reacted toward the challenge of the twentieth century with nonrational stereotypes derived from the imagined experiences of their forebears in the eighteenth and nineteenth centuries. To discard old attitudes and habits was painful. To devise new ones based on a correct perception of external realities was difficult. Whether the transformation was taking place in time to avert the fatal isolation of America in a dangerous world was uncertain as these words were written.

ISOLATIONISM AND REALPOLITIK. All people possess some capacity to learn from experience. But when lessons once learned are embalmed in magic phrases which stir emotions deeply and thereby inhibit rational adjustment to new problems, then the products of experience are obstacles rather than aids to new learning. They render more difficult the task of facing emergencies and achieving that progressive adaptation to environmental change which is the prerequisite of survival for all living things. Still more is this the case when the magic phrases are not only irrelevant today and dangerous tomorrow but false as descriptions of yesterday.

In terms of techniques of communication, transportation, travel, and war, the entire planet on which Americans somewhat reluctantly found themselves in 1941 was a far smaller place than the thirteen states of the Union in 1790. It is simple to say that America's dilemma of the 1930's was the result of the persistence of attitudes toward the world which were relevant and adequate a hundred years and more before but had ceased to be safe guides to action (or inaction) after the revolutionary transformation of the world society effected by science and technology. In terms of *Realpolitik*, however, "isolationism," with its corollary of security through nonintervention and nonentanglement, was never a reality. America was settled by Europeans and was continuously a part of European civilization and of the European State system since the days of Columbus. The United States won its independence only because the rebels of 1776 made a military alliance with France (February 6, 1778) and because Spain and Holland also entered the fray. The Latin American Republics likewise won their independence in consequence of a European war. They preserved their freedom less because of the Monroe Doctrine of 1823 forbidding further European colonization, intervention, or interposition in the Western Hemisphere than because Great Britain, for commercial reasons, favored independence and opposed attempts by Continental Powers to reassert their sovereignty over the New World. After 1815, following the failure of the American attempt to conquer Canada, there was uninterrupted peace between the United States and Britain—and a tacit agreement to abandon all efforts to play the game of power against one another.

For a hundred years thereafter all Americans, North and South, were the almost unconscious beneficiaries of a world balance of power which was unique and temporary but was confused in most American minds (when they were aware of it at all) with the unchanging pattern of the cosmos. The elements of that balance were three: (1) the preponderance of British naval power in the Atlantic and in most other seas; (2) the maintenance of a stable equilibrium on the European Continent by which no one Power could successfully threaten the others with subjugation or seriously endanger the British Empire; and (3) the inability of any Continental or Asiatic Powers, singly or in combination, to challenge the United States or menace Latin America. The first element involved no danger to the Americas; for British "capitalism" and "imperialism," far from harboring territorial designs in the western sphere or cherishing any desire to compete for power with the United States, were inspired by solicitude for Anglo-American collaboration on the basis of a common interest in preserving the world balance and keeping open the world channels of trade and investment. British sea power was therefore a shield between America and Europe rather than a sword pointed toward the New World. The second element in the balance was in part a product of a long-standing British policy of preventing the domination of the Continent by any one Power. The third element was a direct result of the first and second.

So long as Britain stood firm, Americans were safe in "splendid isolation." They could therefore engage safely in the periodic recreation of "twisting the lion's tail," and they could fancy that their security and prosperity were products not of the world balance but of their own wisdom in "minding their own business" and avoiding "foreign entanglements." They could imagine that the Monroe Doctrine kept Latin America free from the impact of European and Asiatic imperialisms. They could define American interests abroad in negative terms of neutrality and abstention from power politics and in positive terms of promoting commerce by championing neutral trading rights, freedom of the seas, most-favored-nation treatment, and the Open Door in the Orient. The underlying facts of power relationships which made these policies practicable were seldom perceived and little appreciated. The verbiage employed was harmless so long as the facts remained unchanged. It was potentially disastrous should the facts be altered and should Americans suppose that their safety was a result of the verbiage rather than of the facts.[1]

1917 AND AFTER. The first serious Continental challenge to Britain since Napoleon put the issue to its first major test. The outbreak of hostilities between the two European coalitions in 1914 caused the United States to proclaim its neutrality, as it had done in 1793 and in all subsequent European wars. An immensely profitable trade in munitions at once developed with the Allies. The effective Allied blockade of Germany prevented this trade from going to both sets of belligerents. But the continuation of this commerce was threatened by the efforts of the warring governments to injure one another economically by cutting off trade between the enemy and the outside world. The United States, in defending the liberty of its traders to do business of this kind, reverted to the principles of neutral rights and freedom of the seas, which it had evolved under comparable circumstances between 1793 and 1812. It protested the British contraband list, the British blockade, and the British interpretation of the doctrine of continuous voyage. It likewise protested the German submarine blockade of the Allies and was soon involved in acrimonious controversy with both sides.

---

[1] Albert K. Weinberg in "The Historical Meaning of the American Doctrine of Isolation," *American Political Science Review,* June, 1940, puts the matter cogently. "The classic definition of American isolation is that it is not a theory but a predicament. . . . Isolation is a theory about a theory of American foreign policy. Because this interpretation is a poor theory, misrepresentative even if taken only semi-literally, it has placed the discussion of American foreign policy in a sad predicament of obfuscation, not without its influence upon national decisions. . . . In appraising meliorative collaboration by the standard of national tradition, Americans may do well to consider that the true objective of their historic caution was not isolation, a friendlessness which may subject their destiny to their enemies, but an ideal interpreted to the nation by Washington as 'the command of its own fortunes.'"

In the sequel the United States leaned more and more toward the Allies, and this not for humanitarian or sentimental reasons expressed in war slogans, but for very tangible considerations connected with business and power politics. American capitalists made huge loans to the Allied Governments, and American exporters sold, at great profit, huge quantities of goods to the borrowers. Allied defeat would probably mean Allied bankruptcy. American business had little to lose and everything to gain from Allied victory. A victory of the Central Powers would not only imperil these economic interests but would completely upset the balance of power and give Germany such a position of overwhelming preponderance on the Continent and throughout the world that even American security might eventually be endangered. Circumstances permitted these economic and political interests to be presented on a high moral plane. Germany was an "autocracy," and the Allies and the United States were "democracies." The Allied cruiser blockade of Germany menaced American property and American legal rights, but the U-boat blockade of the Allies endangered American lives as well. Germany was ruthless, lawless, uncivilized. The Allies were considerate, law-abiding, and virtuous. When Germany announced the resumption of unrestricted submarine warfare, on February 1, 1917, President Wilson severed diplomatic relations. On April 6, 1917, the United States declared war on Germany. Other American States were induced to follow suit. The United States became an "Associate" of the Allies, not an "Ally." A large army was conscripted, trained, and sent to France. A strengthened American navy joined the Allied squadrons. Billions of dollars were raised and loaned to the Allied Governments. The immense economic power of the United States more than overbalanced the defection of Russia, and its support was sufficient to turn the scales. Neutrality had failed to protect American interests, and isolation was abandoned in favor of active participation in the European contest. Victory came in 1918, and the United States shared in the glory thereof.

The disillusioning aftermath produced a violent popular reversion to extreme isolationism. Wilson went to the Paris Peace Conference, participated actively in the making of the treaty, took the initiative in the creation of the League of Nations, and committed the United States to cooperation with other Powers in preserving peace and dealing with post-war problems. On his return home he found himself a prophet without honor in his own land. The Treaty of Versailles was rejected by the Senate, with the Covenant of the League as the chief target of attack. Wilson and all his works were repudiated by Congress and the electorate. He retired from public life a defeated and broken man. The narrow partisanship of some Republicans and the personal animosity of Henry Cabot Lodge, Sr. (who had urged American membership in a league of nations in 1916) were primarily responsible for his defeat, along with his own obstinacy and the doubtful wisdom of the founding fathers in requiring approval of treaties by two-thirds of the Senate. On March 19, 1920, the final vote on the ratifying resolution was taken. It showed 49 Senators for and 35 against. The Covenant thus fell short by 7 votes of securing the necessary two-thirds.

In the election of 1920 the Democratic candidate, James Cox, was overwhelmed by the Republicans under Warren Gamaliel Harding, and the way was prepared for twelve continuous years of Republican rule. In foreign policy, Republican rule meant isolationism with a vengeance. A separate peace was made with Germany on August 25, 1921. The League was first ignored, then recognized as a stubbornly irreducible fact, and later used, through its conferences and commissions, as an agency of cooperation—timidly at the outset and later with more confidence. American entrance into the World Court was pledged, but the pledge remained unfulfilled. The ill-fated intervention in Russia of 1918–1920 was abandoned, but diplomatic recognition was sternly refused to the Soviet Government, even after all the other Great Powers had recognized it. High moral and legal principles were found to justify this attitude, but at bottom it reflected the deep hostility of the businessmen's government of the most capitalistic of modern States toward proletarian Communism. Immigration was cut off, and almost insurmountable tariff walls were erected, for isolationism and economic nationalism were opposite sides of the same coin. The Allies were required to sign on the dotted line for the repayment of their war debts. American dollar diplomacy in the Caribbean was continued in the best tradition, but Latin American sensibilities (which had a relationship to profitable trade) were soothed with assurances that the United States had no imperialistic designs and that the Monroe Doctrine was not what it seemed to be. The Open Door policy in Asia was reiterated. In short, the exclusive pursuit of American national interests was again couched in terms of long-established principles and policies.

During the 1920's the United States, as the most powerful of the Great Powers, helped to make impossible the establishment of a viable world order to supersede the politics of power. Its nonmembership in the League was not in fact, whatever it seemed to be in form, a merely negative policy. The United States had fought four wars in defense of the right of its citizens to trade with belligerents. Should the League Powers commit themselves to an economic boycott of an aggressor, they would face the alternatives of seeing the boycott broken by American ships and goods or of provoking sharp controversy with Washington by challenging the right of Americans to trade with a lawbreaker. Secretary of State Charles E. Hughes and British Ambassador Sir Esme Howard discussed the issue in January, 1925, in connection with the implications of the Covenant, the Geneva Protocol, and the Locarno Treaties. Hughes declared "that there was one thing he believed could be depended upon, and that was that this Government from its very beginning had been insistent upon the rights of neutrals and would continue to maintain them. The Secretary did not believe any Administration, short of a treaty concluded and ratified, could commit the country against assertion of its neutral rights in case there should be occasion to demand their recognition."[1] Under these conditions, it was easy for Anglo-French isolationists to repudiate, and later to betray, collective security on the ground that sanctions against aggressors would mean conflict with America.[2]

Despite this obstructionism, the Republican Administration made various gestures in the direction of peace, disarmament, and international cooperation. In 1921 the United States summoned the Washington Conference, where it secured naval parity with Great Britain in capital ships, in return for a general reduction of naval armaments. It likewise secured a new recognition of the Open Door principle and Japanese withdrawal from Shantung and Siberia, in return for the abandonment of its bid for naval supremacy in the Pacific. In 1937, it sought to promote further naval disarmament in the abortive Coolidge conference at Geneva. In 1928, it sponsored the Kellogg-Briand Pact for the outlawry of war. In 1930, it participated in the five Power naval conference in London, where it acquired complete naval parity with Great Britain but no substantial reduction of naval armaments, because of Anglo-American differences regarding cruisers and Franco-Italian naval rivalry in the Mediterranean. In 1931, it cooperated with the Council of the League of Nations in the Manchurian crisis, though without tangible results. In 1932 the Hoover moratorium proposal for a one-year suspension of all reparation and debt payments was presented as a generous move toward world economic and financial rehabilitation. The United States likewise participated in the General Disarmament Conference of the League of Nations and eloquently urged armament reduction, without being willing to commit itself to consultation or cooperation with other Powers in the interests of peace. By all of these moves, national interests, moral principles, and humanitarian ideals were simultaneously served. And if none of them was served wisely or well in the long run, the cause lay in the refusal of Congress and

[1] *Foreign Relations of the United States*, 1925, U.S. Department of State, December, 1940, 2 vols.

[2] It was this situation which caused Nicholas Murray Butler to write in 1927 in *The Path to Peace*, "Unhappily, the policies as to international affairs—or perhaps the lack of policies—that have been pursued by our Government since the Armistice, have made this nation of ours a dangerous derelict adrift on the high seas of international intercourse, and lying straight across the path of every ship that sails laden with the precious cargo of international friendship and concord."

the country either to implement patriotic power interests with Machiavellian diplomacy or to implement idealistic aspirations with concrete political arrangements contrary to past tradition.

THE NEW DEAL. The diplomatic problems of the first administration of President Franklin D. Roosevelt (1933–1937) necessarily centered in the tasks of restoring commerce in a world sorely afflicted with economic maladjustments and of promoting peace in a world drifting toward war. As a satiated Power, the United States championed peace—and was willing to make minor sacrifices for its preservation within the limits of the isolationist tradition. As a commercial Power and a creditor nation the United States championed a restoration of international trade—within the limits of tariff protectionism. In both cases the gap between hope and achievement was due in part to conditions abroad over which Washington had no control and in part to attitudes and vested interests at home which made impossible a larger degree of cooperation with other States.

In the quest for prosperity, the abandonment of the gold standard and the subsequent depreciation of the dollar by 41 per cent stimulated exports and discouraged imports from countries still on gold. Efforts to secure an international reduction of trade barriers at the London Economic Conference of June and July, 1933, failed because other Powers were unwilling to reduce tariffs without a guarantee against further depreciation of the dollar and Washington was unwilling to accept any agreement for currency stabilization. The abandonment of gold by France, the Netherlands, and Switzerland in September, 1936, was accompanied by provisional Anglo-French-American cooperation to prevent wide currency fluctuations, but no permanent stabilization was achieved. Secretary of State Cordell Hull, under authority of the Tariff Act of 1934, meanwhile negotiated a series of reciprocity agreements for mutual reduction of duties with the benefits extended to all States not discriminating against American goods and having unconditional most-favored-nation clauses in their treaties with the United States. International trade recovered gradually from the low point of 1932. Total American foreign trade declined from $9,640,000,000 in 1929 to $2,935,-000,000 in 1932 and then increased to $4,280,000,000 in 1935 and to approximately $5,000,000,000 in 1936.

The quest for peace was more difficult. Logic posed three alternatives. The United States could protect its interests abroad in an insecure world by overwhelming armaments; it could abandon these interests or refuse them protection and retire into economic as well as political isolationism; or it could cooperate with other Powers interested in maintaining peace, either through alliances against potential aggressors or through participation in international organization and collective security. Unilateral protection of interests by force meant an arms race and eventually war.

Complete abandonment of interests abroad was economically and politically impossible. Cooperation with other Powers was rendered difficult by the isolationist tradition and by the inability of other Powers to cooperate among themselves. Circumstances therefore dictated a policy of illogical compromise among the three possible courses.

Cooperation for peace was promoted by continued advocacy of general disarmament and occasional lip service to the Kellogg Pact and the Stimson Doctrine, all without tangible results. The United States became a member of the I.L.O. in 1934, but Administration efforts to achieve membership in the World Court were defeated by the isolationists. Membership in the I.L.O. was achieved by a Joint Congressional Resolution of June 19, 1934, authorizing the President to make the United States a member provided that no obligations were assumed under the League Covenant. Since no formal treaty was necessary, it was impossible for one-third of the Senators to obstruct action. For twelve years, every President, every Secretary of State, and a large majority in both Houses of Congress favored American membership in the Permanent Court of International Justice. But the isolationist Senators, loudly applauded by the Hearst press, the Chicago *Tribune*, Father Coughlin, and sundry superpatriots, attached five reservations to the Protocols in January, 1926. The last of these forbade the Court to "entertain any request for an advisory opinion touching any dispute or question in which the United States has or claims an interest." Since this proviso, if interpreted broadly, would have given the United States a special veto enjoyed by none of the members of the League Council, whence requests for advisory opinions came, efforts were made by Elihu Root and others to secure agreement on an interpretation which would give the United States only a position of equality. The "Root formula" of 1929 solved the problem. The isolationists, however, had no desire to see it solved. On January 29, 1935, the final Senate vote showed 52 in favor of ratification and 36 opposed. The Protocols failed to secure the required two-thirds by a margin of 7 votes. Father Coughlin declared, "Our thanks are due to Almighty God that America retains her sovereignty. Congratulations to the aroused people of the United States who, by more than two hundred thousand telegrams containing at least one million names, demanded that the principles established by Washington and Jefferson shall keep us clear from foreign entanglements and European hatreds."

Despite this victory for the forces of obfuscation, the Administration found it possible to take certain limited steps toward joint action with other Powers. An obstacle to cooperation was removed by belated recognition of the U.S.S.R. On November 16, 1933, Litvinov and Roosevelt exchanged notes at Washington by which recognition was accorded. The two governments agreed to refrain from hostile propaganda. The religious and civil rights of Americans in the U.S.S.R. were elaborately safeguarded. Moscow waived all counterclaims arising out of American military activities in Siberia. Other claims were left for subsequent settlement. It was understood that American claims against the Soviet[1] would be met by increased interest payments on credits extended by the United States to finance increased trade. William C. Bullitt became the first American Ambassador to Moscow. Alexander Troyanovsky came to Washington as Soviet Ambassador. In January, 1935, however, the claims negotiations which were expected to eventuate in a commercial treaty collapsed, owing to Moscow's refusal to meet claims except through repayments on a long-term loan and Washington's refusal to grant a loan on terms satisfactory to the U.S.S.R. But on July 13, 1935, Litvinov and Bullitt signed a one-year trade agreement which stipulated that Moscow would spend 30 million dollars for American goods. On August 25, 1935, and again on August 31, the United States protested emphatically that the Comintern Congress in Moscow was a violation of the propaganda pledge. The Narkomindel replied that it was not responsible for the activities of the Comintern. Despite this controversy, the trade agreement was renewed from year to year, with questions of loans, claims, and propaganda left in abeyance.

Widespread sentiment in favor of withdrawing diplomatic and military protection from American private interests abroad found expression in the "good-neighbor" policy and in the neutrality legislation. Americans were in effect told that their trade and investments in Latin America would not be protected by interventionist activities. They were forbidden to make loans or to sell arms to countries at war. But the enormous economic interests of Americans in the Latin Republics to the south made the first policy a gesture rather than a reality, although imperialism was renounced and protectorates over Cuba, Haiti, and other States were relinquished. The difficulties in the way of severing all economic ties with belligerents were found to be insuperable. Americans were left free to carry on trade in nonmilitary goods with States at war. The development of new economic ties with belligerents was thus not prevented. Curiously enough, no steps were taken toward withdrawal of protection of American economic interests in the Far East, where trade and investments were negligible as compared with Europe and Latin America. In practice, this meant continued insistence on the Open Door in China and therefore friction with Japan.

The failure of disarmament led to intensified preparations for defense and promised to precipitate a naval race in the Pacific. The Vinson Act

---

[1] In November, 1933, the private claims for confiscated property and defaulted obligations were estimated at 623 million dollars. In addition, Russia owed the United States 192 million dollars in war loans, with accumulated interest at $4\frac{1}{2}$ per cent since 1917.

of March 27, 1934, contemplated building the American Navy up to full Treaty strength. The naval appropriation for 1936 was over $\frac{1}{2}$ billion dollars and constituted the largest peacetime appropriation in the history of the Republic. The army and the air force were likewise enlarged. Total expenditures in preparation for war were approaching 1 billion dollars annually by 1937. The Anglo-French-American Naval Treaty of March 25, 1936, provided for qualitative limitation but not for reductions or even quantitative limitation of fleets. On December 31, 1936, the Washington and London naval treaties expired. No new agreement could be reached because of American unwillingness to grant Japanese demands for parity. In the naval race which ensued, it was clear that the United States could easily outbuild Japan. American possessions west of Hawaii, however, remained within the sphere of effective action of the Japanese fleet, and any effort to render them defensible would also make them available for American offensive operations in Japanese waters. There was danger that Japan might seek to meet this "threat" by sudden attack before being hopelessly outbuilt. In the absence of any new American-Japanese understanding, the danger of war for the United States lay less in prospects of involvement in a European conflict than in an armed clash with Japan. The Japanese-German-Italian entente necessarily made impossible any separation of the problems of Japanese-American relations from those of European politics.

IN QUEST OF CONTINENTAL SOLIDARITY. The position of the United States in the Western Hemisphere gave promise of developing to a point at which all the American Republics might evolve common policies toward Europe and Asia. Latin American resentment against the "Colossus of the North" was mitigated by the new orientation at Washington. Latin America's disposition to seek a counterweight to the United States by giving vigorous support to the League of Nations was weakened not only by the failure of League efforts to end the Chaco war but by the costly futility of sanctions against Italy and by the manifest unwillingness of other League members to create a system of collective security capable of preventing aggression. Brazil had withdrawn from Geneva in 1926, and Guatemala, Honduras, and Nicaragua did likewise in 1936. Argentina's Foreign Minister, Dr. Carlos Saavedra Lamas, presided over the 1936 Assembly but was disappointed that no effective steps were taken toward League reform. The Latin States responded favorably to President Roosevelt's invitation of January 30, 1936, to meet in an Inter-American Conference for the Maintenance of Peace. The Conference program was approved by the Governing Board of the Pan-American Union on July 22. The delegates assembled in Buenos Aires on December 1, 1936, with the American President and Secretary of State both addressing the Conference in person. Whether or not an "American League of Nations" might ultimately emerge from these efforts, the new regional peace system was certain to weaken Latin American ties with Geneva and to promote collaboration with Washington. Inter-American peace machinery was clarified and further developed. A joint neutrality policy, based on the Argentine Anti-War Pact and the legislation of the United States, began to take shape. Commercial and cultural relations were strengthened. With Asia and Europe slipping toward the morass of war, Pan-Americanism breathed a new breath of life and offered new hope of pacific cooperation in the Western Hemisphere.

These aspirations were realized only in part. Friction developed between the United States and Mexico over expropriation of foreign-owned oil properties in 1938, although the United States scrupulously refrained from any threats of intervention. Franco's victories in Spain evoked sympathetic echoes among the propertied classes of the Latin American Republics. The establishment of a "totalitarian" dictatorship in Brazil by President Getulio Vargas in 1937 was not reassuring. Nazi and Fascist agents sowed the seeds of anti-Semitism, anti-Communism, and Yankee-phobia. The Eighth International Conference of American States met in Lima, Peru, in December, 1938. The United States sent a dozen delegates, including Secretary of State Hull and Alfred M. Landon, Republican presidential candidate in 1936. Hull declared that "an ominous shadow falls athwart our own continent" and pleaded for common measures to resist either military or ideological invasion. Foreign Minister Cantilo of Argentina, which had a large Italian population and was dependent upon European markets, opposed any binding commitments or formal treaty. Since unanimity was deemed essential, Washington compromised. The "Declaration of Lima" affirmed "continental solidarity" and "collaboration" but provided only for "consultation" among the foreign ministers, meeting "when deemed desirable and at the initiative of any one of them" whenever the peace, security, or territorial integrity of an American Republic should be threatened. They would use "the measures which in each case the circumstances may make advisable. It is understood that the Governments of the American Republics will act independently in their individual capacity, recognizing fully their juridical equality as sovereign States."

Despite suggestions from Washington, no action was taken in the direction of consolidating and simplifying the confusing array of inter-American peace treaties, such as the Gondra Conciliation Treaty of 1923, the Kellogg Pact, the Pan-American Conciliation and Arbitration Treaties of 1929, the Argentine Anti-War Pact of 1933, the Convention of Montevideo of 1933, and the Buenos Aires Conventions of 1936. Questions of defining aggression and organizing sanctions were also sidetracked. The Stimson Doctrine was reaffirmed, but all hopes of a

Pan-American league or court went glimmering. Sundry innocuous resolutions were passed, but the record of positive achievement toward a genuine solidarity of interests and of deeds, rather than of words, was not impressive.

Following the outbreak of war abroad the foreign ministers met for the first time at Panama in late September, 1939. Sumner Welles asserted that the twenty-one American Republics could not permit "their security, their nationals, or their legitimate commercial rights and interests to be jeopardized by belligerent activities in close proximity to the shores of the New World." He proposed the establishment of a "safety zone." On October 3 a Final Act was approved, embodying sixteen declarations and resolutions. Most of them were clichés (*e.g.*, "maintenance of international activities in accordance with Christian morality") or routine pledges of collaboration. But the "Declaration of Panama" set up a "neutrality zone" including all of South and Central America and North America south of Canada and extending out to sea 300 to 1,000 miles. Within this vast area of ocean, covering more than 5 million square miles, the American Republics asserted "as of inherent right" and "as a measure of continental self-protection" that they were entitled to keep the waters "free from the commission of any hostile acts by any non-American belligerent nation."

That such an attack on belligerent rights and freedom of the seas should be made by twenty-one neutrals, led by the most powerful neutral, all of whom had always insisted on full respect for freedom of the seas and for their own neutral rights, verged upon the preposterous. To relinquish one's own recognized rights, as in the "neutrality" legislation, is in law and fact far different from denying the recognized rights of others, as was done at Panama. Both steps were motivated by an effort to escape involvement in war by fleeing from duty and danger into an imaginary isolationist haven. The President who had proposed on October 5, 1937, to "quarantine" aggressors in the name of upholding international law now sought to "quarantine" the American neutrals by a formula which violated international law in a fashion impartially damaging to aggressors and their victims alike. Wits referred to the zone as a "chastity belt" or a "prophyl-Axis" and predicted that it would fail of its purpose.

It did. The only major Anglo-German naval engagement in the first year of the war took place well inside the "zone." By October 4, Secretary Hull was explaining that the "patrol service," in which United States war vessels were already engaged, was for "information" only and that no effort would be made to compel belligerents to respect the zone. They were merely being requested to respect it. If they did not, no one knew what would be done next, since no method of enforcement had been provided. The State Department hoped that no occasion would arise for enforcement. But on December 13 the pocket battleship *Admiral Graf Spee* under Captain Langsdorff, engaged in commerce raiding in the south Atlantic, encountered three British cruisers, the *Achilles*, the *Ajax*, and the *Exeter* while it was pursuing the French merchantman *Formose*. After a sixteen-hour running fight the *Spee* fled into the harbor of Montevideo while the British cruisers lay in wait outside to renew the encounter. Four days later, following expiration of the time limit granted by Uruguay, the German commander scuttled his ship in the Rio de la Plata and took his own life. Two days later the German freighter *Arauca* fled from a British cruiser into Fort Lauderdale, Florida. On the same day the liner *Columbus*, fleeing from Vera Cruz, encountered a British destroyer 400 miles off the New Jersey coast and was scuttled by her commander. In no instance did any of the belligerents pay the slightest attention to the Declaration of Panama.

On December 21, 1939, the twenty-one American Republics, acting through the President of Panama, protested to Britain, France, and Germany and hinted at barring from American ports belligerent vessels committing acts of war within these zones. On January 14, Downing Street replied politely that the proposed zone could not "on any basis of international law" be imposed on belligerents by "unilateral action." Britain could accept it only if assured that it would not become a "vast sanctuary" for German raiders. "If the American States were to adopt a scheme of sanctions for the enforcement of the zone proposal, they would in effect be offering a sanctuary to German warships, within which H. M. ships would be confronted with the invidious choice of having either to refrain from engaging their enemy or laying themselves open to penalties in American ports and waters." The American Republics should ensure that Germany would send no more war vessels into the zone, and should lay up all German vessels already in the zone for the duration of the war. Without this, Britain would "reserve full belligerent rights." The Quai d'Orsay replied in similar vein on January 23. The German reply held that German vessels already in the zone could be dealt with only on the basis of existing law, not on the basis of unilateral innovations. The Reich could not accept the zone unless assurances were had that British and French possessions within it, including Canada, would not be used as war bases. On March 16, 1940, the American Republics protested to Britain over the pursuit by a British vessel of the German freighter *Wakama*, scuttled by its crew fifteen miles off the Brazilian coast. On May 24 a similar protest was sent to both London and Berlin over the scuttling of the *Hannover* off the Dominican coast. What possible justification there could be in protesting over "violation" of a principle which could by no stretch of the imagination be regarded as good law was not made clear.

The "Second Meeting of Ministers of Foreign Affairs of the American Republics" met in Havana, Cuba, July 21 to 30, 1940, on the initiative of the United States. In the face of the conquest of the northlands, the Low Countries, and France, accompanied by an alarming increase of Nazi activities in Latin America, the delegates were moved to consider countermeasures. On June 17, Hull had informed Berlin and Rome that "the United States would not recognize any transfer, and would not acquiesce in any attempt to transfer, any geographic region of the Western hemisphere from one non-American Power to another non-American Power." The United States Congress had passed a "hands off" resolution, reaffirming the Monroe Doctrine and contemplating immediate consultation with the other American Republics on measures to protect common interests. Washington bespoke economic collaboration and urged common action to thwart all activity arising from non-American sources likely to imperil American economic or political freedom.

The Havana Conference approved a Convention and a Supplementary Act "continentalizing" the Monroe Doctrine and declaring that "when islands or regions in the Americas now under the possession of non-American nations are in danger of becoming the subject of barter of territory or change of sovereignty, the American nations . . . may set up a regime of provisional administration," pending eventual independence ("provided they are capable of self-government") or restitution to their previous status, "whichever of these alternatives shall appear the more practicable and just." The provisional administration should be exercised for the "twofold purpose of contributing to the security and defense of the Continent, and to the economic, political and social progress of such regions." Arrangements were made to establish an emergency committee made up of one delegate from each of the Republics, to be deemed constituted as soon as two-thirds of its members should be appointed, to meet in a crisis at the request of any signatory, and to assume the administration of the threatened region with eventual transfer of authority to an "Inter-American Commission for Territorial Administration." The Convention of July 29, moreover, authorized any one of the Republics to act individually or jointly with others in an urgent emergency in order to safeguard its own defense and that of the continent. Somewhat sketchy resolutions were passed for further economic and financial collaboration. The widely publicized project for an intercontinental marketing cartel was dropped in favor of credits from the Export-Import Bank of the United States for industrialization, agrarian diversification, and holding or marketing of Latin American surpluses.

Some North Americans hoped that such steps as these would eventuate in the creation of a solid "Western Hemisphere" or "continental" coalition which would erect impregnable barriers against foreign attack and successfully defend the ramparts of the New World against dangers from the Old. These hopes, however, had little likelihood of realization. The "Western Hemisphere" or the "American continents" do not constitute a unity, real or potential. Though "Latin America" itself is in no sense a unity, its peoples have much more in common with one another and with Europe than any of them has with the "Colossus of the North." Their ruling *élites* speak the tongues of Latin Europe and look for inspiration to Madrid, Lisbon, Rome, and Paris. Their masses consist of poor peasants, often bound by debt to the soil they till—Indian in race and culture (with a strong Negro strain in Brazil and the Caribbean), often illiterate, half-pagan, half-Catholic, and little touched, save in Mexico, by the tides of change that sweep so swiftly over much of the Western world. Except in Argentina and Chile, there is no middle class and therefore little social basis for democracy save as a form to disguise oligarchy or tyranny. Latin American economy is a colonial economy, based upon crops, herds, and mineral wealth, all of which have value only when sold to the people of industrialized societies who can supply manufactures and capital in exchange. Latin America's great markets, without which no tolerable livelihood is possible for its inhabitants, lie in western Europe rather than in the United States which has long excluded the basic Latin American exports competing with the products of Iowa farmers, Minnesota wheat growers, southern cotton planters, Michigan sugar producers, western cattlemen, and Chicago meat packers. Such imports as coffee, cocoa, bananas, tropical woods, oil, and minerals come into the United States chiefly from Mexico and the Caribbean. They furnish no basis for an exchange of commodities comparable with that which has long taken place between Latin America and Europe. Even in geographical terms, most of South America lies nearer to Eurafrica than to the United States.[1]

Latin American attitudes toward North Americans and Europeans are products of a century of experience. "Yanquis" and Britishers in the southlands have usually been traveling salesmen, unsympathetic with Spanish and Indian ways, living apart and eager to go home. Or they have been bankers or executives or technicians who touch native life either too lightly or too harshly to win good will. They have often symbolized foreign exploitation and "Yankee imperialism." Millions of Germans and Italians live in Latin America as farmers, workers, businessmen, and members of the professions. They are not insensitive to Axis efforts to rally their loyalties to the service of the Caesars. They are respected by Latin Americans, for they have made themselves useful citizens of the countries where they live and work. The native ruling classes, moreover, are insecure in the face of Anglo-American pressures

[1] See Eugene Staley, "The Myth of the Continents," *Foreign Affairs*, April, 1941.

from abroad and social unrest at home from the ranks of the Indian peasantry and proletariat. Despite lip service to democracy, they take kindly and quickly to totalitarian doctrines as conforming to their interests and needs. The preachers of anti-Communism, anti-Semitism, and anti-Yankeeism, whether they be native Fascists, Axis agents, or local members of the Spanish Fascist Falange, receive a ready hearing.

The imperatives of diplomacy and strategy are determined by such facts as these—not, to be sure, beyond all possibility of change, but beyond all probability of decisive change. The British blockade of the Continent after 1939 cut off much of the normal foreign market of Latin America. The United States could not or would not supply an alternative market to the detriment of its own producers. Once hostilities in Europe should cease, Latin America would inevitably resume broken contacts across the Atlantic. Axis defeat would mean that Latin America could remain secure behind the barrier of the British fleet and would cease to be in any sense the "Achilles' heel" of the United States. Peace by stalemate would mean eventual Axis victory. Axis victory would mean the domination of Latin America, economically, ideologically, politically by a Fascist Europe. Neither guns nor planes nor battleships nor gestures of "good neighborliness" nor yet a resumption of imperialistic domination by the United States could possibly prevent this result. Nothing could prevent it save a crusading faith in democracy on the part of the United States, frankly and efficiently directed toward full support of such movements as the Mexican revolution, the People's Front in Chile, and the Apra in Peru and toward the promotion of social revolution elsewhere in the southlands for the purpose of awakening and liberating the Indian masses and the lower classes and thus overthrowing the oligarchies who would at once embrace Fascism. Such a program is scarcely conceivable for the United States of America. Without it, the victory of the Caesars over Britain in the north Atlantic, and inevitably in Africa, would mean Axis victory west of the south Atlantic, followed by the swift penetration of the southern continent by the propagandists, diplomats, and strategists of triumphant Powers bent upon organizing Latin America against the United States and utilizing its resources and its bases to immobilize and possibly conquer the North American Republic.

At the beginning of 1941 the only certain safeguard against this dire peril to the United States appeared to be the defeat of the Axis. Whether the United States would or could or should act relevantly and in time to protect itself was a matter upon which many Americans had not yet made up their minds in the first year of Franklin D. Roosevelt's third term.

THE NEW "NEUTRALITY." In the first year of Franklin D. Roosevelt's first term, most Americans permitted themselves to be persuaded that they could escape involvement in "other people's quarrels" by running away, by "minding their own business," and, if need be, by abandoning business which might "drag them into war." A few voices were from time to time raised in favor of abandoning "freedom of the seas" and "neutral trading rights" in such fashion as to cooperate with, or at least not impede, other Powers which might impose economic sanctions against States resorting to force in violation of the League Covenant or the Kellogg Pact. But all proposals to discriminate between law enforcers and lawbreakers were shouted down by the champions of "impartiality" who urged restrictions on trade with all belligerents in the interest of avoiding "entanglements." That such a program would be based upon a complete misconception of the position and interests of the United States in the world of the mid twentieth century did not prevent it from being eagerly sponsored by millions who wished to believe that war could be escaped by a formula for abandoning rights instead of enforcing them and for insulating America from a dangerous world rather than organizing the world for collective security.

Discussion of these problems was revived by the diplomatic crises of 1935 and by the growing conviction that war abroad had become inevitable. The result was the emergence of a "new" American neutrality policy, largely dictated by isolationists and designed not to facilitate American cooperation with the League States or with the signatories of the Kellogg Pact in preserving peace and restraining aggression, but to ensure American noninvolvement in war when it should come. The complexities, confusions, and frustrations encountered in the course of this effort revealed the impossibility of achieving isolation in a world in which American trade and investments were scattered over the five continents and the seven seas.

The neutrality legislation of 1935–1939 was in part an outgrowth of the investigation of the munitions industry by a committee of seven senators, headed by Gerald P. Nye of North Dakota, pursuant to a Senate resolution of April 12, 1934. The investigators revealed, among other things, that private arms interests had repeatedly defied or circumvented governmental action designed to control the arms traffic, often promoted sales through bribery of officials, employed officials to secure contracts abroad, sold arms to both sides simultaneously in war, armed both factions in civil wars, stimulated armaments races, organized lobbies to oppose arms embargoes and to work for larger military and naval appropriations, reached agreements with foreign competitors for the division of markets and profits, and indulged in sundry other practices designed to enrich the "merchants of death." These revelations stimulated congressional and public interest in the double problem of the arms trade and neutrality, which were linked together in a somewhat artificial fashion. On June 21, 1935, the Senate reratified the 1925 Convention for the Supervision of the International Traffic in Arms, without the curious reservation regarding its application to the Persian Gulf which the Senators had attached on June 15, 1934.

The subsequent consideration of the problem of keeping the United States out of war was conditioned by the prevalence of certain assumptions of dubious validity as judged by past history and current logic. It was generally assumed by Congress, the press, and the public that the United States becomes involved in war by virtue of damage to American interests resulting from hostilities among other States. This was the case in 1798, 1812, and 1917 but not in 1846 or 1898. The possibility that the United States might become involved directly in war with Japan in consequence of the new arms race received almost no discussion, all attention being concentrated on keeping the United States out of the next European war. It was assumed secondly that Americans become involved in European wars by virtue of the machinations of munition makers, bankers, and exporters bent upon making blood money out of the world's woes and determined to make their own profits a national interest for which the United States must fight. This thesis, though in part valid, is too simple an explanation of 1917 or 1812. The United States, like other Powers, becomes involved in war when its interests abroad are jeopardized or injured. These interests are economic, financial, political, social, religious, and humanitarian. If they have any common denominator, it is not profits but power. All nations fight for stakes which are valued because they are envisaged as essential components of power and prestige. Such stakes are often economic in character. But the Nye Committee did not succeed in demonstrating that American entanglement in the Great War was attributable directly or primarily to J. P. Morgan & Co., the duPonts, and other corporate interests. It was assumed in the third place that the price of peace was the sacrifice of profits and that insurance against war was to be had by the abandonment of trade and investments abroad. It was assumed finally that true "neutrality" implied complete impartiality between belligerents, with no distinctions drawn between aggressors and victims of aggression.

These assumptions influenced decisively the new orientation of American policy and, since they were false and unworkable, produced complications scarcely appreciated at the outset. The Neutrality Act of August 31, 1935, hastily formulated in the face of what looked like impending war in Africa and Europe, reflected the beginnings of confusion. The Senate and House resolved "that upon the outbreak or during the progress of war between, or among, two or more foreign States, the President shall proclaim such fact, and it shall thereafter be unlawful to export arms, amunition, or implements of war from any place in the United States, or possessions of the United States to any port of such belligerent States, or to any neutral port for trans-shipment to, or for the use of, a belligerent country . . . The President may from time to time, by proclamation, extend such embargo . . . to other States as and when they may become involved in such war." Violators were to be punished by forfeiture of property and by a $10,000 fine and/or five years imprisonment (Section 1). The act further established a National Munitions Control Board, consisting of the Secretaries of State, Treasury, War, and Navy, with which all manufacturers, exporters, and importers of arms were obliged to register their names, goods, and places of business. A $500 fee was required for a five-year registration certificate. All arms exports from the United States were to be licensed by the Board (Section 2). American vessels were forbidden under penalty to carry arms to belligerents (Sections 3 and 4). The President was authorized at his discretion to close American ports to belligerent submarines (Section 5) and to warn American citizens that travel on belligerent vessels was at their own risk (Section 6).

The public registration and licensing of arms exporters gave rise to no immediate problem. There were difficulties, however, as to Section 1. Far from cutting off all trade with belligerents as a means of keeping the United States at peace, the act only banned arms exports, narrowly defined. This arms embargo, moreover, was to be applied "impartially" with no distinctions among aggressors, victims of aggression, and sanctionist States that might become involved in hostilities in their efforts to uphold international law through the League. The President was given no discretion except in so far as the word "may" with regard to its extension to subsequent belligerents and the phrase "during the progress of" might leave him free to exercise executive judgment. As was pointed out at the time, the United States would be bound to close the American arms market to both Italy and Ethiopia in the event of an attack by the former on the latter. This action would aid the aggressor since Italy, unlike Ethiopia, had no need for American arms. Should Britain or other League States subsequently become involved in hostilities with the aggressor in the course of enforcing League sanctions, the President was presumably bound to aid the aggressor once more by barring American arms to the League States. That such a result could help keep the United States out of war seemed most dubious. In signing the act President Roosevelt asserted, "No Congress and no Executive can foresee all possible future situations. . . . The inflexible provisions might drag us into war instead of keeping us out."

Another feature of the act not generally appreciated at the time was the circumstance that it involved a virtual repudiation of the Kellogg Pact. If all belligerents were to be treated identically regardless of whether they had observed the Pact or violated it, then the pact and its corollary, the Stimson Doctrine—already quite sufficiently emasculated through lack of implementation—would cease to have any concrete meaning at all. America seemed once more on the point of disowning its child. In July, 1935, in response to an appeal from Ethiopia, President Roosevelt had declared that "my Government would be loth to believe that either [Italy or Ethiopia] would resort to other than pacific means as a method of dealing with this controversy or would permit any situation to arise which would be inconsistent with the commitments of the Pact." On July 12, Secretary Hull announced that "the Pact of Paris is no less binding now than when it was entered into by the sixty-three nations that are parties to it." On September 12, as war approached, Mr. Hull said "the American Government asks of those countries which appear to be contemplating armed hostilities that they weigh most solicitously the declaration and pledge given in the Pact of Paris." Thus the Executive was clinging to the Pact, though not prepared to protest in its name against Mussolini's aggression, while Congress was destroying any practical value it might have by proposing to treat the lawless and the law-abiding alike.

On October 5, 1935, two days after the Italian invasion was launched, the President proclaimed that a state of war existed, that exports of American arms, munitions, and implements of war to both belligerents were illegal, and that Americans would henceforth travel on belligerent ships only at their own risk.[1] He further warned that all transactions of any character with either belligerent was at the risk of the trader (Caveat Mercator) and thereby implied, though Congress had not expressly authorized such a step, that the United States would not defend its right as a neutral to trade with Italy in the event of a League blockade. But no mention was made of the fact that Italy had obviously violated the Pact as well as the Covenant. Since Ethiopia had no ships and carried on little trade with the United States, it was assumed that the President's warnings would redound only to the disadvantage of Italy. The arms embargo, however, was a benefit to the aggressor. Ethiopia was penalized by the United States for having been attacked. A lively war trade with Italy soon sprang up in commodities other than arms. Congress had not banned such trade. The warnings issued during October and November by President Roosevelt, Secretaries Hull, Ickes, and Roper, and other officials had little effect since exporters not trading in arms were not subject to punishment. American exports to Italian Africa jumped from a monthly average of $25,403 in 1934 to $367,789 in October and $583,735 in November, 1935. Crude-oil exports to Italy increased 600 per cent and rose over 1 million per cent for Italian Africa. Exports

[1] President Roosevelt revoked these proclamations on June 20, 1936, on the ground that war no longer existed between the belligerents. This action was criticized by some jurists as an implied recognition of the Italian conquest.

to Ethiopia declined. "Moral suasion" failed. Mussolini floated to victory on a sea of oil, much of which came from the United States. American business, as usual, was in the war for profit, and its activities were aiding the aggressor. Congress had obviously failed to build an adequate economic cyclone cellar into which America could flee from foreign hostilities.

Since the Neutrality Act was scheduled to expire on February 29, 1936, Congress began reconsidering it in January. The Administration surrendered to the isolationist forces in Congress on the issue of Executive discretion. Both the Pittman-McReynolds (Administration) bill and the Nye-Clark-Maverick bill sought to tie the President's hands completely. Both bills further sought to carry the cyclone-cellar theory of neutrality to its logical conclusion. The American Government, according to this theory, should itself destroy American foreign trade in order to prevent belligerents from destroying it and thus creating danger of American involvement. To cut off all American foreign trade with all belligerents was unthinkable, however, since it would mean a major economic catastrophe in a general war. The bills therefore sought to limit American trade to "normal" peacetime quotas. But this was seen to be administratively unworkable, and the whole plan was dropped. On February 18 the Senate, following similar action by the House, adopted a joint resolution signed by President Roosevelt on February 28, 1936, amending the Act of the previous summer and extending it to May 1, 1937. The amendments left the President no opportunity for exercising judgment. "Whenever the President shall find that there exists a state of war between" foreign States, he shall proclaim an arms embargo and he "shall" (instead of "may") extend such embargo to other States later involved in the conflict. The new Act also forbade all long-term loans and credits to belligerents and further specified, "This act shall not apply to an American Republic or Republics engaged in war against a non-American State or States, provided that the American Republic is not cooperating with a non-American State or States in such war" (Section 1B).

This act left the situation even more confused than before. The United States would ban arms, ammunition, implements of war, and loans to all belligerents, but all other trade would go on unimpeded and would presumably create all the old problems again in the event of a general and prolonged conflict abroad. Aggressors, victims of aggression, and sanctionist belligerents would be treated alike. But should a Latin American State become involved in war with a non-American State, either as an aggressor or as a victim of aggression, the United States would impose its embargo only against the non-American belligerent—unless the Latin-American States were cooperating in a League war in the enforcement of sanctions, in which case it would receive no preferential treatment. The

States injured by such a policy might be tempted to undertake reprisals against the United States. To old sources of conflict, new ones would be added. Far from ensuring peace the new policy seemed likely to promote war and to throw the economic weight of America into the scales on the side of Covenant-breaking and Pact-breaking aggressors. In December, 1936, at Buenos Aires, Secretary Hull attempted, without success, to commit all the American Republics to a similar policy. "Make the world safe for aggression" might well have been the slogan of the new legislation. This result—which appeared far more likely to drag the United States into war than the traditional American neutrality policy—was the work not of a belligerent Executive but of a peace-seeking Congress, not of internationlists enamored of foreign entanglements but of isolationists who swore by Washington's Farewell Address.

On January 8, 1937, by special amendment sponsored by the Administration, the existing legislation was amplified to extend the arms and loan embargoes to foreign States afflicted by "civil strife." The occasion for this move was the effort of some Americans to sell arms to the Spanish Loyalists. The sensitivity of the Administration to the desires of Downing Street and of certain religious minorities in the United States, reinforced by the sensitivity of Congress to isolationist demands for strict "non-intervention," led to a statutory prohibition on the lending of money or the selling of arms to either side in the Spanish conflict. The Republican régime, whose rights under treaty and customary international law were thereby ignored, was thus deprived of the means of defending itself. The Rebels received all the arms they required from Germany, Italy, and Portugal. When Drew Pearson pointed out a year later that American arms were being sold freely to Germany and that this was a violation of the German-American peace treaty of 1921, and therefore of the Neutrality Act which forbade arms sales contrary to treaty terms, Hull replied weakly that the sales to the Reich were small and that the treaty merely forbade Germany to import arms from the United States without forbidding Americans to export arms to Germany. By May of 1938 even Senator Nye was appalled at the consequences of the "new neutrality" for Spain. He proposed that the Spanish embargo be lifted. But the Administration, more anxious than ever to placate Chamberlain and the Vatican, declined to act. The destruction of Spanish democracy was a direct consequence of "nonintervention" by the European democracies and of a specious "neutrality" on the part of the United States.

Meanwhile the new dispensation had been put into "permanent" form. On May 1, 1937, the President, then fishing in the Gulf of Mexico, signed a new act passed unanimously in the House and by a vote of 41 to 15 in the Senate, following prolonged debate productive of much heat and little light. As before, Americans were forbidden by an impartial and mandatory embargo to sell arms or make loans to foreign belligerents or to factions in civil strife. Travel on belligerent vessels was banned. The arming of American merchant vessels was prohibited. The American Republics were favored. The N.M.C.B. was continued. Section 2 which expired on May 1, 1939, without renewal, gave the President discretionary authority to place trade with belligerents in commodities other than arms on a "cash-and-carry" basis—*i.e.*, specified goods might be sold only on condition that title passed to the purchaser in advance of shipment and that transport be in foreign vessels. This section was never applied, but it furnished a formula for later use. The entire act was not applied to the undeclared war between Japan and China resumed in July, 1937, since its application would obviously injure China more than Japan. In the event of war in Europe, all belligerents would be denied American arms and loans. The United States would thus (in theory) avoid the "deadly parallel" and the "tragic fallacy" of 1917.

THE FAILURE OF NEUTRALITY. Critics of the new course at once pointed out that if the Axis attacked Britain and France the application of the "neutrality" statute would be of incalculable assistance to Hitler and Mussolini. Their heavily armed States would be prevented from securing American arms by the British fleet and would have no need of them in any event. France and Britain might well have desperate need of weapons and money from America, but would be prevented from securing either by American legislation. The United States would thus once more become the economic ally of the aggressors and would contribute to the possible defeat of the Western European Powers whose survival against the Reich had been deemed a major American interest, well worth fighting for, twenty years previously.

In January, 1939, President Roosevelt urged repeal of the arms embargo and resort to methods "short of war" but "stronger than words" to deter aggression. Legislative progress toward this goal was impeded, however, by loud outcries from isolationists over the accidental revelation that the President had released to a French purchasing mission certain types of aircraft intended for the army. Hiram Johnson cried, "Good God, do you not, Gentlemen, think the American people have a right to know if they are going down the road to war?" Herbert Hoover in Chicago on February 1 denounced the President for "his proposal that we make effective protests at acts of aggression against sister nations. . . . The distinction between legitimate expansion and wicked aggression becomes confused." We must not "set ourselves up as an oracle of righteousness." We must not risk war by playing "world-wide power politics." Soon afterward, Roosevelt was quoted in other quarters as having said that the American frontier was on the Rhine. For three days the Anglo-French press rejoiced, only to have the President issue a denial. Moves in Congress to repeal the arms embargo lagged during February and March.

On March 21 Senator Key Pittman moved to amend the Neutrality Act by putting all exports to belligerents, including munitions, on a cash-and-carry basis. Increased military and naval appropriations were voted. Senate hearings on the neutrality legislation opened April 5. Borah argued that aggressors were not violating the Kellogg Pact. Amid confusion worse confounded, the Duce struck down Albania. Hull announced on April 8 that "the forcible and violent invasion of Albania is unquestionably an additional threat to the peace of the world. . . . It is scarcely necessary to add that the inevitable effect of this incident, taken with other similar incidents, is further to destroy confidence and to undermine economic stability in every country of the world, thus affecting our welfare."

The visit to the United States of King George and Queen Elizabeth (June 7 to 12, 1939) strengthened rather than weakened the determination of isolationists and obstructionists to prevent any modification of the Neutrality Act. The Senate Foreign Relations Committee concluded its leisurely hearings on May 8. Pittman's leadership in the upper chamber produced no results. Sol Bloom introduced a resolution into the House to put all trade with belligerents on a cash-and-carry basis. At the end of June, however, the House approved an amendment retaining the impartial and mandatory arms embargo. Hull appealed belatedly to Congress, but the President acknowledged defeat on July 18, 1939. If war came in Europe, the United States would aid the aggressors and penalize their victims. Undeclared war was raging in Asia. Despite notice to Tokio on July 26 of abrogation of the commercial treaty of 1911, the invaders of China continued to purchase 65 per cent of their imported oil, 65 per cent of their motorcars, 77 per cent of their aircraft, and 90 per cent of their copper, scrap iron, and steel from the United States. The aggressors concluded that the world was quite safe for further aggression.

The outbreak of hostilities in Europe found almost all Americans passionately devoted to two desires which were to prove incompatible: Allied victory and American neutrality. On September 5, 1939, the President issued a traditional neutrality proclamation along with a second proclamation under the "Neutrality" Act imposing an embargo on exports of arms, ammunition, and implements of war to Germany, Poland, France, Britain, India, Australia, New Zealand, South Africa (September 8), and Canada (September 10). On September 8, he proclaimed a "limited" national emergency under the National Defense Act. Some 80 million dollars worth of war materials, ordered by Britain and France and already licensed for export, were held up in American harbors by the proclamation. On September 13 the President called Congress into special session. He deemed it expedient to ignore the central issue of aiding the Allies by "methods short of war." When the lawmakers assembled on September 21 the President appealed to the traditional American policy and to the international law which had been departed from in the "neutrality" statute. "I regret that Congress passed that act. I equally regret that I signed that act." He held that the arms embargo was "most vitally dangerous to American neutrality, American security, and American peace." He proposed repeal of the embargo and the substitution of prohibitions on travel by Americans in belligerent vessels, on entry of American vessels into war zones, on lending by Americans to belligerents, and on exports of arms other than those paid for in cash and carried away in foreign vessels.

These proposals were not at all a "return to international law." They constituted a complete abandonment of "freedom of the seas" and "neutral rights" for which America had fought in 1798, 1805, 1812, and 1917. Since isolationists and pacifists chose to believe that America had been "dragged into war" in 1917 by virtue of private loans to the Allies and German destruction of American goods, ships, and lives, the way to peace was obviously to ban loans and to keep American goods, ships, and lives out of danger. The President yielded to this sentiment and sought to make possible the shipment of arms to the Allies by agreeing to prohibit loans, shipping, and travel in the name of "cash and carry." The resultant legislation would aid the Allies so long as they had no need of American money and American shipping. Should Hitler's foes later require funds and vessels from the United States, their rights under customary international law to secure these services would be denied by statute to the immense advantage of the Reich. Under the conditions of September, 1939, however, the President felt that he could secure no more than "cash and carry."

The Senate discussion was tedious. Its low point was reached when Senator Lundeen of Minnesota urged that while the Allies "were pretty busy on the Western front" the United States should demand prompt payment of the war debts and, failing compliance, should seize the British and French West Indies. "Not a shot would be fired. . . . Let us show that there is some red blood in us." The isolationists talked their case to death. Senator Nye agreed with Borah that "there is nothing ahead of America but hell if we repeal the arms embargo." He averred that "the assumption that the British fleet is our first line of defense" was "conceived in the brain of the Mad Hatter." He repeated his favorite thesis that munition makers had pushed America into the Great War, but this argument provoked a belated counterattack, joined by Senator George Norris, lone survivor among the Senators who had voted against war in 1917. Congressman Ludlow pleaded vainly for a total embargo on all trade with the belligerents. Senator Clark of Missouri branded Britain and France as "aggressors" for refusing to make peace on Hitler's terms and thus driving the Germans "into the bosom of Communism."

The President denounced those who were tearing their hair over "American boys dying on European battlefields" for indulging in "a shameless and dishonest fake." The bill was amended to lighten the restrictions on American shipping. On October 27, the Senate passed the bill 63 to 30. Eight Republicans joined 54 Democrats and 1 Independent in voting affirmatively, and 12 Democrats joined 15 Republicans, 2 Farmer Laborites, and 1 Progressive in the opposition. The House assented. After further minor revisions, the Senate voted approval on November 3, 55 to 24, and the House 243 to 172. This result was hastened by the capture of the British-bound American freighter *City of Flint* by the *Deutschland* on October 9. The captors took the vessel to Norway, then to Murmansk, and finally back to Norway where the local authorities interned the prize crew and released the ship. Such incidents would be made impossible by the new statute.

The act which the President signed on November 4, following adjournment of Congress, was entitled "Joint Resolution to Preserve the Neutrality and Peace of the United States and to Secure the Safety of Its Citizens and Their Interests." Its preamble asserted that the United States "waives none of its own rights and privileges, or those of any of its nationals, under international law." Its text abandoned neutral rights and freedom of the seas. The President was required to issue a proclamation naming belligerent States "whenever the President, or the Congress by concurrent resolution, shall find that there exists a state of war between foreign States, and that it is necessary to promote the security or preserve the peace of the United States or to protect the lives of citizens of the United States" (§1). "It shall thereafter be unlawful for any American vessel to carry any passengers or any articles or materials to any State named in such proclamation," subject to a fine of $50,000, five years' imprisonment, or both. "It shall thereafter be unlawful to export or transport, or attempt to export or transport, or cause to be exported or transported, from the United States to any State named in such proclamation, any articles or materials (except copyrighted articles or materials) until all right, title and interest therein shall have been transferred to some foreign government, agency, institution, association, partnership, corporation or national. . . . No loss incurred by any such citizen in connection with the sale or transfer of right, title and interest in any such articles or materials or in connection with the exportation or transportation of any such copyrighted articles or materials shall be made the basis of any claim put forward by the Government of the United States. . . . No insurance policy issued on such articles or materials, or vessels, and no loss incurred thereunder or by the owners of such vessels shall be made the basis of any claims put forward by the Government of the United States" (§2). These prohibitions were not to apply, however, to shipments of goods other than arms by air or inland waters to lands bordering the United States or to ports in the Western Hemisphere south of 35° north latitude or north of 35° and west of 66° west longitude (thereby exempting Canada, except for Halifax, Newfoundland, and Labrador) or to ports in the Pacific or Indian Oceans or to Atlantic ports south of 30° north latitude (cutting across North Africa) unless such ports should be included in "combat areas" proclaimed by the President and barred to American citizens and vessels (§3).

Whenever the President shall have issued a proclamation under the authority of section 1 (a) it shall thereafter be unlawful for any citizen of the United States to travel on any vessel of any State named in such proclamation, except in accordance with such rules and regulations as may be prescribed (§5). . . . It shall thereafter be unlawful, until such proclamation is revoked, for any American vessel, engaged in commerce with any foreign State to be armed (§6). . . . It shall thereafter be unlawful for any person within the United States to purchase, sell, or exchange bonds, securities, or other obligations of the government of any State named in such proclamation, or of any political subdivision of any such State, or of any person acting for or on behalf of the Government of any such State, or political subdivision thereof, issued after the date of such proclamation, or to make any loan or extend any credit (other than necessary credits accruing in connection with the transmission of telegraph, cable, wireless or telephone services) to any such government, political subdivision or person (§7).

For the rest, the new Act varied little from the old. The clause relating to "civil strife" which had helped to destroy the Spanish Republic was omitted. Solicitation and receipt of contributions for belligerent States (save for relief) were banned. American Republics engaged in war against non-American States were exempted from the prohibitions unless "cooperating with a non-American State or States in such war" (§9). The President was given authority to prevent the use of United States ports as bases of supply for belligerent war vessels and, at his discretion, to ban foreign submarines and armed merchant vessels from United States waters. The National Munitions Control Board was retained (§12). The President at once issued proclamations lifting the arms embargo, banning belligerent submarines from United States waters, and defining a "combat area" including the North and Baltic Seas, the Bay of Biscay except for the north coast of Spain, and the eastern Atlantic beyond 20°. American ships and citizens were thus banned not only from European belligerent territories but from the then neutral ports of Eire, Sweden, Denmark, Belgium, the Netherlands, and Norway south of Bergen.

Twenty-two years previously the United States had gone to war rather than accept German terms which would have allowed one American vessel each week to go to Britain. Now the United States itself forbade all its vessels and citizens to go to any European belligerent port or war zone at any time during hostilities, thereby inviting the Reich to sink all neutral shipping on sight without fear of protest from Washington. Berlin at once took advantage of this opportunity. The Nazi leaders realized that the new statute was by no means an unmixed blessing for their enemies. Had it been applied to the wars in Finland and China, it would have aided the cause of the Soviet and Japanese aggressors. Wherever it might be applied, it sounded the death knell of the rights of neutrals to lend, sell, and ship goods to belligerent States—despite ardent defense of these rights by America for over 150 years.

In the terrifying spring of 1940 the fall of Copenhagen, Oslo, Amsterdam, Brussels, and Paris confronted Washington with the necessity of making choices not foreseen in the formulae of 1939. Each new victim of Nazi aggression was dutifully punished for the crime of being weak and neutral by Presidential proclamations barring American ships, citizens, and money from its territory. At the same time the American bank balances of the victims were impounded, lest the victors seize the foreign assets of the vanquished. To Rome and Tokio went warnings and pleas, necessarily unimplemented since Congress and public forbade "commitments" or "entanglements." Rome replied on June 10, Tokio later. On April 13, five days after the event, Roosevelt condemned the German invasion of Denmark and Norway: "If civilization is to survive, the rights of the smaller nations to independence, to their territorial integrity, and to the unimpeded opportunity for self-government must be respected by their more powerful neighbors." On April 17 Hull issued a statement declaring that America had an interest in the rubber and tin of the East Indies and that any violent alteration of the *status quo* would be prejudicial to the "stability, peace, and security" of the "entire Pacific region." He recalled that Japan had promised to respect the rights of the Netherlands. He urged that "policies of force be abandoned." These lofty statements of aspiration produced no visible effect. On May 12 the President warned the American Republics that until recently "too many citizens believed themselves safe." A "definite challenge" had to be faced. "Can we continue our peaceful construction if all the other continents embrace, by preference or by compulsion, a wholly different principle of life?" The President's personal answer to his own question was clear. But his political answer had to be different, since millions of his fellow citizens firmly refused to face the question or insisted upon answering it in a fashion more consonant with spiritual comfort than with mental clarity or moral courage.

On May 16 the President went before Congress to ask for huge defense appropriations and a plane-building capacity of 50,000 units per year. There was no notable dissent until Colonel Charles A. Lindbergh three days later demanded by radio that America "stop this hysterical chatter of calamity and invasion. . . . No one wishes to attack us and no one is in a position to do so." There was little response, however, to the appeals of the man who had aided Hitler to prepare the "peace" of Munich and had subsequently accepted the Service Cross of the Order of the German Eagle with Star, second highest decoration in the Nazi Reich. The President had asked for 1 billion dollars for arms. A few days later, he asked for another billion. The Senate voted almost 2 billion dollars to the army and 1½ billion dollars to the navy, 74 to 0. The House approved, 400 to 1. Wendell Willkie commented on May 29 that Allied victory would save America "billions of dollars, billions of tons of armament, billions of hours of wasted and unfruitful work. Just on the most selfish basis, it is enormously to our advantage to have them win." Vandenberg demanded "insulation," but soon urged full aid to the Allies, "short of war" and "within international law."

THE "ARSENAL OF DEMOCRACY." The collapse of France led to the first step. William Allen White's "Committee to Defend America by Aiding the Allies" grew by leaps and bounds throughout the country and exercised vast influence in arousing the public and mobilizing pressure on Congress, despite the outcries of a few congressmen that it was a "committee to get America into war." Under its auspices, General John J. Pershing made a radio plea on June 8 for "unlimited quantities" of aircraft, guns, and munitions to the Allies. But Senator Claude Pepper's motion to authorize the immediate dispatch of army planes was voted down in the Senate Foreign Relations Committee, 22 to 1. Senator Key Pittman[1] urged a month later that the British Government "end Hitler's ambition for world conquest" by abandoning the British Isles. After reflection and a talk with the President, however, he opined that an "understanding" between the British and American fleets might "localize Hitler in Europe." On June 6 a trickle of army planes to the Allies began by virtue of Presidential exercise of statutory authority to exchange old planes for new ones, with the manufacturers willing enough to sell the traded-in goods to new customers. In his address at the University of Virginia on June 10, denouncing the Duce's "stab in the back," Roosevelt stated a new policy:

Some still hold to the now somewhat obvious delusion that we of the United States can safely permit the United States to become a lone island in a world dominated by the philosophy of force. Such an island may be the dream of those who still talk and vote as isolationists. Such an island represents to me and to the overwhelming majority of Americans today a helpless nightmare, the helpless

[1] Senator Pittman died on November 10, 1940, and was succeeded as chairman of the Committee by Senator Walter F. George of Georgia.

nightmare of a people without freedom; yes, the nightmare of a people lodged in prison, handcuffed, hungry, and fed through the bars from day to day by the contemptuous, unpitying masters of other continents. It is natural also that we should ask ourselves how now we can prevent the building of that prison and the placing of ourselves in the midst of it.

Let us not hesitate—all of us—to proclaim certain truths. Overwhelmingly we, as a nation,—and this applies to all the other American nations—are convinced that military and naval victory for the gods of force and hate would endanger the institutions of democracy in the Western world, and that equally, therefore, the whole of our sympathy lies with those nations that are giving their life blood in combat against these forces. . . .

In our American unity, we will pursue two obvious and simultaneous courses: we will extend to the opponents of force the material resources of this nation and, at the same time, we will harness and speed up the use of those resources in order that we ourselves in the Americas may have equipment and training equal to the task of any emergency and every defense.

All roads leading to the accomplishment of these objectives must be kept clear of obstructions. We will not slow down or detour. Signs and signals call for speed—full speed ahead. . . . I call for effort, courage, sacrifice, devotion. Granting the love of freedom, all of these are possible. And the love of freedom is still fierce, still steady in the nation today.

Colonel Henry L. Stimson declared on June 18 that the world "cannot endure permanently half slave and half free. . . . America can cling to the dreams of a mistaken fiction of neutrality no longer applicable to her interest or her safety; she can leave the British fleet to its fate and face the consequences of a future which may leave her virtually defenseless to a Fascist attack. . . . Or she can frankly realize that now as for many years past our own immediate safety depends in part upon the continuance of British sea power, and she can lend her resources to make our joint sea power effective for that purpose." The former Secretary of State urged repeal of the Neutrality Act, full access to all American ports by British and French vessels, and prompt dispatch of planes and arms "if necessary in our own ships and under convoy." He also urged military conscription and condemned defeatism. "I believe that if we use our brains and curb our prejudices, we can, by keeping command of the sea, beat her [Germany] as we did in 1918." Wendell Willkie, also committed to aid to the Allies, asserted at the same time that "we must stay out of war. . . . No man has the right to use the great powers of the Presidency to lead the people indirectly into war." When Roosevelt on June 20 named Stimson as Secretary of War and another distinguished Republican, Colonel Frank Knox, editor of the Chicago *Daily News*, as Secretary of the Navy, the Republican National Committee "read out" both men from the party.

In his plea to Roosevelt of June 10, Reynaud pledged continued resistance in the provinces and French possessions and asked for all aid "short of an expeditionary force." In his reply, released June 15, the

President extended admiration and sympathy and promised "redoubled efforts" to give material aid. But "only the Congress" could make military commitments. Congress would commit itself to do nothing beyond frantic rearmament. Most Republicans and many Democrats in both Houses gave aid not to the Allies but to the obstructionists who were bent upon preventing aid to the Allies. The President's efforts to transfer a number of small torpedo boats were abandoned after the Attorney General cast doubt on their legality and the Senate Naval Affairs Committee introduced a measure (passed June 28, 1940) designed to forbid any executive transfer of naval vessels. Democratic Chairman David I. Walsh of Massachusetts asked, "Who in God's name thought that these contracts for our own protection would be modified or changed in order to assist one side or the other, or all sides, of belligerents at war? . . . The Committee has inserted into the bill . . . every possible safeguard to see that there is not in the future any attempt made to lessen our defenses so far as the navy is concerned."

On August 18, Ambassador William C. Bullitt spoke in Philadelphia in warning to his countrymen against the strategy of treason by which the French Republic was done to death:

. . . The destruction of the British Navy would be the turning point of our Atlantic Maginot Line. . . . What stands today between the Americas and the unleashed dictatorships? The British fleet and the courage of the British people. . . . It is as clear as anything on this earth that the United States will not go to war, but it is equally clear that war is coming toward the Americas. . . . On the 10th day of last May the people of France were as confident as are the people of the United States today that their country could not be conquered. . . . I am certain that if Great Britain is defeated the attack will come, and that all the strength of this nation will be needed—mobilized, organized, equipped and ready—if we are to parry it and save the independence of our country. Why are we sleeping, Americans? When are we going to wake up? . . . Our fate and the fate of our children depends on what each one of us does—now.

Senator D. Worth Clark of Idaho declared Bullitt's address "very little short of treason." Senator Bennet Champ Clark of Missouri said, "If Ambassador Bullitt should succeed in getting us into the war, he will find a safe place for himself to hide out." Senator Burton K. Wheeler accused him of being a friend of Molotov. Congressman John Schafer of Wisconsin urged that Bullitt be "locked up." These voices represented a minority. But the inert mass of legislators and citizens, blinded by fear of war, believed that America was in no danger or could somehow be defended after the arrival of an invader.

The President could either do nothing, apart from urging measures of defense which he knew could never by themselves defend America, or he could exercise his executive discretion without regard for Congress. He chose the latter course. On August 18 the President and Prime Minister

Mackenzie King of Canada, attending army maneuvers in northern New York, announced their agreement "that a permanent joint board on defense shall be set up at once by the two countries" to "commence immediate studies relating to sea, land, and air problems" and "consider in the broad sense the defenses of the northern part of the Western hemisphere." Since public response was favorable, Roosevelt took another step which was kept secret until completed. On September 3 he sent a communication to Congress:

I transmit herewith for the information of the Congress notes exchanged between the British Ambassador at Washington and the Secretary of State on Sept. 2, 1940, under which this government has acquired the right to lease naval and air bases in Newfoundland and in the Islands of Bermuda, the Bahamas, Jamaica, St. Lucia, Trinidad and Antigua and in British Guiana; also a copy of an opinion of the Attorney General dated Aug. 27, 1940, regarding my authority to consummate this arrangement.

The right to bases in Newfoundland and Bermuda are gifts—generously given and gladly received. The other bases mentioned have been acquired in exchange for fifty of our over-age destroyers.

This is not inconsistent in any sense with our status of peace. Still less is it a threat against any nation. It is an epochal and far-reaching act of preparation for continental defense in the face of grave danger.

Preparation for defense is an inalienable prerogative of a sovereign State. Under present circumstances this exercise of sovereign right is essential to the maintenance of our peace and safety. This is the most important action in the reinforcement of our national defense that has been taken since the Louisiana Purchase. Then, as now, considerations of safety from overseas attack were fundamental.

Lothian's note defined the leaseholds on the Avalon peninsula, on the south coast of Newfoundland, and in Bermuda, granted "freely and without consideration," as well as the West Indies bases, granted "in exchange for naval and military equipment and material." All the leases were for ninety-nine years and "free from all rent or charges" save compensations to owners of private property needed for the bases. Hull's note "gladly" accepted these "generous" proposals and agreed to transfer fifty 1,200-ton destroyers. Robert Jackson's opinion was a masterpiece of legal casuistry, interpreting statutes to mean things never intended by them and finding the transaction consonant with international law by the simple expedient of ignoring the distinction between private and governmental transfers of arms from neutrals to belligerents. A simultaneous exchange of communications conveyed renewed assurances that the British fleet would not be surrendered or scuttled if the British Isles became untenable. This pledge was of dubious value since a successful invasion of England would bring into power a Pétain or a Laval who

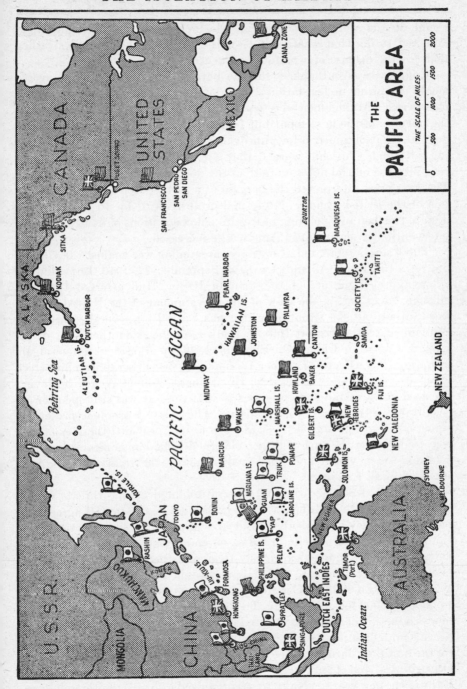

THE
PACIFIC AREA

THE SCALE OF MILES:

0   500   1000 1500 2000

would do the victor's bidding, and the demoralized seamen might be expected to do what was needful for the safety of their families' rather than for the defense of a remote and neutral America.

Congress was outflanked, for the bargain was an "executive agreement," requiring no legislation or appropriations. The anguished outcries of America's Munichmen were less loud than expected. Willkie endorsed the purpose of the agreement but found it "regrettable" that the President had not obtained prior approval from Congress. Britain registered joy, although Churchill warned that "it would be a mistake to try to read into the official notes more than the documents bear on their faces." The Axis press interpreted the bargain as a further step in the disintegration of the British Empire. No formal protest was made to Washington, despite the flagrant violation of traditional conceptions of neutrality, lest interventionist sentiment in America be increased.

The Caesars retaliated at once by threatening war against the United States in the Triple Alliance treaty of September 27, 1940. Immediately following the signature of the Pact of Berlin, Hull asserted that the alliance "does not, in the view of the Government of the United States, substantially alter a situation which has existed for several years." On September 25 the Export-Import Bank announced another loan of 25 million dollars to China. On September 26 the President imposed an embargo, to be effective October 16, on all exports of scrap iron and steel except to Britain and the Western Hemisphere. Sumner Welles, however, declared in Cleveland on September 28 that the way was still open for an "equitable settlement" with Japan. "There is no problem presented which could not be solved through negotiation, provided there existed a sincere desire on the part of those concerned to find an equitable and fair solution which would give just recognition to the rights and the real interests of all concerned."

The United States declined to be intimidated by the threats of the Triplice. Although both major candidates were in substantial agreement on foreign policy, President Roosevelt's unprecedented reelection to a third term was interpreted abroad as an endorsement of the policy of all aid to Britain. He moved cautiously to give further effect to the program laid down and to formulate national purposes in a more forthright fashion. Before the close of 1940, Congress had approved the expenditure of over $12,000,000,000 for defense. By the President's "rule of thumb," half the new production of arms was allotted to Britain. The Compulsory Military Service and Training Law of September 16, 1940, introduced conscription for the first time during "peace" in the history of the Republic. The "Two Ocean Navy" bill of July 19 authorized a 70 per cent increase in sea forces. Early in the new year the Navy was reorganized into an Atlantic squadron, a Pacific squadron, and an Asiatic squadron in an unmistakable gesture of warning to Tokio and the Axis. On January 6, 1941 (two days before proposing a 1941–1942 budget of $17,485,528,000, of which $10,811,000,-000 would go for armaments), President Roosevelt told Congress,

I address you, the members of this new Congress, at a moment unprecedented in the history of the Union. I use the word "unprecedented" because at no previous time has American security been as seriously threatened from without as it is today. . . .

Armed defense of democratic existence is now being gallantly waged in four continents. If that defense fails, all the population and all the resources of Europe, Asia, Africa and Australasia will be dominated by conquerors. And let us remember that the total of those populations and their resources greatly exceeds the sum total of the population and resources of the whole of the Western Hemisphere —many times over.

In times like these it is immature—and incidentally untrue—for anybody to brag that an unprepared America, single-handed, and with one hand tied behind its back, can hold off the whole world.

No realistic American can expect from a dictator's peace international generosity, or return of true independence, or world disarmament, or freedom of expression, or freedom of religion—or even good business. . . .

We are committed to the proposition that principles of morality and considerations for our own security will never permit us to acquiesce in a peace dictated by aggressors and sponsored by appeasers. We know that enduring peace cannot be bought at the cost of other people's freedom.

In the recent national election there was no substantial difference between the two great parties in respect to that national policy. No issue was fought out on this line before the American electorate. Today it is abundantly evident that American citizens everywhere are demanding and supporting speedy and complete action in recognition of obvious danger.

Therefore, the immediate need is a swift and driving increase in our armament production. . . .

For what we send abroad we shall be repaid, within a reasonable time following the close of hostilities, in similar materials, or, at our option, in other goods of many kinds which they can produce and which we need.

Let us say to the democracies: "We Americans are vitally concerned in your defense of freedom. We are putting forth our energies, our resources and our organizing powers to give you the strength to regain and maintain a free world. We shall send you, in ever-increasing numbers, ships, planes, tanks, guns. This is our purpose and our pledge."

In fulfillment of this purpose we will not be intimidated by the threats of dictators that they will regard as a breach of international law and as an act of war our aid to the democracies which dare to resist their aggression. Such aid is not an act of war, even if a dictator should unilaterally proclaim it so to be.

When the dictators, if the dictators, are ready to make war upon us they will not wait for an act of war on our part. They did not wait for Norway or Belgium or the Netherlands to commit an act of war. . . .

In the future days, which we seek to make secure, we look forward to a world founded upon four essential human freedoms.

The first is freedom of speech and expression—everywhere in the world.

The second is freedom of every person to worship God in his own way—everywhere in the world,

The third is freedom from want—which, translated into world terms, means economic understandings which will secure to every nation a healthy peacetime life for its inhabitants—everywhere in the world.

The fourth is freedom from fear—which, translated into world terms, means a world-wide reduction of armaments to such a point and in such a thorough fashion that no nation will be in a position to commit an act of physical aggression against any neighbor—anywhere in the world. . . .

This nation has placed its destiny in the hands and heads and hearts of its millions of free men and women; and its faith in freedom under the guidance of God. Freedom means the supremacy of human rights everywhere. Our support goes to those who struggle to gain those rights and keep them. Our strength is our unity of purpose.

To that high concept there can be no end save victory.

The Administration followed this appeal by the introduction of a "British Aid" bill (House bill 1776) giving the President emergency authority to make the United States the "arsenal of democracy" and to "sell, transfer, exchange, lease, lend or otherwise dispose of" or cause to be manufactured defense materials "for the government of any country whose defense the President deems vital to the defense of the United States." Wendell Willkie endorsed the principle of the bill and carried greetings from Roosevelt to Churchill on his visit to bomb-battered London at the end of January. The bill was attacked, on the ground that it would "lead to war" and create a "dictatorship," by an incongruous congeries of isolationists, Communists, superpatriots, Nazis, Socialists, pacifists, and Fascists.

After leisurely hearings and prolonged debate, the "lease-lend" bill was approved by the Senate, 60-31, and by the House, 317-71, with the addition of minor amendments. The Act was signed by the President on March 11, 1941. He therewith received the authority he sought, "notwithstanding the provisions of any other law," subject to termination on June 30, 1943, or earlier by concurrent resolution of Congress. The Act declared that it did not authorize the convoying of vessels by naval vessels of the United States or the entry of American vessels into combat areas. But Congress and public opinion were now clearly dedicated to the defeat of the Axis. All necessary means to the end in view would follow as a matter of course—unless Americans should acquiesce in the failure of the enterprise to which they had put their hearts and hands and thus invite disaster upon themselves. The President at once requested and received an appropriation of $7,000,000,000 to give effect to the new policy, in addition to the $1,300,000,000 worth of defense articles, procured from funds hitherto appropriated, which he was authorized to transfer by the Act itself.[1]

---

[1] By March, 1941, defense appropriations were approaching a total of $35,000,000,000 for the preceding twelve-month period, a figure comparable to American war expenditures in 1917–1918.

This course was not a declaration of war. It was unlikely to provoke any open retaliation from the Triplice so long as Britain still fought. The initiative in precipitating hostilities with the United States was left to Berlin, Rome, and Tokio. They were likely to accept the challenge only when the advantages of such a course should appear to outweigh the disadvantages. If the new policy was to prove successful, the British Commonwealth and the United States would together face a task far more difficult than that of "national defense" and one which few of their people displayed any eagerness to grapple with: that of crushing the Triplice and rebuilding a world order in which the myths and illusions of neutrality, isolation, and national sovereignty would all alike be abandoned. If, on the other hand, British resistance crumbled, America would face a fight for its life with little hope of peace or plenty ever again in this generation.

SUGGESTED READINGS

Aikman, D.: *The All-American Front*, New York, Doubleday, 1939.
Alsop, J., and R. Kintner: *American White Paper*, New York, Simon & Schuster, 1940.
Angell, Norman: *America's Dilemma: Alone or Allied?*, New York, Harper, 1940.
Bailey, T. A.: *A Diplomatic History of the American People*, New York, Crofts, 1939.
Beals, C.: *America South*, Philadelphia, Lippincott, 1937.
———: *The Coming Struggle for Latin America*, Philadelphia, Lippincott, 1938.
Beard, C. A.: *The Idea of National Interest*, New York, Macmillan, 1934.
———: *The Open Door at Home*, New York, Macmillan, 1934.
——— : *A Foreign Policy for America*, New York, Knopf, 1940.
——— and M. R. Beard: *America in Midpassage*, New York, Macmillan, 1939.
Bemis, S.: *American Secretaries of State and Their Diplomacy*, New York, Knopf, 1920.
Bienstock, G.: *The Struggle for the Pacific*, New York, Macmillan, 1937.
Birdsall, P.: *Versailles Twenty Years After*, New York, Reynal, 1941.
Borchard, E., and W. P. Lage: *Neutrality for the United States*, New Haven, Yale University Press, 1937.
Buell, R. L.: *Isolated America*, New York, Knopf, 1940.
Chamberlain, J.: *The American Stakes*, New York, Carrick and Evans, 1940.
Dennis, L.: *The Coming American Fascism*, New York, Harper, 1936.
Dulles, A. W., and H. F. Armstrong: *Can America Stay Neutral?* New York, Harper, 1939.
Dulles, F. R.: *America in the Pacific*, Boston, Houghton, 1932.
Eliot, G. F.: *The Ramparts We Watch*, New York, Reynal, 1938.
Fagen, M. M.: *The Illusion of Neutrality*, New York, Oxford, 1939.
Fenwick, C. G.: *American Neutrality: Trial and Failure*, New York, New York University Press, 1940.
Fleming, D. F.: *The United States and World Organization*, 1920–1933, New York, Columbia University Press, 1938.
Griswold, A. W.: *The Far Eastern Policy of the United States*, New York, Harcourt, 1938.
Haas, W. H. (ed.): *The American Empire*, Chicago, University of Chicago Press, 1940.
Hallgren, M. A.: *The Tragic Fallacy: A Study of America's War Policies*, New York, Knopf, 1937.
Hill, H., and H. Agar: *Beyond German Victory*, New York, Reynal, 1940.
Johnstone, W. C.: *The United States and Japan's New Order*, New York, Oxford, 1941.
Jones, S., D. P. Myers (eds.): *Documents on American Foreign Relations, January 1938–June 1939*, vol. II, *June, 1939–June 1940*, Boston, World Peace Foundation, 1939.
Latané, J. H. (David W. Wainhouse's 2d revision): *American Foreign Policy*, New York, Odyssey Press, 1940.
Lindley, E. K.: *Half Way with Roosevelt*, New York, Viking, 1936.

Markham, P.: *America Next*, Indianapolis, Bobbs-Merrill, 1940.

Millis, W.: *The Road to War* (1917), Boston, Houghton 1935.

Myers, W. S., and W. H. Newton: *The Hoover Administration*, New York, Scribner, 1936.

Rippy, J. F.: *Caribbean Danger Zone*, New York, Putnam, 1940.

Seymour, Charles: *American Neutrality*, 1914–1917, New Haven, Yale University Press, 1936.

Schuman, F. L., and George Soule: *America Looks Abroad*, New York, Foreign Policy Association, 1938.

Shepardson, W. H. (in collaboration with W. O. Scroggs): *The United States in World Affairs*, New York, Harper, published annually for Council on Foreign Relations.

Sprout, H. and M.: *Toward a New Order of Sea Power*, Princeton, N. J., Princeton University Press, 1940.

Tansill, C. C.: *America Goes to War* (1917), Boston, Little Brown, 1938.

Tobin, H. J., and P. W. Bidwell: *Mobilizing Civilian America*, New York, Council on Foreign Relations, 1940.

White, W. A. (ed.): *Defense for America*, New York, Macmillan, 1940.

Williams, B. H.: *The United States and Disarmament*, New York, Whittlesey House, 1931.

Williams, M. W.: *The People and Politics of Latin America*, Boston, Ginn, 1938.

4. U.S.S.R.: VICTOR OR VICTIM?

> Workers of the world, unite! You have nothing to lose but your chains.
> —Communist Manifesto, 1847.

> Unity of action of the proletariat on a national and international scale is the mighty weapon which renders the working class capable not only of successful defense but also of successful counter-offensive against Fascism, against the class enemy.—GEORGI DIMITROV, August 2, 1935.

> One cannot destroy any ideology by fire and sword. One may respect or hate Hitlerism, just as any other system of political views. This is a matter of taste. But to undertake war for "annihilation of Hitlerism" means to commit criminal folly in politics. . . .
> For whose benefit is this war waged for domination of the world? In any case, not for the benefit of the working class. The working class can only suffer in such a war.—IZVESTIA, October 9, 1939.

A year and a half after the outbreak of the Second World War the only Great Power which was still "neutral" in the old sense of the term was the Union of Socialist Soviet Republics. If Chamberlain and Daladier hoped to win "peace" for their countrymen by standing aside while Hitler led his hosts to an assault upon Stalin's realm, Stalin had the ultimate satisfaction of standing aside while the Third Reich assaulted France and Britain. The course of the Munichmen might well have been ultimately disastrous to the Western Powers even had their initial expectations been realized. The enhancement of Nazi power through the invasion and defeat of Russia would have left France and Britain all but helpless before the victor. Whether Stalin's course in 1939-1941 would prove similarly disastrous to the Soviet Union depended upon whether the Triplice would defeat Britain—for the resulting enhancement of Nazi (and Japanese) power would leave the U.S.S.R. helpless before the victor. In the short run the Kremlin's diplomacy was as brilliantly successful in serving the interests of the Soviet State as the course of Downing Street and the Quai d'Orsay was catastrophic to the Western democracies. What ultimate verdict time might render remained to be seen.

THE ROMANOVS. The old Russian State, stretching in its immensity from the Arctic wastes to the tropic deserts of Turkestan, and from the Baltic and Black Seas across the steppes of Eurasia to the far Pacific, was created by a process of territorial conquest and accretion on the part of the Grand Duchy of Muscovy. Always bearing upon its face the imprint of the Tartar conquest, always half Asiatic and half European, the Russia of the Romanovs remained backward, primitive, isolated from the main currents of Western culture, despite its efforts to secure "windows to the West" and to fashion itself after Western models. In its political and economic institutions and its social life, it was almost medieval. Its government was an arbitrary and unlimited autocracy until 1905, and the Duma, or Parliament, which was the fruit of the first revolution, was a debating society without authority. Its ruling class was a feudal, land-owning aristocracy and a corrupt and irresponsible bureaucracy. The great mass of its population—the "dark people"—consisted of illiterate peasants steeped in ignorance and superstitious religiosity and living in a status of serfdom until 1863. The Industrial Revolution did not come to Russia until the seventies and eighties of the nineteenth century. The urban bourgeoisie which it brought in its wake pleaded for democracy and parliamentary government, but it was given little voice in public affairs. The urban proletariat, recruited from the peasantry, lived in misery under the pressure of ruthless exploitation and had no voice at all in government, except through terrorism and revolutionary violence. While the workers sought salvation in the Western gospel of international Marxian Socialism and the bourgeoisie in the gospel of democratic and patriotic liberalism, the peasantry remained dumb and inert, moved only by blind land hunger and hatred of the landlords.

The foreign policy of this State reflected the interests and attitudes of a ruling class which was aristocratic, religious, and mystically loyal to Holy Russia and to the cult of racial patriotism known as Pan-Slavism. In its quest for power, Tsarist Russia strove for diplomatic stakes expressed not so much in terms of the profit motives of its merchants and industrialists as in terms of the demand for land on the part of its semi-feudal oligarchy of nobles. Some of its nobles were capitalists, and some of its non-noble capitalists were politically influential—and these groups had eyes open for concessions, leaseholds, and markets on the Asiatic fringes of the empire. But Russian economy imported capital and manufactured goods from abroad and exported grain and raw materials. Its imperialism was not a commercial and naval imperialism, but a military and agrarian imperialism of population. As early as the seventeenth century, it reached out across Siberia. In the eighteenth century, it struck Sweden to the north, Poland to the west, Turkey to the south, and extended itself over large areas formerly controlled by these States. In the nineteenth century, it penetrated central Asia, impinged upon Persia, Afghanistan, and China, and encountered the rival imperialisms of Great Britain and Japan. Friction with Britain led to the Crimean War of 1854–1856, in which the progress of the Russian steam roller toward Constantinople and the Straits was temporarily halted. Continued Anglo-Russian rivalry in Asia contributed to the decision to enter into the Dual Alliance with France in 1894. Conflict with Japan led to defeat in Manchuria in 1904–1905 and to internal revolution as the aftermath of defeat. In the years which followed, the continued drive toward the Straits and toward control of the Slavic States of the Balkans made Austria-Hungary and Germany the new enemies—and against these Powers an advantageous combination could be made with France, Great Britain, and even Japan.

The Great War of 1914 was precipitated by the Tsarist Government with the approval of the Quai d'Orsay. The Franco-Russian Alliance had already been "Balkanized," and French support of Russian Balkan policies was secured. Izvolsky, Russian Foreign Minister until 1910 and Russian Ambassador to Paris subsequently, smarted under the diplomatic defeat of 1908 arising out of the Austrian annexation of Bosnia and Herzegovina without compensation to Russia. He was spokesman for those at the Russian Foreign Office determined to acquire the Straits and to block the Teutonic *Drang nach Osten*. In Poincaré, he found a fitting helpmate for the realization of these ambitions. By 1914, Russian military preparations, financed from France, were sufficiently advanced to enable St. Petersburg to risk war over these issues. Russia accordingly championed Serbia in the Austro-Serbian conflict of July, 1914. It was the mobilization of the Russian army against Austria-Hungary and Germany on July 30 which made a general war inevitable; for it was understood in the Franco-Russian Alliance that "mobilization means war," and this was no less clear to Berlin and Vienna. Germany responded to this threat by an ultimatum which remained unanswered. A declaration of war followed on August 1. On September 5, 1914, Russia agreed with Great Britain and France not to conclude peace separately. The inter-Allied secret treaties of 1916 and 1917 promised to the Tsardom, in the prospective division of the spoils, all that it had been striving for and more besides.

But the terrific impact of the German military machine upon Russia brought overwhelming disaster to the entire economic, social, and political structure of the Romanov State. During 1915 and 1916, Galicia and Russian Poland were lost to the enemy, and the ill-equipped and badly led Russian army was driven back in defeat with enormous losses. The transport system collapsed. Food riots broke out in the cities. Mutiny raised its head at the front. "Dark forces" appeared at the court, favoring peace with Germany to save the autocracy. Their spokesman, the mad monk Rasputin, was assassinated by patriotic liberals, but the process of economic and social disintegration went on. The political authority of the reactionaries who surrounded the Tsar was reduced to a nullity as revolution spread throughout the country. In mid-March of 1917, following numerous strikes and revolts, Nicholas II was obliged to abdicate and give way to a "Provisional Government" composed of Duma members of a liberal bourgeois and mildly Socialistic persuasion. This government, under Kerensky's leadership, sought to continue the war and to pave the way for a constituent assembly which would solve all problems and make Russia a middle-class parliamentary democracy. While it deliberated and debated, however, peasants seized the estates of the nobles, workers occupied factories, and soldiers deserted from the front to share in the new freedom. Real power throughout the country passed to spontaneously organized councils, or *soviets*, of workers', soldiers', and peasants' deputies, who spoke for the war-weary masses and insisted upon an end of the imperialist war, the partition of the landed estates, and the socialization of industry.

THE REVOLUTION. There ensued the most revolutionary and far-reaching social upheaval of modern times, demolishing utterly the existing economic and social fabric of Russia and shaking all of Western society to its foundations. Under the leadership of the revolutionary Bolshevik wing of the Social-Democratic party, the trade unions demanded that the political revolution be transformed into a social revolution and that power be transferred to the soviets. The impotent Kerensky régime tottered to its doom, unable either to carry on the war or to withdraw from it, helpless either to avert social revolution or to accept it. With their slogans of "All Power to the Soviets" and "Peace, Land, and Bread," the Bolshevik leaders secured ascendancy in the soviets and organized the new proletarian revolution. On November 7, 1917, the Provisional Government was overthrown by the armed workers of Petrograd, and the Second All-Russian Congress of Soviets approved the creation of a Council of People's Commissars, of which Lenin became president. The Soviet Government, thus established, proceeded at once to expropriate the landlords and the bourgeoisie, to abolish private property in real estate and the means of industrial production, to distribute the land to the villages, to establish workers' control in the factories, mills, and mines, and to lay plans for a socialized economy. In 1918 the Bolsheviki changed their name to the Communist party, in order to distinguish themselves from the Reformist Socialists. The former ruling classes were deprived of their wealth and power and replaced by the workers and peasants, under the leadership of the most class-conscious section of the urban proletariat, organized into the Communist party. This party brushed aside the constituent assembly, assumed a "monopoly of legality" in the Soviet Government, and ruled in the name of "the dictatorship of the proletariat"—a form of political authority intended to prepare the way for a Communistic social order and a classless State.

The foreign policy of the new workers' republic led to immediate friction with the bourgeois governments which were the allies of the old Russia. The Communists regarded their revolution as but a step toward a world revolution of the international proletariat, leading to the universal overthrow of capitalism, nationalism, and imperialism. The bourgeois governments regarded the Communists as a group of dangerous fanatics, whose subversive assault on the existing order must be met by ruthless suppression at the hands of the "sane" elements in Russia, *i.e.*, the expropriated classes, aided by the outside world. Quite apart from this class conflict across national frontiers, there were specific grievances which impelled the Allies and the United States to move against the proletarian dictatorship. The Soviet Government at once opened peace negotiations with the Central Powers. When the Allies refused to participate, the Communists published the secret treaties, in order to reveal to the masses the imperialistic war aims of the Entente. An armistice was concluded on the eastern front in December, 1917; and in March, 1918, the humiliating peace of Brest-Litovsk took Russia out of the war. The Soviet Government, moreover, repudiated the public debts contracted by the Tsarist and Kerensky régimes, including both the pre-war government bonds, held in enormous quantities by French and British investors, and the huge war loans extended by the governments of Great Britain, France, and the United States. It likewise confiscated foreign property and private investments in Russia, along with the holdings of the Russian bourgeoisie. It summoned the workers of the world to revolt against the war and to overthrow the capitalistic governments which were directing it. The Central Powers seized upon the opportunity presented by the revolution to make an advantageous peace in the east. But between the Soviets and the Allies there could be no peace.

In August, 1918, Soviet Russia was subjected to an Allied blockade and to military intervention, participated in by Czechoslovakian, British, French, American, Japanese, and other Allied troops. The intervention coincided with counter-revolutionary uprisings within Russia, subsidized and supported by the Allied Governments, and with the beginning of the civil war. The moderate Socialist enemies of the Communist dictatorship played into the hands of the counter-revolution and were soon swept aside by Tsarist reactionaries, or "Whites," who rallied to their cause the former landowners and business classes. Blockade, intervention, and revolt were supplemented by terrorism and sabotage as weapons against the Soviets. In Finland the workers' government was drowned in blood by White terrorists, with German support. In the north, Allied and American troops seized Archangel and advanced southward toward Vologda and Moscow. In the Caucasus and the Ukraine, Denikin's White Army, with Allied financial and military support, prepared to invade central Russia. In Siberia, Kolchak's White Army, with Allied financial and military support, prepared to do likewise, while Japanese, American, and British troops occupied the Maritime Provinces. In Estonia, Yudenitch's White Army, with Allied financial and military support, prepared to take Petrograd.

The Soviet Government was assaulted on all sides from without and menaced by counter-revolution from within. It met these threats to its existence by suppressing the opposition parties, by inaugurating the Red Terror as a reply to the White terrorism of its enemies, and by organizing the Red Army to defend the revolution. In March, 1919, the Communist, or Third, International was established, with its headquarters at Moscow, as an international federation of the revolutionary Communist parties throughout the world. It was designed to replace the bankrupt Second International of the moderate Socialist parties and to serve as the general staff of the "world revolution" which would attack from the rear the bourgeois governments seeking to strangle the Russian proletarian dictatorship.

The civil strife which followed was long and bloody and characterized by unprecedented savagery and destructiveness; for it was not only an international conflict between Soviet Russia and the Allied and Associated Powers, but a class war between the Russian nobility and bourgeoisie on the one hand and the proletariat and peasantry on the other. The details of the campaigns need not be reviewed here. Suffice it to say that the Red Army, under the direction of Trotsky and his comrades, finally proved more than a match for its enemies, domestic and foreign. Kolchak's forces were driven back from Kazan in the spring of 1919. The Allied and American invaders from the north were finally stopped and later compelled to withdraw. In October, 1919—the darkest month of the revolution—Denikin's divisions approached Moscow from the south, while Yudenitch, with British support, attacked Petrograd. Both offensives were beaten back. Kolchak's army was crushed in central Siberia, and he was captured and executed in February, 1920. The other White Armies were similarly destroyed, despite desperate Allied attempts to save them. Peace seemed in sight in the spring of 1920, when the armies of the new Poland invaded the Ukraine in a mad imperialistic endeavor to restore the Polish frontiers of 1772. Kiev fell to the invaders; but in the summer of 1920 the Polish forces were pushed back, and the Red Army approached the gates of Warsaw and threatened to carry revolution into central Europe. British and French assistance enabled the Poles to counterattack successfully under the direction of General Maxime Weygand, and the war closed in October. Meanwhile, a new White leader, Baron Wrangel, had seized the Crimea, invaded the Ukraine, and secured diplomatic recognition and military and financial support from France. His troops were speedily dispersed by the Red Army in the winter of 1920–1921, and the civil war came to a close with the defeat of intervention and counter-revolution.

The year 1921 marked a definite turning point, both in the internal policies and in the foreign relations of the Soviet Government. The end of the assault from abroad left Russia economically prostrate as a result of six years of almost uninterrupted hostilities. Lenin executed a temporary "strategic retreat toward capitalism" in the New Economic Policy of March, 1921, which permitted a certain amount of individual trade for private profit. At the same time, Great Britain granted *de facto* recognition to the Soviet régime by concluding a trade agreement. The blockade was broken. The *cordon sanitaire* was at an end. A truce prevailed between the proletarian dictatorship and the bourgeois States, and the Communists could turn at last to the difficult task of laying the foundation of the new social order. The restoration of trade relations with the outside world was an integral part of the process, for economic rehabilitation required the importation of machinery, manufactures, and foreign technical skill to be paid for by the export of grain, oil, timber, and other Russian raw materials. At the Genoa Conference of 1922, Chicherin, Commissar for Foreign Affairs, met the representatives of the other European Powers in a general conference for the first time. They demanded payment of Russia's debt and compensation to expropriated investors as the price of recognition, credits, and trade relations. Their bill of 13 billion dollars was met by a Soviet counterclaim of 60 billions for damage done during the intervention. Neither side would yield, and no general agreement was possible. But a bargain was struck with the new Germany in the Treaty of Rapallo, whereby all claims were canceled and mutually advantageous commercial relations were restored. Other States could not afford to ignore the Soviet market. Great Britain extended *de jure* recognition in February, 1924. France, Italy, Japan, and a dozen lesser States followed suit within the next eighteen months, with the United States alone among the Great Powers persisting in its refusal to restore diplomatic relations until 1933. The revolutionary outcast was received again into the community of nations, and a growing foreign commerce hastened the work of internal reconstruction.

THE "SOCIALIST FATHERLAND." Meanwhile the frontiers of the new Russia had been redefined and a territorial reorganization of the Soviet State effected. The Treaty of Brest-Litovsk was liquidated by the defeat of Germany in the Great War and by the express provisions of the Treaty of Versailles. During the intervention, Great Britain and France sought to acquire spheres of influence in southern Russia, for reasons of strategy, oil, and high politics, while Japan seized eastern Siberia and Poland cast covetous eyes on the Ukraine. The United States opposed these territorial acquisitions by championing the integrity of Russia—of a capitalistic "national" Russia, which Washington hoped would emerge. But the Red Army ousted the invaders, and Moscow pursued its own policies. In accordance with its principles of national self-determination, the Soviet Government was quite prepared to recognize the independence of Finland, Estonia, Latvia, Lithuania, and Poland, with boundaries corresponding to the lines of language. The Baltic States became independent. Their boundaries were fixed in a series of treaties of 1920 and 1921. Poland and Rumania, however, were determined to seize Russian territory. Rumania occupied Bessarabia in 1918, with the approval of the Allied Powers, and held it thereafter in the face of the persistent refusal of Moscow to concede the legality of this action. The Polish invasion of 1920 was driven back; but the boundary drawn in the Treaty of Riga of March, 1921, was a compromise which transferred several million Ukrainians and White Russians to Polish rule. Still unsatisfied, Poland seized Vilna from Lithuania in October, 1920; but in this chronic quarrel between her western neighbors, Soviet Russia took no sides save for a certain moral support given to the Lithuanian claims. In the Caucasus the old boundaries were substantially restored by agreements with Turkey and Persia. On the Pacific coast the continued Japanese occupation was met by the creation of the "Far Eastern Republic," a semi-independent Soviet buffer State which was reabsorbed in 1922. In 1925, Japan extended full recognition to Moscow and evacuated all former Russian territory in return for oil and fishing concessions. The agreements with China of 1924 provided for joint ownership and management of the Chinese Eastern Railway across north Manchuria. Outer Mongolia became a Soviet dependency, and Chinese Turkestan was penetrated by Soviet influence. Within Soviet jurisdiction, cultural autonomy was granted to the linguistic minorities; and under the constitution of 1923, creating the U.S.S.R., the Soviet State became a federation of seven units.

The power interests of the U.S.S.R. in international politics, like those of all other States, are intelligible by reference to the attitudes and values of its ruling class. While "capitalistic" States were dominated politically by nationalistic businessmen or landowners, moved by patriotism and by profit motives, these classes were destroyed in Russia and replaced by a new political *élite* speaking in the name of the proletariat. The Russian proletariat, as represented by the Communist party, is antinational, anticapitalist, anti-imperialist. Social and political cohesion in Soviet society was not at first achieved through the symbols of national patriotism, but through those of the revolutionary international proletariat. For the Communists, lines of cleavage and conflict based on language, race, and nationality are effaced by the universal class war between the workers of the world and their exploiters. The Soviet State is composed of numerous linguistic and national groups. It is regarded by its builders, not as a national entity, but as the socialist fatherland, as the citadel of the world proletariat, as the precursor of that world federation of Soviet republics which will follow the world revolution. Its historic mission is the creation of a socialist society and the organization of the class-conscious workers of all countries for the revolutionary seizure of power on a world scale. Its foreign policy is necessarily dominated by the exigencies of this mission.

In view of the "temporary stabilization of capitalism" following the Great War, the U.S.S.R. directed its energies toward building socialism on firm foundations in Russia, rather than toward working for an immediate world revolution. The view of 1917–1919 that a single socialist State could not survive in a hostile capitalistic world was abandoned in favor of the view that political and economic relations with the bourgeois States could be advantageously employed to contribute toward the immediate task in Russia. The world revolution seemed imminent in 1919, with Soviet governments established in Bavaria and Hungary, with all of central Europe in turmoil, and with working-class unrest prevalent throughout the world. By 1921, these hopes had faded. Soviet support was given to the Kuomintang, or revolutionary Nationalist party, in China, but the party came to be dominated by bourgeois and militarist elements and expelled its Soviet advisers in 1927. The Communist movement in China was driven underground, but the seeds which had been sown flowered later in an indigenous Communism among Chinese peasants and workers, who secured control of large areas of the central and southern provinces and successfully resisted the Kuomintang dictatorship. Lenin's disciple, Stalin, and his fellow rulers of the Soviet Union now held that the final cataclysm of capitalism was in the future and that the world proletarian revolution would perhaps come only in the wake of the next great war. The Communist International and its national sections—the Communist parties of the various countries—continued to lay their plans in anticipation of this final event. But, for the present, the greatest service to the international proletariat was envisaged as the strengthening of socialist economy in the U.S.S.R.

The decision to "build socialism" in one country was not reached without sharp conflicts of views among the Soviet leaders, reflected later in foreign policy and in the strategy of the Comintern. The disastrous famine of 1921–1923 and the restoration of productivity achieved by the N.E.P. led to general acceptance of Lenin's tactics of retreat. Following his death in January, 1924, Stalin and Trotsky became rivals, with the latter insisting on world revolution, the immediate liquidation of the kulaks, or wealthy peasants, and the suppression of all private trade. Stalin's control of the party machine and Trotsky's infractions of party discipline led to the latter's dismissal and exile in 1927. He denounced Stalin as a betrayer of the revolution and sought to organize ultra-revolutionary Communists abroad into an anti-Stalinist "Fourth International."[1] After the restoration of production to its pre-war level, Stalin launched the first Five Year Plan in 1928. The N.E.P. was abolished, and a huge program of industrialization was embarked upon. Private trade was suppressed. The kulaks were liquidated with the collectivization of agriculture in 1931–1933. This gigantic agrarian revolution, which abolished individual peasant farms in favor of cooperative collectives and state farms, led to much injustice and suffering, approaching the proportions of famine in some areas; but it was ruthlessly pushed through to a successful conclusion. Industrial and agricultural production rose steadily and paved the way for the second Five Year Plan (1933–1938).

With land in process of socialization and bread of dubious quantity and quality during the transition, Moscow's greatest desire was for peace. Foreign Commissar Chicherin and Maxim Litvinov, his able aide and successor after 1930, bent all their energies toward ensuring peace, securing recognition, fostering trade relations, and forestalling dangers of new attacks on the U.S.S.R. These objectives seemed at times to create a divergence of purposes between the Soviet Foreign Office (the Narko-mindel) and the Comintern. Soviet diplomats offered cooperation, but Comintern agents preached revolution. Acute friction with Britain in 1927–1929, controversies with France in 1929–1930, and continued non-recognition by the United States were in part results of this dualism of Moscow's attitude toward the world. After the Sixth Congress of the Comintern in 1928, no Congresses were held for seven years. Trotsky's fulminations in exile went unheeded. Litvinov gave qualified diplomatic support to the German Republic and to Turkey, Hungary, Italy, and the "revisionist" cause in general against the French bloc, preferring to aid weak potential enemies against strong ones. He championed disarma-

---

[1] Trotsky was assassinated in his home near Mexico City on August 21, 1940, by an alleged follower who was at once accused by Trotskyites of being a "Stalinist agent."

ment, hailed the Kellogg Pact (which the Soviet Union ratified before any of the other Great Powers), and negotiated a series of neutrality and nonaggression agreements with other States.

AGAINST FASCISM. The triumph of Fascism in Germany in 1933 altered fundamentally the peace problem of the U.S.S.R. The German Communist party, largest in the world outside of Russia, had gone down to defeat without a struggle. To the end, it had fought bitterly the largest of Socialist parties. Both had been destroyed, along with German Liberalism and the Weimar Republic. The Nazi leaders were loudly committed to conquest in the east and to an armed crusade against Bolshevism.[1] Militant Fascism threatened Moscow with armed attack and promised to destroy Communists, Socialists, and liberals in other States. To prevent assault from Berlin, Moscow must arm to the teeth and find allies. To prevent destruction of the Communist movement throughout the world, Moscow must cooperate with Socialists and liberals against Fascism. The Narkomindel and the Comintern faced the new task realistically. The result was a revolution in Soviet diplomacy and a reorientation of international Communism.

The Franco-Soviet nonaggression pact of November 29, 1932, was supplemented by a commercial treaty of January 11, 1934, following a diplomatic, commercial, and military *rapprochment* during the year of the Nazi seizure of power in the Reich. Agreements of April and May with Poland and the Baltic States extended these nonaggression pacts to 1945. Closer relations were cultivated with Turkey and Great Britain. In June, 1934, Czechoslovakia and Rumania, on the advice of Louis Barthou, recognized the U.S.S.R., following the example of Hungary in February. On September 18, 1934, the Soviet Union became a member of the League of Nations. Efforts to conclude a nonaggression pact with Berlin and to induce the Reich to enter into an "eastern Locarno" failed. Litvinov strove for a defensive mutual assistance pact with France and the Little Entente, including Germany if she would enter, against Germany if she refused. Tukhachevsky, Vice Commissar of Defense, announced in January, 1935, that the Red army had been increased from 562,000 to 940,000 and that planes, tanks, and artillery had been multiplied many

---

[1] The most popular Nazi philosophical work, *The Myth of the Twentieth Century*, by the Russian émigré, Alfred Rosenberg, contains such passages as the following: "'From West to East' is now the direction from the Rhine to the Vistula, 'from West to East' must resound from Moscow to Tomsk. The 'Russian' who cursed Peter and Catherine was a real Russian. Europe should never have been forced upon him. In the future, after the separation of the non-Russian territories (the western provinces, the Ukraine, the Caucasus) he will have to be content to transfer his center of gravity to Asia. . . . Let him turn his 'word' to the East where there may be room for it, having first cleansed it of that admixture of ideas of Baboeuf, Blank [sic], Bakunin, Tolstoi, Lenin, and Marx, called Bolshevism. In Europe, which is alien to him and which he hates, there is no room for him any more." Munich edition of 1930, p. 601.

fold. Under the impact of Hitler's repudiation of the disarmament clauses of the Treaty of Versailles, Paris signed a mutual assistance pact with Moscow on May 2, and Prague followed suit on May 16, 1935. The U.S.S.R. thus became the ally of France and Czechoslovakia, within the framework of the League, to resist Nazi aggression.

In midsummer, 1935, the Seventh Congress of the Comintern met at Moscow. The old slogan of world revolution—"Turn imperialist war into civil war"—was replaced by a call for union against Fascism. The Comintern resolved to discontinue, or at least defer, its assaults on Socialists and liberals and its efforts to overturn bourgeois democratic governments. The new policy of the "united front" contemplated a strategic retreat toward the right and loyal cooperation not only with Socialist parties but with bourgeois groups opposed to Fascism. Even the Roman Catholics in Germany were invited to join in opposing Nazi rule. An appeal was addressed to the Second International of Socialist Parties at Amsterdam to participate in the new alliance. This policy was met with bitter condemnation on the part of Trotsky and his disciples as a fresh betrayal of the world revolution and a new compromise with capitalism. By Socialists and liberals, it was greeted with suspicion, since the plea of the "united front" (from below) had been made before for the purpose of "boring from within" and seeking to place the organizations which cooperated under Communist domination. Amsterdam spurned fusion with Moscow or even general collaboration. British Laborites as well as Socialists in Czechoslovakia and America likewise declined to cooperate. But in France and Spain, liberals and Socialists joined Communists in Popular Front movements to resist Fascist attacks on democracy.

The new dispensation was accompanied by plans for liberalizing the Soviet régime. In July, 1934, the O.G.P.U., or secret political police, was abolished and its functions transferred to the Commissariat of Internal Affairs. After long deliberation a new Union Constitution was announced in June, 1936, and adopted in November. It created a Parliament or Supreme Soviet of two chambers, one—the Council of the Union—elected by direct and secret ballot every four years with the franchise restored to the former "enemy" classes, and the other—the Council of Nationalities—consisting of elected delegates from the constituent republics, which were increased from seven to eleven. An elected judiciary was also provided, and more adequate protection of individual rights was pledged. This evolution away from dictatorship, however, was transitory. On December 1, 1934, Sergei Kirov, aide of Stalin, was assassinated in Leningrad. Within a few weeks thereafter, 117 persons were executed as terrorists. Zinoviev and Kamenev, former Soviet leaders and once supporters of Trotsky, were implicated in the plot and sentenced to prison. In August, 1936, they, along with 14 others, were charged with conspiring with Trotsky, in his Norwegian exile, to slay Kirov, Stalin, and other Communist functionaries in a Trotskyite-Fascist murder plot. The accused confessed. Trotsky denied all. The defendants were found guilty and shot. Paradoxically, this act—representing a complete break between the Stalin leadership (which was committed to democratization of the régime, to the united front, and to the soft-pedaling of world revolution) and the Trotsky opposition (still bent on proletarian revolt everywhere)— antagonized foreign liberals who otherwise were sympathetic with Stalin rather than Trotsky. As in all dictatorships, ruthless means were held to be justified by ideal ends, but to critics the ends seem to be destroyed by the means.

In January, 1937, in a further trial of Trotskyites (who confessed to attempted assassination, sabotage, espionage, counter-revolution, and conspiracy with Trotsky to aid Germany and Japan in war on the U.S.S.R.), Karl Radek and Gregory Sokolnikov were sentenced to ten years' imprisonment and thirteen other defendants were executed, including Gregory Piatakov and L. Serebriakov, both former prominent officials. Trotsky, then in Mexico after expulsion from Norway, again denied all and cried "frame-up." In April Henry Yagoda, head of the "reformed" G.P.U., was arrested. In June Marshal Tukhachevsky and seven other high officers were court-martialed and shot for treason. In December Leo Kharakhan and other diplomats were executed for allegedly treasonable dealings with Tokio. In March, 1938, Bukharin, Yagoda, Rykov, Krestinsky, and fourteen other former leaders were tried, found guilty, and put to death, while Christian Rakovsky and two other defendants were given prison terms. All internal opposition to Stalin's leadership was thus drowned in blood. All alleged friends and agents of the Axis were "liquidated."

Other defensive measures had long since been devised to meet the danger of Japanese attack in the East. Recognition by the United States on November 16, 1933, was to some degree motivated by common suspicion of Japan. Moscow made repeated but vain efforts to conclude a nonaggression pact with Tokio. As further conciliatory gestures the U.S.S.R. sold the Chinese Eastern Railway to Manchukuo in March, 1935, and in the autumn of 1936 proposed to extend Japanese fishing and oil concessions in eastern Siberia—until the announcement of the German-Japanese anti-Communist accord of November 25 caused a reversal of policy. Japanese penetration of Inner Mongolia, which might place Japanese forces in a position to attack Ulan Bator and the Lake Baikal area, was met by a mutual assistance pact with Outer Mongolia, in force since 1934 and incorporated in a formal agreement on March 12, 1936. More important, a self-sufficient Far Eastern army of 250,000 troops under General Bluecher was established in the Maritime Provinces ready to invade Manchukuo should Japan attack. A thousand warplanes were poised at Vladivostok to give Tokio pause. The Trans-Siberian Railway was double-tracked and supplemented by a road north of Lake Baikal to Khabarovsk. Fears of a combined Nazi-Japanese attack, with possible Finnish and Polish support, led to strengthening frontier fortifications in the east and the west. By January, 1936, the Red Army numbered 1,300,-000 men and had some 6,000 tanks and 7,000 warplanes. Every effort was made to increase the output of mechanized armament. In reply to Hitler's verbal assaults at Nürnberg, Defense Commissar Voroshilov declared on September 17, 1936, "When the enemy attacks the Soviet Ukraine or Soviet White Russia or any other part of the Soviet Union, we will not only prevent his invading our own country, but will defeat him in the territory whence he comes."

THE FAILURE OF THE "POPULAR FRONT." These developments had consequences in terms of the hidden calculations of the Fascist Caesars which were misunderstood by most Western statesmen and commentators. They demonstrated to Hitler and to the war lords of Tokio that the U.S.S.R. was not a weak State but a strong one. They demonstrated that Stalin was prepared to crush internal dissent and to liquidate Nazi and Japanese "Fifth Columnists" and "Trojan Horses" with a ruthlessness worthy of the Führer, the Duce, and the army terrorists of Japan. They demonstrated that the one firm center of vigorous resistance to Fascist aggrandizement was the Soviet Union—not because Communists were converted to "democracy," but because defense of the "Socialist Fatherland" (whether a democracy or a dictatorship or a tyranny ruled by a Red Caesar) was the prime purpose of Communists everywhere. This purpose obviously required opposition to Fascism so long as the Fascist Powers menaced the U.S.S.R. The result was a slow and secret abandonment of Nazi and Japanese dreams of conquest at the expense of the Soviet State and a reorientation of aggressive designs against the Western Powers whose leaders and peoples no longer understood the world. Since these leaders continued to practice appeasement on the assumption that a Fascist-Communist clash was "inevitable," the Caesars found it advantageous to denounce Moscow on all occasions. With each passing year, they took their own threats less seriously, and the Kremlin became less concerned with them. Fascist mouthings of "anti-Bolshevism" were intended for ears in London, Paris, and Washington where they were taken quite seriously—to the ruin of the Western Powers.

Under these conditions, Soviet hopes of a "united front" with the West against the Triplice, and Communist hopes of a "united front" with Socialists and liberals against Fascism, were alike doomed to frustration. Without the support of the Western Powers, Moscow could not thwart

Fascist aggression. Without the support of Western democrats, Moscow could not combat Fascist tactics of disintegration in other States. When the U.S.S.R. sought to use the League to save Ethiopia from Mussolini, London and Paris preferred to save Mussolini at the cost of destroying Ethiopia and the League. When the U.S.S.R. sought to save the Spanish Republic by observing the "nonintervention" agreement only in the measure to which it was observed in Rome and Berlin, the Western appeasers preferred to cooperate with the Axis in destroying the Republican régime. The Spanish People's Front died. The French People's Front followed it to the grave. After *Anschluss*, Litvinov proposed a conference to consider ways and means of halting Hitler. Downing Street and the Quai d'Orsay refused. When Litvinov proposed joint defense of Czechoslovakia in 1938, Chamberlain and Halifax, with the support of Daladier and Bonnet, preferred to abandon Prague. After Munich the *Journal de Moscou* asked, "What now is the value of France's word? . . . What now is the value of the French-Soviet pact since France has just torn up her treaty with Czechoslovakia—a treaty that bound her much more strongly?" Immediately after the fall of Prague, Litvinov proposed a conference to consider joint action to halt aggression. London and Paris refused.

Correct conclusions were drawn from these events in Rome and Berlin. Correct conclusions were also drawn in Moscow. On March 10, 1939, Stalin spoke at length to the Eighteenth Congress of the Communist Party of the U.S.S.R. He ridiculed the Western Munichmen and bespoke friendship with the Caesars:

The majority of the non-aggressive countries, particularly England and France, have rejected the policy of collective security, the policy of collective resistance to the aggressors, and have taken up a position of non-intervention, a position of "neutrality." . . . The policy of non-intervention reveals an eagerness, a desire, not to hinder the aggressors in their nefarious work: not to hinder Japan, say, from embroiling herself in a war with China, or, better still, with the Soviet Union; not to hinder Germany, say, from enmeshing herself in European affairs, from embroiling herself in a war with the Soviet Union. . . . Cheap and easy! . . . Take Germany, for instance. They let her have Austria, despite the undertaking to defend her independence; they let her have the Sudeten region; they abandoned Czechoslovakia to her fate, thereby violating all their obligations; and then they began to lie vociferously in the press about "the weakness of the Russian army," "the demoralization of the Russian air force," and "riots" in the Soviet Union, egging the Germans on to march farther east, promising them easy pickings, and prompting them: "Just start war on the Bolsheviks, and everything will be all right." . . .

The hullabaloo raised by the British, French, and American press over the Soviet Ukraine is characteristic. The gentlemen of the press there shouted until they were hoarse that the Germans were marching on Soviet Ukraine, that they now had what is called the Carpathian Ukraine, with a population of some seven hundred thousand, and that not later than this spring the Germans would annex the Soviet Ukraine, which has a population of over thirty million, to this so-called Carpathian Ukraine. It looks as if the object of this suspicious hullabaloo was to incense the Soviet Union against Germany, to poison the atmosphere and to provoke a conflict with Germany without any visible grounds.

It is quite possible, of course, that there are madmen in Germany who dream of annexing the elephant, that is, the Soviet Ukraine, to the gnat, namely, the so-called Carpathian Ukraine. If there really are such lunatics in Germany, rest assured that we shall find enough straight-jackets for them in our country. But if we ignore the madmen and turn to normal people, is it not clearly absurd and foolish seriously to talk of annexing the Soviet Ukraine to this so-called Carpathian Ukraine? . . .

Far be it from me to moralize on the policy of non-intervention, to talk of treason, treachery, and so on. It would be naïve to preach morals to people who recognize no human morality. Politics is politics, as the old, case-hardened bourgeois diplomats say. It must be remarked, however, that the big and dangerous political game started by the supporters of the policy of non-intervention may end in a serious fiasco for them. . . .

1. We stand for peace and the strengthening of business relations with all countries. That is our position; and we shall adhere to this position as long as these countries maintain like relations with the Soviet Union, and as long as they make no attempt to trespass on the interests of our country.

2. We stand for peaceful, close, and friendly relations with all the neighbouring countries which have common frontiers with the U.S.S.R. That is our position; and we shall adhere to this position as long as these countries maintain like relations with the Soviet Union, and as long as they make no attempt to trespass, directly or indirectly, on the integrity and inviolability of the frontiers of the Soviet state.

3. We stand for the support of nations which are the victims of aggression and are fighting for the independence of their country.

4. We are not afraid of the threats of aggressors, and are ready to deal two blows for every blow delivered by instigators of war who attempt to violate the Soviet borders.

Within a week thereafter, Hitler liquidated Czecho-Slovakia, gave Carpatho-Ukraine to Hungary, and finally convinced the Western Munichmen that their States, rather than the U.S.S.R., were "on the list and would never be missed" after the Reich should strike. They accordingly sought to rebuild a coalition against Germany. The enterprise required Soviet collaboration. Moscow was willing to be wooed and even to be won—for a price. But most of the Western leaders were still motivated by abhorrence of Bolshevism and were by no means convinced that the Nazi threat was so grave as to require acceptance of Moscow's terms. This attitude confirmed the Kremlin's distrust. In the absence of mutual respect and of an equal sense of common danger and a willingness to compromise in order to face it, the obvious logic of *Realpolitik* led nowhere. British willingness to guarantee Poland and even Rumania and Greece before coming to terms with the U.S.S.R. evoked contempt in Moscow. *Pravda's* cartoon of April 4, 1939, showed a silk-hatted British lion in a boat extending a rock-loaded life belt to small nations struggling in a stormy sea swarming with sharks.

When Anglo-Soviet negotiations were initiated in mid-April, Moscow asked a binding alliance. London refused, preferring some more "flexible" formula which would not offend the "anti-Comintern" States and would leave Britain and France free if the Reich after all should attack the U.S.S.R. On May 3 Litvinov resigned his post as Commissar for Foreign Affairs in favor of Premier Vyacheslav Molotov. Chamberlain drew no conclusions from this event, although four days later the French Ambassador in Berlin began a series of ominous reports on the possibility of a Soviet-Nazi *rapprochement* to be followed by a new partition of Poland (*French Yellow Book of* 1939, No. 123*f.*). British counterproposals of May 8 contemplated Soviet aid to Britain and France should they be obliged to fight in defense of Poland or Rumania. Moscow asked Anglo-French aid to the U.S.S.R. should it be attacked or be obliged to fight in defense of the Baltic States. All three Powers should agree to defend one another and should guarantee all the border States between the Reich and the Soviet Union, as well as the border States (Switzerland, Belgium, and the Netherlands) between the Reich and the Western Powers. Churchill and Lloyd George urged acceptance of Molotov's terms. Chamberlain and Halifax refused. The Baltic States worshiped "neutrality" and desired no international guarantee participated in by the U.S.S.R. Downing Street would not guarantee States unwilling to be guaranteed. It proposed "consultation" in the event of any Nazi aggression in the Baltic. But Moscow knew that this was a formula to evade any commitment.

At the end of May Molotov publicly declared that Moscow would make no pact save on the basis of "reciprocity and equality of obligations" and that this required (1) a binding alliance; (2) a joint guarantee of all European countries bordering the U.S.S.R.; and (3) a concrete agreement for mutual aid and defense of the guaranteed States in the event of attack by aggressors. London and Paris now accepted (1) but balked at (2) and (3). The negotiations dragged on inconclusively. At the end of June, Andrei Zhdanov, Leningrad party leader, wrote in *Pravda* that he did not believe that the British and French Governments desired an equal treaty with the U.S.S.R. At the end of July Chamberlain announced that Anglo-French military missions would go to Moscow to initiate staff talks, pending conclusion of a definitive agreement which had been held up by differences of views on the proper definition of "indirect aggression." The missions were of wholly undistinguished personnel. They made a leisurely trip to the Soviet capital. Molotov, Voroshilov, and Stalin expected that they would have authority to sign a pact giving the U.S.S.R. the right to decide when the Baltic States were threatened, to act to meet the threat, to have necessary military access to the Baltic States and Poland, and to summon Britain and France to its support. They had no such authority. Deadlock was complete.

"NEUTRALITY" AND "DEFENSE." A complete revolution in Soviet diplomacy followed the failure of these discussions. Ribbentrop came to Moscow on August 23 and signed a German-Soviet nonaggression pact. Voroshilov declared that the U.S.S.R. could not defend Poland unless the Red Army were permitted to enter Polish territory. Neither Warsaw, Paris, nor London had been willing to grant such permission. Molotov told the Supreme Soviet on August 31, when the pact with Hitler was ratified, that the Western Powers had "plotted to involve us in war" without being willing to see the Soviet Union strengthened. Germany had dropped its anti-Soviet policy. The U.S.S.R. had no need to join either side. It would remain at peace. After several weeks of confusion, due to obvious ignorance of the Kremlin's new decision, the Communist parties of France, Britain, and America dropped all slogans of "People's Front," "Unity against Fascist Aggression," and the like; denounced as an "imperialist war" the new conflict which the pact of Moscow enabled Hitler to unleash; and developed a line of "revolutionary defeatism" which admirably served the purposes of Stalin—and of Hitler.

The Kremlin's policy after the outbreak of hostilities was strict neutrality, tempered by a firm determination to sell neutrality to Hitler at a price which would greatly strengthen the defenses of the U.S.S.R. against the Reich. The first step was to seize the former Russian territories of Poland and to reach an agreement with Berlin on the division of the carcass of the victim of the *Blitzkrieg*. On September 17, 1939, Moscow declared that the Polish State had "virtually ceased to exist" and that the Red Army must untertake the protection of its abandoned "blood brothers," the Ukrainians and the White Russians. Soviet troops were already on the march. They rapidly occupied all eastern Poland not yet in the hands of the Reichswehr. Ribbentrop flew again to Moscow. On September 28 a new German-Soviet agreement partitioned Poland along the ethnographic frontier, the Reich taking the Polish areas and the U.S.S.R. the White Russian and Ukrainian areas, including western Galicia which had been part of Austria-Hungary before 1914. Details of the frontier were defined more precisely by accords of October 5, 1939, and January 10, 1941. This extension of Bolshevism 250 miles westward was but the first of Stalin's victories and the initial installment of the price paid to Moscow by Berlin for "reinsurance" in the east.

The Kremlin's next step was the imposition of protectorates on the Baltic States. Hitler acquiesced not only in Soviet military control of the ancient realm of the Teutonic Knights but in the "voluntary" evacuation to the Reich of the Germans who had lived on the Baltic shore for seven centuries. By a combination of trumped-up accusations, invitations, and threats of invasion, Moscow induced Estonia (September 28), Latvia (October 5), and Lithuania (October 10) to sign mutual assistance pacts pledging common defense "in the event of a direct aggression or threat of aggression on the part of any European Great Power" against the Baltic frontiers of the signatories. Moscow acquired the right to establish garrisons on Baltic territory and to maintain naval and air bases at Paltiski, Oesel, Dago, Libau, and Windau. The Baltic Republics secured in return a short-lived "protection" of their "integrity" and their "sovereign" rights. Lithuania was granted the long-coveted city and region of Vilna.

Moscow now gave moral support to Berlin's bid for "peace" in October, 1939. This attitude, far from being indicative of the Soviet desire to see the Reich win the war, was inspired by the conviction that a "negotiated" settlement on the basis of the new *status quo* would leave the U.S.S.R. secure in its new outposts. Such a development would also save the Western Powers from possible destruction and compel their discredited leaders to seek a new *rapprochement* with the U.S.S.R. on Moscow's terms as the only means of future protection against the victorious Reich. These strictly *Realpolitik* desiderata were rationalized by Communists everywhere in terms of stereotyped eulogies of peace and denunciations of Anglo-French "imperialism." But London and Paris were committed to restoring the *status quo ante bellum* and would neither recognize Moscow's title to the new Soviet territories nor consider peace with Hitler. Stalin therefore considered what further measures he should take to strengthen his State against the bourgeois Powers.

WAR IN FINLAND. Efforts to negotiate a mutual assistance pact with Turkey failed in the autumn of 1939 because of Ankara's reluctance to meet Soviet terms and Turkish determination to remain faithful to the Western Allies. Moscow acquiesced in the Turkish refusal. But when Finland rejected Soviet demands, the Kremlin resorted to force. In mid-October Molotov received a Finnish delegation in Moscow and asked a thirty-year lease for a Red naval base at Hanko and cession to the U.S.S.R. of part of the Karelian Isthmus north of Leningrad, several islands in the Gulf, and a strip of coast near Petsamo on the Arctic in exchange for a larger area of central Karelia midway between Lake Ladoga and the Arctic. Helsinki refused, since the proposals involved the abandonment of the Mannerheim line of fortifications on the Isthmus. Each side was willing to compromise. But Moscow would not relinquish demands for Hanko, for the removal of the alleged "threat" to Leningrad, and for effective military control of the Gulf of Finland and the entire northwestern frontier. Helsinki would not yield to demands which it regarded as incompatible with Finnish security, "neutrality," and "independence." The result was deadlock.

On November 26, 1939, Molotov alleged that Finnish frontier guards had fired on Soviet troops. He demanded that Helsinki withdraw its forces on the Isthmus a distance of twenty to twenty-five kilometers. Finland denied the charge and agreed to withdraw troops from the frontier only if Moscow did likewise. Molotov retorted by denouncing the Soviet-Finnish nonaggression pact of 1932 and ordering Soviet troops and air forces to attack Finland on November 30. On December 1, Moscow granted diplomatic recognition to a "People's Government of the Democratic Republic of Finland," established in the isthmian frontier village of Terijoki and headed by Otto Kuusinen, a Communist refugee from Finland. The U.S.S.R. herewith committed an act of flagrant aggression motivated by strategic considerations regarded as paramount. It sought to imitate the Fascist technique of intimidation and disintegration through support of a puppet régime. The expectation apparently was that Helsinki would yield at the first blow or that the Finnish masses would rally to Kuusinen, with whom Moscow concluded a treaty of mutual assistance (December 2) granting all the Soviet military and territorial demands.

These assumptions were completely mistaken. The Finns rallied to the defense of their country and inflicted heavy losses on the inferior Soviet troops sent against them. Over 100,000 lives were lost in bitter fighting in subzero weather amid the frozen marshes and forests of the sub-Arctic wilderness. During December and January the defenders more than held their own. Early in February, however, the invaders launched a frontal offensive against the Isthmus fortifications with first-class troops under General Gregory Stern. Marshal Gustav Mannerheim's "line" was broken by massed artillery and tanks. His troops were forced out of the island stronghold of Koivisto on February 26 and out of the suburbs of Viipuri (Viborg) on March 5. He had estimated in January that successful defense against the Red giant could be continued if 30,000 foreign troops were available by May. In February, he felt he would need 50,000 foreign troops by April. By early March, he conceded that 100,000 reinforcements were needed at once. Since they were nowhere to be had, he and his colleagues decided to sue for peace.

Meanwhile Finland had appealed to the Western Powers and to the League. On December 14, 1939, the Assembly and Council at Geneva condemned Soviet aggression and for the first time (and the last) expelled an aggressor from membership. Moscow scoffed. The League died. The Council and Assembly never met again. As for aid to Finland outside of the League, Sweden gave generously of arms, supplies, and volunteers but always within the limits of "neutrality." The United States, with nothing to fear, was likewise hypnotized by its own mythology. Private relief funds of more than a million dollars flowed from American pocketbooks to Finland. All Americans loved Finland as the only one of the war debtors to meet its obligations to the United States in full. All Americans hated Bolshevism. On December 10 the Export-Import Bank (created, by a curious irony, to help finance Soviet-American trade) opened a 10 million-dollar credit for Finnish purchases. But the Finns were permitted to buy only "nonmilitary" supplies. Congress failed to act upon the President's plea for further credits until it was too late, when 20 million dollars were made available—also for "nonmilitary" supplies of which the Finns had little need. Although the "Neutrality" Act was not applied, congressional solicitude for "neutrality" forbade any effective assistance.

London and Paris were paralyzed for other reasons. The mad Munichmen relished the thought of fighting the U.S.S.R. far more than that of fighting the Reich. Gamelin and Weygand, then in Syria, made plans for bombing the Baku oil fields, less to aid Finland than to interrupt German imports of Soviet oil. But Turkey would not cooperate. Chamberlain and Daladier made plans for an expeditionary force to cross Scandinavia and go to Finland's support. But Norway and Sweden would not cooperate, lest this departure from "neutrality" provoke a German invasion to forestall Allied control of Scandinavia. After long hesitation the Allied Governments on March 2 formally requested Norway and Sweden to permit passage of Allied troops. Oslo and Stockholm both refused. While Chamberlain and Daladier, primarily for the purpose of cutting the Reich off from iron-ore shipments, via Narvik, from the mines of northern Sweden, contemplated forcible measures to induce compliance, the Finnish Government decided that its situation was hopeless. It asked Moscow for terms. Stalin recognized the error of his original calculations. He had no desire to be involved in hostilities with the Allies. He therefore agreed to drop Kuusinen and grant peace on "moderate" terms. Even after the peace in Finland, the Allied High Command toyed with plans for bombing Baku until the western *Blitzkrieg* put an end to all such schemes.

On March 12, 1940, a Finnish delegation in Moscow signed a peace treaty with the U.S.S.R. Helsinki was obliged to cede without compensation the entire Karelian Isthmus and the shores of Lake Ladoga, most of the Gulf islands, and a strip of northern territory near Petsamo, not including the port, however, or the near-by nickel mines. Moscow secured the right to build a railway in the north, along with free passage to Norway and Sweden. Hanko was leased for thirty years at an annual rental of $330,000. Molotov reaffirmed Soviet neutrality and denounced the Anglo-French "imperialists."

THE KREMLIN'S DILEMMA. The Scandinavian and western *Blitzkriegs* of the spring produced a slight but visible shift of Soviet policy

EXPANSION
OF U.S.S.R.
1939-1940

SCALE OF MILES:
0   100   200   300

in the direction of new defensive measures against the Axis. Allied defeat *per se* would cause no Soviet tears to flow, but German victory over the West would confront the U.S.S.R. with a formidable and probably invincible rival who would undoubtedly follow the precepts of *Mein Kampf* and move against the Ukraine. On June 15 to 17, 1940, Soviet troops abruptly occupied all of Lithuania, Latvia, and Estonia. Following local "elections," the three Baltic Republics were formally incorporated into the U.S.S.R. in August. On June 28 the Red Army occupied Bessarabia and northern Bukovina after Rumanian acceptance of a Soviet ultimatum.

These further enhancements of Soviet power had perforce to be "approved" with good grace by the Fascist Caesars so long as Britain was unbeaten. Moscow would make no direct contribution to the defeat of Britain. Stalin, unlike Mussolini, knew that an alliance with a stronger Power to despoil a third can only lead to ruin. He was confident, moreover, that the United States would not permit British defeat. On this assumption, he could afford to pursue "neutrality" with a vengeance, meanwhile taking care that the Reich did not install its forces in areas where they might prove menacing to the U.S.S.R. Despite its saving clause in Article 5, the Triple Alliance Pact of September 27, 1940, was not comforting to the Kremlin. The swift German occupation of Rumania in early October apparently caught Moscow unawares. A Tass communiqué asserted that reports abroad to the effect that the U.S.S.R. had been consulted and had approved in advance of the German action "did not correspond to the facts." Later reports that Moscow had approved Hungarian adherence to the Triplice elicited the comment that they "did not correspond to the facts to any degree."

Molotov's visit to Berlin, November 12 to 14, 1940, led to no immediate clarification of the Soviet's future role. Moscow buttressed Bulgaria and Turkey in their refusal to join the Triplice or admit German troops. It is probable that Moscow warned Berlin that any Axis attempt to reach the Straits would provoke Soviet countermeasures. The Kremlin apparently offered a mutual assistance pact to Bulgaria, but without immediate results. In the Far East the U.S.S.R. now spurned the projected nonaggression pact with Japan which it had earlier solicited and continued to aid Chungking against Tokio. China might become a vehicle of Soviet-American collaboration, just as Turkey might become a bridge between Moscow and London. But so long as Britain and her Allies could win victories in Albania and Africa and so long as American aid to Britain was being constantly increased, Moscow felt no anxiety about British defeat and therefore felt no need to change its course. Any change of course, moreover, postulated reciprocity. Despite the presence of Ambassador Sir Stafford Cripps in Moscow and the displacement of Halifax by Eden at Downing Street in December, Britain and the United States stubbornly refused to recognize Soviet title to Russia's recovered provinces and declined to release the shipping, bank deposits, and other assets of the Baltic States in their territories to the U.S.S.R. In anxious Washington and beleaguered London, anti-Bolshevism was still a more powerful sentiment than the dictates of *Realpolitik*. Moscow accordingly signed a new trade agreement with the Reich on January 10, 1941, and reaffirmed neutrality and Soviet-German friendship. But when Nazi threats forced Bulgaria on March 1, 1941, to sign the Triple Alliance and to admit German troops for the coercion of Greece and Turkey, Moscow made an oblique and belated protest to Sofia.

The international position of the U.S.S.R. remained simple so long as the Western and Chinese wars were deadlocked. But should Japan finally crush Chinese resistance and should Germany invade and subdue Britain, the U.S.S.R. would be almost inevitably doomed to attack and defeat. Since the Soviet leaders, despite their deceptive verbiage, had no illusions on this score (being well versed in *Mein Kampf* and the Tanaka Memorial), they might be expected to change Soviet policy and the Comintern line as abruptly as they had done in the summer of 1939 should this grim prospect become imminent. In such an event, a Soviet attack on Germany might well bring the Third Reich down in ruins, provided that Britain were still fighting vigorously with full American support. Continued stalemate made continued Soviet neutrality safe. Should Britain and the United States show evidence of ability to defeat the Reich without Soviet aid, Moscow would scarcely intervene to save Hitler. A British defeat would be dangerous to the U.S.S.R., with no compensatory advantages commensurate with the ensuing threat to Muscovy from a victorious Triplice. A German defeat, on the other hand, would involve no grave peril to the U.S.S.R., since the assault against the Soviet realm by the Western Powers was scarcely likely to be resumed. German defeat, moreover, might make possible the extension of Communism into central Europe. Japanese defeat might open similar prospects in Asia. Should Soviet moves in this direction precipitate a clash with the West in the wake of a Fascist débâcle, a new world war would flame out of the still red ashes of the old.

In this eventuality the U.S.S.R. might emerge as the ultimate victor and the residuary legatee of the wreckage of Western civilization. It might equally well find its shaky socialist economy toppling about the heads of its rulers under the impact of blows from the Western Powers. Should the Fascist Triplice be vanquished, reason would seem to dictate a Liberal-Communist *modus vivendi* and Soviet collaboration in a new world order rather than a fight to the death between the U.S.S.R. and the West for mastery of central Europe and eastern Asia. By the spring of 1941, however, it seemed possible that class prejudice and ideological fanaticism on both sides might silence the voices of reason and precipitate a clash. It seemed equally possible that unresolved suspicion and enmity between Muscovy and the West might yet give the Triplice victory over both.[1]

SUGGESTED READINGS

Barbusse, Henri (ed.): *The Soviet Union and Peace*, New York, International Publishers Co., Inc., 1929.

——: *Stalin*, New York, Macmillan, 1934.

Bunyan, J.: *Intervention, Civil War and Communism in Russia, April–December* 1918, Baltimore, Johns Hopkins, 1936.

——, and H. H. Fisher: *The Bolshevik Revolution, 1917–1918*, Stanford University, Calif., Stanford University Press, 1934.

Chamberlin, W. H.: *The Russian Revolution 1917–1921*, New York, Macmillan, 1935.

Cole, G. D. H.: *The People's Front*, London, Gollancz, 1937.

Dimitroff, G. *The United Front, the Struggle against Facism and War*, New York, International Publishers Co., Inc., 1938.

Eastman, Max: *Stalin's Russia and the Crisis in Socialism*, New York, Norton, 1940.

Elliston, H. B.: *Finland Fights*, Boston, Little Brown, 1940.

Fischer, L.: *The Soviets in World Affairs* (2 vols.), New York, Cape & Smith, 1930.

Florinsky, M. T.: *World Revolution and the U.S.S.R.*, New York, Macmillan, 1933.

Graham, M. W.: *The Diplomatic Recognition of the Border States*, Berkeley, University of California, 1939.

Harper, S. N.: *The Government of the Soviet Union*, New York, Van Nostrand, 1938.

Hill, E., and D. Mudie: *The Letters of Lenin*, New York, Harcourt, 1937.

Kohn, H.: *Nationalism in the Soviet Union*, New York, Columbia University Press, 1933.

Litvinov, M.: *Against Aggression*, New York, International Publishers Co., Inc., 1939.

Lyons, E.: *Assignment in Utopia*, New York, Harcourt, 1937.

Norman Wait Harris Memorial Foundation: *The Soviet Union and World Problems*, Chicago, University of Chicago Press, 1938.

Pares, B.: *The Fall of the Russian Monarchy*, New York, Knopf, 1939.

Schuman, F. L.: *American Policy toward Russia since* 1917, New York, International Publishers Co., Inc., 1928.

Souvarine, B.: *Stalin*, New York, Alliance, 1939.

Taracouzio, T. R.: *War and Peace in Soviet Foreign Policy*, New York, Macmillan, 1940.

Valtin, Jan: *Out of the Night*, New York, Alliance, 1941.

Webb, Sidney and Beatrice: *Soviet Communism: A New Civilization?* (2 vols.), New York, Scribner, 1936.

Werner, M. R. (ed.): *Stalin's Kampf*, New York, Howell, Soskin, 1940.

Wilson, E.: *To the Finland Station:* New York, Harcourt, 1940.

Wolfe, H. C.: *The Imperial Soviets*, New York, Doubleday, 1940.

---

[1] Balkan developments in March, 1941, promised increased Soviet-Axis friction. On the 24th Moscow assured Ankara that "if Turkey be attacked and be obliged to enter the war for the purpose of defending her territory, she can rely upon the complete neutrality and understanding of the Soviet Union." On the 25th Premier Dragisha Cvetkovitch and Foreign Minister Alexander Cincar-Markovitch signed a protocol in Vienna making Jugoslavia the eighth signatory of the Triplice pact. Two days later their regime was overthrown by an army coup which ousted Regent Prince Paul and brought General Dushan Simovitch to the Premiership and M. Nincitch to the Foreign Ministry. They defied the Axis. On April 5 Molotov and Ambassador Milan Gavrilovitch signed at Moscow a Soviet-Jugoslav treaty of nonaggression pledging mutual respect of independence and territorial integrity and "a policy of friendly relations" if either party should be attacked by a third Power. The Nazi invasion of Jugoslavia was launched the following day. See pp. 586–587 above.

BOOK FOUR
TOWARD TOMORROW

Chapter XIII

THE AGE OF EMPIRES

1. THE WORLD REVOLUTION

You ought to speak of States in the plural number; none of them is a city, but many cities. . . . For indeed any city, however small, is in fact divided into two; one the city of the poor, the other of the rich; these are at war with one another; and in either there are many smaller divisions, and you would be altogether beside the mark if you treated them all as a single State.—PLATO, *The Republic*.

In the history of the international politics of the Hellenic World, from the time when the Solonian economic revolution first confronted the Hellenic Society with a task of establishing a political world order, we can see that the failure of the Athenian attempt to solve the problem by means of the Delian League led on to Philip of Macedon's attempt to solve it by means of the Corinthian League, and Philip's failure to Augustus's attempt to solve it by means of a *Pax Romana* upheld by a Principate. . . . In this matter of recurrency in rhythm the nature of the disintegrations of civilizations unmistakably resembles the nature of their growths.—ARNOLD J. TOYNBEE, *A Study of History*, Vol. V, p. 12.

LEGEND tells of an ancient monarch who once asked his wise men to supply him with an aphorism which should be appropriate for all possible occasions. After due deliberation they met his request with six short words: "These things too shall pass away." Human beings have always been impressed by the fleeting character of all things mortal and the eternal and changeless rhythm of birth, fulfillment, and death— for societies no less than individuals. In epochs of calamity, men easily see in their own frustrations the symptoms of cultural decay. They readily interpret the disasters they both cause and suffer as portents of doom. Whether such gloomy judgments are warranted, and if so to what degree, can only be known by later generations. Communities, like persons, recover from some disorders and die of others. Accurate analysis of causes makes possible a measure of prediction of results. But only time can tell whether any given disease of the body politic will prove transitory or fatal.

Whether Western civilization after its ten crowded centuries is approaching the end of its allotted life span is still a moot question. The unprecedented mastery over nature which Western man has achieved offers promise of a future less dismal than that which overtook the ancient Egyptians and Chinese, the Greeks and Romans, the Arabs, the Mayas, and the Incas. Yet the genius of Western man for self-defeat and self-destruction, implemented by the very weapons with which nature has been bent to his will, causes numerous observers in the mid twentieth century to postulate a fate for their civilization as cheerless as that which brought all earlier cultures to the grave. All are at least agreed that the world of the West is desperately sick. The nature of the illness demands diagnosis, for recovery is improbable when physicians and patients alike remain ignorant of the malady.

In his comparative study of the decline of civilizations (*The Study of History*, vols. V and VI), Arnold J. Toynbee uses the phrase "schism in the soul" to describe the inner conflicts which characterize the disintegration of every culture and help to bring it to ruin. Through the centuries since the close of the misnamed "middle ages," many schisms have torn the souls of the inheritors of Western civilization. The resulting cleavages and conflicts often took the form of open battle—between kings and barons, Roman Catholics and Protestants, nobles and burghers, monarchists and republicans, reactionaries and liberals, democrats and tyrants. Most of these feuds, although bloody and disruptive to those who participated, were judged by many who came after to have been adventures in liberation along the march of Western mankind from feudalism to freedom. It is possible that the misery and bloodshed of today will seem tomorrow to have been no less productive of ultimate good than were the agonies of yesterday.

The crisis of the twentieth century, however, perhaps springs from deeper sources in the body and soul of Western man than these earlier traumatic experiences. The clashing human purposes which have posed and shaped the problems of the present age and brought its children to frenzy or despair stem from cleavages so profound as to seem all but irreconcilable. They revolve around diametrically opposed conceptions of human society and of the community of nations. Most participant observers long envisaged the struggle as a conflict of "ideologies." The protagonists were Communism, Fascism, Liberalism. Among them no compromise was possible. The adequacy of this explanation became doubtful with the development of a *rapprochement*, albeit stillborn, between Communism and Liberalism in the face of the Fascist peril. It became more doubtful with the connivance of democratic appeasers in Fascist aggression. It collapsed with the Nazi-Soviet pact of 1939 and the unleashing of the war against the West. Thereafter, the issue appeared to be one between Liberalism and "Totalitarianism," whether Black, Brown, Red, or Yellow. But this formulation, too, is much too simple and reveals nothing of the causes or course of the world's disaster.

A more fruitful approach is possibly to be found in the reflection that the oecumenic society of the present age is suffering from a double disorder attributable to the impact of science, technology, and the Industrial Revolution upon peoples unable or unwilling to adapt old habits to the stubborn facts of a changed world. Machine industry produced two consequences which possibly furnish the clue to the frustrations and schisms of a century which began brightly and fell at mid-point upon incredibly evil days of darkness and brutality. One was the creation of a new proletariat at the bottom of the social scale, and the corresponding emergence of a moneyed *élite* of entrepreneurs at the top. All societies in all ages have been divided into poor and rich. The machine has brought to the common man comforts and conveniences beyond the dreams of Croesus. Yet the gap between the wealthy and the impoverished is greater in the industrial societies of today than ever before. Both have become equally insecure in the face of the maladjustments and contradictions of a "capitalism" geared to produce more goods and services than consumers can buy at prices profitable to the producers. The second major result of the machine was the unification of the world with respect to communication, transportation, travel, trade, and war—with no commensurate unification of the separate sovereignties of the Western State System into a world polity. The Industrial Revolution changed a world of isolated, independent societies into a world of integrated, interdependent societies in which every man, woman, and child everywhere in the world was willy-nilly entangled in a web of commerce, finance, and politics spanning the globe. Security, welfare, and life itself therewith became contingent upon the fluctuations of rainfall, unemployment, and political violence in the Antipodes.

The two keys to the chaos of our time may be found on the one hand in the efforts of poor and rich to protect themselves from the effects of the disintegration of a world economy which can no longer function in the face of class conflict and neomercantilism and, on the other hand, in the efforts of patriots to resist the efforts of internationalists to bring to the world a measure of political unity comparable with the technological and economic unity brought about by scientists, engineers, bankers, and merchants. Out of the clash between rich and poor arises much of the political and spiritual confusion of a bewildered generation. Out of the clash between provincial nationalists and cosmopolitan world citizens arises the international anarchy and the democratic defeatism of an unhappy era. Here, as always, a house divided against itself cannot stand. The communities which have remained paralyzed and feckless in the face of this double "schism in the soul" have been quite incapable of protecting themselves against the communities which have in some fashion resolved these inner conflicts.

Western liberals had all the world at their feet in 1919. They could have built for their children and their children's children a new society and a new world order in which poverty and war would alike be abolished forever. But they unwittingly threw away their victory and invited disaster by clinging to symbols and shibboleths irrelevant to the needs of a new epoch. For twenty years and more, they worshiped "peace." But they sought peace not by organizing the world for peace but by deserting or betraying the effort of Woodrow Wilson to organize the world for peace and by taking vain refuge in national patriotism, national sovereignty, and national defense. They thus perpetuated and aggravated the international anarchy which is inevitably the matrix of war. For twenty years and more, they worshiped "democracy," "social justice," and "prosperity." But they sought these goals less by curbing and reconciling the greed of the rich and the envy of the poor in a world economy of abundance than by seeking the advantages of monopoly inside national frontiers. They thus ensured the breakdown of the world economy and engendered the miseries and fears which are the matrix of tyranny.

Poverty and war are the primary afflictions of those unwilling to pay the price of plenty and peace. War is the child of anarchy in the community of nations. This in turn is the offspring of the conflict in every democracy between isolationists and interventionists. It is the ugly spawn of the creed of patriots who hold that their first duty is to serve their own land by avoiding "foreign entanglements." Poverty is the child of anarchy in the relations between producers and consumers. From the poverty of the poor and from the even more terrifying poverty of the rich stems the design for tyranny which breeds autarchy, intolerance, and military aggrandizement.

Those who promise salvation from poverty and war, whatever their ulterior purposes, are assured of a following in a world in which millions of people live in constant dread of economic insecurity and armed violence. Those who achieve solutions of the problems of poverty and war, however vicious or mad the goals may be which their solutions serve, are assured of victory over those who have achieved no solutions. The first secret of success of the totalitarian States is that the despots who rule them have in their own black fashion healed the breach between rich and poor and outlawed class conflict. Their second secret is that they have healed the breach between isolationists and internationalists and embarked boldly upon the political unification of the world. The road they have taken has led their people through violence and want on an appalling scale. But the will-o'-the-wisp at the end of the road is a promise of peace and plenty. Since the promise was for many years more plausible than any which democrats were able to offer, millions who were weary of war and poverty gladly followed the Caesars.

All the totalitarian tyrannies have sprung from class conflict. The first of the new Caesar-states was established in Russia in 1917 in the name of the "dictatorship of the proletariat." It was the instrument and outcome of a class war in which the poor ultimately triumphed over the rich and subjected the vanquished to "expropriation" and "liquidation." This bloody victory of the dispossessed over the former possessing classes sent a paroxysm of fear through all possessors over the world. "Bolshevism" became the great bogy with which the wealthy and wellborn frightened their workers, their children, and themselves. The second of the modern despotisms was established in Italy in 1922 and the third in Germany in 1933. In both cases, tyrants who copied and perfected the political techniques of Lenin were put into power by well-fed gentlemen and ladies to protect their prerogatives from the envy and hatred of the great unwashed.

The ambitious demagogue-despots of the colored shirts persuaded most of the rich that they would save them from "Communism," smash trade-unions, and outlaw strikes. They persuaded some of the poor that they would save them from "capitalism," smash Big Business, and inaugurate "socialism." Classes and masses alike were duped, but in the end both sets of promises were in strange ways fulfilled. Social conflict was terminated as effectively as in the U.S.S.R., though the social ideals and moral purposes (if any) of the new tyrants and their disciples were wholly different from those which had moved the followers of Lenin.

In every totalitarian State the rich who seek to exploit the poor are jailed or shot, since this is no longer a private prerogative of plutocrats but a public privilege of politicians, sternly reserved to the members of the new military élite. In every totalitarian State the poor who denounce the rich are similarly jailed or shot, since this, too, is a pleasure in which only the highest party members may indulge. The cleavage in the body politic between the starving and the glutted is healed. Social schizophrenia is cured by the unifying catharsis of a class myth or a race myth. "Capitalism" is ended. "Socialism" prevails. The authority of Money and Mind gives way to the intoxicating mysticism of Blood and Soil.[1]

All the totalitarian tyrannies have also long since put an end to the interminable and paralyzing debate in the democracies between those who would unify the planet and those who would cultivate only their national land patches. In totalitarian States, isolationists who preach "nonintervention," "neutrality," and "appeasement" are jailed or shot. The tyrant and his aides lay down the party line. Woe to those who challenge it or even deviate from its imperatives! All the new Caesars, despite their trappings of national megalomania, know that the world is one and act

---

[1] The social process which gives rise to Fascism was described clearly and explicitly by Plato in *The Republic. Cf. The Dialogues* in Benjamin Jowett's translation (New York, Random House, Inc., 1937, vol. I, pp. 822–888). See also Spengler's forecast, as compared with Plato's, on pp. 502–503 of *Europe on the Eve* (New York, Alfred A. Knopf, Inc., 1939).

effectively upon their knowledge. Their goal is world unity and world peace—enforced by the conqueror's sword. Here, too, the Russian revolution was the prototype of things to come, for its leaders were avowedly "internationalists" who called upon the workers of the world to unite in throwing off their "chains" and establishing the cooperative commonwealth of all mankind. By conspiracy, by rebellion, and by conquest, they hoped to revolutionize and unite all the peoples of the planet. They failed, but their dream was later borrowed by the followers of Mussolini, Hitler, and the Japanese war lords. By conspiracy, by rebellion, and by conquest, these new world revolutionists hoped to unite and remake the globe. And since they were more clever and more ruthless than their Muscovite rivals, they outlined in plausible guise their "New World Order" (at first in the name of anti-Communism, the better to befuddle the democracies) and then struck down with amazing initial success all who stood in their way.

If the Caesar-States have been strong by virtue of the resolution of the conflict between masses and classes and the silencing of the debate between isolationists and internationalists, the democracies have all been weak precisely because their leaders and peoples achieved no solution of these dissensions. All the democratic Powers without exception were brought to the brink of ruin by 1940 because their politicians were hopelessly split into spokesmen for those who had too much and spokesmen for those who had too little. Their electorates were tragically divided against themselves not only by this cleavage but by the warring faiths of provincial patriots, with little vision and much influence, and of internationalists, with much vision and little influence. The two sources of paralysis converged into one in that strange mosaic of attitudes and acts known as "appeasement."

This all but fatal sickness of the democracies in the late 1930's was of two varieties which may be designated as "appeasement of the Right" and "appeasement of the Left." The latter type will be forever symbolized by Léon Blum, counterpart in the dying days of the French Republic of the Ramsay MacDonalds, the George Lansburys, and the Christian pacifists of Britain and the isolationist liberals and radicals of America. Brought to power as the champion of the poor, Blum devoted himself to "social reforms"—collective bargaining, the forty-hour week, higher wages, longer vacations, and the like. By battling the "200 families" and the Fascist Leagues he hoped to save France. By nationalizing the munitions industries, he hoped to avoid war—for were not the "merchants of death" the instigators of war? Through the attainment of a more perfect democracy at home, he hoped to defend his land against aggression from abroad. His course obviously required avoidance of all foreign "distractions" and "entanglements." He therefore sponsored neutrality, isolation, acquiescence in the remilitarization of the Rhineland, "non-intervention" in Spain, the final betrayal of Ethiopia and the League, and passivity in the face of *Anschluss*. After he had been forced from office and his liberal collaborators had betrayed alike the "People's Front" and the interests of France, he still confessed "cowardly relief" over Munich and joined the chorus in praise of Daladier. But the French poor whom he fancied he was protecting against the French rich became slaves of the Third Reich as the result of his labors. This possibility scarcely occurred to him until appeasement had collapsed in ruins about his ears and he found himself at last in prison and alone in a lost land.

Appeasement of the Right has been a more widespread and more familiar phenomenon. Its eternal symbol is Neville Chamberlain, prototype of the Lavals, the Daladiers, the Bonnets, the Flandins, the Fords, the Lindberghs, and their kind. Despite his reticences and circumlocutions, the man from Birmingham epitomized the interests and the outlook of businessmen everywhere who learned in the years of the Great Depression to fear the power of labor, to dread the misery of the poor, to hate "Communism" with a holy hatred, and to look to the Fascist Caesars as bulwarks of Property, Profits, and Piety. All the Munichmen of the Right shared with Chamberlain, Henderson, Hoare, and Simon a secret envy of the tyrants who "kept labor in its place" and a secret (or not so secret) expectation that they would ultimately attack the U.S.S.R. and thus save "civilization" (*i.e.*, capitalism) from the Bolshevik cutthroats. Misconceived class interest thus dictated isolation, neutrality, and nonintervention in dealing with the Caesars. Chamberlain was also a man of peace. He hated war sincerely and profoundly—not war between Germany and Russia or between Japan and Russia, but war which Britain might have to fight. He and his class feared justly that any war would spell the end of their influence and that a war waged in the name of democracy would eventuate in a Socialist Britain, as almost happened after 1919. In war the poor have nothing to lose but their lives. But the rich may lose their wealth. This sacrifice is far more painful. With the antique ethos of an outworn capitalism as his guide, Chamberlain faced the Caesars in much the same manner as the memorable victim of the bandit who, when asked to surrender his money or his life, replied, "By all means take my life; I need my money for my old age!"

In this manner the pathetic champions of the poor against the rich and the scarcely less pathetic champions of the rich against the poor turned their backs upon the League of Nations and collective security, all alike in the name of "peace." They sought safety for their class and a future for their hopes through futile flight into cramped parochialism and blind patriotism which had no eyes for any "quarrel in a far away country among people of whom we know nothing." The two groups of travelers took the road to Munich for different reasons. They championed isolation, sovereignty, neutrality, pacifism, and a narrowly national "defense" from different motives. But the vale of blood and tears beyond the end of the road was the same. In Prague, Warsaw, Copenhagen, Oslo, Rotterdam, Brussels, Paris, and elsewhere, much the same fate was shared by rich and poor and by isolationists and interventionists alike.

Under these circumstances the peoples of the Western democracies were (and still are at the time of writing) quite incapable of adopting means relevant to their professed ends. Though worshiping "peace," they did none of the things needful to secure it and all of the things certain to destroy it. Though praising "democracy," "toleration," and a "more abundant life," they stubbornly adhered to attitudes and policies mathematically calculated to beget tyranny, intolerance, and impoverishment. When people no longer know what they want or how to obtain what they believe they want, they cease to be effective players of the game of politics (and of life) and become prospective subjects for the psychiatrist. *De gustibus non disputandum est.* But if the democratic peoples genuinely desire patriotism, sovereignty, isolation, neutrality, no "foreign entanglements," and avoidance of "other people's wars," they would be well advised to cease proclaiming their love of "peace" and to recognize that their preferences ensure anarchy and violence among nations on an ever larger scale. And if they are earnestly committed to protectionism, autarchy, monopoly, special privilege, and the economics of scarcity, they would do well to be silent about their fancied devotion to competitive capitalism, individualism, free enterprise, political liberalism, and the economics of plenty. Yet any such logical reordering of ends and means is perhaps precluded by the very "schism in the soul" which has given rise to the initial dilemma.

There is much reason to believe, however, that no real choice remains between competitive capitalism and a new "collectivist" social order, or between international anarchy and world union. In the long run the common mass of men and women everywhere seem likely, after decades of intolerable frustration and misery, to decide that they prefer "socialism" (*any* socialism for *any* purpose administered by *any* group so long as it affords security) to an "individualism" which spells only want and woe. And they appear equally predisposed toward a preference for a "new world order" (*any* order for *any* purpose administered by *any* group so long as it works) as against the endless disorder of anarchic national sovereignty. Should this prove to be the case, it is probable that a new society on a world scale and a new international order all over the planet are both "inevitable" in the correct sense of the much-abused term.

The only unanswered question in this event will be: Who will create and manage the new society and the new world, in the service of what collective ideals, what moral values, what conceptions of Man and the State? Either the Western peoples who still have faith in the postulates of liberalism will assume these tasks and carry them to a successful conclusion in the service of their own purposes, or the Caesars will assume them in the service of purposes which democrats find it hard to distinguish from oppression, brutality, and barbarism. If the peoples of the West assert that they are not interested in or are opposed to the building of a new society and the creation of a new pattern of international life, they will not thereby escape the responsibilities from which they seek to flee. Rather, they will have these things imposed upon them by the sword of conquest. In all likelihood the choice for the Western peoples is not between fashioning a new social structure or not fashioning it. It is between having it in their own way, under their own control and for their own goals, or having it crammed down their throats by the new barbarians within and without. Their choice is probably not between "nationalism" and "internationalism." It is between an internationalism developed and implemented by democrats for liberal purposes and an internationalism imposed by external force in the service of despotism. The peoples of Austria, Czechoslovakia, Poland, Denmark, Norway, the Netherlands, Belgium, Luxemburg, France, Hungary, Rumania, Estonia, Latvia, Lithuania, Finland, etc.—all of whom preferred the "safety" of isolationist neutrality to the "risks" of collective security—have already made this discovery as these words are written. The few surviving democratic communities will also make it before many more years have passed. The double schism in the Western soul will in all probability be healed during the present generation by those who are eager and able to build a new society and to unify the world.

2. THE STAKES OF WAR

If the nineteenth century has been relatively poor in great wars—and revolutions—and has overcome its worst crises diplomatically by means of congresses, this has been due precisely to continuous and terrific war-preparedness. . . . But *ipso facto* this second century will be one of *actually* Contending States. *These* armies are not substitutes for war— they are *for* war, and they want war. Within two generations it will be they whose will prevails over that of all the comfortables put together. In these wars of theirs for the heritage of the whole world, continents will be staked, India, China, South Africa, Russia, Islam called out, new techniques and tactics played and counter-played. The great cosmopolitan foci of power will dispose at their pleasure of smaller States—their territory, their economy and their men alike—all that is now merely province, passive object, means to end. Its destinies are without importance to the great march of things. . . . Again and again between these catastrophes of blood and terror the cry rises up for reconciliation of the peoples and for peace on earth. It is but the background and the echo of the grand happening. . . . Esteem as we may the wish towards all this, we must have the courage to face facts as they are. . . . Life, if it would be great, is hard; it lets choose *only* between victory and ruin—not between war and peace. And to the victors belong the sacrifices of victory.—OSWALD SPENGLER, *The Decline of the West*, vol. II.

The question which group of rulers will unify the world and build the society of the future will be answered by the verdict of arms in the Second World War. The advent of the war itself was the "inevitable" result of the circumstance that the Western peoples threw away the victory of 1918, both at home and abroad, and refused either to reconstruct their own societies or to enforce order in the community of nations. This refusal in turn was the product of chronic strife within the Western States between isolationists and internationalists and between men of money and *les miserables*. These wars within gave the new Caesars their opportunity to overthrow the world balance of power, to disrupt the democratic societies by propaganda and intrigue, to pave their roads to conquest, and to assume the inescapable tasks which the democracies declined to undertake.

The Fascist Triplice sought and found its chance to strike for world hegemony in two sets of attitudes on the part of the rulers of the democracies, both interrelated and both fatal to any hope of keeping peace by halting aggression. In domestic politics, those at the top of the social scale in France, Britain, America, and other democratic States tended to follow the tradition of all insecure and anxious ruling classes. They were more concerned with protecting their own privileges than with extending the frontiers of democracy to the advantage of the unprivileged. In each case, therefore, a small group of persons with blue blood or large bank accounts gave support to the agents of the Caesars and to the indigenous propagandists of Fascism. This sufficed to enable the Triplice, through its far-flung net of professional revolutionists and saboteurs, to fish successfully in troubled waters. The capacity and the will of the democratic Powers to offer resistance to the conquerors was thus slowly dissipated until at the end (and beyond the end) little was left but the shadows of nations whose citizens were divided against themselves, corrupted by anti-Semitism and anti-Communism, and led by leaders who were at worst disloyal and at best witless, feckless, and utterly confused. This formula for defeat was all but perfect.

In foreign policy the democratic spokesmen of these same *élite* groups (with such notable but rare exceptions as Louis Barthou, Anthony Eden, Winston Churchill, Cordell Hull, and Franklin D. Roosevelt) were far more anxious to rescue the Caesars from their own folly and to deflect them against the U.S.S.R. than to stop aggression or build an effective coalition against Japan, Italy, and the Reich. The exceptional leaders and diplomats who sponsored a different course were in every instance undone by their successors or paralyzed until the eleventh hour by forces of isolationism or appeasement which were beyond persuasion or control. The Munichmen won popular support for their cause and rationalized their expectations in terms of patriotism, pacifism, neutrality, and defense against Bolshevism. The result of this attitude was the disintegration of the French bloc on the Continent and the erection of insuperable barriers of class prejudice and reciprocal distrust between the Western Powers and the U.S.S.R.

"Germany," wrote Foch in 1919, "can never win a war on two fronts or lose a war on one front." Without Soviet collaboration, there could be no effective counterweight to the Triplice. Without a counterweight, no balance of power could be preserved. Without a balance of power the Caesars could not be deterred from ever more ambitious adventures. If war came, the absence of an eastern front would spell Axis victory. There could be no eastern front without the U.S.S.R. Before the Ides of March, 1939, the Western appeasers would not join the U.S.S.R. in halting the Axis, for they were confident that only the U.S.S.R. was in danger from the Axis. After the Ides of March, when they perceived their error, they would not pay Moscow's price for an alliance. The consequence was the Nazi-Soviet pact. In this fashion, all the precepts of *Realpolitik* were ignored or violated until nothing was left but a feeble Anglo-French entente confronting a Reich whose rulers had neutralized Russia, conquered Poland, Czechoslovakia, and Austria, and secured predominant influence in Japan, Italy, Hungary, and Spain. The formula for defeat was thus perfected.

The terrors of 1940 wrought an appreciable modification of the formula among the Anglo-Saxon survivors of the holocaust. Whether the change was sufficient to ensure continued survival and, if so, whether it could be carried to the point of winning eventual victory were moot questions in the spring of 1941. Churchill's England had become a land of tears, blood, and indomitable courage. Socialists sat in the Cabinet. Some members of the aristocracy and plutocracy realized that the days of their privileges were done. Some patriots recognized that if Britain were to have hope of victory Britain must abandon the tattered rags of sovereignty and insular aloofness and commit itself irrevocably to a new world order. In America, isolationism waned as citizens perceived belatedly that the world was one; that war was not to be avoided by running away; that the defenses of the Western Hemisphere lay in Europe, Africa, and Asia; and that Britain must be buttressed against the conquerors.

Yet all of this was a far cry from a frank facing of realities, both immediate and remote. Churchill was obliged to collaborate with high Tories and with Continental governments-in-exile whose members (save for Eduard Beneš) learned nothing, forgot nothing, and dreamed of restoring the lost world of 1938. Throughout the year of terror, London and Washington shunned all collaboration with the U.S.S.R. The Kremlin reciprocated their animosity. America gave aid to Britain, at a price, and shrank from war. As in the Mediterranean world of the first century B.C., the Powers menaced by conquest were reluctant to join forces against the conqueror. The ruling classes of Britain hoped for the best and feared the worst without recognizing that the past could never be recaptured. Many men of means in America contended that "socialism" in England and the danger of "socialism" in America were unanswerable arguments in favor of strict isolation. Others hoped to make a profitable "deal" with a Europe under Nazi rule. No considerable body of Americans was mentally or emotionally prepared either to wage total war or to make total peace after victory by policing the world and building a permanent federation of nations.

Thanks to these inhibitions and confusions, neither Churchill nor Roosevelt could formulate war aims or peace aims in terms of a new world order. Neither Britons nor Americans in the spring of 1941 were ready to face the task of rebuilding Western society and unifying the world. Such readiness might come with further lessons in the bitter school of suffering. If it came in time, it might spell victory and reconstruction. If it came too late, victory would go to the Caesars who, for all the barbarism and malevolence of their values, knew (as liberals might never know) that the only means which can serve any purposes effectively in the world of the twentieth century are means which promise an end of conflict among classes and an end of rivalry among national sovereignties.

As the Second World War runs its course, one side will ultimately prove more capable than the other of developing these means and using them to command the future. This side will impose its will by violence upon those unable or unwilling to meet the crisis of a civilization which must be recast in a new mold if it is to survive. The revolutionary will to accomplish this task may well prove to be the decisive weapon of military victory rather than a pious purpose to be translated into acts only at the next peace conference. Here, too, the Triplice marches ahead of its foes, for its "New World Order" was foreshadowed long before war began and was made a weapon of war itself by the pact of September 27, 1940. While London vainly promised to the subjugated peoples of the Continent a restoration of an "independence" and "sovereignty" forever lost, Berlin promised them unity, peace, and ultimate plenty in a federated world ruled by the Nazi sword. Anglo-American leaders could scarcely hope for victory (and, in Churchill's words, "without victory there can be no survival") unless they could offer to Europe and the world some more attractive promise of unity, peace, and plenty. To pledge a restoration of a dead past in the name of "freedom" and a resumption of the anarchy of power politics in the name of "self-determination" was to promise nothing relevant to the needs and wants of desperate and heartsick peoples. Ideas are also weapons. Dynamic and creative ideas, however black the purposes which they serve, cannot be fought save by ideas which are equally dynamic and creative.

There is no law of nature according to which the stupid shall inherit the earth. The future belongs to those who show by deeds that they are aware of the facts of life and are fit to survive, whether they be the civilized defenders of the values of western culture or the barbarian destroyers of those values. Fitness to survive is not measured by vice or virtue. It is not to be tested by good intentions or bad ones or by acceptance or rejection of Western ideals. Fitness to survive depends upon capacity to face realities and upon ability to adapt means to ends. Without these talents, victory and survival are not to be had.

The victors of the days to come will be those who know what must be done and are willing to do it. The hosts of the Caesars are eager and anxious to rebuild society and unify the planet. If victorious, they may clash among themselves and throw away their opportunities. But they may equally well subdue the U.S.S.R., isolate the United States, and build a strange new world—dark, tyrant-ridden, and intolerant but at least free of social strife and united by the sword of the conqueror. The hosts of Anglo-America possess immense superiority of potential physical strength on land and sea and in the air. To couple these resources with knowledge of what must be done and firm will to do it at any cost would be to ensure the defeat of the Caesars. Determination to abandon old ways, however, and to embark upon dangerous and daring enterprises was only slightly in evidence in Anglo-Saxony in 1941. Without such a will, however, any military victory that might be gained would be wasted in the sequel with more chaos to come until new conquerors should at long last make the world one.

3. THE NEW WORLD ORDER

Ours is essentially a tragic age, so we refuse to take it tragically. The cataclysm has happened, we are among the ruins, we start to build up new little habitats, to have new little hopes. It is rather hard work: there is now no smooth road into the future: but we go round, or scramble over the obstacles. We've got to live, no matter how many skies have fallen.— D. H. LAWRENCE.

Out of the present world struggle will finally emerge a world order based upon one of two diametrically opposed conceptions of social organization. The one, the components of which are fairly clear from its history and our experience, will maximize freedom. . . . The other, the components of which are equally clear from its most recent record and from its history in earlier times, represents an order maintained by power and domination. Upon the outcome of this struggle, which is but the most recent phase of an age-old conflict, will depend the character of the institutional framework required by the world order.—WALTER H. C. LAVES.

The position of our Western Society in our age cannot become known with any certainty of knowledge till the voyage has come to an end; and so long as the ship is under way the crew will have no notion whether she is going to founder in mid-ocean through springing a leak or be sent to the bottom by colliding with another vessel or run ashore on the rocks or glide smoothly into a port of which the crew will never have heard before they wake up one fine day to find their ship at rest in dock there. A sailor at sea cannot tell for which, if for any, of these ends the ship is heading as he watches her making headway during the brief period of his own spell of duty. To plot out her course and write up her log from start to finish is a task that can be performed only by observers who are able to wait until the voyage is over, since it will only be then that the unexplored Future, into which the ship is forever sailing so long as she is in motion at all, will have been converted, without any dubious residue, into a traversed and recorded Past; and such observers must, *ex hypothesi*, be members of some other society that will still be alive when ours has ceased to exist, since their post of observation must, again *ex hypothesi*, lie not on board the ship, but somewhere outside of her gunwales.—ARNOLD J. TOYNBEE, *A Study of History*, vol. VI.

To speculate upon the world of tomorrow during the year of disaster, 1941, is to make guesses about events as yet undelivered from the womb of Time. These events are already conceived; but since paternity is in doubt, the probable attributes of the unborn infant are matters of conjecture. With Mars as midwife, even the survival of the child is uncertain. The world of 1815 could not have been foretold in 1810, for Borodino, Leipzig, and Waterloo lay between. A different verdict from the god of war would have led to an outcome utterly different from that which came to pass. The world of 1919 could not have been foreseen in 1915, for the intervening military decision was reached by the narrowest of margins. For similar reasons the world of Julius Caesar was beyond the imagination of Hannibal. By the same token the world of 1945 will be shaped for decades to come by the great decisions of 1941 and 1942. These are still unrevealed as these words are put in print.

But if the father of the future has not yet come forward, the identity of the mother is plain for all to see. She is a woman with a mission which cannot be escaped. That mission is to build a world society in which all nations and all classes and groups within nations will live in ordered peace. The child who is destined to undertake this mission may prove to be the son of the Anglo-Saxon giant who champions freedom and still stands, despite his wounds, astride the north Atlantic seaways. Or the child may be the son of the ogre out of the East who has spat upon freedom and destroyed it, but who has already begotten a breed of men ready and eager to conquer the earth. In either case the child of the future, if he survives at all, will do what fortune demands of him.

It is possible, but scarcely probable, that the child may die. If Britain survives 1941 without inflicting upon Italy a decisive defeat and if America fails to immobilize Tokio or inflict an equally decisive defeat upon Japan, the Second World War may not end abruptly with the collapse of the Nazi empire. It may continue year after year in a hopeless struggle of extermination and exhaustion. All the resources of the Continent may not suffice to break the will of the English-speaking Powers, even though much of Britain be laid in ashes and America be reduced to beggary. All the resources of the north Atlantic world may not suffice to invade and reconquer the Continent, even though tens of thousands of planes and scores of armored land squadrons carry death and ruin over the face of Europe. In this event the only end must be a truce of mutual exhaustion such as finally brought the Thirty Years' War to a close.

Should this prospect materialize, "men, exultant in the technique of homicide, will rage so hotly over the world that every precious thing will be in danger, every book and picture and harmony, every treasure garnered through two millenniums, the small, the delicate, the defenseless —all will be lost or wrecked or utterly destroyed. . . . There will be no safety by arms, no help from authority, no answer in science. The storm will rage until every flower of culture is trampled and all human beings are leveled in a vast chaos."[1] Such a prospect, however, would leave one great

[1] James Hilton's *Lost Horizon*, quoted by President Franklin D. Roosevelt in his "quarantine" speech in Chicago, October 5, 1937.

center of power and order intact. The rulers of this realm would inescapably become the beneficiaries of chaos and the residuary legatees of the wreckage. Such a prospect, and only such a prospect, would bring within the limits of possible realization the Communist dream of proletarian world revolution. In a Europe burned and blasted by years of warfare, in an Asia disorganized by endless strife, in an America bankrupted by the costs of Armageddon, the rulers of Red Muscovy would find their chance. Through a gradual process of intervention and invasion to "rescue" and "liberate" the wretched survivors of catastrophe, the Union of Soviet Socialist Republics might spread itself over much of the earth.

A new world dominated by Communism might conceivably be rebuilt on foundations ultimately promising a large measure of world unity and a resolution of class conflict through the symbols and practices of Red totalitarianism. Such a world would for years be miserable and poor. Much of its capital in human talent and physical assets would be gone before its new rulers could proclaim the new day. Much of what remained would be destroyed in furious combat between the impoverished rich and the starving poor before the conquering sword of the "comrades" could impose upon the world the true faith according to Marx, Lenin, and Stalin. Out of ruin might emerge a new birth of freedom and of hope—or a perpetuation of tyranny in a ramshackle Communist economy more productive of rhetoric than of tangible goods and services.

In all likelihood, however, this is the least probable outcome of today's ordeal. The very prospect of it promises to drive the weaker contestant in the Western war to yield and to be granted mercy of a kind from the victor, before any such grim débâcle becomes imminent. Fear of Communism is quite unlikely to change the appointed course of Berlin, Rome, and Tokio. But it may well influence decisions in London, Washington, and Chungking to the advantage of the Triplice. Any resumption of democratic appeasement would spell ultimate Triplice victory. If the war is not brought to an end in this fashion, it is none the less unlikely to degenerate into a stalemate and a conflict of attrition. The new strategy is mobile, swift, dynamic, decisive. A deadlock between the Triplice and Anglo-America appeared in 1941 less probable than a crushing blow delivered by one of the belligerents to the other long before mutual exhaustion should bring both to common ruin.

By virtue of Soviet neutrality and the possible inability or unwillingness of the United States to reinforce Britain in time, such a blow may be struck successfully by the Fascist war machines against the British Commonwealth. In this eventuality, mastery of the world will be in the hands of the Triplice. The aftermath of a British defeat can be forecast with reasonable certainty. The Soviet Union will be attacked, invaded, and conquered by Greater Germany and Japan. There is no good reason to believe that it can offer effective resistance in a world in which Britain is vanquished and America is helplessly isolated. China, India, and all of Asia will be partitioned between the Reich and Japan. A satellite Italy and an even weaker Spain will be granted such crumbs as the war lords of Berlin may be willing to spare.

Most of Latin America will simultaneously pass into the hands of the victors through bribes, threats, propaganda, conspiracy, intervention, and the connivance of the propertied classes. The United States will be immobilized. Its leaders and people may accept such a subordinate place in a totalitarian world as the rulers of that world will grant them. Or they may offer desperate resistance which will in the end prove futile by virtue of the loss of Latin America and the vastly superior resources for war which will be at the disposal of the masters of Europe, Asia, and Africa. In either case, American "democracy" and "capitalism" will perish. A defeated and demoralized community will resort to such devices of intolerance and tyranny as will bring psychic security to tortured souls and some promise of order and bread to a disintegrating society. The physical conquest of the North American Republic by the Triplice will be improbable and unnecessary. Its economic and strategic position in such a world will ensure its reduction to impotence and its disruption from within.

The manner in which such a world will be reordered and ruled is not in doubt, at least as to its larger aspects. The German "master race" will rule the West. The Japanese "master race" will rule the East. If challenged by a reborn and dynamic America, the masters will wage war in the New World and most probably compel ultimate American capitulation. If left in peace by a defeatist and decadent America, surviving as a kind of new Byzantium in a world controlled by its enemies, the war lords of East and West may deem it pointless to challenge the transatlantic colossus in its own sphere. The millions of Asia and Africa will become helots of the conquerors, granted such security as slaves or serfs enjoy and drugged into complacency through new modes of hypnosis and exploitation which will seem easier to endure than the risks of hopeless resistance. In Europe and Latin America, protectorates and puppet régimes will serve the purposes of the Nazi masters on terms which may not prove too intolerable to those who willingly collaborate. In a hierarchical world society, "inferior" races will occupy an inferior status. A "planned economy," dedicated to new forms of pyramid building, may maintain a low level of material well-being throughout a vast transcontinental and transoceanic empire within which national independence, State sovereignty, protective tariffs, class conflicts, representative government, human freedom, and libertarian ideals will all alike be forever abolished. It is by no means unthinkable that such an imperium may endure, as Hitler promises, for a thousand years. Similar realms have lasted for centuries over vast areas of the earth in the twilight time of all earlier civilizations. What has been before can be again.

It is possible, however, that the verdict of arms in 1941–1942 may lead to a different result. If Britain survives its ordeal by fire; if America or the U.S.S.R. or both act in time to defeat the Triplice; if the vast reserves of the British Empire, the Soviet Union, and the United States are effectively mobilized against Germany and Japan—then the rulers of the world to come will not be the "master races" of central Europe and eastern Asia but the peoples of the North Atlantic Commonwealth and those of Red Muscovy. This victory may not need to be bought with seas of blood. Only the vanquished on whose lands the war will be won will suffer heavily from devastation and death. Victory will go to those who achieve overwhelming superiority in the machines of war. Such a victory costs the victor little in lives, as the campaigns of 1939–1941 in Europe and Africa demonstrated. Yet if Russia and the Western Powers clash for mastery over the vanquished, years of dismal fighting may follow with no result save the ruin of central Europe, of China, of India, and of the contestants as well. Under no imaginable circumstances can Anglo-America strike Russia down. Nor can the U.S.S.R. deal any lethal blow to the Western Powers. Conversely, a *modus vivendi* between the two camps will offer promise of reconstruction on a world scale.

The forms and concrete purposes of such reconstruction in the event of democratic victory are not easy to foresee, since the democratic peoples had not yet faced the issue of remaking the world on the eve of the great decisions of 1941–1942 All that is clear is that any post-victory retreat toward national sovereignty and isolation or toward an empty democracy which merely masks a civil war of rich and poor will of necessity be followed by a new epoch of international anarchy and social disintegration out of which, a decade hence, new Caesars will arise to do what must be done. If, on the other hand, the Western peoples grasp boldly at their chance to remake Western society and reorder the world, with such collaboration from Russia, China, and India as opportunity and mutual respect make possible, then a new epoch will open in mankind's march into the vast and teeming future.

No revival of the League of Nations is likely to prove workable as a basis of world order. The establishment of an international federal government with a common currency, a common commercial régime, and common forces of defense offers far more promise, for only in this fashion can national sovereignty be abolished and the world policed and administered under a régime of law. Such a federation must doubtless be limited in membership at the outset, with the vanquished, the neutrals, and the Soviets free to join later or to collaborate in common tasks without full

membership. The initial scope of such a federation can scarcely be conceived of in terms of "continental blocs." The European Continent west
of Russia is not a self-sufficient entity, economically or politically. Its
peoples are dependent upon, and are depended upon by, those of Africa,
Asia, and the Americas. The "Western Hemisphere" is still less a feasible
unit of world or "hemisphere" organization. Latin America is dependent
upon Europe, not upon the United States, in all of the things of life that
have meaning to its peoples.[1] The only practicable basis for the nucleus
of a world federation is to be found in a union of the United States of
America and the British Commonwealth of Nations. Such a union would
possess overwhelming power to police the world and prevent any restoration of a world balance of power. Such a union could, therefore, abolish
power politics and undertake to unite the world in the service of ideals
of freedom, implemented by a new conception of a collectivist, democratic
society.

In such a world order, colonial areas would of necessity be protected
from unscrupulous exploitation and administered jointly by federal
authorities. The goal of such administration would not be preparation for
a "national independence" which can never again be tolerated if chaos
is to be vanquished. The goal would be eventual membership in the
world federation on the basis of equality and local autonomy. The peoples
of the European Continent and those of Latin America would gravitate
toward full membership in the Union. Russia, Japan, China and India
would doubtless seek some form of liaison which, for an uncertain period,
might well be something less than full membership. Even should this
vision materialize, there would be no easy road into the future. Such a
Union could probably not be secured for posterity save at the cost of
one or more "civil wars" against such communities as might be tempted
from time to time to secede, to challenge federal authority, and to revert
toward the ideology of national sovereignty. But the establishment of
such a Union would at least lay the foundations of a genuine world order
for the centuries to come.

It is of course quite possible that the Western peoples may refuse to
assume any such duties or run any such risks. They may decline to "police
the world" or to pledge irrevocably their blood and treasure to the re-

---

[1] In normal pre-war years, South America sold approximately $2,500,000,000 worth of
goods annually to Europe and bought annually from Europe $1,000,000,000 worth of
goods. It sold to the United States only $300,000,000 worth of goods annually and pur-
chased from the United States (out of the proceeds of sales to Europe) some $600,000,000
worth annually. South America and the European Continent complement one another
economically and could therefore be federated politically without insuperable difficulties.
The same is true of the United States, the British Empire, and Latin America taken together. The United States and Latin America by themselves do not serve one another's
needs, do not understand one another's ways, and cannot constitute a workable federation
of equals under any presently imaginable conditions.

building of the world society and the attainment of a world polity. In this case, their victory in the Second World War is unlikely, and their very survival as self-governing communities is improbable. Should they by some miracle nevertheless vanquish the Triplice with no subsequent desire to reshape the community of nations, the final result will still be their own defeat by the forces of chaos or by new forces dedicated to the abolition of chaos. If such forces should fail in turn to attain the goal, the future of the Great Society of the modern age can scarcely be different from the future of the Great Society of the Mediterranean world after the descent of night fifteen centuries ago. Half a millenium usually passes before a new culture is born out of the savagery and feudal confusions which often overwhelm societies whose citizens are unwilling to do what is necessary to save their heritage.

It is more probable, however, that Western civilization has not yet run its course and that its peoples still have somewhere within them the creative energies needed to rebuild the world of tomorrow. If Western democrats are unwilling to assume the task, others will undertake it. Only the communities willing to venture much will win. Only these are likely to prove fit for survival. The horror of the present and the challenge of the future beckon modern man to new horizons and to an adventure more creative and dynamic than any he has yet known. Those who decline the challenge and look to the lost past will suffer the eternal fate of peoples incapable of perceiving reality and adapting themselves to change.

Those who accept the challenge will rule the planet and shape the days and years to come. Long before this century has passed its midpoint, today's great question will have been answered. Either the free men of the West or the Caesars of the East will do what must be done if the Great Society is to go on. Modern man will say to destiny what Christians say to God: "Thy kingdom come! Thy will be done on earth as it is in heaven!" That which must be done will assuredly be done either in the service of the ideals of freedom or in the service of those who sacrifice freedom to order and see human relations in terms of masters and slaves. In either case the war within the Western soul, the schism between the wealthy and the poor, the politics of power, the anarchic violence of inter-state conflicts will all alike have been resolved. The world community of tomorrow will be pledged to peace. It will be ruled by those prepared to conquer peace and to conserve and cultivate for posterity the fruits of victory.

SUGGESTED READINGS

Beals, C.: *Pan-America*, Boston, Houghton, 1940.
Beneš, Eduard: *Democracy, Today and Tomorrow*, New York, Macmillan, 1939.
———, R. Coulborn, and A. Feiler: *International Security*, Chicago, University of Chicago Press, 1939.

Bernal, J. D.: *The Social Function of Science*, New York, Macmillan, 1939.
Brady, R. A.: *If Night Should Rise*, New York, Viking, 1939.
Burke, Kenneth: *Attitudes toward History*, New York, New Republic, 1937.
The City of Man: A Declaration on World Democracy, New York, Viking, 1940.
Dakin, E. F.: *Today and Destiny* (vital excerpts from *The Decline of the West* by Oswald Spengler), New York, Knopf, 1940.
Dennis, L.: *The Dynamics of War and Revolution*, New York, Weekly Foreign Letter, 1940.
Dewey, J.: *Freedom and Culture*, New York, Putnam, 1939.
Fodor, M. W.: *The Revolution Is On*, Boston, Houghton, 1940.
Fosdick, D.: *What Is Liberty?* New York, Harper, 1939.
Fraenkel, E.: *The Dual State: A Contribution to the Theory of Dictatorship*, New York, Oxford, 1940.
Frank, W.: *Chart for Rough Water*, New York, Doubleday, 1940.
Griffith, E. S.: *The Impasse of Democracy*, New York, Harrison, 1939.
Huizinga, J.: *In the Shadow of Tomorrow*, New York, Norton, 1936.
Jennings, W. I.: *A Federation for Western Europe*, New York, Macmillan, 1940.
Kirkpatrick, F. A.: *Latin-America*, New York, Macmillan, 1939.
Kohn, H.: *Force or Reason*, Cambridge, Mass., Harvard University Press, 1937.
———: *Not by Arms Alone*, Cambridge, Mass., Harvard University Press, 1940.
Lerner, M.: *It Is Later than You Think*, New York, Viking, 1938.
———: *Ideas Are Weapons*, New York, Viking, 1939.
Mumford, Lewis: *Men Must Act*, New York, Harcourt, 1939.
Rader, M.: *No Compromise*, New York, Macmilian, 1939.
Russell, B.: *Freedom versus Organization 1814–1914*, New York, Norton, 1935.
Schevill, F., and others: *The Foundations of a More Stable World Order*, Chicago, University of Chicago Press, 1941.
Strachey, John: *A Faith to Fight For*, London, Gollancz, 1941.
Wells, H. G.: *The Fate of Man*, New York, Alliance, 1939.
Woolf, Leonard: *Barbarians: Within and Without*, New York, Harcourt, 1939.

INDEX

N.B. Entries under major countries are limited to principal treaties and wars. See pp. 93–95 for areas, populations, and capitals. See also names of persons and places. Conferences, treaties, and wars are not individually indexed but are listed chronologically under these headings.

Abbreviations: *c.* = cited or referred to; *q.* = quoted; *n.* = footnote; *d.* = death of; *C.* = conference; *T.* = treaty or agreement; *W.* = war.

INDEX

INDEX

577, 617, 677; Finnish peace (1940), 117, 680; U.S.-Britain (1940), 118, 140, 654; U.S.-Canada (1940), 140, 654; Triple Alliance (1940), 424, 531*f*., 656; U.S.S.R.-Turkish (1941), 684*n*.; U.S.-S.R.-Jugoslav (1941), 648*n*.; U.S.S.R.-Japan (1941), XI (*See also T.* under names of States)

Treitschke, H. von, 561

Trevor, J. B., *c*.366

Triple Alliance (1882–1914), 251, 256, 319, 531, 535

Triple Alliance (1940), 298, 551, 585, 606, 660, 682, 683, 684*n*., 696, 699, VIII; *q*.531–532

Triple Entente, 514

Tripoli, 74, 77

"Trojan Horse," 499*f*., 501, 508

Trondheim, 578

Trotsky, Leon, 669, 671, 672; *d*.669*n*.

Troy, 14

Troyanovsky, Alexander, 631

"Truce of God," 37

Tukachevsky, Marshal, 670, 672

Tunis, 377, 415

Tunisia, 426, 547, 551

Turenne, 57

Turkey, *W.* Italy (1911), 74; World War I, 76–80, peace settlement (1919), 83–85; exchange of minorities *T.*, Greece (1923), 324; and minority *T.*'s, 324; *W.*, Greece (1922–23), 393; nonaggression pact, U.S.S.R., 462, 565; *T.*, France (1939), 599; *T.*, Britain (1939), 615; World War II, 88, 586–587; *T.*, U.S.S.R. (1941), 684*n*., X (*See also* Ottoman Empire)

Turner, R. E., *c*.39

Twenty-one demands, 515

Tyrol, 319*f*.

U

Ual Ual, 236, 237

Ugaki, Gen. Kagushigi, *q*.524

Uganda, 415

Ughet, Serge, 149

Umma, 10

Union of South Africa, 74, 375

U.S.S.R., foreign policy in general, 660–684; *T.*, Brest-Litovsk, 81, 664; peace settlement (1919), 83–85; *W.*, Poland,

666; *T.*, Poland, 667; Anti-Comintern Alliance, 87; recognition by U.S., 107; nonaggression pacts, 462; *T.*, Mongolia (1936), 672; *T.*, Germany (1939), 88, 573, 577, 617, 677; *W.*, Finland, 246, 678*f*.; *T.*, Turkey (March, 1941), 684*n*.; *T.* Jugoslavia (April, 1941), 684*n*.; *T.*, Japan (April, 1941), XI (*See also* Russia)

Union Now, 251, 252, 253, 461, 602

U.S.A., foreign policy in general, 622–659; origin, 63; *T.*, France (1778), 106, 439, 624; *T.*, Britain (1783), 117; Constitution, 122, 124*f*., 127, 128, 166; *q*.169; expansion, 69, 117*f*.; *W.* of 1812, 70; *T.*, China, 404, 328; *W.*, Mexico, 74; Clayton-Bulwer *T.*, 126; Civil *W.*, 74, 106; *W.*, Spain, 74, 102, 380, 383; *T.*, Cuba, 415, 417, 444; *T.*, Panama, 415; *T.*, Dominican Republic, 361; *T.*, Haiti, 361; *T.*, Nicaragua, 191, 361; World War I, 625*f*.; *T.*, Germany, 439, 626, 627; neutrality legislation, 137*f*., 237, 359, 639*f*.; *T.*, Canada, 654; *T.*, Britain, 650

U.S. vs. Curtiss-Wright Export Corporation, *q*.167*n*

United States of Europe, 252

Universal Postal Union, 207*f*.

"Unneutral service," 134

Upper Silesia, 83, 232, 318, 320, 327, 550

Utley, C., *c*.92

Utley, Freda, *c*.534

V

Vagts, A., *c*.299

Valens, Emperor, 29

Valens, Vettius, *q*.3

Vali, F. A., *c*. 142

Valtin, J., *c*.684

Vandenberg, Sen. Arthur, *q*.651

VanKleefens, E. N., *c*.587

VanValkenberg, S., *c*.299

VanZeeland, Paul, 242

Vargas, Getulio, President of Brazil, 633

Vatican City, 146, 538

Vattel, Emeric de, 49; *q*.54, 55, 110

Vauban, Gen., 57

Vavrecka, Hugo, *q*.569

Vayo, Alvarez del, 246, 545; *c*.603

Venice, 40*f*.

[731]